Fifteenth Edition

ACCOUNTING PRINCIPLES

Philip E. Fess, PhD, CPA
Professor of Accountancy
University of Illinois, Champaign-Urbana

Carl S. Warren, PhD, CPA, CMA
Professor of Accounting
University of Georgia, Athens

Published by

A30 **SOUTH-WESTERN PUBLISHING CO.**

CINCINNATI   WEST CHICAGO, IL   DALLAS   LIVERMORE, CA

COVER PHOTO: © David Muench 1986

PREFACE

The fifteenth edition of ACCOUNTING PRINCIPLES is a student-oriented text. It presents the fundamental accounting concepts and principles in a logical, concise, and clear manner. ACCOUNTING PRINCIPLES provides a solid educational foundation that allows instructors to focus on clarifying issues and increasing the student's understanding of accounting and its uses. This student orientation is one of the principal reasons why this text has been used by more students than any other for more than 50 years and why it is still the leader in teaching principles of accounting.

Fundamental accounting concepts and principles are presented in the text in a business setting that allows students to understand accounting as it is applied in serving not only the business world but all of society. Such an approach meets the needs of students planning careers in accounting as well as in business administration, in liberal arts areas, in law, or in other disciplines.

IMPORTANT FEATURES OF THE FIFTEENTH EDITION

The basic foundation of ACCOUNTING PRINCIPLES, which has served instructors and students so well over the years, has been retained in the fifteenth edition. However, many new features have been added. These new features are based on extensive feedback from current users and on independent reviews by numerous scholars and educators. The most significant new features and the quality features introduced in previous editions are:

Chapter Objectives

The chapter objectives have been revised and expanded to enable students and instructors to integrate the chapter materials with the overall learning objectives more successfully.

Illustrations

Many additional charts, graphs, and diagrams have been added throughout the text to enable students to visualize important concepts and principles more efficiently. These charts, graphs, and diagrams are highlighted with color to enhance the learning process.

Real-World Examples

Real-world business examples have been integrated throughout the text to provide students with a flavor for the real-world impact of accounting. These examples add concrete meaning to concepts and principles which might otherwise appear abstract. Many of these examples were taken directly from the latest annual reports of companies such as Pepsico and General Motors. In addition, the American Institute of Certified Public Accountants' publication, *Accounting Trends & Techniques,* is cited where appropriate to indicate the frequency with which alternative accounting presentations and methods are used in the real world.

Enrichment Material

Excerpts from well-known business periodicals, such as the *Journal of Accountancy,* the *Wall Street Journal,* and *Forbes,* have been added to each chapter. Each excerpt was adapted and designed to stir the students' interest and enrich their learning experience by providing real-world information relevant to the topics that are discussed in the chapter.

Chapter Reviews

A chapter review has been added at the end of each chapter. The chapter reviews are designed to increase and enhance student retention of important chapter concepts and principles. Each chapter review includes key points, key terms, self-examination questions, and an illustrative problem and solution.

■ The **key points** summarize the major concepts presented in a chapter. By studying the key points, students can quickly review the major concepts and principles of each chapter.

■ Each **key term** listed in the chapter review is followed by the page number indicating where the key term was first presented in color and discussed in the chapter. Students may also refer to Appendix A, where all the key terms in the text are listed alphabetically and defined.

■ Five **self-examination questions** are provided for each chapter. After studying the chapter, students can answer these questions and compare their answers with the correct ones that appear in Appendix B. An explanation of both the correct and incorrect answers for each question is provided in order to increase students' understanding and enhance the learning process further.

■ The **illustrative problem** with suggested solution focuses on the concepts and principles discussed in the chapter. Students can use these problems as a means of building confidence in their ability to apply a chapter's concepts and principles to a problem situation.

Real-World Focus Questions

A discussion question that requires students to interpret and respond to a real-world business situation is contained in each chapter. In some chapters, a real-world exercise is also included. These questions and exercises, which are labeled "Real World Focus," are based on actual business data.

Comprehensive Problems

Comprehensive problems have been added at appropriate points in the text. These problems integrate and summarize the concepts and principles of several chapters.

Series B Problems

The alternate Series B problems appear at the end of each chapter in order to facilitate student and instructor usage.

Accounting for Merchandise Inventory

The discussion of accounting for merchandise inventory has been revised to facilitate student understanding.

■ The discussion of accounting for merchandise inventory has been expanded into two chapters, so that instructors can cover the material at a slower pace and in more depth.

■ A unique presentation of the work sheet for financial statements enables students to follow easily the various steps in its preparation and use.

■ The accounts *Purchases Returns and Allowances* and *Transportation In* are used in the discussion of accounting for merchandise enterprises.

■ An alternate method of handling merchandise inventory at the end of an accounting period has been added as Appendix C. This method, sometimes referred to as the closing method, can be used instead of the method presented in the merchandising chapters. The Solutions Manual includes solutions for both approaches.

Deferrals and Accruals

The chapter covering deferrals and accruals has been revised. For example, several charts comparing the accounting entries under alternate methods of recording deferrals and accruals have been added.

Periodic and Perpetual Inventories

The discussion of the periodic and perpetual methods of accounting for merchandise inventories has been revised and expanded. A comparison of the journal entries under each method has been added. Also, a discussion of the use of the perpetual inventory system in computerized environments is included.

Price-Level Changes

The discussion of price-level changes has been condensed and is now integrated into Chapter 13, "Concepts and Principles."

Long-Term Liabilities and Investments in Stocks and Bonds

The discussion of accounting for investments in bonds has been separated from the discussion of accounting for investments in stocks, with the latter moved to the succeeding chapter, which also includes the discussion of consolidated statements and international accounting. The long-term liabilities and bond investments chapter has been revised to include a discussion of present value and the use of present value tables.

Statement of Changes in Financial Position

The discussion of the statement of changes in financial position has been revised to emphasize the current trend of using the cash concept of funds as the basis for the statement. The preparation of the funds statement using the cash basis is presented first, followed by the working capital basis.

Financial Statement Analysis

The financial statement analysis chapter has been revised to include a chart summarizing solvency and profitability measures. In addition, a section on corporate annual reports has been added.

Managerial Accounting

The coverage of managerial accounting has been expanded and reorganized.

■ Chapter 21, "Responsibility Accounting," emphasizes responsibility accounting for cost, profit, and investment centers. The discussion of branch accounting has been moved to Appendix E.

■ Chapter 24, "Budgeting and Standard Cost Systems," has been revised to include an integrated example of the master budget and a discussion of budgeting and human behavior. A problem that requires the preparation of all the budgets supporting a budgeted income statement has been added.

■ Chapter 25, "Profit Reporting for Management Analysis," has been revised and expanded to include a section describing the characteristics of managerial accounting reports. In addition, charts and illustrations have been added to the discussion of variable and absorption costing.

■ Chapter 26, "Cost-Volume-Profit Analysis," has been added. The presentation of cost-volume-profit analysis has been significantly expanded to include a more thorough discussion of variable and fixed costs, including graphs to illustrate the costs; the effects of changes in fixed costs, variable costs, and unit selling price on the break-even point; and sales mix considerations. A discussion and illustration of the profit-volume chart has been added. The chapter concludes with a brief discussion of the use of computers and quantitative techniques in managerial accounting.

■ Chapter 27, "Differential Analysis and Capital Investment Analysis," has been added. The discussion of capital investment analysis includes the use of present value tables. Coverage of the discounted internal rate of return is included, along with a discussion of the capital rationing process and methods of planning and controlling capital investment expenditures.

Income Taxes

The coverage of income taxes has been condensed and is presented in Appendix G. This appendix, which incorporates the 1986 changes in the tax law, provides students with an understanding of the basic nature of the federal income tax system and its effects on personal and business income.

End-of-Chapter Materials

The end-of-chapter exercises and problems have been carefully written and revised to be both practical and comprehensive. The variety and volume of the assignment materials presented at the end of each chapter provide a wide choice of subject matter and range of difficulty. In addition, selected problems may be solved using general ledger and spreadsheet software that is available from South-Western Publishing Co. As in previous editions, each chapter contains a mini-case for stimulating student interest. Each case, which presents situations with which students can easily identify, emphasizes important chapter concepts and principles.

SUPPLEMENTARY MATERIALS

ACCOUNTING PRINCIPLES is part of a well-integrated educational package that includes materials designed for the instructor's use and for the students' use. These materials are carefully prepared and reviewed to maintain consistency and high quality throughout.

Available to Instructors

Solutions Manual. This manual contains solutions to all end-of-chapter materials, including the discussion questions, exercises, problems, mini-cases, and comprehensive problems.

Instructor's Manual, prepared by Edward W. Scott, Jr. of Olympic College, Philip E. Fess, and Carl S. Warren. This manual contains a summary of the chapter objectives, terminology, and concepts. In a section organized according to chapter objectives, a basis for developing class lectures and assigning homework is provided. In addition, exercise and problem descriptions, estimated time requirements for the problems, suggestions for use of the appendixes and other supplementary items, and the solutions for the manual practice sets are included.

Transparencies. Transparencies of solutions to all exercises and problems, including the comprehensive problems, are available. The transparencies are packaged in two boxes, one for Chapters 1–14 and one for Chapters 15–28 and Appendixes E, F, and G.

Teaching Transparencies. The teaching transparencies are designed to aid the instructor's focus on key concepts and principles discussed in the text.

Test Bank, prepared by Charles Rohr of Mt. San Jacinto College, Philip E. Fess, and Carl S. Warren. A collection of examination problems, multiple-choice questions, and true or false questions for each chapter, accompanied by solutions, is available in both printed and microcomputer (MicroSWAT II) versions. The Test Bank is designed to save time in preparing and grading periodic and final examinations. Individual items may also be selected for use as short quizzes. The number of questions is sufficient to provide variety from year to year and from class section to class section. The printed version of the Test Bank also contains the solutions for the Achievement Tests.

Achievement Tests, prepared by Charles Rohr, Philip E. Fess, and Carl S. Warren. Three sets of preprinted objective tests are available. Each test in sets A and B covers a single chapter. Each test in set C contains 50 multiple-choice questions covering a group of chapters. Set C, which may be machine graded, also includes a comprehensive test covering each half of the text.

Demonstration Problems and Notes, prepared by L. Paden Neeley of North Texas State University. A set of special problems that emphasize the important accounting concepts and principles of the textbook are available, along with a set of correlating transparencies. As the instructor works through each problem on the transparencies, students can follow the solution as they complete each problem in their workbook.

The Administrator. A software management package is available to adopters. This package is specifically designed for use in maintaining a grade book, creating an interactive testing and/or study guide file, and generating tests.

Available to Students

Solutions: Applications Software, prepared by Warren W. Allen and Dale H. Klooster of Educational Technical Systems. This software, which may be ordered with the textbook, is a general ledger program tailored specifically to ACCOUNTING PRINCIPLES. It may be used with the Apple® //e™ and Apple® //c™,[1] the IBM PC and IBM PCjr,[2] and the Tandy® 1000[3] microcomputers to solve selected end-of-chapter problems and the comprehensive problems, which are identified with the symbol at the right. It may also be used to solve the first two manual practice sets, so that they in effect become computerized practice sets.

Spreadsheet Applications, prepared by Gaylord N. Smith of Albion College. This template diskette is used with Lotus™ 1-2-3™ [4] for solving selected end-of-chapter exercises and problems that are identified with the symbol at the right. This diskette, which also provides for solving these problems using alternative data, may be ordered free of charge from South-Western Publishing Co.

Working Papers. Appropriate printed forms on which to work end-of-chapter problems and mini-cases are available in two bound volumes. The first volume is for use with Chapters 1–14, and the second volume is for use with Chapters 14–28.

Study Guides, prepared by James A. Heintz of Indiana University and Carl S. Warren. The Study Guides are designed to assist in comprehending the concepts and principles presented in the text. These publications, which are printed in two volumes (one for Chapters 1–14 and one for Chapters 15–28), include an outline and a glossary for each chapter as well as brief objective questions and problems. Solutions to these questions and problems are presented at the back of the Study Guides.

Microcomputer Study Guides. These microcomputer versions of the manual Study Guides may be used with the Apple //e and the Apple //c, the IBM PC and the IBM PCjr, and the Tandy 1000.

Audio-Cassette Study Guides, prepared by Wilbur F. Pillsbury of Knox College. Four study guides are available to be used with instructional cassette tapes. The material is self-paced, and immediate feedback is received after step-by-step exercises have been completed.

Check Figures. Instructors may order check figures for distribution to students. These check figures may be used by students in checking their solutions to end-of-chapter problems. Agreement with the check figures is an indication that a significant portion of the solution is basically correct.

Practice Sets, prepared by Herman R. Andress of Santa Fe Community College and Edward E. Stumpf of Fullerton College. Four short practice sets, each requiring the recording, analysis, interpretation, and reporting of accounting data, are available. Set 1, *Top Ten Sporting Goods Co.,* is available with business documents or with a narrative of transactions. The company is a sole proprietorship that uses special journals. Set 2, *Sierra Computer Systems,* is also available with business documents or with a

---

[1]Apple® //e™, Apple® //c™, and Applesoft® are registered or pending trademarks of Apple Computer, Inc. Any reference to Apple //e, Apple //c, or Applesoft refers to this footnote.
[2]IBM is a registered trademark of International Business Machines Corporation. Any reference to the IBM Personal Computer or the IBM PCjr refers to this footnote.
[3]Tandy® 1000 is a registered trademark of the Radio Shack Division of Tandy Corporation. Any reference to the Tandy 1000 microcomputer refers to this footnote.
[4]Lotus™ 1-2-3™ are trademarks of the Lotus Development Corporation. Any reference to Lotus or 1-2-3 refers to this footnote.

narrative of transactions. This company is a sole proprietorship that uses a voucher system. Set 3, *Custom Interiors Inc.,* is available with a narrative of transactions for a corporation operating a departmentalized business. Set 4, *Sunrise Solar Inc.,* is available with a narrative of transactions for a manufacturing company using a job order cost system.

Microcomputer Practice Sets, prepared by Dale H. Klooster and Warren W. Allen. Two automated practice sets — *Custom Auto Parts* and *Sound Ideas* — are available with diskettes. These sets parallel the first two manual practice sets.

Integrated Accounting on Microcomputers, prepared by Dale H. Klooster and Warren W. Allen. This text-workbook with diskette is a stand-alone, automated accounting package that is intended for a first course in microcomputer accounting. Completion time is approximately 45–55 hours.

Electronic Spreadsheet Applications for Accounting Principles, Financial Accounting, and Managerial Accounting, prepared by Gaylord N. Smith. This supplemental text-workbook with template diskette includes accounting applications and a Lotus 1-2-3 tutorial. It requires approximately 20–25 hours for completion, and it requires access to Lotus 1-2-3.

ORGANIZATION OF THE FIFTEENTH EDITION

ACCOUNTING PRINCIPLES has been organized to facilitate the learning of accounting and the overall educational process. Concepts and principles are introduced in a logical, step-by-step way and are reinforced by applications from the business world.

Each chapter builds on the terminology, concepts, and principles introduced in previous chapters. The chapter objectives provide students with a basis for beginning their study of each chapter. In turn, each chapter is organized around the chapter objectives in an educationally sound approach. The chapter reviews provide students with a means for review and a basis for assessing their knowledge of each chapter. The end-of-chapter discussion questions, exercises, problems, and mini-cases provide a vehicle for the instructor to assess the students' knowledge of each chapter's concepts and principles. Periodic assigning of comprehensive problems and the giving of examinations provide instructors with a means for assessing students' cumulative knowledge.

The organization of the fifteenth edition of ACCOUNTING PRINCIPLES is briefly summarized in the following paragraphs.

Introduction: Evolution of Accounting

The introduction presents a summary of the beginnings of accounting in 1494 and its development to the present. This overview provides students of all backgrounds an excellent perspective on the importance and influence of accounting on all phases of society.

Part 1 — Basic Structure of Accounting

Chapters 1–6 focus on the basic concepts and principles of accounting, including accounting for both service enterprises and merchandise enterprises. These chapters are presented without the complexities of special journals and subsidiary ledgers. The emphasis on different forms of organization is minimized by presenting simple owner equity structures and deferring complex owner equity structures to later chapters. Chapter 6 is designed as a self-contained unit, so that instructors have flexibility as to when they cover the chapter. For example, some instructors may prefer to omit the chapter in the first accounting course and include it as a review in beginning the second course.

Part 2 — Accounting Systems

Chapter 7 emphasizes the qualities of a properly designed accounting system, including the principles of internal control and the use of special journals and subsidiary ledgers. Chapters 8–12 build on this systems foundation, beginning with cash in Chapter 8 and, in balance sheet order, proceeding with receivables and temporary investments (Chapter 9), inventories (Chapter 10), plant assets and intangible assets (Chapter 11), and current liabilities and payroll (Chapter 12).

Part 3 — Accounting Principles

Chapter 13, "Concepts and Principles," ties together the generally accepted accounting concepts and principles presented in the first 12 chapters, and expands the discussion to include additional accounting principles. Chapter 13 also includes a discussion of reporting changes in price levels.

Part 4 — Partnerships

Chapter 14 discusses the characteristics of partnerships and the unique accounting concepts and principles related to partnerships.

Part 5 — Corporations

Chapters 15–18 present the special accounting issues related to corporations. These chapters include discussions of stock issuances, dividends, bonds, long-term investments in bonds and stocks, consolidated financial statements, and international accounting.

Part 6 — Additional Statements and Analyses

Chapter 19 presents the basic concepts and principles underlying the statement of changes in financial position. The cash basis is presented first, according to the current trend in emphasizing the cash concept of funds, and is followed by the discussion of the working capital basis. Chapter 20 presents a discussion of solvency and profitability and related analytical procedures useful in assessing these financial statement concepts. Chapter 20 concludes with a discussion of corporate annual reports.

Part 7 — Accounting for Decentralized Operations and Manufacturing Operations

Chapters 21–23 are the beginning of the discussion of managerial accounting concepts and principles. Chapter 21 presents responsibility accounting in relation to cost, profit, and investment centers. Chapters 22 and 23 present accounting concepts and procedures for job order and process cost accounting systems.

Part 8 — Planning, Control, and Decision Making

Chapters 24–27 present managerial accounting concepts and principles that are especially useful for planning, control, and decision making. Chapter 24 presents the concepts of budgeting and standard costs. Chapter 25 presents profit reporting for management analysis, including gross profit analysis and variable and absorption costing. Chapter 26 focuses on cost-volume-profit analysis and quantitative techniques. Differential analysis and capital investment analysis are presented in Chapter 27.

Part 9 — Individuals and Nonprofit Organizations

Chapter 28 presents accounting concepts and principles related to individuals and nonprofit organizations.

Appendixes

- Appendix A contains a glossary of the key terms.
- Appendix B contains the answers to the self-examination questions appearing at the end of each chapter.
- Appendix C presents an alternative method of recording merchandise inventory at the end of an accounting period. This method is sometimes referred to as the closing method. Solutions to problems using this method are presented in the Solutions Manual.
- Appendix D presents a work sheet approach to the preparation of the statement of changes in financial position, using both the cash basis and the working capital basis. The Solutions Manual includes solutions to problems using the work sheet.
- Appendix E presents the accounting concepts and principles related to branch accounting. Problem materials are included with the appendix.
- Appendix F presents a work sheet approach to the preparation of financial statements for manufacturing enterprises using the periodic inventory method. Problem materials are included with the appendix.
- Appendix G discusses income taxes for individuals and business enterprises. Question and exercise materials are included with the appendix.
- Appendix H contains selected financial statements for real companies.

ACKNOWLEDGMENTS

Throughout the textbook, relevant professional statements of the Financial Accounting Standards Board and other authoritative publications are discussed, quoted, paraphrased, or footnoted. We are indebted to the American Accounting Association, the American Institute of Certified Public Accountants, the Financial Accounting Standards Board, and the National Association of Accountants for material from their publications.

We thank the following faculty who reviewed the previous edition or manuscript for this edition and provided helpful suggestions:

Bettie Adams
University of North Florida

Frances Bailey
Grayson County College

J. Basseri
Cuesta College

Robert Battle
Nassau Community College

Henry J. Beck
Danville Community College

Luverne Bierle
Iowa Central Community College

Walter G. DeAguero
Saddleback College

Robert Faulkner
St. Ambrose College

Edward G. Fratantaro
Orange Coast College

Robert C. Furber
College of the Redwoods

Richard B. Griffin
The University of Tennessee at Martin

Joseph M. Hagan
West Georgia College

Jerry A. Kicklighter
Dekalb Community College

Lewis Kolbo
Northeast Wisconsin Technical
    Institute

Willard J. Lawrence
Austin Community College

Michael Layne
Nassau Community College

Larry Lease
Shasta College

James L. Marra
Fulton-Montgomery Community College

Norma V. Meyers
Washtenaw Community College

Charles V. Neal
Alfred State Collage

Gerald J. Peterka
National University

LaDonna Rhodes
Fullerton College

C. Steven Roberts
North Hennepin Community College

Joseph C. Rue
Syracuse University

Roman S. Salazar
Modesto Junior College

Edward S. Scott, Jr.
Olympic College

Steve A. Steed
Tarleton State University

Gregory S. Thom
Parkland College

Jack Whipple
Clinton Community College

We also thank the following faculty who provided suggestions that have been incorporated in this edition: Sandra Byrd, Southwest Missouri State University; Diana Clary, Danville Community College; Steve Doster, Maysville Community College; Mark Griffin, Davenport College; Howard Hendricks, Antelope Valley College; John Hoover, Broward Community College; Edward Krohn, Miami Dade Community College; Rosalee Morgan, Delaware County Community College; Mark Moss, Utah Technical College at Salt Lake; Barbara Pauer, Western Wisconsin Technical Institute; Bill Purdy, Webster Career College; Donald J. Sampson, Foothill College; Roger Sands, Milwaukee Area Technical College; Robert W. Sessoms, Cape Fear Technical Institute; and Frank Zattich, Lincoln Land College.

We continue to welcome your comments and suggestions.

Philip E. Fess
Carl S. Warren

ABOUT THE AUTHORS

Professor Philip E. Fess is the Arthur Andersen & Co. Alumni Professor of Accountancy at the University of Illinois, Champaign-Urbana. Professor Fess received his PhD from the University of Illinois and has been involved in textbook writing for over twenty years. In addition to having more than 30 years of teaching experience, he has won numerous teaching awards, including the University of Illinois, College of Commerce Alumni Association Excellence in Teaching Award.

Professor Fess is a CPA and a member of the American Institute of CPAs and the Illinois Society of CPAs. He has served many professional associations in a variety of ways, including a term as a member of the Auditing Standards Board, editorial advisor to the *Journal of Accountancy,* and chairperson of the American Accounting Association Committee on CPA Examinations. Professor Fess has written more than 100 books and articles, which have appeared in such journals as the *Journal of Accountancy,* the *Accounting Review,* the *CPA Journal,* and *Management Accounting.* He has also served as an expert witness before the U.S. Tax Court.

Professor Fess resides in Champaign, Illinois, with his wife, Suzanne. He has three daughters: Linda, who is completing a PhD in accounting at Arizona State University; Ginny, who is a CPA and is employed by Baxter-Travenol; and Martha, who is majoring in finance at the University of Illinois. Professor Fess' hobby is tennis, and he has represented the United States in international tennis competition.

Professor Carl S. Warren is the Arthur Andersen & Co. Alumni Professor of Accounting at the J. M. Tull School of Accounting at the University of Georgia, Athens. Professor Warren received his PhD from Michigan State University in 1973 and has taught accounting at the University of Iowa, Michigan State University, the University of Chicago, and the University of Georgia. He has received teaching awards from three different student organizations at the University of Georgia.

Professor Warren is a CMA and a CPA. He was awarded a Certificate of Distinguished Performance for his scores on the CMA examination and a Certificate of Honorable Mention for his scores on the CPA examination. He is a member of the National Association of Accountants, the American Institute of CPAs, the Georgia Society of CPAs, the American Accounting Association, the Georgia Association of Accounting Educators, and the Financial Executives Institute. Professor Warren has served on numerous professional committees and editorial boards, including a term as editor of the American Accounting Association publication *Auditing: A Journal of Practice and Theory.* He has written five textbooks and numerous articles in such journals as the *Journal of Accountancy,* the *Accounting Review,* the *Journal of Accounting Research,* the *CPA Journal, Corporate Accounting, Cost and Management,* and *Managerial Planning.* Professor Warren is also the Consulting Editor for South-Western Publishing Co.'s accounting series.

Professor Warren resides in Athens, Georgia, with his wife, Sharon, and two children, Stephanie (age 13) and Jeffrey (age 11). Professor Warren's hobbies include coaching Little League Baseball, golf, tennis, and fishing.

NOTE TO STUDENTS

This text was written with the objective of preparing you for your future professional career. Accounting is a stimulating, rewarding field of study. To be effective, professionals in all areas of business, such as finance, production, marketing, personnel, and general management, must have a good understanding of accounting. In addition, men and women whose careers are in nonbusiness areas can use a knowledge of accounting to perform more effectively in society.

As you begin your study of accounting, you may find the following suggestions helpful:

■ Read each chapter objective before you begin studying a chapter.
■ Take a few minutes and scan the chapter to get a flavor of the material before you begin a detailed reading of the chapter.
■ As you read each chapter, you may wish to underline points that you feel are especially important. Also, you should give special attention to key terms which are identified in color when they first appear in the chapter.
■ After reading the text of the chapter, carefully study the Chapter Review, giving special attention to the following items:

Key Points. You should thoroughly understand each of the key points presented in the chapter. If you have difficulty understanding any of the key points, review the section of the chapter where the key point is discussed and illustrated. The key points are organized as major chapter headings that appear sequentially throughout the chapter.

Key Terms. You should be able to define each key term. If you cannot, refer to the page of the chapter where the key term is first presented and discussed. You may also refer to Appendix A, where all of the key terms are listed in alphabetical order and defined.

Self-Examination Questions. Answer each of the self-examination questions and check your answers by referring to Appendix B. The answers appearing in Appendix B explain the correct response.

Illustrative Problem. Study the illustrative problem and its suggested solution. Each illustrative problem applies the concepts and principles discussed in the chapter to a problem situation. If you have difficulty understanding the illustrative problem, refer to the section of the chapter where the applicable concepts and principles are discussed and illustrated.

■ Work all assigned homework. In many cases, the homework is related to specific chapter illustrations, and you may find it helpful to review the relevant chapter sections before you begin a homework assignment.
■ Take notes during class lectures and discussions and give attention to the topics covered by your instructor.
■ In reviewing for examinations, keep in mind those topics that your instructor has emphasized, and review your class notes and the text.
■ If you feel you need additional aid, you may find the Study Guides that accompany this textbook helpful. The Study Guides can be ordered from South-Western Publishing Co. by your college or university bookstore.

CONTENTS IN BRIEF

CONTENTS

**PRACTICE SET 2   SIERRA COMPUTER
      SYSTEMS**

The narrative accompanies the set, which is available both with and without business papers. This set, which may be assigned after the student has completed Chapter 8, pro-

vides practice in accounting for a sole proprietorship using the voucher system.

3   ACCOUNTING PRINCIPLES

PRACTICE SET 3 CUSTOM INTERIORS INC.

The narrative accompanies the set, which is available without business papers. This set provides practice in account-

ing for a corporation that operates a departmentalized business.

PRACTICE SET 4   SUNRISE SOLAR INC.

The narrative accompanies the set, which is available without business papers. This set provides practice in accounting for a manufacturing business that uses a job order cost system.

TEXT OBJECTIVES

- Describe the evolution of accounting.

- Describe the basic structure of the accounting profession.

- Describe and illustrate the basic financial accounting concepts and principles.

- Describe and illustrate accounting systems for service and merchandising enterprises.

- Describe and illustrate accounting concepts and principles for sole proprietorships, partnerships, and corporations.

- Describe and illustrate financial accounting concepts and principles for analyzing business operations.

- Describe and illustrate managerial accounting concepts and principles for planning and controlling decentralized business operations.

- Describe and illustrate accounting systems for manufacturing enterprises.

- Describe and illustrate managerial accounting concepts and principles for planning, control, and decision making.

- Describe and illustrate the accounting concepts and principles for individuals and nonprofit organizations.

INTRODUCTION: EVOLUTION OF ACCOUNTING

Accounting has evolved, as have medicine, law, and most other fields of human activity, in response to the social and economic needs of society. As business and society have become more complex over the years, accounting has developed new concepts and techniques to meet the ever increasing needs for financial information. Without such information, many complex economic developments and social programs might never have been undertaken. This introduction is devoted to a brief résumé of the evolution of accounting.

PRIMITIVE ACCOUNTING

People in all civilizations have maintained various types of records of business activities. The oldest known are clay tablet records of the payment of wages in Babylonia around 3600 B.C. There are numerous evidences of record keeping and systems of accounting control in ancient Egypt and in the Greek city-states. The earliest known English records were compiled at the direction of William the Conqueror in the eleventh century to ascertain the financial resources of the kingdom.

For the most part, early accounting dealt only with limited aspects of the financial operations of private or governmental enterprises. There was no systematic accounting for all transactions of a particular unit, only for specific types or portions of transactions. Complete accounting for an enterprise developed somewhat later in response to the needs of the commercial republics of Italy.

DOUBLE-ENTRY SYSTEM

The evolution of the system of record keeping which came to be called "double entry" was strongly influenced by Venetian merchants. The first known description of the system was published in Italy in 1494. The author, a Franciscan monk by the name of Luca Pacioli, was a mathematician who taught in various universities in Perugia, Naples, Pisa, and Florence. Evidence of the position that Pacioli occupied among the intellectuals of his day was his

1

close friendship with Leonardo da Vinci, with whom he collaborated on a mathematics book. Pacioli did the text and da Vinci the illustrations.

Goethe, the German poet, novelist, scientist, and universal genius, wrote about double entry as follows: "It is one of the most beautiful inventions of the human spirit, and every good businessman should use it in his economic undertakings."[1] Double entry provides for recording both aspects of a transaction in such a manner as to establish an equilibrium. For example, if an individual borrows $1,000 from a bank, the amount of the loan is recorded both as cash of $1,000 and as an obligation to repay $1,000. Either of the $1,000 amounts is balanced by the other $1,000 amount. As the basic principles are developed further in the early chapters of this book, it will become evident that "double entry" provides for the recording of all business transactions in a systematic manner. It also provides for a set of integrated financial statements reporting in monetary terms the amount of (1) the profit (net income) for a single venture or for a specified period, and (2) the properties (assets) owned by the enterprise and the ownership rights (equities) to the properties.

When the resources of a number of people were pooled to finance a single venture, such as a voyage of a merchant ship, the double-entry system provided records and reports of the income of the venture and the equity of the various participants. As single ventures were replaced by more permanent business organizations, the double-entry system was easily adapted to meet their needs. In spite of the tremendous development of business operations since 1494, and the ever increasing complexities of business and governmental organizations, the basic elements of the double-entry system have continued virtually unchanged.

INDUSTRIAL REVOLUTION

The Industrial Revolution, which occurred in England from the mid-eighteenth to the mid-nineteenth century, brought many social and economic changes, notably a change from the handicraft method of producing marketable goods to the factory system. The use of machinery in turning out many identical products gave rise to the need to determine the cost of a large volume of machine-made products instead of the cost of a relatively small number of individually handcrafted products. The specialized field of cost accounting emerged to meet this need for the analysis of various costs and for recording techniques.

In the early days of manufacturing operations, when business enterprises were relatively small and often isolated geographically, competition was frequently not very keen. Cost accounting was primitive and focused primarily

---

[1]Goethe, Johann Wolfgang von, *Samtliche Werke*, edited by Edward von der Hellen (Stuttgart and Berlin: J. G. Cotta, 1902–07), Vol. XVII, p. 37.

on providing management with records and reports on past operations. Most business decisions were made on the basis of this historical financial information combined with intuition or hunches about the potential success of proposed courses of action.

As manufacturing enterprises became larger and more complex and as competition among manufacturers increased, the "scientific management concept" evolved. This concept emphasized a systematic approach to the solution of management problems. Paralleling this trend was the development of more sophisticated cost accounting concepts to supply management with analytical techniques for measuring the efficiency of current operations and in planning for future operations. This trend was accelerated in the twentieth century by the advent of the electronic computer with its capacity for manipulating large masses of data and its ability to determine the potential effect of alternative courses of action.

CORPORATE ORGANIZATION

The expanded business operations initiated by the Industrial Revolution required increasingly large amounts of money to build factories and purchase machinery. This need for large amounts of capital resulted in the development of the corporate form of organization, which was first legally established in England in 1845. The Industrial Revolution spread rapidly to the United States, which became one of the world's leading industrial nations shortly after the Civil War. The accumulation of large amounts of capital was essential for establishment of new businesses in industries such as manufacturing, transportation, mining, electric power, and communications. In the United States, as in England, the corporation was the form of organization that facilitated the accumulation of the substantial amounts of capital needed.

Almost all large American business enterprises, and many small ones, are organized as corporations largely because ownership is evidenced by readily transferable shares of stock. The shareholders of a corporation control the management of corporate affairs only indirectly. They elect a board of directors, which establishes general policies and selects officers who actively manage the corporation. The development of a class of owners far removed from active participation in the management of the business created an additional dimension for accounting. Accounting information was needed not only by management in directing the affairs of the corporation but also by the shareholders, who required periodic financial statements in order to appraise management's performance.

As corporations became larger, an increasing number of individuals and institutions looked to accountants to provide economic information about these enterprises. Prospective shareholders and creditors sought information about a corporation's financial status and its prospects for the future. Government agencies required financial information for purposes of taxation and regulation. Employees, union representatives, and customers demanded information upon which to judge the stability and profitability of corporate enterprises. Thus accounting began to expand its function of meeting the needs of a relatively few owners to a public role of meeting the needs of a variety of interested parties.

PUBLIC ACCOUNTING

The development of the corporation also created a new social need — the need for an independent audit to provide some assurance that management's financial representations were reliable. This audit function, often referred to as the "attest function," was chiefly responsible for the creation and growth of the public accounting profession. Unlike private accountants, public accountants are independent of the enterprises for which they perform services.

Recognizing the need for accounting services of professional caliber, all of the states provide for the licensing of certified public accountants (CPAs). In 1944, fifty years after the enactment of the first CPA law, there were approximately 25,000 CPAs in the United States. During the next four decades the number increased tenfold, and currently the number exceeds 250,000.

Auditing is still a major service offered by CPAs, but presently they also devote much of their time to assisting their clients with problems related to planning, controlling, and decision making. Such services, known as management advisory services, have increased in volume over the years until today they comprise a significant part of the practice of most public accounting firms.

INCOME TAX

Enactment of the federal income tax law in 1913 resulted in a tremendous stimulus to accounting activity. All business enterprises organized as corporations or partnerships, as well as many individuals, were required to maintain sufficient records to enable them to file accurate tax returns. Since that time the income tax laws and regulations have become increasingly complex, many so-called "loopholes" have been closed, and the impact of the tax liability has generally tended to increase. As a consequence businesses have depended upon both private and public accountants for advice on legal methods of tax minimization, for preparing tax returns, and for representing them in tax disputes with governmental agencies.

It should also be noted that accounting has influenced the development of income tax law to a great degree. Had not accounting progressed to a point where periodic net income could be determined, the enactment and enforcement of any tax law undoubtedly would have been extremely difficult, if not impossible.

GOVERNMENT INFLUENCE

Over the years government at various levels has intervened to an increasing extent in economic and social matters affecting ever greater numbers of people. Accounting has played an important role by providing the financial information needed to achieve the desired goals.

As the number and size of corporate enterprises grew and an ever increasing number of shares of stock were traded in the market place, laws regulating the activities of stock exchanges, stockbrokers, and investment companies were enacted for the protection of investors. These regulations involve accounting requirements. To protect the public from excessive charges by railroads and other monopolies, commissions were established to limit their rates to levels yielding net income considered to be a "fair return" on invested capital. This rate-making process required extensive accounting information. Regulated banks and savings and loan associations also had to meet record-keeping and reporting requirements and permit periodic examination of their records by governmental agencies. As labor unions became larger and more powerful, regulatory laws were enacted requiring them to submit periodic financial reports. With the enactment of social security and medicare legislation came record-keeping and reporting requirements for almost all businesses and many individuals.

As the federal government exercised increasing control over economic activities, accounting information became more essential as a basis for formulating legislation. One of the areas in which the government has influenced economic and social behavior has been through the income tax. For example, contributions to charitable organizations have been encouraged by permitting their deduction in determining taxable income. Controls over wages and prices have also been enacted at various times in attempts to control the economy by reducing the rate of inflation. An enormous volume of accounting data must be reported, summarized, and studied before proceeding with the evaluation of various governmental proposals such as the foregoing.

ACCOUNTING'S CAPACITY FOR SERVICE

Accounting is capable of supplying financial information that is essential for the efficient operation and for the evaluation of performance of any economic unit in society. Changes in the environment in which such organizations operate will inevitably be accompanied by alterations in accounting concepts and techniques. Although long-range predictions as to environmental changes are risky and of doubtful value, there are three areas that promise to receive increased attention in the immediate future— computerized accounting systems, international accounting, and socioeconomic accounting.

Computerized Accounting Systems

Since the electronic computer was first used to process business data in the middle of the twentieth century, it has played an ever increasing role in the design of accounting systems and the processing of economic data. It has generally enabled interested users of accounting information to receive relevant economic data on a more timely basis at a lower cost.

The integration of the electronic computer into accounting systems has created both opportunities and challenges for accountants. The computer provides opportunities for accountants to analyze efficiently a greater quantity of economic data for reporting to users. As the use of computers in business continues to accelerate, there will be an increasing demand for accountants to aid in the analysis, design, and implementation of these systems. This responsibility, in turn, will create ever greater challenges for accountants to obtain a complete understanding of business operations and the principles of designing systems that will gather all accurate, relevant data on a timely basis.

International Accounting

The rapid growth of multinational firms in recent years has had a significant impact on accounting because of the different environments existing in the various countries in which such firms operate. Currently, a major problem is the need to develop more uniform accounting standards among countries. Working toward this end are such international organizations as the International Accounting Standards Committee and the International Federation of Accountants.

Socioeconomic Accounting

The term socioeconomic accounting refers to the measurement and communication of information about the impact of various organizations on society. Three major areas of social measurement can be identified. First, at the societal level the interest is on the total impact of all institutions on matters that affect the quality of life. The second area is concerned with the programs undertaken by the government and socially oriented not-for-profit organizations to accomplish specific social objectives. The third area, sometimes referred to as corporate social responsibility, focuses on the public interest in corporate social performance in such areas as reduction of water and air pollution, conservation of natural resources, improvement in quality of product and customer service, and employment practices regarding minority groups and females. The concept of social measurement is relatively simple as a theory, but much additional study and research will be needed before measurement can be expressed in terms of monetary costs and benefits.

Part 1

BASIC STRUCTURE
OF ACCOUNTING

Chapter 1

ACCOUNTING PRINCIPLES AND PRACTICES

Chapter Objectives:

- Describe accounting as an information system.

- Describe the users of accounting information.

- Describe the profession of accounting and its specialized fields.

- Explain what is meant by the business entity concept and the cost principle.

- Describe a business transaction.

- Identify the accounting equation and its basic elements.

- Describe and illustrate how all business transactions can be stated in terms of the resulting changes in the three basic elements of the accounting equation.

- Identify and describe the financial statements of a sole proprietorship and a corporation.

Accounting plays an important role in our economic and social system. Sound decisions made by individuals, businesses, governments, and other entities are essential for the efficient distribution and use of the nation's scarce resources. To make such decisions, these groups must have reliable information provided by the accounting system. The objective of accounting, therefore, is to record, summarize, report, and interpret economic data for use by many groups within our economic and social system.

ACCOUNTING AS AN INFORMATION SYSTEM

Accounting[1] is often called the "language of business." This language can be viewed as an information system that provides essential information about the financial activities of an entity to various individuals or groups for their use in making informed judgments and decisions. As such, accounting information is composed principally of financial data about business transactions, expressed in terms of money. The recording of transaction data may take various forms, such as pen or pencil markings made by hand, printing by mechanical and electronic devices, or magnetic impressions on tape or disks.

The mere records of transactions are of little use in making informed judgments and decisions. The recorded data must be sorted and summarized and then presented in significant reports. The usefulness of reports is often improved by various kinds of percentage and trend analyses.

USERS OF ACCOUNTING INFORMATION

Accounting provides the techniques for gathering of economic data and the language for communicating these data to different individuals and institutions. Investors in a business enterprise need information about its financial status and its future prospects. Bankers and suppliers appraise the financial soundness of a business organization and assess the risks involved before

---

[1]A glossary of terms appears in Appendix A. The terms included in the glossary are printed in color the first time they appear in the text.

making loans or granting credit. Government agencies are concerned with the financial activities of business organizations for purposes of taxation and regulation. Employees and their union representatives are also vitally interested in the stability and the profitability of the organization that hires them.

The individuals who depend upon and make the most use of accounting are those charged with the responsibility for directing the operations of enterprises. They are often referred to collectively as "management." Many types of data may be needed by management. For example, in the conduct of day-to-day operations, management relies upon accounting to provide the amount owed to each creditor and by each customer and the date each payment is due. Managers also rely upon accounting information to assist them in evaluating current operations and in planning future operations. For example, comparisons of past performance with planned objectives may reveal the means of accelerating favorable trends and reducing those that are unfavorable.

The process of using accounting to provide information to users is illustrated in the following diagram. First, user groups are identified and their information needs determined. These needs determine which economic data are gathered and processed by the accounting system. Finally, the accounting

ACCOUNTING
AS A
PROVIDER
OF INFOR-
MATION TO
USERS

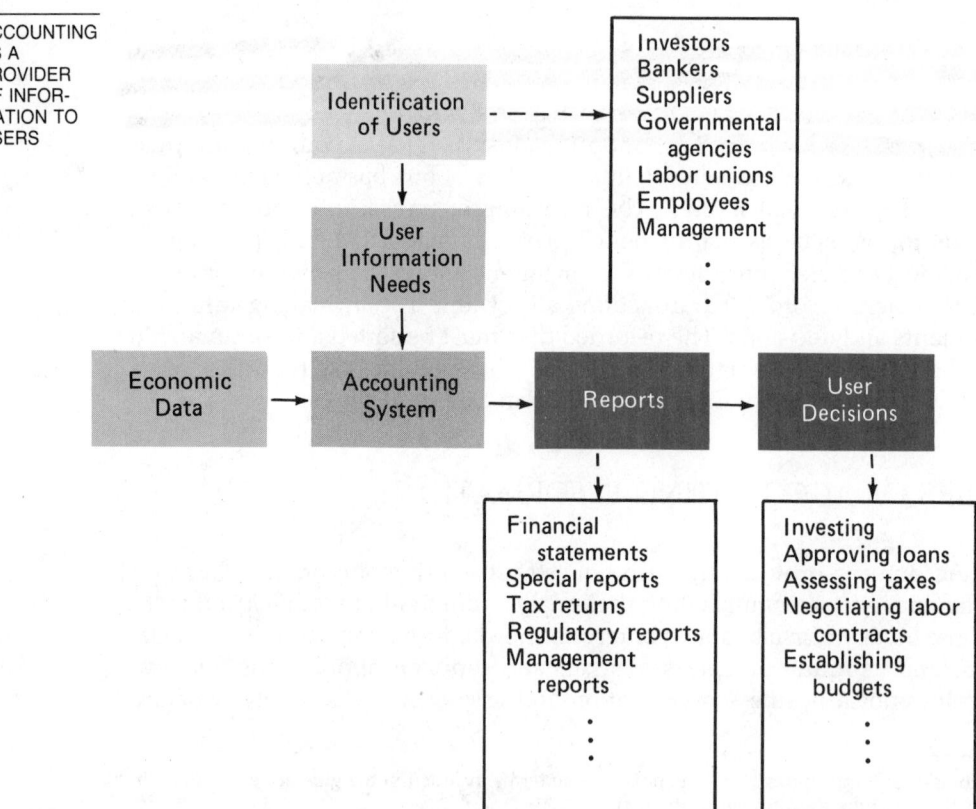

system generates reports that communicate essential information to users. For example, investors need information on the financial condition and results of operations of an enterprise to assess the profitability and riskiness of their investments in the enterprise. The accounting system satisfies these needs by recording essential information and periodically summarizing this information in financial reports. Although the information for one category of users may differ markedly from that needed by other users, accounting can provide each user group with economic information to assist them in making decisions regarding future actions.

RELATIONSHIP OF ACCOUNTING TO OTHER FIELDS

Individuals engaged in such areas of business as finance, production, marketing, personnel, and general management need not be expert accountants, but they are more effective if they have a good understanding of accounting principles. Everyone engaged in business activity, from the youngest employee to the manager and owner, comes into contact with accounting. The higher the level of authority and responsibility, the greater is the need for an understanding of accounting concepts and terminology.

A study of U.S. corporations revealed that finance and accounting was the most common background of chief executive officers. Interviews with corporate executives produced the following comments:[2]

"Today, it's vital that the chief executive officer know the corporation and ... have an understanding of accounting."

"...my training in accounting and auditing practice has been extremely valuable to me throughout."

"A knowledge of accounting carries with it an understanding of the establishment and the maintenance of sound financial controls—an area which is absolutely essential to a chief executive officer."

"I try to have my entire staff understand the financial function and how to use financial data."

The importance of understanding accounting is not limited to the business world. Many employees with specialized training in nonbusiness areas also make use of accounting data and need to understand accounting principles and terminology. For example, an engineer responsible for selecting the most desirable solution to a technical manufacturing problem may consider cost accounting data to be the deciding factor. Lawyers use accounting data in tax cases and in lawsuits involving property ownership and damages from

---

[2]John R. Linden, "Rising Corporate Stars: The Accountant as Chief Executive Officer," *The Journal of Accountancy*, (September, 1978), pp. 64–71.

breach of contract. Governmental agencies rely on accounting data in evaluating the efficiency of government operations and for appraising the feasibility of proposed taxation and spending programs. Finally, every adult engages in business transactions and must necessarily be concerned with the financial aspects of life. Accounting plays an important role in modern society and, broadly speaking, all citizens are affected by accounting in some way.

OPPORTUNITIES IN ACCOUNTING

Accounting can be characterized as a profession that has experienced rapid development during the current century. This has been accompanied by an expansion of the career opportunities in accounting and an increasing number of professionally trained accountants. Among the factors contributing to this growth have been the increase in number, size, and complexity of business corporations; the frequent changes in the tax laws; and other governmental restrictions on business operations.

The following table indicates the projected growth of the profession of accountancy relative to the projected growth of the legal and medical professions:

Profession	Projected Rate of Increase 1982–1995
Accountancy	40.2%
Legal	34.3
Medical	34.0

Source: U. S. Department of Labor, Bureau of Labor Statistics, *Occupational Projections and Training Data: 1984 Edition* (Washington: U. S. Government Printing Office, May, 1984).

During the period 1960–1984, the profession of accountancy grew to approximately double its size in 1960. As the complexity of the business and social environment continues to increase, employment and advancement opportunities in the profession of accountancy are expected to continue to grow and expand.

Profession of Accountancy

Accountancy is a profession whose members may be viewed as engaged in either (1) private accounting or (2) public accounting. Accountants employed by a particular business firm or not-for-profit organization, perhaps as chief accountant, controller, or financial vice-president, are said to be engaged in **private accounting**. Accountants who render accounting services on a fee basis, and staff accountants employed by them, are said to be engaged in **public accounting**.

GROWTH TRENDS IN THE ACCOUNTING PROFESSION

The accounting profession has been growing at a much faster rate than the population of the United States, according to occupational surveys issued by the Bureau of the Census, which count all employed accountants and auditors regardless of the nature of their employer. These figures, which are summarized in the following chart, include accountants in public practice, in industry, and in government, but exclude bookkeepers and other semiprofessionals.

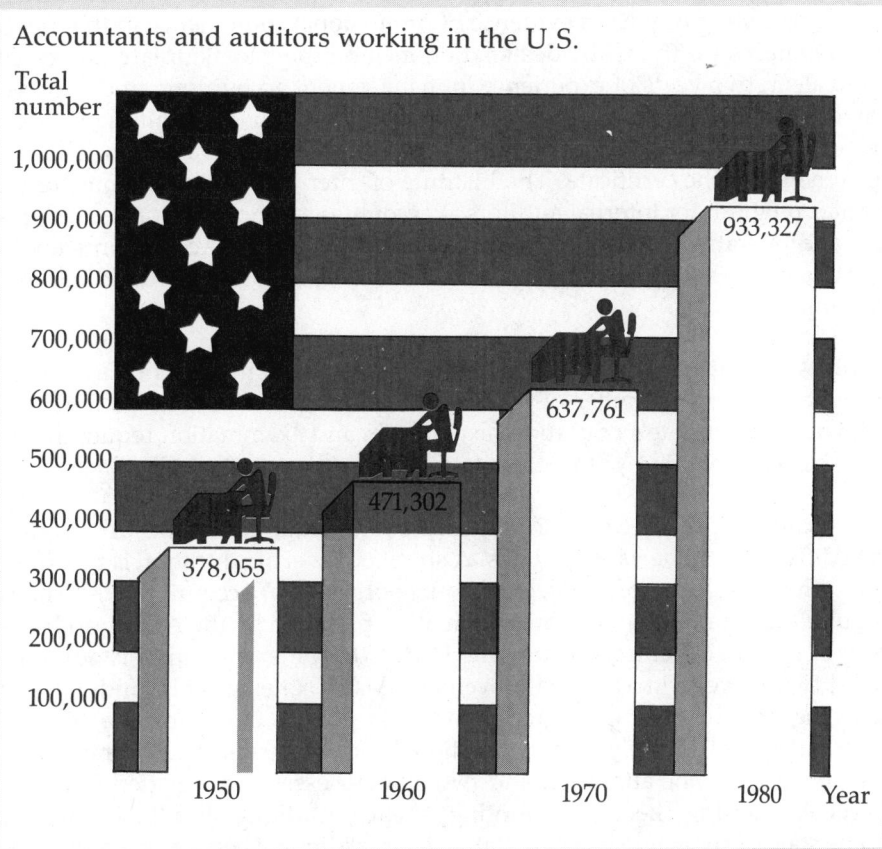

Accountants and auditors working in the U.S.

378,055 — 1950
471,302 — 1960
637,761 — 1970
933,327 — 1980

Source: "Growth Trends in the Accounting Profession," *Journal of Accountancy* (May, 1985), pp. 139–144.

Both private and public accounting have long been recognized as excellent training for top managerial responsibilities. Many executive positions in government and in industry are held by men and women with education and experience in accounting.

Private Accounting. The scope of activities and responsibilities of private accountants varies widely. They are frequently referred to as administrative or managerial accountants, or, if they are employed by a manufacturing concern, as industrial accountants. Various governmental units and other not-for-profit organizations also employ accountants.

The Institute of Certified Management Accounting, which is an affiliate of the National Association of Accountants, grants the certificate in management accounting (CMA) as evidence of professional competence in that field. Requirements for the CMA designation include the baccalaureate degree or equivalent, two years of experience in management accounting, and successful completion of examinations occupying two and one-half days. Participation in a program of continuing professional education is also required for renewal of the certificate. The Institute of Internal Auditors administers a similar program for internal auditors—accountants who review the accounting and operating procedures prescribed by their firms. Accountants qualifying under this program are entitled to use the designation Certified Internal Auditor (CIA).

Public Accounting. In public accounting, an accountant may practice as an individual or as a member of a public accounting firm. Public accountants who have met a state's education, experience, and examination requirements may become certified public accountants, commonly called **CPAs**.

Qualifications of CPAs. The qualifications required for the CPA certificate differ among the various states. A specified level of education is required, often the completion of a collegiate course of study in accounting. All states require that a candidate pass an examination prepared by the **American Institute of Certified Public Accountants (AICPA)**. The examination is administered twice a year, in May and November. Many states permit candidates to take the examination upon graduation from college or during the term in which they will complete the educational requirements. The examination, which occupies one afternoon and two all-day sessions, is divided into four parts: Accounting Theory, Accounting Practice, Auditing, and Business Law. Some states also require an examination in an additional subject, such as Rules of Professional Conduct. Most states do not permit successful candidates to practice as independent CPAs until they have had from one to three years' experience in public accounting or in employment considered equivalent.

In recent years a majority of the states have enacted laws requiring public practitioners to participate in a program of continuing professional education or forfeit their right to continue in public practice. According to the statutes of one of the states, the continuing education must be a "formal program of learning which contributes directly to the professional competence of an individual after he or she has been licensed to practice public accounting." The states differ as to some of the details of the requirement, such as the number of hours of formal education required for renewal of the permit to practice. The rules adopted by a number of State Boards of Accountancy require forty hours per year (a fifty-minute class period counts as one hour).

Details regarding the requirements for practice as a CPA in any particular state can be obtained from the respective State Board of Accountancy.

Professional Ethics for CPAs. CPAs have a duty not only to their clients but to their colleagues and the public to perform services competently and with integrity. However, many clients and much of the public do not have the capability of evaluating a CPA's performance. Therefore, standards of conduct have been established to guide CPAs in the conduct of their practices. These standards, called codes of professional ethics, have been established by professional organizations of CPAs, such as the AICPA and state societies of CPAs, and by regulatory agencies, such as State Boards of Accountancy and the Securities and Exchange Commission.

The purpose of codes of professional ethics is to instill confidence in the quality of services rendered by the profession of public accounting. Such codes establish minimum standards of acceptable conduct, which often extend beyond behavior which is otherwise acceptable under the law. For example, under the current AICPA code of professional ethics, CPAs are prohibited from practicing under a firm name that includes a fictitious name.

A CPA who violates the code of ethics is subject to disciplinary proceedings. The AICPA and state societies of CPAs have authority to revoke a CPA's membership in their organizations. If the violation also involves a regulatory agency, such as a State Board of Accountancy or the Securities and Exchange Commission, the CPA's ability to practice within the agency's jurisdiction may be revoked or otherwise limited. The combination of professional organization and regulatory agency sanctions guards against unethical behavior by the public accounting profession.

To meet the public's expectations of the role and responsibilities of the CPA, codes of professional ethics change as society changes. However, ethical conduct is more than simply conforming to written standards of professional behavior. In a true sense, ethical conduct requires a personal commitment to honorable behavior. This thought was best expressed by Marcus Aurelius, who said, "A man should *be* upright; not be *kept* upright."[3]

Specialized Accounting Fields

As in many other areas of human activity during the twentieth century, a number of specialized fields in accounting have evolved as a result of rapid

---

[3]*The Code of Professional Ethics,* American Institute of Certified Public Accountants (New York, 1986).

technological advances and accelerated economic growth. The most important accounting fields are described briefly in the following paragraphs.

Financial accounting is concerned with the recording of transactions for a business enterprise or other economic unit and the periodic preparation of various reports from such records. The reports, which may be for general purposes or for a special purpose, provide useful information for managers, owners, creditors, governmental agencies, and the general public. Of particular importance to financial accountants are the rules of accounting, termed **generally accepted accounting principles (GAAP)**. Corporate enterprises must employ such principles in preparing their annual reports on profitability and financial status for their stockholders and the investing public. Comparability of financial reports is essential if the nation's resources are to be divided among business organizations in a socially desirable manner.

Auditing is a field of activity involving an independent review of the accounting records. In conducting an audit, public accountants examine the records supporting the financial reports of an enterprise and give an opinion regarding their fairness and reliability. An important element of "fairness and reliability" is adherence to generally accepted accounting principles. In addition to retaining public accountants for a periodic audit, many corporations have their own permanent staff of internal auditors. Their principal responsibility is to determine if the various operating divisions are following management's policies and procedures.

Cost accounting emphasizes the determination and the control of costs. It is concerned primarily with the costs of manufacturing processes and of manufactured products. In addition, one of the most important duties of the cost accountant is to gather and explain cost data, both actual and prospective. Management uses these data in controlling current operations and in planning for the future.

Managerial accounting uses both historical and estimated data in assisting management in daily operations and in planning future operations. It deals with specific problems that confront enterprise managers at various organizational levels. The managerial accountant is frequently concerned with identifying alternative courses of action and then helping to select the best one. For example, the accountant may assist the company treasurer in preparing plans for future financing, or may develop data for use by the sales manager in determining the selling price to be placed on a new product. In recent years, public accountants have realized that their training and experience uniquely qualify them to advise management personnel on policies and administration. This rapidly growing field of specialization by CPAs is frequently called *management advisory services* or *administrative services*.

Tax accounting encompasses the preparation of tax returns and the consideration of the tax consequences of proposed business transactions or alternative courses of action. Accountants specializing in this field, particularly in the area of tax planning, must be familiar with the tax statutes affecting their employer or clients and also must keep up to date on administrative regulations and court decisions on tax cases.

Accounting systems is the special field concerned with the design and implementation of procedures for the accumulation and reporting of financial data. The systems accountant must devise appropriate "checks and balances" to safeguard business assets and provide for information flow that will be efficient and helpful to management. Familiarity with the uses and relative merits of various types of data processing equipment is also essential.

Budgetary accounting presents the plan of financial operations for a period and, through records and summaries, provides comparisons of actual operations with the predetermined plan. A combination of planning and controlling future operations, it is sometimes considered to be a part of managerial accounting.

International accounting is concerned with the special problems associated with the international trade of multinational business organizations. Accountants specializing in this area must be familiar with the influences that custom, law, and taxation of various countries bring to bear on international operations and accounting principles.

Not-for-profit accounting specializes in recording and reporting the transactions of various governmental units and other not-for-profit organizations such as churches, charities, and educational institutions. An essential element is an accounting system that will insure strict adherence on the part of management to restrictions and other requirements imposed by law, by other institutions, or by individual donors.

Social accounting is the newest field of accounting and is the most difficult to describe in a few words. There have been increasing demands on the profession for measurement of social costs and benefits which have previously been considered to be unmeasurable. One of the engagements in this field involved the measurement of traffic patterns in a densely populated section of the nation. This effort was part of a government study to determine the best use of transportation funds, not only in terms of facilitating trade but also of assuring a good environment for the area's residents. Other innovative engagements have dealt with the best use of welfare funds in a large city, with the public use of state parks, with wildlife in state game preserves, and with statewide water and air pollution.

Accounting instruction, as a field of specialization, requires no explanation. However, in addition to teaching, accounting professors often engage in research, auditing, tax accounting, or other areas of accounting on a part-time or consulting basis.

There is some overlapping among the various fields, and leaders in any particular field are likely to be well versed in related areas. There is also a considerable degree of specialization within a particular field. For example, in auditing one may become an expert in a single type of business enterprise such as department stores or public utilities. In tax accounting one may become a specialist in oil and gas producing companies. In systems one may become an expert in electronic data processing equipment.

BOOKKEEPING AND ACCOUNTING

There is some confusion over the difference between "bookkeeping" and "accounting." This is partly due to the fact that the two are related.

Bookkeeping is the recording of business data in a prescribed manner. A bookkeeper may be responsible for keeping all of the records of a business or of only a small segment, such as the records of amounts owed by customers of a department store. Much of the work of the bookkeeper is clerical in nature and is increasingly being handled by computers.

Accounting is primarily concerned with the design of the system of records, the preparation of reports based on the recorded data, and the interpretation of the reports. Accountants often direct and review the work of bookkeepers. The larger the firm, the greater is the number of levels of responsibility and authority. The work of accountants at the beginning levels may possibly include some bookkeeping. In any event, the accountant must have a much higher level of knowledge, conceptual understanding, and analytical skill than is required of the bookkeeper.

PRINCIPLES AND PRACTICE

In accounting, as in the physical and biological sciences, experimentation and change are never-ending. Capable scholars devote their lives and their intellectual energies to the development of accounting principles. Experienced professional accountants contribute their best thinking to the solution of problems continually confronting their clients or employers. Professional accounting associations periodically issue pronouncements on accounting principles. Authoritative accounting pronouncements are issued by such bodies as the Financial Accounting Standards Board (FASB). It is from research, accepted accounting practices, and pronouncements of professional and authoritative bodies that generally accepted accounting principles evolve to form the underlying basis for accounting practice.

This book is devoted primarily to explanations of accounting principles and, to a lesser extent, to demonstrations of related practices or procedures. It is only through this emphasis on the "why" of accounting as well as on the "how" that the full significance of accounting can be learned.

BUSINESS ENTITY CONCEPT

The business entity concept is based on the applicability of accounting to individual economic units in society. These individual economic units include all business enterprises organized for profit; numerous governmental units, such as states, cities, and school districts; other not-for-profit units, such as charities, churches, hospitals, and social clubs; and individual persons and family units. The basic economic data for a unit must first be recorded, followed by analysis and summarization, and finally by periodic reporting. Thus, accounting applies to each separate economic unit.

It is possible, of course, to combine the data for similar economic units to obtain an overall view. For example, accounting data accumulated by each of the airline companies may be assembled and summarized to provide financial information about the entire industry. Similarly, reports on gross national product (GNP) are developed from the accounting records or reports of many separate economic units.

This textbook is concerned primarily with the accounting principles and techniques applicable to profit-making businesses. Such businesses are customarily organized as sole proprietorships, partnerships, or corporations. A **sole proprietorship** is owned by one individual. A **partnership** is owned by two or more individuals in accordance with a contractual arrangement. A **corporation**, organized in accordance with state or federal statutes, is a separate legal entity in which ownership is divided into shares of stock. Although the sole proprietorship is the most common business form, the corporation is the dominant form in terms of dollars of business activity, as indicated in the following charts:

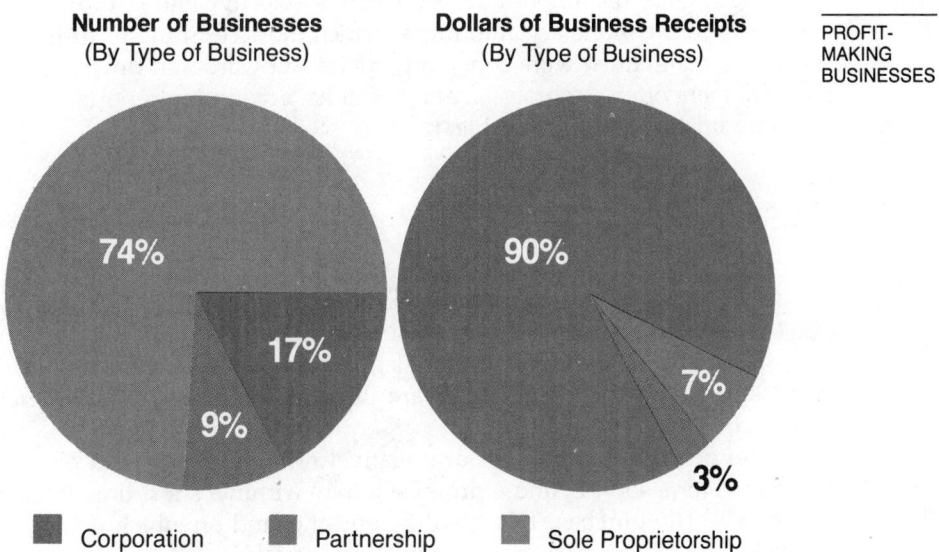

Number of Businesses
(By Type of Business)

Dollars of Business Receipts
(By Type of Business)

PROFIT-
MAKING
BUSINESSES

74%   17%   9%

90%   7%   3%

■ Corporation   ■ Partnership   ■ Sole Proprietorship

SOURCE: U.S. Bureau of the Census, *Statistical Abstract of the United States: 1985* (105th edition; Washington: U.S. Government Printing Office, 1984).

THE COST PRINCIPLE

The records of properties and services purchased by a business are maintained in accordance with the **cost principle**, which requires that the monetary record be in terms of *cost*. For example, if a building is purchased at a cost of $150,000, that is the amount used in the buyer's accounting record. The seller may have been asking $170,000 for the building up to the time of the sale; the buyer may have initially offered $130,000 for it; the building may have been assessed at $125,000 for property tax purposes and insured for $135,000; and the buyer may have received an offer of $175,000 for the building the day after it was acquired. These latter amounts have no effect on the accounting records because they do not originate from an exchange. The exchange price, or cost, of $150,000 determines the monetary amount used in the records for the building.

Continuing the illustration, the $175,000 offer received by the buyer is an indication that the building was a bargain purchase at $150,000. To use $175,000 in the accounting records, however, would give recognition to an illusory or unrealized profit. If, after purchasing the building, the buyer should accept the offer and sell the building for $175,000, a profit of $25,000 would be realized, and the new owner would use $175,000 as the cost of the building.

The determination of costs incurred and revenues earned is fundamental to accounting. In exchanges between buyer and seller, both attempt to get the best price. Only the amount agreed upon is objective enough for accounting purposes. If the monetary amounts at which the accounting records for properties are maintained were constantly revised upward and downward on the basis of mere offers, appraisals, and opinions, accounting reports would soon become unstable and unreliable.

BUSINESS TRANSACTIONS

A **business transaction** is the occurrence of an event or of a condition that must be recorded. For example, the payment of a monthly telephone bill of $68, the purchase of $1,750 of merchandise on credit, and the acquisition of land and a building for $210,000 are illustrative of the variety of business transactions.

The first two transactions are relatively simple: a payment of money in exchange for a service, and a promise to pay within a short time in exchange for goods. The purchase of a building and the land on which it is situated is usually a more complex transaction. The total price agreed upon must be allocated between the land and the building, and the agreement usually provides for spreading the payment of a large part of the price over a period of years and for the payment of interest on the unpaid balance.

A particular business transaction may lead to an event or a condition that results in another transaction. For example, the purchase of merchandise on credit will be followed by payment to the creditor, which is another transaction. Each time a portion of the merchandise is sold, another transaction occurs. Similarly, partial payments for the land and the building are additional transactions, as are periodic payments of interest on the debt. Each of these events must be recorded.

The fact that the life of the building is limited must also be shown in the records. The wearing-out of the building is not an exchange of goods or services between the business and an outsider, but it is nevertheless a significant condition that must be recorded. Transactions of this type, as well as others that are not directly related to outsiders, are sometimes referred to as **internal transactions**.

ASSETS, LIABILITIES, AND OWNER'S EQUITY

The properties owned by a business enterprise are referred to as **assets** and the rights or claims to the properties are referred to as **equities**. If the assets owned by a business amount to $100,000, the equities in the assets must also amount to $100,000. The relationship between the two may be stated in the form of an equation, as follows:

$$\text{Assets} = \text{Equities}$$

Equities may be subdivided into two principal types: the rights of creditors and the rights of owners. The rights of creditors represent *debts* of the business and are called **liabilities**. The rights of the owner or owners are called **owner's equity**. Expansion of the equation to give recognition to the two basic types of equities yields the following, which is known as the **accounting equation**:

$$\text{Assets} = \text{Liabilities} + \text{Owner's Equity}$$

It is customary to place "Liabilities" before "Owner's Equity" in the accounting equation because creditors have preferential rights to the assets. The residual claim of the owner or owners is sometimes given greater emphasis by transposing liabilities to the other side of the equation, yielding:

$$\text{Assets} - \text{Liabilities} = \text{Owner's Equity}$$

TRANSACTIONS AND THE ACCOUNTING EQUATION

All business transactions, from the simplest to the most complex, can be stated in terms of the resulting change in the three basic elements of the accounting equation. The effect of these changes on the accounting equation can be demonstrated by studying some typical transactions. As the basis of the illustration, assume that Jerry Miles establishes a sole proprietorship to be known as Miles Taxi. Each transaction or group of similar transactions during the first month of operations is described, followed by an illustration of its effect on the accounting equation.

Transaction (a)

Miles' first transaction is to deposit $10,000 in a bank account in the name of Miles Taxi. The effect of this transaction is to increase the asset (cash), on the left side of the equation, by $10,000 and to increase the owner's equity, on the other side of the equation, by the same amount. As shown in the following illustration of this transaction's effect on Miles Taxi's accounting equation, the equity of the owner is often referred to by using the owner's name and "Capital," such as "Jerry Miles, Capital."

Assets		Owner's Equity	
Cash	=	**Jerry Miles, Capital**	
(a) 10,000		10,000	Investment

It should be noted that the equation relates only to the business enterprise. Miles' personal assets, such as his home and his personal bank account, and his personal liabilities are excluded from consideration. The business is treated as a separate entity, with cash of $10,000 and owner's equity of $10,000.

Transaction (b)

Miles' next transaction is to purchase land as a future building site, for which $7,500 in cash is paid. This transaction changes the composition of the assets but does not change the total amount. The items in the equation prior to this transaction, the effects of the transaction, and the new balances after the transaction are as follows:

	Assets			Owner's Equity
	Cash	+	**Land**	**Jerry Miles, Capital**
Bal.	10,000			10,000
(b)	−7,500		+7,500	=
Bal.	2,500		7,500	10,000

liabilities = debts

Miles' current plans are to lease automobiles and other equipment and storage facilities from Ross Bus Company for several months until he can arrange financing for the purchase of automobiles and other equipment and for the construction of storage facilities.

Transaction (c)

During the month Miles purchases $850 of gasoline, oil, and other supplies from various suppliers, agreeing to pay in the near future. This type of transaction is called a purchase *on account* and the liability created is termed an **account payable**. Consumable goods purchased, such as supplies, are considered to be **prepaid expenses**, or assets.

In actual practice, each purchase would be treated as a separate transaction. In this illustration, however, the purchases are treated as a group. The effect is to increase assets and liabilities by $850, as follows:

	Assets				Liabilities	+	Owner's Equity
	Cash	+ Supplies	+ Land		Accounts Payable	+	Jerry Miles, Capital
Bal.	2,500		7,500				10,000
(c)		+850			+850		
Bal.	2,500	+850	7,500		+850		10,000

Transaction (d)

During the month $400 is paid to creditors on account, thereby reducing both assets and liabilities. The effect on the equation is as follows:

	Assets				Liabilities	+	Owner's Equity
	Cash	+ Supplies	+ Land		Accounts Payable	+	Jerry Miles, Capital
Bal.	2,500	850	7,500		850		10,000
(d)	−400				−400		
Bal.	2,100	850	7,500		450		10,000

Transaction (e)

In general, the amount charged to customers for goods or services sold to them is called **revenue.** Other terms may be used for certain kinds of revenue, such as *sales* for the sale of merchandise or business services, *fees earned* for charges by a physician to patients, *rent earned* for the use of real estate or other property, and *fares earned* for Miles Taxi.

During the first month of operations, Miles Taxi earned fares of $4,500, receiving the amount in cash. The total effect of these transactions is to increase cash by $4,500 and to increase owner's equity by the same amount. In terms of the accounting equation, the effect of the receipt of cash for services performed is as follows:

	Assets				Liabilities +	Owner's Equity	
	Cash	+ Supplies	+ Land		Accounts Payable	+	Jerry Miles, Capital
Bal.	2,100	850	7,500		450		10,000
(e)	+4,500						+4,500 Fares earned
Bal.	6,600	850	7,500		450		14,500

Instead of requiring the payment of cash at the time goods or services are sold, a business may make sales *on account*, allowing the customer to pay later. In such cases the firm acquires an **account receivable**, which is a claim against the customer. An account receivable is as much an asset as cash, and the revenue is realized in exactly the same manner as if cash had been immediately received. At a later date, when the money is collected, there is only an exchange of one asset for another, with cash increasing and accounts receivable decreasing.

Transaction (f)

In a broad sense, the amount of assets consumed or services used in the process of earning revenue is called **expense**. Expenses would include supplies used, wages of employees, and other assets and services used in operating the business. For Miles Taxi, various business expenses incurred and paid during the month were as follows: wages, $1,125; rent, $850; utilities, $150; miscellaneous, $75. The effect of this group of transactions is to reduce cash and to reduce owner's equity, as follows:

	Assets				Liabilities +	Owner's Equity
	Cash	+ Supplies	+ Land		Accounts Payable +	Jerry Miles, Capital
Bal.	6,600	850	7,500		450	14,500
(f)	−2,200			=		−1,125 Wages exp.
						− 850 Rent expense
						− 150 Utilities exp.
						− 75 Misc. expense
Bal.	4,400	850	7,500		450	12,300

Transaction (g)

At the end of the month it is determined that the cost of the supplies on hand is $250, the remainder ($850 − $250) having been used in the operations of the business. This reduction of $600 in supplies and owner's equity may be shown as follows:

	Assets				Liabilities +	Owner's Equity
	Cash	+ Supplies	+ Land		Accounts Payable +	Jerry Miles, Capital
Bal.	4,400	850	7,500		450	12,300
(g)		−600		=		−600 Supplies exp.
Bal.	4,400	250	7,500		450	11,700

Transaction (h)

At the end of the month Miles withdraws from the business $1,000 in cash for his personal use. This transaction, which reduces cash and reduces owner's equity, is the exact opposite of an investment in the business by the owner. It is not a business expense, but a withdrawal of a portion of the owner's equity. The effect of the $1,000 withdrawal is as follows:

	Assets			=	Liabilities +	Owner's Equity
	Cash +	Supplies +	Land		Accounts Payable +	Jerry Miles, Capital
Bal.	4,400	250	7,500		450	11,700
(h)	−1,000					−1,000 Withdrawal
Bal.	3,400	250	7,500		450	10,700

Summary

The business transactions of Miles Taxi are summarized in tabular form, as follows. The transactions are identified by letter, and the balance of each item is shown after each transaction.

	Assets			=	Liabilities +	Owner's Equity
	Cash +	Supplies +	Land	=	Accounts Payable +	Jerry Miles, Capital
(a)	+10,000					+10,000 Investment
(b)	− 7,500		+7,500			
	2,500		7,500			10,000
(c)		+850			+850	
	2,500	850	7,500		850	10,000
(d)	− 400				−400	
	2,100	850	7,500		450	10,000
(e)	+ 4,500					+ 4,500 Fares earned
	6,600	850	7,500		450	14,500
(f)	− 2,200					− 1,125 Wages exp.
						− 850 Rent expense
						− 150 Utilities exp.
						− 75 Misc. expense
	4,400	850	7,500		450	12,300
(g)		−600				− 600 Supplies exp.
	4,400	250	7,500		450	11,700
(h)	− 1,000					− 1,000 Withdrawal
	3,400	250	7,500		450	10,700

The following observations, which apply to all types of businesses, should be noted:

1. The effect of every transaction can be stated in terms of increases and/or decreases in one or more of the accounting equation elements.
2. The equality of the two sides of the accounting equation is always maintained.
3. The owner's equity is increased by amounts invested by the owner and is decreased by withdrawals by the owner. In addition, owner's equity is increased by revenues and is decreased by expenses. The effect of these four types of transactions on owner's equity is illustrated as follows:

EFFECT OF
TRANS-
ACTIONS ON
OWNER'S
EQUITY

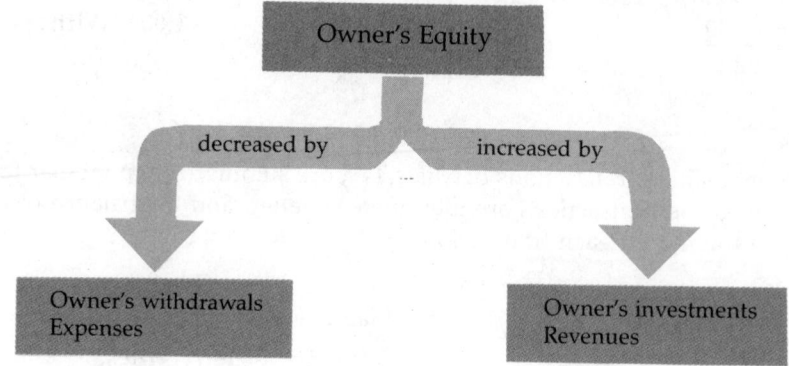

ACCOUNTING STATEMENTS

After the effect of the individual transactions has been determined, the essential information is communicated to users. The principal accounting statements that communicate this information are the income statement, the statement of owner's equity, and the balance sheet. The nature of the data presented in each statement, in general terms, is as follows:

Income statement
> A summary of the revenue and the expenses of a business entity for a specific period of time, such as a month or a year.

Statement of owner's equity
> A summary of the changes in the owner's equity of a business entity that have occurred during a specific period of time, such as a month or a year.

Balance sheet
> A list of the assets, liabilities, and owner's equity of a business entity as of a specific date, usually at the close of the last day of a month or a year.

The basic features of the three statements and their interrelationships are illustrated below. The data for the statements were taken from the summary of transactions of Miles Taxi previously presented.

Miles Taxi
Income Statement
For Month Ended August 31, 1987

Fares earned			$4 5 0 0 00
Operating expenses:			
Wages expense	$1 1 2 5 00		
Rent expense	8 5 0 00		
Supplies expense	6 0 0 00		
Utilities expense	1 5 0 00		
Miscellaneous expense	7 5 00		
Total operating expenses		2 8 0 0 00	
Net income		$1 7 0 0 00	

INCOME STATEMENT

Miles Taxi
Statement of Owner's Equity
For Month Ended August 31, 1987

Investment during the month		$10 0 0 0 00
Net income for the month	$1 7 0 0 00	
Less withdrawals	1 0 0 0 00	
Increase in owner's equity		7 0 0 00
Jerry Miles, capital, August 31, 1987		$10 7 0 0 00

STATEMENT OF OWNER'S EQUITY— SOLE PRO- PRIETORSHIP

Miles Taxi
Balance Sheet
August 31, 1987

Assets		
Cash		$ 3 4 0 0 00
Supplies		2 5 0 00
Land		7 5 0 0 00
Total assets		$11 1 5 0 00
Liabilities		
Accounts payable		$ 4 5 0 00
Owner's Equity		
Jerry Miles, capital		10 7 0 0 00
Total liabilities and owner's equity		$11 1 5 0 00

BALANCE SHEET— SOLE PRO- PRIETORSHIP

An additional statement, referred to as the **statement of changes in financial position,** is also useful in appraising a business enterprise and is an essential part of financial reports to owners and creditors.[4] The preparation and interpretation of the statement of changes in financial position will be considered in a later chapter after various basic concepts and principles have been explained and illustrated.

All financial statements should be identified by the name of the business, the title of the statement, and the date or period of time. The data presented in the income statement, the statement of owner's equity, and the statement of changes in financial position are for a period of time. The data presented in the balance sheet are for a specific date.

The use of indentions, captions, dollar signs, and rulings in the financial statements should be noted. They aid the reader by emphasizing the various distinct sections of the statements.

Income Statement

The excess of the revenue over the expenses incurred in earning the revenue is called **net income** or **net profit**. If the expenses of the enterprise exceed the revenue, the excess is a **net loss**. It is ordinarily impossible to determine the exact amount of expense incurred in connection with each revenue transaction. Therefore, it is considered satisfactory to determine the net income or the net loss for a stated period of time, such as a month or a year, rather than for each sale or small group of sales.

As indicated, the determination of the periodic net income (or net loss) is a two-step process. First, revenues are recognized during the period. Second, the assets consumed in generating the revenues must be matched against the revenues in order to determine the net income or the net loss. Generally, the revenue for the rendering of a service is recognized after the service has been rendered to the customer. The assets consumed in generating revenue during a period must be recognized as expenses. In this way, the expenses are properly matched against the revenues generated.

The effects of revenue earned and expenses incurred during the month for Miles Taxi were shown in the equation as increases and decreases, respectively, in owner's equity. The details, together with net income in the amount of $1,700, are reported in the income statement on page 27.

The order in which the operating expenses are presented in the income statement varies among businesses. One of the arrangements commonly followed is to list them in the order of size, beginning with the larger items. Miscellaneous expense is usually shown as the last item, regardless of the amount.

---

[4]*Opinions of the Accounting Principles Board, No. 19,* "Reporting Changes in Financial Position" (New York: American Institute of Certified Public Accountants, 1971), par. 7.

Statement of Owner's Equity

Three types of transactions affected owner's equity for Miles Taxi during the month: (1) the original investment of $10,000, (2) the revenues and expenses which resulted in net income of $1,700 for the month, and (3) a withdrawal of $1,000 by the owner. This information is presented in the statement of owner's equity on page 27, which serves as a connecting link between the balance sheet and the income statement.

Since Miles Taxi had been in operation for only one month, it had no owner's equity at the beginning of August. For September and most subsequent periods, however, there would be a beginning balance that would be reported on the statement of owner's equity. To illustrate, assume that Miles Taxi reported net income of $2,400, and the owner withdrew $1,250 during September. The statement of owner's equity for Miles Taxi for September would appear as follows:

Miles Taxi		
Statement of Owner's Equity		
For Month Ended September 30, 1987		
Jerry Miles, capital, September 1, 1987		$10 7 0 0 00
Net income for the month	$2 4 0 0 00	
Less withdrawals	1 2 5 0 00	
Increase in owner's equity		1 1 5 0 00
Jerry Miles, capital, September 30, 1987		$11 8 5 0 00

Balance Sheet

The amounts of Miles Taxi's assets, liabilities, and owner's equity at the end of August, the first month of operations, appear on the last line of the summary on page 25. Minor rearrangements of these data and the addition of a heading yield the balance sheet illustrated on page 27. This form of balance sheet, with the liability and owner's equity sections presented below the asset section, is called the **report form**. Another arrangement in common use lists the assets on the left and the liabilities and owner's equity on the right. Because of its similarity to the account, a basic accounting device described in the next chapter, it is referred to as the **account form of balance sheet**.

It is customary to begin the asset section with cash. This item is followed by receivables, supplies, prepaid insurance, and other assets that will be converted into cash or used up in the near future. The assets of a relatively permanent nature, such as land, buildings, and equipment, follow in that order.

In the liabilities and owner's equity section of the balance sheet, it is customary to present the liabilities first, followed by owner's equity. In the illustration on page 27, liabilities are composed entirely of accounts payable.

When there are two or more categories of liabilities, each should be listed and the total amount of liabilities presented in the following manner:

Liabilities

Notes payable	$1,500
Accounts payable	1,100
Salaries payable	300
Total liabilities	$2,900

Statements for Corporations

Business enterprises with large amounts of assets are usually organized as corporations and have many owners, called **stockholders**. The corporate form is also used by many small enterprises with a limited number of stockholders.

If Miles Taxi had been organized as a corporation, with ownership represented by shares of stock, its income statement would be similar to the one shown on page 27. Its report of changes in the **stockholders'** (owner's) **equity** and its balance sheet would be different in some respects from the corresponding statements for a sole proprietorship.

In corporate enterprises, the emphasis in reporting changes in stockholders' equity is on the changes in **retained earnings**, or net income retained in the business. The changes in retained earnings that have occurred during a period are reported in a **retained earnings statement**.[5]

If Miles Taxi had been organized as a corporation, changes in the amount of earnings retained in the business would have resulted from (1) net income and (2) distributions of earnings, called **dividends**, to owners. The retained earnings statement for Miles Taxi Corporation for August would appear as follows:

RETAINED
EARNINGS
STATE-
MENT—
COR-
PORATION

Miles Taxi Corporation Retained Earnings Statement For Month Ended August 31, 1987	
Net income for the month.....................................	$1,700
Less dividends..	1,000
Retained earnings, August 31, 1987........................	$ 700

Having been in existence only one month, Miles Taxi Corporation had no retained earnings at the beginning of August. For September and most sub-

---

[5]If there have been significant changes in capital stock during a period, such data should be reported in a separate additional statement. The details of minor changes need not be reported.

sequent periods, however, there would be a beginning balance of retained earnings that would be reported on the retained earnings statement. To illustrate, assume that Miles Taxi Corporation reported net income of $2,400 and paid dividends of $1,250 during September. The retained earnings statement for Miles Taxi Corporation for September would appear as follows:

Miles Taxi Corporation Retained Earnings Statement For Month Ended September 30, 1987		
Retained earnings, September 1, 1987		$ 700
Net income for the month	$2,400	
Less dividends.	1,250	
Increase in retained earnings		1,150
Retained earnings, September 30, 1987		$1,850

If Miles Taxi had been organized as a corporation, its balance sheet at the end of August, the first month of operations, would appear as follows:

BALANCE SHEET— COR-PORATION

Miles Taxi Corporation Balance Sheet August 31, 1987		
Assets		
Cash		$ 3,400
Supplies		250
Land		7,500
Total assets		$11,150
Liabilities		
Accounts payable		$ 450
Stockholders' Equity		
Capital stock	$10,000	
Retained earnings.	700	
Total stockholders' equity		10,700
Total liabilities and stockholders' equity		$11,150

The only differences between the balance sheet shown above and the one illustrated on page 27 occur in the owner's equity section. In the corporation balance sheet, this section is referred to as the stockholders' equity section. In this section, the investment of the stockholders ($10,000 capital stock) and the net income retained in the business ($700 retained earnings) are reported separately, and the names of the stockholders (owners) are not shown.

CHAPTER REVIEW

KEY POINTS

1. Accounting as an Information System.

The objective of accounting is to record, summarize, report, and interpret economic data for use by many groups within our economic and social system. In this sense, accounting is often called the "language of business." This language can be viewed as an information system that provides essential information about the financial activities of an entity to various individuals or groups for their use in making informed judgments and decisions.

2. Users of Accounting Information.

Accounting provides for the gathering of economic data and the communication of these data to different individuals and institutions. Examples of users of accounting information include investors, bankers, suppliers, government agencies, employees, and managers of the entity.

3. Relationship of Accounting to Other Fields.

To be effective, individuals engaged in such areas of business as finance, production, marketing, personnel, and general management must have a good understanding of accounting concepts, principles, and terminology. In addition, the importance of understanding accounting is not limited to the business world, and many employees with specialized training in non-business areas also make use of accounting data.

4. Opportunities in Accounting

Accountancy is a rapidly expanding profession whose members may be viewed as engaged in either (1) private accounting or (2) public accounting. Accountants employed by a particular business firm or not-for-profit organization, perhaps as a chief accountant, comptroller, or financial vice-president, are said to be engaged in private accounting. Accountants who render accounting services on a fee basis, and staff accountants employed by them, are said to be engaged in public accounting. Public accountants who meet a state's education, experience, and examination requirements may practice as certified public accountants (CPAs).

Specialized fields in accounting have evolved as a result of rapid technological advances and accelerated economic growth. The more important accounting fields are financial accounting, auditing, cost accounting, managerial accounting, tax accounting, accounting systems, budgetary accounting, international accounting, not-for-profit accounting, social accounting, and accounting instruction.

5. Bookkeeping and Accounting.

While bookkeeping is the recording of business data in a prescribed manner, accounting is concerned with the design of the system of records, preparation of reports based upon the recorded data, and the interpretation of reports.

6. Principles and Practice.

Generally accepted accounting principles have evolved to form an underlying basis for accounting practice. Several professional accounting associations, with the dominant one being the Financial Accounting Standards Board, issue pronouncements on accounting principles.

7. Business Entity Concept.

The business entity concept is based upon the applicability of accounting to individual economic units in society. Profit-making businesses are customarily organized as sole proprietorships, partnerships, or corporations.

8. The Cost Principle.

The cost principle requires that properties and services purchased by a business be recorded in terms of cost.

9. Business Transactions.

A business transaction is the occurrence of an event or a condition that must be recorded. Business transactions may be either simple or complex and may lead to an event or a condition that results in yet another transaction.

10. Assets, Liabilities, and Owner's Equity.

The properties owned by a business and the rights or claims to properties may be stated in the form of an equation as follows: Assets = Equities. The expansion of the equation to give recognition to two basic types of equities yields the following, which is known as the accounting equation: Assets = Liabilities + Owner's Equity.

11. Transactions and the Accounting Equation.

All transactions, from the simplest to the most complex, can be stated in terms of the resulting change in the three basic elements of the accounting equation. That is, the effect of every transaction can be stated in terms of increases and/or decreases in one or more of the accounting equation elements such that the equality of the two sides of the accounting equation is always maintained.

12. Accounting Statements.

After the effect of individual transactions has been determined and recorded, reports (accounting statements) summarizing the effects of transactions are prepared and communicated to users. The principal accounting statements of a sole proprietorship are the income statement, the statement of owner's equity, and the balance sheet. An additional statement, the statement of changes in financial position, is also useful in appraising a business enterprise and is an essential part of financial reports to owners and creditors. The accounting statements for a corporation are similar to those of a sole proprietorship, except that a retained earnings statement is prepared instead of a statement of owner's equity. In addition, the owner's equity section of the balance sheet is referred to as stockholders' equity rather than owner's equity.

KEY TERMS

accounting 9
private accounting 12
public accounting 12
certified public accountants
    (CPAs) 14
codes of professional ethics 15
generally accepted accounting
    principles (GAAP) 16
bookkeeping 18
Financial Accounting Standards
    Board (FASB) 18
business entity concept 18
sole proprietorship 19
partnership 19
corporation 19
cost principle 20
business transaction 20
assets 21
equities 21
liabilities 21

owner's equity 21
accounting equation 21
account payable 22
prepaid expenses 22
revenue 23
account receivable 24
expense 24
income statement 26
statement of owner's equity 26
balance sheet 26
statement of changes in financial
    position 28
net income 28
net loss 28
report form of balance sheet 29
account form of balance sheet 29
stockholders' equity 30
retained earnings 30
retained earnings statement 30
dividends 30

SELF-EXAMINATION QUESTIONS
Answers in Appendix B.

1. A profit-making business that is a separate legal entity and in which ownership is divided into shares of stock is known as a:
    A. sole proprietorship   C. partnership
    B. single proprietorship   D. corporation

2. The properties owned by a business enterprise are called:
   A. assets
   B. liabilities
   C. stockholders' equity
   D. owner's equity

3. A list of assets, liabilities, and owner's equity of a business entity as of a specific date is:
   A. a balance sheet
   B. an income statement
   C. a statement of owner's equity
   D. a retained earnings statement

4. If total assets increased $20,000 during a period of time and total liabilities increased by $12,000 during the same period, the amount and direction (increase or decrease) of the period's change in owner's equity is:
   A. $32,000 increase
   B. $32,000 decrease
   C. $8,000 increase
   D. $8,000 decrease

5. If revenue was $45,000, expenses were $37,500, and the owner's withdrawals were $10,000, the amount of net income or net loss was:
   A. $45,000 net income
   B. $7,500 net income
   C. $37,500 net loss
   D. $2,500 net loss

ILLUSTRATIVE PROBLEM

The assets and liabilities of Morgan Dry Cleaners on October 1 of the current year are as follows: Cash, $6,000; Accounts Receivable, $2,200; Supplies, $850; Land, $11,450; Accounts Payable, $2,030. Morgan Dry Cleaners is a sole proprietorship owned and operated by M. A. Morgan. Currently, a building, delivery truck, and equipment are being rented, pending expansion to new facilities. The actual work of dry cleaning is done by another company at wholesale rates. Business transactions during October are summarized as follows:

(a) Received cash from cash customers for dry cleaning sales, $4,928.
(b) Paid creditors on account, $1,755.
(c) Paid personal expenses by checks drawn on the business, $300, and withdrew $1,000 in cash for personal use.
(d) Paid rent for the month, $1,200.
(e) Charged customers for dry cleaning sales on account, $1,025.
(f) Purchased supplies on account, $245.
(g) Received cash from customers on account, $2,000.
(h) Received monthly invoice for dry cleaning expense for October (to be paid on November 10), $1,635.
(i) Paid the following: wages expense, $850; truck expense, $250; utilities expense, $325; miscellaneous expense, $75.
(j) Reimbursed a customer $75 for a garment lost by the cleaning company, which agreed to deduct the amount from the invoice received in transaction (h).
(k) Determined, by taking an inventory, the cost of supplies used during the month, $115.

Instructions:

1. Determine the amount of owner's equity (M. A. Morgan's capital) as of October 1 of the current year.
2. State the assets, liabilities, and owner's equity as of October 1 in equation form similar to that shown in this chapter. In tabular form below the equation, indicate the increases and decreases resulting from each transaction and the new balances after each transaction. Explain the nature of each increase and decrease in owner's equity by an appropriate notation at the right of the amount.
3. Prepare (a) an income statement for October, (b) a statement of owner's equity for October, and (c) a balance sheet as of October 31.

SOLUTION

(1)   Assets − Liabilities = Owner's Equity (M. A. Morgan, capital)
        $20,500 − $2,030 = Owner's Equity (M. A. Morgan, capital)
        $18,470 = Owner's Equity (M. A. Morgan, capital)

(2)

	Assets				=	Liabilities +	Owner's Equity	
	Cash +	Accounts Receivable +	Supplies +	Land =		Accounts Payable +	M. A. Morgan, Capital	
Bal.	6,000	2,200	850	11,450		2,030	18,470	
(a)	+ 4,928						+ 4,928	Dry cleaning sales
Bal.	10,928	2,200	850	11,450		2,030	23,398	
(b)	− 1,755					−1,755		
Bal.	9,173	2,200	850	11,450		275	23,398	
(c)	− 1,300						− 1,300	Withdrawal
Bal.	7,873	2,200	850	11,450		275	22,098	
(d)	− 1,200						− 1,200	Rent expense
Bal.	6,673	2,200	850	11,450		275	20,898	
(e)		+1,025					+ 1,025	Dry cleaning sales
Bal.	6,673	3,225	850	11,450		275	21,923	
(f)			+ 245			+ 245		
Bal.	6,673	3,225	1,095	11,450		520	21,923	
(g)	+ 2,000	−2,000						
Bal.	8,673	1,225	1,095	11,450		520	21,923	
(h)						+1,635	− 1,635	Dry cleaning expense
Bal.	8,673	1,225	1,095	11,450		2,155	20,288	
(i)	− 1,500						− 850	Wages expense
							− 250	Truck expense
							− 325	Utilities expense
							− 75	Miscellaneous exp.
Bal.	7,173	1,225	1,095	11,450		2,155	18,788	
(j)	− 75					− 75		
Bal.	7,098	1,225	1,095	11,450		2,080	18,788	
(k)			− 115				− 115	Supplies expense
Bal.	7,098	1,225	980	11,450		2,080	18,673	

(3)

Morgan Dry Cleaners
Income Statement
For Month Ended October 31, 19--

Dry cleaning sales			$5 9 5 3 00
Operating expenses:			
Dry cleaning expense	$1 6 3 5 00		
Rent expense	1 2 0 0 00		
Wages expense	8 5 0 00		
Utilities expense	3 2 5 00		
Truck expense	2 5 0 00		
Supplies expense	1 1 5 00		
Miscellaneous expense	7 5 00		
Total operating expenses			4 4 5 0 00
Net income			$1 5 0 3 00

Morgan Dry Cleaners
Statement of Owner's Equity
For Month Ended October 31, 19--

M. A. Morgan, capital, October 1, 19--			$18 4 7 0 00
Net income for the month	$1 5 0 3 00		
Withdrawals	1 3 0 0 00		
Increase in owner's equity			2 0 3 00
M. A. Morgan, capital, October 31, 19--			$18 6 7 3 00

Morgan Dry Cleaners
Balance Sheet
October 31, 19--

Assets			
Cash			$ 7 0 9 8 00
Accounts receivable			1 2 2 5 00
Supplies			9 8 0 00
Land			11 4 5 0 00
Total assets			$20 7 5 3 00
Liabilities			
Accounts payable			$ 2 0 8 0 00
Owner's Equity			
M. A. Morgan, capital			18 6 7 3 00
Total liabilities and owner's equity			$20 7 5 3 00

DISCUSSION QUESTIONS

1. What is the objective of accounting?

2. Name some of the categories of individuals and institutions who use accounting information.

3. Why is a knowledge of accounting concepts and terminology useful to all individuals engaged in business activities?

4. Distinguish between public accounting and private accounting.

5. Describe in general terms the requirements that an individual must meet (a) for the CMA designation and (b) for the CPA certificate.

6. Name some of the specialized fields of accounting activity.

7. Distinguish between the terms *bookkeeping* and *accounting*.

8. (a) Name the three principal forms of profit-making business organizations. (b) Which of these forms is identified with the greatest number of businesses?

9. What is meant by the cost principle?

10. (a) Land with an assessed value of $90,000 for property tax purposes is acquired by a business enterprise for $195,000. At what amount should the land be recorded by the purchaser?
    (b) Five years later the plot of land in (a) has an assessed value of $145,000 and the business enterprise receives an offer of $300,000 for it. Should the monetary amount assigned to the land in the business records now be increased and, if so, by what amount?
    (c) Assuming that the land acquired in (a) was sold for $325,000, (1) how much would the owner's equity increase, and (2) at what amount would the purchaser record the land?

11. (a) If the assets owned by a business enterprise total $500,000, what is the amount of the equities of the enterprise? (b) What are the two principal types of equities?

12. (a) An enterprise has assets of $290,000 and liabilities of $175,000. What is the amount of its owner's equity?
    (b) An enterprise has assets of $410,000 and owner's equity of $150,000. What is the total amount of its liabilities?
    (c) A corporation has assets of $970,000, liabilities of $615,000, and capital stock of $200,000. What is the amount of its retained earnings?
    (d) An enterprise has liabilities of $400,000 and owner's equity of $200,000. What is the total amount of its assets?

13. Describe how the following business transactions affect the three elements of the accounting equation.

(a) Invested cash in the business.
(b) Purchased supplies on account.
(c) Received cash for services performed.
(d) Paid for utilities used in the business.

14. (a) A vacant lot acquired for $80,000, on which there is a balance owed of $25,000, is sold for $110,000 in cash. What is the effect of the sale on the total amount of the seller's (1) assets, (2) liabilities, and (3) owner's equity?
   (b) After receiving the $110,000 cash in (a), the seller pays the $25,000 owed. What is the effect of the payment on the total amount of the seller's (1) assets, (2) liabilities, and (3) owner's equity?

15. Operations of a service enterprise for a particular month are summarized as follows:
   Service sales: on account, $42,000; for cash, $82,000
   Expenses incurred: on account, $56,000; for cash, $51,000
   What was the amount of the enterprise's (a) revenue, (b) expenses, and (c) net income?

16. A business enterprise had revenues of $65,000 and operating expenses of $72,750. Did the enterprise (a) incur a net loss or (b) realize a net income?

17. Indicate whether each of the following types of transactions will (a) increase owner's equity or (b) decrease owner's equity:
   (1) owner's investments
   (2) owner's withdrawals
   (3) revenues
   (4) expenses

18. Give the title of a sole proprietorship's three major financial statements illustrated in this chapter, and briefly describe the nature of the information provided by each.

19. What particular item of financial or operating data of a service enterprise, organized as a corporation, appears on (a) both the income statement and the retained earnings statement, and (b) both the balance sheet and the retained earnings statement?

20. The income statement of a sole proprietorship for the month of March indicates a net income of $31,000. During the same period the owner withdrew $40,000 in cash from the business for personal use. Would it be correct to say that the owner incurred a *net loss* of $9,000 during the month? Discuss.

21. Video Center had an owner's equity balance at the beginning of the period of $110,000. At the end of the period, the company had total assets of $198,000 and total liabilities of $93,000. (a) What was the net income or net loss for the period, assuming no additional investments or withdrawals? (b) What was the net income or net loss for the period, assuming a withdrawal of $35,000 had occurred during the period?

22. Real World Focus. Based upon the annual report of the Coca-Cola Company presented in Appendix H, what are (a) the total assets at December 31, 1985, (b) the total liabilities and shareholders' equity at December 31, 1985, (c) the net operating revenues for the year ended December 31, 1985, (d) the net income for the year ended December 31, 1985, (e) the ratio of the net income to the net operating revenues for the year ended December 31, 1985?

EXERCISES

Exercise 1–1.   Balance sheet items. From the following list of selected amounts taken from the records of J. A. Buck Corporation as of a specific date, identify those that would appear on the balance sheet:

(1) Capital Stock –
(2) Fees Earned
(3) Land _
(4) Salaries Expense
(5) Accounts Payable

(6) Retained Earnings
(7) Cash –
(8) Utilities Expense
(9) Supplies _
(10) Salaries Payable

Exercise 1–2.   Transactions of sole proprietorship. The following selected transactions were completed by Owen Delivery Service during May:

(1) Received cash from owner as additional investment, $25,000.
(2) Purchased supplies of gas and oil for cash, $925.
(3) Paid advertising expense, $700.
(4) Received cash from cash customers, $1,500.
(5) Billed customers for delivery services on account, $1,100.
(6) Paid rent for May, $900.
(7) Paid creditors on account, $470.
(8) Received cash from customers on account, $910.
(9) Paid cash to owner for personal use, $1,000.
(10) Determined by taking an inventory that $650 of supplies of gas and oil had been used during the month.

Indicate the effect of each transaction on the accounting equation by listing the numbers identifying the transactions, (1) through (10), in a vertical column, and inserting at the right of each number the appropriate letter from the following list:

(a) Increase in one asset, decrease in another asset.
(b) Increase in an asset, increase in a liability.
(c) Increase in an asset, increase in owner's equity.
(d) Decrease in an asset, decrease in a liability.
(e) Decrease in an asset, decrease in owner's equity.

Exercise 1–3.   Transactions of corporation. Sims Corporation, engaged in a service business, completed the following selected transactions during the period:

(1) Purchased supplies on account.
(2) Issued additional capital stock, receiving cash.
(3) Charged customers for services sold on account.
(4) Paid utilities expense.

(5) Returned defective supplies purchased on account for which payment has not yet been made.
(6) Received cash as a refund from the erroneous overpayment of an expense.
(7) Paid a creditor on account.
(8) Received cash from customers on account.
(9) Determined the amount of supplies used during the month.
(10) Paid cash dividends to stockholders.

Using a tabular form with four column headings entitled Transaction, Assets, Liabilities, and Owner's Equity, respectively, indicate the effect of each transaction. Use + for increase and − for decrease.

Exercise 1–4. Nature of transactions. J. J. Byars is engaged in a service business. Summary financial data for January are presented in equation form as follows. Each line designated by a number indicates the effect of a transaction on the equation. Each increase and decrease in owner's equity, except transaction (5), affects net income.

	Cash	+ Supplies	+ Land	= Liabilities	+ Owner's Equity
Bal.	5,500	740	10,000	6,740	9,500
(1)	+9,000				+ 9,000
(2)	−3,200			−3,200	
(3)	−2,200				− 2,200
(4)		+900		+ 900	
(5)	− 950				− 950
(6)	−4,500		+ 4,500		
(7)		−680			− 680
Bal.	3,650	960	14,500	4,440	14,670

(a) Describe each transaction.
(b) What is the amount of net decrease in cash during the month?
(c) What is the amount of net increase in owner's equity during the month?
(d) What is the amount of the net income for the month?
(e) How much of the net income of the month was retained in the business?

Exercise 1–5. Net income for four sole proprietorships. Four different sole proprietorships, A, B, C, and D, show the same balance sheet data at the beginning and end of a year. These data, exclusive of the amount of owner's equity, are summarized as follows:

	Total Assets	Total Liabilities
Beginning of the year	$350,000	$120,000
End of the year.....................................	410,000	155,000
	60,000	35,000

profit
25000

On the basis of the above data and the following additional information for the year, determine the net income (or loss) of each company for the year. (Suggestion: First determine the amount of increase or decrease in owner's equity during the year.)

Company A: The owner had made no additional investments in the business and had made no withdrawals from the business.

Company B: The owner had made no additional investments in the business but had withdrawn $30,000.   (5000)

Company C: The owner had made an additional investment of $50,000 but had made no withdrawals.   7500 U

Company D: The owner had made an additional investment of $50,000 and had withdrawn $30,000.   45000

Exercise 1–6. Missing amounts from balance sheet and income statement data. One item is omitted in each of the following summaries of balance sheet and income statement data for four different sole proprietorships, A, B, C, and D.

	A	B	C	D
Beginning of the year:				
Assets	$200,000	$60,000	$97,000	(d)
Liabilities	90,000	20,000	76,000	$22,100
End of the year:				
Assets	240,000	95,000	94,000	68,000
Liabilities	110,000	20,000	77,000	37,000
During the year:				
Additional investment in the business ...	(a)	7,000	5,000	30,000
Withdrawals from the business	20,000	12,000	(c)	21,000
Revenue	90,000	(b)	82,100	99,000
Expenses	75,000	40,000	83,600	88,000

Determine the amounts of the missing items, identifying them by letter. (*Suggestion:* First determine the amount of increase or decrease in owner's equity during the year.)

Exercise 1–7. Balance sheets; net income for sole proprietorship. Financial information related to the sole proprietorship of Marilyn Carr Interiors for May and June of the current year is as follows:

	May 31, 19--	June 30, 19--
Accounts Payable	$ 2,520	$ 4,100
Accounts Receivable....................	8,500	12,000
Marilyn Carr, Capital	?	?
Cash...................................	11,500	13,400
Supplies...............................	975	750

(a) Prepare balance sheets for Marilyn Carr Interiors as of May 31 and as of June 30 of the current year.

(b) Determine the amount of net income for June, assuming that the owner had made no additional investments or withdrawals during the month.

(c) Determine the amount of net income for June, assuming that the owner had made no additional investments and had withdrawn $3,000 during the month.

PROBLEMS

Series A

SPREADSHEET
PROBLEM

Problem 1–1A.   Transactions for sole proprietorship. Ann Jones established a sole proprietorship on July 1 of the current year and completed the following transactions during July:

(a) Opened a business bank account with a deposit of $3,000.
(b) Paid rent on office and equipment for the month, $2,000.
(c) Purchased supplies (stationery, stamps, pencils, etc.) on account, $550.
(d) Received cash from fees earned, $2,500.
(e) Paid creditors on account, $250.
(f) Billed customers for fees earned, $1,250.
(g) Paid automobile expenses (including rental charge) for month, $380, and miscellaneous expenses, $275.
(h) Paid office salaries, $1,000.
(i) Determined that the cost of supplies used was $125.
(j) Withdrew cash for personal use, $1,200.

Instructions:

Indicate the effect of each transaction and the balances after each transaction, using the following tabular headings:

Assets	=	Liabilities	+	Owner's Equity
Cash + Accounts Receivable + Supplies	=	Accounts Payable	+	Ann Jones, Capital

By appropriate notations at the right of each change, indicate the nature of each increase and decrease in owner's equity.

Problem 1–2A.   Transactions for sole proprietorship; financial statements. On June 1 of the current year, Carol Plikerd established a sole proprietorship under the name Plikerd Realty. Plikerd completed the following transactions during the month of June:

(a) Opened a business bank account with a deposit of $7,500.
(b) Paid rent on office and equipment for the month, $1,800.
(c) Purchased supplies (stationery, stamps, pencils, etc.) on account, $450.
(d) Paid creditor on account, $250.
(e) Earned sales commissions, receiving cash, $6,100.
(f) Withdrew cash for personal use, $1,500.
(g) Paid automobile expenses (including rental charge) for month, $400, and miscellaneous expenses, $250.
(h) Paid office salaries, $2,150.
(i) Determined that the cost of supplies used was $125.

Instructions:

(1) Indicate the effect of each transaction and the balances after each transaction, using the following tabular headings:

Assets			Liabilities		Owner's Equity
Cash + Supplies		=	Accounts Payable	+	Carol Plikerd, Capital

By appropriate notations at the right of each change, indicate the nature of each increase and decrease in owner's equity.

(2) Prepare an income statement for June, a statement of owner's equity for June, and a balance sheet as of June 30.

Problem 1–3A. Financial statements for sole proprietorship. Following are the amounts of the assets and liabilities of Lane Services, a sole proprietorship, at December 31, the *end* of the current year, and its revenue and expenses for the year ended on that date. The capital of John Lane, owner, was $17,750 at January 1, the *beginning* of the current year, and the owner withdrew $24,000 during the current year.

Cash..	$ 5,750
Accounts receivable	19,250
Supplies..	2,950
Prepaid insurance	1,500
Accounts payable	2,500
Salaries payable	1,750
Sales	99,250
Salary expense	27,100
Rent expense..	12,000
Utilities expense..	8,500
Supplies expense	5,800
Taxes expense..	5,750
Insurance expense	3,500
Advertising expense	3,000
Miscellaneous expense	2,150

Instructions:

(1) Prepare an income statement for the current year ended December 31.
(2) Prepare a statement of owner's equity for the current year ended December 31.
(3) Prepare a balance sheet as of December 31 of the current year.

Problem 1–4A. Financial statements for corporation. Following are the amounts of Fulton Corporation's assets and liabilities at July 31, the end of the current year, and its revenue and expenses for the year ended on that date, listed in alphabetical order. Fulton Corporation had capital stock of $100,000 and retained earnings of $97,890 on August 1, the beginning of the current year. During the current year, the corporation paid cash dividends of $40,000.

Accounts payable	$ 61,250
Accounts receivable	70,500
Advertising expense	30,000
Cash	64,515
Insurance expense	24,000
Land	200,000
Miscellaneous expense	8,125
Notes payable	25,000
Prepaid insurance	6,000
Rent expense	160,500
Salaries payable	9,000
Salary expense	410,500
Sales	845,500
Supplies	5,500
Supplies expense	19,750
Taxes expense	33,500
Utilities expense	65,750

Instructions:

(1) Prepare an income statement for the current year ended July 31.
(2) Prepare a retained earnings statement for the current year ended July 31.
(3) Prepare a balance sheet as of July 31 of the current year. There was no change in the amount of capital stock during the year.

Problem 1–5A. Transactions for sole proprietorship; financial statements. Berry Dry Cleaners is a sole proprietorship owned and operated by R.C. Berry. Currently, a building, delivery truck, and equipment are being rented, pending completion of construction of new facilities. The actual work of dry cleaning is done by another company at wholesale rates. The assets and the liabilities of the business on May 1 of the current year are as follows: Cash, $7,750; Accounts Receivable, $15,600; Supplies, $800; Land, $25,000; Accounts Payable, $9,700. Business transactions during May are summarized as follows:

(a) Received cash from cash customers for dry cleaning sales, $9,150.
(b) Paid rent for the month, $900.
(c) Purchased supplies on account, $220.
(d) Paid creditors on account, $8,000.
(e) Charged customers for dry cleaning sales on account, $3,520.
(f) Received monthly invoice for dry cleaning expense for May (to be paid on June 10), $6,800.
(g) Paid personal expenses by checks drawn on the business, $750, and withdrew $1,000 in cash for personal use.
(h) Reimbursed a customer $100 for a garment lost by the cleaning company, which agreed to deduct the amount from the invoice in transaction (f).
(i) Paid the following: wages expense, $1,400; truck expense, $580; utilities expense, $460; miscellaneous expense, $130.
(j) Received cash from customers on account, $8,100.
(k) Determined the cost of supplies used during the month, $270.

Instructions:

(1) Determine the amount of R. C. Berry's capital as of May 1 of the current year.
(2) State the assets, liabilities, and owner's equity as of May 1 in equation form similar to that shown in this chapter. In tabular form below the equation, indicate the increases and decreases resulting from each transaction and the new balances after each transaction. Explain the nature of each increase and decrease in owner's equity by an appropriate notation at the right of the amount.
(3) Prepare (a) an income statement for May, (b) a statement of owner's equity for May, and (c) a balance sheet as of May 31.

Problem 1–6A. Transactions for corporation; financial statements. On June 1 of the current year, Rapid Delivery Inc. was organized as a corporation. The summarized transactions of the business for its first two months of operations, ending on July 31, are as follows:

(a) Received cash from stockholders for capital stock $60,000

(b) Purchased a portion of a delivery service that had been operating as a sole proprietorship in accordance with the following details:

Assets acquired by the corporation:		
Accounts receivable	$14,000	
Truck supplies	4,550	
Office supplies	750	$19,300
Liabilities assumed by the corporation:		
Accounts payable		9,300
Payment to be made as follows:		
Cash......................................	$ 2,500	
Three non-interest-bearing notes payable of $2,500 each, due at two-month intervals.........	7,500	$10,000

(c) Purchased truck supplies on account..............	$ 1,150
(d) Purchased office supplies for cash.................	250
(e) Paid creditors on account	5,000
(f) Received cash from customers on account	9,500
(g) Paid insurance premiums in advance..............	1,800
(h) Paid advertising expense........................	1,100
(i) Charged delivery service sales to customers on account	39,250
(j) Paid rent expense on office and trucks............	4,100
(k) Paid utilities expense	925
(l) Paid first of the three notes payable	2,500
(m) Paid miscellaneous expenses.....................	1,475
(n) Paid taxes expense	275
(o) Paid wages expense	17,100
(p) Truck supplies used	2,720
(q) Office supplies used.............................	325

(r) Insurance premiums that expired and became an expense...	$ 300
(s) Purchased land as future building site, paying $15,000 cash and giving a note payable due in 5 years for the balance of $25,000................	40,000
(t) Paid cash dividends to stockholders...............	1,000

Instructions:

(1) List the following captions in a single line at the top of a sheet turned sideways.

$$\text{Cash} + \underset{\text{Receivable}}{\text{Accounts}} + \underset{\text{Supplies}}{\text{Truck}} + \underset{\text{Supplies}}{\text{Office}} + \underset{\text{Insurance}}{\text{Prepaid}} + \text{Land} =$$

$$\underset{\text{Payable}}{\text{Notes}} + \underset{\text{Payable}}{\text{Accounts}} + \underset{\text{Stock}}{\text{Capital}} + \underset{\text{Earnings}}{\text{Retained}} \quad \underset{\text{Notations}}{\text{Retained Earnings}}$$

(2) In the appropriate columns, indicate the effect of the original investment and the remaining transactions, identifying each by letter. Indicate increases by + and decreases by −. *Do not determine the new balances of the items after each transaction.* In the space for retained earnings notations, identify each revenue and expense item and dividends paid to stockholders.

(3) Insert the final balances in each column and determine that the equation is in balance at July 31, the end of the period.

(4) Prepare the following: (a) income statement for the two months, (b) retained earnings statement for the two months, and (c) balance sheet as of July 31.

Series B

Problem 1–1B. Transactions for sole proprietorship. John Bower established a sole proprietorship on August 1 of the current year and completed the following transactions during August:

(a) Opened a business bank account with a deposit of $5,000.

(b) Paid rent on office and equipment for the month, $1,800.

(c) Purchased supplies on account, $425.

(d) Paid creditors on account, $225.

(e) Received cash from fees earned, $2,750.

(f) Paid automobile expenses for month, $350, and miscellaneous expenses, $250.

(g) Paid office salaries, $900.

(h) Determined that the cost of supplies used was $250.

(i) Billed customers for fees earned, $1,350.

(j) Withdrew cash for personal use, $1,000.

Instructions:

Indicate the effect of each transaction and the balances after each transaction, using the following tabular headings:

	Assets		Liabilities		Owner's Equity
Cash + Accounts Receivable + Supplies		=	Accounts Payable	+	John Bower, Capital

By appropriate notations at the right of each change, indicate the nature of each increase and decrease in owner's equity.

Problem 1–3B. Financial statements for sole proprietorship. Following are the amounts of the assets and liabilities of Farr's Personnel Service, a sole proprietorship, at June 30, the *end* of the current year, and its revenue and expenses for the year ended on that date. The capital of C. D. Farr, owner, was $11,350 at July 1, the *beginning* of the current year, and the owner withdrew $12,000 during the current year.

Cash..	$ 6,125
Accounts receivable.......................................	7,850
Supplies..	575
Prepaid insurance	500
Accounts payable..	950
Salaries payable..	450
Fees earned	69,525
Salary expense..	29,500
Rent expense	9,000
Advertising expense	6,100
Utilities expense...	4,500
Supplies expense..	2,600
Taxes expense	1,800
Insurance expense...	900
Miscellaneous expense.....................................	825

Instructions:

(1) Prepare an income statement for the current year ended June 30.
(2) Prepare a statement of owner's equity for the current year ended June 30.
(3) Prepare a balance sheet as of June 30 of the current year.

Problem 1–4B. Financial statements for corporation. Following are the amounts of Baker Corporation's assets and liabilities at October 31, the end of the current year, and its revenue and expenses for the year ended on that date, listed in alphabetical order. Baker Corporation had capital stock of $50,000 and retained earnings of $16,765 on November 1, the beginning of the current year. During the current year, the corporation paid cash dividends of $15,000.

Accounts payable...	$ 5,600
Accounts receivable.......................................	19,750
Advertising expense	5,000
Cash...	16,500
Insurance expense...	1,900
Land...	60,000
Miscellaneous expense.....................................	1,250
Notes payable..	5,000
Prepaid insurance	950

Rent expense	$ 42,000
Salaries payable	2,250
Salary expense	90,500
Sales	205,500
Supplies	865
Supplies expense	6,125
Taxes expense	5,775
Utilities expense	19,500

Instructions:

(1) Prepare an income statement for the current year ended October 31.
(2) Prepare a retained earnings statement for the current year ended October 31.
(3) Prepare a balance sheet as of October 31 of the current year. There was no change in the amount of capital stock during the year.

Problem 1–5B. Transactions for sole proprietorship; financial statements.
Berry Dry Cleaners is a sole proprietorship owned and operated by R.C. Berry. Currently, a building and equipment are being rented, pending expansion to new facilities. The actual work of dry cleaning is done by another company at wholesale rates. The assets and the liabilities of the business on June 1 of the current year are as follows: Cash, $9,400; Accounts Receivable, $3,900; Supplies, $410; Land, $15,000; Accounts Payable, $2,880. Business transactions during June are summarized as follows:

(a) Paid rent for the month, $1,050.
(b) Charged customers for dry cleaning sales on account, $6,250.
(c) Paid creditors on account, $1,680.
(d) Purchased supplies on account, $310.
(e) Received cash from cash customers for dry cleaning sales, $3,200.
(f) Received cash from customers on account, $3,750.
(g) Paid personal expenses by checks drawn on the business, $700, and withdrew $1,300 in cash for personal use.
(h) Received monthly invoice for dry cleaning expense for June (to be paid on July 10), $3,200.
(i) Paid the following: wages expense, $1,200; truck expense, $675; utilities expense, $460; miscellaneous expense, $190.
(j) Reimbursed a customer $150 for a garment lost by the cleaning company, which agreed to deduct the amount from the invoice in transaction (h).
(k) Determined the cost of supplies used during the month, $420.

Instructions:

(1) Determine the amount of R.C. Berry's capital as of June 1 of the current year.
(2) State the assets, liabilities, and owner's equity as of June 1 in equation form similar to that shown in this chapter. In tabular form below the equation, indicate increases and decreases resulting from each transaction and the new balances after each transaction. Explain the nature of each increase and decrease in owner's equity by an appropriate notation at the right of the amount.
(3) Prepare (a) an income statement for June, (b) a statement of owner's equity for June, and (c) a balance sheet as of June 30.

MINI-CASE 1

Tennis Services Unlimited

Ann Wolf, a junior in college, has been seeking ways to earn extra spending money. As an active sports enthusiast, Ann plays tennis regularly at the Royal Golf and Tennis Club, where her family has a membership. The president of the club recently approached Ann with the proposal that she manage the club's tennis courts on weekends. Ann's primary duty would be to supervise the operation of the club's two indoor and six outdoor courts, including court reservations. In return for her services, the club would pay Ann $80 per weekend, plus Ann could keep whatever she earned from lessons and the fees from the use of the ball machine. The club and Ann agreed to a one-month trial, after which both would consider an arrangement for the remaining two years of Ann's college career. On this basis, Ann organized Tennis Services Unlimited. During September, Ann managed the tennis courts and entered into the following transactions:

(a) Opened a business account by depositing $500.
(b) Paid $100 for tennis supplies (practice tennis balls, etc.)
(c) Paid $125 for the rental of video tape equipment to be used in offering lessons during September.
(d) Arranged for the rental of a ball machine during September for $50. Paid $25 in advance, with the remaining $25 due October 1.
(e) Received $450 for lessons given during September.
(f) Received $90 in fees from the use of the ball machine during September.
(g) Paid $120 for salaries of part-time employees who answered the telephone and took reservations while Ann was giving lessons.

(h) Paid $75 for miscellaneous expenses.
(i) Received $320 from the club for managing the tennis courts during September.
(j) Supplies on hand at the end of the month totaled $55.
(k) Ann withdrew $400 for personal use on September 30.

As a friend and accounting student, Ann has asked you to aid her in assessing the venture.

Instructions:

(1) Indicate the effect of each transaction and the balances after each transaction, using the following tabular headings:

Assets		Liabilities		Owner's Equity
Cash + Supplies	=	Accounts Payable	+	A. Wolf, Capital

(2) Prepare an income statement for September.
(3) Prepare a statement of owner's equity for September.
(4) Prepare a balance sheet as of September 30.
(5) (a) Assume that Ann Wolf could earn $4.50 per hour working 16 hours per weekend as a waitress. Evaluate which of the two alternatives, working as a waitress or operating Tennis Services Unlimited, would provide Ann with the most income per month.
    (b) Discuss any other factors that you believe Ann should consider before discussing a long-term arrangement with Royal Golf and Tennis Club.

Chapter 2

THE ACCOUNTING CYCLE

Chapter Objectives

■ Describe the nature of an account and the way in which transactions can be presented in an account.

■ Describe what is meant by the double-entry accounting method of recording transactions.

■ Discuss the general rules of debit and credit and normal balances for asset, liability, owner's equity, revenue, expense, drawing, and dividend accounts.

■ Describe the common classification of accounts for a small service enterprise.

■ Describe a chart of accounts for a small service enterprise.

■ Describe and illustrate the flow of data through an accounting system.

■ Describe and illustrate the use of a two-column journal, a two-column account, and a four-column account.

■ Describe and illustrate the posting of transactions to the ledger.

■ Describe and illustrate the preparation of a trial balance and its use in the discovery of errors.

T he transactions completed by an enterprise during a specific period may cause increases and decreases in many different asset, liability, and owner's equity items. To have the details of these transactions readily available and to prepare periodic financial statements, the effects of the transactions must be recorded in a systematic manner.

The nature of transactions and their effect on business enterprises were described and recorded in Chapter 1 by the use of the accounting equation, Assets = Liabilities + Owner's Equity. Although transactions can be analyzed and recorded in terms of their effect on the equation, such a format is not practical as a design for actual accounting systems.

Accountants must have day-to-day information available when they need it and must be able to prepare timely periodic financial statements. Therefore, separate records must be kept for each item that appears on the financial statements. The individual records are then summarized at periodic intervals and the data thus obtained are presented in the financial statements or other reports. For example, it is necessary to have a record used only for recording increases and decreases in cash, another record used only for recording increases and decreases in supplies, another for land, etc. The type of record traditionally used for the purpose of recording individual transactions is called an **account**. A group of related accounts that comprise a complete unit, such as all of the accounts of a specific business enterprise, is called a **ledger**.

NATURE OF AN ACCOUNT

The simplest form of an account has three parts: (1) a title, which is the name of the item recorded in the account; (2) a space for recording increases in the amount of the item, in terms of money; and (3) a space for recording decreases in the amount of the item, also in monetary terms. This form of an account, illustrated below, is known as a **T account** because of its similarity to the letter T.

Title	
Left side	Right side
debit	*credit*

The left side of the account is called the **debit** side and the right side is called the **credit** side.[1] The word **charge** is sometimes used as a synonym for debit. Amounts entered on the left side of an account, regardless of the account title, are called **debits** or **charges** to the account, and the account is said to be **debited** or **charged**. Amounts entered on the right side of an account are called **credits**, and the account is said to be **credited**.

In the following illustration, receipts of cash during a period of time have been listed vertically on the debit side of the cash account. The cash payments for the same period have been listed in similar fashion on the credit side of the account. A memorandum total of the cash receipts for the period to date, $10,950 in the illustration, may be inserted below the last debit at any time the information is desired. The figures should be small and written in pencil in order to avoid mistaking the amount for an additional debit. (The procedure is sometimes referred to as **pencil footing**.) The total of the cash payments, $6,850 in the illustration, may be inserted on the credit side in a similar manner. Subtraction of the smaller sum from the larger, $10,950 − $6,850, yields the amount of cash on hand, which is called the **balance of the account**. The cash account in the illustration has a balance of $4,100. This amount may be inserted in pencil figures next to the larger pencil footing, which identifies it as a **debit balance**. If a balance sheet were to be prepared at this time, the amount of cash reported thereon would be $4,100.

		Cash	
		3,750	850
		4,300	1,400
		2,900	700
4,100	10,950		2,900
			1,000
			6,850

Balance Sheet Accounts

The manner of recording data in the accounts and the relationship of accounts to the balance sheet are presented in the two illustrations that follow. For the first illustration, assume that R. D. Baker establishes a business venture, to be known as Baker Appliance Repair, by initially depositing $3,500 cash in a bank account for the use of the enterprise. Immediately after the deposit, the balance sheet for the business, in account form, would contain the following information:

Assets		Owner's Equity	
Cash	$3,500	R. D. Baker, capital.	$3,500

---

[1]Often abbreviated as *Dr.* for "debit" and *Cr.* for "credit," derived from the Latin *debere* and *credere*.

Every business transaction affects a minimum of two accounts. The effect of the above transaction on accounts in the ledger can be described as a $3,500 debit to Cash and a $3,500 credit to R. D. Baker, Capital. This information is initially entered in a record called a **journal**. In the journal, the information is stated in a formalized manner by listing the title of the account and the amount to be debited, followed by a similar listing, below and to the right of the debit, of the title of the account and the amount to be credited. The process of recording a transaction in the journal is called **journalizing**. The form of presentation is called a **journal entry**, and is illustrated as follows:

```
Cash......................................................  3,500
    R. D. Baker, Capital........................................         3,500
```

The data in the journal entry are transferred to the appropriate accounts by a process known as **posting**. The accounts after posting the above journal entry appear as follows:

Cash		R. D. Baker, Capital	
3,500			3,500

Note that the amount of the asset, which is reported on the left side of the account form of balance sheet, is posted to the left (debit) side of Cash. The owner's equity in the business, which is reported on the right side of the balance sheet, is posted to the right (credit) side of R. D. Baker, Capital. When other assets are acquired, the increases will be recorded as debits to the appropriate accounts. As owner's equity is increased or liabilities are incurred, the increases will be recorded as credits.

For the second illustration, assume that after opening the checking account, Baker purchased equipment and tools at a cost of $2,800. Baker paid $1,800 in cash by writing a check on the bank account, and agreed to pay the remaining $1,000 within thirty days. After this transaction, the data reported in the balance sheet would be as follows:

Assets		Liabilities	
Cash...................	$1,700	Accounts payable	$1,000
Equipment.............	2,800	Owner's Equity	
		R. D. Baker, capital.....	3,500
		Total liabilities and	
Total assets.............	$4,500	owner's equity.......	$4,500

The effect of the transaction can be described as a $2,800 debit (increase) to Equipment, an $1,800 credit (decrease) to Cash, and a $1,000 credit (increase) to Accounts Payable. The same information can be presented in the form of the following journal entry. (An entry composed of two or more debits or of two or more credits is called a **compound journal entry**.)

Equipment..	2,800	
Cash...		1,800
Accounts Payable		1,000

After the journal entry for the second transaction has been posted, the accounts of Baker Appliance Repair appear as follows:

Cash		Accounts Payable	
3,500	1,800		1,000

Equipment		R. D. Baker, Capital	
2,800			3,500

Note that the effect of the transaction was to increase one asset account, decrease another asset account, and increase a liability account. Note also that although the amounts, $2,800, $1,800, and $1,000, are different, the equality of debits and credits was maintained. Regardless of the complexity of a transaction or the number of accounts affected, the sum of the debits is always equal to the sum of the credits. This equality of debit and credit for each transaction is inherent in the equation $A = L + OE$. It is also because of this duality that the system is known as **double-entry accounting**.

In the preceding paragraphs, it was observed that the left side of asset accounts is used for recording increases and the right side is used for recording decreases. It was also observed that the right side of liability and owner's equity accounts is used to record increases. It naturally follows that the left side of such accounts is used to record decreases. The left side of all accounts, whether asset, liability, or owner's equity, is the debit side and the right side is the credit side. Consequently, a debit may be either an increase or a decrease, depending on the nature of the account affected. A credit may likewise be either an increase or a decrease, depending on the nature of the account. The rules of debit and credit may therefore be stated as follows:

GENERAL RULES OF DEBIT AND CREDIT	*Debit* may signify: Increase in asset accounts Decrease in liability accounts Decrease in owner's equity accounts	*Credit* may signify: Decrease in asset accounts Increase in liability accounts Increase in owner's equity accounts

Taking the Human Spirit into Account

Double-entry bookkeeping is one of the most beautiful discoveries of the human spirit. . . . It came from the same spirit which produced the systems of Galileo and Newton and the subject matter of modern physics and chemistry. By the same means, it organizes perceptions into a system, and one can characterize it as the first Cosmos constructed purely on the basis of mechanistic thought. . . . Without too much difficulty, we can recognize in double-entry bookkeeping the ideas of gravitation, of the circulation of the blood and of the conservation of matter.

Source: From the novel, *Wilhelm Meister's Lehrjahre* (Apprenticeship), written in 1795–6 by the German poet Johann Wolfgang von Goethe, translated by the German political economist Werner Sombart (1863–1941)

The rules of debit and credit may also be stated in relationship to the accounting equation and the account form of balance sheet, as in the following diagram:

Balance Sheet Accounts

ASSETS			LIABILITIES	
Asset Accounts			**Liability Accounts**	
Debit for increases	Credit for decreases		Debit for decreases	Credit for increases

OWNER'S EQUITY

Owner's Equity Accounts

Debit for decreases	Credit for increases

57

The owner of a sole proprietorship may from time to time withdraw cash from the business for personal use. This practice is common if the owner devotes full time to the business or if the business is the owner's principal source of income. Such withdrawals have the effect of decreasing owner's equity, and just as decreases in owner's equity are recorded as debits, withdrawals are recorded as debits. Withdrawals are debited to an account bearing the owner's name followed by Drawing or Personal. This account is periodically closed and its balance is transferred to the owner's capital account. Thus, debits to the drawing account may be thought of as either decreasing owner's equity (negative sense) or increasing drawings (positive sense).

The dividends account of a corporation is comparable to the drawing account of a sole proprietorship. Distributions of earnings to the stockholders are debited to Dividends, which is periodically closed and its balance transferred to the retained earnings account. Debits to the dividends account have the effect of decreasing owner's equity (negative sense) or increasing dividends (positive sense).

Income Statement Accounts

The theory of debit and credit in its application to revenue and expense accounts is based on the relationship of these accounts to owner's equity. The net income or the net loss for a period, as reported on the income statement, is the net increase or the net decrease in owner's equity as a result of operations.

Revenue increases owner's equity. Just as increases in owner's equity are recorded as credits, increases in revenues during an accounting period are recorded as credits.

Expenses have the effect of decreasing owner's equity, and just as decreases in owner's equity are recorded as debits, increases in expense accounts are recorded as debits. Debits to expense accounts are usually referred to in the positive sense (as increases in expense) rather than in the negative sense (as decreases in owner's equity). The rules of debit and credit as applied to revenue and expense accounts are shown in the following diagram:

EXPANDED RULES OF DEBIT AND CREDIT—INCOME STATEMENT ACCOUNTS	Income Statement Accounts	
	Debit for *decreases in owner's equity*	*Credit for* *increases in owner's equity*
	Expense Accounts	Revenue Accounts
	Debit for increases	Credit for decreases	Debit for decreases	Credit for increases

At the end of an accounting period, the revenue and expense account balances are reported in the income statement. Periodically, usually at the end of the accounting year, all revenue and expense account balances are transferred to a summarizing account and the accounts are then said to be *closed*. The balance in the summarizing account, which is the net income or net loss for the period, is then transferred to the owner's capital account (to the retained earnings account for a corporation), and the summarizing account is also closed. Because revenue and expense accounts are periodically closed, they are sometimes called **temporary accounts** or **nominal accounts**. The balances of the accounts reported in the balance sheet are carried forward from year to year and because of their permanence are sometimes referred to as **real accounts**.

NORMAL BALANCES OF ACCOUNTS

The sum of the increases recorded in an account is usually equal to or greater than the sum of the decreases recorded in the account. For this reason, the normal balances of all accounts are positive rather than negative. For example, the total debits (increases) in an asset account will ordinarily be greater than the total credits (decreases). Thus, asset accounts normally have debit balances.

The rules of debit and credit and the normal balances of the various types of accounts are summarized as follows. Note that the drawing, dividends, and expense accounts are considered in the positive sense. Increases in these accounts, which represent decreases in owner's equity, are recorded as debits.

	Increase	Decrease	Normal Balance
Balance sheet accounts:			
Asset	Debit	Credit	Debit
Liability	Credit	Debit	Credit
Owner's Equity			
Capital, Capital Stock,			
Retained Earnings	Credit	Debit	Credit
Drawing, Dividends	Debit	Credit	Debit
Income statement accounts:			
Revenue	Credit	Debit	Credit
Expense	Debit	Credit	Debit

NORMAL ACCOUNT BALANCES

When an account that normally has a debit balance actually has a credit balance, or vice versa, it is an indication of an accounting error or of an unusual situation. For example, a credit balance in the office equipment account could result only from an accounting error. On the other hand, a debit balance in an account payable account could result from an overpayment.

CLASSIFICATION OF ACCOUNTS

Accounts in the ledger are customarily listed in the order in which they appear in the financial statements and are classified according to common characteristics. Balance sheet accounts are classified as assets, liabilities, or owner's equity. Income statement accounts are classified as revenues or expenses. In addition, there may be subgroupings within the major categories. The classifications and accounts characteristically used by a small service enterprise are described in the paragraphs that follow. Additional classes and accounts are introduced in later chapters.

Assets

Any physical thing (tangible) or right (intangible) that has a money value is an asset. Assets are customarily divided into groups for presentation on the balance sheet. The two groups used most often are (1) current assets and (2) plant assets.

Current assets. Cash and other assets that may reasonably be expected to be realized in cash or sold or used up usually within a year or less, through the normal operations of the business, are called **current assets**. In addition to cash, the current assets usually owned by a service business are notes receivable and accounts receivable, and supplies and other prepaid expenses.

Cash is any medium of exchange that a bank will accept at face value. It includes bank deposits, currency, checks, bank drafts, and money orders. **Notes receivable** are claims against debtors evidenced by a written promise to pay a sum of money at a definite time to the order of a specified person or to bearer. **Accounts receivable** are also claims against debtors, but are less formal than notes. They arise from sales of services or merchandise on account. **Prepaid expenses** include supplies on hand and advance payments of expenses such as insurance and property taxes.

Plant assets. Tangible assets used in the business that are of a permanent or relatively fixed nature are called **plant assets** or **fixed assets**. Plant assets include equipment, machinery, buildings, and land. With the exception of land, such assets gradually wear out or otherwise lose their usefulness with the passage of time. They are said to *depreciate*. The concept of depreciation is discussed in more detail in Chapter 3.

Liabilities

Liabilities are debts owed to outsiders (creditors) and are frequently described on the balance sheet by titles that include the word "payable." The two categories occurring most frequently are (1) current liabilities and (2) long-term liabilities.

Current liabilities. Liabilities that will be due within a short time (usually one year or less) and that are to be paid out of current assets are called **current liabilities**. The most common liabilities in this group are **notes payable** and **accounts payable**, which are exactly like their receivable counterparts except that the debtor-creditor relationship is reversed. Other current liability accounts commonly found in the ledger are Salaries Payable, Interest Payable, and Taxes Payable.

Long-term liabilities. Liabilities that will not be due for a comparatively long time (usually more than one year) are called **long-term liabilities** or **fixed liabilities**. As they come within the one-year range and are to be paid, such liabilities become current. If the obligation is to be renewed rather than paid at maturity, however, it would continue to be classed as long-term. When payment of a long-term debt is to be spread over a number of years, the installments due within one year from a balance sheet date are classed as a current liability. When a note is accompanied by security in the form of a mortgage, the obligation may be referred to as *mortgage note payable* or *mortgage payable*.

Owner's Equity

Owner's equity is the residual claim against the assets of the business after the total liabilities are deducted. For a corporation, owner's equity is frequently called **stockholders' equity**, *shareholders' equity*, and *stockholders' investment*.

Capital, capital stock, and retained earnings. **Capital** is the owner's equity in a sole proprietorship (and partnership). The owner's equity may also be described as **net worth**. For a corporation, **capital stock** represents the investment of the stockholders, and **retained earnings** represents the net income retained in the business.

Drawing and dividends. **Drawings** represent the amount of withdrawals made by the owner of a sole proprietorship (and partnership). For a corporation, **dividends** represent the distribution of earnings to stockholders.

Revenues

Revenues are the gross increases in owner's equity as a result of the sale of merchandise, the performance of services for a customer or a client, the rental of property, the lending of money, and other business and professional activities entered into for the purpose of earning income. Revenue from sales of merchandise or sales of services is often identified merely as *sales*. Other terms employed to identify sources of revenue include *professional fees, commissions revenue, fares earned,* and *interest income.* If an enterprise has various types of revenue, a separate account should be maintained for each.

Expenses

Costs that have been consumed in the process of producing revenue are **expired costs** or expenses. The number of expense categories and individual expense accounts maintained in the ledger varies with the nature and the size of an enterprise. A large business with authority and responsibility spread among many employees may use an elaborate classification and hundreds of accounts as an aid in controlling expenses. For a small service business, a modest number of expense accounts is satisfactory.

CHART OF ACCOUNTS

The number of accounts maintained by a specific enterprise is affected by the nature of its operations, its volume of business, and the extent to which details are needed for taxing authorities, managerial decisions, credit purposes, etc. For example, one enterprise may have separate accounts for executive salaries, office salaries, and sales salaries, while another may find it satisfactory to record all types of salaries in a single salary expense account.

A listing of the accounts in a ledger is called a **chart of accounts**. Insofar as possible, the order of the accounts in the chart of accounts should agree with the order of the items in the balance sheet and the income statement. The accounts are numbered to permit indexing and also for use as posting references.

Although accounts in the ledger may be numbered consecutively as in the pages of a book, a flexible system of indexing is preferable. In the following chart of accounts for a small service business, Cole Photographic Studio, each account number has two digits. The first digit indicates the major division of the ledger in which the account is placed. Accounts beginning with 1 represent assets; 2, liabilities; 3, owner's equity (owner's capital and drawing); 4, revenue; and 5, expenses. The second digit indicates the position of the account within its division. A numbering system of this type has the advantage of permitting the later insertion of new accounts in their proper sequence without disturbing the other account numbers. For a large enterprise with a number of departments or branches, it is not unusual for each account number to have four or more digits.

Balance Sheet Accounts	Income Statement Accounts
1. Assets *Plant Asset 2*	4. Revenue
11 Cash	41 Sales
12 Accounts Receivable	5. Expenses
14 Supplies	51 Supplies Expense
15 Prepaid Rent	52 Salary Expense
18 Photographic Equipment	53 Rent Expense
19 Accumulated Depreciation[2]	54 Depreciation Expense[2]
2. Liabilities	59 Miscellaneous Expense
21 Accounts Payable	
22 Salaries Payable	
3. Owner's Equity	
31 Sara Cole, Capital	
32 Sara Cole, Drawing	
33 Income Summary[2]	

CHART OF ACCOUNTS FOR COLE PHOTO-GRAPHIC STUDIO

The initial preparation of the ledger based on the chart of accounts is often referred to as *opening the ledger*.

FLOW OF ACCOUNTING DATA

The flow of accounting data from the time a transaction occurs to its recording in the ledger may be diagrammed as follows:

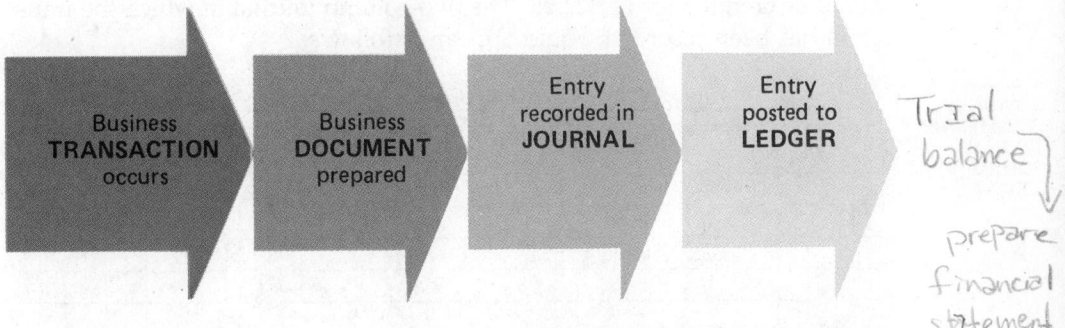

Trial balance → prepare financial statement

The initial record of each transaction, or of a group of similar transactions, is evidenced by a business document, such as a sales ticket, a check stub, or a cash register tape. On the basis of the evidence provided by the business documents, the transactions are entered in chronological order in a journal. The amounts of the debits and the credits in the journal are then transferred or posted to the accounts in the ledger.

[2]The accumulated depreciation, depreciation expense, and income summary accounts are discussed in Chapter 3, when the process of preparing financial statements for Cole Photographic Studio is discussed.

TWO-COLUMN JOURNAL

The basic features of a journal entry were illustrated earlier when the use of debit and credit was introduced. There is great variety in both the design of journals and the number of different journals that can be employed by an enterprise. A business may use a single all-purpose two-column journal, or it may use a number of multicolumn journals, restricting each to a single type of transaction. Examples of more sophisticated journal systems are discussed and illustrated in later chapters. Means by which business documents or various types of automated processing devices may entirely replace journals is also discussed.

Before a transaction is entered in the two-column journal, it should be analyzed according to the following sequence of steps:

1. Determine whether an asset, a liability, owner's equity, revenue, or expense is affected.
2. Determine whether the affected asset, liability, owner's equity, revenue, or expense increases or decreases.
3. Determine whether the effect of the transaction should be recorded as a debit or as a credit in an asset, liability, owner's equity, revenue, or expense account.

To illustrate the results of such analyses, assume that $1,822.25 is received from cash sales for May 1. The asset Cash increases and therefore should be debited for $1,822.25. The revenue account Sales also increases and therefore should be credited for $1,822.25. The two-column journal in which the transaction has been recorded would appear as follows:

STANDARD
FORM OF THE
TWO-
COLUMN
JOURNAL

		JOURNAL							PAGE 17					
	DATE	DESCRIPTION	POST. REF.			DEBIT				CREDIT				
1	1987 May 1	Cash			1	8	2	2	25					1
2		Sales								1	8	2	2	25	2
3		Cash sales for the day.													3
4															4

The process of recording a transaction in a two-column journal is summarized as follows:

1. Record the date:
   a. Insert the year at the top only of the Date column of each page, except when the year date changes.
   b. Insert the month on the first line only of the Date column of each page, except when the month date changes.
   c. Insert the day in the Date column on the first line used for each transaction, regardless of the number of transactions during the day.

2. Record the debit:
   Insert the title of the account to be debited at the extreme left of the Description column and enter the amount in the Debit column.
3. Record the credit:
   Insert the title of the account to be credited below the account debited, moderately indented, and enter the amount in the Credit column.
4. Write an explanation:
   Brief explanations may be written below each entry, moderately indented. Some accountants prefer that the explanation be omitted if the nature of the transaction is obvious. It is also permissible to omit a lengthy explanation of a complex transaction if a reference to the related business document can be substituted.

It should be noted that all transactions are recorded only in terms of debits and credits to specific accounts. The titles used in the entries should be the same as the titles of the accounts in the ledger. For example, supplies purchased should be entered as a debit to Supplies, not to "supplies purchased," and cash received should be entered as a debit to Cash, not to "cash received."

The line following an entry is left blank in order to clearly separate each entry. The column headed Post. Ref. (posting reference) is not used until the debits and credits are posted to the appropriate accounts in the ledger.

TWO-COLUMN ACCOUNTS AND FOUR-COLUMN ACCOUNTS

Accounts in the simple T form are used primarily for illustrative purposes. The addition of special rulings to the T form yields the standard two-column form illustrated as follows:

ACCOUNT Cash								ACCOUNT NO. 11		
DATE	ITEM	POST. REF.	DEBIT	DATE	ITEM	POST. REF.	CREDIT
1987 May 1	Balance	✔	5 2 4 5 00	1987 May 1		17	3 5 0 00
1		17	1 8 2 2 25	1		17	9 9 5 50
3		17	9 6 0 40	3		17	1 9 2 00
				3		17	1 8 8 2 25
	4,607.90		8 0 2 7 65				3 4 1 9 75

STANDARD FORM OF THE TWO-COLUMN ACCOUNT

The standard two-column account form distinguishes to the greatest possible extent between debit entries and credit entries. It is primarily because of this feature that the T form is used at the beginning of introductory accounting courses. In actual practice, there has been a tendency for account forms with balance columns to replace the simpler T form, though the latter is still used. A four-column form is shown as follows:

STANDARD
FORM OF THE
FOUR-
COLUMN
ACCOUNT

ACCOUNT Cash												ACCOUNT NO. 11	
DATE	ITEM	POST. REF.	DEBIT		CREDIT		BALANCE						
							DEBIT			CREDIT			
1987 May 1	Balance	✓					5 2 4 5	00					
1		17	1 8 2 2	25			7 0 6 7	25					
1		17			3 5 0	00	6 7 1 7	25					
1		17			9 9 5	50	5 7 2 1	75					
3		17	9 6 0	40			6 6 8 2	15					
3		17			1 9 2	00	6 4 9 0	15					
3		17			1 8 8 2	25	4 6 0 7	90					

Among the significant advantages of the four-column account form are the following:

1. Only a single date column is required, with each debit and credit appearing in its chronological order.
2. The debit or credit nature of an account balance is more easily determined and more prominently displayed in the account.
3. Having immediately adjacent debit and credit columns makes it easier to examine the data in an account.

When posting is computerized and the four-column format is used, the new balance of an account is automatically computed in the proper column after each posting. The account balance is thus always readily available. The same procedure may be followed when the posting is done manually. An alternative is to postpone the computation of the balance until all postings for the month have been completed. When this is done, only the final month-end balance is inserted in the appropriate balance column. The exact procedure adopted in a particular situation will depend upon such factors as the availability of calculators and the desirability of having current account balances visible at all times.

POSTING

When posting is done manually, the debits and credits in the journal may be posted in the order that they occur or, if many items are to be posted at one time, all the debits may be posted first, followed by the credits. The posting of a debit journal entry or a credit journal entry to an account in the ledger is performed in the following manner:

1. Record the date and the amount of the entry in the account.
2. Insert the number of the journal page in the Posting Reference column of the account.
3. Insert the ledger account number in the Posting Reference column of the journal.

These procedures are illustrated as follows by the posting of a debit to the cash account. The posting of a credit uses the same sequence of procedures.

DIAGRAM OF THE POSTING OF A DEBIT

JOURNAL PAGE 17

	DATE		DESCRIPTION	POST. REF.	DEBIT	CREDIT	
1	1987 May	1	Cash	11	1 8 2 2 25		1
2			Sales			1 8 2 2 25	2
3			Cash sales for the day.				3
4							4

ACCOUNT Cash   ACCOUNT NO. 11

DATE		ITEM	POST. REF.	DEBIT	CREDIT	BALANCE DEBIT	BALANCE CREDIT
1987 May	1	Balance	✔			5 2 4 5 00	
	1		17	1 8 2 2 25		7 0 6 7 25	

ILLUSTRATION OF JOURNALIZING AND POSTING

To illustrate the journalizing and posting process, a month's transactions for Cole Photographic Studio are used. Cole Photographic Studio is the small service business whose chart of accounts was presented on page 63.

To reduce repetition, some of the following transactions are stated as a summary. For example, sales of services for cash are ordinarily recorded on a daily basis, but in the illustration, summary totals are given only at the middle and end of the month. Similarly, all sales of services on account during the month are summarized as a single transaction. In practice, each sale would be recorded separately.

Mar. 1. Sara Cole operated a photographic business in her home on a part-time basis. She decided to move to rented quarters as of March 1 and to devote full time to the business, which was to be known as Cole Photographic Studio. The following assets were invested in the enterprise: cash, $3,500; accounts receivable, $950; supplies, $1,200; and photographic equipment, $15,000. There were no liabilities transferred to the business.

Analysis: The four asset accounts Cash, Accounts Receivable, Supplies, and Photographic Equipment increase and are debited for $3,500, $950, $1,200, and $15,000, respectively. The owner's equity in these assets is equal to the sum of the assets, or $20,650; hence, Sara Cole, Capital is credited for that amount. (The use of individual accounts receivable from customers is described in a later chapter.)

	DATE		DESCRIPTION	POST. REF.	DEBIT	CREDIT	
1	1987 Mar.	1	Cash	11	3 5 0 0 00		1
2			Accounts Receivable	12	9 5 0 00		2
3			Supplies	14	1 2 0 0 00		3
4			Photographic Equipment	18	15 0 0 0 00		4
5			Sara Cole, Capital	31		20 6 5 0 00	5

JOURNAL — PAGE 1

(The ledger to which the illustrative entries are posted is presented on pages 72–74.)

Mar. 1. Paid $2,400 on a lease rental contract, the payment representing three months' rent of quarters for the studio.

Analysis: The asset acquired in exchange for the cash payment is the use of the property for three months. The asset Prepaid Rent increases and is debited for $2,400; the asset Cash decreases and is credited for $2,400. (When rent for a single month is prepaid at the beginning of a month, it is customarily debited to the rent expense account at the time of payment, thus avoiding the necessity of transferring the amount from Prepaid Rent to Rent Expense at the end of the month.)

6							6
7		1	Prepaid Rent	15	2 4 0 0 00		7
8			Cash	11		2 4 0 0 00	8

Mar. 4. Purchased additional photographic equipment on account from Carson Equipment Co. for $2,500.

Analysis: The asset Photographic Equipment increases and is therefore debited for $2,500. The liability Accounts Payable increases and is credited for $2,500. (The use of individual accounts payable to creditors is described in a later chapter.)

9																		9
10		4	Photographic Equipment		18		2	5	0	0	00							10
11			Accounts Payable		21								2	5	0	0	00	11

Mar. 5. Received $850 from customers in payment of their accounts.

Analysis: The asset Cash increases and is debited for $850; the asset Accounts Receivable decreases and is credited for $850.

12																	12
13		5	Cash		11		8	5	0	00							13
14			Accounts Receivable		12							8	5	0	00		14

Mar. 6. Paid $125 for a newspaper advertisement.

Analysis: Expense accounts are subdivisions of owner's equity. Increases in expense are decreases in owner's equity; hence, an expense account is debited for $125. The asset Cash was decreased by the transaction; therefore that account is credited for $125. (Miscellaneous Expense is debited because total expenditures for advertising during an accounting period are expected to be relatively minor.)

15																	15
16		6	Miscellaneous Expense		59		1	2	5	00							16
17			Cash		11							1	2	5	00		17

Mar. 10. Paid $500 to Carson Equipment Co. to apply on the $2,500 debt owed them.

Analysis: This payment decreases the liability Accounts Payable, so that account is debited for $500. It also decreases the asset Cash, which is credited for $500.

18																	18
19		10	Accounts Payable		21		5	0	0	00							19
20			Cash		11							5	0	0	00		20

Mar. 13. Paid receptionist $575 for two weeks' salary.

Analysis: Similar to transaction of March 6.

21									21
22	13	Salary Expense	52	5 7 5 00					22
23		Cash	11			5 7 5 00			23

Mar. 16. Received $1,980 from sales for the first half of March.

Analysis: Cash increases and is debited for $1,980. The revenue account Sales, which is a subdivision of owner's equity, increases and is credited for $1,980.

24									24
25	16	Cash	11	1 9 8 0 00					25
26		Sales	41			1 9 8 0 00			26

Mar. 20. Paid $650 for supplies.

Analysis: The asset Supplies increases and is debited for $650; the asset Cash decreases and is credited for $650.

27									27
28	20	Supplies	14	6 5 0 00					28
29		Cash	11			6 5 0 00			29

Mar. 27. Paid receptionist $575 for two weeks' salary.

Analysis: Similar to transaction of March 6.

30									30
31	27	Salary Expense	52	5 7 5 00					31
32		Cash	11			5 7 5 00			32

Mar. 31. Paid $69 for telephone bill for the month.

Analysis: Similar to transaction of March 6.

33									33
34	31	Miscellaneous Expense	59	6 9 00					34
35		Cash	11			6 9 00			35

Mar. 31. Paid $175 for electric bill for the month.

Analysis: Similar to transaction of March 6.

36																			36
37		31	Miscellaneous Expense		59			1	7	5	00								37
38			Cash		11								1	7	5	00			38

Mar. 31. Received $1,870 from sales for the second half of March.

Analysis: Similar to transaction of March 16.

						JOURNAL								PAGE 2		
	DATE		DESCRIPTION		POST. REF.		DEBIT					CREDIT				
1	1987 Mar.	31	Cash		11		1	8	7	0	00					1
2			Sales		41								1	8	7	0	00	2

Mar. 31. Sales on account totaled $1,675 for the month.

Analysis: The asset Accounts Receivable increases and is debited for $1,675. The revenue account Sales increases and is credited for $1,675. (Note that the revenue is earned even though no cash is received; the claim against the customers is as much an asset as cash. As customers pay their accounts later, Cash will be debited and Accounts Receivable will be credited.)

3																			3
4		31	Accounts Receivable		12			1	6	7	5	00							4
5			Sales		41									1	6	7	5	00	5

Mar. 31. Cole withdrew $1,500 for her personal use.

Analysis: The transaction resulted in a decrease in the amount of owner's equity invested in the business and is recorded by a $1,500 debit to Sara Cole, Drawing; the decrease in business cash is recorded by a $1,500 credit to Cash.

6																			6
7		31	Sara Cole, Drawing		32			1	5	0	0	00							7
8			Cash		11									1	5	0	0	00	8

After all the entries for the month have been posted, the ledger will appear as shown below and on pages 73–74. In practice, each account would appear on a separate page in the ledger. Tracing each entry from the journal to the accounts in the ledger will give a clear understanding of the posting process.

The accounts are numbered in accordance with the chart shown on page 63. However, some of the accounts listed in the chart are not shown in the illustrative ledger. The additional accounts will be used later when the illustration for Cole Photographic Studio is completed in Chapter 3.

LEDGER—
COLE
PHOTO-
GRAPHIC
STUDIO

ACCOUNT Cash   ACCOUNT NO. 11

DATE		ITEM	POST. REF.	DEBIT	CREDIT	BALANCE DEBIT	BALANCE CREDIT
1987 Mar.	1		1	3 5 0 0 00		3 5 0 0 00	
	1		1		2 4 0 0 00	1 1 0 0 00	
	5		1	8 5 0 00		1 9 5 0 00	
	6		1		1 2 5 00	1 8 2 5 00	
	10		1		5 0 0 00	1 3 2 5 00	
	13		1		5 7 5 00	7 5 0 00	
	16		1	1 9 8 0 00		2 7 3 0 00	
	20		1		6 5 0 00	2 0 8 0 00	
	27		1		5 7 5 00	1 5 0 5 00	
	31		1		6 9 00	1 4 3 6 00	
	31		1		1 7 5 00	1 2 6 1 00	
	31		2	1 8 7 0 00		3 1 3 1 00	
	31		2		1 5 0 0 00	1 6 3 1 00	

ACCOUNT Accounts Receivable   ACCOUNT NO. 12

DATE		ITEM	POST. REF.	DEBIT	CREDIT	BALANCE DEBIT	BALANCE CREDIT
1987 Mar.	1		1	9 5 0 00		9 5 0 00	
	5		1		8 5 0 00	1 0 0 00	
	31		2	1 6 7 5 00		1 7 7 5 00	

ACCOUNT Supplies   ACCOUNT NO. 14

DATE		ITEM	POST. REF.	DEBIT	CREDIT	BALANCE DEBIT	BALANCE CREDIT
1987 Mar.	1		1	1 2 0 0 00		1 2 0 0 00	
	20		1	6 5 0 00		1 8 5 0 00	

LEDGER—
COLE
PHOTO-
GRAPHIC
STUDIO
(CONTINUED)

ACCOUNT **Prepaid Rent**   ACCOUNT NO. 15

DATE	ITEM	POST. REF.	DEBIT	CREDIT	BALANCE DEBIT	BALANCE CREDIT
1987 Mar. 1		1	2 4 0 0 00		2 4 0 0 00	

ACCOUNT **Photographic Equipment**   ACCOUNT NO. 18

DATE	ITEM	POST. REF.	DEBIT	CREDIT	BALANCE DEBIT	BALANCE CREDIT
1987 Mar. 1		1	15 0 0 0 00		15 0 0 0 00	
4		1	2 5 0 0 00		17 5 0 0 00	

ACCOUNT **Accounts Payable**   ACCOUNT NO. 21

DATE	ITEM	POST. REF.	DEBIT	CREDIT	BALANCE DEBIT	BALANCE CREDIT
1987 Mar. 4		1		2 5 0 0 00		2 5 0 0 00
10		1	5 0 0 00			2 0 0 0 00

ACCOUNT **Sara Cole, Capital**   ACCOUNT NO. 31

DATE	ITEM	POST. REF.	DEBIT	CREDIT	BALANCE DEBIT	BALANCE CREDIT
1987 Mar. 1		1		20 6 5 0 00		20 6 5 0 00

ACCOUNT **Sara Cole, Drawing**   ACCOUNT NO. 32

DATE	ITEM	POST. REF.	DEBIT	CREDIT	BALANCE DEBIT	BALANCE CREDIT
1987 Mar. 31		2	1 5 0 0 00		1 5 0 0 00	

ACCOUNT **Sales**   ACCOUNT NO. 41

DATE	ITEM	POST. REF.	DEBIT	CREDIT	BALANCE DEBIT	BALANCE CREDIT
1987 Mar. 16		1		1 9 8 0 00		1 9 8 0 00
31		2		1 8 7 0 00		3 8 5 0 00
31		2		1 6 7 5 00		5 5 2 5 00

ACCOUNT **Salary Expense**   ACCOUNT NO. 52

DATE	ITEM	POST. REF.	DEBIT	CREDIT	BALANCE DEBIT	BALANCE CREDIT
1987 Mar. 13		1	5 7 5 00		5 7 5 00	
27		1	5 7 5 00		1 1 5 0 00	

LEDGER—
COLE
PHOTO-
GRAPHIC
STUDIO
(CONCLUDED)

ACCOUNT Miscellaneous Expense								ACCOUNT NO. 59		
DATE	ITEM	POST. REF.	DEBIT	CREDIT	BALANCE					
					DEBIT			CREDIT		
1987 Mar. 6		1	1 2 5 00		1 2 5 00					
31		1	6 9 00		1 9 4 00					
31		1	1 7 5 00		3 6 9 00					

TRIAL BALANCE

The equality of debits and credits in the ledger should be verified at the end of each accounting period, if not more often. Such a verification, which is called a **trial balance**, may be in the form of a calculator tape or in the form illustrated as follows. The summary listing of both the balances and the titles of the accounts is also useful in preparing the financial statements.

Cole Photographic Studio Trial Balance March 31, 1987		
Cash	1 6 3 1 00	
Accounts Receivable	1 7 7 5 00	
Supplies	1 8 5 0 00	
Prepaid Rent	2 4 0 0 00	
Photographic Equipment	17 5 0 0 00	
Accounts Payable		2 0 0 0 00
Sara Cole, Capital		20 6 5 0 00
Sara Cole, Drawing	1 5 0 0 00	
Sales		5 5 2 5 00
Salary Expense	1 1 5 0 00	
Miscellaneous Expense	3 6 9 00	
	28 1 7 5 00	28 1 7 5 00

As the first step in preparing the trial balance, the balance of each account in the ledger should be determined. If two-column accounts are used, memorandum pencil footings and balances are inserted in accordance with the procedure illustrated on page 65. If the four-column account form is employed, the balance of each account must be indicated in the appropriate balance column on the same line as the last posting to the account. (In the illustrative ledger, the balances were extended after each posting.)

Proof Provided by the Trial Balance

The trial balance does not provide complete proof of the accuracy of the ledger. It indicates only that the *debits* and the *credits* are *equal*. This proof is of value, however, because errors frequently affect the equality of debits and credits. If the two totals of a trial balance are not equal, it is probably due to one or more of the following types of errors:

1. Error in preparing the trial balance, such as:
   a. One of the columns of the trial balance was incorrectly added.
   b. The amount of an account balance was incorrectly recorded on the trial balance.
   c. A debit balance was recorded on the trial balance as a credit, or vice versa, or a balance was omitted entirely.
2. Error in determining the account balances, such as:
   a. A balance was incorrectly computed.
   b. A balance was entered in the wrong balance column.
3. Error in recording a transaction in the ledger, such as:
   a. An erroneous amount was posted to the account.
   b. A debit entry was posted as a credit, or vice versa.
   c. A debit or a credit posting was omitted.

Among the types of errors that will not cause an inequality in the trial balance totals are the following:

1. Failure to record a transaction or to post a transaction.
2. Recording the same erroneous amount for both the debit and the credit parts of a transaction.
3. Recording the same transaction more than once.
4. Posting a part of a transaction correctly as a debit or credit but to the wrong account.

It is readily apparent that care should be exercised both in recording transactions in the journal and in posting to the accounts. The desirability of accuracy in determining account balances and reporting them on the trial balance is equally obvious.

Discovery of Errors

The existence of errors in the accounts may be determined in various ways: (1) by audit procedures, (2) by chance discovery, or (3) through the medium of the trial balance. If the debit and the credit totals of the trial balance are not in agreement, the exact amount of the difference between the totals should be determined before proceeding to search for the error.

The amount of the difference between the two totals of a trial balance sometimes gives a clue as to the nature of the error or where it occurred. For example, a difference of 10, 100, or 1,000 between two totals is frequently the result of an error in addition. A difference between totals can also be due to the omission of a debit or a credit posting or, if it is divisible evenly by 2, to the posting of a debit as a credit, or vice versa. For example, if the debit and

ERRORS!

Chasing errors in a trial balance is not a fascinating sport like chasing a golf ball. It is tedious and uninteresting. The only way for an accountant to avoid it is to make no mistakes—and that standard is too high for most of us to maintain continuously. The penalty for one little slip may be a night or two at the office, checking an interminable mass of postings. For this reason, any hint that may aid in tracking an error to its diabolically well concealed lair, any straw that may be floated out for a submerged accountant to grasp, is a kindness and a charity.

Some day, perhaps, the mechanical accountant will entirely supplant the human article, but for a long time yet many a set of accounts will be posted by hand, and many a balance will be taken off without the aid of even an adding machine. Moreover, when the mechanical millennium—or whatever it is—arrives, there will still be balances to chase, for the machine will chew and digest only what is fed to it, and if its diet be not perfectly balanced, neither will be the result, and still will be heard the old familiar question, "How much are you out?"

This quarry is, of course, the mistake that threw out the balance, and it is the difference between what was written and what should have been written. For the sake of brevity, I shall call this the "error", which strictly speaking it is not, for the error is really the mistake itself and not its result.

Now, when a balance doesn't balance, there are several obvious things to be done. The footings all have to be checked; one must be certain that each ledger account is correctly computed and the right amount carried into the trial-balance book in the proper column; one must be assured that the totals have been carried forward correctly from one page to another; that the journal is in balance; that no posting checks are missing. Then all the items that are the same as the error must be looked up for a skipped posting, and, if it happens to be an even number, all items that are one-half the error, in case something has been posted on the wrong side. These things are simple routine, and before the list is complete the cause of the trouble has probably been found, and the happy discoverer has gone contentedly home to help Willie with his arithmetic.

If not, if the two columns simply will not add up the same, things begin to look serious. The accountant phones his wife that he will not be home to dinner. Then he begins to analyze his error and see if there are any sign-posts sticking up out of it. If none is found, he may as well begin to check postings. The sooner he starts, the sooner he gets through, and he has my sympathy, especially if he has to do it by himself.

Source: Adapted from F. Howard Seely, "The Transposition of Figures," *The Journal of Accountancy* (June, 1932).

the credit totals of a trial balance are $20,640 and $20,236 respectively, the difference of $404 may indicate that a credit posting of that amount was omitted or that a credit of $202 was erroneously posted as a debit.

Two other common types of errors are known as **transpositions** and **slides**. A transposition is the erroneous rearrangement of digits, such as writing $542 as $452 or $524. In a slide, the entire number is erroneously moved one or more spaces to the right or the left, such as writing $542.00 as $54.20 or $5,420.00. If an error of either type has occurred and there are no other errors, the discrepancy between the two trial balance totals will be evenly divisible by 9.

A preliminary examination along the lines suggested by the preceding paragraphs will frequently disclose the error. If it does not, the general procedure is to retrace the various steps in the accounting process, beginning with the last step and working back to the original entries in the journal. While there are no rigid rules governing the procedures, the following plan is suggested:

1. Verify the accuracy of the trial balance totals by re-adding the columns.
2. Compare the listings in the trial balance with the balances shown in the ledger, making certain that no accounts have been omitted.
3. Recompute the balance of each account in the ledger.
4. Trace the postings in the ledger back to the journal, placing a small check mark by the item in the ledger and also in the journal. If the error is not found, examine each account to see if there is an entry without a check mark. Do the same with the entries in the journal.
5. Verify the equality of the debits and the credits in the journal.

Ordinarily, errors that have caused the trial balance totals to be unequal will be discovered before all of the procedures outlined above are completed.

CHAPTER REVIEW

KEY POINTS

1. Nature of an Account.

The record traditionally kept for each item that appears on the financial statements is the account. A group of related accounts that comprise a complete

...ll the accounts of a specific business enterprise, is called the

...d decreases in an account are recorded as debits (entries on the ... of the account) and credits (entries on the right side of the account). ...odically, the debits and the credits in an account are summed and the difference between the two sums is determined. This difference is called the balance of the account. General rules of debit and credit have been established for recording increases or decreases to asset, liability, owner's equity, revenue, expense, drawing, and dividend accounts.

The effects of transactions are initially entered in a record called a journal. Periodically, transactions that have been journalized are transferred to the accounts by a process known as posting.

2. Normal Balances of Accounts.

The sum of the increases recorded in an account is usually equal to or greater than the sum of the decreases recorded in the account. For this reason, the normal balance of an account is indicated by the side of the account (debit or credit) that receives the increases.

The rules of debit and credit and normal account balances are summarized in the following table:

	Increase	Decrease	Normal Balance
Balance sheet accounts:			
Asset	Debit	Credit	Debit
Liability	Credit	Debit	Credit
Owner's Equity			
Capital, Capital Stock,			
Retained Earnings	Credit	Debit	Credit
Drawing, Dividends	Debit	Credit	Debit
Income statement accounts:			
Revenue	Credit	Debit	Credit
Expense	Debit	Credit	Debit

3. Classification of Accounts.

Accounts in the ledger are customarily listed in the order in which they appear in the financial statements and are classified according to common characteristics. Balance sheet accounts are classified as asset, liability, or owner's equity accounts. Income statement accounts are classified as revenues or expenses. There may also be subgroupings within the major categories.

4. Chart of Accounts.

Accounts in the ledger are numbered consecutively so as to permit easy indexing and for use in posting. A listing of the accounts used by a specific enterprise in its ledger is referred to as a chart of accounts.

5. Flow of Accounting Data.

The flow of accounting data from the time a transaction occurs to its recording in the ledger is diagrammed as follows:

Business TRANSACTION occurs	→	Business DOCUMENT prepared	→	Entry recorded in JOURNAL	→	Entry posted to LEDGER

6. Two-Column Journal.

A two-column journal with a debit column and a credit column may be used for recording initial transactions in an accounting system. Before a transaction is entered in a journal, it should be analyzed according to the following sequence of steps:
1. Determine whether an asset, a liability, owner's equity, revenue, or expense is affected.
2. Determine whether the affected asset, liability, owner's equity, revenue, or expense increases or decreases.
3. Determine whether the effect of the transaction should be recorded as a debit or as a credit in an asset, liability, owner's equity, revenue, or expense account.

7. Two-Column Accounts and Four-Column Accounts.

T accounts are used primarily for illustrative purposes, but are seldom used in practice. Special rulings may be added to the basic T account form to yield a two-column account. A four-column account that provides debit balance and credit balance columns is used widely in practice.

8. Posting.

Periodically, transaction data are transferred from the journal to the accounts in the ledger through a process known as posting.

9. Trial Balance.

The equality of the debits and credits in a ledger are verified periodically by the preparation of a trial balance. The trial balance does not provide complete proof of accuracy of the ledger, but only indicates that the debits and credits are equal.

KEY TERMS

account 53
ledger 53
T account 53
debit 54
credit 54
balance of the account 54
journal 55
journalizing 55
posting 55
double-entry accounting 56
temporary accounts 59
nominal accounts 59
real accounts 59
current assets 60
cash 60
notes receivable 60
accounts receivable 60
prepaid expenses 60
plant assets 60

current liabilities 61
notes payable 61
accounts payable 61
long-term liabilities 61
owner's equity 61
stockholders' equity 61
capital 61
net worth 61
capital stock 61
retained earnings 61
drawings 61
dividends 61
revenues 61
expenses 62
chart of accounts 62
trial balance 74
transpositions 77
slides 77

SELF-EXAMINATION QUESTIONS

Answers in Appendix B.

1. A debit may signify:
   A. an increase in an asset account
   B. a decrease in an asset account
   C. an increase in a liability account
   D. an increase in the owner's capital account

2. The type of account with a normal credit balance is:
   A. an asset
   B. a drawing
   C. a revenue
   D. an expense

3. The current asset category would include:
   A. cash
   B. accounts receivable
   C. supplies on hand
   D. all of the above

4. The receipt of cash from customers in payment of their accounts would be recorded by a:
   A. debit to Cash; credit to Accounts Receivable
   B. debit to Accounts Receivable; credit to Cash
   C. debit to Cash; credit to Accounts Payable
   D. debit to Accounts Payable; credit to Cash

5. The form listing the balances and the titles of the accounts in the ledger on a given date is the:

   A. income statement   C. retained earnings statement

   B. balance sheet   D. trial balance

ILLUSTRATIVE PROBLEM

Judy K. Schmidt, M.D., has been practicing as a pediatrician for three years. During June, she completed the following transactions in her practice of pediatrics:

June 1. Paid office rent for June, $600.

      2. Purchased equipment on account, $2,100.

      5. Received cash on account from patients, $4,150.

      8. Purchased X-ray film and other supplies on account, $145.

      9. One of the items of equipment purchased on June 2 was defective. It was returned with the permission of the supplier, who agreed to reduce the account for the amount charged for the item, $125.

    12. Paid cash to creditors on account, $1,250.

    16. Sold X-ray film to another doctor at cost, as an accommodation, receiving cash, $63.

    17. Paid cash for renewal of property insurance policy, $370.

    20. Discovered that the balance of the cash account and of the accounts payable account as of June 1 were overstated by $50. A payment of that amount to a creditor in May had not been recorded. Journalize the $50 payment as of June 20.

    23. Paid cash for laboratory analyses, $245.

    27. Paid cash from business bank account for personal and family expenses, $1,250.

    30. Recorded the cash received in payment of services (on a cash basis) to patients during June, $1,720.

    30. Paid salaries of receptionist and nurses, $1,725.

    30. Paid gas and electricity expense, $157.

    30. Paid water expense, $29.

    30. Recorded fees charged to patients on account for services performed in June, $4,145.

    30. Paid telephone expense, $74.

    30. Paid miscellaneous expenses, $132.

Schmidt's account titles, numbers, and balances as of June 1 (all normal balances) are listed as follows: Cash, 11, $3,123; Accounts Receivable, 12, $6,725; Supplies, 13, $290; Prepaid Insurance, 14, $365; Equipment, 18, $19,745; Accounts Payable, 22, $765; Judy K. Schmidt, Capital, 31, $29,483; Judy K. Schmidt, Drawing, 32; Professional Fees, 41; Salary Expense, 51; Rent Expense, 53; Laboratory Expense, 55; Utilities Expense, 56; Miscellaneous Expense, 59.

Instructions:

1. Open a ledger of four-column accounts for Dr. Schmidt as of June 1 of the current year. Enter the balances in the appropriate balance columns and place a check mark ($\checkmark$) in the posting reference column. (It is advisable to verify the equality of the debit and credit balances in the ledger before proceeding with the next instruction.)
2. Record each transaction in a two-column journal.
3. Post the journal to the ledger, extending the month-end balances to the appropriate balance columns after all posting is completed.
4. Prepare a trial balance as of June 30.

SOLUTION

(2) and (3)

JOURNAL   PAGE 27

	DATE		DESCRIPTION	POST. REF.	DEBIT	CREDIT	
1	19-- June	1	Rent Expense	53	6 0 0 00		1
2			Cash	11		6 0 0 00	2
3							3
4		2	Equipment	18	2 1 0 0 00		4
5			Accounts Payable	22		2 1 0 0 00	5
6							6
7		5	Cash	11	4 1 5 0 00		7
8			Accounts Receivable	12		4 1 5 0 00	8
9							9
10		8	Supplies	13	1 4 5 00		10
11			Accounts Payable	22		1 4 5 00	11
12							12

			POST. REF.	DEBIT					CREDIT					
13	9	Accounts Payable	22		1	2	5	00						13
14		Equipment	18							1	2	5	00	14
15														15
16	12	Accounts Payable	22	1	2	5	0	00						16
17		Cash	11						1	2	5	0	00	17
18														18
19	16	Cash	11			6	3	00						19
20		Supplies	13								6	3	00	20
21														21
22	17	Prepaid Insurance	14		3	7	0	00						22
23		Cash	11							3	7	0	00	23
24														24
25	20	Accounts Payable	22			5	0	00						25
26		Cash	11								5	0	00	26
27														27
28	23	Laboratory Expense	55		2	4	5	00						28
29		Cash	11							2	4	5	00	29
30														30
31	27	Judy K. Schmidt, Drawing	32	1	2	5	0	00						31
32		Cash	11						1	2	5	0	00	32
33														33
34	30	Cash	11	1	7	2	0	00						34
35		Professional Fees	41						1	7	2	0	00	35
36														26

JOURNAL PAGE 28

	DATE	DESCRIPTION	POST. REF.	DEBIT					CREDIT					
1	30	Salary Expense	51	1	7	2	5	00						1
2		Cash	11						1	7	2	5	00	2
3														3
4	30	Utilities Expense	56		1	5	7	00						4
5		Cash	11							1	5	7	00	5
6														6
7	30	Utilities Expense	56			2	9	00						7
8		Cash	11								2	9	00	8
9														9
10	30	Accounts Receivable	12	4	1	4	5	00						10
11		Professional Fees	41						4	1	4	5	00	11
12														12
13	30	Utilities Expense	56			7	4	00						13
14		Cash	11								7	4	00	14
15														15
16	30	Miscellaneous Expense	59		1	3	2	00						16
17		Cash	11							1	3	2	00	17

(1) and (3)

ACCOUNT Cash   ACCOUNT NO. 11

DATE		ITEM	POST. REF.	DEBIT	CREDIT	BALANCE DEBIT	BALANCE CREDIT
19-- June	1	Balance	✔			3 1 2 3 00	
	1		27		6 0 0 00		
	5		27	4 1 5 0 00			
	12		27		1 2 5 0 00		
	16		27	6 3 00			
	17		27		3 7 0 00		
	20		27		5 0 00		
	23		27		2 4 5 00		
	27		27		1 2 5 0 00		
	30		27	1 7 2 0 00			
	30		28		1 7 2 5 00		
	30		28		1 5 7 00		
	30		28		2 9 00		
	30		28		7 4 00		
	30		28		1 3 2 00	3 1 7 4 00	

ACCOUNT Accounts Receivable   ACCOUNT NO. 12

DATE		ITEM	POST. REF.	DEBIT	CREDIT	BALANCE DEBIT	BALANCE CREDIT
19-- June	1	Balance	✔			6 7 2 5 00	
	5		27		4 1 5 0 00		
	30		28	4 1 4 5 00		6 7 2 0 00	

ACCOUNT Supplies   ACCOUNT NO. 13

DATE		ITEM	POST. REF.	DEBIT	CREDIT	BALANCE DEBIT	BALANCE CREDIT
19-- June	1	Balance	✔			2 9 0 00	
	8		27	1 4 5 00			
	16		27		6 3 00	3 7 2 00	

ACCOUNT Prepaid Insurance   ACCOUNT NO. 14

DATE		ITEM	POST. REF.	DEBIT	CREDIT	BALANCE DEBIT	BALANCE CREDIT
19-- June	1	Balance	✔			3 6 5 00	
	17		27	3 7 0 00		7 3 5 00	

ACCOUNT Equipment ACCOUNT NO. 18

DATE		ITEM	POST. REF.	DEBIT	CREDIT	BALANCE DEBIT	BALANCE CREDIT
19-- June	1	Balance	✔			19 745 00	
	2		27	2 1 0 0 00			
	9		27		1 2 5 00	21 720 00	

ACCOUNT Accounts Payable ACCOUNT NO. 22

DATE		ITEM	POST. REF.	DEBIT	CREDIT	BALANCE DEBIT	BALANCE CREDIT
19-- June	1	Balance	✔				765 00
	2		27		2 1 0 0 00		
	8		27		1 45 00		
	9		27	1 25 00			
	12		27	1 2 5 0 00			
	20		27	5 0 00			1 585 00

ACCOUNT Judy K. Schmidt, Capital ACCOUNT NO. 31

DATE		ITEM	POST. REF.	DEBIT	CREDIT	BALANCE DEBIT	BALANCE CREDIT
19-- June	1	Balance	✔				29 483 00

ACCOUNT Judy K. Schmidt, Drawing ACCOUNT NO. 32

DATE		ITEM	POST. REF.	DEBIT	CREDIT	BALANCE DEBIT	BALANCE CREDIT
19-- June	27		27	1 2 5 0 00		1 2 5 0 00	

ACCOUNT Professional Fees ACCOUNT NO. 41

DATE		ITEM	POST. REF.	DEBIT	CREDIT	BALANCE DEBIT	BALANCE CREDIT
19-- June	30		27		1 7 2 0 00		
	30		28		4 1 45 00		5 865 00

ACCOUNT Salary Expense ACCOUNT NO. 51

DATE		ITEM	POST. REF.	DEBIT	CREDIT	BALANCE DEBIT	BALANCE CREDIT
19-- June	30		28	1 7 2 5 00		1 7 2 5 00	

ACCOUNT Rent Expense   ACCOUNT NO. 53

DATE	ITEM	POST. REF.	DEBIT	CREDIT	BALANCE DEBIT	BALANCE CREDIT
19-- June 1		27	6 0 0 00		6 0 0 00	

ACCOUNT Laboratory Expense   ACCOUNT NO. 55

DATE	ITEM	POST. REF.	DEBIT	CREDIT	BALANCE DEBIT	BALANCE CREDIT
19-- June 23		27	2 4 5 00		2 4 5 00	

ACCOUNT Utilities Expense   ACCOUNT NO. 56

DATE	ITEM	POST. REF.	DEBIT	CREDIT	BALANCE DEBIT	BALANCE CREDIT
19-- June 30		28	1 5 7 00			
30		28	2 9 00			
30		28	7 4 00		2 6 0 00	

ACCOUNT Miscellaneous Expense   ACCOUNT NO. 59

DATE	ITEM	POST. REF.	DEBIT	CREDIT	BALANCE DEBIT	BALANCE CREDIT
19-- June 30		28	1 3 2 00		1 3 2 00	

(4)

Judy K. Schmidt, M.D.
Trial Balance
June 30, 19--

	DEBIT	CREDIT
Cash	3 1 7 4 00	
Accounts Receivable	6 7 2 0 00	
Supplies	3 7 2 00	
Prepaid Insurance	7 3 5 00	
Equipment	21 7 2 0 00	
Accounts Payable		1 5 8 5 00
Judy K. Schmidt, Capital		29 4 8 3 00
Judy K. Schmidt, Drawing	1 2 5 0 00	
Professional Fees		5 8 6 5 00
Salary Expense	1 7 2 5 00	
Rent Expense	6 0 0 00	
Laboratory Expense	2 4 5 00	
Utilities Expense	2 6 0 00	
Miscellaneous Expense	1 3 2 00	
	36 9 3 3 00	36 9 3 3 00

DISCUSSION QUESTIONS

1. Differentiate between an account and a ledger.

2. Do the terms *debit* and *credit* signify increase or decrease, or may they signify either? Explain.

3. Define posting.

4. Indicate whether each of the following is recorded by a debit or by a credit: (a) increase in an asset account, (b) decrease in a liability account, (c) increase in a revenue account.

5. What is the effect (increase or decrease) of debits to expense accounts (a) in terms of owner's equity; (b) in terms of expense?

6. Identify each of the following accounts as asset, liability, owner's equity, revenue, or expense, and state in each case whether the normal balance is a debit or a credit. If the account is an owner's equity account, also state whether it is capital or drawing. (a) Accounts Receivable, (b) Supplies, (c) Interest Expense, (d) W. A. Dugan, Drawing, (e) Cash, (f) Accounts Payable, (g) Sales, (h) W. A. Dugan, Capital, (i) Equipment, (j) Salary Expense.

7. Chris Eddy Company adheres to a policy of depositing all cash receipts in a bank account and making all payments by check. The cash account as of June 30 has a credit balance of $750 and there is no undeposited cash on hand. (a) Assuming that there were no errors in journalizing or posting, what is the explanation of this unusual balance? (b) Is the $750 credit balance in the cash account an asset, a liability, owner's equity, a revenue, or an expense?

8. Describe the nature of the assets that compose the following categories: (a) current assets, (b) plant assets.

9. As of the time a balance sheet is being prepared, a business enterprise owes a mortgage note payable of $80,000, the terms of which provide for monthly payments of $2,000. How should the liability be classified on the balance sheet?

10. Identify each of the following as (a) a current asset or (b) a plant asset: (1) land, (2) cash, (3) building, (4) accounts receivable, (5) supplies.

11. Describe in general terms the sequence of accounts in the ledger.

12. Rearrange the following in proper sequence: (a) entry recorded in journal, (b) business document prepared, (c) entry posted to ledger, (d) business transaction occurs.

13. During the month, a business enterprise has a substantial number of transactions affecting each of the following accounts. State for each account whether it is likely to have (a) debit entries only, (b) credit entries only, or (c) both debit and credit entries.

   (1) Interest Expense   (5) Cash
   (2) Julia Short, Drawing   (6) Accounts Receivable
   (3) Miscellaneous Expense   (7) Notes Payable
   (4) Accounts Payable   (8) Sales

14. Describe the three procedures required to post the credit portion of the following journal entry (Sales is account No. 41).

JOURNAL   PAGE 20

19-- June	7	Accounts Receivable..........................	12	975	
		Sales......................................			975

15. Twain Company performed services in July for a specific customer for which the fee was $6,500. Payment was received in the following August. (a) Was the revenue earned in July or August? (b) What accounts should be debited and credited in (1) July and (2) August?

16. As of June 1, John Fox, Capital had a credit balance of $25,000. During the year, the owner's withdrawals totaled $18,000, and the business incurred a net loss of $9,000. There were no additional investments in the business. Assuming that there have been no recording errors, will the balance sheet prepared at May 31 balance? Explain.

17. During the month, a business corporation received $725,000 in cash and paid out $675,000 in cash. Do the data indicate that the corporation earned $50,000 during the month? Explain.

18. (a) Describe the form known as a trial balance. (b) What proof is provided by a trial balance?

19. When a trial balance is prepared, an account balance of $36,750 is listed as $3,675, and an account balance of $54,000 is listed as $45,000. Identify the transposition and the slide.

20. When a purchase of supplies of $750 for cash was recorded, both the debit and the credit were journalized and posted as $570. (a) Would this error cause the trial balance to be out of balance? (b) Would the answer be the same if the $750 entry had been journalized correctly, the debit to Supplies had been posted correctly, but the credit to Cash had been posted as $570?

21. Indicate which of the following errors, each considered individually, would cause the trial balance totals to be unequal:
   (a) A fee of $3,500 earned and due from a client was not debited to Accounts Receivable or credited to a revenue account, because the cash had not been received.

(b) A payment of $45,000 for equipment purchased was posted as a debit of $54,000 to Equipment and a credit of $45,000 to Cash.

(c) A withdrawal of $2,100 by the owner was journalized and posted as a debit of $210 to Salary Expense and a credit of $210 to Cash.

(d) A payment of $625 to a creditor was posted as a credit of $625 to Accounts Payable and a credit of $625 to Cash.

(e) A receipt of $550 from an account receivable was journalized and posted as a debit of $550 to Cash and a credit of $550 to Sales.

22. Real World Focus. The current asset and current liability data adapted from the Hershey Food Corporation balance sheet as of December 31, 1985, are as follows:

Current Assets (in thousands):

Cash and short-term investments	$110,636
Accounts receivable	76,617
Inventories	192,678
Other current assets	32,359
Total current assets	$412,290

Current Liabilities (in thousands):

Accounts payable	$ 87,799
Payroll and other compensation costs	37,275
Advertising and promotional expenses	19,828
Income taxes	9,253
Short-term debt and current portion of long-term debt	9,623
Other	31,544
Total current liabilities	$195,322

(a) Based upon the preceding data, determine (1) the difference between the total current assets and the total current liabilities as of December 31, 1985, and (2) the ratio of the total current assets to the total current liabilities as of December 31, 1985. (b) Based upon the solution in (a), is it likely that Hershey Food Corporation will be able to pay its current liabilities as they become due?

EXERCISES

Exercise 2–1. Transactions for sole proprietorship. Cey Company has the following accounts in its ledger: Cash; Accounts Receivable; Supplies; Office Equipment; Accounts Payable; Larry Cey, Capital; Larry Cey, Drawing; Fees Earned; Rent Expense; Advertising Expense; Utilities Expense; Miscellaneous Expense.

Record the following transactions, completed during February of the current year, in a two-column journal:

Feb. 1. Paid advertising expense, $500.
      2. Paid rent for the month, $900.
      5. Paid cash for supplies, $95.
      7. Purchased office equipment on account, $4,100.
     10. Received cash from customers on account, $5,600.
     11. Paid cash for repairs to office equipment, $60.
     12. Paid creditor on account, $2,150.
     14. Withdrew cash for personal use, $1,200.
     24. Paid telephone bill for the month, $160.
     27. Fees earned and billed to customers for the month, $8,550.
     28. Paid electricity bill for the month, $415.

Exercise 2–2. Identify transactions for sole proprietorship. Eight transactions are recorded in the following T accounts:

Cash				Equipment		Ellen Day, Drawing	
(1) 15,000	(2)	7,500		(2) 20,000		(8) 3,000	
(7) 10,600	(3)	950					
	(4)	225					
	(5)	5,000					
	(8)	3,000					

Accounts Receivable		Accounts Payable		Service Revenue	
(6) 27,500	(7) 10,600	(5) 5,000	(2) 12,500		(6) 27,500

Supplies		Ellen Day, Capital		Operating Expenses	
(4) 225			(1) 15,000	(3) 950	

Indicate for each debit and each credit: (a) whether an asset, liability, capital, drawing, revenue, or expense account was affected and (b) whether the account was increased (+) or decreased (−). Answers should be presented in the following form (transaction (1) is given as an example):

	Account Debited		Account Credited	
Transaction	Type	Effect	Type	Effect
(1)	asset	+	capital	+

Exercise 2–3. Chart of accounts for sole proprietorship. J. A. Mitchel Co. is a newly organized enterprise. The list of accounts to be opened in the general ledger is as follows:

Accounts Payable   Depreciation Expense
Accounts Receivable   Equipment
Accumulated Depreciation   J. A. Mitchel, Capital
Cash   J. A. Mitchel, Drawing

Miscellaneous Expense	Salary Expense
Prepaid Rent	Sales
Rent Expense	Supplies
Salaries Payable	Supplies Expense

List the accounts in the order in which they should appear in the ledger of J. A. Mitchel Co. and assign account numbers. Each account number is to have two digits: the first digit is to indicate the major classification ("1" for assets, etc.), and the second digit is to identify the specific account within each major classification ("11" for Cash, etc.).

Exercise 2–4. Chart of accounts for corporation. Alexis Services Co. is a newly organized enterprise. The list of accounts to be opened in the general ledger is as follows:

Retained Earnings	Accounts Receivable
Miscellaneous Expense	Equipment
Sales	Salary Expense
Accumulated Depreciation	Cash
Capital Stock	Accounts Payable
Supplies	Supplies Expense
Prepaid Rent	Salaries Payable
Rent Expense	Depreciation Expense

List the accounts in the order in which they should appear in the ledger of Alexis Services Co. and assign account numbers. Each account number is to have two digits: the first digit is to indicate the major classification ("1" for assets, etc.), and the second digit is to identify the specific account within each major classification ("11" for Cash, etc.).

Exercise 2–5. Trial balance for sole proprietorship. The accounts in the ledger of Corley Realty as of June 30 of the current year are listed in alphabetical order as follows. All accounts have normal balances. The balance of the cash account has been intentionally omitted.

Accounts Payable	$ 18,910
Accounts Receivable	23,750
Cash	?
P. Corley, Capital	150,000
P. Corley, Drawing	28,000
Fees Earned	270,000
Land	120,000
Miscellaneous Expense	9,900
Notes Payable	25,000
Prepaid Insurance	3,850
Salary Expense	210,000
Supplies	3,900
Supplies Expense	6,100
Utilities Expense	21,500

Prepare a trial balance, listing the accounts in their proper order and inserting the missing figure for cash.

Exercise 2–6. *Errors in trial balance.* The following preliminary trial balance of Delmar Company does not balance:

Delmar Company
Trial Balance
October 31, 19--

Cash..		52,140
Accounts Receivable..................................	14,900	
Prepaid Insurance	4,200	
Equipment..	42,100	
Accounts Payable		7,750
Salaries Payable	750	
Vance Delmar, Capital	49,600	
Vance Delmar, Drawing		9,000
Service Revenue		37,900
Salary Expense	18,400	
Advertising Expense	4,200	
Miscellaneous Expense		490
	134,150	107,280

When the ledger and other records are reviewed, you discover the following: (1) the debits and credits in the cash account total $56,150 and $52,140, respectively; (2) a receipt of $500 from a customer on account was not posted to the accounts receivable account; (3) a payment of $1,900 to a creditor on account was not posted to the accounts payable account; (4) the balance of the prepaid insurance account is $2,400; (5) the correct balance of the equipment account is $41,200; and (6) each account has a normal balance. Prepare a corrected trial balance.

Exercise 2–7. *Effect of errors on trial balance.* The following errors occurred in posting from a two-column journal:

(1) A debit of $2,500 to Equipment was posted twice.
(2) A debit of $200 to Cash was posted as $20.
(3) A debit of $810 to Supplies was posted as $180.
(4) A credit of $225 to Accounts Receivable was not posted.
(5) A debit of $1,000 to Cash was posted to Sales.
(6) A credit of $420 to Accounts Payable was posted as a debit.
(7) An entry debiting Rent Expense and crediting Cash for $750 was not posted.

Considering each case individually (i.e., assuming that no other errors had occurred), indicate: (a) by "yes" or "no" whether the trial balance would be out of balance; (b) if answer to (a) is "yes", the amount by which the trial balance totals would differ; and (c) the column of the trial balance that would have the larger total. Answers should be presented in the following form (error (1) is given as an example):

	(a)	(b)	(c)
Error	Out of Balance	Difference	Larger Total
(1)	yes	$2,500	debit

PROBLEMS

Series A

Problem 2–1A. Journal entries and trial balance for sole proprietorship.
Soong Park established a sole proprietorship, to be known as Park Decorators, on
May 11 of the current year. During the remainder of the month, Park completed the fol-
lowing business transactions:

May 11. Park transferred cash from a personal bank account to an account to be
used for the business, $12,000.

11. Paid rent for period of May 11 to end of month, $800.

13. Purchased office equipment on account, $2,500.

15. Purchased a used truck for $10,000, paying $2,500 cash and giving a
note payable for the remainder.

16. Purchased supplies for cash, $525.

17. Received cash for job completed, $300.

17. Paid wages of employees, $400.

20. Paid premiums on property and casualty insurance, $725.

22. Recorded sales on account and sent invoices to customers, $1,650.

23. Paid creditor for equipment purchased on May 13, $2,500.

24. Received an invoice for truck expenses, to be paid in June, $225.

26. Received cash for job completed, $650. This sale had not been recorded
previously.

28. Purchased supplies on account, $178.

29. Paid utilities expense, $390.

29. Paid miscellaneous expenses, $86.

30. Received cash from customers on account, $1,100.

31. Paid wages of employees, $850.

31. Withdrew cash for personal use, $1,000.

Instructions:

(1) Open a ledger of two-column accounts for Park Decorators, using the following titles
and account numbers: Cash, 11; Accounts Receivable, 12; Supplies, 13; Prepaid
Insurance, 14; Equipment, 16; Truck, 18; Notes Payable, 21; Accounts Payable, 22;
Soong Park, Capital, 31; Soong Park, Drawing, 32; Sales, 41; Wages Expense, 51;
Rent Expense, 53; Utilities Expense, 54; Truck Expense, 55; Miscellaneous Ex-
pense, 59.

(2) Record each transaction in a two-column journal, referring to the above list of
accounts or to the ledger in selecting appropriate account titles to be debited and
credited. (Do not insert the account numbers in the journal at this time.)

(3) Post the journal to the ledger, inserting appropriate posting references as each item
is posted.

(4) Determine the balances of the accounts in the ledger, pencil footing all accounts
having two or more debits or credits. A memorandum balance should also be

inserted in accounts having both debits and credits, in the manner illustrated on page 65. For accounts with entries on one side only (such as Sales), there is no need to insert the memorandum balance in the item column. Accounts containing only a single debit and a single credit (such as Accounts Receivable) need no pencil footings; the memorandum balance should be inserted in the appropriate item column. Accounts containing a single entry only (such as Prepaid Insurance) need neither a pencil footing nor a memorandum balance.

(5) Prepare a trial balance for Park Decorators as of May 31.

Problem 2–2A. Journal entries and trial balance for sole proprietorship. Isaac Morhaim, M.D., completed the following transactions in the practice of his profession during June of the current year:

June 1. Paid office rent for June, $1,500.
2. Purchased equipment on account, $7,200.
3. Purchased X-ray film and other supplies on account, $725.
6. Received cash on account from patients, $9,125.
6. Paid cash to creditors on account, $5,240.
8. Sold X-ray film to another doctor at cost, as an accommodation, receiving cash, $75.
10. Paid cash for renewal of property insurance policy, $545.
15. Paid cash for laboratory analyses, $345.
20. Discovered that the balance of the cash account was understated and the accounts receivable account was overstated as of June 1 by $100. A cash receipt of that amount on account from a patient in May had not been recorded. Journalized the $100 receipt as of June 20.
24. One of the items of equipment purchased on June 2 was defective. It was returned with the permission of the supplier, who agreed to reduce the account for the amount charged for the item, $550.
26. Paid cash from business bank account for personal and family expenses, $2,750.
30. Recorded fees charged to patients on account for services performed in June, $7,770.
30. Recorded the cash received in payment of services (on a cash basis) to patients during June, $9,110.
30. Paid salaries of receptionist and nurses, $4,050.
30. Paid miscellaneous expenses, $420.
30. Paid gas and electricity expense, $610.
30. Paid water expense, $130.
30. Paid telephone expense, $280.

Morhaim's account titles, numbers, and balances as of June 1 (all normal balances) are listed as follows: Cash, 11, $5,975; Accounts Receivable, 12, $15,110; Supplies, 13, $1,140; Prepaid Insurance, 14, $3,700; Equipment, 18, $55,500; Accounts Payable, 22, $9,850; Isaac Morhaim, Capital, 31, $71,575; Isaac Morhaim, Drawing, 32; Professional Fees, 41; Salary Expense, 51; Rent Expense, 53; Utilities Expense, 55; Laboratory Expense, 56; Miscellaneous Expense, 59.

Instructions:

(1) Open a ledger of four-column accounts for Dr. Morhaim as of June 1 of the current year. Enter the balances in the appropriate balance columns and place a check mark (√) in the posting reference column. (It is advisable to verify the equality of the debit and credit balances in the ledger before proceeding with the next instruction.)
(2) Record each transaction in a two-column journal.
(3) Post the journal to the ledger, extending the month-end balances to the appropriate balance columns after all posting is completed.
(4) Prepare a trial balance as of June 30.
(5) Assuming that the expenses which have not been recorded (such as supplies expense and insurance expense) amount to a total of $2,450 for the month, determine the following amounts:
  (a) Net income for the month of June.
  (b) Increase or decrease in owner's equity during June.
  (c) Owner's equity as of June 30.

If the working papers correlating with the textbook are not used, omit Problem 2–3A.

✳ Problem 2–3A.   Errors in trial balance for sole proprietorship. The following records of Hutton TV Repair are presented in the working papers:
  Journal containing entries for the period March 1–31.
  Ledger to which the March entries have been posted.
  Preliminary trial balance as of March 31, which does not balance.

Locate the errors, supply the information requested, and prepare a corrected trial balance, proceeding in accordance with the following detailed instructions. The balances recorded in the accounts as of March 1 and the entries in the journal are correctly stated. If it is necessary to correct any posted amounts in the ledger, a line should be drawn through the erroneous figure and the correct amount inserted above. Corrections or notations may be inserted on the preliminary trial balance in any manner desired. It is not necessary to complete all of the instructions if equal trial balance totals can be obtained earlier. However, the requirements of instructions (6) and (7) should be completed in any event.

Instructions:

(1) Verify the totals of the preliminary trial balance, inserting the correct amounts in the schedule provided in the working papers.
(2) Compute the difference between the trial balance totals.
(3) Compare the listings in the trial balance with the balances appearing in the ledger and list the errors found in the space provided in the working papers.
(4) Verify the accuracy of the balance of each account in the ledger and list the errors found in the space provided in the working papers.
(5) Trace the postings in the ledger back to the journal, using small check marks to identify items traced. Correct any amounts in the ledger that may be necessitated by errors in posting, and list the errors in the space provided in the working papers.
(6) Journalize as of March 31 the payment of $160 for gas and electricity. The bill had been paid on March 31 but was inadvertently omitted from the journal. Post to the ledger. (Revise any amounts necessitated by posting this entry.)
(7) Prepare a new trial balance.

Problem 2–4A.   Journal entries and trial balance for corporation. The following business transactions were completed by Dunway Theatre Corporation during May of the current year:

May 3. Deposited in a bank account $65,000 cash received for capital stock.
     4. Purchased the Waddell Drive-In Theatre for $225,000, divided as follows: land, $125,000; buildings, $75,000; equipment, $25,000. Paid $50,000 in cash and gave a mortgage note for the remainder.
     5. Entered into a contract for the operation of the refreshment stand concession at a rental of 25% of the concessionaire's sales, with a guaranteed minimum of $1,000 a month, payable in advance. Received cash of $1,000 as the advance payment for the month of May.
     5. Paid for advertising leaflets for May, $225.
     6. Paid premiums for property and casualty insurance policies, $3,700.
     7. Purchased supplies, $650, and equipment, $3,150, on account.
     8. Paid for May billboard and newspaper advertising, $1,500.
    10. Paid miscellaneous expense, $220.
    12. Cash received from admissions for the week, $5,125.
    17. Paid semimonthly wages, $1,670.
    19. Cash received from admissions for the week, $4,900.
    19. Paid miscellaneous expenses, $210.
    19. Returned a portion of the supplies purchased on May 7 to the supplier, receiving full credit for the cost, $160.
    21. Paid cash to creditors on account, $2,350.
    26. Cash received from admissions for the week, $3,910.
    26. Purchased supplies for cash, $300.
    27. Recorded invoice of $5,800 for rental of film for May. Payment is due on June 6.
    30. Paid electricity and water bills, $625.
    31. Paid semimonthly wages, $1,720.
    31. Cash received from admissions for remainder of the month, $3,100.
    31. Recorded additional amount owed by the concessionaire for the month of May; sales for the month totaled $5,280. Rental charges in excess of the advance payment of $1,000 are not due and payable until June 10.

Instructions:

(1) Open a ledger of four-column accounts for Dunway Theatre Corporation, using the following account titles and numbers: Cash, 11; Accounts Receivable, 12; Prepaid Insurance, 13; Supplies, 14; Land, 17; Buildings, 18; Equipment, 19; Accounts Payable, 21; Mortgage Note Payable, 24; Capital Stock, 31; Admissions Income, 41; Concession Income, 42; Wages Expense, 51; Film Rental Expense, 52; Advertising Expense, 53; Electricity and Water Expense, 54; Miscellaneous Expense, 59.
(2) Record the transactions in a two-column journal.
(3) Post the journal to the ledger, extending the month-end balances to the appropriate balance columns after all posting is completed.
(4) Prepare a trial balance as of May 31.
(5) Determine the following:
    (a) Amount of total revenue recorded in the ledger.
    (b) Amount of total expenses recorded in the ledger.

(c) Amount of net income for May, assuming that additional unrecorded expenses (including supplies used, insurance expired, etc.) totaled $2,450.

(d) The understatement or overstatement of net income for May that would have resulted from failure to record the additional amount owed by the concessionaire for the month of May until it was paid in June (See transaction of May 31.)

(e) The understatement or overstatement of assets as of May 31 that would have resulted from failure to record the additional amount owed by the concessionaire in May. (See transaction of May 31.)

Problem 2–5A. Journal entries and trial balance for corporation. Hill Realty Inc. acts as an agent in buying, selling, renting, and managing real estate. The account balances at the end of March of the current year are as follows:

11	Cash	36,150	
12	Accounts Receivable	28,750	
13	Prepaid Insurance	1,100	
14	Office Supplies	715	
16	Land	—0—	
21	Accounts Payable		6,175
22	Notes Payable		—0—
31	Capital Stock		30,000
32	Retained Earnings		10,840
33	Dividends	2,000	
41	Fees Earned		125,500
51	Salary and Commission Expense	92,100	
52	Rent Expense	4,500	
53	Advertising Expense	3,900	
54	Automobile Expense	2,750	
59	Miscellaneous Expense	550	
		172,515	172,515

The following business transactions were completed by Hill Realty Inc. during April of the current year:

Apr. 1. Paid rent on office for month, $1,500.
3. Purchased office supplies on account, $375.
5. Paid insurance premiums, $1,650.
7. Received cash from clients on account, $18,200.
15. Paid salaries and commissions, $16,650.
15. Purchased land for a future building site for $55,000, paying $11,000 in cash and giving a note payable for the remainder.
15. Recorded revenue earned and billed to clients during first half of month, $19,100.
18. Paid creditors on account, $4,150.
20. Returned a portion of the office supplies purchased on April 3, receiving full credit for their cost, $75.
23. Received cash from clients on account, $16,700.
24. Paid advertising expense, $1,550.
27. Discovered an error in computing a commission; received cash from the salesperson for the overpayment, $350.

28. Paid automobile expense (including rental charges for an automobile), $715.
29. Paid miscellaneous expenses, $215.
30. Recorded revenue earned and billed to clients during second half of month, $16,300.
30. Paid salaries and commissions, $19,850.
30. Paid dividends, $2,000.

Instructions:

(1) Open a ledger of four-column accounts for the accounts listed. Record the balances in the appropriate balance columns as of April 1, write "Balance" in the item section, and place a check mark (√) in the posting reference column.
(2) Record the transactions for April in a two-column journal.
(3) Post to the ledger, extending the month-end balances to the appropriate balance columns after all posting is completed.
(4) Prepare a trial balance of the ledger as of April 30.

Problem 2–6A. Corrected trial balance for sole proprietorship. Martino Photography, a sole proprietorship, prepared the following trial balance as of October 31 of the current year:

Cash	4,735	
Accounts Receivable	9,925	
Supplies	1,277	
Prepaid Insurance	330	
Equipment	12,500	
Notes Payable		5,000
Accounts Payable		3,025
Elaine Martino, Capital		12,490
Elaine Martino, Drawing	6,750	
Sales		80,750
Wages Expense	48,150	
Rent Expense	750	
Advertising Expense	5,250	
Gas, Electricity, and Water Expense	3,150	
	92,817	101,265

The debit and credit totals are not equal as a result of the following errors:

(a) The balance of cash was understated by $1,000.
(b) A cash payment of $450 was posted as a credit to Cash of $540.
(c) A debit of $175 to Accounts Receivable was not posted.
(d) A return of $252 of defective supplies was erroneously posted as a $225 credit to Supplies.
(e) An insurance policy acquired at a cost of $310 was posted as a credit to Prepaid Insurance.
(f) The balance of Notes Payable was understated by $2,500.
(g) A credit of $75 in Accounts Payable was overlooked when the balance of the account was determined.

(h) A debit of $750 for a withdrawal by the owner was posted as a credit to Elaine Martino, Capital.

(i) The balance of $7,500 in Rent Expense was entered as $750 in the trial balance.

(j) Miscellaneous Expense, with a balance of $915, was omitted from the trial balance.

Instructions:

Prepare a corrected trial balance as of October 31 of the current year.

Series B

Problem 2–1B. Journal entries and trial balance for sole proprietorship. Jane Flutie established a sole proprietorship, to be known as Flutie Decorators, on July 10 of the current year. During the remainder of the month, Flutie completed the following business transactions:

July 10. Flutie transferred cash from a personal bank account to an account to be used for the business, $10,000.

10. Paid rent for period of July 10 to end of month, $600.

11. Purchased a truck for $9,000, paying $3,000 cash and giving a note payable for the remainder.

12. Purchased equipment on account, $1,700.

14. Purchased supplies for cash, $885.

14. Paid premiums on property and casualty insurance, $420.

15. Received cash for job completed, $510.

16. Purchased supplies on account, $240.

17. Paid wages of employees, $600.

21. Paid creditor for equipment purchased on July 12, $1,700.

24. Recorded sales on account and sent invoices to customers, $2,100.

26. Received an invoice for truck expenses, to be paid in August, $225.

26. Received cash for job completed, $1,050. This sale had not been recorded previously.

27. Paid utilities expense, $205.

27. Paid miscellaneous expenses, $73.

28. Received cash from customers on account, $1,420.

31. Paid wages of employees, $1,350.

31. Withdrew cash for personal use, $1,500.

Instructions:

(1) Open a ledger of two-column accounts for Flutie Decorators, using the following titles and account numbers: Cash, 11; Accounts Receivable, 12; Supplies, 13; Prepaid Insurance, 14; Equipment, 16; Truck, 18; Notes Payable, 21; Accounts Payable, 22; Jane Flutie, Capital, 31; Jane Flutie, Drawing, 32; Sales, 41; Wages Expense, 51; Rent Expense, 53; Utilities Expense, 54; Truck Expense, 55; Miscellaneous Expense, 59.

(2) Record each transaction in a two-column journal, referring to the above list of accounts or to the ledger in selecting appropriate account titles to be debited and credited. (Do not insert the account numbers in the journal at this time.)

(3) Post the journal to the ledger, inserting appropriate posting references as each item is posted.

(4) Determine the balances of the accounts in the ledger, pencil footing all accounts having two or more debits or credits. A memorandum balance should also be inserted in accounts having both debits and credits, in the manner illustrated on page 65. For accounts with entries on one side only (such as Sales), there is no need to insert the memorandum balance in the item column. Accounts containing only a single debit and a single credit (such as Accounts Receivable) need no pencil footings; the memorandum balance should be inserted in the appropriate item column. Accounts containing a single entry only (such as Prepaid Insurance) need neither a pencil footing nor a memorandum balance.

(5) Prepare a trial balance for Flutie Decorators as of July 31.

If the working papers correlating with the textbook are not used, omit Problem 2–3B.

Problem 2–3B. Errors in trial balance for sole proprietorship. The following records of Hutton TV Repair are presented in the working papers:

    Journal containing entries for the period March 1–31.

    Ledger to which the March entries have been posted.

    Preliminary trial balance as of March 31, which does not balance.

Locate the errors, supply the information requested, and prepare a corrected trial balance, proceeding in accordance with the following detailed instructions. The balances recorded in the accounts as of March 1 and the entries in the journal are correctly stated. If it is necessary to correct any posted amounts in the ledger, a line should be drawn through the erroneous figure and the correct amount inserted above. Corrections or notations may be inserted on the preliminary trial balance in any manner desired. It is not necessary to complete all of the instructions if equal trial balance totals can be obtained earlier. However, the requirements of instructions (6) and (7) should be completed in any event.

Instructions:

(1) Verify the totals of the preliminary trial balance, inserting the correct amounts in the schedule provided in the working papers.

(2) Compute the difference between the trial balance totals.

(3) Compare the listings in the trial balance with the balances appearing in the ledger and list the errors found in the space provided in the working papers.

(4) Verify the accuracy of the balance of each account in the ledger and list the errors found in the space provided in the working papers.

(5) Trace the postings in the ledger back to the journal, using small check marks to identify items traced. Correct any amounts in the ledger that may be necessitated by errors in posting and list the errors in the space provided in the working papers.

(6) Journalize as of March 31 the payment of $125 for advertising expense. The bill had been paid on March 31 but was inadvertently omitted from the journal. Post to the ledger. (Revise any amounts necessitated by posting this entry.)

(7) Prepare a new trial balance.

Problem 2–4B.   Journal entries and trial balance for corporation. The following business transactions were completed by Carr Theatre Corporation during July of the current year:

July 3. Received and deposited in a bank account $50,000 cash for capital stock.

     3. Purchased the Lincoln Drive-In Theatre for $120,000, divided as follows: land, $60,000; buildings, $40,000; equipment, $20,000. Paid $35,000 in cash and gave a mortgage note for the remainder.

     5. Entered into a contract for the operation of the refreshment stand concession at a rental of 20% of the concessionaire's sales, with a guaranteed minimum of $600 a month, payable in advance. Received cash of $600 as the advance payment for the month of July.

     6. Purchased supplies, $390, and equipment, $4,200, on account.

     7. Paid premiums for property and casualty insurance policies, $2,250.

     8. Paid for July billboard and newspaper advertising, $750.

    10. Cash received from admissions for the week, $2,730.

    12. Paid miscellaneous expense, $265.

    17. Paid semimonthly wages, $1,360.

    17. Cash received from admissions for the week, $2,980.

    19. Paid miscellaneous expenses, $310.

    20. Returned a portion of the supplies purchased on July 6 to the supplier, receiving full credit for the cost, $60.

    23. Paid cash to creditors on account, $2,250.

    24. Cash received from admissions for the week, $2,420.

    26. Purchased supplies for cash, $210.

    26. Paid for advertising leaflets for special promotion during last week in July, $375.

    28. Recorded invoice of $4,400 for rental of film for July. Payment is due on August 7.

    29. Paid electricity and water bills, $890.

    31. Paid semimonthly wages, $1,450.

    31. Cash received from admissions for remainder of the month, $3,600.

    31. Recorded additional amount owed by the concessionaire for the month of July; sales for the month totaled $4,500. Rental charges in excess of the advance payment of $600 are not due and payable until August 5.

Instructions:

(1) Open a ledger of four-column accounts for Carr Theatre Corporation, using the following account titles and numbers: Cash, 11; Accounts Receivable, 12; Prepaid Insurance, 13; Supplies, 14; Land, 17; Buildings, 18; Equipment, 19; Accounts Payable, 21; Mortgage Note Payable, 24; Capital Stock, 31; Admissions Income, 41; Concession Income, 42; Wages Expense, 51; Film Rental Expense, 52; Advertising Expense, 53; Electricity and Water Expense, 54; Miscellaneous Expense, 59.

(2) Record the transactions in a two-column journal.

(3) Post the journal to the ledger, extending the month-end balances to the appropriate balance columns after all posting is completed.

(4) Prepare a trial balance as of July 31.

(continued)

(5) Determine the following:
  (a) Amount of total revenue recorded in the ledger.
  (b) Amount of total expenses recorded in the ledger.
  (c) Amount of net income for July, assuming that additional unrecorded expenses (including supplies used, insurance expired, etc.) totaled $610.
  (d) The understatement or overstatement of net income for July that would have resulted from failure to record the invoice for film rental until it was paid in August. (See transaction of July 28.)
  (e) The understatement or overstatement of liabilities as of July 31 that would have resulted from failure to record the invoice for film rental in July. (See transaction of July 28.)

Problem 2–6B.   Corrected trial balance for sole proprietorship. Collins Carpet Installation, a sole proprietorship, has the following trial balance as of August 31 of the current year:

Cash...	4,400	
Accounts Receivable.................................	6,400	
Supplies...	1,010	
Prepaid Insurance ..:...............................	150	
Equipment...	15,500	
Notes Payable		15,000
Accounts Payable		4,620
John Collins, Capital................................		15,300
John Collins, Drawing...............................	7,000	
Sales..		49,980
Wages Expense....................................	28,500	
Rent Expense......................................	6,400	
Advertising Expense	320	
Gas, Electricity, and Water Expense	3,150	
	72,830	84,900

The debit and credit totals are not equal as a result of the following errors:

  (a) The balance of cash was overstated by $500.
  (b) A cash receipt of $240 was posted as a debit to Cash of $420.
  (c) A debit of $1,000 for a withdrawal by the owner was posted as a credit to John Collins, Capital.
  (d) The balance of $3,200 in Advertising Expense was entered as $320 in the trial balance.
  (e) A debit of $725 to Accounts Receivable was not posted.
  (f) A return of $125 of defective supplies was erroneously posted as a $215 credit to Supplies.
  (g) The balance of Notes Payable was overstated by $5,000.
  (h) An insurance policy acquired at a cost of $200 was posted as a credit to Prepaid Insurance.
  (i) Miscellaneous Expense, with a balance of $945, was omitted from the trial balance.

(j) A debit of $710 in Accounts Payable was overlooked when determining the balance of the account.

Instructions:

Prepare a corrected trial balance as of August 31 of the current year.

MINI-CASE 2

beach caddy services

During June through August, Becky Beach is planning to manage and operate Beach Caddy Service at Palm Golf and Country Club. Becky will rent a small maintenance building from the country club for $100 per month and will offer caddy services, including cart rentals, to golfers. Becky has had no formal training in record keeping. During June, she kept notes of all receipts and expenses in a shoe box.

An examination of Becky's shoe box records for June revealed the following:

June 1. Withdrew $1,000 from personal bank account to be used to operate the caddy service.
1. Paid rent to Palm Golf and Country Club, $100.
2. Paid for golf supplies (practice balls, etc.), $190.
2. Paid miscellaneous expenses, $50.
3. Arranged for the rental of forty regular (pulling) golf carts and ten gasoline-driven carts for $1,000 per month. Paid $500 in advance, with the remaining $500 due June 20.
7. Purchased supplies, including gasoline, for the golf carts on account, $325. Palm Golf and Country Club has agreed to allow Becky to store the gasoline in one of their fuel tanks at no cost.
15. Cash receipts for June 1–15, $990.
15. For June 1–15, accepted IOUs from customers on account, $210.
15. Paid salary of part-time employees, $110.
17. Paid cash to creditors on account, $180.
20. Paid remaining rental on golf carts, $500.
22. Purchased supplies, including gasoline, on account, $280.
25. Received cash in payment of IOUs on account, $150.
28. Paid miscellaneous expenses, $60.
30. Cash receipts for June 16–30, $1,475.
30. For June 15–30, accepted IOUs from customers on account, $150.
30. Paid electricity (utilities) expense, $55.
30. Paid telephone (utilities) expense, $30.
30. Paid salary of part-time employees, $110
30. Supplies on hand at the end of June, $170.

Becky has asked you several questions concerning her financial affairs to date, and she has asked you to assist her with her record keeping and reporting of financial data.

Instructions:

(1) To assist Becky with her record keeping, prepare a chart of accounts that would be appropriate for Beach Caddy Service.

(2) Prepare an income statement for June to help Becky assess the profitability of Beach Caddy Service. For this purpose, the use of T accounts may be useful in analyzing the effects of each of the June transactions.

(3) At various times throughout June, Becky took cash from the cash receipts of the caddy service for personal use. If $680 of cash were on hand on June 30, how much did Becky withdraw from the enterprise for personal use?

Chapter 3

COMPLETION OF THE ACCOUNTING CYCLE

Chapter Objectives:

- Discuss the matching principle as it relates to the cash basis and the accrual basis of accounting.

- Describe the nature of the adjusting process.

- Describe and illustrate basic procedures for adjusting the accounting records prior to the preparation of the financial statements.

- Describe and illustrate the work sheet for summarizing the accounting data for use in preparing financial statements.

- Describe and illustrate the preparation of financial statements.

- Describe and illustrate the basic procedures for preparing the accounting records for use in accumulating data for the following accounting period.

- Describe what is meant by a fiscal year and a natural business year.

- Describe and diagram the basic phases of the accounting cycle.

During an accounting period, transactions are recorded as they occur, as was demonstrated in the preceding chapter. At the end of the period, the ledger accounts must be brought up to date, so that revenues and expenses are properly matched and the financial statements fairly present the results of operations for a period and the financial condition at the end of that period.

MATCHING PRINCIPLE

Revenues and expenses may be reported on the income statement by (1) the **cash basis** or (2) the **accrual basis** of accounting. When the cash basis is used, revenues are reported in the period in which cash is received, and expenses are reported in the period in which cash is paid. For example, sales would be recorded only when cash is received from customers, and salaries expense would be recorded only when cash is paid to employees. Net income (or net loss) would be the difference between the cash receipts (revenues) and the cash disbursements (expenses). Small service enterprises which have few receivables and payables, as well as practicing professionals, may use the cash basis. For most businesses, however, the cash basis is not considered an acceptable method. For this reason, the cash basis will not be discussed in the remainder of the text.

Most enterprises use the accrual basis of accounting. Under the accrual method, revenues are reported in the period in which they are earned, and expenses are reported in the period in which they are incurred in an attempt to produce revenues. For example, revenue would be recognized as services are provided to customers and not when the cash is received from customers. Likewise, supplies expense would be recognized when the supplies are used and not when the cash is paid for supplies purchased. Generally accepted accounting principles require the use of the accrual basis, so that revenues recognized are **matched** with the related expenses incurred in producing the revenues.

The accrual basis of accounting requires the use of an adjusting process at the end of the accounting period to match revenues and expenses for the period properly. The common characteristics of the adjusting process are discussed in the following paragraphs.

NATURE OF THE ADJUSTING PROCESS

At the end of the accounting period, many of the amounts listed on the trial balance can be transferred, without change, to the financial statements. For example, the balance of the cash account is normally the amount of that asset owned by the enterprise on the last day of the accounting period. Similarly, the balance in Notes Payable is likely to be the total amount of that type of liability owed by the enterprise on the last day of the accounting period.

All trial balance amounts are not necessarily correct. The amounts listed for prepaid expenses are normally overstated. The reason for the over-statement is that the day-to-day consumption or expiration of these assets has not been recorded. For example, the balance in the supplies account represents the cost of the inventory of supplies at the beginning of the period plus the cost of those acquired during the period. Some of the supplies would have been used during the period; hence, the balance listed on the trial balance is overstated. In the same manner, the balance in Prepaid Insurance represents the beginning balance plus the cost of insurance policies acquired during the period, and no entries were made for the premiums as they expired. To make entries on a day-to-day basis would be costly and unnecessary. There are two effects on the ledger when the daily reduction in prepaid expenses is not recorded: (1) asset accounts are overstated and (2) expense accounts are understated.

Other data needed for the financial statements may be entirely omitted from the trial balance because revenue or expense related to the period has not been recorded. For example, salary expense incurred between the last payday and the end of the accounting period would not ordinarily be recorded in the accounts because salaries are customarily recorded only when they are paid. However, such accrued salaries are an expense of the period because the services were rendered during the period. They also represent a liability as of the last day of the period because they are owed to the employees.

The entries required at the end of an accounting period to bring the accounts up to date and to assure the proper matching of revenues and expenses are called **adjusting entries.** In a broad sense, they may be called corrections to the ledger. But bringing the ledger up to date at the end of a period is part of the accounting procedure; it is not caused by errors. The term "adjusting entries" is therefore more appropriate than the term "correcting entries."

The illustrations of adjusting entries that follow are based on the ledger of Cole Photographic Studio. T accounts are used for illustrative purposes and the adjusting entries, which are shown in the accounts, appear in color to separate them from items that were posted during the month.

Prepaid Expenses

According to Cole's trial balance appearing on page 74, the balance in the supplies account on March 31 is $1,850. Some of these supplies (film, developing agents, etc.) have been used during the past month and some are still in stock. If the amount of either is known, the other can be readily determined. It is more practical to determine the cost of the supplies on hand at the end of the month than it is to keep a record of those used from day to day. Assuming that the inventory of supplies on March 31 is determined to be $890, the amount to be moved from the asset account to the expense account is computed as follows:

Supplies available (balance of account)	$1,850
Supplies on hand (inventory)	890
Supplies used (amount of adjustment)	$ 960

Increases in expense accounts are recorded as debits and decreases in asset accounts are recorded as credits. Hence at the end of March, the supplies expense account should be debited for $960 and the supplies account should be credited for $960. The adjusting entry is illustrated in the following T accounts:

Supplies				Supplies Expense			
Mar. 1	1,200	Mar. 31	960	Mar. 31	960		
20	650						
	1,850						

ADJUSTMENT OF PREPAID EXPENSE— SUPPLIES

After the adjustment, the asset account has a debit balance of $890, and the expense account has a debit balance of $960.

The debit balance of $2,400 in Cole's prepaid rent account represents a prepayment on March 1 of rent for three months, March, April, and May. At the end of March, the rent expense account should be increased (debited) and the prepaid rent account should be decreased (credited) by $800, the rental for one month. The adjusting entry is illustrated in the following T accounts:

Prepaid Rent				Rent Expense		
Mar. 1	2,400	Mar. 31	800	Mar. 31	800	

The prepaid rent account now has a debit balance of $1,600, which is an asset. The rent expense account has a debit balance of $800, which is an expense.

If the preceding adjustments for supplies ($960) and rent ($800) are not recorded, the financial statements prepared as of March 31 will be incorrect to the extent indicated as follows:

Income statement
Expenses will be understated............................. $1,760
Net income will be overstated 1,760

Statement of owner's equity
Net income will be overstated $1,760
Ending owner's equity will be overstated.................. 1,760

Balance sheet
Assets will be overstated................................. $1,760
Owner's equity will be overstated 1,760

The cost of supplies, prepaid rent, and other prepayments of expenses of future periods may be recorded as expenses at the time of payment, rather than as assets. This alternative treatment will be considered in a later chapter. Meanwhile, all such expenditures will be assumed to be recorded first as assets, as in the preceding illustration.

Prepayments of expenses of one accounting period are sometimes made at the beginning of the period to which they apply. When this is the case, the expenditure is ordinarily recorded as an expense rather than as an asset. During the accounting period, the expense account debited will include an amount that represents an asset, but it will be wholly expense at the end of the period. For example, if rent for March is paid on March 1, it is an asset at the time of payment. The asset expires gradually from day to day, and at the end of the month the entire amount has become an expense. Therefore, if the expenditure is initially recorded as a debit to Rent Expense, no additional entries are needed at the close of the period.

Plant Assets

Like supplies, the photographic equipment was used in the operations of Cole Photographic Studio. Unlike supplies, there is no visible reduction in the quantity of the equipment. As time passes, however, equipment does lose its capacity to provide useful services. This decrease in usefulness is a business expense, which is called **depreciation**. The factors involved in computing depreciation are discussed in a later chapter.

The adjusting entry to record depreciation is similar in effect to those illustrated in the preceding section. An amount is transferred from an asset account to an expense account. However, for reasons to be described in a later chapter, it is not practical to reduce plant asset accounts by the amount estimated as depreciation. In addition, it is common practice to show on the balance sheet both the original cost of plant assets and the amount of depreciation accumulated since their acquisition. Accordingly, the cost of a plant asset is recorded as a debit to the appropriate asset account and the decrease in usefulness is recorded as a credit to the related **accumulated depreciation** account. The unexpired or remaining cost of a plant asset is determined by subtracting the credit balance in an accumulated depreciation account from the debit balance in the related plant asset account.

An accumulated depreciation account is a **contra account** because it is "offset against" another account. Accumulated depreciation accounts may be referred to as **contra asset accounts** because they are offset against asset accounts.

Typical titles for plant asset accounts and their related contra asset accounts are as follows:

Plant Asset	*Contra Asset*
Land	———
Buildings	Accumulated Depreciation — Buildings
Equipment	Accumulated Depreciation — Equipment

The ledger could show more detail by having a separate account for each of a number of buildings. Equipment may also be subdivided according to function, such as Delivery Equipment, Store Equipment, and Office Equipment, with a related accumulated depreciation account for each plant asset account.

The adjusting entry to record depreciation for March for Cole Photographic Studio is illustrated in the following T accounts. The estimated amount of depreciation for the month is assumed to be $175.

Photographic Equipment			Accumulated Depreciation			ADJUSTMENT FOR DEPRECIATION
Mar. 1	15,000				Mar. 31 175	
4	2,500					
	17,500					

	Depreciation Expense	
Mar. 31	175	

The $175 increase in the accumulated depreciation account represents a subtraction from the $17,500 cost recorded in the related plant asset account. The difference between the two balances is called the **book value of the asset**, which may be presented on the balance sheet in the following manner:

Plant assets:
Photographic equipment $17,500
    Less accumulated depreciation 175 $17,325

If the previous adjustment for depreciation ($175) is not recorded, the financial statements as of March 31 will be incorrect to the extent indicated as follows:

Income statement
Expenses will be understated. $175
Net income will be overstated   175

Statement of owner's equity
Net income will be overstated $175
Ending owner's equity will be overstated   175

Balance Sheet
Assets will be overstated. $175
Owner's equity will be overstated   175

Accrued Expenses (Liabilities)

It is customary to pay for some types of services, such as insurance and rent, before they are used. Other types of services are paid for after the service has been performed. Services performed by employees is an example of this type of situation. The wage or salary expense accumulates or accrues as a legal claim hour by hour and day by day, but payment is made only weekly, biweekly, or in accordance with some other period of time. Such an accumulated expense that is unpaid and unrecorded is referred to as an **accrued expense**. In the case of the wage or salary expense, if the last day of a pay period is not the last day of the accounting period, the accrued expense and the related liability must be recorded in the accounts by an adjusting entry.

The data in the following T accounts were taken from the ledger of Cole Photographic Studio. The debits of $575 on March 13 and 27 in the salary expense account were biweekly payments on alternate Fridays for the payroll periods ended on those days. The salaries earned on Monday and Tuesday, March 30 and 31, total $115. This amount is an additional expense of March and is debited to the salary expense account. It is also a liability as of March 31 and is therefore credited to Salaries Payable.

Salaries Payable			Salary Expense			ADJUSTMENT FOR ACCRUED EXPENSE
	Mar. 31	115	Mar. 13	575		
			27	575		
				1,150		
			31	115		

After the adjustment, the debit balance of the salary expense account is $1,265, which is the actual expense for the month. The credit balance of $115 in Salaries Payable is the amount of the liability for salaries owed as of March 31. If the previous adjustment for salaries ($115) is not recorded, the financial statements as of March 31 will be incorrect to the extent indicated as follows:

Income statement

Expenses will be understated...................................	$115
Net income will be overstated...................................	115

Statement of owner's equity

Net income will be overstated...................................	$115
Ending owner's equity will be overstated	115

Balance sheet

Liabilities will be understated	$115
Owner's equity will be overstated...............................	115

WORK SHEET FOR FINANCIAL STATEMENTS

Before journalizing and posting adjustments similar to those just described, it is necessary to determine and assemble the relevant data. For example, it is necessary to determine the cost of supplies on hand and the salaries accrued at the end of the period. Such collections of data, preliminary drafts of financial statements, and other useful analyses prepared by accountants are generally called **working papers**.

A type of working paper frequently used by accountants prior to the preparation of financial statements is called a **work sheet**. Its use reduces the possibility of overlooking the need for an adjustment, provides a convenient means of verifying arithmetical accuracy, provides for the arrangement of data in a logical form, and provides the source data for the financial statements.

The work sheet is identified by (1) the name of the enterprise, (2) the nature of the form (work sheet), and (3) the period of time involved. A form commonly used has an account title column and ten money columns arranged in five pairs of debit and credit columns. The main headings of the five sets of money columns are:

1. Trial Balance
2. Adjustments
3. Adjusted Trial Balance

4. Income Statement
5. Balance Sheet

The use of the work sheet is described and illustrated in the paragraphs that follow.

Trial Balance Columns

The trial balance data may be assembled directly on the work sheet form or they may be prepared on another sheet first and then copied on the work sheet form. The work sheet for Cole Photographic Studio, with the trial balance data recorded, is presented below.

WORK SHEET WITH TRIAL BALANCE ADDED

Cole Photographic
Work
For Month Ended

	ACCOUNT TITLE	TRIAL BALANCE DEBIT	TRIAL BALANCE CREDIT	ADJUSTMENTS DEBIT	ADJUSTMENTS CREDIT
1	Cash	1 631 00			
2	Accounts Receivable	1 775 00			
3	Supplies	1 850 00			
4	Prepaid Rent	2 400 00			
5	Photographic Equipment	17 500 00			
6	Accounts Payable		2 000 00		
7	Sara Cole, Capital		20 650 00		
8	Sara Cole, Drawing	1 500 00			
9	Sales		5 525 00		
10	Salary Expense	1 150 00			
11	Miscellaneous Expense	369 00			
12		28 175 00	28 175 00		

Adjustments Columns

Both the debit and the credit parts of an adjustment should be inserted on the appropriate lines before going on to another adjustment, as indicated on the work sheet for Cole Photographic Studio appearing on pages 116–117. Cross-referencing the related debit and credit of each adjustment by letters is useful to anyone who may have occasion to review the work sheet. It is also helpful later when the adjusting entries are recorded in the journal. The sequence of adjustments is not important, except that there is a time and accuracy advantage in following the order in which the adjustment data are assembled. If the titles of some of the accounts to be adjusted do not appear in the trial balance because they had no balance prior to adjustment, they

Studio

Sheet

March 31, 1987

ADJUSTED TRIAL BALANCE		INCOME STATEMENT		BALANCE SHEET	
DEBIT	CREDIT	DEBIT	CREDIT	DEBIT	CREDIT

should be inserted in the Account Title column, below the trial balance totals, as they are needed.

The adjusting entries for Cole Photographic Studio were explained and illustrated by T accounts earlier in the chapter. In practice, the adjustments are inserted directly on the work sheet on the basis of the data assembled by the accounting department.

Explanatory notes for the entries in the Adjustments columns of the work sheet follow:

(a) Supplies. The supplies account has a debit balance of $1,850; the cost of the supplies on hand at the end of the period is $890; therefore, the supplies expense for March is the difference between the two amounts, or $960. The adjustment is entered by writing (1) *Supplies Expense* in the Account Title column, (2) *$960* in the Adjustments Debit column on the

WORK SHEET WITH TRIAL BALANCE AND ADJUSTMENTS RECORDED

Cole Photographic
Work
For Month Ended

	ACCOUNT TITLE	TRIAL BALANCE DEBIT	TRIAL BALANCE CREDIT	ADJUSTMENTS DEBIT	ADJUSTMENTS CREDIT
1	Cash	1 6 3 1 00			
2	Accounts Receivable	1 7 7 5 00			
3	Supplies	1 8 5 0 00			(a) 9 6 0 00
4	Prepaid Rent	2 4 0 0 00			(b) 8 0 0 00
5	Photographic Equipment	1 7 5 0 0 00			
6	Accounts Payable		2 0 0 0 00		
7	Sara Cole, Capital		2 0 6 5 0 00		
8	Sara Cole, Drawing	1 5 0 0 00			
9	Sales		5 5 2 5 00		
10	Salary Expense	1 1 5 0 00		(d) 1 1 5 00	
11	Miscellaneous Expense	3 6 9 00			
12		2 8 1 7 5 00	2 8 1 7 5 00		
13	Supplies Expense			(a) 9 6 0 00	
14	Rent Expense			(b) 8 0 0 00	
15	Depreciation Expense			(c) 1 7 5 00	
16	Accumulated Depreciation				(c) 1 7 5 00
17	Salaries Payable				(d) 1 1 5 00
18				2 0 5 0 00	2 0 5 0 00
19					
20					
21					
22					
23					

same line, and (3) *$960* in the Adjustments Credit column on the line with Supplies.

(b) Rent. The prepaid rent account has a debit balance of $2,400, which represents a payment for three months beginning with March; therefore, the rent expense for March is $800. The adjustment is entered by writing (1) *Rent Expense* in the Account Title column, (2) *$800* in the Adjustments Debit column on the same line, and (3) *$800* in the Adjustments Credit column on the line with Prepaid Rent.

(c) Depreciation. Depreciation of the photographic equipment is estimated at $175 for the month. This expired portion of the cost of the equipment is both an expense and a reduction in the asset. The adjustment is entered by writing (1) *Depreciation Expense* in the Account Title column, (2) *$175* in

Studio

Sheet

March 31, 1987

ADJUSTED TRIAL BALANCE		INCOME STATEMENT		BALANCE SHEET		
DEBIT	CREDIT	DEBIT	CREDIT	DEBIT	CREDIT	
						1
						2
						3
						4
						5
						6
						7
						8
						9
						10
						11
						12
						13
						14
						15
						16
						17
						18
						19
						20
						21
						22
						23

the Adjustments Debit column on the same line, (3) *Accumulated Depreciation* in the Account Title column, and (4) *$175* in the Adjustments Credit column on the same line.

(d) Salaries. Salaries accrued but not paid at the end of March amount to $115. This is an increase in expense and an increase in liabilities. The adjustment is entered by writing (1) *$115* in the Adjustments Debit column on the same line with Salary Expense, (2) *Salaries Payable* in the Account Title column, and (3) *$115* in the Adjustments Credit column on the same line.

The final step in completing the Adjustments columns is to prove the equality of debits and credits by totaling and ruling the two columns.

WORK SHEET WITH TRIAL BALANCE, ADJUSTMENTS, AND ADJUSTED TRIAL BALANCE RECORDED

Cole Photographic
Work
For Month Ended

	ACCOUNT TITLE	TRIAL BALANCE		ADJUSTMENTS	
		DEBIT	CREDIT	DEBIT	CREDIT
1	Cash	1631 00			
2	Accounts Receivable	1775 00			
3	Supplies	1850 00			(a) 960 00
4	Prepaid Rent	2400 00			(b) 800 00
5	Photographic Equipment	17500 00			
6	Accounts Payable		2000 00		
7	Sara Cole, Capital		20650 00		
8	Sara Cole, Drawing	1500 00			
9	Sales		5525 00		
10	Salary Expense	1150 00		(d) 115 00	
11	Miscellaneous Expense	369 00			
12		28175 00	28175 00		
13	Supplies Expense			(a) 960 00	
14	Rent Expense			(b) 800 00	
15	Depreciation Expense			(c) 175 00	
16	Accumulated Depreciation				(c) 175 00
17	Salaries Payable				(d) 115 00
18				2050 00	2050 00
19					
20					
21					
22					
23					

Adjusted Trial Balance Columns

The data in the Trial Balance columns are combined with the adjustments data and extended to the Adjusted Trial Balance columns as indicated on the work sheet for Cole Photographic Studio below. For example, the cash and accounts receivable accounts are extended at their original amounts of $1,631 and $1,775, since no adjustments affected either account. Supplies has an initial balance of $1,850 and a credit adjustment (decrease) of $960. The amount to be extended is the debit balance of $890. The same procedure is continued until all account balances have been extended to the Adjusted Trial Balance columns. The Debit and Credit columns are then totaled to prove that no arithmetical errors have been made up to this point.

Studio
Sheet
March 31, 1987

ADJUSTED TRIAL BALANCE		INCOME STATEMENT		BALANCE SHEET		
DEBIT	CREDIT	DEBIT	CREDIT	DEBIT	CREDIT	
1 631 00						1
1 775 00						2
890 00						3
1 600 00						4
17 500 00						5
	2 000 00					6
	20 650 00					7
1 500 00						8
	5 525 00					9
1 265 00						10
369 00						11
						12
960 00						13
800 00						14
175 00						15
	175 00					16
	115 00					17
28 465 00	28 465 00					18
						19
						20
						21
						22
						23

Income Statement and Balance Sheet Columns

The data in the Adjusted Trial Balance columns are extended to one of the remaining four columns as indicated on the work sheet for Cole Photographic Studio appearing below. The amounts of assets, liabilities, owner's equity, and drawing (or dividends) are extended to the Balance Sheet columns, and the revenues and expenses are extended to the Income Statement columns. An advantage in time and accuracy can be achieved by beginning at the top and proceeding down the page in sequential order.

In the illustrative work sheet, the first account listed is Cash and the balance appearing in the Adjusted Trial Balance Debit column is $1,631. This amount should be extended to the appropriate column. Cash is an asset, it is

WORK SHEET COMPLETED FOR COLE PHOTO-GRAPHIC STUDIO

Cole Photographic
Work
For Month Ended

	ACCOUNT TITLE	TRIAL BALANCE		ADJUSTMENTS	
		DEBIT	CREDIT	DEBIT	CREDIT
1	Cash	1631 00			
2	Accounts Receivable	1775 00			
3	Supplies	1850 00			(a) 960 00
4	Prepaid Rent	2400 00			(b) 800 00
5	Photographic Equipment	17500 00			
6	Accounts Payable		2000 00		
7	Sara Cole, Capital		20650 00		
8	Sara Cole, Drawing	1500 00			
9	Sales		5525 00		
10	Salary Expense	1150 00		(d) 115 00	
11	Miscellaneous Expense	369 00			
12		28175 00	28175 00		
13	Supplies Expense			(a) 960 00	
14	Rent Expense			(b) 800 00	
15	Depreciation Expense			(c) 175 00	
16	Accumulated Depreciation				(c) 175 00
17	Salaries Payable				(d) 115 00
18				2050 00	2050 00
19	Net Income				
20					
21					
22					
23					

listed on the balance sheet, and it has a debit balance. Accordingly, the $1,631 amount is extended to the Debit column of the balance sheet section. The balance of Accounts Receivable is extended in similar fashion. The $890 adjusted balance of Supplies is extended to the Balance Sheet Debit column. The same procedure is continued until all account balances have been extended to the appropriate columns. The balances of the capital and drawing accounts are extended to the Balance Sheet columns, because this work sheet does not provide for separate Statement of Owner's Equity columns.

After all of the balances have been extended, each of the four columns is totaled. The net income or the net loss for the period is the amount of the difference between the totals of the two Income Statement columns. If the Credit column total is greater than the Debit column total, the excess is the net

Studio
Sheet
March 31, 1987

ADJUSTED TRIAL BALANCE		INCOME STATEMENT		BALANCE SHEET		
DEBIT	CREDIT	DEBIT	CREDIT	DEBIT	CREDIT	
1 631 00				1 631 00		1
1 775 00				1 775 00		2
890 00				890 00		3
1 600 00				1 600 00		4
17 500 00				17 500 00		5
	2 000 00				2 000 00	6
	20 650 00				20 650 00	7
1 500 00				1 500 00		8
	5 525 00		5 525 00			9
1 265 00		1 265 00				10
369 00		369 00				11
						12
960 00		960 00				13
800 00		800 00				14
175 00		175 00				15
	175 00				175 00	16
	115 00				115 00	17
28 465 00	28 465 00	3 569 00	5 525 00	24 896 00	22 940 00	18
		1 956 00			1 956 00	19
		5 525 00	5 525 00	24 896 00	24 896 00	20
						21
						22
						23

income. For the work sheet presented on pages 120–121, the computation of net income is as follows:

Total of Credit column (revenue)	$5,525
Total of Debit column (expenses).	3,569
Net income (excess of revenue over expenses)	$1,956

Revenue and expense accounts, which are subdivisions of owner's equity, are temporary in nature. They are used during the accounting period to aid in the accumulation of detailed operating data. After they have served their purpose, the net balance will be transferred to the capital account (or the retained earnings account) in the ledger. This transfer is accomplished on the work sheet by entries in the Income Statement Debit column and the Balance Sheet Credit column, with the description of the amount, "Net Income," inserted in the Account Title column, as illustrated on pages 120–121. If there had been a net loss instead of a net income, the amount would have been entered in the Income Statement Credit column and the Balance Sheet Debit column, and described as "Net Loss" in the Account Title column.

After the final entry is made on the work sheet, each of the four statement columns is totaled to verify the arithmetic accuracy of the amount of net income or net loss transferred from the income statement to the balance sheet. The totals of the two Income Statement columns must be equal, as must the totals of the two Balance Sheet columns. The work sheet may be expanded by the addition of a pair of columns solely for the statement of owner's equity (or retained earnings statement) data. However, because of the very few items involved, this variation is not illustrated.

FINANCIAL STATEMENTS

The work sheet is an aid in preparing the financial statements. The income statement, statement of owner's equity, and balance sheet prepared from the work sheet of Cole Photographic Studio appear on page 123. Their basic forms correspond to the statements presented in Chapter 1. Some minor variations are illustrated; others will be introduced in later chapters. The remaining portions of this section are devoted to the sources of the data and the manner in which they are reported on the statements.

Income Statement

The work sheet is the source of all of the data reported on the income statement. The sequence of expenses as listed on the work sheet may be changed in order to present them on the income statement in the order of size.

Cole Photographic Studio
Income Statement
For Month Ended March 31, 1987

Sales..		$ 5,525.00
Operating expenses:		
Salary expense............................	$ 1,265.00	
Supplies expense	960.00	
Rent expense	800.00	
Depreciation expense.....................	175.00	
Miscellaneous expense	369.00	
Total operating expenses................		3,569.00
Net income		$ 1,956.00

Cole Photographic Studio
Statement of Owner's Equity
For Month Ended March 31, 1987

Sara Cole, capital, March 1, 1987		$20,650.00
Net income for the month........................	$ 1,956.00	
Less withdrawals	1,500.00	
Increase in owner's equity		456.00
Sara Cole, capital, March 31, 1987		$21,106.00

Cole Photographic Studio
Balance Sheet
March 31, 1987

Assets

Current assets:		
Cash..	$ 1,631.00	
Accounts receivable	1,775.00	
Supplies....................................	890.00	
Prepaid rent	1,600.00	
Total current assets		$ 5,896.00
Plant assets:		
Photographic equipment	$17,500.00	
Less accumulated depreciation	175.00	17,325.00
Total assets...................................		$23,221.00

Liabilities

Current liabilities:		
Accounts payable	$ 2,000.00	
Salaries payable...........................	115.00	
Total liabilities		$ 2,115.00

Owner's Equity

Sara Cole, capital		21,106.00
Total liabilities and owner's equity		$23,221.00

Statement of Owner's Equity

The amount listed on the work sheet as the capital of a sole proprietor does not always represent the account balance at the beginning of the accounting period. The proprietor may have invested additional assets in the business during the period. Hence, it is necessary to refer to the account in the ledger to determine the beginning balance and any additional investments. The amount of net income (or net loss) and the amount of the drawings appearing in the Balance Sheet columns of the work sheet are then used to determine the ending capital account balance.

The form of the statement of owner's equity can be changed to meet the circumstances of any particular case. In the illustration on page 123, the amount withdrawn by the owner was less than the net income. If the withdrawals had exceeded the net income, the order of the two items could have been reversed. The difference between the two would then be deducted from the beginning capital account balance.

Other factors, such as additional investments or a net loss, also require changes in form, as in the following example:

Frank White, capital, January 1, 19--.............	$45,000.00	
Additional investment during the year	6,000.00	
Total......................................		$51,000.00
Net loss for the year.........................	$ 7,500.00	
Withdrawals................................	8,600.00	
Decrease in owner's equity		16,100.00
Frank White, capital, December 31, 19--..........		$34,900.00

In an incorporated business, it is necessary to show the difference between changes in capital stock and changes in retained earnings. If the change in the amount of capital stock issued during the period is significant, a capital stock statement should be prepared. Otherwise, such a statement is unnecessary.

Balance Sheet

The balance sheet illustrated on page 123 was expanded by the addition of subcaptions for current assets, plant assets, and current liabilities. If there were any liabilities that were not due until more than a year from the balance sheet date, they would be listed under the caption "Long-term liabilities." An example of a balance sheet illustrating a long-term liabilities section appears on page 207.

In the illustration on page 123, the plant assets are made up entirely of photographic equipment. When there are two or more categories of plant assets, the cost, accumulated depreciation, and book value of each category should be listed, and the total amount of plant assets should be shown. This presentation is illustrated as follows:

Plant assets:

Equipment.............................	$40,600	
Less accumulated depreciation..........	12,100	$28,500
Automobiles...........................	$22,500	
Less accumulated depreciation..........	9,600	12,900
Total plant assets...................		$41,400

The work sheet is the source of all the data reported on the balance sheet, with the exception of the amount of the sole proprietor's capital, which can be obtained from the statement of owner's equity. The stockholder's equity section of the balance sheet of a corporation is subdivided into capital stock and retained earnings. The amount to be reported for the latter is obtained from the retained earnings statement.

Retained Earnings Statement

The basic form of a retained earnings statement for a corporation was illustrated on page 31. If dividend payments are debited to Dividends, the amount will appear on the work sheet. However, some accountants prefer to debit dividends directly to Retained Earnings. When this is the case, it is necessary to refer to the ledger to determine the beginning balance of Retained Earnings and the amount of the dividends debited during the period.

JOURNALIZING AND POSTING ADJUSTING ENTRIES

At the end of the accounting period, the adjusting entries appearing in the work sheet are recorded in the journal and posted to the ledger. This procedure brings the ledger into agreement with the data reported on the financial statements. The adjusting entries are dated as of the last day of the period, even though they are usually recorded at a later date. Each entry may be supported by an explanation, but a suitable caption above the first adjusting entry is sufficient.

The adjusting entries in the journal of Cole Photographic Studio are presented as follows. The accounts to which they have been posted appear in the ledger beginning on page 129.

	DATE		DESCRIPTION	POST. REF.	DEBIT	CREDIT	
			JOURNAL			PAGE 2	
11			Adjusting Entries				11
12	Mar.	31	Supplies Expense	51	9 6 0 00		12
13			Supplies	14		9 6 0 00	13
14							14
15		31	Rent Expense	53	8 0 0 00		15
16			Prepaid Rent	15		8 0 0 00	16
17							17
18		31	Depreciation Expense	54	1 7 5 00		18
19			Accumulated Depreciation	19		1 7 5 00	19
20							20
21		31	Salary Expense	52	1 1 5 00		21
22			Salaries Payable	22		1 1 5 00	22
23							23

NATURE OF THE CLOSING PROCESS

The revenue, expense, and drawing (or dividends) accounts are tempo-rary accounts used in classifying and summarizing changes in the owner's equity during the accounting period. At the end of the period, the net effect of the balances in these accounts must be recorded in the permanent capital (or retained earnings) account. The balances must also be removed from the temporary accounts, so that they will be ready for use in accumulating data for the following accounting period. Both of these goals are accomplished by a series of entries called closing entries.

JOURNALIZING AND POSTING CLOSING ENTRIES

An account titled Income Summary is used for summarizing the data in the revenue and expense accounts. It is used only at the end of the accounting period and is both opened and closed during the closing process. Other account titles used for the summarizing account are Expense and Revenue Summary, Profit and Loss Summary, and Income and Expense Summary.

Four entries are required in order to close the temporary accounts of a sole proprietorship at the end of the period. They are as follows:

1. Each revenue account is debited for the amount of its balance, and Income Summary is credited for the total revenue.

2. Each expense account is credited for the amount of its balance, and Income Summary is debited for the total expense.
3. Income Summary is debited for the amount of its balance (net income), and the capital account is credited for the same amount. (Debit and credit are reversed if there is a net loss.)
4. The drawing account is credited for the amount of its balance, and the capital account is debited for the same amount.

The process of closing the temporary accounts of Cole Photographic Studio is illustrated by the following flowchart:

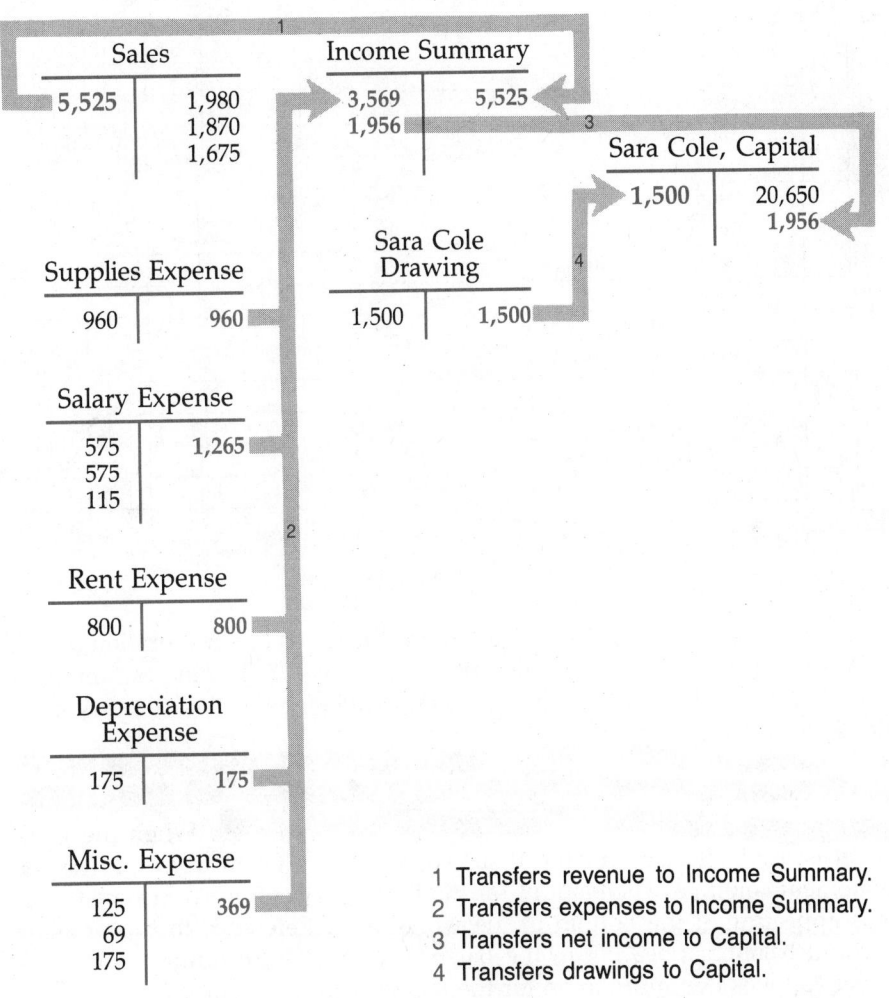

1 Transfers revenue to Income Summary.
2 Transfers expenses to Income Summary.
3 Transfers net income to Capital.
4 Transfers drawings to Capital.

After the closing entries have been journalized, illustrated as follows, and posted to the ledger, the balance in the capital account will correspond to the amounts reported on the statement of owner's equity and balance sheet. In addition, the revenue, expense, and drawing accounts will have zero balances.

CLOSING
ENTRIES

JOURNAL				PAGE 2						
	DATE	DESCRIPTION	POST. REF.	DEBIT			CREDIT			
24		Closing Entries								24
25	Mar. 31	Sales	41	5 5 2 5	00					25
26		Income Summary	33				5 5 2 5	00		26
27										27
28	31	Income Summary	33	3 5 6 9	00					28
29		Salary Expense	52				1 2 6 5	00		29
30		Miscellaneous Expense	59				3 6 9	00		30
31		Supplies Expense	51				9 6 0	00		31
32		Rent Expense	53				8 0 0	00		32
33		Depreciation Expense	54				1 7 5	00		33
34										34
35	31	Income Summary	33	1 9 5 6	00					35
36		Sara Cole, Capital	31				1 9 5 6	00		26
37										37
38	31	Sara Cole, Capital	31	1 5 0 0	00					38
39		Sara Cole, Drawing	32				1 5 0 0	00		39
40										40
41										41

The procedure for closing the temporary accounts of a corporation differs only slightly from the outline described on page 127. Income Summary is closed (entry 3) to Retained Earnings, and Dividends is closed (entry 4) to Retained Earnings.

The account titles and amounts needed in journalizing the closing entries may be obtained from any one of three sources: (1) work sheet, (2) income statement and statement of owner's equity, and (3) ledger. When the work sheet is used, the data for the first two entries are taken from the Income Statement columns. The amount for the third entry is the net income or net loss appearing at the bottom of the work sheet. Reference to the drawing account balance appearing in the Balance Sheet Debit column of the work sheet supplies the information for the fourth, and final, entry.

The ledger of Cole Photographic Studio after the adjusting and closing entries have been posted is presented on pages 129–131. Each posting of an adjusting entry and a closing entry is identified in the item section of the account as an aid to the student. It is not necessary that this be done in actual practice.

LEDGER AFTER THE ACCOUNTS HAVE BEEN ADJUSTED AND CLOSED

ACCOUNT Cash   ACCOUNT NO. 11

DATE		ITEM	POST. REF.	DEBIT	CREDIT	BALANCE DEBIT	BALANCE CREDIT
1987 Mar.	1		1	3 5 0 0 00		3 5 0 0 00	
	1		1		2 4 0 0 00	1 1 0 0 00	
	5		1	8 5 0 00		1 9 5 0 00	
	6		1		1 2 5 00	1 8 2 5 00	
	10		1		5 0 0 00	1 3 2 5 00	
	13		1		5 7 5 00	7 5 0 00	
	16		1	1 9 8 0 00		2 7 3 0 00	
	20		1		6 5 0 00	2 0 8 0 00	
	27		1		5 7 5 00	1 5 0 5 00	
	31		1		6 9 00	1 4 3 6 00	
	31		1		1 7 5 00	1 2 6 1 00	
	31		2	1 8 7 0 00		3 1 3 1 00	
	31		2		1 5 0 0 00	1 6 3 1 00	

ACCOUNT Accounts Receivable   ACCOUNT NO. 12

DATE		ITEM	POST. REF.	DEBIT	CREDIT	BALANCE DEBIT	BALANCE CREDIT
1987 Mar.	1		1	9 5 0 00		9 5 0 00	
	5		1		8 5 0 00	1 0 0 00	
	31		2	1 6 7 5 00		1 7 7 5 00	

ACCOUNT Supplies   ACCOUNT NO. 14

DATE		ITEM	POST. REF.	DEBIT	CREDIT	BALANCE DEBIT	BALANCE CREDIT
1987 Mar.	1		1	1 2 0 0 00		1 2 0 0 00	
	20		1	6 5 0 00		1 8 5 0 00	
	31	Adjusting	2		9 6 0 00	8 9 0 00	

ACCOUNT Prepaid Rent   ACCOUNT NO. 15

DATE		ITEM	POST. REF.	DEBIT	CREDIT	BALANCE DEBIT	BALANCE CREDIT
1987 Mar.	1		1	2 4 0 0 00		2 4 0 0 00	
	31	Adjusting	2		8 0 0 00	1 6 0 0 00	

ACCOUNT **Photographic Equipment** ACCOUNT NO. 18

DATE		ITEM	POST. REF.	DEBIT	CREDIT	BALANCE DEBIT	BALANCE CREDIT
1987 Mar.	1	Balance	1	15 000 00		15 000 00	
	4		1	2 500 00		17 500 00	

ACCOUNT **Accumulated Depreciation** ACCOUNT NO. 19

DATE		ITEM	POST. REF.	DEBIT	CREDIT	BALANCE DEBIT	BALANCE CREDIT
1987 Mar.	31	Adjusting	2		1 75 00		1 75 00

ACCOUNT **Accounts Payable** ACCOUNT NO. 21

DATE		ITEM	POST. REF.	DEBIT	CREDIT	BALANCE DEBIT	BALANCE CREDIT
1987 Mar.	4		1		2 500 00		2 500 00
	10		1	5 00 00			2 000 00

ACCOUNT **Salaries Payable** ACCOUNT NO. 22

DATE		ITEM	POST. REF.	DEBIT	CREDIT	BALANCE DEBIT	BALANCE CREDIT
1987 Mar.	31	Adjusting	2		1 1 5 00		1 1 5 00

ACCOUNT **Sara Cole, Capital** ACCOUNT NO. 31

DATE		ITEM	POST. REF.	DEBIT	CREDIT	BALANCE DEBIT	BALANCE CREDIT
1987 Mar.	1		1		20 650 00		20 650 00
	31	Closing	2		1 956 00		22 606 00
	31	Closing	2	1 500 00			21 106 00

ACCOUNT **Sara Cole, Drawing** ACCOUNT NO. 32

DATE		ITEM	POST. REF.	DEBIT	CREDIT	BALANCE DEBIT	BALANCE CREDIT
1987 Mar.	31		2	1 500 00		1 500 00	
	31	Closing	2		1 500 00		

ACCOUNT **Income Summary** ACCOUNT NO. 33

DATE		ITEM	POST. REF.	DEBIT	CREDIT	BALANCE DEBIT	BALANCE CREDIT
1987 Mar.	31	Closing	2		5 525 00		5 525 00
	31	Closing	2	3 569 00			1 956 00
	31	Closing	2	1 956 00			

LEDGER AFTER THE ACCOUNTS HAVE BEEN ADJUSTED AND CLOSED— CONCLUDED

ACCOUNT Sales — ACCOUNT NO. 41

DATE	ITEM	POST. REF.	DEBIT	CREDIT	BALANCE DEBIT	BALANCE CREDIT
1987 Mar. 16		1		1 9 8 0 00		1 9 8 0 00
31		2		1 8 7 0 00		3 8 5 0 00
31		2		1 6 7 5 00		5 5 2 5 00
31	Closing	2	5 5 2 5 00		—	—

ACCOUNT Supplies Expense — ACCOUNT NO. 51

DATE	ITEM	POST. REF.	DEBIT	CREDIT	BALANCE DEBIT	BALANCE CREDIT
1987 Mar. 31	Adjusting	2	9 6 0 00		9 6 0 00	
31	Closing	2		9 6 0 00	—	—

ACCOUNT Salary Expense — ACCOUNT NO. 52

DATE	ITEM	POST. REF.	DEBIT	CREDIT	BALANCE DEBIT	BALANCE CREDIT
1987 Mar. 13		1	5 7 5 00		5 7 5 00	
27		1	5 7 5 00		1 1 5 0 00	
31	Adjusting	2	1 1 5 00		1 2 6 5 00	
31	Closing	2		1 2 6 5 00	—	—

ACCOUNT Rent Expense — ACCOUNT NO. 53

DATE	ITEM	POST. REF.	DEBIT	CREDIT	BALANCE DEBIT	BALANCE CREDIT
1987 Mar. 31	Adjusting	2	8 0 0 00		8 0 0 00	
31	Closing	2		8 0 0 00	—	—

ACCOUNT Depreciation Expense — ACCOUNT NO. 54

DATE	ITEM	POST. REF.	DEBIT	CREDIT	BALANCE DEBIT	BALANCE CREDIT
1987 Mar. 31	Adjusting	2	1 7 5 00		1 7 5 00	
31	Closing	2		1 7 5 00	—	—

ACCOUNT Miscellaneous Expense — ACCOUNT NO. 59

DATE	ITEM	POST. REF.	DEBIT	CREDIT	BALANCE DEBIT	BALANCE CREDIT
1987 Mar. 6		1	1 2 5 00		1 2 5 00	
31		1	6 9 00		1 9 4 00	
31		1	1 7 5 00		3 6 9 00	
31	Closing	2		3 6 9 00	—	—

As the entry to close an account is posted, a line should be inserted in both Balance columns opposite the final entry, as illustrated by Sara Cole, Drawing and the remaining temporary accounts. Transactions affecting the accounts in the following period will be posted in the spaces immediately below the closing entry.

POST-CLOSING TRIAL BALANCE

The last procedure of the accounting cycle is the preparation of a trial balance after all of the temporary accounts have been closed. The purpose of the **post-closing** (after closing) **trial balance**, which is illustrated as follows, is to make sure that the ledger is in balance at the beginning of the new accounting period. The accounts and amounts should agree exactly with the accounts and amounts listed on the balance sheet at the end of the period.

POST-
CLOSING
TRIAL
BALANCE

Cole Photographic Studio									
Post-Closing Trial Balance									
March 31, 1987									
Cash	1	6	3	1	00				
Accounts Receivable	1	7	7	5	00				
Supplies		8	9	0	00				
Prepaid Rent	1	6	0	0	00				
Photographic Equipment	17	5	0	0	00				
Accumulated Depreciation							1	7	5	00
Accounts Payable						2	0	0	0	00
Salaries Payable							1	1	5	00
Sara Cole, Capital						21	1	0	6	00
	23	3	9	6	00	23	3	9	6	00

Instead of preparing a formalized post-closing trial balance, it is possible to proceed directly from the ledger to a calculator to determine the equality of debit and credit balances in the ledger. Equipment providing a tape record of the amounts introduced into the device should be used — the tape becoming, in effect, the post-closing trial balance. Without such a tape, there are no efficient means of determining whether the cause of an inequality of trial balance totals is due to errors in manipulating the keys or to errors in the ledger.

FISCAL YEAR

The maximum length of an accounting period is usually one year, which includes a complete cycle of the seasons and of business activities. Income and property taxes are also based on yearly periods and thus require that annual determinations be made.

The annual accounting period adopted by an enterprise is known as its **fiscal year**. Fiscal years ordinarily begin with the first day of the particular month selected and end on the last day of the twelfth month hence. The period most commonly adopted is the calendar year, although other periods are not unusual, particularly for incorporated businesses.

The 1985 edition of *Accounting Trends & Techniques*, published by the American Institute of Certified Public Accountants, reported the following results of a survey of 600 industrial and merchandising companies concerning the month of their fiscal year end:

Percentage of companies with fiscal years ending in the month of:

Month	Percentage
January	4%
February	2
March	2
April	1
May	2
June	7
July	3
August	3
September	7
October	5
November	2
December	62

A period ending when a business's activities have reached the lowest point in its annual operating cycle is termed the **natural business year**.

The long-term financial history of a business enterprise may be shown by a succession of balance sheets, prepared every year. The history of operations for the intervening periods is presented in a series of income statements. If the life of a business enterprise is represented by a line moving from left to right, a series of balance sheets and income statements may be diagrammed as follows:

THE LIFE OF A BUSINESS

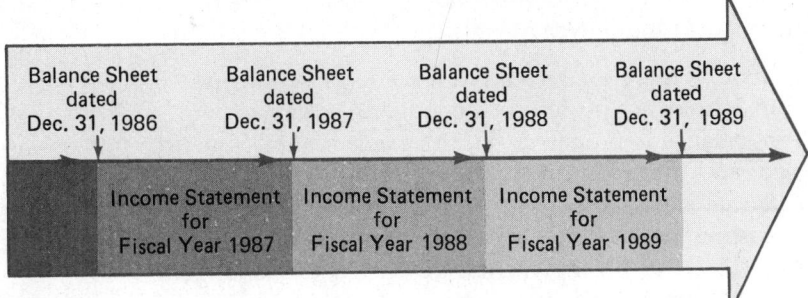

CLOSING THE BOOKS

Habit is a wonderful saver of mental effort. But too close adherence to habit in business limits efficiency by shutting off initiative.

This is particularly true in the adherence of general business to the habit of following a fixed date for closing the so-called "fiscal" year.

The best date for closing the books and preparing financial statements for the "fiscal" year is when business is in its most liquid condition—when bank loans and other liabilities are lowest, accounts receivable reduced, and, especially, when the inventory is at a minimum.

The most logical date for closing *your* "fiscal" year is that time when *your* business is logically over for the twelve months—when stocks are lowest—when prices are normal—when selling is not being forced—when you are not buying heavily—when profits can be most accurately determined—when your accounting department is not working nights, or your bank is not burdened with December 31st reports. In other words, close *your* books when *your* business is most naturally through with the rush of *your* year, when proper time and attention can be given, and your public accountants can serve you best.

SOURCE: *Management and Administration* (May, 1924), p. 503.

ACCOUNTING CYCLE

The principal accounting procedures of a fiscal period have been presented in this and the preceding chapter. The sequence of procedures is frequently called the **accounting cycle**. It begins with the analysis and the journalizing of transactions and ends with the post-closing trial balance. The most significant output of the accounting cycle is, of course, the financial statements.

An understanding of all phases of the accounting cycle is essential as a foundation for further study of accounting principles and the uses of accounting data by management. The following basic phases of the cycle are shown, by number, in the flowchart on page 135:

1. Transactions are analyzed and recorded in a journal.
2. Transactions are posted to the ledger.
3. Trial balance is prepared, data needed to adjust the accounts are assembled, and the work sheet is completed.
4. Financial statements are prepared.
5. Adjusting and closing entries are journalized.
6. Adjusting and closing entries are posted to the ledger.
7. Post-closing trial balance is prepared.

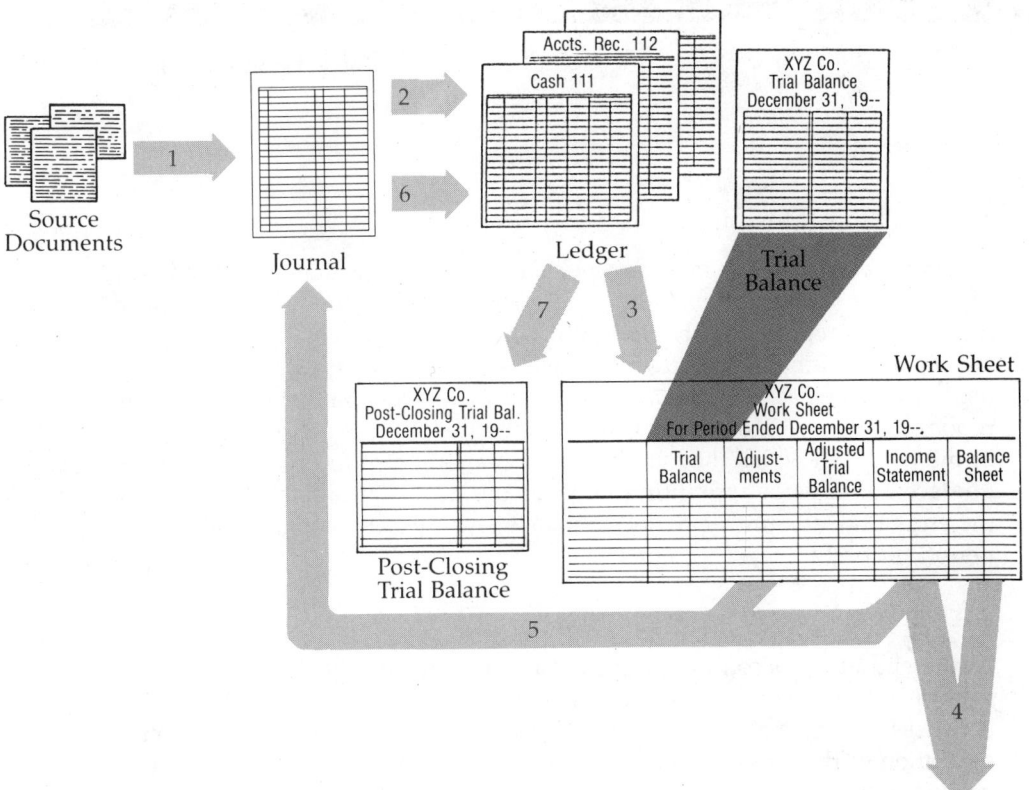

1. Transactions analyzed and recorded in journal.
2. Transactions posted to ledger.
3. Trial balance prepared, adjustment data assembled, and work sheet completed.
4. Financial statements prepared.
5. Adjusting and closing entries journalized.
6. Adjusting and closing entries posted to ledger.
7. Post-closing trial balance prepared.

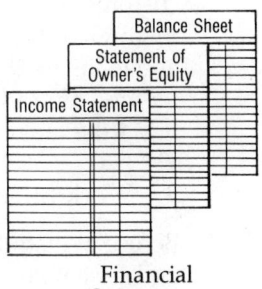

Financial
Statements

ACCOUNTING CYCLE

CHAPTER REVIEW

KEY POINTS

1. Matching Principle.

Revenues and expenses may be reported on the income statement by (1) the cash basis or (2) the accrual basis of accounting. When the cash basis is used, revenues are reported in the period in which cash is received, and expenses are reported in the period in which cash is paid. Most enterprises, however, use the accrual basis of accounting. Under the accrual method, revenues are reported in the period in which they are earned, and expenses are reported in the period in which they are incurred in an attempt to produce revenues. The accrual basis of accounting requires the use of an adjusting process at the end of the accounting period to match revenues and expenses within the period properly.

2. Nature of the Adjusting Process.

At the end of the accounting period, some of the amounts listed on the trial balance are not necessarily correct. For example, amounts listed for prepaid expenses are normally overstated because the day-to-day consumption or expiration of these assets has not been recorded. Likewise, some revenue or expense items related to the period may not be recorded, since these items are customarily recorded only when cash has been received or paid. The entries required at the end of the accounting period to bring the accounts up to date and to insure the proper matching of revenues and expenses under the accrual method are called adjusting entries. The posting of the adjusting entries will bring the ledger up to date as a planned part of the accounting cycle.

3. Work Sheet and Financial Statements.

Before adjustments are journalized and posted, it is necessary to determine and assemble the relevant data. A type of working paper that is used frequently by accountants to summarize these data is called a work sheet. The work sheet is also an aid in preparing the financial statements, including the income statement, statement of owner's equity, and balance sheet. For a corporation, a retained earnings statement can be prepared from the work sheet.

4. Journalizing and Posting Adjusting Entries.

At the end of the accounting period, the adjusting entries are recorded in the journal and posted to the ledger. This procedure brings the ledger into agreement with the data reported on the financial statements.

5. Nature of the Closing Process.

The revenue, expense, and drawing (dividends) accounts are temporary accounts used in classifying and summarizing changes in owner's equity during an accounting period. At the end of the period, the net effect of the balances in these accounts must be recorded in a permanent capital (or retained earnings) account. The balances must also be removed from the temporary accounts so that they will be ready for use to accumulate data for the following accounting period. Both of these goals are accomplished by the journalizing and posting of closing entries.

6. Journalizing and Posting Closing Entries.

In preparing the closing entries, an account titled Income Summary is used for summarizing the data in the revenue and expense accounts. The balance of this account is then closed to the owner's capital account (or retained earnings account for a corporation). Finally, the drawing (dividends) account is closed to the capital account (retained earnings account for a corporation). After the closing entries have been journalized and posted to the ledger, the balance in the owner's capital account (or retained earnings account for a corporation) will correspond to the amounts reported on the statement of owner's equity (retained earnings statement for a corporation) and balance sheet.

7. Post-Closing Trial Balance.

The last procedure of the accounting cycle is the preparation of a trial balance after all of the temporary accounts have been closed. The purpose of the post-closing trial balance is to make sure the ledger is in balance at the beginning of the new accounting period. The accounts and amounts should agree exactly with the accounts and amounts listed on the balance sheet at the end of the period.

8. Fiscal Year.

The annual accounting period adopted by an enterprise is known as the fiscal year. The period most commonly adopted is the calendar year, although other periods corresponding to the enterprise's natural business year may be used, particularly for incorporated enterprises.

9. Accounting Cycle.

The sequence of accounting procedures during a fiscal period is called the accounting cycle. It begins with the analysis of transactions and ends with the post-closing trial balance. The most significant output of the accounting cycle is the financial statements.

KEY TERMS

matching principle 107
cash basis 107
accrual basis 107
adjusting entries 108
depreciation 111
accumulated depreciation 111
contra account 111
accrued expense 112

work sheet 113
closing entries 126
Income Summary 126
post-closing trial balance 132
fiscal year 133
natural business year 133
accounting cycle 134

SELF-EXAMINATION QUESTIONS
Answers in Appendix B.

1. If the supplies account, before adjustment on May 31, indicated a balance
    of $2,250, and an inventory of supplies on hand at May 31 totaled $950,
    the adjusting entry would be:
    A. debit Supplies, $950; credit Supplies Expense, $950
    B. debit Supplies, $1,300; credit Supplies Expense, $1,300
    C. debit Supplies Expense, $950; credit Supplies, $950
    D. debit Supplies Expense, $1,300; credit Supplies, $1,300

2. If the estimated amount of depreciation on equipment for a period is
    $2,000, the adjusting entry to record depreciation would be:
    A. debit Depreciation Expense, $2,000; credit Equipment, $2,000
    B. debit Equipment, $2,000; credit Depreciation Expense, $2,000
    C. debit Depreciation Expense, $2,000; credit Accumulated Depreciation,
        $2,000
    D. debit Accumulated Depreciation, $2,000; credit Depreciation Expense,
        $2,000

3. If the equipment account has a balance of $22,500 and its accumulated
    depreciation account has a balance of $14,000, the book value of the
    equipment is:
    A. $36,500   C. $14,000
    B. $22,500   D. $8,500

4. Which of the following accounts would be closed to the income summary
    account at the end of a period?
    A. Sales   C. Both Sales and Salary Expense
    B. Salary Expense   D. Neither Sales nor Salary Expense

5. The post-closing trial balance would include which of the following accounts?
   A. Cash
   B. Sales
   C. Salary Expense
   D. All of the above

ILLUSTRATIVE PROBLEM

Two years ago, K. L. Waters organized Star Laundromat as a sole proprietorship. At March 31, 1988, the end of the current fiscal year, the trial balance of Star Laundromat is as follows:

Star Laundromat
Trial Balance
March 31, 1988

	Debit	Credit
Cash	2 4 2 5 00	
Laundry Supplies	1 8 7 0 00	
Prepaid Insurance	6 2 0 00	
Laundry Equipment	37 6 5 0 00	
Accumulated Depreciation		9 7 0 0 00
Accounts Payable		9 2 5 00
K. L. Waters, Capital		22 1 8 0 00
K. L. Waters, Drawing	10 2 0 0 00	
Laundry Revenue		39 1 2 5 00
Wages Expense	12 4 1 5 00	
Rent Expense	3 6 0 0 00	
Utilities Expense	2 7 1 5 00	
Miscellaneous Expense	4 3 5 00	
	71 9 3 0 00	71 9 3 0 00

The data needed to determine year-end adjustments are as follows:

(a) Inventory of laundry supplies at March 31, 1988	$ 480
(b) Insurance premiums expired during the year	315
(c) Depreciation on equipment during the year	1,950
(d) Wages accrued but not paid at March 31, 1988	140

Instructions:

1. Record the trial balance on a ten-column work sheet and complete the work sheet.
2. Prepare an income statement, a statement of owner's equity (no additional investments were made during the year), and a balance sheet.
3. On the basis of the adjustments data in the work sheet, journalize the adjusting entries.
4. On the basis of the data in the work sheet, journalize the closing entries.

(1)

Star
Work
For Year Ended

	ACCOUNT TITLE	TRIAL BALANCE		ADJUSTMENTS	
		DEBIT	CREDIT	DEBIT	CREDIT
1	Cash	2 4 2 5 00			
2	Laundry Supplies	1 8 7 0 00			(a) 1 3 9 0 00
3	Prepaid Insurance	6 2 0 00			(b) 3 1 5 00
4	Laundry Equipment	3 7 6 5 0 00			
5	Accumulated Depreciation		9 7 0 0 00		(c) 1 9 5 0 00
6	Accounts Payable		9 2 5 00		
7	K. L. Waters, Capital		2 2 1 8 0 00		
8	K. L. Waters, Drawing	1 0 2 0 0 00			
9	Laundry Revenue		3 9 1 2 5 00		
10	Wages Expense	1 2 4 1 5 00		(d) 1 4 0 00	
11	Rent Expense	3 6 0 0 00			
12	Utilities Expense	2 7 1 5 00			
13	Miscellaneous Expense	4 3 5 00			
14		7 1 9 3 0 00	7 1 9 3 0 00		
15	Laundry Supplies Expense			(a) 1 3 9 0 00	
16	Insurance Expense			(b) 3 1 5 00	
17	Depreciation Expense			(c) 1 9 5 0 00	
18	Wages Payable				(d) 1 4 0 00
19				3 7 9 5 00	3 7 9 5 00
20	Net Income				
21					
22					
23					

(2)

Star Laundromat
Income Statement
For Year Ended March 31, 1988

Laundry revenue		$39 1 2 5 00
Operating expenses:		
Wages expense	$12 5 5 5 00	
Rent expense	3 6 0 0 00	
Utilities expense	2 7 1 5 00	
Depreciation expense	1 9 5 0 00	
Laundry supplies expense	1 3 9 0 00	
Insurance expense	3 1 5 00	
Miscellaneous expense	4 3 5 00	
Total operating expenses		22 9 6 0 00
Net income		$16 1 6 5 00

Laundromat

Sheet

March 31, 1988

ADJUSTED TRIAL BALANCE DEBIT	ADJUSTED TRIAL BALANCE CREDIT	INCOME STATEMENT DEBIT	INCOME STATEMENT CREDIT	BALANCE SHEET DEBIT	BALANCE SHEET CREDIT	
2 4 2 5 00				2 4 2 5 00		1
4 8 0 00				4 8 0 00		2
3 0 5 00				3 0 5 00		3
3 7 6 5 0 00				3 7 6 5 0 00		4
	1 1 6 5 0 00				1 1 6 5 0 00	5
	9 2 5 00				9 2 5 00	6
	2 2 1 8 0 00				2 2 1 8 0 00	7
1 0 2 0 0 00				1 0 2 0 0 00		8
	3 9 1 2 5 00		3 9 1 2 5 00			9
1 2 5 5 5 00		1 2 5 5 5 00				10
3 6 0 0 00		3 6 0 0 00				11
2 7 1 5 00		2 7 1 5 00				12
4 3 5 00		4 3 5 00				13
						14
1 3 9 0 00		1 3 9 0 00				15
3 1 5 00		3 1 5 00				16
1 9 5 0 00		1 9 5 0 00				17
	1 4 0 00				1 4 0 00	18
7 4 0 2 0 00	7 4 0 2 0 00	2 2 9 6 0 00	3 9 1 2 5 00	5 1 0 6 0 00	3 4 8 9 5 00	19
		1 6 1 6 5 00			1 6 1 6 5 00	20
		3 9 1 2 5 00	3 9 1 2 5 00	5 1 0 6 0 00	5 1 0 6 0 00	21
						22
						23

Star Laundromat

Statement of Owner's Equity

For Year Ended March 31, 1988

K. L. Waters, capital, April 1, 1987		$22 1 8 0 00
Net income for the year	$16 1 6 5 00	
Less withdrawals	10 2 0 0 00	
Increase in owner's equity		5 9 6 5 00
K. L. Waters, capital, March 31, 1988		$28 1 4 5 00

Star Laundromat
Balance Sheet
March 31, 1988

Assets										
Current assets:										
Cash	$ 2	4	2	5	00					
Laundry supplies		4	8	0	00					
Prepaid insurance		3	0	5	00					
Total current assets						$ 3	2	1	0	00
Plant assets:										
Laundry equipment	$37	6	5	0	00					
Less accumulated depreciation	11	6	5	0	00	26	0	0	0	00
Total assets						$29	2	1	0	00
Liabilities										
Current liabilities:										
Accounts payable	$	9	2	5	00					
Wages payable		1	4	0	00					
Total liabilities						$ 1	0	6	5	00
Owner's Equity										
K. L. Waters, capital						28	1	4	5	00
Total liabilities and owner's equity						$29	2	1	0	00

(3)

JOURNAL   PAGE

	DATE		DESCRIPTION	POST. REF.	DEBIT					CREDIT					
1			Adjusting Entries												1
2	1988 Mar.	31	Laundry Supplies Expense		1	3	9	0	00						2
3			Laundry Supplies							1	3	9	0	00	3
4															4
5		31	Insurance Expense			3	1	5	00						5
6			Prepaid Insurance								3	1	5	00	6
7															7
8		31	Depreciation Expense		1	9	5	0	00						8
9			Accumulated Depreciation							1	9	5	0	00	9
10															10
11		31	Wages Expense			1	4	0	00						11
12			Wages Payable								1	4	0	00	12

(4)

14			Closing Entries														14
15	1988 Mar.	31	Laundry Revenue		39	1	2	5	00								15
16			Income Summary								39	1	2	5	00		16
17																	17
18		31	Income Summary		22	9	6	0	00								18
19			Wages Expense								12	5	5	5	00		19
20			Rent Expense								3	6	0	0	00		20
21			Utilities Expense								2	7	1	5	00		21
22			Miscellaneous Expense									4	3	5	00		22
23			Laundry Supplies Expense								1	3	9	0	00		23
24			Insurance Expense									3	1	5	00		24
25			Depreciation Expense								1	9	5	0	00		25
26																	26
27		31	Income Summary		16	1	6	5	00								27
28			K. L. Waters, Capital								16	1	6	5	00		28
29																	29
30		31	K. L. Waters, Capital		10	2	0	0	00								30
31			K. L. Waters, Drawing								10	2	0	0	00		31

DISCUSSION QUESTIONS

1. Is the balance listed on the trial balance for supplies, before the accounts have been adjusted, normally the amount that should be reported on the balance sheet? Explain.

2. Why are adjusting entries needed at the end of an accounting period?

3. What is the nature of the balance in the prepaid insurance account at the end of the accounting period (a) before adjustment? (b) after adjustment?

4. If the effect of the credit portion of an adjusting entry is to decrease the balance of an asset account, which of the following statements describes the effect of the debit portion of the entry?
   (a) Decreases the balance of a liability account.
   (b) Increases the balance of an expense account.
   (c) Increases the balance of an asset account.

5. Does every adjusting entry have an effect on the determination of the amount of net income for a period? Explain.

6. On March 1 of the current year, an enterprise paid the March rent on the building that it occupies. (a) Do the rights acquired at March 1 represent an asset or an expense? (b) What is the justification for debiting Rent Expense at the time of payment?

7. At the end of July, the first month of the fiscal year, the usual adjusting entry transferring supplies used to an expense account is inadvertently omitted. Which items will be incorrectly stated, because of the error, on (a) the income statement for July and (b) the balance sheet as of July 31? Also indicate whether the items in error will be overstated or understated.

8. In accounting for depreciation on equipment, what is the name of the account that would be referred to as a contra asset account?

9. (a) Explain the purpose of the two accounts: Depreciation Expense and Accumulated Depreciation. (b) What is the normal balance of each account? (c) Is it customary for the balances of the two accounts to be equal in amount? (d) In what financial statements, if any, will each account appear?

10. What term is applied to the difference between the balance in a plant asset account and its related accumulated depreciation account?

11. Accrued salaries of $5,500 owed to employees for December 29, 30, and 31 are not taken into consideration in preparing the financial statements for the fiscal year ended December 31. Which items will be erroneously stated, because of the error, on (a) the income statement for the year and (b) the balance sheet as of December 31? Also indicate whether the items in error will be overstated or understated.

12. Assume that the error in Question 11 was not corrected and that the $5,500 of accrued salaries was included in the first salary payment in January. Which items will be erroneously stated, because of failure to correct the initial error, on (a) the income statement for the month of January and (b) the balance sheet as of January 31?

13. Is the work sheet a substitute for the financial statements? Discuss.

14. In the Balance Sheet columns of the work sheet for Fox Company for the current year, the Debit column total is $22,150 greater than the Credit column total. Would the income statement report a net income or a net loss? Explain.

15. Why are closing entries required at the end of an accounting period?

16. What type of accounts are closed by transferring their balances to Income Summary (a) as a debit, (b) as a credit?

17. To what account is the income summary account closed for (a) a sole proprietorship? (b) a corporation?

18. To what account in the ledger of a corporation is the account Dividends periodically closed?

19. From the following list, identify the accounts that should be closed to Income Summary at the end of the fiscal year: (a) Accounts Receivable, (b) Salaries

Expense, (c) Capital Stock, (d) Salaries Payable, (e) Depreciation Expense—Equipment, (f) Utilities Expense, (g) Equipment, (h) Supplies, (i) Retained Earnings, (j) Sales, (k) Land, (l) Accumulated Depreciation—Equipment.

20. Are adjusting and closing entries in the journal dated as of the last day of the fiscal period or as of the day the entries are actually made? Explain.

21. Which of the following accounts in the ledger of a corporation will ordinarily appear in the post-closing trial balance? (a) Accounts Payable, (b) Accumulated Depreciation, (c) Capital Stock, (d) Supplies, (e) Depreciation Expense, (f) Sales, (g) Equipment, (h) Retained Earnings, (i) Dividends, (j) Cash, (k) Wages Expense, (l) Wages Payable.

22. What term is applied to the annual accounting period adopted by a business enterprise?

23. Real World Focus. The fiscal years for several well-known companies were as follows:

Company	Fiscal Year Ending
K Mart	January 30
J. C. Penney	January 26
Zayre Corp.	January 26
Toys "R" Us, Inc.	February 3
Federated Department Stores	February 2
The Limited, Inc.	February 2

What general characteristic of these companies explains why they do not have fiscal years ending December 31?

EXERCISES

Exercise 3–1. Adjusting entries for prepaid insurance. The balance in the prepaid insurance account, before adjustment at the end of the year, is $4,525. Journalize the adjusting entry required under each of the following alternatives: (a) the amount of insurance expired during the year is $3,225; (b) the amount of unexpired insurance applicable to future periods is $1,300.

Exercise 3–2. Adjusting entries for accrued salaries. A business enterprise pays weekly salaries of $11,300 on Friday for a five-day week ending on that day. Journalize the necessary adjusting entry at the end of the fiscal period, assuming that the fiscal period ends (a) on Monday, (b) on Wednesday.

Exercise 3–3.   Adjusting entries for prepaid and accrued taxes. A business enterprise was organized on July 1 of the current year. On July 2, the enterprise paid $3,600 to the city for taxes (license fees) for the next 12 months, and debited the prepaid taxes account. The same enterprise is also required to pay in January an annual tax (on property) for the previous calendar year. The estimated amount of the property tax for the current year is $3,950. (a) Journalize the two adjusting entries required to bring the accounts affected by the two taxes up to date as of December 31, the end of the current year. (b) What is the amount of tax expense for the current year?

Exercise 3–4.   Adjusting entries for depreciation; effect of error. On December 31, a business enterprise estimates depreciation on equipment used during the first year of operations to be $2,910. (a) Journalize the adjusting entry required as of December 31. (b) If the adjusting entry in (a) were omitted, which items would be erroneously stated on (1) the income statement for the year, and (2) the balance sheet as of December 31?

Exercise 3–5.   Closing entries for sole proprietorship. After all revenue and expense accounts have been closed at the end of the fiscal year, Income Summary has a debit of $792,500 and a credit of $845,500. As of the same date, Alice Henson, Capital has a credit balance of $160,250, and Alice Henson, Drawing has a balance of $32,000. (a) Journalize the entries required to complete the closing of the accounts. (b) State the amount of Henson's capital at the end of the period.

Exercise 3–6.   Closing entries for corporation. After all revenue and expense accounts have been closed at the end of the fiscal year, Income Summary has a debit of $919,750 and a credit of $889,250. As of the same date, Retained Earnings has a credit balance of $310,600, and Dividends has a balance of $25,000. (a) Journalize the entries required to complete the closing of the accounts. (b) State the amount of Retained Earnings at the end of the period.

Exercise 3–7.   Balance sheet for sole proprietorship. After all of the accounts have been closed on July 31, the end of the current fiscal year, the balances of selected accounts from the ledger of Townsend Company are as follows:

Accounts Payable	$ 4,250
Accounts Receivable	6,850
Accumulated Depreciation—Equipment	18,200
Cash	3,795
Equipment	38,900
Prepaid Insurance	1,050
Prepaid Rent	975
Salaries Payable	750
Supplies	1,100
Thomas Townsend, Capital	29,470

Prepare a balance sheet in report form.

Exercise 3–8.   Retained earnings statement. Selected accounts from the ledger of W. C. Barnett Inc., for the current fiscal year ended June 30, 1988, are as follows:

Capital Stock			Dividends			
	July 1	100,000	Aug. 1	4,000	June 30	18,000
			Nov. 1	4,000		
			Feb. 1	5,000		
			May 1	5,000		

Retained Earnings				Income Summary			
June 30	18,000	July 1	133,450	June 30	604,650	June 30	647,500
		June 30	42,850	30	42,850		

Prepare a retained earnings statement for the year.

Exercise 3–9.   Statement of owner's equity. Selected accounts from the ledger of E. G. Grant Company, for the current fiscal year ended December 31, are as follows:

E. G. Grant, Capital				E. G. Grant, Drawing			
Dec. 31	40,000	Jan. 1	90,500	Mar. 31	10,000	Dec. 31	40,000
		Dec. 31	33,250	June 30	10,000		
				Sept. 30	10,000		
				Dec. 31	10,000		

Income Summary			
Dec. 31	412,350	Dec. 31	445,600
31	33,250		

Prepare a statement of owner's equity for the year.

PROBLEMS

Series A

Problem 3–1A.   Work sheet and related items for sole proprietorship. The trial balance of Ozier Coin Laundry at October 31, 1988, the end of the current fiscal year, and the data needed to determine year-end adjustments are as follows:

Ozier Coin Laundry
Trial Balance
October 31, 1988

Cash..	13,100	
Laundry Supplies...................................	6,560	
Prepaid Insurance..................................	2,750	
Laundry Equipment.................................	84,100	
Accumulated Depreciation...........................		45,200
Accounts Payable.................................		6,100
D. L. Ozier, Capital................................		36,060
D. L. Ozier, Drawing...............................	18,000	
Laundry Revenue..................................		140,900
Wages Expense...................................	51,400	
Rent Expense.....................................	36,000	
Utilities Expense..................................	13,650	
Miscellaneous Expense	2,700	
	228,260	228,260

Adjustment data:

(a) Inventory of laundry supplies at October 31	$3,050
(b) Insurance premiums expired during the year	1,800
(c) Depreciation on equipment during the year....................	4,600
(d) Wages accrued but not paid at October 31....................	1,750

Instructions:

(1) Record the trial balance on a ten-column work sheet and complete the work sheet.
(2) Prepare an income statement, a statement of owner's equity (no additional investments were made during the year), and a balance sheet.
(3) On the basis of the adjustment data in the work sheet, journalize the adjusting entries.
(4) On the basis of the data in the work sheet, journalize the closing entries.

Problem 3–2A. Adjusting and closing entries; statement of owner's equity.
As of April 30, 1988, the end of the current fiscal year, the accountant for Benedict Company prepared a trial balance, journalized and posted the adjusting entries, prepared an adjusted trial balance, prepared the statements, and completed the other procedures required at the end of the accounting cycle. The two trial balances as of April 30, one before adjustments and the other after adjustments, are shown on page 149.

Instructions:

(1) Present the eight journal entries that were required to adjust the accounts at April 30. None of the accounts was affected by more than one adjusting entry.
(2) Present the journal entries that were required to close the accounts at April 30.
(3) Prepare a statement of owner's equity for the fiscal year ended April 30, 1988. There were no additional investments during the year.

Benedict Company
Trial Balance
April 30, 1988

	Unadjusted		Adjusted	
Cash..............................	7,325		7,325	
Supplies...........................	6,920		1,610	
Prepaid Rent	16,900		1,300	
Prepaid Insurance...................	1,275		350	
Equipment..........................	69,750		69,750	
Accumulated Depreciation—Equipment..		33,480		36,270
Automobiles	36,500		36,500	
Accumulated Depreciation—Automobiles.		18,250		21,900
Accounts Payable		4,310		4,530
Salaries Payable		—		3,480
Taxes Payable		—		1,200
B. C. Benedict, Capital		37,375		37,375
B. C. Benedict, Drawing	18,300		18,300	
Service Fees Earned		181,200		181,200
Salary Expense	112,300		115,780	
Rent Expense.......................	—		15,600	
Supplies Expense	—		5,310	
Depreciation Expense—Equipment	—		2,790	
Depreciation Expense—Automobiles.....	—		3,650	
Utilities Expense	2,720		2,940	
Taxes Expense	915		2,115	
Insurance Expense...................	—		925	
Miscellaneous Expense	1,710		1,710	
	274,615	274,615	285,955	285,955

If the working papers correlating with this textbook are not used, omit problem 3–3A.

Problem 3–3A. Ledger accounts and work sheet and related items for sole proprietorship. The ledger and trial balance of Horner Carpet Cleaning as of January 31, 1988, the end of the first month of its current fiscal year, are presented in the working papers.

Instructions:

(1) Complete the ten-column work sheet. Data needed to determine the necessary adjusting entries are as follows:

    a Inventory of supplies at January 31 .... $ 550.60

    b Insurance premiums expired during January 72.50

    c Depreciation on the building during January.................... 125.00

    d Depreciation on equipment during January..................... 95.00

    e Wages accrued but not paid at January 31 .... 1,006.50

(2) Prepare an income statement, a statement of owner's equity, and a balance sheet. (Note: The owner made an additional investment during the period.)

(3) Journalize and post the adjusting entries, inserting balances in the accounts affected.

(4) Journalize and post the closing entries. Indicate closed accounts by inserting a line in both Balance columns opposite the closing entry. Insert the new balance of the capital account.

(5) Prepare a post-closing trial balance.

Problem 3–4A.   Ledger accounts, work sheet, and related items for sole proprietorship. The trial balance of Victor Machine Repairs at July 31, 1988, the end of the current year, and the data needed to determine year-end adjustments are as follows:

Victor Machine Repairs
Trial Balance
July 31, 1988

Cash..	6,491	
Supplies..	4,295	
Prepaid Insurance	1,735	
Equipment...	30,650	
Accumulated Depreciation—Equipment...................		9,750
Trucks..	23,300	
Accumulated Depreciation—Trucks		6,400
Accounts Payable		2,015
D. D. Victor, Capital.......................................		30,426
D. D. Victor, Drawing.....................................	18,000	
Service Revenue		89,950
Wages Expense...	33,925	
Rent Expense..	9,600	
Truck Expense	8,350	
Miscellaneous Expense	2,195	
	138,541	138,541

Adjustment data:

(a) Inventory of supplies at July 31	$ 302
(b) Insurance premiums expired during year......................	990
(c) Depreciation on equipment during year	3,380
(d) Depreciation on truck during year	4,400
(e) Wages accrued but not paid at July 31	693

Instructions:

(1) Open a ledger of four-column accounts, using the following account titles and numbers: Cash, 11; Supplies, 13; Prepaid Insurance, 14; Equipment, 16; Accumulated Depreciation—Equipment, 17; Trucks, 18; Accumulated Depreciation—Trucks, 19; Accounts Payable, 21; Wages Payable, 22; D. D. Victor, Capital, 31; D. D. Victor, Drawing, 32; Income Summary, 33; Service Revenue, 41; Wages Expense, 51; Supplies Expense, 52; Rent Expense, 53; Depreciation Expense—Equipment, 54; Truck Expense, 55; Depreciation Expense—Trucks, 56; Insurance Expense, 57; Miscellaneous Expense, 59.

(2) For the accounts listed in the trial balance, enter the balances in the appropriate balance columns and place a check mark (√) in the posting reference column.

(3) Record the trial balance on a ten-column work sheet and complete the work sheet.

(4) Prepare an income statement, statement of changes in owner's equity (no additional investments were made during the year), and a balance sheet.

(5) Journalize and post the adjusting entries, inserting balances in the accounts affected.

(6) Journalize and post the closing entries. Indicate closed accounts by inserting a line in both Balance columns opposite the closing entry. Insert the new balance of the capital account.
(7) Prepare a post-closing trial balance.

Problem 3–5A.   Work sheet and statements for corporation. Beacon Bowl Inc. prepared the following trial balance at June 30, 1988, the end of the current fiscal year:

Beacon Bowl Inc.
Trial Balance
June 30, 1988

Cash...	11,500	
Prepaid Insurance	2,400	
Supplies...	1,950	
Land...	40,000	
Building	122,000	
Accumulated Depreciation—Building		31,700
Equipment...	72,400	
Accumulated Depreciation—Equipment................		15,300
Accounts Payable		6,100
Capital Stock..		100,000
Retained Earnings		60,500
Dividends..	15,000	
Bowling Revenue.....................................		161,200
Salaries and Wages Expense	60,200	
Advertising Expense	19,000	
Utilities Expense.....................................	18,200	
Repairs Expense	8,100	
Miscellaneous Expense	4,050	
	374,800	374,800

The data needed to determine year-end adjustments are as follows:

(a) Insurance expired during the year............................	$1,050
(b) Inventory of supplies at June 30	450
(c) Depreciation of building for the year..........................	1,620
(d) Depreciation of equipment for the year........................	5,160
(e) Accrued salaries and wages at June 30.......................	1,950

Instructions:

(1) Record the trial balance on a ten-column work sheet and complete the work sheet.
(2) Prepare an income statement for the year ended June 30.
(3) Prepare a retained earnings statement for the year ended June 30.
(4) Prepare a balance sheet as of June 30.
(5) Compute the percent of net income to revenue for the year.
(6) Compute the percent of net income for the year ended June 30 to total stockholders' equity as of the beginning of the fiscal year. The capital stock account remained unchanged during the year.

Series B

Problem 3–1B.   Work sheet and related items for sole proprietorship. The trial balance of Island Laundromat at July 31, 1988, the end of the current fiscal year, and the data needed to determine year-end adjustments are as follows:

Island Laundromat
Trial Balance
July 31, 1988

Cash...	6,290	
Laundry Supplies................................	3,850	
Prepaid Insurance	2,400	
Laundry Equipment..............................	81,600	
Accumulated Depreciation.......................		52,700
Accounts Payable		3,950
Ellen Cole, Capital.............................		33,900
Ellen Cole, Drawing............................	16,600	
Laundry Revenue...............................		66,900
Wages Expense................................	22,900	
Rent Expense..................................	14,400	
Utilities Expense................................	8,500	
Miscellaneous Expense	910	
	157,450	157,450

Adjustment data:

(a) Inventory of laundry supplies at July 31...........................	$ 940
(b) Insurance premiums expired during the year	1,500
(c) Depreciation on equipment during the year.......................	5,220
(d) Wages accrued but not paid at July 31	850

Instructions:

(1) Record the trial balance on a ten-column work sheet and complete the work sheet.
(2) Prepare an income statement, a statement of owner's equity (no additional investments were made during the year), and a balance sheet.
(3) On the basis of the adjustment data in the work sheet, journalize the adjusting entries.
(4) On the basis of the data in the work sheet, journalize the closing entries.

Problem 3–2B.   Adjusting and closing entries; statement of owner's equity. As of December 31, the end of the current fiscal year, the accountant for Bonner Company prepared a trial balance, journalized and posted the adjusting entries, prepared an adjusted trial balance, prepared the statements, and completed the other procedures required at the end of the accounting cycle. The two trial balances as of December 31, one before adjustments and the other after adjustments, are as follows:

Bonner Company
Trial Balance
December 31, 19--

	Unadjusted		Adjusted	
Cash................................	13,650		13,650	
Supplies............................	10,380		3,960	
Prepaid Rent	9,750		750	
Prepaid Insurance...................	2,400		800	
Land................................	42,500		42,500	
Buildings	116,000		116,000	
Accumulated Depreciation—Buildings ...		77,600		82,400
Trucks	82,000		82,000	
Accumulated Depreciation—Trucks		32,800		50,900
Accounts Payable		7,120		7,520
Salaries Payable		—		1,450
Taxes Payable		—		920
C. C. Bonner, Capital		116,790		116,790
C. C. Bonner, Drawing	21,000		21,000	
Service Fees Earned		140,680		140,680
Salary Expense	71,200		72,650	
Depreciation Expense—Trucks	—		18,100	
Rent Expense.......................	—		9,000	
Supplies Expense	—		6,420	
Utilities Expense	4,550		4,950	
Depreciation Expense—Buildings.......	—		4,800	
Taxes Expense	600		1,520	
Insurance Expense..................	—		1,600	
Miscellaneous Expense	960		960	
	374,990	374,990	400,660	400,660

Instructions:

(1) Present the eight journal entries that were required to adjust the accounts at December 31. None of the accounts was affected by more than one adjusting entry.
(2) Present the journal entries that were required to close the accounts at December 31.
(3) Prepare a statement of owner's equity for the fiscal year ended December 31. There were no additional investments during the year.

If the working papers correlating with this textbook are not used, omit Problem 3–3B.

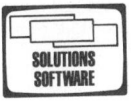

Problem 3–3B. Ledger accounts and work sheet and related items for sole proprietorship. The ledger and trial balance of Horner Carpet Cleaning as of January 31, 1988, the end of the first month of its current fiscal year, are presented in the working papers.

Instructions:

(1) Complete the ten-column work sheet. Data needed to determine the necessary adjusting entries are as follows:

Inventory of supplies at January 31	$450.00
Insurance premiums expired during January	80.00
Depreciation on the building during January.................	110.00
Depreciation on equipment during January.................	115.00
Wages accrued but not paid at January 31.................	975.00

(2) Prepare an income statement, a statement of owner's equity, and a balance sheet. (Note: The owner made an additional investment during the period.)

(3) Journalize and post the adjusting entries, inserting balances in the accounts affected.

(4) Journalize and post the closing entries. Indicate closed accounts by inserting a line in both Balance columns opposite the closing entry. Insert the new balance of the capital account.

(5) Prepare a post-closing trial balance.

MINI-CASE 3

Assume that you recently accepted a position with the American National Bank as an assistant loan officer. As one of your first duties, you have been assigned the responsibility of evaluating a loan request for $75,000 from Antipest, a small sole proprietorship. In support of the loan application, Donna Polk, owner, submitted the following "Statement of Accounts" (trial balance) for the first year of operations ended December 31, 1987:

Antipest
Statement of Accounts
December 31, 1987

Cash............................	4,120	
Billings Due from Others.............	7,740	
Supplies (chemicals, etc.)............	14,950	
Trucks...........................	32,750	
Equipment........................	16,150	
Amounts Owed to Others.............		4,700
Investment in Business..............		47,500
Service Revenue		97,650
Wages Expense....................	60,100	
Utilities Expense...................	6,900	
Rent Expense.....................	4,800	
Insurance Expense	1,400	
Other Expenses	940	
	149,850	149,850

Instructions:

(1) Explain to Donna Polk why a set of financial statements (income statement, statement of owner's equity, and a balance sheet) would be useful to you in evaluating the loan request.

(2) In discussing the "Statement of Accounts" with Donna Polk, you discovered that the accounts had not been adjusted at December 31. Through analysis of the "Statement of Accounts," indicate possible adjusting entries that might be necessary before an accurate set of financial statements could be prepared.

(3) Assuming that an accurate set of financial statements will be submitted by Donna Polk in a few days, what other considerations or information would you require before making a decision on the loan request?

COMPREHENSIVE PROBLEM 1

SOLUTIONS
SOFTWARE

For the past several years, Allen M. Sutton has operated a television repair service in his home on a part-time basis. As of September 1, Sutton decided to move to rented quarters and to devote full time to the business, which was to be known as Sutton TV. Sutton TV entered into the following transactions during September:

Sept. 1. The following assets were received from Allen Sutton: cash $6,000; accounts receivable, $1,000; supplies, $1,250; and service equipment, $6,200. There were no liabilities received.
2. Paid three months' rent on a lease rental contract, $2,400.
2. Paid the premiums on property and casualty insurance policies, $1,800.
4. Purchased additional service equipment on account from Payne Company, $2,000.
6. Received cash from customers on account, $600.
9. Paid cash for a newspaper advertisement, $80.
11. Paid Payne Company for part of the debt incurred on September 4, $1,100.
12. Recorded sales on account for the period September 1–12, $1,200.
13. Paid receptionist for two weeks' salary, $400.
17. Recorded cash from cash customers for service revenue earned during the first half of September, $2,100.
17. Paid cash for supplies, $950.
20. Recorded sales on account for the period September 13–20, $1,100.
24. Recorded cash from cash customers for service revenue earned for the period September 17–24, $1,850.
27. Received cash from customers on account, $1,200.
27. Paid receptionist for two weeks' salary, $400.
30. Paid telephone bill for September, $65.
30. Paid electricity bill for September, $140.
30. Recorded cash from cash customers for service revenue earned for the period September 25–30, $850.
30. Recorded sales on account for the remainder of September, $500.
30. Sutton withdrew $1,200 for personal use.

Instructions:

(1) Open a ledger of four-column accounts for Sutton TV, using the following titles and account numbers: Cash, 11; Accounts Receivable, 12; Supplies, 14; Prepaid Rent, 15; Prepaid Insurance, 16; Service Equipment, 18; Accumulated Depreciation, 19; Accounts Payable, 21; Salaries Payable, 22; Allen M. Sutton, Capital, 31; Allen M. Sutton, Drawing, 32; Income Summary, 33; Service Revenue, 41; Salary Expense, 51; Rent Expense, 52; Supplies Expense, 53; Depreciation Expense, 54; Insurance Expense, 55; Miscellaneous Expense, 59.
(2) Record the transactions in a two-column journal.
(3) Post the journal to the ledger, extending the month-end balances to the appropriate balance columns after all posting is completed.
(4) Prepare a trial balance as of September 30, on a ten-column work sheet, listing all the accounts in the order given in the ledger. Complete the work sheet, using the following adjustment data:

(a) Insurance expired during September	$ 250
(b) Inventory of supplies on September 30	1,420
(c) Depreciation of store equipment for September	750
(d) Accrued receptionist salary on September 30..................	100
(e) Rent expired during September............................	800

(5) Prepare an income statement, a statement of owner's equity, and a balance sheet.

(6) Journalize and post the adjusting entries.

(7) Journalize and post the closing entries. Indicate closed accounts by inserting a line in both balance columns opposite the closing entry. Insert the new balance in the capital account.

(8) Prepare a post-closing trial balance.

Chapter 4

ACCOUNTING FOR A MERCHANDISING ENTERPRISE

CHAPTER OBJECTIVES

■ Describe and illustrate the accounting for purchases by a merchandising enterprise.

■ Describe and illustrate the accounting for sales by a merchandising enterprise.

■ Describe the sequence of year-end procedures for a merchandising enterprise.

■ Describe two merchandise inventory systems.

■ Describe and illustrate the cost of merchandise sold section of an income statement.

■ Describe and illustrate the journal entries for merchandise inventory adjustments at year end.

■ Describe and illustrate the preparation and completion of a work sheet for a merchandising enterprise.

Merchandising enterprises acquire merchandise for resale to customers. It is the selling of merchandise, instead of a service, that makes the activities of merchandising enterprises differ from the activities of service enterprises. This chapter focuses on the accounting principles and concepts that are unique to merchandising enterprises—accounting for the purchase and sale of merchandise. In addition, the necessary year-end adjustments and the work sheet for a merchandising enterprise are presented.

PURCHASING AND SELLING PROCEDURES

The procedures followed in purchasing and selling merchandise may vary from business to business. For example, purchases and sales may be made for cash or on credit (on account), and many different arrangements may be made for making payments on account. In addition, policies for the return of merchandise and for the payment of transportation costs may be different. The common procedures for recording transactions between buyers and sellers of merchandise are discussed in the following paragraphs.

ACCOUNTING FOR PURCHASES

Purchases of merchandise are usually identified in the ledger as *Purchases*. A more exact account title, such as "Purchases of Merchandise," could be used, but the briefer title is customarily used. Thus a merchandising enterprise can accumulate in the purchases account the cost of all merchandise purchased for resale during the accounting period.

When purchases are made for cash, the transaction may be recorded as follows:

Jan. 3	Purchases..............................	510	
	Cash		510
	Purchases from supplier, Bowen Co.		

Most purchases of merchandise are made on account and may be recorded as follows:

Jan. 4	Purchases.............................	925	
	Accounts Payable......................		925
	Purchases from supplier,		
	Thomas Corporation.		

Purchases Discounts

The arrangements agreed upon by the buyer and the seller as to when payments for merchandise are to be made are called the **credit terms**. If payment is required immediately upon delivery, the terms are said to be "cash" or "net cash." Otherwise, the buyer is allowed a certain amount of time, known as the **credit period**, in which to pay.

It is usual for the credit period to begin with the date of the sale as shown by the date of the **invoice** or **bill**. If payment is due within a stated number of days after the date of the invoice, for example 30 days, the terms are said to be "net 30 days," which may be written as "n/30."[1] If payment is due by the end of the month in which the sale was made, it may be expressed as "n/eom."

As a means of encouraging payment before the end of the credit period, the seller may offer a discount for the early payment of cash. Thus the expression "2/10, n/30" means that, although the credit period is 30 days, the buyer may deduct 2% of the amount of the invoice if payment is made within 10 days of the invoice date. This deduction is known as a **cash discount**. The essentials of credit terms of 2/10, n/30 are summarized in the following diagram:

cash discount promotes early payment

CREDIT
TERMS

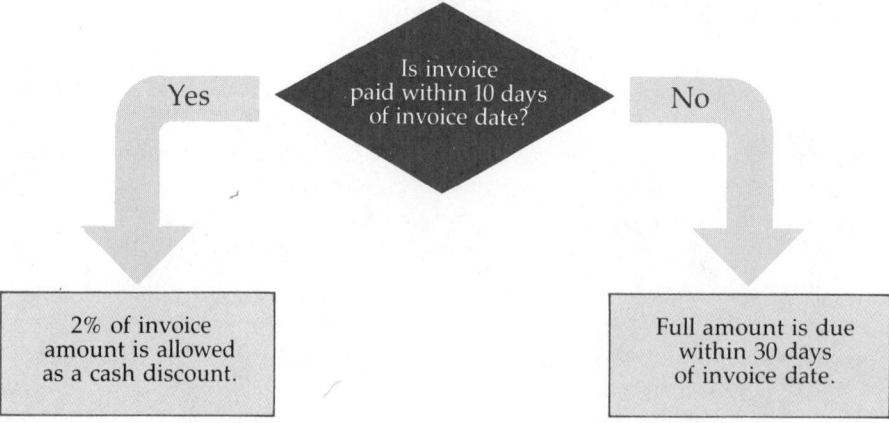

_____

[1]The word "net" in this context does not have the usual meaning of a remainder after all relevant deductions have been subtracted, as in "net income," for example.

From the buyer's standpoint, it is important to take advantage of all available discounts, even though it may be necessary to borrow the money to make the payment. To illustrate, assume that the following invoice for $1,500 is received by Midtown Electric Corporation:

Wallace Electronics Supply
3800 MISSION STREET
SAN FRANCISCO, CA 94110-1732

FOR CUSTOMER'S USE ONLY	
Calculations Checked *W. M. L.*	Price Approved
Material Received 10-13 19 87 *a. S.* Rec. Cl.	
Date / Signature / Title	
Audited *L. R. a.*	Final Approval

Customer's Order No. & Date 412 Oct. 9, 1987

Refer to Invoice No. 106-8

Invoice Date Oct. 11, 1987

Vendor's Nos.

SOLD TO Midtown Electric Corporation
1200 San Vicente Blvd.
Los Angeles, CA 90019-2350

Date Shipped Oct. 11, 1987   From San Francisco   Prepaid or Collect?

How Shipped and Route Western Trucking Co.   F.O.B. Los Angeles   Prepaid

Terms 2/10, n/30   Made in U.S.A.

QUANTITY	DESCRIPTION	UNIT PRICE	AMOUNT
20	392E Transformers	75.00	1,500.00

The invoice, with terms of 2/10, n/30, is to be paid within the discount period with money borrowed for the remaining 20 days of the credit period. If an annual interest rate of 12% is assumed, the net savings to the buyer is $20.20, determined as follows:

Discount of 2% on $1,500	$30.00
Interest for 20 days, at rate of 12% on $1,470 ($1,500 − $30)	9.80
Savings effected by borrowing	$20.20

Discounts taken by the buyer for early payment of an invoice are called **purchases discounts**. They are recorded by crediting the purchases discounts account and are usually viewed as a deduction from the amount initially recorded as Purchases. In this sense, the purchases discounts account is a contra (or offsetting) account to Purchases. To illustrate, the receipt of the purchase invoice presented above and its payment at the end of the discount period may be recorded as follows:

Oct. 11	Purchases.............................	1,500	
	Accounts Payable....................		1,500
	Invoice 106-8 from Wallace Electronics Supply.		
Oct. 21	Accounts Payable......................	1,500	
	Cash		1,470
	Purchases Discounts		30
	Invoice 106-8 from Wallace Electronics Supply.		

Purchases Returns and Allowances

When merchandise is returned **(purchases return)** or a price adjustment **(purchases allowance)** is requested, the buyer usually communicates with the seller in writing. The details may be stated in a letter, or the buyer (debtor) may use a **debit memorandum** form. This form, illustrated as follows, is a convenient medium for informing the seller (creditor) of the amount the buyer proposes to debit to the accounts payable account. It also states the reasons for the return or request for a price reduction.

DEBIT
MEMO-
RANDUM

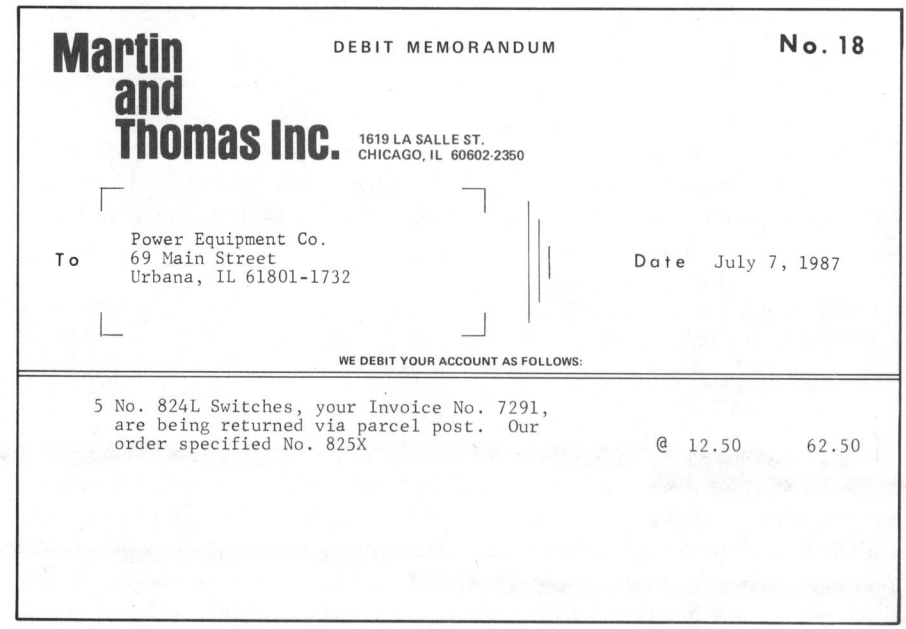

The debtor may use a copy of the debit memorandum as the basis for an entry or may wait for confirmation from the creditor, which is usually in the form of a **credit memorandum.** In either event, Accounts Payable must be debited and Purchases Returns and Allowances must be credited.[2] The purchases returns and allowances account can be viewed as a deduction from the amount initially recorded as Purchases. In this sense, like Purchases Discounts, the purchases returns and allowances account is a contra (or offsetting) account to Purchases. To illustrate, the entry by Martin and Thomas Inc. to record the return of the merchandise identified in the debit memo above would be as follows:

July 7	Accounts Payable........................	62.50	
	Purchases Returns and Allowances		62.50
	Debit Memo No. 18.		

When a buyer returns merchandise or has been granted an allowance prior to the payment of the invoice, the amount of the debit memorandum is deducted from the invoice amount before the purchases discount is computed. For example, assume that the details related to the amount payable to Power Equipment Co., for which the debit memo illustrated above was issued, are as follows:

Invoice No. 7291 dated July 1 (terms 2/10, n/30)	$2,045.00
Debit Memo No. 18 dated July 7	62.50
Balance of account	$1,982.50
Discount (2% of $1,982.50)..................................	39.65
Cash payment, July 11	$1,942.85

The cash payment could be recorded by Martin and Thomas Inc. as follows:

July 11	Accounts Payable........................	1,982.50	
	Cash		1,942.85
	Purchases Discounts		39.65
	Payment of Invoice No. 7291 from Power		
	Equipment Co., less Debit Memo No. 18.		

[2]Many businesses credit the purchases returns and allowances account for merchandise returned and allowances granted. However, some businesses prefer to credit the purchases account. If this alternative is used, the balance of the purchases account will be a net amount—the total purchases less the total returns and allowances for the period.

ACCOUNTING FOR SALES

Merchandise sales are usually identified in the ledger as *Sales*. A more exact title, such as "Sales of Merchandise," could be used.

A business may sell merchandise for cash. These sales are generally "rung up" on a cash register and totaled at the end of the day. Such sales may be recorded as follows:

Jan. 7	Cash	1,872.50	
	Sales		1,872.50
	Cash sales for the day.		

Sales to customers who use bank credit cards (such as MasterCard and VISA) are generally treated as cash sales. The credit card invoices representing these sales are deposited by the seller directly into the bank, along with the currency and checks received from customers. Periodically, the bank charges a service fee for handling these credit card sales. The service fee should be debited to an expense account.

A business may also sell merchandise on account. Such sales result in a debit to Accounts Receivable and a credit to Sales, as illustrated in the following entry:

Jan. 12	Accounts Receivable	510	
	Sales		510
	Invoice No. 7172 to Sims Co.		

Sales made by the use of nonbank credit cards (such as American Express) generally must be reported periodically to the card company before cash is received. Therefore, such sales create a receivable with the card company. Before the card company remits cash, it normally deducts a service fee. To illustrate, assume that nonbank credit card sales of $1,000 are made and reported to the card company on January 20. On January 27, the company deducts a service fee of $50 and remits $950. The transactions may be recorded as follows:

Jan. 20	Accounts Receivable	1,000	
	Sales		1,000
	American Express credit sales.		
Jan. 27	Cash	950	
	Credit Card Collection Expense............	50	
	Accounts Receivable		1,000
	Receipt of cash from American Express for sales reported on January 20.		

CREDIT CARDS AND CASH DISCOUNTS

Calls for a cashless society appeared regularly in the business press in the 1970s. Many predicted that plastic cards, both credit and debit, would replace green paper. Alas, polish for the crystal ball is in order. High interest rates and state usury laws have caused many retailers to examine their consumer credit policies for ways to wipe out red ink.

Exxon, Amoco, Sohio, and Mobil have been trying out various ways of offering discounts for cash in lieu of credit card sales. Mobil has lowered its wholesale price while adding a 3% processing fee for credit sales to induce station managers to favor cash sales. As a result, Mobil stations are offering consumers gasoline at 4 cents a gallon less if they pay cash.

The idea received a boost in the summer of 1981 when Congress passed the Cash Discount Act, permitting businesses to give discounts exceeding 5% to consumers paying cash. Previously, a rebate of more than 5% was considered a finance charge levied against credit card users and was therefore illegal.

The retailer incurs two costs in each credit card transaction: the collection fee to convert the charge to cash and the interest expense arising from the time lag between the sale and collection of funds. If, for example, his cost of funds is 20%, if an average six days elapse between the sale and collection of the proceeds, and if the collector's fee is 5%, then $10,000 in credit sales are equivalent to $9,472 in cash sales. The retailer could offer a cash discount of 5.3% and still be as well off as with a credit card sale.

Although many retailers might like to reject credit cards altogether because of their expense, up to now they have been ill-advised to take this step unless most of their competitors followed suit. Otherwise, they could suffer a disadvantage.

The retailer should consider four elements before adopting a discount-for-cash policy:

The reasons why his customers use credit cards. If it's just because they like the convenience of not carrying cash or consider it an advantage to buy now and pay later, they are candidates for a cash discount strategy. If, however, customers *need* the credit in order to make a purchase, a small cash reduction for cash payment probably would not deter their use of credit cards.

The proportion of his volume made up by cash sales. If the proportion is high, a discount-for-cash policy would give many customers who would have paid cash anyway a "free" deduction. Obviously, the effect on the retailer's earnings would not be healthy.

The cost of implementing the new policy. Computerized cash registers permit programming of a discount. Without electronic cash-handling technology, calculating the rebates could result in slower checkouts and clerical errors.

His customers' attitudes toward such an incentive—if he can ascertain them. If his competitors have a cash discount policy, the retailer could match this and wait for customer reaction. This "competitive parity" assumes, however, that rivals have determined an optimal discount policy that is applicable to others.

SOURCE: Adapted from Michael Levy and Charles A. Ingene, "Retailers: Head off Credit Cards with Cash Discounts," *Harvard Business Review* (May–June, 1983).

Sales Discounts

The seller refers to the discounts taken by the buyer for early payment of an invoice as **sales discounts**. They are recorded by debiting the sales discounts account and are considered to be a reduction in the amount initially recorded as Sales. In this sense, the balance of the sales discounts account is viewed as a contra (or offsetting) account to Sales. To illustrate, if cash is received within the discount period from a previously recorded credit sale of $500, 2/10, n/30, the transaction may be recorded as follows:

June 10	Cash	490	
	Sales Discounts.........................	10	
	Accounts Receivable		500
	Collection on Invoice No. 8722 to		
	Carver Co., less discount.		

Sales Returns and Allowances

Merchandise sold may be returned by the buyer **(sales return)** or, because of defects or for other reasons, the buyer may be allowed a reduction from the original price at which the goods were sold **(sales allowance)**. If the return or allowance is for a sale on account, the seller usually gives the buyer a **credit memorandum**. This memorandum shows the amount for which the buyer is to be credited and the reason therefor. A typical credit memorandum is illustrated as follows:

CREDIT
MEMO-
RANDUM

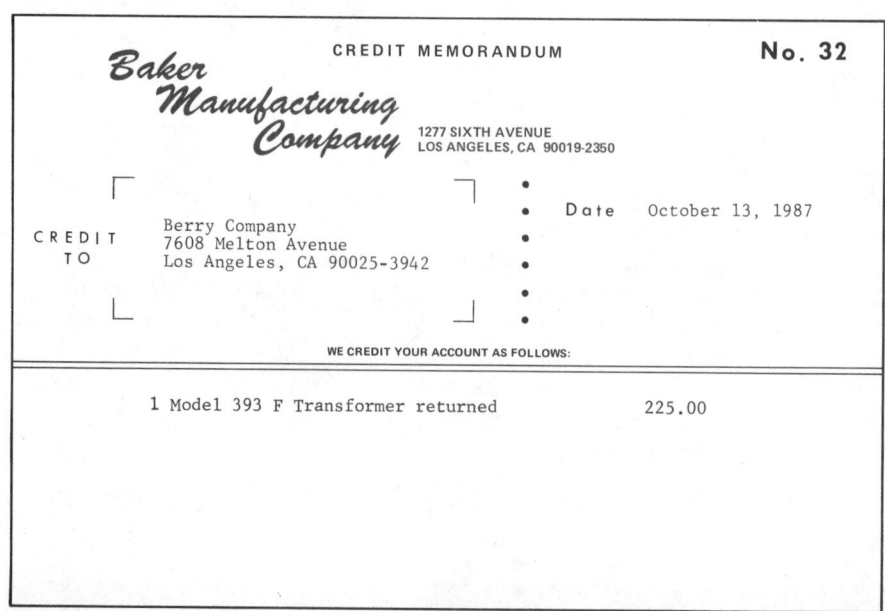

CREDIT MEMORANDUM   No. 32

Baker Manufacturing Company
1277 SIXTH AVENUE
LOS ANGELES, CA 90019-2350

CREDIT TO
Berry Company
7608 Melton Avenue
Los Angeles, CA 90025-3942

Date   October 13, 1987

WE CREDIT YOUR ACCOUNT AS FOLLOWS:

1 Model 393 F Transformer returned   225.00

The effect of a sales return or allowance is a reduction in sales revenue and a reduction in cash or accounts receivable. If the sales account is debited, however, the balance of the account at the end of the period will represent net sales, and the volume of returns and allowances will not be disclosed. Because of the loss in revenue resulting from allowances, and the various expenses (transportation, unpacking, repairing, reselling, etc.) related to returns, it is advisable that management know the amount of such transactions. Such a policy will allow management to determine the causes of returns and allowances, should they become excessive, and to take corrective action. It is therefore preferable to debit an account entitled Sales Returns and Allowances. If the original sale is on account, the remainder of the transaction is recorded as a credit to Accounts Receivable. Because sales returns and allowances are viewed as reductions of the amount initially recorded as Sales, the sales returns and allowances account is a contra (or offsetting) account to Sales. To illustrate, the following entry would be made by Baker Manufacturing Company to record the credit memo presented above:

Oct. 13	Sales Returns and Allowances.............	225	
	Accounts Receivable		225
	Credit Memo No. 32.		

If a cash refund is made because of merchandise returned or for an allowance, Sales Returns and Allowances is debited and Cash is credited.

TRADE DISCOUNTS

Manufacturers and wholesalers of certain types of merchandise frequently give large reductions from the *list prices* quoted in their catalogs. Such reductions in price are called **trade discounts**. Trade discounts are an easy method of making changes in prices without reprinting catalogs. As prices go up or down, new schedules of discounts may be issued. Trade discounts may also be used to give various classes of customers different prices.

There is no need to record list prices and their related trade discounts in the accounts. For example, the seller of an article listed at $100 with a trade discount of $40 would record the transaction as a sale of $60. Similarly, the buyer would record the transaction as a purchase of $60. For accounting purposes it is only the agreed price, which in the example is $60, that is important.

TRANSPORTATION COSTS

The terms of the agreement between buyer and seller include provisions concerning (1) when the ownership (title) of the merchandise passes to the buyer and (2) which party is to bear the cost of delivering the merchandise to the buyer. If the ownership passes to the buyer when the seller delivers the merchandise to the shipper, the buyer is to absorb the transportation costs, and the terms are said to be **FOB shipping point**. If ownership passes to the buyer when the merchandise is received by the buyer, the seller is to assume the costs of transportation, and the terms are said to be **FOB destination**. The relationship of the shipping terms to the passage of ownership and who is to bear the costs of transportation is summarized in the following table:

SHIPPING TERMS	FOB shipping point	FOB destination
Ownership (title) passes to buyer when merchandise is............	delivered to shipper	delivered to buyer
Transportation costs are borne by..............	buyer	seller

When merchandise is purchased on terms of FOB shipping point, the transportation costs paid by the buyer should be debited to Transportation In or Freight In and credited to Cash. The balance of the transportation in or freight in account should be added to net purchases in determining the total cost of merchandise purchased.[3]

In some cases, the seller may prepay the transportation costs and add them to the invoice, as an accommodation or courtesy to the buyer, even though the agreement states that the buyer bear such costs (terms FOB shipping point). If the seller prepays the transportation charges, the buyer will debit Transportation In for the transportation costs. To illustrate, assume that on June 10, Durban Co. purchases merchandise from Bell Corp. on account, $900, terms FOB shipping point, 2/10, n/30, with prepaid transportation costs of $50 added to the invoice. The entry by Durban Co. would be as follows:

June 10	Purchases...............................	900	
	Transportation In	50	
	Accounts Payable		950

When the terms provide for a discount for early payment, the discount is based on the amount of the sale rather than on the invoice total. To illustrate,

---

[3]Some businesses prefer to debit the purchases account for transportation charges paid on merchandise purchased FOB shipping point. If this alternative is used, the balance of the purchases account will include the transportation costs borne by the buyer. The total cost of merchandise purchased will be the same as when a separate transportation in or freight in account is used.

if Durban Co. pays the amount due on the purchase of June 10 within 10 days, the amount of the discount and the amount of the payment may be determined as follows:

Invoice from Bell Corp., including prepaid transportation of $50...		$950
Amount subject to discount	$900	
Rate of discount...	2%	
Amount of purchases discount		18
Amount of payment.......................................		$932

Durban Co. may record the payment as follows:

June 20	Accounts Payable........................	950	
	Cash		932
	Purchases Discounts		18
	Invoice 73B from Bell Corp.		

When the seller prepays the transportation costs and the terms are FOB shipping point, as in the illustration above, the seller adds these costs to the invoice that is sent to the buyer. Therefore, the seller records the payment of the transportation costs by debiting Accounts Receivable. In the illustration above, for example, Bell Corp. would record the following entry on June 10, in addition to the entry to record the sale to Durban Co.:

June 10	Accounts Receivable	50	
	Cash		50

When the agreement states that the seller is to bear the delivery costs (FOB destination), the amounts paid by the seller for delivery are debited to Transportation Out, Delivery Expense, or a similarly titled account. The total of such costs incurred during a period is reported on the seller's income statement as a selling expense.

SALES TAXES

Almost all states and many other taxing units levy a tax on sales of merchandise. The liability for the sales tax is ordinarily incurred at the time the sale is made, regardless of the terms of the sale.

Sales Tax for Seller

At the time of a cash sale, the seller collects the sales tax. When a sale is made on account, the buyer is charged for the tax. The seller credits the sales account for only the amount of the sale, and credits the tax to Sales Tax Payable. For example, a sale of $100 on account, subject to a tax of 4%, may be recorded by the following entry:

Aug. 12	Accounts Receivable	104	
	Sales		100
	Sales Tax Payable		4
	Invoice No. 339.		

Periodically, the appropriate amount of the sales tax is paid to the taxing unit, and Sales Tax Payable is debited.

Sales Tax for Buyer

The buyer debits the purchases account for the full amount of the merchandise acquired, including the sales tax. For example, a purchase of $100 on account, subject to a tax of 4%, may be recorded by the following entry:

Aug. 12	Purchases.	104	
	Accounts Payable		104
	Invoice No. 339.		

PERIODIC REPORTING FOR MERCHANDISING ENTERPRISES

At yearly intervals throughout the life of a business enterprise, the operating data for the fiscal year must be summarized and reported for the use of managers, owners, creditors, various governmental agencies, and other interested persons. Summaries of the various assets of the enterprise on the last day of the fiscal year, together with the status of the equities of creditors and owners, must also be reported. The ledger, which contains the basic data for the reports, must then be brought up to date through proper adjusting entries. Finally, the accounts must be prepared to receive entries for transactions that will occur in the following year. The sequence of year-end procedures may be changed slightly, but in general the following outline is typical:

1. Prepare a trial balance of the ledger on a work sheet form.
2. Review the accounts and gather the data required for the adjustments.
3. Insert the adjustments and complete the work sheet.
4. Prepare financial statements from the data in the work sheet.
5. Journalize the adjusting entries and post to the ledger.
6. Journalize the closing entries and post to the ledger.
7. Prepare a post-closing trial balance of the ledger.

Although the summarizing and reporting procedures presented in the remainder of this chapter and in Chapter 5 are similar to those discussed in the preceding chapter, a number of differences should be noted. In a merchandising business, merchandise purchased during the period has been recorded in the purchases account. Some of this merchandise may have been sold during the period, and some may be unsold at the end of the period (ending inventory). This ending inventory becomes the beginning inventory for the next period.

MERCHANDISE INVENTORY SYSTEMS

There are two main systems for accounting for merchandise held for sale: **periodic** and **perpetual**. Many merchandising enterprises use the periodic system. In this system, the revenues from sales are recorded when sales are made, but no attempt is made on the sales date to record the cost of the merchandise sold. It is only by a detailed listing of the merchandise on hand (called a **physical inventory**) at the end of the accounting period that a determination is made of (1) the cost of the merchandise sold during the period and (2) the cost of the inventory on hand at the end of the period. The periodic method is used in illustrations in this chapter.

Under the perpetual system, both the sales amount and the cost of merchandise sold amount are recorded when each item of merchandise is sold. In this manner, the accounting records continuously (perpetually) disclose the inventory on hand. The perpetual system is discussed in later chapters.

used for large or expensive merchandise

COST OF MERCHANDISE SOLD

For merchandising enterprises that use the periodic system, the cost of merchandise sold during a period is reported in a separate section in the income statement. To illustrate, assume that Cox Co. began its business operations on January 3, 1986, and purchased $340,000 of merchandise during the year. If the inventory at December 31, 1986, the end of the year, is $59,700, the cost of merchandise sold during 1986 would be reported as follows:

COST OF
MERCHAN-
DISE SOLD—
ENDING
INVENTORY
BUT NO
BEGINNING
INVENTORY

Cost of merchandise sold:

Purchases...	$340,000	
Less merchandise inventory, December 31, 1986	59,700	
Cost of merchandise sold		$280,300

To continue the illustration, assume that during 1987 Cox Co. purchases additional merchandise of $521,980, receives credit for purchases returns and allowances of $9,100, takes purchases discounts of $2,525, and pays transportation costs of $17,400. The purchases returns and allowances and the purchases discounts are deducted from the total purchases to yield the **net purchases**, and the transportation costs are added to the net purchases to yield the **cost of merchandise purchased**. These amounts would be reported in the cost of merchandise sold section of Cox Co.'s income statement for 1987 as follows:

Purchases		$521,980
Less: Purchases returns and allowances....	$9,100	
Purchases discounts	2,525	11,625
Net purchases............................		$510,355
Add transportation in.....................		17,400
Cost of merchandise purchased		$527,755

The ending inventory of Cox Co. on December 31, 1986, $59,700, becomes the beginning inventory for 1987. In the cost of merchandise sold section of the income statement for 1987, this beginning inventory is added to the cost of merchandise purchased to yield the **merchandise available for sale**. The ending inventory, which is assumed to be $62,150, is then subtracted from the merchandise available for sale to yield the cost of merchandise sold. The cost of merchandise sold during 1987 would be reported as follows:

COST OF
MERCHAN-
DISE SOLD—
BEGINNING
AND ENDING
INVENTORIES

Cost of merchandise sold:

Merchandise inventory, January 1, 1987.................			$ 59,700
Purchases.......................		$521,980	
Less: Purchases returns and allowances................	$9,100		
Purchases discounts.........	2,525	11,625	
Net purchases		$510,355	
Add transportation in...............		17,400	
Cost of merchandise purchased...			527,755
Merchandise available for sale......			$587,455
Less merchandise inventory, December 31, 1987..............			62,150
Cost of merchandise sold			$525,305

MERCHANDISE INVENTORY ADJUSTMENTS

The best method of making the data readily available for reporting the cost of merchandise sold is to maintain a separate account entitled Merchandise Inventory. Throughout an accounting period, this account shows the inventory at the beginning of the period. Purchases of merchandise during the period are then debited to the account entitled Purchases. As explained previously, returns and allowances are recorded in the purchases returns and allowances account. Cash discounts are recorded in a purchases discounts account, and transportation costs are recorded in the transportation in account.

At the end of the period it is necessary to remove from Merchandise Inventory the amount representing the inventory at the beginning of the period and to replace it with the amount representing the inventory at the end of the period. This is accomplished by two adjusting entries.[4] The first entry transfers the beginning inventory to Income Summary. Since this beginning inventory is part of the cost of merchandise sold, it is debited to Income Summary. It is also a subtraction from the asset account, Merchandise Inventory, and hence is credited to that account. The first adjusting entry is as follows:

Dec. 31	Income Summary	59,700	
	Merchandise Inventory................		59,700

The second adjusting entry debits the cost of the merchandise inventory at the end of the period to the asset account, Merchandise Inventory. The credit portion of the entry effects a deduction of the unsold merchandise from the total cost of the merchandise available for sale during the period. In terms of the illustration of the partial income statement above, the credit portion of the second entry accomplishes the subtraction of $62,150 from $587,455 to yield the $525,305 cost of merchandise sold. The second adjusting entry is as follows:

Dec. 31	Merchandise Inventory....................	62,150	
	Income Summary		62,150

---

[4]An alternative method of recording merchandise inventory is presented in Appendix C. This alternative method is sometimes referred to as the closing method.

The effect of the two inventory adjustments is indicated by the following T accounts for Merchandise Inventory and Income Summary:

Merchandise Inventory

Dec. 31 Preceding year	59,700	Dec. 31 Current year	59,700
Dec. 31 Current year	62,150		

Income Summary

Dec. 31 Current year	59,700	Dec. 31 Current year	62,150

In the accounts, the inventory of $59,700 at the end of the preceding year (beginning of current year) has been transferred to Income Summary as a part of the cost of merchandise available for sale. It is replaced by a debit of $62,150, the merchandise inventory at the end of the current year. The credit of the same amount to Income Summary is a deduction from the cost of merchandise available for sale.

TRIAL BALANCE AND ADJUSTMENTS ON THE WORK SHEET

After year-end posting of the journal has been completed, a trial balance of the ledger is taken. The trial balance for Midtown Electric Corporation as of December 31, 1987, appears on the work sheet presented on pages 176 and 177. It differs slightly from trial balances illustrated earlier. All of the accounts in the ledger are listed in sequential order, including titles of accounts that have no balances. This variation in format has the advantage of listing accounts in the order in which they will be used when the statements are prepared.

The data needed for adjusting the accounts of Midtown Electric Corporation are summarized as follows:

Merchandise inventory as of December 31, 1987		$62,150
Office supplies as of December 31, 1987		480
Insurance expired during 1987		1,910
Depreciation during 1987 on:		
Store equipment		3,100
Office equipment		2,490
Salaries accrued on December 31, 1987:		
Sales salaries	$780	
Office salaries	360	1,140

Explanations of the adjusting entries in the work sheet above are given in the paragraphs that follow.

(a), (b) **Merchandise Inventory.** As discussed previously, the $59,700 balance of merchandise inventory appearing in the trial balance represents the amount of the inventory at the end of the preceding year (beginning of the current year). It is part of the merchandise available for sale during the year and is hence transferred to Income Summary, where it will be combined with the net cost of merchandise purchased during the year [entry (a)].

The merchandise on hand at the end of the current year, as determined by a physical inventory, is an asset and must be debited to the asset account, Merchandise Inventory. It must also be deducted from the cost of merchandise available for sale to yield the cost of merchandise sold. These objectives are accomplished by debiting Merchandise Inventory and crediting Income Summary for $62,150 [entry (b)].

(c) **Office Supplies.** The $1,090 balance of the office supplies account in the trial balance is the combined cost of office supplies on hand at the beginning of the year and the cost of office supplies purchased during the year. The physical inventory at the end of the year indicates office supplies on hand totaling $480. The excess of $1,090 over the inventory of $480 is $610, which is the cost of the office supplies used during the period. The accounts are adjusted by debiting Office Supplies Expense and crediting Office Supplies for $610.

(d) **Prepaid Insurance.** The adjustment for insurance expired is similar to the adjustment for supplies consumed. The balance in Prepaid Insurance is the amount prepaid at the beginning of the year plus the additional premium costs incurred during the year. Analysis of the various insurance policies reveals that a total of $1,910 in premiums has expired. Insurance Expense is debited and Prepaid Insurance is credited for $1,910.

(e), (f) **Depreciation of Plant Assets.** The expired cost of a plant asset is debited to a depreciation expense account and credited to an accumulated depreciation account. A separate account for the current period's expense and for the accumulation of prior periods is maintained for each plant asset account. Thus, the adjustment for depreciation of the store equipment is recorded by a debit to Depreciation Expense — Store Equipment and a credit to Accumulated Depreciation — Store Equipment for $3,100 [entry (e)]. The adjustment for depreciation of the office equipment is recorded in a similar manner [entry (f)].

(g) **Salaries Payable.** The liability for salaries earned by employees but not yet paid is recorded by a credit of $1,140 to Salaries Payable and debits of $780 and $360 to Sales Salaries Expense and Office Salaries Expense respectively.

WORK SHEET

Midtown Electric
Work
For Year Ended

ACCOUNT TITLE	TRIAL BALANCE		ADJUSTMENTS	
	DEBIT	CREDIT	DEBIT	CREDIT
Cash...	62,950			
Notes Receivable................................	40,000			
Accounts Receivable............................	60,880			
Merchandise Inventory	59,700		(b) 62,150	(a) 59,700
Office Supplies..................................	1,090			(c) 610
Prepaid Insurance	4,560			(d) 1,910
Store Equipment.................................	27,100			
Accumulated Depreciation—Store Equipment		12,600		(e) 3,100
Office Equipment	15,570			
Accumulated Depreciation—Office Equipment		7,230		(f) 2,490
Accounts Payable		22,420		
Salaries Payable				(g) 1,140
Mortgage Note Payable		25,000		7807360
Capital Stock....................................		100,000		
Retained Earnings		41,200		
Dividends..	18,000			
Income Summary................................			(a) 59,700	(b) 62,150
Sales..		720,185		
Sales Returns and Allowances	6,140			
Sales Discounts	5,790			
Purchases	521,980			
Purchases Returns and Allowances.................		9,100		
Purchases Discounts.............................		2,525		
Transportation In	17,400			
Sales Salaries Expense	59,250		(g) 780	
Advertising Expense	10,860			
Depreciation Expense—Store Equipment			(e) 3,100	
Miscellaneous Selling Expense....................	630			
Office Salaries Expense	20,660		(g) 360	
Rent Expense....................................	8,100			
Depreciation Expense—Office Equipment...........			(f) 2,490	
Insurance Expense			(d) 1,910	
Office Supplies Expense..........................			(c) 610	
Miscellaneous General Expense...................	760			
Interest Income..................................		3,600		
Interest Expense	2,440			
	943,860	943,860	131,100	131,100
Net Income				

COMPLETING THE WORK SHEET

    After all of the necessary adjustments are entered on the work sheet, the two adjustments columns are totaled to prove the equality of debits and credits. As illustrated in the preceding chapter, the balances of the accounts in the trial balance columns and the amount of any adjustments are added or deducted as appropriate. The adjusted balances are then extended into the

Corporation
Sheet
December 31, 1987

ADJUSTED TRIAL BALANCE		INCOME STATEMENT		BALANCE SHEET	
DEBIT	CREDIT	DEBIT	CREDIT	DEBIT	CREDIT
62,950				62,950	
40,000				40,000	
60,880				60,880	
62,150				62,150	
480				480	
2,650				2,650	
27,100				27,100	
	15,700				15,700
15,570				15,570	
	9,720				9,720
	22,420				22,420
	1,140				1,140
	25,000				25,000
	100,000				100,000
	41,200				41,200
18,000				18,000	
59,700	62,150	59,700	62,150		
	720,185		720,185		
6,140		6,140			
5,790		5,790			
521,980		521,980			
	9,100		9,100		
	2,525		2,525		
17,400		17,400			
60,030		60,030			
10,860		10,860			
3,100		3,100			
630		630			
21,020		21,020			
8,100		8,100			
2,490		2,490			
1,910		1,910			
610		610			
760		760			
	3,600		3,600		
2,440		2,440			
1,012,740	1,012,740	722,960	797,560	289,780	215,180
		74,600			74,600
		797,560	797,560	289,780	289,780

adjusted trial balance columns, which are totaled to prove the equality of debits and credits. Both the debit and credit amounts for Income Summary are extended.

Some accountants prefer to eliminate the adjusted trial balance columns and to extend the adjusted account balances directly to the appropriate statement column. Such an alternative form of work sheet is especially popular if there are only a few items involved.

The process of extending the balances, as adjusted, to the statement columns is accomplished best by beginning with Cash at the top and moving down the work sheet, item by item, in sequential order. An exception to the usual practice of extending only the account balances should be noted. Both the debit and credit amounts for Income Summary are extended to the Income Statement columns. Since both the amount of the debit adjustment (beginning inventory of $59,700) and the amount of the credit adjustment (ending inventory of $62,150) may be reported on the income statement, there is no need to determine the difference between the two amounts.

After all of the items have been extended into the statement sections of the work sheet, the four columns are totaled and the net income or net loss is determined. In the illustration, the difference between the credit and the debit columns of the Income Statement section is $74,600, the amount of the net income. The difference between the debit and the credit columns of the Balance Sheet section is also $74,600, which is the increase in owner's equity as a result of the net income. Agreement between the two balancing amounts is evidence of debit-credit equality and arithmetical accuracy.

COMPLETION OF YEAR-END PROCEDURES

The year-end accounting procedures that are necessary for a merchandising enterprise include the preparation of financial statements, adjusting entries, and closing entries. These items, which are discussed and illustrated in Chapter 5, are prepared from the data in the statement sections of the work sheet.

CHAPTER REVIEW

KEY POINTS

1. Purchasing and Selling Procedures.

Merchandising enterprises acquire merchandise for resale to customers. It is the selling of merchandise, instead of a service, that makes the activities of merchandising enterprises differ from the activities of service enterprises.

2. Accounting for Purchases.

Purchases of merchandise, which may be made for cash or on account, are usually identified in the ledger as Purchases. For purchases of merchandise on account, the credit terms may allow cash discounts for early payment. Such discounts are recorded by the buyer as purchases discounts and are usually viewed as a deduction from the amount initially recorded as Purchases. Likewise, when merchandise is returned or a price adjustment is granted, the buyer records the adjustment as a purchases return and allowance.

3. Accounting for Sales.

Merchandise sales, which may be for cash or on account, are usually identified in the ledger as Sales. The seller refers to the discounts taken by the buyer for early payment as sales discounts, which are viewed as a reduction in the amount initially recorded as Sales. Merchandise returned or an allowance for reduction in the original price at which the goods were sold is treated as a sales return or allowance. Like sales discounts, sales returns and allowances are treated as a reduction in the initial amount recorded as Sales.

4. Trade Discounts.

Large reductions from list prices quoted in catalogs issued by manufacturers and wholesalers are referred to as trade discounts. The sellers and buyers of merchandise subject to trade discounts record the amount of the sales and purchases net of the trade discounts.

5. Transportation Costs.

The terms of a sale between a buyer and seller will include provisions concerning when ownership of the merchandise passes to the buyer and which party is to bear the cost of delivering merchandise to the buyer. If the ownership passes to the buyer when the seller delivers the merchandise to the shipper, the buyer is to absorb the transportation costs, and the terms are said to be FOB shipping point. If the ownership passes to the buyer when the merchandise is received by the buyer, the seller is to assume the cost of transportation, and the terms are said to be FOB destination.

6. Sales Taxes.

The liability for the sales tax is ordinarily incurred at the time the sale is made and is recorded by the seller as a credit to the sales tax payable account. The offsetting debit will be to Accounts Receivable if the merchandise is purchased on account, or to Cash if the cash is collected at the time of the sale. From the buyer's perspective, the cost of the purchases will include the original list price of the merchandise plus the sales tax.

7. Periodic Reporting for Merchandising Enterprises.

The summarization and reporting procedures for a merchandising enterprise are similar to those of a service enterprise. In a merchandising enterprise, however, merchandise purchased during the period will be recorded in a purchases account. Because some of this merchandise may be unsold at the end of the period, an adjustment to the merchandise inventory account is necessary.

8. Merchandise Inventory Systems.

Under the periodic system of accounting for merchandise, no attempt is made to record the cost of merchandise sold until the end of the period. It is only by a detailed listing of merchandise on hand (called a physical inventory) at the end of the accounting period that a determination is made of (1) the cost of merchandise sold during the period and (2) the cost of inventory on hand at the end of the period. Under the perpetual system of accounting for merchandise inventory, both the sales amount and the cost of merchandise sold amount are recorded when each item of merchandise is sold.

9. Cost of Merchandise Sold and Inventory Adjustments.

For merchandising enterprises using the periodic system, the cost of merchandise sold and the beginning and ending inventories are reported in the income statement. Two adjusting entries are required to adjust the merchandise inventory to its proper balance as of the end of the accounting period. These adjusting entries are recorded through the use of the income summary account.

10. Work Sheet.

The work sheet for a merchandising enterprise is completed in a similar fashion to that of a service enterprise. The primary difference is that the beginning and ending merchandise inventories, which are shown in the income summary account, appear in both the debit and credit income statement columns of the work sheet.

KEY TERMS

invoice 160

cash discount 160

purchases discounts 161

purchases returns and
  allowances 162

debit memorandum 162

credit memorandum 163

sales discounts 166

sales returns and allowances 166

trade discounts 167

FOB shipping point 168

FOB destination 168

periodic inventory system 171

perpetual inventory system 171

physical inventory 171

SELF-EXAMINATION QUESTIONS

Answers in Appendix B.

1. If merchandise purchased on account is returned, the buyer may inform the seller of the details by issuing:
   A. a debit memorandum   C. an invoice
   B. a credit memorandum   D. a bill

2. If merchandise is sold on account to a customer for $1,000, terms FOB shipping point, 1/10, n/30, and the seller prepays $50 in transportation costs, the amount of the discount for early payment would be:
   A. $0   C. $10.00
   B. $5.00   D. $10.50

3. Merchandise is sold on account to a customer for $1,000, terms FOB destination, 1/10, n/30. If the seller pays $50 in transportation costs and the customer returns $100 of the merchandise prior to payment, what is the amount of the discount for early payment?
   A. $0   C. $10.00
   B. $9.00   D. $10.50

4. For an enterprise using the periodic inventory system, which of the following is added to merchandise inventory at the beginning of the period in computing the cost of merchandise sold?
   A. Purchases discounts
   B. Purchases returns and allowances
   C. Merchandise inventory at the end of the period
   D. None of the above

5. The amount for merchandise inventory that appears in the trial balance columns of the work sheet represents:
   A. inventory at the beginning of the current period
   B. inventory at the end of the current period
   C. cost of merchandise sold during the current period
   D. none of the above

ILLUSTRATIVE PROBLEM

MacBride Discount Stores Inc. entered into the following selected transactions during August of the current year:

Aug. 1. Purchased merchandise on account, terms 2/10, n/30, FOB shipping point, $28,500.
      1. Paid rent for August, $4,500.
      2. Paid transportation charges on purchase of August 1, $1,180.
      5. Purchased office supplies for cash, $600.
      7. Sold merchandise on account, terms 1/10, n/30, FOB destination, $12,400.
      8. Paid transportation charges on sale of August 7, $550.
     11. Paid for merchandise purchased on August 1, less discount.
     12. Received merchandise returned from sale of August 7, $3,200.
     14. Purchased merchandise on account, terms 4/15, n/30, FOB destination, $18,300.
     15. Paid transportation charges on purchase of August 14, $750.
     16. Returned merchandise purchased on August 14, $5,200.
     17. Received cash on account from sale of August 7, less return and discount.
     18. Sold merchandise on account, terms 1/10, n/30, FOB shipping point, $8,800. Prepaid transportation costs as an accommodation to the customer, $250.
     26. Sold merchandise on bank credit cards, $3,700.
     29. Paid for merchandise purchased on August 14, less prepaid transportation charges, return, and discount.
     31. Received cash on account from sale of August 18, $9,050.

Instructions:

1. Record the August transactions in a two-column journal.
2. The merchandise inventory on hand at September 1, 1987, the beginning of the current fiscal year, was $250,000. A physical inventory taken on August 31, 1988, determined that merchandise on hand was $274,600. Prepare the adjusting entries for merchandise inventory for the current fiscal year ended August 31, 1988.

SOLUTION

(1)

Aug.	1 Purchases	28,500	
	Accounts Payable		28,500
	1 Rent Expense	4,500	
	Cash		4,500

2 Transportation In	1,180	
Cash		1,180
5 Office Supplies	600	
Cash		600
7 Accounts Receivable	12,400	
Sales		12,400
8 Transportation Out	550	
Cash		550
11 Accounts Payable	28,500	
Purchases Discounts		570
Cash		27,930
12 Sales Returns and Allowances	3,200	
Accounts Receivable		3,200
14 Purchases	18,300	
Accounts Payable		18,300
15 Accounts Payable	750	
Cash		750
16 Accounts Payable	5,200	
Purchases Returns and Allowances		5,200
17 Cash	9,108	
Sales Discounts	92	
Accounts Receivable		9,200
18 Accounts Receivable	8,800	
Sales		8,800
18 Accounts Receivable	250	
Cash		250
26 Cash	3,700	
Sales		3,700
29 Accounts Payable	12,350	
Purchases Discounts		524
Cash		11,826
31 Cash	9,050	
Accounts Receivable		9,050

(2)

Aug. 31 Income Summary	250,000	
Merchandise Inventory		250,000
31 Merchandise Inventory	274,600	
Income Summary		274,600

DISCUSSION QUESTIONS

1. What distinguishes a merchandising enterprise from a service enterprise?

2. The credit period during which the purchaser of merchandise is allowed to pay usually begins with what date?

3. Nash Inc. ordered $3,000 of merchandise on account on October 2, terms 2/10, n/30. Although the supplier shipped the merchandise on October 3, the merchandise was not received by Nash Inc. until October 6. The invoice received with the merchandise by Nash Inc. was dated October 3. What is the last date Nash Inc. could pay the invoice and still receive the discount?

4. What is the meaning of (a) 2/10, n/30; (b) n/60; (c) n/eom?

5. What is the term applied to discounts for early payment by (a) the buyer; (b) the seller?

6. Thomas Company purchased merchandise on account from a supplier for $4,000, terms 1/10, n/30. Thomas Company returned $500 of the merchandise and received full credit. (a) If Thomas Company pays the invoice within the discount period, what is the amount of cash required for the payment? (b) What accounts are credited to record the return and the cash discount?

7. The debits and credits from three related transactions are presented in the following T accounts. (a) Describe each transaction. (b) What is the rate of the discount and on what amount was it computed?

Cash				Accounts Payable		
	(2)	250	(3)	400	(1)	7,200
	(4)	6,664	(4)	6,800		

Purchases			Purchases Discounts	
(1)	7,200		(4)	136

Transportation In			Purchases Returns and Allowances	
(2)	250		(3)	400

8. How does the accounting for sales to customers using bank credit cards, such as MasterCard and VISA, differ from accounting for sales to customers using nonbank credit cards, such as American Express?

9. At what amount would a seller record the sale of an item of merchandise with a list price of $5,000 and subject to a trade discount of 40%?

10. After the amount due on a sale of $2,000, terms 2/10, n/eom, is received from a customer within the discount period, the seller consents to the return of the entire shipment. (a) What is the amount of the refund owed to the customer? (b) What accounts should be debited and credited by the seller to record the return and the refund?

11. Who bears the transportation costs when the terms of sale are (a) FOB shipping point, (b) FOB destination?

12. Merchandise is sold on account to a customer for $8,000, terms FOB shipping point, 2/10, n/30, the seller paying the transportation costs of $300. Determine the following: (a) amount of the sale, (b) amount debited to Accounts Receivable, (c) amount of the discount for early payment, (d) amount of the remittance due within the discount period.

13. A retailer is considering the purchase of 10 units of a specific commodity from either of two suppliers. Their offers are as follows:
A: $200 a unit, total of $2,000, 2/10, n/30, plus transportation costs of $250.
B: $220 a unit, total of $2,200, 1/10, n/30, no charge for transportation.
Which of the two offers, A or B, yields the lower price?

14. A sale of merchandise on account for $400 is subject to a 6% sales tax. (a) Should the sales tax be recorded at the time of sale or when payment is received? (b) What is the amount of the sale? (c) What is the amount debited to Accounts Receivable? (d) What is the title of the account to which the $24 is credited?

15. What is the name of the account in which unsold merchandise at the end of a period is recorded?

16. In which type of system for accounting for merchandise held for sale is there no attempt to record the cost of merchandise sold until the end of the period, when a physical inventory is taken?

17. In the following questions, identify the items designated by "X":
(a) Purchases − (X + X) = Net purchases
(b) Net purchases + X = Cost of merchandise purchased
(c) X + Cost of merchandise purchased = Merchandise available for sale
(d) Merchandise available for sale − X = Cost of merchandise sold

18. The account Merchandise Inventory is listed at $150,000 on, the trial balance (before adjustments) as of October 31, the end of the first month in the fiscal year. Which one of the following phrases describes the item correctly?
(a) Inventory of merchandise at October 1, beginning of the month.
(b) Purchases of merchandise during October.
(c) Merchandise available for sale during October.
(d) Inventory of merchandise at October 31, end of the month.
(e) Cost of merchandise sold during October.

19. What account is used in a periodic inventory system to remove from the merchandise inventory account the inventory at the beginning of the period and replace it with the amount representing the inventory at the end of the period?

20. The following data appear in a work sheet as of December 31, the end of the fiscal year:

		Adjustments			Income Statement	
		Dr.	Cr.		Dr.	Cr.
Income Summary		(a) 120,000	(b) 145,000		120,000	145,000

(a) To what account was the $120,000 credited in adjustment (a)?

(b) To what account was the $145,000 debited in adjustment (b)?

(c) What was the amount of the merchandise inventory at January 1, the beginning of the fiscal year?

(d) What amount will be listed for merchandise inventory on the balance sheet at December 31, the end of the fiscal year?

(e) If the totals of the Income Statement columns of the work sheet are $1,340,000 debit and $1,510,000 credit, what is the amount of the net income for the year?

(f) Would the amount determined to be net income be affected by extending only the net amount of $25,000 ($145,000−$120,000) into the Income Statement column?

21. Real World Focus. It is not unusual for a customer to drive into a Texaco, Mobil, or Gulf gasoline station and discover that the cash price per gallon is 3 or 4 cents lower than the credit price per gallon. As a result, many customers pay cash rather than use their credit cards. Why would a gasoline station owner establish such a policy?

EXERCISES

○ Exercise 4–1.   Purchase-related transactions. Sutton Co. purchases $4,000 of merchandise from a supplier on account, terms FOB shipping point, 1/10, n/30. The supplier adds transportation charges of $150 to the invoice. Sutton Co. returns some of the merchandise, receiving a credit memorandum for $500, and then pays the amount due within the discount period. Present Sutton Co.'s entries to record (a) the purchase, (b) the merchandise return, and (c) the payment.

Exercise 4–2. Determination of amounts to be paid on invoices. **Determine the amount to be paid in full settlement of each of the following invoices, assuming that credit for returns and allowances was received prior to payment and that all invoices were paid within the discount period.**

| | Purchase Invoice | | | Returns and |
	Merchandise	Transportation	Terms	Allowances
(a)	$5,000	—	FOB destination, n/30	$1,000
(b)	4,000	—	FOB destination, 2/10, n/30	—
(c)	7,500	—	FOB shipping point, 1/10, n/30	500
(d)	3,200	$ 80	FOB shipping point, 1/10, n/30	100
(e)	6,000	240	FOB shipping point, 2/10, n/30	800

Exercise 4–3. Sales-related transactions, including the use of credit cards. **Present entries for the following transactions of Hodges Inc.:**

(a) Sold merchandise for cash, $5,200.

(b) Sold merchandise on account, $6,800.

(c) Sold merchandise to customers who used MasterCard and VISA, $2,600.

(d) Sold merchandise to customers who used American Express, $1,300.

(e) Paid an invoice from First National Bank for $130, representing a service fee for processing of MasterCard and VISA sales.

(f) Received $1,235 from American Express Company after a $65 collection fee had been deducted.

Exercise 4–4. Sales-related transactions. **Present entries for the following related transactions.**

Feb. 4. Sold merchandise to a customer for $12,000, terms FOB shipping point, 2/10, n/30.

4. Paid the transportation charges of $310, debiting the amount to Accounts Receivable.

8. Issued a credit memorandum for $1,500 to the customer for merchandise returned.

14. Received a check for the amount due from the sale.

Exercise 4–5. Sales-related transactions with trade discount. **Lowe Corp. sells merchandise to Howard Co. on account, list price $8,500, trade discount 20%, FOB shipping point, 1/10, n/30. Lowe Corp. pays the transportation charges of $400 as an accommodation and adds it to the invoice. Lowe Corp. issues a credit memorandum for $800 for merchandise returned and subsequently receives the amount due within the discount period. Present Lowe Corp.'s entries to record (a) the sale and the transportation costs, (b) the credit memorandum, and (c) the receipt of the check for the amount due.**

Exercise 4–6. Purchase-related transactions. Based upon the data presented in Exercise 4–5, present Howard Co.'s entries to record (a) the purchase, including the transportation charges, (b) the return of the merchandise for credit, and (c) the payment of the invoice within the discount period.

Exercise 4–7. Purchase-related transactions. Present entries for the following related transactions of Thompson Inc.:

(a) Purchased $3,000 of merchandise from Delano Co. on account, terms 2/10, n/30.
(b) Paid the amount owed on the invoice within the discount period.
(c) Discovered that some of the merchandise was defective and returned items with an invoice price of $1,000, receiving credit.
(d) Purchased an additional $800 of fabrics from Delano Co. on account, terms 2/10, n/30.
(e) Received a check for the balance owed from the return in (c), after deducting for the purchase in (d).

Exercise 4–8. Sales tax-related transactions. Present entries to record the following related transactions of Sanders Co.:

(a) Purchased merchandise on account, $3,200, terms 2/10, n/30. The merchandise was subject to a sales tax of 6%.
(b) Sold $2,000 of merchandise on account, subject to a sales tax of 6%.
(c) Paid the amount owed in (a) within the discount period.
(d) Paid $1,200 to the state revenue department for sales taxes collected.

Exercise 4–9. Merchandising adjusting entries. Data needed for adjusting the periodic merchandise inventory for E & M Drapery Inc. for the fiscal year ended December 31, 1987, are as follows:

Merchandise inventory as of January 1, 1987 . . . . $240,000
Merchandise inventory as of December 31, 1987 310,000

Journalize the necessary adjusting entries for merchandise inventory.

SPREADSHEET PROBLEM

Exercise 4–10. Cost of merchandise sold section of income statement. On the basis of the following data, prepare the cost of merchandise sold section of the income statement for the fiscal year ended March 31, 1987, for Dysan Inc.

Merchandise Inventory, March 31, 1987 . . . . $150,000
Merchandise Inventory, April 1, 1986 120,000
Purchases 600,000
Purchases Returns and Allowances 5,500
Purchases Discounts 3,200
Transportation In 2,800

PROBLEMS

Series A

Problem 4–1A. Purchase-related and sales-related transactions. The following selected transactions were completed during June between Hogan Company and Sneed Inc.:

June 3. Hogan Company sold merchandise on account to Sneed Inc., $12,500, terms FOB shipping point, 2/10, n/30. Hogan Company prepaid transportation costs of $600 which were added to the invoice.

   8. Hogan Company sold merchandise on account to Sneed Inc., $16,000, terms FOB destination, 1/15, n/eom.

   8. Hogan Company paid transportation costs of $800 for delivery of merchandise sold to Sneed Inc. on June 8.

   11. Sneed Inc. returned merchandise purchased on account on June 8 from Hogan Company, $4,000.

   13. Sneed Inc. paid Hogan Company for purchases of June 3, less discount.

   23. Sneed Inc. paid Hogan Company for purchases of June 8, less discount and less return of June 11.

   24. Hogan Company sold merchandise on account to Sneed Inc., $8,000, terms FOB destination, n/eom.

   27. Sneed Inc. paid transportation charges of $300 on June 24 purchase from Hogan Company. Hogan Company was not notified of this transaction until June 30.

   30. Sneed Inc. paid Hogan Company on account for purchases of June 24, less transportation charges paid.

Instructions:

Journalize the June transactions in a two-column journal for (1) Hogan Company and (2) Sneed Inc.

Problem 4–2A. Purchase-related and sales-related transactions. The following were selected from among the transactions completed by Kline Company during May of the current year:

May 3. Purchased merchandise on account from Floyd Inc., $4,000, terms FOB shipping point, 2/10, n/30, with prepaid transportation costs of $120 added to the invoice.

   5. Purchased merchandise on account from Kramer Co., $8,500, terms FOB destination, 1/10, n/30.

   6. Sold merchandise on account to C.F. Howell Co., $2,800, terms 2/10, n/30.

   8. Purchased office supplies for cash, $650.

10. Returned merchandise purchased on May 5 from Kramer Co., $1,300.
13. Paid Floyd Inc. on account for purchases of May 3, less discount.
14. Purchased merchandise for cash, $14,000, less trade discount of 25%.
15. Paid Kramer Co. on account for purchases of May 5, less return of May 10 and discount.
16. Received cash on account from sale of May 6 to C. F. Howell Co., less discount.
19. Sold merchandise on nonbank credit cards and reported accounts to the card company, $2,450.
22. Sold merchandise on account to Comer Co., $3,480, terms 2/10, n/30.
24. Sold merchandise for cash, $4,350.
25. Received merchandise returned by Comer Co. from sale of May 22, $1,480.
31. Received cash from card company for nonbank credit card sales of May 19, less $140 service fee.

Instructions:

Journalize the transactions for Kline Company in a two-column journal.

Problem 4–3A.   Purchase-related and sales-related transactions for a sole proprietorship. The account balances at July 1 of the current year of Haynes Company are as follows:

11	Cash	$ 15,540
12	Accounts Receivable	31,800
13	Merchandise Inventory	82,600
14	Prepaid Insurance	2,500
15	Store Supplies	1,700
21	Accounts Payable	28,300
31	L. Haynes, Capital	105,840
32	L. Haynes, Drawing	—
33	Income Summary	—
41	Sales	—
42	Sales Returns and Allowances	—
43	Sales Discounts	—
51	Purchases	—
52	Purchases Returns and Allowances	—
53	Purchases Discounts	—
54	Transportation In	—
55	Sales Salaries Expense	—
56	Advertising Expense	—
57	Store Supplies Expense	—
58	Miscellaneous Selling Expense	—
59	Office Salaries Expense	—
60	Rent Expense	—
61	Insurance Expense	—
62	Miscellaneous General Expense	—

The following transactions were completed during July of the current year:

July 1. Paid rent for month, $2,500.
3. Purchased merchandise on account, $11,200.
5. Purchased merchandise on account, FOB shipping point, $18,600.
8. Sold merchandise on account, $12,300.
9. Paid transportation charges on the purchase of July 5, $450.
10. Received $14,750 cash from customers on account, after discounts of $250 were deducted.
11. Paid creditors $16,700 on account, after discounts of $280 had been deducted.
14. Sold merchandise for cash, $9,500.
15. Received merchandise returned on account, $800.
16. Paid sales salaries of $3,400 and office salaries of $1,100.
17. Paid creditors $12,750 on account, after discounts of $200 had been deducted.
18. Received $9,500 cash from customers on account, after discounts of $120 had been deducted.
21. Purchased merchandise on account, $15,200.
22. Paid advertising expense, $3,000.
23. Sold merchandise for cash, $8,100.
24. Returned merchandise purchased on account, $6,800.
25. Sold merchandise for cash, $4,600.
28. Sold merchandise on account, $27,300.
28. Refunded $350 cash on sales made for cash.
29. Paid sales salaries of $2,800 and office salaries of $1,100.
30. Paid creditors $10,900 on account, no discount.
31. Received $12,500 cash from customers on account, no discount.

Instructions:

(1) Open a ledger of four-column accounts for the accounts listed. Record the balances in the appropriate balance column as of July 1, write "Balance" in the item section, and place a check mark (√) in the posting reference column.
(2) Record the transactions for July in a two-column journal.
(3) Post to the ledger, extending the month-end balances to the appropriate balance columns after all posting is completed.
(4) Prepare a trial balance of the ledger as of July 31.

done

Problem 4–4A. Work sheet for merchandising corporation. The accounts in the ledger of Bemis Company, with the unadjusted balances on August 31, the end of the current fiscal year, are as follows:

Cash.	$ 17,760	Accounts Payable	$ 32,000
Accounts Receivable	53,340	Salaries Payable	—
Merchandise Inventory	121,400	Capital Stock	100,000
Prepaid Insurance	2,480	Retained Earnings.	99,550
Store Supplies	2,120	Dividends	16,000
Store Equipment	166,200	Income Summary	—
Accumulated Depreciation — Store		Sales	790,500
Equipment.	84,600	Purchases	513,700

Sales Salaries Expense.............	$ 82,800	Office Salaries Expense	$ 52,200
Advertising Expense................	23,300	Rent Expense	25,000
Depreciation Expense—Store		Heating and Lighting Expense.......	17,400
Equipment	—	Taxes Expense	7,850
Store Supplies Expense	—	Insurance Expense................	—
Miscellaneous Selling Expense	1,600	Miscellaneous General Expense	3,500

The data needed for year end adjustments on August 31 are as follows:

Merchandise inventory on August 31...................		$100,000
Insurance expired during the year		1,560
Store supplies inventory on August 31		520
Depreciation for the current year		9,300
Accrued salaries on August 31:		
Sales salaries.....................................	$1,500	
Office salaries....................................	1,200	2,700

Instructions:

(1) Prepare a work sheet for the fiscal year ended August 31. List all accounts in the order given.
(2) Compute the percent of net income to sales.

Problem 4–5A. Work sheet for merchandising sole proprietorship. The accounts and their balances in the ledger of Carlson Company on December 31 of the current year are as follows:

Cash..	$ 36,900
Accounts Receivable.......................................	85,800
Merchandise Inventory	111,300
Prepaid Insurance	9,500
Store Supplies	1,800
Office Supplies	1,200
Store Equipment...	84,600
Accumulated Depreciation—Store Equipment	28,000
Office Equipment	27,300
Accumulated Depreciation—Office Equipment	12,000
Accounts Payable	50,500
Salaries Payable	—
Mortgage Note Payable (due 1999)	100,000
W. B. Carlson, Capital......................................	87,800
W. B. Carlson, Drawing.....................................	40,000
Income Summary..	—
Sales..	750,000
Sales Returns and Allowances	6,000
Sales Discounts	3,500
Purchases..	500,000
Purchases Returns and Allowances...........................	12,500
Purchases Discounts.......................................	6,500
Transportation In	2,400

Sales Salaries Expense	$ 60,000
Advertising Expense	18,000
Depreciation Expense—Store Equipment	—
Store Supplies Expense	—
Miscellaneous Selling Expense	1,400
Office Salaries Expense	35,000
Rent Expense	10,000
Depreciation Expense—Office Equipment	—
Insurance Expense	—
Office Supplies Expense	—
Miscellaneous General Expense	1,100
Interest Expense	11,500

The data for year-end adjustments on December 31 are as follows:

Merchandise inventory on December 31		$105,000
Insurance expired during the year		3,600
Inventory of supplies on December 31:		
Store supplies		900
Office supplies		500
Depreciation for the year:		
Store equipment		8,100
Office equipment		3,000
Salaries payable on December 31:		
Sales salaries	$2,500	
Office salaries	1,200	3,700

Instructions:

(1) Prepare a work sheet for the fiscal year ended December 31. List all accounts in the order given.
(2) Prepare the cost of merchandise sold section of the income statement from the data presented in the income statement columns of the work sheet.

Series B

Problem 4–1B. Purchase-related and sales-related transactions. The following selected transactions were completed during October between Early Company and Flynn Inc.:

Oct. 4. Early Company sold merchandise on account to Flynn Inc., $10,000, terms FOB destination, 1/15, n/eom.

Oct. 4. Early Company paid transportation costs of $600 for delivery of merchandise sold to Flynn Inc. on October 4.

10. Early Company sold merchandise on account to Flynn Inc., $15,000, terms FOB destination, n/eom.

12. Flynn Inc. returned merchandise purchased on account on October 4 from Early Company, $2,000.

14. Flynn Inc. paid transportation charges of $1,200 on October 10 purchase from Early Company.

18. Early Company sold merchandise on account to Flynn Inc., $18,000, terms FOB shipping point, 2/10, n/30. Early Company prepaid transportation costs of $1,500 which were added to the invoice.

19. Flynn Inc. paid Early Company on account for purchases of October 4, less discount and less return of October 12.

28. Flynn Inc. paid Early Company on account for purchases of October 18, less discount.

31. Flynn Inc. paid Early Company on account for purchases of October 10, less transportation charges paid.

Instructions:

Journalize the October transactions in a two-column journal for (1) Early Company and (2) Flynn Inc.

SOLUTIONS
SOFTWARE

Problem 4–2B. Purchase-related and sales-related transactions. The following were selected from among the transactions completed by Brooks Co. during November of the current year:

Nov. 3. Purchased office supplies for cash, $720.

5. Purchased merchandise on account from Butler Co., $12,500, terms FOB destination, 1/10, n/30.

6. Sold merchandise for cash, $2,950.

7. Purchased merchandise on account from Mattox Co., $6,400, terms FOB shipping point, 2/10, n/30, with prepaid transportation costs of $190 added to the invoice.

7. Returned merchandise purchased on November 5 from Butler Co., $2,500.

11. Sold merchandise on account to Bowles Co., $1,800, terms 1/10, n/30.

15. Paid Butler Co. on account for purchases of November 5, less return of November 7 and discount.

16. Sold merchandise on nonbank credit cards and reported accounts to the card company, $3,850.

17. Paid Mattox Co. on account for purchases of November 7, less discount.

19. Purchased merchandise for cash, $5,000, less trade discount of 30%.

21. Received cash on account from sale of November 11 to Bowles Co., less discount.

24. Sold merchandise on account to Clemons Inc., $4,200, terms 1/10, n/30.

28. Received cash from card company for nonbank credit card sales of November 16, less $190 service fee.

30. Received merchandise returned by Clemons Inc. from sale of November 24, $2,700.

Instructions:

Journalize the transactions for Brooks Co. in a two-column journal.

Problem 4–4B. Work sheet for merchandising corporation. **The accounts in the ledger of Argo Company, with the unadjusted balances on April 30, the end of the current fiscal year, are as follows:**

Cash...................	$ 26,250	Purchases	$360,000
Accounts Receivable	57,600	Sales Salaries Expense	46,500
Merchandise Inventory...........	87,150	Advertising Expense	15,800
Prepaid Insurance...............	7,600	Depreciation Expense—	
Store Supplies	4,950	Store Equipment...............	—
Store Equipment	53,700	Store Supplies Expense	—
Accumulated Depreciation—		Miscellaneous Selling Expense.....	2,750
Store Equipment	15,180	Office Salaries Expense	30,000
Accounts Payable...............	26,800	Rent Expense	24,000
Salaries Payable................	—	Heating and Lighting Expense	9,660
Capital Stock	75,000	Taxes Expense..................	5,100
Retained Earnings	69,020	Insurance Expense	—
Dividends	15,000	Miscellaneous General Expense....	2,140
Income Summary	—		
Sales	562,200		

The data needed for year-end adjustments on April 30 are as follows:

Merchandise inventory on April 30.....................		$90,000
Insurance expired during the year		3,800
Store supplies inventory on April 30....................		1,250
Depreciation for the current year		11,500
Accrued salaries on April 30:		
Sales salaries.....................................	$1,600	
Office salaries.....................................	750	2,350

Instructions:

(1) Prepare a work sheet for the fiscal year ended April 30, listing all of the accounts in the order given.
(2) Compute the percent of net income to sales.

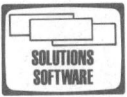

Problem 4–5B. Work sheet for merchandising sole proprietorship. **The accounts and their balances in the ledger of Carlson Company on December 31 of the current year are as follows:**

Cash...	$ 36,900
Accounts Receivable.............................	85,800
Merchandise Inventory	111,300
Prepaid Insurance	9,500
Store Supplies	1,800

Office Supplies	$ 1,200
Store Equipment	84,600
Accumulated Depreciation—Store Equipment	28,000
Office Equipment	27,300
Accumulated Depreciation—Office Equipment	12,000
Accounts Payable	50,500
Salaries Payable	—
Mortgage Note Payable (due 1999)	100,000
W. B. Carlson, Capital	87,800
W. B. Carlson, Drawing	40,000
Income Summary	—
Sales	750,000
Sales Returns and Allowances	6,000
Sales Discounts	3,500
Purchases	500,000
Purchases Returns and Allowances	12,500
Purchases Discounts	6,500
Transportation In	2,400
Sales Salaries Expense	60,000
Advertising Expense	18,000
Depreciation Expense—Store Equipment	—
Store Supplies Expense	—
Miscellaneous Selling Expense	1,400
Office Salaries Expense	35,000
Rent Expense	10,000
Depreciation Expense—Office Equipment	—
Insurance Expense	—
Office Supplies Expense	—
Miscellaneous General Expense	1,100
Interest Expense	11,500

The data for year-end adjustments on December 31 are as follows:

Merchandise inventory on December 31		$115,200
Insurance expired during the year		2,500
Inventory of supplies on December 31:		
Store supplies		600
Office supplies		450
Depreciation for the year:		
Store equipment		7,500
Office equipment		2,800
Salaries payable on December 31:		
Sales salaries	$3,200	
Office salaries	900	4,100

Instructions:

(1) Prepare a work sheet for the fiscal year ended December 31. List all accounts in the order given.

(2) Prepare the cost of merchandise sold section of the income statement from the data presented in the income statement columns of the work sheet.

GIBBONS
DISCOUNT INC.

For the past twenty years, your father has managed and operated Gibbons Discount Inc., a regional chain of retail stores. You have recently accepted a position with Gibbons Discount Inc. as a special assistant to the president. As a first assignment, you are to review the purchasing and disbursing policies of the enterprise.

For your analysis, the controller has gathered the following data covering the past three years:

	19X3	19X2	19X1
Purchases	$20,400,000	$18,200,000	$16,300,000
Purchases returns and allowances.....	204,000	136,500	81,500
Transportation in	591,600	564,200	489,000

After reviewing these data, you ask the controller why no purchases discounts are shown for the three-year period. The controller responded as follows:

> Your father won't let us take purchases discounts. It doesn't make sense to me. The industry standard is 2/10, n/30. Your father always has believed in paying the bills on the final due date and not a day before. I've tried to convince him that we should take the discounts, but he won't budge.

The controller also indicated that the company has recently entered into a store expansion program that will likely create a cash shortage. Because of this situation, the company has negotiated a $500,000 line of credit with its bank at an interest rate of 11%.

Instructions:

(1) Prepare an analysis indicating the net savings that the company could have earned from taking all discounts for the past three years. Assume that discounts are available on all purchases. In addition, assume that the company had sufficient cash to pay all invoices without borrowing and that the average rates at which the excess cash could have been invested in each of the past three years were as follows:

19X3...................	11%
19X2...................	12%
19X1...................	14%

(Hint: You should take into consideration the interest income the company would have forgone by paying the invoices within the discount period.)

(2) Assume that you are able to convince your father to use the new line of credit to pay all invoices within the discount period during 19X4. The net purchases for 19X4 are projected to increase 15% over the net purchases for 19X3. Compute the expected net savings for 19X4 by taking all the available purchases discounts.

(3) Based upon the purchase data for 19X3, 19X2, and 19X1, what other questions might you raise concerning the company's purchasing and disbursing policies?

Chapter 5

PERIODIC REPORTING FOR A MERCHANDISING ENTERPRISE

CHAPTER OBJECTIVES

- Describe alternative formats and terminology for the income statement, retained earnings statement, and balance sheet of a merchandising enterprise.

- Illustrate the preparation of an income statement, retained earnings statement, and balance sheet from the work sheet of a merchandising enterprise.

- Describe and illustrate the preparation of adjusting entries and closing entries for a merchandising enterprise.

- Describe and illustrate the preparation of reversing entries for a merchandising enterprise.

- Describe the preparation of interim financial statements.

- Describe and illustrate the procedures for correcting errors in accounting records.

5

Accounting for merchandising enterprises, including the year-end adjustment procedures and the preparation of the work sheet, was discussed in Chapter 4. The discussion is continued in this chapter by describing and illustrating the preparation of financial statements, adjusting entries, closing entries, and a post-closing trial balance for a merchandising enterprise. Alternative formats and terminology which can be used in preparing financial statements are also described and illustrated.

In connection with the discussion of adjusting entries, the purpose and use of reversing entries is presented and illustrated. A discussion of interim financial statements and their preparation is also presented. Finally, recognition is given to the fact that occasional errors in journalizing and posting transactions will occur. Procedures necessary to correct such errors are discussed and illustrated.

FINANCIAL STATEMENTS FOR MERCHANDISING ENTERPRISES

The basic financial statements for a merchandising enterprise, including the income statement, statement of owner's equity, and balance sheet, are similar to those of a service enterprise. For a corporate enterprise, the financial statements would include the retained earnings statement rather than the statement of owner's equity. The basic differences between the financial statements of a merchandising enterprise and a service enterprise include the cost of merchandise sold section of the income statement, which was illustrated in Chapter 4, and the inclusion of merchandise inventory on the balance sheet as a current asset.

To simplify the presentation, the work sheet of Midtown Electric Corporation, presented in Chapter 4, and reproduced on page 201, is used as a basis for illustration and discussion. From this work sheet, alternative formats and terminology for the financial statements of Midtown Electric Corporation are illustrated.[1]

---

[1]Examples of alternative forms are also presented in Appendix H, Specimen Financial Statements.

Midtown Electric Corporation
Work Sheet
For Year Ended December 31, 1987

ACCOUNT TITLE	TRIAL BALANCE DEBIT	TRIAL BALANCE CREDIT	ADJUSTMENTS DEBIT	ADJUSTMENTS CREDIT	ADJUSTED TRIAL BALANCE DEBIT	ADJUSTED TRIAL BALANCE CREDIT	INCOME STATEMENT DEBIT	INCOME STATEMENT CREDIT	BALANCE SHEET DEBIT	BALANCE SHEET CREDIT
Cash	62,950				62,950				62,950	
Notes Receivable	40,000				40,000				40,000	
Accounts Receivable	60,880				60,880				60,880	
Merchandise Inventory	59,700		(b) 62,150	(a) 59,700	62,150				62,150	
Office Supplies	1,090			(c) 610	480				480	
Prepaid Insurance	4,560			(d) 1,910	2,650				2,650	
Store Equipment	27,100				27,100				27,100	
Accumulated Depreciation — Store Equipment		12,600		(e) 3,100		15,700				15,700
Office Equipment	15,570				15,570				15,570	
Accumulated Depreciation — Office Equipment		7,230		(f) 2,490		9,720				9,720
Accounts Payable		22,420				22,420				22,420
Salaries Payable				(g) 1,140		1,140				1,140
Mortgage Note Payable		25,000				25,000				25,000
Capital Stock		100,000				100,000				100,000
Retained Earnings		41,200				41,200				41,200
Dividends	18,000				18,000				18,000	
Income Summary			(a) 59,700	(b) 62,150	59,700	62,150	59,700	62,150		
Sales		720,185				720,185		720,185		
Sales Returns and Allowances	6,140				6,140		6,140			
Sales Discounts	5,790				5,790		5,790			
Purchases	521,980				521,980		521,980			
Purchases Returns and Allowances		9,100				9,100		9,100		
Purchases Discounts		2,525				2,525		2,525		
Transportation In	17,400				17,400		17,400			
Sales Salaries Expense	59,250		(g) 780		60,030		60,030			
Advertising Expense	10,860				10,860		10,860			
Depreciation Expense — Store Equipment			(e) 3,100		3,100		3,100			
Miscellaneous Selling Expense	630				630		630			
Office Salaries Expense	20,660		(g) 360		21,020		21,020			
Rent Expense	8,100				8,100		8,100			
Depreciation Expense — Office Equipment			(f) 2,490		2,490		2,490			
Insurance Expense			(d) 1,910		1,910		1,910			
Office Supplies Expense			(c) 610		610		610			
Miscellaneous General Expense	760				760		760			
Interest Income		3,600				3,600		3,600		
Interest Expense	2,440				2,440		2,440			
	943,860	943,860	131,100	131,100	1,012,740	1,012,740	722,960	797,560	289,780	215,180
Net income							74,600			74,600
							797,560	797,560	289,780	289,780

201

Income Statement

There are two widely used forms for the income statement: **multiple-step** and **single-step**. Both forms are used with approximately the same frequency among large corporations. The 1985 edition of *Accounting Trends & Techniques* reported that 51% of the 600 industrial and merchandising companies surveyed use the multiple-step form, while 49% use the single-step form.

Multiple-Step Form. The multiple-step income statement is so called because of its many sections, subsections, and intermediate balances. In practice, there is considerable variation in the amount of detail presented in these sections. For example, instead of reporting separately gross sales and the related returns, allowances, and discounts, the statement may begin with net sales. Similarly, the supporting data for the determination of the cost of merchandise sold may be omitted from the statement. A multiple-step income statement for Midtown Electric Corporation is presented on page 203.

The various sections of a conventional multiple-step income statement for Midtown Electric Corporation are discussed briefly in the paragraphs that follow.

Revenue from sales. The total of all charges to customers for merchandise sold, both for cash and on account, is reported in this section. Sales returns and allowances and sales discounts are deducted from the gross amount to yield net sales.

Cost of merchandise sold. The determination of this important figure was explained and illustrated in Chapter 4. Other descriptive terms frequently employed are **cost of goods sold** and **cost of sales**.

Gross profit. The excess of the net revenue from sales over the cost of merchandise sold is called **gross profit, gross profit on sales**, or **gross margin**. It is called *gross* because operating expenses must be deducted from it.

Operating expenses. The operating expenses of a business may be grouped under any desired number of headings and subheadings. In a retail business of the kind that has been used for illustrative purposes, it is usually satisfactory to subdivide operating expenses into two categories, selling and general.

Expenses that are incurred directly and entirely in connection with the sale of merchandise are classified as **selling expenses**. They include such expenses as salaries of the sales force, store supplies used, depreciation of store equipment, and advertising.

Expenses incurred in the general operations of the business are classified as **general expenses** or **administrative expenses**. Examples of these expenses are office salaries, depreciation of office equipment, and office supplies used.

Midtown Electric Corporation
Income Statement
For Year Ended December 31, 1987

Revenue from sales:			
Sales..............................		$720,185	
Less: Sales returns and allowances ...	$ 6,140		
Sales discounts................	5,790	11,930	
Net sales.........................			$708,255
Cost of merchandise sold:			
Merchandise inventory,			
January 1, 1987..................		$ 59,700	
Purchases.........................	$521,980		
Less: Purchases returns			
and allowances	$9,100		
Purchases discounts	2,525	11,625	
Net purchases	$510,355		
Add transportation in	17,400		
Cost of merchandise purchased		527,755	
Merchandise available for sale........		$587,455	
Less merchandise inventory,			
December 31, 1987		62,150	
Cost of merchandise sold			525,305
Gross profit...........................			$182,950
Operating expenses:			
Selling expenses:			
Sales salaries expense............	$ 60,030		
Advertising expense..............	10,860		
Depreciation expense—			
store equipment.................	3,100		
Miscellaneous selling expense......	630		
Total selling expenses		$ 74,620	
General expenses:			
Office salaries expense	$ 21,020		
Rent expense	8,100		
Depreciation expense—			
office equipment	2,490		
Insurance expense	1,910		
Office supplies expense	610		
Miscellaneous general expense.....	760		
Total general expenses		34,890	
Total operating expenses.............			109,510
Income from operations			$ 73,440
Other income:			
Interest income.....................		$ 3,600	
Other expense:			
Interest expense		2,440	1,160
Net income[2]			$ 74,600

---

[2]This amount is further reduced by corporation income tax. The discussion of income taxes levied on corporate entities is reserved for later chapters.

Expenses that are partly connected with selling and partly connected with the general operations of the business may be divided between the two categories. In a small business, however, such expenses as rent, insurance, and taxes are commonly reported as general expenses.

Expenses of relatively small amounts that cannot be identified with the principal accounts are usually accumulated in accounts entitled Miscellaneous Selling Expense and Miscellaneous General Expense.

Income from operations. The excess of gross profit over total operating expenses is called **income from operations**, or **operating income**. The amount of the income from operations and its relationship to capital investment and to net sales are important factors in judging the efficiency of management and the degree of profitability of an enterprise. If operating expenses are greater than the gross profit, the excess is called **loss from operations**.

Other income. Revenue from sources other than the principal activity of a business is classified as **other income**, or **nonoperating income**. In a merchandising business, this category often includes income from interest, rent, dividends, and gains resulting from the sale of plant assets.

Other expense. Expenses that cannot be associated definitely with operations are identified as **other expense**, or **nonoperating expense**. Interest expense that results from financing activities and losses incurred in the disposal of plant assets are examples of items that are reported in this section.

The two categories of nonoperating items are offset against each other on the income statement. If the total of other income exceeds the total of other expense, the difference is added to income from operations. If the reverse is true, the difference is subtracted from income from operations.

Net income. The final figure on the income statement is labeled **net income** (or **net loss**). It is the net increase (or net decrease) in owner's equity as a result of profit-making activities. (As noted on the preceding page, the reporting of corporation income tax is discussed later.)

Single-Step Form. The single-step form of income statement derives its name from the fact that the total of all expenses is deducted from the total of all revenues. Such a statement is illustrated as follows for Midtown Electric Corporation. The illustration has been condensed to focus attention on its principal features. Such condensation is not an essential characteristic of the form.

Midtown Electric Corporation
Income Statement
For Year Ended December 31, 1987

Revenues:		
Net sales		$708,255
Interest income		3,600
Total revenues		$711,855
Expenses:		
Cost of merchandise sold	$525,305	
Selling expenses	74,620	
General expenses	34,890	
Interest expense	2,440	
Total expenses		637,255
Net income		$ 74,600

The single-step form has the advantage of being simple and it emphasizes total revenues and total expenses as the factors that determine net income. An objection to the single-step form is that such relationships as gross profit to sales and income from operations to sales are not as readily determinable as they are when the multiple-step form is used.

Retained Earnings Statement

The **retained earnings statement** summarizes the changes which have occurred in the retained earnings account during the fiscal period. It serves as a connecting link between the income statement and the balance sheet. The retained earnings statement for Midtown Electric Corporation is illustrated as follows:

Midtown Electric Corporation
Retained Earnings Statement
For Year Ended December 31, 1987

Retained earnings, January 1, 1987		$41,200
Net income for the year	$74,600	
Less dividends	18,000	
Increase in retained earnings		56,600
Retained earnings, December 31, 1987		$97,800

It is not unusual to add the analysis of retained earnings at the bottom of the income statement to form a **combined income and retained earnings statement**. This combined form was used by 12% of the 600 industrial and merchandising companies surveyed in the 1985 edition of *Accounting Trends & Techniques*. The income statement portion of the combined statement may be shown either in multiple-step form or in a single-step form, as in the following illustration:

COMBINED
INCOME AND
RETAINED
EARNINGS
STATEMENT

Midtown Electric Corporation Income and Retained Earnings Statement For Year Ended December 31, 1987		
Revenues:		
Net sales..		$708,255
Interest income................................		3,600
Total revenues		$711,855
Expenses:		
Cost of merchandise sold	$525,305	
Selling expenses	74,620	
General expenses	34,890	
Interest expense...............................	2,440	
Total expenses.............................		637,255
Net income		$ 74,600
Retained earnings, January 1, 1987		41,200
		$115,800
Less dividends..................................		18,000
Retained earnings, December 31, 1987		$ 97,800

The combined statement form emphasizes net income as the connecting link between the income statement and the retained earnings portion of owner's equity and thus helps the reader's understanding. A criticism of the combined statement is that the net income figure is buried in the body of the statement.

Balance Sheet

The traditional arrangement of assets on the left-hand side of the balance sheet, with the liabilities and owner's equity on the right-hand side, is referred to as the **account form**.[3] If the entire statement is presented on a single page,

---

[3]An account form of balance sheet is illustrated on pages 792 and 793.

it is customary to present the three sections in a downward sequence, with the total of the assets section equaling the combined totals of the other two sections. The latter form, called the **report form**, is illustrated in the following balance sheet for Midtown Electric Corporation:

REPORT
FORM OF
BALANCE
SHEET

Midtown Electric Corporation
Balance Sheet
December 31, 1987

Assets

Current assets:

Cash	$ 62,950	
Notes receivable	40,000	
Accounts receivable	60,880	
Merchandise inventory	62,150	
Office supplies	480	
Prepaid insurance	2,650	
Total current assets		$229,110

Plant assets:

Office equipment	$15,570		
Less accumulated depreciation	9,720	$ 5,850	
Store equipment	$27,100		
Less accumulated depreciation	15,700	11,400	
Total plant assets			17,250
Total assets			$246,360

Liabilities

Current liabilities:

Accounts payable	$ 22,420	
Mortgage note payable (current portion)	5,000	
Salaries payable	1,140	
Total current liabilities		$ 28,560

Long-term liabilities:

Mortgage note payable (final payment, 1999)		20,000
Total liabilities		$ 48,560

Stockholders' Equity

Capital stock	$100,000	
Retained earnings	97,800	
Total stockholders' equity		197,800
Total liabilities and stockholders' equity		$246,360

ADJUSTING ENTRIES

The analyses required to make the adjustments were completed during the process of preparing the work sheet. It is therefore unnecessary to refer again to the basic data when recording the adjusting entries in the journal. After the entries are posted, the balances of all asset, liability, revenue, and expense accounts correspond exactly to the amounts reported in the financial statements. The adjusting entries for Midtown Electric Corporation are as follows:[4]

	DATE		DESCRIPTION	POST. REF.	DEBIT	CREDIT	
			JOURNAL			PAGE 28	
1			Adjusting Entries				1
2	1987 Dec.	31	Income Summary	313	59 7 0 0 00		2
3			Merchandise Inventory	114		59 7 0 0 00	3
4							4
5		31	Merchandise Inventory	114	62 1 5 0 00		5
6			Income Summary	313		62 1 5 0 00	6
7							7
8		31	Office Supplies Expense	717	6 1 0 00		8
9			Office Supplies	116		6 1 0 00	9
10							10
11		31	Insurance Expense	716	1 9 1 0 00		11
12			Prepaid Insurance	117		1 9 1 0 00	12
13							13
14		31	Depreciation Expense—Store Equip.	613	3 1 0 0 00		14
15			Accumulated Depr.—Store Equip.	122		3 1 0 0 00	15
16							16
17		31	Depreciation Expense—Office Equip.	715	2 4 9 0 00		17
18			Accumulated Depr.—Office Equip.	124		2 4 9 0 00	18
19							19
20		31	Sales Salaries Expense	611	7 8 0 00		20
21			Office Salaries Expense	711	3 6 0 00		21
22			Salaries Payable	213		1 1 4 0 00	22
23							23
24							24

[4]An alternative method of recording merchandise inventory is presented in Appendix C. This alternative method is sometimes referred to as the closing method. Under this method, the entries for beginning and ending merchandise inventory are classified as closing entries rather than adjusting entries.

CLOSING ENTRIES

The closing entries are recorded in the journal immediately following the adjusting entries. All of the temporary owner's equity accounts are cleared of their balances, reducing them to zero. The final effect of closing out such balances is a net increase or a net decrease in the retained earnings account. The closing entries for Midtown Electric Corporation are as follows:

	DATE		DESCRIPTION	POST. REF.	DEBIT	CREDIT	
1			Closing Entries				1
2	1987 Dec.	31	Sales	411	720 1 8 5 00		2
3			Purchases Returns and Allowances	512	9 1 0 0 00		3
4			Purchases Discounts	518	2 5 2 5 00		4
5			Interest Income	812	3 6 0 0 00		5
6			Income Summary	313		735 4 1 0 00	6
7							7
8		31	Income Summary	313	663 2 6 0 00		8
9			Sales Returns and Allowances	412		6 1 4 0 00	9
10			Sales Discounts	413		5 7 9 0 00	10
11			Purchases	511		521 9 8 0 00	11
12			Transportation In	514		17 4 0 0 00	12
13			Sales Salaries Expense	611		60 0 3 0 00	13
14			Advertising Expense	612		10 8 6 0 00	14
15			Depreciation Exp.—Store Equip.	613		3 1 0 0 00	15
16			Miscellaneous Selling Expense	619		6 3 0 00	16
17			Office Salaries Expense	711		21 0 2 0 00	17
18			Rent Expense	712		8 1 0 0 00	18
19			Depreciation Exp.—Office Equip.	715		2 4 9 0 00	19
20			Insurance Expense	716		1 9 1 0 00	20
21			Office Supplies Expense	717		6 1 0 00	21
22			Miscellaneous General Expense	719		7 6 0 00	22
23			Interest Expense	911		2 4 4 0 00	23
24							24
25		31	Income Summary	313	74 6 0 0 00		25
26			Retained Earnings	311		74 6 0 0 00	26
27							27
28		31	Retained Earnings	311	18 0 0 0 00		28
29			Dividends	312		18 0 0 0 00	29
30							30
31							31
32							32

JOURNAL   PAGE 29

CLOSING ENTRIES

The effect of each of these four entries may be described as follows:

1. The first entry closes all income statement accounts with *credit* balances by transferring the total to the *credit* side of Income Summary.
2. The second entry closes all income statement accounts with *debit* balances by transferring the total to the *debit* side of Income Summary.
3. The third entry closes Income Summary by transferring its balance, the net income for the year, to Retained Earnings.
4. The fourth entry closes Dividends by transferring its balance to Retained Earnings.

The income summary account, as it will appear after the merchandise inventory adjustments and the closing entries have been posted, is as follows. Each item in the account is identified as an aid to understanding. Such notations are not an essential part of the posting procedure.

INCOME
SUMMARY
ACCOUNT

ACCOUNT Income Summary   ACCOUNT NO. 313

DATE		ITEM	POST. REF.	DEBIT	CREDIT	BALANCE	
						DEBIT	CREDIT
1987 Dec.	31	Mer. inv.,					
		Jan. 1	28	59 7 0 0 00		59 7 0 0 00	
	31	Mer. inv.,					
		Dec. 31	28		62 1 5 0 00		2 4 5 0 00
	31	Revenue, etc.	29		735 4 1 0 00		737 8 6 0 00
	31	Expense, etc.	29	663 2 6 0 00			74 6 0 0 00
	31	Net income	29	74 6 0 0 00			

After all temporary owner's equity accounts have been closed, the only accounts with balances are the asset, contra asset, liability, capital stock, and retained earnings accounts. The balances of these accounts in the ledger will correspond exactly with the amounts appearing on the balance sheet on page 207.

POST-CLOSING TRIAL BALANCE

After the adjusting and closing entries have been recorded, it is advisable to take another trial balance to verify the debit-credit equality of the ledger at the beginning of the following year. This post-closing trial balance may consist of two calculator tape listings, one for the debit balances and the other for the credit balances, or its details may be shown in a more formal fashion, as was illustrated in Chapter 3 on page 132.

REVERSING ENTRIES

Some of the adjusting entries recorded at the end of a fiscal year have an important effect on otherwise routine transactions that occur in the following year. A typical example is the adjusting entry for accrued salaries owed to employees at the end of the year. The wage or salary expense of an enterprise and the accompanying liability to employees actually accumulates or accrues day by day, or even hour by hour, during any part of the fiscal year. Nevertheless, the practice of recording the expense only at the time of payment is more efficient. When salaries are paid weekly, an entry debiting Salary Expense and crediting Cash will be recorded 52 or 53 times during the year. If there has been an adjusting entry for accrued salaries at the end of the year, however, the first payment of salaries in the following year will include such year-end accrual. In the absence of some special provision, it will be necessary to debit Salaries Payable for the amount owed for the earlier year and Salary Expense for the portion of the payroll that represents expense for the later year.

To illustrate, assume the following facts for an enterprise that pays salaries weekly and ends its fiscal year on December 31:

1. Salaries are paid on Friday for the five-day week ending on Friday.
2. The balance in Salary Expense as of Friday, December 27, is $62,500.
3. Salaries accrued for Monday and Tuesday, December 30 and 31, total $500.
4. Salaries paid on Friday, January 3, of the following year total $1,250.

The foregoing data may be diagrammed as follows:

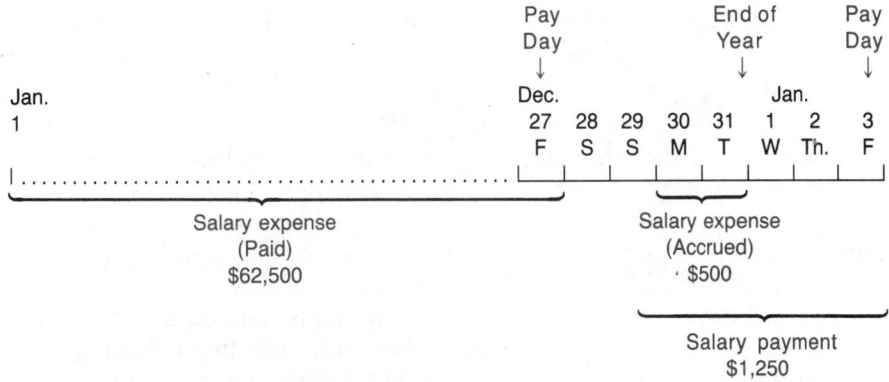

The adjusting entry to record the accrued salary expense and salaries payable for Monday and Tuesday, December 30 and 31, is as follows:

| Dec. 31 | Salary Expense...................... | 611 | 500 | |
| | Salaries Payable................... | 213 | | 500 |

After the adjusting entry has been posted, Salary Expense will have a debit balance of $63,000 ($62,500 + $500) and Salaries Payable will have a credit balance of $500. After the closing process is completed, Salary Expense is in balance and ready for entries of the following year, but Salaries Payable continues to have a credit balance of $500. As matters now stand, it would be necessary to record the $1,250 payroll on January 3 as a debit of $500 to Salaries Payable and a debit of $750 to Salary Expense. This means that the employee who records payroll entries must not only record this particular payroll in a different manner from all other weekly payrolls for the year but must also refer to the adjusting entries in the journal or the ledger to determine the amount of the $1,250 payment to be debited to each of the two accounts.

The need to refer to earlier entries and to divide the debit between two accounts can be avoided by an optional procedure of recording a **reversing entry** as of the first day of the following fiscal period. As the term implies, such an entry is the exact reverse of the adjusting entry to which it relates. The amounts and the accounts are the same; the debits and credits are merely reversed.

Continuing with the illustration, the reversing entry for the accrued salaries is as follows:

| Jan. 1 | Salaries Payable.................... | 213 | 500 | |
| | Salary Expense................... | 611 | | 500 |

The effect of the reversing entry is to transfer the $500 liability from Salaries Payable to the credit side of Salary Expense. The real nature of the $500 balance is unchanged; it remains a liability. When the payroll is paid on January 3, Salary Expense will be debited and Cash will be credited for $1,250, the entire amount of the weekly salaries. After the entry is posted, Salary Expense will have a debit balance of $750, which is the amount of expense incurred for January 1–3. The sequence of entries, including adjusting, closing, and reversing entries, may be traced in the following accounts:

ACCOUNT SALARY EXPENSE   ACCOUNT NO. 611

Date		Item	Post. Ref.	Debit	Credit	Balance	
						Debit	Credit
1987 Jan.	5		1	1,240		1,240	
Dec.	6		25	1,300		58,440	
	13		26	1,450		59,890	
	20		27	1,260		61,150	
	27		28	1,350		62,500	
	31	Adjusting	28	500		63,000	
	31	Closing	29		63,000	—	—
1988 Jan.	1	Reversing	29		500		500
	3		29	1,250		750	

ACCOUNT SALARIES PAYABLE   ACCOUNT NO. 213

Date		Item	Post. Ref.	Debit	Credit	Balance	
						Debit	Credit
1987 Dec.	31	Adjusting	28		500		500
1988 Jan.	1	Reversing	29	500		—	—

The year-end procedures for Midtown Electric Corporation are completed by journalizing and posting the reversing entry for accrued salaries. The entry is as follows:

	DATE		DESCRIPTION	POST. REF.	DEBIT	CREDIT	
30			Reversing Entry				30
31	1988 Jan.	1	Salaries Payable	213	1 1 4 0 00		31
32			Sales Salaries Expense	611		7 8 0 00	32
33			Office Salaries Expense	711		3 6 0 00	33
34							34
35							35

JOURNAL   PAGE 29

After the reversing entry is posted, Salaries Payable is in balance and the liabilities for sales and office salaries appear as credits in the respective expense accounts. The entire amount of the first payroll in January will be debited to the salary expense accounts, and the balances of the accounts will then automatically represent the expense of the new period.

Reversing Entries: Once or Twice?

The use of reversing entries is an optional procedure designed to simplify the recording of transactions that follow, reduce the time required to record such transactions, avoid errors, and promote efficiency in general. In one case, however, a reversing entry created rather than prevented an error from occurring.

The error occurred when two companies merged and combined their accounting systems. The accounting systems for the two companies were incompatible—and so, unfortunately, were the chief accounting personnel of the two companies, who were jockeying for position and scarcely speaking to each other. Competent enough to perform routine functions for the separate companies, they were unable to cope with the change brought about by the merger. Furthermore, the basic data which the accounting systems provided were suspect; one company's computerized accounting system was badly programmed and almost nightmarishly erratic.

Amid the confusion of closing and opening the books while the two accounting departments were being combined, an accrued liability was reversed twice instead of once. The net effect was that earnings were overstated by $790,000 and accounts payable were understated by the same amount.

Source: Adapted from Richard J. Whalen, "The Big Skid at Yale Express," *Fortune* (November, 1965).

INTERIM STATEMENTS

Service and merchandising enterprises frequently prepare financial statements at intervals within the fiscal year, such as monthly, quarterly, or semiannually. Statements issued for periods covering less than a fiscal year are called **interim statements**.

The analysis and recording of transactions is performed on a continuous basis throughout the fiscal year, regardless of when financial statements are to be prepared. When interim financial statements are to be prepared, the adjustment data are assembled and a work sheet is completed as of the end of the interim period. The work sheet then serves as a basis for preparing the interim statements. However, adjusting and closing entries are not recorded in the accounts. These entries are recorded only at the end of the fiscal year.

The amounts of the asset and liability accounts appearing in the balance sheet section of the work sheet for an interim period are the balances as of the last day of that period. The amounts of the revenue and expenses appearing in the income statement section, however, are the total amounts accumulated since the beginning of the fiscal year. To illustrate, assume that the fiscal year of an enterprise is the calendar year. The work sheet prepared at the end of February provides data for an income statement for the two-month period, January–February, and data for a balance sheet as of February 28(29). The

214 work sheet at the end of March provides data for an income statement for the

three-month period, January–March, and data for a balance sheet as of March 31. Data for the income statement for a single month only are obtained by subtracting from the amount of each revenue and expense of the current cumulative income statement the corresponding amount from the preceding cumulative income statement. Continuing the illustration, if sales are reported at $190,000 on the cumulative January–March income statement and at $120,000 on the cumulative January–February income statement, the sales reported on the March income statement will be $70,000 ($190,000 − $120,000). The amount of each expense incurred in March and the net income for March is determined in the same manner.

CORRECTION OF ERRORS

Occasional errors in journalizing and posting transactions are unavoidable. Procedures used to correct errors in the journal and ledger vary according to the nature of the error and the phase of the accounting cycle in which it is discovered.

When an error in an account title or amount in the journal is discovered before the entry is posted, the correction may be made by drawing a line through the error and inserting the correct title or amount immediately above. If there is any likelihood of questions arising later, the person responsible may initial the correction. To illustrate, assume that a purchase of office equipment for cash was erroneously journalized as a $500 debit to Office Supplies but correctly journalized as a $500 credit to Cash. If the journal entry has not been posted to the ledger, then the correction may be made as follows:

	DATE		DESCRIPTION	POST. REF.	DEBIT	CREDIT	
1	1987 Oct.	5	Office Equipment ~~Office Supplies~~	DC	5 0 0 00		1
2			Cash			5 0 0 00	2
3							3

JOURNAL   PAGE 1

JOURNAL WITH CORRECTED ENTRY

When an entry in the journal is prepared correctly, but the debit portion is incorrectly posted to the account as a credit (or vice versa), the incorrect posting may be corrected by drawing a line through the error and posting the item correctly. If the amount of a single debit or credit posting is in error, such as posting a journal debit of $500 as $50, the correction may be made in a similar manner. As indicated in the preceding paragraph, if there is any likelihood of questions arising later, the person responsible may initial the correction, as in the following illustration in which a debit of $500 for office equipment was erroneously posted as a $50 debit.

ACCOUNT
WITH
CORRECTED
POSTING

ACCOUNT	Office Equipment						ACCOUNT NO. 18	
DATE	ITEM	POST. REF.	DEBIT	CREDIT	BALANCE			
					DEBIT		CREDIT	
1987 Oct. 5	DC	1	500 00 500 00		500 00 500 00			

When an erroneous account title appears in a journal entry and the error is not discovered until after posting is completed, the preferable procedure is to journalize and post a correcting entry. To illustrate, assume that a purchase of office equipment, which was paid in cash, was erroneously journalized and posted as a $500 debit to Office Supplies but correctly journalized and posted as a $500 credit to Cash. Before a correcting entry is made, it is advisable to establish clearly both (1) the debit(s) and credit(s) of the entry in which the error occurred and (2) the debit(s) and credit(s) that should have been recorded. T accounts may be helpful in making this analysis, as in the following example:

Entry in which error occurred:

Office Supplies		Cash	
500			500

Entry that should have been recorded:

Office Equipment		Cash	
500			500

Comparison of the two sets of T accounts shows that the erroneous debit of $500 to Office Supplies may be corrected by a $500 credit to that account and that Office Equipment should be debited for $500. The following correcting entry is then journalized and posted:

CORRECTING
ENTRY

	JOURNAL					PAGE 22		
	DATE	DESCRIPTION	POST. REF.	DEBIT		CREDIT		
1	1987 Oct. 31	Office Equipment	18	5 0 0 00				1
2		Office Supplies	15			5 0 0 00		2
3		To correct erroneous debit to						3
4		Office Supplies on Oct. 5.						4
5		See invoice from Allen						5
6		Supply Company. CRN						6
7								7

The preceding procedures for correction of errors are summarized in the following table:

Error	Correction Procedure	
Journal entry incorrect, but not posted.	Draw line through the error and insert correct title or amount.	PROCEDURES FOR CORRECTING ERRORS
Journal entry correct, but posted incorrectly.	Draw line through the error and post correctly.	
Journal entry incorrect and posted.	Journalize and post a correcting entry.	

CHAPTER REVIEW

KEY POINTS

1. Financial Statements for Merchandising Enterprises.

The basic financial statements for a merchandising enterprise are the income statement, statement of owner's equity or retained earnings statement, and balance sheet.

There are two widely used forms for the income statement: multiple-step and single-step. The multiple-step income statement is so called because of its many sections, subsections, and intermediate balances. The single-step income statement derives its name from the fact that the total of all expenses is deducted from the total of all revenues.

The retained earnings statement summarizes the changes that have occurred in the retained earnings account during a fiscal period. It is not unusual to add the analysis of retained earnings at the bottom of the income statement to form a combined income and retained earnings statement.

The balance sheet may be prepared using the account form or the report form. The account form lists assets on the left-hand side of the statement, with liabilities and owner's equity on the right-hand side. The report form lists assets, liabilities, and owner's equity in a downward sequence.

2. Adjusting Entries.

The adjusting entries are prepared for a merchandising enterprise from the work sheet adjustments columns. After the adjusting entries have been posted, the balances of all asset, liability, revenue, and expense accounts correspond exactly to the amounts reported in the financial statements.

3. Closing Entries.

The closing entries are recorded in the journal immediately following the adjusting entries. All the temporary owner's equity accounts are cleared of their balances, reducing them to zero. The final effect of closing out such balances is a net increase or decrease in the retained earnings (owner's capital) account. The final closing entry reduces the dividends (drawing) account to a zero balance by transferring it to retained earnings (owner's capital).

4. Post-Closing Trial Balance.

After the adjusting and closing entries have been recorded, it is advisable to take another trial balance to verify the debit-credit equality of the ledger as of the beginning of the following year.

5. Reversing Entries.

Some of the adjusting entries recorded at the end of the fiscal year have an important effect on otherwise routine transactions that occur in the following year. To simplify the recording of transactions in the following year, to reduce the time required to record such transactions, to avoid errors, and to promote efficiency, reversing entries may be prepared. As the term implies, a reversing entry is the exact reverse of the adjusting entry to which it relates. The amounts are the same; the debits and credits are merely reversed.

6. Interim Statements.

Financial statements issued for periods covering less than a fiscal year are called interim statements. When interim financial statements are to be prepared, the adjustment data are assembled and a work sheet is completed as of the end of the interim period. Interim adjusting and closing entries are not recorded in the accounts.

7. Correction of Errors.

Occasional errors in journalizing and posting transactions are unavoidable. The procedures for correction of errors are summarized in the following table:

Error	Correction Procedure
Journal entry incorrect, but not posted.	Draw line through the error and insert correct title or amount.
Journal entry correct, but posted incorrectly.	Draw line through the error and post correctly.
Journal entry incorrect and posted.	Journalize and post a correcting entry.

KEY TERMS

multiple-step income statement 202
single-step income statement 202
cost of merchandise sold 202
gross profit 202
selling expenses 202
general expenses 202
income from operations 204
other income 204

other expense 204
net income   204
net loss 204
retained earnings statement 205
account form of balance sheet 206
report form of balance sheet 207
reversing entry 212
interim statements 214

SELF-EXAMINATION QUESTIONS
Answers in Appendix B.

1. The income statement in which the total of all expenses is deducted from the total of all revenues is termed:
   A. multiple-step form
   ⊁ B. single-step form
   C. account form
   D. report form

2. On a multiple-step income statement, the excess of net sales over the cost of merchandise sold is called:
   A. operating income
   B. income from operations
   ⊁ C. gross profit
   D. net income

3. Which of the following expenses would normally be classified as "other expense" on a multiple-step income statement?
   A. Depreciation expense—   C. Insurance expense
      office equipment   x D. Interest expense
   B. Sales salaries expense

4. On July 1, the first day of the fiscal year, Salary Expense has a credit balance of $5,500. On July 3, the first payday in the year, salaries of $21,700 are paid. What is the salary expense for July 1–3?
   A. $5,500   C. $21,700
   B. $16,200   D. $27,200

5. At the end of the fiscal year, the adjusting entry for accrued salaries was inadvertently omitted. The effect of the error (assuming that it is not corrected) would be to:
   A. understate expenses for the year
   B. overstate net income for the year
   C. understate liabilities at the end of the year
   D. all of the above

ILLUSTRATIVE PROBLEM

A partially completed work sheet for Hadley Inc., including all adjustments, is presented on page 221.

Instructions:

1. Complete the work sheet for Hadley Inc.
2. Prepare a multiple-step income statement.
3. Prepare a retained earnings statement.
4. Prepare a report form of balance sheet, assuming that the current portion of the mortgage note payable is $7,500.
5. Journalize the adjusting entries.
6. Journalize the closing entries.
7. Journalize any reversing entries as of November 1, 1988.

Hadley Inc.

Work Sheet

For Year Ended October 31, 1988

	ACCOUNT TITLE	TRIAL BALANCE Debit	TRIAL BALANCE Credit	ADJUSTMENTS Debit	ADJUSTMENTS Credit
1	Cash	2 640 00			
2	Accounts Receivable	6 220 00			
3	Merchandise Inventory	14 130 00		(b) 15 600 00	(a) 14 130 00
4	Prepaid Insurance	6 800 00			(c) 4 300 00
5	Store Supplies	1 250 00			(d) 660 00
6	Office Supplies	800 00			(e) 480 00
7	Store Equipment	6 500 00			
8	Accumulated Depreciation — Store Equipment		2 010 00		(f) 5 850 00
9	Office Equipment	1 960 00			
10	Accumulated Depreciation — Office Equipment		810 00		(g) 2 160 00
11	Accounts Payable		3 640 00		
12	Salaries Payable				(h) 2 700 00
13	Mortgage Note Payable (final payment, 1998)		7 500 00		
14	Capital Stock		5 000 00		
15	Retained Earnings		6 342 00		
16	Dividends	8 000 00			
17	Income Summary			(a) 14 130 00	(b) 15 600 00
18	Sales		54 000 00		
19	Sales Returns and Allowances	4 300 00			
20	Sales Discounts	2 500 00			
21	Purchases	36 000 00			
22	Purchases Returns and Allowances		9 000 00		
23	Purchases Discounts		4 680 00		
24	Transportation In	1 800 00			
25	Sales Salaries Expense	4 320 00		(h) 1 800 00	
26	Advertising Expense	1 500 00			
27	Depreciation Expense — Store Equipment			(f) 5 850 00	
28	Store Supplies Expense			(d) 660 00	
29	Miscellaneous Selling Expense	970 00			
30	Office Salaries Expense	3 000 00		(h) 900 00	
31	Rent Expense	8 500 00			
32	Insurance Expense			(c) 4 300 00	
33	Depreciation Expense — Office Equipment			(g) 2 160 00	
34	Office Supplies Expense			(e) 480 00	
35	Miscellaneous General Expense	830 00			
36	Interest Expense	8 250 00			
37		80 670 00	80 670 00	31 345 00	31 345 00
38	Net Income				

SOLUTION

	ACCOUNT TITLE	TRIAL BALANCE DEBIT	TRIAL BALANCE CREDIT	ADJUSTMENTS DEBIT	ADJUSTMENTS CREDIT
1	Cash	2 6 4 0 0 00			
2	Accounts Receivable	6 2 2 0 0 00			
3	Merchandise Inventory	14 1 3 0 0 00		(b) 15 6 0 0 0 00	(a) 14 1 3 0 0 00
4	Prepaid Insurance	6 8 0 0 00			(c) 4 3 0 0 00
5	Store Supplies	1 2 5 0 00			(d) 6 6 0 00
6	Office Supplies	8 0 0 00			(e) 4 8 0 00
7	Store Equipment	6 5 0 0 0 00			
8	Accumulated Depreciation — Store Equipment		2 0 1 0 0 00		(f) 5 8 5 0 00
9	Office Equipment	1 9 6 0 0 00			
10	Accumulated Depreciation — Office Equipment		8 1 0 0 00		(g) 2 1 6 0 00
11	Accounts Payable		3 6 4 0 0 00		
12	Salaries Payable				(h) 2 7 0 0 00
13	Mortgage Note Payable (final payment, 1998)		7 5 0 0 0 00		
14	Capital Stock		5 0 0 0 0 00		
15	Retained Earnings		6 3 4 2 0 00		
16	Dividends	8 0 0 0 00			
17	Income Summary			(a) 14 1 3 0 0 00	(b) 15 6 0 0 0 00
18	Sales		54 0 0 0 0 00		
19	Sales Returns and Allowances	4 3 0 0 00			
20	Sales Discounts	2 5 0 0 00			
21	Purchases	36 0 0 0 0 00			
22	Purchases Returns and Allowances		9 0 0 0 00		
23	Purchases Discounts		4 6 8 0 00		
24	Transportation In	1 8 0 0 00			
25	Sales Salaries Expense	4 3 2 0 0 00		(h) 1 8 0 0 00	
26	Advertising Expense	1 5 0 0 0 00			
27	Depreciation Expense — Store Equipment			(f) 5 8 5 0 00	
28	Store Supplies Expense			(d) 6 6 0 00	
29	Miscellaneous Selling Expense	9 7 0 00			
30	Office Salaries Expense	3 0 0 0 0 00		(h) 9 0 0 00	
31	Rent Expense	8 5 0 0 00			
32	Insurance Expense			(c) 4 3 0 0 00	
33	Depreciation Expense — Office Equipment			(g) 2 1 6 0 00	
34	Office Supplies Expense			(e) 4 8 0 00	
35	Miscellaneous General Expense	8 3 0 00			
36	Interest Expense	8 2 5 0 00			
37		80 6 7 0 0 00	80 6 7 0 0 00	31 3 4 5 0 00	31 3 4 5 0 00
38	Net Income				
39					
40					

Inc.

Sheet

October 31, 1988

ADJUSTED TRIAL BALANCE		INCOME STATEMENT		BALANCE SHEET		
DEBIT	CREDIT	DEBIT	CREDIT	DEBIT	CREDIT	
2 6 4 0 0 00				2 6 4 0 0 00		1
6 2 2 0 0 00				6 2 2 0 0 00		2
15 6 0 0 0 00				15 6 0 0 0 00		3
2 5 0 0 00				2 5 0 0 00		4
5 9 0 00				5 9 0 00		5
3 2 0 00				3 2 0 00		6
6 5 0 0 0 00				6 5 0 0 0 00		7
	2 5 9 5 0 00				2 5 9 5 0 00	8
1 9 6 0 0 00				1 9 6 0 0 00		9
	1 0 2 6 0 00				1 0 2 6 0 00	10
	3 6 4 0 0 00				3 6 4 0 0 00	11
	2 7 0 0 00				2 7 0 0 00	12
	7 5 0 0 0 00				7 5 0 0 0 00	13
	5 0 0 0 0 00				5 0 0 0 0 00	14
	6 3 4 2 0 00				6 3 4 2 0 00	15
8 0 0 0 00				8 0 0 0 00		16
14 1 3 0 0 00	15 6 0 0 0 00	14 1 3 0 0 00	15 6 0 0 0 00			17
	54 0 0 0 0 00		54 0 0 0 0 00			18
4 3 0 0 00		4 3 0 0 00				19
2 5 0 0 00		2 5 0 0 00				20
36 0 0 0 0 00		36 0 0 0 0 00				21
	9 0 0 0 00		9 0 0 0 00			22
	4 6 8 0 00		4 6 8 0 00			23
1 8 0 0 00		1 8 0 0 00				24
4 5 0 0 0 00		4 5 0 0 0 00				25
1 5 0 0 0 00		1 5 0 0 0 00				26
5 8 5 0 00		5 8 5 0 00				27
6 6 0 00		6 6 0 00				28
9 7 0 00		9 7 0 00				29
3 0 9 0 0 00		3 0 9 0 0 00				30
8 5 0 0 00		8 5 0 0 00				31
4 3 0 0 00		4 3 0 0 00				32
2 1 6 0 00		2 1 6 0 00				33
4 8 0 00		4 8 0 00				34
8 3 0 00		8 3 0 00				35
8 2 5 0 00		8 2 5 0 00				36
97 3 4 1 0 00	97 3 4 1 0 00	63 2 8 0 0 00	70 9 6 8 0 00	34 0 6 1 0 00	26 3 7 3 0 00	37
		7 6 8 8 0 00			7 6 8 8 0 00	38
		70 9 6 8 0 00	70 9 6 8 0 00	34 0 6 1 0 00	34 0 6 1 0 00	39
						40

223

(2)

Hadley Inc.
Income Statement
For Year Ended October 31, 1988

Revenue from sales:			
Sales...................................		$540,000	
Less: Sales returns and allowances	$ 4,300		
Sales discounts.....................	2,500	6,800	
Net sales................................			$533,200
Cost of merchandise sold:			
Merchandise inventory, November 1, 1987 ...		$141,300	
Purchases...............................	$360,000		
Less: Purchases returns and allowances..... $9,000			
Purchases discounts 4,680	13,680		
Net purchases	$346,320		
Add transportation in.....................	1,800		
Cost of merchandise purchased...........		348,120	
Merchandise available for sale..............		$489,420	
Less merchandise inventory,			
October 31, 1988.....................		156,000	
Cost of merchandise sold			333,420
Gross profit................................			$199,780
Operating expenses:			
Selling expenses:			
Sales salaries expense...................	$ 45,000		
Advertising expense	15,000		
Depreciation expense—store equipment...	5,850		
Store supplies expense	660		
Miscellaneous selling expense	970		
Total selling expenses		$ 67,480	
General expenses:			
Office salaries expense	$ 30,900		
Rent expense...........................	8,500		
Insurance expense	4,300		
Depreciation expense—office equipment ..	2,160		
Office supplies expense..................	480		
Miscellaneous general expense	830		
Total general expenses		47,170	
Total operating expenses..................			114,650
Income from operations			$ 85,130
Other expense:			
Interest expense..........................			8,250
Net income			$ 76,880

(3)

Hadley Inc.
Retained Earnings Statement
For Year Ended October 31, 1988

Retained earnings, November 1, 1987		$ 63,420
Net income for the year....................................	$76,880	
Less dividends..	8,000	
Increase in retained earnings		68,880
Retained earnings, October 31, 1988		$132,300

(4)

Hadley Inc.
Balance Sheet
October 31, 1988

Assets

Current assets:
Cash....................................		$ 26,400
Accounts receivable		62,200
Merchandise inventory.....................		156,000
Prepaid insurance.........................		2,500
Store supplies		590
Office supplies...........................		320
Total current assets		$248,010

Plant assets:
Store equipment	$65,000	
Less accumulated depreciation	25,950	$ 39,050
Office equipment..........................	$19,600	
Less accumulated depreciation	10,260	9,340
Total plant assets		48,390
Total assets		$296,400

Liabilities

Current liabilities:
Accounts payable		$ 36,400
Mortgage note payable (current portion)........		7,500
Salaries payable		2,700
Total current liabilities...................		$ 46,600

Long-term liabilities:
Mortgage note payable (final payment, 1998) ...		67,500
Total liabilities................................		$114,100

Stockholders' Equity

Capital stock.................................		$ 50,000
Retained earnings............................		132,300
Total stockholders' equity......................		182,300
Total liabilities and stockholders' equity		$296,400

(5)

	JOURNAL			PAGE 27

	DATE		DESCRIPTION	POST. REF.	DEBIT	CREDIT	
1			Adjusting Entries				1
2	1988 Oct.	31	Income Summary		141 3 0 0 00		2
3			Merchandise Inventory			141 3 0 0 00	3
4							4
5		31	Merchandise Inventory		156 0 0 0 00		5
6			Income Summary			156 0 0 0 00	6
7							7
8		31	Insurance Expense		4 3 0 0 00		8
9			Prepaid Insurance			4 3 0 0 00	9

	Date	Account	Debit	Credit
11	31	Store Supplies Expense	6 6 0 00	
12		Store Supplies		6 6 0 00
14	31	Office Supplies Expense	4 8 0 00	
15		Office Supplies		4 8 0 00
17	31	Depr. Expense—Store Equipment	5 8 5 0 00	
18		Accumulated Depr.—Store Equip.		5 8 5 0 00
20	31	Depr. Expense—Office Equipment	2 1 6 0 00	
21		Accumulated Depr.—Office Equip.		2 1 6 0 00
23	31	Sales Salaries Expense	1 8 0 0 00	
24		Office Salaries Expense	9 0 0 00	
25		Salaries Payable		2 7 0 0 00

(6)

	Date	Account	Debit	Credit
27		Closing Entries		
28	31	Sales	540 0 0 0 00	
29		Purchases Returns and Allowances	9 0 0 0 00	
30		Purchases Discounts	4 6 8 0 00	
31		Income Summary		553 6 8 0 00
33	31	Income Summary	491 5 0 0 00	
34		Sales Returns and Allowances		4 3 0 0 00
35		Sales Discounts		2 5 0 0 00
36		Purchases		360 0 0 0 00
37		Transportation In		1 8 0 0 00
38		Sales Salaries Expense		45 0 0 0 00
39		Advertising Expense		15 0 0 0 00
40		Depr. Expense—Store Equipment		5 8 5 0 00
41		Store Supplies Expense		6 6 0 00
42		Miscellaneous Selling Expense		9 7 0 00
43		Office Salaries Expense		30 9 0 0 00
44		Rent Expense		8 5 0 0 00
45		Insurance Expense		4 3 0 0 00
46		Depr. Expense—Office Equipment		2 1 6 0 00
47		Office Supplies Expense		4 8 0 00
48		Miscellaneous General Expense		8 3 0 00
49		Interest Expense		8 2 5 0 00
51		Income Summary	76 8 8 0 00	
52		Retained Earnings		76 8 8 0 00
54		Retained Earnings	8 0 0 0 00	
55		Dividends		8 0 0 0 00

(7)

					DEBIT							CREDIT					
	DATE		DESCRIPTION	POST. REF.													
1			Reversing Entry														1
2	1988 Nov.	1	Salaries Payable		2 7 0 0	00											2
3			Sales Salaries Expense								1 8 0 0	00					3
4			Office Salaries Expense								9 0 0	00					4

JOURNAL   PAGE 28

DISCUSSION QUESTIONS

1. What is the primary characteristic of the multiple-step income statement?

2. Is there uniformity in the amount of detail presented in a multiple-step income statement? Explain.

3. For the fiscal year, net sales were $780,000 and the cost of merchandise purchased was $520,000. Merchandise inventory at the beginning of the year was $60,000, and at the end of the year it was $70,000. Determine the following amounts:
   (a) Merchandise available for sale.
   (b) Cost of merchandise sold.
   (c) Gross profit.
   (d) Merchandise inventory listed on the balance sheet as of the end of the year.

4. Into what two categories are operating expenses of a merchandising enterprise usually separated?

5. The following expenses were incurred by a merchandising enterprise during the year. In which expense section of the income statement should each be reported: (a) selling, (b) general, or (c) other?
   (1) Interest expense on notes payable.
   (2) Salaries of salespersons.
   (3) Insurance expense on office equipment.
   (4) Advertising expense.
   (5) Office supplies used.
   (6) Depreciation expense on store equipment.
   (7) Rent expense.
   (8) Salary of general manager.

6. Differentiate between the multiple-step and the single-step forms of the income statement.

7. What major advantages and disadvantages does the single-step form of income statement have in comparison to the multiple-step statement?

8. (a) What two financial statements are frequently combined and presented as a single statement? (b) What is the major criticism directed at the combined statement?

9. Differentiate between the account form and the report form of balance sheet.

10. Before adjustment at October 31, the end of the fiscal year, the salary expense account has a debit balance of $370,000. The amount of salary accrued (owed but not paid) on the same date is $7,800. Indicate the necessary (a) adjusting entry, (b) closing entry, and (c) reversing entry.

11. Describe the four entries to close the accounts of a corporation.

12. (a) What is the effect of closing the revenue, expense, and dividends accounts of a corporation at the end of a fiscal year? (b) After the closing entries have been posted, what type of accounts remain with balances?

13. Why is it advisable, after closing the accounts at the end of a year, to reverse the adjusting entries that had been made for accrued salaries and other accrued expenses?

14. Immediately after the reversing entries have been recorded, Salary Expense has a credit balance of $7,500. Assuming that there have been no errors, does the balance represent an asset, expense, revenue, liability, contra asset, or contra expense?

15. As of November 1, the first day of the fiscal year, Salary Expense has a credit balance of $4,800. On November 4, the first payday of the year, salaries of $13,100 are paid. (a) What is the salary expense for November 1–4? (b) What entry should be made to record the payment on November 4?

16. What are financial statements issued for periods covering less than a fiscal year called?

17. How is a correction made when an error in an account title or amount in the journal is discovered before the entry is posted?

18. In preparing and posting the journal entry to record the purchase of land by issuing a mortgage note payable, the capital stock account was erroneously credited. What is the preferred procedure to correct the error?

19. Real World Focus. A recent trend in retailing is the establishment of warehouse clubs. These clubs offer name-brand merchandise at prices ranging from 20 to 40 percent below discount store prices to their members who pay a nominal yearly fee. The Price Club, with projected 1985 sales of $1.8 billion, is one of the leaders in this growing area of retailing. The following graph compares the gross profit as a percent of sales of The Price Club with that of K Mart Corp.:

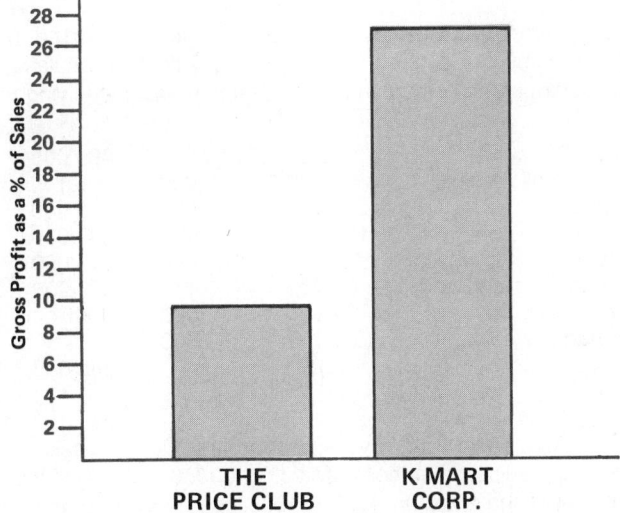

How can the Price Club remain profitable with a gross profit percentage less than one half that of K Mart Corp.?

EXERCISES

Exercise 5–1. Identification of items missing from income statement. For (a) through (i), identify the items designated by "X".

(a) Sales − (X + X) = Net sales
(b) Purchases − (X + X) = Net purchases
(c) Net purchases + X = Cost of merchandise purchased
(d) Merchandise inventory (beginning) + cost of merchandise purchased = X
(e) Merchandise available for sale − X = Cost of merchandise sold
(f) Net sales − cost of merchandise sold = X
(g) X + X = Operating expenses
(h) Gross profit − operating expenses = X
(i) Income from operations + X − X = Net income

Exercise 5–2. Determination of amounts for items omitted from income statement. Three items are omitted in each of the following tabulations of income statement data. Determine the amounts of the missing items, identifying them by letter.

Sales......................	$ (a)	$560,000	$880,000	$750,000
Sales returns and allowances .	8,000	20,000	(g)	18,000
Sales discounts	2,000	10,000	5,000	(j)
Net sales	100,000	(d)	860,000	(k)
Beginning inventory..........	(b)	120,000	215,000	(l)
Cost of merchandise purchased	60,000	(e)	500,000	580,000
Ending inventory.............	30,000	100,000	(h)	120,000
Cost of merchandise sold.....	50,000	340,000	(i)	540,000
Gross profit	(c)	(f)	385,000	180,000

Exercise 5–3. Adjusting and reversing entries. On the basis of the following data, journalize (a) the adjusting entries at March 31, 1988, the end of the current fiscal year, and (b) the reversing entry on April 1, 1988, the first day of the following year.

(1) Sales salaries are uniformly $9,000 for a five-day workweek, ending on Friday. The last payday of the year was Friday, March 28.

(2) Merchandise inventory: April 1, 1987 (beginning), $70,800; March 31, 1988 (ending), $65,400.

(3) Store supplies account balance before adjusting, $1,250; store supplies physical inventory, March 31, $470.

(4) The prepaid insurance account before adjustment on March 31 has a balance of $8,270. An analysis of the policies indicates that $5,230 of premiums has expired during the year.

Exercise 5–4. Entries posted to the salary expense account. Portions of the salary expense account of an enterprise are as follows:

ACCOUNT Salary Expense   ACCOUNT NO. 54

Date		Item	Post Ref.	Dr.	Cr.	Balance Dr.	Balance Cr.
19--							
Jan.	2		24		1,250		1,250
	6		24	6,000		4,750	
~~							
Dec.	27	(1)	51	7,500		245,500	
	31	(2)	51	3,000		248,500	
	31	(3)	52		248,500	—	—
19--							
Jan.	2	(4)	52		3,000		3,000
	5	(5)	53	7,500		4,500	

(a) Indicate the nature of the entry (payment, adjusting, closing, reversing) from which each numbered posting was made. (b) Present the complete journal entry from which each numbered posting was made.

Exercise 5–5. Multiple-step income statement, merchandise inventory adjustments, and closing entries. Selected account titles and related amounts appearing in the income statement and balance sheet columns of the work sheet of North Company for the year ended December 31 are listed in alphabetical order as follows:

Building	$260,000	Purchases Discounts	$ 10,000
Capital Stock	100,000	Purchases Returns and Allowances	15,000
Cash.	57,800	Retained Earnings	300,000
Dividends	15,000	Salaries Payable.	3,720
General Expenses.	87,200	Sales.	1,200,000
Interest Expense	7,500	Sales Discounts	9,500
Merchandise Inventory (1/1)	200,000	Sales Returns and Allowances . . .	28,000
Merchandise Inventory (12/31).	230,000	Selling Expenses	125,000
Office Supplies.	8,500	Store Supplies.	7,200
Purchases.	850,000	Transportation In.	6,300

All selling expenses have been recorded in the account entitled "Selling Expenses," and all general expenses have been recorded in the account entitled "General Expenses."

(a) Prepare a multiple-step income statement for the year.
(b) Determine the amount of retained earnings to be reported in the balance sheet at the end of the year.
(c) Journalize the entries to adjust the merchandise inventory.
(d) Journalize the closing entries.

Exercise 5–6. Single-step income statement. Summary operating data for Ronald Childers Inc. during the current year ended August 31, 1988, are as follows: cost of merchandise sold, $850,000; general expenses, $150,000; interest expense, $30,000; rent income, $50,000; net sales, $1,400,000; and selling expenses, $200,000. Prepare a single-step income statement.

Exercise 5–7. Combined income and retained earnings statement. From the data presented in Exercise 5–6 and assuming that the balance of Retained Earnings was $610,000 on September 1, 1987, and that $40,000 of dividends were paid during the year, prepare a combined income and retained earnings statement for Ronald Childers Inc. (Use the single-step form for the income statement portion).

Exercise 5–8. Entries to correct errors. A number of errors in journalizing and posting transactions are described as follows:

(a) A $180 purchase of supplies on account was recorded as a debit to Supplies and a credit to Cash.

(b) A payment of $1,200 to a supplier on account, terms 2/10, n/30, within the discount period was recorded as a debit to Accounts Receivable, $1,200, a credit to Cash, $1,176, and a credit to Purchases Discounts, $24.

(c) Payment of $2,500 cash to V.E. Haskins, owner of the enterprise, was recorded as a debit to Miscellaneous Expense and a credit to Cash.

(d) Rent of $500 paid for the current month was recorded as a debit to Insurance Expense and a credit to Cash.

(e) Land of $60,000 purchased through the issuance of a mortgage note payable was recorded as a debit to Buildings and a credit to Accounts Payable.

Present the journal entries to correct the errors.

PROBLEMS

Series A

Problem 5–1A.   Preparation of multiple-step income statement and report form of balance sheet for corporation. The following selected accounts and their normal balances appear in the income statement and balance sheet columns of the work sheet of Thaxton Inc. for the fiscal year ended November 30, 1988:

Cash	$ 95,000
Notes Receivable	60,000
Accounts Receivable	92,000
Merchandise Inventory, Dec. 1, 1987	90,000
Merchandise Inventory, Nov. 30, 1988	100,000
Office Supplies	1,600
Prepaid Insurance	6,800
Office Equipment	24,000
Accumulated Depreciation — Office Equipment	10,800
Store Equipment	40,500
Accumulated Depreciation — Store Equipment	18,900
Accounts Payable	32,000
Salaries Payable	1,700
Mortgage Note Payable (final payment, 1998)	35,000
Capital Stock	150,000
Retained Earnings	144,010
Dividends	25,000
Sales	1,000,000
Sales Returns and Allowances	9,000
Sales Discounts	8,500

Purchases	$ 790,000
Purchases Returns and Allowances	16,200
Purchases Discounts	3,800
Transportation In	10,300
Sales Salaries Expense	88,000
Advertising Expense	16,300
Depreciation Expense—Store Equipment	4,600
Miscellaneous Selling Expense	1,000
Office Salaries Expense	30,900
Rent Expense	12,150
Depreciation Expense—Office Equipment	3,700
Insurance Expense	2,750
Office Supplies Expense	900
Miscellaneous General Expense	1,150
Interest Income	5,400
Interest Expense	3,660

Instructions:

(1) Prepare a multiple-step income statement.
(2) Prepare a retained earnings statement.
(3) Prepare a report form of balance sheet, assuming that the current portion of the mortgage note payable is $3,500.

Problem 5–2A. Preparation of single-step income statement and combined income and retained earnings statement. Selected accounts and related amounts for Thaxton Inc. for the fiscal year ended November 30, 1988, are presented in Problem 5–1A.

Instructions:

(1) Prepare a single-step income statement.
(2) Prepare a combined income and retained earnings statement, using the single-step form for the income statement portion.

Problem 5–3A. Combined income and retained earnings statement; balance sheet. The following data for Tift Co. were selected from the ledger after adjustment at December 31, the end of the current fiscal year:

Accounts payable	$ 50,700
Accounts receivable	161,100
Accumulated depreciation—office equipment	40,800
Accumulated depreciation—store equipment	75,200
Capital stock	150,000
Cash	105,600
Cost of merchandise sold	726,600
Dividends	40,000
Dividends payable	10,000
General expenses	207,300
Interest expense	18,250

Interest income

Merchandise inventory	$ 175,000
Mortgage note payable (due in 1995)	150,000
Office equipment	72,200
Prepaid insurance	10,700
Rent income	15,500
Retained earnings	156,100
Salaries payable	9,750
Sales	1,267,000
Selling expenses	233,500
Store equipment	174,800

Instructions:

(1) Prepare a combined income and retained earnings statement, using the single-step form for the income statement portion.
(2) Prepare a balance sheet in report form.

If the working papers correlating with this textbook are not used, omit Problem 5–4A.

Problem 5–4A. Completion of work sheet and preparation of financial statements for corporation. A partially completed work sheet for Feldman Inc. is presented in the working papers. All adjustments have been entered on the work sheet.

Instructions:

(1) Complete the work sheet for Feldman Inc.
(2) Prepare a multiple-step income statement.
(3) Prepare a retained earnings statement.
(4) Prepare a report form of balance sheet, assuming that the current portion of the mortgage note payable is $10,000.

Problem 5–5A. Preparation of work sheet, financial statements, and adjusting, closing, and reversing entries for sole proprietorship. The accounts and their balances in the ledger of Fischer Company on December 31 of the current year are as follows:

Cash	$ 53,160
Accounts Receivable	125,000
Merchandise Inventory	180,000
Prepaid Insurance	9,540
Store Supplies	2,500
Office Supplies	1,700
Store Equipment	134,000
Accumulated Depreciation—Store Equipment	40,300
Office Equipment	40,000
Accumulated Depreciation—Office Equipment	17,200
Accounts Payable	62,540
Salaries Payable	—
Note Payable (final payment, 1994)	105,000
F. E. Fischer, Capital	220,510
F. E. Fischer, Drawing	40,000

Income Summary..	—
Sales..	$1,080,000
Sales Returns and Allowances	12,500
Sales Discounts	6,500
Purchases	720,000
Purchases Returns and Allowances..........................	8,200
Purchases Discounts..	6,800
Transportation In	5,000
Sales Salaries Expense	86,400
Advertising Expense	30,000
Depreciation Expense—Store Equipment	—
Store Supplies Expense.......................................	—
Miscellaneous Selling Expense..............................	2,000
Office Salaries Expense	60,000
Rent Expense..	18,000
Insurance Expense	—
Depreciation Expense—Office Equipment...................	—
Office Supplies Expense......................................	—
Miscellaneous General Expense.............................	1,650
Interest Expense	12,600

The data for year-end adjustments on December 31 are as follows:

Merchandise inventory on December 31................		$220,000
Insurance expired during the year		6,200
Inventory of supplies on December 31:		
Store supplies.....................................		800
Office supplies		400
Depreciation for the year:		
Store equipment....................................		13,400
Office equipment		5,200
Salaries payable on December 31:		
Sales salaries.....................................	$2,750	
Office salaries.....................................	1,150	3,900

Instructions:

(1) Prepare a work sheet for the fiscal year ended December 31, listing all accounts in the order given.
(2) Prepare a multiple-step income statement.
(3) Prepare a statement of owner's equity.
(4) Prepare a report form of balance sheet, assuming that the current portion of the note payable is $15,000.
(5) Journalize the adjusting entries.
(6) Journalize the closing entries.
(7) Journalize the reversing entries as of January 1.

Problem 5–6A. Adjusting entries from work sheet for sole proprietorship. A portion of the work sheet of Monfort Co. for the current year ended October 31 is as follows:

Account Title	Income Statement		Balance Sheet	
	Debit	Credit	Debit	Credit
Cash..			57,900	
Accounts Receivable......................			122,500	
Merchandise Inventory			335,000	
Prepaid Rent..............................			3,000	
Prepaid Insurance			2,340	
Supplies...................................			1,380	
Store Equipment..........................			152,300	
Accumulated Depr.—Store Equipment.......				51,000
Office Equipment			44,520	
Accumulated Depr.—Office Equipment				35,000
Accounts Payable				115,600
Sales Salaries Payable....................				4,500
Mortgage Note Payable				250,000
F. G. Monfort, Capital......................				240,850
F. G. Monfort, Drawing			43,200	
Income Summary..........................	354,000	335,000		
Sales......................................		1,020,000		
Sales Returns and Allowances	12,000			
Sales Discounts	8,500			
Purchases	617,720			
Purchases Returns and Allowances.........		14,650		
Purchases Discounts......................		10,140		
Transportation In	7,230			
Sales Salaries Expense	124,000			
Depreciation Expense—Store Equipment	16,460			
Supplies Expense	960			
Miscellaneous Selling Expense.............	3,800			
Office Salaries Expense...................	70,000			
Rent Expense.............................	36,000			
Heating and Lighting Expense..............	21,750			
Insurance Expense	4,100			
Depreciation Expense—Office Equipment....	5,180			
Miscellaneous General Expense.............	2,900			
Interest Expense	30,000			
	1,314,600	1,379,790	762,140	696,950

Instructions:

(1) From the partial work sheet, determine the eight entries that appeared in the adjustments columns and present them in journal form. The only accounts affected by more than one adjusting entry were Merchandise Inventory and Income Summary. The balance in Prepaid Rent before adjustment was $39,000, representing 13 months' rent at $3,000 per month.
(2) Determine the following:
   (a) Amount of net income for the year.
   (b) Balance of the owner's capital account at the end of the year.

Problem 5–7A.   Work sheet and interim financial statements for sole proprietorship. R & R Services prepares interim statements at the end of each month and closes its accounts annually as of December 31. The trial balance at September 30 of the current year, the adjustment data needed at September 30, and the interim income statement for the eight months ended August 31 of the current year are as follows:

R & R Services
Trial Balance
September 30, 19--

Cash.	7,990	
Prepaid Insurance	1,200	
Supplies.	1,120	
Land.	30,000	
Building	79,500	
Accumulated Depreciation—Building		31,725
Equipment.	61,250	
Accumulated Depreciation—Equipment.		35,200
Accounts Payable		3,170
Richard Rundle, Capital		86,255
Richard Rundle, Drawing	13,500	
Service Revenue		80,600
Salaries and Wages Expense	31,150	
Advertising Expense	4,500	
Utilities Expense.	4,380	
Repairs Expense	1,320	
Miscellaneous Expense	1,040	
	236,950	236,950

Adjustment data at September 30:

(a) Insurance expired for the period January 1–September 30 . . . . . . $ 900
(b) Inventory of supplies on September 30.   270
(c) Depreciation of building for the period January 1–September 30. .   1,620
(d) Depreciation of equipment for the period
    January 1–September 30   5,150
(e) Accrued salaries and wages on September 30   1,820

R & R Services
Income Statement
For Eight Months Ended August 31, 19--

Service revenue		$68,500
Operating expenses:		
Salaries and wages expense.	$28,750	
Depreciation expense—equipment	4,400	
Advertising expense	3,755	
Utilities expense.	3,702	
Depreciation expense—building.	1,440	
Repairs expense	1,148	
Insurance expense.	750	
Supplies expense.	700	
Miscellaneous expense.	827	
Total operating expenses		45,472
Net income		$23,028

Instructions:

(1) Record the trial balance on a ten-column work sheet and complete the work sheet.
(2) Prepare an interim income statement for the nine months ended September 30. (For this problem, it is not necessary to distinguish between selling and general expenses.)
(3) Prepare an interim statement of owner's equity for the nine months ended September 30.
(4) Prepare an interim balance sheet as of September 30.
(5) On the basis of the income statement for the nine-month period and the income statement for the eight-month period, prepare an interim income statement for the month of September.

Problem 5–8A. Entries for transactions and corrections. The following selected transactions and errors relate to the accounts of Lanier Co. during the current fiscal year:

April 1. Betty Lanier established the business with an investment of $35,000 in cash and $12,000 in store equipment, on which there was a balance owed of $6,400. The account payable is to be recorded in the ledger of the enterprise.

May 5. Acquired land to be used as a future building site at a contract price of $60,000. The property was encumbered by a mortgage of $40,000. Paid the seller $20,000 in cash and agreed to assume the responsibility for paying the mortgage note.

July 18. Discovered that a withdrawal of $2,000 by the owner had been debited to Salary Expense.

Aug. 20. Discovered that a cash payment of $1,200 in partial payment of the account payable incurred with the equipment acquired on April 1 had been journalized and posted as a debit to Accounts Payable of $1,200 and a credit to Equipment of $1,200.

Sept. 15. Discovered that a payment of a $3,000 invoice, terms 2/10, n/30, within the discount period had been recorded as a debit to Accounts Payable of $2,940 and a credit to Cash of $2,940.

Oct. 3. Discovered that cash of $5,000, received from a customer on account, had been journalized and posted as a debit to Cash and a credit to Sales.

30. Sold to an employee for cash $400 of store supplies at cost for the employee's personal use.

Nov. 23. Discovered that a purchase of merchandise of $4,200 returned to the supplier for credit had been journalized and posted as a debit to Cash and a credit to Miscellaneous Expense.

Dec. 31. Discovered that depreciation of $850 on the equipment acquired on April 1 had been journalized and posted as a debit to Miscellaneous Expense of $580 and a credit to Equipment of $580.

Instructions:

Journalize the transactions and the corrections. When there are more than two items in an entry, present the entry in compound form.

Series B

SOLUTIONS SOFTWARE

Problem 5–1B. Preparation of multiple-step income statement and report form of balance sheet for corporation. The following selected accounts and their normal balances appear in the income statement and balance sheet columns of the work sheet of Daisy Inc. for the fiscal year ended January 31, 1988:

Cash	$ 41,000
Notes Receivable	120,000
Accounts Receivable	210,000
Merchandise Inventory, Feb. 1, 1987	125,000
Merchandise Inventory, Jan. 31, 1988	100,000
Office Supplies	5,600
Prepaid Insurance	3,400
Office Equipment	35,000
Accumulated Depreciation—Office Equipment	12,800
Store Equipment	72,000
Accumulated Depreciation—Store Equipment	24,200
Accounts Payable	45,600
Salaries Payable	2,400
Mortgage Note Payable (final payment, 1998)	56,000
Capital Stock	100,000
Retained Earnings	291,000
Dividends	15,000
Sales	1,400,000
Sales Returns and Allowances	12,100
Sales Discounts	11,900
Purchases	1,100,000
Purchases Returns and Allowances	24,600
Purchases Discounts	15,400
Transportation In	15,000
Sales Salaries Expense	123,200
Advertising Expense	22,800
Depreciation Expense—Store Equipment	6,400
Miscellaneous Selling Expense	1,600
Office Salaries Expense	31,150
Rent Expense	16,350
Depreciation Expense—Office Equipment	12,700
Insurance Expense	3,900
Office Supplies Expense	1,300
Miscellaneous General Expense	1,600
Interest Income	21,000
Interest Expense	6,000

Instructions:

(1) Prepare a multiple-step income statement.
(2) Prepare a retained earnings statement.
(3) Prepare a report form balance sheet, assuming that the current portion of the mortgage note payable is $6,000.

Problem 5–2B. Preparation of single-step income statement and combined income and retained earnings statement. Selected accounts and related amounts for Daisy Inc. for the fiscal year ended January 31, 1988, are presented in Problem 5–1B.

Instructions:

(1) Prepare a single-step income statement.
(2) Prepare a combined income and retained earnings statement, using the single-step form for the income statement portion.

Problem 5–3B. Combined income and retained earnings statement; balance sheet. The following data for Jenner Co. were selected from the ledger after adjustment at April 30, 1988, the end of the current fiscal year:

Accounts payable.	$ 68,700
Accounts receivable.	132,100
Accumulated depreciation—office equipment	30,750
Accumulated depreciation—store equipment	91,050
Capital stock	100,000
Cash.	45,300
Cost of merchandise sold.	860,400
Dividends.	20,000
Dividends payable	5,000
General expenses	108,720
Interest expense.	18,000
Merchandise inventory	280,200
Mortgage note payable (due in 1998)	150,000
Office equipment	110,800
Prepaid insurance	5,250
Rent income	19,260
Retained earnings	281,500
Salaries payable.	4,640
Sales.	1,240,700
Selling expenses	170,580
Store equipment.	240,250

Instructions:

(1) Prepare a combined income and retained earnings statement, using the single-step form for the income statement portion.
(2) Prepare a balance sheet in report form.

Problem 5–6B. Adjusting entries from work sheet for corporation. A portion of the work sheet of Shriver Inc. for the current year ended November 30 is as follows:

Account Title	Income Statement Debit	Income Statement Credit	Balance Sheet Debit	Balance Sheet Credit
Cash			62,650	
Accounts Receivable.			210,800	
Merchandise Inventory.			241,650	
Prepaid Rent			8,400	
Prepaid Insurance.			17,200	
Supplies			3,360	
Store Equipment.			87,750	
Accumulated Depr.—Store Equipment.				33,490
Office Equipment			45,600	
Accumulated Depr.—Office Equipment				15,750
Accounts Payable.				93,750
Sales Salaries Payable				4,500
Mortgage Note Payable				180,000
Capital Stock				100,000
Retained Earnings				117,160
Dividends			15,000	
Income Summary	260,500	241,650		
Sales		1,240,700		
Sales Returns and Allowances	31,400			
Sales Discounts	12,900			
Purchases.	770,650			
Purchases Returns and Allowances		18,050		
Purchases Discounts.		8,600		
Transportation In	12,100			
Sales Salaries Expense.	120,750			
Depreciation Expense—Store Equipment. . .	11,800			
Supplies Expense.	2,040			
Miscellaneous Selling Expense	1,600			
Office Salaries Expense.	50,300			
Rent Expense	33,600			
Heating and Lighting Expense.	13,420			
Insurance Expense	11,500			
Depreciation Expense—Office Equipment . .	5,180			
Miscellaneous General Expense	1,900			
Interest Expense	21,600			
	1,361,240	1,509,000	692,410	544,650

Instructions:

(1) From the partial work sheet, determine the eight entries that appeared in the adjustments columns and present them in journal form. The only accounts affected by more than one adjusting entry were Merchandise Inventory and Income Summary. The balance in Prepaid Rent before adjustment was $42,000, representing 15 months' rent at $2,800 per month.

(2) Determine the following:
   (a) Amount of net income for the year.
   (b) Balance of the retained earnings account at the end of the year.

MINI-CASE 5

VIDEO CONNECTION INC.

Your brother operates Video Connection Inc., a video tape distributorship that is in its third year of operation. Recently, Jane Crawley, the firm's accountant, resigned to enter nursing school. Before leaving, she completed the work sheet for the year ended May 31, 1988, and recorded the necessary adjusting entries. From this work sheet, your brother prepared the following financial statements:

Video Connection Inc.
Income Statement
For Year Ended May 31, 1988

Sales.		$308,200
Less cost of merchandise sold:		
Purchases	$231,600	
Net increase in merchandise inventory . . .	17,500	214,100
Gross profit		$ 94,100
Operating expenses:		
Salaries expense	$ 29,600	
Heat and lighting expense	5,750	
Insurance expense.	4,050	
Depreciation expense—building.	2,880	
Depreciation expense—office equipment. .	1,260	
Depreciation expense—store equipment .	2,160	
Supplies expense.	2,440	
Miscellaneous expense.	1,620	
Transportation in.	7,100	56,860
		$ 37,240
Selling expenses:		
Advertising expense	$ 6,940	
Transportation out	14,160	21,100
Income from operations		$ 16,140
Other income:		
Purchases discounts	$ 2,480	
Purchases returns and allowances.	3,820	
Interest income.	500	6,800
		$ 22,940
Other expenses:		
Sales returns.	$ 1,200	
Dividends.	15,000	
Interest expense.	6,000	22,200
Net income		$ 740

Video Connection Inc.
Retained Earnings Statement
For Year Ended May 31, 1988

Retained earnings June 1, 1987	$30,760
Net income for the year.........................	740
Retained earnings, May 31, 1988	$31,500

Video Connection Inc.
Balance Sheet
May 31, 1988

Assets

Cash...	$ 15,100
Merchandise inventory	62,300
Supplies.....................................	1,820
Prepaid insurance	1,680
Accounts receivable..........................	25,600
Store equipment..............................	12,800
Office equipment	6,300
Building	58,900
Land	30,000
Notes receivable.............................	5,000
Total assets.............................	$219,500

Liabilities and Stockholders' Equity

Accumulated depreciation—store equipment	$ 4,320
Accumulated depreciation—office equipment	2,520
Accumulated depreciation—building	5,760
Accounts payable.............................	13,800
Salaries payable.............................	1,600
Mortgage note payable—	
First National Bank (due in 1996)	60,000
Capital stock	100,000
Retained earnings	31,500
Total liabilities and stockholders' equity	$219,500

As part of the existing loan agreement with First National Bank, Video Connection Inc. must submit financial statements annually to the bank. In reviewing your brother's statements and supporting records before he submits the statements to the bank, you discover the following information:

Merchandise inventory:	
June 1, 1987...............................	$44,800
May 31, 1988	62,300

Salaries expense:
   Sales salaries $20,200
   Office salaries   9,400
Supplies expense:
   Store supplies . . . . $ 1,600
   Office supplies   840
Miscellaneous expense:
   Selling . . . . $ 1,020
   General   600

Instructions:

(1) Revise your brother's statements as necessary to conform to proper form for a multiple-step income statement, a retained earnings statement, and a report form of balance sheet.

(2) Prepare a projected single-step income statement based upon the following data:

Your brother is considering a proposal to increase net income by offering sales discounts of 2/15, n/30, and by shipping all merchandise FOB shipping point. Currently, no sales discounts are allowed and merchandise is shipped FOB destination. It is estimated that these credit terms will increase net sales by 10%. The ratio of cost of merchandise sold to net sales is 70% and is not expected to change under the proposed plan. All selling and general expenses are expected to remain unchanged, except for store supplies, miscellaneous selling, office supplies, and miscellaneous general expenses, which are expected to increase proportionately with increased net sales. The other income and other expense items will remain unchanged. The shipment of all merchandise FOB shipping point will eliminate all transportation out expenses.

(3) (a) Based upon the projected income statement in (2), would you recommend the implementation of the proposed changes?

(b) Describe any possible concerns you may have related to the proposed changes described in (2).

COMPREHENSIVE PROBLEM 2

SOLUTIONS
SOFTWARE

The account balances for Lyons Inc. are as follows. All balances are stated as of May 1, 1988, unless otherwise indicated.

11	Cash..	39,160
12	Accounts Receivable............................	50,220
13	Merchandise Inventory, June 1, 1987	123,900
14	Prepaid Insurance.............................	3,750
15	Store Supplies	2,550
18	Store Equipment	44,300
19	Accumulated Depreciation......................	12,600
21	Accounts Payable	38,500
22	Salaries Payable	—
31	Capital Stock	50,000
32	Retained Earnings, June 1, 1987..............	113,270
33	Dividends.....................................	4,500
34	Income Summary...............................	—
41	Sales	741,600
42	Sales Returns and Allowances.................	13,600
43	Sales Discounts..............................	5,200
51	Purchases....................................	540,000
52	Purchases Returns and Allowances	21,600
53	Purchases Discounts	5,760
54	Transportation In	5,400
55	Sales Salaries Expense.......................	74,400
56	Advertising Expense..........................	18,000
57	Depreciation Expense.........................	—
58	Store Supplies Expense.......................	—
59	Miscellaneous Selling Expense................	2,800
60	Office Salaries Expense......................	29,400
61	Rent Expense.................................	24,500
62	Insurance Expense	—
63	Miscellaneous General Expense	1,650

During May, the last month of Lyons Inc.'s fiscal year, the following transactions were completed:

May 1. Paid rent for May, $2,500.
   2. Purchased merchandise on account, terms 2/10, n/30, FOB shipping point, $22,000.
   3. Paid transportation charges on purchase of May 2, $860.
   4. Purchased merchandise on account, terms 1/10, n/30, FOB destination, $16,200.
   5. Sold merchandise on account, terms 2/10, n/30, FOB shipping point, $8,500.
   8. Received $14,900 cash from customers on account, no discount.
   10. Sold merchandise for cash, $18,300.
   11. Paid $12,800 to creditors on account, after discounts of $200 had been deducted.
   12. Paid for merchandise purchased on May 2, less discount.
   13. Received merchandise returned on sale of May 5, $1,000.
   14. Paid advertising expense for last half of May, $2,000.
   15. Received cash from sale of May 5, less return and discount.

May 18. Paid sales salaries of $1,500 and office salaries of $500.

18. Received $28,500 cash from customers on account, after discounts of $400 had been deducted.

19. Purchased merchandise for cash, $6,400.

19. Paid $13,150 to creditors on account, after discounts of $250 had been deducted.

20. Sold merchandise on account, terms 1/10, n/30, FOB shipping point, $16,000.

21. As an accommodation to the customer, paid shipping charges on sale of May 20, $600.

21. Purchased merchandise on account, terms 1/10, n/30, FOB destination, $15,000.

22. Paid for merchandise purchased on May 4.

24. Returned damaged merchandise purchased on May 21, receiving credit from the seller, $3,000.

25. Refunded cash on sales made for cash, $400.

27. Paid sales salaries of $1,200 and office salaries of $400.

28. Sold merchandise on account, terms 2/10, n/30, FOB shipping point, $24,700.

29. Purchased store supplies for cash, $350.

30. Received cash from sale of May 20, less discount, plus transportation paid on May 21.

31. Paid for purchase of May 21, less return and discount.

31. Sold merchandise on account, terms 2/10, n/30, FOB shipping point, $17,400.

31. Purchased merchandise on account, terms 1/10, n/30, FOB destination, $19,700.

Instructions:

(1) Record the balances of each of the accounts as of May 1 in the appropriate balance column of a four-column account. Write "Balance" in the item section, and place a check mark (√) in the posting reference column.

(2) Record the transactions for May in a two-column journal.

(3) Post to the ledger, extending the month-end balances to the appropriate balance columns after all posting is completed.

(4) Prepare a trial balance as of May 31 on a ten-column work sheet, listing all the accounts in the order given in the ledger. Complete the work sheet for the fiscal year ended May 31, using the following adjustment data:

(a) Merchandise inventory on May 31		$134,150
(b) Insurance expired during the year		2,250
(c) Store supplies inventory on May 31		750
(d) Depreciation for the current year		8,860
(e) Accrued salaries on May 31:		
Sales salaries	$400	
Office salaries	140	540

(5) Prepare a multiple-step income statement, a retained earnings statement, and a report form of balance sheet.

(6) Journalize and post the adjusting entries.
(7) Journalize and post the closing entries. Indicate closed accounts by inserting a line in both balance columns opposite the closing entry. Insert the new balance in the retained earnings account.
(8) Prepare a post-closing trial balance.
(9) Journalize and post any reversing entries as of June 1, 1988.

DEFERRALS AND ACCRUALS

Chapter 6

CHAPTER OBJECTIVES

- Identify and describe common classifications of deferrals and accruals.

- Describe and illustrate two alternative systems for accounting for prepaid expenses (deferrals).

- Describe and illustrate two alternative systems for accounting for unearned revenues (deferrals).

- Describe and illustrate the accounting for accrued liabilities (accrued expenses).

- Describe and illustrate the accounting for accrued assets (accrued revenues).

Data on revenues earned and expenses incurred by a business enterprise are periodically assembled and reported in an income statement. Such statements always cover a definite period of time, such as a specific month, quarter, half year, or year. The periodic matching of revenues and expenses yields not only the amount of net income or net loss but also the amounts for assets, liabilities, and owner's equity to be reported in the balance sheet as of the end of the period.

When cash is received for revenue within the same period that the revenue is earned, there is no question about the period to which the revenue relates. Similarly, when an expense is paid during the period in which the benefits from incurring the expense are received, there can be no doubt concerning the period to which the expense should be allocated. Problems of allocation occur when there are differences in the time between the earning of revenues or the incurrence of expenses and the recognition of their respective effects on assets and equities.

The use of adjusting entries helps to allocate expenses to appropriate periods, as was demonstrated in earlier chapters. Deferrals and accruals of some expenses, including insurance, supplies, rent, and wages, have been described and illustrated. This chapter further discusses deferrals and accruals of expenses as well as revenues. The underlying purpose of their recognition is to match revenues and expenses in order to determine net income for a specific period of time and the assets and equities as of the last day of that period.

CLASSIFICATION AND TERMINOLOGY

Many kinds of revenues and expenses may require deferral or accrual in certain instances. When such is the case, they are recorded as adjusting entries on the work sheet used in preparing financial statements. If the work sheet is for the fiscal year, the adjustments are also journalized and posted to the ledger. For interim statements, the adjustments may appear only on the work sheet.

Every adjusting entry affects both a balance sheet account and an income statement account. To illustrate, assume that the effect of the credit portion of a particular adjusting entry is to increase a liability account (balance sheet). It follows that the effect of the debit portion of the entry will be either (1) to increase an expense account (income statement) or (2) to decrease a revenue account (income statement). In no case will an adjustment affect only an asset and a liability (both balance sheet) or only an expense and a revenue (both income statement).

Deferral   *Prepaid Insurance*

A **deferral** is a delay of the recognition of an expense already paid or of a revenue already received.

Deferred expenses expected to benefit a short period of time are listed on the balance sheet among the current assets, where they are called **prepaid expenses**. Long-term prepayments that can be charged to the operations of several years are presented on the balance sheet in a section called **deferred charges**.

Deferred revenues may be listed on the balance sheet as a current liability, where they are called **unearned revenues** or **revenues received in advance**. If a long period of time is involved, they are presented on the balance sheet in a section called **deferred credits**.

Accrual   *Wages Payable, Fees Earned*

An **accrual** is an expense that has not been paid or a revenue that has not been received. Unrecorded accruals must be recognized before financial statements are prepared.

Accrued expenses may also be described on the balance sheet as **accrued liabilities**, or reference to the accrual may be omitted from the title, as in "Wages payable." The liabilities for accrued expenses are ordinarily due within a year and are listed as current liabilities.

Accrued revenues may also be described on the balance sheet as **accrued assets**, or reference to the accrual may be omitted from the title, as in "Fees receivable." The amounts receivable for accrued revenues are usually due within a short time and are classified as current assets.

PREPAID EXPENSES (DEFERRALS)

Prepaid expenses are the costs of goods and services that have been purchased but not used at the end of the accounting period. The portion of the asset that has been used during the period has become an expense; the remainder will not become an expense until some time in the future. Prepaid expenses include such items as prepaid insurance, prepaid rent, prepaid advertising, prepaid interest, and various kinds of supplies.

At the time an expense is prepaid, it may be debited to either an asset account or an expense account. The two alternative systems are explained and illustrated in the paragraphs that follow. In any particular situation, either alternative may be elected. The only difference between the systems is in the procedure used. Their effect on the financial statements is the same.

Prepaid Expenses Recorded Initially as Assets

Insurance premiums or other services or supplies that are used may be debited to asset accounts when purchased, even though all or a part of them are expected to be consumed during the accounting period. The amount actually used is then determined at the end of the period and the accounts adjusted accordingly.

To illustrate, assume that the prepaid insurance account has a balance of $2,034 at the end of the year. This amount represents the unexpired insurance at the beginning of the year plus the total of premiums on policies purchased during the year. Assume further that $906 of insurance premiums have expired during the year. The adjusting entry to record the $906 decrease of the asset and the corresponding increase in expense is as follows:

	Adjusting Entry			
Dec. 31	Insurance Expense..................	716	906	
	Prepaid Insurance.................	118		906

After this entry has been posted, the two accounts affected appear as follows:

ACCOUNT INSURANCE EXPENSE ACCOUNT NO. 716

Date		Item	Post. Ref.	Debit	Credit	Balance	
						Debit	Credit
1987 Dec.	31	Adjusting	25	906		906	

ADJUSTMENT FOR PREPAID EXPENSE RECORDED AS ASSET

ACCOUNT PREPAID INSURANCE ACCOUNT NO. 118

Date		Item	Post. Ref.	Debit	Credit	Balance	
						Debit	Credit
1987 Jan.	1	Balance	✓	1,250		1,250	
Mar.	18		6	225		1,475	
Aug.	26		16	379		1,854	
Nov.	11		20	180		2,034	
Dec.	31	Adjusting	25		906	1,128	

After the $906 of expired insurance is transferred to the expense account, the balance of $1,128 in Prepaid Insurance represents the cost of premiums on various policies that apply to future periods. The $906 expense appears on the income statement for the period and the $1,128 asset appears on the balance sheet as of the end of the period.

Prepaid Expenses Recorded Initially as Expenses *requires reversing entry*

Instead of being debited to an asset account, prepaid expenses may be debited to an expense account at the time of the expenditure, even though all or a part of the prepayment is expected to be unused at the end of the accounting period. The amount actually unused is then determined at the end of the period and the accounts are adjusted accordingly.

To illustrate this alternative system, assume that the insurance expense account has a balance of $2,034 at the end of the year. This amount represents the unexpired insurance at the beginning of the year plus the total premiums on policies purchased during the year. Assume further that $1,128 of the insurance premiums applies to future periods. The adjusting entry to record the $1,128 decrease of the expense and the corresponding increase in the asset is as follows:

	Adjusting Entry			
Dec. 31	Prepaid Insurance....................	118	1,128	
	Insurance Expense................	716		1,128

After this entry has been posted, the two accounts affected appear as follows:

ADJUSTMENT FOR PREPAID EXPENSE RECORDED AS EXPENSE

ACCOUNT PREPAID INSURANCE   ACCOUNT NO. 118

Date	Item	Post. Ref.	Debit	Credit	Balance Debit	Balance Credit
1987						
Dec. 31	Adjusting	25	1,128		1,128	

ACCOUNT INSURANCE EXPENSE   ACCOUNT NO. 716

Date	Item	Post. Ref.	Debit	Credit	Balance Debit	Balance Credit
1987						
Jan. 1	Reversing	1	1,250		1,250	
Mar. 18		6	225		1,475	
Aug. 26		16	379		1,854	
Nov. 11		20	180		2,034	
Dec. 31	Adjusting	25		1,128	906	

After the $1,128 of unexpired insurance is transferred to the asset account, the balance of $906 in Insurance Expense represents the cost of premiums on various policies that has expired during the year. The $1,128 asset appears on the balance sheet at the end of the period and the $906 expense appears on the income statement for the period.

In future periods, the unexpired insurance becomes insurance expense. Therefore, some provision must be made in future periods to transfer the expiration of the insurance from the asset account to the expense account. Although it would be possible to transfer daily the cost of the expiration, a more efficient way of assuring proper allocations in future periods is to add **reversing entries** to the summarizing procedures. Their use eliminates the need to refer to earlier adjustment data to record the expiration of insurance. It also lessens the possibilities of error. The effect of the reversing entry is to transfer the entire balance of the asset account to the expense account immediately after the temporary accounts have been closed for the period. Continuing with the illustration, the reversing entry is as follows:

	Reversing Entry			
Jan. 1	Insurance Expense..................	716	1,128	
	Prepaid Insurance................	118		1,128

After the reversing entry has been posted to the two accounts, they will appear as follows:

ACCOUNT PREPAID INSURANCE   ACCOUNT NO. 118

Date		Item	Post. Ref.	Debit	Credit	Balance Debit	Balance Credit
1987							
Dec.	31	Adjusting	25	1,128		1,128	
1988							
Jan.	1	Reversing	26		1,128	—	—

ACCOUNT INSURANCE EXPENSE   ACCOUNT NO. 716

Date		Item	Post. Ref.	Debit	Credit	Balance Debit	Balance Credit
1987							
Jan.	1	Reversing	1	1,250		1,250	
Mar.	18		6	225		1,475	
Aug.	26		16	379		1,854	
Nov.	11		20	180		2,034	
Dec.	31	Adjusting	25		1,128	906	
	31	Closing	25		906	—	
1988							
Jan.	1	Reversing	26	1,128		1,128	

ADJUSTMENT AND REVERSAL FOR PREPAID EXPENSE RECORDED AS EXPENSE

The reversing entry does not change the basic nature of the $1,128, only its location in the ledger. It is unexpired insurance on January 1, just as it was unexpired insurance on December 31.

After the reversing entry has been posted, the unexpired insurance at January 1 is in the expense account. Furthermore, since past expenditures were debited to the expense account, all expenditures for insurance policies in force during the following year may also be recorded in the expense account. At the end of the following year, the adjusting and reversing procedures would be repeated in the manner illustrated.

Comparison of the Two Systems

The basic features of the two systems of recording prepaid expenses, including the related entries at the end of the accounting period, can be summarized as follows, using the data in the preceding illustration:

SYSTEMS OF RECORDING PREPAID EXPENSES

Prepaid Expense **Recorded Initially as Asset**	Prepaid Expense **Recorded Initially as Expense**

Initial entries (to record initial expenditures):
Prepaid Insurance.......... 225
   Cash 225
	Initial entries (to record initial expenditures):
	Insurance Expense.......... 225
	   Cash 225

Prepaid Insurance.......... 180
   Cash 180
	Insurance Expense.......... 180
	   Cash 180

Adjusting entry (to transfer amount **used** to appropriate **expense** account):
Insurance Expense.......... 906
   Prepaid Insurance......... 906
	Adjusting entry (to transfer amount **unused** to the appropriate **asset** account):
	Prepaid Insurance.......... 1,128
	   Insurance Expense........ 1,128

Closing entry (to close statement accounts with debit balances):
Income Summary XXXXXX
   Purchases................ XXXXXX
 	
Insurance Expense....... 906
	Closing entry (to close income statement accounts with debit balances):
	Income Summary XXXXXX
	   Purchases................ XXXXXX
	
	Insurance Expense....... 906

Reversing entry (**not required** because amount prepaid at beginning of new period is in the asset account None.	Reversing entry (to transfer amount **unused** back to **expense** account for the beginning of the new period): Insurance Expense.......... 1,128 Prepaid Insurance......... 1,128

NOTE: Both methods will result in the same account balances.

Either of the two systems may be used for all of the prepaid expenses of an enterprise, or one system may be used for prepayment of some kinds of expenses and the other system for other kinds. Initial debits to the asset account seem to be logical for prepayments of insurance, which are usually for periods of from one to three years. On the other hand, interest charges on notes payable are usually for short periods. Some charges may be recorded when a note is issued; other charges may be recorded when a note is paid; and few, if any, of the debits for interest may require adjustment at the end of the period. It therefore seems logical to record all interest charges initially by debiting the expense account rather than the asset account.[1]

As was noted earlier, the amounts reported as expenses in the income statement and as assets on the balance sheet will not be affected by the system used. To avoid confusion, the system adopted by an enterprise for each kind of prepaid expense should be followed consistently from year to year.

UNEARNED REVENUES (DEFERRALS)

Revenue received during a particular period may be only partly earned by the end of the period. Items of revenue that are received in advance represent a liability that may be termed **unearned revenue**. The portion of the liability that is discharged during the period through delivery of goods or services has been earned; the remainder will be earned in the future. For example, magazine publishers usually receive advance payment for subscriptions covering periods ranging from a few months to a number of years. At the end of an accounting period, that portion of the receipts which is related to future periods has not been earned and should, therefore, appear in the balance sheet as a liability.

Other examples of unearned revenue are rent received in advance on property owned, premiums received in advance by an insurance company, tuition received in advance by a school, an annual retainer fee received in advance by an attorney, and amounts received in advance by an advertising firm for advertising services to be rendered in the future.

By accepting advance payment for a good or service, a business commits itself to furnish the good or the service at some future time. At the end of the accounting period, if some portion of the good or the service has been furnished, part of the revenue has been earned. The earned portion appears in the income statement. The unearned portion represents a liability of the business to furnish the good or the service in a future period and is reported in the balance sheet as a liability. As in the case of prepaid expenses, two systems of accounting are explained and illustrated.

Unearned Revenues Recorded Initially as Liabilities

When revenue is received in advance, it may be credited to a liability account. To illustrate, assume that on October 1 a business rents a portion of

---

[1]Notes payable and related interest charges are discussed in more detail in Chapter 12.

its building for a period of one year, receiving $7,200 in payment for the entire term of the lease. Assume also that the transaction was originally recorded by a debit to Cash and a credit to the liability account Unearned Rent. On December 31, the end of the fiscal year, one fourth of the amount has been earned and three fourths of the amount remains a liability. The entry to record the revenue and reduce the liability appears as follows:

	Adjusting Entry			
Dec. 31	Unearned Rent	218	1,800	
	Rent Income...............	812		1,800

After this entry has been posted, the unearned rent account and the rent income account appear as follows:

ADJUSTMENT FOR UNEARNED REVENUE RECORDED AS LIABILITY

ACCOUNT UNEARNED RENT   ACCOUNT NO. 218

| | | | Post. | | | Balance | |
Date		Item	Ref.	Debit	Credit	Debit	Credit
1987							
Oct.	1		18		7,200		7,200
Dec.	31	Adjusting	25	1,800			5,400

ACCOUNT RENT INCOME   ACCOUNT NO. 812

| | | | Post. | | | Balance | |
Date		Item	Ref.	Debit	Credit	Debit	Credit
1987							
Dec.	31	Adjusting	25		1,800		1,800

After the amount earned, $1,800, is transferred to Rent Income, the balance of $5,400 remaining in Unearned Rent is a liability to render a service in the future. It appears as a current liability in the balance sheet because the service is to be rendered within the next accounting period. Rent Income is reported in the Other Income section of the income statement.

Unearned Revenues Recorded Initially as Revenues

Instead of being credited to a liability account, unearned revenue may be credited to a revenue account as the cash is received. To illustrate this alternative, assume the same facts as in the preceding illustration, except that the transaction was originally recorded on October 1 by a debit to Cash and a credit to Rent Income. On December 31, the end of the fiscal year, three fourths of the balance in Rent Income is still unearned and the remaining one fourth has been earned. The entry to record the transfer to the liability account appears as follows:

	Adjusting Entry			
Dec. 31	Rent Income........................	812	5,400	
	Unearned Rent	218		5,400

After this entry has been posted, the unearned rent account and the rent income account appear as follows:

ACCOUNT UNEARNED RENT   ACCOUNT NO. 218

Date		Item	Post. Ref.	Debit	Credit	Balance Debit	Balance Credit
1987							
Dec.	31	Adjusting	25		5,400		5,400

ACCOUNT RENT INCOME   ACCOUNT NO. 812

Date		Item	Post. Ref.	Debit	Credit	Balance Debit	Balance Credit
1987							
Oct.	1		18		7,200		7,200
Dec.	31	Adjusting	25	5,400			1,800

ADJUSTMENT FOR UNEARNED REVENUE RECORDED AS REVENUE

The unearned rent of $5,400 is listed in the current liability section of the balance sheet, and the rent income of $1,800 is reported in the income statement.

The $5,400 of unearned rent at the end of the year will be earned during the following year. If it is transferred to the income account by a reversing entry immediately after the accounts are closed, no further action will be needed either month by month or at the end of the nine-month period. Furthermore, since the $7,200 rent was credited initially to the income account, all such payments received in the following year may also be treated the same way. If a reversing entry is not made, there may be balances in both the liability account and the income account at the end of the following year. This would require analysis of both accounts and possibly cause confusion. The reversing entry for the unearned rent, which is the exact reverse of the adjusting entry, is as follows:

	Reversing Entry			
Jan. 1	Unearned Rent	218	5,400	
	Rent Income......................	812		5,400

After the foregoing entry is posted to the two accounts, they will appear as follows:

ADJUSTMENT AND REVERSAL FOR UNEARNED REVENUE RECORDED AS REVENUE

ACCOUNT UNEARNED RENT   ACCOUNT NO. 218

Date		Item	Post. Ref.	Debit	Credit	Balance Debit	Balance Credit
1987 Dec.	31	Adjusting	25		5,400		5,400
1988 Jan.	1	Reversing	26	5,400		—	—

ACCOUNT RENT INCOME   ACCOUNT NO. 812

Date		Item	Post. Ref.	Debit	Credit	Balance Debit	Balance Credit
1987 Oct.	1		18		7,200		7,200
Dec.	31	Adjusting	25	5,400			1,800
	31	Closing	25	1,800		—	—
1988 Jan.	1	Reversing	26		5,400		5,400

At the beginning of the new fiscal year, there is a credit balance of $5,400 in Rent Income. Although the balance is in reality a liability at this time, it will become revenue before the end of the year. Whenever a revenue account needs adjustment for an unearned amount at the end of a period, the adjusting entry should be reversed after the accounts have been closed.

Comparison of the Two Systems

The basic features of the two systems of recording unearned revenue, including the related entries at the end of the accounting period, can be summarized as follows, using the data in the preceding illustration:

Unearned Revenue **Recorded Initially as Liability**		Unearned Revenue **Recorded Initially as Revenue**	
Initial entries (to record initial receipt):		Initial entries (to record initial receipt):	
Cash	7,200	Cash	7,200
Unearned Rent	7,200	Rent Income	7,200
Adjusting entry (to transfer amount **earned** to appropriate **revenue** account):		Adjusting entry (to transfer amount **unearned** to appropriate **liability** account):	
Unearned Rent	1,800	Rent Income	5,400
Rent Income	1,800	Unearned Rent	5,400
Closing entry (to close income statement accounts with credit balances):		Closing entry (to close income statement accounts with credit balances):	
Sales	XXXXXX	Sales	XXXXXX
~~	~~~	~~~	~~~
Rent Income	1,800	Rent Income	1,800
Income Summary	XXXXXX	Income Summary	XXXXXX
Reversing entry (**not required** because amount unearned at beginning of new period is in the liability account):		Reversing entry (to transfer amount **unearned** back to **revenue** account for the beginning of the new period):	
None		Unearned Rent	5,400
		Rent Income	5,400

NOTE: Both methods will result in the same account balances.

Either of the systems may be used for all revenues received in advance, or the first system may be used for advance receipts of some kinds of revenue and the second system for other kinds. The results obtained are the same under both systems, but to avoid confusion the system used should be followed consistently from year to year.

ACCRUED LIABILITIES (ACCRUED EXPENSES) *Are paid*

Some expenses accrue from day to day but are usually recorded only when they are paid. Examples are salaries paid to employees and interest paid on notes payable. The amounts of such accrued but unpaid items at the end of the fiscal period are both an expense and a liability. It is for this reason that such accruals are called **accrued liabilities** or **accrued expenses**.

To illustrate the adjusting entry for an accrued liability, assume that on December 31, the end of the fiscal year, the salary expense account has a debit balance of $72,800. During the year, salaries have been paid each Friday for the five-day week then ended. For this particular fiscal year, December 31 falls on Wednesday. The records of the business show that the salary accrued for these last three days of the year amounts to $940. The entry to record the additional expense and the liability is as follows:

	Adjusting Entry					
Dec. 31	Salary Expense.....................	611	940			
	Salaries Payable.................	214			940	

After the adjusting entry has been posted to the two accounts, they appear as follows:

ACCOUNT SALARIES PAYABLE   ACCOUNT NO. 214

Date	Item	Post. Ref.	Debit	Credit	Balance Debit	Balance Credit
1987 Dec. 31	Adjusting	25		940		940

ACCOUNT SALARY EXPENSE   ACCOUNT NO. 611

Date	Item	Post. Ref.	Debit	Credit	Balance Debit	Balance Credit
1987						
Dec. 26		23	1,425		72,800	
31	Adjusting	25	940		73,740	

The accrued salaries of $940 recorded in Salaries Payable will appear in the balance sheet of December 31 as a current liability. The balance of $73,740 now recorded in Salary Expense will appear in the income statement for the year ended December 31.

When the weekly salaries are paid on January 2 of the following year, part of the payment will discharge the liability of $940 and the remainder will represent salary expense incurred in January. To avoid the need of analyzing the payment, a reversing entry is made at the beginning of the new year. The effect of the entry, which is illustrated as follows, is to transfer the credit balance in the salaries payable account to the credit side of the salary expense account.

	Reversing Entry					
Jan. 1	Salaries Payable.....................	214	940			
	Salary Expense.................	611			940	

What Happened to the Accrued Liabilities?

The accounting systems and procedures for recording accruals and the related adjusting entries for one company are not always applicable to another company. This was never better illustrated than in a court case involving the Yale Express and Republic Carloading companies.

Yale Express was a New York-based short-haul trucker specializing in carrying less than truckload freight to points along the east coast within 500 miles of New York. Yale Express kept its books on a semi-cash basis and recorded all adjusting entries for accrued liabilities based upon a cutoff period ending twenty days into the following period. Any bills for unpaid expenses related to the prior accounting period received during this twenty-day period would be recorded through the use of adjusting entries. Over the years, this procedure had proven adequate for preparing the financial statements of Yale Express, since few bills relating to a prior period were received beyond the twenty-day cutoff point.

Republic Carloading was basically a sales organization that held an ICC certificate authorizing it to serve as a freight forwarder in all fifty states. As a freight forwarder, Republic moved little freight itself, but contracted for others to actually move the freight. Republic kept its books on a full accrual basis and recorded adjusting entries for accrued liabilities at the end of its fiscal year for anticipated expenses and transportation bills that often arrived months into the new accounting period. These accrued liabilities were recorded as debits to various expense accounts and credits to Accounts Payable and other liability accounts.

When Yale Express acquired Republic in a merger, the administrative vice-president of Yale Express decided to use Yale Express' semi-cash, twenty-day cutoff procedure for accrued liabilities for Republic. Later it was discovered that millions of dollars of accrued liabilities had not been recorded by Republic. These accrued liabilities, along with other miscellaneous errors, misstated the financial statements of the combined companies, such that an original profit of $1.14 million was restated to a loss of $1.88 million. As a result of the misstated financial statements, several lawsuits were filed by the stockholders and creditors against the management and auditor for Yale Express.

Source: Adapted from Richard J. Whalen, "The Big Skid at Yale Express," *Fortune* (November, 1965).

After the reversing entry has been posted, the salaries payable account and the salary expense account appear as follows:

ACCOUNT SALARIES PAYABLE   ACCOUNT NO. 214

| Date | | Item | Post. Ref. | Debit | Credit | Balance | |
						Debit	Credit
1987 Dec.	31	Adjusting	25		940		940
1988 Jan.	1	Reversing	26	940		—	—

ACCOUNT SALARY EXPENSE   ACCOUNT NO. 611

| Date | | Item | Post. Ref. | Debit | Credit | Balance | |
						Debit	Credit
1987							

Date		Item	Post. Ref.	Debit	Credit	Debit	Credit
Dec.	26		23	1,425		72,800	
	31	Adjusting	25	940		73,740	
	31	Closing	25		73,740	—	—
1988 Jan	1	Reversing	26		940		940

The liability for salaries on December 31 now appears as a credit in Salary Expense. Assuming that the salaries paid on Friday, January 2, amount to $1,470, the debit to Salary Expense will automatically record the discharge of the liability of $940 and an expense of $530 ($1,470 − $940) for the new period.

The discussion of the treatment of accrued salary expense is illustrative of the method of handling accrued liabilities in general. If, in addition to accrued salaries, there are other accrued liabilities at the end of a fiscal period, separate liability accounts may be set up for each type. When there are many accrued liability items, however, a single account entitled Accrued Payables or Accrued Liabilities may be used. All accrued liabilities may then be recorded as credits to this account instead of to separate accounts.

ACCRUED ASSETS (ACCRUED REVENUES)

All assets belonging to the business at the end of an accounting period and all revenues earned during the period should be recorded in the ledger. But during a fiscal period it is common to record some types of revenue only as the cash is received; consequently, at the end of the period there may be items of revenue that have not been recorded. In such cases, the amount of the accrued revenue must be recorded by debiting an asset account and crediting a revenue account. Because of the dual nature of such accruals, they are called **accrued assets** or **accrued revenues**.

To illustrate the adjusting entry for an accrued asset, assume that on December 31, the end of the fiscal year, the fees earned account has a credit balance of $50,500. Assume further that on the same date unbilled services have been performed for a client for $8,050. The entry to record this increase in the amount due from clients and the additional revenue earned is as follows:

	Adjusting Entry			
Dec. 31	Fees Receivable	114	8,050	
	Fees Earned	401		8,050

After this entry has been posted, the fees receivable account and the fees earned account appear as follows:

ACCOUNT FEES RECEIVABLE ACCOUNT NO. 114

Date		Item	Post. Ref.	Debit	Credit	Balance	
						Debit	Credit
1987 Dec.	31	Adjusting	25	8,050		8,050	

ACCOUNT FEES EARNED ACCOUNT NO. 401

Date		Item	Post. Ref.	Debit	Credit	Balance	
						Debit	Credit
1987							
Dec.	12		22		4,750		50,500
	31	Adjusting	25		8,050		58,550

ADJUSTMENT FOR ACCRUED ASSET

The accrued fees of $8,050 recorded in Fees Receivable will appear in the balance sheet of December 31 as a current asset. The credit balance of $58,550 in Fees Earned will appear in the income statement for the year ended December 31.

In the following year, the services for the client, for which the accrued fees of $8,050 were recorded at the end of the year, will be completed and the client billed. Part of the fee collected will cause a reduction in fees receivable and the remainder will represent revenue for the new year. To avoid the inconvenience of analyzing each receipt of fees in the new year, a reversing entry is made immediately after the accounts are closed. The effect of the entry, which is illustrated as follows, is to transfer the debit balance in the fees receivable account to the debit side of the fees earned account.

	Reversing Entry				
Jan. 1	Fees Earned......................	401	8,050		
	Fees Receivable	114		8,050	

After this entry has been posted, the fees receivable account and the fees earned account appear as follows:

ADJUSTMENT
AND
REVERSAL
FOR
ACCRUED
ASSET

ACCOUNT FEES RECEIVABLE   ACCOUNT NO. 114

Date		Item	Post. Ref.	Debit	Credit	Balance Debit	Balance Credit
1987 Dec.	31	Adjusting	25	8,050		8,050	
1988 Jan.	1	Reversing	26		8,050	—	—

ACCOUNT FEES EARNED   ACCOUNT NO. 401

Date		Item	Post. Ref.	Debit	Credit	Balance Debit	Balance Credit
1987							
Dec.	12		22		4,750		50,500
	31	Adjusting	25		8,050		58,550
	31	Closing	25	58,550		—	—
1988 Jan.	1	Reversing	26	8,050		8,050	

The accrual of fees on December 31, $8,050, now appears as a debit in Fees Earned. At the time the client is billed in the following year, the entire amount of the billing will be credited to Fees Earned. This credit will in part represent a reduction in the receivable and in part a revenue of the following period. To illustrate, assume that the client with the unbilled fees of $8,050 on December 31 is billed for $10,000 in the following year. The total amount of fees billed, $10,000, will be credited to Fees Earned, regardless of the amount representing the collection of the receivable and the amount representing revenue of the new period. The effect of the $10,000 credit to Fees Earned is to automatically adjust Fees Earned, so that the balance of the account, $1,950 ($10,000 credit less $8,050 debit), represents revenue for the new year.

The treatment of accrued fees illustrates the method of handling accrued assets in general. If there are other accrued assets at the end of a fiscal period, separate accounts may be set up. Each of these accounts will be similar to the account with fees receivable. When such items are numerous, a single account entitled Accrued Receivables or Accrued Assets may be used. All accrued assets may then be recorded as debits to this account.

SUMMARY OF USE OF REVERSING ENTRIES

As discussed in Chapter 5, the use of reversing entries is optional. However, the use of reversing entries generally simplifies the analysis of transactions and reduces the likelihood of errors in the subsequent recording of transactions. Thus, in this text, it will be assumed that the necessary reversing entries will be prepared when applicable. The following table summarizes those situations in which reversing entries will be prepared:

Reversing entries should be prepared:

■ when a prepaid expense has been initially recorded as an expense;
■ when an unearned revenue has been initially recorded as a revenue;
■ when an accrued liability has been recorded;
■ when an accrued asset has been recorded.

REVERSING
ENTRY
SUMMARY

CHAPTER REVIEW

KEY POINTS

1. Classification and Terminology.

A deferral is a delay of the recognition of an expense already paid or a revenue already received. Deferred expenses expected to benefit a short period of time are called prepaid expenses, while long-term prepayments are called deferred charges. Deferred revenues are called unearned revenues. Unearned revenues to be earned over a short period of time are current liabilities, while long-term deferred revenues are classified as deferred credits.

An accrual is an expense that has not been paid or a revenue that has not been received. Accrued expenses may be referred to as accrued liabilities, and accrued revenues may be called accrued assets.

2. Prepaid Expenses (Deferrals).

Prepaid expenses are the costs of goods and services that have been purchased but not used. The portion of the asset that has been used during the period has become an expense; the remainder will not become an expense until some time in the future. At the time an expense is prepaid, it may be debited to either an asset account or an expense account. Either alternative may be elected, since the effect on the financial statements, after adjusting entries, is the same. If a prepaid expense is initially recorded as an asset, no reversing entry is required. If, however, the prepaid expense is recorded initially as an expense, a reversing entry would be applicable.

3. Unearned Revenues (Deferrals).

Items of revenue that are received in advance represent a liability that may be termed unearned revenue. The portion of the liability that is discharged during the period, through the delivery of goods or services, has been earned; the remainder will be earned in the future. When revenue is received in advance, it may be credited to either a liability account or a revenue account. Either alternative may be used, since the effect on the financial statements, after adjusting entries, is the same. If unearned revenue is initially recorded as a liability, no reversing entry is required. If the unearned revenue is recorded initially as revenue, a reversing entry would be applicable.

4. Accrued Liabilities (Accrued Expenses).

Some expenses accrue from day to day but are usually recorded only when paid. The amounts of such accrued but unpaid items at the end of the fiscal period are both an expense and a liability. It is for this reason that accruals are called accrued liabilities or accrued expenses. At the end of the accounting period, the amount of the accrued liability must be recorded by an adjusting entry that debits an expense account and credits a liability account. Reversing entries are applicable for accrued liabilities.

5. Accrued Assets (Accrued Revenues).

All assets belonging to the business at the end of an accounting period and all revenues earned during the period should be recorded in the ledger. But during a fiscal period it is common to record some types of revenue only as cash is received; consequently, at the end of the period there may be items of revenue that have not been recorded. In such cases, the amount of the accrued revenue must be recorded by an adjusting entry which debits an asset account and credits a revenue account. Reversing entries are applicable for accrued assets.

KEY TERMS

deferral 250
accrual 250
prepaid expenses 250
reversing entry 253
unearned revenues 255

accrued liabilities 259
accrued expenses 259
accrued assets 263
accrued revenue 263

SELF-EXAMINATION QUESTIONS
Answers in Appendix B.

1. If the effect of the debit portion of a specific adjusting entry is to increase an asset account, the effect of the credit portion of the entry would be to:
    A. decrease an asset account
    B. increase a liability account
    C. decrease a liability account
    D. decrease an expense account

2. Deferred expenses expected to benefit a relatively short period of time are listed on the balance sheet under:
    A. current assets
    B. plant assets
    C. current liabilities
    D. long-term liabilities

3. The balance in Unearned Rent at the end of a period represents:
    A. an asset
    B. a liability
    C. a revenue
    D. an expense

4. The office supplies inventory at the beginning of the year was $660, purchases of office supplies during the year were $2,250, and inventory at the end of the year was $595. If office supplies are initially recorded as an expense, the adjusting entry at the end of the year would be:
   A. Dr. Office Supplies, $595; Cr. Office Supplies Expense, $595
   B. Dr. Office Supplies, $2,315; Cr. Office Supplies Expense, $2,315
   C. Dr. Office Supplies Expense, $595; Cr. Office Supplies, $595
   D. Dr. Office Supplies Expense, $2,315; Cr. Office Supplies, $2,315

5. The salary expense account has a credit balance of $500 on January 1, the beginning of the fiscal year, after reversing entries have been posted but before any transactions have occurred. The balance represents:
   A. an asset   C. a revenue
   B. a liability   D. an expense

ILLUSTRATIVE PROBLEM

From a review of the ledger (before adjustment) and other records of Epstein Company, the following data were obtained for the current fiscal year ending May 31:

(a) As insurance premiums are paid, they have been debited to Prepaid Insurance, which has a balance of $4,120 at May 31. An analysis of the insurance policies and premiums indicates that $2,940 of the insurance has expired during the year.

(b) Rent Income has a balance at May 31 of $20,320, composed of the following:
   (1) the beginning balance at June 1 of $7,420, representing rent prepaid for six months;
   (2) a credit of $12,900, representing advance payment of rent for twelve months beginning December 1.

(c) Sales salaries are uniformly $16,800 for a six-day workweek ending on Saturday. The last payday of the year was Saturday, May 27.

(d) Unbilled service fees total $13,600 at May 31.

Instructions:

1. Journalize the adjusting entries as of May 31 of the current fiscal year, identifying each entry by letter.

2. Journalize the reversing entries that should be made on June 1 of the succeeding fiscal year, identifying each entry by the corresponding letter used in (1).

SOLUTION

(1)

(a) Insurance Expense	2,940	
Prepaid Insurance		2,940
(b) Rent Income	6,450	
Unearned Rent		6,450
(c) Sales Salaries Expense	8,400	
Sales Salaries Payable		8,400
(d) Service Fees Receivable	13,600	
Service Fee Revenue		13,600

(2)

(b) Unearned Rent	6,450	
Rent Income		6,450
(c) Sales Salaries Payable	8,400	
Sales Salaries Expense		8,400
(d) Service Fee Revenue	13,600	
Service Fees Receivable		13,600

DISCUSSION QUESTIONS

1. What term is used to describe a delay of the recognition of an expense already paid or of a revenue already received?

2. What term is used to describe an expense that has not been paid or a revenue that has not been received?

3. Where would (a) accrued expenses and (b) accrued revenues, both due within a year, appear on the balance sheet?

4. Describe the effect of the debit portion of a specific adjusting entry when the effect of the credit portion decreases an asset account.

5. A purchase of office supplies can be debited to one of two types of accounts. Name the two types of accounts that can be debited.

6. (a) Will a business enterprise almost always have prepaid property and casualty insurance at the end of each fiscal year? Explain.
   (b) Will a business enterprise that occasionally places advertisements in the local newspaper, for which it makes advance payments, always have prepaid advertising at the end of each fiscal year? Explain.
   (c) Would it be logical to record prepayments of the type referred to in (a) as assets and prepayments of the type referred to in (b) as expenses? Discuss.

7. On September 30, the end of its fiscal year, an enterprise owed salaries of $11,200 for an incomplete payroll period. On the first payday in October, salaries of $18,600 are paid. (a) Is the $11,200 a deferral or an accrual as of September 30? (b) Which of the following types of accounts will be affected by the related adjusting entry: (1) asset, (2) liability, (3) revenue, (4) expense? (c) How much of the $18,600 salary payment should be allocated to October?

8. On January 2, an enterprise receives $18,600 from a tenant as rent for the current calendar year. The fiscal year of the enterprise is from April 1 to March 31. (a) Will the enterprise's adjusting entry for the rent as of March 31 of the current year be a deferral or an accrual? (b) Which of the following types of accounts will be affected by the adjusting entry as of March 31: (1) asset, (2) liability, (3) revenue, (4) expense? (c) How much of the $18,600 rent should be allocated to the current fiscal year ending March 31?

9. From time to time during the fiscal year, an enterprise makes an advance payment of premiums on three-year and one-year property insurance policies. (a) At the end of such fiscal year, will there be a deferral or an accrual for the enterprise? (b) Which of the following types of accounts will be affected by the related adjusting entry at the end of the fiscal year: (1) asset, (2) liability, (3) revenue, (4) expense?

10. Classify the following items as (a) prepaid expense, (b) unearned revenue, (c) accrued expense, or (d) accrued revenue.
    (1) Salary owed but not yet due.
    (2) Fees received but not yet earned.
    (3) Utilities owed but not yet paid.
    (4) Fees earned but not yet received.
    (5) Storage fees earned but not yet received.
    (6) Taxes owed but payable in the following period.
    (7) Receipts from sales of meal tickets by a restaurant.
    (8) Property taxes paid in advance.
    (9) Supplies on hand.
    (10) Tuition collected in advance by a university.
    (11) A two-year premium paid on a fire insurance policy.
    (12) Life insurance premiums received by an insurance company.

11. The debit portion of a particular adjustment is to an asset account. (a) If the adjustment is for a deferral, which of the following types of accounts will be credited: (1) asset, (2) liability, (3) revenue, (4) expense? (b) If the adjustment is for an accrual, which of the following types of accounts will be credited: (1) asset, (2) liability, (3) revenue, (4) expense?

12. Each of the following debits and credits represents one half of an adjusting entry. Name the title of the account that would be used for the remaining half of the entry.
(a) Prepaid Insurance is credited.
(b) Unearned Rent is debited.
(c) Fees Earned is debited.
(d) Office Supplies Expense is debited.
(e) Unearned Subscriptions is credited.
(f) Salary Expense is debited.
(g) Property Tax Payable is credited.

13. There are balances in each of the following accounts after adjustments have been made at the end of the fiscal year. Identify each as (a) asset, (b) liability, (c) revenue, or (d) expense.
(1) Prepaid Advertising
(2) Rent Receivable
(3) Salary Expense
(4) Rent Income
(5) Prepaid Insurance
(6) Insurance Expense
(7) Taxes Payable
(8) Supplies
(9) Fees Receivable
(10) Supplies Expense
(11) Unearned Subscriptions
(12) Fees Earned

14. Explain how the reversing of adjustments for accrued assets and accrued liabilities facilitates the recording of transactions.

15. The accountant for a real estate brokerage and management company uses the following uniform procedures in recording certain transactions:
(1) Premiums on fire insurance are debited to Prepaid Insurance.
(2) Advertising, which is paid in advance, is debited to Advertising Expense.
(3) Management fees, which are collected for one year in advance, are credited to Unearned Management Fees when received.
Assuming that an adjusting entry is required at the end of the fiscal year as a result of each of the foregoing recording procedures, (a) give the accounts to be debited and credited for each adjustment and (b) state whether or not each of the adjusting entries should be reversed as of the beginning of the following year.

16. The status of the following accounts is as of the beginning of the fiscal year, after reversing entries have been posted but before any transactions have occurred. Identify each balance as (a) an asset or (b) a liability.
(1) Insurance Expense, debit balance of $1,875.
(2) Unearned Subscriptions, credit balance of $3,394.
(3) Office Supplies, debit balance of $680.
(4) Utilities Expense, credit balance of $1,120.
(5) Rent Income, debit balance of $840.

17. If a particular type of revenue usually collected in advance is always credited to an income account at the time received, why should the year-end adjusting entry be reversed?

18. Briefly summarize the situations in which reversing entries should be prepared.

19. Real World Focus. The balance sheet for Tandy Corporation as of June 30, 1985, includes the following accrued expenses as current liabilities:

Accrued payroll and bonuses..............................	$61,492,000
Accrued sales and payroll taxes	15,240,000
Accrued insurance	13,924,000
Accrued interest	14,211,000

The net income for Tandy Corporation for the year ended June 30, 1985, was $189,060,000. (a) If the accrued expenses and unearned income had *not* been recorded at June 30, 1985, how much would net income have been misstated for the fiscal year ended June 30, 1985? (b) What is the percentage of the misstatement in (a) to the actual net income of $189,060,000?

EXERCISES

Exercise 6–1.   Two methods of recording store supplies. The store supplies inventory at the beginning of the fiscal year is $1,240, purchases of store supplies during the year total $3,670, and the inventory at the end of the year is $1,485.

(a) Set up T accounts for Store Supplies and Store Supplies Expense and record the following directly in the accounts, employing the system of initially recording store supplies as an expense (identify each entry by number): (1) beginning balance; (2) purchases for the period; (3) adjusting entry at end of the period; (4) closing entry.

(b) Set up T accounts for Store Supplies and Store Supplies Expense and record the following directly in the accounts, employing the system of initially recording store supplies as an asset (identify each entry by number): (1) beginning balance; (2) purchases for the period; (3) adjusting entry at the end of the period; (4) closing entry.

Exercise 6–2.   Two methods of recording insurance expense. Because of a lack of consistency by the bookkeeper in recording the payment of premiums on property and casualty insurance, there are balances in both the asset and expense accounts at the end of the year, before adjustments. Prepaid Insurance has a debit balance of $2,415, and Insurance Expense has a debit balance of $3,710. You determine that the total amount of insurance premiums allocable to future periods is $2,940.

(a) Assuming that you will instruct the bookkeeper to record all future insurance premiums as an asset, present journal entries: (1) to adjust the accounts and (2) to close the appropriate account.
(b) Assuming that you will instruct the bookkeeper to record all future insurance premiums as an expense, present journal entries: (1) to adjust the accounts, (2) to close the appropriate account, and (3) transfer the balance in Prepaid Insurance to Insurance Expense.
(c) (1) What is the amount of insurance expense for the year?
(2) What is the amount of prepaid insurance at the end of the year?

Exercise 6–3.   Year-end entries for deferred revenues. In their first year of operations, Roper Publishing Co. received $400,000 from advertising contracts and $875,000 from magazine subscriptions, crediting the two amounts to Advertising Revenue and Circulation Revenue respectively. At the end of the year, the deferral of advertising revenue amounts to $75,000, and the deferral of circulation revenue amounts to $250,000. (a) If no adjustments are made at the end of the year, will revenue for the year be overstated or understated, and by what amount? (b) Present the adjusting entries that should be made at the end of the year. (c) Present the entries to close the two revenue accounts. (d) Present the reversing entries if appropriate.

Exercise 6–4.   Two methods of recording advertising revenue. The unearned advertising revenue of Seagraves Advertising Agency at the beginning of the fiscal year is $38,850, revenues received during the year total $390,500, and the unearned advertising revenue at the end of the year is $43,120.

(a) Set up T accounts for Unearned Advertising Revenue and Advertising Revenue and record the following directly in the accounts, employing the system of initially recording advertising fees as a revenue (identify each entry by number): (1) beginning balance; (2) revenues received during the period; (3) adjusting entry at the end of the period; (4) closing entry.
(b) Set up T accounts for Unearned Advertising Revenue and Advertising Revenue and record the following directly in the accounts, employing the system of initially recording advertising fees as a liability (identify each entry by number): (1) beginning balance; (2) revenues received during the period; (3) adjusting entry at the end of the period; (4) closing entry.

Exercise 6–5.   Identification of entries in Rent Expense. The entries identified by numbers in the following account are related to the summarizing process at the end of the year. (a) Identify each entry as adjusting, closing, or reversing, and (b) present for each entry the title of the account to which the related debit or credit was posted.

RENT EXPENSE

Date		Item	Debit	Credit	Balance Debit	Balance Credit
Jan.	1	(1)	1,200		1,200	
Jan.	1	Transactions				
to		during the	14,400		15,600	
Dec.	31	year				
	31	(2)		1,400	14,200	
	31	(3)		14,200	—	—
Jan.	1	(4)	1,400		1,400	

Exercise 6–6. Year-end entries for salary expense. Salary Expense has a balance of $577,720 as of October 27.

(a) Present entries for the following:

    Oct. 31 Recorded accrued salaries, $8,150.

        31 Closed the salaries expense account.

    Nov. 1 Recorded a reversing entry for accrued salaries.

        2 Recorded salaries paid, $12,300.

(b) Answer the following questions:

    (1) What is the balance of the salary expense account on November 1?

    (2) Is the balance of the salary expense account on November 1 an asset, a liability, a revenue, or an expense?

    (3) What is the balance of the salary expense account on November 2?

    (4) Of the $12,300 salary payment on November 2, how much is expense in November?

    (5) If there had been no reversing entry on November 1, how should the debit for the salary payment on November 2 have been recorded?

PROBLEMS

Series A

Problem 6–1A. Year-end adjusting, closing, and reversing entries; general ledger accounts. The following accounts appear in the ledger of Frost Inc. at January 31, the end of the current fiscal year. None of the year-end adjustments have been recorded.

113	Fees Receivable..............	_12400_ —	411	Fees Earned................	$99,600
114	Supplies	$1,080 _-320_	511	Salary Expense	66,720
115	Prepaid Insurance	5,960 _-3360_	513	Advertising Expense..........	16,540 _-2000_
116	Prepaid Advertising	_2—0_	514	Insurance Expense	—
213	Salaries Payable.............	_—1850_	515	Supplies Expense	—
215	Unearned Rent	_—1120_	611	Rent Income................	14,560
313	Income Summary............	—			

The following information relating to adjustments at January 31 is obtained from physical inventories, supplementary records, and other sources:

(a) Unbilled fees at January 31, $12,400.
(b) Inventory of supplies at January 31, $320.
(c) The insurance record indicates that $3,360 of insurance has expired during the year.
(d) Of a prepayment of $2,500 for advertising space on a billboard, 80% of the time has expired, and the remainder will expire in the following year. The payment of the $2,500 was recorded in Advertising Expense.
(e) Salaries accrued at January 31, $1,850.
(f) Rent collected in advance that will not be earned until the following year, $1,120.

Instructions:

(1) Open the accounts listed and record the balances in the appropriate balance columns, as of January 31.
(2) Journalize the adjusting entries and post to the appropriate accounts after each entry, extending the balances. Identify the postings by writing "Adjusting" in the item columns.
(3) Prepare a compound journal entry to close the revenue accounts and another compound entry to close the expense accounts.
(4) Post the closing entries, inserting a short line in both balance columns of accounts that are closed. Identify the postings by writing "Closing" in the item columns.
(5) Prepare the reversing journal entries that should be made on February 1 and post to the appropriate accounts after each entry, inserting a short line in both balance columns of accounts that now have zero balances. Write "Reversing" in the item columns.

If the working papers correlating with the textbook are not used, omit Problem 6–2A.

Problem 6–2A. Work sheet and financial statements for sole proprietorship. Jerry Hutchins Company prepares interim financial statements at the end of each month and closes its accounts annually on December 31. Its income statement for the two-month period, January and February of the current year, is presented in the working papers. In addition, the trial balance of the ledger as of one month later is presented on a ten-column work sheet in the working papers. Data needed for adjusting entries at March 31, the end of the three-month period, are as follows:

(a) Estimated merchandise inventory at March 31, $220,600.

(b) Salaries accrued at March 31:
Sales salaries, $1,320.
Office salaries, $200.
(c) Unearned rent income at March 31, $280.
(d) Insurance expired during the three-month period:
Allocable as selling expense, $290.
Allocable as general expense, $110.
(e) Estimated inventory of store supplies at March 31, $130.
(f) Depreciation for the three-month period:
Store equipment, $1,140.
Office equipment, $450.

Instructions:

(1) Complete the work sheet for the three-month period ended March 31 of the current year.
(2) Prepare an income statement for the three-month period, using the last three-column group of the nine-column form in the working papers.
(3) Prepare an income statement for the month of March, using the middle three-column group of the nine-column form in the working papers.
(4) Prepare a statement of owner's equity for the three-month period. There were no additional investments during the period.
(5) Prepare a balance sheet as of March 31.

Problem 6–3A. Adjusting and reversing entries. The following information was obtained from a review of the ledger (before adjustments) and other records of Hass Company at December 31, the end of the current fiscal year:

(a) As advance premiums have been paid on insurance policies during the year, they have been debited to Prepaid Insurance, which has a balance of $3,258 at December 31. Details of premium expirations are as follows:

Policy No.	Premium Cost per Month	Period in Effect During Year
SB106	$50	Jan. 1–June 30
84162	20	Feb. 1–Dec. 31
C84DE	45	Jan. 1–Oct. 31
01CF2	32	Mar. 1–Dec. 31
Z149C	15	Aug. 1–Dec. 31

(b) Management Fees Earned has a credit balance of $156,900 at December 31. The unbilled fees at December 31 total $9,500.
(c) As office supplies have been purchased during the year, they have been debited to Office Supplies Expense, which has a balance of $1,280 at December 31. The inventory of supplies at that date totals $390.
(d) On December 31, Rent Expense has a debit balance of $19,500, which includes rent of $1,500 for January of the following year, paid on December 31 of the preceding year.

(e) Sales commissions are uniformly 2% of net sales and are paid on the tenth of the month following the sales. Net sales for the month ended December 31 were $108,600. Only commissions paid have been recorded during the year.

(f) Prepaid Advertising has a debit balance of $13,000 at December 31, which represents the advance payment on April 1 of a yearly contract for a uniform amount of space in 52 consecutive issues of a weekly publication. As of December 31, advertisements had appeared in 39 issues.

(g) Unearned Rent has a credit balance of $18,900, composed of the following: (1) January 1 balance of $4,500, representing rent prepaid for four months, January through April, and (2) a credit of $14,400, representing advance payment of rent for twelve months at $1,200 a month, beginning with May.

Instructions:

(1) Determine the amount of each adjustment, identifying all principal figures used in the computations.

(2) Journalize the adjusting entries as of December 31 of the current fiscal year, identifying each entry by letter.

(3) Journalize the reversing entries that should be made as of January 1 of the succeeding fiscal year, identifying each entry by the corresponding letter used in (2).

Problem 6–4A. Two methods of recording advertising expense and rent income; financial statement presentation. The following transactions relate to advertising and rent. Accounts are adjusted and closed only at December 31, the end of the fiscal year.

Advertising

Jan. 1. Debit balance of $1,850 (allocable to January–May).
June 1. Payment of $6,600 (allocable at $550 a month for 12 months beginning June 1).

Rent

Jan. 1. Credit balance of $12,220 ($2,300 allocable to January–February; $9,920 allocable to January–August).
Mar. 1. Receipt of $14,400 (allocable at $1,200 a month for 12 months beginning March 1).
Sept. 1. Receipt of $15,300 (allocable at $1,275 a month for 12 months beginning September 1).

Instructions:

(1) Open accounts for Prepaid Advertising, Advertising Expense, Unearned Rent, and Rent Income. Using the system of initially recording prepaid expense as an asset and unearned revenue as a liability, record the following directly in the accounts: (a) beginning balances as of January 1; (b) transactions of March 1, June 1, and September 1; (c) adjusting entries at December 31; (d) closing entries at December 31; and (e) reversing entries at January 1, if appropriate. Identify each entry in the item section of the accounts as balance, transaction, adjusting, closing, or reversing, and extend the balance after each entry.

(2) Open a duplicate set of accounts and follow the remaining instructions in Instruction (1), except to employ the system of initially recording prepaid expense as an expense and unearned revenue as revenue.

(3) Determine the amounts that would appear in the balance sheet at December 31 as asset and liability respectively, and in the income statement for the year as expense and revenue respectively, according to the system employed in Instruction (1) and the system employed in Instruction (2). Present your answers in the following form:

System	Asset	Expense	Liability	Revenue
Instruction (1)	$	$	$	$
Instruction (2)				

Problem 6–5A.   Adjusting entries from ledger account balances. Selected accounts from the ledger of Jesse Moody Inc. at the end of the fiscal year are as follows. The account balances are shown before and after adjustment.

	Unadjusted Balance	Adjusted Balance
Fees Receivable..............................	—	$ 3,900
Supplies.......................................	$ 2,550	810
Prepaid Insurance	6,720	2,940
Wages Payable...............................	—	3,560
Utilities Payable	—	570
Unearned Rent...............................	—	720
Fees Earned..................................	109,200	113,100
Wages Expense..............................	72,600	76,160
Utilities Expense.............................	5,940	6,510
Insurance Expense	—	3,780
Supplies Expense	—	1,740
Rent Income	9,360	8,640

Instructions:

(1) Journalize the adjusting entries that were posted to the ledger at the end of the fiscal year.
(2) Insert the letter "R" in the date column opposite each adjusting entry that should be reversed as of the first day of the following fiscal year.

Series B

Problem 6–1B.   Year-end adjusting, closing, and reversing entries; general ledger accounts. The following accounts appear in the ledger of Jackson Company at April 30, the end of the current fiscal year. None of the year-end adjustments have been recorded.

113	Fees Receivable..............	—	411	Fees Earned...............		$152,000
114	Supplies	$1,560	511	Salary Expense		92,600
115	Prepaid Insurance.............	3,840	513	Advertising Expense		20,400
116	Prepaid Advertising	—	514	Insurance Expense		—
213	Salaries Payable.............	—	515	Supplies Expense		—
215	Unearned Rent	—	611	Rent Income		15,600
313	Income Summary	—				

The following information relating to adjustments at April 30 is obtained from physical inventories, supplementary records, and other sources:

(a) Salaries accrued at April 30, $2,380.
(b) Unbilled fees at April 30, $6,800.
(c) Rent collected in advance that will not be earned until the following year, $1,200.
(d) The insurance record indicates that $1,300 of insurance relates to future years.
(e) Inventory of supplies at April 30, $540.
(f) Of a prepayment of $6,000 for advertising space on a billboard, 60% of the time has expired, and the remainder will expire in the following year. The payment of the $6,000 was recorded in Advertising Expense.

Instructions:

(1) Open the accounts listed and record the balances in the appropriate balance columns, as of April 30.
(2) Journalize the adjusting entries and post to the appropriate accounts after each entry, extending the balances. Identify the postings by writing "Adjusting" in the item columns.
(3) Prepare a compound journal entry to close the revenue accounts and another compound entry to close the expense accounts.
(4) Post the closing entries, inserting a short line in both balance columns of accounts that are closed. Identify the postings by writing "Closing" in the item columns.
(5) Prepare the reversing journal entries that should be made on May 1 and post to the appropriate accounts after each entry, inserting a short line in both balance columns of accounts that now have zero balances. Write "Reversing" in the item columns.

If the working papers correlating with the textbook are not used, omit Problem 6–2B.

Problem 6–2B. Work sheet and financial statements for sole proprietorship. Jerry Hutchins Company prepares interim financial statements at the end of each month and closes its accounts annually on December 31. Its income statement for the two-month period, January and February of the current year, is presented in the working papers. In addition, the trial balance of the ledger as of one month later is presented on a ten-column work sheet in the working papers. Data needed for adjusting entries at March 31, the end of the three-month period, are as follows:

(a) Depreciation for the three-month period:
    Store equipment, $1,140.
    Office equipment, $450.
(b) Insurance expired during the three-month period:
    Allocable as selling expense, $300.
    Allocable as general expense, $120.
(c) Estimated merchandise inventory at March 31, $200,500.
(d) Unearned rent income at March 31, $270.
(e) Estimated inventory of store supplies at March 31, $140.
(f) Salaries accrued at March 31:
    Sales salaries, $1,330.
    Office salaries, $180.

Instructions:

(1) Complete the work sheet for the three-month period ended March 31 of the current year.
(2) Prepare an income statement for the three-month period, using the last three-column group of the nine-column form in the working papers.
(3) Prepare an income statement for the month of March, using the middle three-column group of the nine-column form in the working papers.
(4) Prepare a statement of owner's equity for the three-month period. There were no additional investments during the period.
(5) Prepare a balance sheet as of March 31.

Problem 6–5B.   Adjusting entries from ledger account balances. Selected accounts from the ledger of Groves Company at the end of the fiscal year are as follows. The account balances are shown before and after adjustment.

	Unadjusted Balance	Adjusted Balance
Fees Receivable...................................	—	$ 9,000
Supplies..	$ 1,860	780
Prepaid Insurance	4,720	2,120
Wages Payable..................................	—	2,472
Advertising Payable.............................	—	3,000
Unearned Rent..................................	—	400
Fees Earned....................................	149,600	158,600
Wages Expense.................................	63,280	65,752
Insurance Expense	—	2,600
Advertising Expense	16,200	19,200
Supplies Expense	—	1,080
Rent Income....................................	5,200	4,800

Instructions:

(1) Journalize the adjusting entries that were posted to the ledger at the end of the fiscal year.
(2) Insert the letter "R" in the date column opposite each adjusting entry that should be reversed as of the first day of the following fiscal year.

MINI-CASE 6

WILLARD APPLIANCE COMPANY

A close friend of your family organized Willard Appliance Company on March 1, 1987. Having little training in record keeping, the owner, Jeffrey Willard, kept only cash receipts and disbursements records along with a folder of bills to be paid and a folder listing amounts due from customers. To expand his business, Willard has applied for a bank loan of $100,000 with which to purchase a warehouse and land. The bank has requested financial statements, and Willard has asked you to aid him in preparing such statements. Following is a summary of Willard's records:

Cash receipts (March 1, 1987–August 31, 1988):
(1)	Cash received from Jeffrey Willard to begin the enterprise	$200,000
(2)	Sales (after deducting sales returns and allowances of $7,000 and sales discounts of $4,920)	500,700

Cash disbursements (March 1, 1987–August 31, 1988):
(1)	Rent	$ 11,520
(2)	Insurance premiums	4,320
(3)	Purchases (after deducting purchases discounts of $2,940)	398,880
(4)	Utilities	16,800
(5)	Salaries	129,450
(6)	Store equipment	48,000
(7)	Delivery equipment	13,200
(8)	Advertisements in the Carroll Daily News	1,515
(9)	Taxes	5,700
(10)	Supplies	2,775
(11)	Miscellaneous expenses	6,480
(12)	Withdrawals by Jeffrey Willard	15,000

Total of amounts due on August 31, 1988 from customers	38,100
Total of unpaid bills on August 31, 1988 from purchases	27,960

Further analysis of the records, reveals the following data:

(a) Merchandise inventory,
  August 31, 1988................... $104,100
(b) Supplies on hand, August 31, 1988.... 1,370
(c) Prepaid rent, August 31, 1988......... 720
(d) Prepaid insurance, August 31, 1988 ... 800
(e) Depreciation to date on store equipment. 4,800
(f) Depreciation to date on delivery
  equipment....................... 1,650
(g) Accrued salaries, August 31, 1988..... 3,240

Instructions:

(1) Prepare a multiple-step income statement and a statement of owner's equity for the 18-month period ended August 31, 1988, and a balance sheet as of August 31, 1988, in report form. For purposes of this case, it is not necessary to distinguish between general and selling expenses.

(2) After receiving the statements in (1), the bank requested a balance sheet as of February 29, 1988, and an income statement and statement of owner's equity ended February 29, 1988. Is it possible to prepare such statements? Discuss.

ACCOUNTING SYSTEMS

Part

Chapter 7

ACCOUNTING SYSTEMS DESIGN

Chapter Objectives:

■ Describe the principles of properly designed accounting systems.

■ Describe the three phases of accounting system installation and revision.

■ Describe and illustrate the principles of internal control.

■ Describe data processing methods that may be used in accounting systems.

■ Describe and illustrate the use of the following special journals to process accounting data more efficiently:
    Purchases journal
    Cash payments journal
    Sales journal
    Cash receipts journal

■ Describe and illustrate the use of subsidiary ledgers in accounting systems.

■ Describe the use of electronic data processing (EDP) systems to process accounting data.

The way in which management is given the information for use in conducting the affairs of the business and in reporting to owners, creditors, and other interested parties is called the **accounting system**. In a general sense, an accounting system includes the entire network of communications used by a business organization to provide needed information.

PRINCIPLES OF ACCOUNTING SYSTEMS

Because of differences in businesses, in the number of transactions to be processed, and in the uses made of accounting data, accounting systems will vary from business to business. However, there are a number of broad principles discussed in the paragraphs that follow that apply to all systems.

Cost-Effectiveness Balance

An accounting system must be tailored to meet the specific needs of each business. Since costs must be incurred in meeting these needs, one of the major considerations in developing an accounting system is cost effectiveness. For example, although the reports produced by an accounting system are a valuable end product of the system, the value of the reports produced should be at least equal to the cost of producing them. No matter how detailed or informational a report may be, it should not be produced if it costs more than the benefits received by those who use it.

Flexibility to Meet Future Needs

A characteristic of the modern business environment is change. Each business must adapt to the constantly changing environment in which it operates. Whether the changes are the result of new government regulations, changes in accounting principles, organizational changes necessary to meet practices of competing businesses, changes in data processing technology, or other factors, the accounting system must be flexible enough to meet the 285 changing demands made of it. For example, when granting credit to customers became a common practice, it was necessary for many businesses to maintain accounts receivable, accounts payable, and related statistical and other useful information. Regulatory agencies, such as the Securities and Exchange Commission, often require a continually changing variety of reports that require changes in the accounting system.

Adequate Internal Controls

An accounting system must provide the information needed by management in reporting to owners, creditors, and other interested parties and in conducting the affairs of the business. In addition, the system should aid management in controlling operations. The detailed procedures used by management to control operations are called **internal controls**. The broad principles of internal control are discussed later in the chapter.

Effective Reporting

Users of the information provided by the accounting system rely on various reports for relevant information presented in an understandable manner. When these reports are prepared, the requirements and knowledge of the user should be recognized. For example, management may need detailed reports for controlling operations on a weekly or even daily basis, and regulatory agencies often require uniform data and establish certain deadlines for the submission of certain reports.

Adaptation to Organizational Structure

Only by effectively using and adapting to the human resources of a business can the accounting system meet information needs at the lowest cost. Since no two businesses are structured alike, the accounting system must be tailored to the organizational structure of each business. The lines of authority and responsibility will affect the information requirements of each business. In addition, an effective system needs the approval and support of all levels of management.

ACCOUNTING SYSTEM INSTALLATION AND REVISION

Before designing and installing an accounting system for an enterprise, the designer must have a complete knowledge of the business' operations. However, the designer should recognize that some areas of the system, such as the types and design of the forms needed and the number and titles of the accounts required, may be affected by factors that are not known when a business is first organized. As new information about a business is obtained and as a business "outgrows" its accounting system when it expands to new operational areas, the system will need to be revised.

Many large businesses continually review their accounting system and may constantly be involved in changing some part of it. The job of installing or changing an accounting system, either in its entirety or only in part, is made up of three phases: (1) analysis, (2) design, and (3) implementation.

Systems Analysis

The goal of **systems analysis** is to determine information needs, the sources of such information, and the deficiencies in procedures and data processing methods presently used. The analysis usually begins with a review of the organizational structure and the job descriptions of the personnel affected. This review is followed by a study of the forms, records, procedures, processing methods, and reports used by the enterprise. The source of such information is usually the firm's *Systems Manual*.

In addition to looking at the shortcomings of the present system, the analyst should determine management's plans for changes in operations (volume, products, territories, etc.) in the foreseeable future.

Systems Design

Accounting systems are changed as a result of the kind of analysis previously described. The design of the new system may involve only minor changes from the existing system, such as revision of a particular form and the related procedures and processing methods, or it may be a complete revision of the entire system. Systems designers must have a general knowledge of the qualities of different kinds of data processing equipment, and the ability to evaluate alternatives. Although successful systems design depends to a large extent upon the creativity, imagination, and general capabilities of the designer, observance of the broad principles previously discussed is necessary.

Systems Implementation

The final phase of the creation or revision of an accounting system is to carry out, or implement, the proposals. New or revised forms, records, procedures, and equipment must be installed, and any that are no longer useful must be withdrawn. All personnel responsible for operating the system must be carefully trained and closely supervised until satisfactory efficiency is achieved.

Accounting Systems, Profit Measurement, and Management

A Greek restaurant owner in Canada had his own system of accounting. He kept his accounts payable in a cigar box on the left-hand side of his cash register, his daily cash returns on the cash register, and his receipts for paid bills in another cigar box on the right.

When his youngest son graduated as an accountant, he was appalled by his father's primitive methods. "I don't know how you can run a business that way," he said. "How do you know what your profits are?"

"Well, son," the father replied, "when I got off the boat from Greece, I had nothing but the pants I was wearing. Today, your brother is a doctor. You are an accountant. Your sister is a speech therapist. Your mother and I have a nice car, and city house, a country home. We have a good business, and everything is paid for. . ."

"So, you add all that together, subtract the pants, and there's your profit!"

Source: Anonymous.

In 1950, Congress passed the Budget and Accounting Procedures Act, which required the comptroller general to prescribe accounting principles for federal executive agencies to follow in designing their accounting systems. However, the full and satisfactory implementation of this Act was a slow process and, in the interim, serious deficiencies were noted.

In a speech before a group of government accountants, the comptroller general cited examples of some of the problems that resulted from failing to use a good accounting system. The Department of the Army, for instance, experienced a breakdown in the control over its procurements in the late 1970s, resulting in excess obligations totaling about $225 million. Some top officials were reprimanded, and more than 28,000 staff days were used in unraveling the accounting records. In 1975, the Social Security Administration estimated that it had made nearly a billion dollars in erroneous Supplemental Security income payments. In commenting on this case, the comptroller general indicated that "if more effort had been devoted to better accounting systems, these errors might have been lessened."

The comptroller general noted that those agencies which devote the time and effort required to design and implement a good accounting system, in accordance with prescribed principles, generally have less problems and are able to manage their operations more efficiently and economically. In addition, agency management is provided with better accounting data on which to base decisions, control funds and property, and make full disclosure of financial results.

Source: Adapted from "A Good Accounting System—A Key to Good Management," *Journal of Accountancy,* (February, 1978), pp. 66–69.

For a large organization, a major revision such as a change from an obsolete to a modern computer processing system is usually done gradually over an extended period rather than all at once. With such a procedure, there is less likelihood that the flow of useful data will be seriously slowed down during the critical phase of implementation. Weaknesses and conflicting or unnecessary elements in the design may also become apparent during the implementation phase. They are more easily seen and corrected when changes in a system are adopted gradually, and possible chaos is thereby avoided.

INTERNAL CONTROLS

Internal controls are classified as (1) administrative controls and (2) accounting controls. **Internal administrative controls** consist of procedures and records that aid management in achieving business goals. For example, with records of defective work by production employees, management can evaluate personnel performance and thus control the quality of the product manufactured. **Internal accounting controls** consist of procedures and records that are mainly concerned with the reliability of financial records and reports and with the safeguarding of assets. For example, procedures established to make sure that all transactions are recorded according to generally accepted accounting principles help assure reliable financial records. A way of safeguarding assets is to limit access to assets to authorized personnel.

Details of a system of internal control will vary according to the size and type of business enterprise. In a small business where it is possible for the owner-manager to personally supervise the employees and to direct the affairs of the business, few controls are necessary. As the number of employees and the complexities of an enterprise increase, it becomes more difficult for management to maintain control over all phases of operations. As a firm grows, management needs to delegate authority and to place more reliance on the accounting system in controlling operations.

Several broad principles of internal control are discussed in the following paragraphs. Many of these principles should be considered by all businesses, large and small.

Competent Personnel and Rotation of Duties

The successful operation of an accounting system requires people who are able to perform the duties to which they are assigned. Hence, it is necessary that all accounting employees be adequately trained and supervised to perform their jobs. It is also advisable to rotate clerical personnel periodically from job to job. In addition to broadening their understanding of the system, the knowledge that others may in the future perform their jobs tends to discourage deviations from prescribed procedures. Rotation of duties is also very helpful in disclosing any irregularities that may have occurred.

Assignment of Responsibility

If employees are to work efficiently, their responsibilities must be clearly defined. There should be no overlapping or undefined areas of responsibility. For example, if a certain cash register is to be used by two or more salesclerks, each one should be assigned a separate cash drawer and register key. Thus, daily proof of the handling of cash can be obtained for each clerk.

Separation of Responsibility for Related Operations

To decrease the possibility of inefficiency, errors, and fraud, responsibility for a sequence of related operations should be divided among two or more persons. For example, no one individual should be authorized to order merchandise, verify the receipt of the goods, and pay the supplier. To do so would invite abuses such as the following:

1. Placing orders with a supplier on the basis of friendship rather than on price, quality, and other objective factors.
2. Indifferent and routine verification of the quantity and the quality of goods received.
3. Conversion of goods to the personal use of the employee.
4. Carelessness in verifying the validity and the accuracy of invoices.
5. Payment of false invoices.

When the responsibility for purchasing, receiving, and paying are divided among three persons or departments, the possibilities of such abuses are minimized.

The "checks and balances" provided by distributing responsibility among various departments requires no duplication of effort. The business documents prepared as a result of the work of each department must "fit" with those prepared by the other departments.

Separation of Operations and Accounting

Responsibility for maintaining the accounting records should be separated from the responsibility for engaging in business transactions and for the custody of the firm's assets. By so doing, the accounting records serve as an independent check on the business operations. For example, the employees entrusted with handling cash receipts from credit customers should not have access to the journal or ledger. Separation of the two functions reduces the possibilities of errors and embezzlement.

Proofs and Security Measures

Proofs and security measures should be used to safeguard business assets and assure reliable accounting data. This principle applies to many different techniques and procedures, such as the use of a bank account and other safekeeping measures for cash and other valuable documents. Cash registers are widely used in making the initial record of cash sales. The conditioning of the public to observe the amount recorded as the sale or to accept a printed receipt from the salesclerk increases the machine's effectiveness as a part of internal control.

The use of fidelity insurance is also an aid to internal control. It insures against losses caused by fraud on the part of employees who are entrusted with company assets.

Independent Review

To determine whether the other internal control principles are being effectively applied, the system should be periodically reviewed and evaluated by internal auditors. These auditors must be independent of the employees responsible for operations. An example of the use of internal auditors for review of internal controls is described in the annual report of Rose's Stores Inc., as follows:

> To meet its responsibilities with respect to financial information, management maintains and enforces internal accounting policies, procedures, and controls which are designed to provide reasonable assurance that assets are safeguarded and that transactions are properly recorded and executed in accordance with management's authorization. The concept of reasonable assurance is based on the recognition that the cost of controls should not exceed the expected benefits. Management maintains an internal audit function and an internal control function which are responsible for evaluating the adequacy and application of financial and operating controls and for testing compliance with Company policies and procedures.

Internal auditors should report any weaknesses and recommend changes to correct them. For example, a review of cash disbursements may disclose that invoices were not paid within the discount period, even though enough cash was available.

DATA PROCESSING METHODS

The entire amount of data needed by an enterprise is called its **data base**. Depending upon the variety and the amount of data included in the data base, various processing methods—manual and computerized—may be used. Whether the accounting system for a particular enterprise uses one or a combination of these methods, the basic principles of accounting systems as discussed are applicable.

In preceding chapters, manual accounting systems were used to process accounting data, because they are the easiest systems to understand. If the data base is relatively small, manually kept records may serve a business reasonably well. However, as the data base increases, manual processing becomes too costly and takes too much time. In such a case, the manual system can be changed, or it may be replaced or supplemented by a computerized system in order to reduce costs and process accounting data more efficiently. In the following paragraphs, changes that can make a manual system more efficient will be described and illustrated.

SUBSIDIARY LEDGERS AND SPECIAL JOURNALS

In preceding chapters, all transactions were initially recorded in a two-column journal, then posted individually to the appropriate accounts in the ledger. Applying such detailed procedures to a large number of transactions that are often repeated is impractical. For example, if many credit sales are made, each of these transactions would require an entry debiting Accounts Receivable and crediting Sales. In addition, the accounts receivable account in the ledger would include receivables from a large number of customers. In such cases, subsidiary ledgers and special journals may be useful.

Subsidiary Ledgers

As the number of purchases and sales on account increase, the need for maintaining a separate account for each creditor and debtor is clear. If such accounts are numerous, their inclusion in the same ledger with all other accounts would cause the ledger to become unmanageable. The chance of posting errors would also be increased and the preparation of the trial balance and the financial statements would be delayed.

When there are a large number of individual accounts with a common characteristic, it is common to place them in a separate ledger called a **subsidiary ledger**. The principal ledger, which contains all of the balance sheet and income statement accounts, is then called the **general ledger**. Each subsidiary ledger is represented in the general ledger by a summarizing account, called a **controlling account**. The sum of the balances of the accounts in a subsidiary ledger must agree with the balance of the related controlling account. Thus, a subsidiary ledger may be said to be *controlled* by its controlling account.

The individual accounts with creditors are arranged in alphabetical order in a subsidiary ledger called the **accounts payable ledger** or **creditors ledger**.

The related controlling account in the general ledger is Accounts Payable. The subsidiary ledger containing the individual accounts for credit customers is called the **accounts receivable ledger** or **customers ledger**. The controlling account in the general ledger that summarizes the debits and credits to the individual customers accounts is Accounts Receivable. The accounts payable ledger is illustrated and further discussed on pages 300–303, and the accounts receivable ledger is further discussed on page 307.

Special Journals

One of the simplest methods of processing data more efficiently in a manual accounting system is to expand the two-column journal to a **multi-column** journal. Each amount column included in a multicolumn journal is restricted to the recording of transactions affecting a certain account. For example, a special column could be used only for recording debits to the cash account and another special column could be used only for recording credits to the cash account. The addition of the two special columns would eliminate the writing of "Cash" in the journal for every receipt and payment of cash. Furthermore, there would be no need to post each individual debit and credit to the cash account. Instead, the "Cash Dr." and "Cash Cr." columns could be totaled periodically and only the totals posted, yielding additional economies. In a similar manner, special columns could be added for recording credits to Sales, debits and credits to Accounts Receivable and Accounts Payable, and for other entries that are repeated. Although there is no exact number of columns that may be effectively used in a multicolumn journal, there is a maximum number beyond which the journal would become unmanageable. Also, the possibilities of errors in recording become greater as the number of columns and the width of the page increase.

An all-purpose multicolumn journal is usually satisfactory for a small business enterprise that needs the services of only one bookkeeper. If the number of transactions is enough to require two or more bookkeepers, the use of a single journal is usually not efficient. The next logical development in expanding the system is to replace an all-purpose journal with a number of **special journals,** each designed to record a single kind of transaction. Special journals would be needed only for the kinds of transactions that occur frequently. Since most enterprises have many transactions in which cash is received and many in which cash is paid out, it is common practice to use a special journal for recording cash receipts and another special journal for recording cash payments. An enterprise that sells services or merchandise to customers on account might use a special journal designed for recording only such transactions. On the other hand, a business that does not give credit would have no need for such a journal.

The transactions that occur most often in a medium-size merchandising firm and the special journals in which they are recorded are as follows:

Purchase of merchandise or
  other items *on account*   recorded in   ➤ Purchases journal

Payments of cash for
  any purpose   recorded in   ➤ Cash payments journal

Sale of merchandise
  on account   recorded in   ➤ Sales journal

Receipt of cash from
  any source   recorded in   ➤ Cash receipts journal

    Sometimes the business documents evidencing purchases and sales transactions are used as special journals. When there are a large number of such transactions on a credit basis, the use of this procedure may result in a substantial savings in bookkeeping expenses and a reduction of bookkeeping errors.

    The two-column form illustrated in earlier chapters can be used for miscellaneous entries, such as adjusting and closing entries, that do not "fit" in any of the special journals. The two-column form is commonly called the **general journal** or simply the **journal**.

Purchases Journal

    Property most frequently purchased on account by a merchandising concern is of the following types: (1) merchandise for resale to customers, (2)

PURCHASES JOURNAL

PAGE 19   PURCHASES

	DATE		ACCOUNT CREDITED	POST. REF.	ACCOUNTS PAYABLE CR.
1	1987 Oct.	2	Video Co.	✓	5 7 2 4 00
2		3	Marsh Inc.	✓	7 4 0 6 00
3		9	Parker Supply Co.	✓	2 5 7 00
4		11	Marsh Inc.	✓	3 2 0 8 00
5		16	Dunlap Corporation	✓	3 5 9 3 00
6		17	Robinson Supply	✓	1 5 0 0 00
7		20	Walton Co.	✓	15 1 2 5 00
8		23	Parker Supply Co.	✓	1 3 2 00
9		27	Dunlap Corporation	✓	6 3 7 5 00
10		31			43 3 2 0 00
11					(2 1 1)

supplies for use in conducting the business, and (3) equipment and other plant assets. Because of the variety of items acquired on credit terms, the purchases journal should be designed to allow for the recording of everything purchased on account. The form of purchases journal used by Kannon Corporation is illustrated below.

For each transaction recorded in the purchases journal, the credit is entered in the Accounts Payable Cr. column. The next three amount columns are used for accumulating debits to the particular accounts most frequently affected. Invoice amounts for merchandise purchased for sale to customers are recorded in the Purchases Dr. column. The purpose of the Store Supplies Dr. and Office Supplies Dr. columns is readily apparent. If supplies of these two categories were purchased only once in a while, the two columns could be omitted from the journal.

The final set of columns, under the main heading Sundry Accounts Dr., is used to record acquisitions, on account, of items not provided for in the special debit columns. The title of the account to be debited is entered in the Account column and the amount is entered in the Amount column. A separate posting reference column is provided for this section of the purchases journal.

Posting the Purchases Journal. The special journals used in recording most of the transactions affecting creditors accounts are designed to allow the posting of individual transactions to the accounts payable ledger and a single monthly total to Accounts Payable. The basic techniques of posting credits from a purchases journal to an accounts payable ledger and the controlling account are shown in the flowchart on page 296.

JOURNAL								PAGE 19	
PURCHASES DR.	STORE SUPPLIES DR.	OFFICE SUPPLIES DR.	SUNDRY ACCOUNTS DR.						
			ACCOUNT	POST. REF.	AMOUNT				
5 7 2 4 00									1
7 4 0 6 00									2
	1 3 1 00	1 2 6 00							3
3 2 0 8 00									4
3 5 9 3 00									5
1 5 0 0 00									6
			Store Equipment	121	15 1 2 5 00				7
	7 5 00	5 7 00							8
6 3 7 5 00									9
27 8 0 6 00	2 0 6 00	1 8 3 00			15 1 2 5 00				10
(5 1 1)	(1 1 5)	(1 1 6)			(✓)				11

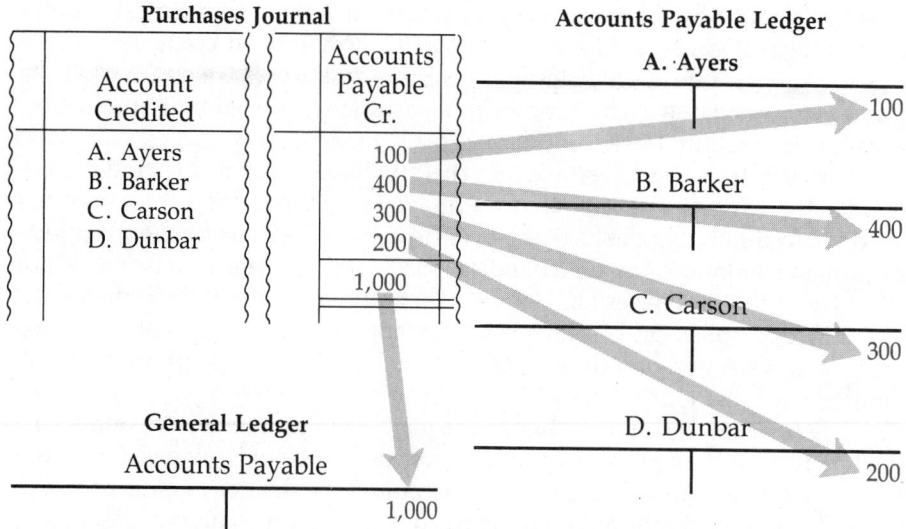

The individual credits of $100, $400, $300, and $200 to Ayers, Barker, Carson, and Dunbar respectively are posted to their accounts in the accounts payable ledger. The sum of the credits to the four individual accounts in the subsidiary ledger is posted as a single $1,000 credit to Accounts Payable, the controlling account in the general ledger.

The source of the entries posted to the subsidiary and general ledgers is indicated in the posting reference column of each account by inserting the letter "P" and the page number of the purchases journal. An account in the accounts payable ledger of Kannon Corporation is presented as an example.

NAME Robinson Supply

ADDRESS 3800 Mission Street, San Francisco, CA 94110-1732

DATE	ITEM	POST. REF.	DEBIT	CREDIT	BALANCE
1987 Oct. 17		P19		1 5 0 0 00	1 5 0 0 00

Since the balances in the creditors accounts are usually credit balances, a three-column account form is used instead of the four-column account form illustrated earlier. When a creditor's account is overpaid and a debit balance occurs, that fact should be indicated by an asterisk or parentheses in the Balance column. When an account's balance is zero, a line may be drawn in the Balance column.

The creditors accounts in the subsidiary ledger are not numbered, because the order changes each time a new account is inserted alphabetically or an old account is removed. Thus, instead of a number, a check mark (✔) is inserted in the posting reference column of the purchases journal after a credit is posted.

The amounts in the Sundry Accounts Dr. column of the purchases journal are posted to the appropriate accounts in the general ledger and the posting reference ("P" and page number) are inserted in the accounts. As each amount is posted, the related general ledger account number is inserted in the posting reference column of the Sundry Accounts section.

At the end of each month, the purchases journal is totaled and ruled in the manner illustrated on pages 294 and 295. Before posting the totals to the general ledger, the sum of the totals of the four debit columns should be compared with the total of the credit column to prove their equality.

The totals of the four special columns are posted to the appropriate general ledger accounts in the usual manner, with the related account numbers inserted below the columnar totals. Because each amount in the Sundry Accounts Dr. was posted individually, a check mark is placed below the $15,125 total to show that no further action is needed.

Two of the general ledger accounts to which postings were made are presented as examples. The debit posting to Store Equipment was from the Sundry Accounts Dr. column; the credit posting to Accounts Payable was from the total of the Accounts Payable Cr. column.

ACCOUNT Store Equipment						ACCOUNT NO. 121	
DATE	ITEM	POST. REF.	DEBIT	CREDIT	BALANCE DEBIT	BALANCE CREDIT	
1987 Oct 1	Balance	✔			11 975 00		
20		P19	15 125 00		27 100 00		

GENERAL LEDGER ACCOUNTS AFTER POSTING FROM PURCHASES JOURNAL

ACCOUNT Accounts Payable						ACCOUNT NO. 211	
DATE	ITEM	POST. REF.	DEBIT	CREDIT	BALANCE DEBIT	BALANCE CREDIT	
1987 Oct 1	Balance	✔				21 975 00	
31		P19		43 320 00		65 295 00	

The flow of data from the purchases journal of Kannon Corporation to its two related ledgers is presented graphically in the diagram on page 298. Two procedures revealed by the flow diagram should be given special attention:

1. Postings are made from the purchases journal to both (a) accounts in the subsidiary ledger and (b) accounts in the general ledger.
2. The sum of the postings to individual accounts payable in the subsidiary ledger equals the columnar total posted to Accounts Payable (controlling account) in the general ledger.

Purchases Journal

Account Credited	P. R.	Accts. Payable Cr.	Pur-chases Dr.	Store Sup. Dr.	Office Sup. Dr.	Sundry Accounts Debit		
						Account	P. R.	Amount
Video Co.	✓	5,724	5,724					
Marsh Inc.	✓	7,406	7,406					
Parker Supply Co.	✓	257		131	126			
Walton Co.	✓	15,125				Store Equip.	121	15,125
Parker Supply Co.	✓	132		75	57			
Dunlap Corporation	✓	6,375	6,375					
		43,320	27,806	206	183			15,125

General Ledger

Accounts Payable   Store Supplies   Office Supplies

| 43,320 | 206 | | 183 |

Purchases   Store Equipment

| 27,806 | | 15,125 |

Accounts Payable Ledger

Each individual entry is posted as a credit to an account in the accounts payable ledger, making a total of $43,320.

Purchases Returns and Allowances. When merchandise purchased is returned or a price adjustment is granted, an entry is made in the general journal according to the principles described in Chapter 4. To illustrate, assume that during October, Kannon Corporation issued a debit memorandum for a return of merchandise. The entry may be recorded in a two-column general journal, as follows:

GENERAL
JOURNAL
ENTRY FOR
RETURNS
AND
ALLOWANCES

	DATE		DESCRIPTION	POST. REF.	DEBIT	CREDIT	
17	Oct.	20	Accounts Payable — Dunlap Corp.	211 ✓	9 7 50		17
18			Purchases Returns and Allowances	512		9 7 50	18
19			Debit Memo No. 20.				19

JOURNAL   PAGE 18

The debit portion of the entry is posted to the accounts payable account in the general ledger (No. 211) and also to the creditor's account in the subsidiary ledger (✓). The need for posting the debits to two different accounts is indicated, at the time these entries are journalized, by drawing a *diagonal line* in the posting reference column. The account number and check mark are inserted, in the usual manner, at the time the entry is posted.

After the entry has been recorded, the memorandum is attached to the related unpaid invoice. If the invoice had been paid before the return or allowance was granted, the settlement might be a cash refund.

If goods other than merchandise are returned or a price adjustment is granted, the account to which the goods were first debited should be credited. For example, if a purchase of office equipment is returned, the credit would be to Office Equipment rather than Purchases Returns and Allowances.

Cash Payments Journal

The standards for determining the special columns to be provided in the **cash payments journal** are the same as for the purchases journal, namely, the kind of transactions to be recorded and the frequency of their occurrence. It is necessary to have a Cash Cr. column. Payments to creditors on account happen often enough to require columns for Accounts Payable Dr. and Purchases Discounts Cr. The cash payments journal illustrated below has these three columns and an additional column for Sundry Accounts Dr.

Cash Cr ↓ decrease

	DATE	CK. NO.	ACCOUNT DEBITED	POST. REF.	SUNDRY ACCOUNTS DR	ACCOUNTS PAYABLE DR	PURCHASES DISCOUNTS CR	CASH CR	
1	1987 Oct. 2	312	Purchases	511	1 2 7 5 00			1 2 7 5 00	1
2	4	313	Store Equipment	121	3 5 0 00			3 5 0 00	2
3	12	314	Marsh Inc.	✓		7 4 0 6 00	7 4 06	7 3 3 1 94	3
4	12	315	Sales Salaries Exp.	611	2 5 6 0 00			2 5 6 0 00	4
5	12	316	Office Salaries Exp.	711	8 8 0 00			8 8 0 00	5
6	14	317	Misc. Gen. Exp.	719	5 6 40			5 6 40	6
7	16	318	Prepaid Insurance	117	9 8 4 00			9 8 4 00	7
8	20	319	Marsh Inc.	✓		3 2 0 8 00	3 2 08	3 1 7 5 92	8
9	20	320	Heath Co.	✓		4 8 5 0 00		4 8 5 0 00	9
10	21	321	Sales Ret. & Allow.	412	4 6 2 00			4 6 2 00	10
11	23	322	Robinson Supply	✓		1 5 0 0 00	3 0 00	1 4 7 0 00	11
12	23	323	Video Co.	✓		7 6 0 0 00		7 6 0 0 00	12
13	23	324	Rent Expense	712	7 8 9 20			7 8 9 20	13
14	24	325	Walton Co.	✓		9 5 2 5 00		9 5 2 5 00	14
15	26	326	Sales Salaries Exp.	611	2 5 6 0 00			2 5 6 0 00	15
16	26	327	Office Salaries Exp.	711	8 8 0 00			8 8 0 00	16
17	26	328	Advertising Expense	612	7 8 6 00			7 8 6 00	17
18	27	329	Misc. Selling Exp.	619	4 1 50			4 1 50	18
19	28	330	Office Equipment	123	9 0 0 00			9 0 0 00	19
20	31				12 5 2 4 10	34 0 8 9 00	1 3 6 14	46 4 7 6 96	20
21					(✓)	(2 1 1)	(5 1 3)	(1 1 1)	21

CASH PAYMENTS JOURNAL PAGE 16

CASH PAYMENTS JOURNAL AFTER POSTING

All payments by Kannon Corporation are made by check. As each transaction is recorded in the cash payments journal, the related check number is entered in the column at the right of the Date column. The check numbers provide a convenient cross-reference, and their use also is helpful in controlling cash payments.

The Sundry Accounts Dr. column is used to record debits to any account for which there is no special column. On October 2, for example, Kannon Corporation paid $1,275 for a cash purchase of merchandise. The transaction was recorded by writing "Purchases" in the space provided and $1,275 in the Sundry Accounts Dr. and the Cash Cr. columns. The posting reference (511) was inserted later, at the time the debit was posted.

Debits to creditors accounts for invoices paid are recorded in the Accounts Payable Dr. column and credits for the amounts paid are recorded in the Cash Cr. column. If a discount is taken, the debit to the account payable will, of course, differ from the amount of the payment. Cash discounts taken on merchandise purchased for resale are recorded in the Purchases Discounts Cr. column.

At frequent intervals during the month, the amounts entered in the Accounts Payable Dr. column are posted to the creditors accounts in the accounts payable ledger. After each posting, "CP" and the page number of the journal are inserted in the posting reference column of the account. Check marks are placed in the posting reference column of the cash payments journal to indicate that the amounts have been posted. The items in the Sundry Accounts Dr. column are also posted to the appropriate accounts in the general ledger at frequent intervals. The posting is indicated by writing the account numbers in the posting reference column of the cash payments journal. At the end of the month, each of the amount columns in the cash payments journal is footed, the sum of the two debit totals is compared with the sum of the two credit totals to determine their equality, and the journal is ruled.

A check mark is placed below the total of the Sundry Accounts Dr. column to indicate that it is not posted. As each of the totals of the other three columns is posted to a general ledger account, the proper account numbers are inserted below the column totals.

Accounts Payable Control and Subsidiary Ledger

During October, the following postings were made to Accounts Payable in the general ledger of Kannon Corporation:

Credits to Accounts Payable

Oct. 31 Total purchases on account (purchases journal)........ $43,320.00

Debits to Accounts Payable

Oct. 20 A return of merchandise (general journal)............. 97.50
31 Total cash payments on account
(cash payments journal) 34,089.00

The accounts payable controlling account and the subsidiary accounts payable ledger of Kannon Corporation as of October 31 are presented below and on the following page.

GENERAL LEDGER

DATE		ITEM	POST. REF.	DEBIT	CREDIT	BALANCE DEBIT	BALANCE CREDIT
ACCOUNT Accounts Payable						ACCOUNT NO. 211	
1987 Oct.	1	Balance	✔				21 975 00
	20		J18	97 50			21 877 50
	31		P19		43 320 00		65 197 50
	31		CP16	34 089 00			31 108 50

ACCOUNTS PAYABLE ACCOUNT IN THE GENERAL LEDGER AT THE END OF THE MONTH

ACCOUNTS PAYABLE LEDGER

NAME Dunlap Corporation
ADDRESS 521 Scottsdale Blvd., Phoenix, AZ 85004-1100

DATE		ITEM	POST. REF.	DEBIT	CREDIT	BALANCE
1987 Oct.	16		P19		3 593 00	3 593 00
	20		J18	97 50		3 495 50
	27		P19		6 375 00	9 870 50

ACCOUNTS PAYABLE LEDGER AT THE END OF THE MONTH

NAME Heath Co.
ADDRESS 9950 Ridge Ave., Los Angeles, CA 90048-3694

DATE		ITEM	POST. REF.	DEBIT	CREDIT	BALANCE
1987 Sept.	21		P18		4 850 00	4 850 00
Oct.	20		CP16	4 850 00		—

NAME Marsh Inc.
ADDRESS 650 Wilson, Portland, OR 97209-1406

DATE		ITEM	POST. REF.	DEBIT	CREDIT	BALANCE
1987 Oct.	3		P19		7 406 00	7 406 00
	11		P19		3 208 00	10 614 00
	12		CP16	7 406 00		3 208 00
	20		CP16	3 208 00		—

ACCOUNTS PAYABLE LEDGER AT THE END OF THE MONTH—CONCLUDED

NAME Parker Supply Co.
ADDRESS 142 West 8th, Los Angeles, CA 90014-1225

DATE		ITEM	POST. REF.	DEBIT	CREDIT	BALANCE
1987 Oct.	9		P19		257 00	257 00
	23		P19		132 00	389 00

NAME Robinson Supply
ADDRESS 3800 Mission Street, San Francisco, CA 94110-1732

DATE		ITEM	POST. REF.	DEBIT	CREDIT	BALANCE
1987 Oct.	17		P19		1500 00	1500 00
	23		CP16	1500 00		—

NAME Video Co.
ADDRESS 1200 Capital Ave., Sacramento, CA 95814-1048

DATE		ITEM	POST. REF.	DEBIT	CREDIT	BALANCE
1987 Sept.	25		P18		7600 00	7600 00
Oct.	2		P19		5724 00	13324 00
	23		CP16	7600 00		5724 00

NAME Walton Co.
ADDRESS 9554 W. Colorado Blvd., Pasadena, CA 91107-1318

DATE		ITEM	POST. REF.	DEBIT	CREDIT	BALANCE
1987 Sept.	28		P18		9525 00	9525 00
Oct.	20		P19		15125 00	24650 00
	24		CP16	9525 00		15125 00

After all posting has been completed for the month, the sum of the balances in the accounts payable ledger should be compared with the balance of the accounts payable account in the general ledger. If the controlling account and the subsidiary ledger do not agree, the error or errors must be located and corrected. The balances of the individual creditors accounts may be summarized on a calculator tape, or a schedule such as the following may be prepared. The total of the schedule, $31,108.50, agrees with the balance of the accounts payable account shown on page 301.

SCHEDULE
OF
ACCOUNTS
PAYABLE

| Kannon Corporation | |
| Schedule of Accounts Payable | |
October 31, 1987	
Dunlap Corporation.	$ 9,870.50
Parker Supply Co..	389.00
Video Co..	5,724.00
Walton Co..	15,125.00
Total accounts payable.	$31,108.50

Sales Journal *on account (recording) acct/R — asset acct*

The **sales journal** is used only for recording *sales of merchandise on account;* sales of merchandise for cash are recorded in the cash receipts journal. Sales of non-merchandise assets are recorded in the cash receipts journal or the general journal, depending upon whether the sale was made for cash or on account. The sales journal of Kannon Corporation for October is as follows:

SALES
JOURNAL
AFTER
POSTING

	DATE		INVOICE NO.	ACCOUNT DEBITED	POST. REF.	ACCTS. REC. DR. SALES CR.	
1	1987 Oct.	2	615	Barnes Inc.	✓	9 3 5 0 00	1
2		3	616	Standard Supply Co.	✓	1 6 0 4 00	2
3		5	617	David T. Mattox	✓	15 3 0 5 00	3
4		9	618	Barnes Inc.	✓	1 3 9 6 00	4
5		10	619	Adler Company	✓	6 7 5 0 00	5
6		17	620	Hamilton Inc.	✓	7 8 6 5 00	6
7		23	621	Cooper & Co.	✓	1 5 0 2 00	7
8		26	622	Tracy & Lee Inc.	✓	3 2 6 0 00	8
9		27	623	Standard Supply Co.	✓	1 9 0 8 00	9
10		31				48 9 4 0 00	10
11						(113) (411)	11

SALES JOURNAL   PAGE 35

Details of the first sale recorded by Kannon Corporation in October are taken from Invoice No. 615. The customer is Barnes Inc., and the invoice total is $9,350. Since the amount of the debit to Accounts Receivable is the same as the credit to Sales, a single amount column in the sales journal is sufficient. However, if sales are subject to a sales tax, a special column may be added to the sales journal for recording the credit to Sales Tax Payable.

Posting the Sales Journal. The principles used in posting the sales journal compare to those used in posting the purchases journal. The source of the entry being posted is shown in the posting reference column of an account by the letter "S" and the proper page number. A customer's account with a posting from the sales journal is as follows:

**AN ACCOUNT
IN THE
ACCOUNTS
RECEIVABLE
LEDGER**

NAME Adler Company

ADDRESS 7608 Melton Ave., Los Angeles, CA 90025-3942

DATE	ITEM	POST. REF.	DEBIT	CREDIT	BALANCE
1987 Oct. 10		S35	6 7 5 0 00		6 7 5 0 00

As each debit to a customer's account is posted, a check mark (✔) is inserted in the posting reference column of the sales journal. At the end of each month, the amount column of the sales journal is added, the journal is ruled, and the total is posted as a debit to Accounts Receivable and a credit to Sales. The respective account numbers are then inserted below the total to indicate that the posting is completed.

Sales Returns and Allowances. When merchandise sold is returned or a price adjustment is granted, an entry is made in the general journal according to the principles described in Chapter 4. During October, Kannon Corporation issued credit memorandum and prepared the following entry in a two-column general journal:

**GENERAL
JOURNAL
ENTRY
FOR SALES
RETURNS
AND
ALLOWANCES**

		JOURNAL			PAGE 18	
	DATE	DESCRIPTION	POST. REF.	DEBIT	CREDIT	
1	1987 Oct. 13	Sales Returns and Allowances	412	2 2 5 00		1
2		Accounts Receivable—				2
3		Adler Company	113 ✔		2 2 5 00	3
4		Credit Memo No. 32				4

Note the *diagonal line* and *double posting* in the entry to record the credit memorandum. The diagonal line is placed in the posting reference column *at the time the entry is recorded in the general journal.*

If a cash refund is made because of merchandise returned or for an allowance, Sales Returns and Allowances is debited and Cash is credited. The entry would be recorded in the cash payments journal.

Cash Receipts Journal

All transactions that increase the amount of cash are recorded in a **cash receipts journal**. In a typical merchandising business, the most frequent sources of cash receipts are likely to be cash sales and collections from customers on account.

The cash receipts journal has a special column entitled Cash Dr. The frequency of the various kinds of transactions in which cash is received determines the titles of the other columns. The cash receipts journal of Kannon Corporation for October is as follows:

receened cash cash sales account (handwritten)

CASH RECEIPTS JOURNAL							PAGE 14	
	DATE	ACCOUNT CREDITED	POST. REF.	SUNDRY ACCOUNTS CR.	SALES CR.	ACCOUNTS REC. CR.	SALES DISCOUNTS DR.	CASH DR.
1	1987 Oct. 2	Notes Receivable	112	2400 00				2544 00	1
2		Interest Income	812	144 00					2
3	5	Barnes Inc.	✓			5800 00	116 00	5684 00	3
4	6	Fogarty & Jacobs	✓			2625 00	52 50	2572 50	4
5	7	Sales	✓		3700 00			3700 00	5
6	10	David T. Mattox	✓			600 00	12 00	588 00	6
7	13	Standard Supply Co.	✓			1604 00	32 08	1571 92	7
8	14	Sales	✓		1632 00			1632 00	8
9	17	Adler Company	✓			6525 00	130 50	6394 50	9
10	19	Hamilton Inc.	✓			4850 00		4850 00	10
11	21	Sales	✓		1920 30			1920 30	11
12	23	Purchases Returns							12
13		and Allowances	512	86 20				86 20	13
14	24	Wallace Corporation	✓			2200 00		2200 00	14
15	27	Hamilton Inc.	✓			7865 00	157 30	7707 70	15
16	28	Sales	✓		2086 00			2086 00	16
17	31	Sales	✓		2423 40			2423 40	17
18	31			2630 20	11761 70	32069 00	500 38	45960 52	18
19				(✓)	(411)	(113)	(413)	(111)	19

The Sundry Accounts Cr. column is used for recording credits to any account for which there is no special column. For example, as of October 2, in the illustration, the receipt of $2,544 in payment of an interest-bearing note was recorded by a credit to Notes Receivable of $2,400 and a credit to Interest Income of $144. Both amounts were entered in the Sundry Accounts Cr. column. The posting references for the credits were inserted at the time the amounts were posted.

The Sales Cr. column is used for recording sales of merchandise for cash. Each individual sale is recorded on a cash register, and the totals thus accumulated are recorded in the cash receipts journal daily, weekly, or at other regular intervals. This is illustrated by the entry of October 7 recording weekly sales and cash receipts of $3,700. Since the total of the Sales Cr. column will be posted at the end of the month, a check mark is inserted in the posting reference column to show that the $3,700 item needs no further attention.

Credits to customers accounts for payments of invoices are recorded in the Accounts Receivable Cr. column. The amount of the cash discount granted, if any, is recorded in the Sales Discounts Dr. column, and the amount of cash actually received is recorded in the Cash Dr. column. The entry on October 5 illustrates the use of these columns. Cash in the amount of $5,684 was received from Barnes Inc. in payment of its account of $5,800, the cash discount being 2% of $5,800, or $116.

Each amount in the Sundry Accounts Cr. column of the cash receipts journal is posted to the proper account in the general ledger at frequent intervals during the month. The posting is indicated by inserting the account number in the posting reference column. At regular intervals the amounts in the Accounts Receivable Cr. column are posted to the customers accounts in the subsidiary ledger, and "CR" and the proper page number are inserted in the posting reference columns of the accounts. Check marks are placed in the posting reference column of the journal to show that the amounts have been posted. None of the individual amounts in the remaining three columns of the cash receipts journal are posted.

At the end of the month, all of the amount columns are footed, the equality of the debits and credits is proved, and the journal is ruled. Because each amount in the Sundry Accounts Cr. column has been posted individually to a general ledger account, a check mark is inserted below the column total to indicate that no further action is needed. The totals of the other four columns are posted to the proper accounts in the general ledger and their account numbers are inserted below the totals to show that the posting has been completed.

The flow of data from the cash receipts journal to the ledgers of Kannon Corporation is illustrated in the following diagram:

FLOW OF DATA FROM CASH RECEIPTS JOURNAL TO LEDGERS

Cash Receipts Journal

Account Credited	P. R.	Sundry Accounts Cr.	Sales Cr.	Accounts Receivable Cr.	Sales Discounts Dr.	Cash Dr.
Notes Receivable	112	2,400.00				2,544.00
Interest Income	811	144.00				
Barnes Inc.	✔			5,800.00	116.00	5,684.00
Fogarty & Jacobs	✔			2,625.00	52.50	2,572.50
Sales	✔		3,700.00			3,700.00
David T. Mattox	✔			600.00	12.00	588.00
Sales	✔		2,423.40			2,423.40
		2,630.20	11,761.70	32,069.00	500.38	45,960.52

General Ledger

Notes Receivable		Sales		Sales Discounts
2,400.00		11,761.70		500.38

Interest Income		Accounts Receivable		Cash
144.00		32,069.00		45,960.52

Accounts Receivable Ledger

Each individual entry is posted as a credit to an account in the accounts receivable ledger, making a total of $32,069.

Accounts Receivable Control and Subsidiary Ledger

During October, the following postings were made to Accounts Receivable in the general ledger of Kannon Corporation:

Debits

Oct. 31 Total sales on account (sales journal) $48,940.00

Credits

Oct. 13 A sales return (general journal) 225.00
Oct. 31 Total cash received on account (cash receipts journal) .. 32,069.00

The accounts receivable controlling account of Kannon Corporation as of October 31 is as follows:

GENERAL LEDGER

ACCOUNT Accounts Receivable								ACCOUNT NO. 113	
DATE	ITEM	POST. REF.	DEBIT	CREDIT	BALANCE				
					DEBIT		CREDIT		
1987 Oct. 1	Balance	✔			17 2 6 0 00				
13		J18		2 2 5 00	17 0 3 5 00				
31		S35	48 9 4 0 00		65 9 7 5 00				
31		CR14		32 0 6 9 00	33 9 0 6 00				

ACCOUNTS RECEIVABLE ACCOUNT IN THE GENERAL LEDGER AT THE END OF THE MONTH

The posting procedures and determination of the balances of the accounts in the accounts receivable ledger and the preparation of the schedule of accounts receivable are comparable to those for accounts payable and are therefore not illustrated.

ELECTRONIC DATA PROCESSING SYSTEMS

A system that uses an electronic computer to process accounting data may be termed an **electronic data processing (EDP)** system. An electronic data processing system processes accounting data in much the same way as does a manual system but with greater speed and accuracy. For example, electronic cash registers are being used with the computer to process both cash and credit sales. For cash sales, the data entered by the salesclerk in the electronic cash register provide the basis for the computer to update the accounting records, including the cash receipts journal and the general ledger accounts. For credit sales, the salesclerk enters the customer's account number and other relevant data in the electronic cash register. The computer then updates the customer's account in the subsidiary ledger and the other accounting records. Printouts of the updated general ledger and subsidiary account balances, the sales journal, and customers statements of account can be obtained when needed.

In recent years, microcomputers and minicomputers have made electronic data processing affordable to small and medium-size businesses. Some small businesses have been able to gain the use of electronic data processing through computer service centers, which provide computer services on a fee basis.

CHAPTER REVIEW

KEY POINTS

1. Principles of Accounting Systems.

Although accounting systems will vary from business to business, the following broad principles will apply to all systems: cost-effectiveness balance; flexibility to meet future needs; adequate internal controls; effective reporting; and adaptation to organizational structure.

2. Accounting System Installation and Revision.

Accounting system installation and revision involves three phases: (1) analysis of information needs, (2) design of the new system, and (3) implementation of proposals.

3. Internal Controls.

Internal controls are classified as (1) administrative controls and (2) accounting controls. Although the details of the system of internal control will vary according to size and type of business, the following broad principles of internal control apply to most businesses: competent personnel and rotation of duties, assignment of responsibility, separation of responsibility for related operations, separation of operations and accounting, proofs and security measures, and independent review.

4. Data Processing Methods.

The entire amount of data needed by an enterprise is called its data base. Depending upon the variety and the amount of data included in the data base, various processing methods—manual and computerized—may be used.

5. Subsidiary Ledgers and Special Journals.

Subsidiary ledgers may be used to maintain separate records for each creditor and debtor. When subsidiary ledgers are used, each subsidiary ledger is represented in the general ledger by a summarizing account, called a controlling account. The sum of the balances of the accounts in a subsidiary ledger must agree with the balance of the related controlling account.

One of the simplest methods of reducing the processing time and expense of recording a large number of transactions in a manual system is to use special journals. Special journals commonly used in medium-size merchandising firms include the following: purchases journal, cash payments journal, sales journal, and cash receipts journal.

The purchases journal is used to record purchases of merchandise or other items on account. The cash payments journal is used to record the payment of cash for any purpose. The sales journal is used to record the sale of merchandise on account. The cash receipts journal is used to record the receipt of cash from any source. The two-column general journal is used for recording transactions that do not "fit" in any of the four special journals.

6. Electronic Data Processing Systems.

Electronic data processing systems (computerized systems) may be employed to process data quickly and efficiently. In recent years, microcomputers and minicomputers have made electronic data processing available to businesses of all sizes.

KEY TERMS

accounting system 285
internal controls 286
internal administrative controls 289
internal accounting controls 289
subsidiary ledger 292
general ledger 292
controlling account 292
accounts payable ledger 292

accounts receivable ledger 293
special journals 293
general journal 294
purchases journal 294
cash payments journal 299
sales journal 303
cash receipts journal 304
electronic data processing
(EDP) 307

SELF-EXAMINATION QUESTIONS

Answers in Appendix B.

1. The final phase of the revision of an accounting system that involves carrying out the proposals for changes in the system is termed:
   A. systems analysis   C. systems implementation
   B. systems design   D. none of the above

2. The detailed procedures adopted by management to control operations are collectively termed:
   A. internal controls   C. internal administrative controls
   B. internal accounting controls   D. none of the above

3. A payment of cash for the purchase of merchandise would be recorded in the:
   A. purchases journal   C. sales journal
   B. cash payments journal   D. cash receipts journal

4. When there are a large number of individual accounts with a common characteristic, it is common to place them in a separate ledger called a:
   A. subsidiary ledger   C. accounts payable ledger
   B. creditors ledger   D. accounts receivable ledger

5. The controlling account in the general ledger that summarizes the debits and credits to the individual customers accounts in the subsidiary ledger is entitled:
   A. Accounts Payable   C. Sales
   B. Accounts Receivable   D. Purchases

ILLUSTRATIVE PROBLEM

Selected transactions of O'Malley Inc. for the month of May are as follows:

(a) May 1 Issued Check No. 1001 in payment of rent for May, $1,200.

(b)   2 Purchased merchandise on account from McMillan Co., terms 2/10, n/30, FOB shipping point, $3,600.

(c)   4 Issued Check No. 1003 in payment of transportation charges on the merchandise purchased on May 2, $320.

(d)   8 Sold merchandise on account to Waller Inc., Invoice No. 51, terms 1/10, n/eom, FOB shipping point, $4,500.

(e)   9 Issued Check No. 1005 for office supplies purchased, $450.

(f)   10 Received cash for office supplies sold to employees at cost, $120.

(g)   11 Purchased office equipment on account from Fender Office Products, $15,000.

(h)   12 Issued Credit Memorandum No. 801 for $400 to Waller Inc. for merchandise returned.

(i) 12 Issued Check No. 1010 in payment of the merchandise pur-
     chased from McMillan Co. on May 2, less discount, $3,528.

(j) 16 Sold merchandise on account to Riepe Co., Invoice No. 58,
     terms 1/10, n/30, FOB shipping point, $8,000.

(k) 18 Received $4,059 from Waller Inc. in payment of May 8 invoice,
     less return of May 12 and discount.

(l) 20 Issued additional capital stock for cash, $100,000.

(m) 23 Issued Credit Memorandum No. 802 for $220 to Riepe Co. for a
     price adjustment on damaged merchandise sold on May 16.

(n) 24 Sold merchandise on nonbank credit cards, $16,700.

(o) 25 Sold merchandise for cash, $15,900.

(p) 30 Issued Check No. 1040 in payment of dividends to stock-
     holders, $10,000.

(q) 30 Issued Check No. 1041 in payment of electricity and water bills,
     $690.

(r) 30 Issued Check No. 1042 in payment of office and sales salaries
     for May, $15,800.

(s) 31 Recorded adjusting entries from the work sheet prepared for
     the fiscal year ended May 31.

O'Malley Inc. maintains a purchases journal, a cash payments journal, a sales journal, a cash receipts journal, and a general journal. In addition, accounts receivable and accounts payable subsidiary ledgers are used.

Instructions:

1. Indicate the journal in which each of the preceding transactions [(a) through (s)] would be recorded.
2. Indicate whether an account in the accounts receivable or accounts payable subsidiary ledgers would be affected for each of the preceding transactions.
3. Record transactions (b), (c), (d), (h), (i) and (k) in the appropriate journals.

SOLUTION

(1)	(2)
(a) Cash payments journal	
(b) Purchases journal	Accounts payable ledger
(c) Cash payments journal	
(d) Sales journal	Accounts receivable ledger
(e) Cash payments journal	
(f) Cash receipts journal	
(g) Purchases journal	Accounts payable ledger
(h) General journal	Accounts receivable ledger
(i) Cash payments journal	Accounts payable ledger

	(1)	(2)
(j)	Sales journal	Accounts receivable ledger
(k)	Cash receipts journal	Accounts receivable ledger
(l)	Cash receipts journal	
(m)	General journal	Accounts receivable ledger
(n)	Sales journal	Accounts receivable ledger
(o)	Cash receipts journal	
(p)	Cash payments journal	
(q)	Cash payments journal	
(r)	Cash payments journal	
(s)	General journal	

(3)
Transaction (b):

PURCHASES JOURNAL

DATE	ACCOUNT CREDITED	POST. REF.	ACCOUNTS PAYABLE CR.	PURCHASES DR.	STORE SUPPLIES DR.
May 2	McMillan Co.		3 6 0 0 00	3 6 0 0 00	

Transactions (c) and (i):

CASH PAYMENTS JOURNAL

DATE	CK. NO.	ACCOUNT DEBITED	POST. REF.	SUNDRY ACCOUNTS DR.	ACCOUNTS PAYABLE DR.	PURCHASES DISCOUNTS CR.	CASH CR.
May 4	1003	Transportation In		3 2 0 00			3 2 0 00
12	1010	McMillan Co.			3 6 0 0 00	7 2 00	3 5 2 8 00

Transaction (d):

SALES JOURNAL

DATE	INVOICE NO.	ACCOUNT DEBITED	POST. REF.	ACCTS. REC. DR. SALES CR.
May 8	51	Waller Inc.		4 5 0 0 00

Transaction (h):

JOURNAL

DATE	DESCRIPTION	POST. REF.	DEBIT	CREDIT
May 12	Sales Returns and Allowances		4 0 0 00	
	Accounts Receivable — Waller Inc.			4 0 0 00
	Credit Memo No. 801.			

Transaction (k):

CASH RECEIPTS JOURNAL

DATE	ACCOUNT CREDITED	POST. REF.	SUNDRY ACCOUNTS CR.	SALES CR.	ACCOUNTS REC. CR.	SALES DISCOUNTS DR.	CASH DR.
May 18	Waller Inc.				4 1 0 0 00	4 1 00	4 0 5 9 00

DISCUSSION QUESTIONS

1. Why is the accounting system of an enterprise an information system?

2. What are internal controls?

3. What is the objective of systems analysis?

4. How do internal administrative controls and internal accounting controls differ?

5. How does a policy of rotating clerical employees from job to job aid in strengthening internal control?

6. Why should the responsibility for a sequence of related operations be divided among different persons?

7. The ticket seller at a movie theater doubles as ticket taker for a few minutes each day while the ticket taker is on a "break." Which principle of internal control is violated in this situation?

8. Why should the responsibility for maintaining the accounting records be separated from the responsibility for operations?

9. How can the use of fidelity insurance aid internal control?

10. How does a periodic review by internal auditors strengthen the system of internal control?

11. What is the term applied (a) to the ledger containing the individual customers accounts and (b) to the single account summarizing accounts receivable?

12. The following items were purchased on account by a retail hardware store. Indicate the account to which each purchase should be debited.
    (a) Five lawnmowers
    (b) Two dozen hammers
    (c) One display case
    (d) One gross of pads of sales tickets
    (e) Two gross of flashlight batteries
    (f) Two kegs of nails
    (g) Two-year fire insurance policy on building
    (h) One electronic calculator for office use
    (i) One cash register

13. During the current month, the following errors occurred in recording transactions in the purchases journal or in posting therefrom:
    (a) An invoice for merchandise of $1,725 from Harris Corp. was recorded as having been received from Harrison Co., another supplier.
    (b) An invoice for merchandise of $6,400 was recorded as $4,600.
    (c) A credit of $65 to Cuthbert Bros. was posted as $56 in the subsidiary ledger.
    (d) The accounts payable column of the purchases journal was underadded by $100.
    How will each error come to the bookkeeper's attention, other than by chance discovery?

14. The accounts payable and cash columns in the cash payments journal were unknowingly overadded by $1,000 at the end of the month. (a) Assuming no other errors in recording or posting, will the error cause the trial balance totals to be unequal? (b) Will the creditors ledger agree with the accounts payable controlling account?

15. In recording a cash payment, the bookkeeper enters the correct amount of $600 in the Accounts Payable Dr. column and the correct amount of $588 in the Cash Cr. column, but omits the entry for Purchases Discounts. How will the error be found, other than by chance discovery?

16. Assuming the use of a two-column general journal and a purchases journal and a cash payments journal as illustrated in this chapter, indicate the journal in which each of the following transactions should be recorded:

(a) Purchase of merchandise for cash.
(b) Purchase of store equipment on account.
(c) Payment of cash on account to creditor.
(d) Return of portion of merchandise purchased in (a).
(e) Purchase of office supplies on account.
(f) Withdrawal of cash by owner.

17. In recording 100 sales of merchandise on account during a single month, how many times will it be necessary to write "Sales" (a) if each transaction, including sales, is recorded individually in a two-column general journal; (b) if each sale is recorded in a sales journal?

18. How many individual postings to Sales for the month would be needed in Question 17, if the procedure described in (a) had been used; if the procedure described in (b) had been used?

19. In posting the following general journal entry, the bookkeeper posted correctly to Capel's account but failed to post to the controlling account.

    June 9 Sales Returns and Allowances   402   150
            Accounts Receivable — C. H. Capel. . . . .   ✔   150

    (a) How will the error be discovered? (b) Describe the procedure that is designed to prevent oversights of this type.

20. What does a check mark (✔) in the posting reference column of the cash receipts journal, which is illustrated in this chapter, signify (a) when the account being credited is an account receivable; (b) when the account credited is Sales?

21. Assuming the use of a two-column general journal and a sales journal and a cash receipts journal as illustrated in this chapter, indicate the journal in which each of the following transactions should be recorded:
    (a) Sale of merchandise for cash.
    (b) Investment of additional cash in the business by the owner.
    (c) Receipt of cash refund for an overcharge on a purchase of merchandise.
    (d) Sale of office supplies on account, at cost, to a neighboring business.
    (e) Receipt of cash on account from customer.
    (f) Receipt of cash from sale of office equipment.
    (g) Sale of merchandise on account.
    (h) Issuance of credit memorandum to customer.
    (i) Adjustment to record accrued salaries at the end of the year.
    (j) Closing of the owner's drawing account at the end of the year.

22. Real World Focus. One of the largest single company frauds in history was perpetrated against Equity Funding Corporation of America. Approximately $2 billion of insurance policies that were claimed to have been sold by the company were bogus. The bogus policies, which were supported by falsified policy applications, were listed along with real policies on Equity Funding's computer tapes (records). These computer tapes were kept in a separate room where they were easily accessible by Equity Funding personnel, including the computer programmers. In addition, computer programmers and other company personnel had access to the computer. What general weaknesses in Equity Funding's internal controls contributed to the occurrence and the size of the fraud?

EXERCISES

Exercise 7–1. **Identification of postings from purchases journal.** Using the following purchases journal, identify each of the posting references, indicated by a letter, as representing (1) a posting to a general ledger account, (2) a posting to a subsidiary ledger account, or (3) that no posting is required.

(Left Page)   PURCHASES JOURNAL

Date	Account Credited	Post. Ref.	Accounts Payable Cr.
19--			
Jan. 4	Cowan Auto Supply	(a)	4,525
6	Porter Supply Inc.	(b)	3,000
11	Baker Products	(d)	1,950
13	Wilson and Wilson	(e)	6,800
20	Cowan Auto Supply	(f)	3,775
27	Porter Supply Inc.	(g)	9,100
31			29,150
			(i)

(Right Page) 31

Purchases Dr.	Store Supplies Dr.	Office Supplies Dr.	Sundry Accounts Dr. Account	Post. Ref.	Amount
4,525	......	......			......
......	......	......	Office Equipment.....	(c)	3,000
......	1,500	450	....	...	......
6,800	......	......	....	...	......
3,775	......	......	....	...	......
......	......	......	Store Equipment	(h)	9,100
15,100	1,500	450			12,100
(j)	(k)	(l)			(m)

post reference n v.

Exercise 7–2. **Identification of postings from cash payments journal.** Using the following cash payments journal, identify each of the posting references, indicated by a letter, as representing (1) a posting to a general ledger account, (2) a posting to a subsidiary ledger account, or (3) that no posting is required.

CASH PAYMENTS JOURNAL   Page 35

Date	Ck. No.	Account Debited	Post. Ref.	Sundry Accounts Dr.	Accounts Payable Dr.	Purchases Discounts Cr.	Cash Cr.
19--							
May 3	611	W. A. Davis Co.........	(a)	.....	4,000	40	3,960
5	612	Sales Returns and					
		Allowances..........	(b)	325	.....	.....	325
10	613	Purchases	(c)	3,200	.....	.....	3,200
17	614	Coe Bros..............	(d)	.....	2,500	50	2,450
20	615	Office Equipment	(e)	2,100	.....	.....	2,100
22	616	Advertising Expense	(f)	400	.....	.....	400
25	617	Office Supplies	(g)	250	.....	.....	250
27	618	Evans Co..............	(h)	.....	5,500	55	5,445
31	619	Salaries Expense	(i)	1,750	.....	.....	1,750
31				8,025	12,000	145	19,880
				(j)	(k)	(l)	(m)

Exercise 7–3. Identification of transactions in accounts payable ledger account. The debits and credits from three related transactions are presented in the following account taken from the accounts payable ledger:

NAME Eastwood Supplies

ADDRESS 1600 Neil Street

Date	Item	Post. Ref.	Debit	Credit	Balance
19--					
July 6		P34		12,500.00	12,500.00
10		J10	500.00		12,000.00
16		CP37	12,000.00		—

Describe each transaction.

Exercise 7–4. Error in accounts payable ledger and schedule of accounts payable. After Collins Company had completed all posting for the month of October in the current year, the sum of the balances in the following accounts payable ledger did not agree with the balance of the appropriate controlling account in the general ledger.

NAME C. D. Adams Co.

ADDRESS 1240 W. Main Street

Date	Item	Post. Ref.	Debit	Credit	Balance
19--					
Oct. 1	Balance	✔			4,750
10		CP22	4,750		—
17		P30		3,250	3,250
25		J7	250		2,000

NAME Baker and Powell

ADDRESS 717 Elm Street

Date	Item	Post. Ref.	Debit	Credit	Balance
Oct. 1	Balance	✔			6,100
18		CP23	6,100		—
29		P31		7,500	7,500

NAME C. D. Davis and Son

ADDRESS 972 S. Tenth Street

Date	Item	Post. Ref.	Debit	Credit	Balance
Oct. 17		P30		3,750	3,750
27		P31		7,000	10,750

NAME John Reese Supply

ADDRESS 1170 Mattis Avenue

Date	Item	Post. Ref.	Debit	Credit	Balance
Oct. 1	Balance	✔			8,250
7		P30		4,900	13,050
12		J7	250		12,800
20		CP23	5,700		7,100

NAME C. B. Wilcox Co.

ADDRESS 915 E. Walnut Street

Date	Item	Post. Ref.	Debit	Credit	Balance
Oct. 5		P30		2,750	2,750

Assuming that the controlling account balance of $31,200 has been verified as correct, (a) determine the error(s) in the preceding accounts and (b) prepare a schedule of accounts payable.

Exercise 7–5.   Identification of transactions in accounts receivable ledger. The debits and credits from three related transactions are presented in the following account taken from the accounts receivable ledger:

NAME P. G. Williams

ADDRESS 1319 Oriole Circle

Date	Item	Post. Ref.	Debit	Credit	Balance
19--					
Sept. 3		S50	5,000.00		5,000.00
9		J9		700.00	4,300.00
13		CR38		4,300.00	—

Describe each transaction.

Exercise 7–6.   Entries to record memorandums and correction of errors. Present general journal entries to record the following transactions:

July 5. Received credit memorandum for return of equipment purchased on account from Ladd Equipment Co. on July 1, $2,500.

8. Issued credit memorandum for return of merchandise sold on account to R. D. Sharp Co. on June 30, $900.

12. Issued debit memorandum for return of merchandise purchased on account from L. L. Linke Inc. on July 7, $1,100.

19. Issued credit memorandum for allowance made to C. C. Palmer for defective merchandise sold on account on July 13, $220.

24. Corrected error of June 30 when a note received from JMB Co. for $5,000 on account was not recorded.

Exercise 7–7.   Entries to correct errors. Present the general journal entries to correct the following errors, assuming that the incorrect entries had been posted and that the corrections are recorded in the same period in which the errors occurred.

(a) A cash receipt of $735 ($750 less 2% discount) from Ann Ponds was recorded as a $735 debit to Cash and a $735 credit to the subsidiary account Ann Ponds (and to Accounts Receivable).

(b) A cash remittance of $220 received from Flowers Co. as payment on account was recorded as a cash sale.

(c) A cash sale of $410 to O. C. Neale was recorded as a sale on account.

(d) Transportation costs of $72 incurred on purchases of merchandise had been debited to Office Equipment.

(e) A $490 cash purchase of merchandise from C. D. Richards Co. had been recorded as a purchase on account.

PROBLEMS

Series A

Problem 7–1A. Chart of accounts for sole proprietorship. Janet Abrams acquired the assets and assumed the liabilities of two competing businesses and organized Westview Supply Co. The new enterprise will use the following asset, liability, and owner's equity accounts, arranged in alphabetical order:

Janet Abrams, Capital	Land
Janet Abrams, Drawing	Merchandise Inventory
Accounts Payable	Mortgage Note Payable
Accounts Receivable	(long-term)
Accumulated Depreciation—Building	Notes Payable (short-term)
Accumulated Depreciation—Delivery Equipment	Office Equipment
Accumulated Depreciation—Office Equipment	Office Supplies
Accumulated Depreciation—Store Equipment	Prepaid Insurance
Building	Salaries Payable
Cash	Store Equipment
Delivery Equipment	Store Supplies
Interest Payable	Taxes Payable

Instructions:

Construct a chart of accounts, assigning account numbers and arranging the accounts in balance sheet order, as illustrated on page 63. Each account number is to be composed of three digits: the first digit is to indicate the major classification ("1" for assets, etc.), the second digit is to indicate the subclassification ("11" for current assets, etc.), and the third digit is to identify the specific account ("111" for Cash, etc.).

Problem 7–2A. Purchases and purchases returns, accounts payable account, and accounts payable ledger. Purchases on account and related returns and allowances completed by Video Sales during May of the current year are as follows:

May 2. Purchased merchandise on account from Yu Co., $6,150.50
     4. Purchased merchandise on account from O'Grady Corp. $9,250.
     5. Received a credit memorandum from Yu Co. for merchandise returned, $200.
     9. Purchased office supplies on account from Tyler Supply, $175.30.
   13. Purchased merchandise on account from Yu Co., $4,370.50.
   14. Purchased office equipment on account from Diamond Equipment Co., $5,500.
   17. Purchased merchandise on account from James Co., $3,100.

May 19. Received a credit memorandum from Tyler Supply for office supplies returned, $22.50.

20. Purchased merchandise on account from Craig Co., $1,130.30.

24. Purchased store supplies on account from Tyler Supply, $325.

27. Received a credit memorandum from O'Grady Corp. as an allowance for damaged merchandise, $500.

29. Purchased merchandise on account from James Co., $475.15

31. Purchased office supplies on account from Tyler Supply, $210.50.

Instructions:

(1) Open the following accounts in the general ledger and enter the balances as of May 1:

114	Store Supplies	$ 460.00
115	Office Supplies	327.40
122	Office Equipment	32,500.00
211	Accounts Payable	12,212.30
511	Purchases	89,917.40
512	Purchases Returns and Allowances	2,170.10

(2) Open the following accounts in the accounts payable ledger and enter the balances in the balance columns as of May 1: Craig Co., $2,177.70; Diamond Equipment Co.; James Co., $4,550.25; O'Grady Corp., $5,484.35; Tyler Supply; Yu Co.

(3) Record the transactions for May, posting to the creditors accounts in the accounts payable ledger immediately after each entry. Use a purchases journal, similar to the one illustrated on pages 294 and 295, and a two-column general journal.

(4) Post the general journal and the purchases journal to the accounts in the general ledger.

(5) (a) What is the sum of the balances in the subsidiary ledger at May 31?
    (b) What is the balance of the controlling account at May 31?

Problem 7–3A.   Purchases and cash payments journals; accounts payable and general ledgers. Ladd Co. was established on March 15 of the current year. Transactions related to purchases, returns and allowances, and cash payments during the remainder of March are as follows:

Mar. 16. Issued Check No. 1 in payment of rent for March, $1,000.

16. Purchased store equipment on account from Harper Equipment Corp., $9,900.

17. Purchased merchandise on account from Carter Clothing, $3,250.

18. Issued Check No. 2 in payment of store supplies, $140, and office supplies, $75.

19. Purchased merchandise on account from Hernandez Clothing Co., $5,920.

20. Purchased merchandise on account from Adams Co., $4,600.

22. Received a credit memorandum from Hernandez Clothing Co. for returned merchandise, $220.
    Post the journals to the accounts payable ledger.

Mar. 24. Issued Check No. 3 to Harper Equipment Corp. in payment of invoice of $9,900.

25. Received a credit memorandum from Adams Co. for defective merchandise, $300.

26. Issued Check No. 4 to Carter Clothing in payment of invoice of $3,250, less 2% discount.

28. Issued Check No. 5 to a cash customer for merchandise returned, $65.

28. Issued Check No. 6 to Hernandez Clothing Co. in payment of the balance owed, less 2% discount.

28. Purchased merchandise on account from Adams Co., $5,250.
Post the journals to the accounts payable ledger.

30. Purchased the following from Harper Equipment Corp. on account: store supplies, $110; office supplies, $42; office equipment, $3,450.

30. Issued Check No. 7 to Adams Co. in payment of invoice of $4,600, less the credit of $300 and 1% discount.

30. Purchased merchandise on account from Carter Clothing, $1,200.

31. Issued Check No. 8 in payment of store supplies, $170.

31. Issued Check No. 9 in payment of sales salaries, $2,200.

31. Received a credit memorandum from Harper Equipment Corp. for defect in office equipment, $50.
Post the journals to the accounts payable ledger.

Instructions:

(1) Open the following accounts in the general ledger, using the account numbers indicated:

111	Cash	412	Sales Returns and Allowances
116	Store Supplies	511	Purchases
117	Office Supplies	512	Purchases Returns and Allowances
121	Store Equipment	513	Purchases Discounts
122	Office Equipment	611	Sales Salaries Expense
211	Accounts Payable	712	Rent Expense

(2) Open the following accounts in the accounts payable ledger: Adams Co.; Carter Clothing; Harper Equipment Corp.; Hernandez Clothing Co.

(3) Record the transactions for March, using a purchases journal similar to the one illustrated on pages 294 and 295, a cash payments journal similar to the one illustrated on page 299, and a two-column general journal. Post to the accounts payable ledger at the points indicated in the narrative of transactions.

(4) Post the appropriate individual entries to the general ledger (Sundry Accounts columns of the purchases journal and the cash payments journal; both columns of the general journal).

(5) Total each of the columns of the purchases journal and the cash payments journal, and post the appropriate totals to the general ledger. (Because the problem does not include transactions related to cash receipts, the cash account in the ledger will have a credit balance.)

(6) Prepare a schedule of accounts payable.

Problem 7–4A. Sales journal; accounts receivable and general ledgers.

RGM Company was established on May 15 of the current year. Its sales of merchandise on account and related returns and allowances during the remainder of the month are as follows. Terms of all sales were 1/10, n/30, FOB destination.

May 20. Sold merchandise on account to Bows Co., Invoice No. 1, $1,200.
    22. Sold merchandise on account to Stark Inc., Invoice No. 2, $2,750.
    24. Sold merchandise on account to Morris Co., Invoice No. 3, $3,175.
    25. Issued Credit Memorandum No. 1 for $100 to Bows Co. for merchandise returned.
    27. Sold merchandise on account to C. D. Walters Co., Invoice No. 4, $2,500.
    28. Sold merchandise on account to Unisac Inc., Invoice No. 5, $1,500.
    28. Issued Credit Memorandum No. 2 for $150 to Stark Inc. for merchandise returned.
    30. Sold merchandise on account to Stark Inc., Invoice No. 6, $2,925.
    30. Issued Credit Memorandum No. 3 for $75 to C. D. Walters Co. for damages to merchandise caused by faulty packing.
    31. Sold merchandise on account to Morris Co., Invoice No. 7, $995.

Instructions:

(1) Open the following accounts in the general ledger, using the account numbers indicated: Accounts Receivable, 113; Sales, 411; Sales Returns and Allowances, 412.
(2) Open the following accounts in the accounts receivable ledger: Bows Co.; Morris Co.; Stark Inc.; Unisac Inc.; C. D. Walters Co.
(3) Record the transactions for May, posting to the customers accounts in the accounts receivable ledger and inserting the balance immediately after recording each entry. Use a sales journal, similar to the one illustrated on page 303, and a two-column general journal.
(4) Post the general journal and the sales journal to the three accounts opened in the general ledger, inserting the account balances only after the last postings.
(5) (a) What is the sum of the balances of the accounts in the subsidiary ledger at May 31?
    (b) What is the balance of the controlling account at May 31?

If the working papers correlating with the textbook are not used, omit Problem 7–5A.

Problem 7–5A. Sales and cash receipts journals; accounts receivable and general ledgers. Three journals, the accounts receivable ledger, and portions of the general ledger of White Company are presented in the working papers. Sales invoices and credit memorandums were entered in the journals by an assistant. Terms of sales on account are 1/10, n/30, FOB shipping point. Transactions in which cash and notes receivable were received during July are as follows:

July 2. Received $5,940 from C. D. Martin Co. in payment of June 22 invoice, less discount.
    3. Received $20,200 in payment of $20,000 note receivable and interest of $200.
    Post transactions of July 2 and 6 to accounts receivable ledger.
    8. Received $6,435 from Janet Rowe Co. in payment of June 28 invoice, less discount.

July 10. Received $2,200 from R. C. Fellows Inc. in payment of June 10 invoice, no discount.

15. Cash sales for first half of July totaled $14,915.
Post transactions of July 8, 10, 12, and 15 to accounts receivable ledger.

19. Received $1,250 refund for return of defective equipment purchased for cash in June.

20. Received $2,871 from C. D. Martin Co. in payment of balance due on July 10 invoice, less discount.

22. Received $5,742 from R. C. Fellows Inc. in payment of July 12 invoice, less discount.
Post transactions of July 17, 20, 22, and 23 to accounts receivable ledger.

28. Received $50 for sale of office supplies at cost.

31. Received $1,750 cash and a $2,500 note receivable from Ignacio and Co. in settlement of the balance due on the invoice of July 2, no discount. (Record receipt of note in the general journal.)

31. Cash sales for the second half of July totaled $16,100.
Post transactions of July 27, 28, 30, and 31 to accounts receivable ledger.

Instructions:

(1) Record the cash receipts in the cash receipts journal and the note in the general journal. Before recording a receipt of cash on account, determine the balance of the customer's account. Post the entries from the three journals, in date sequence, to the accounts receivable ledger in accordance with the instructions in the narrative of transactions. Insert the new balance after each posting to an account.

(2) Post the appropriate individual entries from the cash receipts journal and the general journal to the general ledger.

(3) Total each of the columns of the sales journal and the cash receipts journal and post the appropriate totals to the general ledger. Insert the balance of each account after the last posting.

(4) Prepare a schedule of the accounts receivable as of July 31 and compare the total with the balance of the controlling account.

Problem 7–6A. Sales and cash receipts journals; accounts receivable and general ledgers. Transactions related to sales and cash receipts completed by W. A. Duke Company during the period June 15–30 of the current year are as follows. The terms of all sales on account are 1/10, n/30, FOB shipping point.

June 15. Issued Invoice No. 717 to Towers Co., $6,100.

16. Received cash from F. G. Black Co. for the balance owed on its account, less discount.

17. Issued Invoice No. 718 to Halloway Co., $7,700.

18. Issued Invoice No. 719 to Ross and Son, $2,600.
Post all journals to the accounts receivable ledger.

21. Received cash from Halloway Co. for the balance owed on June 15, no discount.

June 22. Issued Credit Memorandum No. 55 to Towers Co., $200.
    24. Issued Invoice No. 720 to Halloway Co., $7,000.
    24. Received $1,050 in payment of a $1,000 note receivable and interest of $50.
    Post all journals to the accounts receivable ledger.
    25. Received cash from Towers Co. for the balance due on invoice of June 15, less discount.
    27. Received cash from Halloway Co. for invoice of June 17, less discount.
    29. Issued Invoice No. 721 to F. G. Black Co., $8,500.
    30. Recorded cash sales for the second half of the month, $11,750.
    30. Issued Credit Memorandum No. 56 to F. G. Black Co., $150.
    Post all journals to the accounts receivable ledger.

Instructions:

(1) Open the following accounts in the general ledger, inserting the balances indicated, as of June 1:

111	Cash	$13,705
112	Notes Receivable	7,500
113	Accounts Receivable	15,975
411	Sales	—
412	Sales Returns and Allowances	—
413	Sales Discounts	—
811	Interest Income	—

(2) Open the following accounts in the accounts receivable ledger, inserting the balances indicated, as of June 15: F. G. Black Co., $8,900; Halloway Co., $9,825; Ross and Son; Towers Co.

(3) In a sales journal similar to the one illustrated on page 303 and a cash receipts journal similar to the one illustrated on page 305, insert "June 15 Total(s) Forwarded" on the first line of the Account Debited or Account Credited column, "✔" in the Post. Ref. column, and the following dollar figures in the respective amount columns:

    Sales journal: 25,350
    Cash receipts journal: 3,467; 13,470; 22,600; 366; 39,171.

(4) Using the two special journals and a two-column general journal, record the transactions for the remainder of June. Post to the accounts receivable ledger, and insert the balances at the points indicated in the narrative of transactions. *Determine the balance in the customer's account before recording a cash receipt.*

(5) Total each of the columns of the special journals and post the individual entries and totals to the general ledger. Insert account balances after the last posting.

(6) Determine that the subsidiary ledger agrees with the controlling account in the general ledger.

Problem 7–7A. All journals and general ledger for a sole proprietorship; trial balance. The transactions completed by C. E. Dunn Co. during July, the first month of the current fiscal year, were as follows:

July 1. Issued Check No. 920 for July rent, $2,000.
    2. Purchased equipment on account from Mann Co., $7,500.

July 2. Purchased merchandise on account from Evans Corp., $4,250.

     3. Issued Invoice No. 832 to Black Co., $1,975.

     7. Received check for $2,475 from Owens Corp. in payment of $2,500 invoice, less discount.

     7. Issued Check No. 921 for miscellaneous selling expense, $190.

     7. Received credit memorandum from Evans Corp. for returned merchandise, $250.

     8. Issued Invoice No. 833 to Kane Co., $5,000.

     9. Issued Check No. 922 for $9,310 to Frank Inc. in payment of $9,500 invoice, less 2% discount.

     9. Received check for $7,425 from Baker Manufacturing Co. in payment of $7,500 invoice, less discount.

    10. Issued Check No. 923 to Davis Enterprises in payment of $3,100 invoice, no discount.

    12. Issued Invoice No. 834 to Owens Corp., $3,500.

    12. Issued Check No. 924 for $930 to Ross Corp. in payment of account, no discount.

    12. Received check for $775 from Black Co. on account, no discount.

    14. Issued credit memorandum to Owens Corp. for damaged merchandise, $500.

    15. Issued Check No. 925 for $3,920 to Evans Corp. in payment of $4,000 balance, less 2% discount.

    15. Issued Check No. 926 for $2,250 for cash purchase of merchandise.

    15. Cash sales for July 1–15, $23,750.

    18. Purchased merchandise on account from Davis Enterprises, $6,420.

    19. Received check for return of merchandise that had been purchased for cash, $90.

    19. Issued Check No. 927 for miscellaneous general expense, $145.

    21. Purchased the following on account from Cass Supply Inc.: store supplies, $225; office supplies, $195.

    22. Issued Check No. 928 in payment of advertising expense, $945.

    23. Issued Invoice No. 835 to Baker Manufacturing Co., $1,950.

    24. Purchased the following on account from Frank Inc.: merchandise, $4,170; store supplies, $130.

    25. Issued Invoice No. 836 to Jackson Co., $3,290.

    25. Received check for $2,970 from Owens Corp. in payment of $3,000 balance, less discount.

    29. Issued Check No. 929 for $7,500 to Mann Co. in payment of invoice of July 2, no discount

    30. Issued Check No. 930 to C. E. Dunn as a personal withdrawal, $3,000.

    31. Issued Check No. 931 for monthly salaries as follows: sales salaries, $11,100; office salaries, $4,500.

    31. Cash sales for July 16–31, $26,150.

    31. Issued Check No. 932 in payment of transportation charges for merchandise purchased during the month, $465.

Instructions:

(1) Open the following accounts in the general ledger, entering the balances indicated as of July 1:

111	Cash	$ 9,850
113	Accounts Receivable	12,975
114	Merchandise Inventory	35,500
115	Store Supplies	545
116	Office Supplies	360
117	Prepaid Insurance	2,100
121	Equipment	47,250
122	Accumulated Depreciation	22,250
211	Accounts Payable	13,530
311	C. E. Dunn, Capital	72,800
312	C. E. Dunn, Drawing	—
411	Sales	—
412	Sales Returns and Allowances	—
413	Sales Discounts	—
511	Purchases	—
512	Purchases Returns and Allowances	—
513	Purchases Discounts	—
514	Transportation In	—
611	Sales Salaries Expense	—
612	Advertising Expense	—
619	Miscellaneous Selling Expense	—
711	Office Salaries Expense	—
712	Rent Expense	—
719	Miscellaneous General Expense	—

(2) Record the transactions for July, using a purchases journal (as on pages 294 and 295), a sales journal (as on page 303), a cash payments journal (as on page 299), a cash receipts journal (as on page 305), and a two-column general journal. The terms of all sales on account are FOB shipping point, 1/10, n/30. Assume that an assistant makes daily postings to the individual accounts in the accounts payable ledger and the accounts receivable ledger.

(3) Post the appropriate individual entries to the general ledger.

(4) Total each of the columns of the special journals and post the appropriate totals to the general ledger; insert the account balances.

(5) Prepare a trial balance.

(6) Balances of the accounts in the subsidiary ledgers as of July 31 are as follows:

Accounts receivable: 2,200; 1,975; 5,000; 1,950; 3,290.
Accounts payable: 6,420; 420; 4,300.

Verify the agreement of the subsidiary ledgers with their respective controlling accounts.

Series B

Problem 7–1B.   Chart of accounts for sole proprietorship. Clark Fashions is a newly organized enterprise with the following list of asset, liability, and owner's equity accounts, arranged in alphabetical order:

Accounts Payable
Accounts Receivable
Accumulated Depreciation—Building
Accumulated Depreciation—Office Equipment
Accumulated Depreciation—Store Equipment
Building
Cash
Susan Clark, Capital
Susan Clark, Drawing
Land
Merchandise Inventory
Notes Payable (long-term)

Notes Receivable (short-term)
Office Equipment
Office Supplies
Prepaid Insurance
Salaries Payable
Sales Commissions Payable
Store Equipment
Store Supplies
Taxes Payable

Instructions:

Construct a chart of accounts, assigning account numbers and arranging the accounts in balance sheet order, as illustrated on page 63. Each account number is to be composed of three digits: the first digit is to indicate the major classification ("1" for assets, etc.), the second digit is to indicate the subclassification ("11" for current assets, etc.), and the third digit is to identify the specific account ("111" for Cash, etc.).

Problem 7–3B. Purchases and cash payments journals; accounts payable and general ledgers. Bachman Clothiers began operations on June 16 of the current year. Transactions related to purchases, returns and allowances, and cash payments during the remainder of June are as follows:

June 16. Issued Check No. 1 in payment of rent for the remainder of June, $900.
   16. Purchased office equipment on account from Harper Equipment Corp., $7,250.
   16. Purchased merchandise on account from Hernandez Clothing Co., $15,500.
   17. Issued Check No. 2 in payment of store supplies, $410, and office supplies, $290.
   18. Purchased merchandise on account from Carter Clothing, $9,720.
   19. Purchased merchandise on account from Adams Co., $2,150.
   20. Received a credit memorandum from Carter Clothing for returned merchandise, $720.
       Post the journals to the accounts payable ledger.
   23. Issued Check No. 3 to Harper Equipment Corp. in payment of invoice of $7,250.
   23. Received a credit memorandum from Adams Co. for defective merchandise, $465.
   24. Issued Check No. 4 to Hernandez Clothing Co., in payment of invoice of $15,500, less 1% discount.
   25. Issued Check No. 5 to a cash customer for merchandise returned, $215.
   26. Issued Check No. 6 to Carter Clothing in payment of the balance owed, less 2% discount.
   27. Purchased merchandise on account from Adams Co., $1,610.
       Post the journals to the accounts payable ledger.

June 30. Purchased the following from Harper Equipment Corp. on account: store supplies, $150; office supplies, $75; store equipment, $1,500.

30. Issued Check No. 7 to Adams Co. in payment of invoice of $2,150, less the credit of $465.

30. Purchased merchandise on account from Hernandez Clothing Co., $6,200.

30. Issued Check No. 8 in payment of sales salaries, $1,775.

30. Received a credit memorandum from Harper Equipment Corp. for defect in office equipment, $75.

Post the journals to the accounts payable ledger.

Instructions:

(1) Open the following accounts in the general ledger, using the account numbers indicated:

111	Cash	412	Sales Returns and Allowances
116	Store Supplies	511	Purchases
117	Office Supplies	512	Purchases Returns and Allowances
121	Store Equipment	513	Purchases Discounts
122	Office Equipment	611	Sales Salaries Expense
211	Accounts Payable	712	Rent Expense

(2) Open the following accounts in the accounts payable ledger: Adams Co.; Carter Clothing; Harper Equipment Corp.; and Hernandez Clothing Co.

(3) Record the transactions for June, using a purchases journal similar to the one illustrated on pages 294 and 295, a cash payments journal similar to the one illustrated on page 299, and a two-column general journal. Post to the accounts payable ledger at the points indicated in the narrative of transactions.

(4) Post the appropriate individual entries to the general ledger (Sundry Accounts columns of the purchases journal and the cash payments journal; both columns of the general journal).

(5) Total each of the columns of the purchases journal and the cash payments journal, and post the appropriate totals to the general ledger. (Because the problem does not include transactions related to cash receipts, the cash account in the ledger will have a credit balance.)

(6) Prepare a schedule of accounts payable.

If the working papers correlating with the textbook are not used, omit Problem 7–5B.

Problem 7–5B. Sales and cash receipts journals; accounts receivable and general ledgers. Three journals, the accounts receivable ledger, and portions of the general ledger of Chase Company are presented in the working papers. Sales invoices and credit memorandums were entered in the journals by an assistant. Terms of sales on account are 2/10, n/30, FOB shipping point. Transactions in which cash and notes receivable were received during July are as follows:

July 2. Received $5,880 from C. D. Martin Co. in payment of June 22 invoice, less discount.

3. Received $10,300 in payment of $10,000 note receivable and interest of $300.

Post transactions of July 2 and 6 to accounts receivable ledger.

July 7. Received $6,370 from Janet Rowe Co. in payment of June 28 invoice, less discount.

8. Received $2,200 from R. C. Fellows Inc. in payment of June 10 invoice, no discount.

Post transactions of July 7, 8, 10, 12, and 15 to accounts receivable ledger.

16. Cash sales for first half of July totaled $4,610.

19. Received $1,000 refund for return of defective equipment purchased for cash in June.

20. Received $2,842 from C. D. Martin Co. in payment of balance due on July 10 invoice, less discount.

22. Received $5,684 from R. C. Fellows Inc. in payment of July 12 invoice, less discount.

Post transactions of July 17, 20, 22 and 23 to accounts receivable ledger.

27. Received $40 for sale of office supplies at cost.

31. Received $1,750 cash and a $2,500 note receivable from Ignacio and Co. in settlement of the balance due on the invoice of July 2, no discount. (Record receipt of note in the general journal.)

31. Cash sales for second half of July totaled $4,150.

Post transactions of July 27, 28, 30, and 31 to accounts receivable ledger.

Instructions:

(1) Record the cash receipts in the cash receipts journal and the note in the general journal. Before recording a receipt of cash on account, determine the balance of the customer's account. Post the entries from the three journals, in date sequence, to the accounts receivable ledger in accordance with the instructions in the narrative of transactions. Insert the new balance after each posting to an account.

(2) Post the appropriate individual entries from the cash receipts journal and the general journal to the general ledger.

(3) Total each of the columns of the sales journal and the cash receipts journal and post the appropriate totals to the general ledger. Insert the balance of each account after the last posting.

(4) Prepare a schedule of the accounts receivable as of July 31 and compare the total with the balance of the controlling account.

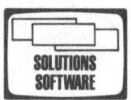

Problem 7–6B.   Sales and cash receipts journals; accounts receivable and general ledgers. Transactions related to sales and cash receipts completed by Ross Company during the period June 15–30 of the current year are as follows. The terms of all sales on account are 2/10, n/30, FOB shipping point.

June 15. Issued Invoice No. 793 to Towers Co., $4,425.

16. Received cash from F. G. Black Co. for the balance due on its account, less discount.

19. Issued Invoice No. 794 to Halloway Co., $7,500.

June 20. Issued Invoice No. 795 to Ross and Son, $2,975.
Post all journals to the accounts receivable ledger.
23. Received cash from Halloway Co. for the balance owed on June 15, no discount.
24. Issued Credit Memorandum No. 35 to Towers Co., $275.
24. Issued Invoice No. 796 to Halloway Co., $4,950.
24. Received $1,560 in payment of a $1,500 note receivable and interest of $60.
Post all journals to the accounts receivable ledger.
25. Received cash from Towers Co. for the balance due on invoice of June 15, less discount.
28. Received cash from Halloway Co. for invoice of June 19, less discount.
28. Issued Invoice No. 797 to F. G. Black Co., $2,100.
30. Issued Credit Memorandum No. 36 to F. G. Black Co., $250.
30. Recorded cash sales for the second half of the month, $8,155.
Post all journals to the accounts receivable ledger.

Instructions:

(1) Open the following accounts in the general ledger, inserting the balances indicated, as of June 1:

111	Cash.	$13,705
112	Notes Receivable.	7,500
113	Accounts Receivable.	15,975
411	Sales	—
412	Sales Returns and Allowances.	—
413	Sales Discounts.	—
811	Interest Income.	—

(2) Open the following accounts in the accounts receivable ledger, inserting the balances indicated, as of June 15: F. G. Black Co., $8,900; Halloway Co., $9,825; Ross and Son; Towers Co.

(3) In a sales journal similar to the one illustrated on page 303 and a cash receipts journal similar to the one illustrated on page 305, insert "June 15 Total(s) Forwarded" on the first line of the Account Debited or Account Credited column, "✔" in the Post. Ref. column, and the following dollar figures in the respective amount columns:

Sales journal: 25,350
Cash receipts journal: 3,467; 13,470; 22,600; 366; 39,171.

(4) Using the two special journals and a two-column general journal, record the transactions for the remainder of June. Post to the accounts receivable ledger, and insert the balances at the points indicated in the narrative of transactions. *Determine the balance in the customer's account before recording a cash receipt.*
(5) Total each of the columns of the special journals and post the individual entries and totals to the general ledger. Insert account balances after the last posting.
(6) Determine that the subsidiary ledger agrees with the controlling account in the general ledger.

Problem 7–7B. All journals and general ledger for sole proprietorship; trial balance. The transactions completed by C. E. Dunn Co. during July, the first month of the current fiscal year, were as follows:

July   1. Issued Check No. 610 for July rent, $1,400.

      2. Purchased merchandise on account from Bidwell Co., $2,590.

      3. Purchased equipment on account from Glass Equipment Co., $9,600.

      5. Issued Invoice No. 940 to W. Cox Inc., $1,700.

      6. Received check for $2,772 from Powell Corp. in payment of $2,800 invoice, less discount.

      6. Issued Check No. 611 for miscellaneous selling expense, $310.

      9. Received credit memorandum from Bidwell Co. for returned merchandise, $290.

      9. Issued Invoice No. 941 to Collins Corp., $8,500.

    10. Issued Check No. 612 for $9,405 to Howell Inc. in payment of $9,500 invoice, less 1% discount.

    10. Received check for $7,375 from Sax Manufacturing Co. in payment of $7,375 invoice, no discount.

    10. Issued Check No. 613 to Bone Enterprises in payment of $2,120 invoice, no discount.

    11. Issued Invoice No. 942 to Joy Corp., $3,120.

    11. Issued Check No. 614 for $705 to Porter Corp. in payment of account, no discount.

    12. Received check for $1,683 from W. Cox Inc. in payment of $1,700 invoice, less discount.

    13. Issued credit memorandum to Joy Corp. for damaged merchandise, $320.

    13. Issued Check No. 615 for $2,254 to Bidwell Co. in payment of $2,300 balance, less 2% discount.

    16. Issued Check No. 616 for $2,725 for cash purchase of merchandise.

    16. Cash sales for July 1–16, $21,520.

    17. Purchased merchandise on account from Bone Enterprises, $7,920.

    18. Received check for return of merchandise that had been purchased for cash, $790.

    18. Issued Check No. 617 for miscellaneous general expense, $238.

    19. Purchased the following on account from Moore Supply Inc.: store supplies, $248; office supplies, $197.

    20. Issued Check No. 618 in payment of advertising expense, $1,850.

    23. Issued Invoice No. 943 to Sax Manufacturing Co., $8,172.

    24. Purchased the following on account from Howell Inc.: merchandise, $5,127; store supplies, $292.

    25. Issued Invoice No. 944 to Collins Corp., $4,650.

    25. Received check for $2,800 from Powell Corp. in payment of $2,800 balance, no discount.

    26. Issued Check No. 619 to Glass Equipment Co. in payment of $9,600 invoice of July 3, no discount.

    27. Issued Check No. 620 to C. E. Dunn as a personal withdrawal, $3,500.

    30. Issued Check No. 621 for monthly salaries as follows: sales salaries, $9,100; office salaries, $3,800.

July 31. Cash sales for July 17–31, $18,150.
    31. Issued Check No. 622 in payment of transportation charges for merchandise purchased during the month, $930.

Instructions:

(1) Open the following accounts in the general ledger, entering the balances indicated as of July 1:

111	Cash	$ 9,850
113	Accounts Receivable	12,975
114	Merchandise Inventory	35,500
115	Store Supplies	545
116	Office Supplies	360
117	Prepaid Insurance	2,100
121	Equipment	47,250
122	Accumulated Depreciation	22,250
211	Accounts Payable	13,530
311	C. E. Dunn, Capital	72,800
312	C. E. Dunn, Drawing	—
411	Sales	—
412	Sales Returns and Allowances	—
413	Sales Discounts	—
511	Purchases	—
512	Purchases Returns and Allowances	—
513	Purchases Discounts	—
514	Transportation In	—
611	Sales Salaries Expense	—
612	Advertising Expense	—
619	Miscellaneous Selling Expense	—
711	Office Salaries Expense	—
712	Rent Expense	—
719	Miscellaneous General Expense	—

(2) Record the transactions for July, using a purchases journal (as on pages 294 and 295), a sales journal (as on page 303), a cash payments journal (as on page 299), a cash receipts journal (as on page 305), and a two-column general journal. The terms of all sales on account are FOB shipping point, 1/10, n/30. Assume that an assistant makes daily postings to the individual accounts in the accounts payable ledger and the accounts receivable ledger.

(3) Post the appropriate individual entries to the general ledger.

(4) Total each of the columns of the special journals and post the appropriate totals to the general ledger; insert the account balances.

(5) Prepare a trial balance.

(6) Balances of the accounts in the subsidiary ledgers as of July 31 are as follows:

      Accounts receivable: 13,150; 8,172; 2,800.
      Accounts payable: 5,419; 7,920; 1,650.

Verify the agreement of the subsidiary ledgers with their respective controlling accounts.

KAY JEWELERS

For the past few years, your aunt has operated a small jewelry store, Kay Jewelers. Its current annual revenues are approximately $450,000. Because the company's bookkeeper has been taking more and more time each month to record all transactions in a two-column journal and to prepare the financial statements, your aunt is considering improving the company's accounting system by adding special journals and subsidiary ledgers. Your aunt has asked you to help her with this project. She has compiled the following information:

(1)

Type of Transaction	Estimated Frequency per Month
Purchases of merchandise on account	200
Sales on account	175
Cash receipts from customers on account	150
Daily cash register summaries of cash sales	25
Purchases of merchandise for cash	20
Purchases of office supplies on account	5
Purchases of store supplies on account	5
Cash payments for utilities expenses	4
Cash purchases of office supplies	4
Cash purchases of store supplies	4

(2) For merchandise purchases of high dollar-value items, Kay Jewelers issues notes payable at current

interest rates to vendors. These notes are issued because many of the high-value items may not sell
immediately and the issuance of the notes reduces
the need to maintain large balances of cash or assets
that can be readily converted to cash. Notes are
issued for approximately 10% of the purchases on
account.

(3) All purchases discounts are taken when available.
(4) A sales discount of 1/10, n/30 is offered to all credit
customers.
(5) A local sales tax of 6% is collected on all intrastate
sales of merchandise.
(6) Monthly financial statements are prepared.

Instructions:

(1) Based upon the preceding description of Kay Jewelers, indicate which special journals you would recommend as part of Kay Jewelers' accounting system.
(2) Assume that your aunt has decided to use a sales
journal and a purchases journal. Design the format
for each journal, giving special consideration to the
needs of Kay Jewelers.
(3) Which subsidiary ledgers would you recommend for
Kay Jewelers?

COMPREHENSIVE PROBLEM 3

The transactions completed by Redmond Supply Co. during January, the first month of the current fiscal year, were as follows:

Jan. 2. Issued Check No. 810 for January rent, $1,500.
2. Purchased merchandise on account from Dane Corp., $2,250.
2. Purchased equipment on account from Lee Equipment Co., $3,700.
3. Issued Invoice No. 942 to C. Block Inc., $1,320.
7. Received check for $2,744 from Nichols Corp. in payment of $2,800 invoice, less discount.
7. Issued Check No. 811 for miscellaneous selling expense, $205.
8. Received credit memorandum from Dane Corp. for merchandise returned to them, $150.
8. Issued Invoice No. 943 to Jackson Co., $5,000.
9. Issued Check No. 812 for $9,310 to Easterly Inc. in payment of $9,500 invoice, less 2% discount.
9. Received check for $9,604 from Baker Manufacturing Co. in payment of $9,800 invoice, less discount.
10. Issued Check No. 813 to Collins Enterprises in payment of $2,120 invoice, no discount.
10. Issued Invoice No. 944 to Nichols Corp., $3,225.
11. Issued Check No. 814 to Peak Corp. in payment of account, $705, no discount.
12. Received check for $775 from C. Block Inc. on account, no discount.
14. Issued credit memorandum to Nichols Corp. for damaged merchandise, $225.
15. Issued Check No. 815 for $2,058 to Dane Corp. in payment of $2,100 balance, less 2% discount.
15. Issued Check No. 816 for $1,250 for cash purchase of merchandise.
15. Cash sales for January 2–15, $18,942.
17. Purchased merchandise on account from Collins Enterprises, $6,420.
18. Received check for return of merchandise that had been purchased for cash, $75.
18. Issued Check No. 817 for miscellaneous general expense, $130.
21. Purchased the following on account from Bunn Supply Inc.: store supplies, $215; office supplies, $170.
22. Issued Check No. 818 in payment of advertising expense, $610.
23. Issued Invoice No. 945 to Baker Manufacturing Co., $1,950.
24. Purchased the following on account from Easterly Inc.: merchandise, $3,125; store supplies, $110.
25. Issued Invoice No. 946 to Jackson Co., $3,290.
25. Received check for $2,940 from Nichols Corp. in payment of $3,000 balance, less discount.
26. Issued Check No. 819 to Lee Equipment Co. in payment of $3,700 invoice of January 2, no discount.
29. Issued Check No. 820 to Ann Day as a personal withdrawal, $2,500.
30. Issued Check No. 821 for monthly salaries as follows; sales salaries, $9,600; office salaries, $3,800.
31. Cash sales for January 16–31, $19,250.
31. Issued Check No. 822 for cash purchase of merchandise, $390.

Instructions:

(1) Open the following accounts in the general ledger, entering the balances indicated as of January 1:

111	Cash	$ 9,100
113	Accounts Receivable	16,200
114	Merchandise Inventory	31,500
115	Store Supplies	410
116	Office Supplies	225
117	Prepaid Insurance	2,100
121	Equipment	40,650
122	Accumulated Depreciation	12,350
211	Accounts Payable	12,325
311	Ann Day, Capital	75,510
312	Ann Day, Drawing	—
411	Sales	—
412	Sales Returns and Allowances	—
413	Sales Discounts	—
511	Purchases	—
512	Purchases Returns and Allowances	—
513	Purchases Discounts	—
611	Sales Salaries Expense	—
612	Advertising Expense	—
619	Miscellaneous Selling Expense	—
711	Office Salaries Expense	—
712	Rent Expense	—
719	Miscellaneous General Expense	—

Open the following accounts in the accounts receivable ledger and enter the balances in the balance columns as of January 1: Baker Manufacturing Co., $9,800; C. Block Inc., $775; Jackson Co.; Nichols Corp., $2,800; Wilson and Son, $2,825. Open the following accounts in the accounts payable ledger and enter the balances in the balance columns as of January 1: Bunn Supply Inc.; Collins Enterprises, $2,120; Dane Corp.; Easterly Inc., $9,500; Lee Equipment Co.; Peak Corp., $705.

(2) Record the transactions for January, using a purchases journal (as on pages 294 and 295), a sales journal (as on page 303), a cash payments journal (as on page 299), a cash receipts journal (as on page 305), and a two-column general journal. The terms of all sales on account are 2/15, n/60, FOB shipping point. Post to the accounts receivable and accounts payable ledgers and insert the balances immediately after recording each entry.

(3) Post the appropriate individual entries to the general ledger.

(4) Add the columns of the special journals and post the appropriate totals to the general ledger; insert the account balances.

(5) Prepare a trial balance.

(6) Prepare schedules of accounts receivable and accounts payable as of January 31 and compare the total of each schedule with the balance of the appropriate controlling account.

Chapter 8

CASH

Chapter Objectives:

- Describe and illustrate the use of a bank account for controlling cash, including the preparation of a bank reconciliation.

- Describe internal controls for cash receipts, including the handling of mail receipts, the use of a cash short and over account, and the use of cash change funds.

- Describe and illustrate the use of the voucher system for controlling cash payments.

- Describe and illustrate the use of a discounts lost account and a petty cash account for controlling cash payments.

- Describe recent trends in the use of electronic funds transfer to process cash transactions.

In Chapter 7, the qualities of a properly designed accounting system and the principles of internal control for directing operations were discussed. This chapter presents the application of these internal control principles to the design of an effective system for controlling cash and the accounting for cash transactions.

CONTROL OVER CASH

Because of the ease with which money can be transferred, cash is the asset most likely to be diverted and used improperly by employees. In addition, many transactions either directly or indirectly affect the receipt or payment of cash. It is therefore necessary that cash be effectively safeguarded by special controls.

The Bank Account as a Tool for Controlling Cash

One of the major devices for maintaining control over cash is the bank account. To get the most benefit from a bank account, all cash received must be deposited in the bank and all payments must be made by checks drawn on the bank or from special cash funds. When such a system is strictly followed, there is a double record of cash, one maintained by the business and the other by the bank.

In some cases, a bank may require a business to maintain a minimum cash balance in a bank account. This requirement for a minimum balance, called a **compensating balance**, is generally imposed by the bank as a part of a loan agreement. Compensating balance requirements should be disclosed in notes to the financial statements, as indicated in the following note taken from the 1984 financial statements for Lockheed Corporation:

Formal compensating balance arrangements under a 1984 Credit Agreement require the company either to maintain compensating balances or to pay an agreed-upon fee. There are no other formal or informal compensating balance arrangements.

The forms used by a business in connection with a bank account are a signature card, deposit ticket, check, and a record of checks drawn.

Signature Card. At the time an account is opened, an identifying number is assigned to the account, and a **signature card** must be signed by each person authorized to sign checks drawn on the account. The card is used by the bank to determine the authenticity of the signature on checks presented to it for payment.

Deposit Ticket. The details of a deposit are listed by the depositor on a printed form supplied by the bank. **Deposit tickets** may be prepared in duplicate, in which case the copy is stamped or initialed by the bank's teller and given to the depositor as a receipt. The receipt of a deposit may be indicated by means other than a duplicate deposit ticket, but all methods give the depositor written proof of the date and the total amount of the deposit.

Check. A **check** is a written instrument signed by the depositor, ordering the bank to pay a certain sum of money to the order of a designated person. There are three parties to a check: the **drawer**, the one who signs the check; the **drawee**, the bank on which the check is drawn; and the **payee**, the one to whose order the check is drawn. When checks are issued to pay bills, they are recorded as credits to Cash on the day issued, even though they are not presented to the drawer's bank until some later time. When checks are received from customers, they are recorded as debits to Cash, on the assumption that the customer has enough money on deposit.

Check forms may be obtained in many styles. The name and the address of the depositor are often printed on each check, and the checks are usually numbered in sequence to facilitate the depositor's internal control. Most banks use automatic sorting and posting equipment and, therefore, provide check forms on which the bank's identification number and the depositor's account number are printed along the lower margin in machine-readable magnetic ink. When the check is presented for payment, the amount for which it is drawn is inserted next to the account number, also in magnetic ink.

Record of Checks Drawn. A memorandum record of the basic details of a check should be prepared at the time the check is written. The record may be a stub from which the check is detached or it may be a small booklet designed to be kept with the check forms. Each type of record also provides spaces for recording deposits and the current bank balance.

Business firms may prepare a copy of each check drawn and then use it as a basis for recording the transaction in the cash payments journal. Checks issued to a creditor on account are usually accompanied by a notification of the specific invoice that is being paid. The purpose of such notification, sometimes called a **remittance advice**, is to make sure that proper credit is recorded in the accounts of the creditor. Mistakes are less likely to happen and the possible need for exchanges of correspondence is reduced. The invoice number or other descriptive data may be inserted in spaces provided on the face or on the back of the check or on an attachment to the check, as in the following illustration:

```
                                                                        363
  MONROE COMPANY
  813 Greenwood Street      Detroit, MI 48206-4070    April 12        19 87   9-42
                                                                              720

  Pay to the
  Order of        Hammond Office Products Inc.                      $ 921.20

  Nine hundred twenty-one 20/100--------------------------------------- Dollars

   A
   NB   AMERICAN NATIONAL BANK        K. R. Simms          Treasurer
        OF DETROIT
   DETROIT, MI 48201-2500  (313)933-8547  MEMBER FDIC    Earl M. Hartman    Vice President

   ⑈0720004231⑈  1627042 363
  DETACH THIS PORTION BEFORE CASHING
```

DATE	DESCRIPTION	GROSS AMOUNT	DEDUCTIONS	NET AMOUNT
4/12/87	Invoice No. 529482	940.00	18.80	921.20

MONROE COMPANY

Before depositing the check at the bank, the payee removes the part of the check containing the remittance information. The removed part may then be used by the payee as written proof of the details of the cash receipt.

Bank Statement

Although there are some differences in procedure, banks usually maintain an original and a copy of all checking account transactions. When this is done, the original becomes the statement of account that is mailed to the depositor, usually once each month. Like any account with a customer or a creditor, the bank statement shows the beginning balance, checks and other debits (deductions by the bank), deposits and other credits (additions by the bank), and the balance at the end of the period. The depositor's checks received by the bank during the period may accompany the bank statement, arranged in the order of payment. The paid or canceled checks are perforated or stamped "Paid," together with the date of payment.

Debit or credit memorandums describing other entries in the depositor's account may also be enclosed with the statement. For example, the bank may have debited the depositor's account for service charges or for deposited checks returned because of insufficient funds. It may have credited the account for receipts from notes receivable left for collection, for loans to the depositor, or for interest.[1] A typical bank statement is illustrated as follows:

---

[1]Although interest-bearing checking accounts are common for individuals, Federal Reserve Regulation Q prohibits the paying of interest on corporate checking accounts.

BANK STATEMENT

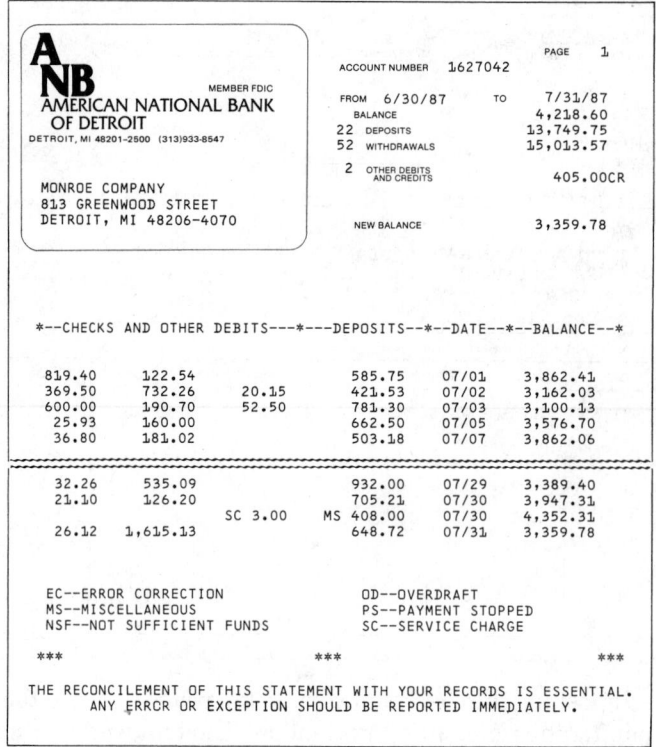

Bank Reconciliation

When all cash receipts are deposited in the bank and all payments are made by check, the cash account is often called Cash in Bank. This account in the depositor's ledger is the reciprocal of the account with the depositor in the bank's ledger. Cash in Bank in the depositor's ledger is an asset with a debit balance, and the account with the depositor in the bank's ledger is a liability with a credit balance.

It might seem that the two balances should be equal, but they are not likely to be equal on any specific date because of either or both of the following: (1) delay by either party in recording transactions, and (2) errors by either party in recording transactions. Ordinarily, there is a time lag of one day or more between the date a check is written and the date that it is presented to the bank for payment. If the depositor mails deposits to the bank or uses the night depository, a time lag between the date of the deposit and the date that it is recorded by the bank is also probable. Conversely, the bank may debit or credit the depositor's account for transactions about which the depositor will not be informed until later. Examples are service or collection fees charged by the bank and the proceeds of notes receivable sent to the bank for collection.

To determine the reasons for any difference and to correct any errors that may have been made by the bank or the depositor, the depositor's own records should be reconciled with the bank statement. The **bank reconciliation** is divided into two major sections: one section begins with the balance according to the bank statement and ends with the adjusted balance; the other section begins with the balance according to the depositor's records and also ends with the adjusted balance. The two amounts designated as the adjusted balance must be equal. The form and the content of the bank reconciliation are outlined as follows:

Bank balance according to bank statement		$XXX	**FORMAT FOR BANK RECONCILIATION**
Add: Additions by depositor not on bank statement	$XX		
Bank errors	XX	XX	
		$XXX	
Deduct: Deductions by depositor not on bank statement	$XX		
Bank errors	XX	XX	
Adjusted balance		$XXX	
Bank balance according to depositor's records		$XXX	
Add: Additions by bank not recorded by depositor	$XX		
Depositor errors	XX	XX	
		$XXX	
Deduct: Deductions by bank not recorded by depositor	$XX		
Depositor errors	XX	XX	
Adjusted balance		$XXX	

The following procedures are used in finding the reconciling items and determining the adjusted balance of Cash in Bank:

1. Individual deposits listed on the bank statement are compared with unrecorded deposits appearing in the preceding reconciliation and with deposit receipts or other records of deposits. Deposits not recorded by the bank are added to the balance according to the bank statement.
2. Paid checks are compared with outstanding checks appearing on the preceding reconciliation and with checks listed in the cash payments journal. Checks issued that have not been paid by the bank are outstanding and are deducted from the balance according to the bank statement.
3. Bank credit memorandums are traced to the cash receipts journal. Credit memorandums not recorded in the cash receipts journal are added to the balance according to the depositor's records.
4. Bank debit memorandums are traced to the cash payments journal. Debit memorandums not recorded in the cash payments journal are deducted from the balance according to the depositor's records.
5. Errors discovered during the process of making the foregoing comparisons are listed separately on the reconciliation. For example, if the amount for

which a check was written had been recorded erroneously by the depositor, the amount of the error should be added to or deducted from the balance according to the depositor's records. Similarly, errors by the bank should be added to or deducted from the balance according to the bank statement.

Illustration of Bank Reconcilation. The bank statement for Monroe Company, reproduced on page 342, indicates a balance of $3,359.78 as of July 31. The balance in Cash in Bank in Monroe Company's ledger as of the same date is $2,234.99. Use of the procedures outlined above reveals the following reconciling items:

Deposit of July 31 not recorded on bank statement	$ 816.20
Checks outstanding: No. 812, $1,061.00; No.878, $435.39;	
No. 883, $48.60	1,544.99
Note plus interest of $8 collected by bank (credit memorandum),	
not recorded in cash receipts journal	408.00
Bank service charges (debit memorandum) not recorded in cash	
payments journal	3.00
Check No. 879 for $732.26 to Taylor Co. on account, recorded in	
cash payments journal as $723.26	9.00

The bank reconciliation based on the bank statement and the reconciling items is as follows:

Monroe Company
Bank Reconciliation
July 31, 1987

Balance per bank statement		$3,359.78
Add deposit of July 31, not recorded by bank		816.20
		$4,175.98
Deduct outstanding checks:		
No. 812	$1,061.00	
No. 878	435.39	
No. 883	48.60	1,544.99
Adjusted balance		$2,630.99
Balance per depositor's records		$2,234.99
Add note and interest collected by bank		408.00
		$2,642.99
Deduct: Bank service charges	$ 3.00	
Error in recording Check No. 879	9.00	12.00
Adjusted balance		$2,630.99

Entries Based on Bank Reconciliation. Bank memorandums not recorded by the depositor and depositor's errors shown by the bank reconciliation require that entries be made in the accounts. The entries may be recorded in the appropriate special journals if they have not already been posted for the month, or they may be recorded in the general journal.

The entries for Monroe Company, based on the bank reconciliation on page 344, are as follows:

July 31	Cash in Bank............................	408	
	Notes Receivable		400
	Interest Income		8
	Note collected by bank.		
31	Miscellaneous General Expense	3	
	Accounts Payable—Taylor Co.............	9	
	Cash in Bank........................		12
	Bank service charges and error in recording Check No. 879.		

The data needed for these adjustments are provided by the section of the bank reconciliation that begins with the balance per depositor's records. No adjusting entries are necessary on the depositor's books as a result of the information included in the section that begins with the balance per bank statement.

After the foregoing entries are posted, the cash in bank account will have a debit balance of $2,630.99, which agrees with the adjusted balance shown on the bank reconciliation. This is the amount of cash available for use as of July 31 and the amount that would be reported on the balance sheet on that date.

Importance of Bank Reconciliation. The bank reconciliation is an important part of the system of internal control because it is a means of comparing recorded cash, as shown by the accounting records, with the amount of cash reported by the bank. It thus provides for finding and correcting errors and irregularities. Greater internal control is achieved when the bank reconciliation is prepared by an employee who does not take part in or record cash transactions with the bank. Without a proper separation of these duties, cash is more likely to be embezzled. For example, an employee who takes part in all of these duties could prepare an unauthorized check, omit it from the accounts, and cash it. Then to account for the canceled check when returned by the bank, the employee could understate the amount of the outstanding checks on future bank reconciliations by the amount of the embezzlement.

Check-Churning Frenzy

Cash managers wire their bank balances to New York and other money centers every night, so that they may be invested in government securities and commercial paper (ironically including bank commercial paper). The money is wired back to the banks in the morning and during the day as needed. The result is that the majority of all corporate deposits are turned over every day.

The nation's cash managers and bankers transact more than $600 billion a day in wire transfers alone. The great majority of this is on Fedwire — the wire service operated by the Federal Reserve System. This daily dollar volume is triple the federal budget deficit for 1985 and annually amounts to more than $170 trillion, which makes our annual gross national product of close to $4 trillion look small.

The technological and management sophistication required to churn money on this massive scale has led many in the banking industry to boast that we have the most advanced payments system in the world. This is true. But this sophistication is largely a direct result of efforts to *abuse* existing clearing rules, which are the most backward and wasteful of any developed country, and to avoid Regulation Q's nonsensical prohibition against paying interest on deposits of corporations, including banks and other depository institutions. Congressional deregulation has phased out Regulation Q as it relates to consumers, but it still applies to corporations.

Another important reason for the heavy use of Fedwire is that it grants interest-free loans, or float. In an effort to attract business, the Fed (which competes directly against banks in both check clearing and wire transfers) gives immediate and irrevocable credit and availability of funds to recipients of wires but does not require senders to pay until the end of the day. Such a policy causes the Fed to extend unsecured, and to a large extent uncontrollable, intraday loans to some wire users. Recent estimates are that such loans, called "daylight overdrafts" or float, often exceed $100 billion by day's end.

Float is the principal reason for the existence of cash management. A cash manager's job is to make payments to others clear as slowly as possible and to clear payments received from others as quickly as possible. The clearing of payments to others is slowed through techniques such as remote disbursement. This involves issuing corporate checks on, say, First National Remote Bank. Almost everyone has received a check from a local company written on a bank in Butte, Mont., or Bangor, Maine. The clearing of checks from other banks is expedited through the use of a sophisticated and expensive network of jets, helicopters and couriers (First National Remote Bank is always located far from an airport, and ideally has a parking lot too small for a helicopter).

Source: Adapted from "End the Check-Churning Frenzy," *Wall Street Journal*, May 5, 1985.

INTERNAL CONTROL OF CASH RECEIPTS

Department stores and other retail businesses ordinarily receive cash from two main sources: (1) over the counter from cash customers and (2) by mail from charge customers making payments on account. At the end of the business day, each salesclerk counts the cash in the assigned cash drawer and records the amount on a memorandum form. An employee from the cashier's department removes the cash register tapes on which total receipts were recorded for each cash drawer, counts the cash, and compares the total with the memorandum and the tape, noting any differences. The cash is then taken to the cashier's office and the tapes and memorandum forms are forwarded to the accounting department, where they become the basis for entries in the cash receipts journal.

The employees who open incoming mail compare the amount of cash received with the amount shown on the accompanying remittance advice to be certain that the two amounts agree. If there is no separate remittance advice, an employee prepares one on a form designed for such use. All cash received, usually in the form of checks and money orders, is sent to the cashier's department, where it is combined with the receipts from cash sales and a deposit ticket is prepared. The remittance advices are delivered to the accounting department, where they become the basis for entries in the cash receipts journal and for posting to the customers accounts in the subsidiary ledger.

The duplicate deposit tickets or other bank receipt forms obtained by the cashier are sent to the controller or other financial officer, who compares the total amount with that reported by the accounting department as the total debit to Cash in Bank for the period.

Cash Short and Over

The amount of cash actually received during a day often does not agree with the record of cash receipts. Whenever there is a difference between the record and the actual cash and no error can be found in the record, it must be assumed that the mistake occurred in making change. The cash shortage or overage is recorded in an account entitled Cash Short and Over. A common method for handling such mistakes is to include in the cash receipts journal a Cash Short and Over Debit column into which all cash shortages are entered, and a Cash Short and Over Credit column into which all cash overages are entered. For example, if the actual cash received from cash sales is less than the amount indicated by the cash register tally, the entry in the cash receipts journal would include a debit to Cash Short and Over. An example for one day's receipts, in general journal form, follows:

Cash in Bank	4,577.60	
Cash Short and Over	3.16	
Sales		4,580.76

If there is a debit balance in the cash short and over account at the end of the fiscal period, it is an expense and may be included in "Miscellaneous general expense" on the income statement. If there is a credit balance, it is revenue and may be listed in the "Other income" section. If the balance becomes larger than may be accounted for by minor errors in making change, the management should take corrective measures.

Cash Change Funds

Retail stores and other businesses that receive cash directly from customers must maintain a fund of currency and coins in order to make change. The fund may be established by drawing a check for the required amount, debiting the account Cash on Hand and crediting Cash in Bank. No additional charges or credits to the cash on hand account are necessary unless the amount of the fund is to be increased or decreased. At the end of each business day, the total amount of cash received during the day is deposited and the original amount of the change fund is retained. The desired composition of the fund is maintained by exchanging bills or coins for those of other denominations at the bank.

INTERNAL CONTROL OF CASH PAYMENTS

It is common practice for business enterprises to require that every payment of cash be evidenced by a check signed by a designated official. As an additional control, some firms require two signatures on all checks or only on checks which are larger than a certain amount. It is also common to use a check protector, which produces amounts on the check that are not easily removed or changed.

When the owner of a business has personal knowledge of all goods and services purchased, the owner may sign checks, with the assurance that the creditors have followed the terms of their contracts and that the exact amount of the obligation is being paid. Disbursing officials are seldom able to have such a complete knowledge of affairs, however. In enterprises of even moderate size, the responsibility for issuing purchase orders, inspecting goods received, and verifying contractual and arithmetical details of invoices is divided among the employees of several departments. It is desirable, therefore, to coordinate these related activities and to link them with the final issuance of checks to creditors. One of the best systems used for this purpose is the voucher system.

will not be on test

Basic Features of the Voucher System

A **voucher system** is made up of records, methods, and procedures used in proving and recording liabilities and in making and recording cash payments. A voucher system uses (1) vouchers, (2) a voucher register, (3) a file for unpaid vouchers, (4) a check register, and (5) a file for paid vouchers. As in all areas of accounting systems and internal controls, many differences in detail are possible. The discussion that follows refers to a medium-size merchandising enterprise with separate departments for purchasing, receiving, accounting, and disbursing.

Vouchers. The term **voucher** is widely used in accounting. In a general sense, it means any document that serves as proof of authority to pay cash, such as an invoice approved for payment, or as evidence that cash has been paid, such as a canceled check. The term has a narrower meaning when applied to the voucher system: a voucher is a special form on which is recorded relevant data about a liability and the details of its payment.

An important characteristic of the voucher system is the requirement that a voucher be prepared for each expenditure. In fact, a check may not be issued except in payment of a properly authorized voucher. Vouchers may be paid immediately after they are prepared or at a later date, depending upon the circumstances and the credit terms.

A voucher form is illustrated below. The face of the voucher provides space for the name and address of the creditor, the date and number of the voucher, and basic details of the invoice or other supporting document, such as the vendor's invoice number and the amount and terms of the invoice. One half of the back of the voucher is devoted to the account distribution and the other half to summaries of the voucher and the details of payment. Spaces are also provided for the signature or initials of certain employees.

JANSEN AUTO SUPPLY INC.

VOUCHER

Date July 1, 1987   Voucher No. 451

Payee   Allied Manufacturing Company
683 Fairmont Road
Chicago, IL 60630-3168

DATE	DETAILS	AMOUNT
June 28, 1987	Invoice No. 4693-C FOB Chicago, 2/10, n/30	450.00

Attach Supporting Documents

ACCOUNT DISTRIBUTION

DEBIT	AMOUNT
PURCHASES	450 00
SUPPLIES	
ADVERTISING EXPENSE	
DELIVERY EXPENSE	
MISC. SELLING EXPENSE	
MISC. GENERAL EXPENSE	
CREDIT ACCOUNTS PAYABLE	450 00

DISTRIBUTION APPROVED   *L. Donnelly*

VOUCHER   NO. 451

DATE 7/1/87   DUE 7/8/87

PAYEE
Allied Manufacturing Company
683 Fairmont Road
Chicago, IL 60630-3168

VOUCHER SUMMARY

AMOUNT		450 00
ADJUSTMENT		
DISCOUNT		9 00
NET		441 00
APPROVED *H. C. Leshen*	CONTROLLER	
RECORDED *H.B.*		

PAYMENT SUMMARY

DATE	7/8/87
AMOUNT	441.00
CHECK NO.	863
APPROVED	*a. T. Wood*
RECORDED	*L. K. R.* *a. s.*

VOUCHER

Vouchers are customarily prepared by the accounting department on the basis of an invoice or a memorandum that serves as proof of an expenditure. This is usually done only after the following comparisons and verifications have been completed and noted on the invoice:

1. Comparison of the invoice with a copy of the purchase order to verify quantities, prices, and terms.
2. Comparison of the invoice with the receiving report to verify receipt of the items billed.
3. Verification of the arithmetical accuracy of the invoice.

After all data except details of payment have been inserted, the invoice or other supporting evidence is attached to the face of the voucher, which is then folded with the account distribution and summaries on the outside. The voucher is then given to the designated official or officials for final approval.

Voucher Register.   After approval by the designated official, each voucher is recorded in a journal known as a **voucher register**. It is similar to and replaces the purchases journal described in Chapter 7.

A typical form of a voucher register is illustrated below. The vouchers are entered in numerical order, each being recorded as a credit to Accounts Payable (sometimes entitled Vouchers Payable) and as a debit to the account or accounts to be charged for the expenditure.

VOUCHER
REGISTER

PAGE 11							VOUCHER
DATE	VOU. NO.	PAYEE	DATE PAID	CK. NO.	ACCOUNTS PAYABLE CR.	PURCHASES DR.
19--						
JULY 1	451	ALLIED MFG. CO.	7-8	863	450.00	450.00
1	452	CHAVEZ REALTORS	7-1	856	600.00	
2	453	FOSTER PUBLICATIONS	7-2	857	52.50	
3	454	BENSON EXPRESS CO.	7-3	859	36.80	24.20
3	455	ROBERSON'S SUPPLY CO.			784.20	
3	456	MOORE & CO.	7-11	866	1,236.00	1,236.00
6	457	J. L. BROWN CO.	7-6	860	22.50	
6	458	TURNER CORP.			395.30	395.30
31	477	CENTRAL MOTORS			112.20	
31	478	PETTY CASH	7-31	883	48.60	
31					15,551.60 (212)	11,640.30 (511)

When a voucher is paid, the date of payment and the number of the check are inserted in the proper columns in the voucher register. These notations provide a ready means of determining at any time the amount of an individual unpaid voucher or of the total amount of unpaid vouchers.

Unpaid Voucher File. After a voucher has been recorded in the voucher register, it is filed in an unpaid voucher file, where it remains until it is paid. The amount due on each voucher represents the credit balance of an account payable, and the voucher itself is like an individual account in a subsidiary accounts payable ledger. Accordingly, a separate subsidiary ledger is not needed.

All voucher systems include some way to assure payment within the discount period or on the last day of the credit period. A simple but effective method is to file each voucher in the unpaid voucher file according to the earliest date that consideration should be given to its payment. The file may be made up of a group of folders, numbered from 1 to 31, the numbers representing the days of a month. Such a system brings to the attention of the disbursing official the vouchers that are to be paid on each day. It also provides management with a convenient means of forecasting the amount of cash needed to meet maturing obligations.

When a voucher is to be paid, it is removed from the unpaid voucher file and a check is issued in payment. The date, the number, and the amount of the check are listed on the back of the voucher for use in recording the

REGISTER							PAGE 11
STORE SUPPLIES DR.	ADV. EXP. DR.	DEL. EXP. DR.	MISC. SELLING EXP. DR.	MISC. GENERAL EXP. DR.	SUNDRY ACCOUNTS DR.		
					ACCOUNT	POST. REF.	AMOUNT
					RENT EXPENSE	712	600.00
	52.50						
		12.60					
34.20					OFFICE EQUIPMENT	122	750.00
				22.50			
		112.20					
4.30		16.20	19.50	8.60			
59.80	176.40	286.10	48.30	64.90			3,275.80
(116)	(612)	(613)	(618)	(718)			(✔)

payment in the check register. Paid vouchers and the supporting documents are often run through a canceling machine to prevent accidental or intentional reuse.

An exception to the general rule that vouchers be prepared for all expenditures may be made for bank charges shown by debit memorandums or notations on the bank statement. For example, such items as bank service charges, safe-deposit box rentals, and returned NSF (Not Sufficient Funds) checks from customers may be charged to the depositor's account without either a formal voucher or a check. For large expenditures, such as the repayment of a bank loan, a supporting voucher may be prepared, if desired, even though a check is not written. The paid note may then be attached to the voucher as evidence of the obligation. All bank debit memorandums are the equivalent of checks as evidence of payment.

Check Register.   The payment of a voucher is recorded in a check register, an example of which is illustrated below. The **check register** is a modified form of the cash payments journal and is so called because it is a complete record of all checks. It is common to record all checks in the check register in sequential order, including occasional checks that are voided because of an error in their preparation.

Each check issued is in payment of a voucher that has previously been recorded as an account payable in the voucher register. The effect of each entry in the check register is a debit to Accounts Payable and a credit to Cash in Bank (and Purchases Discounts, when appropriate).

			CHECK REGISTER					PAGE 14
DATE	CK. NO.	PAYEE	VOU. NO.	ACCOUNTS PAYABLE DR.	PURCHASES DISCOUNTS CR.	CASH IN BANK CR.	BANK DEPOSITS	BANK BALANCE
19--								8,743.10
JULY 1	856	CHAVEZ REALTORS	452	600.00		600.00	1,240.30	9,383.40
2	857	FOSTER PUBLICATIONS	453	52.50		52.50		9,330.90
2	858	HILL AND DAVIS	436	1,420.00	14.20	1,405.80	865.70	8,790.80
3	859	BENSON EXPRESS CO.	454	36.80		36.80	942.20	9,696.20
30	879	VOIDED						
30	880	STONE & CO.	460	14.30		14.30		9,521.80
30	881	EVANS CORP.	448	1,015.00		1,015.00	765.50	9,272.30
31	882	GRAHAM & CO.	469	830.00	16.60	813.40		8,458.90
31	883	PETTY CASH	478	48.60		48.60	938.10	9,348.40
31				17,322.90 (212)	198.20 (513)	17,124.70 (111)		

CHECK REGISTER

The memorandum columns for Bank Deposits and Bank Balance appearing in the illustration of the check register are optional. They provide a convenient means of determining the cash available at all times.

When check forms with a remittance advice are prepared in duplicate, the copies retained may make up the check register. At the end of each month, summary totals can be readily obtained for Accounts Payable debit, Purchases Discounts credit, and Cash credit, and the entry recorded in the general journal. If the volume of checks issued is large, a significant amount of clerical expenses may be saved by eliminating the copying of data in a columnar check register.

Paid Voucher File. After payment, vouchers are usually filed in numerical order in a paid voucher file. They are then readily available for examination by employees or independent auditors needing information about a certain expenditure. Eventually the paid vouchers are destroyed according to the firm's policies concerning the retention of records.

The Voucher System and Management. The voucher system not only provides effective accounting controls but also aids management in discharging other responsibilities. For example, the voucher system gives greater assurance that all payments are in liquidation of valid liabilities. In addition, current information is always available for use in determining future cash requirements. This in turn enables management to make the best use of cash resources. Invoices on which cash discounts are allowed can be paid within the discount period and other invoices can be paid on the final day of the credit period, thus reducing costs and maintaining a favorable credit standing. Seasonal borrowing can also be planned more accurately, with a consequent saving in interest costs.

Purchases Discounts

In earlier chapters, purchases of merchandise were recorded at the invoice price, and cash discounts taken were credited to the purchases discounts account at the time of payment. There are two opposing views on how discounts taken should be reported in the income statement.

The most widely accepted view, which has been followed in this textbook, is that purchases discounts should be reported as a deduction from purchases. For example, the cost of merchandise with an invoice price of $1,000, subject to terms of 2/10, n/30, is recorded initially at $1,000. If payment is made within the discount period, the discount of $20 reduces the cost to $980. If the invoice is not paid within the discount period, the cost of the merchandise remains $1,000. This treatment of purchases discounts may be attacked on the grounds that the date of payment should not affect the cost of a commodity. The additional payment required beyond the discount period adds nothing to the value of the commodities purchased.

The second view reports discounts taken as "other income." In terms of the preceding example, the cost of the merchandise is considered to be $1,000, regardless of the time of payment. If payment is made within the discount period, revenue of $20 is considered to be realized. The objection to this procedure lies in the recognition of revenue from the act of purchasing and paying for a commodity. Theoretically, an enterprise might make no sales of merchandise during an accounting period and yet might report as revenue the amount of cash discounts taken.

A major disadvantage of recording purchases at the invoice price and recognizing purchases discounts at the time of payment is that this method does not measure the cost of failing to take discounts. Well-managed enterprises maintain enough cash to pay within the discount period all invoices subject to a discount, and view the failure to take a discount as an inefficiency. To measure the cost of this inefficiency, purchases invoices may be recorded at the net amount, assuming that all discounts will be taken. Any discounts *not* taken are then recorded in an expense account called Discounts Lost. This method measures the cost of failure to take cash discounts and gives management an opportunity to take remedial action. Again assuming the same data, the invoice for $1,000 would be recorded as a debit to Purchases of $980 and a credit to Accounts Payable for the same amount. If the invoice is not paid until after the discount period has passed, the entry in general journal form would be as follows:

Accounts Payable	980	
Discounts Lost	20	
Cash in Bank		1,000

When this method is used with the voucher system, all vouchers are prepared and recorded at the net amount. Any discount lost is noted on the related voucher and recorded in a special column in the check register when the voucher is paid.

Another advantage of this treatment of purchases discounts is that all merchandise purchased is recorded initially at the net price, and hence no later adjustments to cost are necessary. An objection, however, is that the amount reported as accounts payable in the balance sheet may be less than the amount needed to discharge the liability.

Petty Cash

In most businesses there is a frequent need for the payment of relatively small amounts, such as for postage due, for transportation charges, or for the purchase of urgently needed supplies at a nearby retail store. Payment by check in such cases would result in delay, annoyance, and excessive expense of maintaining the records. Yet because these small payments may occur frequently and therefore amount to a considerable total sum, it is desirable to retain close control over such payments. This may be done by maintaining a special cash fund called **petty cash.**

In establishing a petty cash fund, the first step is to estimate the amount of cash needed for disbursements of relatively small amounts during a certain period, such as a week or a month. If the voucher system is used, a voucher is then prepared for this amount and it is recorded in the voucher register as a debit to Petty Cash and a credit to Accounts Payable. The check drawn to pay the voucher is recorded in the check register as a debit to Accounts Payable and a credit to Cash in Bank.

The money obtained from cashing the check is placed in the custody of a specific employee who is authorized to disburse the fund according to restrictions as to maximum amount and purpose. Each time a disbursement is made from the fund, the employee records the essential details on a receipt form, obtains the signature of the payee as proof of the payment, and initials the completed form. A typical petty cash receipt is illustrated as follows:

PETTY CASH RECEIPT

	PETTY CASH RECEIPT		
NO. ___121___	DATE ___August 1, 1987___		
PAID TO ___Metropolitan Times___		AMOUNT	
FOR ___Daily newspaper___		3	70
CHARGE TO ___Miscellaneous General Expense___			
PAYMENT RECEIVED:			
___S. O. Hall___	APPROVED BY ___N.E.R.___		

When the amount of money in the petty cash fund is reduced to the predetermined minimum amount, the fund is replenished. If the voucher system is used, the accounts debited on the replenishing voucher are those indicated by a summary of expenditures. The voucher is then recorded in the voucher register as a debit to the various expense and asset accounts and a credit to Accounts Payable. The check in payment of the voucher is recorded in the check register in the usual manner.

To illustrate the entries that would be made in accounting for petty cash, assume that a voucher system is used and that a petty cash fund of $100 is established on August 1. At the end of August, the petty cash receipts indicate expenditures for the following items: office supplies, $28; postage (office supplies), $22; store supplies, $35; and daily newspaper (miscellaneous general expense), $3.70. To record the establishment and replenishment of the petty cash fund, the entries in general journal form would be as follows:

Aug.	1	Petty Cash.....................................	100.00	
		Accounts Payable		100.00
	1	Accounts Payable	100.00	
		Cash in Bank		100.00
	31	Office Supplies.............................	50.00	
		Store Supplies	35.00	
		Miscellaneous General Expense...............	3.70	
		Accounts Payable		88.70
	31	Accounts Payable	88.70	
		Cash in Bank		88.70

Replenishing the petty cash fund restores it to its original amount. It should be noted that the only entry in the petty cash account will be the initial debit, unless at some later time the standard amount of the fund is increased or decreased.

Because disbursements are not recorded in the accounts until the fund is replenished, petty cash funds and other special funds that operate in a like manner should always be replenished at the end of an accounting period. The amount of money actually in the fund will then agree with the balance in the related fund account, and the expenses and the assets for which payment has been made will be recorded in the proper period.

Other Cash Funds

Cash funds may also be established to meet other special needs of a business. For example, money may be advanced for travel expenses as needed. Then periodically, after expense reports have been received, the expenses are recorded and the fund is replenished. A similar procedure may be used to provide a working fund for a sales office located in another city. The amount of the fund may be deposited in a local bank and the sales representative may be authorized to draw checks for payment of rent, salaries, and other operating expenses. Each month, the representative sends the invoices, bank statement, paid checks, bank reconciliation, and other business documents to the home office. The data are audited, the expenditures are recorded, and a reimbursing check is returned for deposit in the local bank.

CASH TRANSACTIONS AND ELECTRONIC FUNDS TRANSFER

Currently most cash transactions are in the form of currency or check. The broad principles discussed in earlier sections provide the basis for developing an effective system to control such cash transactions. However, the development of **electronic funds transfer (EFT)** may eventually change the form in which many cash transactions are executed and could affect the processing and controlling of cash transactions.

EFT can be defined as a payment system that uses computerized electronic impulses rather than paper (money, checks, etc.) to effect a cash transaction. For example, a business may pay its employees by means of EFT. Under such a system, employees who want their payroll checks deposited directly in a checking account sign an authorization form. For each pay period, the business' computer produces a magnetic tape with computer-sensitive notations for relevant payroll data. The magnetic tape is delivered to the bank, or the data are transmitted over telephone lines. The bank then debits the business' account for the entire payroll and credits the checking account of each employee. Similar cash payments might be made for other preauthorized payments. The federal government currently processes several million social security checks through EFT.

EFT is also beginning to play a role in retail sales. Through a point-of-sale (POS) system, a customer pays for goods at the time of purchase by presenting a plastic card. The card is used to activate a terminal in the store and thereby effect an immediate transfer from the customer's checking account to the retailer's account at the bank.

Studies have indicated that EFT systems may reduce the cost of processing certain cash transactions and contribute to better control over cash receipts and cash payments. Offsetting these potential advantages are problems of protecting the privacy of information stored in computers, and difficulties in documenting purchase and sale transactions. In any event, developments with EFT systems are likely to be followed very closely by most businesses over the next few years.

CHAPTER REVIEW

KEY POINTS

1. Control Over Cash.

It is necessary to safeguard cash effectively because of the ease with which it can be transferred. One of the major devices for maintaining control over cash is the bank account. To obtain the most benefit from a bank account, all cash received must be deposited in the bank and all payments must be made by checks drawn on the bank or from special cash funds.

Periodically, the bank mails to the depositor a statement of account. This statement of account should be reconciled with the depositor's records by preparing a bank reconciliation. The bank reconciliation is divided into two major sections: one section begins with the balance according to the bank statement and ends with an adjusted balance; the other section begins with the balance according to the depositor's records and also ends with an adjusted balance. After all reconciling items have been considered, the two amounts designated as the adjusted balance must be equal.

After a bank reconciliation has been prepared, the items which appear in the section of the bank reconciliation beginning with the balance according to the depositor's records must be entered into the accounting records through the use of adjusting journal entries.

2. Internal Control of Cash Receipts.

The bank reconciliation is an important part of the system of internal control over cash. Other controls of cash receipts include the separation of responsibilities for recording cash transactions from the handling of cash, the use of a cash short and over account for differences between recorded receipts and actual receipts, and the use of cash change funds.

3. Internal Control of Cash Payments.

One of the best systems for establishing control of cash payments is the use of a voucher system. A voucher system is made up of records, methods, and procedures used in proving and recording liabilities and in making and recording cash payments. A voucher system uses (1) vouchers, (2) a voucher register, (3) a file for unpaid vouchers, (4) a check register, and (5) a file for paid vouchers.

Because of the importance of taking advantage of all purchases discounts, a business may use a separate account, called Discounts Lost, to account for any discounts not taken during the discount period. When this method is used with the voucher system, all vouchers are prepared and recorded at the net amount, assuming that the discount will be taken.

A special cash fund, called petty cash, may be used by a business to make small payments that occur frequently, for which payment by check would cause delay, annoyance, and excessive expense of maintaining records. The amount of money maintained in a petty cash fund is placed in the custody of a specific employee, who authorizes disbursement of the fund according to specific restrictions as to maximum amount and purpose. When the amount of money in the petty cash fund is reduced to a predetermined minimum amount, the fund is replenished. Other cash funds may be established by businesses for purposes such as travel expenses, selling expenses, and other operating expenses.

4. Cash Transactions and Electronic Funds Transfer.

Electronic funds transfer is a payment system that uses computerized electronic impulses rather than paper (money, checks, etc.) to effect cash transactions. EFT is beginning to play an important role in retail sales.

KEY TERMS

bank reconciliation 343
voucher system 349
voucher 349
voucher register 350

check register 352
petty cash 355
electronic funds transfer (EFT) 357

SELF-EXAMINATION QUESTIONS
Answers in Appendix B.

1. In preparing a bank reconciliation, the amount of checks outstanding would be:
   A. added to the bank balance according to the bank statement
   B. deducted from the bank balance according to the bank statement
   C. added to the bank balance according to the depositor's records
   D. deducted from the bank balance according to the depositor's records

2. Journal entries based on the bank reconciliation are required for:
   A. additions to the bank balance according to the depositor's records
   B. deductions from the bank balance according to the depositor's records
   C. both A and B
   D. neither A nor B

3. The journal used to record liabilities when a voucher system is used is called:
   A. a voucher
   B. an unpaid voucher file
   C. a check register
   D. a voucher register

4. A voucher system is used, all vouchers for purchases are recorded at the net amount, and a purchase is made for $500 under terms 1/10, n/30.
   A. Purchases would be debited for $495 to record the purchase.
   B. Discounts Lost would be debited for $5 if the voucher is not paid within the discount period.
   C. If the voucher is not paid until after the discount period has expired, the discount lost would be reported as an expense on the income statement.
   D. All of the above

5. A petty cash fund is:
   A. used to pay relatively small amounts
   B. established by estimating the amount of cash needed for disbursements of relatively small amounts during a specified period
   C. reimbursed when the amount of money in the fund is reduced to a predetermined minimum amount
   D. all of the above

ILLUSTRATIVE PROBLEM

The bank statement for Dunlap Company for April 30 indicates a balance of $10,443.11. The Dunlap Company employs the voucher system in controlling expenditures and disbursements. All cash receipts are deposited each evening in a night depository, after banking hours. The accounting records indicate the following summary data for cash receipts and disbursements for April:

CASH IN BANK ACCOUNT
   Balance as of April 1 . . . . $ 5,143.50

CASH RECEIPTS JOURNAL
   Total cash receipts for April $28,971.60

CHECK REGISTER
   Total amount of checks issued in April $26,060.85

Comparison of the bank statement and the accompanying canceled checks and memorandums with the records revealed the following reconciling items:

(a) The bank had collected for Dunlap Company $912 on a note left for collection. The face of the note was $900.
(b) A deposit of $1,852.21, representing receipts of April 30, had been made too late to appear on the bank statement.
(c) Checks outstanding totaled $3,265.27.
(d) A check drawn for $79 had been erroneously charged by the bank as $97.
(e) A check for $10 returned with the statement had been recorded in the check register as $100. The check was for the payment of an obligation to Davis Equipment Company for the purchase of office supplies on account.
(f) Bank service charges for April amounted to $8.20.

Instructions:

1. Prepare a bank reconciliation for April.
2. Journalize the entries that should be made by Dunlap Company.

SOLUTION

(1)

Dunlap Company
Bank Reconciliation
April 30, 19--

Balance per bank statement		$10,443.11
Add: Deposit of April 30 not recorded		
by bank........................	$1,852.21	
Bank error in charging check for $97		
instead of $79..................	18.00	1,870.21
		$12,313.32
Deduct: Outstanding checks		3,265.27
Adjusted balance		$ 9,048.05
Balance per depositor's records		$ 8,054.25*
Add: Proceeds of note collected by bank		
including $12 interest..............	$ 912.00	
Error in recording check.............	90.00	1,002.00
		$ 9,056.25
Deduct: Bank service charges.............		8.20
Adjusted balance		$ 9,048.05

*$5,143.50 + $28,971.60 − $26,060.85

(2)

Cash in Bank	1,002.00	
Notes Receivable		900.00
Interest Income		12.00
Accounts Payable......................		90.00
Miscellaneous General Expense	8.20	
Cash in Bank		8.20

DISCUSSION QUESTIONS

1. Why is cash the asset that often warrants the most attention in the design of an effective internal control system?

2. (a) What is meant by the term *compensating balance* as applied to the checking account of a firm? (b) How is the compensating balance reported in the financial statements?

3. What name is often given to the notification attached to a check that indicates the specific invoice that is being paid?

4. When checks are received, they are recorded as debits to Cash, the assumption being that the drawer has sufficient funds on deposit. What entry should be made if a check received from a customer and deposited is returned by the bank for lack of sufficient funds (NSF)?

5. Do items reported on the bank statement as debits represent (a) deductions made by the bank from the depositor's balance, or (b) additions made by the bank to the depositor's balance?

6. What is the purpose of preparing a bank reconciliation?

7. Identify each of the following reconciling items as: (a) an addition to the balance per bank statement, (b) a deduction from the balance per bank statement, (c) an addition to the balance per depositor's records, or (d) a deduction from the balance per depositor's records. (None of the transactions reported by bank debit and credit memorandums have been recorded by the depositor.)
   (1) Outstanding checks, $4,210.50.
   (2) Note collected by bank, $5,150.
   (3) Deposit in transit, $3,305.75.
   (4) Check for $2,000 charged by bank as $200.
   (5) Check drawn by depositor for $520 but recorded as $250.
   (6) Check of a customer returned by bank to depositor because of insufficient funds, $92.55.
   (7) Bank service charges, $22.50.

8. Which of the reconciling items listed in Question 7 necessitate an entry in the depositor's accounts?

9. The procedures employed by Garcia's for over-the-counter receipts are as follows: At the close of each day's business, the salesclerks count the cash in their respective cash drawers, after which they determine the amount recorded by the register and prepare the memorandum cash form, noting any discrepancies. An employee from the cashier's office counts the cash, compares the total with the memorandum, and takes the cash to the cashier's office. (a) Indicate the weak link in internal control. (b) How can the weakness be corrected?

10. The mailroom employees of C.L. Dunn Co. send all remittances and remittance advices to the cashier. The cashier deposits the cash in the bank and forwards the remittance advices and duplicate deposit slips to the accounting department. (a) Indicate the weak link in internal control in the handling of cash receipts. (b) How can the weakness be corrected?

11. The combined cash count of all cash registers at the close of business is $4.35 less than the cash sales indicated by the cash register tapes. (a) In what account is the cash shortage recorded? (b) Are cash shortages debited or credited to this account?

12. The bookkeeper pays all obligations by prenumbered checks. What are the strengths and weaknesses in the internal control over cash disbursements in this situation?

13. What is meant by the term *voucher* as applied to the voucher system?

14. Before a voucher for the purchase of merchandise is approved for payment, three documents should be compared to verify the accuracy of the liability. Name these three documents.

15. (a) When the voucher system is employed, is the accounts payable account in the general ledger a controlling account? (b) Is there a subsidiary creditors ledger?

16. Ann Jacobs, controller of D. D. West and Company, approves all vouchers before they are submitted to the treasurer for payment. What procedure can Jacobs add to the system to assure that the documents accompanying the vouchers and supporting the expenditures are not "reused" to support future vouchers improperly?

17. In what order are vouchers ordinarily filed (a) in the unpaid voucher file, and (b) in the paid voucher file? Give reasons for answers.

18. What are the two possibilities for reporting purchases discounts on the income statement?

19. Merchandise with an invoice price of $5,000 is purchased subject to terms of 2/10, n/30. Determine the cost of the merchandise according to each of the following systems:

(a) Discounts taken are treated as deductions from the invoice price.
   (1) The invoice is paid within the discount period.
   (2) The invoice is paid after the discount period has expired.
(b) Discounts taken are treated as other income.
   (1) The invoice is paid within the discount period.
   (2) The invoice is paid after the discount period has expired.
(c) Discounts allowable are treated as deductions from the invoice price, regardless of when payment is made.
   (1) The invoice is paid within the discount period.
   (2) The invoice is paid after the discount period has expired.

20. What account or accounts are debited when recording the voucher (a) establishing a petty cash fund and (b) replenishing a petty cash fund?

21. The petty cash account has a debit balance of $250. At the end of the accounting period, there is $33 in the petty cash fund along with petty cash receipts totaling $217. Should the fund be replenished as of the last day of the period? Discuss.

22. What is meant by electronic funds transfer?

23. Real World Focus. Between September 3 and September 22, seventeen prenumbered checks totaling $1,129,232.39 were forged and cashed on the accounts of Perini Corporation, a construction company based in the Boston suburb of Framingham. Perini Corporation kept its supply of blank prenumbered checks in an unlocked storeroom with items such as styrofoam coffee cups. Every clerk and secretary had access to this storeroom. It was later discovered that someone had apparently stolen two boxes of prenumbered checks. The numbers of the missing checks matched the numbers of the out-of-sequence checks cashed by the banks. What fundamental principle of control over cash was violated in this case?

EXERCISES

SPREADSHEET PROBLEM

Exercise 8–1.   Bank reconciliation. The following data are accumulated for use in reconciling the bank account of Lambert and Mann Inc. for June:

    (a) Balance per bank statement at June 30, $8,791.22.
    (b) Balance per depositor's records at June 30, $7,548.02.
    (c) Checks outstanding, $1,955.25.
    (d) Deposit in transit, not recorded by bank, $787.50.
    (e) A check for $122 in payment of a voucher was erroneously recorded in the check register as $212.
    (f) Bank debit memorandum for service charges, $14.55.

    Prepare a bank reconciliation.

Exercise 8–2.   Entries for bank reconciliation. Using the data presented in Exercise 8–1, prepare in general journal form the entry or entries that should be made by the depositor.

Exercise 8–3.   Entries for note collected by bank. Accompanying a bank statement for DeMaris and Son is a credit memorandum for $5,150, representing the principal ($5,000) and interest ($150) on a note that had been collected by the bank. The depositor had been notified by the bank at the time of the collection, but had made no entries. In general journal form, present the entry that should be made by the depositor.

Exercise 8–4.   Entry for cash sales. The actual cash received from cash sales for Susan Clark Company was $3,745.75, and the amount indicated by the cash register tally was $3,750.25. Prepare the entry, in general journal form, to record the cash receipts and cash sales.

Exercise 8–5.   Entries for vouchers and checks; purchases at gross amount. Record in general journal form the following selected transactions, indicating above each entry the name of the register in which it should be recorded. Assume the use of a voucher register and a check register similar to those illustrated in this chapter. All invoices are recorded at invoice price.

    July   1. Recorded Voucher No. 792 for $2,000, payable to Corley Co., for merchandise purchased, terms 2/10, n/30.

July 2. Recorded Voucher No. 793 for $300, payable to B. M. Systems, for merchandise purchased, terms 1/10, n/30.

11. Issued Check No. 779 in payment of Voucher No. 793.

13. Recorded Voucher No. 812 for $2,500, payable to Glos Inc., for merchandise purchased, terms 2/10, n/30.

23. Issued Check No. 799 in payment of Voucher No. 812.

30. Recorded Voucher No. 840 for $212.10 to replenish the petty cash fund for the following disbursements: store supplies, $72.50; office supplies, $51.25; miscellaneous general expense, $46.10; miscellaneous selling expense, $42.25.

30. Issued Check No. 815 in payment of Voucher No. 840.

30. Issued Check No. 816 in payment of Voucher No. 792.

Exercise 8–6. Entries for purchases at net amount. Record in general journal form the following related transactions, assuming that invoices for commodities purchased are recorded at their net price after deducting the allowable discount:

June 10. Voucher No. 801 is prepared for merchandise purchased from Klein Co., $3,000, terms 2/10, n/30.

15. Voucher No. 811 is prepared for merchandise purchased from Zimmer Co., $1,500, terms 1/10, n/30.

25. Check No. 798 is issued in payment of Voucher No. 811.

July 10. Check No. 808 is issued in payment of Voucher No. 801.

Exercise 8–7. Petty cash fund entries. Prepare in general journal form the entries to record the following:

(a) Voucher No. 19 is prepared to establish a petty cash fund of $200.

(b) Check No. 15 is issued in payment of Voucher No. 19.

(c) The amount of cash in the petty cash fund is now $19.90. Voucher No. 80 is prepared to replenish the fund, based on the following summary of petty cash receipts: office supplies $62.20; miscellaneous selling expense, $59.15; miscellaneous general expense, $57.50. (Since the amount of the check to replenish the fund plus the balance in the fund do not equal $200, record the discrepancy in the cash short and over account.)

(d) Check No. 73 is issued by the disbursing officer in payment of Voucher No. 80. The check is cashed and the money is placed in the fund.

Exercise 8–8. Cash change fund entries. Record in general journal form the following transactions:

(a) Voucher No. 440 is prepared to establish a change fund of $250.

(b) Check No. 419 is issued in payment of Voucher No. 440.

(c) Cash sales for the day, according to the cash register tapes, were $1,900.05, and cash on hand is $2,152.15. A bank deposit ticket was prepared for $1,902.15.

PROBLEMS

Series A

SPREADSHEET
PROBLEM

Problem 8–1A.   Bank reconciliation and entries. The cash in bank account for J. C. Peters Co. at June 30 of the current year indicated a balance of $18,500.30 after both the cash receipts journal and the check register for June had been posted. The bank statement indicated a balance of $29,106.30 on June 30. Comparison of the bank statement and the accompanying canceled checks and memorandums with the records revealed the following reconciling items:

(a) Checks outstanding totaled $13,441.50.
(b) A deposit of $6,917.75, representing receipts of June 30, had been made too late to appear on the bank statement.
(c) The bank had collected for J. C. Peters Co. $4,240 on a note left for collection. The face of the note was $4,000.
(d) A check for $92.50 returned with the statement had been recorded erroneously in the check register as $9.25. The check was for the payment of an obligation to Allen Supply Company for the purchase of office equipment on account.
(e) A check drawn for $505 had been erroneously charged by the bank as $550.
(f) Bank service charges for June amounted to $29.50.

Instructions:

(1) Prepare a bank reconciliation.
(2) Record the necessary entries in general journal form. The accounts have not been closed. The voucher system is used.

Problem 8–2A.   Transactions for petty cash, advances to salespersons fund; cash short and over. Martin Company has just adopted the policy of depositing all cash receipts in the bank and of making all payments by check in conjunction with the voucher system. The following transactions were selected from those completed in June of the current year:

June 1. Recorded Voucher No. 1 to establish a petty cash fund of $200 and a change fund of $500.
      1. Issued Check No. 909 in payment of Voucher No. 1.
      4. Recorded Voucher No. 5 to establish an advances to salespersons fund of $1,000.

June 4. Issued Check No. 912 in payment of Voucher No. 5.
10. The cash sales for the day, according to the cash register tapes, totaled $3,107.90. The combined count of all cash on hand (including the change fund) totaled $3,610.50.
25. Recorded Voucher No. 35 to reimburse the petty cash fund for the following disbursements, each evidenced by a petty cash receipt:

June 5. Store supplies, $15.50.
6. Express charges on merchandise purchased, $14.50.
8. Office supplies, $12.75
9. Office supplies, $9.20.
12. Postage stamps, $22 (Office Supplies).
12. Repair to adding machine, $27.50 (Miscellaneous General Expense).
16. Repair to typewriter, $20.50 (Miscellaneous General Expense).
18. Postage due on special delivery letter, $1.05 (Miscellaneous General Expense).
20. Express charges on merchandise purchased, $19.50.
24. Telegram charges, $7.75 (Miscellaneous Selling Expense).
25. Issued Check No. 942 in payment of Voucher No. 35.
28. The cash sales for the day, according to the cash register tapes, totaled $2,605.50. The count of all cash on hand (including the change fund) totaled $3,101.60.
30. Recorded Voucher No. 40 to replenish the advances to salespersons fund for the following expenditures for travel: Ann Brennon, $197.50; John Kottes, $297.40; Jane Palmer, $311.15.
30. Issued Check No. 948 in payment of Voucher No. 40.

Instructions:

Record the transactions in general journal form.

Problem 8–3A. Voucher and check registers; accounts payable account; schedule of unpaid vouchers. A. Getz Co. had the following vouchers in its unpaid voucher file at May 31 of the current year:

Due Date	Voucher No.	Creditor	Date of Invoice	Amount	Terms
June 5	586	King Co.	May 26	$1,350	2/10, n/30
June 14	570	White Inc.	May 15	2,550	n/30
June 26	599	Royal Co.	May 27	1,125	n/30

The vouchers prepared and the checks issued during the month of June were as follows:

VOUCHERS

Date	Voucher No.	Payee	Amount	Terms	Account(s) Debited
June 1	603	Glaze Co.	$1,200	1/10, n/30	Purchases
2	604	Adams and Fox	90	cash	Office supplies
6	605	Walls Co.	750	2/10, n/30	Purchases
7	606	Mann Supply	105	cash	Store supplies
9	607	Ramos Co.	1,250	2/10, n/30	Purchases
12	608	Ace Express	52	cash	Delivery expense
15	609	Commercial Savings	5,300		Note payable, $5,000 Interest, $300
18	610	Baker Office Co.	1,550	n/30	Office equipment
19	611	Ross & Co.	950	2/10, n/30	Purchases
23	612	L. M. Carr Co.	2,200	cash	Store equipment
25	613	Herr Co.	3,100	2/10, n/30	Purchases
29	614	Petty Cash	130		Store supplies, $27 Office supplies, $25 Miscellaneous selling expense, $38 Miscellaneous general expense, $40

CHECKS

Date	Check No.	Payee	Voucher Paid	Amount
June 2	570	Adams and Fox	604	$ 90
5	571	King Co.	586	1,323
7	572	Mann Supply	606	105
11	573	Glaze Co.	603	1,188
12	574	Ace Express	608	52
14	575	White Inc.	570	2,550
15	576	Commercial Savings	609	5,300
16	577	Walls Co.	605	735
19	578	Ramos Co.	607	1,225
23	579	L. M. Carr Co.	612	2,200
26	580	Royal Co.	599	1,125
29	581	Ross & Co.	611	931
29	582	Petty Cash	614	130

Instructions:

(1) Set up a four-column account for Accounts Payable, Account No. 205, and record the balance of $5,025 as of June 1. Place a ✔ in the Post. Ref. column.

(2) Record the June vouchers in a voucher register similar to the one illustrated in this chapter, with the following amount columns: Accounts Payable Cr., Purchases Dr., Store Supplies Dr., Office Supplies Dr., and Sundry Accounts Dr. Purchases invoices are recorded at the gross amount.

(3) Record the June checks in a check register similar to the one illustrated in this chapter, but omit the Bank Deposits and Balance columns. As each check is recorded in the check register, the date and check number should be inserted in the appropriate columns of the voucher register. (Assume that notations for payment of the May vouchers are made in the voucher register for May.)

(4) Total and rule the registers and post to Accounts Payable.

(5) Prepare a schedule of unpaid vouchers.

If the working papers correlating with the textbook are not used, omit Problem 8–4A.

Problem 8–4A. Voucher and check registers; accounts payable account; bank reconciliation. Portions of the voucher register, check register, and accounts payable account of Tarkey Co. are presented in the working papers. Cash disbursements and other selected transactions completed during the period May 25–31 of the current year are described as follows:

May 25. Issued Check No. 754 to Dolan Co. in payment of Voucher No. 609 for $3,000, less cash discount of 1%.

25. Recorded Voucher No. 617, payable to Cannon Co. for merchandise, $5,000, terms 2/10, n/30. (Purchases invoices are recorded at the invoice price.)

26. Recorded Voucher No. 618, payable to Bain Auto Insurance Co. for an insurance policy, $2,150.

26. Issued Check No. 755 in payment of Voucher No. 618.

27. Recorded Voucher No. 619, payable to Palmer Co. for merchandise, $4,200, terms, 1/10, n/30.

27. Recorded Voucher No. 620 for $10,400, payable to Noble National Bank for note payable, $10,000, and interest, $400.

27. Issued Check No. 756 in payment of Voucher No. 620.

28. Recorded Voucher No. 621, payable to Midway Press for advertising, $475.

28. Issued Check No. 757 in payment of Voucher No. 621.

29. Recorded Voucher No. 622, payable to Petty Cash for $193.05, distributed as follows: office supplies, $54.40; advertising expense, $18.35; delivery expense, $40.10; miscellaneous selling expense, $38.15; miscellaneous general expense, $42.05.

29. Issued Check No. 758 in payment of Voucher No. 622.

31. Issued Check No. 759 to Marcus Co. in payment of Voucher No. 608 for $1,050, no discount.

After the journals are posted at the end of the month, the cash in bank account has a debit balance of $20,098.55.

The bank statement indicates a May 31 balance of $23,125.10. A comparison of paid checks with the check register reveals that Check Nos. 755 and 759 are outstanding. Check No. 723 for $175.00, which appeared on the April reconciliation as outstanding, is still outstanding. Debit memorandums accompanying the bank statement indicate a charge of $335.25 for a check drawn by R. N. Corley, a customer, which was returned because of insufficient funds, and $13.20 for service charges.

Instructions:

(1) Record the transactions for May 25–31 in the appropriate journals.
(2) Total and rule the voucher register and the check register, and post totals to the accounts payable account.
(3) Complete the schedule of unpaid vouchers. (Compare the total with the balance of the accounts payable account as of May 31.)
(4) Prepare a bank reconciliation and journalize any necessary entries.

Problem 8–5A.   Bank reconciliation from listings in check register and bank statement; related entries. Quartz Company employs the voucher system in controlling expenditures and disbursements. All cash receipts are deposited each Wednesday and Friday in a night depository after banking hours. The data required to reconcile the bank statement as of April 30 have been abstracted from various documents and records and are reproduced as follows. To facilitate identification, the sources of the data are printed in capital letters.

CASH IN BANK ACCOUNT:
    Balance as of April 1. . . . . $8,217.40

CASH RECEIPTS JOURNAL:
    Total of Cash in Bank Debit column for month of April 7,829.58

DUPLICATE DEPOSIT TICKETS:
    Date and amount of each deposit in April:

Date	Amount	Date	Amount	Date	Amount
April 1	$798.63	April 10	$971.71	April 22	$972.34
3	894.04	15	957.85	24	867.71
8	910.50	17	946.74	29	510.06

CHECK REGISTER:
    Number and amount of each check issued in April:

Check No.	Amount	Check No.	Amount	Check No.	Amount
725	$327.50	732	$490.90	739	$172.75
726	515.15	733	Void	740	249.75
727	401.90	734	640.13	741	113.95
728	771.30	735	376.77	742	907.95
729	506.88	736	299.37	743	359.60
730	117.25	737	537.01	744	601.50
731	298.66	738	380.95	745	486.39

    Total amount of checks issued in April $8,555.66

APRIL BANK STATEMENT:
    Balance as of April 1. . . . . $ 8,347.20
    Deposits and other credits . . . : 10,602.77
    Checks and other debits. . . . .   (8,182.21)
    Balance as of April 30. . . . . $10,767.76

Date and amount of each deposit in April:

Date	Amount	Date	Amount	Date	Amount
April 1	$690.25	April 9	$910.50	April 18	$946.74
2	798.63	11	971.71	23	972.34
4	894.04	16	975.85	25	867.71

CHECKS ACCOMPANYING APRIL BANK STATEMENT:

Number and amount of each check, rearranged in numerical sequence:

Check No.	Amount	Check No.	Amount	Check No.	Amount
716	$112.15	729	$506.88	736	$299.37
723	301.40	730	117.25	737	537.01
724	60.55	731	298.66	738	380.95
725	327.50	732	490.90	740	249.75
726	515.15	734	640.13	741	113.95
727	401.90	735	376.77	742	907.95
728	771.30			745	486.39

BANK MEMORANDUMS ACCOMPANYING APRIL BANK STATEMENT:

Date, description, and amount of each memorandum:

Date	Description	Amount
April 4	Bank credit memo for note collected:	
	Principal	$2,500.00
	Interest	75.00
24	Bank debit memo for check returned because of insufficient funds.	266.80
30	Bank debit memo for service charges	19.50

BANK RECONCILIATION FOR PRECEDING MONTH:

Quartz Company
Bank Reconciliation
March 31, 19--

Balance per bank statement		$8,347.20
Add deposit for March 31, not recorded by bank		690.25
		$9,037.45
Deduct outstanding checks:		
No. 716	$112.15	
721	345.95	
723	301.40	
724	60.55	820.05
Adjusted balance		$8,217.40
Balance per depositor's records		$8,230.50
Deduct service charges		13.10
Adjusted balance		$8,217.40

Instructions:

(1) Prepare a bank reconciliation as of April 30. If errors in recording deposits or checks are discovered, assume that the errors were made by the company. Assume that all deposits are from cash sales. All checks are in payment of vouchers.

(2) Record the necessary entries in general journal form. The accounts have not been closed.
(3) What is the amount of cash in bank that should appear on the balance sheet as of April 30?

Series B

Problem 8–1B. Bank reconciliation and entries. The cash in bank account for L. L. Holmes Co. at May 31 of the current year indicated a balance of $12,643.35 after both the cash receipts journal and the check register for May had been posted. The bank statement indicated a balance of $17,762.90 on May 31. Comparison of the bank statement and the accompanying canceled checks and memorandums with the records revealed the following reconciling items:

(a) Checks outstanding totaled $6,172.25.
(b) A deposit of $3,770.10, representing receipts of May 31, had been made too late to appear on the bank statement.
(c) The bank had collected for L. L. Holmes Co. $2,575 on an interest-bearing note left for collection. The face of the note was $2,500.
(d) A check for $47 returned with the statement had been recorded erroneously in the check register as $74. The check was for the payment of an obligation to Durham Bros. for the purchase of office supplies on account.
(e) A check drawn for $150 had been erroneously charged by the bank as $15.
(f) Bank service charges for May amounted to $19.60.

Instructions:

(1) Prepare a bank reconciliation.
(2) Record the necessary entries in general journal form. The accounts have not been closed. The voucher system is used.

Problem 8–3B. Voucher and check registers; accounts payable account; schedule of unpaid vouchers. Tennis 'N Things had the following vouchers in its unpaid voucher file at May 31 of the current year:

Due Date	Voucher No.	Creditor	Date of Invoice	Amount	Terms
June 5	470	Tennis Fashions	May 26	$4,500	1/10, n/30
June 12	458	Ace Shoes	May 13	2,100	n/30
June 13	460	Davis Co.	May 14	1,750	n/30

The vouchers prepared and the checks issued during the month of June were as follows:

VOUCHERS

Date	Voucher No.	Payee	Amount	Terms	Account(s) Debited
June 1	478	Funk Sporting Goods	$ 2,500	2/10, n/30	Purchases
4	479	R and M Supply	90	n/10	Store supplies
5	480	Powell Co.	1,250	2/10, n/30	Purchases
8	481	The Trophy Shop	500	1/10, n/30	Purchases
13	482	Busey National Bank	5,500		Note payable, $5,000 Interest, $500
15	483	Evans Office Supply	4,100	n/30	Office equipment
20	484	Sax Printers	215	cash	Office supplies
22	485	Bach Sportswear	1,250	2/10, n/30	Purchases
25	486	The Ski Shop	1,900	1/10, n/30	Purchases
28	487	Eastman Sports Inc.	550	n/30	Purchases
30	488	Parkhill Motors	15,000	cash	Delivery equipment
30	489	Petty Cash	110		Office supplies, $30 Store supplies, $24 Miscellaneous selling expense, $29 Miscellaneous general expense, $27

CHECKS

Date	Check No.	Payee	Voucher Paid	Amount
June 1	350	Funk Sporting Goods	478	$ 2,450
5	351	Tennis Fashions	470	4,455
12	352	Ace Shoes	458	2,100
13	353	Davis Co.	460	1,750
13	354	Busey National Bank	482	5,500
14	355	R and M Supply	479	90
15	356	Powell Co.	480	1,225
18	357	The Trophy Shop	481	495
20	358	Sax Printers	484	215
30	359	Parkhill Motors	488	15,000
30	360	Petty Cash	489	110

Instructions:

(1) Set up a four-column account for Accounts Payable, Account No. 205, and record the balance of $8,350 as of June 1. Place a ✔ in the Post. Ref. column.

(2) Record the June vouchers in a voucher register similar to the one illustrated in this chapter, with the following amount columns: Accounts Payable Cr., Purchases Dr., Store Supplies Dr., Office Supplies Dr., and Sundry Accounts Dr. Purchases invoices are recorded at the gross amount.

(3) Record the June checks in a check register similar to the one illustrated in this chapter, but omit the Bank Deposits and Balance columns. As each check is recorded in the check register, the date and check number should be inserted in the appropriate columns of the voucher register. (Assume that notations for payment of the May vouchers are made in the voucher register for May.)

(4) Total and rule the registers and post to Accounts Payable.

(5) Prepare a schedule of unpaid vouchers.

If the working papers correlating with the textbook are not used, omit Problem 8–4B.

Problem 8–4B.   Voucher and check registers; accounts payable account; bank reconciliation. Portions of the voucher register, check register, and accounts payable account of Tarkey Co. are presented in the working papers. Cash disbursements and other selected transactions completed during the period May 25–31 of the current year are described as follows:

May 25. Recorded Voucher No. 595, payable to Tempo Co. for merchandise, $5,000, terms 2/10, n/30. (Purchases invoices are recorded at the invoice price.)

25. Issued Check No. 576 to Morris Co. in payment of Voucher No. 583 for $2,500, less cash discount of 1%.

26. Recorded Voucher No. 596, payable to United Automobile Insurance Co. for an insurance policy, $1,584.

26. Issued Check No. 577 in payment of Voucher No. 596.

26. Recorded Voucher No. 597, payable to Howard Co. for merchandise, $1,500, terms 2/10, n/30.

27. Recorded Voucher No. 598 for $5,100, payable to Queens National Bank for note payable, $5,000, and interest, $100.

27. Issued Check No. 578 in payment of Voucher No. 598.

28. Issued Check No. 579 to Henry Stevens Co. in payment of Voucher No. 591 for $1,550, less cash discount of 2%.

29. Recorded Voucher No. 599, payable to Urbana News for advertising, $500.

29. Issued Check No. 580 in payment of Voucher No. 599.

31. Recorded Voucher No. 600, payable to Petty Cash for $179.90, distributed as follows: office supplies, $42.50; advertising expense, $31.45; delivery expense, $22.50; miscellaneous selling expense, $47.22; miscellaneous general expense, $36.23

31. Issued Check No. 581 in payment of Voucher No. 600.

After the journals are posted at the end of the month, the cash in bank account has a debit balance of $18,067.50.

The bank statement indicates a May 31 balance of $21,871.20. A comparison of paid checks with the check register reveals that Check Nos. 577, 579, and 580 are outstanding. Check No. 553 for $850.70, which appeared on the April reconciliation as outstanding, is still outstanding. A debit memorandum accompanying the bank statement indicates a charge of $650 for a check drawn by Cowen and Cowen, a customer, which was returned because of insufficient funds.

Instructions:

(1) Record the transactions for May 25–31 in the appropriate journals.
(2) Total and rule the voucher register and the check register, and post totals to the accounts payable account.

(3) Complete the schedule of unpaid vouchers. (Compare the total with the balance of the accounts payable account as of May 31.)

(4) Prepare a bank reconciliation and journalize any necessary entries.

Problem 8–5B. Bank reconciliation determined from listings in check register and bank statement; related entries. Venice Company employs the voucher system in controlling expenditures and disbursements. All cash receipts are deposited each Wednesday and Friday in a night depository after banking hours. The data required to reconcile the bank statement as of July 31 have been abstracted from various documents and records and are reproduced as follows. To facilitate identification, the sources of the data are printed in capital letters.

CASH IN BANK ACCOUNT:

Balance as of July 1...................................... $10,905.50

CASH RECEIPTS JOURNAL:

Total of Cash in Bank Debit column for month of July .... $ 7,005.10

DUPLICATE DEPOSIT TICKETS:

Date and amount of each deposit in July:

Date	Amount	Date	Amount	Date	Amount
July 2	$850.40	July 12	$616.70	July 23	$881.45
5	709.90	16	797.60	26	601.50
9	919.24	19	701.26	30	927.05

CHECK REGISTER:

Number and amount of each check issued in July:

Check No.	Amount	Check No.	Amount	Check No.	Amount
414	$152.50	421	$399.50	428	$717.70
415	710.10	422	VOID	429	349.90
416	289.90	423	VOID	430	882.20
417	595.50	424	918.01	431	982.16
418	335.40	425	558.63	432	62.40
419	220.10	426	530.03	433	675.48
420	238.87	427	338.73	434	97.90

Total amount of checks issued in July........................ $9,055.01

JULY BANK STATEMENT:

Balance as of July 1	$11,017.02
Deposits and other credits...................................	14,508.85
Checks and other debits.....................................	(9,559.03)
Balance as of July 31	$15,966.84

Date and amount of each deposit in July:

Date	Amount	Date	Amount	Date	Amount
July 1	$780.80	July 11	$919.24	July 21	$701.26
3	850.40	13	616.70	24	881.45
6	709.90	17	797.60	28	601.50

CHECKS ACCOMPANYING JULY BANK STATEMENT:

Number and amount of each check, rearranged in numerical sequence:

Check No.	Amount	Check No.	Amount	Check No.	Amount
400	$390.40	418	$335.40	426	$530.03
412	110.25	419	220.10	427	338.73
413	219.17	420	238.87	429	359.90
414	152.50	421	399.50	430	882.20
415	710.10	424	918.01	431	982.16
416	289.90	425	558.63	432	62.40
417	595.50			433	675.48

BANK MEMORANDUMS ACCOMPANYING JULY BANK STATEMENT:

Date, description, and amount of each memorandum:

Date	Description	Amount
July 3	Bank credit memo for note collected:	
	Principal	$7,500.00
	Interest	150.00
16	Bank debit memo for check returned because of insufficient funds	575.50
31	Bank debit memo for service charges.................	14.30

BANK RECONCILIATION FOR PRECEDING MONTH:

Venice Company
Bank Reconciliation
June 30, 19--

Balance per bank statement		$11,017.02
Add deposit of June 30, not recorded by bank		780.80
		$11,797.82
Deduct outstanding checks:		
No. 400	$390.40	
406	172.50	
412	110.25	
413	219.17	892.32
Adjusted balance		$10,905.50
Balance per depositor's records		$10,917.75
Deduct service charges		12.25
Adjusted balance		$10,905.50

Instructions:

(1) Prepare a bank reconciliation as of July 31. If errors in recording deposits or checks are discovered, assume that the errors were made by the company. Assume that all deposits are from cash sales. All checks are in payment of vouchers.

(2) Record the necessary entries in general journal form. The accounts have not been closed.

(3) What is the amount of cash in bank that should appear on the balance sheet as of July 31?

MINI-CASE 8

PEREZ
COMPANY

The records of Perez Company indicate an April 30 cash in bank balance of $30,777.35, which includes undeposited receipts for April 29 and 30. The cash balance on the bank statement as of April 30 is $27,196.30. This balance includes a note of $1,500 plus $60 interest collected by the bank but not recorded in the cash receipts journal. Checks outstanding on April 30 were as follows: No. 110, $713.40; No. 177, $300.00; No. 201, $522.40; No. 882, $825.15; No. 885, $327.70; and No. 886, $466.10.

On April 10, the Perez Company cashier resigned, effective at the end of the month. Before leaving on April 30, the cashier prepared the following bank reconciliation:

Balance per books, April 30........		$30,777.35
Add outstanding checks:		
882	$825.15	
885	327.70	
886	466.10	1,418.95
		$32,196.30
Less undeposited receipts		5,000.00
Balance per bank, April 30........		$27,196.30
Deduct unrecorded note with interest.		1,560.00
True cash, April 30		$25,636.30

Calculator Tape of Outstanding Checks

0.	*
825.15	+
327.70	+
466.10	+
1,418.95	*

Subsequently, the owner of Perez Company discovered that the cashier had stolen all undeposited receipts on hand on April 30 in excess of $5,000. The owner, a close family friend, has asked your help in determining the amount that the former cashier has stolen.

Instructions:

(1) Determine the amount the cashier stole from Perez Company. Show your computations in good form.
(2) How did the cashier attempt to conceal the theft?
(3) (a) Identify two major weaknesses in Perez Company's internal accounting controls, which allowed the cashier to steal the undeposited cash receipts. (b) Recommend improvements in Perez Company's internal accounting controls, so that similar types of thefts of undeposited cash receipts could be prevented.

(AICPA adapted)

Chapter 9

RECEIVABLES AND TEMPORARY INVESTMENTS

Chapter Objectives:

- Describe the common classifications of receivables.

- Describe the basic principles of internal control over receivables.

- Describe and illustrate the accounting for notes receivable, including the determination of interest and proceeds from discounting notes.

- Describe and illustrate the allowance method of accounting for uncollectible receivables, including the estimation of uncollectibles based on sales and an analysis of receivables.

- Describe and illustrate the direct write-off method of accounting for uncollectible receivables.

- Describe and illustrate the accounting for temporary investments.

- Describe and illustrate the presentation of temporary investments and receivables in the balance sheet.

F or many businesses, the revenue from sales on a credit basis is the largest factor influencing the amount of net income. As credit is granted, businesses must account for the resulting receivables, which may represent a substantial portion of the total current assets. As the receivables are collected, the cash realized is accounted for in the manner discussed in Chapter 8. If the amount of cash on hand exceeds immediate cash requirements, the excess cash might be invested in securities until needed. These securities are accounted for as temporary investments.

CLASSIFICATION OF RECEIVABLES

The term **receivables** includes all money claims against people, organizations, or other debtors. Receivables are acquired by a business enterprise in various kinds of transactions, the most common being the sale of merchandise or services on a credit basis.

Credit may be granted on open account or on the basis of a formal instrument of credit, such as a promissory note. Promissory notes are usually used for credit periods of more than sixty days, as in sales of equipment on the installment plan, and for transactions of relatively large dollar amounts. Promissory notes may also be used in settlement of an open account and in borrowing or lending money.

A **promissory note**, frequently referred to simply as a **note**, is a written promise to pay a sum of money on demand or at a definite time. As in the case of a check, it must be payable to the order of a certain person or firm, or to bearer. It must also be signed by the person or firm that makes the promise. The one to whose order the note is payable is called the **payee**, and the one making the promise is called the **maker**. The enterprise owning a note refers to it as a note receivable and records it as an asset at its face amount.

A note that provides for the payment of interest for the period between the issuance date and the due date is called an **interest-bearing note**. If a note makes no provision for interest, it is said to be **non-interest-bearing**. In the following illustration of an interest-bearing note, Pearland Company is the payee, and Selig Corporation is the maker.

```
$ 2,500.00                          Fresno, California  October 2    19 87

  Sixty days                     AFTER DATE  We     PROMISE TO PAY TO

THE ORDER OF   Pearland Company

  Two thousand five hundred 00/100-------------------- DOLLARS

PAYABLE AT   First National Bank
                                          SELIG CORPORATION
VALUE RECEIVED WITH INTEREST AT   10%
NO.  14  DUE  December 1, 1987              H. B. Lane
                                              TREASURER
```

The amount that is due at the maturity or due date is called the **maturity value**. The maturity value of a non-interest-bearing note is the face amount. The maturity value of an interest-bearing note is the sum of the face amount and the interest.

From the point of view of the creditor, a claim evidenced by a note has some advantages over a claim in the form of an account receivable. By signing a note, the debtor acknowledges the debt and agrees to pay it according to the terms given. The note is therefore a stronger legal claim if there is court action. It is also more liquid than an open account because the holder can usually transfer it more readily to a bank or other financial agency in exchange for cash.

Accounts and notes receivable originating from sales transactions are sometimes called **trade receivables**. In the absence of other descriptive words or phrases, accounts and notes receivable may be assumed to have originated from sales in the usual course of the business.

Other receivables include interest receivable, loans to officers or employees, and loans to affiliated companies. To facilitate their classification and presentation on the balance sheet, a general ledger account should be maintained for each type of receivable, with proper subsidiary ledgers.

All receivables that are expected to be realized in cash within a year are presented in the current assets section of the balance sheet. Those that are not currently collectible, such as long-term loans, should be listed under the caption "Investments" below the current assets section.

CONTROL OVER RECEIVABLES

As is the case for all assets, the broad principles of internal control discussed in Chapter 7 can be used to establish procedures to safeguard receivables. These controls would include the separation of the business operations and the accounting for receivables, so that the accounting records can serve as an independent check on operations. Thus the employee who handles the accounting for notes and accounts receivable should not be involved with credit approvals or collections of receivables. Separation of these functions reduces the possibility of errors and embezzlement. The controls would also include the separation of responsibility for related functions, so that the work of one employee can serve as a check on the work of another employee. For example, the handling of the accounts receivable ledger and the general ledger should be separated. In this way, the work of the accounts receivable clerk can be checked by comparing the total of the individual account balances in the accounts receivable subsidiary ledger with the balance of the accounts receivable controlling account that is maintained by the general ledger clerk.

For most businesses, the principal receivables are notes receivable and accounts receivable. Generally, notes receivable are recorded in a single general ledger account. If there are numerous notes, the general ledger account can be supported by a notes receivable register. The register would contain details of each note, such as the name of the maker, place of payment, amount, term, interest rate, and due date. Frequent reference to the due date section directs attention to those notes that are due for payment. In this way, the maker of the note can be notified when the note is due, and the risk that the maker will overlook the due date can be minimized.

Adequate control over accounts receivable begins with the approval of the sale by a responsible company official or the credit department, after the customer's credit rating has been reviewed. Likewise, adjustments of accounts receivable, such as for sales returns and allowances and sales discounts, should be authorized or reviewed by a responsible party. Effective collection procedures should also be established to ensure timely collection of accounts receivable and to minimize losses from uncollectible accounts. The proper use of the controlling account and the accounts receivable ledger, as discussed in Chapter 7, also increases the effectiveness of the control over accounts receivable.

DETERMINING INTEREST

Interest rates are usually stated in terms of a period of a year, regardless of the actual period of time involved. Thus the interest on $2,000 for a year at 12% would be $240 (12% of $2,000); the interest on $2,000 for one fourth of a year at 12% would be $60 (¼ of $240).

Notes covering a period of time longer than a year ordinarily provide that the interest be paid semiannually, quarterly, or at some other stated interval. The time involved in commercial credit transactions is usually less than a year, and the interest provided for by a note is payable at the time the note is paid. In computing interest for a period of less than a year, agencies of the federal government use the actual number of days in the year. For example, 90 days is considered to be 90/365 of a year. The usual commercial practice is to use 360 as the denominator of the fraction; thus 90 days is considered to be 90/360 of a year.

Effective Control of Accounts Receivable

Here's a familiar scene: "Many times, we'll say to a small-company client, 'You guys are doing pretty well; you show $100,000 in profits this year,'" says Anthony Timiraos, manager of the accounting and business advisory service department in Laventhol & Horwath's Boston office, "and they'll say to us, 'Where is it, then?'" The frequent problem, of course, is that accounts receivable is cash-poor.

None of this is news to most financial managers. The question is, how do you improve your cash flow?

A common mistake is having customers send payments to the company. "Checks sit on someone's desk for a few days, then they are sent through the mail, then they are processed at the bank, and then they sit for a while until they clear," says Andrea Bierce, manager for Peat, Marwick, Mitchell & Co.'s financial management division in New York City. Instead, she says, have customers send payments directly to a bank lockbox. "I've seen companies free up $100,000 to $1 million this way," says Bierce.

Timiraos tells clients strapped for financial manpower to split up the cash management responsibilities. "Sometimes the salespeople make a sale to someone just to make their department look good," he observes. "They don't always check with the credit manager to approve the sale." Next thing you know, says Timiraos, goods are going out to customers who can't pay their bills. Instead, he says, "Small companies need to split up cash management responsibilities among different departments." Managers should work out collection goals for the sales and marketing department, for instance, to help them determine the validity of sales.

Source: Adapted from Leslie Schultz, "Which Way the Cash Flows," *CFO* (March, 1986), p. 20.

The basic formula for computing interest is as follows:

$$\text{Principal} \times \text{Rate} \times \text{Time} = \text{Interest}$$

To illustrate the use of the formula, assume that a note for $1,500 is payable in 20 days with interest at 12%. The interest would be $10, computed as follows:

$$\$1,500 \times \frac{12}{100} \times \frac{20}{360} = \$10 \quad \text{interest}$$

One of the commonly used shortcut methods of computing interest is called the 60-day, 6% method. The 6% annual rate is converted to the effective rate of 1% for a 60-day period (60/360 of 6%). Accordingly, the interest on any amount for 60 days at 6% is determined by moving the decimal point in the principal two places to the left. For example, the interest on $1,500 at 6% for 60 days is $15. The amount obtained by moving the decimal point must be adjusted (1) for interest rates greater or less than 6% and (2) for periods of time greater or less than 60 days. For example, the interest on $1,500 at 6% for 90 days is $22.50 (90/60 of $15). The interest on $1,500 at 12% for 60 days is $30 (12/6 of $15).

Comprehensive interest tables are available and are commonly used by financial institutions and other enterprises that require frequent interest calculations. Nevertheless, students of business should know the mechanics of interest computations well enough to use them with complete accuracy and to recognize major errors in interest amounts that come to their attention.

When the term of a note is stated in months instead of in days, each month may be considered as being 1/12 of a year, or, alternatively, the actual number of days in the term may be counted. For example, the interest on a 3-month note dated June 1 could be computed on the basis of 3/12 of a year or on the basis of 92/360 of a year. It is the usual commercial practice to use the first method, while banks usually charge interest for the exact number of days. For the sake of simplicity, the usual commercial practice will be assumed in all cases.

DETERMINING DUE DATE

The period of time between the issuance date and the maturity date of a short-term note may be stated in either days or months. When the term of a note is stated in days, the due date is the specified number of days after its

The Bobtailed Year

In 46 B.C., Julius Caesar proclaimed that a year would be pegged at 365 days, with an extra day added every fourth year. What was good enough for Caesar has been good enough for the rest of us ever since except for the nation's bankers.

A lot of bankers are using a 360-day year to compute the interest they charge to borrowers on commercial and corporate loans. This means, in effect, that they are collecting a smidgin more interest on these loans than their stated "annual" interest rates would indicate.

Though only small amounts of money are involved in the difference between 365- and 360-day charges on any one loan, the nickels and dimes add up to an impressive pile. In fact, the overcharges that result from the use of the bobtailed year have been estimated to be at least $145 million a year.

According to the bankers, use of the bobtailed year began before the widespread use of adding machines; clerks who had to do the computations with pencil and paper found it a lot easier to multiply and divide by 360 rather than 365 or 366. Since nobody seemed to care much, the 360-day base continued in use through the age of calculators and now is imbedded in the banks' computer programs. "Converting our computers to a 365-day year would be a massive job," says one officer of a major bank.

Source: Adapted from James F. Carberry, "365 Days May Have Been Good Enough For Caesar, But Lenders Find That 360 Provide More Profit," *The Wall Street Journal,* March 30, 1973.

issuance. To illustrate, the due date of a 90-day note dated March 16 may be determined as follows:

Term of the note		90
March (days)	31	
Date of note	16	15
Number of days remaining		75
April (days)		30
		45
May (days)		31
Due date, June		14

DETERMINATION OF DUE DATE OF NOTE

determine no. of day in discount period

When the term of a note is stated as a certain number of months after the issuance date, the due date is determined by counting the number of months from the issuance date. Thus, a 3-month note dated June 5 would be due on September 5. In those cases in which there is no date in the month of maturity that corresponds to the issuance date, the due date becomes the last day of the month. For example, a 2-month note dated July 31 would be due on September 30.

NOTES RECEIVABLE AND INTEREST INCOME

The typical retail enterprise makes most of its sales for cash or on account. If the account of a customer becomes delinquent, the creditor may insist that the account be converted into a note. In this way, the debtor is given more time, and if the creditor needs more funds, the note may be endorsed and transferred to a bank or other financial agency. Notes may also be received by retail firms that sell merchandise on long-term credit. For example, a dealer in household appliances may require a down payment at the time of sale and accept a note or a series of notes for the remainder. Such arrangements usually provide for monthly payments. Wholesale firms and manufacturers are likely to receive notes more often than retailers, although here, too, much depends upon the kind of product and the length of the credit period.

When a note is received from a customer to apply on account, the facts are recorded by debiting the notes receivable account and crediting the accounts receivable controlling account and the account of the customer from whom the note is received. If the note is interest-bearing, interest must also be recorded as appropriate.

To illustrate, assume that the account of W. A. Bunn Co., which has a debit balance of $6,000, is past due. A 30-day, 12% note for that amount, dated December 21, 1987, is accepted in settlement of the account. The entry to record the transaction is as follows:

Dec. 21	Notes Receivable	6,000	
	Accounts Receivable — W. A. Bunn Co.		6,000
	Received a 30-day, 12% note dated		
	December 21, 1987.		

On December 31, 1987, the end of the fiscal year, an adjusting entry would be recorded for the accrual of the interest from December 21 to December 31. The entry to record the accrued revenue of $20 ($6,000 $\times$ 12/100 $\times$ 10/360) is as follows:

	Adjusting Entry		
Dec. 31	Interest Receivable......................	20	
	Interest Income		20

Interest receivable is reported on the balance sheet at December 31, 1987, as a current asset. The interest income account is closed at December 31 and the amount is reported in the Other Income section of the income statement for the year ended December 31, 1987.

When the amount due on the note is collected in 1988, part of the interest received will effect a reduction of the interest that was receivable at December 31, 1987, and the remainder will represent revenue for 1988. To avoid the possibility of failing to recognize this division and to avoid the inconvenience of analyzing the receipt of interest in 1988, a reversing entry is made after the accounts are closed. The effect of the entry, which is illustrated as follows, is to transfer the debit balance in the interest receivable account to the debit side of the interest income account.

	Reversing Entry		
Jan. 1	Interest Income	20	
	Interest Receivable.....................		20

At the time the note matures and payment is received, the entire amount of the interest received is credited to Interest Income, as illustrated by the following entry that would be recorded in the cash receipts journal:

Jan. 20	Cash	6,060	
	Notes Receivable		6,000
	Interest Income		60

After the foregoing entries are posted, the interest income account will appear as follows:

ACCOUNT INTEREST INCOME					ACCOUNT NO. 811	
					Balance	
Date	Item	Post. Ref.	Debit	Credit	Debit	Credit
1987						
Dec. 12		CR20		120		946
31	Adjusting	J17		20		966
31	Closing	J17	966		—	—
1988 Jan. 1	Reversing	J18	20		20	
20		CR21		60		40

The adjusting and reversing process divided the $60 of interest received on January 20, 1988, into two parts for accounting purposes: (1) $20 representing the interest income for 1987 (recorded by the adjusting entry) and (2) $40 representing the interest income for 1988 (the balance in the interest income account at January 20, 1988).

Discounting Notes Receivable

Although it is not a common transaction, a company in need of cash may transfer its notes receivable to a bank by endorsement. The **discount** (interest) charged by the bank is computed on the maturity value of the note for the period of time the bank must hold the note, namely the time that will pass between the date of the transfer and the due date of the note. The amount of the **proceeds** paid to the endorser is the excess of the maturity value over the discount.

To illustrate, assume that a 90-day, 12% note receivable for $1,800, dated November 8, is discounted at the payee's bank on December 3 at the rate of 14%. The data used in determining the effect of the transaction are as follows:

Face value of note dated Nov. 8	$1,800.00
Interest on note—90 days at 12%	54.00
Maturity value of note due Feb. 6	$1,854.00
Discount period—Dec. 3 to Feb. 6 ....65 days	
Discount on maturity value—65 days at 14%	46.87 *bank charge*
Proceeds	$1,807.13

The same information is presented graphically in the following flow diagram. In reading the data, follow the direction of the arrows.

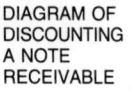
DIAGRAM OF DISCOUNTING A NOTE RECEIVABLE

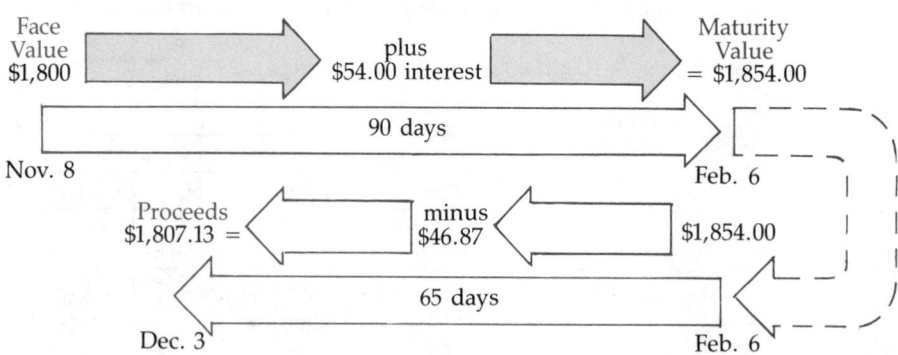

The excess of the proceeds from discounting the note, $1,807.13, over its face value, $1,800, is recorded as interest income. The entry for the transaction, in general journal form, is as follows:

Dec. 3	Cash	1,807.13	
	Notes Receivable		1,800.00
	Interest Income		7.13

It should be observed that the proceeds from discounting a note receivable may be less than the face value. When this situation occurs, the excess of the face value over the proceeds is recorded as interest expense. The amount and direction of the difference between the interest rate and the discount rate will affect the result, as will the relationship between the full term of the note and the length of the discount period.

Without a statement limiting responsibility, the endorser of a note is committed to paying the note if the maker should default. Such potential obligations that will become actual liabilities only if certain events occur in the future are called contingent liabilities. Thus, the endorser of a note that has been discounted has a contingent liability that is in effect until the due date. If the maker pays the promised amount at maturity, the contingent liability is removed without any action on the part of the endorser. If, on the other hand, the maker defaults and the endorser is notified according to legal requirements, the liability becomes an actual one.

Significant contingent liabilities should be disclosed on the balance sheet or in an accompanying note. Disclosure requirements for contingent liabilities are discussed and illustrated in Chapter 13.

Dishonored Notes Receivable

If the maker of a note fails to pay the debt on the due date, the note is said to be dishonored. A dishonored note receivable is no longer negotiable, and for that reason the holder usually transfers the claim, including any interest due, to the accounts receivable account. For example, if the $6,000, 30-day, 12% note received and recorded on December 21 (page 386) had been dishonored at maturity, the entry to charge the note, including the interest, back to the customer's account would have been as follows:

Jan. 20	Accounts Receivable — W. A. Bunn Co.	6,060	
	Notes Receivable		6,000
	Interest Income		60
	Dishonored note and interest.		

If there had been some assurance that the maker would pay the note within a relatively short time, action would have been delayed until the matter was resolved. However, for future guidance in extending credit, it may be desirable that the customer's account in the subsidiary ledger disclose the dishonor of the note.

When a discounted note receivable is dishonored, the holder usually notifies the endorser of such fact and asks for payment. If the request for payment and notification of dishonor are timely, the endorser is legally obligated to pay the amount due on the note. The entire amount paid to the holder by the endorser, including the interest, should be debited to the account receivable of the maker. To illustrate, assume that the $1,800, 90-day, 12% note discounted on December 3 (page 388) is dishonored at maturity by the maker, Pryor & Co. The entry to record the payment by the endorser, in general journal form, would be as follows:

Feb. 6	Accounts Receivable—Pryor & Co.................	1,854	
	Cash...		1,854

In some cases, the holder of a dishonored note gives the endorser a notarized statement of the facts of the dishonor. The fee for this statement, known as a **protest fee**, is charged to the endorser, who in turn charges it to the maker of the note. If there had been a protest fee of $6 in connection with the dishonor and the payment previously recorded, the debit to the maker's account and the credit to Cash would have been $1,860.

UNCOLLECTIBLE RECEIVABLES

When merchandise or services are sold without the immediate receipt of cash, a part of the claims against customers usually proves to be uncollectible. This situation is common, regardless of the care used in granting credit and the effectiveness of the collection procedures used. The operating expense incurred because of the failure to collect receivables is called an expense or a loss from **uncollectible accounts**, **doubtful accounts**, or **bad debts**.[1]

There is no single general rule for determining when an account or a note becomes uncollectible. The fact that a debtor fails to pay an account according to a sales contract or dishonors a note on the due date does not necessarily mean that the account will be uncollectible. Bankruptcy of the debtor is one of the most positive indications of partial or complete worthlessness of a receivable. Other evidence includes closing of the debtor's business, disappearance of the debtor, failure of repeated attempts to collect, and the barring of collection by the statute of limitations.

There are two methods of accounting for receivables that are believed to be uncollectible. The allowance method, which is sometimes called the **reserve method**, provides in advance for uncollectible receivables. The other procedure, called the direct write-off method or **direct charge-off method**, recognizes the expense only when certain accounts are judged to be worthless.

---

[1] If both notes and accounts are involved, both may be included in the title, as in "uncollectible notes and accounts expense," or the general term "uncollectible receivables expense" may be substituted. Because of its wide usage and simplicity, "uncollectible accounts expense" will be used in this text.

ALLOWANCE METHOD OF ACCOUNTING FOR UNCOLLECTIBLES

Most large business enterprises provide currently for the amount of their trade receivables estimated to become uncollectible in the future. The advance provision for future uncollectibility is made by an adjusting entry at the end of the fiscal period. As with all periodic adjustments, the entry serves two purposes. In this instance, it provides for (1) the reduction of the value of the receivables to the amount of cash expected to be realized from them in the future, and (2) the allocation to the current period of the expected expense resulting from such reduction.

Assumed data for a new business firm, Richards Company, will be used to explain and illustrate the allowance method. The enterprise began business in August and chose to use the calendar year as its fiscal year. The accounts receivable account, illustrated as follows, has a balance of $105,000 at the end of the period.

ACCOUNT ACCOUNTS RECEIVABLE   ACCOUNT NO. 114

Date		Item	Post. Ref.	Debit	Credit	Balance Debit	Balance Credit
19--							
Aug.	31		S3	20,000		20,000	
Sept.	30		S6	25,000		45,000	
	30		CR4		15,000	30,000	
Oct.	31		S10	40,000		70,000	
	31		CR7		25,000	45,000	
Nov.	30		S13	38,000		83,000	
	30		CR10		23,000	60,000	
Dec.	31		S16	75,000		135,000	
	31		CR13		30,000	105,000	

Among the individual customers accounts making up the $105,000 balance in Accounts Receivable are a number of balances which are a varying number of days past due. No specific accounts are believed to be wholly uncollectible at this time, but it seems likely that some will be collected only in part and that others are likely to become entirely worthless. Based on a careful study, it is estimated that a total of $3,000 will eventually prove to be uncollectible. The amount expected to be realized from the accounts receivable is, therefore, $102,000 ($105,000 − $3,000), and the $3,000 reduction in value is the uncollectible accounts expense for the period.

The $3,000 reduction in accounts receivable cannot yet be identified with specific customers accounts in the subsidiary ledger and should therefore not be credited to the controlling account in the general ledger. The customary practice is to use a contra asset account entitled Allowance for Doubtful Accounts. The adjusting entry to record the expense and the reduction in the asset is as follows:

			Post.				
Dec. 31	*Adjusting Entry* Uncollectible Accounts Expense		717	3,000			
	Allowance for Doubtful Accounts ..		115			3,000	

The two accounts to which the entry is posted are illustrated as follows:

ACCOUNT UNCOLLECTIBLE ACCOUNTS EXPENSE   ACCOUNT NO. 717

Date		Item	Post. Ref.	Debit	Credit	Balance	
						Debit	Credit
19-- Dec.	31	Adjusting	J4	3,000		3,000	

ACCOUNT ALLOWANCE FOR DOUBTFUL ACCOUNTS   ACCOUNT NO. 115

Date		Item	Post. Ref.	Debit	Credit	Balance	
						Debit	Credit
19-- Dec.	31	Adjusting	J4		3,000		3,000

The debit balance of $105,000 in Accounts Receivable is the amount of the total claims against customers on open account, and the credit balance of $3,000 in Allowance for Doubtful Accounts is the amount to be deducted from Accounts Receivable to determine the **expected realizable value**. The $3,000 reduction in the asset was transferred to Uncollectible Accounts Expense, which will in turn be closed to Income Summary.

Uncollectible accounts expense is generally reported on the income statement as a general expense, because the credit-granting and collection duties are the responsibilities of departments within the general administrative framework. The accounts receivable may be listed on the balance sheet at the net amount of $102,000, with a notation in parentheses showing the amount of the allowance, or the details may be presented as shown on the following partial balance sheet. When the allowance account includes provision for doubtful notes as well as accounts, it should be deducted from the total of Notes Receivable and Accounts Receivable.

ACCOUNTS
RECEIVABLE
ON THE
BALANCE
SHEET

Richards Company
Balance Sheet
December 31, 19--

Assets

Current assets:

Cash...		$ 21,600
Accounts receivable	$105,000	
Less allowance for doubtful accounts............	3,000	102,000

Write-Offs to the Allowance Account

When an account is believed to be uncollectible, it is written off against the allowance account as in the following entry:

Jan. 21	Allowance for Doubtful Accounts	110	
	Accounts Receivable — John Parker		110
	To write off the uncollectible account.		

During the year, as more accounts or portions of accounts are determined to be uncollectible, they are written off against Allowance for Doubtful Accounts in the same manner. Instructions for write-offs should originate with the credit manager or other designated official. The authorizations, which should always be written, serve as objective evidence in support of the accounting entry.

Naturally enough, the total amount written off against the allowance account during the period will rarely be equal to the amount in the account at the beginning of the period. The allowance account will have a credit balance at the end of the period if the write-offs during the period amount to less than the beginning balance. It will have a debit balance if the write-offs exceed the beginning balance. After the year-end adjusting entry is recorded, the allowance account will have a credit balance.

An account receivable that has been written off against the allowance account may later be collected. In such cases, the account should be reinstated by an entry that is the exact reverse of the write-off entry. For example, assume that the account of $110 written off in the preceding journal entry is later collected. The entry to reinstate the account would be as follows:

June 10	Accounts Receivable — John Parker	110	
	Allowance for Doubtful Accounts		110
	To reinstate account written off earlier		
	in the year.		

The cash received in payment would be recorded as a receipt on account. Although it is possible to combine the reinstatement and the receipt of cash into a single debit and credit, the entries in the customer's account, with a proper notation, provide useful credit information.

Estimating Uncollectibles

The estimate of uncollectibles at the end of the fiscal period is based on past experience and forecasts of future business activity. When the trend of general sales volume is upward and there is relatively full employment, the amount of the expense should usually be less than when the trend is in the opposite direction. The estimate is customarily based on either (1) the amount of sales for the entire fiscal period or (2) the amount and the age of the receivable accounts at the end of the fiscal period.

Estimate Based on Sales. Accounts receivable are acquired as a result of sales on account. The amount of such sales during the year may therefore be used to determine the probable amount of the accounts that will be uncollectible. The amount of this estimate is added to whatever balance exists in Allowance for Doubtful Accounts. To illustrate, assume that the allowance account has a credit balance of $700 before adjustment. If it is known from past experience that about 1% of charge sales will be uncollectible and the charge sales for a certain year amount to $300,000, the adjusting entry for uncollectible accounts at the end of the year would be as follows:

	Adjusting Entry		
Dec. 31	Uncollectible Accounts Expense	3,000	
	Allowance for Doubtful Accounts		3,000

After the adjusting entry is posted, the balance in the allowance account is $3,700. If there had been a debit balance of $200 in the allowance account before the year-end adjustment, the amount of the adjustment would still have been $3,000. The balance in the allowance account, after the adjusting entry is posted, would be $2,800 ($3,000 − $200).

Instead of charge sales, total sales (including those made for cash) may be used in developing the percentage. Total sales is obtainable from the ledger without the analysis that may be needed to determine charge sales. If the ratio of sales on account to cash sales does not change very much from year to year, the results obtained will be equally satisfactory. If in the above example the balance of the sales account at the end of the year is assumed to be $400,000, the application of 3/4 of 1% to that amount would also yield an estimate of $3,000.

If it becomes apparent over a period of time that the amount of write-offs is always greater or less than the amount provided by the adjusting entry, the percentage applied to sales data should be changed accordingly. A newly established business enterprise, having no record of credit experience, may obtain data on the probable amount of the expense from trade association journals and other publications containing information on credit and collections.

The estimate-based-on-sales method of determining the uncollectible accounts expense is widely used. It is simple and it provides the best basis for charging uncollectible accounts expense to the period in which the related sales were made.

Estimate Based on Analysis of Receivables. The process of analyzing the receivable accounts in terms of the length of time past due is sometimes called **aging the receivables.** The base point for determining age is the due date of the account. The number and breadth of the time intervals used will vary according to the credit terms granted to customers. A portion of a typical analysis is as follows:

CUSTOMER	BALANCE	NOT DUE	1–30	31–60	61–90	91–180	181–365	over 365
			DAYS PAST DUE					
Ashby & Co....	$ 150			$ 150				
B. T. Barr	610					$ 350	$260	
Brock Co.	470	$ 470						
J. Zimmer Co...	160							160
Total	$86,300	$75,000	$4,000	$3,100	$1,900	$1,200	$800	$300

ANALYSIS OF ACCOUNTS RECEIVABLE

The analysis is completed by adding the columns to determine the total amount of receivables in each age group. A sliding scale of percentages, based on experience, is next applied to obtain the estimated amount of uncollectibles in each group. The manner in which the data may be presented is illustrated as follows:

Age Interval	Balance	Estimated Uncollectible Accounts	
		Percent	Amount
Not due	$75,000	2%	$1,500
1–30 days past due	4,000	5	200
31–60 days past due	3,100	10	310
61–90 days past due	1,900	20	380
91–180 days past due	1,200	30	360
181–365 days past due ...	800	50	400
Over 365 days past due...	300	80	240
Total	$86,300		$3,390

ESTIMATE OF UNCOLLECTIBLE ACCOUNTS

The estimate of uncollectible accounts, $3,390 in the example above, is the amount to be deducted from accounts receivable to yield their expected realizable value. It is thus the amount of the desired balance of the allowance account after adjustment. The excess of this figure over the balance of the allowance account before adjustment is the amount of the current provision to be made for uncollectible accounts expense.

To continue the illustration, assume that the allowance account has a credit balance of $510 before adjustment. The amount to be added to this balance is therefore $2,880 ($3,390 − $510), and the adjusting entry is as follows:

	Adjusting Entry		
Dec. 31	Uncollectible Accounts Expense	2,880	
	Allowance for Doubtful Accounts		2,880

After the adjusting entry is posted, the credit balance in the allowance account will be $3,390, which is the desired amount. If there had been a debit balance of $300 in the allowance account before the year-end adjustment, the amount of the adjustment would have been $3,690 ($3,390 desired balance + $300 negative balance).

Estimations of uncollectible accounts expense based on an analysis of receivables are less common than estimations based on sales volume. Estimations based on receivables analyses are sometimes preferred because they give more accurate estimates of the current realizable values of the receivables.

DIRECT WRITE-OFF METHOD OF ACCOUNTING FOR UNCOLLECTIBLES

The use of the allowance method, as previously illustrated, results in the uncollectible accounts expense being reported in the period in which the sales are made. This matching of expenses with related revenue is the preferred method of accounting for uncollectible receivables. However, there are situations in which it is impossible to estimate, with reasonable accuracy, the uncollectibles at the end of the period. Also if an enterprise sells most of its goods or services on a cash basis, the amount of its expense from uncollectible accounts is usually small in relation to its revenue. The amount of its receivables at any time is also likely to represent a relatively small part of its total current assets. In such cases, it is satisfactory to delay recognition of uncollectibility until the period in which certain amounts are believed to be worthless and are actually written off as an expense. Accordingly, an allowance account or an adjusting entry is not needed at the end of the period. The entry to write off an account when it is believed to be uncollectible is as follows:

May 10	Uncollectible Accounts Expense	42	
	Accounts Receivable — D. L. Ross		42
	To write off uncollectible account.		

If an account that has been written off is collected later, the account should be reinstated. If the recovery is in the same fiscal year as the write-off, the earlier entry should be reversed to reinstate the account. To illustrate, assume that the account written off in the May 10 entry is collected in November of the same fiscal year. The entry to reinstate the account would be as follows:

Nov. 21	Accounts Receivable — D. L. Ross	42	
	Uncollectible Accounts Expense		42
	To reinstate account written off earlier in the year.		

The receipt of cash in payment of the reinstated amount would be recorded in the usual manner.

When an account that has been written off is collected in a later fiscal year, it may be reinstated by an entry like that just illustrated. An alternative is to credit some other appropriately titled account, such as Recovery of Uncollectible Accounts Written Off. The credit balance in such an account at the end of the year may then be reported on the income statement as a deduction from Uncollectible Accounts Expense, or the net expense only may be reported. Such amounts are likely to be small compared to net income.

TEMPORARY INVESTMENTS

A business may have a large amount of cash on hand that is not needed immediately, but this cash may be needed later in operating the business, possibly within the coming year. Rather than allow this excess cash to lie idle until it is actually needed, the business may put all or a part of it into income-yielding investments, such as certificates of deposit and money market funds. In many cases, the idle cash is invested in securities that can be quickly sold when cash is needed. Such securities are known as **temporary investments** or **marketable securities**. Although they may be retained as an investment for a number of years, they continue to be classified as temporary, provided that: (1) the securities are readily marketable and thus can be sold for cash at any time, and (2) management intends to sell them at such time as the enterprise needs more cash for normal operations.

Temporary investments in securities include stocks and bonds. **Stocks** are equity securities issued by corporations, and **bonds** are debt securities issued by corporations and various government agencies. Stocks and bonds held as temporary investments are classified on the balance sheet as current assets. They may be listed after "Cash," or they may be combined with cash and described as "Cash and marketable securities."

A temporary investment in a portfolio of debt securities is usually carried at cost. However, the **carrying amount** (also called **basis**) of a temporary investment in a portfolio of equity securities is the lower of its total cost or market value, determined at the date of the balance sheet.[2] Note that in the following illustration, the carrying amount is based on the comparison between the *total* cost and the *total* market value of the portfolio, rather than the lower of cost or market price of *each item*.

Temporary Investment Portfolio	Cost	Market	Unrealized Gain (Loss)
Equity security A	$150,000	$100,000	$(50,000)
Equity security B	200,000	200,000	—
Equity security C	180,000	210,000	30,000
Equity security D	160,000	150,000	(10,000)
Total	$690,000	$660,000	$(30,000)

The marketable equity securities would be reported in the current assets section of the balance sheet at a cost of $690,000 less an allowance for decline to market value of $30,000 to yield a carrying amount of $660,000. The unrealized loss of $30,000 is included in the determination of net income and reported as a separate item on the income statement. If the market value of the portfolio later rises, the unrealized loss is reversed and included in net income, but only to the extent that it does not exceed the original cost. In such cases, the increase is reported separately in the Other Income section of the income statement, and the amount reported on the balance sheet is likewise adjusted.[3]

TEMPORARY INVESTMENTS AND RECEIVABLES IN THE BALANCE SHEET

Temporary investments and all receivables that are expected to be realized in cash within a year are presented in the current assets section of the balance sheet. It is customary to list the assets in the order of their liquidity, that is, in the order in which they can be converted to cash in normal operations. An illustration of the presentation of receivables and temporary investments is shown in the following partial balance sheet for Pilar Enterprises Inc.:

---

[2]*Statement of Financial Accounting Standards, No. 12,* "Accounting for Certain Marketable Securities" (Stamford: Financial Accounting Standards Board, 1975), par. 8.
[3]*Ibid.,* par. 11.

Pilar Enterprises Inc.
Balance Sheet
December 31, 19--

Assets

Current assets:

Cash		$119,500
Marketable equity securities	$690,000	
Less allowance for decline to market	30,000	660,000
Notes receivable		250,000
Accounts receivable	$445,000	
Less allowance for doubtful accounts	15,000	430,000
Interest receivable		14,500

CHAPTER REVIEW

KEY POINTS

1. Classification of Receivables.

The term receivables includes all money claims against people, organizations, or other debtors. A promissory note is a written promise to pay a sum of money on demand or at a definite time. Accounts and notes receivable originating from sales transactions are called trade receivables.

2. Control Over Receivables.

The internal controls that apply to receivables include the separation of responsibility for related functions, so that the work of one employee can serve as a check on the work of another employee. For most businesses, the principal receivables are notes receivable and accounts receivable. If there are numerous notes receivable, a general ledger account for notes receivable should be supported by a notes receivable register.

3. Determining Interest.

Interest rates are usually stated in terms of a period of a year, regardless of the actual period of time involved. Notes covering a period of time longer than a year ordinarily provide that the interest be paid semiannually, quarterly, or at some other stated interval. The basic formula for computing interest is as follows: Principal × Rate × Time = Interest

4. Determining Due Date.

The period of time between the issuance date and the maturity date of a short-term note may be stated in either days or months. When the term of a note is stated in days, the due date is the specified number of days after its issuance. When the term of a note is stated as a number of months after the issuance date, the due date is determined by counting the number of months from the issuance date.

5. Notes Receivable and Interest Income.

Notes may be received by retail firms that sell merchandise on long-term credit. Such notes usually provide for monthly payments. In addition, if an account receivable becomes delinquent, the account may be converted to a note. Instead of retaining the note receivable until maturity, a note receivable may be transferred to a bank by endorsement. This transfer to a bank is called discounting the note receivable. The discount (interest) charged by the bank is computed on the maturity value of the note for the period of time the bank must hold the note until the due date. The amount of the proceeds paid to the endorser is the excess of the maturity value over the discount. Without a statement limiting responsibility, the endorser of a note is committed to paying the note if the maker should default. Such potential obligations that will become actual liabilities only if certain events occur in the future are called contingent liabilities.

If the maker of a note fails to pay the debt on the due date, the note is said to be dishonored. A dishonored note receivable is no longer negotiable, and the amount of the claim against the maker is transferred to an accounts receivable account.

6. Uncollectible Receivables.

When merchandise or services are sold on credit, a part of the claims against customers may prove to be uncollectible. The operating expense incurred because of the failure to collect receivables is called uncollectible accounts expense. There are two methods of accounting for receivables that are believed to be uncollectible: the allowance method and the direct write-off method.

7. Allowance Method of Accounting for Uncollectibles.

Most large business enterprises provide currently for the amount of their trade receivables estimated to become uncollectible. The estimate of the amount of uncollectibles may be based on either (1) the amount of sales for the entire fiscal period, or (2) the amount and the age of the receivable accounts at the end of the fiscal period. An adjusting entry made at the end of the fiscal period provides for (1) the reduction of the value of the receivables to the amount of cash expected to be realized from them in the future and (2) the allocation to the current period of the expected expense resulting from such reduction. The adjusting entry debits Uncollectible Accounts Expense and credits Allowance for Doubtful Accounts. When an account is believed to be uncollectible, it is written off against the allowance account.

The allowance account, which will normally have a credit balance after the adjusting entry has been posted, is a contra asset account. The uncollectible accounts expense is generally reported on the income statement as a general expense.

8. Direct Write-Off Method of Accounting for Uncollectibles.

If it is impossible to estimate uncollectibles with reasonable accuracy or if most sales are made on a cash basis, it is satisfactory to delay recognition of the uncollectibility of accounts receivable until the period in which certain accounts are believed to be worthless and are actually written off as an expense. Accordingly, under this method neither an allowance account nor an adjusting entry is needed at the end of the period. The entry in this case to write off an account debits Uncollectible Accounts Expense and credits Accounts Receivable.

9. Temporary Investments.

A business may put all or part of any excess cash on hand into income-yielding investments that are readily marketable and are known as temporary investments or marketable securities. These investments may include stocks and bonds. Stocks are equity securities and bonds are debt securities issued by corporations and various governmental agencies. A temporary investment of debt securities is usually carried in the records at cost. However, a temporary investment in equity securities must be carried at the lower of its total cost or market value at the balance sheet date.

10. Temporary Investments and Receivables in the Balance Sheet.

Temporary investments and all receivables that are expected to be realized in cash within a year are presented in the current assets section of the balance sheet. It is customary to list the assets in the order of their liquidity, that is, in the order in which they can be converted to cash in normal operations.

KEY TERMS

promissory note 380
note receivable 380
maturity value 381
discount 388
proceeds 388
contingent liabilities 389
dishonored 389

allowance method 390
direct write-off method 390
aging the receivables 395
temporary investments 397
marketable securities 397
carrying amount 398

SELF-EXAMINATION QUESTIONS

Answers in Appendix B.

prt = c

1. What is the maturity value of a 90-day, 12% note for $10,000?
   A. $8,800   C. $10,300
   B. $10,000   D. $11,200

2. On June 16, an enterprise discounts a 60-day, 10% note receivable for $15,000, dated June 1, at the rate of 12%. The proceeds are:
   A. $15,000.00   C. $15,250.00
   B. $15,021.25   D. $15,478.75

3. At the end of the fiscal year, before the accounts are adjusted, Accounts Receivable has a balance of $200,000 and Allowance for Doubtful Accounts has a credit balance of $2,500. If the estimate of uncollectible accounts determined by aging the receivables is $8,500, the current provision to be made for uncollectible accounts expense would be:
   A. $2,500   C. $8,500
   B. $6,000   D. $200,000

4. At the end of the fiscal year, Accounts Receivable has a balance of $100,000 and Allowance for Doubtful Accounts has a balance of $7,000. The expected realizable value of the accounts receivable is:
   A. $7,000   C. $100,000
   B. $93,000   D. $107,000

5. Under what caption would a temporary investment in stock be reported in the balance sheet?
   A. Current assets   C. Investments
   B. Plant assets   D. None of the above

ILLUSTRATIVE PROBLEM

Selected transactions completed by Rodriguez Company are as follows. Rodriguez Company uses the allowance method of accounting for uncollectible accounts receivable.

Jan. 28. Sold merchandise on account to Lakeland Inc., $10,000.

Mar. 1. Accepted a 60-day, 12% note for $10,000 from Lakeland Inc. on account.

Apr. 11. Wrote off a $4,500 account from Exdel Inc. as uncollectible.

16. Loaned $7,500 cash to Thomas Glazer, receiving a 90-day, 14% note.

30. Received the interest due from Lakeland Inc. and a new 90-day, 14% note as a renewal of the loan. (Record both the debit and credit to the notes receivable account.)

May 1. Discounted the note from Thomas Glazer at the First National Bank at 10%.

June 13. Reinstated the account of Exdel Inc., written off on April 11, and received $4,500 in full payment.

July 15. Received notice from First National Bank that Thomas Glazer dishonored his note. Paid the bank the maturity value of the note plus a $20 protest fee.

29. Received from Lakeland Inc. the amount due on its note of April 30.

Aug. 14. Received from Thomas Glazer the amount owed on the dishonored note, plus interest for 30 days at 15%, computed on the maturity value of the note and the protest fee.

Dec. 31. It is estimated that 2% of the credit sales of $958,600 for the year ended December 31 will be uncollectible.

Instructions:

Record the transactions in general journal form.

SOLUTION

Jan.	28	Accounts Receivable — Lakeland Inc. . 10,000.00	
		Sales	10,000.00
Mar.	1	Notes Receivable — Lakeland Inc. 10,000.00	
		Accounts Receivable — Lakeland Inc. .	10,000.00
Apr.	11	Allowance for Doubtful Accounts 4,500.00	
		Accounts Receivable — Exdel Inc....	4,500.00
	16	Notes Receivable — Thomas Glazer ... 7,500.00	
		Cash	7,500.00
	30	Notes Receivable — Lakeland Inc. 10,000.00	
		Cash 200.00	
		Notes Receivable — Lakeland Inc. ..	10,000.00
		Interest Income..................	200.00

May 1 Cash 7,600.78

    Notes Receivable—Thomas Glazer .　　　　　　7,500.00

    Interest Income................... 　　　　　　100.78

Face value	$7,500.00
Interest on note (90 days at 14%)	262.50
Maturity value............	$7,762.50
Discount on maturity value (75 days at 10%)	161.72
Proceeds.................	$7,600.78

June 13 Accounts Receivable—Exdel Inc...... 4,500.00

    Allowance for Doubtful Accounts .. 　　　　　　4,500.00

   13 Cash 4,500.00

    Accounts Receivable—Exdel Inc.... 　　　　　　4,500.00

July 15 Accounts Receivable—Thomas Glazer . 7,782.50

    Cash .... 　　　　　　7,782.50

   29 Cash 10,350.00

    Notes Receivable—Lakeland Inc. .. 　　　　　　10,000.00

    Interest Income................... 　　　　　　350.00

Aug. 14 Cash 7,879.78

    Accounts Receivable— Thomas Glazer .... 　　　　　　7,782.50

    Interest Income ($7,782.50 × 15% × 30/360)...... 　　　　　　97.28

Dec. 31 Uncollectible Accounts Expense 19,172.00

    Allowance for Doubtful Accounts .. 　　　　　　19,172.00

DISCUSSION QUESTIONS

1. Johnson Corporation issued a promissory note to Madrid Company. (a) Who is the payee? (b) What is the title of the account employed by Madrid Company in recording the note?

2. What are the advantages, to the creditor, of a note receivable in comparison to an account receivable?

3. In what section of the balance sheet should a note receivable be listed if its term is (a) 90 days, (b) 5 years?

4. The accounts receivable clerk is also responsible for handling cash receipts. Which principle of internal control is violated in this situation?

5. If a note provides for payment of principal of $1,000 and interest at the rate of 10%, will the interest amount to $100? Explain.

6. The following questions refer to a 60-day, 12% note for $20,000, dated April 1: (a) What is the face value of the note? (b) What is the amount of interest payable at maturity? (c) What is the maturity value of the note? (d) What is the due date of the note?

7. At the end of the fiscal year, an enterprise holds a 90-day note receivable accepted from a customer fifteen days earlier. (a) Which of the following types of accounts will be affected by the related adjusting entry at the end of the year: (1) asset, (2) liability, (3) revenue, (4) expense? (b) If the note is held until maturity, what fraction of the total interest should be allocated to the year in which the note is collected?

8. The payee of a 90-day, 10% note for $4,000, dated May 1, endorses it to a bank on May 31. The bank discounts the note at 12%, paying the endorser $4,018. Identify or determine the following as they relate to the note: (a) face value, (b) maturity value, (c) due date, (d) number of days in the discount period, (e) proceeds, (f) interest income or expense recorded by endorser, (g) amount payable to the bank if the maker should default.

9. During the year, notes receivable of $250,000 were discounted at a bank by an enterprise. By the end of the year, $220,000 of these notes have matured. What is the amount of the endorser's contingent liability for notes receivable discounted at the end of the year?

10. The maker of a $5,000, 12%, 30-day note receivable failed to pay the note on the due date. What entry should be made in the accounts of the payee to record the dishonored note receivable?

11. A discounted note receivable is dishonored by the maker and the endorser pays the bank the face of the note, $10,000, the interest, $150, and a protest fee of $8. What entry should be made in the accounts of the endorser to record the payment?

12. The series of six transactions recorded in the following T accounts were related to a sale to a customer on account and receipt of the amount owed. Briefly describe each transaction.

Cash		
(4) 4,854	(5) 4,956	
(6) 4,980		

Notes Receivable	
(3) 4,900	(4) 4,900

Accounts Receivable	
(1) 5,000	(2) 100
(5) 4,956	(3) 4,900
	(6) 4,956

Sales	
(2) 100	(1) 5,000

Interest Income
(6) 24

Interest Expense
(4) 46

13. Which of the two methods of accounting for uncollectible accounts provides for the recognition of the expense at the earlier date?

14. What kind of an account (asset, liability, etc.) is Allowance for Doubtful Accounts, and is its normal balance a debit or a credit?

15. Give the adjusting entry to increase Allowance for Doubtful Accounts by $9,450.

16. After the accounts are adjusted and closed at the end of the fiscal year, Accounts Receivable has a balance of $260,500 and Allowance for Doubtful Accounts has a balance of $9,900.
    (a) What is the expected realizable value of the accounts receivable?
    (b) If an account receivable of $1,500 is written off against the allowance account, what will be the expected realizable value of the accounts receivable after the write-off, assuming that no other changes in either account have occurred in the meantime?

17. A firm has consistently adjusted its allowance account at the end of the fiscal year by adding a fixed percent of the period's net sales on account. After five years, the balance in Allowance for Doubtful Accounts has become disproportionately large in relationship to the balance in Accounts Receivable. Give two possible explanations.

18. The $250 balance of an account owed by a customer is considered to be uncollectible and is to be written off. Give the entry to record the write-off in the general ledger, (a) assuming that the allowance method is used and (b) assuming that the direct write-off method is used.

19. Which of the two methods of estimating uncollectibles, when advance provision for uncollectible receivables is made, provides for the most accurate estimate of the current realizable value of the receivables?

20. Under what caption should securities held as a temporary investment be reported on the balance sheet?

21. A corporation has two equity securities which it holds as a temporary investment. If they have a total cost of $210,000 and a fair market value of $200,000, at what amount should these securities be reported in the current assets section of the corporation's balance sheet?

22. Real World Focus. Receivables and related allowances for doubtful accounts for fiscal years ending in 1984 and 1983 for six corporations are as follows:

	1984		1983	
	Receivables	Allowance for Doubtful Accounts	Receivables	Allowance for Doubtful Accounts
Chrysler Corp.	$ 346,000,000	$13,800,000	$ 316,700,000	$ 25,500,000
PepsiCo, Inc.	672,047,000	31,966,000	681,067,000	33,738,000
General Electric	5,602,000,000	93,000,000	5,351,000,000	102,000,000
W. R. Grace & Co....	678,200,000	25,700,000	670,900,000	28,000,000
Fuqua Industries	181,071,000	8,096,000	155,653,000	7,383,000
Gannett Co., Inc.....	262,918,000	7,748,000	220,386,000	7,051,000

For 1984 and 1983, compute for each company (a) the realizable value of the receivables and (b) the percent of the allowance for doubtful accounts to the total receivables, rounding to the nearest tenth of a percent. (c) What might explain the general decrease from 1983 to 1984 in the percentages computed in (b)?

EXERCISES

Exercise 9–1.   Determination of due date and interest on notes. Determine the due date and the amount of interest due at maturity on the following notes:

Date of Note	Face Amount	Term of Note	Interest Rate
(a) March 1	$12,000	60 days	10%
(b) April 10	3,000	60 days	12%
(c) May 16	6,000	75 days	14%
(d) June 5	4,000	90 days	15%
(e) July 22	7,200	120 days	10%

Exercise 9–2.   Entries for notes receivable. Leigh Company issues a 90-day, 12% note for $5,000, dated July 20, to Lakes Corporation on account.

(a) Determine the due date of the note.
(b) Determine the maturity value of the note.
(c) Present entries, in general journal form, to record the following:
   (1) Receipt of the note by the payee.
   (2) Receipt by payee of payment of the note at maturity.

Exercise 9–3.   Entries for note receivable and related year-end adjustments. The following selected transactions were completed by Bering Co. during the current year:

May   1. Received from Adams Co., on account, an $8,000, 90-day, 12% note dated May 1.
      31. Recorded an adjusting entry for accrued interest on the note of May 1.
      31. Closed the interest income account. The only entry in this account originated from the May 31 adjustment.

June 1. Recorded a reversing entry for accrued interest.
July 30. Received $8,240 from Adams Co. for the note due today.

(a) Record the transactions in general journal form.
(b) What is the balance in interest income after the entry of July 30?
(c) How many days' interest on $8,000 at 12% does the amount reported in (b) represent?

Exercise 9–4.   Discounting note receivable. Lincoln Co. holds a 60-day, 12% note for $7,500, dated April 20, that was received from a customer on account. On May 10, the note is discounted at the Franklin National Bank at the rate of 15%.

(a) Determine the maturity value of the note.
(b) Determine the number of days in the discount period.
(c) Determine the amount of the discount.
(d) Determine the amount of the proceeds.
(e) Present the entry, in general journal form, to record the discounting of the note on May 10.

Exercise 9–5.   Entries for receipt and discounting of note receivable and dishonored note. Record the following transactions, in general journal form, in the accounts of D. Shuman and Son.

April 6. Received a $9,000, 60-day, 14% note dated April 6 from B. C. Andrews on account.
      26. Discounted the note at Paxton National Bank at 15%.
June 5. The note is dishonored; paid the bank the amount due on the note plus a protest fee of $10.
      25. Received the amount due on the dishonored note plus interest for 20 days at 14% on the total amount charged to B. C. Andrews on June 5.

Exercise 9–6.   Entries for receipt and dishonor of notes receivable. Record the following transactions, in general journal form, in the accounts of Jane Thomas and Daughter.

May   1. Received a $40,000, 90-day, 14% note dated May 1 from A. B. James Corp. on account.
      10. Received a $12,000, 60-day, 15% note dated May 10 from Clark and Dodds on account.
July 9. The note dated May 10 from Clark and Dodds is dishonored and the customer's account is charged for the note, including interest.
      30. The note dated May 1 from A. B. James Corp. is dishonored and the customer's account is charged for the note, including interest.
Aug. 29. Cash is received for the amount due on the dishonored note dated May 1 plus interest for 30 days at 14% on the total amount debited to A. B. James Corp. on July 30.
Sept. 30. Wrote off against the allowance account the amount charged to Clark and Dodds on July 9 for the dishonored note dated May 10.

Exercise 9–7. Provision for doubtful accounts. At the end of the current year, the accounts receivable account has a debit balance of $95,000, and net sales for the year total $900,000. Determine the amount of the adjusting entry to record the provision for doubtful accounts under each of the following assumptions:

(a) The allowance account before adjustment has a credit balance of $500.
  (1) Uncollectible accounts expense is estimated at 1% of net sales.
  (2) Analysis of the accounts in the customers ledger indicates doubtful accounts of $9,950.

(b) The allowance account before adjustment has a debit balance of $250.
  (1) Uncollectible accounts expense is estimated at 3/4 of 1% of net sales.
  (2) Analysis of the accounts in the customers ledger indicates doubtful accounts of $5,900.

Exercise 9–8. Entries for uncollectible receivables using allowance method. In general journal form, record the following transactions in the accounts of Baker Corporation, which uses the allowance method of accounting for uncollectible receivables.

Feb. 10. Sold merchandise on account to J. A. Jacobs, $2,500.
June 30. Received $1,250 from J. A. Jacobs and wrote off the remainder owed on the sale of February 10 as uncollectible.
Dec. 15. Reinstated the account of J. A. Jacobs that had been written off on June 30 and received $1,250 cash in full payment.

Exercise 9–9. Entries for uncollectible accounts, using direct write-off method. In general journal form, record the following transactions in the accounts of Dexter and Parker, which uses the direct write-off method of accounting for uncollectible receivables.

Jan. 5. Sold merchandise on account to P. P. Rossi, $1,000.
May 12. Received $600 from P. P. Rossi and wrote off the remainder owed on the sale of January 5 as uncollectible.
Nov. 30. Reinstated the account of P. P. Rossi that had been written off on May 12 and received $400 cash in full payment.

Exercise 9–10. Temporary equity securities in financial statements. As of December 31 of the first year of operations, Royal Corporation has the following portfolio of temporary equity securities:

	Cost	Market
Security A	$22,100	$19,750
Security B	18,000	16,200
Security C	17,750	19,500
Security D	85,800	81,000

Describe how the portfolio of temporary equity securities would affect the year-end balance sheet and income statement of Royal Corporation.

PROBLEMS

Series A

Problem 9–1A.   Sales, notes receivable, discounting notes receivable transactions. The following were selected from among the transactions completed by Alex Gomez and Co. during the current year:

Jan. 20. Loaned $5,000 cash to Ann Santos, receiving a 90-day, 12% note.

Mar.   1. Sold merchandise on account to J. A. Block Co., $10,000.

      20. Sold merchandise on account to C. D. Connors Co., $7,100.

      30. Received from C. D. Conners Co. the amount of the invoice of March 20, less 2% discount.

      31. Accepted a 30-day, 15% note for $10,000 from J. A. Block Co. on account.

Apr. 20. Received the interest due from Ann Santos and a new 90-day, 14% note as a renewal of the loan of January 20. (Record both the debit and the credit to the notes receivable account.)

      30. Received from J. A. Block Co. the amount due on the note of March 31.

July 12. Sold merchandise on account to Swartz and Sons, $20,000.

      19. Received from Ann Santos the amount due on her note of April 20.

Aug. 11. Accepted a 60-day, 12% note for $20,000 from Swartz and Sons on account.

Sept. 10. Discounted the note from Swartz and Sons at the American National Bank at 14%.

Oct. 10. Received notice from the American National Bank that Swartz and Sons had dishonored its note. Paid the bank the maturity value of the note.

Nov.   9. Received from Swartz and Sons the amount owed on the dishonored note, plus interest for 30 days at 12% computed on the maturity value of the note.

Instructions:

Record the transactions in general journal form.

Problem 9–2A.   Details of notes receivable, including discounting. During the last three months of the current fiscal year, Atkins Co. received the following notes. Notes (1), (2), (3), and (4) were discounted on the dates and at the rates indicated.

	Date	Face Amount	Term	Interest Rate	Date Discounted	Discount Rate
(1)	Oct. 1	$7,200	60 days	14%	Oct. 21	12%
(2)	Oct. 11	9,500	30 days	12%	Oct. 26	14%
(3)	Oct. 28	3,100	90 days	14%	Dec. 27	15%

	Date	Face Amount	Term	Interest Rate	Date Discounted	Discount Rate
(4)	Nov. 8	$8,000	60 days	12%	Nov. 23	16%
(5)	Dec. 11	9,000	60 days	11%	—	—
(6)	Dec. 21	8,700	30 days	12%	—	—

Instructions:

(1) Determine for each note (a) the due date and (b) the amount of interest due at maturity, identifying each note by number.
(2) Determine for each of the first four notes (a) the maturity value, (b) the discount period, (c) the discount, (d) the proceeds, and (e) the interest income or interest expense, identifying each note by number.
(3) Present, in general journal form, the entries to record the discounting of notes (2) and (4) at a bank.
(4) Assuming that notes (5) and (6) are held until maturity, determine for each the amount of interest earned (a) in the current fiscal year and (b) in the following fiscal year.

Problem 9–3A. Note receivable entries and year-end entries; general ledger accounts. A. C. Cohen Co. closes its accounts annually as of December 31, the end of the fiscal year. The following data relate to notes receivable and interest from November 1, 1987, through March 10, 1988. (All notes are dated as of the day they are received.)

Nov. 1. Received a $6,750, 12%, 60-day note on account. *135*
     11. Received a $30,000, 15%, 120-day note on account. *1500*
Dec. 16. Received a $12,000, 13%, 60-day note on account. *260*
     21. Received an $18,000, 12%, 30-day note on account. *180*
     31. Received $6,885 on note of November 1.
     31. Recorded an adjusting entry for the interest accrued on the notes dated November 11, December 16, and December 21. There are no other notes receivable on this date.
     31. Closed the interest income account.
Jan. 1. Recorded a reversing entry for the accrued interest.
     20. Received $18,180 on note of December 21.
     26. Received a $7,000, 12%, 30-day note on account. *70*
Feb. 14. Received $12,260 on note of December 16.
     25. Received $7,070 on note of January 26.
Mar. 10. Received $31,500 on note of November 11.

1500
260
1760
180
1940

Instructions:

(1) Open accounts for Interest Receivable (Account No. 116) and Interest Income (Account No. 611), and record a credit balance of $4,450 in the latter account as of November 1 of the current year.
(2) Present entries in general journal form to record the transactions and other data, posting to the two accounts after each entry affecting them.
(3) If the reversing entry had not been recorded as of January 1, indicate how each interest receipt in January, February, and March should be allocated. Submit the data in the following form:

Note (Face Amount)	Total Interest Received	Cr. Interest Receivable	Cr. Interest Income
$18,000	$ 180	$ 135	$
12,000	260		
7,000	70		
30,000	1500		
Total	$ 2010	$ 2145	$

(4) Do the March 10 balances of Interest Receivable and Interest Income obtained by use of the reversing entry technique correspond to the balances that would have been obtained by analyzing each receipt?

Problem 9–4A. Entries related to uncollectible accounts. The following transactions, adjusting entries, and closing entries were completed during the current fiscal year ended December 31.

Feb. 8. Received 60% of the $5,000 balance owed by Flowers Co., a bankrupt business, and wrote off the remainder as uncollectible.

May 29. Reinstated the account of James Gray, which had been written off in the preceding year as uncollectible. Recorded the receipt of $990 cash in full payment of Gray's account.

Aug. 16. Wrote off the $5,300 balance owed by Shaw Corp., which has no assets.

Oct. 1. Reinstated the account of W. Ricardo Inc. which had been written off in the preceding year as uncollectible. Recorded the receipt of $2,950 cash in full payment of W. Ricardo Inc.'s account.

Dec. 30. Wrote off the following accounts as uncollectible (compound entry): Mertz and Dodds, $4,920; Nance Inc., $3,975; Powell Distributors, $9,700; J. J. Stevens, $4,200.

31. Based on an analysis of the $610,000 of accounts receivable, it was estimated that $31,250 will be uncollectible. Recorded the adjusting entry.

31. Recorded the entry to close the appropriate account to Income Summary.

Instructions:

(1) Open the following selected accounts, recording the credit balance indicated as of January 1 of the current fiscal year:

115	Allowance for Doubtful Accounts.....................	$29,500
313	Income Summary	—
718	Uncollectible Accounts Expense	—

(2) Record in general journal form the transactions and the adjusting and closing entries previously described. After each entry, post to the three selected accounts affected and extend the new balances.

(3) Determine the expected realizable value of the accounts receivable as of December 31.

(4) Assuming that, instead of basing the provision for uncollectible accounts on an analysis of receivables, the adjusting entry on December 31 had been based on an estimated loss of 1/2 of 1% of the net sales of $5,700,000 for the year, determine the following:

(a) Uncollectible accounts expense for the year.

(b) Balance in the allowance account after the adjustment of December 31.

(c) Expected realizable value of the accounts receivable as of December 31.

Problem 9–5A.   Comparison of two methods of accounting for receivables.

SPREADSHEET
PROBLEM

AID Corporation has just completed its fourth year of operations. The direct write-off method of recording uncollectible accounts expense has been employed during the entire period. Because of substantial increases in sales volume and amount of uncollectible accounts, the firm is considering the possibility of changing to the allowance method. Information is requested as to the effect that an annual provision of 1% of sales would have had on the amount of uncollectible accounts expense reported for each of the past four years. It is also considered desirable to know what the balance of Allowance for Doubtful Accounts would have been at the end of each year. The following data have been obtained from the accounts:

Year	Sales	Uncollectible Accounts Written Off	Year of Origin of Accounts Receivable Written off as Uncollectible			
			1st	2d	3d	4th
1st	$450,000	$2,500	$2,500			
2d	600,000	2,950	1,500	$1,450		
3d	850,000	4,700	700	2,400	$1,600	
4th	950,000	6,450		1,900	2,950	$1,600

Instructions:

(1) Assemble the desired data, using the following columnar captions:

	Uncollectible Accounts Expense			Balance of
Year	Expense Actually Reported	Expense Based on Estimate	Increase in Amount of Expense	Allowance Account, End of Year

(2) Experience during the first four years of operation indicated that the receivables were either collected within two years or had to be written off as uncollectible. Does the estimate of 1% of sales appear to be reasonably close to the actual experience with uncollectible accounts originating during the first two years?

Problem 9–6A.   Financial statements for corporation. The following data for N. B. Neter Company were selected from the ledger, after adjustment at December 31, the end of the current fiscal year.

Accounts payable.. $ 25,750

Accounts receivable.. 51,500

Accumulated depreciation—building...........................	$175,000
Accumulated depreciation—office equipment....................	49,750
Allowance for decline to market of marketable securities..........	1,100
Allowance for doubtful accounts..............................	1,500
Building...	325,000
Capital stock..	250,000
Cash..	35,500
Cost of merchandise sold....................................	510,000
Dividends...	60,000
General expenses..	73,500
Interest and dividend income................................	6,100
Land..	75,000
Marketable equity securities................................	60,000
Merchandise inventory......................................	72,500
Notes receivable...	40,000
Office equipment...	79,750
Office supplies..	7,500
Prepaid insurance...	5,000
Retained earnings...	205,900
Salaries payable...	3,250
Sales...	795,000
Sales discounts...	6,500
Selling expenses..	110,500
Unrealized loss from decline to market of marketable securities....	1,100

Instructions:

(1) Prepare an income statement in multiple-step form.
(2) Prepare a retained earnings statement.
(3) Prepare a balance sheet in report form.

Series B

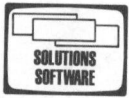

Problem 9–1B. Sales, notes receivable, discounting notes receivable transactions. The following were selected from among the transactions completed by D. L. Parton Co. during the current year:

Jan. 20. Sold merchandise on account to Grant Co., $10,000.
     30. Accepted a 60-day, 12% note for $10,000 from Grant Co. on account.
Mar. 31. Received from Grant Co. the amount due on the note of January 30.
May 1. Sold merchandise on account to W. A. Lewis Co. for $2,000.
     5. Loaned $6,000 cash to Frank Nelson, receiving a 30-day, 14% note.
   11. Received from W. A. Lewis Co. the amount due on the invoice of May 1, less 1% discount.
June 4. Received the interest due from Frank Nelson and a new 60-day, 14% note as a renewal of the loan of May 5. (Record both the debit and the credit to the notes receivable account.)
Aug. 3. Received from Frank Nelson the amount due on his note of June 4.
   16. Sold merchandise on account to J. A. Rohr, $8,000.
Sept. 10. Accepted a 60-day, 12% note for $8,000 from J. A. Rohr on account.
Oct. 10. Discounted the note from J. A. Rohr at the Collier National Bank at 10%.

Nov. 9. Received notice from Collier National Bank that J. A. Rohr had dishonored its note. Paid the bank the maturity value of the note.

Dec. 9. Received from J. A. Rohr the amount owed on the dishonored note, plus interest for 30 days at 10% computed on the maturity value of the note.

Instructions:

Record the transactions in general journal form.

Problem 9–2B.   Details of notes receivable, including discounting. During the last six months of the current fiscal year, Amos Co. received the following notes. Notes (1), (2), (3), and (4) were discounted on the dates and at the rates indicated.

Date	Face Amount	Term	Interest Rate	Date Discounted	Discount Rate
(1) June 5	$13,500	60 days	12%	June 25	10%
(2) July 30	8,000	60 days	12%	Aug. 9	15%
(3) Aug. 19	15,000	90 days	10%	Sept. 18	12%
(4) Sept. 1	10,800	60 days	11%	Oct. 11	12%
(5) Dec. 11	9,000	30 days	14%	—	—
(6) Dec. 16	12,000	60 days	13%	—	—

Instructions:

(1) Determine for each note (a) the due date and (b) the amount of interest due at maturity, identifying each note by number.

(2) Determine for each of the first four notes (a) the maturity value, (b) the discount period, (c) the discount, (d) the proceeds, and (e) the interest income or interest expense, identifying each note by number.

(3) Present, in general journal form, the entries to record the discounting of notes (2) and (3) at a bank.

(4) Assuming that notes (5) and (6) are held until maturity, determine for each the amount of interest earned (a) in the current fiscal year and (b) in the following fiscal year.

Problem 9–3B.   Notes receivable entries and year-end entries; general ledger accounts. Tracy Co. closes its accounts annually as of December 31, the end of the fiscal year. The following data relate to notes receivable and interest from November 1, 1987, through March 16, 1988. (All notes are dated as of the day they are received.)

Nov. 1. Received a $20,000, 12%, 60-day note on account.

21. Received a $9,000, 14%, 90-day note on account.

Dec. 16. Received a $12,000, 15%, 90-day note on account.

21. Received a $3,600, 13%, 30-day note on account.

31. Received $20,400 on note of November 1.

31. Recorded an adjusting entry for the interest accrued on the notes dated November 21, December 16, and December 21. There are no other notes receivable on this date.

31. Closed the interest income account.

Jan. 1. Recorded a reversing entry for the accrued interest.
     20. Received $3,639 on note of December 21.
     21. Received a $7,000, 12%, 30-day note on account.
Feb. 19. Received $9,315 on note of November 21.
     20. Received $7,070 on note of January 21.
Mar. 16. Received $12,450 on note of December 16.

Instructions:

(1) Open accounts for Interest Receivable (Account No. 116) and Interest Income (Account No. 611), and record a credit balance of $2,050 in the latter account as of November 1 of the current year.
(2) Present entries in general journal form to record the transactions and other data, posting to the two accounts after each entry affecting them.
(3) If the reversing entry had not been recorded as of January 1, indicate how each interest receipt in January, February, and March should be allocated. Submit the data in the following form:

Note (Face Amount)	Total Interest Received	Cr. Interest Receivable	Cr. Interest Income
$ 9,000	$	$	$
12,000			
3,600			
7,000			
Total	$	$	$

(4) Do the March 16 balances of Interest Receivable and Interest Income obtained by the use of the reversing entry technique correspond to the balances that would have been obtained by analyzing each receipt?

Problem 9–4B. Entries related to uncollectible accounts. The following transactions, adjusting entries, and closing entries were completed during the current fiscal year ended December 31:

Feb. 22. Reinstated the account of Bob Lowe, which had been written off in the preceding year as uncollectible. Recorded the receipt of $610 cash in full payment of Lowe's account.
May   3. Wrote off the $3,925 balance owed by Licci Co., which has no assets.
Aug. 7. Received 30% of the $5,000 balance owed by C. O'Rourke Corp., a bankrupt business, and wrote off the remainder as uncollectible.
Oct. 19. Reinstated the account of John Nowak, which had been written off two years earlier as uncollectible. Recorded the receipt of $925 cash in full payment.
Dec. 20. Wrote off the following accounts as uncollectible (compound entry): Cain Bros., $480; Gerber and Hertz, $1,900; Jenson Furniture, $2,775; Charles Menke, $840.
     31. Based on an analysis of the $234,250 of accounts receivable, it was estimated that $15,000 will be uncollectible. Recorded the adjusting entry.
     31. Recorded the entry to close the appropriate account to Income Summary.

Instructions:

(1) Open the following selected accounts, recording the credit balance indicated as of January 1 of the current fiscal year:

115 Allowance for Doubtful Accounts $13,050
313 Income Summary..................................... —
718 Uncollectible Accounts Expense..................... —

(2) Record in general journal form the transactions and the adjusting and closing entries described. After each entry, post to the three selected accounts affected and extend the new balances.

(3) Determine the expected realizable value of the accounts receivable as of December 31.

(4) Assuming that, instead of basing the provision for uncollectible accounts on an analysis of receivables, the adjusting entry on December 31 had been based on an estimated loss of 1/2 of 1% of the net sales of $2,700,000 for the year, determine the following:

(a) Uncollectible accounts expense for the year.

(b) Balance in the allowance account after the adjustment of December 31.

(c) Expected realizable value of the accounts receivable as of December 31.

MINI-CASE 9

CANNONS

For several years, Cannons' sales have been on a "cash only" basis. On January 1, 1984, however, Cannons began offering credit on terms of n/30. The amount of the adjusting entry to record the estimated uncollectible receivables at the end of each year has been 1/2 of 1% of credit sales, which is the rate reported as the average for the industry. Credit sales and the year-end credit balances in Allowance for Doubtful Accounts for the past four years are as follows:

Year	Credit Sales	Allowance for Doubtful Accounts
1984	$3,900,000	$ 6,000
1985	3,600,000	8,000
1986	4,000,000	11,500
1987	3,750,000	14,000

Jane Cannon, president of Cannons, is concerned that the method used to account for and write off uncollectible receivables is unsatisfactory. She has asked for your advice in the analysis of past operations in this area and for recommendations for change.

Instructions:

(1) Determine the amount of (a) the addition to Allowance for Doubtful Accounts and (b) the accounts written off for each of the four years.
(2) Advise Jane Cannon as to whether the estimate of 1/2 of 1% of credit sales appears reasonable.
(3) Assume that after discussing item (2) with Jane Cannon, she asked you what action might be taken to determine what the balance of Allowance for Doubtful Accounts should be at December 31, 1987, and possible changes, if any, you might recommend in accounting for uncollectible receivables. How would you respond?

Chapter 10

INVENTORIES

Chapter Objectives:

- Describe and illustrate the effect of inventory on the financial statements of the current period and the following period.

- Identify and describe the two principal inventory systems.

- Identify and illustrate the procedures for determining the actual quantity in inventory.

- Describe and illustrate the most common methods of determining the cost of inventory, including the comparison of the effect of the methods on operating results.

- Describe and illustrate the valuation of inventory at the lower of cost or market.

- Describe and illustrate the perpetual inventory system.

- Identify and illustrate the proper presentation of inventory in the financial statements.

- Describe and illustrate methods of estimating the cost of inventory.

Inventory
Balance sheet item

The term **inventories** is used to designate (1) merchandise held for sale in the normal course of business, and (2) materials in the process of production or held for such use. This chapter discusses the determination of the inventory of merchandise purchased for resale, commonly called **merchandise inventory**. Inventories of raw materials and partially processed materials of a manufacturing enterprise will be considered in a later chapter.

IMPORTANCE OF INVENTORIES

Merchandise, being continually purchased and sold, is one of the most active elements in the operation of wholesale and retail businesses. The sale of merchandise provides the principal source of revenue for such enterprises. When the net income is determined, the cost of merchandise sold is normally the largest deduction from sales. In fact, it is usually larger than all other deductions combined. In addition, a substantial part of a merchandising firm's resources is invested in inventory. It is frequently the largest of the current assets of such a firm.

The Effect of Inventory on the Current Period's Statements

Inventory determination plays an important role in matching expired costs with revenues of the period. As was explained and illustrated in Chapter 4, the total cost of merchandise available for sale during a period of time must be divided into two parts at the end of the period. The cost of the merchandise determined to be in the inventory will appear on the balance sheet as a current asset. The other element, which is the cost of the merchandise sold, will be reported on the income statement as a deduction from net sales to yield gross profit. An error in the determination of the inventory amount at the end of the period will cause an equal misstatement of gross profit and net income, and the amount reported for both assets and owner's equity in the balance sheet will be incorrect by the same amount. The effects of understatements and overstatements of merchandise inventory at the end of the period are demonstrated in the following three sets of condensed

420

income statements and balance sheets. The first set of statements is based on a correct ending inventory of $20,000; the second set, on an *incorrect ending inventory of $12,000*; and the third set, on an *incorrect ending inventory of $27,000*. In all three cases, net sales are $200,000, merchandise available for sale is $140,000, and expenses are $55,000.

Income Statement for the Year   Balance Sheet at End of Year

1. Inventory at end of period correctly stated at $20,000.

Income Statement		Balance Sheet	
Net sales.................	$200,000	Merchandise inventory......	$ 20,000
Cost of merchandise sold ...	120,000	Other assets..............	80,000
Gross profit.............	$ 80,000	Total....................	$100,000
Expenses	55,000	Liabilities.................	$ 30,000
Net income.............	$ 25,000	Owner's equity............	70,000
		Total....................	$100,000

2. Inventory at end of period incorrectly stated at $12,000; (understated by $8,000).

Income Statement		Balance Sheet	
Net sales.................	$200,000	Merchandise inventory......	$ 12,000
Cost of merchandise sold ...	128,000	Other assets..............	80,000
Gross profit.............	$ 72,000	Total....................	$ 92,000
Expenses	55,000	Liabilities.................	$ 30,000
Net income.............	$ 17,000	Owner's equity............	62,000
		Total....................	$ 92,000

3. Inventory at end of period incorrectly stated at $27,000; (overstated by $7,000).

Income Statement		Balance Sheet	
Net sales.................	$200,000	Merchandise inventory......	$ 27,000
Cost of merchandise sold ...	113,000	Other assets..............	80,000
Gross profit.............	$ 87,000	Total....................	$107,000
Expenses	55,000	Liabilities.................	$ 30,000
Net income.............	$ 32,000	Owner's equity............	77,000
		Total....................	$107,000

Note that in the illustration the total cost of merchandise available for sale was constant at $140,000. It was the way in which the cost was allocated that varied. The variations in allocating the $140,000 of merchandise cost are summarized as follows:

	Merchandise Available		
	Total	*Inventory*	*Sold*
1. Inventory correctly stated	$140,000	$20,000	$120,000
2. Inventory understated by $8,000.......	140,000	12,000	128,000
3. Inventory overstated by $7,000	140,000	27,000	113,000

The effect of the errors on net income, assets, and owner's equity may also be summarized. Comparison of the financial statements in 2 and 3 with the financial statements in 1 yields the following:

	Net Income	Assets	Owner's Equity
2. Ending inventory understated $8,000	Understated $8,000	Understated $8,000	Understated $8,000
3. Ending inventory overstated $7,000	Overstated $7,000	Overstated $7,000	Overstated $7,000

The Effect of Inventory on the Following Period's Statements

The inventory at the end of one period becomes the inventory for the beginning of the following period. Thus, if the inventory is incorrectly stated at the end of the period, the net income of that period will be misstated and so will the net income for the following period. The amount of the two misstatements will be equal and in opposite directions. Therefore, the effect on net income of an incorrectly stated inventory, if not corrected, is limited to the period of the error and the following period. At the end of this following period, assuming no additional errors, both assets and owner's equity will be correctly stated. To illustrate, assume that the ending inventory for period 1 was understated by $10,000, and no other errors are made. The gross profit (and net income) would be understated for period 1 and overstated for period 2 by $10,000, indicated as follows:

	Period 1		Period 2	
	No Error	Error	Error	No Error
Net sales.....................	$90,000	$90,000	$85,000	$85,000
Cost of merchandise sold:				
Beginning inventory...........	$25,000	$25,000	$20,000	$30,000
Purchases	70,000	70,000	65,000	65,000
Merchandise available for sale .	$95,000	$95,000	$85,000	$95,000
Less ending inventory.........	30,000	20,000	28,000	28,000
Cost of merchandise sold ...	65,000	75,000	57,000	67,000
Gross profit...................	$25,000	$15,000	$28,000	$18,000

Understated $10,000   Overstated $10,000

In the illustration, the $10,000 understatement of inventory at the end of period 1 resulted in an overstatement of the cost of merchandise sold and thus an understatement of gross profit by $10,000. On the balance sheet, merchandise inventory and owner's equity would both be understated by $10,000. Because the ending inventory of period 1 becomes the beginning inventory for period 2, the cost of merchandise sold was understated and gross profit was overstated by $10,000 for period 2. Both merchandise inventory and owner's equity will be correct at the end of period 2.

INVENTORY SYSTEMS

There are two principal systems of inventory accounting — periodic and perpetual. When the **periodic inventory system** is used, only the revenue from sales is recorded each time a sale is made. No entry is made at the time of the sale to record the cost of the merchandise that has been sold. Consequently, a **physical inventory** must be taken in order to determine the cost of the inventory at the end of an accounting period. Ordinarily, it is practical to take a complete physical inventory only at the end of the fiscal year. In the earlier chapters dealing with purchases and sales of merchandise, the use of the periodic system was assumed.

In contrast to the periodic system, the **perpetual inventory system** uses accounting records that continuously disclose the amount of the inventory. A separate account for each type of merchandise is maintained in a subsidiary ledger. Increases in inventory items are recorded as debits to the proper accounts, and decreases are recorded as credits. The balances of the accounts are called the **book inventories** of the items on hand. Regardless of the care with which the perpetual inventory records are maintained, their accuracy must be tested by taking a physical inventory of each type of commodity at least once a year. The records are then compared with the actual quantities on hand and any differences are corrected.

The periodic inventory system is often used by retail enterprises that sell many kinds of low unit cost merchandise, such as groceries, hardware, and drugs. The expense of maintaining perpetual inventory records may be prohibitive in such cases. In recent years, however, the use of computerized systems in such businesses has reduced this expense considerably. Firms selling a relatively small number of high unit cost items, such as office equipment, automobiles, or fur garments, are more likely to use the perpetual system.

Although much of the discussion that follows applies to both systems, the use of the periodic inventory system will be assumed. Later in the chapter, principles and procedures related only to the perpetual inventory system will be presented.

DETERMINING ACTUAL QUANTITIES IN THE INVENTORY

The first stage in the process of "taking" an inventory is to determine the quantity of each kind of merchandise owned by the enterprise. When the periodic system is used, the counting, weighing, and measuring should be done at the end of the accounting period. To accomplish this, the inventory crew may work during the night, or business operations may be stopped until the count is finished.

The details of the specific procedures for determining quantities and assembling the data differ among companies. A common practice is to use teams made up of two persons. One person counts, weighs, or otherwise determines quantity, and the other lists the description and the quantity on inventory sheets. The quantity indicated for high-cost items is verified by a third person at some time during the inventory-taking period. It is also advisable for the third person to verify other items selected at random from the inventory sheets.

All of the merchandise owned by the business on the inventory date, and only such merchandise, should be included in the inventory. It may be necessary to examine purchase and sales invoices of the last few days of the accounting period and the first few days of the following period to determine who has legal title to merchandise in transit on the inventory date. When goods are purchased or sold **FOB shipping point**, title usually passes to the buyer when the goods are shipped. When the terms are **FOB destination**, title usually does not pass to the buyer until the goods are delivered. To illustrate, assume that merchandise purchased FOB shipping point is shipped by the seller on the last day of the buyer's fiscal period. The merchandise does not arrive until the following period and hence is not available for "counting" by the inventory crew. However, such merchandise should be included in the buyer's inventory because title has passed. It is also evident that a debit to Purchases and a credit to Accounts Payable should be recorded by the buyer as of the end of the period, rather than recording it as a transaction of the following period.

Another example, although less common, will further show the importance of closely examining transactions involving shipments of merchandise. Manufacturers sometimes ship merchandise on a consignment basis to retailers who act as the manufacturer's agent when selling the merchandise. The manufacturer retains title until the goods are sold. Obviously, such unsold merchandise is a part of the manufacturer's (consignor's) inventory, even though the manufacturer does not have physical possession. It is just as obvious that the consigned merchandise should not be included in the retailer's (consignee's) inventory.

DETERMINING THE COST OF INVENTORY

The cost of merchandise inventory is made up of the purchase price and all expenditures incurred in acquiring such merchandise, including transportation, customs duties, and insurance against losses in transit. The purchase price can be readily determined, as may some of the other costs. Those that are difficult to associate with specific inventory items may be prorated on some equitable basis. Minor costs that are difficult to allocate may be left out entirely from inventory cost and treated as operating expenses of the period.

If purchases discounts are treated as a deduction from purchases on the income statement, they should also be deducted from the purchase price of items in the inventory. If it is not possible to determine the exact amount of discount applicable to each inventory item, a pro rata amount of the total discount for the period may be deducted instead. For example, if net purchases and purchases discounts for the period amount to $200,000 and $3,000 respectively, the discounts represent 1½% of net purchases. If the inventory cost, before considering the cash discounts is $30,000, the amount may be reduced by 1½%, or $450, to yield an inventory cost of $29,550.

INVENTORY COSTING METHODS UNDER A PERIODIC SYSTEM

One of the most significant problems in determining inventory cost comes about when identical units of a certain commodity have been acquired at different unit cost prices during the period. In such cases, it is necessary to determine the unit prices of the items still on hand. To illustrate this problem and its relationship to the determination of net income and inventory cost, assume that three identical units of Commodity X were available for sale to customers during the fiscal year. One of these units was in the inventory at the beginning of the year, and the other two were purchased on March 4 and May 9 respectively. The costs per unit are as follows:

Commodity X	Units	Cost
Jan. 1 Inventory	1	$ 9
Mar. 4 Purchase	1	13
May 9 Purchase	1	14
Total................................	3	$36
Average cost per unit		$12

During the year, two units of Commodity X were sold, leaving one unit in the inventory at the end of the year. In the illustration and in actual practice, it may be possible to identify units with specific expenditures if both the variety of merchandise carried in stock and the volume of sales are relatively small. Ordinarily, however, **specific identification** procedures are too costly and too time consuming to justify their use. It is customary, therefore, to use an arbitrary assumption as to the *flow of costs* of merchandise through the enterprise. The three most common assumptions of determining the cost of the merchandise sold are as follows:

1. Cost flow is in the order in which the expenditures were made—first-in, first-out.
2. Cost flow is in the reverse order in which the expenditures were made—last-in, first-out.
3. Cost flow is an average of the expenditures.

Details of the cost of the two units of Commodity X assumed to be sold and the cost of the one unit remaining, determined in accordance with each of these assumptions, are as follows:

	Commodity X Costs		
	Units Available	Units Sold	Unit Remaining
1. In order of expenditures (first-in, first-out)........	$36	− ($ 9 + $13) =	$14
2. In reverse order of expenditures (last-in, first-out)	36	− (14 + 13) =	9
3. In accordance with average expenditures........	36	− (12 + 12) =	12

The three most widely used inventory costing methods (which correspond to the three assumptions of cost flows illustrated) are:

1. **First-in, first-out (fifo)**
2. **Last-in, first-out (lifo)**
3. **Average**

The extent of the use of these three methods is indicated by the following chart:

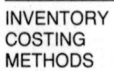

INVENTORY
COSTING
METHODS

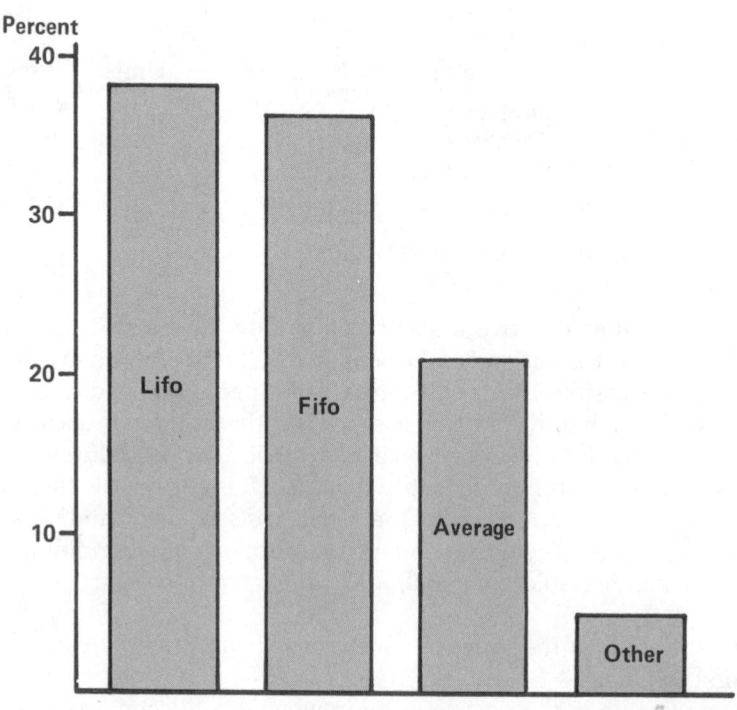

Source: Accounting Trends & Techniques, 39th ed. (New York: American Institute of Certified Public Accountants, 1985).

First-In, First-Out Method

The first-in, first-out (fifo) method of costing inventory is based on the assumption that costs should be charged against revenue in the order in which they were incurred. Hence the inventory remaining is assumed to be made up of the most recent costs. The illustration of the application of this method is based on the following data for a particular commodity:

Jan. 1	Inventory	200 units at $ 9	$ 1,800
Mar. 10	Purchase	300 units at 10	3,000
Sept. 21	Purchase	400 units at 11	4,400
Nov. 18	Purchase	100 units at 12	1,200
	Available for sale during year	1,000	$10,400

The physical count on December 31 shows that 300 units of the particular commodity are on hand. In accordance with the assumption that the inventory is composed of the most recent costs, the cost of the 300 units is determined as follows:

Most recent costs, Nov. 18	100 units at $12	$1,200
Next most recent costs, Sept. 21	200 units at 11	2,200
Inventory, Dec. 31	300	$3,400

Deduction of the inventory of **$3,400** from the **$10,400** of merchandise available for sale yields **$7,000** as the cost of merchandise sold, which represents the earliest costs incurred for this commodity. The relationship of the inventory at December 31 and the cost of merchandise sold during the year is illustrated in the following diagram:

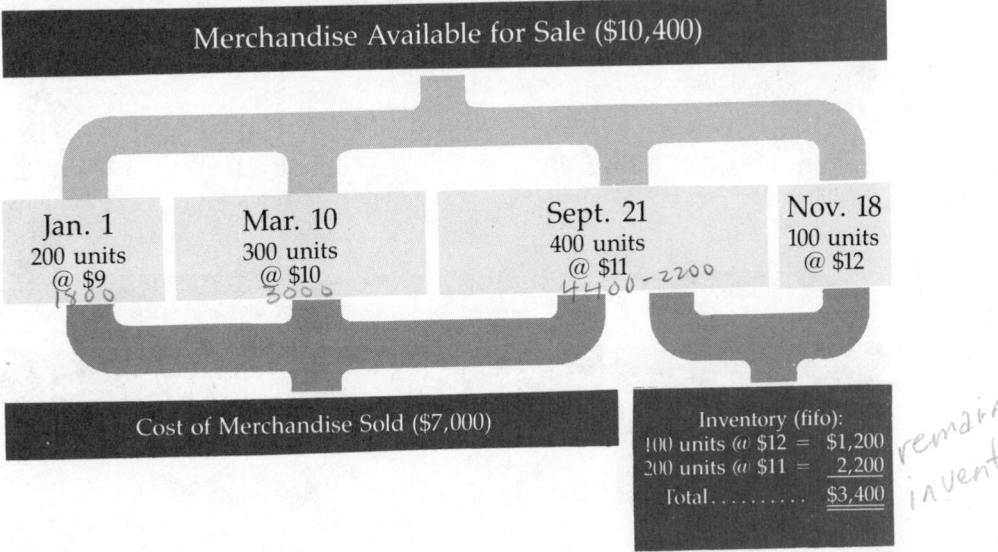

In most businesses, there is a tendency to dispose of goods in the order of their acquisition. This would be particularly true of perishable merchandise and goods in which style or model changes are frequent. Thus, the fifo method is generally in harmony with the physical movement of merchandise in an enterprise. To the extent that this is the case, the fifo method approximates the results that would be obtained by the specific identification of costs.

Last-In, First-Out Method

The last-in, first-out (lifo) method is based on the assumption that the most recent costs incurred should be charged against revenue. Hence the inventory remaining is assumed to be composed of the earliest costs. Based on the illustrative data presented in the preceding section, the cost of the 300 units of inventory is determined in the following manner:

Earliest costs, Jan. 1...............	200 units at $ 9	$1,800
Next earliest costs, Mar. 10........	100 units at 10	1,000
Inventory, Dec. 31	300	$2,800

Deduction of the inventory of $2,800 from the $10,400 of merchandise available for sale yields $7,600 as the cost of merchandise sold, which represents the most recent costs incurred for this particular commodity. The relationship of the inventory at December 31 and the cost of merchandise sold during the year is illustrated in the following diagram:

The use of the lifo method was originally confined to the relatively rare situations in which the units sold were taken from the most recently acquired stock. Its use has greatly increased during the past few decades, and it is now often used even when it does not represent the physical flow of goods.

Average Cost Method

$$\frac{Total\ cost}{Total\ units} = Avg\ cost/unit$$

The average cost method, sometimes called the **weighted average method**, is based on the assumption that costs should be charged against revenue according to the weighted average unit costs of the goods sold. The same weighted average unit costs are used in determining the cost of the merchandise remaining in the inventory. The weighted average unit cost is determined by dividing the total cost of the identical units of each commodity available for sale during the period by the related number of units of that commodity. Assuming the same cost data as in the preceding illustrations, the average cost of the 1,000 units and the cost of the 300 units in inventory are determined as follows:

```
Average unit cost.......... $10,400 ÷ 1,000 = $10.40
Inventory, Dec. 31 ........ 300 units at $10.40................. $3,120
```

Deduction of the inventory of **$3,120** from the **$10,400** of merchandise available for sale yields **$7,280** as the cost of merchandise sold, which represents the average of the costs incurred for this commodity.

For businesses in which various purchases of identical units of a commodity are mingled, the average method has some relationship to the physical flow of goods.

Comparison of Inventory Costing Methods

Each of the three alternative methods of costing inventories under the periodic system is based on a different assumption as to the flow of costs. If the cost of units and prices at which they were sold had remained stable, all three methods would have yielded the same results. Prices do change, however, and as a consequence the three methods will usually yield different amounts for (1) the inventory reported on the balance sheet at the end of the period, (2) the cost of the merchandise sold for the period, and (3) the gross profit (and net income) reported for the period. Using the examples presented in the preceding sections and assuming that net sales were $15,000, the following partial income statements indicate the effects of each method when prices are rising:

	First-In, First-Out	Average Cost	Last-In, First-Out
Net sales.........................	$15,000	$15,000	$15,000
Cost of merchandise sold:			
Beginning inventory..............	$ 1,800	$ 1,800	$ 1,800
Purchases.....................	8,600	8,600	8,600
Merchandise available for sale....	$10,400	$10,400	$10,400
Less ending inventory..........	3,400	3,120	2,800
Cost of merchandise sold	7,000	7,280	7,600
Gross profit.....................	$ 8,000	$ 7,720	$ 7,400

As shown in the income statements, the fifo method yielded the lowest amount for the cost of merchandise sold and the highest amount for gross profit (and net income). It also yielded the highest amount for the ending inventory. On the other hand, the lifo method yielded the highest amount for the cost of merchandise sold, the lowest amount for gross profit (and net income), and the lowest amount for ending inventory. The average cost method yielded results that were between those of fifo and lifo.

Use of the first-in, first-out method. During a period of inflation or rising prices, the use of the fifo method will result in the effects shown in the illustration because the costs of the units sold are assumed to be in the order in which they were incurred, and the earlier unit costs were lower than the more recent unit costs. Much of the benefit of the larger amount of gross profit is lost, however, as the inventory is continually replenished at ever higher prices. During the 1970s, when the rate of inflation increased to double-digit percentages, the larger gross profits that resulted were frequently referred to as *inventory profits* or *illusory profits.*

In a period of deflation or declining prices, the effect described above is reversed, and the fifo method yields the lowest amount of gross profit. The major criticism of the fifo method is this tendency to maximize the effect of inflationary and deflationary trends on amounts reported as gross profit. However, the dollar amount reported as merchandise inventory on the balance sheet will usually be about the same as its current replacement cost.

Use of the last-in, first-out method. During a period of rising prices, the use of the last-in, first-out method will result in a lower amount of inventory at the end of the period, a higher amount of cost of merchandise sold, and a lower amount of gross profit than the other two methods. The reason for these effects is that the cost of the most recently acquired units most nearly approximates the cost of their replacement, and the more recent unit costs were higher than the earlier unit costs. Thus, it can be argued that the use of the lifo method more nearly matches current costs with current revenues. This latter point was one reason that Chrysler Corporation changed from the fifo method to the lifo method in 1984, as stated in the following footnote that accompanied Chrysler's financial statements for 1984:

> Effective January 1, 1984, Chrysler changed its method of accounting from first-in, first-out (fifo) to last-in, first-out (lifo) for substantially all of its domestic productive inventories. The change to lifo was made to more accurately match current costs with current revenues. Had the inventory, at December 31, 1984, been valued on the fifo basis, it would have been $29.7 million higher than reported.

During periods of rising prices, the use of lifo offers a savings in income taxes. The income tax savings results because lifo reports the lowest amount of net income of the three methods. During the accelerated inflationary trend of the 1970s, many business enterprises changed from fifo to lifo to take advantage of this tax savings.

In a period of deflation or falling price levels, the effect described above is reversed and the lifo method yields the highest amount of gross profit. The major justification for lifo is this tendency to minimize the effect of price trends on reported gross profit and, therefore, to exert a stabilizing influence on the economy. A criticism of the use of lifo is that the dollar amount reported for merchandise inventory on the balance sheet may be quite far removed from the current replacement cost. In such situations, however, it is customary to indicate in a note accompanying the published financial statements the approximate difference between the lifo inventory amount and the inventory amount if fifo had been used. The following note accompanying the 1984 statements of Magic Chef Inc. is illustrative:

> Inventories are generally computed using the lifo inventory method, which the Company believes more realistically matches current costs and current revenues. Had the Company's inventories been valued on the fifo method, inventories would have been $29,247,000, $27,491,000 and $29,130,000 higher at June 30, 1984, July 2, 1983, and July 3, 1982, respectively.

Use of the average cost method. The average cost method of inventory costing is, in a sense, a compromise between fifo and lifo. The effect of price trends is averaged, both in the determination of gross profit and in the determination of inventory cost. For any given series of acquisitions, the average cost will be the same, regardless of the direction of price trends. For example, a complete reversal of the sequence of unit costs presented in the illustration on page 427 would not affect the reported gross profit or the inventory cost. The time required to assemble the data is likely to be greater for the average cost method than for the other two methods. The additional expense incurred could be large if there are many purchases of a wide variety of merchandise items.

Inflation and Adoption of Lifo

As inflation began heating up in the 1970s, corporate managers turned with increasing interest to the last-in, first-out (lifo) method of inventory valuation as a means of improving the quality of reported earnings and deferring income taxes.

The primary advantage of lifo is that in today's inflationary environment lifo defers (not avoids) income taxes by reducing income. The improved cash flow, then, can be profitably invested or used to reduce borrowings.

In addition to deferring income taxes, though, lifo has a great deal of theoretical justification. By matching current costs against current sales, lifo produces a truer picture of income; that is, the quality of income produced by the use of lifo is higher because it more nearly approximates disposable income.

Even though the primary advantage of lifo—reduced tax payments—is a function of lower income, the negative earnings impact ironically continues to cloud corporate managers' decisions about the adoption of lifo. Managers fear that lower reported earnings will have unfavorable effects on the stock price, executive compensation contracts, and credit ratings. However, there is little evidence to suggest that stock price is adversely affected by lifo adoption. Furthermore, lifo should have no effect on executive compensation contracts or credit ratings.

The Internal Revenue Code and Treasury Regulations mandate that taxpayers who avail themselves of the federal income tax benefits of the lifo method also must use lifo "...for credit purposes or for purposes of reports to shareholders, partners, or other proprietors, or to beneficiaries...." Thus, the lifo conformity requirement is the culprit behind the negative earnings impact issue. However, regulations adopted in January, 1981, although not going to the extent of allowing the use of lifo in tax returns and a non-lifo method elsewhere, did relax the conformity requirement significantly, such that it is now possible to present non-lifo information very favorably in lifo-based reports.

The non-lifo data may be presented in the notes to the financial statements as in the 1981 Merck & Co. Inc. Annual Report:

> ...Lifo had the effect of reducing 1981 net income by $21,108,000 ($.28 per share)...with a positive increase to cash flow of $19,500,000...as a result of decreased U.S. taxes.

Another concern about lifo commonly expressed by corporate managers is misstatement of the inventories on the lifo balance sheet. Particularly over a period of rapidly rising inventory quantities and prices, the use of lifo can lead to a valuation of inventories that is significantly less than current replacement cost. However, this misstatement can be mitigated by presenting inventories valued on a non-lifo basis and deducting the lifo valuation allowance to reduce the balance sheet inventory to the lifo amount, as follows:

Inventory	XXX
Less reduction to lifo cost	XXX
Total	XXX

Source: Adapted from Clayton T. Rumble, "So You Still Have Not Adopted Lifo," *Management Accounting* (October, 1983), pp. 59–67.

Selection of an inventory costing method. The foregoing comparisons show the importance attached to the selection of the inventory costing method. It is not unusual for manufacturing enterprises to apply one method to a particular class of inventory, such as merchandise ready for sale, and a different method to another class, such as raw materials purchased. The method(s) used may be changed for a valid reason. The effect of any change in method and the reason for the change should be fully disclosed in the financial statements for the fiscal period in which the change occurred.

VALUATION OF INVENTORY AT OTHER THAN COST

As discussed in the preceding section, cost is the primary basis for the valuation of inventories. Under certain circumstances, however, inventory may be valued at other than cost. Two such circumstances arise when (1) the cost of replacing items in inventory is below recorded cost, and (2) the inventory is not salable at normal sales prices because of imperfections, shop wear, style changes, or other causes.

Valuation at Lower of Cost or Market

If the market price of an item in inventory is lower than its cost, an alternative to valuing inventory at cost is to use the **lower of cost or market** method. It should be noted that regardless of the method used (cost, or lower of cost or market), it is first necessary to determine the cost of the inventory. "Market," as used in the phrase lower of cost or market, is interpreted to mean the cost to replace the merchandise on the inventory date, based on quantities typically purchased from the usual source of supply. In the discussion that follows, the salability of the merchandise at normal sales prices will be assumed. Articles that have to be sold at a price below their cost would be valued at their net realizable value, as described on page 434.

If the replacement price of an item in the inventory is lower than its cost, the use of the lower of cost or market method provides two advantages: (1) the gross profit (and net income) are reduced for the period in which the decline occurred and (2) an approximately normal gross profit is realized during the period in which the item is sold. To illustrate, assume that merchandise with a unit cost of $70 has sold at $100 during the period, yielding a gross profit of $30 a unit, or 30% of sales. Assume also that at the end of the year, there is a single unit of the commodity in the inventory and that its replacement price has declined to $63. Under such circumstances it would be reasonable to expect that the selling price would also decline, if indeed it had not already done so. Assuming a reduction in selling price to $90, the gross profit based on replacement cost of $63 would be $27, which is also 30% of the selling price. Accordingly, valuation of the unit in the inventory at $63 reduces gross profit of the past period by $7 and permits a normal gross profit of $27 to be realized on its sale in the following period. If the unit had been valued at its original cost of $70, the gross profit determined for the past year would have been $7 greater, and the gross profit attributable to the sale of the item in the following period would have been $7 less.

It would be possible to apply the lower of cost or market basis (1) to each item in the inventory, (2) to major classes or categories, or (3) to the inventory as a whole. The first procedure is the one usually followed in practice. To illustrate the application of the lower of cost or market to individual items, assume that there are 400 identical units of Commodity A in the inventory, each acquired at a unit cost of $10.25. If at the inventory date the commodity would cost $10.50 to replace, the cost price of $10.25 would be multiplied by 400 to determine the inventory value. On the other hand, if the commodity could be replaced at $9.50 a unit, the replacement price of $9.50 would be used for valuation purposes. The following tabulation illustrates one of the forms that may be followed in assembling inventory data.

DETERMI-
NATION OF
INVENTORY
AT LOWER
OF COST OR
MARKET

Description	Quantity	Unit Cost Price	Unit Market Price	Total Cost	Total Lower of C or M
Commodity A	400	$10.25	$ 9.50	$ 4,100	$ 3,800
Commodity B	120	22.50	24.10	2,700	2,700
Commodity C	600	8.00	7.75	4,800	4,650
Commodity D	280	14.00	14.00	3,920	3,920
Total...				$15,520	$15,070

Although it is not essential to accumulate the data for total cost, as in the illustration, it permits the measurement of the reduction in inventory value as a result of a decline in market prices. When the amount of the market decline is known ($15,520 − $15,070, or $450), it may be reported as a separate item on the income statement. Otherwise, the market decline will be included in the amount reported as the cost of merchandise sold and will reduce gross profit by a corresponding amount. In any event, the amount reported as net income will not be affected. It will be the same, regardless of whether the amount of the market decline is determined and separately stated.

As with the method elected for the determination of inventory cost (first-in, first-out; last-in, first-out; or average cost), the method elected for inventory valuation (cost, or lower of cost or market) must be followed consistently from year to year.

Valuation at Net Realizable Value

Obsolete, spoiled, or damaged merchandise and other merchandise that can be sold only at prices below cost should be valued at **net realizable value**. For this purpose, net realizable value is the estimated selling price less any direct cost of disposition, such as sales commissions. To illustrate, assume that damaged merchandise that had a cost of $1,000 can be sold for only $800, and direct selling expenses are estimated at $150. This inventory would be valued at $650 ($800−$150), which is its net realizable value.

ACCOUNTING FOR AND REPORTING INVENTORY UNDER A PERPETUAL SYSTEM

The use of a perpetual inventory system for merchandise provides the most effective means of control over this important asset. Although it is possible to maintain a perpetual inventory in memorandum records only or to limit the data to quantities, a complete set of records integrated with the general ledger is preferable. With the widespread use of computers, integrated perpetual inventory systems are being used by more and more companies.

Under the periodic inventory system, as described in earlier chapters, the merchandise inventory account at the beginning of an accounting period reflects the merchandise on hand on that date. Purchases of merchandise are recorded in the purchases account, and sales of merchandise are recorded in the sales account. The cost of the merchandise sold is not determined for each sale. Instead, at the end of an accounting period, when a physical inventory is taken, two adjusting entries are made.[1] With these entries, the beginning inventory is removed from the merchandise inventory account and is replaced by the ending inventory. This adjusted balance of merchandise inventory is reported on the balance sheet. The cost of merchandise sold is then determined, and this amount is reported on the income statement.

Under the perpetual inventory system, all merchandise increases and decreases are recorded in a manner somewhat similar to the recording of increases and decreases in cash. The merchandise inventory account at the beginning of an accounting period reflects the merchandise on hand on that date. Sales are recorded in the sales account and, on the date of each sale, the cost of the merchandise sold is recorded by debiting Cost of Merchandise Sold and crediting Merchandise Inventory. Thus, in the perpetual system, the merchandise inventory account continuously (perpetually) discloses the balance of merchandise on hand. At the end of the period, the balance in the merchandise inventory account is reported on the balance sheet, and the balance in the cost of merchandise sold account is reported on the income statement.

---

[1]An alternative method of recording merchandise inventory is presented in Appendix C.

The accounting for and reporting of merchandise inventory transactions under the periodic and perpetual systems are compared and illustrated as follows:

Inventory, Purchases, and Sales Data

January	1	Merchandise inventory (beginning)............................	$52,500
	1–31	Purchases (on account)	26,200
	1–31	Sales (on account) — selling price	49,750
		Sales — cost price	28,000
	31	Merchandise inventory (ending)	50,700

Periodic	Perpetual

January 1 Merchandise Inventory

Periodic	Perpetual
Merchandise inventory account reflects inventory on hand, $52,500.	Merchandise inventory account reflects inventory on hand, $52,500.

Entries to Record Purchases, January 1–31

Periodic			Perpetual		
Purchases	26,200		Merchandise Inventory ..	26,200	
Accounts Payable		26,200	Accounts Payable		26,200

Entries to Record Sales, January 1–31

Periodic			Perpetual		
Accounts Receivable....	49,750		Accounts Receivable....	49,750	
Sales................		49,750	Sales................		49,750
			Cost of Merchandise Sold	28,000	
			Merchandise Inventory .		28,000

Adjusting Entries for January 31 Merchandise Inventory

Periodic			Perpetual
Income Summary.......	52,500		No entries necessary
Merchandise Inventory		52,500	
Merchandise Inventory ..	50,700		
Income Summary.....		50,700	

Reporting Cost of Merchandise Sold in January on Income Statement

Periodic			Perpetual	
Cost of merchandise sold:			Cost of merchandise sold.........	$28,000
Jan. 1 inventory	$52,500			
January purchases....	26,200			
Merchandise available				
for sale...........	$78,700			
Less Jan. 31 inventory .	50,700			
Cost of merchandise				
sold..............		$28,000		

Reporting Merchandise Inventory, January 31, on Balance Sheet

Periodic		Perpetual	
Merchandise inventory	$50,700	Merchandise inventory	$50,700

INVENTORY COSTING METHODS UNDER A PERPETUAL SYSTEM

Unlike cash, merchandise is a mixed mass of goods. Details of the cost of each type of merchandise purchased and sold, together with such related transactions as returns and allowances, must be maintained in a subsidiary **inventory ledger**, with a separate account for each type. Whether this ledger is computerized or maintained manually, it is customary to use one of the three costing methods—first-in, first out; last-in, first-out; or average.

In the following paragraphs, the fifo and lifo methods in a perpetual system are discussed and illustrated. The average cost method is briefly discussed also, but an illustration is reserved for advanced texts.

The basis for the fifo and lifo illustrations is the following data for merchandise identified as Commodity 127B:

			Units	Cost
Jan.	1	Inventory	10	$20
	4	Sale	7	
	10	Purchase	8	21
	22	Sale	4	
	28	Sale	2	
	30	Purchase	10	22

First-In, First-Out Method

To illustrate the first-in, first-out method of cost flow in a perpetual inventory system, the inventory ledger account for Commodity 127B is as follows. The number of units on hand after each transaction, together with total costs and unit costs, appears in the inventory section of the account.

Commodity 127B

Date	Purchases			Cost of Merchandise Sold			Inventory		
	Quantity	Unit Cost	Total Cost	Quantity	Unit Cost	Total Cost	Quantity	Unit Cost	Total Cost
Jan. 1							10	20	200
4				7	20	140	3	20	60
10	8	21	168				3	20	60
							8	21	168
22				3	20	60			
				1	21	21	7	21	147
28				2	21	42	5	21	105
30	10	22	220				5	21	105
							10	22	220

PERPETUAL INVENTORY ACCOUNT (FIFO)

Note that after the 7 units of the commodity were sold on January 4, there was a remaining inventory of 3 units at $20 each. The 8 units purchased on January 10 were acquired at a unit cost of $21, instead of $20, and hence could not be combined with the 3 units. The inventory after the January 10 purchase is therefore reported on two lines, 3 units at $20 each and 8 units at $21 each. Next, it should be noted that the $81 cost of the 4 units sold on January 22 is composed of the remaining 3 units at $20 each and 1 unit at $21. At this point, 7 units remain in inventory at a cost of $21 per unit. The remainder of the illustration is explained in a similar manner.

Last-In, First-Out Method

When the last-in, first-out method is used in a perpetual inventory system, the cost of the units sold is the cost of the most recent purchases. To illustrate, the ledger account for Commodity 127B, prepared on a lifo basis, is as follows:

PERPETUAL INVENTORY ACCOUNT (LIFO)

Commodity 127B

Date	Purchases			Cost of Merchandise Sold			Inventory		
	Quantity	Unit Cost	Total Cost	Quantity	Unit Cost	Total Cost	Quantity	Unit Cost	Total Cost
Jan. 1							10	20	200
4				7	20	140	3	20	60
10	8	21	168				3 8	20 21	60 .168
22				4	21	84	3 4	20 21	60 84
28				2	21	42	3 2	20 21	60 42
30	10	22	220				3 2 10	20 21 22	60 42 220

A comparison of the ledger accounts for the fifo perpetual system and the lifo perpetual system indicates that the accounts are the same through the January 10 purchase. Using the lifo perpetual system, however, the cost of the 4 units sold on January 22 is the cost of the units from the January 10 purchase ($21 per unit). The cost of the 7 units in inventory after the sale on January 22 is the cost of the 3 units remaining from the beginning inventory and the cost of the 4 units remaining from the January 10 purchase. The remainder of the lifo illustration is explained in a similar manner.

Average Cost Method

When the average cost method is used in a perpetual inventory system, an average unit cost for each type of commodity is computed each time a purchase is made, rather than at the end of the period. This unit cost is then used to determine the cost of each sale, until another purchase is made and a new average is computed. This averaging technique is called a **moving average**.

INTERNAL CONTROL AND PERPETUAL INVENTORY SYSTEMS

The control feature is the most important advantage of the perpetual system. The inventory of each type of merchandise is always readily available in the subsidiary ledger. A physical count of any type of merchandise can be made at any time and compared with the balance of the subsidiary account to determine the existence and seriousness of any shortages. When a shortage is discovered, an entry is made debiting Inventory Shortages and crediting Merchandise Inventory for the cost. If the balance of the inventory shortages account at the end of a fiscal period is relatively small, it may be included in miscellaneous general expense on the income statement. Otherwise it may be separately reported in the general expense section.

In addition to the usefulness of the perpetual inventory system in the preparation of interim statements, the subsidiary ledger can be an aid in maintaining inventory quantities at an optimum level. Frequent comparisons of balances with predetermined maximum and minimum levels facilitate both (1) the timely reordering of merchandise to avoid the loss of sales and (2) the avoidance of excess inventory.

AUTOMATED PERPETUAL INVENTORY RECORDS

A perpetual inventory system may be maintained using manually kept records. However, such a system is often too costly and too time consuming for enterprises with a large number of inventory items and/or with many purchase and sales transactions. In such cases, because of the mass of data to be processed, the frequently recurring and routine nature of the processing, and the importance of speed and accuracy, the record keeping is often computerized. A computerized inventory system operates with little human intervention.

One use of computers in maintaining perpetual inventory records for retail stores is described in the following outline:

1. The quantity of inventory for each commodity, along with its color, unit size or other descriptive data, and any other information desired, is stored in the computer.
2. Each time a commodity is purchased, or is returned by a customer, the data are recorded and processed by the computer, so that the inventory records are updated.
3. Each time a commodity is sold, a salesclerk passes an electronic wand over the price tag attached to the merchandise. The electronic wand "reads" the magnetic code on the price tag. The information provided in the magnetic code is used by the computer to update the inventory records.
4. Data from a physical inventory count are periodically entered into the computer. These data are compared with the current balances and a listing of the overages and shortages is printed. The appropriate commodity balances are adjusted to the quantities determined by the physical count.

By entering additional data, the system described can be extended to aid in maintaining inventory quantities at optimum levels. For example, data on the most economical quantity to be purchased in a single order and the minimum quantity to be maintained for each commodity can be entered into the computer. The equipment is then programmed to compare these data with data on actual inventory and to start the purchasing activity by preparing purchase orders.

The system can also be extended to aid in processing the related accounting transactions. For example, as cash sales are entered on an electronic cash register, the sales data can be accumulated and used for the appropriate accounting entries. These entries would include a debit to Cash and a credit to Sales as well as a debit to Cost of Merchandise Sold and a credit to Merchandise Inventory.

PRESENTATION OF MERCHANDISE INVENTORY ON THE BALANCE SHEET

Merchandise inventory is usually presented on the balance sheet immediately following receivables. Both the method of determining the cost of the inventory (fifo, lifo, or average) and the method of valuing the inventory (cost, or lower of cost or market) should be shown. Both are important to the reader. The details may be disclosed by a parenthetical notation or a footnote. The use of a parenthetical notation is illustrated by the following partial balance sheet:

Afro-Arts Company
Balance Sheet
December 31, 1987

Assets

Current assets:

Cash...		$ 19,400
Accounts receivable.............................	$80,000	
Less allowance for doubtful accounts.............	3,000	77,000
Merchandise inventory—at lower of cost (first-in, first-out method) or market......................		216,300

It is not unusual for large enterprises with diversified activities to use different costing methods for different segments of their inventories. The following note taken from the 1984 financial statements of Black and Decker Manufacturing Company is illustrative:

> Inventories are stated at the lower of cost or market. The cost of United States inventories is based on the last-in, first-out (lifo) method; all other inventories are based on the first-in, first-out (fifo) method.

ESTIMATING INVENTORY COST

In practice, an inventory amount may be needed in order to prepare an income statement when it is impractical or impossible to take a physical inventory or to maintain perpetual inventory records. For example, taking a physical inventory each month may be too costly, even though monthly income statements are desired. Taking a physical inventory may be impossible when a catastrophe, such as a fire, has destroyed the inventory. In such cases, the inventory cost might be estimated for use in preparing the income statement. Two commonly used methods of estimating inventory cost are (1) the retail method and (2) the gross profit method.

Retail Method of Inventory Costing

The **retail inventory method** of inventory costing is widely used by retail businesses, particularly department stores. It is based on the relationship of the cost of merchandise available for sale to the retail price of the same merchandise. The retail prices of all merchandise acquired are accumulated in supplementary records, and the inventory at retail is determined by deducting sales for the period from the retail price of the goods that were available for sale during the period. The inventory at retail is then converted to cost on the basis of the ratio of cost to selling (retail) price for the merchandise available for sale. Determination of inventory by the retail method is illustrated as follows:

DETERMI-
NATION OF
INVENTORY
BY RETAIL
METHOD

	Cost	Retail
Merchandise inventory, January 1	$19,400	$ 36,000
Purchases in January (net)	42,600	64,000
Merchandise available for sale	$62,000	$100,000

Ratio of cost to retail price: $\dfrac{\$62,000}{\$100,000} = 62\%$

Sales for January (net)		70,000
Merchandise inventory, January 31, at retail		$ 30,000
Merchandise inventory, January 31, at estimated cost		
($30,000 × 62%)		$ 18,600

subtract Sales (Jan) from MAS → (handwritten annotation)

There is an inherent assumption in the retail method of inventory costing that the composition or "mix" of the commodities in the ending inventory, in terms of percent of cost to selling price, is comparable to the entire stock of merchandise available for sale. In the illustration, for example, it is unlikely that the retail price of every item was composed of exactly 62% cost and 38% gross profit. It is assumed, however, that the weighted average of the cost percentages of the merchandise in the inventory ($30,000) is the same as in the merchandise available for sale ($100,000). When the inventory is made up of different classes of merchandise with very different gross profit rates, the cost percentages and the inventory should be developed separately for each class.

One of the major advantages of the retail method is that it provides inventory figures for use in preparing interim statements. Department stores and similar merchandisers usually determine gross profit and operating income each month but take a physical inventory only once a year. In addition to facilitating frequent income determinations, a comparison of the computed ending inventory with the physical ending inventory, both at retail prices, will help identify inventory shortages resulting from shoplifting and other causes. The appropriate corrective measures can then be taken.

The retail method can also be used in conjunction with the periodic system when a physical inventory is taken at the end of the year. In such a case, the items counted are recorded on the inventory sheets at their selling prices instead of their cost prices. The physical inventory at selling price is then converted to cost by applying the ratio of cost to selling (retail) price for the merchandise available for sale. To illustrate, assume that the data presented in the example above are for an entire fiscal year rather than for the first month of the year only. If the physical inventory taken on December 31 totaled $29,000, priced at retail, it would be this amount rather than the $30,000 that would be converted to cost. Accordingly, the inventory at cost would be $17,980 ($29,000 × 62%) instead of $18,600 ($30,000 × 62%). The

$17,980 is generally accepted for use on the year-end financial statements and for income tax purposes.

Gross Profit Method of Estimating Inventories

[handwritten: can use reciprocal]

The **gross profit method** uses an estimate of the gross profit realized during the period to estimate the inventory at the end of the period. By using the rate of gross profit, the dollar amount of sales for a period can be divided into its two components: (1) gross profit and (2) cost of merchandise sold. The latter may then be deducted from the cost of merchandise available for sale to yield the estimated inventory of merchandise on hand.

To illustrate this method, assume that the inventory on January 1 is $57,000, that net purchases during the month are $180,000, that net sales during the month are $250,000, and finally that gross profit is *estimated* to be 30% of net sales. The inventory on January 31 may be estimated as follows:

Merchandise inventory, January 1.		$ 57,000	ESTIMATE OF INVENTORY
Purchases in January (net).		180,000	BY GROSS
Merchandise available for sale.		$237,000	PROFIT METHOD
Sales in January (net)	$250,000		
Less estimated gross profit ($250,000 × 30%) . .	75,000		
Estimated cost of merchandise sold.		175,000	
Estimated merchandise inventory, January 31 . . .		$ 62,000	

[handwritten annotation: at cost]

The estimate of the rate of gross profit is ordinarily based on the actual rate for the preceding year, adjusted for any changes made in the cost and sales prices during the current period. Inventories estimated in this manner are useful in preparing interim statements. The method may also be used in establishing an estimate of the cost of merchandise destroyed by fire or other disaster.

[handwritten: profit margin? = should be given or known by company]

CHAPTER REVIEW

KEY POINTS

1. Importance of Inventories.

Inventory determination plays an important role in matching expired costs with revenues of the period. An error in the determination of the inventory amount at the end of the period will cause an equal misstatement of gross profit and net income. The amount reported for both assets and owner's equity in the balance sheet will also be incorrect by the same amount. In addition, because the inventory at the end of one period becomes the inventory for the beginning of the following period, an error in inventory at the end of the period will cause the net income of the following period to be misstated. The effect of the two misstatements in income will be equal and in opposite directions. Therefore, the effect on net income of an incorrectly stated inventory is limited to the period of the error and the following period. At the end of this following period, assuming no additional errors, both assets and owner's equity will be correctly stated.

2. Inventory Systems.

There are two principal systems of inventory accounting — periodic and perpetual. In the periodic system, only the revenue from sales is recorded at the time a sale is made. No entry is made until the end of the period to record the cost of merchandise sold. In the perpetual inventory system, sales and cost of merchandise sold are recorded at the time each sale is made. In this way, the accounting records continuously disclose the amount of inventory on hand. In a perpetual inventory system, a subsidiary ledger is maintained with a separate account first each type of merchandise.

3. Determining Actual Quantities in the Inventory.

All the merchandise owned by a business on the inventory date, and only such merchandise, should be included in the inventory. The first step in "taking" an inventory is to count the merchandise on hand. To this count is added merchandise in transit that is owned. Therefore, it is normally necessary to examine purchases and sales invoices of the last few days of the accounting period and the first few days of the following period to determine who has legal title to merchandise in transit on the inventory date.

4. Determining the Cost of Inventory.

The cost of merchandise inventory is made up of the purchase price and all expenditures incurred in acquiring such merchandise, including transportation, customs duties, and insurance against losses in transit.

5. Inventory Costing Methods Under a Periodic System.

In determining the cost of merchandise sold and the inventory cost at the end of the period, it is customary to use an assumption as to the flow of costs of merchandise through an enterprise. The three most common assumptions of determining the cost of merchandise sold are as follows: first-in, first-out (fifo), last-in, first-out (lifo), and average cost. The fifo method of costing inventory is based on the assumption that costs should be charged against revenue in the order in which they were incurred. The lifo method is based on the assumption that the most recent costs incurred should be charged against revenues. The average cost method, sometimes called the weighted average method, is based on the assumption that costs should be charged against revenue according to the weighted average unit costs of the goods sold.

If the cost of units and the prices at which they are sold remain stable, all three inventory costing methods will yield the same results. However, during a period of rising prices, the use of the fifo method will result in a higher amount of gross profit than the other two methods. In a period of declining prices, the use of the lifo method will result in a higher amount of gross profit than the other two methods. The average cost method of inventory costing is often viewed as a compromise between the fifo and lifo methods.

6. Valuation of Inventory at Other than Cost.

An alternative to valuing inventory at cost is to compare cost with market price and use the lower of the two. Market, as used in the phrase *lower of cost or market*, is interpreted to mean the cost to replace the merchandise on the inventory date. It is possible to apply the lower of cost or market basis to each item in the inventory, to major classes or categories, or to the inventory as a whole.

Merchandise that can be sold only at prices below cost should be valued at net realizable value, which is the estimated selling price less any direct cost of disposition.

7. Accounting for and Reporting Inventory Under a Perpetual System.

The use of a perpetual inventory system for merchandise provides the most effective means of control over this important asset. Under this system, sales are recorded in the sales account and, on the date of each sale, the cost of the merchandise sold is recorded by debiting Cost of Merchandise Sold and crediting Merchandise Inventory.

8. Inventory Costing Methods Under a Perpetual System.

In a perpetual system, the details of merchandise increases and decreases are maintained in a subsidiary ledger, called an inventory ledger, with a separate account for each type of merchandise. As in a periodic system, it is customary to use one of the three costing methods—fifo, lifo, or average.

9. Internal Control and Perpetual Inventory Systems.

In a perpetual system, the existence of shortages can be determined by taking a physical count of the merchandise and comparing the count with the balance of the subsidiary ledger. The timely reordering of merchandise and the avoidance of excess inventory can be accomplished by comparing the balance of the subsidiary ledger with predetermined maximum and minimum levels of inventory.

10. Automated Perpetual Inventory Records.

The basic inventory records in a perpetual inventory system may be maintained by using a computer. The system can be extended to aid in maintaining inventory quantities at optimum levels and in processing the inventory-related accounting transactions.

11. Presentation of Merchandise Inventory on the Balance Sheet.

Merchandise inventory is usually presented in the current assets section of the balance sheet immediately following receivables. Both the method of determining the cost of the inventory (lifo, fifo, or average) and the method of valuing the inventory (cost, or lower of cost or market) should be shown.

12. Estimating Inventory Cost.

When it is impractical or impossible to take a physical inventory or to maintain perpetual inventory records, two commonly used methods of estimating inventory may be used: (1) the retail method, and (2) the gross profit method. The retail method of inventory estimation is based on the relationship of the cost of merchandise available for sale to the retail price of the same merchandise. The inventory at retail is determined by deducting sales for the period from the retail price of the goods that were available for sale during the period. The inventory at retail is then converted to cost on the basis of the ratio of cost to selling (retail) price for the merchandise available for sale.

The gross profit method of estimating inventory is based upon the historical relationship of the gross profit to the dollar amount of sales. The rate of gross profit is multiplied by the current period sales in order to estimate the gross profit for the period. To determine the estimate of the cost of merchandise sold, the estimated gross profit is then subtracted from the sales of the period. The estimated cost of merchandise sold can then be subtracted from the merchandise available for sale for the period to determine an estimate of the ending inventory.

KEY TERMS

merchandise inventory 420
periodic inventory system 423
physical inventory 423

perpetual inventory system 423
first-in, first-out (fifo) method 427
last-in, first-out (lifo) method 428

SELF-EXAMINATION QUESTIONS
Answers in Appendix B.

1. If the merchandise inventory at the end of the year is overstated by $7,500, the error will cause an:
   A. overstatement of cost of merchandise sold for the year by $7,500
   B. understatement of gross profit for the year by $7,500
   C. overstatement of net income for the year by $7,500
   D. understatement of net income for the year by $7,500

2. The inventory system employing accounting records that continuously disclose the amount of inventory is called:
   A. periodic
   B. perpetual
   C. physical
   D. retail

3. The inventory costing method that is based on the assumption that costs should be charged against revenue in the order in which they were incurred is:
   A. fifo
   B. lifo
   C. average cost
   D. perpetual inventory

4. The following units of a particular commodity were available for sale during the period:

Beginning inventory..	40 units at $20
First purchase	50 units at $21
Second purchase..	50 units at $22
Third purchase...	50 units at $23

   What is the unit cost of the 35 units on hand at the end of the period as determined under the periodic system by the fifo costing method?
   A. $20
   B. $21
   C. $22
   D. $23

5. If merchandise inventory is being valued at cost and the price level is steadily rising, the method of costing that will yield the highest net income is:
   A. lifo
   B. fifo
   C. average
   D. periodic

ILLUSTRATIVE PROBLEM

Stewart Inc.'s beginning inventory and purchases during the fiscal year ended March 31, 1987, were as follows:

		Units	Unit Cost	Total Cost
April 1, 1987	Inventory	1,000	$50.00	$ 50,000
April 10, 1987	Purchase	1,200	52.50	63,000
May 30, 1987	Purchase	800	55.00	44,000
August 26, 1987	Purchase	2,000	56.00	112,000
October 15, 1987	Purchase	1,500	57.00	85,500
December 31, 1987	Purchase	700	58.00	40,600
January 18, 1988	Purchase	1,350	60.00	81,000
March 21, 1988	Purchase	450	62.00	27,900
Total		9,000		$504,000

Stewart Inc. uses the periodic inventory system, and there are 3,200 units of inventory on hand on March 31, 1988.

Instructions:

1. Determine the cost of inventory on March 31, 1988, under each of the following inventory costing methods:
   a. First-in, first-out
   b. Last-in, first-out
   c. Average cost
2. Assume that during the fiscal year ended March 31, 1988, sales of $536,000 were made at an estimated gross profit rate of 40%. Estimate the ending inventory at March 31, 1988, using the gross profit method.

SOLUTION

(1)
   (a) First-in, first-out method:

450 units @ $62	$ 27,900
1,350 units @ $60	81,000
700 units @ $58	40,600
700 units @ $57	39,900
3,200 units	$189,400

(b) Last-in, first-out method:

1,000 units @ $50.00	$ 50,000
1,200 units @ $52.50	63,000
800 units @ $55.00	44,000
200 units @ $56.00	11,200
3,200 units	$168,200

(c) Average cost method:

Average cost per unit..$504,000 ÷ 9,000 units = $56
Inventory, March 31...3,200 units at $56............ $179,200

(2)

Merchandise inventory, April 1, 1987............		$ 50,000
Purchases (net), April 1, 1987–March 31, 1988		454,000
Merchandise available for sale		$504,000
Sales (net), April 1, 1987–March 31, 1988........	$536,000	
Less estimated gross profit ($536,000 × 40%).....	214,400	
Estimated cost of merchandise sold		321,600
Estimated merchandise inventory, March 31, 1988..		$182,400

DISCUSSION QUESTIONS

1. The merchandise inventory at the end of the year was inadvertently overstated by $5,000. (a) Did the error cause an overstatement or an understatement of the gross profit for the year? (b) Which items on the balance sheet at the end of the year were overstated or understated as a result of the error?

2. The $5,000 inventory error in Question 1 was not discovered, and the inventory at the end of the following year was correctly stated. (a) Will the earlier error cause an overstatement or an understatement of the gross profit for the following year? (b) Which items on the balance sheet at the end of the following year will be overstated or understated as a result of the error in the earlier year?

3. (a) Differentiate between the periodic system and the perpetual system of inventory determination. (b) Which system is more costly to maintain?

4. If the perpetual inventory system is used, is it necessary to take a physical inventory? Discuss.

5. What is the meaning of the following terms: (a) physical inventory; (b) book inventory?

6. In which of the following types of businesses would a perpetual inventory system ordinarily be used: (a) retail hardware store, (b) retail yacht dealer, (c) grocery store, (d) retail sports car dealer, (e) retail drugstore?

7. When does title to merchandise pass from the seller to the buyer if the terms of shipment are (a) FOB shipping point; (b) FOB destination?

8. Which of the three methods of inventory costing—fifo, lifo, or average cost—is based on the assumption that costs should be charged against revenue in the reverse order in which they were incurred?

9. Do the terms *fifo* and *lifo* refer to techniques employed in determining quantities of the various classes of merchandise on hand? Explain.

10. Does the term *last-in* in the lifo method mean that the items in the inventory are assumed to be the most recent (last) acquisitions? Explain.

11. Under which method of cost flow are (a) the earliest costs assigned to inventory; (b) the most recent costs assigned to inventory; (c) average costs assigned to inventory?

12. The following units of a particular commodity were available for sale during the year:

Beginning inventory.......................	10 units at $50
First purchase...........................	15 units at $54
Second purchase........................	20 units at $65

The firm uses the periodic system, and there are 9 units of the commodity on hand at the end of the year. What is their unit cost according to (a) fifo, (b) lifo, (c) average cost?

13. If merchandise inventory is being valued at cost and the price level is steadily rising, which of the three methods of costing—fifo, lifo, or average cost—will yield (a) the highest inventory cost, (b) the lowest inventory cost, (c) the highest gross profit, (d) the lowest gross profit?

14. Which of the three methods of inventory costing—fifo, lifo, or average cost—will in general yield an inventory cost most nearly approximating current replacement cost?

15. In the phrase *lower of cost or market,* what is meant by "market"?

16. The cost of a particular inventory item is $125, the current replacement cost is $115, and the selling price is $180. At what amount should the item be included in the inventory according to the lower of cost or market basis?

17. Because of imperfections, an item of merchandise cannot be sold at its normal selling price. How should this item be valued for financial statement purposes?

18. An enterprise using a perpetual inventory system sells merchandise to a customer on account for $475; the cost of the merchandise was $300.
    (a) What entries would be made on the general ledger accounts as a result of the transaction?
    (b) What is the amount and direction of the net change in the amount of assets and owner's equity resulting from the transaction?

19. What are the three most important advantages of the perpetual inventory system over the periodic system?

20. An enterprise using the retail method of inventory costing determines that merchandise inventory at retail is $100,000. If the ratio of cost to retail price is 70%, what is the amount of inventory to be reported on the financial statements?

21. What uses can be made of the estimate of the cost of inventory determined by the gross profit method?

22. Real World Focus. The following footnote was taken from the 1985 financial statements of Adolph Coors Company:

> Inventories are stated at the lower of cost or market. Cost is determined by the last-in, first-out (lifo) method for substantially all inventories.
>   Current cost, as determined principally on the first-in, first-out method, exceeded lifo cost by $56,630,000 and $55,354,000 at December 29, 1985, and December 30, 1984, respectively.

Additional data are as follows:

Operating income for 1985................	$ 90,208,000
Total inventories, December 29, 1985.......	142,950,000

Based on the preceding data, determine (a) what the total inventories at December 29, 1985, would have been, using the fifo method, and (b) what the operating income for 1985 would have been if fifo had been used instead of lifo.

EXERCISES

Exercise 10–1.   Periodic inventory by three methods. The beginning inventory and the purchases of an item during the year were as follows:

Jan. 1	Inventory..................	15 units at $60	
Feb. 12	Purchase.....3.1.0..........	10 units at $62	
June 24	Purchase...1390.........5	20 units at $65	
Oct. 8	Purchase.................	15 units at $70	

There are 20 units of the commodity in the physical inventory at December 31. The periodic system is used. Determine the inventory cost and the cost of merchandise sold by three methods, presenting your answers in the following form:

	Cost	
Inventory Method	Merchandise Inventory	Merchandise Sold
(1) First-in, first-out	$ 1375	$ 2495
(2) Last-in, first-out	1210	2660
(3) Average cost	1290	2580

Exercise 10–2. Lower of cost or market inventory. On the basis of the following data, determine the value of the inventory at the lower of cost or market. Assemble the data in the form illustrated on page 434.

Commodity	Inventory Quantity	Unit Cost	Unit Market Price
12A	8	$340	$350
78G	17	110	105
33P	12	275	260
90R	35	60	65
45T	20	95	100

Exercise 10–3. Perpetual inventory using fifo. Beginning inventory, purchases, and sales data for Commodity A12 are as follows:

Jan. 1. Inventory................... 20 units at $45
4. Sold...................... 10 units
9. Purchased .... 15 units at $47
15. Sold...................... 18 units
22. Sold...................... 3 units
30. Purchased .... 10 units at $48

The enterprise maintains a perpetual inventory system, costing by the first-in, first-out method. Determine the cost of the merchandise sold in each sale and the inventory balance after each sale, presenting the data in the form illustrated on page 437.

Exercise 10–4. Perpetual inventory using lifo. Beginning inventory, purchases, and sales data for Commodity C33 for June are as follows:

Inventory:
June 1.......................... 30 units at $30
Sales:
June 8.......................... 15 units
17.......................... 10 units
27.......................... 10 units
Purchases:
June 5.......................... 20 units at $31
20.......................... 15 units at $32

Assuming that the perpetual inventory system is used, costing by the lifo method, determine the cost of the inventory balance at June 30, presenting data in the form illustrated on page 438.

Exercise 10–5. Perpetual inventory entries. The perpetual inventory system is used, and the merchandise inventory account (controlling) had a balance of $394,250 on January 1, the beginning of the current year. The account was debited for $776,750 for purchases made during the year.

(a) Journalize the entries required to record sales for the year (all sales are made on account): sales price, $1,150,000; cost, $782,500.
(b) If a physical count of inventory on December 31 revealed a cost of $381,200, prepare the entry to record the inventory shortage.

Exercise 10–6. Retail inventory method. On the basis of the following data, estimate the cost of the merchandise inventory at October 31 by the retail method:

		Cost	Retail
October 1	Merchandise inventory............	$244,500	$370,500
October 1–31	Purchases (net)...................	164,700	249,500
October 1–31	Sales (net)		259,000

Exercise 10–7. Gross profit inventory method. The merchandise inventory of Joop Company was destroyed by fire on June 10. The following data were obtained from the accounting records:

Jan. 1	Merchandise inventory	$172,250
Jan. 1–June 10	Purchases (net)	212,250
	Sales (net).................................	380,000
	Estimated gross profit rate..................	40%

Estimate the cost of the merchandise destroyed.

cost is reciporical of gross profit rate

PROBLEMS

Series A

Problem 10–1A. Periodic inventory by three methods. B & M Television employs the periodic inventory system. Details regarding the inventory of television sets at July 1, 1987, purchases invoices during the year, and the inventory count at June 30, 1988, are summarized as follows:

Model	Inventory, July 1	Purchases Invoices 1st	2d	3d	Inventory Count, June 30
C10	6 at $238	4 at $250	8 at $260	10 at $266	12
D05	6 at 77	5 at 82	8 at 89	8 at 99	10
L10	2 at 108	2 at 110	3 at 128	3 at 130	3
O18	8 at 88	4 at 79	3 at 85	6 at 92	8
K72	2 at 250	2 at 260	4 at 271	4 at 275	4
S91	5 at 160	4 at 170	4 at 175	7 at 180	8
V17	—	4 at 150	4 at 200	2 at 205	5

Instructions:

(1) Determine the cost of the inventory on June 30, 1988, by the first-in, first-out method. Present data in columnar form, using the following headings:

Model   Quantity   Unit Cost   Total Cost

If the inventory of a particular model is composed of an entire lot plus a portion of another lot acquired at a different unit cost, use a separate line for each lot.

(2) Determine the cost of the inventory on June 30, 1988, by the last-in, first-out method, following the procedures indicated in (1).

(3) Determine the cost of the inventory on June 30, 1988, by the average cost method, using the columnar headings indicated in (1).

Problem 10–2A.   Fifo and lifo perpetual inventory. The beginning inventory of soybeans at the Urbana Co-Op and data on purchases and sales for a three-month period are as follows:

Date	Transaction	Number of Bushels	Per Unit	Total
July 1.	Inventory	25,000	$6.10	$152,500
10.	Purchase	75,000	6.15	461,250
15.	Sale	35,000	7.00	245,000
25.	Sale	30,000	7.00	210,000
Aug. 8.	Sale	10,000	7.10	71,000
12.	Purchase	50,000	6.20	310,000
17.	Sale	35,000	7.20	252,000
28.	Sale	20,000	7.15	143,000
Sept. 5.	Purchase	60,000	6.10	366,000
17.	Sale	40,000	7.00	280,000
20.	Purchase	30,000	6.00	180,000
30.	Sale	45,000	7.00	315,000

Instructions:

(1) Record the inventory, purchases, and cost of merchandise sold data in a perpetual inventory record similar to the one illustrated on page 437, using the first-in, first-out method.

(2) Determine the total sales and the total cost of soybeans sold for the period and indicate their effect on the general ledger by two entries in general journal form. Assume that all sales were on account.

(3) Determine the gross profit from sales of soybeans for the period.

(4) Record the inventory, purchases, and cost of merchandise sold data in a perpetual inventory record similar to the one illustrated on page 438, using the last-in, first-out method.

If the working papers correlating with the textbook are not used, omit Problem 10–3A.

Problem 10–3A. Lower of cost or market inventory. Data on the physical inventory of Dent Corporation as of April 30, the end of the current fiscal year, are presented in the working papers. The quantity of each commodity on hand has been determined and recorded on the inventory sheet. Unit market prices have also been determined as of April 30 and recorded on the sheet. The inventory is to be determined at cost and also at the lower of cost or market, using the first-in, first-out method. Quantity and cost data from the last purchases invoice of the year and the next-to-the-last purchases invoice are summarized as follows:

	Last Purchases Invoice		Next-to-the-Last Purchases Invoice	
Description	Quantity Purchased	Unit Cost	Quantity Purchased	Unit Cost
A71	20	$ 60	30	$ 59
C22	25	210	20	205
D82	10	145	25	142
E34	150	25	100	24
F17	10	560	10	570
J19	100	15	100	14
K41	10	380	5	385
P21	500	6	500	6
R72	80	17	50	18
T15	5	250	4	260
V55	700	9	500	9
AC2	100	45	50	46
BB7	5	420	5	425
BD1	100	20	75	19
CC1	60	16	40	17
EB2	. 50	29	25	28
FF7	75	26	60	25
GE4	5	710	5	715

Instructions:

Record the appropriate unit costs on the inventory sheet and complete the pricing of the inventory. When there are two different unit costs applicable to a commodity, proceed as follows:

(1) Draw a line through the quantity and insert the quantity and unit cost of the last purchase.

(2) On the following line, insert the quantity and unit cost of the next-to-the-last purchase. The first item on the inventory sheet has been completed as an example.

Problem 10–4A.   Retail method; gross profit method. Selected data on merchandise inventory, purchases, and sales for Payton Co. and Reese Co. are as follows:

Payton Co.

	Cost	Retail
Merchandise inventory, July 1	$259,800	$370,000
Transactions during July:		
Purchases	366,840⎱	521,000
Purchases discounts	2,940⎰	
Sales		600,000
Sales returns and allowances		5,000

Reese Co.

Merchandise inventory, April 1	$317,500
Transactions during April and May:	
Purchases	410,250
Purchases discounts	5,250
Sales	625,000
Sales returns and allowances	5,000
Estimated gross profit rate	40%

Instructions:

(1) Determine the estimated cost of the merchandise inventory of Payton Co. on July 31 by the retail method, presenting details of the computations.
(2) Estimate the cost of the merchandise inventory of Reese Co. on May 31 by the gross profit method, presenting details of the computations.

Problem 10–5A.   Adjusting entries; statements for sole proprietorship. Dixon Sales is a distributor of imported motorcycles. Its unadjusted trial balance as of the end of the current fiscal year is as follows:

Cash	17,900	
Accounts Receivable	29,500	
Allowance for Doubtful Accounts		275
Merchandise Inventory	90,200	
Equipment	30,000	
Accumulated Depreciation—Equipment		12,250
Accounts Payable		24,500
Notes Payable		10,000
John Dixon, Capital		71,750
John Dixon, Drawing	36,000	
Sales		535,700
Purchases	395,800	
Operating Expenses (controlling account)	55,175	
Rent Income		1,200
Interest Expense	1,100	
	655,675	655,675

Data needed for adjustments at December 31:

(a) Merchandise inventory at December 31, at lower of cost (first-in, first-out method) or market, $84,600.
(b) Uncollectible accounts expense for current year, estimated at $1,725.
(c) Depreciation on equipment for current year, $5,500.

Instructions:

(1) Journalize the necessary adjusting entries.
(2) Prepare the following without the use of a conventional work sheet: (a) an income statement, (b) a statement of owner's equity, and (c) a balance sheet in report form.

Problem 10-6A. Corrections to inventory; revised income statement. The following preliminary income statement of Jordan Enterprises Inc. was prepared before the accounts were adjusted or closed at the end of the fiscal year. The company uses the periodic inventory system.

Jordan Enterprises Inc.
Income Statement
For Year Ended December 31, 19--

Sales (net)......................................		$985,750
Cost of merchandise sold:		
Merchandise inventory, January 1, 19--............	$230,000	
Purchases (net)	695,000	
Merchandise available for sale	$925,000	
Less merchandise inventory, December 31, 19--	245,000	
Cost of merchandise sold.....................		680,000
Gross profit......................................		$305,750
Operating expenses.............................		202,250
Net income		$103,500

The following errors in the ledger and on the inventory sheets were discovered by the independent CPA retained to conduct the annual audit:

(a) A number of errors were discovered in pricing inventory items, in extending amounts, and in footing inventory sheets. The net effect of the errors, exclusive of those described below, was to overstate by $5,000 the amount of ending inventory on the income statement.
(b) A purchases invoice for merchandise of $1,500, dated December 30, had been received and correctly recorded, but the merchandise was not received until January 3 and had not been included in the December 31 inventory. Title had passed to Jordan Enterprises Inc. on December 30.
(c) A purchases invoice for merchandise of $3,000, dated December 31, was not received until January 4 and had not been recorded by December 31. However, the merchandise, to which title had passed, had arrived and had been included in the December 31 inventory.

(d) A sales order for $10,000, dated December 31, had been recorded as a sale on that date, but title did not pass to the buyer until shipment was made on January 3. The merchandise, which had cost $6,500, was excluded from the December 31 inventory.

(e) A sales invoice for $1,250, dated December 30, had not been recorded. The merchandise was shipped on December 30, FOB shipping point, and its cost, $775, was excluded from the December 31 inventory.

(f) An item of office equipment, received on December 27, was erroneously included in the December 31 merchandise inventory at its cost of $8,500. The invoice had been recorded correctly.

Instructions:

(1) Journalize the entries to correct the general ledger accounts as of December 31, inserting the identifying letters in the date column. All purchases and sales were made on account.

(2) Determine the correct inventory for December 31, beginning your analysis with the $245,000 inventory shown on the preliminary income statement. Assemble the corrections in two groupings, "Additions" and "Deductions," allowing six lines for each group. Identify each correction by the appropriate letter.

(3) Prepare a revised income statement.

Series B

Problem 10–1B.   Periodic inventory by three methods. Allen Stereo employs the periodic inventory system. Details regarding the inventory of television sets at January 1, purchases invoices during the year, and the inventory count at December 31 are summarized as follows:

Model	Inventory, January 1	Purchases Invoices 1st	Purchases Invoices 2d	Purchases Invoices 3d	Inventory Count, December 31
B91	4 at $150	6 at $150	8 at $155	7 at $155	5
F10	3 at 210	3 at 215	5 at 213	4 at 225	3
H21	2 at 520	2 at 530	2 at ·530	2 at 536	3
J39	6 at 520	8 at 531	4 at 549	6 at 542	8
P80	9 at 213	7 at 215	6 at 222	6 at 225	8
T15	6 at 305	3 at 310	3 at 316	4 at 321	5
V11	—	4 at 220	4 at 230	—	2

Instructions:

(1) Determine the cost of the inventory on December 31 by the first-in, first-out method. Present data in columnar form, using the following headings:

Model	Quantity	Unit Cost	Total Cost

If the inventory of a particular model is composed of an entire lot plus a portion of another lot acquired at a different unit cost, use a separate line for each lot.

(2) Determine the cost of the inventory on December 31 by the last-in, first-out method, following the procedures indicated in (1).
(3) Determine the cost of the inventory on December 31 by the average cost method, using the columnar headings indicated in (1).

Problem 10–2B. Fifo and lifo perpetual inventory. The beginning inventory of Commodity 12A and data on purchases and sales for a three-month period are as follows:

Date	Transaction	Number of Units	Per Unit	Total
April 1.	Inventory	9	$220	$1,980
5.	Purchase	25	225	5,625
12.	Sale	10	300	3,000
22.	Sale	6	300	1,800
May 4.	Purchase	10	230	2,300
6.	Sale	8	310	2,480
21.	Sale	5	310	1,550
28.	Purchase	15	235	3,525
June 5.	Sale	9	315	2,835
13.	Sale	10	315	3,150
19.	Purchase	10	240	2,400
26.	Sale	8	320	2,560

Instructions:

(1) Record the inventory, purchases, and cost of merchandise sold data in a perpetual inventory record similar to the one illustrated on page 437, using the first-in, first-out method.
(2) Determine the total sales and the total cost of Commodity 12A sold for the period and indicate their effect on the general ledger by two entries in general journal form. Assume that all sales were on account.
(3) Determine the gross profit from sales of Commodity 12A for the period.
(4) Record the inventory, purchases, and cost of merchandise sold data in a perpetual inventory record similar to the one illustrated on page 438, using the last-in, first-out method.

If the working papers correlating with the textbook are not used, omit Problem 10–3B.

Problem 10–3B. Lower of cost or market inventory. Data on the physical inventory of W. A. Anderson Co. as of December 31, the end of the current fiscal year, are presented in the working papers. The quantity of each commodity on hand has been determined and recorded on the inventory sheet. Unit market prices have also been determined as of December 31 and recorded on the sheet. The inventory is to be determined at cost and also at the lower of cost or market, using the first-in, first-out method. Quantity and cost data from the last purchases invoice of the year and the next-to-the last purchases invoice are summarized as follows:

| Description | Last Purchases Invoice | | Next-to-the-Last Purchases Invoice | |
	Quantity Purchased	Unit Cost	Quantity Purchased	Unit Cost
A71	20	$ 60	40	$ 59
C22	25	190	15	190
D82	15	145	15	142
E34	150	25	100	27
F17	6	550	15	540
J19	75	16	100	17
K41	8	400	5	410
P21	500	6	500	7
P72	70	17	50	16
T15	5	250	4	260
V55	1,000	10	500	10
AC2	100	45	100	46
BB7	5	410	5	400
BD1	100	20	100	19
CC1	50	15	40	16
EB2	40	29	50	28
FF7	55	28	50	28
GE4	6	690	5	700

Instructions:

Record the appropriate unit costs on the inventory sheet and complete the pricing of the inventory. When there are two different unit costs applicable to a commodity, proceed as follows:

(1) Draw a line through the quantity and insert the quantity and unit cost of the last purchase.

(2) On the following line, insert the quantity and unit cost of the next-to-the-last purchase. The first item on the inventory sheet has been completed as an example.

Problem 10–4B. Retail method; gross profit method. Selected data on merchandise inventory, purchases, and sales for Boyd Co. and Carson Supply Co. are as follows:

Boyd Co.

	Cost	Retail
Merchandise inventory, January 1	$377,100	$579,100
Transactions during January:		
Purchases	186,600	
Purchases discounts	2,100	298,400
Sales		340,500
Sales returns and allowances		5,500

Carson Supply Co.

Merchandise inventory, July 1	$517,900
Transactions during July and August:	
Purchases	425,500
Purchases discounts	3,600
Sales	570,250
Sales returns and allowances	5,250
Estimated gross profit rate	35%

Instructions:

(1) Determine the estimated cost of the merchandise inventory of Boyd Co. on January 31 by the retail method, presenting details of the computations.
(2) Estimate the cost of the merchandise inventory of Carson Supply Co. on August 31 by the gross profit method, presenting details of the computations.

MINI-CASE 10

 DREW company

Drew Company began operations in 1987 by selling a single product. Data on purchases and sales for the year were as follows:

Purchases

Date	Units Purchased	Unit Cost	Total Cost
April 5	5,000	$13.20	$ 66,000
May 2	5,000	14.00	70,000
June 4	5,000	14.20	71,000
July 10	5,000	15.00	75,000
August 7	3,000	15.25	45,750
October 5	2,000	15.50	31,000
November 1	1,000	15.75	15,750
December 10	1,000	17.00	17,000
	27,000		$391,500

Sales

April........	2,000 units	September.....	3,500 units
May........	2,000	October........	2,250
June	3,500	November	2,250
July........	4,000	December	1,000
August	3,500		

Total sales.. $454,000

On January 2, 1988, the president of the company, Ann Drew, asked for your advice on costing the 3,000-unit physical inventory that was taken on December 31, 1987. Also, since the firm plans to expand its product line, she asked for your advice on the use of a perpetual inventory system in the future.

Instructions:

(1) Determine the cost of the December 31, 1987 inventory under the periodic system, using the (a) first-in, first-out method, (b) last-in, first-out method, and (c) average cost method.

(2) Determine the gross profit for the year under each of the three methods in (1).

(3) (a) In your opinion, which of the three inventory costing methods best reflects the results of operations for 1987? Why?

   (b) In your opinion, which of the three inventory costing methods best reflects the replacement cost of the inventory on the balance sheet as of December 31, 1987? Why?

   (c) Which inventory costing method would you choose to use for income tax purposes? Why?

(4) Discuss the advantages and disadvantages of using a perpetual inventory system. From the data presented in this case, is there any indication of the adequacy of inventory levels during the year?

Chapter 11

PLANT ASSETS AND INTANGIBLE ASSETS

Chapter Objectives

■ Describe the characteristics of plant assets and illustrate the accounting for the acquisition of plant assets.

■ Describe the nature of depreciation and illustrate the accounting for depreciation.

■ Describe and illustrate the accounting for plant asset disposals.

■ Describe and illustrate the accounting for the leasing of plant assets.

■ Describe and illustrate the accounting for depletion.

■ Describe and illustrate the accounting for intangible assets.

■ Describe and illustrate the reporting of depreciation expense, plant assets, and intangible assets in the financial statements.

L*ong-lived* is a general term that may be applied to assets of a relatively fixed or permanent nature owned by a business enterprise. Such assets that are tangible in nature, used in the operations of the business, and not held for sale in the ordinary course of the business are classified on the balance sheet as **plant assets** or **fixed assets**. Other descriptive titles frequently used are **property, plant, and equipment**, used either alone or in various combinations. The properties most frequently included in plant assets may be described in more specific terms as equipment, furniture, tools, machinery, buildings, and land. Although there is no standard criterion as to the minimum length of life necessary for classification as plant assets, such assets must be capable of repeated use and are ordinarily expected to last more than a year. However, the asset need not actually be used continuously or even often. Items of standby equipment held for use in the event of a breakdown of regular equipment or for use only during peak periods of activity are included in plant assets.

Assets acquired for resale in the normal course of business cannot be characterized as plant assets, regardless of their durability or the length of time they are held. For example, undeveloped land or other real estate acquired as a speculation should be listed on the balance sheet in the asset section entitled "Investments."

INITIAL COSTS OF PLANT ASSETS

The initial cost of a plant asset includes all expenditures *necessary* to get it in place and ready for use. Sales tax, transportation charges, insurance on the asset while in transit, special foundations, and installation costs should be added to the purchase price of the related plant asset. Similarly, when a secondhand asset is purchased, the initial costs of getting it ready for use, such as expenditures for new parts, repairs, and painting, are debited to the asset account. On the other hand, costs associated with the acquisition of a plant asset should be excluded from the asset account if they are not necessary for getting the asset ready for use and therefore do not increase the asset's usefulness. Expenditures resulting from carelessness or errors in installing the asset, from vandalism, or from other unusual occurrences do not increase the usefulness of the asset and should be allocated to the period as an expense.

The cost of constructing a building includes the fees paid to architects and engineers for plans and supervision, insurance incurred during construction, and all other needed expenditures related to the project. Generally, interest incurred during the construction period on money borrowed to finance construction should also be treated as part of the cost of the building.[1]

The cost of land includes not only the negotiated price but also broker's commissions, title fees, surveying fees, and other expenditures connected with securing title. If delinquent real estate taxes are assumed by the buyer, they also are chargeable to the land account. If unwanted buildings are located on land acquired for a plant site, the cost of their razing or removal, less any salvage recovered, is properly chargeable to the land account. The cost of leveling or otherwise permanently changing the contour is also an additional cost of the land.

Other expenditures related to the land may be charged to Land, Buildings, or Land Improvements, depending upon the circumstances. If the property owner bears the initial cost of paving the public street bordering the land, either by direct payment or by special tax assessment, the paving may be considered to be as permanent as the land. On the other hand, the cost of constructing walkways to and around the building may be added to the building account if the walkways are expected to last as long as the building. Expenditures for improvements that are neither as permanent as the land nor directly associated with the building may be set apart in a land improvements account and depreciated according to their different life spans. Some of the more usual items of this nature are trees and shrubs, fences, outdoor lighting systems, and paved parking areas.

NATURE OF DEPRECIATION

As time passes, all plant assets with the exception of land lose their capacity to yield services.[2] Accordingly, the cost of such assets should be transferred to the related expense accounts in an orderly manner during their expected useful life. This periodic cost expiration is called **depreciation**.

---

[1]*Statement of Financial Accounting Standards, No. 34,* "Capitalization of Interest Cost" (Stamford: Financial Accounting Standards Board, 1979), par. 6.
[2]Land is here assumed to be used only as a site. Consideration will be given later in the chapter to land acquired for its mineral deposits or other natural resources.

Factors contributing to a decline in usefulness may be divided into two categories: *physical* depreciation, which includes wear from use and deterioration from the action of the elements, and *functional* depreciation, which includes inadequacy and obsolescence. A plant asset becomes inadequate if its capacity is not sufficient to meet the demands of increased production. A plant asset is obsolete if the commodity that it produces is no longer in demand or if a newer machine can produce a commodity of better quality or at a great reduction in cost. The continued growth of technological progress during this century has made obsolescence an increasingly important part of depreciation. Although the several factors comprising depreciation can be defined, it is not feasible to identify them when recording depreciation expense.

The meaning of the term "depreciation" as used in accounting is often misunderstood because the same term is also commonly used in business to mean a decline in the market value of an asset. The amount of unexpired cost of plant assets reported in the balance sheet is not likely to agree with the amount that could be realized from their sale. Plant assets are held for use in the enterprise rather than for sale. It is assumed that the enterprise will continue forever as a **going concern**. Consequently, the decision to dispose of a plant asset is based mainly on its usefulness to the enterprise and not on its market value.

Another common misunderstanding is that depreciation accounting automatically provides the cash needed to replace plant assets as they wear out. The cash account is neither increased nor decreased by the periodic entries that transfer the cost of plant assets to depreciation expense accounts. The misconception probably occurs because depreciation expense, unlike most expenses, does not require an equivalent outlay of cash in the period in which the expense is recorded.

DETERMINING DEPRECIATION

If a plant asset is expected to have no value at the time that it is retired from service, its entire initial cost should be spread over the expected useful life of the asset as depreciation expense. Also, if a plant asset's value at the time of retirement is expected to be very small in comparison with the cost of the asset, this value may be ignored and the entire cost spread over the asset's expected useful life. If a plant asset is expected to have a significant value at the time that it is retired from service, the difference between its initial cost and this value is the cost (depreciable cost) that should be spread over the useful life of the asset as depreciation expense. The plant asset's estimated value at the time that it is to be retired from service is called its **residual value, scrap value, salvage value,** or **trade-in value.**

In determining the amount of depreciable cost that is to be recognized as periodic depreciation expense, three factors need to be considered: the plant asset's (a) initial cost, (b) residual value, and (c) useful life. The relationship between these three factors and the periodic depreciation expense is presented in the following diagram:

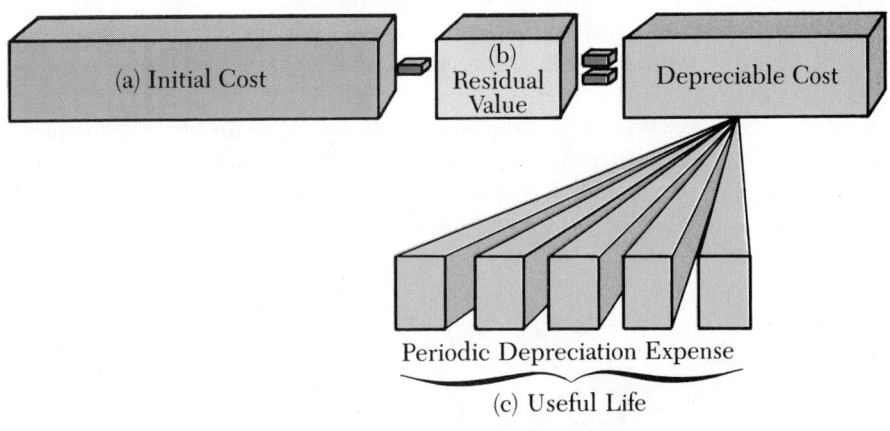

Periodic Depreciation Expense

(c) Useful Life

FACTORS THAT DETERMINE DEPRECIATION EXPENSE

Neither the period of usefulness of a plant asset nor its residual value at the end of that period can be accurately determined until the asset is retired. However, in determining the amount of the periodic depreciation, these two related factors must be estimated at the time the asset is placed in service.

There are no hard-and-fast rules for estimating either factor, and both factors may be greatly affected by management policies. For example, the estimates of a company that provides its sales representatives with a new automobile every year will differ from those of a firm that keeps its cars for three years. Such variables as climate, frequency of use, maintenance, and minimum standards of efficiency will also affect the estimates.

Life estimates for depreciable assets are available in various trade association and other publications. For federal income tax purposes, the Internal Revenue Service has also established guidelines for life estimates. These guidelines may be useful in determining depreciation for financial reporting purposes.

In addition to the many factors that may influence the life estimate of an asset, there is a wide range in the degree of exactness used in the computation. A calendar month is ordinarily the smallest unit of time used. When this period of time is used, all assets placed in service or retired from service during the first half of a month are treated as if the event had occurred on the first day of that month. Similarly, all plant asset additions and reductions during the second half of a month are considered to have occurred on the first day of the next month. In the absence of any statement to the contrary, this practice will be assumed throughout this chapter.

It is not necessary that an enterprise use a single method of computing depreciation for all classes of its depreciable assets. The methods used in the accounts and financial statements may also differ from the methods used in determining income taxes and property taxes. The four methods used most often are straight-line, units-of-production, declining-balance, and sum-of-the-years-digits. The extent of the use of these methods in financial statements is presented in the following chart:

USE OF
DEPRECIA-
TION
METHODS

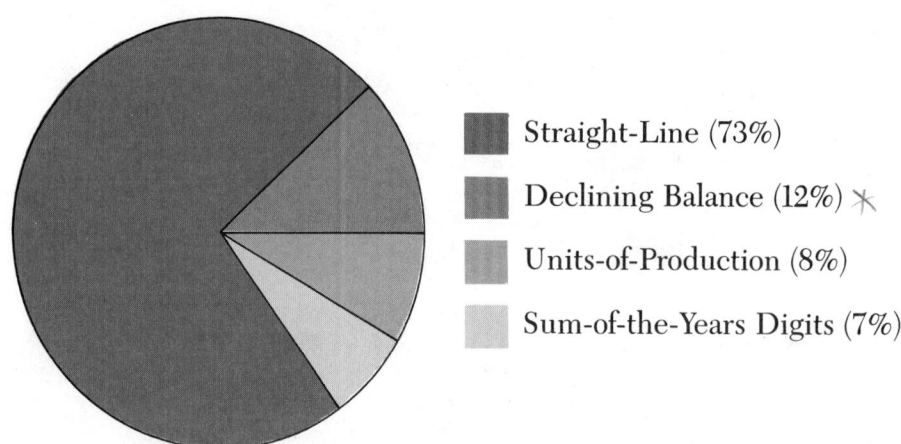

Straight-Line (73%)

Declining Balance (12%)

Units-of-Production (8%)

Sum-of-the-Years Digits (7%)

Source: *Accounting Trends & Techniques,* 39th ed. (New York: American Institute of Certified Public Accountants, 1985).

Straight-Line Method

The **straight-line method** of determining depreciation provides for equal periodic charges to expense over the estimated life of the asset. To illustrate this method, assume that the cost of a depreciable asset is $16,000, its estimated residual value is $1,000, and its estimated life is 5 years. The annual depreciation is computed as follows:

$$\frac{\$16,000 \text{ cost} - \$1,000 \text{ estimated residual value}}{5 \text{ years estimated life}} = \$3,000 \text{ annual depreciation}$$

The annual depreciation of $3,000 would be prorated for the first and the last partial years of use. Assuming a fiscal year ending on December 31 and first use of the asset on October 15, the depreciation for that fiscal year would be $750 (3 months). If usage had begun on October 16, the depreciation for the year would be $500 (2 months).

The annual straight-line depreciation may be converted to a percentage rate, determined on the basis of cost and the estimated life of the asset without regard to residual value. The conversion to an annual percentage rate is accomplished by dividing 100 by the number of years of life. Thus a life of 50 years is equivalent to a 2% depreciation rate, 20 years is equivalent to a 5% rate, 8 years is equivalent to a 12½% rate, and so on.

The straight-line method is widely used because of its simplicity. In addition, it provides a reasonable allocation of costs to periodic revenue when usage is relatively the same from period to period.

Units-of-Production Method

The **units-of-production method** yields a depreciation charge that varies with the amount of asset usage. To apply this method, the length of life of the asset is expressed in terms of productive capacity, such as hours, miles, or number of units. Depreciation is first computed for the appropriate unit of production, and the depreciation for each accounting period is then determined by multiplying the unit depreciation by the number of units used during the period. To illustrate, assume that a machine with a cost of $16,000 and estimated residual value of $1,000 is expected to have an estimated life of 10,000 operating hours. The depreciation for a unit of one hour is computed as follows:

$$\frac{\$16,000 \text{ cost} - \$1,000 \text{ estimated residual value}}{10,000 \text{ estimated hours}} = \$1.50 \text{ hourly depreciation}$$

Assuming that the machine was in operation for 2,200 hours during a particular year, the depreciation for that year would be $3,300 ($1.50 × 2,200).

When the amount of usage of a plant asset changes from year to year, the units-of-production method is more logical than the straight-line method. It may yield fairer allocations of cost against periodic revenue.

Declining-Balance Method

The **declining-balance method** yields a declining periodic depreciation charge over the estimated life of the asset. The most common technique is to double the straight-line depreciation rate, computed as explained previously, and apply the resulting rate to the cost of the asset less its accumulated depreciation. For example, the declining-balance rate for an asset with an estimated life of five years would be double the straight-line rate of 20%, or 40%. This rate is then applied to the cost of the asset for the first year of its use and thereafter to the declining book value (cost minus accumulated depreciation). The method is illustrated in the following table:

DECLINING-
BALANCE
METHOD OF
DEPRECI-
ATION

Year	Cost	Accumulated Depreciation at Beginning of Year	Book Value at Beginning of Year	Rate	Depreciation for Year	Book Value at End of Year
1	$16,000	—	$16,000.00	40%	$6,400.00	$9,600.00
2	16,000	$ 6,400.00	9,600.00	40%	3,840.00	5,760.00
3	16,000	10,240.00	5,760.00	40%	2,304.00	3,456.00
4	16,000	12,544.00	3,456.00	40%	1,382.40	2,073.60
5	16,000	13,926.40	2,073.60	40%	829.44	1,244.16

Note that estimated residual value is not considered in determining the depreciation rate. It is also ignored in computing periodic depreciation, except that the asset should not be depreciated below the estimated residual value. In the above example, it was assumed that the estimated residual value at the end of the fifth year approximates the book value of $1,244.16. If the residual value had been estimated at $1,500, the depreciation for the fifth year would have been $573.60 ($2,073.60 − $1,500) instead of $829.44.

There was an implicit assumption in the above illustration that the first use of the asset coincided with the beginning of the fiscal year. This would usually not occur in actual practice, however, and would require a slight change in the computation for the first partial year of use. If the asset in the example had been placed in service at the end of the third month of the fiscal year, only the pro rata portion of the first full year's depreciation, $4,800 (9/12 × 40% × $16,000), would be allocated to the first fiscal year. The method of computing the depreciation for the following years would not be affected. Thus, the depreciation for the second fiscal year would be $4,480 [40% × ($16,000 − $4,800)].

Sum-of-the-Years-Digits Method

The **sum-of-the-years-digits method** yields results like those obtained by use of the declining-balance method. The periodic charge for depreciation declines steadily over the estimated life of the asset because a successively smaller fraction is applied each year to the original cost of the asset less the estimated residual value. The denominator of the fraction, which remains the same, is the sum of the digits representing the years of life. The numerator of the fraction, which changes each year, is the number of years of life remaining at the beginning of the year for which depreciation is being computed. For an asset with an estimated life of 5 years, the denominator is $5 + 4 + 3 + 2 + 1$, or 15.[3] For the first year, the numerator is 5, for the second year 4, and so on. The method is illustrated by the following depreciation schedule for an asset with an assumed cost of $16,000, residual value of $1,000, and life of 5 years:

Year	Cost Less Residual Value	Rate	Depreciation for Year	Accumulated Depreciation at End of Year	Book Value at End of Year	SUM-OF-THE-YEARS-DIGITS METHOD OF DEPRECIATION
1	$15,000	5/15	$5,000	$ 5,000	$11,000	
2	15,000	4/15	4,000	9,000	7,000	
3	15,000	3/15	3,000	12,000	4,000	
4	15,000	2/15	2,000	14,000	2,000	
5	15,000	1/15	1,000	15,000	1,000	

When the first use of the asset does not coincide with the beginning of a fiscal year, it is necessary to allocate each full year's depreciation between the two fiscal years benefited. Assuming that the asset in the example was placed in service after three months of the fiscal year had elapsed, the depreciation for that fiscal year would be $3,750 ($9/12 \times 5/15 \times \$15,000$). The depreciation for the second year would be $4,250, computed as follows:

$$3/12 \times 5/15 \times \$15,000 \ldots\ldots\ldots\ldots\ldots\ldots \quad \$1,250$$
$$9/12 \times 4/15 \times \$15,000 \ldots\ldots\ldots\ldots\ldots\ldots \quad \underline{3,000}$$
$$\text{Total, second fiscal year} \ldots\ldots\ldots\ldots\ldots \quad \$4,250$$

Comparison of Depreciation Methods

The straight-line method provides for uniform periodic charges to depreciation expense over the life of the asset. The units-of-production method provides for periodic charges to depreciation expense that may vary considerably, depending upon the amount of usage of the asset.

---

[3]The denominator can also be determined from the following formula, where S = sum of the digits and N = number of years of estimated life: $S = N[(N + 1) \div 2]$.

Both the declining-balance and the sum-of-the-years-digits methods provide for a higher depreciation charge in the first year of use of the asset and a gradually declining periodic charge thereafter. For this reason they are frequently referred to as **accelerated depreciation methods**. These methods are most appropriate for situations in which the decline in productivity or earning power of the asset is proportionately greater in the early years of its use than in later years. Further justification for their use is based on the tendency of repairs to increase with the age of an asset. The reduced amounts of depreciation in later years are therefore offset to some extent by increased maintenance expenses.

The periodic depreciation charges for the straight-line method and the accelerated methods are compared in the following chart. This chart is based on an asset cost of $16,000, an estimated life of 5 years, and an estimated residual value of $1,000.

COMPARISON
OF DEPRECI-
ATION
METHODS

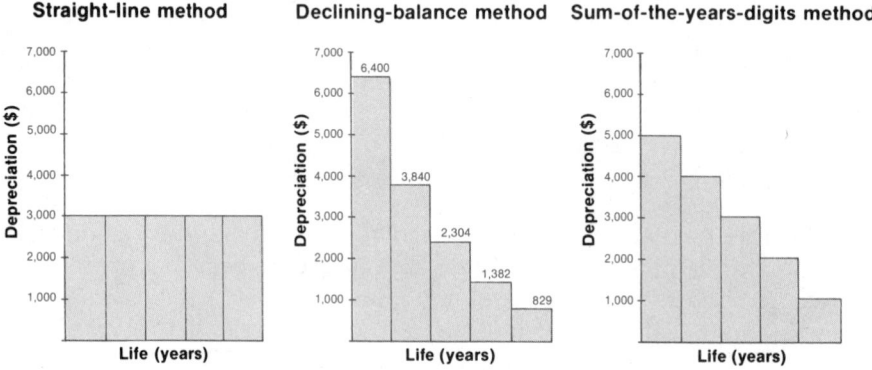

DEPRECIATION FOR FEDERAL INCOME TAX

Each of the four depreciation methods described in the preceding paragraphs can be used to determine the amount of depreciation for federal income tax purposes for plant assets acquired prior to 1981. The accelerated depreciation methods are widely used. Acceleration of the "write-off" of the asset reduces the income tax liability in the earlier years and thus increases the amount of cash available in those years to pay for the asset or for other purposes.

For plant assets acquired after 1980 and before 1987, either the straight-line method or the Accelerated Cost Recovery System (ACRS) could be used for federal income tax purposes. ACRS provided for depreciation deductions that approximated the depreciation calculated by the 150-percent declining-balance method. For most business property, ACRS also provided for three classes of useful life. Each class of useful life was often much shorter than the actual useful life of the asset in that class.

The Tax Reform Act of 1986 revised ACRS by providing for eight classes of useful life for plant assets acquired after 1986. The two most common classes, other than real estate, are the 5-year class and the 7-year class.[4] The 5-year class includes automobiles and light-duty trucks, and the 7-year class includes most machinery and equipment. The depreciation deduction for these two classes approximates the use of the 200-percent declining-balance method.

The Internal Revenue Service has prescribed methods that result in annual percentages to be used in determining depreciation for each class. In using these rates, salvage value is ignored, and all plant assets are assumed to be placed in service in the middle of the year and taken out of service in the middle of the year. Thus, for the 5-year-class assets, for example, depreciation is spread over six years, as shown in the following schedule of ACRS depreciation rates:

Year	5-Year-Class Depreciation Rates
1	20.0%
2	32.0
3	19.2
4	11.5
5	11.5
6	5.8
	100.0%

ACRS DEPRECIATION RATE SCHEDULE

REVISION OF PERIODIC DEPRECIATION

Earlier in this chapter, it was noted that two of the factors that must be considered in computing the periodic depreciation of a plant asset—its residual value at the time it is retired from service and its useful life—must be estimated at the time the asset is placed in service. Minor errors resulting from the use of these estimates are normal and tend to be recurring.[5] When such errors occur, the revised estimates are used to determine the amount of the remaining undepreciated asset cost to be charged as an expense in future periods.

To illustrate, assume that a plant asset purchased for $130,000 and originally estimated to have a useful life of 30 years and a residual value of $10,000 has been depreciated for 10 years by the straight-line method. At the end of

[4]Real estate is classified into 27 1/2-year classes and 31 1/2-year classes and is depreciated by the straight-line method.
[5]The correction of material or large errors made in computing depreciation is discussed in Chapter 16.

ten years, its book value (undepreciated cost) would be $90,000, determined as follows:

Asset cost.	$130,000
Less accumulated depreciation ($4,000 per year×10 years). . .	40,000
Book value (undepreciated cost), end of tenth year	$ 90,000

If during the eleventh year it is estimated that the remaining useful life is 25 years (instead of 20) and that the residual value is $5,000 (instead of $10,000), the depreciation expense for each of the remaining 25 years would be $3,400, determined as follows:

Book value (undepreciated cost), end of tenth year	$90,000
Less revised estimated residual value	5,000
Revised remaining depreciation.	$85,000
Revised annual depreciation expense ($85,000 ÷ 25).	$ 3,400

Note that the correction of minor errors in the estimates used in the determination of depreciation does not affect the amounts of depreciation expense recorded in earlier years. The use of estimates, and the resulting likelihood of minor errors in such estimates, is inherent in the accounting process. Therefore when such errors do occur, the amounts recorded for depreciation expense in the past are not corrected; only future depreciation expense amounts are affected.

RECORDING DEPRECIATION

Depreciation may be recorded by an entry at the end of each month, or the adjustment may be delayed until the end of the year. As illustrated on page 111, the part of the entry that records the decrease in the plant asset is credited to a contra asset account entitled Accumulated Depreciation or Allowance for Depreciation. The use of a contra asset account permits the original cost to remain unchanged in the plant asset account. This facilitates the computation of periodic depreciation, the listing of both cost and accumulated depreciation on the balance sheet, and the reporting required for property tax and income tax purposes.

An exception to the general procedure of recording depreciation monthly or annually is often made when a plant asset is sold, traded in, or scrapped. As discussed and illustrated later in the chapter, the disposal is recorded by removing from the accounts both the cost of the asset and its related accumulated depreciation as of the date of the disposal. Hence, it is advisable to record the additional depreciation on the item for the current period before recording the transaction disposing of the asset. A further advantage of recording the depreciation at the time of the disposal of the asset is that no additional attention need be given the transaction when the amount of the periodic depreciation adjustment for the other plant assets is later determined.

CAPITAL AND REVENUE EXPENDITURES

In addition to the initial cost of acquiring a plant asset, costs for additions made to the asset and other costs related to its efficiency or capacity may be incurred during its service life. Expenditures for additions to a plant asset or expenditures that add to the utility of the asset for more than one accounting period are called capital expenditures. Such expenditures are debited to the asset account or to a related accumulated depreciation account. Expenditures that benefit only the current period and that are made in order to maintain normal operating efficiency are called revenue expenditures. Such expenditures are debited to expense accounts. Although it may be difficult to distinguish between capital and revenue expenditures, care should be exercised so that revenues and expenses will be matched properly. Capital expenditures will affect the depreciation expense of more than one period, while revenue expenditures will affect the expenses of only the current period.

Capital Expenditures

Expenditures for an addition to a plant asset are capital expenditures and should be debited to the plant asset account. For example, the cost of installing an air conditioning unit in an automobile or of adding a wing to a building should be debited to the respective asset account.

Expenditures that increase operating efficiency or capacity for the remaining useful life of an asset should be treated as capital expenditures. For example, if the power unit attached to a machine is replaced by one of greater capacity, the cost should be added to the plant asset account. Also, the cost and the accumulated depreciation related to the old motor should be removed from the accounts. The cost of the new power unit would be depreciated over its estimated useful life.

Expenditures that increase the useful life of an asset beyond the original estimate are also capital expenditures. They should be debited to the appropriate accumulated depreciation account, however, rather than to the asset account. In such circumstances, the expenditures may be said to restore or "make good" a portion of the depreciation accumulated in prior years. To illustrate, assume that a machine with an estimated life of ten years is substantially rebuilt at the end of its seventh year of use, and that the extraordinary repairs are expected to extend the life of the machine an additional three years beyond the original estimate. In this case, the expenditure would be debited to the accumulated depreciation account. In addition, the periodic depreciation for future periods would be redetermined on the basis of the new book value of the asset and the new estimate of the remaining useful life.

Revenue Expenditures

Expenditures for ordinary maintenance and repairs of a recurring nature should be classified as revenue expenditures and debited to expense accounts. For example, the cost of replacing spark plugs in an automobile or the cost of repainting a building should be debited to proper expense accounts.

Small expenditures are usually treated as repair expense, even though they may have the characteristics of capital expenditures. The saving in time and clerical expenses justifies the sacrifice of the small degree of accuracy. Some businesses establish a minimum amount required to classify an item as a capital expenditure.

Summary of Capital and Revenue Expenditures

The initial cost of acquiring a plant asset is debited to a plant asset account. Subsequent to the initial expenditures, the accounting for expenditures related to the plant asset is summarized in the following diagram:

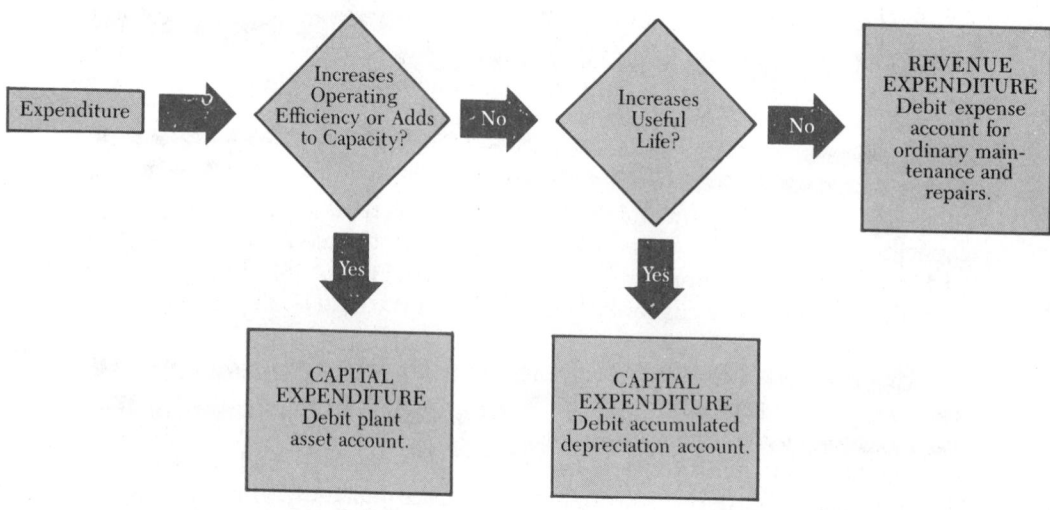

CAPITAL AND REVENUE EXPENDITURES

DISPOSAL OF PLANT ASSETS

Plant assets that are no longer useful may be discarded, sold, or applied toward the purchase of other plant assets. The details of the entry to record a disposal will vary, but in all cases it is necessary to remove the book value of the asset from the accounts. This is done by debiting the proper accumulated depreciation account for the total depreciation to the date of disposal and crediting the asset account for the cost of the asset.

A plant asset should not be removed from the accounts only because it has been depreciated for the full period of its estimated life. If the asset is still useful to the enterprise, the cost and accumulated depreciation should remain in the ledger. Otherwise the accounts would contain no evidence of the continued existence of such plant assets and the control function of the ledger would be impaired. In addition, the cost and the accumulated depreciation data on such assets are often needed in reporting for property tax and income tax purposes.

Discarding Plant Assets   *at book value*

When plant assets are no longer useful to the business and have no market value, they are discarded. If the asset has been fully depreciated, no loss is realized. To illustrate, assume that an item of equipment acquired at a cost of $6,000 became fully depreciated at December 31, the end of the preceding fiscal year, and is now to be discarded as worthless. The entry to record the disposal is as follows:

Mar. 24	Accumulated Depreciation—Equipment . . . . Equipment. . . . . To write off equipment discarded.	6,000	6,000

600 × 7 = 4200

If the accumulated depreciation applicable to the $6,000 of discarded equipment had been less than $6,000, there would have been a loss on its disposal. Furthermore, it would have been necessary to record depreciation for the three months of use in the current period before recording the disposal. To illustrate these differences, assume that annual depreciation on the equipment is computed at 10% of cost and that the accumulated depreciation balance is $4,750 after the annual adjusting entry at the end of the preceding year. The entry to record depreciation of $150 for the three months of the current period is as follows:

450

4200
450
4650

$$\frac{600}{1} \times \frac{3}{12} = 150$$

from Jan 1 to March 24

Mar. 24	Depreciation Expense — Equipment	150	
	Accumulated Depreciation — Equipment ..		150
	To record current depreciation on		
	equipment discarded.		

The equipment is then removed from the accounts and the loss is recorded by the following entry:

4750+150=4900

Mar. 24	Accumulated Depreciation — Equipment	4,900	
	Loss on Disposal of Plant Assets	1,100	
	Equipment...........................		6,000
	To write off equipment discarded.		

Ordinary losses and gains on the disposal of plant assets are non-operating items and may be reported in the Other Expense and Other Income sections, respectively, of the income statement.

Sale of Plant Assets

The entry to record the sale of a plant asset is like the entries illustrated in the preceding section, except that the cash or other asset received must also be recorded. If the selling price is more than the book value of the asset, the transaction results in a gain; if the selling price is less than the book value, there is a loss. To illustrate some possibilities, assume that equipment acquired at a cost of $10,000 and depreciated at the annual rate of 10% of cost is sold for cash on October 12 of the eighth year of its use. The accumulated depreciation in the account as of the preceding December 31 is $7,000. The entry to record the depreciation for the nine months of the current year is as follows:

7000
750
7750

Oct. 12	Depreciation Expense — Equipment	750	
	Accumulated Depreciation — Equipment ..		750
	To record current depreciation on		
	equipment sold.		

After the current depreciation is recorded, the book value of the asset is $2,250. In general journal form, entries to record the sale under three different assumptions as to selling price are as follows:

Sold at book value, for $2,250. No gain or loss.

Oct. 12	Cash	2,250	
	Accumulated Depreciation—Equipment	7,750	
	Equipment		10,000

Sold below book value, for $1,000. Loss of $1,250.

Oct. 12	Cash	1,000	
	Accumulated Depreciation—Equipment	7,750	
	Loss on Disposal of Plant Assets	1,250	
	Equipment		10,000

Sold above book value, for $3,000. Gain of $750.

Oct. 12	Cash	3,000	
	Accumulated Depreciation—Equipment	7,750	
	Equipment		10,000
	Gain on Disposal of Plant Assets		750

Exchange of Plant Assets

Old equipment is often traded in for new equipment having a similar use. The trade-in allowance is deducted from the price of the new equipment, and the balance owed (boot) is paid according to the credit terms. The trade-in allowance given by the seller is often greater or less than the book value of the old equipment traded in. In the past, it was acceptable for financial reporting purposes to recognize the difference between the trade-in allowance and the book value as a gain or a loss. For example, a trade-in allowance of $1,500 on equipment with a book value of $1,000 would have yielded a recognized gain of $500. Such treatment is no longer acceptable for financial reporting purposes on the theory that revenue occurs from the production and sale of items produced by plant assets and not from the exchange of similar plant assets. However, if the trade-in allowance is less than the book value of the old equipment, the loss is recognized immediately.

Nonrecognition of Gain. The acceptable method of accounting for an exchange in which the trade-in allowance exceeds the book value of the old plant asset requires that the cost of the new asset be determined by adding the amount of boot given to the book value of the old asset. To illustrate, assume an exchange based on the following data:

Equipment traded in (old):

Cost of old equipment	$4,000
Accumulated depreciation at date of exchange	3,200
Book value at June 19, date of exchange	$ 800

Similar equipment acquired (new):

Price of new equipment............................	$5,000
Trade-in allowance on old equipment................	1,100
Boot given (cash)	$3,900

The cost basis of the new equipment is **$4,700**, which is determined by adding the boot given (**$3,900**) to the book value of the old equipment (**$800**). The compound entry to record the exchange and the payment of cash, in general journal form, is as follows:

June 19 Accumulated Depreciation—Equipment.............	3,200	
Equipment..	4,700	
Equipment....................................		4,000
Cash...		3,900

[handwritten margin note: adjust the basis reduce equipment by gain]

It should be noted that the nonrecognition of the $300 gain ($1,100 trade-in allowance minus $800 book value) at the time of the exchange is really a postponement. The periodic depreciation expense is based on a cost of $4,700 rather than on the quoted price of $5,000. The unrecognized gain of $300 at the time of the exchange will be matched by a reduction of $300 in the total amount of depreciation taken during the life of the equipment.

Recognition of Loss. To illustrate the accounting for a loss on the exchange of one plant asset for another which is similar in use, assume an exchange based on the following data:

Equipment traded in (old):

Cost of old equipment	$ 7,000
Accumulated depreciation at date of exchange	4,600
Book value at September 7, date of exchange.......	$ 2,400

Similar equipment acquired (new):

Price of new equipment...........................	$10,000
Trade-in allowance on old equipment..............	2,000
Boot given (cash)	$ 8,000

The amount of the loss to be recognized on the exchange is the excess of the book value of the equipment traded in (**$2,400**) over the trade-in allowance (**$2,000**), or **$400**. The entry to record the exchange, in general journal form, is as follows:

Sept. 7 Accumulated Depreciation—Equipment	4,600	
Equipment..	10,000	
Loss on Disposal of Plant Assets	400	
Equipment....................................		7,000
Cash		8,000

Federal Income Tax Requirements. The Internal Revenue Code (IRC) requires that neither gains nor losses be recognized for income tax purposes if (1) the asset acquired by the taxpayer is similar in use to the asset given in exchange and (2) any boot involved is given (rather than received) by the taxpayer. Thus, the treatment of a nonrecognized gain corresponds to the acceptable method prescribed for financial reporting purposes, the boot given being added to the book value of the old equipment. In the first illustration, the cost basis for federal income tax purposes corresponds to the amount recorded as the cost of the new equipment, namely $4,700.

The cost basis of the new equipment in the second illustration, for federal income tax purposes, is determined in a like manner. The boot given ($8,000) is added to the book value of the old equipment ($2,400), yielding a cost basis of $10,400. The unrecognized loss of $400 at the time of the exchange will be matched by an increase of $400 in the total amount of depreciation allowed for income tax purposes during the life of the asset.

SUBSIDIARY LEDGERS FOR PLANT ASSETS

When depreciation is to be computed individually on a large number of assets making up a functional group, it is advisable to maintain a subsidiary ledger. To illustrate, assume that an enterprise owns about 200 items of office equipment with a total cost of about $100,000. Unless the business is newly organized, the equipment would have been acquired over a number of years. The individual cost, estimated residual value, and estimated useful life would be different in each case, and the makeup of the group will continually change because of acquisitions and disposals.

There are many variations in the form of subsidiary records for depreciable assets. Multicolumn analysis sheets may be used, or a separate ledger account may be maintained for each asset. The form should be designed to provide spaces for recording the acquisition and the disposal of the asset, the depreciation charged each period, the accumulated depreciation to date, and any other pertinent data desired. Following is an example of a subsidiary ledger account for a plant asset:

AN ACCOUNT IN THE OFFICE EQUIPMENT LEDGER

Plant Asset Record

Account No.: 123-215
General Ledger Account: Office Equipment
Item: SF 490 COPIER

Serial No.: AT 47-3926
From Whom Purchased: Hamilton Office Machines Co. Inc.
Estimated Useful Life: 10 Years Estimated Residual Value: $500 Depreciation per Year: $240

	Asset			Accumulated Depreciation			Book
Date	Debit	Credit	Balance	Debit	Credit	Balance	Value
04/08/87	2,900		2,900				2,900
12/31/87					180	180	2,720
12/31/88					240	420	2,480

The number assigned to the account illustrated is made up of the number of the office equipment account in the general ledger (123) followed by the number assigned to the specific item of office equipment purchased (215). An identification tag or plaque with the corresponding account number is attached to the asset. Depreciation for the year in which the asset was acquired, computed for nine months on a straight-line basis, is $180; for the following year it is $240. These amounts, together with the corresponding amounts from all other accounts in the subsidiary ledger, provide the figures for the respective year-end adjusting entries debiting the depreciation expense account and crediting the accumulated depreciation account.

The sum of the asset balances and the sum of the accumulated depreciation balances in all of the accounts should be compared periodically with the balances of their respective controlling accounts in the general ledger. When a certain asset is disposed of, the asset section of the subsidiary account is credited and the accumulated depreciation section is debited. This reduces the balances of both sections to zero. The account is then removed from the ledger and filed for possible future reference.

Subsidiary ledgers for plant assets are useful to the accounting department in (1) determining the periodic depreciation expense, (2) recording the disposal of individual items, (3) preparing tax returns, and (4) preparing insurance claims in the event of insured losses. The forms may also be expanded to provide spaces for accumulating data on the operating efficiency of the asset. Such information as number of breakdowns, length of time out of service, and cost of repairs is useful in comparing similar equipment produced by different manufacturers. When new equipment is to be purchased, the data are useful to management in deciding upon size, model, and other specifications and the best source of supply.

Regardless of whether subsidiary equipment ledgers are maintained, plant assets should be inspected periodically in order to determine their state of repair and whether or not they are still in use.

COMPOSITE-RATE DEPRECIATION METHOD

In the preceding illustrations, depreciation has been computed on each individual plant asset and, unless otherwise stated, this procedure will be assumed in the problem materials at the end of the chapter. Another procedure, called the composite-rate depreciation method, is to determine depreciation for entire groups of assets by use of a single rate. The basis for grouping may be similarity in life estimates or other common traits, or it may be broadened to include all assets within a functional class, such as office equipment or factory equipment.

When depreciation is computed on the basis of a composite group of assets of differing life spans, a rate based on averages must be developed. This may be done by (1) computing the annual depreciation for each asset,

(2) determining the total annual depreciation, and (3) dividing the sum thus determined by the total cost of the assets. The procedure is illustrated as follows:

Asset No.	Cost	Estimated Residual Value	Estimated Life	Annual Depreciation
101	$ 20,000	$4,000	10 years	$ 1,600
102	15,600	1,500	15 years	940
147	41,000	1,000	8 years	5,000
Total	$473,400			$49,707

$$\frac{\$49,707 \text{ annual depreciation}}{\$473,400 \text{ cost}} = 10.5\% \text{ composite rate}$$

Although new assets of differing life spans and residual values will be added to the group and old assets will be retired, the "mix" is assumed to remain relatively unchanged. Accordingly, a depreciation rate based on averages (10.5% in the illustration) also remains unchanged for an indefinite time in the future.

When a composite rate is used, it may be applied against total asset cost on a monthly basis, or some reasonable assumption may be made regarding the timing of increases and decreases in the group. A common practice is to assume that all additions and retirements have occurred uniformly throughout the year. The composite rate is then applied to the average of the beginning and the ending balances of the account. Another acceptable averaging technique is to assume that all additions and retirements during the first half of the year occurred as of the first day of the year, and that all additions and retirements during the second half of the year occurred on the first day of the following year.

When assets within the composite group are retired, no gain or loss should be recognized. Instead, the asset account is credited for the cost of the asset and the accumulated depreciation account is debited for the excess of cost over the amount realized from the disposal. Any deficiency in the amount of depreciation recorded on the shorter-lived assets is presumed to be balanced by excessive depreciation on the longer-lived assets.

Regardless of whether depreciation is computed for each individual unit or for composite groups, the periodic depreciation charge is based on estimates. The effect of obsolescence and inadequacy on the life of plant assets is particularly difficult to forecast. Any system that provides for the allocation of depreciation in a systematic and rational manner fulfills the requirements of good accounting.

AT&T-Line Depreciation

Ever hear the term "reserve deficiency"? It's a term that the nation's 1,400 local telephone companies are using quite a bit these days. What it means is a $26 billion-plus time bomb on their balance sheets — the amount by which they have underdepreciated old equipment that they will have to replace to keep from becoming obsolete in the age of deregulation.

That $26 billion represents over 10% of the operating companies' $195.8 billion physical plant — telephone poles, miles of copper wire and giant switching stations, all built in the days when telecommunications was dominated by a monopoly jointly overseen by the Bell system and the government. Indeed, the 22 Bell operating companies account for over $20 billion of the total shortfall.

In the monopoly days, Bell executives sat down with state and federal regulators, estimated how long a new piece of equipment would last, and stretched the depreciation accordingly — sometimes for longer than 40 years. Independent companies followed the pattern. That cozy arrangement suited everybody's purposes: The companies could count on a steady revenue stream, shareholders got a stable return, and consumers benefited from low telephone rates.

Result: As Cornell's Alfred E. Kahn puts it: "Depreciation lives were set under a monopoly that was in a position to control the rate of innovation." No matter how long the costs were stretched out, they were certain to be recovered. And if the geniuses at Bell Labs came up with something new — improved fiber optics, say — it was unlikely that billions of dollars' worth of copper wire would be pulled out until it was fully depreciated.

No more. With deregulation, anybody with the wherewithal can put in a state-of-the-art telephone system vastly more efficient and cheaper than old-fashioned copper wires and mechanical switching. Some of the telephone companies' biggest customers are doing just that.

All in all, says a study by the U.S. Telephone Association, local operating companies could lose $8.4 billion in annual revenues by 1995 because big customers are bypassing them.

So the local companies are spending big — an estimated $18 billion this year on capital construction — in a rush to install digital switching and fiber optics before their big customers desert them for good. Trouble is, they still have that $26 billion in old plant on their books that won't be depreciated for years.

While most states are gradually phasing in higher depreciation rates, few states approach 10% composite annual depreciation, a rate that could begin to redress the capital recovery problem.

What will happen? Unless somebody comes up with a better solution, which isn't likely, the telephone companies are going to have to write off some of that $26 billion, probably a lot of it. Alfred Kahn compares their plight to that of a utility with an abandoned nuclear plant. "You just have to eat some of that deficiency," he says. "You have to write down the assets to something more closely approximating what you can hope to get back in the future, write down your equity on the other side of the balance sheet, and take your loss."

Source: Adapted from "The $26 Billion Solution," *Forbes* (July 29, 1985), pp. 40–41.

DEPRECIATION OF PLANT ASSETS OF LOW UNIT COST

Subsidiary ledgers are not usually maintained for classes of plant assets that are made up of individual items of low unit cost. Hand tools and other portable equipment of small size and value are typical examples. Because of hard usage, breakage, and pilferage, such assets may be relatively short-lived and may require constant replacement. In such cases, the usual depreciation methods are not practical. One common method of determining cost expiration is to take a periodic inventory of the items on hand, estimate their fair value based on original cost, and transfer the remaining amount from the asset account to an appropriately titled account, such as Tools Expense. Other categories to which the same method is often applied are dies, molds, patterns, and spare parts.

ACQUISITION OF PLANT ASSETS THROUGH LEASING

Instead of owning a plant asset, a business may acquire the use of a plant asset through a lease. A **lease** is a contractual agreement that conveys the right to use an asset for a stated period of time. The two parties to a lease contract are the **lessor** and the **lessee**. The lessor is the party who legally owns the asset and who conveys the rights to use the asset to the lessee. Typical lease transactions include the leasing of automobiles, computers, airplanes, and communication satellites.

In agreeing to a lease, the lessee incurs an obligation to make periodic rent payments for the lease term. In accounting for lease obligations, all leases are classified by the lessee as either capital leases or operating leases. **Capital leases** are defined as leases which include one or more of the following provisions: (1) the lease transfers ownership of the leased asset to the lessee at the end of the lease term; (2) the lease contains an option for a bargain purchase of the leased asset by the lessee; (3) the lease term extends over most of the economic life of the leased asset; or (4) the lease requires rental payments which approximate the fair market value of the leased asset.[6] Leases which do not meet the preceding criteria for a capital lease are classified as **operating leases**.

A capital lease is accounted for as if the lessee has, in fact, purchased the asset. Accordingly, when a lease is executed, the lessee would debit an asset account for the fair market value of the leased asset and would credit a long-term lease liability account. The complex accounting procedures applicable to capital leases are discussed in detail in more advanced accounting texts.

---

[6]*Statement of Financial Accounting Standards, No. 13,* "Accounting for Leases" (Stamford: Financial Accounting Standards Board, 1976), par. 7.

In accounting for operating leases, rent expense is recognized as the leased asset is used. Neither future lease obligations nor the future rights to use the leased asset are recognized in the accounts. However, the lessee must disclose future lease commitments in footnotes to the financial statements.[7]

DEPLETION

The periodic allocation of the cost of metal ores and other minerals removed from the earth is called depletion. The amount of the periodic cost allocation is based on the relationship of the cost to the estimated size of the mineral deposit and on the quantity extracted during the particular period. To illustrate, assume that the cost of certain mineral rights is $400,000 and that the deposit is estimated at 1,000,000 tons of ore of uniform grade. The depletion rate would be $400,000 ÷ 1,000,000, or $.40 a ton. If 90,000 tons are mined during the year, the depletion, amounting to $36,000, would be recorded by the following entry:

	Adjusting Entry		
Dec. 31	Depletion Expense	36,000	
	Accumulated Depletion		36,000

The accumulated depletion account is a contra asset account and is presented in the balance sheet as a deduction from the cost of the mineral deposit.

In determining income subject to the federal income tax, the IRC permits, with certain limitations, a depletion deduction equal to a specified percent of gross income from the extractive operations. Thus, for income tax purposes, it is possible for total depletion deductions to be more than the cost of the property. A detailed examination of the tax law and regulations regarding "percentage depletion" is beyond the scope of this discussion, however.

INTANGIBLE ASSETS

Long-lived assets that are useful in the operations of an enterprise, not held for sale, and without physical qualities are usually classified as intangible assets. The basic principles of accounting for intangible assets are like those described earlier for plant assets. The major concerns are the determination of the initial costs and the recognition of periodic cost expiration, called amortization, due to the passage of time or a decline in usefulness. Intangible assets often include patents, copyrights, and goodwill.

---

[7]*Ibid.*, par. 16.

Patents

Manufacturers may acquire exclusive rights to produce and sell goods with one or more unique features. Such rights are evidenced by **patents**, which are issued to inventors by the federal government. They continue in effect for 17 years. An enterprise may purchase patent rights from others or it may obtain patents on new products developed in its own research laboratories.

The initial cost of a purchased patent should be debited to an asset account and then written off, or amortized, over the years of its expected usefulness. This period of time may be less than the remaining legal life of the patent, and the expectations are also subject to change in the future. The straight-line method of amortization should be used unless it can be shown that another method is more appropriate.[8]

A separate contra asset account is normally not credited for the write-off or amortization of patents. In most situations, the credit is recorded directly in the patents account. This practice is common for all intangible assets. To illustrate, assume that at the beginning of its fiscal year an enterprise acquires for $100,000 a patent granted six years earlier. Although the patent will not expire for another eleven years, it is expected to be of value for only five years. The entry to amortize the patent at the end of the fiscal year is as follows:

	Adjusting Entry		
Dec. 31	Amortization Expense—Patents	20,000	
	Patents		20,000

Continuing the illustration, assume that after two years of use it appears that the patent will have no value at the end of an additional two years. The cost to be amortized in the third year would be the balance of the asset account, $60,000, divided by the remaining two years, or $30,000.

An enterprise that develops patentable products in its own research laboratories often incurs substantial costs for the experimental work involved. In theory, some accountants believe that such costs, normally referred to as **research and development costs**, should be treated as an asset in the same manner as patent rights purchased from others. However, business enterprises are generally required to treat expenditures for research and development as current operating expenses.[9] The reason for this requirement is

---

[8]*Opinions of the Accounting Principles Board, No. 17*, "Intangible Assets" (New York: American Institute of Certified Public Accountants, 1970), par. 30.
[9]*Statement of Financial Accounting Standards, No. 2*, "Accounting for Research and Development Costs" (Stamford: Financial Accounting Standards Board, 1974), par. 12.

that there is a high degree of uncertainty about their future benefits, and therefore expensing these costs as incurred seems most appropriate. In addition, from a practical standpoint, a reasonably fair cost figure for each patent is difficult to establish because a number of research projects may be in process at the same time or work on some projects may extend over a number of years. As a result, a specific relationship between research and development costs and future revenue seldom can be established.

Whether patent rights are purchased from others or result from the effort of its own research laboratories, an enterprise often incurs substantial legal fees related to the patents. For example, legal fees may be incurred in establishing the legal validity of the patents. Such fees should be debited to an asset account and then amortized over the years of the usefulness of the patents.

Copyrights

The exclusive right to publish and sell a literary, artistic, or musical composition is obtained by a **copyright**. Copyrights are issued by the federal government and extend for 50 years beyond the author's death. The costs assigned to a copyright include all costs of creating the work plus the cost of obtaining the copyright. A copyright that is purchased from another should be recorded at the price paid for it. Because of the uncertainty regarding the useful life of a copyright, it is usually amortized over a relatively short period of time.

Goodwill

In the sense that it is used in business, **goodwill** is an intangible asset that attaches to a business as a result of such favorable factors as location, product superiority, reputation, and managerial skill. Its existence is evidenced by the ability of the business to earn a rate of return on the investment that is in excess of the normal rate for other firms in the same line of business.

Accountants are in general agreement that goodwill should be recognized in the accounts only if it can be objectively determined by an event or transaction, such as the purchase or sale of a business. Accountants also agree that the value of goodwill eventually disappears and that the recorded costs should be amortized over the years during which the goodwill is expected to be of value. This period should not, however, exceed 40 years.[10]

---

[10]*Opinions of the Accounting Principles Board, No. 17,* "Intangible Assets," *op. cit.,* par. 29.

REPORTING DEPRECIATION EXPENSE, PLANT ASSETS, AND INTANGIBLE ASSETS IN THE FINANCIAL STATEMENTS

The amount of depreciation expense of a period should be set forth separately in the income statement or disclosed in some other manner. A general description of the method or methods used in computing depreciation should also accompany the financial statements.[11]

The balance of each major class of depreciable assets should be disclosed in the balance sheet or in notes thereto, together with the related accumulated depreciation, either by major class or in total.[12] When there are too many classes of plant assets to permit such a detailed listing in the balance sheet, a single figure may be presented, supported by a separate schedule.

Intangible assets are usually presented in the balance sheet in a separate section immediately following plant assets. The balance of each major class of intangible assets should be disclosed at an amount net of amortization taken to date.

An illustration of the presentation of plant assets and intangible assets is shown in the following partial balance sheet:

Clinton Door Inc.
Balance Sheet
December 31, 19--

Assets

	Cost	Accumulated Depreciation	Book Value	
Total current assets..				$462,500
Plant assets:				
Land.................	$ 30,000	—	$ 30,000	
Buildings	110,000	$ 26,000	84,000	
Factory equipment.....	650,000	192,000	458,000	
Office equipment......	120,000	13,000	107,000	
Total plant assets....	$910,000	$231,000		679,000
Intangible assets:				
Patents...............			$ 75,000	
Goodwill.............			50,000	
Total intangible assets				125,000

---

[11]*Opinions of the Accounting Principles Board, No. 22,* "Disclosure of Accounting Policies" (New York: American Institute of Certified Public Accountants, 1972), par. 13.

[12]*Opinions of the Accounting Principles Board, No. 12,* "Omnibus Opinion—1967" (New York: American Institute of Certified Public Accountants, 1967), par. 5.

CHAPTER REVIEW

KEY POINTS

1. Initial Costs of Plant Assets.

The initial cost of a plant asset includes all expenditures necessary to get it in place and ready for use. Such expenditures include sales taxes, transportation charges, insurance on the asset while in transit, special foundations, installation costs, broker's commissions, and title fees.

2. Nature of Depreciation.

As time passes, all plant assets with the exception of land lose their capacity to yield services. This expiration of the cost of plant assets is called depreciation.

3. Determining Depreciation.

In determining the amount of depreciation, three factors need to be considered: (1) the plant asset's initial cost, (2) the residual value of the asset, and (3) the useful life of the asset. The difference between a plant asset's initial cost and its residual value is the cost that is to be spread over the useful life of the asset.

The four methods of depreciation used most often are summarized as follows:

Straight-line...............	Provides for equal periodic charges to expense over the estimated useful life of the asset.
Units-of-production	Yields a depreciation charge that varies with the amount of asset usage. Length of useful life of asset expressed in terms of productive capacity.
Declining-balance	Yields a declining periodic depreciation charge over the estimated useful life of the asset. Rate of depreciation usually twice the straight-line rate. Computed without regard to residual value. Resulting rate applied to cost of asset less accumulated depreciation.
Sum-of-the-year-digits	Yields a steadily declining periodic depreciation charge over the estimated useful life of the asset. Successively smaller fraction applied each year to the original cost of the asset less the estimated residual value.

All four depreciation methods will yield a total depreciation over the life of the asset which is the same. However, each method will yield periodic charges which may vary significantly. Because the declining-balance and the sum-of-the-years-digits methods provide a higher depreciation charge in the early years of the life of the asset and a gradually declining charge thereafter, they are referred to as accelerated depreciation methods.

4. Depreciation for Federal Income Tax.

Each of the four depreciation methods described in this chapter can be used to determine the amount of depreciation for federal income tax purposes for plant assets acquired prior to 1981. For plant assets acquired after 1980 and before 1987, either the straight-line method or the Accelerated Cost Recovery System (ACRS) may be used. The Tax Reform Act of 1986 revised ACRS for plant assets acquired after 1986.

5. Revision of Periodic Depreciation.

Minor errors resulting from incorrect estimates of a plant asset's useful life and residual value are corrected by revising estimates used to determine the amount of remaining undepreciated asset cost to be charged to expense in future periods.

6. Recording Depreciation.

Depreciation is recorded periodically by debiting depreciation expense and crediting a contra asset account entitled accumulated depreciation. The use of a contra asset account permits the original cost to remain unchanged in the plant asset account.

7. Capital and Revenue Expenditures.

In addition to the initial cost of acquiring a plant asset, costs for additions made to the asset and other costs related to its efficiency or capacity may be incurred during its service life. Costs for additions or costs that add to the utility of the asset for more than one period are chargeable to an asset account or to a related accumulated depreciation account and are called capital expenditures. Expenditures that benefit only the current period and that are made in order to maintain normal operating efficiency are chargeable to expense accounts and are called revenue expenditures.

8. Disposal of Plant Assets.

Plant assets that are no longer useful may be discarded, sold, or traded in on other plant assets. When disposal of a plant asset occurs, the cost of the plant asset and the accumulated depreciation must be removed from the accounts and any related gain or loss recognized.

9. Subsidiary Ledgers for Plant Assets.

When depreciation is to be computed individually on a large number of assets making up a functional group, it is advisable to maintain a subsidiary ledger. Subsidiary ledgers for plant assets are useful in determining the periodic depreciation expense, recording the disposal of individual items, preparing tax returns, and preparing insurance claims in the event of insured losses.

10. Composite-Rate Depreciation Method.

Depreciation determined for an entire group of assets by use of a single rate is referred to as composite-rate depreciation. When this method is used to compute depreciation on a group of assets of differing life spans, a rate based on averages must be developed.

11. Depreciation of Plant Assets of Low Unit Cost.

For classes of plant assets that are made up of individual items of low unit cost, depreciation is often determined by periodically taking an inventory of items on hand, estimating their fair value based on original cost, and transferring the remaining amount from the asset account to an expense account.

12. Acquisition of Plant Assets Through Leasing.

Instead of owning a plant asset, a business may acquire the use of a plant asset through a lease. A lease agreement conveys the right to use an asset for a stated period of time. A capital lease is accounted for as if the lessee has, in fact, purchased the asset. An operating lease recognizes lease payments as rent expense for the lessee and as rent income for the lessor.

13. Depletion.

The periodic allocation of the cost of metal ores and other minerals removed from the earth is called depletion. The amount of the periodic cost allocation is based on the relationship of the cost to the estimated size of the mineral deposit, and on the quantity extracted during the particular period. An accumulated depletion account is maintained as a contra account to the original cost of the mineral deposit.

14. Intangible Assets.

Long-lived assets that are useful in the operations of an enterprise, not held for sale, and without physical qualities are usually classified as intangible assets. The initial cost of an intangible asset is normally amortized over its useful life. Intangible assets include patents, copyrights, and goodwill.

15. Reporting Depreciation Expense, Plant Assets, and Intangible Assets in the Financial Statements.

The amount of depreciation expense and the method or methods used in computing depreciation should be disclosed in the financial statements. In addition, each major class of depreciable assets should be disclosed, along with the related accumulated depreciation. Intangible assets are usually presented in the balance sheet in a separate section immediately following plant assets. Each major class of intangible assets should be disclosed at an amount net of amortization taken to date.

KEY TERMS

plant assets 464
depreciation 465
residual value 466
straight-line method 468
units-of-production method 469
declining-balance method 470
sum-of-the-years-digits
    method 470
accelerated depreciation
    method 472
capital expenditures 475

revenue expenditures 475
boot 479
composite-rate depreciation
    method 482
capital leases 485
operating leases 485
depletion 486
intangible assets 486
amortization 486
goodwill 488

SELF-EXAMINATION QUESTIONS

Answers in Appendix B.

1. Which of the following expenditures incurred in connection with the acquisition of machinery is a proper charge to the asset account?
   A. Transportation charges   C. Both A and B
   B. Installation costs   D. Neither A nor B

2. What is the amount of depreciation, using the sum-of-the-years-digits method, for the first year of use for equipment costing $9,500, with an estimated residual value of $500 and an estimated life of 3 years?
   A. $4,500.00   C. $3,000.00
   B. $3,166.67   D. None of the above

3. An example of an accelerated depreciation method is:
   A. straight-line   C. units-of-production
   B. sum-of-the-years-digits   D. none of the above

4. A plant asset priced at $100,000 is acquired by trading in a similar asset that has a book value of $25,000. Assuming that the trade-in allowance is $30,000 and that $70,000 cash is paid for the new asset, what is the cost basis for the new asset for financial reporting purposes?
   A. $100,000   C. $30,000
   B. $70,000   D. None of the above

5. Which of the following is an example of an intangible asset?
   A. Patents   C. Copyrights
   B. Goodwill   D. All of the above

ILLUSTRATIVE PROBLEM

Florence Company acquired new equipment at a cost of $75,000 at the beginning of the fiscal year. The equipment has an estimated life of five years and an estimated residual value of $6,000. The president, John C. Florence, has requested information regarding the alternative depreciation methods.

Instructions:

1. Determine the annual depreciation for each of the five years of estimated useful life of the equipment, the accumulated depreciation at the end of each year, and the book value of the equipment at the end of each year by (a) the straight-line method, (b) the declining-balance method (at twice the straight-line rate), and (c) the sum-of-the-years-digits method.
2. Assume that the equipment was depreciated under the declining-balance method. In the first week of the fifth year, the equipment was traded in for similar equipment priced at $90,000. The trade-in allowance on the old equipment was $8,000, and cash was paid for the balance.
   a. Prepare the journal entry to record the exchange.
   b. What is the cost basis of the new equipment for computing the amount of depreciation allowable for income tax purposes?

SOLUTION

(1)

	Year	Depreciation Expense	Accumulated Depreciation, End of Year	Book Value, End of Year
(a)	1	$13,800	$13,800	$61,200
	2	13,800	27,600	47,400
	3	13,800	41,400	33,600
	4	13,800	55,200	19,800
	5	13,800	69,000	6,000
(b)	1	$30,000	$30,000	$45,000
	2	18,000	48,000	27,000
	3	10,800	58,800	16,200
	4	6,480	65,280	9,720
	5	3,720*	69,000	6,000
(c)	1	$23,000	$23,000	$52,000
	2	18,400	41,400	33,600
	3	13,800	55,200	19,800
	4	9,200	64,400	10,600
	5	4,600	69,000	6,000

*The asset is not depreciated below the estimated residual value of $6,000.

(2)(a) Accumulated Depreciation — Equipment....... 65,280
      Equipment.................................. 90,000   *157000*
      Loss on Disposal of Plant Assets............. 1,720
        Equipment..............................   75,000   *157006*
        Cash....................................   82,000

(b) Book value of old equipment...................... $ 9,720
    Boot given (cash)................................ 82,000
    Cost basis of new equipment for income tax purposes .. $91,720

or

    Price of new equipment............................ $90,000
    Plus unrecognized loss on old equipment............ 1,720
    Cost basis of new equipment for income tax purposes .. $91,720

DISCUSSION QUESTIONS

1. Which of the following qualities are characteristic of plant assets? (a) tangible, (b) intangible, (c) capable of repeated use in the operations of the business, (d) long-lived, (e) held for sale in the normal course of business, (f) used continuously in the operations of the business.

2. Shay Office Equipment Co. has a fleet of automobiles and trucks for use by salespersons and for delivery of office supplies and equipment. Martin Auto Sales Inc. has automobiles and trucks for sale. Under what caption would the automobiles and trucks be reported on the balance sheet of (a) Shay Office Equipment Co., (b) Martin Auto Sales Inc.?

3. Roarke and Simons Co. acquired an adjacent vacant lot as a speculation. The lot will hopefully be sold in the future at a gain. Where should such real estate be listed in the balance sheet?

4. Which of the following expenditures incurred in connection with the acquisition of a lathe should be charged to the asset account? (a) sales tax on purchase price, (b) freight charges, (c) insurance while in transit, (d) cost of special foundation (e) new parts to replace those damaged in unloading, (f) fee paid to factory representative for installation.

5. Which of the following expenditures incurred in connection with the purchase of a secondhand printing press should be debited to the asset account? (a) freight

charges, (b) installation costs, (c) repair of vandalism damages that occurred during installation, (d) replacement of worn-out parts.

6. To increase its parking area, Market Place Shopping Center acquired adjoining land for $80,000 and a building located on the land for $40,000. The net cost of razing the building and leveling the land was $10,000, after amounts received from the sale of salvaged building materials were deducted. What accounts should be debited for (a) the cost of the land ($80,000), (b) the cost of the building ($40,000), (c) the net cost of preparing the land ($10,000)?

7. Are the amounts at which plant assets are reported in the balance sheet their approximate market values as of the balance sheet date? Discuss.

8. (a) Does the recognition of depreciation in the accounts provide a special cash fund for the replacement of plant assets? Explain. (b) Describe the nature of depreciation as the term is used in accounting.

9. Name the three factors that need to be considered in determining the amount of periodic depreciation.

10. Is it necessary for an enterprise to use the same method of computing depreciation (a) for all classes of its depreciable assets, (b) in the financial statements and in the determination of income taxes?

11. Of the four common depreciation methods, which is most widely used?

12. Convert each of the following estimates of useful life to a straight-line depreciation rate, stated as a percent, assuming that the residual value of the plant assset is to be ignored: (a) 4 years, (b) 5 years, (c) 10 years, (d) 20 years, (e) 25 years, (f) 40 years, (g) 50 years.

13. A plant asset with a cost of $85,000 has an estimated residual value of $5,000 and an estimated useful life of 4 years. What is the amount of the annual depreciation, computed by the straight-line method?

14. A plant asset with a cost of $95,000 has an estimated residual value of $5,000 and an estimated productive capacity of 900,000 units. What is the amount of annual depreciation, computed by the units-of-production method, for a year in which production is (a) 90,000 units, (b) 60,000 units?

15. The declining-balance method, at double the straight-line rate, is to be used for an asset with a cost of $100,000, estimated residual value of $10,000, and estimated useful life of 10 years. What is the depreciation for the first fiscal year, assuming that the asset was placed in service at the beginning of the year?

16. An asset with a cost of $26,000, an estimated residual value of $1,000, and an estimated useful life of 4 years is to be depreciated by the sum-of-the-years-digits method. (a) What is the denominator of the depreciation fraction? (b) What is the amount of depreciation for the first full year of use? (c) What is the amount of depreciation for the second full year of use?

17. (a) Name the two accelerated depreciation methods described in this chapter. (b) Why are the accelerated depreciation methods used frequently for income tax purposes?

18. A plant asset with a cost of $205,000 has an estimated residual value of $5,000, an estimated useful life of 40 years, and is depreciated by the straight-line method. (a) What is the amount of the annual depreciation? (b) What is the book value at the end of the twentieth year of use? (c) If at the start of the twenty-first year it is estimated that the remaining life is 25 years and that the residual value is $5,000, what is the depreciation expense for each of the remaining 25 years?

19. (a) Differentiate between capital expenditures and revenue expenditures. (b) Why are some items that have the characteristics of capital expenditures treated as revenue expenditures?

20. Immediately after a used truck is acquired, a new motor is installed and the tires are replaced at a total cost of $3,500. Is this a capital expenditure or a revenue expenditure?

21. For a number of subsidiary plant ledger accounts of an enterprise, the balance in accumulated depreciation is exactly equal to the cost of the asset. (a) Is it permissible to record additional depreciation on the assets if they are still useful to the enterprise? Explain. (b) When should an entry be made to remove the cost and accumulated depreciation from the accounts?

22. In what sections of the income statement are gains and losses from the disposal of plant assets presented?

23. A plant asset priced at $120,000 is acquired by trading in a similar asset and paying cash for the remainder. (a) Assuming that the trade-in allowance is $50,000, what is the amount of boot given? (b) Assuming that the book value of the asset traded in is $40,000, what is the cost basis of the new asset for financial reporting purposes? (c) What is the cost basis of the new asset for the computation of depreciation for federal income tax purposes?

24. Assume the same facts as in Question 23, except that the book value of the asset traded in is $60,000. (a) What is the cost basis of the new asset for financial reporting purposes? (b) What is the cost basis of the new asset for the computation of depreciation for federal income tax purposes?

25. The cost of a composite group of equipment is $700,000 and the annual depreciation, computed on the individual items, totals $77,000 (a) What is the composite straight-line depreciation rate? (b) What would the rate be if the total depreciation amounted to $56,000 instead of $77,000?

26. Differentiate between a capital lease and an operating lease.

27. What is the term applied to the periodic charge for (a) ore removed from a mine, (b) the write-off of the cost of an intangible asset?

28. (a) Over what period of time should the cost of a patent acquired by purchase be amortized? (b) In general, what is the required treatment for research and development costs?

29. Real World Focus. The 1985 financial statements of La-Z-Boy Chair Company contain the following footnote:

The Company has several long-term leases covering manufacturing facilities. The lease agreements require the Company to insure and maintain the facilities and provide for annual payments, which include interest. These leases give the Company the option to purchase the facilities for nominal amounts, or in some instances to renew the leases for extended periods at nominal annual rentals.

Would these leases be classified as operating or capital leases? Discuss.

EXERCISES

Exercise 11–1. Depreciation by three methods. A plant asset acquired on January 2 at a cost of $220,000 has an estimated useful life of 10 years. Assuming that it will have no residual value, determine the depreciation for each of the first two years (a) by the straight-line method, (b) by the declining-balance method, using twice the straight-line rate, and (c) by the sum-of-the-years-digits method.

Exercise 11–2. Depreciation by units-of-production method. A diesel-powered generator with a cost of $160,000 and estimated salvage value of $10,000 is expected to have a useful operating life of 50,000 hours. During June, the generator was operated 360 hours. Determine the depreciation for the month. *1080*

Exercise 11–3. Depreciation by units-of-production method. Balances in Trucks and in Accumulated Depreciation—Trucks at the end of the year, prior to adjustment, are $109,600 and $53,500, respectively. Details of the subsidiary ledger are as follows:

Truck No.	Cost	Estimated Residual Value	Estimated Useful Life in Miles	Accumulated Depreciation at Beginning of Year	Miles Operated During Year
1	$45,000	$5,000	200,000	$22,500	25,000
2	17,600	2,600	100,000	7,700	20,000
3	28,000	4,000	150,000	23,300	4,500
4	19,000	1,000	200,000	—	12,000

(a) Determine the depreciation rates per mile and the amount to be credited to the accumulated depreciation section of each of the subsidiary accounts for the current year. (b) Present the journal entry to record depreciation for the year.

Exercise 11–4.   Depreciation by three methods. An item of equipment acquired at the beginning of the fiscal year at a cost of $45,200 has an estimated residual value of $2,000 and an estimated useful life of 8 years. Determine the following: (a) the amount of annual depreciation by the straight-line method, (b) the amount of depreciation for the second year computed by the declining-balance method (at twice the straight-line rate), (c) the amount of depreciation for the second year computed by the sum-of-the-years-digits method.

Exercise 11–5.   Depreciation by accelerated depreciation methods. A piece of machinery acquired at a cost of $33,000 has an estimated residual value of $3,000 and an estimated useful life of 5 years. It was placed in service on April 1 of the current fiscal year, which ends on December 31. Determine the depreciation for the current fiscal year and for the following fiscal year by (a) the declining-balance method, at twice the straight-line rate, and (b) the sum-of-the-years-digits method.

Exercise 11–6.   Revision of depreciation. An item of equipment acquired on January 3, 1984, at a cost of $32,500 has an estimated residual value of $2,500 and an estimated useful life of 10 years. Depreciation has been recorded for the first four years ended December 31, 1987, by the straight-line method. Determine the amount of depreciation for the current year ended December 31, 1988, if the revised estimated residual value is $2,100 and the revised estimated remaining useful life (including the current year) is 8 years.

Exercise 11–7.   Major repair to plant asset. A number of major structural repairs completed at the beginning of the current fiscal year at a cost of $90,000 are expected to extend the life of a building 10 years beyond the original estimate. The original cost of the building was $800,000, and it has been depreciated by the straight-line method for 25 years. Residual value is expected to be negligible and has been ignored. The balance of the related accumulated depreciation account after the depreciation adjustment at the end of the preceding year is $400,000. (a) What has the amount of annual depreciation been in past years? (b) To what account should the cost of repairs ($90,000) be debited? (c) What is the book value of the building after the repairs have been recorded? (d) What is the amount of depreciation for the current year, using the straight-line method (assume that the repairs were completed at the very beginning of the year)?

Exercise 11–8.   Entries for loss on trade of plant asset. On July 1, Ross Co. acquired a new computer with a list price of $125,000. Ross received a trade-in allowance of $15,000 on an old computer of a similar type, paid cash of $30,000, and gave a series of five notes payable for the remainder. The following information about the old computer is obtained from the account in the office equipment ledger: cost, $82,500; accumulated depreciation on December 31, the end of the preceding fiscal year, $50,000; annual depreciation, $15,000. Present entries to record: (a) the current depreciation on the old computer to the date of trade-in; (b) the transaction on July 1 for financial reporting purposes.

Exercise 11–9.   Depreciation on asset acquired by exchange. On the first day of the fiscal year, a delivery truck with a list price of $30,000 was acquired in an exchange for an old delivery truck and $26,000 cash. The old truck has a book value of $2,500 at the date of the exchange. The new truck is to be depreciated over 5 years by the straight-line method. The estimated residual value is $2,000. Determine the following: (a) annual depreciation for financial reporting purposes, (b) annual depreciation for income tax purposes, (c) annual depreciation for financial reporting purposes, assuming that the book value of the old delivery truck was $5,000, (d) annual depreciation for income tax purposes, assuming the same book value as indicated in (c).

Exercise 11–10.   Composite depreciation rate. A composite depreciation rate of 15% is applied annually to a plant asset account. Details of the account for the fiscal year ended December 31 are as follows:

Delivery Equipment

Jan.	1	Balance	297,750	May	1		16,500
Mar.	2		27,250	Sept.	7		11,750
Apr.	29		14,000	Dec.	15		15,500
Aug.	22		20,500				
Nov.	14		17,500				

Determine the depreciation for the year according to each of the following assumptions: (a) that all additions and retirements have occurred uniformly throughout the year, (b) that additions and retirements during the first half of the year occurred on the first day of that year and those during the second half occurred on the first day of the succeeding year.

Exercise 11–11.   Amortization and depletion entries. On July 1 of the current fiscal year ended December 31, Huff Co. acquired a patent for $75,000 and mineral rights for $200,000. The patent, which expires in 9 years, is expected to have value for 6 years. The mineral deposit is estimated at 500,000 tons of ore of uniform grade. Present entries to record the following for the current year: (a) amortization of the patent, (b) depletion, assuming that 50,000 tons were mined during the year.

Exercise 11–12.   Amortization and depletion entries. For each of the following unrelated transactions, (a) determine the amount of the amortization or depletion expense for the current year, and (b) present the adjusting entries required to record each expense.

(1) Timber rights on a tract of land were purchased for $50,000. The stand of timber is estimated at 500,000 board feet. During the current year, 75,000 board feet of timber were cut.

(2) Goodwill in the amount of $160,000 was purchased on January 4, the first month of the fiscal year. It is decided to amortize over the maximum period allowable.

(3) Governmental and legal costs of $24,800 were incurred at midyear in obtaining a patent with an estimated economic life of 8 years. Amortization is to be for one-half year.

PROBLEMS

Series A

Problem 11-1A. Allocation of expenditures and receipts to plant asset accounts. The following expenditures and receipts are related to land, land improvements, and buildings acquired for use in a business enterprise. The receipts are identified by an asterisk.

(a)	Cost of real estate acquired as a plant site: Land..................	$125,000
	Building	45,000
(b)	Delinquent real estate taxes on property assumed by purchaser	8,750
(c)	Cost of razing and removing the building	5,800
(d)	Fee paid to attorney for title search	900
(e)	Cost of land fill and grading....................................	9,700
(f)	Architect's and engineer's fees for plans and supervision...........	60,000
(g)	Premium on 1-year insurance policy during construction	5,500
(h)	Paid to building contractor for new building	750,000
(i)	Cost of repairing windstorm damage during construction	1,500
(j)	Cost of paving parking lot to be used by customers................	12,500
(k)	Cost of trees and shrubbery planted	15,000
(l)	Special assessment paid to city for extension of water main to	
	the property...	2,500
(m)	Cost of repairing vandalism damage during construction	500
(n)	Interest incurred on building loan during construction	39,000
(o)	Cost of floodlights installed on parking lot	13,500
(p)	Proceeds from sale of salvage materials from old building..........	1,100*
(q)	Money borrowed to pay building contractor	600,000*
(r)	Proceeds from insurance company for windstorm damage..........	1,000*
(s)	Refund of premium on insurance policy (g) canceled after	
	11 months	350*

Instructions:

Assign each expenditure and receipt (indicate receipts by an asterisk) to Land (permanently capitalized), Land Improvements (limited life), Building, or Other Accounts. Identify each item by letter and list the amounts in columnar form, as follows:

Item	Land	Land Improvements	Building	Other Accounts
	$	$	$	$

Problem 11-2A. Depreciation by four methods. North Company purchased equipment on January 1, 1988, for $75,000. The equipment was expected to have a useful life of 4 years, or 14,000 operating hours, and a residual value of $5,000. The equipment was used for 3,200 hours during 1988 and for 4,000, 3,800, and 3,000 hours for 1989, 1990, and 1991 respectively. The equipment was sold for $5,000 on January 4, 1992.

Instructions:

Determine the amount of depreciation expense for 1988, 1989, 1990, and 1991 by (a) the straight-line method, (b) the declining-balance method, using twice the straight-line rate, (c) the sum-of-the-years-digits method, and (d) the units-of-production method.

Problem 11–3A. Depreciation by three methods; trade of plant asset. An item of new equipment, acquired at a cost of $125,000 at the beginning of a fiscal year, has an estimated useful life of 5 years and an estimated residual value of $5,000. The manager requested information regarding the effect of alternative methods on the amount of depreciation expense each year. Upon the basis of the data presented to the manager, the declining-balance method was elected.

In the first week of the fifth year, the equipment was traded in for similar equipment priced at $170,000. The trade-in allowance on the old equipment was $20,000, cash of $25,000 was paid, and a note payable was issued for the balance.

Instructions:

(1) Determine the annual depreciation expense for each of the estimated 5 years of use, the accumulated depreciation at the end of each year, and the book value of the equipment at the end of each year by (a) the straight-line method. (b) the sum-of-the-years-digits method, and (c) the declining-balance method (at twice the straight-line rate). The following columnar headings are suggested for each schedule:

Year	Depreciation Expense	Accumulated Depreciation, End of Year	Book Value, End of Year

(2) For financial reporting purposes, determine the cost basis of the new equipment acquired in the exchange.
(3) Present the entries to record the exchange.
(4) What is the cost basis of the new equipment for purposes of computing the amount of depreciation allowable for income tax purposes?
(5) Present the entries to record the exchange, assuming that the trade-in allowance was $10,000 instead of $20,000.
(6) What is the cost basis of the new equipment for purposes of computing the amount of depreciation allowable for income tax purposes, assuming the data presented in Instruction (5)?

If the working papers correlating with the textbook are not used, omit Problem 11–4A.

Problem 11–4A. Plant asset transactions and subsidiary plant asset ledger. Victor Press Inc. maintains a subsidiary equipment ledger for the printing equipment and accumulated depreciation accounts in the general ledger. A small portion of the subsidiary ledger, the two controlling accounts, and a journal are presented in the working papers. The company computes depreciation on each individual item of equipment. Transaction and adjusting entries affecting the printing equipment are described as follows:

1987

Sept. 1. Purchased a power binder (Model 4C, Serial No. 7765) from Ryan Manufacturing Co. on account for $60,000. The estimated useful life of the asset is 10 years, it is expected to have no residual value, and the straight-line method of depreciation is to be used. (This is the only transaction of the year that directly affected the printing equipment account.)

Dec. 31. Recorded depreciation for the year in subsidiary accounts 125-30 to 125-32, and inserted the balances. (An assistant recorded the depreciation and the new balances in accounts 125-1 to 125-29.)

31. Journalized and posted the annual adjusting entry for depreciation on printing equipment. The depreciation for the year, recorded in subsidiary accounts 125-1 to 125-29, totaled $68,200, to which was added the depreciation entered in accounts 125-30 to 125-32.

1988

Mar. 31 Purchased a Model 32 rotary press from Jackson Press Inc., priced at $50,000, giving the Model G3 flatbed press (Account No. 125-31) in exchange plus $7,500 cash and a series of four $5,000 notes payable, maturing at 6-month intervals. The estimated useful life of the new press is 10 years, and it is expected to have a residual value of $2,000. (Recorded depreciation to date in 1988 on item traded in.)

Instructions:

(1) Journalize the transaction of September 1. Post to Printing Equipment in the general ledger and to Account No. 125-32 in the subsidiary ledger.

(2) Journalize the adjusting entry required on December 31 and post to Accumulated Depreciation — Printing Equipment in the general ledger.

(3) Journalize the entries required by the purchase of printing equipment on March 31. Post to Printing Equipment and to Accumulated Depreciation — Printing Equipment in the general ledger and to Account Nos. 125-31 and 125-33 in the subsidiary ledger.

(4) If the rotary press purchased on March 31 had been depreciated by the declining-balance method at twice the straight-line rate, determine the depreciation on this press for the fiscal years ending (a) December 31, 1988, and (b) December 31, 1989.

Problem 11–5A. Transactions for plant assets, including trade. The following transactions, adjusting entries, and closing entries were completed by Urbana Furniture Co. during a 3-year period. All are related to the use of delivery equipment. The declining-balance method (twice the straight-line rate) of depreciation is used.

1987

Jan. 2. Purchased a used delivery truck for $10,800, paying cash.

5. Paid $1,200 for major repairs to the truck.

Sept. 17. Paid garage $225 for miscellaneous repairs to the truck.

Dec. 31. Recorded depreciation on the truck for the fiscal year. The estimated useful life of the truck is 4 years, with a residual value of $1,800.

31. Closed the appropriate accounts to the income summary account.

1988
June 30. Traded in the used truck for a new truck priced at $25,000, receiving a trade-in allowance of $5,000 and paying the balance in cash. (Record depreciation to date in 1988.)
Nov. 4. Paid garage $195 for miscellaneous repairs to the truck.
Dec. 31. Recorded depreciation on the truck. It has an estimated residual value of $4,500 and an estimated useful life of 5 years.
   31. Closed the appropriate accounts to the income summary account.
1989
Oct. 1. Purchased a new truck for $24,400, paying cash.
   2. Sold the truck purchased in 1988 for $15,000. (Record depreciation to date in 1989.)
Dec. 31. Recorded depreciation on the remaining truck. It has an estimated residual value of $1,500 and an estimated useful life of 8 years.
   31. Closed the appropriate accounts to the income summary account.

Instructions:

(1) Open the following accounts in the ledger:

122 Delivery Equipment
123 Accumulated Depreciation—Delivery Equipment
616 Depreciation Expense—Delivery Equipment
617 Truck Repair Expense
812 Gain on Disposal of Plant Assets

(2) Record the transactions and the adjusting and closing entries. Post to the accounts and extend the balances after each posting.

Problem 11–6A.   Correcting entries. The following recording errors occurred and were discovered during the current year:

(a) The $750 cost of repairing factory equipment damaged in the process of installation was charged to Factory Equipment.
(b) The sale of an electronic typewriter for $475 was recorded by a $475 credit to Office Equipment. The original cost of the machine was $1,450, and the related balance in Accumulated Depreciation at the beginning of the current year was $925. Depreciation of $100 accrued during the current year, prior to the sale, had not been recorded.
(c) Property taxes of $5,000 were paid on real estate acquired during the year and were debited to Property Tax Expense. Of this amount, $4,000 was for taxes that were delinquent at the time the property was acquired.
(d) Office equipment with a book value of $11,200 was traded in for similar equipment with a list price of $60,000. The trade-in allowance on the old equipment was $15,000, and a note payable was given for the balance. A gain on disposal of plant assets of $3,800 was recorded.
(e) The $1,100 cost of a major motor overhaul expected to prolong the life of a truck two years beyond the original estimate was debited to Delivery Expense. The truck was acquired new four years earlier.
(f) A $450 charge for incoming transportation on an item of factory equipment was debited to Transportation In.

(g) The cost of a razed building, $30,000, was debited to Loss on Disposal of Plant Assets and credited to Building. The building and the land on which it was located had been acquired at a total cost of $110,000 ($80,000 debited to Land, $30,000 debited to Building) as a parking area for the adjacent plant.

(h) The fee of $7,500 paid to the wrecking contractor to raze the building in (g) was debited to Miscellaneous Expense.

(i) The $7,750 cost of repainting several interior rooms of a building was debited to Building. The building had been owned and occupied for 20 years.

Instructions:

Journalize the entries to correct the errors during the current year. Identify each entry by letter.

Problem 11–7A. Income statement and balance sheet for corporation. The trial balance of Shaul Corporation at the end of the current fiscal year, before adjustments, is as follows:

Cash.	29,600	
Accounts Receivable	60,700	
Allowance for Doubtful Accounts		500
Merchandise Inventory.	178,700	
Prepaid Expense.	11,250	
Land.	50,000	
Buildings	225,000	
Accumulated Depreciation—Buildings		86,000
Office Equipment.	31,100	
Accumulated Depreciation—Office Equipment.		11,600
Store Equipment	51,500	
Accumulated Depreciation—Store Equipment		21,400
Delivery Equipment.	57,850	
Accumulated Depreciation—Delivery Equipment.		21,750
Patents	18,000	
Accounts Payable		40,200
Notes Payable (short-term).		20,000
Capital Stock		250,000
Retained Earnings.		179,750
Dividends	70,000	
Sales (net)		996,950
Purchases (net).	702,350	
Operating Expenses (controlling account)	140,500	
Interest Expense	1,600	
	1,628,150	1,628,150

Data needed for year-end adjustments:

(a) Estimated uncollectible accounts at December 31, $6,100.
(b) Insurance and other prepaid operating expenses expired during the year, $7,250.
(c) Merchandise inventory at December 31, $171,000.

(d) Depreciation is computed at composite rates on the average of the beginning and the ending balances of the plant asset accounts. The beginning balances and rates are as follows:

Office Equipment, $27,900; 10%   Delivery Equipment, $57,150; 20%
Store Equipment, $48,500; 8%   Buildings, $225,000; 2%

(e) Amortization of patents computed for the year, $3,000.
(f) Accrued liabilities at the end of the year, $3,000, of which $300 is for interest on the notes and $2,700 is for wages and other operating expenses.

Instructions:

(1) Prepare a multiple-step income statement for the current year.
(2) Prepare a balance sheet in report form, presenting the plant assets in the manner illustrated in this chapter.

Series B

Problem 11–1B. Allocation of expenditures and receipts to plant asset accounts. The following expenditures and receipts are related to land, land improvements, and buildings acquired for use in a business enterprise. The receipts are identified by an asterisk.

(a)	Cost of real estate acquired as a plant site: Land	$ 225,000
	Building	65,000
(b)	Finder's fee paid to real estate agency	15,000
(c)	Fee paid to attorney for title search	900
(d)	Delinquent real estate taxes on property, assumed by purchaser	18,500
(e)	Cost of razing and removing the building	11,250
(f)	Proceeds from sale of salvage materials from old building	1,500*
(g)	Cost of land fill and grading	13,500
(h)	Architect's and engineer's fees for plans and supervision	105,000
(i)	Premium on 1-year insurance policy during construction	9,000
(j)	Cost of paving parking lot to be used by customers	17,500
(k)	Cost of trees and shrubbery planted	10,000
(l)	Special assessment paid to city for extension of water main to the property	4,500
(m)	Cost of repairing windstorm damage during construction	3,500
(n)	Cost of repairing vandalism damage during construction	800
(o)	Proceeds from insurance company for windstorm and vandalism damage	3,300*
(p)	Interest incurred on building loan during construction	85,000
(q)	Money borrowed to pay building contractor	1,000,000*
(r)	Paid to building contractor for new building	1,250,000
(s)	Refund of premium on insurance policy (i) canceled after 10 months	750*

Instructions:

Assign each expenditure and receipt (indicate receipts by an asterisk) to Land (permanently capitalized), Land Improvements (limited life), Building, or Other Accounts. Identify each item by letter and list the amounts in columnar form, as follows:

Item	Land $	Land Improvements $	Building $	Other Accounts $

Problem 11–2B.   Depreciation by four methods. Colby Company purchased equipment on July 1, 1987, for $72,000. The equipment was expected to have a useful life of 3 years, or 6,900 operating hours, and a residual value of $3,000. The equipment was used for 700 hours during 1987 and for 2,800, 2,400 and 1,000 hours for 1988, 1989, and 1990 respectively. The equipment was sold for $3,000 on July 3, 1990.

Instructions:

Determine the amount of depreciation expense for 1987, 1988, 1989, and 1990 by (a) the straight-line method, (b) the declining-balance method, using twice the straight-line rate, (c) the sum-of-the-years-digits method, and (d) the units-of-production method.

Problem 11–3B.   Determination of depreciation by three methods; trade of plant asset. An item of new equipment, acquired at a cost of $80,000 at the beginning of a fiscal year, has an estimated useful life of 4 years and an estimated residual value of $5,000. The manager requested information regarding the effect of alternative methods on the amount of depreciation expense each year. Upon the basis of the data presented to the manager, the declining-balance method was elected.

In the first week of the fourth year, the equipment was traded in for similar equipment priced at $200,000. The trade-in allowance on the old equipment was $15,000, cash of $15,000 was paid, and a note payable was issued for the balance.

Instructions:

(1) Determine the annual depreciation expense for each of the estimated 4 years of use, the accumulated depreciation at the end of each year, and the book value of the equipment at the end of each year by (a) the straight-line method, (b) the declining-balance method (at twice the straight-line rate), and (c) the sum-of-the-years-digits method. The following columnar headings are suggested for each schedule:

Year	Depreciation Expense	Accumulated Depreciation, End of Year	Book Value, End of Year

(2) For financial reporting purposes, determine the cost basis of the new equipment acquired in the exchange.
(3) Present the entries to record the exchange.

(continued)

(4) What is the cost basis of the new equipment for purposes of computing the amount of depreciation allowable for income tax purposes?

(5) Present the entries to record the exchange, assuming that the trade-in allowance was $5,000 instead of $15,000.

(6) What is the cost basis of the new equipment for purposes of computing the amount of depreciation allowable for income tax purposes, assuming the data presented in Instruction (5)?

If the working papers correlating with the textbook are not used, omit Problem 11–4B.

Problem 11–4B.   Plant asset transactions and subsidiary plant asset ledger.

Hamilton Press Co. maintains a subsidiary equipment ledger for the printing equipment and accumulated depreciation accounts in the general ledger. A small portion of the subsidiary ledger, the two controlling accounts, and a journal are presented in the working papers. The company computes depreciation on each individual item of equipment. Transactions and adjusting entries affecting the printing equipment are described as follows:

1987

June 30. Purchased a power binder (Model 14, Serial No. D7351) from Evans Manufacturing Co. on account for $108,000. The estimated useful life of the asset is 12 years, it is expected to have no residual value, and the straight-line method of depreciation is to be used. (This is the only transaction of the year that directly affected the printing equipment account.)

Dec. 31. Recorded depreciation for the year in subsidiary accounts 125-30 to 125-32, and inserted the new balances. (An assistant recorded the depreciation and the new balances in accounts 125-1 to 125-29.)

31. Journalized and posted the annual adjusting entry for depreciation on printing equipment. The depreciation for the year, recorded in subsidiary accounts 125-1 to 125-29, totaled $61,200, to which was added the depreciation entered in accounts 125-30 to 125-32.

1988

Sept. 30. Purchased a Model F5 rotary press from Wei Press Inc., priced at $60,000, giving the Model G3 flatbed press (Account No. 125-31) in exchange plus $20,000 cash and a series of ten $2,500 notes payable, maturing at 6-month intervals. The estimated useful life of the new press is 10 years, and it is expected to have a residual value of $6,250. (Recorded depreciation to date in 1988 on item traded in.)

Instructions:

(1) Journalize the transaction of June 30. Post to Printing Equipment in the general ledger and to Account No. 125-32 in the subsidiary ledger.

(2) Journalize the adjusting entry on December 31 and post to Accumulated Depreciation — Printing Equipment in the general ledger.

(3) Journalize the entries required by the purchase of printing equipment on September 30. Post to Printing Equipment and to Accumulated Depreciation — Printing Equipment in the general ledger and to Account Nos. 125-31 and 125-33 in the subsidiary ledger.

(4) If the rotary press purchased on September 30 had been depreciated by the declining-balance method at twice the straight-line rate, determine the depreciation on this press for the fiscal years ending (a) December 31, 1988, and (b) December 31, 1989.

Problem 11–5B. Transactions for plant assets, including trade. The following transactions, adjusting entries, and closing entries were completed by Reliable Furniture Co. during 3 fiscal years ending on June 30. All are related to the use of delivery equipment. The declining-balance method (twice the straight-line rate) of depreciation is used.

1987–1988 Fiscal Year

July 3. Purchased a used delivery truck for $15,000, paying cash.
6. Paid $1,000 to replace the automatic transmission and install new brakes on the truck. (Debit Delivery Equipment.)
Dec. 7. Paid garage $215 for changing the oil, replacing the oil filter, and tuning the engine on the delivery truck.
June 30. Recorded depreciation on the truck for the fiscal year. The estimated useful life of the truck is 8 years, with a residual value of $3,000.
30. Closed the appropriate accounts to the income summary account.

1988–1989 Fiscal Year

Aug. 29. Paid garage $240 to tune the engine and make other minor repairs on the truck.
Oct. 31. Traded in the used truck for a new truck priced at $28,000, receiving a trade-in allowance of $12,000 and paying the balance in cash. (Record depreciation to date in 1988.)
June 30. Recorded depreciation on the truck. It has an estimated trade-in value of $2,750 and an estimated life of 10 years.
30. Closed the appropriate accounts to the income summary account.

1989–1990 Fiscal Year

Apr. 1. Purchased a new truck for $30,000, paying cash.
2. Sold the truck purchased October 31, 1988, for $20,500. (Record depreciation for the year.)
June 30. Recorded depreciation on the remaining truck. It has an estimated residual value of $4,500 and an estimated useful life of 8 years.
30. Closed the appropriate accounts to the income summary account.

Instructions:
(1) Open the following accounts in the ledger:
122 Delivery Equipment
123 Accumulated Depreciation—Delivery Equipment
616 Depreciation Expense—Delivery Equipment
617 Truck Repair Expense
812 Gain on Disposal of Plant assets
(2) Record the transactions and the adjusting and closing entries. Post to the accounts and extend the balances after each posting.

MINI-CASE 11

FRANK
CRAMER
& company

Frank Cramer, president of Frank Cramer and Company, is considering the purchase of machinery for $120,000. The machinery has a useful life of 5 years and no residual value. In the past, all plant assets have been leased. Cramer is considering depreciating the machinery by either the straight-line method or the sum-of-the-years-digits method, and has asked for your advice as to which method to use.

Instructions:

(1) Compute depreciation for each of the five years of useful life by (a) the straight-line method and (b) the sum-of-the-years-digits method.
(2) Assuming that income before depreciation and income tax is estimated to be uniformly $100,000 per year, that the depreciation method selected will be used for both financial reporting and income tax purposes, and that the income tax rate is 30%, compute the net income for each of the five years of useful life if (a) the straight-line method is used and (b) the sum-of-the-years-digits method is used.
(3) What factors would you present for Cramer's consideration in the selection of a depreciation method?

Chapter 12

PAYROLL, NOTES PAYABLE, AND OTHER CURRENT LIABILITIES

Chapter Objectives

■ Describe and illustrate accounting for payrolls, including liabilities arising from employee earnings, deductions from earnings, and employer's payroll taxes.

■ Describe and illustrate accounting systems for payroll and payroll taxes.

■ Describe the principles of internal control for payroll systems.

■ Describe and illustrate accounting for employee fringe benefits, including vacation pay and pensions.

■ Describe and illustrate accounting for short-term notes payable.

■ Describe and illustrate accounting for product warranties.

P ayables are the opposite of receivables. They are debts owed by an enterprise to its creditors. Money claims against a firm may originate in many ways, such as purchases of merchandise or services on account, loans from banks, and purchases of equipment and marketable securities on a credit basis. At any particular moment, a business may also owe its employees for wages or salaries accrued, banks or other creditors for interest accrued on notes, and governmental agencies for taxes.

Some types of current liabilities, such as accounts payable, have been discussed in earlier chapters. Additional types of current liabilities, including liabilities arising from payrolls, vacation pay, pensions, notes payable, and product warranties, are discussed in this chapter.

PAYROLL

The term **payroll** is often used to refer to the total amount paid to employees for a certain period. Payroll expenditures are usually significant for several reasons. First, employees are sensitive to payroll errors or irregularities, and maintaining good employee morale requires that the payroll be paid on a timely, accurate basis. Second, payroll expenditures are subject to various federal and state regulations. Finally, the amount of these payroll expenditures and related payroll taxes has a significant effect on the net income of most business enterprises. Although the degree of importance of such expenses varies widely, it is not unusual for a business to expend nearly a third of its sales revenue for payroll and payroll-related expenses. These expenses and their related liabilities are discussed in the following sections.

LIABILITY FOR PAYROLL

The term **salary** is usually applied to payment for managerial, administrative, or similar services. The rate of salary is ordinarily expressed in terms of a month or a year. Remuneration for manual labor, both skilled and unskilled, is commonly called **wages** and is stated on an hourly, weekly, or piecework basis. In practice, the terms salary and wages are often used interchangeably.

The basic salary or wage of an employee may be supplemented by commissions, bonuses, profit sharing, or cost-of-living adjustments. The form in which remuneration is paid generally has no effect on the manner in which it is treated by either the employer or the employee. Although payment is usually in terms of cash, it may take such forms as securities, notes, lodging, or other property or services.

Salary and wage rates are determined, in general, by agreement between the employer and the employees. Enterprises engaged in interstate commerce must also follow the requirements of the Fair Labor Standards Act. Employers covered by this legislation, which is commonly called the Federal Wage and Hour Law, are required to pay a minimum rate of 1½ times the regular rate for all hours worked in excess of 40 hours per week. Exemptions from the requirements are provided for executive, administrative, and certain supervisory positions. Premium rates for overtime or for working at night or other less desirable times are fairly common, even when not required by law, and the premium rates may be as much as twice the base rate.

Determination of Employee Earnings

To illustrate the computation of the earnings of an employee, it is assumed that Thomas C. Johnson is employed at the rate of $20 per hour for the first 40 hours in the weekly pay period and at $30 ($20 + $10) per hour for any additional hours. His time card shows that he worked 43 hours during the week ended December 27. His earnings for that week are computed as follows:

Earnings at base rate (40 × $20)	$800.00
Earnings at overtime rate (3 × $30)	90.00
Total earnings..............................	$890.00

The foregoing computations can be stated in generalized arithmetic formulas or algorithms. If the hours worked during the week are less than or equal to (≤) 40, the formula may be expressed by the following equation, where E represents total earnings, H represents hours worked, and R represents hourly rate:

$$E = H \times R$$

This equation cannot be used to determine the earnings of an employee who has worked more than (>) 40 hours during the week, because the overtime rate differs from the basic rate. The expansion of the equation to include the additional factor of overtime yields the following:

$$E = 40\ R + 1.5\ R(H - 40)$$

The two equations can be expressed as shown in the following algorithm:

If	Then
$H \le 40$	$E = H \times R$
$H > 40$	$E = 40R + 1.5R(H - 40)$

After the value of H and R are known for each employee at the end of a payroll period, the earnings of each employee can be computed accurately and speedily. Application of the standardized procedure of the algorithm to computers makes it possible to process a payroll routinely, regardless of its size.

Determination of Profit-Sharing Bonuses

Many enterprises pay their employees an annual bonus in addition to their regular salary or wage. The amount of the bonus is often based on the productivity of the employees, as measured by the net income of the enterprise. Such profit-sharing bonuses are treated in the same manner as wages and salaries.

The method used in determining the amount of a profit-sharing bonus is usually stated in the agreement between the employer and the employees. When the amount of the bonus is measured by a certain percentage of income, there are four basic formulas for the computation. The percentage may be applied (1) to income before deducting the bonus and income taxes, (2) to income after deducting the bonus but before deducting income taxes, (3) to income before deducting the bonus but after deducting income taxes, or (4) to net income after deducting both the bonus and income taxes.

Determination of a 10% bonus according to each of the four methods is illustrated as follows, based on the assumption that the employer's income before deducting the bonus and income taxes amounts to $150,000, and that income taxes are levied at the rate of 40% of income. Bonus and income taxes are abbreviated as B and T respectively.

(1) Bonus based on income before deducting bonus and taxes.

$$B = .10\ (\$150,000)$$
$$\text{Bonus} = \$15,000$$

(2) Bonus based on income after deducting bonus but before deducting taxes.

$$B = .10 (\$150,000 - B)$$

Simplifying: $\quad B = \$15,000 - .10B$

Transposing: $\quad 1.10B = \$15,000$

$$\text{Bonus} = \$13,636.36$$

(3) Bonus based on income before deducting bonus but after deducting taxes.

B equation: $\qquad B = .10 (\$150,000 - T)$

T equation: $\qquad T = .40 (\$150,000 - B)$

Substituting for T in the B equation and solving for B:

$$B = .10 [\$150,000 - .40 (\$150,000 - B)]$$

Simplifying: $\qquad B = .10 (\$150,000 - \$60,000 + .40B)$

Simplifying: $\qquad B = \$15,000 - \$6,000 + .04B$

Transposing: $\quad .96B = \$9,000$

$$\text{Bonus} = \$9,375$$

(4) Bonus based on net income after deducting bonus and taxes.

B equation: $\qquad B = .10 (\$150,000 - B - T)$

T equation: $\qquad T = .40 (\$150,000 - B)$

Substituting for T in the B equation and solving for B:

$$B = .10 [\$150,000 - B - .40 (\$150,000 - B)]$$

Simplifying: $\qquad B = .10 (\$150,000 - B - \$60,000 + .40B)$

Simplifying: $\qquad B = \$15,000 - .10B - \$6,000 + .04B$

Transposing: $\quad 1.06B = \$9,000$

$$\text{Bonus} = \$8,490.57$$

With the amount of the bonus possibilities ranging from the high of $15,000 to the low of $8,490.57, the importance of strictly following the agreement is evident. If the bonus is to be shared by all of the employees, the agreement must also provide for the manner by which the bonus is divided among them. A common method is to express the bonus as a percentage of total earnings for the year. For example, if the bonus were computed to be $15,000 and employee earnings before the bonus had been $100,000, the bonus for each of the employees could be stated as 15% of their earnings.

DEDUCTIONS FROM EMPLOYEE EARNINGS

The total earnings of an employee for a payroll period, including bonuses and overtime pay, are often called the **gross pay**. From this amount is subtracted one or more **deductions** to arrive at the **net pay**, which is the amount the employer must pay the employee. The deductions for federal taxes are of the widest applicability and usually the largest in amount. Deductions may also be needed for state or local income taxes and for contributions to state unemployment compensation programs. Other deductions may be made for contributions to pension plans and for items authorized by individual employees.

Managers' Rewards for Corporate Performance

David Margolis works for a very generous company. In 1985, Mr. Margolis, the president, chairman and chief executive officer of Colt Industries Inc., received a bonus of $555,000, more than double the average bonus for chief executives of similar-sized companies. And that bonus was $115,680 *more* than his base salary. Total compensation: close to $1 million.

Colt says its generosity was well-founded. In 1984, the year on which the bonus was based, the company had a record income.

"We have no shame or trepidation about the fact that our people are highly paid," says Karyl Lynn, Colt's personnel director. "They've earned it."

A similar attitude can be found in increasing numbers of board rooms across the country. After years of regularly receiving hefty increases in salary and bonus—regardless of their company's success or failure—more top executives are now finding their compensation linked directly to corporate performance.

"There's been so much scrutiny that boards have been taking a closer look" at compensation, says Pete Smith, national director of Wyatt Co.'s compensation consulting business. As a result, companies are relying less on salary and more on bonuses and other performance-linked compensation to reward executives. They are also tightening the criteria for earning those rewards. For example, more compensation is being pegged to three-year or five-year gains in performance.

Some companies also want to extend bonuses, which are usually limited to senior executives, to lower-level managers. Specialists believe that bonuses work successfully as incentives only if they amount to 15% or more of total compensation. But most lower-level managers are unwilling to risk that large a proportion of their income. "If you're a $40,000-a-year executive, can you afford to have $6,000 at risk?" asks Colt's Mr. Lynn.

The solution—adding bonuses to existing salaries—means a big increase in costs. But some executives say those costs are worth it to retain first-class management. Says David Jones, chairman and chief executive of Humana Corp.: "You don't pay executives with cornflakes. There's always costs of employing executives. If the costs are reasonable, you pay them. You have to pay what the marketplace demands."

Source: Adapted from "More Managers Find Salary, Bonus Are Tied Directly to Performance," *The Wall Street Journal,* February 28, 1986.

FICA Tax

Most employers are required by the Federal Insurance Contributions Act (FICA) to withhold a portion of the earnings of each of their employees. The amount of **FICA tax** withheld is the employees' contribution to the combined federal programs for old-age and disability benefits, insurance benefits to survivors, and health insurance for the aged (medicare). With very few exceptions, employers are required to withhold from each employee a tax at a specified rate on earnings up to a specified amount paid in the calendar year. Although both the schedule of future tax rates and the maximum amount subject to tax are revised often by Congress, such changes have no effect on the basic outline of the payroll system.[1] For purposes of illustration, a rate of 7.5% on maximum annual earnings of $45,000, or a maximum annual tax of $3,375, will be assumed.

Federal Income Tax

Except for certain types of employment, all employers must withhold a portion of the earnings of their employees for payment of the employees' liability for federal income tax. The amount that must be withheld from each employee differs according to the amount of gross pay, marital status, and the estimated deductions and exemptions claimed when filing the annual income tax return.

Other Deductions

Deductions from gross earnings for payment of taxes are compulsory. Neither the employer nor the employee has any choice in the matter. In addition, however, there may be other deductions authorized by individual employees or by the union representing them. For example, an employee may authorize deductions for the purchase of United States savings bonds, for contributions to a United Fund or other charitable organization, for payment of premiums on various types of employee insurance, or for the purchase of a retirement annuity. The union contract may also require the deduction of union dues or other deductions for group benefits.

---

[1] Current tax rates and the amount of earnings subject to tax may be located in Internal Revenue Service publications and in standard tax reporting services.

COMPUTATION OF EMPLOYEE NET PAY

Gross earnings for a payroll period less the payroll deductions yields the amount to be paid to the employee, which is often called the **net pay** or **take-home pay**. The amount to be paid Thomas C. Johnson for the week ended December 27 is $640.80, based on the following summary:

Gross earnings for the week........		$890.00
Deductions:		
FICA tax	$ 37.50	
Federal income tax..............	186.70	
U.S. savings bonds..............	20.00	
United Fund	5.00	
Total deductions..............		249.20
Net pay		$640.80

As has been indicated, there is a ceiling on the annual earnings subject to the FICA tax, and consequently the amount of the annual tax is also limited. Therefore, when the amount of FICA tax to withhold from an employee is determined for a payroll period, it is necessary to refer to one of the following cumulative amounts:

1. Employee gross earnings for the year up to, but not including, the current payroll period, or
2. Employee tax withheld for the year up to, but not including, the current payroll period.

To continue with the illustration, reference to Johnson's earnings record shows cumulative earnings of $44,500 prior to the current week's earnings of $890. The amount of the current week's earnings subject to FICA tax is therefore the maximum of $500 ($45,000 − $44,500), and the FICA tax to be withheld is $37.50 (7.5% of $500). Alternatively, the determination could be based on the amount of FICA tax withheld from Johnson prior to the current payroll period. This amount, according to the employee record, is $3,337.50, and the amount to be withheld is the maximum of $37.50 ($3,375 − $3,337.50).

There is no ceiling on the amount of earnings subject to withholding for income taxes and hence no need to consider the cumulative earnings. The amount of federal income tax withheld would be determined by reference to official withholding tax tables issued by the Internal Revenue Service. For purposes of this illustration, the amount of federal income tax withheld was assumed to be $186.70. The deductions for the purchase of bonds and for the charitable contribution were in accordance with Johnson's authorizations.

As in the determination of gross earnings when overtime rates are a factor, the computation of some deductions can be generalized in the form of algorithms. The algorithm for the determination of the FICA tax deduction, based on the maximum deduction approach, is as follows, where E represents current period's earnings, F represents current period's FICA deduction, and f represents cumulative FICA deductions prior to the current period:

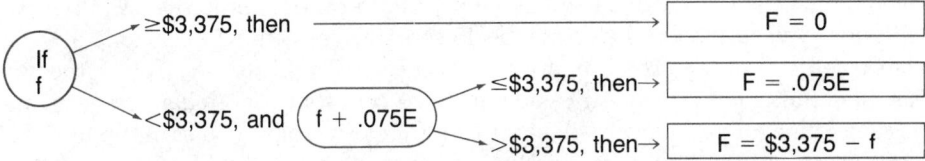

An alternative generalization of the method of determining FICA deductions, based on the maximum taxable earnings approach, is illustrated by the following decision diagram. The additional symbol "e" represents cumulative earnings prior to the current period.

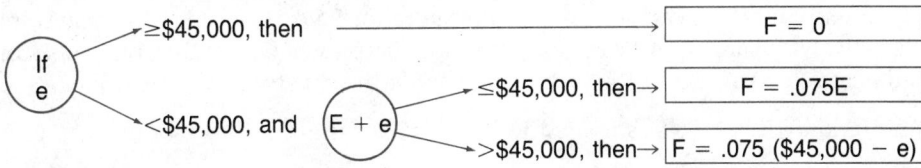

The elements of the decision diagram are examples of standardized instructions that can be applied to computations involving many variables. They are used in many situations as an aid to routine processing of repetitive data, regardless of whether the processing is performed manually or with a computer.

LIABILITY FOR EMPLOYER'S PAYROLL TAXES

Thus far the discussion of taxes has been limited to those levied against employees and withheld by employers. Most employers are subject to federal and state taxes based on the amount of remuneration earned by their employees. Such taxes are an operating expense of the business and may amount to a relatively large sum.

FICA Tax

Employers are required to contribute to the Federal Insurance Contributions Act program for each employee. The tax rate and the maximum amount of employee remuneration entering into an employer's tax base are the same as those applicable to employees, which for purposes of illustration are assumed to be 7.5% and $45,000 respectively.

Your Social Security Taxes

In its 1936 publication, *Security in Your Old Age,* the Social Security Board set forth the following explanation of how the social security tax would affect a worker's paycheck:

> The taxes called for in this law will be paid both by your employer and by you. For the next 3 years you will pay maybe 15 cents a week, maybe 25 cents a week, maybe 30 cents or more, according to what you earn. That is to say, during the next 3 years, beginning January 1, 1937, you will pay 1 cent for every dollar you earn, and at the same time your employer will pay 1 cent for every dollar you earn, up to $3,000 a year. Twenty-six million other workers and their employers will be paying at the same time.
>
> After the first 3 years — that is to say, beginning in 1940 — you will pay, and your employer will pay, 1½ cents for each dollar you earn, up to $3,000 a year. This will be the tax for 3 years, and then beginning in 1943, you will pay 2 cents, and so will your employer, for every dollar you earn for the next three years. After that, you and your employer will each pay half a cent more for 3 years, and finally, beginning in 1949, twelve years from now, you and your employer will each pay 3 cents on each dollar you earn, up to $3,000 a year. That is the most you will ever pay.

The rate on January 1, 1987, is estimated to be 7.15% of the first $44,100 of earnings.

Source: Adapted from Arthur Lodge, "That Is the Most You Will Ever Pay," *Journal of Accountancy* (October, 1985), p. 44.

Federal Unemployment Compensation Tax

Unemployment insurance provides temporary relief to those who become unemployed as a result of economic forces beyond their control. Types of employment subject to the unemployment insurance program are similar to those covered by the FICA tax. The tax of .8% is levied on employers only, rather than on both employers and employees. It is applicable only to the first $7,000 of the remuneration of each covered employee during a calendar year. As with the FICA tax, the rate and the maximum amount subject to federal unemployment compensation tax are revised often by Congress. The funds collected by the federal government are not paid out as benefits to the unemployed, but are allocated among the states for use in administering state programs.

State Unemployment Compensation Tax

The amounts paid as benefits to unemployed persons are obtained, for the most part, by taxes levied upon employers only. A very few states also require employee contributions. The rates of tax and the tax base vary, and in most states, employers who provide steady employment for their employees are awarded reduced rates. The employment experience and the status of each employer's tax account are reviewed annually, and the merit ratings and tax rates are revised accordingly.[2]

ACCOUNTING SYSTEMS FOR PAYROLL AND PAYROLL TAXES

Accounting systems for payroll and payroll taxes are concerned with the records and reports associated with the employer-employee relationship. It is important that the accounting system provide safeguards to insure that payments are in accord with management's general plans and its specific authorizations.

All employees of a firm expect and are entitled to receive their remuneration at regular intervals following the close of each payroll period. Regardless of the number of employees and the difficulties in computing the amounts to be paid, the payroll system must be designed to process the necessary data quickly and assure payment of the correct amount to each employee. The system must also provide adequate safeguards against payments to fictitious persons and other misappropriations of funds.

Various federal, state, and local laws require that employers accumulate certain specified data in their payroll records, not only for each payroll period but also for each employee. Periodic reports of such data must be submitted to the appropriate governmental agencies and remittances made for amounts withheld from employees and for taxes levied on the employer. The records must be retained for specified periods of time and be available for inspection by those responsible for enforcement of the laws. In addition, payroll data may be useful in negotiations with labor unions, in settling employee grievances, and in determining rights to vacations, sick leaves, and retirement pensions.

Although complex organizational structures may necessitate the use of detailed subsystems, the major parts common to most payroll systems are the payroll register, employee's earnings record, and payroll checks. Each of these major payroll components is illustrated and discussed in the following sections. Although the illustrations are relatively simple, many modifications might be introduced in actual practice.

---

[2]As of January 1, 1987, the maximum state rate recognized by the federal unemployment system was 5.4% of the first $7,000 of each employee's earnings during a calendar year.

Payroll Register

The multicolumn form used in assembling and summarizing the data needed at the end of each payroll period is called the **payroll register**. Its design varies according to the number and classes of employees and the extent to which computers are used. A form suitable for a small number of employees is illustrated below.

The nature of most of the data appearing in the illustrative payroll register is evident from the columnar headings. The number of hours worked and the earnings and deduction data are inserted in the appropriate columns. The sum of the deductions applicable to an employee is then deducted from the total earnings to yield the amount to be paid. Recording the check numbers in the payroll register as the checks are written eliminates the need to maintain other detailed records of the payments.

The two columns under the general heading of Taxable Earnings are used in accumulating data needed to compute the employer's payroll taxes. The last two columns of the payroll register are used to accumulate the total wages or salaries to be charged to the expense accounts. This process is usually termed **payroll distribution**. If there is an extensive account classification of labor expense, the charges may be analyzed on a separate payroll distribution sheet.

The format of the illustrative payroll register aids the determination of arithmetic accuracy before checks are issued to employees and before the

PAYROLL
REGISTER

					PAYROLL FOR WEEK ENDING	
		EARNINGS			TAXABLE EARNINGS	
NAME	TOTAL HOURS	REGULAR	OVERTIME	TOTAL	UNEMPLOY-MENT COMP.	FICA
ARKIN, JOAN E.	40	500.00		500.00	500.00	500.00
DAWSON, LOREN A.	44	392.00	58.80	450.80		450.80
GREEN, MINDY M.		840.00		840.00		
JOHNSON, THOMAS C.	43	800.00	90.00	890.00		500.00
WYATT, WILLIAM R.	40	480.00		480.00		480.00
ZACHS, ANNA H.		600.00		600.00	150.00	600.00
TOTAL		13,328.70	574.00	13,902.70	2,710.00	11,354.70

summary amounts are formally recorded. Specifically, all columnar totals except those in the Taxable Earnings columns should be cross-verified. The miscellaneous deductions must also be summarized by account classification. The following tabulation illustrates the method of cross-verification:

Earnings:		
Regular	$13,328.70	
Overtime	574.00	
Total		$13,902.70
Deductions:		
FICA tax	$ 851.60	
Federal income tax	3,332.18	
U.S. savings bonds	680.00	
United Fund	470.00	
Accounts receivable	50.00	
Total		5,383.78
Paid—net amount		$ 8,518.92
Accounts debited:		
Sales Salaries Expense		$11,122.16
Office Salaries Expense		2,780.54
Total (as above)		$13,902.70

DECEMBER 27, 19--

	DEDUCTIONS					PAID		ACCOUNTS DEBITED	
FICA TAX	FEDERAL INCOME TAX	U.S. SAVINGS BONDS	MISCEL-LANEOUS		TOTAL	NET AMOUNT	CHECK NO.	SALES SALARIES EXPENSE	OFFICE SALARIES EXPENSE
37.50	74.10	20.00	UF	10.00	141.60	358.40	6857	500.00	
33.81	62.60		AR	50.00	146.41	304.39	6858		450.80
	186.30	25.00	UF	10.00	221.30	618.70	6859	840.00	
37.50	186.70	20.00	UF	5.00	249.20	640.80	6860	890.00	
36.00	69.20	10.00			115.20	364.80	6880	480.00	
45.00	71.36	5.00	UF	2.00	123.36	476.64	6881		600.00
851.60	3,332.18	680.00	UF	470.00	5,383.78	8,518.92		11,122.16	2,780.54
			AR	50.00					

MISCELLANEOUS DEDUCTIONS: AR—ACCOUNTS RECEIVABLE   UF—UNITED FUND

Recording Employees' Earnings. The payroll register may be used as a posting medium in a manner like that in which the voucher register and check register are used. Alternatively, it may be used as a supporting record for a compound journal entry that records the payroll data. The entry based on the payroll register illustrated is as follows:

Dec. 27	Sales Salaries Expense....................	11,122.16	
	Office Salaries Expense	2,780.54	
	FICA Tax Payable......................		851.60
	Employees Federal Income Tax Payable...		3,332.18
	Bond Deductions Payable..............		680.00
?	United Fund Deductions Payable		470.00
	Accounts Receivable—Loren A. Dawson ..		50.00
	Salaries Payable......................		8,518.92
	Payroll for week ended December 27.		

The total expense incurred for the services of employees is recorded by the debits to the salary expense accounts. Amounts withheld from employees' earnings have no effect on the debits to these accounts. Five of the credits in the entry represent increases in specific liability accounts and one represents a decrease in the accounts receivable account.

Recording and Paying Payroll Taxes. Each time the payroll register is prepared, the amounts of all employees' current earnings entering the tax base are listed in the respective taxable earnings columns. As explained earlier, the cumulative amounts of each employee's earnings just prior to the current period are available in the employee's earnings record.

According to the payroll register illustrated for the week ended December 27, the amount of remuneration subject to FICA tax was $11,354.70, and the amount subject to state and federal unemployment compensation taxes was $2,710. Multiplication by the applicable tax rates yields the following amounts:

FICA tax...	$ 851.60
State unemployment compensation tax (5.4% × $2,710)	146.34
Federal unemployment compensation tax (.8% × $2,710)	21.68
Total payroll taxes expense	$1,019.62

The journal entry to record the payroll tax expense for the week and the liability for the taxes accrued is as follows:

Dec. 27	Payroll Taxes Expense....................	1,019.62	
	FICA Tax Payable......................		851.60
	State Unemployment Tax Payable........		146.34
	Federal Unemployment Tax Payable		21.68
	Payroll taxes for week ended		
	December 27.		

Payment of the liability for each of the taxes is recorded in the same manner as the payment of other liabilities. Employers are required to compute and report all payroll taxes on the calendar-year basis, regardless of the fiscal year they may use for financial reporting and income tax purposes. Details of the federal income tax and FICA tax withheld from employees are combined with the employer's FICA tax on a single return accompanied by the amount of tax due. Payments are required on a weekly, semimonthly, monthly, or quarterly basis, depending on the amount of the combined taxes. Unemployment compensation tax returns and payments are required by the federal government on an annual basis. Earlier payments are required when the tax exceeds a certain minimum. Unemployment compensation tax returns and payments are required by most states on a basis similar to that required by the federal government.

All payroll taxes levied against employers become liabilities at the time the related remuneration is *paid* to employees, rather than at the time the liability to the employees is incurred. Observance of this requirement may cause a problem of expense allocation between fiscal periods. To illustrate, assume that an enterprise using the calendar year as its fiscal year pays its employees on Friday for a weekly payroll period ending the preceding Wednesday, the two-day lag between Wednesday and Friday being needed to process the payroll. Regardless of the day of the week on which the year ends, there will be some accrued wages. If it ends on a Thursday, the accrual will cover a full week plus an extra day. Logically, the unpaid wages and the related payroll taxes should both be charged to the period that benefited from the services performed by the employees. On the other hand, there is legally no liability for the payroll taxes until the wages are paid in January, when a new cycle of earnings subject to tax is begun. The distortion of net income that would result from failure to accrue the payroll taxes might well be insignificant. The practice adopted should be followed consistently.

Employee's Earnings Record

The necessity of having the cumulative amount of each employee's earnings readily available at the end of each payroll period was discussed earlier. Without such information or the related data on the cumulative amount of FICA tax previously withheld, there would be no means of determining the appropriate amount to withhold from current earnings. It is essential, therefore, that detailed records be maintained for each employee.

A portion of the **employee's earnings record** is illustrated below. The relationship between this record and the payroll register can be seen by tracing the amounts entered on Johnson's earnings record for December 27 back to its source, which is the fourth line of the payroll register illustrated on pages 522 and 523.

In addition to spaces for recording data for each payroll period and the cumulative total of earnings, there are spaces for quarterly totals and the yearly total. These totals are used in various reports for tax, insurance, and other purposes. Copies of one such annual report, known as Form W-2 Wage and Tax Statement, must be given to each employee as well as to the Social Security Administration.

EMPLOYEE'S EARNINGS RECORD

THOMAS C. JOHNSON
4990 COLUMBUS AVENUE   PHONE: 555-3148
STATESVILLE, IA 52732-6142

MARRIED   NUMBER OF
                 WITHHOLDING   PAY
                 ALLOWANCES: 4   RATE: $800.00 PER WEEK

OCCUPATION: SALESPERSON   EQUIVALENT HOURLY RATE: $20

LINE NO.	PERIOD ENDED	TOTAL HOURS	EARNINGS REGULAR EARNINGS	OVERTIME	TOTAL EARNINGS	CUMULATIVE TOTAL
39	SEPT. 27	41	800.00	30.00	830.00	34,690.00
THIRD QUARTER			10,400.00	270.00	10,670.00	
40	OCT. 4	40	800.00		800.00	35,490.00
46	NOV. 15	41	800.00	30.00	830.00	40,320.00
47	NOV. 22	40	800.00		800.00	41,120.00
48	NOV. 29	42	800.00	60.00	860.00	41,980.00
49	DEC. 6	40	800.00		800.00	42,780.00
50	DEC. 13	40	800.00		800.00	43,580.00
51	DEC. 20	44	800.00	120.00	920.00	44,500.00
52	DEC. 27	43	800.00	90.00	890.00	45,390.00
FOURTH QUARTER			10,400.00	300.00	10,700.00	
YEARLY TOTAL			41,600.00	3,790.00	45,390.00	

The source of the amounts inserted in the following statement was the employee's earnings record.

1 Control number	44012	For Paperwork Reduction Act Notice, see back of Copy D. OMB No. 1545–0008	For Official Use Only		WAGE AND TAX STATEMENT

2 Employer's name, address, and ZIP code	3 Employer's identification number 61-843652		4 Employer's State number

Langford Supply Co.
560 Hudson Avenue
Cedar Rapids, IA 52731-6148

5 Stat. em-ployee	De-ceased	Legal rep.	942 emp.	Sub-total	Void

6 Allocated tips	7 Advance EIC payment

8 Employee's social security number 381-48-9120	9 Federal income tax withheld $8,942.06	10 Wages, tips, other compensation $45,390.00	11 Social security tax withheld $3,375.00

12 Employee's name (first, middle, last)	13 Social security wages $45,000.00	14 Social security tips

	16 °	

Thomas C. Johnson
4990 Columbus Avenue
Statesville, IA 52732-6142

17 State income tax	18 State wages, tips, etc.	19 Name of State
20 Local income tax	21 Local wages, tips, etc.	22 Name of locality

15 Employee's address and ZIP code

Form **W-2 Wage and Tax Statement 19**-- · Copy A For Social Security Administration · See Instructions for Forms W–2 and W–2P · Department of the Treasury Internal Revenue Service

---

SOC. SEC. NO.: 381-48-9120	EMPLOYEE NO.: 814

DATE EMPLOYED: FEBRUARY 15, 1974

DATE OF BIRTH: OCTOBER 4, 1952

DATE EMPLOYMENT TERMINATED:

	DEDUCTIONS				PAID		
FICA TAX	FEDERAL INCOME TAX	U.S. BONDS	OTHER	TOTAL	NET AMOUNT	CHECK NO.	LINE NO.
62.25	174.11	20.00		256.36	573.64	6175	39
800.25	2,238.30	260.00	AR 40.00	3,338.55	7,331.45		
60.00	167.82	20.00	UF 5.00	252.82	547.18	6225	40
62.25	174.11	20.00		256.36	573.64	6530	46
60.00	167.82	20.00		247.82	552.18	6582	47
64.50	180.41	20.00		264.91	595.09	6640	48
60.00	167.82	20.00	UF 5.00	252.82	547.18	6688	49
60.00	167.82	20.00		247.82	552.18	6743	50
69.00	192.99	20.00		281.99	638.01	6801	51
37.50	186.70	20.00	UF 5.00	249.20	640.80	6860	52
773.25	2,244.60	260.00	UF 15.00	3,292.85	7,407.15		
3,375.00	8,942.06	1,040.00	AR 40.00 UF 60.00	13,457.06	31,932.94		

Payroll Checks

One of the principal outputs of most payroll systems is a series of **payroll checks** at the end of each pay period. The data needed for this purpose are provided by the payroll register, each line of which applies to an individual employee. It is possible to prepare the checks solely by reference to the Net Amount column of the register. However, the customary practice is to provide each employee with a statement of the details of the computation. The statement may be entirely separate from the check or it may be in the form of a detachable stub attached to the check.

When employees are paid by checks drawn on the regular bank account and the voucher system is used, it is necessary to prepare a voucher for the net amount to be paid the employees. The voucher is then recorded in the voucher register as a debit to Salaries Payable and a credit to Accounts Payable, and payment is recorded in the check register in the usual manner. If the voucher system is not used, the payment would be recorded by a debit to Salaries Payable and a credit to Cash.

It should be understood that the journal entry derived from the payroll register, such as the compound entry illustrated on page 525, would precede the entries just described. It should also be noted that the entire amount paid may be recorded as a single item, regardless of the number of employees. There is no need to record each check separately because all of the details are available in the payroll register for future reference.

Most employers with a large number of employees use a special bank account and payroll checks designed specifically for the purpose. After the data for the payroll period have been recorded and summarized in the payroll register, a single check for the total amount to be paid is drawn on the firm's regular bank account and deposited in a special account. The individual payroll checks are then drawn against the special payroll account, and the numbers of the payroll checks are inserted in the payroll register.

The use of special payroll checks relieves the treasurer or other executives of the task of signing a large number of regular checks each payday. The responsibility for signing payroll checks may be given to the paymaster, or mechanical means of signing the checks may be used. Another advantage of this system is that reconciling the regular bank statement is simplified. The paid payroll checks are returned by the bank separately from regular checks and are accompanied by a statement of the special bank account. Any balance shown on the bank's statement will correspond to the sum of the payroll checks outstanding because the amount of each deposit is exactly the same as the total amount of checks drawn. The recording procedures are the same as when checks on the regular bank account are used.

Currency is sometimes used as the medium of payment when the payroll is paid each week or when the business location or the time of payment is such that banking or check-cashing facilities are not readily available to employees. In such cases, a single check, payable to Payroll, is drawn for the entire amount to be paid. The check is then cashed at the bank and the money is inserted in individual pay envelopes. Each employee should be required to sign a receipt which serves as evidence of payment. The procedures for recording the payment correspond to those outlined for payroll checks.

PAYROLL SYSTEM DIAGRAM *start*

The flow of data within segments of an accounting system may be shown by diagrams such as the one illustrated below. It depicts the interrelationships of the principal parts of the payroll system described in this chapter. The requirement of constant updating of the employee's earnings record is indicated by the dotted line.

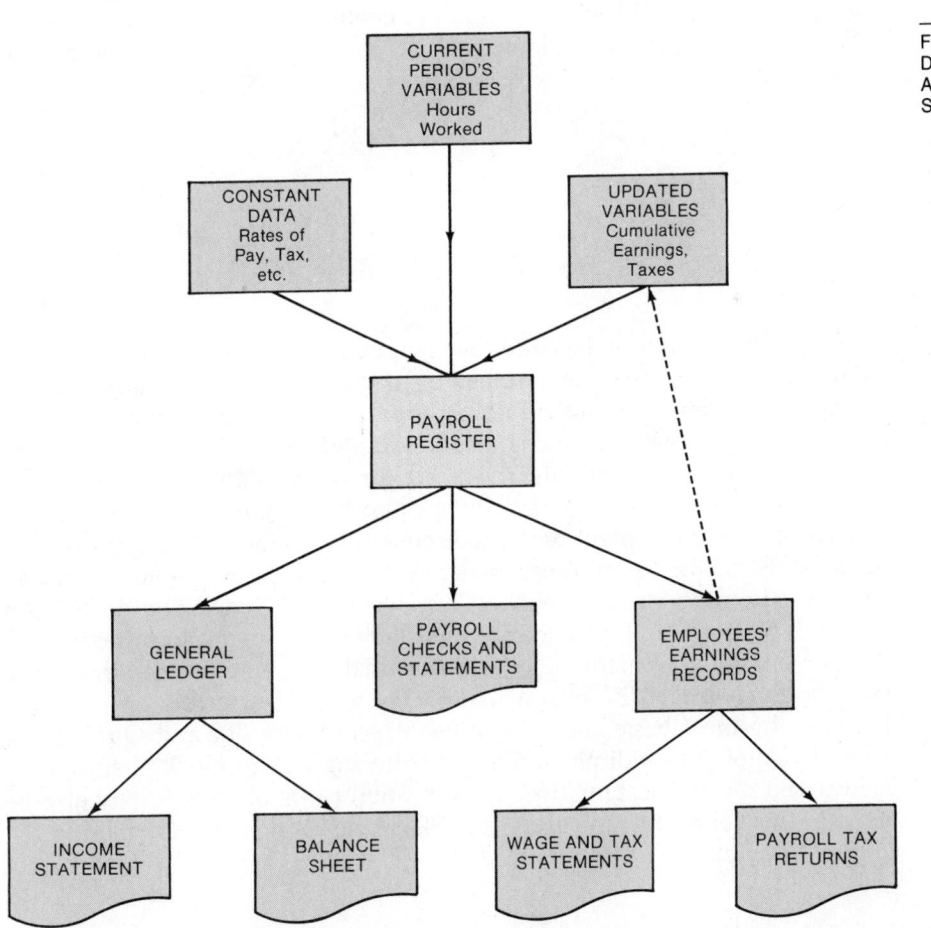

FLOW DIAGRAM OF A PAYROLL SYSTEM

Attention thus far has been directed to the end product or *output* of a payroll system, namely the payroll register, the checks payable to individual employees, the earnings records for each employee, and reports for tax and other purposes. The basic data entering the payroll systems are sometimes called the *input* of the system. Input data that remain relatively unchanged and do not need to be reintroduced into the system for each payroll period are characterized as *constants*. Those data that differ from period to period are termed *variables*.

Constants include such data for each employee as name and social security number, marital status, number of income tax withholding allowances claimed, rate of pay, functional category (office, sales, etc.), and department where employed. The FICA tax rate, maximum earnings subject to tax, and various tax tables are also constants which apply to all employees. The variable data for each employee include the number of hours or days worked during each payroll period, days of sick leave with pay, vacation credits, and cumulative amounts of earnings and taxes withheld. If salespersons are employed on a commission basis, the amount of their sales would also vary from period to period. The forms used in initially recording both the constant and the variable data vary widely according to the complexities of the payroll system and the processing methods used.

INTERNAL CONTROLS FOR PAYROLL SYSTEMS

The large amount of data and the computations necessary to process the payroll are evident. As the number of employees and the mass of data increase, the number of individuals needed to manage and process payroll data likewise increases. Such characteristics, together with the relative magnitude of labor costs, indicate the need for controls that will assure the reliability of the data and minimize the opportunity for misuse of funds.

The cash disbursement controls discussed in Chapter 8 are applicable to payrolls. Thus, the use of the voucher system and the requirement that all payments be supported by vouchers are desirable. The addition or deletion of names on the payroll should be supported by written authorizations from the personnel department. It is also essential that employees' attendance records be controlled in such a manner as to prevent errors and abuses. Perhaps the most basic and widely used records are "In and Out" cards, whereby employees indicate, often by "punching" a time clock, their time of arrival and departure. Employee identification cards or badges may also be used in this connection to assure that all salaries and wages are paid to the proper individuals.

LIABILITY FOR EMPLOYEES' FRINGE BENEFITS

Many companies provide their employees a variety of benefits in addition to salary and wages earned. These benefits, often referred to as **fringe benefits**, may take many forms, such as vacations, employee pension plans, and health, life, and disability insurance. If the employer pays part or all of the cost of the fringe benefits and revenues and expenses are to be matched properly, the estimated cost of these benefits must be recognized as an expense of the period during which the employee earns the benefit. The application of accounting principles to fringe benefits is described in the following paragraphs, using vacation pay and pensions as examples.

Liability for Vacation Pay

Most employees are granted some vacation privileges. To match revenue and expense properly, the employer should accrue the vacation pay liability as the vacation privilege is earned, if the payment is probable and can be reasonably estimated.[3] To illustrate the accounting for vacation absences, frequently referred to as compensated absences, assume that all employees earn two weeks of vacation for each 50 weeks worked during the year, and the total vacation pay expense for the year is $100,000. Since this expense is actually incurred during the 50 weeks the employees work during the year, the expense and the liability could be recorded by an adjusting entry at the end of the accounting period, or recorded each pay period, illustrated as follows:

May 5	Vacation Pay Expense....................	2,000	
	Vacation Pay Payable		2,000
	Vacation pay for week ended May 5		
	(1/50 of annual vacation pay of $100,000)		

Depending upon when it is to be paid, the vacation liability will be classified in the balance sheet as either a current liability or a long-term liability. When the payroll in which the employees are paid for their vacations is prepared, Vacation Pay Payable would be debited, and Salaries Payable and the appropriate accounts for recording taxes and withholdings would be credited.

---

[3]*Statement of Financial Accounting Standards, No. 43,* "Accounting for Compensated Absences" (Stamford: Financial Accounting Standards Board, 1980), par. 6.

Liability for Pensions

In recent years, retirement pension plans have increased rapidly in number, variety, and complexity. Although the details of the plans vary from employer to employer, pension benefits are usually based on factors such as employee age, years of service, and salary level. In 1974, Congress enacted the Employee Retirement Income Security Act (ERISA), which established guidelines for safeguarding employee benefits.

Pension plans may be classified as contributory or noncontributory, funded or unfunded, and qualified or unqualified. A **contributory plan** requires the employer to withhold a portion of each employee's earnings as a contribution to the plan. The employer then makes a contribution according to the provisions of the plan. A **noncontributory plan** requires the employer to bear the entire cost. A **funded plan** requires the employer to set aside funds to meet future pension benefits by making payments to an independent funding agency. The funding agency is responsible for managing the assets of the pension fund and for disbursing the pension benefits to employees. For many pension plans, insurance companies serve as the funding agency. An **unfunded plan** is managed entirely by the employer instead of by an independent agency. A **qualified plan** is designed to comply with federal income tax requirements which allow the employer to deduct pension contributions for tax purposes and which exempt pension fund income from tax. Most pension plans are qualified.

The accounting for pension plans can be complex due to the uncertainties of projecting future pension obligations. Future pension obligations depend upon such factors as employee life expectancies, expected employee compensation levels, and investment income on pension contributions. Pension funding requirements are estimated by individuals known as actuaries, who use sophisticated mathematical and statistical models.

The employer's cost of an employee's pension plan in a given year, referred to as the **net periodic pension cost**, is debited to an operating expense account, Pension Expense.[4] The credit is to Cash if the pension cost is fully funded. If the pension cost is partially funded, any unfunded amount is credited to Unfunded Accrued Pension Cost. To illustrate, assume that the pension plan of Flossmoor Industries requires an annual pension cost of $25,000, and Flossmoor Industries pays $15,000 to the fund trustee, Equity Insurance Company. The entry to record the transaction is as follows:

Pension Expense	25,000	
Cash		15,000
Unfunded Accrued Pension Cost		10,000

---

[4]*Statement of Financial Accounting Standards, No. 87,* "Employers' Accounting for Pensions" (Stamford: Financial Accounting Standards Board, 1985), par. 6.

Depending upon when the pension liability (unfunded accrued pension cost) is to be paid, the $10,000 will be classified on the balance sheet as either a long-term or a current liability.

An entity's financial statements should fully disclose the nature of its pension plans and pension obligations. The financial statement disclosures should include the net periodic pension cost for the year and a description of the pension plan, including such items as the employee groups covered, the entity's accounting and funding policies, and any pension changes affecting comparability among years.

When an employer first adopts or changes a pension plan, the employer must consider whether to grant employees credit for prior years service. If a company does grant credit to employees for prior service, a prior service cost obligation must be recognized. The funding of prior service cost is normally provided for over a number of years, thus creating a long-term prior service pension cost liability. The complex nature of accounting for prior service costs is left for more advanced accounting study.

NOTES PAYABLE AND INTEREST EXPENSE

Notes may be issued to creditors in temporary satisfaction of an account payable created earlier, or they may be issued at the time merchandise or other assets are purchased. To illustrate the former, assume that an enterprise issues to Murray Co. a 90-day, 12% note for $1,000, dated December 1, 1987, in settlement of a $1,000 overdue account. The entry to record the transaction is as follows:

Dec. 1	Accounts Payable—Murray Co.	1,000	
	Notes Payable.		1,000
	Issued a 90-day, 12% note on account.		

On December 31, 1987, the end of the fiscal year, an adjusting entry would be recorded for the accrual of the interest from December 1 to December 31. The entry to record the accrued expense of $10 ($1,000 × 12/100 × 30/360) is as follows:

	Adjusting Entry		
Dec. 31	Interest Expense.	10	
	Interest Payable		10

Interest payable is reported on the balance sheet at December 31, 1987, as a current liability. The interest expense account is closed at December 31, and the amount is reported in the Other Expense section of the income statement for the year ended December 31, 1987.

When the amount due on the note is paid in 1988, part of the interest paid will effect a reduction of the interest that was payable at December 31, 1987, and the remainder will represent expense for 1988. To avoid the possibility of failing to recognize this division and to avoid the inconvenience of analyzing the payment of interest in 1988, a reversing entry is made after the accounts are closed. The effect of the entry, illustrated as follows, is to transfer the credit balance in the interest payable account to the credit side of the interest expense account.

	Reversing Entry		
Jan. 1	Interest Payable............	10	
	Interest Expense..........		10

At the time the note matures and payment is made, the entire amount of the interest payment is debited to Interest Expense, as illustrated by the following entry:

Mar. 1	Notes Payable..............	1,000	
	Interest Expense...........	30	
	Cash.....................		1,030

After the foregoing entries are posted, the interest expense account will appear as follows:

ACCOUNT INTEREST EXPENSE   ACCOUNT NO. 911

Date	Item	Post. Ref.	Debit	Credit	Balance	
					Debit	Credit
1987						
Nov. 10		CP40	250		890	
Dec. 31	Adjusting	J17	10		900	
31	Closing	J17		900	—	—
1988						
Jan. 1	Reversing	J18		10		10
Mar. 1		CP42	30		20	

The adjusting and reversing process divided the $30 of interest paid on March 1, 1988, into two parts for accounting purposes: (1) $10 representing the interest expense for 1987 (recorded by the adjusting entry) and (2) $20 representing the interest expense for 1988 (the balance in the interest expense account at March 1, 1988).

Notes may also be issued when money is borrowed from banks. Although there are many variations in interest and repayment terms, the most direct procedure is for the borrower to issue an interest-bearing note for the amount of the loan. For example, assume that on September 19 a firm borrows $4,000 from the First National Bank, with the loan evidenced by the firm's 90-day, 15% note. The effect of this transaction is as follows:

Sept. 19	Cash..	4,000	
	Notes Payable..................................		4,000

On the due date of the note, ninety days later, the borrower owes $4,000, the face amount of the note, and interest of $150. The accounts are affected by the payment as follows:

Dec. 18	Notes Payable...................................	4,000	
	Interest Expense................................	150	
	Cash......................................		4,150

A variant of the bank loan transaction just illustrated is to issue a non-interest-bearing note for the amount that is to be paid at maturity. Although the note issued is non-interest-bearing, interest is deducted from the maturity value of the note and the borrower receives the remainder. The deduction of interest from a future value is termed **discounting**. The rate used in computing the interest may be termed the **discount rate**, the deduction may be called the **discount**, and the net amount available to the borrower is called the **proceeds**.

To illustrate the discounting of a note payable, assume that on August 10 an enterprise issued to a bank a $4,000, 90-day, non-interest-bearing note and that the bank discount rate is 15%. The amount of the discount is $150, and the proceeds are $3,850. The entry to record the transaction is as follows:

Aug. 10	Cash..	3,850	
	Interest Expense................................	150	
	Notes Payable..................................		4,000

The note payable is recorded at its face value, which is also its maturity value, and the interest expense is recorded at the time the note is issued. When the note is paid, the following entry is recorded:

Nov. 8	Notes Payable...................................	4,000	
	Cash......................................		4,000

PRODUCT WARRANTY LIABILITY

At the time of sale, a company may grant a warranty on a product. If revenues and expenses are to be matched properly, a liability to cover the warranty must be recorded in the period of the sale.[5] Later, when the product is repaired or replaced, the liability will be reduced. To illustrate, assume that during June a company sells $60,000 of a product, on which there is a 36-month warranty for repairing defects in the product. If past experience indicates that the average cost to repair defects is 5% of the sales price, the entry to record the product warranty liability would be as follows:

June 30	Product Warranty Expense	3,000	
	Product Warranty Payable.		3,000
	Product warranty for June, 5% × $60,000.		

When the defective product is repaired, the repair costs would be recorded by debiting Product Warranty Payable and crediting Cash, Supplies, or other appropriate account.

CHAPTER REVIEW

KEY POINTS

1. Payroll and Liability for Payroll.

The term payroll is used to refer to the total amount paid to employees for a certain period. Payroll includes amounts paid for salaries to managerial or administrative employees as well as wages paid for manual labor.

Many enterprises pay their employees an annual bonus in addition to their regular salary or wage. The amount of the bonus may be measured by a certain percentage of income, which may be computed in a variety of ways.

---

[5]*Statement of Financial Accounting Standards, No. 5,* "Accounting for Contingencies" (Stamford: Financial Accounting Standards Board, 1975), pars. 8, 24.

2. Deductions from Employee Earnings and Computation of Employee Net Pay.

The total earnings of an employee for a payroll period, including bonuses and overtime pay, are often called the gross pay. From this amount is subtracted one or more deductions to arrive at the net pay. Deductions normally include FICA tax, federal income tax, and state and local income taxes, and may include union dues, charitable contributions, or employee insurance.

3. Liability for Employer's Payroll Taxes.

Most employers are subject to federal and state taxes based on the amount of remuneration earned by their employees. Such taxes include FICA tax, federal unemployment compensation tax, and state unemployment compensation tax.

4. Accounting Systems for Payroll and Payroll Taxes.

Although payroll systems will vary, the major parts common to most payroll systems include the payroll register, payroll checks, and employee's earnings record. Based upon the data in the payroll register, a compound journal entry is usually prepared to record the payroll for a period. This entry recognizes employer and employee payroll taxes as well as the liability for the net pay to the employees. The payment of the payroll liabilities is recorded in the usual manner. The payment of the payroll is usually accomplished through the use of payroll checks.

The employee's earnings record is updated after each payroll period and is used for preparing reports for tax, insurance, and other purposes.

5. Internal Controls for Payroll Systems.

Cash disbursement controls are applicable to payrolls. Thus, the use of the voucher system and the requirement that all payments be supported by vouchers is desirable. Additional controls, such as the maintenance of employees' attendance records, are also desirable.

6. Liability for Employees' Fringe Benefits.

Most companies provide their employees a variety of benefits in addition to salary and wages earned. These benefits are referred to as fringe benefits and may take the form of vacations, employee pension plans, health insurance, etc. The estimated cost of these benefits should be recognized as an expense of the period during which the employee earns the benefit.

7. Notes Payable and Interest Expense.

Notes may be issued to creditors in temporary satisfaction of an account payable created earlier, or they may be issued at the time merchandise or other assets are purchased. At the end of the fiscal period, an adjusting entry is normally prepared for the accrual of interest. The interest payable is reported on the balance sheet as a current liability. The adjusting entry for accrued interest at the end of the period is normally reversed to simplify the accounting process in the following period.

Notes may also be issued to borrow money from banks. The notes may be interest-bearing or non-interest-bearing. In the case of non-interest-bearing notes, the interest (discount) is deducted from the face of the note and the borrower receives the balance (proceeds).

8. Product Warranty Liability.

At the time of sale, a company may grant a warranty on a product. A liability to cover the warranty should be recorded during the period of the sale.

KEY TERMS

payroll 512
gross pay 515
net pay 515
FICA tax 517
payroll register 522

employee's earnings record 526
discount rate 535
discount 535
proceeds 535

SELF-EXAMINATION QUESTIONS

Answers in Appendix B.

1. An employee's rate of pay is $20 per hour, with time and a half for all hours worked in excess of 40 during a week. The following data are available:

Hours worked during current week.	45
Year's cumulative earnings prior to current week	$44,400
FICA rate, on maximum of $45,000 of annual earnings.	7.5%
Federal income tax withheld	$ 212

   Based on these data, the amount of the employee's net pay for the current week is:
   A. $600   C. $800
   B. $693   D. $950

2. Which of the following taxes are employers usually required to withhold from employees?
   A. Federal income tax
   B. Federal unemployment compensation tax
   C. State unemployment compensation tax
   D. All of the above

3. With limitations on the maximum earnings subject to the tax, employers incur operating costs for which of the following payroll taxes?
   A. FICA tax
   B. Federal unemployment compensation tax
   C. State unemployment compensation tax
   D. All of the above

4. The unpaid balance of a mortgage note payable is $50,000 at the end of the current fiscal year. If the terms of the note provide for monthly principal payments of $1,000, how should the liability for the principal be presented on the balance sheet?
   A. $50,000 current liability
   B. $50,000 long-term liability
   C. $12,000 current liability; $38,000 long-term liability
   D. $12,000 long-term liability; $38,000 current liability

5. An enterprise issued a $5,000, 60-day, non-interest-bearing note to the bank, and the bank discounts the note at 12%. The proceeds are:
   A. $4,400   C. $5,000
   B. $4,900   D. $5,100

ILLUSTRATIVE PROBLEM

Selected transactions of Grainger Company, completed during the fiscal year ended December 31, are as follows:

Mar. 1. Purchased merchandise on account from Perry Inc., $15,000.
Apr. 10. Issued a 60-day, 12% note for $15,000 to Perry Inc., on account.
June 9. Paid Perry Inc. the amount owed on the note of April 10.
Aug. 1. Issued a 90-day, non-interest-bearing note for $30,000 to Atlantic Coast National Bank. The bank discounted the note at 15%.
Oct. 30. Paid Atlantic Coast National Bank the amount due on the note of August 1.
Dec. 15. Prepared the journal entry to record the biweekly payroll. A summary of the payroll record follows:

Deductions:	
FICA tax	$ 4,820
Federal income tax withheld.	13,280
State income tax withheld.	3,840
Savings bond deductions.	630
Medical insurance deductions	960
Salary distribution:	
Sales	$50,800
Officers	25,800
Office	6,400
Net amount.	$59,470

Dec. 30. Issued a check in payment of employees' federal income tax of
$68,550 and FICA tax of $24,650 due.
31. Issued a check for $8,600 to the pension fund trustee to fully fund the
pension cost for December.
31. Prepared a journal entry to record the employees' accrued vacation
pay, $32,200.
31. Prepared a journal entry to record the estimated accrued product
warranty liability, $41,360.

Instructions:

Record the preceding transactions, using a general journal.

SOLUTION

Mar. 1	Purchases............................	15,000	
	Accounts Payable — Perry Inc.		15,000
Apr. 10	Accounts Payable — Perry Inc.	15,000	
	Notes Payable		15,000
June 9	Notes Payable	15,000	
	Interest Expense......................	300	
	Cash		15,300
Aug. 1	Cash	28,875	
	Interest Expense......................	1,125	
	Notes Payable		30,000
Oct. 30	Notes Payable	30,000	
	Cash		30,000
Dec. 15	Sales Salaries Expense..................	50,800	
	Officers Salaries Expense	25,800	
	Office Salaries Expense.................	6,400	
	FICA Tax Payable...................		4,820
	Employees Federal Income Tax Payable..		13,280
	Employees State Income Tax Payable ...		3,840
	Bond Deductions Payable.............		630
	Medical Insurance Payable............		960
	Salaries Payable		59,470
30	Employees Federal Income Tax Payable ...	68,550	
	FICA Tax Payable.....................	24,650	
	Cash		93,200
31	Pension Expense.......................	8,600	
	Cash		8,600

Dec. 31	Vacation Pay Expense	32,200	
	Vacation Pay Payable.................		32,200
31	Product Warranty Expense...............	41,360	
	Product Warranty Payable		41,360

DISCUSSION QUESTIONS

1. If an employee is granted a profit-sharing bonus, is the amount of the bonus (a) part of the employee's earnings and (b) deductible as an expense of the enterprise in determining the federal income tax?

2. The general manager of a business enterprise is entitled to an annual profit-sharing bonus of 8%. For the current year, income before bonus and income taxes is $202,500, and income taxes are estimated at 40% of income before income taxes. Determine the amount of the bonus, assuming that the bonus is based on net income after deducting both bonus and income taxes.

3. What is (a) gross pay? (b) net or take-home pay?

4. (a) Identify the federal taxes that most employers are required to withhold from employees. (b) Give the titles of the accounts to which the amounts withheld are credited.

5. For each of the following payroll-related taxes, indicate whether there is a ceiling on the annual earnings subject to the tax: (a) FICA tax, (b) federal income tax, (c) federal unemployment compensation tax.

6. Identify the payroll taxes levied against employers.

7. Do payroll taxes levied against employers become liabilities at the time the liabilities for wages are incurred or at the time the wages are paid?

8. Prior to the last weekly payroll period of the calendar year, the cumulative earnings of employees A and B are $44,800 and $45,500, respectively. Their earnings for the last completed payroll period of the year are $900 each, which will be paid in January. If the amount of earnings subject to FICA tax is $45,000 and the tax rate is 7.5%, (a) what will be the employer's FICA tax on the earnings of employees A and B in the last payroll period; (b) what is the employer's total FICA tax expense for employees A and B for the calendar year just ended?

9. Indicate the principal functions served by the employee's earnings record.

10. Explain how a payroll system that is properly designed and operated tends to give assurance (a) that wages paid are based upon hours actually worked, and (b) that payroll checks are not issued to fictitious employees.

11. An employer pays the employees in currency and the pay envelopes are prepared by an employee rather than by the bank. (a) Why would it be advisable to obtain from the bank the exact amount of money needed for a payroll? (b) How could the exact number of each bill and coin denomination needed be determined efficiently in advance?

12. A company uses a weekly payroll period and a special bank account for payroll. (a) When should deposits be made in the account? (b) How is the amount of the deposit determined? (c) Is it necessary to have in the general ledger an account entitled "Cash—Special Payroll Account"? Explain. (d) The bank statement for the payroll bank account for the month ended November 30 indicates a bank balance of $11,705.50. Assuming that the bank has made no errors, what does this amount represent?

13. To match revenues and expenses properly, should the expense for employee vacation pay be recorded in the period during which the vacation privilege is earned or during the period in which the vacation is taken? Discuss.

14. Differentiate between a contributory and a noncontributory pension plan.

15. Identify several factors which influence the future pension obligation of an enterprise.

16. How does prior service cost arise in a new or revised pension plan?

17. The unpaid balance of a mortgage note payable is $500,000 at the end of the current fiscal year. The terms of the note provide for quarterly principal payments of $20,000. How should the liability for the principal be presented on the balance sheet as of this date?

18. A business enterprise issued a 90-day, 12% note for $10,000 to a creditor on account. Give the entries to record (a) the issuance of the note and (b) the payment of the note at maturity, including interest of $300.

19. In borrowing money from a bank, an enterprise issued a $50,000, 60-day, non-interest-bearing note, which the bank discounted at 15%. Are the proceeds $50,000? Explain.

20. When should the liability associated with a product warranty be recorded? Discuss.

21. Real World Focus. The 1984 annual report for Ranco Inc. contains the following footnote disclosures concerning product warranties:

> Product Warranty: The Company accrues product warranty costs based upon sales levels, warranty terms, and actual experience. . . . Accrued product warranty costs were $642,000 . . . at September 30, 1984. . . .

What journal entry would be made to record the accrued product warranty costs at September 30, 1984?

EXERCISES

Exercise 12–1. Algorithm. Develop an algorithm, in the form illustrated in this chapter, to compute the amount of each employee's weekly earnings subject to state unemployment compensation tax. Assume that the tax is 4.2% on the first $7,000 of each employee's earnings during the year and that the following symbols are to be used:

    e—Cumulative earnings subject to state unemployment compensation tax prior to current week

    E—Current week's earnings

    S—Amount of current week's earnings subject to state unemployment compensation tax

Exercise 12–2. Profit-sharing bonus. The general manager of a business enterprise is entitled to an annual profit-sharing bonus of 5%. For the current year, income before bonus and income taxes is $400,000, and income taxes are estimated at 40% of income before income taxes. Determine the amount of the bonus, assuming that (a) the bonus is based on income before deductions for bonus and income taxes and (b) the bonus is based on income after deduction for both bonus and income taxes.

Exercise 12–3. Summary payroll data. In the following summary of data for a payroll period, some amounts have been intentionally omitted:

Earnings:		Deductions:	
(1) At regular rate	—	(4) FICA tax.	$ 4,315.20
(2) At overtime rate . . .	$ 4,144.00	(5) Income tax withheld	9,281.60
(3) Total earnings	—	(6) Medical insurance .	710.00
		(7) Union dues	—
		(8) Total deductions . . .	15,766.40
		(9) Net amount paid. . .	59,116.80

Accounts debited:
    (10) Factory Wages . . $53,984.40
    (11) Sales Salaries . . .   —
    (12) Office Salaries . . .   4,872.00

(a) Determine the amounts omitted in lines (1), (3), (7), and (11). (b) Present the journal entry to record the payroll. (c) Present, in general journal form, the entry to record the voucher for the payroll. (d) Present, in general journal form, the entry to record the payment of the voucher. (e) From the data given in this exercise and your answer to (a), would you conclude that this payroll was paid sometime during the first few weeks of the calendar year? Explain.

Exercise 12–4. Payroll tax entries. According to a summary of the payroll of McMann Distributing Co., the amount of earnings for the four weekly payrolls paid in December of the current year was $360,000, of which $25,000 was not subject to FICA tax and $345,000 was not subject to state and federal unemployment taxes. (a) Determine the employer's payroll taxes expense for the month, using the following rates: FICA, 7.5%; state unemployment, 4.8%; federal unemployment, .8%. (b) Present the general journal entry to record the accrual of payroll taxes for the month of December.

Exercise 12–5. Accrued vacation pay and product warranty. A business enterprise provides its employees with varying amounts of vacation per year, depending on the length of employment. It also warrants its products for one year. The estimated total amount of the current year's vacation pay is $180,000, and the estimated product warranty is 2% of sales. If sales were $650,000 for January, prepare the adjusting entries required at January 31, the end of the first month of the current year, to record (a) the accrued vacation pay and (b) the accrued product warranty.

Exercise 12–6. Pension plan entries. Jefferson Corporation maintains a funded pension plan for its employees. The plan requires quarterly installments to be paid to the funding agent, Curtin Insurance Company, by the fifteenth of the month following the end of each quarter. If for the quarter ended December 31, the pension cost is $45,000, prepare entries to record (a) the accrued pension liability on December 31 and (b) the payment to the funding agent on January 15.

Exercise 12–7. Entries for discounting notes. Newhart Co. issues a 90-day, non-interest-bearing note for $100,000 to Roberts Bank and Trust Co., and the bank discounts the note at 15%. (a) Present the maker's entries to record (1) the issuance of the note and (2) the payment of the note at maturity. (b) Present the payee's entries to record (1) the receipt of the note and (2) the receipt of payment of the note at maturity.

Exercise 12–8. Determination of interest on notes issued. In negotiating a 120-day loan, an enterprise has the option of either (1) issuing a $200,000, non-interest-bearing note that will be discounted at the rate of 12%, or (2) issuing a $200,000 note that bears interest at the rate of 12% and that will be accepted at face value.

  (a) Determine the amount of the interest expense for each option.
  (b) Determine the amount of the proceeds for each option.
  (c) Indicate the option that is more favorable to the borrower.

Exercise 12–9. Plant asset purchases with note. On September 1, Oliver Company purchased land for $150,000 and a building for $500,000, paying $130,000 cash and issuing a 12% note for the balance, secured by a mortgage on the property. The terms of the note provide for 26 semiannual payments of $20,000 on the principal plus the interest accrued from the date of the preceding payment. Present the entry to record (a) the transaction on September 1, (b) the adjustment for accrued interest on December 31, (c) the reversal of the adjustment on January 1, (d) the payment of the first installment on February 28, and (e) the payment of the second installment the following August 31.

PROBLEMS

Series A

Problem 12–1A. Profit-sharing bonuses. The president of Wagner Company is entitled to an annual profit-sharing bonus of 4%. For the current year, income before bonus and income taxes is $720,000, and income taxes are estimated at 40% of income before income taxes.

Instructions:

(1) Determine the amount of the bonus, assuming that:
  (a) The bonus is based on income before deductions for bonus and income taxes.
  (b) The bonus is based on income after deduction for bonus but before deduction for income taxes.
  (c) The bonus is based on income after deduction for income taxes but before deduction for bonus.
  (d) The bonus is based on income after deduction for both bonus and income taxes.
(2) (a) Which bonus plan would the president prefer? (b) Would this plan always be the president's choice, regardless of Wagner Company's income level?

Problem 12–2A. Entries for payroll and payroll taxes. The following information relative to the payroll for the week ended December 30 was obtained from the records of E. Thurmond Inc.:

Salaries:		Deductions:	
Sales salaries...........	$148,700	Income tax withheld.......	$33,850
Warehouse salaries......	21,280	U.S. savings bonds	4,400
Office salaries..........	12,020	Group insurance..........	2,800
	$182,000	FICA tax withheld totals the same amount as the employer's tax.	

Tax rates assumed:
  FICA, 7.5%
  State unemployment (employer only), 3.8%
  Federal unemployment, .8%

Instructions:

(1) Assuming that the payroll for the last week of the year is to be paid on December 31, present the following entries:
  (a) December 30, to record the payroll. Of the total payroll for the last week of the year, $112,800 is subject to FICA tax and $15,000 is subject to unemployment compensation taxes.
  (b) December 30, to record the employer's payroll taxes on the payroll to be paid on December 31.
  (continued)

(2) Assuming that the payroll for the last week of the year is to be paid on January 4 of the following year, present the following entries:
    (a) December 30, to record the payroll.
    (b) January 4, to record the employer's payroll taxes on the payroll to be paid on January 4.

If the working papers correlating with the textbook are not used, omit Problem 12–3A.

Problem 12–3A.   Payroll register. The payroll register for H. A. Howe Company for the week ended December 7 of the current fiscal year is presented in the working papers.

Instructions:

(1) Journalize the entry to record the payroll for the week.
(2) Assuming the use of a voucher system and payment by regular check, present the entries, in general journal form, to record the payroll voucher and the issuance of the checks to employees.
(3) Journalize the entry to record the employer's payroll taxes for the week. Assume the following tax rates: FICA, 7.5%; state unemployment, 3.8%; federal unemployment, .8%.
(4) Present the entries, in general journal form, to record the following selected transactions:

    Dec. 15. Prepared a voucher, payable to First National Bank, for employees income taxes, $3,750.60, and FICA taxes, $2,369.15, on salaries paid in November.
         15. Issued a check to First National Bank in payment of the voucher.

Problem 12–4A.   Payroll accounts, entries with voucher and check registers, and year-end entries. The following accounts, with the balances indicated, appear in the ledger of Monico Company on December 1 of the current year:

212	Salaries Payable	—
213	FICA Tax Payable	$ 14,910
214	Employees Federal Income Tax Payable	44,800
215	Employees State Income Tax Payable	13,260
216	State Unemployment Tax Payable	1,710
217	Federal Unemployment Tax Payable	360
218	Bond Deductions Payable	715
219	Medical Insurance Payable	3,875
611	Sales Salaries Expense	631,300
711	Officers Salaries Expense	311,800
712	Office Salaries Expense	85,500
719	Payroll Taxes Expense	92,430

The following transactions relating to payroll, payroll deductions, and payroll taxes occurred during December:

Dec. 2. Prepared Voucher No. 638 for $715, payable to Marine National Bank, to purchase United States savings bonds for employees.

2. Issued Check No. 621 in payment of Voucher No. 638.

14. Prepared a journal entry to record the biweekly payroll. A summary of the payroll record follows:

Deductions:

FICA tax	$ 3,250
Federal income tax withheld	7,790
State income tax withheld	1,920
Savings bond deductions	315
Medical insurance deductions	480

Salary distributions:

Sales	$30,600
Officers	15,200
Office	3,800
Net amount	$35,845

14. Prepared Voucher No. 646, payable to Payroll Bank Account, for the net amount of the biweekly payroll.

14. Issued Check No. 627 in payment of Voucher No. 646.

15. Prepared Voucher No. 647 for $59,710, payable to Marine National Bank for $44,800 of employees' federal income tax and $14,910 of FICA tax due on December 15.

15. Issued Check No. 633 in payment of Voucher No. 647.

18. Prepared Voucher No. 650 for $3,875, payable to Wilson Insurance Company, for the semiannual premium on the group medical insurance policy.

19. Issued Check No. 639 in payment of Voucher No. 650.

28. Prepared a journal entry to record the biweekly payroll. A summary of the payroll record follows:

Deductions:

FICA tax	$ 3,010
Federal income tax withheld	7,565
State income tax withheld	1,845
Savings bond deductions	315

Salary distribution:

Sales	$28,500
Officers	15,200
Office	3,800
Net amount	$34,765

28. Prepared Voucher No. 684, payable to Payroll Bank Account, for the net amount of the biweekly payroll.

28. Issued check No. 671 in payment of Voucher No. 684.

30. Prepared Voucher No. 690 for $630, payable to Marine National Bank, to purchase United States savings bonds for employees.

30. Issued Check No. 680 in payment of Voucher No. 690.

30. Prepared Voucher No. 691 for $13,260, payable to Marine National Bank, for employees' state income tax due on December 31.

Dec. 30. Issued Check No. 681 in payment of Voucher No. 691.

31. Prepared a journal entry to record the employer's payroll taxes on earnings paid in December. FICA tax totals $6,260, and taxable earnings subject to unemployment compensation tax are $8,500. Assume the following tax rates: state unemployment, 3.8%; federal unemployment, .8%.

Instructions:

(1) Open the accounts listed and enter the account balances as of December 1.

(2) Record the transactions, using a voucher register, a check register, and a general journal. The only amount columns needed in the voucher register are Accounts Payable Cr. and Sundry Accounts Dr. (subdivided into Account, Post. Ref., and Amount). The only amount columns needed in the check register are Accounts Payable Dr. and Cash in Bank Cr. Post to the accounts.

(3) Journalize the adjusting entry on December 31 to record salaries for the incomplete payroll period. Salaries accrued are as follows: sales salaries, $2,950; officers salaries, $1,640; office salaries, $410. The payroll taxes are immaterial and are not accrued. Post to the accounts.

(4) Journalize the entry to close the salary expense and payroll taxes expense accounts to Income Summary, and post to the accounts.

(5) Journalize the entry on January 1 to reverse the adjustment of December 31 and post to the accounts.

Problem 12–5A.   Wage and Tax Statement data and employer FICA tax.
Griffin Company began business on January 2 of last year. Salaries were paid to employees on the last day of each month, and both FICA tax and federal income tax were withheld in the required amounts. An employee who is hired in the middle of the month receives half the monthly salary for that month. All required payroll tax reports were filed and the correct amount of payroll taxes was remitted by the company for the calendar year. Before the Wage and Tax Statements (Form W-2) could be prepared for distributing to employees and filing with the Social Security Administration, the employees' earnings records were inadvertently destroyed.

None of the employees resigned or were discharged during the year, and there were no changes in salary rates. The FICA tax was withheld at the rate of 7.5% on the first $45,000 of salary. Data on dates of employment, salary rates, and employees' income taxes withheld, which are summarized as follows, were obtained from personnel records and payroll records.

Employee	Date First Employed	Monthly Salary	Monthly Income Tax Withheld
Allen	June 2	$2,500	$ 417.50
Cox	Jan. 2	4,200	854.50
Gower	Mar. 1	3,800	748.15
Nunn	Jan. 2	4,000	810.10
Quinn	Nov. 15	3,600	652.30
Ruiz	Apr. 15	2,800	461.10
Wu	Jan. 16	5,200	1,261.40

Instructions:

(1) Determine the amounts to be reported on each employee's Wage and Tax Statement (Form W-2) for the year, arranging the data in the following form:

Employee	Gross Earnings	Federal Income Tax Withheld	Earnings Subject to FICA Tax	FICA Tax Withheld

(2) Determine the following employer payroll taxes for the year: (a) FICA; (b) state unemployment compensation at 3.8% on the first $7,000 of each employee's earnings; (c) federal unemployment compensation at .8% of the first $7,000 of each employee's earnings; (d) total.
(3) In a manner similar to the illustrations in this chapter, develop four algorithms to describe the computations required to determine the four amounts in (1), using the following symbols:

n = Number of payroll periods
g = Monthly gross earnings
f = Monthly federal income tax withheld
G = Total gross earnings

F = Total federal income tax withheld
T = Total earnings subject to FICA tax
S = Total FICA tax withheld

Problem 12–6A. Purchases and notes payable transactions. The following items were selected from among the transactions completed by Flowers Co. during the current year:

Mar. 2. Purchased merchandise on account from Hines and York, $5,400.
      8. Purchased merchandise on account from Malone Co., $10,000.
      12. Paid Hines and York for the invoice of March 2, less 2% discount.
Apr. 1. Issued a 60-day, 12% note for $10,000 to Malone Co., on account.
May 10. Issued a 120-day, non-interest-bearing note for $45,000 to Garden City Bank. The bank discounted the note at the rate of 14%.
      31. Paid Malone Co. the amount owed on the note of April 1.
Aug. 5. Borrowed $7,500 from First Financial Corporation, issuing a 60-day, 14% note for that amount.
Sept. 7. Paid Garden City Bank the amount due on the note of May 10.
Oct. 4. Paid First Financial Corporation the interest due on the note of August 5 and renewed the loan by issuing a new 30-day, 16% note for $7,500. (Record both the debit and the credit to the notes payable account.)
Nov. 3. Paid First Financial Corporation the amount due on the note of October 4.
      15. Purchased store equipment from Sims Equipment Co. for $50,000, paying $8,000 and issuing a series of seven 12% notes for $6,000 each, coming due at 30-day intervals.
Dec. 15. Paid the amount due Sims Equipment Co. on the first note in the series issued on November 15.

Instructions:

(1) Record the transactions.
(2) Determine the total amount of interest accrued as of December 31 on the six notes owed to Sims Equipment Co.
(continued)

(3) Record the adjusting journal entry for the accrued interest at December 31 and the reversing entry on January 1.

(4) Assume that a single note for $42,000 had been issued on November 15 instead of the series of seven notes, and that its terms required principal payments of $6,000 each 30 days, with interest at 12% on the principal balance before applying the $6,000 payment. Determine the amount that would have been due and payable on December 15.

Series B

Problem 12–1B. *Profit-sharing bonuses.* The president of Wilson Products is entitled to an annual profit-sharing bonus of 5%. For the current year, income before bonus and income taxes is $309,000, and income taxes are estimated at 40% of income before income taxes.

Instructions:

(1) Determine the amount of the bonus, assuming that:
  (a) The bonus is based on income before deductions for bonus and income taxes.
  (b) The bonus is based on income after deduction for bonus but before deduction for income taxes.
  (c) The bonus is based on income after deduction for income taxes but before deduction for bonus.
  (d) The bonus is based on income after deduction for both bonus and income taxes.

(2) (a) Which bonus plan would the president prefer? (b) Would this plan always be the president's choice, regardless of Wilson Products' income level?

SOLUTIONS SOFTWARE

Problem 12–2B. *Entries for payroll and payroll taxes.* The following information relative to the payroll for the week ended December 30 was obtained from the records of C. H. Beal Inc.:

Salaries:		Deductions:	
Sales salaries............	$ 86,500	Income tax withheld	$18,050
Warehouse salaries.......	18,980	Group insurance	1,350
Office salaries	9,520	U.S. savings bonds........	1,200
	$115,000	FICA tax withheld totals the same amount as the employer's tax.	

Tax rates assumed:
  FICA, 7.5%
  State unemployment (employer only), 4.2%
  Federal unemployment, .8%

Instructions:

(1) Assuming that the payroll for the last week of the year is to be paid on December 31, present the following entries:
  (a) December 30, to record the payroll. Of the total payroll for the last week of the year, $109,000 is subject to FICA tax and $9,000 is subject to unemployment compensation taxes.

(b) December 30, to record the employer's payroll taxes on the payroll to be paid on December 31.

(2) Assuming that the payroll for the last week of the year is to be paid on January 5 of the following fiscal year, present the following entries:

(a) December 31, to record the payroll.

(b) January 5, to record the employer's payroll taxes on the payroll to be paid on January 5.

If the working papers correlating with the textbook are not used, omit Problem 12–3B.

Problem 12–3B.   Payroll register. The payroll register for Ann Murphy Co. for the week ending December 7 of the current fiscal year is presented in the working papers.

Instructions:

(1) Journalize the entry to record the payroll for the week.

(2) Assuming the use of a voucher system and payment by regular check, present the entries, in general journal form, to record the payroll voucher and the issuance of the checks to employees.

(3) Journalize the entry to record the employer's payroll taxes for the week. Assume the following tax rates: FICA, 7.5%; state unemployment, 3.1%; federal unemployment, .8%.

(4) Present the entries, in general journal form, to record the following selected transactions:

Dec. 16. Prepared a voucher, payable to Palmer National Bank, for employees income taxes, $3,192.50, and FICA taxes, $2,172.25, on salaries paid in November.

16. Issued a check to Palmer National Bank in payment of the above voucher.

Problem 12–5B.   Wage and Tax Statement data and employer FICA tax. Stoner Company began business on January 2 of last year. Salaries were paid to employees on the last day of each month, and both FICA tax and federal income tax were withheld in the required amounts. An employee who is hired in the middle of the month receives half the monthly salary for that month. All required payroll tax reports were filed and the correct amount of payroll taxes was remitted by the company for the calendar year. Before the Wage and Tax Statements (Form W-2) could be prepared for distributing to employees and filing with the Social Security Administration, the employees' earnings records were inadvertently destroyed.

None of the employees resigned or were discharged during the year, and there were no changes in salary rates. The FICA tax was withheld at the rate of 7.5% on the first $45,000 of salary. Data on dates of employment, salary rates, and employees' income taxes withheld, which are summarized as follows, were obtained from personnel records and payroll records.

Employee	Date First Employed	Monthly Salary	Monthly Income Tax Withheld
Alvarez	Jan. 16	$2,800	$ 471.20
Cruz	Nov. 1	2,500	394.25
Funk	Jan. 2	4,200	895.60
Little	July 16	3,400	636.50

Employee	Date First Employed	Monthly Salary	Monthly Income Tax Withheld
Powell	Jan. 2	$5,400	$1,374.10
Soong	May 1	3,600	652.30
Wilson	Feb. 16	4,000	864.10

Instructions:

(1) Determine the amounts to be reported on each employee's Wage and Tax Statement (Form W-2) for the year, arranging the data in the following form:

Employee	Gross Earnings	Federal Income Tax Withheld	Earnings Subject to FICA Tax	FICA Tax Withheld

(2) Determine the following employer payroll taxes for the year: (a) FICA; (b) state unemployment compensation at 4.2% on the first $7,000 of each employee's earnings; (c) federal unemployment compensation at .8% on the first $7,000 of each employee's earnings; (d) total.

(3) In a manner similar to the illustrations in this chapter, develop four algorithms to describe the computations required to determine the four amounts in (1), using the following symbols:

n = Number of payroll periods F = Total federal income tax withheld
g = Monthly gross earnings T = Total earnings subject to FICA tax
f = Monthly federal income tax withheld S = Total FICA tax withheld
G = Total gross earnings

SOLUTIONS
SOFTWARE

Problem 12–6B. Purchases and notes payable transactions. The following items were selected from among the transactions completed by Douglas Co. during the current year:

Jan. 15. Purchased merchandise on account from Davis Co., $7,800.
Mar. 1. Purchased merchandise on account from Evans Co., $9,600.
    6. Issued a 30-day, 12% note for $7,800 to Davis Co., on account.
   10. Paid Evans Co. for the invoice of March 1, less 1% discount.
Apr. 5. Paid Evans Co. the amount owed on the note of March 6.
July 15. Borrowed $8,000 from Royal National Bank, issuing a 90-day, 13% note for that amount.
   25. Issued a 120-day, non-interest-bearing note for $20,000 to Barnett State Bank. The bank discounted the note at the rate of 15%.
Oct. 13. Paid Royal National Bank the interest due on the note of July 15 and renewed the loan by issuing a new 30-day, 15% note for $8,000. (Record both the debit and credit to the notes payable account.)
Nov. 12. Paid Royal National Bank the amount due on the note of October 13.
   22. Paid Barnett State Bank the amount due on the note of July 25.
Dec. 1. Purchased office equipment from Bunn Equipment Co. for $57,500, paying $7,500 and issuing a series of ten 12% notes for $5,000 each, coming due at 30-day intervals.
   31. Paid the amount due Bunn Equipment Co. on the first note in the series issued on December 1.

Instructions:

(1) Record the transactions.
(2) Determine the total amount of interest accrued as of December 31 on the nine notes owed to Bunn Equipment Co.
(3) Record the adjusting entry for the accrued interest at December 31 and the reversing entry on January 1.
(4) Assume that a single note for $50,000 had been issued on December 1 instead of the series of ten notes, and that its terms required principal payments of $5,000 each 30 days, with interest at 12% on the principal balance before applying the $5,000 payment. Determine the amount that would have been due and payable on December 31.

MINI-CASE 12

In 1986, your father retired as president of the family-owned business, MG Inc., and a new president was recruited by an executive search firm. The new president's contract called for an annual base salary of $50,000 plus a bonus of 12% of income after deducting the bonus but before deducting income taxes.

In 1987, the first full year under the new president, MG Inc. reported income of $910,000 before deducting the bonus and income taxes. After being fired on January 3, 1988, the new president demanded immediate payment of a $109,200 bonus for 1987.

Your father was concerned about the accounting practices used during 1987, and he has asked you to help him in reviewing the accounting records before the bonus is paid. Upon investigation, you have discovered the following facts:

(a) The payroll for December 27–31, 1987, was not accrued at the end of the year. The salaries for the five-day period and the applicable payroll taxes are as follows:

Sales salaries	$5,500
Warehouse salaries	3,500
Office salaries	3,000
FICA tax	7.5%
State unemployment tax (employer only)	3.2%
Federal unemployment tax	.8%

The payroll was paid on January 9, 1988, for the period December 27, 1987, through January 7, 1988.

(b) The semiannual pension cost of $25,000 was not accrued for the last half of 1987. The pension cost was paid to Equity Insurance Company on January 12, 1988, and was recorded by a debit to Pension Expense and a credit to Cash for $25,000.

(c) The estimated product warranty liability of $10,000 for products sold during the year ended December 31, 1987, was not recorded.

(d) On July 1, 1987, MG Inc. purchased a one-year insurance policy for $9,640, debiting the cost to Prepaid Insurance. No adjusting entry was made for insurance expired at December 31, 1987.

(e) The vacation pay liability of $12,000 for December, 1987, was not recorded.

Instructions:

(1) Based on reported 1987 income of $910,000 before deducting the bonus and income taxes, was the president's calculation of the $109,200 bonus correct? Explain.

(2) What accounting errors were made in 1987 which would affect the amount of the president's bonus?

(3) Based on the employment contract and your answer to (2), what is the correct amount of the president's bonus for 1987?

(4) How much did the president's demand for a $109,200 bonus exceed the correct amount of the bonus under the employment contract?

(5) Late in 1988, MG Inc. paid the president the amount of the bonus computed in (3), after which the president sued MG Inc. for breach of contract. The suit requested compensatory and punitive damages of $500,000. Should the lawsuit be reported on the 1988 financial statements?

(6) Describe the major advantage and disadvantage of using profit-sharing bonuses in employment contracts.

Part 3

ACCOUNTING PRINCIPLES

Chapter 13

CONCEPTS AND PRINCIPLES

Chapter Objectives:

■ Describe the development of accounting concepts and principles.

■ Identify and illustrate the application of ten basic accounting concepts and principles:

> Business entity
> Going concern
> Objective evidence
> Unit of measurement
> Accounting period
> Matching revenue and expired costs
> Adequate disclosure
> Consistency
> Materiality
> Conservatism

The historical development of accounting practice has been closely related to the economic development of the country. In the earlier stages of the American economy, a business enterprise was very often managed by its owner, and the accounting records and reports were used mainly by the owner-manager in conducting the business. Bankers and other lenders often relied on their personal relationship with the owner rather than on financial statements as the basis for making loans for business purposes. If a large amount was owed to a bank or supplier, the creditor often participated in management decisions.

As business organizations grew in size and complexity, "management" and "outsiders" became more clearly differentiated. From the latter group, which includes owners (stockholders), creditors, government, labor unions, customers, and the general public, came the demand for accurate financial information for use in judging the performance of management. In addition, as the size and complexity of the business unit increased, the accounting problems involved in the issuance of financial statements became more and more complex. With these developments came an awareness of the need for a framework of concepts and generally accepted accounting principles to serve as guidelines for the preparation of the basic financial statements.

DEVELOPMENT OF CONCEPTS AND PRINCIPLES

The word "principle" as used in the context of generally accepted accounting principles does not have the same authoritativeness as universal principles or natural laws relating to the study of astronomy, physics, or other physical sciences. Accounting principles have been developed by individuals to help make accounting data more useful in an ever-changing society. They represent the best possible guides, based on reason, observation, and experimentation, to the achievement of the desired results. The selection of the best method from among many alternatives has come about gradually, and in some subject matter areas a clear consensus is still lacking. These principles are continually reexamined and revised to keep pace with the increasing complexity of business operations. General acceptance among the members of the accounting profession is the criterion for determining an accounting principle.

The Importance of Accounting Standards

No amount of policing by the public accounting profession or regulatory agencies to prevent abuses in financial reporting can satisfy the public need for comparable information from all companies. Only financial accounting and reporting standards can satisfy that need. The challenge to the FASB is to strike a reasonable balance between the prevention of abuses and the portrayal of economic reality. As standard setters, we must try to avoid the concern about potential abuses leading to standards that make significantly different situations look the same — in other words, forcing square pegs into round holes.

Source: Adapted from Donald J. Kirk, FASB chairman (From a speech before the National Association of Accountants Second Annual International-European Conference, Paris, April 19, 1985).

Responsibility for the development of accounting principles has rested primarily on practicing accountants and accounting educators, working both independently and under the sponsorship of various accounting organizations. These principles are also influenced by business practices and customs, ideas and beliefs of the users of the financial statements, governmental agencies, stock exchanges, and other business groups.

Financial Accounting Standards Board

In 1973, the **Financial Accounting Standards Board (FASB)** was appointed by the Financial Accounting Foundation (FAF). The FAF is an independent, nonprofit organization that was created in 1972 to oversee the standard-setting process, to appoint members of standard-setting boards (the FASB and the Governmental Accounting Standards Board) and advisory councils, and to raise funds for the operation of the standard-setting process.

The FASB replaced the **Accounting Principles Board (APB)**, which provided much of the leadership in the development of generally accepted accounting principles from 1959 to 1973. The APB was composed of eighteen accountants who were members of the American Institute of Certified Public Accountants and who served without pay and continued their affiliations with their firms or institutions. The FASB, which is presently the dominant body in the development of generally accepted accounting principles, is composed of seven members, four of whom must be CPAs drawn from public practice. These seven members serve full time, receive a salary, and must resign from the firm or institution with which they have been affiliated. The FASB is assisted by an advisory council of approximately forty members, whose major responsibilities include the recommendation of priorities and agenda and the review of FASB plans, activities, and statements proposed for issuance. The FASB employs a full-time research staff and administrative staff as well as task forces to study specific matters from time to time.

As problems in financial reporting are identified, the FASB conducts extensive research to identify the principal issues involved and the possible solutions. Generally, after issuing discussion memoranda and preliminary proposals and evaluating comments from interested parties, the Board issues *Statements of Financial Accounting Standards*, which become part of generally accepted accounting principles. To explain, clarify, or elaborate on existing pronouncements, the Board also issues *Interpretations*, which have the same authority as the standards.

Presently, the Board is in the process of developing a broad conceptual framework for financial accounting. This project, which is expected to take many years to complete, is an attempt to develop a "constitution" that can be used to evaluate current standards and can serve as the basis for future standards. The results of the completed portion of this project have been published as six *Statements of Financial Accounting Concepts*, which are briefly described as follows:

■ **Objectives of Financial Reporting by Business Enterprises (No. 1)**
Sets forth three broad objectives of financial reporting:
1. To provide financial information that is useful in making rational investment, credit, and similar decisions;
2. To provide financial information to enable users to predict cash flows to the business and subsequently to themselves;
3. To provide financial information about business resources (assets), claims to these resources (liabilities and owner's equity), and changes in these resources and claims.

■ **Qualitative Characteristics of Accounting Information (No. 2)**
Identifies the essential qualities of the accounting information included in financial reports as follows: usefulness, understandability, relevance, reliability, verifiability, timeliness, neutrality, completeness, and comparability.

■ **Elements of Financial Statements of Business Enterprises (No. 3)**
Replaced by Statement No. 6.

■ **Objectives of Financial Reporting by Nonbusiness Organizations (No. 4)**
Sets forth the objectives that guide the preparation of the financial statements for nonbusiness organizations.

■ **Recognition and Measurement in Financial Statements of Business Enterprises (No. 5)**
   Identifies the financial statements that should be prepared to meet the objectives of financial reporting for business enterprises.

■ **Elements of Financial Statements (No. 6)**
   Replaces Statement No. 3 and defines the interrelated elements of financial statements that are directly related to measuring the performance and status of businesses and nonprofit organizations.

Governmental Accounting Standards Board

The **Governmental Accounting Standards Board (GASB)** was formed in 1984 as an arm of the Financial Accounting Foundation. The GASB has a full-time chairperson and four part-time members who have responsibility for establishing the accounting standards to be followed by state and municipal governments. The GASB employs a full-time research staff and administrative staff. An advisory council of approximately 20 members assists the GASB and also has fund-raising responsibilities.

Accounting Organizations

Among the oldest and most influential organizations of accountants are the **American Institute of Certified Public Accountants (AICPA)** and the **American Accounting Association (AAA)**. Each organization publishes a monthly or quarterly periodical and, from time to time, issues other publications in the form of research studies, technical opinions, and monographs. There are also other national accounting organizations as well as many state societies and local chapters of the national and state organizations. These groups provide forums for the interchange of ideas and discussion of accounting principles.

Government Organizations

Of the various governmental agencies with an interest in the development of accounting principles, the **Securities and Exchange Commission (SEC)** has been the most influential. Established by an act of Congress in 1934, the SEC issues regulations that must be observed in the preparation of financial statements and other reports filed with the Commission.

The **Internal Revenue Service (IRS)** issues regulations that govern the determination of income for purposes of federal income taxation. Because these regulations sometimes conflict with financial accounting principles, many enterprises maintain two sets of accounts to satisfy both reporting requirements. To avoid this increased record keeping, there have been times when firms have adopted practices that are acceptable for tax purposes as generally accepted accounting principles. A discussion of the nature of the income tax is presented in more detail in Appendix G.

Other regulatory agencies exercise a dominant influence on the accounting principles of the industries under their jurisdiction. In rare situations, Congress may also enact legislation that dictates accounting principles. These situations usually involve controversial issues on which no clear consensus has been reached within the profession.

Other Influential Organizations

The **Financial Executives Institute (FEI)** has influenced the development of accounting principles by encouraging and sponsoring accounting research. The FEI also comments on proposed pronouncements of the FASB, the SEC, and other organizations.

The **National Association of Accountants (NAA)** is one of the largest organizations of accountants. It is primarily concerned with management's use of accounting information in directing business operations. Since management is responsible for the preparation of the basic financial statements, however, the NAA communicates its recommendations on generally accepted accounting principles to appropriate organizations.

Although the organizations mentioned above have traditionally had the most influence upon the establishment of accounting principles, other organizations representing users of accounting reports are increasingly making their views known. Prominent in this group are the **Financial Analysts Federation** (investors and investment advisors) and the **Securities Industry Associates** (investment bankers).

Many accounting principles have been introduced and integrated with discussions in earlier chapters. The remainder of this chapter is devoted to the underlying assumptions, concepts, and principles of the greatest importance and widest applicability. Attention will also be directed to applications of principles to specific situations in order to facilitate better understanding of accounting practices.

BUSINESS ENTITY

The **business entity concept** assumes that a business enterprise is separate and distinct from the persons who supply its assets. This distinction exists regardless of the legal form of the business organization. The accounting equation, Assets = Equities, or Assets = Liabilities + Owner's Equity, is an expression of the entity concept; i.e., the business owns the assets and owes the various claimants. Thus, the accounting process is primarily concerned with the enterprise as a productive economic unit and only secondarily concerned with the investor as a claimant to the assets of the business.

The business entity concept used in accounting for a sole proprietorship is distinct from the legal concept of a sole proprietorship. The nonbusiness assets, liabilities, revenues, and expenses of a sole proprietor are excluded from the business accounts. If a sole proprietor owns two or more dissimilar enterprises, each one is treated as a separate business entity for accounting purposes. Legally, however, a sole proprietor is personally liable for all business debts and may be required to use nonbusiness assets to satisfy the business creditors. Conversely, business assets are not immune from the claims of the sole proprietor's personal creditors.

Differences between the business entity concept and the legal nature of other forms of business organization will be considered in later chapters. For accounting purposes, however, revenues and expenses of any enterprise are viewed as affecting the business assets and liabilities, not the investors' assets and liabilities.

GOING CONCERN

Only in rare cases is a business organized with the expectation of operating for only a certain period of time. In most cases, it is not possible to determine in advance the length of life of an enterprise, and so an assumption must be made. The nature of the assumption will affect the manner of recording some of the business transactions, which in turn will affect the data reported in the financial statements.

It is customary to assume that a business entity has a reasonable expectation of continuing in business at a profit for an indefinite period of time. This **going concern concept** provides much of the justification for recording plant assets at acquisition cost and depreciating them in an orderly manner without reference to their current realizable values. If there is no immediate expectation of selling them, plant assets should not be reported on the balance sheet at their estimated realizable values regardless of whether their current market value is less than their book value or greater than their book value. If the firm continues to use the assets, the change in market value causes no gain or loss, nor does it increase or decrease the usefulness of the assets. Thus, if the going concern assumption is a valid concept, the investment in plant assets will serve the purpose for which it was made — the investment in the assets will be recovered even though they may be individually marketable only at a loss.

The going concern assumption similarly supports the treatment of prepaid expenses as assets, even though they may not be salable. To illustrate, assume that on the last day of its fiscal year, a wholesale firm receives from a printer a $20,000 order of sales catalogs. If there were no assumption that the firm is to continue in business, the catalogs would be merely scrap paper and the value reported for them on the balance sheet would be small.

Doubt as to the continued existence of a firm may be disclosed in a note to the financial statements, as indicated in the following adaptation from the 1984 statements of International Harvester Company:[1]

> The Company's financial statements have been presented on the basis that the Company is a going concern, which contemplates the realization of assets and a satisfaction of liabilities in the normal course of business.

> Although it cannot be assured that the Company will be able to continue as a going concern in view of its weakened financial condition and the uncertainties with respect to an agreement to sell substantially all of the assets of its agricultural equipment business, management believes that the successful completion of the sale will enable the Company to realize a return on its assets, satisfy its liabilities, and return to profitability.

When there is conclusive evidence that a business entity has a limited life, the accounting procedures should be appropriate to the expected terminal date of the entity. Changes in the application of normal accounting procedures may be needed for business organizations in receivership or bankruptcy, for example. In such cases, the financial statements should clearly disclose the limited life of the enterprise and should be prepared from the "quitting concern" or liquidation point of view, rather than from a "going concern" point of view.

OBJECTIVE EVIDENCE   *tangible*

Entries in the accounting records and data reported on financial statements must be based on objectively determined evidence. If this principle is not followed, the confidence of the many users of the financial statements could not be maintained. For example, objective evidence such as invoices and vouchers for purchases, bank statements for the amount of cash in bank, and physical counts for merchandise on hand supports much of accounting. Such evidence is completely objective and can be verified.

Evidence is not always conclusively objective, for there are many cases in accounting in which judgments, estimates, and other subjective factors must be taken into account. In such situations, the most objective evidence available should be used. For example, the provision for doubtful accounts is an estimate of the losses expected from failure to collect sales made on account. The estimation of this amount should be based on such objective factors as past experience in collecting accounts receivable and reliable forecasts of future business activities. To provide accounting reports that can be accepted with confidence, evidence should be developed that will minimize the possibility of error, intentional bias, or fraud.

---

[1]After International Harvester sold its agricultural equipment business, its name was changed to Navistar International.

UNIT OF MEASUREMENT

All business transactions are recorded in terms of money. Other pertinent information of a nonfinancial nature may also be recorded, such as the description of assets acquired, the terms of purchase and sale contracts, and the purpose, amount, and term of insurance policies. But it is only through the record of dollar amounts that the diverse transactions and activities of a business may be measured, reported, and periodically compared. Money is both the common factor of all business transactions and the only feasible unit of measurement that can be used to achieve uniform financial data.

The generally accepted use of the monetary unit for accounting for and reporting the activities of an enterprise has two major limitations: (1) it limits the scope of accounting reports and (2) it assumes a stability of the measurement unit.

Scope of Accounting Reports

Many factors affecting the activities and the future prospects of an enterprise cannot be expressed in monetary terms. In general, accounting does not attempt to report such factors. For example, information regarding the capabilities of the management, the state of repair of the plant assets, the effectiveness of the employee welfare program, the attitude of the labor union, the effectiveness of antipollution measures, and the relative strengths and weaknesses of the firm's competitors cannot be expressed in monetary terms. Although such matters are important to those concerned with enterprise operations, at the present time, accountancy does not assume responsibility for reporting information of this kind.

Changes in Price Levels.

As a unit of measurement, the dollar differs from such quantitative standards as the kilogram, liter, or meter, which have not changed for centuries. The instability of the purchasing power of the dollar is well known, and the disruptive effect of the declining value of the dollar is acknowledged by accountants. In the past, however, this declining value generally has not been given recognition in the accounts or in conventional financial statements.

To indicate the nature of the problem, assume that the plant assets acquired by an enterprise for $100,000 twenty years ago are now to be replaced with similar assets which will cost $200,000 at present price levels. Assume further that during the twenty-year period the plant assets had been fully depreciated and the net income of the enterprise had amounted to $300,000. Although the initial outlay of $100,000 for the plant assets was recovered through depreciation charges, the amount represents only half of the cost of replacing the assets. Instead of considering the current value of the new assets to have increased to double the value of two decades earlier, the dollars recovered can be said to have declined to one half of their earlier value. From either point of view, the firm has suffered a loss in purchasing power, which is the same as a loss of capital. In addition, $100,000 of the net income reported during the period might be said to be illusory, since it must be used to replace the assets.

The use of a monetary unit that is assumed to be stable insures objectivity. In spite of the inflationary trend in the United States, historical-dollar financial statements are considered to be better than statements based on movements of the general price level. There are, however, two widely discussed recommendations for supplementing conventional statements and thus resolving financial reporting problems created by increasing price levels: (1) supplemental financial data based on current costs, and (2) supplemental financial data based on constant dollars. The discussion in the following sections is confined to the basic concepts and problems of these recommendations.

Current Cost Data. Current cost is the amount of cash that would have to be paid currently to acquire assets of the same age and in the same condition as existing assets. When current costs are used as the basis for financial reporting, assets, liabilities, and owner's equity are stated at current values, and expenses are stated at the current cost of doing business. The use of current costs permits the identification of gains and losses that result from holding assets during periods of changes in price levels. To illustrate, assume that a firm acquired land at the beginning of the fiscal year for $50,000 and that at the end of the year its current cost (value) is $60,000. The land could be reported at its current cost of $60,000, and the $10,000 increase in value could be reported as an unrealized gain from holding the land.

The major disadvantage in the use of current costs is the absence of established standards and procedures for determining such costs. However, many accountants believe that adequate standards and procedures will evolve through experimentation with actual applications.

Constant Dollar Data. Constant dollar data, also known as general price-level data, are historical costs that have been converted to constant dollars through the use of a price-level index. In this manner, financial statement elements are reported in dollars, each of which has the same (that is, constant) general purchasing power.

A price-level index is the ratio of the total cost of a group of commodities prevailing at a particular time to the total cost of the same group of commodities at an earlier base time. The total cost of the commodities at the base time is assigned a value of 100 and the price-level indexes for all later times are expressed as a ratio to 100. For example, assume that the cost of a selected group of commodities amounted to $12,000 at a particular time and $13,200 today. The price index for the earlier, or base, time becomes 100 and the current price index is 110 [(13,200 ÷ 12,000) × 100].

A general price-level index may be used to determine the effect of changes in price levels on certain financial statement items. To illustrate, assume a price index of 120 at the time of purchase of a plot of land for $10,000 and a current price index of 150. The **constant dollar equivalent** of the original cost of $10,000 may be computed as follows:

$$\frac{\text{Current Price Index}}{\text{Price Index at Date of Purchase}} \times \text{Original Cost} = \text{Constant Dollar Equivalent}$$

$$\frac{150}{120} \times \$10,000 = \$12,500$$

Current Annual Reporting Requirements for Price-Level Changes. In 1979, the Financial Accounting Standards Board undertook an experimental program for reporting the effects of changing prices by requiring approximately 1,300 large, publicly held enterprises to disclose certain current cost information and constant dollar information annually as supplemental data.[2] In 1984, after reviewing the experiences with these 1979 disclosure requirements, the FASB concluded that current cost information was more useful than constant dollar information as a supplement to the basic financial statements. In addition, the FASB concluded that requiring two different methods of reporting the effects of changing prices may detract from the usefulness of the information. As a result, the requirement to report constant dollar information was dropped for those companies that report current cost information.[3]

The adherence to the FASB recommendation is indicated in the following note that accompanied the 1985 financial statements of The Dun and Bradstreet Corporation:

> Supplemental Financial Information, Effects of Inflation on Financial Statements
>
> The supplementary financial data...present the Company's primary...financial statements adjusted to eliminate the effects of inflation under the current cost method. This method of inflation accounting has been established by the Financial Accounting Standards Board (FASB), which considers it experimental.

ACCOUNTING PERIOD

A complete and accurate picture of an enterprise's success or failure cannot be obtained until it discontinues operations, converts its assets into cash, and pays off its debts. Then, and only then, is it possible to determine its true net income. But many decisions regarding the business must be made

---

[2]*Statement of Financial Accounting Standards, No. 33*, "Financial Reporting and Changing Prices" (Stamford: Financial Accounting Standards Board, 1979).
[3]*Statement of Financial Accounting Standards, No. 82*, "Financial Reporting and Changing Prices: Elimination of Certain Disclosures" (Stamford: Financial Accounting Standards Board, 1984).

by management and interested outsiders during its existence. It is therefore necessary to prepare periodic reports on operations, financial position, and changes in financial position.

Reports may be prepared when a certain job or project is completed, but more often they are prepared at specified time intervals. For a number of reasons, including custom and various legal requirements, the longest interval between reports is one year.

This element of periodicity creates many of the problems of accountancy. The basic problem is the determination of periodic net income. For example, the need for adjusting entries discussed in earlier chapters is directly attributable to the division of the life of an enterprise into arbitrary time periods. Problems of inventory costing, of recognizing the uncollectibility of receivables, and of selecting depreciation methods are also directly related to the periodic measurement process. Furthermore, the amounts of the assets and the equities reported on the balance sheet will also be affected by the methods used in determining net income. For example, the cost flow assumption used in determining the cost of merchandise sold during the accounting period will have a direct effect on the amount of cost assigned to the remaining inventory.

MATCHING REVENUE AND EXPIRED COSTS   *accural based accounting*

During the early stages of accounting development, accountants viewed the balance sheet as the principal financial statement. Over the years, the emphasis has shifted to the income statement as the users of financial statements have become more concerned with the results of business operations than with financial position.

The determination of periodic net income is a two-fold problem involving (1) the revenue recognized during the period and (2) the expired costs to be allocated to the period. It is thus a problem of **matching** revenues and expired costs, the residual amount being the net income or net loss for the period.

Recognition of Revenue

Revenue is measured by the amount charged to customers for merchandise delivered or services rendered to them. The problem created by periodicity is one of timing; that is, at what point is the revenue realized? For any particular accounting period, the question is whether revenue items should be recognized and reported as such in the current period or whether their recognition should be delayed to a future period.

Various criteria are acceptable for determining when revenue is realized. In any case, the criteria used should reasonably agree with the terms of the contractual arrangements with the customer and be based insofar as possible on objective evidence. The criteria most often used are described in the remaining paragraphs of this section.

revenue recognizes when title passed to buyer

Point of Sale. Revenue from the sale of merchandise is usually determined by the **point of sale method**, under which revenue is realized at the time title passes to the buyer. At point of sale, the sale price has been agreed upon, the buyer acquires the right of ownership in the merchandise, and the seller has a legal claim against the buyer. The realization of revenue from the sale of services may be determined in a like manner, although there is often a time lag between the time of the initial agreement and the completion of the service. For example, assume that a contract provides that certain repair services be performed, either for a specified price or on a time and materials basis. The price or terms agreed upon in the initial contract does not become revenue until the work has been performed.

Theoretically, revenue from the production and sale of merchandise and services emerges continuously as effort is expended. As a practical matter, however, it is usually not possible to make an objective determination until both (1) the contract price has been agreed upon and (2) the seller's portion of the contract has been completed.

Receipt of Payment. The recognition of revenue may be delayed until payment is received. When this criterion is used, revenue is considered to be realized at the time the cash is collected, regardless of when the sale was made. The cash basis is widely used by physicians, attorneys, and other enterprises in which professional services are the source of revenue. It has little theoretical justification but has the practical advantage of simplicity of operation and avoidance of the problem of estimating losses from uncollectible accounts. Its acceptability as a fair method of timing the recognition of revenue from personal services is influenced somewhat by the fact that it may be used in determining income subject to the federal income tax. It is not an appropriate method of measuring revenue from the sale of merchandise.

Installment Method. In some businesses, especially in the retail field, it is common to make sales on the installment plan. In the typical installment sale, the buyer makes a down payment and agrees to pay the remainder in specified amounts at stated intervals over a period of time. The seller may retain technical title to the goods or may take other means to make repossession easier in the event that the buyer defaults on the payments. Despite such provisions, installment sales should ordinarily be treated in the same manner as any other sale on account, in which case the revenue is considered to be realized at the point of sale.[4]

In some exceptional cases, the circumstances are such that the collection of receivables is not reasonably assured. In these cases, the **installment method** of determining revenue may be used.[5] Under this method, each receipt of cash is considered to be revenue and to be composed of partial amounts of (1) the cost of merchandise sold and (2) gross profit on the sale.

---

[4]*Opinions of the Accounting Principles Board, No. 10,* "Omnibus Opinion—1966" (New York: American Institute of Certified Public Accountants, 1966), par. 12.
[5]*Ibid.*

As a basis for illustration, assume that in the first year of operations, a dealer in household appliances had total installment sales of $300,000, and the cost of the merchandise sold amounted to $180,000. Assume also that collections of the installment accounts receivable were spread over three years as follows: 1st year, $140,000; 2d year, $100,000; 3d year, $60,000. According to the point of sale method, all of the revenue would be recognized in the first year and the gross profit realized in that year would be determined as follows:

Installment sales	$300,000	POINT OF SALE METHOD
Cost of merchandise sold	180,000	
Gross profit..............................	$120,000	

Under the installment method, gross profit is allocated according to the amount of receivables collected in each year, based on the percent of gross profit to sales. The rate of gross profit to sales is determined as follows:

$$\frac{\text{Gross Profit}}{\text{Installment Sales}} = \frac{\$120,000}{\$300,000} = 40\%$$

The amounts reported as gross profit for each of the three years in the illustration, based on collections of installment accounts receivable, are as follows:

1st year collections:	$140,000 × 40%	$ 56,000	INSTALLMENT METHOD
2d year collections:	$100,000 × 40%	40,000	
3d year collections:	$ 60,000 × 40%	24,000	
Total	$300,000	$120,000	

Percentage of Completion. Enterprises engaged in large construction projects may devote several years to the completion of a particular contract. To illustrate, assume that a contractor engages in a project that will require three years to complete, for a contract price of $50,000,000. Further assume that the total cost to be incurred, which will also be spread over the three-year period, is estimated at $44,000,000. According to the point of sale criterion, neither the revenue nor the related costs would be recognized until the project is completed. Therefore, using the **completed-contract method** of determining revenue, the entire net income from the contract would be reported in the third year.

Whenever the total cost of a long-term contract and the extent of the project's progress can be reasonably estimated, it is preferable to consider the revenue as being realized over the entire life of the contract.[6] The amount of revenue to be recognized in any particular period is then determined on the

[6]*Accounting Research and Terminology Bulletins—Final Edition,* "No. 45, Long-term Construction-type Contracts" (New York: American Institute of Certified Public Accountants, 1961), par. 15.

basis of the estimated percentage of the contract that has been completed during the period. The estimated percentage of completion can be developed by comparing the incurred costs with the most recent estimates of total costs or by estimates by engineers, architects, or other qualified personnel of the progress of the work performed. To continue with the illustration, assume that by the end of the first fiscal year the contract is estimated to be one-fourth completed and the costs incurred during the year were $11,200,000. According to the **percentage-of-completion method**, the revenue to be recognized and the income for the year would be determined as follows:

Revenue ($50,000,000 × 25%)	$12,500,000
Costs incurred	11,200,000
Income (Year 1)	$ 1,300,000

The costs actually incurred during the year (rather than one fourth of the original cost estimate of $44,000,000, or $11,000,000) are deducted from the revenue recognized.

The 1985 edition of *Accounting Trends & Techniques* indicated that 90% of the surveyed companies with long-term contracts used the percentage-of-completion method. Although the use of this method involves some subjectivity, and hence possible error, in the determination of the amount of reported revenue, the financial statements may be more informative and more useful than they would be if none of the revenue was recognized until completion of the contract.

The method used to recognize revenue on a long-term contract should be noted in the financial statements, as indicated in the following excerpt taken from a note to the 1985 financial statements of Martin Marietta Corporation:

Revenue Recognition. Sales under long-term contracts generally are recognized under the percentage-of-completion method, and include a proportion of the earnings expected to be realized on the contract. . . . Other sales are recorded upon shipment of products or performance of services.

Allocation of Costs

Properties and services acquired by an enterprise are generally recorded at cost. "Cost" is the amount of cash or equivalent given to acquire the property or the service. If property other than cash is given to acquire properties or services, the cost is the cash equivalent of the property given. When the properties or the services acquired are sold or used, the costs are deducted from the related revenue to determine the amount of net income or net loss. The costs of properties or services acquired and on hand at any particular time represent assets. Such costs may also be called "unexpired costs." As the assets are sold or used, they become "expired costs" or "expenses."

The techniques of determining and recording cost expirations have been described and illustrated in earlier chapters. In general, there are two approaches to cost allocations: (1) compute the amount of the expired cost or (2) compute the amount of the unexpired cost. For example, it is customary to determine the portion of plant assets that have expired. After the depreciation for the period has been recorded, the balances of the plant asset accounts minus the balances of the related accumulated depreciation accounts represent the unexpired cost of the assets. The alternative approach must be used for merchandise and supplies, unless perpetual inventory records are maintained. If the cost of the merchandise or supplies on hand at the end of the period is determined by taking a physical inventory, the remaining costs in the related accounts are assumed to have expired. It might appear that the first approach emphasizes expired costs and the second emphasizes unexpired costs. This is not the case, however, since the selection of the method is based merely on convenience or practicality.

Many of the costs allocable to a period are treated as an expense at the time of incurrence because they will be wholly expired at the end of the period. For example, when a monthly rent is paid at the beginning of a month, the cost incurred is unexpired and hence it is an asset; but since the cost incurred will be wholly expired at the end of the month, the rental is usually charged directly to the appropriate expense account. This process makes a subsequent adjusting entry unnecessary. The proper allocation of costs among periods is the most important consideration. Any one of many accounting techniques may be used in achieving this objective.

ADEQUATE DISCLOSURE   *inform reader of financial status*

Financial statements and their accompanying footnotes or other explanatory materials should contain all of the pertinent data believed essential to the reader's understanding of the enterprise's financial status. Criteria for **adequate disclosure** often must be based on value judgments rather than on objective facts.

Financial statements are made more useful by the use of headings and subheadings and by merging items in significant categories. For example, detailed information as to the amount of cash in various special and general funds, the amount on deposit in each of several banks, and the amount invested in various marketable government securities is not needed by the reader of financial statements. Such information displayed on the balance sheet would impede rather than aid understanding. On the other hand, significant details should be disclosed. For example, if the terms of significant loan agreements provide for a secured claim through a mortgage on an asset, those terms should be disclosed.

Some of the matters that accountants agree should be adequately disclosed in the financial statements or the accompanying notes are briefly described and illustrated in the following paragraphs. The illustrations quoted were taken from corporations' annual reports to stockholders, where they appeared in a section often titled "Notes to Financial Statements."

Accounting Methods Employed

When there are several acceptable alternative methods that could have a significant effect on amounts reported on the statements, the particular method used should be disclosed. Examples include inventory cost flow and pricing methods, depreciation methods, and various criteria of revenue recognition. There is considerable variation in the format used to disclose accounting methods employed. One form of disclosure is to use a separate "Summary of Significant Accounting Policies" section preceding the notes to financial statements or as the initial note. Some of the variations are illustrated by the following examples extracted from selected financial statements for 1984:

Digital Equipment Corporation

Note A — Significant Accounting Policies

Inventories — Inventories are stated at the lower of cost (first-in, first-out) or market.

Property, Plant and Equipment — Depreciation expense is computed principally on the following basis:

Classification	Depreciation Lives and Methods
Buildings	33 years (straight-line)
Machinery and equipment	8 and 10 years (sum-of-years), 4 and 5 years (double declining-balance)

Atico Financial Corporation

Sales of homesites are recorded under the installment method of accounting.

All depreciable assets are recorded at cost; depreciation is calculated using the straight-line method.

Changes in Accounting Estimates

There are many cases in accounting in which the use of estimates is necessary. These estimates should be revised when additional information or subsequent developments permit better insight or improved judgment upon which to base the estimates. If the effect of such a change on net income is material, it should be disclosed in the financial statements for the year in which the change is adopted.[7] An example of such a disclosure appeared in the 1985 financial statements of Murphy Oil Corporation:

> Note I (In Part): Property, Plant and Equipment—... The estimated useful life of offshore drilling barges was extended, based on experience, from 12 to 16 years effective January 1, 1984. Extending the useful life reduced depreciation in 1984 by $42,721,000 and increased net income $13,696,000, $.37 a share.

Contingent Liabilities

As discussed previously, contingent liabilities are potential obligations that will materialize only if certain events occur in the future. They arise from discounting notes receivable, litigation, possible tax assessments, or other causes. If the liability is probable and the amount of the liability can be reasonably estimated, it should be recorded in the accounts. If the amount cannot be reasonably estimated, the details of the contingency should be disclosed.[8] Following is an example of a note disclosing a contingent liability in the 1985 financial statements of Florida Steel Corporation:

> The Company is defending various claims and legal actions which are common to its operations. This includes a suit in the Commonwealth of Puerto Rico against the Company and others for alleged violations of Puerto Rican antidumping statutes asking damages in excess of $5,000,000. While it is not feasible to predict or determine the ultimate outcome of these matters, none of them, in the opinion of management, will have a material effect on the Company's financial position or results of operations.

Segment of a Business

Many companies diversify their operations; that is, they are involved in more than one type of business activity. These companies may also operate in foreign markets. The individual segments of such diversified companies ordinarily experience differing rates of profitability, degrees of risk, and opportunities for growth. To help financial statement users in assessing past performance and future potential of diversified companies, financial statements should disclose such information as the enterprise's operations in different industries, its foreign markets, and its major customers. The required information for each significant reporting segment includes the following: revenue, income from operations, and identifiable assets associated with the

---

[7]*Opinions of the Accounting Principles Board, No. 20,* "Accounting Changes" (New York: American Institute of Certified Public Accountants, 1971), pars. 31–33.

[8]*Statement of Financial Accounting Standards, No. 5,* "Accounting for Contingencies" (Stamford: Financial Accounting Standards Board, 1975), pars. 8, 10, 12.

segment.[9] An example of financial reporting for segments of a business is illustrated by the following note adapted from the 1985 financial statements of The Coca-Cola Company:

15. Lines of Business. The Company operates principally in the soft drink industry. The Entertainment Business Sector is engaged in the production and distribution of motion picture and television products and other entertainment related activities. Citrus, fruit drinks, coffee and other products are included in the Foods Business Sector. Information concerning operations in different lines of business is as follows (in millions):

Year Ended December 31,	1985
Net operating revenues:	
Soft drinks	$5,510.0
Entertainment	1,072.1
Foods	1,321.8
Consolidated net operating revenues	$7,903.9
Operating income:	
Soft drinks	$ 880.7
Entertainment	160.6
Foods	117.5
General expenses	(113.4)
Consolidated operating income	$1,045.4
Identifiable assets at year-end:	
Soft drinks	$3,679.5
Entertainment	1,802.4
Foods	473.5
Corporate assets (principally marketable securities, investments and fixed assets)	942.3
Consolidated assets	$6,897.7

Net Operating Revenues
($ Millions)

Entertainment	1,072
Foods	1,322
Soft Drinks	5,510

Operating Income
($ Millions)

Entertainment	161
Foods	118
Soft Drinks	881

---

[9]*Statement of Financial Accounting Standards, No. 14,* "Financial Reporting for Segments of a Business Enterprise" (Stamford: Financial Accounting Standards Board, 1976). Nonpublic corporations are exempted from this requirement by *Statement of Financial Accounting Standards, No. 21,* "Suspension of the Reporting of Earnings per Share and Segment Information by Nonpublic Enterprises" (Stamford: Financial Accounting Standards Board, 1978).

Events Subsequent to Date of Statements

Events occuring or becoming known after the close of the period may have a significant effect on the financial statements and should be disclosed.[10] For example, if an enterprise should suffer a crippling loss from a fire or other catastrophe between the end of the year and the issuance of the statements, the facts should be disclosed. Similarly, such occurrences as the issuance of long-term debt or capital stock, or the purchase of another business enterprise after the close of the period should be made known. American Bakeries Company reported a subsequent event in a note to its 1984 financial statements as follows:

14. Subsequent Events:

In January 1985, the Company acquired Cotton Brothers, Inc. and Coast-to-Coast Resorts. Cotton Brothers, Inc. was purchased for $13 million and consists of three bakery operations in Louisiana with sales in 1984 of approximately $52 million. Coast-to-Coast Resorts was purchased for $15.5 million plus a contingent payment of up to $4.5 million depending on the number of members in excess of 400,000 by 1987. Coast-to-Coast services the membership campground resorts segment of the travel and leisure industry and had sales of $5.1 million in 1984.

CONSISTENCY *apply same accounting methods from year to year*

A number of accepted alternative principles affecting the determination of income statement and balance sheet amounts have been presented in earlier sections of the text. Recognizing that different methods may be used under varying circumstances and that the comparison of an enterprise's current financial statements with those of the preceding year is common practice, some guide or standard is needed to assure that the enterprise's periodic financial statements can be compared.

The amount and the direction of change in net income and financial position from period to period is very important to readers and may greatly influence their decisions. Therefore, interested persons should be able to assume that successive financial statements of an enterprise are based consistently on the same generally accepted accounting principles. If the principles are not applied consistently, the trends indicated could be the result of changes in the principles used rather than the result of changes in business conditions or managerial effectiveness.

---

[10]*Statement on Auditing Standards, No. 1,* "Codification of Auditing Standards and Procedures" (New York: American Institute of Certified Public Accountants, 1986), section 560.

The concept of **consistency** does not completely prohibit changes in the accounting principles used. Changes are permissible when it is believed that the use of a different principle will more fairly state net income and financial position. Examples of changes in accounting principles include a change in the method of inventory pricing, a change in depreciation method for previously recorded assets, and a change in the method of accounting for long-term construction contracts. Consideration of changes in accounting principles must be accompanied by consideration of the general rule for disclosure of such changes, which is as follows:

> *The nature of and justification for a change in accounting principle and its effect on income should be disclosed in the financial statements of the period in which the change is made. The justification for the change should explain clearly why the newly adopted accounting principle is preferable.* [11]

There are various methods of reporting the effect of a change in accounting principle on net income. The cumulative effect of the change on net income may be reported on the income statement of the period in which the change is adopted. In some cases, the effect of the change could be applied retroactively to past periods by presenting revised income statements for the earlier years affected. The methods of disclosure are discussed in more detail in Chapter 16.

The application of the consistency concept does not require that a specific accounting method be used uniformly throughout an enterprise. For example, it is not unusual for large enterprises to use different costing and pricing methods for different segments of their inventories, as illustrated by the following note that appeared in the 1984 financial statements of National Can Corporation:

> Inventories: Inventories are stated at the lower of cost or market. Cost of inventories determined on a last-in, first-out (lifo) basis was approximately 53% of the inventory in 1984 and 61% in 1983. Cost of remaining inventories is determined on a first-in, first-out (fifo) basis.

MATERIALITY *effect of error*

In following generally accepted accounting principles, the accountant must consider the relative importance of any event, accounting procedure, or change in procedure that affects items on the financial statements. Absolute

---

[11]*Opinions of the Accounting Principles Board*, No. 20, "Accounting Changes" (New York: American Institute of Certified Public Accountants, 1971), par. 17.

accuracy in accounting and full disclosure in reporting are not ends in themselves, and there is no need to exceed the limits of practicality. The determination of what is significant and what is not requires the exercise of judgment. Precise criteria cannot be formulated.

To determine **materiality**, the size of an item and its nature must be considered in relationship to the size and the nature of other items. The erroneous classification of a $10,000 asset on a balance sheet exhibiting total assets of $10,000,000 would probably be immaterial. If the assets totaled only $100,000, however, it would certainly be material. If the $10,000 represented a note receivable from an officer of the enterprise, it might well be material even in the first assumption. If the loan was increased to $100,000 between the close of the period and the issuance of the statements, both the nature of the item at the balance sheet date and the subsequent increase in amount would require disclosure.

The concept of materiality may be applied to procedures used in recording transactions. As was stated in an earlier chapter, small expenditures for plant assets may be treated as an expense of the period rather than as an asset. The saving in clerical costs is justified if the practice does not materially affect the financial statements. In establishing a dollar amount as the dividing line between a revenue expenditure and a capital expenditure, consideration would need to be given to such factors as: (1) amount of total plant assets, (2) amount of plant assets in relationship to other assets, (3) frequency of occurrence of expenditures for plant assets, (4) nature and expected life of plant assets, and (5) probable effect on the amount of periodic net income reported.

Custom and practicality also influence criteria of materiality. Corporate financial statements seldom report the cents amounts or even the hundreds of dollars. A common practice is to round to the nearest thousand. For large corporations, there is an increasing tendency to report the financial data in terms of millions, carrying figures to one decimal. For example, the 1985 edition of *Accounting Trends of Techniques* indicated that 72 of 600 companies reported amounts to the nearest dollar, 407 to the nearest thousand dollars, and 121 to the nearest million dollars.

A technique known as "whole-dollar" accounting, which is used by some businesses, eliminates the cents amounts from accounting entries at the earliest possible point in the accounting sequence. There are some accounts, such as those with customers and creditors, in which it is not feasible to round to the nearest dollar. Nevertheless, the technique yields savings in office costs and improved productivity. The errors introduced into other accounts by rounding the amounts of individual entries at the time of recording tend to be compensating in nature, and the amount of the final error is not material.

It should not be inferred from the foregoing that whole-dollar accounting encourages or condones errors. The unrecorded cents are not lost; they are merely reported in a manner that reduces bookkeeping costs without materially affecting the accuracy of accounting data.

Concerning the Gnat and the Camel

This is the story as it comes to us: An accountant was asked to check the cash of a concern, which may be called the XYZ Corporation. This concern among its activities included a selling department where goods of small value were sold in fairly large quantities. When the cash of the selling department was counted it was found that the amount on hand was, let us say, $2.04 — a fictitious amount greater than the actual sum — more than it should have been. Now this incident happened in the city of New York where, as all citizens know to their sorrow, there is a two per cent tax on sales. Evidently, therefore, this excessive sum of $2.04 represented the sale of some article for $2, plus a tax of four cents. Apparently a careless member of the staff had sold such an article, placed the proceeds in the till, and forgot to make the proper record of the whole stupendous transaction. The carelessness was unpardonable, of course. No member of any staff anywhere should forget anything. However, the error occurred and the perspicacious young accountant discovered it, as he could not very well avoid doing. He found the unaccountable excess and, like a well-trained man, conscious of his complete efficiency, he set to work to trace the mistake and to expose the guilty person. Here was a chance for him to demonstrate his incalculable value to his firm. Such wrong-doing must not escape unchallenged. Relying upon his supposed authority he began a search, a veritable inquisition, and after two or three days of earnest effort, during which he had interrupted the work of the entire office and had considerable time expended, he was compelled to admit that he could not find a shortage in the inventory to account for the surplus cash, nor could he rightfully determine who had committed the crime. At last he regretfully reported the matter to his superior and confessed himself defeated. What the superior had to say about the matter is not recorded; but one can imagine the attitude of the superior and can form a reasonably accurate notion of the comments which were made.

This little story bears a moral which every accountant may well take to heart. It might be unwise to say that errors should be overlooked or that carelessness should be condoned. But surely there is no sense whatever in a ridiculous adherence to meticulous detail when the sole purpose is to trace something which is not worth tracing. What the accountant should have done in the present case is clear. He should have made a note of the excess, and after spending a few minutes in trying to trace it to its source, he should have gone on to weightier things. It is a great pity that this sort of incident ever occurs; but we are told that the case before us is not unique. There are many little fellows who revel in the most microscopic minutiae. They can't help it. They probably were born that way, but they should never, never, be employed in the work of accountancy, which, after all, is a matter of principles, not of pin points.

Source: Adapted from A. P. Richardson, *The Journal of Accountancy* (October, 1936), pp. 233–235.

CONSERVATISM

concerns/ approach to net income

Periodic statements are affected to a great degree by the selection of accounting procedures and other value judgments. Historically, accountants have tended to be conservative, and in selecting among alternatives they have often favored the method or the procedure that yielded the lesser amount of net income or of asset value. This attitude of **conservatism** was often expressed in the statement to "anticipate no profits and provide for all losses." For example, it is acceptable to price merchandise inventory at lower of cost or market. If market price is higher than cost, the higher amount is ignored in the accounts and, if presented in the financial statements, is presented parenthetically. Such an attitude of pessimism has been due in part to the need for an offset to the optimism of business management. It could also be argued that potential future losses to an enterprise from poor management decisions would be lessened if net income and assets were understated.

Current accounting thought has shifted somewhat from this philosophy of conservatism. Conservatism is no longer considered to be a dominant factor in selecting among alternatives. Revenue should be recognized when realized, and expired costs should be matched against revenue according to the principles based on reason and logic. The element of conservatism may be considered only when other factors affecting a choice of alternatives are neutral. The concepts of objectivity, consistency, disclosure, and materiality are more important than conservatism, and the latter should be a factor only when the others do not play a significant role.

CHAPTER REVIEW

KEY POINTS

1. Development of Concepts and Principles.

As the American economy developed and as business organizations grew in size and complexity, there came an awareness of the need for a framework of concepts and generally accepted accounting principles to serve as guidelines for the preparation of the basic financial statements. These principles represent the best possible guides, based on reason, observation, and experimentation, to help make accounting data more useful in an ever-changing society.

Currently, the Financial Accounting Standards Board establishes accounting standards for business enterprises. The Governmental Accounting Standards Board has responsibility for establishing accounting standards to be followed by state and municipal governments.

Among the other organizations which have had an effect on the development of accounting principles are the American Institute of Certified Public Accountants, the American Accounting Association, the Securities and Exchange Commission, the Internal Revenue Service, the Financial Executives Institute, and the National Association of Accountants.

2. Business Entity.

The business entity concept assumes that a business enterprise is separate and distinct from the persons who supply its assets. This distinction exists regardless of the legal form of the organization.

3. Going Concern.

In most cases, it is not possible to determine in advance the length of life of an enterprise, and so an assumption must be made. It is customary to assume that a business entity has a reasonable expectation of continuing in business at a profit for an indefinite period of time.

4. Objective Evidence.

Entries in the accounting records and data reported on financial statements must be based on objectively determined evidence. If this principle is not followed, the confidence of the many users of the financial statements could not be maintained.

5. Unit of Measurement.

All business transactions are recorded in terms of money. The use of the monetary unit in accounting for and reporting the activities of an enterprise has two major limitations: (1) it limits the scope of accounting reports, and (2) it assumes stability of the measurement unit. Factors affecting the activities and the future prospects of an enterprise that cannot be expressed in monetary terms may be disclosed in descriptions in notes to the financial statements. There are two widely discussed recommendations for supplementing conventional financial statements and thus resolving financial reporting problems created by the instability of the monetary unit: (1) supplemental financial data based on current costs and (2) supplemental financial data based on constant dollars.

6. Accounting Period.

A complete and accurate picture of an enterprise's success or failure cannot be obtained until it discontinues operations, converts its assets into cash, and pays off its debts. However, many decisions regarding the business must be made by management and interested outsiders during its existence. It is therefore necessary to prepare periodic reports on operations, financial position, and changes in financial position.

7. Matching Revenue and Expired Costs.

The determination of periodic net income is a two-fold problem involving (1) the revenue recognized during the period and (2) the expired costs to be allocated to the period. Thus, revenues and expired costs must be matched to determine net income or net loss for the period.

Revenue may be recognized at the point of sale, upon receipt of payment, or under the installment method. In addition, for enterprises engaged in large construction projects, revenue may be recognized under the percentage-of-completion method.

Properties and services acquired by an enterprise are generally recorded at cost. As the cost expires, it must be recognized as an expense of the period. Many costs are treated as an expense at the time of occurrence because they will be wholly expired at the end of the period.

8. Adequate Disclosure.

Financial statements and their accompanying footnotes or other explanatory materials should contain all of the pertinent data believed essential to the reader's understanding of the enterprise's financial status. When there are several acceptable alternative accounting methods that could have a significant effect on amounts reported on the statements, the particular method used should be disclosed. When accounting estimates are revised because of additional information or subsequent developments, their effect on net income should be disclosed in the financial statements for the period in which the change is adopted. Any contingent liabilities that exist and are significant in nature should also be disclosed in financial statements. Companies with diversified segments should disclose their operations in different industries, their foreign markets, and their major customers. Events occurring or becoming known after the close of the period that have a significant effect on the financial statements should be disclosed.

9. Consistency.

A number of acceptable alternative principles affecting the determination of income statement and balance sheet amounts exist. The concept of consistency implies that the financial statements should be prepared by applying the same principles year after year. If changes in principles do occur, their effect on the financial statements should be disclosed.

10. Materiality.

In following generally accepted accounting principles, the accountant must consider the relative importance of any event, accounting procedure, or change in procedure that affects items on the financial statements. The concept of materiality implies that accountants need not strictly adhere to generally accepted accounting principles if the amounts involved are not significant.

11. Conservatism.

The concept of conservatism implies that, in selecting among alternative accounting principles, the principle that yields the lesser amount of net income or asset value should be chosen. Current accounting thought has shifted somewhat from this philosophy of conservatism, and it is no longer considered to be a dominant factor in selecting among alternatives.

KEY TERMS

Financial Accounting Standards
  Board (FASB) 558
Governmental Accounting
  Standards Board (GASB) 560
American Institute of Certified
  Public Accountants (AICPA) 560
Securities and Exchange
  Commission (SEC) 560
Internal Revenue Service (IRS) 560
business entity concept 561
going concern concept 562
current cost 565

constant dollar 565
price-level index 565
matching 567
point of sale method 568
installment method 568
completed-contract method 569
percentage-of-completion
  method 570
adequate disclosure 571
consistency 576
materiality 577
conservatism 579

SELF-EXAMINATION QUESTIONS

Answers in Appendix B.

1. Equipment that was acquired for $250,000 has a current book value of $100,000 and an estimated market value of $120,000. If the replacement cost of the equipment is $350,000, at what amount should the equipment be reported in the balance sheet?
    A. $120,000
    B. $150,000
    C. $350,000
    D. None of the above

2. Merchandise costing $140,000 was sold on the installment plan for $200,000 during the current year. Down payments of $40,000 and installment payments of $35,000 were received during the current year. If the installment method of accounting is employed, what is the amount of gross profit to be realized in the current year?
   A. $22,500   C. $75,000
   B. $60,000   D. None of the above

3. The total contract price for the construction of an ocean liner was $20,000,000, and the estimated construction costs were $17,000,000. During the current year, the project was estimated to be 40% completed and the costs incurred totaled $7,050,000. Under the percentage-of-completion method of accounting, what amount of income would be recognized for the current year?
   A. $950,000   C. $3,000,000
   B. $1,200,000   D. None of the above

4. The concept of consistency requires that the nature of and justification for a change in accounting principle and its effect on income be disclosed in the financial statements of the period in which a change is made. An example of a change in accounting principle is a:
   A. change in method of inventory pricing
   B. change in depreciation method for previously recorded plant assets
   C. change in method of accounting for installment sales
   D. all of the above

5. A corporation's financial statements do not report cents amounts. This is an example of the application of which of the following concepts?
   A. Business entity   C. Consistency
   B. Going concern   D. Materiality

ILLUSTRATIVE PROBLEM

Town and Country Furniture Company makes all sales on the installment basis and recognizes revenue at the point of sale. Condensed income statements and the amounts collected from customers for each of the first three years of operations are as follows:

	1987	1988	1989
Sales.	$190,000	$240,000	$170,000
Cost of merchandise sold.	133,000	163,200	122,400
Gross profit	$ 57,000	$ 76,800	$ 47,600
Operating expenses.	33,900	41,500	30,000
Net income	$ 23,100	$ 35,300	$ 17,600

	1987	1988	1989
Collected from sales of first year	$ 50,000	$110,000	$ 30,000
Collected from sales of second year		80,000	120,000
Collected from sales of third year............................			60,000

Instructions:

Determine the amount of net income that would have been reported in each year if the installment method of recognizing revenue had been used. Ignore the possible effects of uncollectible accounts on the computations.

SOLUTION

		1987	1988	1989
Gross profit realized on collections from sales of:				
First year:	30%[1] × $ 50,000	$ 15,000		
	30% × $110,000		$33,000	
	30% × $ 30,000			$ 9,000
Second year:	32%[2] × $ 80,000		25,600	
	32% × $120,000			38,400
Third year:	28%[3] × $ 60,000			16,800
Total gross profit realized		$ 15,000	$58,600	$64,200
Operating expenses.................		33,900	41,500	30,000
Income (loss) from operations		$(18,900)	$17,100	$34,200

[1]$57,000 ÷ $190,000 = 30% gross profit
[2]$76,800 ÷ $240,000 = 32% gross profit
[3]$47,600 ÷ $170,000 = 28% gross profit

DISCUSSION QUESTIONS

1. Accounting principles are broad guides to accounting practice. (a) How do these principles differ from the principles relating to the physical sciences? (b) Of what significance is acceptability in the development of accounting principles? (c) Why must accounting principles be continually reexamined and revised?

2. What role does the Financial Accounting Foundation play in the development of accounting principles?

3. What body is currently dominant in the development of (a) generally accepted accounting principles for business enterprises and (b) principles for state and municipal governments?

4. For accounting purposes, what is the nature of the assumption as to the length of life of an enterprise?

5. Plant assets are reported on the balance sheet at a total cost of $500,000, less accumulated depreciation of $300,000. (a) Is it possible that the assets might realize considerably more or considerably less than $200,000 if the business were discontinued and the assets were sold separately? (b) Why aren't plant assets reported on the balance sheet at their estimated market values?

6. During the current year, a mortgage note payable for $250,000, issued by Parson Company 10 years ago, became due and was paid. Assuming that the general price level had increased by 50% during the 10-year period, did the loan result in an increase or a decrease in Parson Company's purchasing power? Explain.

7. A machine with a cost of $75,000 and accumulated depreciation of $60,000 will soon need to be replaced by a similar machine that will cost $125,000. (a) At what amount should the machine presently owned be reported on the balance sheet? (b) What amount should management use in planning for the cash required to replace the machine?

8. During July, merchandise costing $150,000 was sold for $225,000 in cash. Because the purchasing power of the dollar has declined, it will cost $160,000 to replace the merchandise. (a)What is the amount of gross profit in July? (b) Assuming that all operating expenses for the month are paid in cash and that the owner withdraws cash in the amount of the net income, would there be enough cash remaining from the $225,000 of sales to replace the merchandise sold? Discuss.

9. Conventional financial statements do not give recognition to the instability of the purchasing power of the dollar. How can the effect of the fluctuating dollar on business operations be presented to the users of the financial statements?

10. What is the current cost of an asset?

11. If land was purchased for $80,000 when the general price-level index was 220, and the general price-level index has risen to 242, what is the constant dollar equivalent of the original cost of the land?

12. Is revenue from sales of merchandise on account more commonly recognized at the time of sale or at the time of cash receipt?

13. During the current year, merchandise costing $150,000 was sold on the installment plan for $250,000. The down payments and the installment payments received during the current year totaled $125,000. What is the amount of gross profit considered to be realized in the current year, applying (a) the point of sale method and (b) the installment method of revenue recognition?

14. During the current year, Evans Construction Company obtained a contract to build an apartment building. The total contract price was $6,000,000, and the estimated construction costs were $4,950,000. During the current year, the project was estimated to be 40% completed, and the costs incurred totaled $2,290,000. Under the percentage-of-completion method of revenue recognition, what amount of (a) revenue, (b) cost, and (c) income should be recognized from the contract for the current year?

15. On January 7 of the current year, Nixon Realty Company acquired a 10-acre tract of land for $150,000. Before the end of the year, $50,000 was spent in subdividing the tract and in paving streets. The market value of the land at the end of the year was estimated at $250,000. Although no lots were sold during the year, the income statement for the year reported revenue of $100,000, expenses of $50,000, and net income of $50,000 from the project. Were generally accepted accounting principles followed? Discuss.

16. Mini-Storage Company constructed a warehouse at a cost of $175,000, after a local contractor had submitted a bid of $200,000. The building was recorded at $200,000, and income of $25,000 was recognized. Were generally accepted accounting principles followed? Discuss.

17. Farr Company purchased equipment for $250,000 at the beginning of a fiscal year. The equipment could be sold for $260,000 at the end of the fiscal year. It was proposed that since the equipment was worth more at the end of the year than at the beginning of the year, (a) no depreciation should be recorded for the current year, and (b) the gain of $10,000 should be recorded. Discuss the propriety of the proposals.

18. When there are several acceptable alternative accounting methods that could be used, the method used by an enterprise should be disclosed in the financial statements. Give examples of accounting methods that fall in this category.

19. If significant changes are made in the accounting principles applied from one period to the next, why should the effect of these changes be disclosed in the financial statements?

20. You have just been employed by a relatively small merchandising business that records its revenues only when cash is received and its expenses only when cash is paid. You are aware of the fact that the enterprise should record its revenues and expenses on the accrual basis. Would changing to the accrual basis violate the principle of consistency? Discuss.

21. For many years, Yost Company has used the sum-of-the-years-digits method of computing depreciation. For the current year, the straight-line method was used, depreciation expense amounted to $50,000, and net income amounted to $60,000. Depreciation computed by the sum-of-the-years-digits method would have been $65,000. (a) What is the quantitative effect of the change in method on the net income for the current year? (b) Is the effect of the change material? (c) Should the effect of the change in method be disclosed in the financial statements?

22. The accountant for a large department store charged the acquisition of a pencil sharpener to an expense account, even though the asset had an estimated useful life of 8 years. Which accounting concept supports this treatment of the expenditure?

23. In 1960, Allen Corporation acquired a building, with a useful life of 40 years, and depreciated it by the declining-balance method. Is this practice conservative (a) for the year 1960 and (b) for the year 1999? Explain.

24. Real World Focus. The following financial data (in millions) were taken from the 1985 annual report of General Electric Company:

	As Reported in the Financial Statements	As Adjusted for Current Costs
Sales..............................	$28,285	$28,285
Cost of merchandise sold............	19,775	19,907
Selling, general, and administrative expense	4,349	4,349
Depreciation, depletion, and amortization.....................	1,226	1,476

Determine for 1985 (a) the operating income as reported in the financial statements, (b) the operating income on a current cost basis, and (c) the difference between (a) and (b).

EXERCISES

Exercise 13–1.   Recognition of revenue. Indicate for each of the following items the amount of revenue that should be reported for the current year and the amount of revenue that should be postponed to a future period. Give a reason for your answer.

(a) Sales of merchandise made on terms 1/10, n/60 and delivered during the current year totaled $975,000. Cash received on credit sales totaled $935,000 during the current year.

(b) Merchandise on hand at the end of the current fiscal year, costing $172,500, is expected to be sold in the following year for $242,250.

(c) Thirty days before the end of the current fiscal year, $100,000 was loaned at 12% for 60 days.

(d) Season tickets for a series of four concerts were sold for $90,000. Three concerts were played during the current year.

(e) The contract price for building a bridge is $11,000,000. During the current year, the first year of construction, the bridge is estimated to be 20% completed and the costs incurred totaled $1,950,000. Revenue is to be recognized by the percentage-of-completion method.

(f) A tract of land was leased on the first day of the fourth month of the current year, and one year's rent of $40,000 was received.

(g) Sixty days before the end of the current fiscal year, a $100,000, 90-day, non-interest-bearing note was accepted at a discount of 12%. Proceeds in the amount of $97,000 were given to the maker of the note.

(h) Salespersons submitted orders in the current year for merchandise to be delivered in the following year. The merchandise had a cost of $20,000 and a selling price of $27,250.

(i) Cash of $25,000 was received in the current year on the sale of gift certificates to be redeemed in merchandise in the following year.

Exercise 13–2.   Effect of price-level change on investment in land. Several years ago, Manley Company purchased land as a future building site for $60,000. The price-level index at that time was 120. On October 11 of the current year, when the price-level index was 132, the land was sold for $71,500.

(a) Determine the amount of the gain that would be realized according to conventional accounting.

(b) Indicate the amount of the gain that may be (1) attributed to the change in purchasing power and (2) considered a true gain in terms of current dollars.

Exercise 13–3.   Gross profit by point of sale and installment methods. Sexton Company makes all sales on the installment plan. Data related to merchandise sold during the current fiscal year are as follows:

Sales...	$900,000
Cash received on the $900,000 of installment contracts	340,000
Merchandise inventory, beginning of year..................	102,500
Merchandise inventory, end of year	107,500
Purchases	635,000

Determine the amount of gross profit that would be recognized for the current fiscal year according to (a) the point of sale method and (b) the installment method.

Exercise 13–4.   Determination of cost of products and services acquired. Properties and services acquired by an enterprise are generally recorded at cost. For each of the following, determine the cost.

(a) Materials and supplies costing $3,600 were purchased for the construction of a display case. An additional $2,000 was paid to hire a carpenter to build the display case. A similar case would cost $6,300 if purchased from a manufacturer.

(b) Equipment was purchased for $35,500 under terms of n/30, FOB shipping point. The freight charge amounted to $550, and installation costs totaled $375.

(c) An adjacent tract of land was acquired for $46,500 to provide additional parking for customers. The structures on the land were removed at a cost of $4,250. The salvaged material from the structures was sold for $750. The cost of grading the land was $1,250.

Exercise 13–5.   Effect of different inventory cost methods on net income. The cost of merchandise inventory at the end of the first fiscal year of operations, according to three different methods, is as follows: fifo, $95,500; average, $91,000; lifo, $83,500. If the average cost method is employed, the net income reported will be $75,000. (a) What will be the amount of net income reported if the lifo method is adopted? (b) What will be the amount of net income reported if the fifo method is adopted? (c) Which of the three methods is the most conservative in terms of net income? (d) Is the particular method adopted of sufficient materiality to require disclosure in the financial statements?

Exercise 13–6.   Effects on financial statements of failure to accrue commission. Salespersons for Pelican Realty receive a commission of 4% of sales, the amount due on sales of one month being paid in the middle of the following month. At the end of each of the first three years of operations, the accountant failed to record accrued sales commissions expense as follows: first year, $15,000; second year, $12,500; third year, $13,500. In each case, the commissions were paid during the first month of the succeeding year and were charged as an expense of that year. Accrued sales commissions expense was properly recorded at the end of the fourth year. (a) Determine the amount by which net income was overstated or understated for each of the four years. (b) Determine the items on the balance sheet that would have been overstated or understated at the end of each of the four years, and the amount of overstatement or understatement.

Exercise 13–7.   Effect on financial statements of failure to record sales. Altenberger Company sells most of its products on a cash basis, but extends short-term credit to a few of its customers. Invoices for sales on account are placed in a file and are not recorded until cash is received, at which time the sale is recorded in the same manner as a cash sale. The net income reported for the first three years of operations was $69,500, $58,000, and $95,000, respectively. The total amount of the uncollected sales invoices in the file at the end of each of the three years was $7,800, $6,750, and $8,500, respectively. In each case, the entire amount was collected during the first month of the succeeding year. (a) Determine the amount by which net income was overstated or understated for each of the three years. (b) Determine the items on the balance sheet that were overstated or understated, and the amount of overstatement or understatement, as of the end of each year.

Exercise 13–8.   Determination of materiality. Of the following matters, considered individually, indicate those that are material and that should be disclosed either in the financial statements or in accompanying explanatory notes.

(a) A change in accounting for depreciation of plant assets was adopted in the current year. The amount of net income that would otherwise have been reported decreased from $795,000 to $575,000.

(b) A company is facing litigation involving restraint of trade. Damages might amount to $5,000,000. Annual net income reported in the past few years has ranged from $12,000,000 to $15,000,000.

(c) A change in estimates of the remaining usefulness of computer equipment decreased the amount of net income that would otherwise have been reported from $1,900,000 to $1,870,000.

(d) A merchandising company employs the first-in, first-out cost flow assumption and prices its inventory at the lower of cost or market.

(e) Between the end of the fiscal year and the date of publication of the annual report, a fire completely destroyed one of three principal plants. The loss was estimated at $2,000,000 and was fully covered by insurance. The net income for the fiscal year was $475,000.

Exercise 13–9.   Identification of generally accepted accounting principles. Each of the following statements represents a decision made by an accountant. State whether or not you agree with the decision. Support your answer with reference to generally accepted accounting principles that are applicable in the circumstances.

(a) In preparing the balance sheet, detailed information as to the amount due to hundreds of creditors was omitted. The total amount was presented under the caption "Accounts Payable."

(b) Used electronic data processing equipment, with an estimated useful life of 5 years and no salvage value, was purchased early in the current fiscal year for $250,000. Since the company planned to purchase new equipment, costing $450,000, to replace this equipment at the end of three years, depreciation expense of $150,000 was recorded for the current year. The depreciation expense thus provided for one third of the cost of the replacement.

(c) All minor expenditures for office equipment are charged to an expense account.

(d) Merchandise transferred to other parties on a consignment basis and not sold was included in merchandise inventory.

(e) Land, used as a parking lot, was purchased 5 years ago for $50,000. Since its market value is now $80,000, the land account is debited for $30,000 and a gain account is credited for a like amount. The gain is presented as an "Other income" item in the income statement.

PROBLEMS

Series A

Problem 13–1A. Adjusting and correcting entries. You are engaged to review the accounting records of Eason Company prior to the closing of the revenue and expense accounts as of December 31, the end of the current fiscal year. The following information comes to your attention during the review.

(a) Accounts receivable include $6,500 owed by I. D. Inc., a bankrupt company. There is no prospect of collecting any of the receivable. The allowance method of accounting for receivables is employed.

(b) Land recorded in the accounts at a cost of $75,000 was appraised at $112,500 by two expert appraisers.

(c) The company is being sued for $2,000,000 by a customer who claims damages for personal injury allegedly caused by a defective product. Company attorneys and outside legal counsel retained by Eason Company feel extremely confident that the company will have no liability for damages resulting from this case.

(d) The prepaid insurance account has a balance of $7,175. At December 31, the unexpired premiums were $2,200.

(e) Since net income for the current year is expected to be considerably less than it was for the preceding year, depreciation on equipment has not been recorded. Equipment depreciation for the year, determined in a manner consistent with the preceding year, amounts to $52,100.

(f) No interest has been accrued on a $100,000, 12%, 90-day note receivable, dated November 1 of the current year.

(g) Merchandise inventory on hand at December 31 of the current year has been recorded in the accounts at cost, $277,150. Current market price of the inventory is $286,500.

Instructions:

Journalize any entries required to adjust or correct the accounts, identifying each by letter.

Problem 13–2A. Installment sales. R. C. Nunn Inc. makes all sales on the installment basis and recognizes revenue at the point of sale. Condensed income statements and the amounts collected from customers for each of the first three years of operations are as follows:

	First Year	Second Year	Third Year
Sales..............................	$300,000	$340,000	$440,000
Cost of merchandise sold...............	195,000	224,400	281,600
Gross profit...........................	$105,000	$115,600	$158,400
Operating expenses....................	62,500	68,500	98,400
Net income	$ 42,500	$ 47,100	$ 60,000
Collected from sales of first year	$ 75,000	$125,000	$100,000
Collected from sales of second year		110,000	180,000
Collected from sales of third year.........			115,000

Instructions:

Determine the amount of net income that would have been reported in each year if the installment method of recognizing revenue had been employed, ignoring the possible effects of uncollectible accounts on the computation. Present figures in good order.

Problem 13–3A.   Installment sale and repossession. Fuller Video employs the installment method of recognizing gross profit for sales made on the installment plan. Details of a particular installment sale, amounts collected from the buyer, and the repossession of the item sold are as follows:

First year:
> Sold for $900 a color television set having a cost of $720; received a down payment of $150.

Second year:
> Received 12 monthly payments of $30 each.

Third year:
> The buyer defaulted on the monthly payments, the set was repossessed, and the remaining 13 installments were canceled. The set was estimated to be worth $350.

Instructions:

(1) Determine the gross profit to be recognized in the first year.
(2) Determine the gross profit to be recognized in the second year.
(3) Determine the gain or loss to be recognized from the repossession of the set. (*Suggestion:* First determine the amount of the unrecovered cost in the canceled installments. The gain or loss on repossession will then be the difference between this unrecovered cost and the value of the repossessed set.)

Problem 13–4A.   Percentage-of-completion method. Newell Company began construction on three contracts during 1987. The contract prices and construction activities for each of the years 1987, 1988, and 1989 were as follows:

Contract	Contract Price	1987 Costs Incurred	1987 Percent Completed	1988 Costs Incurred	1988 Percent Completed	1989 Costs Incurred	1989 Percent Completed
1	$6,000,000	$2,175,000	40%	$3,250,000	60%	—	—
2	4,000,000	600,000	20	1,375,000	40	$1,500,000	40%
3	3,500,000	455,000	15	985,000	30	1,575,000	50

Instructions:

Determine the amount of revenue and income to be recognized from the contracts for each of the years 1987, 1988, and 1989. Revenue is to be recognized by the percentage-of-completion method. Present computations in good order.

Problem 13–5A. Effect on net income from changes in three accounting principles. Olson Company was organized on January 3, 1986. During its first three years of operations, the company determined uncollectible accounts expense by the direct write-off method, the cost of the merchandise inventory at the end of the period by the first-in, first-out method, and depreciation expense by the straight-line method. The amounts of net income reported and the amounts of the foregoing items for each of the three years were as follows:

	First Year	Second Year	Third Year
Net income reported	$39,700	$60,750	$71,400
Uncollectible accounts expense	1,050	2,350	4,250
Ending merchandise inventory	49,750	54,000	58,150
Depreciation expense	19,000	19,900	20,900

The firm is considering the possibility of changing to the following methods in determining net income for the fourth and subsequent years: provision for doubtful accounts through the use of an allowance account, last-in, first-out inventory, and declining-balance depreciation at twice the straight-line rate. To consider the probable future effect of these changes on the determination of net income, the management requests that net income of the past three years be recomputed on the basis of the proposed methods. The uncollectible accounts expense, inventory, and depreciation expense for the past three years, computed in accordance with the proposed methods, are as follows:

	First Year	Second Year	Third Year
Uncollectible accounts expense	$ 1,625	$ 2,900	$ 4,000
Ending merchandise inventory	53,000	52,900	59,650
Depreciation expense	38,000	32,000	27,520

Instructions:

Recompute the net income for each of the three years, presenting the figures in an orderly manner.

Problem 13–6A.   Adjustments and corrections on work sheet; statements for sole proprietorship. John Reeves owns and manages The Gallery on a full-time basis. He also maintains the accounting records. At the end of the first year of operations, he prepared the following balance sheet and income statement:

The Gallery
Balance Sheet
December 31, 19--

Cash...	$ 7,750
Equipment.....................................	17,250
John Reeves....................................	$25,000

The Gallery
Income Statement
For Year Ended December 31, 19--

Sales...		$98,700
Purchases.....................................		73,500
Gross profit...................................		$25,200
Operating expenses:		
Salary expense............................	$17,850	
Rent expense.............................	13,000	
Utilities expense..........................	5,100	
Miscellaneous expense.....................	1,750	
Total operating expenses.................		37,700
Net loss......................................		$12,500

Because of the large net loss reported on the income statement, Reeves is considering discontinuing operations. Before making a decision, he asks you to review the accounting methods employed and, if material errors are found, to prepare revised statements. The following information is discovered during the course of the review:

(a) The only transactions recorded have been those in which cash was received or disbursed.
(b) The accounts have not been closed for the year.
(c) The business was established on January 4 by an investment of $30,000 in cash by the owner. An additional investment of $7,500 was made in cash on July 20.
(d) The equipment listed on the balance sheet at $17,250 was purchased for cash on January 5. Equipment purchased July 1 for $5,000 in cash was debited to Purchases. Equipment purchased on December 31 for $4,000, for which a 60-day, 12% note was issued, was not recorded.
(e) Depreciation on equipment has not been recorded. The equipment is estimated to have a useful life of 10 years and no salvage value. (Use straight-line method.)
(f) Accounts receivable from customers at December 31 total $6,700.
(g) Uncollectible accounts are estimated at $475.
(h) The merchandise inventory at December 31, as nearly as can be determined, has a cost of $12,750.

(i) Insurance premiums of $850 were debited to Miscellaneous Expense during the year. The unexpired portion at December 31 is $350.

(j) Supplies of $1,000 purchased during the year were debited to Purchases. An estimated $250 of supplies were on hand at December 31.

(k) A total of $5,000 is owed to merchandise creditors on account at December 31.

(l) Rent Expense includes an advance payment of $1,000 for the month of January in the subsequent year.

(m) Salaries owed but not paid on December 31 total $350.

(n) The classification of operating expenses as "selling" and "general" is not considered to be sufficiently important to justify the cost of the analysis.

(o) The proprietor made no withdrawals during the year.

Instructions:

(1) On the basis of the financial statements presented, prepare an unadjusted trial balance, as of December 31, on an eight-column work sheet.

(2) Record the adjustments and the corrections in the Adjustments columns. Complete the work sheet by extending the adjusted trial balance amounts directly to the appropriate Income Statement or Balance Sheet column.

(3) Prepare a multiple-step income statement, a statement of owner's equity, and a report form balance sheet.

Series B

Problem 13–1B. Adjusting and correcting entries. You are engaged to review the accounting records of C. D. Jacobs Company prior to the closing of the revenue and expense accounts as of June 30, the end of the current fiscal year. The following information comes to your attention during the review:

(a) Since net income for the current year is expected to be considerably less than it was for the preceding year, depreciation on machinery has not been recorded. Machinery depreciation for the year, determined in a manner consistent with the preceding year, amounts to $31,500.

(b) Land recorded in the accounts at a cost of $75,000 was appraised at $120,000 by two expert appraisers.

(c) No interest has been accrued on a $50,000, 12%, 90-day note payable, dated May 31 of the current year.

(d) The office supplies account has a balance of $7,250. The cost of the office supplies on hand at June 30, as determined by a physical count, was $1,250.

(e) Merchandise inventory on hand at June 30 of the current year has been recorded in the accounts at cost, $215,200. Current market price of the inventory is $218,750.

(f) Accounts receivable include $14,625 owed by Baker and Wilson Inc., a bankrupt. C. D. Jacobs Company expects to receive twenty cents on each dollar owed. The allowance method of accounting for receivables is employed.

(g) The company is being sued for $1,500,000 by a customer who claims damages for personal injury allegedly caused by a defective product. Company attorneys and outside legal counsel feel extremely confident that the company will have no liability for damages resulting from this case.

(h) The company received a debit memorandum with the bank statement from Palmer National Bank, indicating that a customer note discounted at the bank has been dishonored. The 12%, 90-day note is from Cowens Co. and has a $40,000 face value. C. D. Jacobs Company has not recorded the memorandum, which included a protest fee of $15.

Instructions:

Journalize any entries required to adjust or correct the accounts, identifying each entry by letter.

Problem 13–2B.   Installment sales. Watson Co. makes all sales on the installment basis and recognizes revenue at the point of sale. Condensed income statements and the amounts collected from customers for each of the first three years of operations are as follows:

	First Year	Second Year	Third Year
Sales.	$398,750	$340,000	$382,000
Cost of merchandise sold.	271,150	227,800	248,300
Gross profit	$127,600	$112,200	$133,700
Operating expenses.	60,000	51,500	62,250
Net income	$ 67,600	$ 60,700	$ 71,450
Collected from sales of first year	$121,250	$157,500	$120,000
Collected from sales of second year		95,000	145,000
Collected from sales of third year.			99,000

Instructions:

Determine the amount of net income that would have been reported in each year if the installment method of recognizing revenue had been employed, ignoring the possible effects of uncollectible accounts on the computation. Present figures in good order.

Problem 13–4B.   Percentage-of-completion method. Sheppard Company began construction on three contracts during 1987. The contract prices and construction activities for 1987, 1988, and 1989 were as follows:

		1987		1988		1989	
Contract	Contract Price	Costs Incurred	Percent Completed	Costs Incurred	Percent Completed	Costs Incurred	Percent Completed
1	$ 5,000,000	$1,810,000	40%	$1,575,000	35%	$1,090,000	25%
2	10,000,000	2,550,000	30	2,625,000	30	2,695,000	30
3	8,000,000	3,710,000	50	3,815,000	50	—	—

Instructions:

Determine the amount of revenue and the income to be recognized for each of the years, 1987, 1988, and 1989. Revenue is to be recognized by the percentage-of-completion method. Present computations in good order.

Problem 13–5B. Effect on net income from changes in three accounting principles. Palmer Corporation was organized on January 3, 1987. During its first three years of operations, the company determined uncollectible accounts expense by the direct write-off method, the cost of the merchandise inventory at the end of the period by the first-in, first-out method, and depreciation expense by the straight-line method. The amount of net income reported and the amounts of the foregoing items for each of the three years were as follows:

	First Year	Second Year	Third Year
Net income reported	$97,500	$142,000	$200,000
Uncollectible accounts expense	1,125	2,800	5,950
Ending merchandise inventory	60,750	82,000	112,000
Depreciation expense	20,000	26,800	35,000

The firm is considering the possibility of changing to the following methods in determining net income for the fourth and subsequent years: provision for doubtful accounts through the use of an allowance account, last-in, first-out inventory, and declining-balance depreciation at twice the straight-line rate. To consider the probable future effect of these changes on the determination of net income, the management requests that net income of the past three years be recomputed on the basis of the proposed methods. The uncollectible accounts expense, inventory, and depreciation expense for the past three years, computed in accordance with the proposed methods, are as follows:

	First Year	Second Year	Third Year
Uncollectible accounts expense	$ 2,625	$ 3,500	$ 4,250
Ending merchandise inventory	59,000	70,100	92,750
Depreciation expense	40,000	38,840	34,100

Instructions:

Recompute the net income for each of the three years, presenting the figures in an orderly manner.

Problem 13–6B. Adjustments and corrections on work sheet; statements for sole proprietorship. Jane Dillow owns and manages The Art Mart on a full-time basis. She also maintains the accounting records. At the end of the first year of operations, she prepared the following balance sheet and income statement:

The Art Mart
Balance Sheet
December 31, 19--

Cash..	$ 8,000
Equipment......................................	12,000
Jane Dillow	$ 20,000

The Art Mart
Income Statement
For Year Ended December 31, 19--

Sales..		$146,750
Purchases		90,500
Gross profit		$ 56,250
Operating expenses:		
Salary expense.................................	$38,410	
Rent expense	16,800	
Utilities expense................................	4,225	
Miscellaneous expense..........................	2,315	
Total operating expenses.......................		61,750
Net loss		$ 5,500

Because of the large net loss reported on the income statement, Dillow is considering discontinuing operations. Before making a decision, she asks you to review the accounting methods employed and, if material errors are found, to prepare revised statements. The following information is elicited during the course of the review:

(a) The only transactions recorded have been those in which cash was received or disbursed.
(b) The accounts have not been closed for the year.
(c) The classification of operating expenses as "selling" and "general" is not considered to be sufficiently important to justify the cost of the analysis.
(d) The proprietor made no withdrawals during the year.
(e) The business was established on January 26 by an investment of $17,500 in cash by the owner. An additional investment of $8,000 was made in cash on June 1.
(f) Accounts receivable from customers at December 31 total $10,250.
(g) The merchandise inventory at December 31, as nearly as can be determined, has a cost of $23,425.
(h) Rent Expense includes an advance payment of $1,400 for the month of January in the subsequent year.
(i) Salaries owed but not paid on December 31 total $925.
(j) The equipment listed on the balance sheet at $12,000 was purchased for cash on February 1. Equipment purchased April 1 for $6,000 in cash was debited to Purchases. Equipment purchased on December 31 for $7,000, for which a 90-day, 12% note was issued, was not recorded.
(k) Uncollectible accounts are estimated at $950.
(l) A total of $17,500 is owed to merchandise creditors on account at December 31.

(m) Depreciation on equipment has not been recorded. The equipment is esti-mated to have a useful life of 10 years and no salvage value. (Use straight-line method.)

(n) Insurance premiums of $1,250 were debited to Miscellaneous Expense during the year. The unexpired portion at December 31 is $400.

(o) Supplies of $2,400 purchased during the year were debited to Purchases. An estimated $800 of supplies were on hand at December 31.

Instructions:

(1) On the basis of the financial statements presented, prepare an unadjusted trial balance, as of December 31, on an eight-column work sheet.

(2) Record the adjustments and the corrections in the Adjustments columns. Complete the work sheet by extending the adjusted trial balance amounts directly to the appro-priate Income Statement or Balance Sheet column.

(3) Prepare a multiple-step income statement, a statement of owner's equity, and a report form balance sheet.

MINI-CASE 13

R&M Parts Inc. operates twelve "cash and carry" auto parts stores in the southeast. In an effort to expand sales, the company has decided to offer two additional sales plans:

(1) credit sales to commercial enterprises, such as body and repair shops, with free twenty-four-hour delivery

(2) installment sales of major dollar items, with payments spread over 36 months.

The company president has asked you when the revenue from each of the two new plans would be recog-nized in the accounting records and statements.

Instructions:

(1) Indicate to the president when the revenue from each type of sale should be recorded in the accounting records.

(2) While discussing the concepts in (1), the president raised the following questions related to various accounting concepts. How would you respond to each?

(a) "Many businesses cease operating each year; so why do accountants assume a going concern concept when preparing the financial statements?"

(b) "To assume that the value of the dollar does not change and that we don't have inflation is wrong! An automatic transmission that cost $300 five years ago costs $400 today. Why wouldn't it be better to use current dollars, at least for the inventory?"

(c) "With so many different accounting methods that can be used, how can I switch methods to improve net income this year?"

(d) "Our annual bonuses to store managers are based on store profits. It is not fair to 'anticipate no profits and provide for all losses.'"

PARTNERSHIPS

Part

4

Chapter **14**

PARTNERSHIP FORMATION, INCOME DIVISION, AND LIQUIDATION

Chapter Objectives:

- Identify basic characteristics of partnership organization and operation which have accounting implications.

- Describe and illustrate the accounting for partnerships from formation to final liquidation.

- Describe and illustrate the accounting for admission of new partners.

- Describe and illustrate the accounting for the withdrawal of partners.

- Describe and illustrate the preparation of financial statements for partnerships.

T he Uniform Partnership Act, which has been adopted by more than ninety percent of the states, defines a partnership as "an association of two or more persons to carry on as co-owners a business for profit." The partnership form of business organization is widely used for comparatively small businesses that wish to take advantage of the combined capital, managerial talent, and experience of two or more persons. In many cases, the alternative to securing the amount of investment or the various skills needed to operate a business is to adopt the corporate form of organization. The typical corporate form of organization is sometimes not permitted, however, because of restrictions in state laws. In addition, a group of physicians, attorneys, or certified public accountants who wish to band together to practice a profession often organize as a partnership. Medical and legal partnerships made up of 20 or more partners are not unusual, and the number of partners in some CPA firms exceeds 1,000.

CHARACTERISTICS OF PARTNERSHIPS

Partnerships have several characteristics that have accounting implications. These characteristics are described in the following paragraphs.

A partnership has a **limited life**. Dissolution of a partnership occurs whenever a partner ceases to be a member of the firm for any reason, including withdrawal, bankruptcy, incapacity, or death. Similarly, admission of a new partner dissolves the old partnership. In case of dissolution, a new partnership must be formed if the operations of the business are to be continued without interruption. This situation frequently occurs with professional partnerships. Their composition may change often as new partners are admitted and others are retired.

Most partnerships are *general partnerships*, in which the partners have **unlimited liability**. Each partner is individually liable to creditors for debts incurred by the partnership. Thus, if a partnership becomes insolvent, the partners must contribute sufficient personal assets to settle the debts of the partnership. In some states, a *limited partnership* may be formed, in which the liability of some partners may be limited to the amount of their 603 capital investment. However, a limited partnership must have at least one general partner who has unlimited liability. In this chapter, the discussion is focused on the general partnership.

Partners have **co-ownership of partnership property**. The property invested in a partnership by a partner becomes the property of all the partners jointly. Upon dissolution of the partnership and distribution of its assets, the partners' claims against the assets are measured by the amount of the balances in their capital accounts.

Another characteristic of a partnership is **mutual agency**. This feature means that each partner is an agent of the partnership, with the authority to enter into contracts for the partnership. Thus, the acts of each partner bind the partnership and become the responsibility of all partners.

A significant right of partners is **participation in income** of the partnership. Net income and net loss are distributed among the partners according to their agreement. In the absence of any agreement, all partners share equally. If the agreement specifies profit distribution but is silent as to losses, the losses are shared in the same manner as profits.

A partnership, like a sole proprietorship, is a **nontaxable entity** and is therefore not required to pay federal income taxes. However, revenue and expense and other financial details of partnership operations must be reported annually on official Internal Revenue Service forms known as *information returns*. The individual partners must report their distributive share of partnership income on their personal tax returns.

A partnership is created by a voluntary contract containing all the elements essential to any other enforceable contract. It is not necessary that this contract be in writing, nor even that its terms be specifically expressed. However, good business practice dictates that the contract should be in writing and should clearly express the intentions of the partners. The contract, known as the **articles of partnership** or **partnership agreement**, should contain provisions regarding such matters as the amount of investment to be made, limitations on withdrawals of funds, the manner in which net income and net loss are to be divided, and the admission and withdrawal of partners.

ADVANTAGES AND DISADVANTAGES OF PARTNERSHIPS

The partnership form of business organization is less widely used than are the sole proprietorship and corporate forms. For a particular business endeavor, however, the advantages of the partnership form may outweigh the disadvantages.

A partnership is relatively easy and inexpensive to organize, requiring only an agreement between two or more persons. A partnership has the advantage of being able to bring together more capital, more managerial skills, and more experience than would a sole proprietorship. Because the partnership is a nontaxable entity, the combined income taxes paid by the individual partners may be lower than the income taxes that would be paid by a corporation, which is a taxable entity.

The disadvantages of a partnership are that its life is limited, each partner has unlimited liability, and one partner can bind the partnership to contracts. Also, raising large amounts of capital is more difficult for a partnership than for a corporation.

ACCOUNTING FOR PARTNERSHIPS

Most of the day-to-day accounting for a partnership is the same as the accounting for any other form of business organization. The system described in earlier chapters may, with little change, be used by a partnership. For example, the journals described may be used without alteration. The chart of accounts, with the exception of drawing and capital accounts for each partner, does not differ from the chart of accounts of a similar business conducted by a single owner. It is in the areas of the formation, income distribution, dissolution, and liquidation of partnerships that transactions peculiar to partnerships arise. The remainder of the chapter is devoted to the accounting principles and procedures applicable to these areas.

RECORDING INVESTMENTS

A separate entry is made for the investment of each partner in a partnership. The various assets contributed by a partner are debited to the proper asset accounts. If liabilities are assumed by the partnership, the appropriate liability accounts are credited. The partner's capital account is credited for the net amount.

To illustrate the entry to record an initial investment, assume that Robert A. Stevens and Earl S. Foster, who are sole owners of competing hardware stores, agree to combine their businesses in a partnership. Each is to contribute certain amounts of cash and other business assets. It is also agreed that the partnership is to assume the liabilities of the separate businesses. The entry to record the assets contributed and the liabilities transferred by Stevens is as follows:

Apr. 1	Cash	7,200	
	Accounts Receivable	16,300	
	Merchandise Inventory	28,700	
	Store Equipment	5,400	
	Office Equipment	1,500	
	Allowance for Doubtful Accounts		1,500
	Accounts Payable		2,600
	Robert A. Stevens, Capital		55,000

A similar entry would record the assets contributed and the liabilities transferred by Foster. In each entry, the monetary amounts at which the noncash assets are stated are those agreed upon by the partners. In arriving at an appropriate amount for such assets, consideration should be given to their market values at the time the partnership is formed. The values agreed upon represent the acquisition cost to the accounting entity created by the formation of the partnership. These amounts may differ from the balances appearing in the accounts of the separate businesses before the partnership was organized. For example, the store equipment stated at $5,400 in the entry above may have had a book value of $3,500, appearing in Stevens' ledger at its original cost of $10,000 with accumulated depreciation of $6,500.

Receivables contributed to the partnership are recorded at their face amount, with a credit to a contra account if provision is to be made for possible future uncollectibility. Ordinarily, only accounts with reasonable chances of collection are transferred to the partnership. Again referring to the preceding entry, the accounts receivable on Stevens' ledger may have totaled $17,600, of which $1,300 was considered to be completely worthless. The remaining $16,300 of receivables was recorded in the partnership accounts by a debit to Accounts Receivable and by debits to the individual accounts in the subsidiary ledger. The credit of $1,500 to Allowance for Doubtful Accounts is the provision for possible future uncollectibility of the accounts receivable contributed to the partnership by Stevens.

DIVISION OF NET INCOME OR NET LOSS

As in the case of a sole proprietorship, the net income of a partnership may be said to include a return for the services of the owners, for the capital invested, and for economic or pure profit. Partners are not legally employees of the partnership, nor are their capital contributions a loan. If each of two partners is to contribute equal services and amounts of capital, an equal sharing in partnership net income would be equitable. But if one partner is to contribute a larger portion of capital than the other, provision for unequal capital contributions should be given recognition in the agreement for dividing net income. Or, if the services of one partner are much more valuable to the partnership than those of the other, provision for unequal service contributions should be given recognition in their agreement.

To illustrate the division of net income and the accounting for this division, two possible agreements are to be considered. It should be noted that division of the net income or the net loss among the partners in exact accordance with their partnership agreement is of the utmost importance. If the agreement is silent on the matter, the law provides that all partners share equally, regardless of differences in amounts of capital contributed, of special skills possessed, or of time devoted to the business. The partners may, however, make any agreement they wish in regard to the division of net income and net losses.

Executive Compensation—A Partnership Vs. A Corporation

Generally, and specifically in the case of Deloitte, Haskins & Sells (a public accounting partnership), compensation to partners is, in both form and substance, different from corporate executive compensation.

As a general rule, compensation in major mid-sized corporations (to which we might be compared based on revenue size, number of personnel, etc.) consists of current cash, deferred payments, payments made on behalf of an individual for retirement benefits, and perquisites. In addition, options to purchase stock at potentially favorable prices may also be an attractive compensation component. Unlike a corporation, partners must provide from their own earnings for their own retirement benefits, as well as paying for self-employment taxes, group insurance, and other benefit programs. As a partnership, of course, our partners do not have stock options available.

Each year the majority of the firm's earnings are distributed to the partners. Some small percentage is usually retained for working capital needs. No amounts are guaranteed, like a "pre-set" annual salary. If earnings decline, partners' individual earnings also decline. Partners are also required to invest capital in the firm. As such, part of their earnings represent a return on their investment. With regard to their firm activities, partners have a much broader exposure to personal liability than do most corporate officers.

The factors mentioned above must be considered in making meaningful comparisons of partners' compensation with other business executives. To simply compare amounts would be misleading.

Our partnership is a private organization and many of the partners feel strongly that their compensation should not be disclosed. Nonetheless, firm management has concluded that the public may be better served if we disclose selective compensation data. We hope this disclosure demonstrates to the public that our earnings enable us to retain competent professionals, that we do not earn excessive amounts, and that we have no special agreements that would compromise our integrity or our independence.

The average earnings of all of our partners for fiscal year 1985 was approximately $143,000. As to our five most highly compensated partners, their individual earnings ranged from $385,000 to $725,000, and their average was $500,000.

Source: Deloitte, Haskins & Sells, *A Report for Congress and the Public* (September, 1985).

Income Division Recognizing Services of Partners

As a means of recognizing differences in ability and in amount of time devoted to the business, articles of partnership often provide for the division of a portion of net income to the partners in the form of a salary allowance. The articles may also provide for withdrawals of cash by the partners in lieu of salary payments. A clear distinction must therefore be made between the division of net income, which is credited to the capital accounts, and payments to the partners, which are debited to the drawing accounts.

As a basis for illustration, assume that the articles of partnership of Jennifer L. Stone and Crystal R. Mills provide for monthly salary allowances of $2,500 and $2,000 respectively, with the balance of the net income to be divided equally, and that the net income for the year is $75,000. A report of the division of net income may be presented as a separate statement accompanying the balance sheet and the income statement, or it may be added at the bottom of the income statement. If the latter procedure is used, the lower part of the income statement would appear as follows:

	J. L. Stone	C. R. Mills	Total
Net income			$75,000
Division of net income:			
Salary allowance	$30,000	$24,000	$54,000
Remaining income...................	10,500	10,500	21,000
Net income	$40,500	$34,500	$75,000

The division of net income is recorded as a closing entry, regardless of whether the partners actually withdraw the amounts of their salary allowances. The entry for the division of net income is as follows:

Dec. 31	Income Summary	75,000	
	Jennifer L. Stone, Capital		40,500
	Crystal R. Mills, Capital		34,500

If Stone and Mills had withdrawn their salary allowances monthly, the withdrawals would have accumulated as debits in the drawing accounts during the year. At the end of the year, the debit balances of $30,000 and $24,000 in their drawing accounts would be transferred to their respective capital accounts.

Income Division Recognizing Services of Partners and Investment

Partners may agree that the most equitable plan of income sharing is to allow salaries based on the services rendered and also to allow interest on the capital investments. The remainder is then shared in an arbitrary ratio. To illustrate, assume that Stone and Mills (1) are allowed monthly salaries of $2,500 and $2,000 respectively; (2) are allowed interest at 12% on capital balances at January 1 of the current fiscal year, which amounted to $80,000 and $60,000 respectively; and (3) divide the remainder of net income equally. The division of $75,000 net income for the year could then be reported on the income statement as follows:

Net income			$75,000

Division of net income:	J. L. Stone	C. R. Mills	Total
Salary allowance	$30,000	$24,000	$54,000
Interest allowance	9,600	7,200	16,800
Remaining income..................	2,100	2,100	4,200
Net income	$41,700	$33,300	$75,000

On the basis of the information in the foregoing income statement, the entry to close the income summary account would be recorded as follows:

Dec. 31	Income Summary	75,000	
	Jennifer L. Stone, Capital		41,700
	Crystal R. Mills, Capital		33,300

Income Division — Allowances Exceed Net Income

In the illustrations presented thus far, the net income has exceeded the sum of the allowances for salary and interest. If the net income is less than the total of the special allowances, the "remaining balance" will be a negative figure that must be divided among the partners as though it were a net loss. The effect of this situation may be illustrated by assuming the same salary and interest allowances as in the preceding illustration, but changing the amount of net income to $50,000. The salary and interest allowances to Stone total $39,600, and the comparable figure for Mills is $31,200. The sum of these amounts, $70,800, exceeds the net income of $50,000 by $20,800. It is therefore necessary to deduct $10,400 (1/2 of $20,800) from each partner's share to arrive at the net income, as follows:

Net income $50,000

Division of net income:	J. L. Stone	C. R. Mills	Total
Salary allowance	$30,000	$24,000	$54,000
Interest allowance	9,600	7,200	16,800
Total	$39,600	$31,200	$70,800
Excess of allowances over income.....	10,400	10,400	20,800
Net income	$29,200	$20,800	$50,000

In closing Income Summary at the end of the year, $29,200 would be credited to Jennifer L. Stone, Capital, and $20,800 would be credited to Crystal R. Mills, Capital.

STATEMENTS FOR PARTNERSHIPS

Details of the division of net income should be disclosed in the financial statements prepared at the end of the fiscal period. This disclosure may be made by adding a section to the income statement, as illustrated in the preceding pages, or by presenting the data in a separate statement.

Details of the changes in the owner's equity of a partnership during the period should also be presented in a statement of owner's equity. The purposes of this statement and the data included in it correspond to those of the statement of owner's equity for a sole proprietorship. There are a number of variations in form. One of these variations is illustrated as follows for the Stone and Mills partnership, using assumed data and the income division shown on page 609:

STATEMENT
OF OWNER'S
EQUITY

Stone and Mills
Statement of Owner's Equity
For Year Ended December 31, 19--

	Jennifer L. Stone	Crystal R. Mills	Total
Capital, January 1, 19--	$ 80,000	$60,000	$140,000
Additional investment during the year....		5,000	5,000
	$ 80,000	$65,000	$145,000
Net income for the year	41,700	33,300	75,000
	$121,700	$98,300	$220,000
Withdrawals during the year	24,000	20,000	44,000
Capital, December 31, 19--	$ 97,700	$78,300	$176,000

PARTNERSHIP DISSOLUTION

One of the basic characteristics of the partnership form of organization is its limited life. Any change in the personnel of the ownership results in the dissolution of the partnership. Thus, admission of a new partner dissolves the old firm. Similarly, death, bankruptcy, or withdrawal of a partner causes dissolution.

Dissolution of the partnership is not necessarily followed by the winding up of the affairs of the business. For example, a partnership composed of two partners may admit an additional partner. Or if one of three partners in a business withdraws, the remaining two partners may continue to operate the business. In all such cases, a new partnership is formed and new articles of partnership should be prepared.

Admission of a Partner

An additional person may be admitted to a partnership enterprise only with the consent of all the current partners. It does not follow, however, that a partner's interest, or part of that interest, cannot be disposed of without the consent of the remaining partners. Under common law, if a partner's interest was assigned to an outside party, the partnership was automatically dissolved. Under the Uniform Partnership Act, a partner's interest can be disposed of without the consent of the remaining partners. The person who buys the interest acquires the selling partner's rights to share in net income and in assets upon liquidation. The buyer does not automatically become a partner, however, and has no voice in partnership affairs unless admitted to the firm.

An additional person may be admitted to a partnership through either of two procedures:

1. Purchase of an interest from one or more of the current partners.
2. Contribution of assets to the partnership.

When the first procedure is followed, the capital interest of the incoming partner is obtained from current partners, and *neither the total assets nor the total owner's equity of the business is affected*. When the second procedure is followed, *both the total assets and the total owner's equity of the business are increased*.

Admission by Purchase of an Interest. When an additional person is admitted to a firm by purchasing an interest from one or more of the partners, the purchase price is paid directly to the selling partners. Payment is for partnership equity owned by the partners as individuals, and hence the cash or other consideration paid is not recorded in the accounts of the partnership. The only entry needed is the transfer of the proper amounts of owner's equity from the capital accounts of the selling partners to the capital account established for the incoming partner.

As an example, assume that partners Tom Andrews and George Bell have capital balances of $50,000 each. On June 1, each sells one fifth of his respective equity to Joe Canter for $10,000 in cash. The exchange of cash is not a partnership transaction and thus is not recorded by the partnership. The only entry required in the partnership accounts is as follows:

June 1	Tom Andrews, Capital	10,000	
	George Bell, Capital	10,000	
	Joe Canter, Capital		20,000

The effect of the transaction on the partnership accounts is presented in the following diagram:

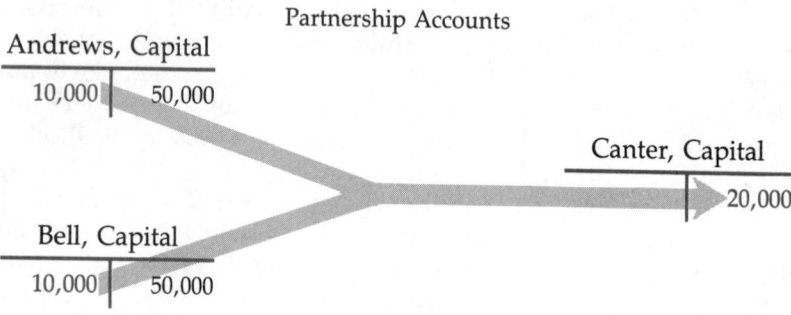

Partnership Accounts

The foregoing entry is not affected by the amount paid by Canter for the one-fifth interest. If the firm had been earning a high rate of return on the investment and Canter had been very eager to obtain the one-fifth interest, he might have paid considerably more than $20,000. Had other circumstances prevailed, he might have acquired the one-fifth interest for considerably less than $20,000. In either event, the entry to transfer the capital interests would be as illustrated.

After the admission of Canter, the total owner's equity of the firm is $100,000, of which Canter has a one-fifth interest, or $20,000. It does not necessarily follow that he will be entitled to a similar share of the partnership net income. Division of net income or net loss will be in accordance with the new partnership agreement.

Admission by Contribution of Assets. Instead of buying an interest from the current partners, the incoming partner may contribute assets to the partnership. In this case, both the assets and the owner's equity of the firm are increased. To illustrate, assume that Donald Lewis and Gerald Morton are partners with capital accounts of $35,000 and $25,000 respectively. On June 1, Sharon Nelson invests $20,000 cash in the business, for which she is to receive an ownership equity of $20,000. The entry to record this transaction is as follows:

June 1	Cash...	20,000	
	Sharon Nelson, Capital.....................		20,000

The major difference between the circumstances of the admission of Nelson and the admission of Canter in the preceding example may be observed by comparing the following diagram with the one on the preceding page:

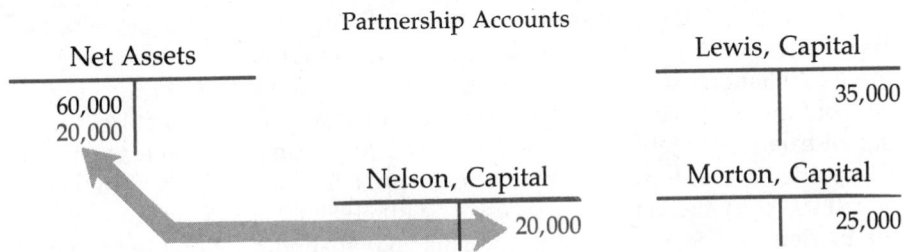

Partnership Accounts

With the admission of Nelson, the total owners' equity of the new partnership becomes $80,000, of which Nelson has a one-fourth interest, or $20,000. The extent of her participation in partnership net income will be governed by the articles of partnership.

Revaluation of assets. If the partnership assets are not fairly stated in terms of current market value at the time a new partner is admitted, the accounts may be adjusted accordingly. The net amount of the increases and decreases in asset values are then allocated to the capital accounts of the old partners according to their income-sharing ratio. To illustrate, assume that in the preceding illustration for the Lewis and Morton partnership, the balance of the merchandise inventory account had been $14,000 and the current replacement price had been $17,000. Prior to Nelson's admission, the revaluation would be recorded as follows, assuming that Lewis and Morton share net income equally:

June 1	Merchandise Inventory.....................	3,000	
	Donald Lewis, Capital.....................		1,500
	Gerald Morton, Capital....................		1,500

If a number of assets are revalued, the adjustments may be debited or credited to a temporary account entitled Asset Revaluations. After all adjustments are made, the account is closed to the capital accounts.

It is important that the assets be stated in terms of current prices at the time of admission of a new partner. Failure to recognize current prices may result in the new partner participating in gains or losses attributable to the period prior to admission.

Goodwill. When a new partner is admitted to a partnership, goodwill attributable either to the old partnership or to the incoming partner may be recognized. Although there are various methods of estimating goodwill, such factors as the respective shares owned by the partners and the relative bargaining abilities of the partners will influence the final determination. The amount of goodwill agreed upon is recorded as an asset, with a corresponding credit to the appropriate capital accounts.

To illustrate the recognition of goodwill to the old partners, assume that on March 1 the partnership of Marsha Jenkins and Helen Kramer admits William Larson, who is to contribute cash of $15,000. After the tangible assets of the old partnership have been adjusted to current market prices, the capital balances of Jenkins and Kramer are $20,000 and $24,000 respectively. The parties agree, however, that the enterprise is worth $50,000. The excess of $50,000 over the capital balances of $44,000 ($20,000 + $24,000) indicates the existence of $6,000 of goodwill. This $6,000 should be divided between the capital accounts of the original partners according to their income-sharing agreement.

The entries to record the goodwill and the admission of the new partner, assuming that the original partners share equally in net income, are as follows:

Mar. 1	Goodwill	6,000	
	Marsha Jenkins, Capital		3,000
	Helen Kramer, Capital		3,000
1	Cash	15,000	
	William Larson, Capital		15,000

If a partnership admits a new partner who is expected to improve the fortunes of the firm, the parties might agree to recognize this high earnings potential. To illustrate, assume that Sandra Ellis is to be admitted to the partnership of Cowen and Dodd for an investment of $30,000. If the parties agree to recognize $5,000 of goodwill attributable to Ellis, the entry to record her admission is as follows:

July 1	Cash	30,000	
	Goodwill	5,000	
	Sandra Ellis, Capital		35,000

Withdrawal of a Partner

When a partner retires or for some other reason wishes to withdraw from the firm, one or more of the remaining partners may purchase the withdrawing partner's interest and the business may be continued without apparent interruption. In such cases, settlement for the purchase and sale is made between the partners as individuals, in a manner similar to the admission of a new partner by purchase of an interest, and thus is not recorded by the partnership. The only entry required by the partnership is a debit to the capital account of the partner withdrawing and a credit to the capital account of the partner or partners acquiring the interest.

If the settlement with the withdrawing partner is made by the partnership, the effect is to reduce the assets and the owner's equity of the firm. To determine the ownership equity of the withdrawing partner, the asset accounts should be adjusted to current market prices. The net amount of the adjustments should be divided among the capital accounts of the partners according to the income-sharing ratio. In the event that the cash or the other available assets are insufficient to make complete payment at the time of withdrawal, a liability account should be credited for the balance owed to the withdrawing partner.

Death of a Partner

The death of a partner dissolves the partnership. In the absence of any contrary agreement, the accounts should be closed as of the date of death, and the net income for the fractional part of the year should be transferred to the capital accounts. It is not unusual, however, for the partnership agreement to stipulate that the accounts remain open to the end of the fiscal year or until the affairs are wound up, if that should occur earlier. The net income of the entire period is then divided, as provided by the agreement, between the respective periods occurring before and after dissolution.

The balance in the capital account of the deceased partner is then transferred to a liability account with the deceased's estate. The surviving partner or partners may continue the business or the affairs may be wound up. If the former course is followed, the procedures for settling with the estate will conform to those outlined earlier for the withdrawal of a partner from the business.

LIQUIDATION OF A PARTNERSHIP

When a partnership goes out of business, it usually sells the assets, pays the creditors, and distributes the remaining cash or other assets to the partners according to their claims. The winding-up process may generally be called

liquidation. Although liquidation refers specifically to the payment of liabilities, it is often used in a broader sense to include the entire winding-up process.

When the ordinary business activities are discontinued as the partnership goes out of business, the accounts should be adjusted and closed according to the customary procedures of the periodic summary. The only accounts remaining open then will be the various asset, contra asset, liability, and owner's equity accounts.

The sale of the assets is called **realization.** As cash is realized, it is applied first to the payment of the claims of creditors. After all liabilities have been paid, the remaining cash is distributed to the partners, based on their ownership equities as indicated by their capital accounts.

If the assets are sold piecemeal, the liquidation process may extend over a considerable period of time. This situation creates no special problem, however, if the distribution of cash to the partners is delayed until all of the assets have been sold, as assumed in the following illustrations. As a basis for the illustrations, assume that Farley, Greene, and Hill share income and losses in a ratio of 5:3:2 (5/10, 3/10, 2/10). On April 9, after discontinuing the ordinary business operations of their partnership and closing the accounts, the following summary of the general ledger is prepared:

Cash...........................	$11,000	
Noncash Assets...................	64,000	
Liabilities		$ 9,000
Jane Farley, Capital		22,000
Brad Greene, Capital		22,000
Alice Hill, Capital.................		22,000
Total.........................	$75,000	$75,000

Based on these facts, accounting for the liquidation of the partnership will be illustrated using three different selling prices for the noncash assets. For the sake of brevity, it will be assumed for each selling price that all noncash assets are disposed of in a single transaction, and that all liabilities are paid at one time. In addition, Noncash Assets and Liabilities will be used as account titles in place of the various asset, contra asset, and liability accounts that in actual practice would be affected by the transactions.

Gain on Realization

Between April 10 and April 30 of the current year, Farley, Greene, and Hill sell all noncash assets for $72,000, realizing a gain of $8,000 ($72,000 − $64,000). The gain is divided among the capital accounts in the income-sharing ratio of 5:3:2. The liabilities are paid, and *the remaining cash is distributed to the partners according to the balances in their capital accounts.* A statement of partnership liquidation, which summarizes the liquidation process, follows:

	Cash	+	Noncash Assets	=	Liabilities	+	Capital		
							Farley (50%)	Greene (30%)	Hill (20%)
Balances before realization . . .	$11,000		$64,000		$9,000		$22,000	$22,000	$22,000
Sale of noncash assets and division of gain	+72,000		−64,000		—		+ 4,000	+ 2,400	+ 1,600
Balances after realization	$83,000		0		$9,000		$26,000	$24,400	$23,600
Payment of liabilities.	− 9,000		—		−9,000		—	—	—
Balances after payment of liabilities	$74,000		0		0		$26,000	$24,400	$23,600
Distribution of cash to partners .	−74,000		—		—		−26,000	−24,400	−23,600
Final balances	0		0		0		0	0	0

Farley, Greene, and Hill
Statement of Partnership Liquidation
For Period April 10–30, 19--

The entries to record the several steps in the liquidation procedure are as follows:

Sale of assets

Cash.	72,000	
Noncash Assets		64,000
Loss and Gain on Realization		8,000

Division of gain

Loss and Gain on Realization	8,000	
Jane Farley, Capital.		4,000
Brad Greene, Capital.		2,400
Alice Hill, Capital		1,600

Payment of liabilities

Liabilities	9,000	
Cash.		9,000

Distribution of cash to partners

Jane Farley, Capital.	26,000	
Brad Greene, Capital.	24,400	
Alice Hill, Capital	23,600	
Cash.		74,000

As shown in the foregoing statement of partnership liquidation, the distribution of the cash to the partners is determined by reference to the balances of their respective capital accounts after the gain on realization has been divided among the partners. *Under no circumstances should the income-sharing ratio be used as a basis for distributing the cash.*

Loss on Realization; No Capital Deficiencies

Assume that in the foregoing example, Farley, Greene, and Hill dispose of all noncash assets for $44,000, incurring a loss of $20,000 ($64,000 − $44,000). The various steps in the liquidation of the partnership are summarized in the following statement:

		Cash +	Noncash Assets	= Liabilities +	Capital		
					Farley (50%) +	Greene (30%) +	Hill (20%)
Balances before realization		$11,000	$64,000	$9,000	$22,000	$22,000	$22,000
Sale of assets and division of loss		+44,000	−64,000	—	−10,000	− 6,000	− 4,000
Balances after realization		$55,000	0	$9,000	$12,000	$16,000	$18,000
Payment of liabilities		− 9,000	—	−9,000	—	—	—
Balances after payment of liabilities		$46,000	0	0	$12,000	$16,000	$18,000
Distribution of cash to partners		−46,000	—	—	−12,000	−16,000	−18,000
Final balances		0	0	0	0	0	0

Farley, Greene, and Hill
Statement of Partnership Liquidation
For Period April 10–30, 19--

The entries to record the liquidation are as follows:

Sale of assets
Cash	44,000	
Loss and Gain on Realization	20,000	
Noncash Assets		64,000

Division of loss
Jane Farley, Capital	10,000	
Brad Greene, Capital	6,000	
Alice Hill, Capital	4,000	
Loss and Gain on Realization		20,000

Payment of liabilities
| Liabilities | 9,000 | |
| Cash | | 9,000 |

Distribution of cash to partners
Jane Farley, Capital................................	12,000	
Brad Greene, Capital...............................	16,000	
Alice Hill, Capital	18,000	
Cash...		46,000

Loss on Realization; Capital Deficiency

In the preceding illustration, the capital account of each partner was more than sufficient to absorb the appropriate share of the loss from realization. The partners shared in the distribution of cash to the extent of the remaining credit balance in their respective capital accounts. However, the share of the loss chargeable to a partner may be such that it exceeds that partner's ownership equity. The resulting debit balance in the capital account, called a **deficiency**, is a claim of the partnership against the partner. Pending collection from the deficient partner, the partnership cash will not be sufficient to pay the other partners in full. In such cases, the available cash should be distributed in such a manner that, if the claim against the deficient partner cannot be collected, each of the remaining capital balances will be sufficient to absorb the appropriate share of the deficiency.

To illustrate a situation of this type, assume that Farley, Greene, and Hill sell all of the noncash assets for $10,000, incurring a loss of $54,000 ($64,000 − $10,000). It is readily apparent that the part of the loss allocable to Farley, $27,000 (50% of $54,000), exceeds the $22,000 balance in Farley's capital account. This $5,000 deficiency of Farley is a potential deficiency to Greene and Hill and must be tentatively divided between them in their income-sharing ratio of 3:2 (3/5 and 2/5). The capital balances remaining represent their claims on the partnership cash. The computations may be summarized in the following manner:

	Capital			
	Farley (50%)	*Greene (30%)*	*Hill (20%)*	*Total*
Balances before realization......	$ 22,000	$ 22,000	$ 22,000	$ 66,000
Division of loss on realization....	−27,000	−16,200	−10,800	−54,000
Balances after realization	$− 5,000	$ 5,800	$ 11,200	$ 12,000
Division of potential additional deficiency	5,000	− 3,000	− 2,000	—
Claims to partnership cash......	0	$ 2,800	$ 9,200	$ 12,000

The various transactions that have occurred thus far in the liquidation are summarized in the following statement:

	Cash	+	Noncash Assets	=	Liabilities	+	Capital		
							Farley (50%) +	Greene (30%) +	Hill (20%)
Balances before realization	$11,000		$64,000		$9,000		$22,000	$22,000	$22,000
Sale of assets and division of loss.	+10,000		−64,000		—		−27,000	−16,200	−10,800
Balances after realization	$21,000		0		$9,000		$ 5,000 (Dr.)	$ 5,800	$11,200
Payment of liabilities............	− 9,000		—		−9,000		—	—	—
Balances after payment of liabilities	$12,000		0		0		$ 5,000 (Dr.)	$ 5,800	$11,200
Distribution of cash to partners ..	−12,000		—		—		—	− 2,800	− 9,200
Balances.....................	0		0		0		$ 5,000 (Dr.)	$ 3,000	$ 2,000

Farley, Greene, and Hill
Statement of Partnership Liquidation
For Period April 10–30, 19--

The entries to record the liquidation to this point are as follows:

Sale of assets

Cash..	10,000	
Loss and Gain on Realization........................	54,000	
Noncash Assets..................................		64,000

Division of loss

Jane Farley, Capital.................................	27,000	
Brad Greene, Capital................................	16,200	
Alice Hill, Capital	10,800	
Loss and Gain on Realization		54,000

Payment of liabilities

| Liabilities .... | 9,000 | |
| Cash... | | 9,000 |

Distribution of cash to partners

Brad Greene, Capital...............................	2,800	
Alice Hill, Capital	9,200	
Cash...		12,000

The affairs of the partnership are not completely wound up until the claims among the partners are settled. Payments to the firm by the deficient partner are credited to that partner's capital account. Any uncollectible deficiency becomes a loss to the partnership and is written off against the capital balances of the remaining partners. Finally, the cash received from the deficient partner is distributed to the other partners according to their ownership claims.

To continue with the preceding illustration, the capital balances remaining after the $12,000 cash distribution are as follows: Farley, $5,000 debit; Greene, $3,000 credit; Hill, $2,000 credit. The various steps in the final settlement and the entries for the partnership under three different assumptions as to the final settlement are illustrated in the following paragraphs.

Assumption 1:

Farley pays the entire amount of the $5,000 deficiency to the partnership (no loss).

The receipt of the $5,000 paid by Farley to the partnership and the distribution of the $5,000 to the partners are indicated in the following statement of partnership liquidation:

<table>
<tr><td colspan="9" align="center">Farley, Greene, and Hill
Statement of Partnership Liquidation
For Period April 10–30, 19--</td></tr>
<tr><td></td><td></td><td></td><td></td><td></td><td colspan="5" align="center">Capital</td></tr>
<tr><td></td><td>Cash</td><td>+</td><td>Noncash
Assets</td><td>= Liabilities +</td><td>Farley
(50%)</td><td>+</td><td>Greene
(30%)</td><td>+ Hill
(20%)</td></tr>
<tr><td>Balances.....................</td><td>0</td><td></td><td>0</td><td>0</td><td>$5,000 (Dr.)</td><td></td><td>$3,000</td><td>$2,000</td></tr>
<tr><td>Receipt of deficiency...........</td><td>+5,000</td><td></td><td>—</td><td>—</td><td>+5,000</td><td></td><td>—</td><td>—</td></tr>
<tr><td>Balances.....................</td><td>$5,000</td><td></td><td>0</td><td>0</td><td>0</td><td></td><td>$3,000</td><td>$2,000</td></tr>
<tr><td>Distribution of cash to partners ..</td><td>−5,000</td><td></td><td>—</td><td>—</td><td>—</td><td></td><td>−3,000</td><td>−2,000</td></tr>
<tr><td>Final balances.................</td><td>0</td><td></td><td>0</td><td>0</td><td>0</td><td></td><td>0</td><td>0</td></tr>
</table>

The entries to record the final settlement are as follows:

Receipt of deficiency
Cash..	5,000	
Jane Farley, Capital....................................		5,000

Distribution of cash to partners
Brad Greene, Capital....................................	3,000	
Alice Hill, Capital	2,000	
Cash..		5,000

After the two transactions above are completed, all of the partnership's assets will have been distributed, the liabilities paid, and the partner's capital balances reduced to zero.

Assumption 2:

Farley pays $3,000 of the deficiency to the partnership, and
the remainder is considered to be uncollectible ($2,000 loss).

The receipt of the $3,000 paid by Farley to the partnership, the division of the $2,000 loss, and the distribution of the $3,000 to the partners are indicated in the following statement of partnership liquidation:

					Capital		
	Cash +	Noncash Assets =	Liabilities +	Farley (50%) +	Greene (30%) +	Hill (20%)
Balances...........	0	0	0	$5,000 (Dr.)	$3,000	$2,000
Receipt of part of deficiency ..	+3,000	—	—	+3,000	—	—
Balances.................	$3,000	0	0	$2,000 (Dr.)	$3,000	$2,000
Division of loss	—	—	—	+2,000	−1,200	− 800
Balances.................	$3,000	0	0	0	$1,800	$1,200
Distribution of cash to partners .	−3,000	—	—	—	−1,800	−1,200
Final balances.............	0	0	0	0	0	0

Farley, Greene, and Hill
Statement of Partnership Liquidation
For Period April 10–30, 19--

It should be noted that the $2,000 loss was divided between Greene and Hill in their income-sharing ratio of 3:2 (3/5 and 2/5). The entries to record the final settlement are as follows:

Receipt of part of deficiency

| Cash... | 3,000 | |
| Jane Farley, Capital................................. | | 3,000 |

Division of loss

Brad Greene, Capital.................................	1,200	
Alice Hill, Capital	800	
Jane Farley, Capital.................................		2,000

Distribution of cash to partners

Brad Greene, Capital.................................	1,800	
Alice Hill, Capital	1,200	
Cash...		3,000

After the three transactions above are completed, all of the partnership's assets will have been distributed, the liabilities paid, and the partners' capital balances reduced to zero.

Assumption 3:

Farley is unable to pay any part of the $5,000 deficiency ($5,000 loss).

The division of the $5,000 loss is indicated in the following statement of partnership liquidation:

							Capital				
	Cash	+	Noncash Assets	=	Liabilities	+	Farley (50%)	+	Greene (30%)	+	Hill (20%)
Balances..............	0		0		0		$5,000 (Dr.)		$3,000		$2,000
Division of loss	—		—		—		+5,000		−3,000		−2,000
Final balances	0		0		0		0		0		0

Farley, Greene, and Hill
Statement of Partnership Liquidation
For Period April 10–30, 19--

The $5,000 loss was divided between Greene and Hill in their income-sharing ratio 3:2 (3/5 and 2/5). The entry to record this final step in the liquidation is as follows:

Division of loss
    Brad Greene, Capital..................................... 3,000
    Alice Hill, Capital 2,000
        Jane Farley, Capital....................................   5,000

After this transaction has been recorded, the partnership account balances will have been reduced to zero.

It should be noted that the type of error most likely to occur in the liquidation of a partnership is an improper distribution of cash to the partners. Errors of this type result from confusing the distribution of cash with the division of gains and losses on realization.

Gains and losses on realization result from the disposal of assets to outsiders. *These gains and losses represent changes in partnership equity and should be divided among the capital accounts in the same manner as net income or net loss from ordinary business operations, namely, in the income-sharing ratio.* On the other hand, the distribution of cash (or other assets) to the partners is an entirely different matter and has no direct relationship to the income-sharing ratio. The distribution of assets to the partners upon liquidation is the exact reverse of the contribution of assets by the partners at the time the partnership was established. The distribution of assets to the partners is *equal to the credit balances in their respective capital accounts* after all gains and losses on realization have been divided and proper allowance has been made for any potential deficiencies.

CHAPTER REVIEW

KEY POINTS

1. Characteristics of Partnerships.

Partnership characteristics that have accounting implications are: limited life, unlimited liability, co-ownership of property, mutual agency, and participation in income. In addition, a partnership is a nontaxable entity and is therefore not required to pay federal income taxes. Individual partners must report their distributive share of partnership income on their personal returns.

2. Advantages and Disadvantages of Partnerships.

The principal advantages of a partnership include the fact that it is easy and inexpensive to organize, brings together capital of one or more individuals, and is a nontaxable entity. The major disadvantages of a partnership are that its life is limited, each partner has unlimited liability, one partner can bind the partnership to contracts, and it may be difficult to raise large amounts of capital.

3. Accounting for Partnerships.

Most of the day-to-day accounting for partnerships is the same as the accounting for any other form of business organization. It is in the areas of formation, income distribution, dissolution, and liquidation of partnerships that transactions peculiar to partnerships arise.

4. Recording Investments.

To record the investment of each partner in a partnership, the various assets contributed by a partner are debited to the proper asset accounts, the liabilities assumed are credited to the appropriate liability accounts, and the partner's capital account is credited for the net amount. The monetary amounts at which noncash assets are stated are those agreed upon by the partners.

5. Division of Net Income or Net Loss.

The net income of a partnership can be divided among the partners in any manner agreed to by the partners. The net income is often divided on the basis of services rendered by individual partners and/or on the basis of the investments of the individual partners. In the absence of any agreement, net income is divided equally among the partners.

6. Statements for Partnerships.

Details of the division of partnership net income should be disclosed in the financial statements prepared at the end of the fiscal period. In addition, details of changes in the owner's equity of a partnership during the period should be presented in the statement of owner's equity.

7. Partnership Dissolution.

Any change in the personnel of ownership results in the dissolution of the partnership. However, dissolution of the partnership is not necessarily followed by a winding up of the affairs of the business. A partnership may be dissolved by admission of a new partner, withdrawal of a partner, or death of a partner.

8. Liquidation of a Partnership.

When a partnership goes out of business, it usually sells the noncash assets, pays the creditors, and distributes the remaining cash or other assets to the partners according to the balances of the partners' capital accounts. Any gain or loss on the realization of the assets should be allocated to the partners' capital accounts in the income-sharing ratio. The distribution of assets to the partners is equal to the credit balances in their respective capital accounts after all gains and losses on realization have been divided and proper allowance has been made for any potential losses.

KEY TERMS

articles of partnership 604
liquidation 616

realization 616
deficiency 619

SELF-EXAMINATION QUESTIONS
Answers in Appendix B.

1. As part of the initial investment, a partner contributes office equipment that had originally cost $20,000 and on which accumulated depreciation of $12,500 had been recorded. If the partners agree on a valuation of $9,000 for the equipment, what amount should be debited to the office equipment account?
   A. $7,500   C. $12,500
   B. $9,000   D. $20,000

2. X and Y agree to form a partnership. X is to contribute $50,000 in assets and to devote one-half time to the partnership. Y is to contribute $20,000 and to devote full time to the partnership. How will X and Y share in the division of net income or net loss?
   A. 5:2   C. 1:1
   B. 1:2   D. None of the above

3. X and Y invest $100,000 and $50,000 respectively in a partnership and agree to a division of net income that provides for an allowance of interest at 10% on original investments, salary allowances of $12,000 and $24,000 respectively, with the remainder divided equally. What would be X's share of a periodic net income of $45,000?
   A. $22,500   C. $19,000
   B. $22,000   D. $10,000

4. X and Y are partners who share income in the ratio of 2:1 and who have capital balances of $65,000 and $35,000 respectively. If P, with the consent of Y, acquired one half of X's interest for $40,000, for what amount would P's capital account be credited?
   A. $32,500   C. $50,000
   B. $40,000   D. None of the above

5. X and Y share gains and losses in the ratio of 2:1. After selling all assets for cash, dividing the losses on realization, and paying liabilities, the balances in the capital accounts were: X, $10,000 Cr.; Y, $2,000 Dr. How much of the cash would be distributed to X?
   A. $2,000   C. $10,000
   B. $8,000   D. $12,000

ILLUSTRATIVE PROBLEM

Ryan, Shaw, and Todd, who share in income and losses in the ratio of 4:2:4, decided to discontinue business operations as of April 30 and liquidate their partnership. After the accounts were closed on April 30, the following summary of the general ledger was prepared:

Cash	$ 8,100	
Noncash Assets	70,600	
Liabilities.....................................		$27,500
Ryan, Capital.................................		23,300
Shaw, Capital		12,100
Todd, Capital.................................		15,800
Total.......................................	$78,700	$78,700

Between May 1 and May 18, the noncash assets were sold for $20,600, and the liabilities were paid.

Instructions:

1. Assuming that the available cash is to be distributed to the partners, prepare a statement of partnership liquidation.
2. Present entries to record (a) the sale of the assets, (b) the division of loss on the sale of the assets, (c) the payment of the liabilities, and (d) the distribution of cash to the partners.
3. Assuming that Todd pays $2,400 of the deficiency to the partnership and the remainder is considered to be uncollectible, present entries to record (a) the receipt of part of the deficiency, (b) the division of loss, and (c) the distribution of cash to the partners.

SOLUTION

(1)

Ryan, Shaw, and Todd
Statement of Partnership Liquidation
For Period May 1–18, 19--

	Cash	+	Noncash Assets	=	Liabilities	+	Ryan (40%)	+	Shaw (20%)	+	Todd (40%)
									Capital		
Balances before realization ..	$ 8,100		$70,600		$27,500		$23,300		$12,100		$15,800
Sale of assets and division of loss..................	+20,600		−70,600		—		−20,000		−10,000		−20,000
Balances after realization....	$28,700		0		$27,500		$ 3,300		$ 2,100		$ 4,200 (Dr.)
Payment of liabilities	−27,500		—		−27,500		—		—		—
Balances after payment of liabilities................	$ 1,200		0		0		$ 3,300		$ 2,100		$ 4,200 (Dr.)
Distribution of cash to partners.................	− 1,200		—		—		− 500		− 700		—
Final balances,............	0		0		0		$ 2,800		$ 1,400		$ 4,200 (Dr.)

(2) (a) Cash.. 20,600
    Loss and Gain on Realization 50,000
        Noncash Assets........................ 70,600

(b) Ryan, Capital............................ 20,000
    Shaw, Capital............................ 10,000
    Todd, Capital............................ 20,000
        Loss and Gain on Realization   50,000

(c) Liabilities................................ 27,500
        Cash.................................   27,500

(d) Ryan, Capital............................   500
    Shaw, Capital............................   700
        Cash.................................   1,200

(3) (a) Cash..................................... 2,400
        Todd, Capital............................   2,400

(b) Ryan, Capital............................ 1,200
    Shaw, Capital............................   600
        Todd, Capital............................   1,800

(c) Ryan, Capital............................ 1,600
    Shaw, Captial............................   800
        Cash.................................   2,400

DISCUSSION QUESTIONS

1. Lisa Doherty and John Ellet joined together to form a partnership. Is it possible for them to lose a greater amount than the amount of their investment in the partnership enterprise? Explain.

2. Must a partnership (a) file a federal income tax return or (b) pay federal income taxes? Explain.

3. The partnership agreement between Weiss and Young provides for the sharing of partnership net income in the ratio of 2:1. Since the agreement is silent concerning the sharing of net losses, in what ratio will they be shared?

4. In the absence of an agreement, how will the net income be distributed between Joe Morris and Ann Peters, partners in the firm of Morris and Peters Consultants?

5. John Powers, John Rivera, and Bob Victor are contemplating the formation of a partnership. According to the partnership agreement, Powers is to invest $90,000 and devote one-half time, Rivera is to invest $50,000 and devote three-fourths time, and Victor is to make no investment and devote full time. Would Victor be correct in assuming that, since he is not contributing any assets to the firm, he is risking nothing? Explain.

6. As a part of the initial investment, a partner contributes delivery equipment that had originally cost $25,000 and on which accumulated depreciation of $17,500 had been recorded. The partners agree on a valuation of $10,000. How should the delivery equipment be recorded in the accounts of the partnership?

7. All partners agree that $100,000 of accounts receivable invested by a partner will be collectible to the extent of 80%. How should the accounts receivable be recorded in the general ledger of the partnership?

8. Martha Shaul and Barbara Towne are contemplating the formation of a partnership in which Shaul is to devote full time and Towne is to devote one-half time. In the absence of any agreement, will the partners share in net income or net loss in the ratio of 2:1? Explain.

9. (a) What accounts are debited or credited to record a partner's cash withdrawal in lieu of salary? (b) At the end of the fiscal year, what accounts are debited or credited to record the division of net income among partners? (c) The articles of partnership provide for a salary allowance of $4,000 per month to partner C. If C withdrew only $2,500 per month, would this affect the division of the partnership net income?

10. James Coe, a partner in the firm of Coe, Davis, and Edwards, sells his investment (capital balance of $75,000) to Loraine Yates. (a) Does the withdrawal of Coe dissolve the partnership? (b) Are Davis and Edwards required to admit Yates as a partner?

11. Explain the difference between the admission of a new partner to a partnership (a) by purchase of an interest from another partner and (b) by contribution of assets to the partnership.

12. Sue Ness and Frank Owens are partners who share in net income equally and have capital balances of $80,000 and $62,500 respectively. Ness, with the consent of Owens, sells one fourth of her interest to Joe Atles. What entry is required by the partnership if the sale price is (a) $20,000? (b) $30,000?

13. Why is it important to state all partnership assets in terms of current prices at the time of the admission of a new partner?

14. When a new partner is admitted to a partnership and goodwill is attributable to the old partnership, how should the amount of the goodwill be allocated to the capital accounts of the original partners?

15. Why might a partnership attribute goodwill to a newly admitted partner?

16. (a) Differentiate between *dissolution* and *liquidation* of a partnership. (b) What does *realization* mean when used in connection with liquidation of a partnership?

17. In the liquidation process, (a) how are losses and gains on realization divided among the partners, and (b) how is cash distributed among the partners?

18. Vance and Wallace are partners, sharing gains and losses equally. At the time they decide to terminate their partnership, their capital balances are $55,000 and $30,000 respectively. After all noncash assets are sold and all liabilities are paid, there is a cash balance of $70,000. (a) What is the amount of gain or loss on realization? (b) How should the gain or loss be divided between Vance and Wallace? (c) How should the cash be divided between Vance and Wallace?

19. Bowen, Carr, and Delbert share equally in net income and net loss. After the partnership sells all the assets for cash, divides the losses on realization, and pays the liabilities, the balances in the capital accounts are as follows: Bowen, $10,000 Cr.; Carr, $25,000 Cr.; Delbert, $9,000 Dr. (a) What is the amount of cash on hand? (b) How should the cash be distributed?

20. Power, Quinn, and Roberts are partners sharing income 3:2:1. After the firm's loss from liquidation is distributed, Power's capital account has a debit balance of $15,000. If Power is personally bankrupt and unable to pay any of the $15,000, how will the loss be divided between Quinn and Roberts?

21. Real World Focus. The national public accounting partnership of Deloitte, Haskins & Sells disclosed net income of $111,000,000 for the year ended June 1, 1985. The net income was attributable to 765 active partners, whose total capital as of June 1, 1985, was $116,000,000. (a) What was the average net income per active partner for the fiscal year ended June 1, 1985? (b) If the partners' total capital approximates the fair market value of the firm's net assets, what would be considered a minimum contribution for the admission of a new partner to the firm? (c) Why might the amount to be contributed by a new partner for admission to the firm exceed the amount determined in (b)?

EXERCISES

Exercise 14–1. Entry for partner's original investment. Alice Adams and Paul Baker decide to form a partnership by combining the assets of their separate businesses. Baker contributes the following assets to the partnership: cash, $8,500; accounts receivable with a face amount of $97,500 and an allowance for doubtful accounts of $8,500; merchandise inventory with a cost of $90,000; and equipment with a cost of $125,000 and accumulated depreciation of $70,000. The partners agree that $5,000 of the accounts receivable are completely worthless and are not to be accepted by the partnership, that $7,500 is a reasonable allowance for the uncollectibility of the remaining accounts, that the merchandise inventory is to be recorded at the current market price of $81,500, and that the equipment is to be priced at $75,000. Present the partnership's entry to record Baker's investment.

Exercise 14–2. Division of partnership income. John Martin and Larry North formed a partnership, investing $100,000 and $50,000 respectively. Determine their participation in the year's net income of $60,000 under each of the following assumptions: (a) no agreement concerning division of net income; (b) divided in the ratio of original capital investment; (c) interest at the rate of 12% allowed on original investments and the remainder divided in the ratio of 2:3; (d) salary allowances of $15,000 and $30,000 respectively, and the balance divided equally; (e) allowance of interest at the rate of 12% on original investments, salary allowances of $15,000 and $30,000 respectively, and the remainder divided equally.

Exercise 14–3. Division of partnership income. Determine the participation of Martin and North in the year's net income of $90,000, according to each of the five assumptions as to income division listed in Exercise 14–2.

Exercise 14–4. Partnership entries and statement of owner's equity. The capital accounts of Lee Lacy and Juan Marrino have balances of $75,000 and $95,000 respectively on January 1, the beginning of the current fiscal year. On March 1, Lacy invested an additional $15,000. During the year, Lacy and Marrino withdrew $36,000 and $42,000 respectively, and net income for the year was $80,000. The articles of partnership make no reference to the division of net income. (a) Present the journal entries to close (1) the income summary account and (2) the drawing accounts. (b) Prepare a statement of owner's equity for the current year.

Exercise 14–5. Admission of new partners. The capital accounts of Alan Evans and Mary Farr have balances of $60,000 and $100,000 respectively. Don Reese and Gloria Swain are to be admitted to the partnership. Reese purchases one fourth of Evans' interest for $22,500 and one fifth of Farr's interest for $30,000. Swain contributes $60,000 cash to the partnership, for which she is to receive an ownership equity of $60,000. (a) Present the entries to record the admission of (1) Reese and (2) Swain. (b) What are the capital balances of each partner after the admission of Reese and Swain?

Exercise 14–6. Withdrawal of partner. Alan Wicks is to retire from the partnership of Wicks and Associates as of July 31, the end of the current fiscal year. After closing the accounts, the capital balances of the partners are as follows: Alan Wicks, $200,000; Sandra Young, $125,000; and Ralph Zimmer, $140,000. They have shared net income and net losses in the ratio of 3:2:2. The partners agreed that the merchandise inventory should be increased by $7,000, and the allowance for doubtful accounts should be increased by $1,050. Wicks agreed to accept an interest-bearing note for

$150,000 in partial settlement of his ownership equity. The remainder of his claim is to be paid in cash. Young and Zimmer are to share equally in the net income or net loss of the new partnership. Present entries to record (a) the adjustment of the assets to bring them into agreement with current market prices, and (b) the withdrawal of Wicks from the partnership.

Exercise 14–7. Distribution of cash on liquidation. John Gann and Juan Herr, with capital balances of $51,000 and $36,000 respectively, decided to liquidate their partnership. After selling the noncash assets and paying the liabilities, there is $67,000 of cash remaining. If the partners share income and losses equally, how should the cash be distributed?

Exercise 14–8. Distribution of cash on liquidation. Ellen Gray, Elmer Hall, and Sam Ivey arranged to import and sell orchid corsages for a university dance. They agreed to share equally the net income or net loss on the venture. Gray and Hall advanced $175 and $125 of their own respective funds to pay for advertising and other expenses. After collecting for all sales and paying creditors, they have $525 in cash. (a) How should the money be distributed? (b) Assuming that they have only $150 instead of $525, how should the money be distributed? (c) Assuming that the money was distributed as determined in (b), do any of the three have claims against another? If so, how much?

Exercise 14–9. Statement of partnership liquidation. After closing the accounts on August 1, prior to liquidating the partnership, the capital account balances of Gertz, Hart, and Imes are $21,000, $26,000, and $13,000 respectively. Cash, noncash assets, and liabilities total $11,000, $79,000, and $30,000 respectively. Between August 1 and August 30, the noncash assets are sold for $49,000, the liabilities are paid, and the remaining cash is distributed to the partners. The partners share net income and loss in the ratio of 3:2:1. Prepare a statement of partnership liquidation for the period August 1–30.

PROBLEMS

Series A

Problem 14–1A. Division of partnership income. Martha Cole and Ann Dunn have decided to form a partnership. They have agreed that Cole is to invest $60,000 and that Dunn is to invest $90,000. Cole is to devote full time to the business and Dunn is to devote one-half time. The following plans for the division of income are being considered:

(a) Equal division.
(b) In the ratio of original investments.
(c) In the ratio of time devoted to the business.
(d) Interest of 10% on original investments and the remainder in the ratio of 3:2.
(e) Interest of 10% on original investments, salary allowances of $30,000 to Cole and $15,000 to Dunn, and the remainder equally.
(f) Plan (e), except that Cole is also to be allowed a bonus equal to 20% of the amount by which net income exceeds the salary allowances.

Instructions:

For each plan, determine the division of the net income under each of the following assumptions: (1) net income of $75,000; and (2) net income of $45,000. Present the data in tabular form, using the following columnar headings:

	$75,000		$45,000	
Plan	Cole	Dunn	Cole	Dunn

Problem 14–2A. Entries and balance sheet for partnership. On June 1 of the current year, Louis Alou and Ron Bowen form a partnership. Alou agrees to invest $10,000 cash and merchandise inventory valued at $55,000. Bowen invests certain business assets at valuations agreed upon, transfers business liabilities, and contributes sufficient cash to bring his total capital to $85,000. Details regarding the book values of the business assets and liabilities, and the agreed valuations, follow:

	Bowen's Ledger Balance	Agreed Valuation
Accounts Receivable..............................	$33,250	$30,500
Allowance for Doubtful Accounts	500	1,000
Merchandise Inventory	42,500	40,900
Equipment.......................................	50,000 }	27,750
Accumulated Depreciation—Equipment...............	29,700 }	
Accounts Payable	9,700	9,700
Notes Payable	10,000	10,000

The articles of partnership include the following provisions regarding the division of net income: interest of 10% on original investments, salary allowances of $24,000 and $18,000 respectively, and the remainder equally.

Instructions:

(1) Prepare the entries to record the investments of Alou and Bowen in the partnership accounts.
(2) Prepare a balance sheet as of June 1, the date of formation of the partnership.
(3) After adjustments and the closing of revenue and expense accounts at May 31, the end of the first full year of operations, the income summary account has a credit

balance of $65,000, and the drawing accounts have debit balances of $26,000 (Alou) and $17,500 (Bowen). Present the journal entries to close the income summary account and the drawing accounts at May 31.

Problem 14–3A.   Financial statements for partnership.

The ledger of Little and Morris, attorneys-at-law, contains the following accounts and balances after adjustments have been recorded on December 31, the end of the current fiscal year:

Cash	$ 19,500
Accounts Receivable	26,900
Supplies	1,400
Land	30,000
Building	125,000
Accumulated Depreciation—Building	69,200
Office Equipment	39,000
Accumulated Depreciation—Office Equipment	21,500
Accounts Payable	2,100
Salaries Payable	2,000
Roger Little, Capital	75,000
Roger Little, Drawing	60,000
Marsha Morris, Capital	55,000
Marsha Morris, Drawing	75,000
Professional Fees	265,650
Salary Expense	75,500
Depreciation Expense—Building	10,500
Property Tax Expense	8,000
Heating and Lighting Expense	7,900
Supplies Expense	2,850
Depreciation Expense—Office Equipment	2,800
Miscellaneous Expense	6,100

An additional investment of $5,000 was made by Morris on July 2 of the current year.

Instructions:

(1) Prepare an income statement for the current fiscal year, indicating the division of net income. The articles of partnership provide for salary allowances of $30,000 to Little and $40,000 to Morris; allowances of 12% on each partner's capital balance at the beginning of the fiscal year; and equal division of the remaining net income or net loss.
(2) Prepare a statement of owner's equity for the current fiscal year.
(3) Prepare a balance sheet as of the end of the current fiscal year.

Problem 14–4A.   Admission of new partner.

Ann Thorpe and Carol Unser have operated a successful firm for many years, sharing net income and net losses equally. Sue Baxter is to be admitted to the partnership on July 1 of the current year, in accordance with the following agreement:

(a) Assets and liabilities of the old partnership are to be valued at their book values as of June 30, except for the following:
- Accounts receivable amounting to $2,500 are to be written off, and the allowance for doubtful accounts is to be increased to 5% of the remaining accounts.
- Merchandise inventory is to be valued at $52,900.
- Equipment is to be valued at $95,000.

(b) Goodwill of $30,000 is to be recognized as attributable to the firm of Thorpe and Unser.

(c) Baxter is to purchase $20,000 of the ownership interest of Unser for $25,000 cash and to contribute $20,000 cash to the partnership for a total ownership equity of $40,000.

(d) The income-sharing ratio of Thorpe, Unser, and Baxter is to be 2:1:1.

The post-closing trial balance of Thorpe and Unser as of June 30 is as follows:

Thorpe and Unser
Post-Closing Trial Balance
June 30, 19--

Cash..	8,800	
Accounts Receivable................................	22,500	
Allowance for Doubtful Accounts		550
Merchandise Inventory	50,600	
Prepaid Insurance	750	
Equipment.......................................	145,000	
Accumulated Depreciation—Equipment................		65,000
Accounts Payable		12,100
Notes Payable		10,000
Ann Thorpe, Capital...............................		80,000
Carol Unser, Capital		60,000
	227,650	227,650

Instructions:

(1) Present journal entries as of June 30 to record the revaluations, using a temporary account entitled Asset Revaluations. The balance in the accumulated depreciation account is to be eliminated.

(2) Present the additional entries to record the remaining transactions relating to the formation of the new partnership. Assume that all transactions occur on July 1.

(3) Present a balance sheet for the new partnership as of July 1.

Problem 14–5A. Statement of partnership liquidation. After the accounts are closed on July 15, prior to liquidating the partnership, the capital accounts of Charles Kaps, Robert Ling, and Sara May are $27,800, $8,300, and $13,900 respectively. Cash and noncash assets total $6,500 and $89,100 respectively. Amounts owed to creditors total $45,600. The partners share income and losses in the ratio of 2:1:1. Between July 15 and July 30, the noncash assets are sold for $33,500, the partner with the capital deficiency pays his or her deficiency to the partnership, and the liabilities are paid.

Instructions:

Prepare a statement of partnership liquidation indicating (1) the sale of assets and division of loss, (2) the receipt of the deficiency (from the appropriate partner), and (3) the payment of liabilities.

If the working papers correlating with the textbook are not used, omit Problem 14–6A.

Problem 14–6A.   Partnership liquidation. John Hall, Frank Ides, and Lori Jain decided to discontinue business operations and liquidate their partnership. A summary of the various transactions that have occurred thus far is presented in the working papers in a partial statement of liquidation.

Instructions:

(1) Assuming that the available cash is to be distributed to the partners, complete the statement of partnership liquidation through the distribution of available cash to the partners.
(2) Present entries to record (a) the sale of assets, (b) the division of loss on the sale of assets, (c) the payment of liabilities, and (d) the distribution of cash to partners.
(3) Assuming that Ides pays $3,500 of his deficiency to the partnership and the remainder is considered to be uncollectible, complete the statement of partnership liquidation.
(4) Present entries to record (a) the receipt of part of the deficiency from Ides, (b) the division of loss, and (c) the distribution of cash to partners.

Problem 14–7A.   Statement of partnership liquidation. On May 1, the date the firm of Farr, Goss, and Hale decided to liquidate the partnership, the partners have capital balances of $100,000, $90,000, and $30,000 respectively. The cash balance is $20,000, the book values of noncash assets total $250,000, and liabilities total $50,000. The partners share income and losses in the ratio of 2:2:1.

Instructions:

Prepare a statement of partnership liquidation covering the period May 1 through May 30 for each of the following assumptions:

(1) All of the noncash assets are sold for $300,000 in cash, the creditors are paid, and the remaining cash is distributed to the partners.
(2) All of the noncash assets are sold for $150,000 in cash, the creditors are paid, and the remaining cash is distributed to the partners.
(3) All of the noncash assets are sold for $80,000 in cash, the creditors are paid, and the remaining cash is distributed to the partners. After the available cash is paid to the partners:
    (a) The partner with the debit capital balance pays the amount owed to the firm.
    (b) The additional cash is distributed.
(4) All of the noncash assets are sold for $70,000 in cash, the creditors are paid, and the remaining cash is distributed to the partners. After the available cash is paid to the partners:

(a) The partner with the debit capital balance pays 50% of his or her deficiency to the firm.
(b) The remaining partners absorb the remaining deficiency as a loss.
(c) The additional cash is distributed.

Series B

Problem 14–1B.   Division of partnership income. Chin and Dyke have decided to form a partnership. They have agreed that Chin is to invest $100,000 and that Dyke is to invest $50,000. Chin is to devote one-half time to the business and Dyke is to devote full time. The following plans for the division of income are being considered:

(a) Equal division.
(b) In the ratio of original investments.
(c) In the ratio of time devoted to the business.
(d) Interest of 12% on original investments and the remainder equally.
(e) Interest of 12% on original investments, salaries of $15,000 to Chin and $30,000 to Dyke, and the remainder equally.
(f) Plan (e), except that Dyke is also to be allowed a bonus equal to 20% of the amount by which net income exceeds the salary allowances.

Instructions:

For each plan, determine the division of the net income under each of the following assumptions: (1) net income of $45,000; (2) net income of $120,000. Present the data in tabular form, using the following columnar headings:

	$45,000		$120,000	
Plan	Chin	Dyke	Chin	Dyke

Problem 14–2B.   Entries and balance sheet for partnership. On July 1 of the current year, Chris Victor and Dave Walls form a partnership. Victor agrees to invest $10,500 in cash and merchandise inventory valued at $39,500. Walls invests certain business assets at valuations agreed upon, transfers business liabilities, and contributes sufficient cash to bring his total capital to $40,000. Details regarding the book values of the business assets and liabilities, and the agreed valuations, follow:

	Walls' Ledger Balance	Agreed Valuation
Accounts Receivable................................	$20,750	$19,500
Allowance for Doubtful Accounts	950	800
Equipment..	79,100	45,000
Accumulated Depreciation — Equipment................	35,200	
Accounts Payable	14,000	14,000
Notes Payable	15,000	15,000

The articles of partnership include the following provisions regarding the division of net income: interest on original investments at 10%, salary allowances of $18,000 and $21,000 respectively, and the remainder equally.

Instructions:

(1) Prepare the entries to record the investments of Victor and Walls in the partnership accounts.
(2) Prepare a balance sheet as of July 1, the date of formation of the partnership.
(3) After adjustments and the closing of revenue and expense accounts at June 30, the end of the first full year of operations, the income summary account has a credit balance of $68,000, and the drawing accounts have debit balances of $18,000 (Victor) and $24,000 (Walls). Present the journal entries to close the income summary account and the drawing accounts at June 30.

Problem 14–5B. Statement of partnership liquidation. After the accounts are closed on March 5, prior to liquidating the partnership, the capital accounts of Nancy Ames, Mary Betts, and Sue Cone are $20,000, $3,900, and $10,000 respectively. Cash and noncash assets total $1,900 and $62,000 respectively. Amounts owed to creditors total $30,000. The partners share income and losses in the ratio of 2:1:1. Between March 5 and March 25, the noncash assets are sold for $22,000, the partner with the capital deficiency pays her deficiency to the partnership, and the liabilities are paid.

Instructions:

Prepare a statement of partnership liquidation, indicating (1) the sale of assets and division of loss, (2) the receipt of the deficiency (from the appropriate partner), and (3) the payment of liabilities.

If the working papers correlating with the textbook are not used, omit Problem 14–6B.

Problem 14–6B. Partnership liquidation. John Hall, Frank Ides, and Lori Jain decided to discontinue business operations and liquidate their partnership. A summary of the various transactions that have occurred thus far is presented in the working papers in a partial statement of liquidation.

(1) Assuming that the available cash is to be distributed to the partners, complete the statement of partnership liquidation through the distribution of available cash to partners.
(2) Present entries to record (a) the sale of assets, (b) the division of loss on the sale of assets, (c) the payment of liabilities, and (d) the distribution of cash to partners.
(3) Assuming that Ides pays $2,100 of his deficiency to the partnership and the remainder is considered to be uncollectible, complete the statement of partnership liquidation.
(4) Present entries to record (a) the receipt of part of the deficiency from Ides, (b) the division of loss, and (c) the distribution of cash to partners.

MINI-CASE 14

& COMPANY

Sharon Lin and John Marr formed L and M Company as a partnership ten years ago by each contributing $50,000 in capital. The partnership agreement indicated the following division of net income: salary allowances of $20,000 and $30,000 to Lin and Marr respectively, and all remaining net income divided equally.

Marr recently expressed concern with the manner in which profits are being divided. Specifically, the profit-sharing agreement did not consider changes in the amounts invested by each partner as reflected in the balances of their capital accounts. Over the years, Lin has consistently withdrawn more from the partnership than Marr, with the result that the capital balances as of January 1, 1988, indicated an investment of $160,000 by Lin and $290,000 by Marr.

Lin agreed with Marr that a change in the profit-sharing agreement was warranted and accordingly proposed the following two alternatives:

Proposal I
(a) The salary allowances of Lin and Marr would be increased to $30,000 and $45,000 respectively.
(b) Interest of 10% would be allowed on the January 1 balances of the capital accounts.
(c) All remaining income would be divided equally.

Proposal II
(a) The salary allowances of Lin and Marr would not be changed.
(b) No interest would be allowed on the capital balances.
(c) Marr would be allowed a bonus of 20% of the amount by which net income exceeds salary allowances, and the remainder would be divided equally.

Marr has asked for your advice on which of the two proposals he should accept.

Instructions:

(1) For each proposal, prepare an analysis of the distribution of net income between Lin and Marr for 1988 for net income levels of $100,000, $140,000, and $200,000.

(2) Which proposal would you recommend that Marr accept?

(3) Anna Chung has offered to purchase for $200,000 a one-third interest in the partnership capital and net income. Assuming that the net tangible assets of the partnership approximate their fair market values at January 1, 1988, how much total goodwill for the partnership is implied by Chung's offer?

CORPORATIONS

Part

5

Chapter **15**

CORPORATIONS: ORGANIZATION AND OPERATION

Chapter Objectives:

■ Identify basic corporation characteristics which have accounting implications.

■ Describe and illustrate the accounting for stockholders' equity.

■ Describe and illustrate the computation of equity per share of stock.

■ Describe and illustrate the accounting for organization costs.

I n the Dartmouth College case in 1819, Chief Justice Marshall stated: "A corporation is an artificial being, invisible, intangible, and existing only in contemplation of the law." The concept underlying this definition has become the foundation for the prevailing legal doctrine that a corporation is an artificial person, created by law and having a distinct existence separate and apart from the natural persons who are responsible for its creation and operation. Almost all large business enterprises in the United States are organized as corporations.

Corporations may be classified as **nonprofit** or **profit**. Nonprofit corporations include those organized for recreational, educational, charitable, or other philanthropic purposes. For their continuation, they depend upon dues from their members or upon gifts and grants from the public at large. Other nonprofit corporations include those which render services to the public for a fee, such as cooperative-owned utility companies, but whose objective is rendering services to the public on a cost basis rather than earning a profit.[1]

Profit corporations are engaged in business activities. They depend upon profitable operations for their continued existence. Large, profit corporations whose shares of stock are widely distributed and traded in a public market are often called **public corporations**. Corporations whose shares are owned by a small group are often called **nonpublic corporations**. Regardless of their nature or purpose, profit corporations are created according to state or federal statutes and are separate legal entities.

CHARACTERISTICS OF A CORPORATION

As a legal entity, the corporation has certain characteristics that make it different from other types of business organizations. The most important

---

[1]Nonprofit organizations are discussed in more detail in Chapter 28.

charactistics with accounting implications are described briefly in the following paragraphs.

A corporation has a **separate legal existence**. It may acquire, own, and dispose of property in its corporate name. It may also incur liabilities and enter into other types of contracts according to the provisions of its **charter** (also called **articles of incorporation**).

The ownership of a corporation, of which there may be several categories or classes, is divided into **transferable units** known as **shares of stock**. Each share of stock of a certain class has the same rights and privileges as every other share of the same class. The owners of the corporation, or **stockholders** (also called **shareholders**), may buy and sell shares without interfering with the activities of the corporation. The millions of transactions that occur daily on stock exchanges are independent transactions between buyers and sellers. Thus, in contrast to the partnership, the existence of the corporation is not affected by changes in ownership.

The stockholders of a corporation have **limited liability**. A corporation is responsible for its own acts and obligations, and therefore its creditors usually may not look beyond the assets of the corporation for satisfaction of their claims. Thus, the financial loss that a stockholder may suffer is limited to the amount invested. The phenomenal growth of the corporate form of business would not have been possible without this limited liability feature.

The stockholders, who are, in fact, the owners of the corporation, exercise control over the management of corporate affairs indirectly by electing a **board of directors**. It is the responsibility of the board of directors to meet from time to time to determine the corporate policies and to select the officers who manage the corporation. The following chart shows the **organizational structure** of a corporation:

ORGANIZATIONAL STRUCTURE OF A CORPORATE ENTERPRISE

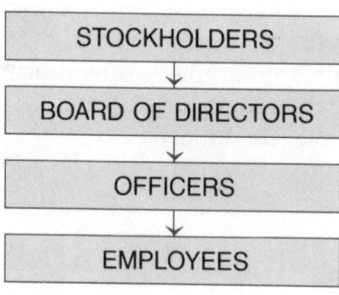

As a separate entity, a corporation is subject to **additional taxes**. It must pay a charter fee to the state at the time of its organization and annual taxes thereafter. If the corporation does business in states other than the one in which it is incorporated, it may also be required to pay annual taxes to such states. The earnings of a corporation may also be subject to a state income tax.

The earnings of a corporation are subject to the federal income tax. When the remaining earnings are distributed to stockholders as dividends, they are again taxed as income to the individuals receiving them. Under certain conditions specified in the Internal Revenue Code, a corporation with a few stockholders may elect to be treated in a manner similar to a partnership for income tax purposes. A corporation electing this optional treatment does not pay federal income taxes. Instead, its stockholders include their distributive shares of corporate income in their own taxable income, regardless of whether the income is distributed to them.

Being a creature of the state and being owned by stockholders who have limited liability, a corporation has less freedom of action than a sole proprietorship and a partnership. There may be **government regulations** in such matters as ownership of real estate, retention of earnings, and purchase of its own stock.

STOCKHOLDERS' EQUITY

The owners' equity in a corporation is commonly called **stockholders' equity, shareholders' equity, shareholders' investment**, or **capital**. The two main sources of stockholders' equity are (1) investments contributed by the stockholders, called **paid-in capital** or **contributed capital**, and (2) net income retained in the business, called **retained earnings**. As shown in the following illustration, the stockholders' equity section of corporation balance sheets is divided into subsections based on these two sources.

Stockholders' Equity

Paid-in capital:	
Common stock	$330,000
Retained earnings	80,000
Total stockholders' equity	$410,000

The paid-in capital contributed by the stockholders is recorded in accounts maintained for each class of stock. If there is only one class of stock, the account is entitled Common Stock or Capital Stock.

The retained earnings amount results from transferring the balance in the income summary account (the net income) to a retained earnings account at the end of a fiscal year. The dividends account, to which distributions of earnings to stockholders have been debited, is also closed to Retained Earnings. If the occurrence of net losses results in a debit balance in Retained Earnings, it is termed a **deficit**. In the stockholders' equity section of the balance sheet, a deficit is deducted from paid-in capital to determine total stockholders' equity.

There are a number of acceptable variants of the term "retained earnings," among which are *earnings retained for use in the business, earnings reinvested in the business, earnings employed in the business,* and *accumulated earnings.* For many years, the term applied to retained earnings was *earned surplus.* However, the use of this term in published financial statements has generally been discontinued.[2] Because of its connotation as an excess, or something left over, "surplus" was sometimes erroneously interpreted by readers of financial statements to mean "cash available for dividends."

CHARACTERISTICS OF STOCK

The general term applied to the shares of ownership of a corporation is **capital stock**. The number of shares that a corporation is *authorized* to issue is set forth in its charter. The term *issued* is applied to the shares issued to the stockholders. A corporation may, under circumstances discussed later in the chapter, reacquire some of the stock that it has issued. The stock remaining in the hands of the stockholders is then referred to as the stock outstanding.

The shares of capital stock are often assigned an arbitrary monetary figure, known as **par**. The par amount is printed on the **stock certificate**, which is the evidence of ownership issued to the stockholder. Stock may also be issued without par, in which case it is called **no-par** stock. Many states provide that the board of directors must assign a **stated value** to no-par stock, which makes it similar to par stock.

Because of the limited liability feature, the creditors of a corporation have no claim against the personal assets of stockholders. However, the law requires that some specific minimum contribution by the stockholders be retained by the corporation for the protection of its creditors. This amount, called **legal capital**, varies among the states but usually includes the par or stated value of the shares of capital stock issued.

Classes of Stock

The major basic rights that accompany ownership of a share of stock are (1) the right to vote in matters concerning the corporation, (2) the right to share in distributions of earnings, (3) the **preemptive right**, which is the right to maintain the same fractional interest in the corporation by purchasing a

---

[2]*Accounting Research and Terminology Bulletins—Final Edition.* "Accounting Terminology Bulletins, No. 1, Review and Résumé" (New York: American Institute of Certified Public Accountants, 1961), par. 65–69.

proportionate number of shares of any additional issuances of stock[3] and (4) the right to share in assets upon liquidation.

If a corporation issues only **common stock**, each share generally has equal rights. In order to appeal to a broader investment market, a corporation may provide for one or more classes of stock with various preferential rights. The preference usually relates to the right to share in distributions of earnings. Such stock is generally called **preferred stock**.

The board of directors has the sole authority to distribute earnings to the stockholders. When such action is taken, the directors are said to *declare a dividend*. A corporation cannot guarantee that its operations will be profitable and hence it cannot guarantee dividends to its stockholders. Furthermore, the directors have wide discretionary powers in determining the extent to which earnings should be retained by the corporation to provide for expansion, to offset possible future losses, or to provide for other contingencies.

A corporation with both preferred stock and common stock may declare dividends on the common only after it meets the requirements of the stated dividend on the preferred (which may be stated in monetary terms or as a percent of par). To illustrate, assume that a corporation has 1,000 shares of $10 preferred stock (that is, the preferred has a prior claim to an annual $10 per share dividend) and 4,000 shares of common stock outstanding. Assume also that in the first three years of operations, net income was $30,000, $55,000, and $100,000 respectively. The directors authorize the retention of a portion of each year's earnings and the distribution of the remainder. Details of the dividend distribution are presented in the following tabulation:

	First Year	Second Year	Third Year
Net income	$30,000	$55,000	$100,000
Amount retained	10,000	20,000	40,000
Amount distributed	$20,000	$35,000	$ 60,000
Preferred dividend (1,000 shares)	10,000	10,000	10,000
Common dividend (4,000 shares)	$10,000	$25,000	$ 50,000
Dividends per share:			
Preferred	$10.00	$10.00	$10.00
Common	$ 2.50	$ 6.25	$12.50

Participating and Nonparticipating Preferred Stock

In the foregoing illustration, the holders of preferred stock received an annual dividend of $10 per share, in contrast to the common stockholders,

---

[3]In recent years the stockholders of a significant number of corporations have, by formal action, given up their preemptive rights.

whose annual per share dividends were $2.50, $6.25, and $12.50 respectively. It is apparent from the example that holders of preferred stock have relatively greater assurance than common stockholders of receiving dividends regularly. On the other hand, holders of common stock have the possibility of receiving larger dividends than preferred stockholders. The preferred stockholders' preferential right to dividends is usually limited to a certain amount, which was assumed to be the case in the preceding example. Such stock is said to be **nonparticipating.**

Preferred stock which provides for the possibility of dividends in excess of a certain amount is said to be **participating.** Preferred shares may participate with common shares to varying degrees, and the agreement with the shareholders must be examined to determine the extent of this participation. To illustrate, assume that the contract covering the preferred stock of the corporation in the preceding illustration provides that if the total dividends to be distributed exceed the regular preferred dividend and a comparable dividend on common, the preferred shall share in the excess ratably on a share-for-share basis with the common. According to such terms, the $60,000 dividend distribution in the third year would be allocated as follows:

	Preferred Dividend	Common Dividend	Total Dividends
Regular dividend to preferred (1,000 × $10).........................	$10,000	—	$10,000
Comparable dividend to common (4,000 × $10).........................	—	$40,000	40,000
Remainder to 5,000 shares ratably ($2 per share).........................	2,000	8,000	10,000
Total	$12,000	$48,000	$60,000
Dividends per share	$12	$12	

Cumulative and Noncumulative Preferred Stock

As was indicated in the preceding section, most preferred stock is nonparticipating. Provision is usually made, however, to assure the continuation of the preferential dividend right if at any time the directors *pass* (do not declare) the usual dividend. The preferential dividend right is assured by providing that dividends may not be paid on the common stock if any preferred dividends have been passed (are in *arrears*). Such preferred stock is said to be **cumulative.** To illustrate, assume that a corporation has outstanding 5,000 shares of cumulative preferred 9% stock of $100 par (that is, the preferred stockholders have a prior claim to an annual 9% dividend, or $9 per share). In addition, assume that dividends have been passed for the preceding two years. In the current year, no dividend may be declared on the common stock unless the directors first declare preferred dividends of $90,000 for the past two years and $45,000 for the current year. Preferred stock not having this cumulative right is called **noncumulative**.

Other Preferential Rights

Thus far the discussion of preferential rights of preferred stock has related to dividend distributions. Preferred stock may also be given a preference in its claim to assets upon liquidation of the corporation. If the assets remaining after payment of creditors are not sufficient to return the capital contributions of both classes of stock, payment would first be made to the preferred stockholders and any balance remaining would go to the common stockholders. Another difference between preferred and common stock is that the former may have no voting rights. A corporation may also have more than one class of preferred stock, with differences as to the amount of dividends, priority of claims upon liquidation, and voting rights. In any particular case, the rights of a class of stock may be determined by reference to the charter, the stock certificate, or some other abstract of the agreement.

ISSUING STOCK

The entries to record investments of stockholders in a corporation are like those for investments by owners of other types of business organizations, in that cash and other assets received are debited and any liabilities assumed are credited. The credit to stockholders' equity differs, however, in that there are accounts for each class of stock. To illustrate, assume that a corporation, with an authorization of 10,000 shares of preferred stock of $100 par and 100,000 shares of common stock of $20 par, issues one half of each authorization at par for cash. The entry to record the stockholders' investment and the receipt of the cash is as follows:

Cash.	1,500,000	
Preferred Stock.		500,000
Common Stock.		1,000,000

The capital stock accounts (Preferred Stock, Common Stock) are controlling accounts. It is necessary to maintain records of each stockholder's name, address, and number of shares held in order to issue dividend checks, proxy forms, and financial reports. Individual stockholders accounts are kept in a subsidiary ledger known as the **stockholders ledger**.

Par stock is often issued by a corporation at a price other than par. When it is issued for more than par, the excess of the contract price over par is termed a **premium** on stock. When it is issued at a price that is below par, the difference is called a **discount** on stock. Thus, if stock with a par of $50 is issued at $60, the amount of the premium is $10. If the same stock is issued at $45, the amount of the discount is $5.

Theoretically, there is no reason for a newly organized corporation to issue stock at a price other than par. The par designation is merely a part of the plan of dividing owners' equity into a number of units of ownership. Hence, a group of persons investing their funds in a new corporation might all be expected to pay par for the shares. The fortunes of an enterprise do not remain the same, however, even when it is still in the process of organizing. The changing prospects for its future success may affect the price per share at which the incorporators can secure other investors.

A need for additional paid-in capital may arise long after a corporation has become established. Losses during prior fiscal periods may have depleted operating funds or the operations may have been successful enough to warrant a substantial expansion of plant and equipment. If the funds are to be obtained by the issuance of additional stock, it is apparent that the current price at which the original stock is selling in the market will affect the price that can be obtained for the new shares.

Generally speaking, the price at which stock can be sold by a corporation is influenced by (1) the financial condition, the earnings record, and the dividend record of the corporation, (2) its potential earning power, (3) the availability of money for investment purposes, and (4) general business and economic conditions and prospects.

Premium on Stock

When capital stock is issued at a premium, cash or other assets are debited for the amount received. The stock account is then credited for the par amount, and a premium account, sometimes called Paid-In Capital in Excess of Par, is credited for the amount of the premium. For example, if Caldwell Company issues 2,000 shares of $50 par preferred stock for cash at $55, the entry to record the transaction would be as follows:

Cash..	110,000	
Preferred Stock....................................		100,000
Premium on Preferred Stock.......................		10,000

The premium of $10,000 is a part of the investment of the stockholders and is therefore a part of paid-in capital. It is distinguished from the capital stock account because usually it is not a part of legal capital and in many states may be used as a basis for dividends to stockholders. However, if the premium is returned to stockholders as a dividend at a later date, it should be emphasized that the dividend is a return of paid-in capital rather than a distribution of earnings.

Discount on Stock

Some states do not permit the issuance of stock at a discount. In others, it may be done only under certain conditions. When stock is issued at less than its par, it is considered to be fully paid as between the corporation and the stockholder. In some states, however, the stockholders are contingently liable to creditors for the amount of the discount. If the corporation is liquidated and there are not enough assets to pay creditors in full, the stockholders may be assessed for an additional contribution up to the amount of the discount on their stock.

When capital stock is issued at a discount, cash or other assets are debited for the amount received, and a discount account is debited for the amount of the discount. The capital stock account is then credited for the par amount. For example, if Caldwell Company issues 20,000 shares of $25 par common stock for cash at $23, the entry to record the transaction would be as follows:

Cash..	460,000	*— issue price*
Discount on Common Stock	40,000	
Common Stock.....................................		500,000

The discount of $40,000 is a contra paid-in capital account and must be offset against Common Stock to arrive at the amount actually invested by the holders of common stock. The discount is not an asset, nor should it be amortized against revenue as though it were an expense.

Premiums and Discounts on the Balance Sheet

The manner in which premiums and discounts may be presented in the stockholders' equity section of the balance sheet is illustrated as follows, based on the two illustrative entries for Caldwell Company:

Stockholders' Equity

$5.00   *10% percentage of par value*

Paid-in capital:		
Preferred 10% stock, cumulative, $50 par		
(2,000 shares authorized and issued)..	$100,000	
Premium on preferred stock...........	10,000	$110,000
Common stock, $25 par (50,000 shares		
authorized, 20,000 shares issued)....	$500,000	
Less discount on common stock	40,000	460,000
Total paid-in capital.................		$570,000
Retained earnings		175,000
Total stockholders' equity.............		$745,000

issued for more than par

The following stockholders' equity section illustrates the reporting of a deficit and some differences in terminology from that in the foregoing example:

Shareholders' Equity

Paid-in capital:		
Preferred $3 stock, cumulative, $25 par (10,000 shares authorized and issued).........	$ 250,000	
Excess of issuance price over par..	20,000	$ 270,000
Common stock, $10 par (200,000 shares authorized, 100,000 shares issued)	$1,000,000	
Less excess of par over issuance price	100,000	900,000
Total paid in by stockholders ...		$1,170,000
Less deficit		75,000
Total shareholders' equity		$1,095,000

[handwritten margin notes: excess = premium; deficit = discount]

Issuing Stock for Assets Other Than Cash

When capital stock is issued in exchange for assets other than cash, such as land, buildings, and equipment, the assets acquired should be recorded at their fair market price or at the fair market price of the stock issued, whichever is more objectively determinable. The determination of the values to be assigned to the assets is the responsibility of the board of directors.

As a basis for illustration, assume that a corporation acquired land for which the fair market price is not determinable. In exchange, the corporation issued 10,000 shares of its $10 par common stock with a current market price of $12 per share. The transaction could be recorded as follows:

Dec. 5	Land......................................	120,000	
	Common Stock		100,000
	Premium on Common Stock.............		20,000

No-Par Stock

In the early days of rapid industrial expansion and increasing use of the corporate form of business organization, it was customary to assign a par of $100 to shares of stock. It is not surprising that unsophisticated investors, mistakenly considering "par value" to be the equivalent of "value," were often induced to invest in mining and other highly speculative enterprises by the simple means of being offered $100 par stock at "bargain" prices. Another misleading practice was the use of par in assigning highly inflated values to assets acquired in exchange for stock. For example, stock with a total par of $1,000,000 might be issued in exchange for patents, mineral rights, or other properties with a conservatively estimated value of $50,000. The assets would be recorded at the full par of $1,000,000, whereas in reality the stock had been issued at a discount of $950,000. Balance sheets that were "window-dressed" in this manner were obviously deceptive.

To combat such abuses and also to eliminate the troublesome discount liability of stockholders, stock without par was conceived. The issuance of stock without par was first permitted by New York in 1912. Its use is now authorized in nearly all of the states.

Over the years, questionable practices in the issuance of securities have been virtually eliminated. Today federal and state laws and rules imposed by organized stock exchanges and governmental agencies such as the Securities and Exchange Commission combine to protect the investor from misrepresentations that were common in earlier days.

In most states, both preferred and common stock may be issued without a par designation. However, preferred stock is usually assigned a par. When no-par stock is issued, the entire proceeds may be credited to the capital stock account, even though the issuance price varies from time to time. For example, if at the time of organization a corporation issues no-par common stock at $40 a share and at a later date issues additional shares at $36, the entries would be as follows:

1. *Original issuance of 10,000 shares of no-par common at $40:*

Cash	400,000	
Common Stock		400,000

2. *Subsequent issuance of 1,000 shares of no-par common at $36:*

Cash	36,000	
Common Stock		36,000

The laws of some states require that the entire proceeds from the issuance of no-par stock be regarded as legal capital. The preceding entries conform to this principle, which also conforms to the original concept of no-par stock. In other states, no-par stock may be assigned a stated value per share, and the excess of the proceeds over the stated value may be credited to Paid-In Capital in Excess of Stated Value. Assuming that in the previous example the stated value is $25 and the board of directors wishes to credit the common stock for stated value, the transactions would be recorded as follows:

1. *Original issuance of 10,000 shares of no-par common, stated value $25, at $40:*

Cash	400,000	
Common Stock		250,000
Paid-In Capital in Excess of Stated Value		150,000

2. *Subsequent issuance of 1,000 shares of no-par common, stated value $25, at $36:*

Cash	36,000	
Common Stock		25,000
Paid-In Capital in Excess of Stated Value		11,000

It is readily apparent that the accounting for no-par stock with a stated value may follow the same pattern as the accounting for par stock.

SUBSCRIPTIONS AND STOCK ISSUANCE *temporary account*

In some situations involving the initial issue of capital stock or subsequent issuances where the stockholders have waived the preemptive right, a corporation may sell its stock to an **underwriter**. The underwriter then resells the shares to investors at a price high enough to earn a profit from the sale. Under these circumstances, the corporation is relieved of the task of marketing the stock. It receives the entire amount of cash without delay and can proceed immediately with its plans for the use of the funds.

In other situations, a corporation may sell its stock directly to investors or others, such as employees, under stock purchase plans. In such cases, the buyer may enter into an agreement with the corporation to subscribe to shares at a certain price per share. The terms may provide for payment in full at some future date or for installment payments over a period of time.

When stock is subscribed for at par, the subscription price is debited to the asset account Stock Subscriptions Receivable and credited to the capital stock account Stock Subscribed. When stock is subscribed for at a price above or below par, the stock subscriptions receivable account is debited for the subscription price. The stock subscribed account is credited at par, and the difference between the subscription price and par is debited to a discount account or credited to a premium account, as the case may be.

After a subscriber has completed the agreed payments, the corporation issues the stock certificate. The stock subscribed account is then debited for the total par of the shares issued, and the capital stock account is credited for the same amount.

As the basis for illustrating the entries for subscriptions and stock issuance, assume that the newly organized Ledway Corporation receives subscriptions, collects cash, and issues stock certificates according to the following transactions. The required entries appear after the statement of the transaction.

1. *Received subscriptions to 10,000 shares of $20 par common stock from various subscribers at $21 per share, with a down payment of 50% of the subscription price.*

[handwritten margin note: preemptive right: right of each shareholder to maintain the same fractional interest in the corp. by purchasing a proportionate number of any additional issuance of stock.]

? temporary accts

Mar. 1	Common Stock Subscriptions Receivable . . . . . *recorded for par*	210,000	
	Common Stock Subscribed. . . .		200,000
	Premium on Common Stock.		10,000
1	Cash	105,000	
	Common Stock Subscriptions Receivable . .		105,000

2. Received 25% of subscription price from all subscribers.

| May 1 | Cash . . . . | 52,500 | |
| | Common Stock Subscriptions Receivable . . | | 52,500 |

3. Received final 25% of subscription price from all subscribers and issued the stock certificates.

July 1	Cash	52,500	
	Common Stock Subscriptions Receivable . .		52,500
1	Common Stock Subscribed.	200,000	
	Common Stock		200,000

premanent account

A balance sheet prepared after the transactions of March 1 would list the subscriptions receivable as a current asset and the stock subscribed and the premium as paid-in capital. While it is true that the entire amount has not been "paid in" in cash, the claim against the subscribers is an asset of equivalent value. The presentation of the items in the balance sheet of the Ledway Corporation as of March 1 is as follows:

Ledway Corporation Balance Sheet March 1, 19--			
Assets		**Stockholders' Equity**	
Current assets:		Paid-in capital:	
Cash.	$105,000	Common stock *temporary acct*	
Common stock subscrip-		subscribed	$200,000
tions receivable . . . . . . *temporary acct*	105,000	Premium on common	
		stock.	10,000
Total assets.	$210,000	Total stockholders' equity.	$210,000

The stock subscriptions receivable account is a controlling account. The individual accounts with each subscriber are maintained in a subsidiary ledger known as a **subscribers ledger**. It is used in much the same manner as the accounts receivable ledger.

After all the subscriptions have been collected, the common stock subscriptions receivable account will have a zero balance. The stock certificates will then be issued and the common stock subscribed account will have a zero balance. The ultimate effect of the series of transactions is a debit to Cash of $210,000, a credit to Common Stock of $200,000, and a credit to Premium on Common Stock of $10,000.

End to Paper Stock Certificates

Securities and Exchange Commission Chairman John Shad is doing his best to go down in history as the man who pushed the mysterious business of issuing and selling securities into the computer era. In speeches, personal letters, and meetings, Mr. Shad has been jawboning issuers and dealers, urging them to adopt computerized "book entry" clearing systems. Mr. Shad acknowledges that his goal — complete elimination of the paper certificate — won't come any time soon. His ideal is to limit each security issue to a single, "global" certificate that would rest, forever immobilized, in a central depository. All sales and purchases of the issue would be tracked by computer.

"Billion-dollar benefits," Mr. Shad says, "will be realized by gradually turning off the flow of new paper into the system." The SEC says computerized clearing would cost brokers six to 10 times less than physically transferring certificates from sellers to buyers.

Mr. Shad promises book-entry systems will improve the market's speed, simplicity, and safety. Certificates, he says, waste time and energy. "They are inspected, counted, and sorted over and over again, repackaged and sent by couriers and insured mail to investors and depositories, and stored in vaults and safety deposit boxes. Millions of dollars of securities are counterfeited, lost, stolen, and accidentally mutilated and destroyed annually."

Issuers agree. "It's a real pain in the neck to print certificates," says Weyland F. Blood, vice president and treasurer of Ford Motor Credit Co.

Many issuers worry that investors might balk at buying book-entry securities, making it more difficult to sell the issue. "All other things being equal, Citicorp favors the book-entry notion," says Robert M. Butcher, vice president. But he would want to find out if the lack of a certificate would hurt the distribution of a book-entry issue. "If the answer is no, fine. If it's yes, forget it. If it's maybe, forget it."

Some investors do face obstacles in buying book-entry issues. Some states require government pension funds and insurance companies to keep their certificates on hand. At the SEC's urging, most of the states that require certificates are considering changing their regulations.

Other investors, suspicious of computer glitches, take comfort in holding paper. Chrysler Corp. would gladly issue book-entry securities, says Frederick W. Zuckerman, treasurer, but would hesitate before buying them. When Chrysler holds certificates, he explains, he can make a "surprise visit" to the bank that holds them. "In a world where not everybody is always honest and always careful, that gives me a sense of comfort."

Unlike the French government, which has mandated the conversion of all securities to electronic book entry, the SEC has relied on persuasion. Most market participants agree that although a book-entry system is painfully slow in coming, it's inevitable.

Source: Adapted from Ann Monroe and Bruce Ingersoll, "SEC Chief Seeks End to Paper Securities," *Wall Street Journal* (April 28, 1986), p. 6.

TREASURY STOCK

[handwritten: lost identity of common or perferred stock,]

[handwritten: corp buys back its stock]
[handwritten: upon re-issuing by company stock regains identity]

Although there are some legal restrictions on the practice, a corporation may purchase shares of its own outstanding stock from stockholders. It may also accept shares of its own stock in payment of a debt owed by a stockholder, which in essence is much the same as acquisition by purchase. A corporation may buy its own stock in order to provide shares for resale to employees, to provide shares for reissuance to employees as a bonus, or to support the market price of the stock. In March, 1986, for example, General Motors announced that it would buy back as much as $1.95 billion of its common stock. General Motors officials stated that two primary uses of the treasury stock would be for incentive compensation plans and employee savings plans.

The term treasury stock may be applied only to the issuing corporation's stock that (1) has been issued as fully paid, (2) has later been reacquired by the corporation, and (3) has not been canceled or reissued. In the past, corporations would occasionally list treasury stock on the balance sheet as an asset. The justification for such treatment was that the stock could be reissued and was thus like an investment in the stock of another corporation. The same argument, though indefensible, might well be extended to authorized but unissued stock.

Today, it is generally agreed among accountants that treasury stock should not be reported as an asset. A corporation cannot own a part of itself. Treasury stock has no voting rights, it does not have the preemptive right to participate in additional issuances of stock, nor does it generally participate in cash dividends. When a corporation purchases its own stock, it is returning capital to the stockholders from whom the purchase was made.

There are several methods of accounting for the purchase and the resale of treasury stock. A commonly used method is the **cost basis**. When the stock is purchased by the corporation, the account Treasury Stock is debited for the price paid for it. The par and the price at which the stock was originally issued are ignored. When the stock is resold, Treasury Stock is credited at the price paid for it, and the difference between the price paid and the selling price is debited or credited to an account entitled Paid-In Capital from Sale of Treasury Stock.

As a basis for illustrating the cost method, assume that the paid-in capital of a corporation is composed of common stock issued at a premium, detailed as follows:

Common stock, $25 par (20,000 shares authorized and issued)....	$500,000
Premium on common stock....................................	150,000

The assumed transactions involving treasury stock and the required entries are as follows:

1. *Purchased 1,000 shares of treasury stock at $45.*

Treasury Stock	45,000	
Cash		45,000

2. *Sold 200 shares of treasury stock at $55.*

Cash	11,000	
Treasury Stock . . . . . . ~~purchase price~~		9,000
Paid-In Capital from Sale of Treasury Stock . . . ~~premium~~		2,000

3. *Sold 200 shares of treasury stock at $40.*

Cash	8,000	
Paid-In Capital from Sale of Treasury Stock	1,000	
Treasury Stock		9,000

Paid-In Capital from Sale of Treasury Stock is reported in the paid-in capital section of the balance sheet. Treasury Stock is deducted from the total of the paid-in capital and retained earnings. After the foregoing transactions are completed, the stockholders' equity section of the balance sheet would appear as follows:

Stockholders' Equity

Paid-in capital:		
Common stock, $25 par (20,000 shares		
authorized and issued)	$500,000	
Premium on common stock	150,000	$650,000
From sale of treasury stock		1,000
Total paid-in capital		$651,000
Retained earnings		130,000
Total		$781,000
Deduct treasury stock (600 shares		
at cost)		27,000
Total stockholders' equity		$754,000

The stockholders' equity section of the balance sheet indicates that 20,000 shares of stock were issued, of which 600 are held as treasury stock. The number of shares outstanding is therefore 19,400. If cash dividends are declared at this time, the declaration would apply to only 19,400 shares of stock. Similarly, 19,400 shares could be voted at a stockholders' meeting.

If sales of treasury stock result in a net decrease in paid-in capital, the decrease may be reported on the balance sheet as a reduction of paid-in capital or it may be debited to the retained earnings account.

EQUITY PER SHARE

total shareholder's equity ÷ outstanding shares

The amount appearing on the balance sheet as total stockholders' equity can be stated in terms of the **equity per share**. Another term sometimes used in referring to the equity allocable to a single share of stock is **book value per share**. The latter term is not only less accurate but its use of "value" may also be interpreted by nonaccountants to mean "market value" or "actual worth."

When there is only one class of stock, the equity per share is determined by dividing total stockholders' equity by the number of shares outstanding. For a corporation with both preferred and common stock, it is necessary first to allocate the total equity between the two classes. In making the allocation, consideration must be given to the liquidation rights of the preferred stock, including any participating and cumulative dividend features. After the total is allocated to the two classes, the equity per share of each class may then be determined by dividing the respective amounts by the related number of shares outstanding.

To illustrate, assume that as of the end of the current fiscal year, a corporation has both preferred and common shares outstanding, that there are no preferred dividends in arrears, and that the preferred stock is entitled to receive $105 per share upon liquidation. The amounts of the stockholders' equity accounts of the corporation and the computation of the equity per share are as follows:

Stockholders' Equity

Preferred $9 stock, cumulative, $100 par (1,000 shares outstanding)	$100,000
Premium on preferred stock	2,000
Common stock, $10 par (50,000 shares outstanding)	500,000
Premium on common stock	50,000
Retained earnings	253,000
Total equity	$905,000

Allocation of Total Equity to Preferred and Common Stock

Total equity	$905,000
Allocated to preferred stock: Liquidation price	105,000
Allocated to common stock	$800,000

Equity Per Share

Preferred stock: $105,000 ÷ 1,000 shares = $105 per share
Common stock: $800,000 ÷ 50,000 shares = $ 16 per share

If it is assumed that the preferred stock is entitled to dividends in arrears in the event of liquidation, and that there is an arrearage of two years, the computations for the foregoing illustration would be as follows:

Allocation of Total Equity to Preferred and Common Stock

Total equity		$905,000
Allocated to preferred stock:		
Liquidation price	$105,000	
Dividends in arrears	18,000	123,000
Allocated to common stock		$782,000

Equity Per Share

Preferred stock: $123,000 ÷   1,000 shares = $123.00 per share
Common stock: $782,000 ÷ 50,000 shares = $ 15.64 per share

Equity per share, particularly of common stock, is often stated in corporation reports to stockholders and quoted in the financial press. It is one of the many factors affecting the **market price**, that is, the price at which a share is bought and sold at a particular moment. However, it should be noted that earning capacity, dividend rates, and prospects for the future usually affect the market price of listed stocks to a much greater extent than does equity per share. So-called "glamour" stocks may at times sell at more than ten times the amount of the equity per share. On the other hand, stock in corporations that have suffered severe declines in earnings or whose future prospects appear to be unfavorable may sell at prices which are much less than the equity per share.

ORGANIZATION COSTS

Expenditures incurred in organizing a corporation, such as legal fees, taxes and fees paid to the state, and promotional costs, are charged to an intangible asset account entitled Organization Costs. Although such costs have no realizable value upon liquidation, they are as essential as plant and equipment, for without the expenditures the corporation could not have been created. If the life of a corporation is limited to a definite period of time, the organization costs should be amortized over the period by annual charges to an expense account. However, at the time of incorporation the length of life of most corporations is indeterminate.

There are two possible extreme viewpoints on the proper accounting for organization costs and other intangibles of indeterminate life. One extreme would consider the cost of intangibles as a permanent asset until there was convincing evidence of loss in value. The other extreme would consider the cost of intangibles as an expense in the period in which the cost is incurred. The practical solution to the problem is expressed in the following quotation:

. . . . Allocating the cost of goodwill or other intangible assets with an indeterminate life over time is necessary because the value almost inevitably becomes zero at some future date. Since the date at which the value becomes zero is indeterminate, the end of the useful life must necessarily be set arbitrarily at some point or within some range of time for accounting purposes.[4]

The Internal Revenue Code permits the amortization of organization costs equally over a period of not less than sixty months beginning with the month the corporation commences business. Since the amount of such costs is generally small in relation to total assets and the effect on net income is ordinarily not significant, amortization of organization costs over sixty months is generally accepted in accounting practice.

CHAPTER REVIEW

KEY POINTS

1. Characteristics of a Corporation.

The most important corporation characteristics with accounting implications are the following: separate legal existence, transferable units of stock, limited liability, and organizational structure. In addition, a corporation as a separate entity is subject to federal income taxes.

2. Stockholders' Equity.

The stockholders' equity section of a corporation balance sheet is divided into two subsections: paid-in capital and retained earnings.

3. Characteristics of Stock.

The stock of a corporation may be classified according to its par, right to vote, preference as to dividends, and preference as to liquidation rights. Various types of stock include par common stock, no-par common stock, participating

---

[4]*Opinions of the Accounting Principles Board*, No. 17, "Intangible Assets" (New York: American Institute of Certified Public Accountants, 1970), par. 23.

preferred stock, nonparticipating preferred stock, cumulative preferred stock, and noncumulative preferred stock.

4. Issuing Stock.

When a corporation issues stock at par, each class of stock is credited for its par amount. When a corporation issues stock at more than par, a premium is recognized in the records, and when stock is issued at less than par, a discount is recognized. Balances in the premium and discount accounts appear with their related class of stock in the stockholders' equity section of the balance sheet.

When capital stock is issued and exchanged for assets other than cash, the assets acquired should be recorded at their fair market price or at the fair market price of the stock issued, whichever is more objectively determinable.

When no-par stock is issued, the entire proceeds may be credited to the capital stock account, even though the issue price varies from time to time. In some cases, no-par stock may be assigned a stated value per share, and the excess of the proceeds over the stated value may be credited to a separate paid-in capital account.

5. Subscriptions and Stock Issuance.

In some cases, investors may subscribe to shares of stock directly from a corporation. The terms of the sale usually provide for the payment in full at some future date or for installment payments over a period of time. When stock is initially subscribed, the subscription price is debited to an asset account, Stock Subscriptions Receivable, and credited to a capital stock account, Stock Subscribed. Any difference between the subscription price and the par or stated value of the stock is debited or credited to a premium or discount account. After a subscriber has completed the agreed payments, the corporation issues the stock certificate. The stock subscribed account is then debited for the total par of the shares issued, and the capital stock account is credited for the same amount.

6. Treasury Stock.

A corporation may purchase shares of its own outstanding stock from stockholders. Any treasury stock held at the end of an accounting period is deducted from the total of the paid-in capital and retained earnings of the corporation. Any difference between the price paid for and the selling price of the treasury stock is usually recorded in a paid-in capital account for treasury stock transactions.

7. Equity per Share.

The amount appearing on the balance sheet as total stockholders' equity can be stated in terms of the equity per share. For a corporation with both preferred and common stock outstanding, it is necessary to allocate the total equity between the two classes of stock. The equity allocated to each class is divided by the number of shares outstanding of the respective class to determine the equity per share.

8. Organization Costs.

Expenditures incurred in organizing a corporation are charged to an intangible asset account entitled Organization Costs. The generally accepted accounting practice is to amortize organization costs over a period of sixty months, which conforms with federal income tax regulations.

KEY TERMS

stockholders 644
stockholders' equity 645
paid-in capital 645
retained earnings 645
deficit 645
capital stock 646
stock outstanding 646
par 646
stated value 646

preemptive right 646
common stock 647
preferred stock 647
participating preferred stock 648
cumulative preferred stock 648
premium on stock 649
discount on stock 649
treasury stock 657
equity per share 658

SELF-EXAMINATION QUESTIONS
Answers in Appendix B.

1. The owners' equity in a corporation is commonly called:
   A. stockholders' equity   C. capital
   B. shareholders' investment   D. all of the above

2. If a corporation has outstanding 1,000 shares of $9 cumulative preferred stock of $100 par and dividends have been passed for the preceding three years, what is the amount of preferred dividends that must be declared in the current year before a dividend can be declared on common stock?
   A. $9,000   C. $36,000
   B. $27,000   D. None of the above

3. The stockholders' equity section of the balance sheet may include:
   A. Discount on Common Stock   C. Premium on Preferred Stock
   B. Common Stock Subscribed   D. all of the above

4. If a corporation reacquires its own stock, the stock is listed on the balance
    sheet in the:
    A. current assets section   C. stockholders' equity section
    B. long-term liabilities section   D. none of the above

5. A corporation's balance sheet includes 10,000 outstanding shares of $8
    cumulative preferred stock of $100 par; 100,000 outstanding shares of $20
    par common stock; premium on common stock of $100,000; and retained
    earnings of $540,000. If preferred dividends are three years in arrears and
    the preferred stock is entitled to dividends in arrears plus $110 per share
    in the event of liquidation, what is the equity per common share?
    A. $20.00   C. $25.40
    B. $23.00   D. None of the above

ILLUSTRATIVE PROBLEM

The stockholders' equity and related accounts of Rockton Manufacturing
Corporation as of November 1, 1987, the beginning of the fiscal year, are as
follows:

Preferred Stock Subscriptions Receivable	$ 120,000
Preferred 8% Stock, $50 par (100,000 shares authorized, 20,000 shares issued)...................................	1,000,000
Preferred Stock Subscribed (3,000 shares)	150,000
Premium on Preferred Stock	80,000
Common Stock, $25 par (500,000 shares authorized, 100,000 shares issued)...................................	2,500,000
Premium on Common Stock	600,000
Retained Earnings	3,150,000

During the fiscal year ended October 31, 1988, Rockton Manufacturing
Corporation completed the following transactions affecting stockholders'
equity:

(a) Purchased 5,000 shares of treasury common for $130,000.
(b) Received balance due on preferred stock subscribed and issued the
    certificates.
(c) Sold 3,000 shares of treasury common for $81,000.
(d) Received subscriptions to 4,000 shares of preferred 8% stock at $51,
    collecting one third of the subscription price.
(e) Issued 40,000 shares of common stock at $27, receiving cash.
(f) Sold 1,000 shares of treasury common for $24,000.

Instructions:

1. Prepare the journal entries to record the transactions listed, identifying each transaction by the appropriate letter.
2. Prepare the stockholders' equity section for the October 31, 1988 balance sheet. The beginning retained earnings balance must be increased by the net income for the year, $710,000, and reduced by the dividends declared and paid, $280,000.

SOLUTION

(1)

(a)	Treasury Stock *(cost)*	130,000	
	Cash		130,000
(b)	Cash	120,000	
	Preferred Stock Subscriptions Receivable		120,000
	Preferred Stock Subscribed	150,000	
	Preferred Stock.		150,000
(c)	Cash	81,000	
	Treasury Stock .... 3,000 X 26		78,000
	Paid-In Capital from Sale of Treasury Stock .... *premium*		3,000
(d)	Preferred Stock Subscriptions Receivable .	204,000	
	Preferred Stock Subscribed		200,000
	Premium on Preferred Stock.		4,000
	Cash	68,000	
	Preferred Stock Subscriptions Receivable		68,000
(e)	Cash	1,080,000	
	Common Stock.		1,000,000
	Premium on Common Stock.		80,000
(f)	Cash	24,000	
	Paid-In Capital from Sale of Treasury Stock.	2,000	
	Treasury Stock		26,000

(2)

Stockholders' Equity

Paid-in capital:

Preferred 8% stock, $50 par
(100,000 shares authorized,
23,000 shares issued) $1,150,000

Preferred stock subscribed,
$50 par (4,000 shares)   200,000

Premium on preferred stock .   84,000 $1,434,000

Common stock, $25 par
(500,000 shares authorized,
140,000 shares issued). $3,500,000

Premium on common stock .   680,000   4,180,000

From sale of treasury stock . .   1,000

Total paid-in capital. $5,615,000
Retained earnings   3,580,000

Total $9,195,000
Deduct treasury common stock
(1,000 shares at cost).   26,000

Total stockholders' equity $9,169,000

DISCUSSION QUESTIONS

1. Why are most large business enterprises organized as corporations?

2. Contrast the owners' liability to creditors of (a) a partnership (partners) and (b) a corporation (stockholders).

3. Why is it said that the earnings of a corporation are subject to "double taxation"? Discuss.

4. What are the two principal sources of stockholders' equity?

5. The retained earnings account of a corporation at the beginning of the year had a credit balance of $60,000. The only other entry in the account during the year was a debit of $75,000 transferred from the income summary account at the end of the year. (a) What is the term applied to the $75,000 debit? (b) What is the balance in Retained Earnings at the end of the year? (c) What is the term applied to the balance determined in (b)?

6. The charter of a corporation provides for the issuance of a maximum of 50,000 shares of common stock. The corporation issued 40,000 shares of common stock, and two years later it reacquired 5,000 shares. After the reacquisition, what is the number of shares of stock (a) authorized, (b) issued, and (c) outstanding?

7. Of two corporations organized at approximately the same time and engaged in competing businesses, one issued $20 par common stock and the other issued $50 par common stock. Do the par designations provide any indication as to which stock is preferable as an investment? Explain.

8. (a) Differentiate between common stock and preferred stock. (b) Describe briefly (1) participating preferred stock and (2) cumulative preferred stock.

9. Assume that a corporation has had outstanding 100,000 shares of $5 cumulative preferred stock of $50 par and dividends were passed for the preceding three years. What amount of total dividends must be paid to the preferred stockholders before the common stockholders are entitled to any dividends in the current year?

10. What are some of the factors that influence the market price of a corporation's stock?

11. When a corporation issues stock at a premium, does the premium constitute income? Explain.

12. In which section of the corporation balance sheet would Discount on Preferred Stock appear?

13. The stockholders' equity section of a corporation balance sheet is composed of the following items:

Preferred $10 stock........	$400,000		
Premium on preferred stock .	40,000	$440,000	
Common stock...........	$800,000		
Discount on common stock .	70,000	730,000	$1,170,000
Retained earnings.........		330,000	$1,500,000

Determine the following amounts: (a) paid-in capital attributable to preferred stock, (b) paid-in capital attributable to common stock, (c) earnings retained for use in the business, and (d) total stockholders' equity.

14. Land is acquired by a corporation for 10,000 shares of its $20 par common stock, which is currently selling for $35 per share on a national stock exchange. (a) At what value should the land be recorded? (b) What accounts and amounts should be credited to record the transaction? Land 350,00 0 Common Stoc 200 00 0 pre 150 00 0

15. A corporation receives subscriptions to 1,000 shares of $50 par common stock from various subscribers at $60 per share, with a down payment of 25% of the subscription price. Subsequently, another payment of 25% of the subscription price was received. Assuming that financial statements are prepared at this point, determine the following account balances: (a) Subscriptions Receivable, (b) Common Stock Subscribed, (c) Premium on Common Stock, and (d) Common Stock.

16. (a) In what respect does treasury stock differ from unissued stock? (b) For what reasons might a company purchase treasury stock? (c) How should treasury stock be presented on the balance sheet?

17. A corporation reacquires 1,000 shares of its own $20 par common stock for $30,000, recording it at cost. (a) What effect does this transaction have on revenue or expense of the period? (b) What effect does it have on stockholders' equity? NONE reduces by 30,000

18. The treasury stock in Question 17 is resold for $35,000. (a) What is the effect on the corporation's revenue of the period? (b) What is the effect on stockholders' equity?

19. A corporation that had issued 80,000 shares of $10 par common stock subsequently reacquired 10,000 shares, which it now holds as treasury stock. If the board of directors declares a cash dividend of $1 per share, what will be the total amount of the dividend?

20. At the end of the current period, a corporation has 10,000 shares of preferred stock and 100,000 shares of common stock outstanding. Assuming that there are no preferred dividends in arrears, that the preferred stock is entitled to receive $55 per share upon liquidation, and that total stockholders' equity is $2,750,000, determine the following amounts: (a) equity per share of preferred stock, and (b) equity per share of common stock.

21. Common stock has a par of $10 per share, the current equity per share is $37.25, and the market price per share is $45. Suggest reasons for the comparatively high market price in relation to par and to equity per share.

22. (a) What type of expenditure is charged to the organization costs account? (b) Give examples of such expenditures. (c) In what section of the balance sheet is the balance of Organization Costs listed?

23. Identify each of the following accounts as asset, liability, stockholders' equity, revenue, or expense, and indicate the normal balance of each:
    (1) Preferred Stock
    (2) Paid-In Capital from Sale of Treasury Stock
    (3) Common Stock Subscribed
    (4) Common Stock Subscriptions Receivable
    (5) Treasury Stock
    (6) Organization Costs
    (7) Discount on Common Stock
    (8) Common Stock
    (9) Premium on Preferred Stock
    (10) Retained Earnings

24. Real World Focus. The following excerpt was taken from the January 31, 1986 balance sheet of Deb Shops Inc.

Shareholders' Equity
   Series A Preferred Stock, par value $1.00 a share:
      Authorized—5,000,000 shares
      Issued and outstanding—460 shares..................... $ 460
   Common Stock, par value $.01 a share:
      Authorized—25,000,000 shares
      Issued and outstanding—7,579,321 shares   75,793
   Additional paid-in capital   1,282,634
   Retained earnings.....................................   38,287,626
                                                              $39,646,513
   Less: 26,631 common treasury shares at cost   519,927
   Total... $39,126,586

Notes to the financial statements indicate that the holders of the Series A Preferred Stock are entitled to a $1,000 per share liquidation preference and a $120 per share annual dividend, which is cumulative. (a) If no dividends are in arrears on January 31, 1986, what is the total liquidation value of the Series A Preferred Stock? (b) What is the equity per share of the outstanding common stock as of January 31, 1986?

EXERCISES

Exercise 15–1.   Dividends per share. A. P. Nelson Company has stock outstanding as follows: 10,000 shares of $8 cumulative, nonparticipating preferred stock of $100 par, and 100,000 shares of $20 par common. During its first five years of operations, the following amounts were distributed as dividends: first year, none; second year, $120,000; third year, $180,000; fourth year, $230,000; fifth year, $200,000. Determine the dividends per share on each class of stock for each of the five years.

Exercise 15–2.   Dividends per share. CDP Inc. has outstanding stock composed of 1,000 shares of 10%, $100 par, participating preferred stock and 10,000 shares of no-par common stock. The preferred stock is entitled to participate equally with the common, on a share-for-share basis, in any dividend distributions which exceed the regular preferred dividend and a $2 per share common dividend. The directors declare dividends of $41,000 for the current year. Determine the amount of the dividend per share on (a) the preferred stock and (b) the common stock.

Exercise 15–3.   Entries for stock issuance. On February 20, Adams Company issued for cash 5,000 shares of no-par common stock (with a stated value of $20) at $22, and on August 7 it issued for cash 2,000 shares of $50 par preferred stock at $52. (a) Give the entries for February 20 and August 7, assuming that the common stock is to be credited with the stated value. (b) What is the total amount invested by all stockholders as of August 7?

Exercise 15–4.   Stock subscriptions. On January 15, Chow Company received its charter authorizing 10,000 shares of $50 par common stock. On March 5, the corporation received subscriptions to 5,000 shares of stock at $60. Cash for one half of the subscription price accompanied the subscriptions. On June 5, the remaining half was received from all subscribers and the stock was issued. (a) Present entries to record the transactions of March 5. (b) Present entries to record the transactions of June 5. (c) By what amount did the corporation's stockholders' equity increase on January 15, March 5, and June 5? (d) Name two controlling accounts used in the transactions and identify the related subsidiary ledgers.

Exercise 15–5. Issuance of stock; stockholders' equity section. C. D. Buckley Company, with an authorization of 5,000 shares of preferred stock and 50,000 shares of common stock, completed several transactions involving its capital stock on April 1, the first day of operations. The trial balance at the close of the day follows:

Cash...	390,000	
Common Stock Subscriptions Receivable............	260,000	
Land...	90,000	
Buildings	410,000	
Preferred $12 Stock, $100 par......................		450,000
Premium on Preferred Stock........................		50,000
Common Stock, $20 par.............................		300,000
Premium on Common Stock		150,000
Common Stock Subscribed		200,000
	1,150,000	1,150,000

All shares within each class of stock were sold or subscribed at the same price, the preferred stock was issued in exchange for the land and buildings, and no cash was received on the unissued common stock subscribed. (a) Present the three compound entries to record the transactions summarized in the trial balance. (b) Prepare the stockholders' equity section of the balance sheet as of April 1.

Exercise 15–6. Corporate organization; stockholders' equity section. Sanderson Products Inc. was organized on January 9 of the current year, with an authorization of 10,000 shares of $11 cumulative preferred stock, $100 par, and 100,000 shares of $10 par common stock. └dividend

The following selected transactions were completed during the first year of operations:

Jan. 9. Issued 20,000 shares of common stock at par for cash.
      9. Issued 950 shares of common stock to an attorney in payment of legal fees for organizing the corporation.
Feb. 4. Issued 20,000 shares of common stock in exchange for land, buildings, and equipment with fair market prices of $40,000, $120,000, and $45,000 respectively.
Oct. 15. Issued 2,000 shares of preferred stock at $96 for cash.

(a) Record the transactions. (b) Prepare the stockholders' equity section of the balance sheet as of December 31, the end of the current year. The net income for the year amounted to $37,500.

Exercise 15–7. Treasury stock transactions. On January 11 of the current year, Lang Company reacquired 1,000 shares of its common stock at $22 per share. On July 2, 500 of the reacquired shares were sold at $25 per share. The remaining 500 shares were sold at $20 per share on December 19. (a) Record the transactions of January 11, July 2, and December 19. (b) What is the balance in Paid-In Capital from Sale of Treasury Stock on December 31 of the current year? (c) Where will the balance in Paid-In Capital from Sale of Treasury Stock be reported on the balance sheet?

SPREADSHEET PROBLEM

Exercise 15–8.   Equity per share. The stockholders' equity accounts of Diaz Company at the end of the current fiscal year are as follows: Preferred $5 Stock, $50 par, $1,000,000; Common Stock, $25 par, $5,000,000; Premium on Common Stock, $200,000; Premium on Preferred Stock, $40,000; Retained Earnings, $860,000. (a) Determine the equity per share of each class of stock, assuming that the preferred stock is entitled to receive $60 upon liquidation. (b) Determine the equity per share of each class of stock, assuming that the preferred stock is to receive $60 per share plus the dividends in arrears in the event of liquidation, and that only the dividends for the current year are in arrears.

Exercise 15–9.   Treasury stock and equity per share. The following items were listed in the stockholders' equity section of the balance sheet of June 30: Common stock, $10 par (50,000 shares outstanding), $500,000; Premium on common stock, $150,000; Retained earnings, $190,000. On July 1, the corporation purchased 2,000 shares of its stock for $24,000. (a) Determine the equity per share of stock on June 30. (b) Present the entry to record the purchase of the stock on July 1. (c) Determine the equity per share on July 1.

Exercise 15–10.   Equity per share; liquidation amounts. The following items were listed in the stockholders' equity section of the balance sheet on July 31: Preferred stock, $50 par, $500,000; Common stock, $20 par, $1,500,000; Premium on common stock, $150,000; Deficit, $250,000. On August 1, the board of directors voted to dissolve the corporation immediately. A short time later, after all noncash assets were sold and liabilities were paid, cash of $1,525,000 remained for distribution to stockholders. (a) Assuming that preferred stock is entitled to preference in liquidation of $55 per share, determine the equity per share on July 31 of (1) preferred stock and (2) common stock. (b) Determine the amount of the $1,525,000 that will be distributed for each share of (1) preferred stock and (2) common stock. (c) Explain the reason for the difference between the common stock equity per share on July 31 and the amount of the cash distribution per common share.

PROBLEMS

Series A

Problem 15–1A.   Corporation organization; stockholders' equity section. Lincolnshire West Corp. was organized by Dunn, Howe, and Radner. The charter authorized 50,000 shares of common stock with a par of $10. The following transactions affecting stockholders' equity were completed during the first year of operations:

(handwritten notes in left margin:)
equity = FMV - liability
add FMV
of land & bldg
minus liabilities

(a) Issued 5,000 shares of stock at par to Dunn for cash.
(b) Issued 500 shares of stock at par to Howe for promotional services rendered in connection with the organization of the corporation, and issued 4,500 shares of stock at par to Howe for cash.
(c) Purchased land and a building from Radner. The building is encumbered by a 13%, 16-year mortgage of $95,500, and there is accrued interest of $4,000 on the mortgage note at the time of the purchase. It is agreed that the land is to be priced at $40,000 and the building at $125,000, and that Radner's equity will be exchanged for stock at par. The corporation agreed to assume responsibility for paying the mortgage note and the accrued interest.
(d) Issued 10,000 shares of stock at $12 to various investors for cash.
(e) Purchased equipment for $75,000. The seller accepted a 6-month, 11% note for $25,000 and 5,000 shares of stock in exchange for the equipment.

Instructions: *i = prt*

(1) Prepare entries to record the transactions.
(2) Prepare the stockholders' equity section of the balance sheet as of the end of the first year of operations. The retained earnings balance is the net income for the year, $77,500, less dividends declared and paid during the year, $1 per share.

Problem 15–2A. Dividends on preferred and common stock. The annual dividends declared by Cullum Company during a six-year period are presented in the following table:

Year	Total Dividends	Preferred Dividends		Common Dividends	
		Total	Per Share	Total	Per Share
1984	$ 62,000	*133,330*	*5*		*2.60*
1985	128,000				*0.40*
1986	12,000				*.60*
1987	5,000				*25*
1988	6,000				*30*
1989	45,000				*2.25*

During the entire period, the outstanding stock of the company was composed of 2,000 shares of cumulative, participating, $5 preferred stock, $50 par, and 20,000 shares of common stock, $10 par. The preferred stock contract provides that the preferred stock shall participate in distributions of additional dividends after allowance of a $2 dividend per share on the common stock, the additional dividends to be prorated among common and preferred shares on the basis of the total par of the stock outstanding.

Instructions:

(1) Determine the total dividends and the per-share dividends declared on each class of stock for each of the six years, using the headings presented above. There were no dividends in arrears on January 1, 1984.
(2) Determine the average annual dividend per share for each class of stock for the six-year period.

(3) Assuming that the preferred stock was sold at par and common stock was sold at $28 at the beginning of the six-year period, determine the percentage return on initial shareholders' investment, based on the average annual dividend per share (a) for preferred stock and (b) for common stock.

Problem 15–3A.   Equity per share. Selected data from the balance sheets of six corporations, identified by letter, are as follows:

A. Common stock, no par, 50,000 shares outstanding . . . . $ 750,000
   Deficit   90,000

B. Preferred $2 stock, $25 par . . . . $ 750,000
   Common stock, $10 par   2,000,000
   Premium on common stock   50,000
   Retained earnings   450,000
   Preferred stock has prior claim to assets on liquidation to the extent of par.

C. Preferred $12 stock, $100 par . . . . $ 500,000
   Premium on preferred stock   30,000
   Common stock, $5 par   1,000,000
   Discount on common stock   55,000
   Deficit   95,000
   Preferred stock has prior claim to assets on liquidation to the extent of par.

D. Preferred 10% stock, $100 par . . . . $ 750,000
   Premium on preferred stock   100,000
   Common stock, $20 par   2,500,000
   Deficit   75,000
   Preferred stock has prior claim to assets on liquidation to the extent of 110% of par.

E. Preferred 11% stock, $100 par . . . . $ 800,000
   Common stock, $5 par   2,000,000
   Premium on common stock   300,000
   Retained earnings   104,000
   Dividends on preferred stock are in arrears for 2 years, including the dividend passed during the current year. Preferred stock is entitled to par plus unpaid cumulative dividends upon liquidation to the extent of retained earnings.

F. Preferred $2 stock, $25 par . . . . $ 500,000
   Premium on preferred stock   10,000
   Common stock, $10 par   1,500,000
   Deficit   55,000
   Dividends on preferred stock are in arrears for 3 years, including the dividend passed during the current year. Preferred stock is entitled to par plus unpaid cumulative dividends upon liquidation, regardless of the availability of retained earnings.

Instructions:

Determine for each corporation the equity per share of each class of stock, presenting the total stockholders' equity allocated to each class and the number of shares outstanding.

Problem 15–4A. Corporate expansion; stockholders' equity section. The following accounts and their balances appear in the ledger of Fred Sims and Co. on June 30 of the current year:

Preferred $9 Stock, $100 par (10,000 shares authorized, 8,000 shares issued)	$ 800,000
Premium on Preferred Stock	16,000
Common Stock, $20 par (100,000 shares authorized, 75,000 shares issued)	1,500,000
Premium on Common Stock	210,000
Retained Earnings	305,000

At the annual stockholders' meeting on July 9, the board of directors presented a plan for modernizing and expanding plant operations at a cost of approximately $500,000. The plan provided (a) that the corporation borrow $200,000, (b) that 1,000 shares of the unissued preferred stock be issued through an underwriter, and (c) that a building, valued at $155,000, and the land on which it is located, valued at $40,000, be acquired in accordance with preliminary negotiations by the issuance of 8,000 shares of common stock. The plan was approved by the stockholders and accomplished by the following transactions:

July 24. Issued 8,000 shares of common stock in exchange for land and building in accordance with the plan.
　　30. Issued 1,000 shares of preferred stock, receiving $105 per share in cash from the underwriter.
　　31. Borrowed $200,000 from Palmer National Bank, giving a 14% mortgage note.

Instructions:

Assuming for the purpose of the problem that no other transactions occurred during July:

(1) Prepare the entries to record the foregoing transactions.
(2) Prepare the stockholders' equity section of the balance sheet as of July 31.

Problem 15–5A. Stock transactions; stockholders' equity section. The following selected accounts appear in the ledger of Wayne Corporation on July 1, the beginning of the current fiscal year:

Preferred Stock Subscriptions Receivable	$ 65,900
Preferred $12 Stock, $100 par (20,000 shares authorized, 10,000 shares issued)	1,000,000
Preferred Stock Subscribed (2,500 shares)	250,000
Premium on Preferred Stock	62,500
Common Stock, $10 par (500,000 shares authorized, 300,000 shares issued)	3,000,000
Premium on Common Stock	600,000
Retained Earnings	1,450,000

During the year, the corporation completed a number of transactions affecting the stockholders' equity. They are summarized as follows:

(a) Received balance due on preferred stock subscribed and issued the certificates.
(b) Purchased 10,000 shares of treasury common for $120,000.
(c) Sold 3,000 shares of treasury common for $45,000.
(d) Received subscriptions to 2,000 shares of preferred $12 stock at $105, collecting 25% of the subscription price.
(e) Issued 50,000 shares of common stock at $15, receiving cash.
(f) Sold 2,000 shares of treasury common for $22,000.

Instructions:

(1) Prepare entries to record the transactions. Identify each entry by letter. (The use of T accounts for the stockholders' equity accounts will facilitate the determination of the amounts needed in recording some of the transactions and in completing Instruction (2).)
(2) Prepare the stockholders' equity section of the balance sheet as of June 30, the end of the current fiscal year. The net income for the year was $550,000, and cash dividends declared and paid during the year were $420,000.

Problem 15–6A. Stock transactions and corrections; balance sheet. Reese Company was organized on April 1 of the current year and prepared its first financial statement, a balance sheet, the following December 31, the date that had been adopted as the end of the fiscal year. The balance sheet that was prepared by the bookkeeper is as follows:

Reese Company
Balance Sheet
April 1 to December 31, 19--

Assets		Liabilities	
Cash...................	$ 65,750	Accounts payable.........	$ 85,000
Accounts receivable	215,000	Preferred stock...........	200,000
Merchandise inventory....	145,250	Common stock	300,000
Prepaid insurance........	6,500	Premium on common stock	30,000
Treasury common stock...	20,000		
Equipment..............	130,000		
Retained earnings (deficit) .	32,500		
Total assets	$615,000	Total liabilities..........	$615,000

You are retained by the board of directors to audit the accounts and to prepare a revised balance sheet. The relevant facts developed during the course of your engagement are:

(a) Stock authorized: 5,000 shares of $100 par, $11 preferred, and 50,000 shares of $20 par common.
(b) Stock issued: 1,000 shares of fully paid preferred at $105 and 15,000 shares of common at $22. The premium on preferred stock was credited to Retained Earnings.
(c) Stock subscribed but not issued: 1,000 shares of preferred at par, on which all subscribers have paid one half of the subscription price. Unpaid subscriptions are included in accounts receivable and are collectible in 60 days.

(d) The company reacquired 1,000 shares of the issued common stock at $30. The difference between par and the price paid was debited to Retained Earnings. (It is decided that the treasury stock is to be recorded at cost.)

(e) Included in merchandise inventory is $1,500 of office supplies.

(f) Land to be used as a future building site cost $30,000 and was debited to Equipment.

(g) No depreciation has been recognized. The equipment is to be depreciated for 9 months by the straight-line method, using an estimated life of 10 years.

(h) Organization costs of $6,000 were debited to Advertising Expense. (The organization costs are to be amortized over 60 months beginning with April 1 of the current year.)

(i) No dividends have been declared or paid.

(j) In balancing the common stockholders ledger with the common stock controlling account, it was discovered that the account with James Wade contained a posting for an issuance of 100 shares, while the copy of the stock certificate indicated that 1,000 shares had been issued. The stock certificate was found to be correct.

Instructions:

(1) Prepare journal entries where necessary to record the corrections. Corrections of net income should be recorded as adjustments to retained earnings.

(2) Prepare a six-column work sheet, with columns for (a) balances per balance sheet, (b) corrections, and (c) corrected balances. In listing the accounts, leave an extra line blank following the retained earnings account. Complete the work sheet.

(3) Prepare a corrected balance sheet in report form as of the end of the fiscal year.

Series B

Problem 15–2B. Dividends on preferred and common stock. The annual dividends declared by A. W. Twig Company during a six-year period are presented in the following table:

Year	Total Dividends	Preferred Dividends Total	Preferred Dividends Per Share	Common Dividends Total	Common Dividends Per Share
1984	$ 4,000				
1985	11,000				
1986	30,000				
1987	84,000				
1988	72,000				
1989	21,000				

During the entire period, the outstanding stock of the company was composed of 1,000 shares of cumulative, participating, 10% preferred stock, $100 par, and 10,000 shares of common stock, $50 par. The preferred stock contract provides that the preferred stock shall participate in distributions of additional dividends after allowance of a $5 dividend per share on the common stock, the additional dividends to be prorated among common and preferred shares on the basis of the total par of the stock outstanding.

Instructions:

(1) Determine the total dividends and the per share dividends declared on each class of stock for each of the six years, using the headings presented above. There were no dividends in arrears on January 1, 1984.
(2) Determine the average annual dividend per share for each class of stock for the six-year period.
(3) Assuming that the preferred stock was sold at par and common stock was sold at $40 at the beginning of the six-year period, determine the percentage return on initial shareholders' investment, based on the average annual dividend per share (a) for preferred stock and (b) for common stock.

Problem 15–3B.   Equity per share. Selected data from the balance sheets of six corporations, identified by letter, are as follows:

A. Common stock, $10 par................................... $ 500,000
    Premium on common stock.............................   100,000
    Deficit..   75,000

B. Preferred $10 stock, $25 par............................ $ 500,000
    Common stock, $20 par...............................   1,500,000
    Premium on common stock.............................   130,000
    Retained earnings   410,000
    Preferred stock has prior claim to assets on liquidation to the extent of par.

C. Preferred $9 stock, $100 par........................... $1,000,000
    Premium on preferred stock   50,000
    Common stock, no par, 25,000 shares outstanding   1,250,000
    Deficit..   200,000
    Preferred stock has prior claim to assets on liquidation to the extent of par.

D. Preferred 11% stock, $50 par........................... $2,000,000
    Premium on preferred stock   275,000
    Common stock, $25 par...............................   3,750,000
    Retained earnings   450,000
    Preferred stock has prior claim to assets on liquidation to the extent of 110% of par.

E. Preferred 9% stock, $100 par........................... $1,200,000
    Common stock, $50 par...............................   4,000,000
    Premium on common stock.............................   340,000
    Retained earnings   108,000
    Dividends on preferred stock are in arrears for 2 years, including the dividend passed during the current year. Preferred stock is entitled to par plus unpaid cumulative dividends upon liquidation to the extent of retained earnings.

F. Preferred $2 stock, $25 par.............................. $ 500,000
Discount on preferred stock............................... 40,000
Common stock, $10 par.................................. 2,000,000
Deficit... 130,000

Dividends on preferred stock are in arrears for 3 years, including the dividend passed during the current year. Preferred stock is entitled to par plus unpaid cumulative dividends upon liquidation, regardless of the availability of retained earnings.

Instructions:

Determine for each corporation the equity per share of each class of stock, presenting the total stockholders' equity allocated to each class and the number of shares outstanding.

Problem 15–5B. Stock transactions; stockholders' equity section. The following selected accounts appear in the ledger of Perez Corporation on July 1, the beginning of the current fiscal year:

Preferred Stock Subscriptions Receivable .... $ 26,750
Preferred 10% Stock, $50 par (10,000 shares authorized,
   5,000 shares issued).. 250,000
Preferred Stock Subscribed (2,000 shares) 100,000
Premium on Preferred Stock................................... 28,000
Common Stock, $20 par (50,000 shares authorized,
   25,000 shares issued)..................................... 500,000
Premium on Common Stock 90,000
Retained Earnings.. 337,000

During the year, the corporation completed a number of transactions affecting the stockholders' equity. They are summarized as follows:

(a) Purchased 1,000 shares of treasury common for $27,500.
(b) Received balance due on preferred stock subscribed and issued the certificates.
(c) Sold 500 shares of treasury common for $15,000.
(d) Issued 2,500 shares of common stock at $30, receiving cash.
(e) Received subscriptions to 1,000 shares of preferred 10% stock at $52.50, collecting 25% of the subscription price.
(f) Sold 250 shares of treasury common for $6,500.

Instructions:

(1) Prepare entries to record the transactions. Identify each entry by letter. (The use of T accounts for stockholders' equity accounts will facilitate the determination of the amounts needed in recording some of the transactions and in completing Instruction (2).)
(2) Prepare the stockholders' equity section of the balance sheet as of June 30, the end of the current fiscal year. The net income for the year was $185,000, and cash dividends declared and paid during the year were $105,000.

MINI-CASE 15

Miami Valley Cooperative Electric Corporation needs $2,000,000 to finance a major plant expansion. To raise the $2,000,000, the chairman of the board of directors suggested that the cooperative first offer common stock for sale at a price equal to the January 1, 1988 equity per share of common stock. The chairman indicated that by setting the price in this way, the value of the current common stockholders' interest in the cooperative would be preserved. Any additional funds that might be needed after this offer expired could be obtained from the issuance of preferred stock.

Since no preferred stock is authorized, the board is considering characteristics of the stock, such as the dividend rate and the cumulative and participating features. So as not to jeopardize common stockholder dividends, the board of directors tentatively approved a dividend rate of 4% for the preferred stock. The board agreed to delay any final action on other aspects of the financing plan until the legal counsel can be contacted to determine the procedures necessary to seek authorization of the preferred stock.

As of January 1, 1988, the stockholders' equity is as follows:

Paid-in capital:		
Common stock, $50 par (100,000 shares authorized, 60,000 shares issued).......	$3,000,000	
Premium on common stock....	450,000	
Total paid-in capital........		$3,450,000
Retained earnings..............		1,350,000
Total stockholders' equity........		$4,800,000

Instructions:

(1) Determine the equity per share of common stock on January 1, 1988.   *80.00*

(2) During the board meeting, the chairman asked for your opinion of the suggestion for determining the selling price of the common stock. How would you respond?

(3) What characteristics might you suggest the board consider in designing the preferred stock? Comment on the low preferred stock dividend rate tentatively approved by the board.

increase dividend rate because 4% is less than pass book savings rate

Chapter 16

STOCKHOLDERS' EQUITY, EARNINGS, AND DIVIDENDS

Chapter Objectives:

- Identify and illustrate alternative terminology used in preparing the stockholders' equity section of the balance sheet.

- Describe and illustrate the accounting for corporate income taxes.

- Describe and illustrate the accounting for unusual items in the financial statements.

- Describe and illustrate the computation of earnings per share.

- Describe and illustrate the accounting for appropriations of retained earnings and the preparation of a retained earnings statement.

- Describe and illustrate the accounting for dividends, including cash dividends, stock dividends, and liquidating dividends.

- Describe and illustrate the accounting for stock splits.

16

As has been indicated, the stockholders' equity section of the balance sheet is divided into two major subdivisions, *paid-in capital* (or contributed capital) and *retained earnings*. Although in practice there is wide variation in the amount of detail presented and the descriptive captions used, sources of significant amounts of stockholders' equity should be properly disclosed.

The emphasis on disclosure and clarity of expression by the accounting profession has been relatively recent. In earlier days, it was not unusual to present for stockholders' equity only the amount of the par of the preferred and common stock outstanding and a balancing amount described simply as "Surplus." Readers of the balance sheet could only assume that par represented the amount paid in by stockholders and that surplus represented retained earnings. Although it was possible for a "surplus" of $1,000,000, for example, to be composed solely of retained earnings, it could represent paid-in capital from premiums on stock issued or even an excess of $1,200,000 of such premiums over an accumulated deficit of $200,000 of retained earnings.

PAID-IN CAPITAL

As illustrated in Chapter 15, the main credits to paid-in capital accounts result from the issuance of stock. If par stock is issued at a price above or below par, the difference is recorded in a separate premium or discount account. It is also common to use two accounts in recording the issuance of no-par stock, one for the stated value and the other for the excess over stated value. Another account for paid-in capital discussed in the preceding chapter was Paid-In Capital from Sale of Treasury Stock.

Paid-in capital may also originate from donated real estate and redemptions of a corporation's own stock. Civic organizations sometimes give land or land and buildings to a corporate enterprise as an inducement to locate in the community. In such cases, the assets are recorded in the corporate accounts at fair market value, with a credit to Donated Capital. Preferred stock contracts may give to the issuing corporation the right to redeem the stock at varying redemption prices at varying future dates. If the redemption price paid to the stockholder is greater than the original issuance price, the excess is considered to be a distribution of retained earnings. On the other hand, if the amount paid is less than the amount originally received by the corporation, the difference is a retention of capital and should be credited to Paid-In Capital from Preferred Stock Redemption or a similarly titled account.

As with other sections of the balance sheet, there are many variations in terminology and arrangement of the paid-in capital section. Some of these variations are illustrated by the following three examples. The details of each class of stock, including related stock premium or discount, are commonly listed first, followed by the other paid-in capital accounts. Instead of describing the source of each amount in excess of par or stated value, a common practice is to combine all such accounts into a single amount. It is then listed below the capital stock accounts and described as "Additional paid-in capital," "Capital in excess of par (or stated value) of shares," or by a similarly descriptive phrase.

Stockholders' Equity

Paid-in capital:			
Common stock, $20 par			
(50,000 shares authorized,			
45,000 shares issued)		$900,000	
Premium on common stock		132,000	$1,032,000
From stock redemption			60,000
From sale of treasury stock			25,000
Total paid-in capital			$1,117,000

Shareholders' Equity

Paid-in capital:			
Common stock, $20 par			
(50,000 shares authorized,			
45,000 shares issued)			$ 900,000
Excess of issuance price over par		$132,000	
From redemption of common stock		60,000	
From transactions in own stock		25,000	217,000
Total paid-in capital			$1,117,000

Shareholders' Investment

Contributed capital:			
Common stock, $20 par			
(50,000 shares authorized,			
45,000 shares issued)			$ 900,000
Additional paid-in capital			217,000
Total contributed capital			$1,117,000

Significant changes in paid-in capital during the period should also be disclosed. The details of these changes may be presented either in a separate paid-in capital statement or in notes to other financial statements.

CORPORATE EARNINGS AND INCOME TAXES

The determination of the net income or net loss of a corporation is comparable, in most respects, to that of other forms of business organization. Unlike sole proprietorships and partnerships, however, corporations are distinct legal entities. In general, they are subject to the federal income tax and, in many cases, to income taxes levied by states or other political subdivisions. Although the discussion that follows is limited to the income tax levied by the federal government, the basic concepts apply also to state and local income taxes.

For several years, most corporations have been required to estimate the amount of their federal income tax expense for the year and to make advance payments, usually in four installments. To illustrate, assume that a calendar-year corporation estimates its income tax expense for the year to be $84,000. The required entry for each of the four payments of $21,000 (1/4 of $84,000) would be as follows:

Income Tax	21,000	
Cash		21,000

At year end, the actual taxable income and the actual tax are determined. If an additional amount is owed, this liability must be recorded. Continuing with the illustration, assume that the corporation's actual tax, based on actual taxable income, is $86,000 instead of $84,000. The following entry would be required in order to include the income tax expense in the fiscal year in which the related income was earned:

Dec. 31	Income Tax	2,000	
	Income Tax Payable		2,000

If the amount of the advance payments exceeds the tax liability based on actual income, the amount of the overpayment would be debited to a receivable account and credited to Income Tax.

Income tax returns and related records and documents are subject to review by the taxing authority, usually for a period of three years after the return is filed. Consequently, the determination made by the taxpayer is provisional rather than final. In recognition of the possibility of an assessment for a tax deficiency, the liability for income taxes is sometimes described in the current liability section of the balance sheet as "Estimated income tax payable."

Because of its substantial size in relationship to net income, income tax is often reported on the income statement as a special deduction, as follows:

Palmer Corporation Income Statement For Year Ended December 31, 19--	
Sales...	$980,000

Income before income tax......................................	$200,000
Income tax..	82,500
Net income..	$117,500

ALLOCATION OF INCOME TAX BETWEEN PERIODS

The **taxable income** of a corporation, determined according to the tax laws, is often different from the amount of income (before income tax) determined from the accounts and reported in the income statement. This difference may need to be allocated between periods, depending upon whether it is a permanent difference or a timing difference.[1]

Permanent Differences

The tax laws provide for special treatment of certain revenue and expense items. This special treatment results in permanent differences between the amount of income tax actually owed and the amount that would be owed if the tax were based on income before income tax. These items may be described as follows:

1. An expense for a specified purpose is not deductible in determining taxable income, or revenue from a specified source is excludable from taxable income. Example: Interest income on tax-exempt municipal bonds.
2. A deduction is allowed in determining taxable income, but there is no actual expenditure and hence no expense. Example: The excess of the allowable deduction for percentage depletion of natural resources over depletion expense based on cost.

Permanent differences cause no problem for financial reporting. The amount of income tax determined in accordance with the tax laws is the amount reported on the income statement.

---

[1]*Opinions of the Accounting Principles Board, No. 11,*"Accounting for Income Taxes" (New York: American Institute of Certified Public Accountants, 1967), par. 13.

Timing Differences   *ex. depreciation*

The treatment of certain items results in differences between income before income tax and taxable income, because the items are recognized in one period for income statement purposes and in another period for tax purposes. These timing differences reverse or turn around in later years. The cases in which such differences occur are described as follows:

1. The method used in determining the amount of a specified revenue or expense for income tax purposes differs from the method used in determining net income for reporting purposes. Example: The installment method of determining revenue is used in determining taxable income and the point of sale method is used for reporting purposes.
2. The manner prescribed for the treatment of a specified revenue or expense in determining taxable income is contrary to generally accepted accounting principles and hence not acceptable in determining net income for reporting purposes. Example: Revenue received in advance that is to be earned in future years must be included in taxable income in the year received, which is contrary to the basic accounting principle that such revenue be allocated to the years benefited.

Timing differences require special treatment in the accounts. To illustrate the effect of timing differences and their related effect on the amount of income tax reported in corporate financial statements, assume that a corporation that sells its product on the installment basis recognizes the revenue at the time of sale and maintains its accounts accordingly. At the end of the first year of operations, the income before income tax according to the ledger is $300,000. Realizing the advantage of reducing current income tax, the corporation elects the installment method of determining revenue and cost of merchandise sold, which yields taxable income of only $100,000. Assuming an income tax rate of 45%, the income tax on $300,000 of income would amount to $135,000. The income tax actually due for the year would only be $45,000 (45% of $100,000). The $90,000 difference between the two amounts is due to the timing difference in recognizing revenue. It represents a deferment of $90,000 of income tax to future years. As the installment accounts receivable are collected in later years, the additional $200,000 of income will be included in the taxable income and the $90,000 deferment will become a tax liability of those years. The situation may be summarized as follows:

Income before income tax according to ledger	$300,000	
Income tax based on $300,000 at 45%.............		$135,000
Taxable income according to tax return...............	$100,000	
Income tax based on $100,000 at 45%.............		45,000
Income tax deferred to future years..................		$ 90,000

The income tax to be reported on the income statement should be the total tax ($135,000 in the illustration) expected to result from the net income of the year. In this manner, the revenue reported on the income statement will be matched with the expenses (including income tax) related to that revenue, regardless of when the tax will become an actual liability to be paid.[2] Applying the concept of the allocation of income tax between periods to the illustrative data yields the following results, stated in terms of a journal entry:

debit expenses

Income Tax	135,000	
Income Tax Payable		45,000
Deferred Income Tax Payable		90,000

Continuing with the illustration, the $90,000 in Deferred Income Tax Payable will be transferred to Income Tax Payable as the remaining $200,000 of income becomes taxable in later years. If, for example, $120,000 of untaxed income of the first year of the corporation's operations becomes taxable in the second year, the effect would be as follows, stated as a journal entry:

Deferred Income Tax Payable	54,000	
Income Tax Payable		54,000

In the illustration, the amount in Deferred Income Tax Payable at the end of a year will be reported as a liability. The amount due within one year will be classified as a current liability, and the remainder will be classified as a long-term liability or reported in a Deferred Credits section following the Long-Term Liabilities section.

If installment sales are made in later years, there will be more differences between taxable income and reported income, and an accompanying deferment of tax liability. During periods of growth, the amount of deferred income taxes for an enterprise may increase rapidly and can become a significant amount. The amounts of deferred income taxes listed as long-term liabilities on the 1984 annual reports of nine major companies were as follows:

	Deferred Income Taxes (in millions)
IBM	$2,057
DuPont	1,627
Pepsico Inc.	621
Alcoa	489
Coca-Cola Company	241
American Can	105
Colgate-Palmolive	80
Xerox Corporation	54
Chrysler Corporation	22

[2]*Ibid.*, par. 29.

Are Deferred Taxes Really a Liability?

The liability side of Anheuser-Busch's 1980 balance sheet shows "deferred income taxes, $267.7 million." That's no small sum—equal to 19% of total liabilities and 26% of stockholders' equity. Anheuser is not an isolated case. But are deferred taxes really a *liability*?

That's a question many accountants are asking themselves these days. Says Harvey D. Moskowitz, national director of accounting and auditing for Seidman & Seidman, "The deferred taxes on the balance sheet bear no relationship to what is actually going to be owed. So the current method of income tax accounting makes it impossible for the investor to evaluate a company's liquidity, solvency or cash flow."

Here's the explanation for this curious state of affairs: Anheuser-Busch had pretax income of $271.5 million, so, using standard corporate tax rates (less credits), it owed $99.7 million to Uncle Sam. That's what it set aside as "provision for income taxes" on its income statement. But it's not what the company actually paid. Like most businesses Anheuser keeps two sets of books, one for tax purposes, one for stock owners. It uses accelerated depreciation for taxes but straight line for reporting to investors. So, out-of-pocket, it really had to pay only $31.9 million in taxes in 1980—the line marked "current" on the income statement. The other $67.8 million, called "deferred," represents cash that's squirreled away in liabilities on the balance sheet, under the assumption that the company will pay those taxes *eventually*—when accelerated depreciation runs out, for example.

That assumption is probably wrong, though. As long as the company keeps growing—in real terms or because of inflation—it will keep adding new assets and new interest costs to replace the ones that are running out. That means those deferred taxes, instead of getting paid, will simply roll over. And over and over and over. It could almost make you dizzy.

Source: Adapted from Jane Carmichael, "Rollover," *Forbes* (January 18, 1982), pp. 75, 78.

REPORTING UNUSUAL ITEMS IN THE FINANCIAL STATEMENTS

In recent years, professional accounting organizations have devoted much time to the development of guidelines for reporting unusual items relating to the determination of net income. These items may be divided into four relatively well-defined categories, as follows:

1. Adjustments or corrections of net income of prior fiscal periods.
2. Segregation of the results of discontinued operations from the results of continuing operations.
3. Recognition of extraordinary items of gain or loss.
4. Change from one generally accepted accounting principle to another.

Before examining the guidelines that are presently in effect, a brief summary of earlier viewpoints is in order. For several years, there were two conflicting theories about the proper function of the income statement: (1) to report the *current operating performance* and (2) to be *all-inclusive*. According to the first theory, only the effects of the ordinary, normal, and recurring operations were to be reported in the income statement. It was considered better to report nonrecurring items of significant amount in the retained earnings statement. By so doing, it was argued that readers of the income statement would not draw incorrect conclusions about the "normal operating performance" of an enterprise.

On the other hand, the all-inclusive point of view was exactly the opposite of the current operating performance viewpoint. It required that all revenue and expense items recorded in the current period be reported in the income statement, with significant amounts of a nonrecurring nature properly identified. If nonrecurring items were "buried" in the retained earnings statement, they were likely to be overlooked and the total amount of the periodic net income reported over the entire life of an enterprise could not be determined from its income statements. The all-inclusive viewpoint has prevailed, and most professional accountants agree that it is preferable. The generally accepted guidelines on the subject are discussed briefly in the subsections that follow.

Prior Period Adjustments

Minor accounting errors often result from the use of estimates that are inherent in the accounting process. For example, relatively small errors in amounts provided for income taxes of one or more periods are not unusual. Similarly, annual provisions for the uncollectibility of receivables seldom agree with the amounts of the accounts actually written off. Such minor errors are normal and tend to be recurring. The effect of these errors should be included in determining amounts for the current period.

Material errors may result from mathematical mistakes and from mistakes in the application of accounting principles or oversight or misuse of facts that existed at the time transactions were recorded. The treatment of material errors depends on when they are discovered. Errors that are discovered in the same period in which they occurred were discussed in Chapter 5. The procedure recommended there for correcting erroneous entries that have been posted to the ledger is summarized as follows: (1) set forth the entire entry in which the error occurred by the use of memorandum T accounts or a journal entry; (2) set forth the entry that should have been made, using a second set of T accounts or a journal entry; and (3) formulate the debits and credits needed to bring the erroneous entry into agreement with the correct entry. This procedure is entirely a matter of technique, and no question of principle is involved. After the correction has been made, the account balances are the same as they would have been in the absence of error, and the information given in the income statement and the balance sheet is unaffected.

The effect of material errors that are not discovered within the same fiscal period in which they occurred should not be included in the determination of net income for the current period.[3] Corrections of this type of error, usually called prior period adjustments, should be reported as an adjustment of the retained earnings balance at the beginning of the period in which the correction is made. Prior period adjustments would include, for example, the correction of a material error in computing depreciation expense for a prior period. In addition, a change from an unacceptable accounting principle to an acceptable accounting principle is considered to be a correction of a material error and should be treated as a prior period adjustment. An example of such a situation would be the correction resulting from changing from the cash basis to the accrual basis of accounting for a business enterprise that buys and sells merchandise. The manner in which a prior period adjustment is presented in the retained earnings statement is illustrated as follows:

Palmer Company		
Retained Earnings Statement		
For Year Ended December 31, 1987		
Retained earnings, January 1, 1987		$310,500
Less prior period adjustment:		
Correction of error in depreciation expense in 1986,		
net of applicable income tax of $13,000.		29,200
Corrected retained earnings, January 1, 1987		$281,300
Net income for year.	$77,350	
Less dividends.	40,000	
Increase in retained earnings		37,350
Retained earnings, December 31, 1987		$318,650

[3]*Statement of Financial Accounting Standards*, No. 16, "Prior Period Adjustments" (Stamford: Financial Accounting Standards Board, 1977), par. 11.

Note that the amount reported as a prior period adjustment is reported net of the related income tax. In addition, if financial statements are presented only for the current period, the effect of the adjustment on the net income of the preceding period should also be disclosed. If financial statements for prior periods are presented, as is preferable, the statements should be adjusted and the amount of each adjustment should be disclosed.

Adjustments applicable to prior periods that meet the criteria for a prior period adjustment are rare in modern financial accounting. Annual audits by independent public accountants, combined with the internal control features of accounting systems, lessen the chances of errors justifying such treatment.

Discontinued Operations

A gain or loss resulting from the disposal of a segment of a business should be identified on the income statement as a gain or loss from **discontinued operations**. The term *discontinued* refers to "the operations of a segment of a business . . . that has been sold, abandoned, spun off, or otherwise disposed of or . . . is the subject of a formal plan for disposal."[4] The term "segment of a business" refers to a part of an enterprise whose activities represent a major line of business, such as a division or department or a certain class of customer.[5] For example, if an enterprise owning newspapers, television stations, and radio stations were to sell its radio stations, the results of the sale would be reported as a gain or loss on discontinued operations.

When an enterprise discontinues a segment of its operations and identifies the gain or loss therefrom, the results of "continuing operations" should also be identified in the income statement. The net income or loss from continuing operations is presented first, beginning with sales and followed by the enterprise's customary analysis of its costs and expenses. In addition to the data on discontinued operations presented in the body of the statement, such details as the identity of the segment disposed of, the disposal date, a description of the assets and liabilities involved, and the manner of disposal should be disclosed in a note to the financial statements.[6]

Extraordinary Items

Extraordinary gains and losses result from "events and transactions that are distinguished by their unusual nature *and* by the infrequency of their occurrence."[7] Such gains and losses, other than those from the disposal of

---

[4]*Opinions of the Accounting Principles Board, No. 30,* "Reporting the Results of Operations" (New York: American Institute of Certified Public Accountants, 1973), par. 8.
[5]*Ibid.,* par. 13.
[6]*Ibid.,* par. 18.
[7]*Ibid.,* par. 20.

a segment of a business, should be identified in the income statement as **extraordinary items**. To be so classified, an event or transaction must meet both of the following criteria:

1. *Unusual nature — the underlying event or transaction should possess a high degree of abnormality and be of a type clearly unrelated to, or only incidentally related to, the ordinary and typical activities of the entity, taking into account the environment in which the entity operates.*

2. *Infrequency of occurrence — the underlying event or transaction should be of a type that would not reasonably be expected to recur in the foreseeable future, taking into account the environment in which the entity operates.*[8]

Transactions that meet both of the criteria are rare. For example, the 1985 edition of *Accounting Trends & Techniques* indicated that only 74 of the 600 industrial and merchandising companies surveyed reported extraordinary items on their income statements. Usually, extraordinary items result from major casualties, such as floods, earthquakes, and other rare catastrophes not expected to recur. In addition, gains or losses that result when land or buildings are condemned for public use are considered extraordinary.

Gains and losses on the disposal of plant assets do not qualify as extraordinary items because (1) they are not unusual and (2) they recur from time to time in the ordinary course of business activities. Similarly, gains and losses incurred on the sale of investments are usual and recurring for most enterprises. However, if a company had owned only one investment during its entire existence, a gain or loss on its sale might qualify as an extraordinary item, provided there was no intention of acquiring other investments in the foreseeable future.

Changes in Accounting Principles

A change in accounting principle "results from adoption of a generally accepted accounting principle different from the one used previously for reporting purposes."[9] The concept of consistency and its relationship to changes in accounting methods were discussed in Chapter 13. A change from one generally accepted accounting principle or method to another generally accepted principle or method should be disclosed in the financial statements of the period in which the change is made. In addition to describing the nature of the change, the justification for the change should be stated and the effect of the change on net income should be disclosed.

---

[8]*Ibid.*
[9]*Opinions of the Accounting Principles Board, No. 20,* "Accounting Changes" (New York: American Institute of Certified Public Accountants, 1971), par. 7.

The generally accepted procedures for disclosing the effect on net income of a change in principle are as follows: (1) report the cumulative effect of the change on net income of prior periods as a special item on the income statement, and (2) report the effect of the change on net income of the current period. If the financial statements for prior periods are presented in conjunction with the current statements, the effect of the change in accounting principle should also be applied retroactively to the published statements of the prior periods and reported either on their face or in accompanying notes.

The amount of the cumulative effect on net income of prior periods should be reported in a special section of the income statement located immediately prior to the net income. If an extraordinary item or items are reported on the statement, the amount related to the change in principle should follow the extraordinary items.

The procedures should be modified for a change from the lifo assumption for inventory costing to another method or for a change in the method of accounting for long-term construction contracts. For these changes in principle, the cumulative effect on prior years' income is not reported as a special item on the income statement. Instead, the newly adopted principle should be applied retroactively to the income statements of the prior periods and the effect on income disclosed, either on the face of the statements or in accompanying notes. Financial statements of subsequent periods need not repeat the disclosures.[10]

Allocation of Income Tax to Unusual Items

The amount reported as a prior period adjustment, a gain or loss from a discontinued operation, an extraordinary item, or the cumulative effect of a change in accounting principle should be net of the related income tax. The amount of income tax allocable to each of these items may be disclosed on the face of the appropriate financial statement or by an accompanying note.

Presentation of Unusual Items in the Income Statement

The manner in which gains or losses from discontinued operations, extraordinary items, and the cumulative effect of a change in accounting principle may be presented in the income statement is illustrated for CAP Corporation as follows. Many variations in terminology and format are possible.

---

[10]*Ibid.*, pars. 27 and 28.

CAP Corporation
Income Statement
For the Year Ended August 31, 19--

Net sales	$9,600,950

Income from continuing operations before income tax		$1,310,000
Income tax..		620,000
Income from continuing operations		$ 690,000
Loss on discontinued operations (Note A).......................		100,000
Income before extraordinary item and cumulative effect of a change in accounting principle		$ 590,000
Extraordinary item:		
Gain on condemnation of land, net of applicable income tax of $65,000		150,000
Cumulative effect on prior years of changing to a different depreciation method (Note B)...............................		92,000
Net income		$ 832,000

Note A. On July 1 of the current year, the entire electrical products division of the corporation was sold at a loss of $100,000, net of applicable income tax of $50,000. The net sales of the division for the current year were $2,900,000. The assets sold were composed of inventories, equipment, and plant totaling $2,100,000, and the liabilities' assumed by the purchaser amounted to $600,000.

Note B. Depreciation of property, plant, and equipment has been computed by the straight-line method at all manufacturing facilities in 19--. Prior to 19--, depreciation of equipment for one of the divisions had been computed on the double-declining balance method. In 19--, the straight-line method was adopted for this division in order to achieve uniformity and to more appropriately match the remaining depreciation charges with the estimated economic utility of such assets. Pursuant to APB Opinion 20, this change in depreciation has been applied retroactively to prior years. The effect of the change was to increase income before extraordinary items for 19-- by approximately $30,000. The adjustment of $92,000 (after reduction for income tax of $88,000) to apply retroactively the new method is also included in income for 19--.

EARNINGS PER COMMON SHARE

The absolute amounts of net income are often useful in evaluating a company's profitability. However, these absolute amounts are difficult to use in comparing companies of different sizes. For example, a net income of $750,000 may be very satisfactory for a small computer manufacturer, but it may be very unsatisfactory for a very large computer manufacturer. Likewise, the absolute amount of net income is difficult to use in evaluating a company's profitability when the amount of stockholders' equity changes significantly. In such cases, the profitability of a company may be expressed as earnings per share. The term **earnings per share** refers to the net income per share of common stock outstanding during a given period. For public corporations, data on earnings per share of common stock must be reported on the income statement.[11] Earnings per share is often the item of greatest interest contained in corporate financial statements. These data are also often reported by the financial press and by various statistical services.

If a company has only common stock outstanding, the earnings per share of common stock is determined by dividing net income by the number of common shares outstanding. If preferred stock is outstanding, the net income must be reduced by the amount of any preferred dividend requirements before dividing by the number of common shares outstanding.

The effect of nonrecurring additions to or deductions from income of a period should be considered in computing earnings per share. Otherwise, a single per share amount based on net income would be misleading. To illustrate this point, assume that CAP Corporation, whose partial income statement for the current year was presented on page 694, reported net income of $700,000 for the preceding year, with no extraordinary or other special items. Assume also that the corporation's capital stock was composed of 200,000 common shares outstanding during the entire two-year period. If the earnings per share of $3.50 ($700,000 ÷ 200,000) for the preceding year were compared with the earnings per share of $4.16 ($832,000 ÷ 200,000) for the current year, it would appear that operations had greatly improved. However, the current year's per share amount that is comparable to $3.50 is in reality $3.45 ($690,000 ÷ 200,000), which indicates a slight downward trend in normal operations.

Data on earnings per share should be presented in conjunction with the income statement. If there are nonrecurring items on the statement, the per share amounts should be presented for (1) income from continuing operations, (2) income before extraordinary items and the cumulative effect of a change in accounting principle, (3) the cumulative effect of a change in accounting principle, and (4) net income.[12] Presentation of per share amounts is optional for the gain or loss on discontinued operations and for extraordinary items. The per share data may be shown in parentheses or added at the bottom of the statement, as in the following illustration for CAP Corporation:

---

[11]Nonpublic corporations are exempt from this requirement, according to *Statement of Financial Accounting Standards, No. 21,* "Suspension of the Reporting of Earnings per Share and Segment Information by Nonpublic Enterprises" (Stamford: Financial Accounting Standards Board, 1978).

[12]*Opinions of the Accounting Principles Board, No. 15,* "Earnings per Share" (New York: American Institute of Certified Public Accountants, 1969) as amended by *Opinions of the Accounting Principles Board, No. 20,* and *Opinions of the Accounting Principles Board, No. 30.*

```
                           CAP Corporation
                           Income Statement
                    For the Year Ended August 31, 19--
```

Income from continuing operations $690,000

Net income $832,000

Earnings per common share:
   Income from continuing operations $3.45
   Loss on discontinued operations 50
   Income before extraordinary item and cumulative effect of a
      change in accounting principle $2.95
   Extraordinary item 75
   Cumulative effect on prior years of changing to a different
      depreciation method 46
   Net income $4.16

In computing the earnings per share of common stock, all factors that affect the number of common shares outstanding must be considered. If there is an issue of preferred stock or bonds (debt) with the privilege of converting to common stock, two different amounts of per share earnings should ordinarily be reported. One amount is computed without regard to the conversion privilege and is referred to as "Earnings per common share—assuming no dilution" or "Primary earnings per share." The other computation is based on the assumption that the convertible preferred stock or bonds are converted to common stock, and the amount is referred to as "Earnings per common share—assuming full dilution" or "Fully diluted earnings per share."[13]

The details of the computation of earnings per share should be disclosed in notes to the financial statements, as indicated by the following note adapted from the 1984 statements of Pan Am Corporation:

11. Earnings Per Common Share

Primary earnings per common share is computed by dividing net income by the average number of common shares outstanding during each year. Fully diluted earnings per common share is computed by dividing net income, adjusted to eliminate interest expense on convertible bonds, by the total of the average number of common shares outstanding and the average number of common shares reserved for issuance on conversion of such bonds.

---

[13]*Opinions of the Accounting Principles Board, No. 15,* "Earnings per Share" (New York: American Institute of Certified Public Accountants, 1969) par. 16.

The complexities of the computation of earnings per share and other complexities of capital structure are discussed in more advanced accounting texts.

APPROPRIATION OF RETAINED EARNINGS *unappropriated appropriated / not restrictive*

The amount of a corporation's retained earnings available for distribution to its shareholders may be limited by action of the board of directors. The amount restricted, which is called an **appropriation** or a **reserve**, remains a part of retained earnings and should be so classified in the financial statements. An appropriation can be effected by transferring the desired amount from Retained Earnings to a special account designating its purpose, such as Appropriation for Plant Expansion.

Appropriations may be initiated by the directors, or they may be required by law or contract. Some states require that a corporation retain earnings equal to the amount paid for treasury stock. For example, if a corporation with accumulated earnings of $200,000 purchases shares of its own issued stock for $50,000, the corporation would not be permitted to pay more than $150,000 in dividends. The restriction is equal to the $50,000 paid for the treasury stock and assures that legal capital will not be impaired by a declaration of dividends. The entry to record the appropriation would be:

| Apr. 24 | Retained Earnings. . . . . | 50,000 | |
| | Appropriation for Treasury Stock . . . . | | 50,000 |

When a part or all of an appropriation is no longer needed, the amount should be transferred back to the retained earnings account. Thus, if the corporation in the above illustration sells the treasury stock, the appropriation would be eliminated by the following entry:

| Nov. 10 | Appropriation for Treasury Stock . . . . | 50,000 | |
| | Retained Earnings. . . . . | | 50,000 |

When a corporation borrows a large amount through the issuance of bonds (debt), the agreement may provide for restrictions on dividends until the debt is paid. The contract may stipulate that retained earnings equal to the amount borrowed be restricted during the entire period of the loan, or it may require that the restriction be built up by annual appropriations. For example, assume that a corporation borrows $700,000 on ten-year bonds. If equal annual appropriations were to be made over the life of the bonds, there would be a series of ten entries, each in the amount of $70,000, debiting Retained Earnings and crediting an appropriation account entitled Appropriation for Bonded Indebtedness. Even if the bond agreement did not require the restriction on retained earnings, the directors might decide to establish the appropriation. In that case, it would be a *discretionary* rather than a *contractual* appropriation. The entries would be the same in either case.

It must be clearly understood that the appropriation account is not directly related to any certain group of asset accounts. Its existence does not imply that there is an equivalent amount of cash or other assets set aside in a special fund. The appropriation serves the purpose of restricting dividends, but it does not assure that the cash that might otherwise be distributed as dividends will not be invested in additional inventories or other assets, or used to reduce liabilities.

Appropriations of retained earnings may be accompanied by a segregation of cash or marketable securities, in which case the appropriation is said to be **funded**. Accumulation of such funds is discussed in Chapter 17.

There are other purposes for which the directors may consider appropriations desirable. A company may earmark earnings for specific contingencies, such as inventory price declines or an adverse decision on a pending lawsuit. Some companies with properties in many locations may assume their own risk of losses from fire, windstorm, and other casualties rather than obtain protection from insurance companies. In such cases, the appropriation account would be entitled Appropriation for Self-Insurance. Such an appropriation is likely to be permanent, although its amount may vary as the total value of properties and the extent of casualty protection change. If a loss occurs, it should be debited to a special loss account rather than to the appropriation account. It is definitely a loss of the particular period and should be reported in the income statement.

The details of retained earnings may be presented in the balance sheet in the following manner. The item designated "Unappropriated" is the balance of the retained earnings account.

```
Retained earnings:
  Appropriated:
    For plant expansion.......................  $  250,000
  Unappropriated.............................   1,800,000
    Total retained earnings...................             $2,050,000
```

Restrictions on retained earnings do not need to be formalized in the ledger. However, following legal requirements and contractual restrictions is necessary, and the nature and the amount of all restrictions should always be disclosed in the balance sheet. For example, the appropriations data appearing in the foregoing illustration could be presented in a note accompanying the balance sheet. Such an alternative might also be used as a means of simplifying or condensing the balance sheet, even though appropriation accounts are maintained in the ledger. The alternative balance sheet presentation, including the note, might appear as follows:

Retained earnings (see note) $2,050,000

Note: Retained earnings in the amount of $250,000 are appropriated for expansion of plant facilities; the remaining $1,800,000 is unrestricted.

When there are accounts for appropriations, it is customary to divide the retained earnings statement into two major sections: (1) appropriated and (2) unappropriated. The first section is composed of an analysis of all appropriation accounts, beginning with the opening balance, followed by the additions or the deductions during the period, and ending with the closing balance. The second section is composed of an analysis of the retained earnings account, beginning with the opening balance, followed by the period's net income, dividends, and transfers to and from the appropriation accounts, and ending with the closing balance. The final figure on the statement is the total retained earnings as of the last day of the period. This form of the statement is illustrated for Shaw Corporation as follows:

Shaw Corporation
Retained Earnings Statement
For Year Ended December 31, 19--

Appropriated:			
Appropriation for plant expansion, January 1, 19--......		$ 180,000	
Additional appropriation (see below)................		100,000	
Retained earnings appropriated, December 31, 19--...			$ 280,000
Unappropriated:			
Balance, January 1, 19--...........................	$1,414,500		
Net income for the year........................	580,000	$1,994,500	
Cash dividends declared.........................	$ 125,000		
Transfer to appropriation for plant expansion (see above).................................	100,000	225,000	
Retained earnings unappropriated, December 31, 19--.			1,769,500
Total retained earnings, December 31, 19--...........			$2,049,500

RETAINED EARNINGS STATEMENT

There are many possible variations in the form of the retained earnings statement. It may also be added to the income statement to form a combined statement of income and retained earnings, as illustrated in Chapter 5.

NATURE OF DIVIDENDS

A **dividend** is a distribution by a corporation to its shareholders. On common shares, the dividend is usually stated in terms of dollars and cents rather than as a percentage of par. On preferred shares, the dividend may be stated either in monetary terms or as a percentage of par. For example, the annual dividend rate on a particular $100 par preferred stock may be stated as either $10 or 10%.

A dividend usually represents a distribution from retained earnings, and may be paid in cash, in stock of the company, or in other property. A dividend may also represent a distribution from paid-in capital. The types of dividends are discussed in the following paragraphs.

Cash Dividends

A cash distribution of earnings by a corporation to its shareholders is called a **cash dividend**. Cash dividends are the most usual form of dividend. Usually there are three prerequisites to paying a cash dividend:

1. Sufficient unappropriated retained earnings,
2. Sufficient cash, and
3. Formal action by the board of directors.

A large amount of accumulated earnings does not always mean that a corporation is able to pay dividends. There must also be enough cash in excess of routine requirements. The amount of retained earnings, which represents net income retained in the business, is not directly related to cash. The cash provided by the net income may have been used to purchase assets, to reduce liabilities, or for other purposes. The directors are not required by law to declare dividends, even when both retained earnings and cash appear to be sufficient. When a dividend has been declared, however, it becomes a liability of the corporation.

Corporations with a wide distribution of stock usually try to maintain a stable dividend record. They may retain a large part of earnings in good years in order to be able to continue dividend payments in lean years. Dividends may be paid once a year or on a semiannual or quarterly basis. The tendency is to pay quarterly dividends on both common and preferred stock. In particularly good years, the directors may declare an "extra" dividend on common stock. It may be paid at one of the usual dividend dates or at some other date. The designation "extra" indicates that the board of directors does not anticipate an increase in the amount of the "regular" dividend.

Notice of a dividend declaration is usually reported in financial publications and newspapers. The notice identifies three different dates related to a declaration:

1. The date of declaration,
2. The date of record, and
3. The date of payment.

The first is the date the directors take formal action declaring the dividend, the second is the date as of which ownership of shares is to be determined, and the third is the date payment is to be made. For example, a notice read: "On June 26, the board of directors of Campbell Soup Co. declared a quarterly cash dividend of $.33 per common share to stockholders of record as of the close of business on July 8, payable on July 31."

The liability for a dividend is recorded on the declaration date, when the formal action is taken by the directors. No entry is required on the date of record, which merely fixes the date for determining the identity of the stockholders entitled to receive the dividend. The period of time between the record date and the payment date is provided to permit completion of postings to the stockholders ledger and preparation of the dividend checks. The liability of the corporation is paid by the mailing of the checks.

To illustrate the entries required in the declaration and the payment of cash dividends, assume that on December 1 the board of directors of Hiber Corporation declares the regular quarterly dividend of $2.50 on the 5,000 shares of $100 par, 10% preferred stock outstanding (total dividend of $12,500), and a quarterly dividend of 30¢ on the 100,000 shares of $10 par common stock outstanding (total dividend of $30,000). Both dividends are to stockholders of record on December 10, and checks are to be issued to stockholders on January 2. The entry to record the declaration of the dividends is as follows:

| Dec. 1 | Cash Dividends............................ | 42,500 | |
| | Cash Dividends Payable .... | | 42,500 |

The balance in Cash Dividends would be transferred to Retained Earnings as a part of the closing process and Cash Dividends Payable would be listed on the balance sheet as a current liability. Payment of the liability on January 2 would be recorded in the usual manner as a debit to Cash Dividends Payable and a credit to Cash for $42,500.

Dividends on cumulative preferred stock do not become a liability of the corporation until formal action is taken by the board of directors. However, dividends in arrears at a balance sheet date should be disclosed by a footnote, a parenthetical notation, or a segregation of retained earnings similar to the following:

Retained earnings:
Required to meet dividends in arrears on		
preferred stock	$30,000	
Remainder, unrestricted	16,000	
Total retained earnings...........................		$46,000

Stock Dividends   *an additional issuance of stock based on a % of the outstanding stock*

A pro rata distribution of shares of stock of a company to the stockholders, accompanied by a transfer of retained earnings to paid-in capital accounts, is called a **stock dividend**. Such distributions are usually in common stock and are issued to holders of common stock. It is possible to issue common stock to preferred stockholders or vice versa, but such stock dividends are too unusual to warrant their consideration here.

Stock dividends are quite unlike cash dividends, in that there is no distribution of cash or other corporate assets to the stockholders. They are ordinarily issued by corporations that "plow back" (retain) earnings for use in acquiring new facilities or for expanding their operations.

The effect of a stock dividend on the capital structure of the issuing corporation is to transfer accumulated earnings to paid-in capital. The statutes of most states require that an amount equivalent to the par or stated value of a stock dividend be transferred from the retained earnings account to the common stock account. Compliance with this minimum requirement is considered by accountants to be satisfactory for a nonpublic corporation, whose stockholders are presumed to have enough knowledge of the corporation's affairs to recognize the true import of the dividend. However, many investors in the stock of public corporations are often less knowledgeable. An analysis of this latter situation, and the widely accepted viewpoint of professional accountants, has been expressed as follows:

> ... many recipients of stock dividends look upon them as distributions of corporate earnings and usually in an amount equivalent to the fair value of the additional shares received. Furthermore, it is to be presumed that such views of recipients are materially strengthened in those instances, which are by far the most numerous, where the issuances are so small in comparison with the shares previously outstanding that they do not have any apparent effect upon the share market price and, consequently, the market value of the shares previously held remains substantially unchanged. The committee therefore believes that where these circumstances exist the corporation should in the public interest account for the transaction by transferring from [retained earnings] to the category of permanent capitalization ... an amount equal to the fair value of the additional shares issued. Unless this is done, the amount of earnings which the shareholder may believe to have been distributed to him will be left, except to the extent otherwise dictated by legal requirements, in [retained earnings] subject to possible further similar stock issuances or cash distributions. [14]

To illustrate the issuance of a stock dividend according to the procedure recommended above, assume the following balances in the stockholders' equity accounts of Montag Corporation as of December 15:

Common Stock, $20 par (2,000,000 shares issued) $40,000,000
Premium on Common Stock............................. 9,000,000
Retained Earnings 26,600,000

5% of outstanding shares

[14]*Accounting Research and Terminology Bulletins—Final Edition*, "No. 43, Restatement and Revision of Accounting Research Bulletins" (New York: American Institute of Certified Public Accountants, 1961), Ch. 7, Sec. B, par. 10.

5% X shares issued = 100,000 shares

On December 15, the board of directors declares a 5% stock dividend (100,000 shares, $20 par), to be issued on January 10. Assuming that the average of the high and low market prices on the declaration date is $31 a share, the entry to record the declaration would be as follows:

always recorded at market value

Dec. 15	Stock Dividends................	3,100,000		31
	Stock Dividends Distributable........		2,000,000	−20
	Premium on Common Stock.........		1,100,000	11

recorded at par

100,000 X 11

The $3,100,000 debit to Stock Dividends would be transferred to Retained Earnings as a part of the closing process. The issuance of the stock certificates would be recorded on January 10 as follows:

100,000 X 20

Jan. 10	Stock Dividends Distributable..........	2,000,000	
	Common Stock		2,000,000

The effect of the stock dividend is to transfer $3,100,000 from the retained earnings account to paid-in capital accounts and to increase by 100,000 the number of shares outstanding. There is no change in the assets, liabilities, or total stockholders' equity of the corporation. If financial statements are prepared between the date of declaration and the date of issuance, the stock dividends distributable account should be listed in the paid-in capital section of the balance sheet.

The issuance of the additional shares does not affect the total amount of a stockholder's equity and proportionate interest in the corporation. The effect of the stock dividend on the accounts of a corporation and on the equity of a stockholder owning 1,000 shares is demonstrated by the following tabulation:

The Corporation	Before Stock Dividend	After Stock Dividend
Common Stock	$40,000,000	$42,000,000
Premium on common stock	9,000,000	10,100,000
Retained earnings....................	26,600,000	23,500,000
Total stockholders' equity	$75,600,000	$75,600,000
Number of shares outstanding..........	2,000,000	2,100,000
Equity per share	$37.80	$36.00
A Stockholder		
Number of shares owned	1,000	1,050
Total equity........................	$37,800	$37,800
Portion of corporation owned..........	.05%	.05%

transfer from one equity account to another

Liquidating Dividends

The term **liquidating dividend** is applied to a distribution to stockholders from paid-in capital. Such dividends are unusual, but in many states they may be declared from the excess of paid-in capital over par or stated value. Liquidating dividends are usually paid when a corporation permanently reduces its operations or winds up its affairs completely. Since dividends are normally paid from retained earnings, dividends that reduce paid-in capital should be identified as liquidating dividends when paid.

STOCK SPLITS

cancel all old stock — *purpose to reduce market price to make stock afforable to ordinary investors*

Corporations sometimes reduce the par or stated value of their common stock and issue a proportionate number of additional shares. Such a procedure is called a **stock split** or **stock split-up**. The primary purpose of a stock split is to bring about a reduction in the market price per share and thus to encourage more investors to enter the market for the company's shares.

To illustrate a stock split, assume that the board of directors of Riley Corporation, which has 10,000 shares of $100 par stock outstanding, reduces the par to $20 and increases the number of shares to 50,000. The amount of stock outstanding is $1,000,000 both before and after the stock split. Only the number of shares and the par per share are changed. Since there are no changes in the balances of any of the corporation's accounts, no entry to record the stock split is required.

Each shareholder in a corporation whose stock is split owns the same total par amount of stock before and after the stock split. For example, a Riley Corporation stockholder who owned 100 shares of $100 par stock before the split (total par of $10,000) would own 500 shares of $20 par stock after the split (total par of $10,000).

DIVIDENDS AND STOCK SPLITS FOR TREASURY STOCK

Cash or property dividends are not paid on treasury stock. To do so would place the corporation in the position of earning income through dealing with itself. Accordingly, the total amount of a cash (or property) dividend should be based on the number of shares outstanding at the record date.

When a corporation holding treasury stock declares a stock dividend, the number of shares to be issued may be based on either (1) the number of shares outstanding or (2) the number of shares issued. In practice, the number of shares held as treasury stock represents a small percent of the number of shares issued. Also, the rate of dividend is usually small, so that the difference between the end results of both methods is usually not significant.

There is no legal, theoretical, or practical reason for excluding treasury stock when computing the number of shares to be issued in a stock split. The reduction in par or stated value would apply to all shares of the class, including the unissued, issued, and treasury shares.

CHAPTER REVIEW

KEY POINTS

1. Paid-In Capital.

Although paid-in capital usually results from the issuance of stock, it may also originate from donated assets and redemptions of a corporation's own stock. Many variations in terminology and arrangement of the paid-in capital section of the balance sheet exist. Significant changes in paid-in capital during a period should be disclosed.

2. Corporate Earnings and Income Taxes.

Unlike sole proprietorships and partnerships, corporations are subject to federal income tax and, in many cases, to income taxes levied by states or other political subdivisions. Most corporations are required to estimate the amount of their federal income tax expense for the year and make advance payment, usually in four installments. At the end of the year, the actual taxable income and the actual tax are determined. If an additional amount is owed, a liability is recorded. If an overpayment occurs, the amount would be debited to a receivable account and credited to Income Tax.

3. Allocation of Income Tax Between Periods.

The taxable income of a corporation, determined according to the tax laws, is often different from the amount of income (before income tax) determined from the accounts and reported in the income statement. This difference may need to be allocated between periods, depending upon whether it is a permanent difference or a timing difference.

The tax laws provide for special treatment of certain revenue and expense items. This special treatment results in permanent differences between the amount of income tax actually owed and the amount that would be owed if the tax laws were based on income before income tax. Permanent differences cause no problems for financial reporting. The amount of income tax determined in accordance with the tax laws is the amount reported on the income statement.

The treatment of certain items results in differences between income before income tax and taxable income, because the items are recognized in one period for income statement purposes and in another period for tax purposes. These timing differences turn around in later years. Timing differences require special treatment in the accounts. The income tax to be reported on the income statement should be the total tax expected to result from the net income reported for that period. The difference between the amount of income tax based on reported net income and the amount based on taxable income is debited or credited to a deferred income tax account. The deferred income tax account will normally have a credit balance and is reported on the balance sheet as a current liability or a long-term liability, depending on when the items to which it relates will reverse their effects on taxable income.

4.   Reporting Unusual Items in the Financial Statements.

General guidelines have been developed for reporting unusual items related to the determination of net income. Material errors related to a prior period are reported as an adjustment to the retained earnings balance at the beginning of the period in which the correction is made. Any financial statements presented for the prior period should be restated, and the current period financial statements should clearly set forth the adjustment necessary to the retained earnings account.

A gain or loss resulting from the disposal of a segment of a business should be identified on the income statement as a gain or loss from discontinued operations. In addition, the results of continuing operations should be identified in the income statement. Details of the discontinued operations should also be disclosed in a note to the financial statements.

Extraordinary gains and losses result from events and transactions that are distinguished by their unusual nature and the infrequency of their occurrence. Such gains and losses, other than those from the disposal of a segment of a business, should be identified in the income statement as extraordinary items.

A change in accounting principle results from the adoption of a generally accepted accounting principle different from the one used previously for reporting purposes. The effect of the change in principle on net income in the current period, as well as the cumulative effect on income of prior periods, should be disclosed. Details describing the change in accounting principle are also normally disclosed in an accompanying note to the financial statements.

The amount reported as a prior period adjustment, a gain or loss from discontinued operations, an extraordinary item, or the cumulative effect of a change in accounting principle should be net of the related income tax. The amount of income tax allocable to each of these items should be disclosed on the face of the appropriate financial statement or by an accompanying note.

5. Earnings per Common Share.

Data on earnings per share of common stock are reported on the income statements of public corporations. If preferred stock is outstanding, the net income must be reduced by the amount of any preferred dividend requirements before dividing by the number of common shares outstanding. If there are nonrecurring items on the income statement, the per share amount should be presented for (1) income from continuing operations, (2) income before extraordinary items and the cumulative effect of a change in accounting principle, (3) the cumulative effect of a change in accounting principle, and (4) net income. Presentation of per share amounts is optional for a gain or loss on discontinued operations and for extraordinary items.

6. Appropriation of Retained Earnings.

The amount of a corporation's retained earnings available for distribution to its shareholders may be limited by action of the board of directors or by law or contract. The amount restricted, called an appropriation or a reserve, remains a part of retained earnings. An appropriation of retained earnings is not directly related to any certain group of assets, and its existence does not imply that there is an equivalent amount of cash or other assets set aside in a special fund. However, appropriations may be accompanied by a segregation of cash or marketable securities, in which case the appropriation is said to be funded. Appropriations of retained earnings should be clearly set forth in the retained earnings statement and should be properly identified on the face of the balance sheet or in an accompanying note.

It is customary to divide the retained earnings statement into two major sections: (1) appropriated and (2) unappropriated. Each of these sections should identify the beginning balance and any additions or deductions during the period.

7. Nature of Dividends.

A dividend is a distribution by a corporation to its shareholders. Dividends may be paid in cash, in stock of the company, or in other property. Three dates are important in the distribution of dividends. (1) The date of declaration is the date on which the directors take formal action to declare the dividend and on which the dividend is recorded in the accounting records. (2) The date of record is the date on which ownership of shares is to be determined for purposes of distribution of the dividend. (3) The date of payment is the date on which the dividend is to be distributed or paid.

Dividends on cumulative preferred stock do not become a liability of the corporation until formal action is taken by the board of directors. However, dividends in arrears at a balance sheet date should be disclosed by a footnote, a parenthetical notation, or a segregation of retained earnings.

A stock dividend is a pro rata distribution of shares of stock to stockholders. The effect of a stock dividend on the capital structure of the issuing corporation is to transfer accumulated earnings to paid-in capital. There is no change in the assets, liabilities, or total stockholders' equity of the corporation.

A dividend distribution to stockholders from paid-in capital is known as a liquidating dividend. Such dividends are usually paid when a corporation permanently reduces its operations or winds up its affairs completely. Because of the unusual nature of liquidating dividends, they should be clearly identified in the financial statements.

8. Stock Splits.

When a corporation reduces the par or stated value of its common stock and issues a proportionate number of additional shares, a stock split or stock split-up has occurred. Because only the number of shares and the par amount per share of stock is changed during a stock split, there are no changes in the balances of any corporation accounts, and no entry is required. Each shareholder owns the same total par amount of stock before and after a stock split. The primary purpose of a stock split is to reduce the market price per share and encourage more investors to enter the market for the company's shares.

9. Dividends and Stock Splits for Treasury Stock.

Cash or property dividends are not paid on treasury stock. To do so would place the corporation in a position of earning income through dealing with itself. However, when a stock dividend or a stock split occurs, treasury shares may or may not participate, depending upon action of the board of directors.

KEY TERMS

taxable income 685
prior period adjustments 690
discontinued operations 691
extraordinary items 692
earnings per share 695
appropriation of
   retained earnings 697

funded 698
dividend 699
cash dividend 700
stock dividend 702
liquidating dividend 704
stock split 704

SELF-EXAMINATION QUESTIONS
Answers in Appendix B.

1. Paid-in capital for a corporation may originate from which of the following sources?
    A. Real estate donated to the corporation
    B. Redemption of the corporation's own stock
    C. Sale of the corporation's treasury stock
    D. All of the above

2. During its first year of operations, a corporation elected to use the straight-line method of depreciation for financial reporting purposes and the sum-of-the-years-digits method in determining taxable income. If the income tax is 45% and the amount of depreciation expense is $60,000 under the straight-line method and $100,000 under the sum-of-the-years-digits method, what is the amount of income tax deferred to future years?
   A. $18,000
   B. $27,000
   C. $45,000
   D. None of the above

3. An item treated as a prior period adjustment should be reported in the financial statements as:
   A. an extraordinary item
   B. an other expense item
   C. an adjustment of the beginning balance of retained earnings
   D. none of the above

4. A material gain resulting from the condemnation of land for public use would be reported on the income statement as:
   A. an extraordinary item
   B. an other income item
   C. an item of revenue from sales
   D. none of the above

5. An appropriation for plant expansion would be reported on the balance sheet in:
   A. the plant assets section
   B. the long-term liabilities section
   C. the stockholders' equity section
   D. none of the above

ILLUSTRATIVE PROBLEM

During its current fiscal year ended December 31, 1987, Block Inc. completed the following selected transactions:

Jan. 9. Purchased 1,500 shares of own common stock at $16, recording the stock at cost. (Prior to the purchase there were 70,000 shares of $10 par common stock outstanding.)

Mar. 16. Discovered that a receipt of $500 cash on account from I. Jonson had been posted in error to the account of I. Johnson. The transaction was recorded correctly in the journal.

May 18. Declared a semiannual dividend of $1 on the 10,000 shares of preferred stock and a 20¢ dividend on the common stock to stockholders of record on May 28, payable on June 10.

June 10. Paid the cash dividends.

Aug. 23. Sold 1,000 shares of treasury stock at $18, receiving cash.

Nov. 12. Declared semiannual dividends of $1 on the preferred stock and 20¢ on the common stock. In addition, a 5% common stock dividend was declared on the common stock outstanding, to be capitalized at the fair market value of the common stock, which is estimated at $16.

Dec.   4. Paid the cash dividends and issued the certificates for the common
          stock dividend.
      31. Recorded $75,000 additional federal income tax allocable to net
          income for the year. Of this amount, $65,600 is a current liability and
          $9,400 is deferred.
      31. The board of directors authorized the appropriation necessitated by
          the holding of treasury stock.

Instructions:

Prepare the journal entries to record the transactions for Block Inc.

SOLUTION

1987
Jan.   9 Treasury Stock   24,000
           Cash   24,000

Mar. 16 No entry. Error can be corrected by revising
          the postings in the subsidiary accounts
          receivable ledger.

May 18 Cash Dividends   23,700
           Cash Dividends Payable   23,700

June 10 Cash Dividends Payable   23,700
           Cash   23,700

Aug. 23 Cash   18,000
           Treasury Stock   16,000
           Paid-In Capital from Sale of
             Treasury Stock   2,000

Nov. 12 Cash Dividends   23,900
           Stock Dividends. . . 3475 X 16 55,600
           Cash Dividends Payable   23,900
           Stock Dividends Distributable . . . . *par value*   34,750
           Premium on Common Stock.   20,850

Dec.   4 Cash Dividends Payable   23,900
           Stock Dividends Distributable   34,750
           Cash.   23,900
           Common Stock.   34,750

      31 Income Tax   75,000
           Income Tax Payable   65,600
           Deferred Income Tax Payable...........   9,400

      31 Retained Earnings. . . . . 500 X 16   8,000
           Appropriation for Treasury Stock   8,000

DISCUSSION QUESTIONS

1. What are the titles of the two principal subdivisions of the stockholders' equity section of a corporate balance sheet?

2. If a corporation is given land as an inducement to locate in a particular community, (a) how should the amount of the debit to the land account be determined, and (b) what is the title of the account that should be credited for the same amount?

3. A corporation has paid $300,000 of federal income tax during the year on the basis of its estimated income. What entry should be recorded as of the end of the year if it determines that (a) it owes an additional $10,000? (b) it overpaid its tax by $20,000?

4. The income before income tax reported on the income statement for the year is $600,000. Because of timing differences between accounting and tax methods, the taxable income for the same year is $450,000. Assuming an income tax rate of 50%, state (a) the amount of income tax to be deducted from the $600,000 on the income statement, (b) the amount of the actual income tax that should be paid for the year, and (c) the amount of the deferred income tax liability.

5. How would the amount of deferred income tax payable be reported in the balance sheet if (a) it is payable within one year, and (b) if it is payable beyond one year?

6. Indicate how prior period adjustments would be reported on the financial statements presented only for the current period.

7. Indicate where the following should be reported in the financial statements, assuming that financial statements are presented only for the current year:
   (a) Loss on disposal of equipment considered to be obsolete.
   (b) Uninsured loss on building due to hurricane damage. The firm was organized in 1905, and had not previously incurred hurricane damage.

8. Classify each of the following revenue and expense items as either (a) normally recurring or (b) extraordinary. Assume that the amount of each item is material.
   (1) Uninsured flood loss. (Flood insurance is unavailable because of periodic flooding in the area.)
   (2) Uncollectible accounts expense.
   (3) Interest income on notes receivable.
   (4) Gain on sale of land condemned for public use.
   (5) Loss on sale of plant assets.
   (6) Salaries of corporate officers.

9. During the current year, ten acres of land which cost $75,000 were condemned for construction of an interstate highway. Assuming that an award of $125,000 in cash was received and that the applicable income tax on this transaction is 25%, how would this information be presented in the income statement?

10. A corporation reports earnings per share of $5.75 for the most recent year and $4.75 for the preceding year. The $5.75 includes $1.50 per share gain from a sale of the only investment owned since the business was organized in 1939. (a) Should the composition of the $5.75 be disclosed in the financial reports? (b) What is the earnings per share amount for the most recent year that is comparable to the $4.75 earnings per share of the preceding year? (c) On the basis of the limited information presented, would you conclude that operations had improved or declined?

11. Appropriations of retained earnings may be (a) required by law, (b) required by contract, or (c) made at the discretion of the board of directors. Give an illustration of each type of appropriation.

12. A credit balance in Retained Earnings does not represent cash. Explain.

13. The board of directors votes to appropriate $100,000 of retained earnings for bonded indebtedness. What is the effect of this action on (a) cash, (b) total retained earnings, and (c) retained earnings available for dividends?

14. What are the three prerequisites of the declaration and the payment of a cash dividend?

15. The dates in connection with the declaration of a cash dividend are June 15, July 1, and July 15. Identify each date.

16. A corporation with both cumulative preferred stock and common stock outstanding has a substantial credit balance in its retained earnings account at the beginning of the current fiscal year. Although net income for the current year is sufficient to pay the preferred dividend of $25,000 each quarter and a common dividend of $40,000 each quarter, the board of directors declares dividends only on the preferred stock. Suggest possible reasons for passing the dividends on the common stock.

17. State the effect of the following actions on a corporation's assets, liabilities, and stockholders' equity: (a) declaration of a cash dividend; (b) payment of the cash dividend declared in (a); (c) declaration of a stock dividend; (d) issuance of stock certificates for the stock dividend declared in (c); (e) authorization and issuance of stock certificates in a stock split.

18. An owner of 100 shares of Randall Company common stock receives a stock dividend of 5 shares. (a) What is the effect of the stock dividend on the equity per share of the stock? (b) How does the total equity of 105 shares compare with the total equity of 100 shares before the stock dividend?

19. What term is used to identify a distribution to stockholders from paid-in capital?

20. A corporation with 5,000 shares of no-par common stock issued, of which 200 shares are held as treasury stock, declares a cash dividend of $1 a share. What is the total amount of the dividend?

21. If a corporation with 10,000 shares of common stock outstanding has a 4-for-1 stock split (3 additional shares for each share issued), what will be the number of shares outstanding after the split?

22. If the common stock in Question 21 had a market price of $200 per share before the stock split, what would be an approximate market price per share after the split?

23. Real World Focus. The 1984 annual report of Xerox Corporation disclosed the discontinuance of its Shugart operations, which manufactured and marketed disk drives primarily for use with personal computers and word processors. A summary of information relating to the discontinuance of the Shugart operations for 1984 is as follows:

	(In millions)
Operating revenues...............................	$179.7
Income (loss) before taxes	$ (72.4)
Income (taxes) benefits	37.2
Income (loss) from operations	(35.2)
Estimated loss on disposition	(49.9)
Income (loss) from discontinued operations...........	$ (85.1)

Indicate how the income (loss) from discontinued operations should be reported by Xerox Corporation on its income statement for the year ended December 31, 1984.

EXERCISES

Exercise 16–1.   Income tax entries. Present entries to record the following selected transactions of CPD Inc.:

Apr. 15. Paid the first installment of the estimated income tax for the current fiscal year ending December 31, $175,000. No entry had been made to record the liability.

June 15. Paid the second installment of $175,000.

Dec. 31. Recorded the additional income tax liability for the year just ended and the deferred income tax liability, based on the two transactions above and the following data:

Income tax rate	45%
Income before income tax...........................	$1,700,000
Taxable income according to tax return	1,575,000
Third installment paid on September 15...............	175,000
Fourth installment paid on December 15	175,000

Exercise 16–2.   Retained earnings statement with prior period adjustment. Howard Trier and Company reported the following results of transactions affecting retained earnings for the current year ended December 31, 1987:

Net income..	$97,500
Dividends	50,000
Prior period adjustment for understatement of merchandise inventory on December 31, 1986, net of applicable income tax of $9,000	11,000

Assuming that the retained earnings balance reported on the retained earnings statement as of December 31, 1986, was $212,500, prepare a retained earnings statement for the year ended December 31, 1987.

Exercise 16–3. Income statement. On the basis of the following data for the current fiscal year ended September 30, prepare an income statement for Stein Company, including an analysis of earnings per share in the form illustrated in this chapter. There were 50,000 shares of $25 par common stock outstanding throughout the year.

Cost of merchandise sold.	$609,600
Cumulative effect on prior years of changing to a different depreciation method	68,500
Gain on condemnation of land (extraordinary item)	57,750
General expenses	46,250
Income tax applicable to change in depreciation method	20,500
Income tax applicable to gain on condemnation of land	16,750
Income tax reduction applicable to loss from discontinued operations	22,500
Income tax applicable to ordinary income.	108,000
Loss on discontinued operations.	74,500
Sales.	979,600
Selling expenses	74,750

Exercise 16–4. Entries for treasury stock. A corporation purchased for cash 5,000 shares of its own $10 par common stock at $15 a share. In the following year, it sold 2,000 of the treasury shares at $18 a share for cash. (a) Present the entries (1) to record the purchase (treasury stock is recorded at cost) and (2) to provide for the appropriation of retained earnings. (b) Present the entries (1) to record the sale of the stock and (2) to reduce the appropriation.

Exercise 16–5. Entries for cash dividends. The dates in connection with a cash dividend of $25,000 on a corporation's common stock are January 9, January 28, and February 14. Present the entries required on each date.

Exercise 16–6. Stock dividends; equity per share. The following account balances appear on the balance sheet of Haris Company: Common stock (10,000 shares authorized), $50 par, $400,000; Premium on common stock, $52,250; and Retained earnings, $219,750. The board of directors declared a 5% stock dividend when the market price of the stock was $65 a share. (a) Present entries to record (1) the declaration of the dividend, capitalizing an amount equal to market value, and (2) the issuance of the stock certificates. (b) Determine the equity per share (1) before the stock dividend and (2) after the stock dividend. (c) Linda Celise owned 100 shares of the common stock before the stock dividend was declared. Determine the total equity of her holdings (1) before the stock dividend and (2) after the stock dividend.

Exercise 16–7. Stock split. The board of directors of Magno Corporation authorized the reduction of par of its common shares from $100 to $25, increasing the number of outstanding shares to 400,000. The market price of the stock immediately before the

no entry required

100,000

stock split was $180 a share. (a) Determine the number of outstanding shares prior to the stock split. (b) Present the entry to record the stock split. (c) At approximately what price would a share of stock be expected to sell immediately after the stock split? 45.00

Exercise 16–8. Retained earnings statement. Rittenhouse Corporation reports the following results of transactions affecting net income and retained earnings for its first fiscal year of operations ended on December 31:

Appropriation for plant expansion	$ 25,000
Cash dividends declared.................................	50,000
Income before income tax..............................	147,500
Income tax...	49,500

Prepare a retained earnings statement for the fiscal year ended December 31.

PROBLEMS

Series A

Problem 16–1A. Income tax allocation. Differences between the accounting methods applied to accounts and financial reports and those used in determining taxable income yielded the following amounts for the first four years of a corporation's operations:

	First Year	Second Year	Third Year	Fourth Year
Income before income tax	$290,000	$370,000	$460,000	$440,000
Taxable income	240,000	340,000	470,000	480,000

The income tax rate for each of the four years was 45% of taxable income, and each year's taxes were promptly paid.

Instructions:

(1) Determine for each year the amounts described in the following columnar captions, presenting the information in the form indicated:

Year	Income Tax Deducted on Income Statement	Income Tax Payments for the Year	Deferred Income Tax Payable	
			Year's Addition (Deduction)	Year-End Balance

(2) Total the first three amount columns.

347 750

6154

Problem 16–2A.   Entries for selected corporate transactions. **Selected transactions completed by Golan Corporation during the current fiscal year are as follows:**

Jan.   4. Split the common stock 5 for 1 and reduced the par from $50 to $10 per share. After the split, there were 80,000 common shares outstanding.

25. Declared semiannual dividends of $5 on 10,000 shares of preferred stock and 50¢ on the 80,000 shares of $10 par common stock to stockholders of record on February 14, payable on February 22.

Feb. 22. Paid the cash dividends.

Mar. 6. Purchased 5,000 shares of the corporation's own common stock at $16, recording the stock at cost.

Apr. 29. Discovered that a receipt of $1,725 cash on account from C. W. Smith Co. had been posted in error to the account of John Smid Inc. The transaction was recorded correctly in the journal.

July 10. Sold 1,000 shares of treasury stock at $22, receiving cash.

23. Declared semiannual dividends of $5 on the preferred stock and 50¢ on the common stock. In addition, a 2% common stock dividend was declared on the common stock outstanding, to be capitalized at the fair market value of the common stock, which is estimated at $20.

Aug. 25. Paid the cash dividends and issued the certificates for the common stock dividend.

Nov. 8. Discovered that an invoice of $825 for utilities expense for the month of October was debited to Office Supplies.

Dec. 31. Recorded $112,500 additional federal income tax allocable to net income for the year. Of this amount, $83,000 is a current liability and $29,500 is deferred.

31. The board of directors authorized the appropriation necessitated by the holding of treasury stock.

Instructions:

Record the transactions.

Problem 16–3A.   Retained earnings statement. **The retained earnings accounts of Tardy Corporation for the current fiscal year ended December 31 are as follows:**

ACCOUNT		APPROPRIATION FOR PLANT EXPANSION			ACCOUNT NO.	3201
					Balance	
Date		Item	Debit	Credit	Debit	Credit
19-- Jan.	1	Balance				200,000
Dec.	31	Retained earnings		50,000		250,000

ACCOUNT		APPROPRIATION FOR TREASURY STOCK			ACCOUNT NO.	3202
					Balance	
Date		Item	Debit	Credit	Debit	Credit
19-- Jan.	1	Balance				300,000
Dec.	31	Retained earnings	30,000			270,000

ACCOUNT RETAINED EARNINGS ACCOUNT NO. 3301

Date			Item	Debit	Credit	Balance Debit	Balance Credit
19--							
Jan.	1		Balance				515,000
Dec.	31		Income summary		190,000		705,000
	31		Appropriation for plant expansion	50,000			655,000
	31		Appropriation for treasury stock		30,000		685,000
	31		Cash dividends	50,000			635,000
	31		Stock dividends	100,000			535,000

ACCOUNT CASH DIVIDENDS ACCOUNT NO. 3302

Date			Item	Debit	Credit	Balance Debit	Balance Credit
19--							
Mar.	2			25,000		25,000	
Sept.	7			25,000		50,000	
Dec.	31		Retained earnings		50,000	—	—

ACCOUNT STOCK DIVIDENDS ACCOUNT NO. 3303

Date			Item	Debit	Credit	Balance Debit	Balance Credit
19--							
Sept.	7			100,000		100,000	
Dec.	31		Retained earnings		100,000	—	—

Instructions:

Prepare a retained earnings statement for the fiscal year ended December 31.

Problem 16–4A.   Income statement. The following data were selected from the records of A. Jones Inc. for the current fiscal year ended December 31:

Advertising expense	$ 24,000
Delivery expense	9,900
Depreciation expense—office equipment	4,250
Depreciation expense—store equipment	11,000
Gain on condemnation of land	50,000
Income tax:	
Applicable to continuing operations	55,000
Applicable to loss from disposal of a segment of a business (reduction)	5,000
Applicable to gain on condemnation of land	15,000
Insurance expense	9,100
Interest income	13,700

Loss from disposal of a segment of the business	$ 25,000
Merchandise inventory (January 1)	97,750
Merchandise inventory (December 31)	105,000
Miscellaneous general expense	2,800
Miscellaneous selling expense	3,500
Office salaries expense	46,000
Office supplies expense	1,750
Purchases	602,250
Rent expense	30,000
Sales	987,500
Sales commissions expense	44,900
Sales salaries expense	56,400
Store supplies expense	2,600

Instructions:

Prepare a multiple-step income statement, concluding with a section for earnings per share in the form illustrated in this chapter. There were 50,000 shares of common stock (no preferred) outstanding throughout the year. Assume that the condemnation of land is an extraordinary item.

Problem 16–5A.   Entries for selected corporate transactions. The stockholders' equity accounts of Wright Enterprises Inc., with balances on January 1 of the current fiscal year, are as follows:

Common Stock, stated value $10 (100,000 shares authorized, 80,000 shares issued)	$800,000
Paid-In Capital in Excess of Stated Value	70,000
Appropriation for Plant Expansion	100,000
Appropriation for Treasury Stock	37,500
Retained Earnings	422,750
Treasury Stock (3,000 shares, at cost)	37,500

The following selected transactions occurred during the year:

Jan. 29. Paid cash dividends of $1 per share on the common stock. The dividend had been properly recorded when declared on December 28 of the preceding fiscal year.

Feb. 25. Sold all of the treasury stock for $45,000.

May 5. Issued 10,000 shares of common stock for $130,000 cash.

June 11. Received land with an estimated fair market value of $50,000 from the Naples City Council as a donation.

July 30. Declared a 5% stock dividend on common stock, to be capitalized at the market price of the stock, which is $15 a share.

Aug. 27. Issued the certificates for the dividend declared on July 30.

Oct. 8. Purchased 2,500 shares of treasury stock for $25,000.

Dec. 20. Declared a $1 per share dividend on common stock.

   20. The board of directors authorized the increase of the appropriation for plant expansion by $25,000.

   20. Decreased the appropriation for treasury stock to $25,000.

   31. Closed the credit balance of the income summary account, $132,500.

   31. Closed the two dividends accounts to Retained Earnings.

Instructions:

(1) Open T accounts for the stockholders' equity accounts listed and enter the balances as of January 1. Also open T accounts for the following: Paid-In Capital from Sale of Treasury Stock; Donated Capital; Stock Dividends Distributable; Stock Dividends; Cash Dividends.
(2) Prepare entries to record the transactions and post to the eleven selected accounts.
(3) Prepare the stockholders' equity section of the balance sheet as of December 31 of the current fiscal year.

Problem 16–6A. Stockholders' equity transactions and statements. **The** stockholders' equity section of the balance sheet of KGM Industries as of January 1 is as follows:

Stockholders' Equity

Paid-in capital:

Common stock, $20 par (100,000 shares authorized, 40,000 shares issued)......	$800,000	
Premium on common stock.............	150,000 +	
Total paid-in capital..................		$ 950,000
Retained earnings:		
Appropriated for bonded indebtedness....	$275,000	
Unappropriated	530,000	
Total retained earnings...............		805,000
Total.....................................		$1,755,000
Deduct treasury stock (5,000 shares at cost) .		125,000
Total stockholders' equity.................		$1,630,000

The following selected transactions occurred during the fiscal year:

Feb. 2. Issued 10,000 shares of stock in exchange for land and buildings with an estimated fair market value of $75,000 and $300,000 respectively. The property was encumbered by a mortgage of $125,000, and the company *mortgage note payable 250,000* agreed to assume the responsibility for paying the mortgage note.

May 30. Sold all of the treasury stock for $150,000.

June 25. Declared a cash dividend of $2 per share to stockholders of record on July 15, payable on July 30.

July 30. Paid the cash dividend declared on June 25.

Sept. 2. Received additional land valued at $50,000. The land was donated for *Land 50,000 Donated Capital* a plant site by the Bonita Industrial Development Council.

Dec. 1. Issued 1,000 shares of stock to officers as a salary bonus. Market price *cash Office Salaries* of the stock is $30 a share. (Debit Officers Salaries Expense.)

10. Declared a 4% stock dividend on the stock outstanding to stockholders of record on December 30 to be issued on January 20. The stock dividend is to be capitalized at the market price of $30 a share.

31. Increased the appropriation for bonded indebtedness by $25,000. *—P. 697*

31. Closed the income summary account. After closing all revenue and *Income Summary* expense accounts, Income Summary has a credit balance of $195,000. *Retained*

31. Closed the two dividends accounts to Retained Earnings. *Earning*

Retained Earning Earnings

Dividends

Instructions:

(1) Open T accounts for the accounts appearing in the stockholders' equity section of the balance sheet and enter the balances as of January 1. Also open T accounts for the following: Paid-In Capital from Sale of Treasury Stock; Donated Capital; Cash Dividends; Stock Dividends; Stock Dividends Distributable.
(2) Prepare entries to record the transactions and post to the ten selected accounts.
(3) Prepare the stockholders' equity section of the balance sheet as of December 31, the end of the fiscal year.
(4) Prepare a retained earnings statement for the fiscal year ended December 31.

Problem 16–7A. Correcting entries and financial statements. C. L. Eddy Company is in need of additional cash to expand operations. To raise the needed funds, the company is applying to the Collier County Bank for a loan. For this purpose, the bank requests that the financial statements be audited. To assist the auditor, C. L. Eddy Company's accountant prepared the following financial statements related to the current year:

C. L. Eddy Company
Balance Sheet
December 31, 19--

Current assets:		
Cash.	$ 56,250	
Accounts receivable	64,500	
Merchandise inventory	85,750	
Supplies.	7,250	$213,750
Plant assets:		
Land.	$ 90,000	
Buildings	325,000	
Equipment.	132,500	
Patents	45,000	592,500
Total assets		$806,250
Current liabilities:		
Accounts payable	$ 46,500	
Salaries payable	3,500	$ 50,000
Deferred charges:		
Accumulated depreciation — buildings.	$ 72,500	
Accumulated depreciation — equipment	37,500	
Allowance for doubtful accounts.	3,700	113,700
Stockholders' equity:		
Common stock (100,000 shares authorized, $10 par)	$350,000	
Premium on common stock.	45,000	
Retained earnings.	165,000	
Net income.	82,550	642,550
Total liabilities and stockholders' equity		$806,250

C. L. Eddy Company
Income Statement
For Year Ended December 31, 19--

Revenues:		
Net sales..	$722,500	
Gain on expropriation of land	42,000	
Total revenues.....................................		$764,500
Expenses:		
Cost of merchandise sold	$440,500	
Salary expense	60,250	
Depreciation expense—buildings	36,900	
Loss on discontinued operations	35,550	
Utilities expense....................................	20,750	
Insurance expense	10,400	
Depreciation expense—equipment.....................	8,500	
Amortization expense—patents.......................	5,000	
Uncollectible accounts expense	3,750	
Miscellaneous general expense......................	3,350	
Income tax	32,000	
Dividends expense	25,000	
Total expenses.....................................		681,950
Net income.......................................		$ 82,550

In the course of the audit, the auditor examined the common stock and retained earnings accounts, which appeared as follows:

ACCOUNT	COMMON STOCK ($10 Par)				ACCOUNT NO. 3200	
					Balance	
Date	Item	Debit	Credit	Debit	Credit	
19--						
Jan. 1	Balance—30,000 shares				300,000	
2	Issued 3,000 shares for patents		50,000		350,000	

ACCOUNT	RETAINED EARNINGS				ACCOUNT NO. 3300	
					Balance	
Date	Item	Debit	Credit	Debit	Credit	
19--						
Jan. 1	Balance				97,500	
Feb. 1	Donation of land		50,000		147,500	
10	Error correction	7,500			140,000	
Dec. 28	Appropriation for land acquisition		25,000		165,000	

A closer examination of the transactions in these and other accounts revealed the following details:

(a) The patent acquired on January 2 by an issuance of 3,000 shares of common stock had a fair market value of $50,000 and an estimated useful life of 10 years.

(b) On February 1, the company received a donation of land. The land account was debited for $50,000, the fair market value of the land at that date.

(c) A computational error was made in the calculation of a prior year's dividend. The corrected amount of the dividend was paid on February 10 and debited to the retained earnings account.

(d) In anticipation of further land acquisition, the board of directors on December 28 authorized a $25,000 appropriation of retained earnings that resulted in a debit to Land and a credit to Retained Earnings.

(e) After three years of using the straight-line method of depreciation for the buildings, the company changed to the sum-of-the-years-digits method. The following entry recorded this change:

Depreciation Expense—Buildings	26,900	
Accumulated Depreciation—Buildings		26,900

(f) A $1 cash dividend declared on December 28 and payable on February 9 of the next fiscal year was not recorded. The $25,000 of dividends expense represents the mid-year cash dividend paid on July 30 of the current year.

(g) The income tax of $32,000 is the estimated tax paid during the year. The tax based on the corrected net income was determined to be $33,950, allocated as follows:

(1)	Income from continuing operations	$44,500
(2)	Loss from discontinued operations	14,100
(3)	Gain on expropriation of land	12,300
(4)	Cumulative effect of change in depreciation method	8,750

The tax owed of $1,950 at December 31 had not been recorded.

Instructions:

(1) Prepare the necessary correcting entries for the items discovered by the independent auditor. Assume that the accounts have not been closed for the current fiscal year.

(2) Prepare a multiple-step income statement for the current fiscal year, including the appropriate earnings per share disclosure. Operating expenses need not be divided into selling and general expense categories.

(3) Prepare the retained earnings statement for the current fiscal year.

(4) Prepare a balance sheet as of the end of the current fiscal year.

Series B

Problem 16–1B. Income tax allocation. Differences between the accounting methods applied to accounts and financial reports and those used in determining taxable income yielded the following amounts for the first four years of a corporation's operations:

	First Year	Second Year	Third Year	Fourth Year
Income before income tax	$210,000	$300,000	$450,000	$488,000
Taxable income	150,000	260,000	430,000	518,000

The income tax rate for each of the four years was 45% of taxable income, and each year's taxes were promptly paid.

Instructions:

(1) Determine for each year the amounts described in the following columnar captions, presenting the information in the form indicated:

Year	Income Tax Deducted on Income Statement	Income Tax Payments for the Year	Deferred Income Tax Payable	
			Year's Addition (Deduction)	Year-End Balance

(2) Total the first three amount columns.

Problem 16–2B. Entries for selected corporate transactions. Selected transactions completed by Odell Company during the current fiscal year are as follows:

Jan. 2. Split the common stock 4 for 1 and reduced the par from $100 to $25 per share. After the split, there were 40,000 common shares outstanding.

Feb. 3. Purchased 1,000 shares of the corporation's own common stock at $62, recording the stock at cost.

Mar. 2. Discovered that a receipt of $600 cash on account from A. Baker had been posted in error to the account of C. Barker. The transaction was recorded correctly in the journal.

May 1. Declared semiannual dividends of $5 on 5,000 shares of preferred stock and $1 on the common stock to stockholders of record on May 20, payable on July 15.

July 15. Paid the cash dividends.

Aug. 22. Sold 500 shares of treasury stock at $70, receiving cash.

Nov. 30. Declared semiannual dividends of $5 on the preferred stock and $1.25 on the common stock. In addition, a 5% common stock dividend was declared on the common stock outstanding, to be capitalized at the fair market value of the common stock, which is estimated at $72.

Dec. 30. Paid the cash dividends and issued the certificates for the common stock dividend.

30. Recorded $76,500 additional federal income tax allocable to net income for the year. Of this amount, $51,500 is a current liability and $25,000 is deferred.

30. The board of directors authorized the appropriation necessitated by the holding of treasury stock.

Instructions:

Record the transactions.

Problem 16–3B.   Retained earnings statement. The retained earnings accounts of Pena Corporation for the current fiscal year ended December 31 are as follows:

ACCOUNT   APPROPRIATION FOR PLANT EXPANSION   ACCOUNT NO. 3201

Date		Item	Debit	Credit	Balance Debit	Balance Credit
19--						
Jan.	1	Balance				300,000
Dec.	31	Retained earnings		50,000		350,000

ACCOUNT   APPROPRIATION FOR TREASURY STOCK   ACCOUNT NO. 3202

Date		Item	Debit	Credit	Balance Debit	Balance Credit
19--						
Jan.	1	Balance				225,000
Dec.	31	Retained earnings	125,000			100,000

ACCOUNT   RETAINED EARNINGS   ACCOUNT NO. 3301

Date		Item	Debit	Credit	Balance Debit	Balance Credit
19--						
Jan.	1	Balance				515,000
Dec.	31	Income summary		175,000		690,000
	31	Appropriation for plant expansion	50,000			640,000
	31	Appropriation for treasury stock		125,000		765,000
	31	Cash dividends	150,000			615,000
	31	Stock dividends	125,000			490,000

ACCOUNT   CASH DIVIDENDS   ACCOUNT NO. 3302

Date		Item	Debit	Credit	Balance Debit	Balance Credit
19--						
Oct.	11		150,000		150,000	
Dec.	31	Retained earnings		150,000	—	—

ACCOUNT   STOCK DIVIDENDS   ACCOUNT NO. 3303

Date		Item	Debit	Credit	Balance Debit	Balance Credit
19--						
Oct.	11		125,000		125,000	
Dec.	31	Retained earnings		125,000	—	—

Instructions:

Prepare a retained earnings statement for the fiscal year ended December 31.

Problem 16–4B.   Income statement. The following data were selected from the records of A. P. Davis Co. for the current fiscal year ended December 31:

Merchandise inventory (January 1)	$130,000
Merchandise inventory (December 31)	135,500
Office salaries expense...	42,750
Depreciation expense—store equipment	9,000
Sales...	997,500
Sales salaries expense...	42,500
Sales commissions expense	53,500
Advertising expense	27,250
Purchases	605,500
Rent expense	21,000
Delivery expense	19,750
Store supplies expense...	7,500
Office supplies expense	1,700
Insurance expense...	9,000
Depreciation expense—office equipment.......................	5,200
Miscellaneous selling expense	8,600
Miscellaneous general expense	4,550
Interest expense...	25,200
Loss from disposal of a segment of the business................	40,200
Gain on condemnation of land	20,000
Income tax:	
Applicable to continuing operations	35,000
Applicable to loss from disposal of a segment of	
the business (reduction)......................................	8,200
Applicable to gain on condemnation of land...................	4,000

Instructions:

Prepare a multiple-step income statement, concluding with a section for earnings per share in the form illustrated in this chapter. There were 25,000 shares of common stock (no preferred) outstanding throughout the year. Assume that the gain on condemnation of land is an extraordinary item.

Problem 16–5B.   Entries for selected corporate transactions. The stockholders' equity accounts of Anderson Enterprises Inc., with balances on January 1 of the current fiscal year, are as follows:

Common Stock, stated value $25 (100,000 shares authorized,	
50,000 shares issued).......................................	$1,250,000
Paid-In Capital in Excess of Stated Value......................	450,000
Appropriation for Plant Expansion	250,000
Appropriation for Treasury Stock..............................	120,000
Retained Earnings	575,000
Treasury Stock (4,000 shares, at cost)	120,000

The following selected transactions occurred during the year:

Jan. 15. Received land with an estimated fair market value of $65,000 from the city as a donation.

     30. Paid cash dividends of $1 per share on the common stock. The dividend had been properly recorded when declared on December 20 of the preceding fiscal year for $46,000.

Feb. 25. Sold all of the treasury stock for $150,000.

Apr. 1. Issued 5,000 shares of common stock for $190,000.

July   1. Declared a 4% stock dividend on common stock, to be capitalized at the market price of the stock, which is $40 a share.

Aug. 11. Issued the certificates for the dividend declared on July 1.

Nov. 20. Purchased 2,000 shares of treasury stock for $72,000.

Dec. 21. The board of directors authorized an increase of the appropriation for plant expansion by $50,000.

     21. Declared a $1.10 per share dividend on common stock.

     21. Decreased the appropriation for treasury stock to $72,000.

     31. Closed the credit balance of the income summary account, $196,700.

     31. Closed the two dividends accounts to Retained Earnings.

Instructions:

(1) Open T accounts for the stockholders' equity accounts listed and enter the balances as of January 1. Also open T accounts for the following: Paid-in Capital from Sale of Treasury Stock; Donated Capital; Stock Dividends Distributable; Stock Dividends; Cash Dividends.

(2) Prepare entries to record the transactions and post to the eleven selected accounts.

(3) Prepare the stockholders' equity section of the balance sheet as of December 31 of the current fiscal year.

MINI-CASE 16

COMPANY

    Kahn Co. has paid quarterly cash dividends since 1980. These dividends have steadily increased from $.20 per share to the latest dividend declaration of $.50 per share. The board of directors would like to continue this trend and are hesitant to suspend or decrease the amount of quarterly dividends. Unfortunately, sales of Kahn Co. dropped sharply in the fourth quarter of 1987 due to worsening economic conditions and increased competition. As a result, the board is uncertain as to whether it should declare a dividend for the last quarter of 1987.

On November 1, 1987, Kahn Co. borrowed $500,000 from Citizens National Bank to use in modernizing its retail stores and to expand its product line in reaction to its competition. The terms of the 10-year, 12% loan require Kahn Co. to:

(a) Pay monthly the total interest due, 500.00
(b) Pay $50,000 of the principal each November 1, beginning in 1988,
(c) Maintain a current ratio (current assets ÷ current liabilities) of 2:1,
(d) Appropriate $500,000 of retained earnings until the loan is fully paid, and
(e) Maintain a minimum balance of $25,000 (called a compensating balance) in its Citizens National Bank account.

On December 31, 1987, 25% of the $500,000 loan had been disbursed in modernization of the retail stores and in expansion of the product line, and the remainder is temporarily invested in U.S. Treasury notes. Kahn Co.'s balance sheet as of December 31, 1987, is as follows:

Kahn Co.
Balance Sheet
December 31, 1987

Assets

Current assets:		
Cash..............................		$ 40,000
Marketable securities, at cost (market price, $379,500)...........		375,000
Accounts receivable..................	$ 91,500	
Less allowance for doubtful accounts..............	6,500	85,000
Merchandise inventory		120,500
Prepaid expenses		4,500
Total current assets..............		$ 625,000
Plant assets:		
Land.............................		$150,000
Buildings	$950,000	
Less accumulated depreciation.....	215,000	735,000
Equipment........................	$460,000	
Less accumulated depreciation.....	110,000	350,000
Total plant assets..............		1,235,000
Total assets........................		$1,860,000

Liabilities

Current liabilities:
Accounts payable.................. $ 71,800
Notes payable
  (Citizens National Bank)........... 50,000
Salaries payable.................. 3,200
  Total current liabilities $125,000
Long-term liabilities:
Notes payable
  (Citizens National Bank).......... 450,000
Total liabilities....................... $ 575,000

Stockholders' Equity

Paid-in capital:
Common stock, $20 par
  (50,000 shares authorized,
  25,000 shares issued)............. $500,000
Premium on common stock 40,000
  Total paid-in capital $540,000
Retained earnings:
Appropriated for provision of
  Citizens National Bank loan........ $500,000
Unappropriated.................... 245,000
  Total retained earnings 745,000
Total stockholders' equity............. 1,285,000
Total liabilities and
  stockholders' equity................ $1,860,000

The board of directors is scheduled to meet January 10, 1988, to discuss the results of operations for 1987 and to consider the declaration of dividends for the fourth quarter of 1987. The chairman of the board has asked for your advice on the declaration of dividends.

Instructions:

(1) What factors should the board consider in deciding whether to declare a cash dividend?
(2) The board is considering the declaration of a stock dividend instead of a cash dividend. Discuss the issuance of a stock dividend from the point of view of (a) a stockholder and (b) the board of directors.

Chapter 17

LONG-TERM
LIABILITIES AND
INVESTMENTS
IN BONDS

Chapter Objectives:

- Describe and illustrate the impact of borrowing on a long-term basis as a means of financing corporations.

- Describe the characteristics of bonds.

- Describe and illustrate the concept of present value and how it relates to bonds.

- Describe and illustrate the accounting for bonds payable.

- Describe and illustrate the accounting for bond sinking funds.

- Describe and illustrate the accounting for long-term investments in bonds.

bonds = debt
bond holders can force a corp
to liquidate

T he acquisition of cash and other assets by a corporation through the issuance of its stock has been discussed in earlier chapters. Expansion of corporate enterprises through the retention of earnings, in some instances accompanied by the issuance of stock dividends, has also been explored. In addition to these two methods of obtaining relatively permanent funds, corporations may also borrow money on a long-term basis by issuing notes or bonds, which are a form of interest-bearing note. Long-term notes may be issued to relatively few lending agencies or to a single investor such as an insurance company. Bonds are usually sold to underwriters (dealers and brokers in securities), who in turn sell them to investors. Although the discussion that follows will be limited to bonds, the accounting principles involved apply equally to long-term notes.

When funds are borrowed through the issuance of bonds, there is a definite commitment to pay interest and to repay the principal at a stated future date. Bondholders are creditors of the issuing corporation and their claims for interest and for repayment of principal rank ahead of the claims of stockholders.

FINANCING CORPORATIONS

Many factors influence the incorporators or the board of directors in deciding upon the best means of obtaining funds. The subject will be limited here to a brief illustration of the effect of different financing methods on the income of a corporation and the common stockholders. To illustrate, assume that three different plans for financing a $4,000,000 corporation are under consideration by its organizers, and that in each case the securities will be issued at their par or face amount. The incorporators estimate that the enterprise will earn $800,000 annually, before deducting interest on the bonds and income tax estimated at 40% of income. The following tabulation indicates the amount of earnings that would be available to common stockholders under each of the three plans:

	Plan 1	Plan 2	Plan 3
12% bonds	—	—	$2,000,000
Preferred 9% stock, $50 par	—	$2,000,000	1,000,000
Common stock, $10 par	$4,000,000	2,000,000	1,000,000
Total	$4,000,000	$4,000,000	$4,000,000

730

	Plan 1	Plan 2	Plan 3
Earnings before interest and income tax ...	$ 800,000	$ 800,000	$ 800,000
Deduct interest on bonds	—	—	240,000
Income before income tax..............	$ 800,000	$ 800,000	$ 560,000
Deduct income tax	320,000	320,000	224,000
Net income.........................	$ 480,000	$ 480,000	$ 336,000
Dividends on preferred stock	—	180,000	90,000
Available for dividends on common stock ..	$ 480,000	$ 300,000	$ 246,000
Shares of common stock outstanding......	400,000	200,000	100,000
Earnings per share on common stock	$1.20	$1.50	$2.46

If Plan 1 is adopted and the entire financing is from the issuance of common stock, the earnings per share on the common stock would be $1.20 per share. Under Plan 2, the effect of using 9% preferred stock for half of the capitalization would result in $1.50 earnings per common share. The issuance of 12% bonds in Plan 3, with the remaining capitalization split between preferred and common stock, would yield a return of $2.46 per share on common stock.

Under the assumed conditions, Plan 3 would obviously be the most attractive for common stockholders. If the anticipated earnings should increase beyond $800,000, the spread between the earnings per share to common stockholders under Plan 1 and Plan 3 would become even greater. But if successively smaller amounts of earnings are assumed, the attractiveness of Plan 2 and Plan 3 decreases. The effect of lower earnings is illustrated by the following tabulation, in which earnings, before interest and income tax are deducted, are assumed to be $440,000 instead of $800,000:

	Plan 1	Plan 2	Plan 3
12% bonds	—	—	$2,000,000
Preferred 9% stock, $50 par.............	—	$2,000,000	1,000,000
Common stock, $10 par.................	$4,000,000	2,000,000	1,000,000
Total.....................................	$4,000,000	$4,000,000	$4,000,000
Earnings before interest and income tax ...	$ 440,000	$ 440,000	$ 440,000
Deduct interest on bonds	—	—	240,000
Income before income tax..............	$ 440,000	$ 440,000	$ 200,000
Deduct income tax	176,000	176,000	80,000
Net income.........................	$ 264,000	$ 264,000	$ 120,000
Dividends on preferred stock	—	180,000	90,000
Available for dividends on common stock ..	$ 264,000	$ 84,000	$ 30,000
Shares of common stock outstanding......	400,000	200,000	100,000
Earnings per share on common stock	$.66	$.42	$.30

The preceding analysis focused attention on the effect of the different plans on earnings per share of common stock. There are other factors that must be considered when different methods of financing are evaluated. The issuance of bonds represents a fixed annual interest charge that, in contrast to dividends, is not subject to corporate control. Provision must also be made for the eventual repayment of the principal amount of the bonds, in contrast to the absence of any such obligation to stockholders. On the other hand, a decision to finance entirely by an issuance of common stock would require substantial investment by a single stockholder or small group of stockholders who desire to control the corporation.

CHARACTERISTICS OF BONDS

When a corporation issues bonds, it executes a contract with the bond-holders known as a **bond indenture** or **trust indenture**. The entire issue is divided into a number of individual bonds, which may be of varying denominations. Usually the principal of each bond, also called the **face value**, is $1,000 or a multiple thereof. The interest on bonds may be payable at annual, semiannual, or quarterly intervals. Most bonds provide for payment on a semiannual basis.

Registered bonds may be transferred from one owner to another only by endorsement on the bond certificate, and the issuing corporation must maintain a record of the name and the address of each bond holder. Interest payments are made by check to the owner of record. Title to **bearer bonds**, which are also called **coupon bonds**, is transferred merely by delivery, and the issuing corporation does not know the identity of the bondholders. Interest coupons for the entire term, in the form of checks or drafts payable to bearer, are attached to the bond certificate. At each interest date, the holder detaches the appropriate coupon and presents it to a bank for payment.

When all bonds of an issue mature at the same time, they are called **term bonds**. If the maturities are spread over several dates, they are called **serial bonds**. For example, one tenth of an issue of $1,000,000, or $100,000, may mature eleven years from the issuance date, another $100,000 may mature twelve years from the issuance date, and so on until the final $100,000 matures at the end of the twentieth year.

Bonds that may be exchanged for other securities under certain conditions are called **convertible bonds**. Bonds issued by a corporation that reserves the right to redeem them before maturity are referred to as **callable bonds**.

A **secured bond** is one that gives the bondholder a claim on specific assets in case the issuing corporation fails to meet its obligations on the bonds. The properties mortgaged or pledged may be specific buildings and equipment, the entire plant, or stocks and bonds of other companies owned by the debtor corporation. Unsecured bonds issued on the basis of the general credit of the corporation are called **debenture bonds**.

Pepsi's Zero-Coupon Bonds

On the surface it looks like a terrible deal for PepsiCo. The company gets just under $54 million for bonds that bear no interest but pay $850 million between 1988 and 2012. That's more than the company's total debt at present.

But appearances can be deceiving. On a zero-coupon bond like PepsiCo's, the interest is built into the face value. It is estimated that PepsiCo will be paying an average yield to investors of 13.4%. If PepsiCo had issued an ordinary 30-year interest-bearing bond, the company would have had to pay about 15.5%. PepsiCo is getting its money for less because zero-coupon bonds are, for all practical purposes, noncallable. Yes, they can be called. But only at full value at maturity. So it makes no sense to call them.

In effect, PepsiCo is betting on double-digit interest rates continuing for the next three decades. Other companies have placed the same bet but for nowhere near 30 years out. Buyers of PepsiCo zeros (as they are known on Wall Street) are betting that rates will drop back to single digits.

By financing with zeros, PepsiCo neatly sidesteps the cash drain of semiannual interest payments. PepsiCo, a pioneer of zeros, is also hedging its bet on interest rates by using serial maturities. In no year will it have to pay out more than $75 million.

Pepsi's new long-term zero is an early warning that corporate America does not believe inflation will be brought under control in the foreseeable future. Politicians and economists predict interest rates with their mouths. PepsiCo is putting its money where its mouth is.

Source: Adapted from Subrata N. Chakravarty, "Things Won't Go Better with Pepsi," *Forbes* (May 24, 1982), p. 177.

PRESENT VALUE CONCEPTS

The concept of present value plays an important role in many accounting analyses and business decisions. For example, accounting analyses based on the present value concept are useful for evaluating proposals for long-term investments in plant and equipment. Such analyses will be discussed in a later chapter. In this chapter, the concept of present value will be discussed in the context of the role that it plays in determining the selling price of bonds.

The concept of **present value** is that an amount of cash to be received at some date in the future is not the equivalent of the same amount of cash held at an earlier date. In other words, a sum of cash to be received in the future is not as valuable as the same sum on hand today, because cash on hand today can be invested to earn income. For example, $100 on hand today would be more valuable than $100 to be received a year from today. In this case, if the $100 cash on hand today can be invested to earn 10% per year, the $100 will accumulate to $110 ($100 plus $10 earnings) by one year from today. The $100 on hand today can be referred to as the present value amount that is equivalent to $110 to be received a year from today.

PRESENT VALUE CONCEPTS FOR BONDS PAYABLE

When a corporation issues bonds, it usually incurs two distinct obligations: (1) to pay the face amount of the bonds at a specified maturity date, and (2) to pay periodic interest at a specified percentage of the face amount. The price that a buyer is willing to pay for these future benefits is the sum of (1) the *present value* of the face amount of the bonds at the maturity date and (2) the *present value* of the periodic interest payments.

Present Value of $1

The present value of the face amount of bonds at the maturity date is the value today of the promise to pay the face amount at some future date. To illustrate, assume that $1,000 is to be paid in one year and that the rate of earnings is 12%. The present value amount is $892.86 ($1,000 ÷ 1.12). If the $1,000 is to be paid one year later (two years in all), with the earnings compounded at the end of the first year, the present value amount would be $797.20 ($892.86 ÷ 1.12).

Instead of determining the present value of a future cash sum by a series of divisions in the manner just illustrated, it is customary to use a table of present values to find the present value of $1 for the appropriate number of periods, and to multiply that present value factor by the amount of the future cash sum. A partial table of the present value of $1 appears as follows:[1]

Discount of face

Periods	5%	5½%	6%	6½%	7%	10%	11%	12%	13%	14%
1	0.9524	0.9479	0.9434	0.9390	0.9346	0.9091	0.9009	0.8929	0.8850	0.8772
2	0.9070	0.8985	0.8900	0.8817	0.8734	0.8264	0.8116	0.7972	0.7831	0.7695
3	0.8638	0.8516	0.8396	0.8278	0.8163	0.7513	0.7312	0.7118	0.6931	0.6750
4	0.8227	0.8072	0.7921	0.7773	0.7629	0.6830	0.6587	0.6355	0.6133	0.5921
5	0.7835	0.7651	0.7473	0.7299	0.7130	0.6209	0.5935	0.5674	0.5428	0.5194
6	0.7462	0.7252	0.7050	0.6853	0.6663	0.5645	0.5346	0.5066	0.4803	0.4556
7	0.7107	0.6874	0.6651	0.6435	0.6228	0.5132	0.4817	0.4523	0.4251	0.3996
8	0.6768	0.6516	0.6274	0.6042	0.5820	0.4665	0.4339	0.4039	0.3762	0.3506
9	0.6446	0.6176	0.5919	0.5674	0.5439	0.4241	0.3909	0.3606	0.3329	0.3075
10	0.6139	0.5854	0.5584	0.5327	0.5083	0.3855	0.3522	0.3220	0.2946	0.2697
11	0.5847	0.5549	0.5268	0.5002	0.4751	0.3505	0.3173	0.2875	0.2607	0.2366
12	0.5568	0.5260	0.4970	0.4697	0.4440	0.3186	0.2858	0.2567	0.2307	0.2076
13	0.5303	0.4986	0.4688	0.4410	0.4150	0.2897	0.2575	0.2292	0.2042	0.1821
14	0.5051	0.4726	0.4423	0.4141	0.3878	0.2633	0.2320	0.2046	0.1807	0.1597
15	0.4810	0.4479	0.4173	0.3888	0.3624	0.2394	0.2090	0.1827	0.1599	0.1401
16	0.4581	0.4246	0.3936	0.3651	0.3387	0.2176	0.1883	0.1631	0.1415	0.1229
17	0.4363	0.4024	0.3714	0.3428	0.3166	0.1978	0.1696	0.1456	0.1252	0.1078
18	0.4155	0.3815	0.3503	0.3219	0.2959	0.1799	0.1528	0.1300	0.1108	0.0946
19	0.3957	0.3616	0.3305	0.3022	0.2765	0.1635	0.1377	0.1161	0.0981	0.0829
20	0.3769	0.3427	0.3118	0.2838	0.2584	0.1486	0.1240	0.1037	0.0868	0.0728

market rate

PRESENT VALUE OF $1 AT COMPOUND INTEREST   *use to determine present amount of face value*

For the previous example, the table indicates that the present value of $1 to be received two years hence, with earnings at the rate of 12% a year, is .7972. Multiplying $1,000 by .7972 yields $797.20, which is the same amount that was determined previously by two successive divisions. In using the table, it should be noted that the "periods" column represents the number of compounding periods, while the "percentage" columns represent the compound interest rate per period. For example, 12% for two years compounded annually, as in the preceding illustration, is 12% for two periods; 12% for two years compounded semiannually would be 6% (12% per year ÷ 2 semiannual periods) for four periods (2 years × 2 semiannual periods); and 12% for three years compounded semiannually would be 6% (12% ÷ 2) for six periods (3 years × 2 semiannual periods).

Present Value of Annuity of $1

The present value of the periodic interest payments on bonds is the value today of the promise to pay a fixed amount of interest at the end of each of a

---

[1]The tables illustrated are limited to 20 periods for a small number of interest rates, and the amounts are carried to only four decimal places. Books of tables are available with as many as 360 periods, 45 interest rates (including many fractional rates), and amounts carried to eight decimal places.

number of periods. Such a series of fixed payments at fixed intervals is called an **annuity**.

The following partial table of the present value of an annuity of $1 at compound interest indicates the value now (present value) of $1 to be received at the end of *each* period at various compound rates of interest. For example, the present value of $1,000 to be received at the end of each of the next 5 periods at 10% compound interest per period is $3,790.80 (3.7908 × $1,000).

Discount of interest

Periods	5%	5½%	6%	6½%	7%	10%	11%	12%	13%	14%
1	0.9524	0.9479	0.9434	0.9390	0.9346	0.9091	0.9009	0.8929	0.8850	0.8772
2	1.8594	1.8463	1.8334	1.8206	1.8080	1.7355	1.7125	1.6901	1.6681	1.6467
3	2.7232	2.6979	2.6730	2.6485	2.6243	2.4869	2.4437	2.4018	2.3612	2.3216
4	3.5460	3.5052	3.4651	3.4258	3.3872	3.1699	3.1024	3.0373	2.9745	2.9137
5	4.3295	4.2703	4.2124	4.1557	4.1002	**3.7908**	3.6959	3.6048	3.5172	3.4331
6	5.0757	4.9955	4.9173	4.8410	4.7665	4.3553	4.2305	4.1114	3.9976	3.8887
7	5.7864	5.6830	5.5824	5.4845	5.3893	4.8684	4.7122	4.5638	4.4226	4.2883
8	6.4632	6.3346	6.2098	6.0888	5.9713	5.3349	5.1461	4.9676	4.7988	4.6389
9	7.1078	6.9522	6.8017	6.6561	6.5152	5.7590	5.5370	5.3283	5.1317	4.9464
10	7.7217	7.5376	7.3601	7.1888	7.0236	6.1446	5.8892	5.6502	5.4262	5.2161
11	8.3064	8.0925	7.8869	7.6890	7.4987	6.4951	6.2065	5.9377	5.6869	5.4527
12	8.8633	8.6185	8.3838	8.1587	7.9427	6.8137	6.4924	6.1944	5.9176	5.6603
13	9.3936	9.1171	8.8527	8.5997	8.3577	7.1034	6.7499	6.4235	6.1218	5.8424
14	9.8986	9.5896	9.2950	9.0138	8.7455	7.3667	6.9819	6.6282	6.3025	6.0021
15	10.3797	10.0376	9.7123	9.4027	9.1079	7.6061	7.1909	6.8109	6.4624	6.1422
16	10.8378	10.4622	10.1059	9.7678	9.4467	7.8237	7.3792	6.9740	6.6039	6.2651
17	11.2741	10.8646	10.4773	10.1106	9.7632	8.0216	7.5488	7.1196	6.7291	6.3729
18	11.6896	11.2461	10.8276	10.4325	10.0591	8.2014	7.7016	7.2497	6.8399	6.4674
19	12.0853	11.6077	11.1581	10.7347	10.3356	8.3649	7.8393	7.3658	6.9380	6.5504
20	12.4622	11.9504	11.4699	11.0185	10.5940	8.5136	7.9633	7.4694	7.0248	6.6231

PRESENT VALUE OF ANNUITY OF $1 AT COMPOUND INTEREST

use to determine the present value of interest payments

ACCOUNTING FOR BONDS PAYABLE

The interest rate specified in the bond indenture is called the **contract** or **coupon rate**, which may differ from the rate prevailing in the market at the time the bonds are issued. If the **market** or **effective rate** is higher than the contract rate, the bonds will sell at a **discount**, or less than their face amount. This discount results because buyers are unwilling to pay the face amount for bonds whose contract rate is lower than the prevailing market rate. The discount, therefore, represents the amount necessary to make up for the difference in the market and the contract interest rates. Conversely, if the market rate is lower than the contract rate, the bonds will sell at a **premium**, or more than their face amount. In this case, buyers are willing to pay more than the face amount for bonds whose contract rate is higher than the market rate.

Bonds Issued at Face Amount

To illustrate an issuance of bonds, assume that on January 1 a corporation issues for cash $100,000 of 12%, five-year bonds, with interest of $6,000 payable semiannually. The market rate of interest at the time the bonds are issued is 12%. Since the contract rate and the market rate of interest are the same, the bonds will sell at their face amount. This amount, calculated as follows, is the sum of (1) the present value of the face amount of $100,000 to be repaid in 5 years and (2) the present value of 10 semiannual interest payments of $6,000 each.[2]

Present value of face amount of $100,000 due in 5 years, at 12%
   compounded semiannually: $100,000 × .5584 (present value of $1 for
   10 periods at 6%) .... $ 55,840
Present value of 10 semiannual interest payments of $6,000, at 12%
   compounded semiannually: $6,000 × 7.3601 (present value of annuity
   of $1 for 10 periods at 6%) 44,160
Total present value of bonds....................................... $100,000

The basic data for computing the two present values totaling $100,000 were obtained from the two present value tables presented on pages 735 and 736. The first of the two amounts, **$55,840**, is the present value of the $100,000 that is to be repaid in 5 years. The $55,840 is determined by locating the present value of $1 for 10 periods (5 years of semiannual payments) at 6% semiannually (12% annual rate) in the present value of $1 table and multiplying by $100,000. If the bond indenture provided that no interest would be paid during the entire 5-year period, the bonds would be worth only $55,840 at the time of their issuance. To express the concept of present value from a different viewpoint, if $55,840 were invested today, with interest at 12% compounded semiannually, the sum accumulated at the end of 10 semiannual periods would be $100,000.

The second of the two amounts, **$44,160**, is the present value of the series of ten $6,000 payments. The $44,160 is determined by locating the present value of an annuity of $1 for 10 periods (5 years of semiannual payments) at 6% semiannually (12% annual rate) in the present value of an annuity of $1 table and multiplying by $6,000. The present value of $44,160 can also be viewed as the amount of a current deposit earning 12% that would yield ten semiannual withdrawals of $6,000, with the original deposit being reduced to zero by the tenth withdrawal.

---

[2]Because the present value tables are rounded to four decimal places, minor rounding errors may appear in the illustrations.

The entry to record the issuance of the $100,000 bonds at their face amount is as follows:

```
Jan. 1  Cash ......................................  100,000
           Bonds Payable ...........................              100,000
```

At six-month intervals following the issuance of the 12% bonds, the interest payment of $6,000 is recorded in the usual manner by a debit to Interest Expense and a credit to Cash. At the maturity date, the payment of the principal sum of $100,000 would be recorded by a debit to Bonds Payable and a credit to Cash.

Bonds Issued at a Discount

If the market rate of interest is 13% and the contract rate is 12%, the bonds will sell at a discount. The present value of the five-year, $100,000 bonds with a market rate of 13% may be calculated as follows:

Present value of $100,000 due in 5 years, at 13% compounded semiannually:
   $100,000 × .5327 (present value of $1 for 10 periods at 6 1/2%)....... $53,270
Present value of 10 semiannual interest payments of $6,000 at 13% com-
   pounded semiannually: $6,000 × 7.1888 (present value of an annuity of
   $1 for 10 periods at 6 1/2%).....................................   43,133
Total present value of bonds....................................... $96,403

[handwritten note: contract rate × face value = 6,000]

The two present values that make up the total are both somewhat less than the comparable amounts in the first illustration, where the contract rate and the market rate were exactly the same. The reason for the lesser present value is that the value now of a future amount becomes less and less as the interest rate rises. In other words, the sum that would have to be invested today to equal a fixed future amount becomes less and less as the interest rate earned on the investment rises.

[handwritten note: inflation]

In the following entry to record the issuance of the 12% bonds, the bond liability is recorded at the face amount, and the discount is recorded in a separate contra account:

```
Jan. 1  Cash ......................................   96,403
           Discount on Bonds Payable ...................    3,597
           Bonds Payable ...........................              100,000
```

The $3,597 discount may be viewed as the amount that is needed to compensate the investor for accepting a contract rate of interest that is below the prevailing market rate. From another view, the $3,597 represents the additional amount that must be returned by the issuer at maturity; that is, the issuer received $96,403 at the sale date but must return $100,000 at the maturity date. The $3,597 discount must therefore be amortized as additional interest expense over the five-year life of the bonds. There are two widely used methods of allocating bond discount to the various periods: (1) **straight-line** and (2) **interest**. Although the interest method is the recommended method, the straight-line method is acceptable if the results obtained by its use do not materially differ from the results that would be obtained by the use of the interest method.[3]

Amortization of Discount by the Straight-Line Method. The straight-line method is the simpler of the two methods and provides for amortization in equal periodic amounts. Application of this method to the illustration would yield amortization of 1/10 of $3,597, or $359.70, each half year. The amount of the interest expense on the bonds would remain constant for each half year at $6,000 plus $359.70, or $6,359.70. The entry to record the first interest payment and the amortization of the related amount of discount is as follows:

July 1	Interest Expense	6,359.70	
	Discount on Bonds Payable		359.70
	Cash		6,000.00

As an alternative to recording the amortization each time the interest is paid, it may be recorded only at the end of the year. When this procedure is used, each interest payment is recorded as a debit to Interest Expense and a credit to Cash. In terms of the illustration, the entry to amortize the discount at the end of the first year would be as follows:

Dec. 31	Interest Expense	719.40	
	Discount on Bonds Payable		719.40

The amount of the discount amortized, $719.40, is made up of the two semiannual amortization amounts of $359.70.

Amortization of Discount by the Interest Method. In contrast to the straight-line method, which provides for a constant *amount* of interest expense, the interest method provides for a constant *rate* of interest on the **carrying amount** (also called **book value**) of the bonds at the beginning of each period. The interest rate used in the computation is the market rate as of the date the bonds were issued, and the carrying amount of the bonds is their face amount minus the unamortized discount. The difference between the interest expense

---

[3]*Opinions of the Accounting Principles Board, No. 21,* "Interest on Receivables and Payables" (New York: American Institute of Certified Public Accountants, 1971), par. 14.

computed in this manner and the amount of the periodic interest payment is the amount of discount to be amortized for the period. Application of this method to the illustration yields the following data:

AMORTIZA-
TION OF
DISCOUNT
ON BONDS
PAYABLE

Interest Payment	A Interest Paid (6% of Face Amount)	B Interest Expense (6½% of Bond Carrying Amount)	C Discount Amortization (B–A)	D Unamortized Discount (D–C)	E Bond Carrying Amount ($100,000–D)
				$3,597	$ 96,403
1	$6,000	$6,266(6½% of $96,403)	$266	3,331	96,669
2	6,000	6,284(6½% of $96,669)	284	3,047	96,953
3	6,000	6,302(6½% of $96,953)	302	2,745	97,255
4	6,000	6,322(6½% of $97,255)	322	2,423	97,577
5	6,000	6,343(6½% of $97,577)	343	2,080	97,920
6	6,000	6,365(6½% of $97,920)	365	1,715	98,285
7	6,000	6,389(6½% of $98,285)	389	1,326	98,674
8	6,000	6,415(6½% of $98,674)	415	911	99,089
9	6,000	6,441(6½% of $99,089)	441	470	99,530
10	6,000	6,470(6½% of $99,530)	470	—	100,000

The following important details should be observed:

1. The interest paid (column A) remains constant at 6% of $100,000, the face amount of the bonds.
2. The interest expense (column B) is computed at 6 1/2% of the bond carrying amount at the beginning of each period, yielding a gradually increasing amount.
3. The excess of the interest expense over the interest payment of $6,000 is the amount of discount to be amortized (column C).
4. The unamortized discount (column D) decreases from the initial balance, $3,597, to a zero balance at the maturity date of the bonds.
5. The carrying amount (column E) increases from $96,403, the amount received for the bonds, to $100,000 at maturity.

The entry to record the first interest payment and the amortization of the related amount of discount is as follows:

July 1	Interest Expense	6,266	
	Discount on Bonds Payable		266
	Cash		6,000

If the amortization is recorded only at the end of the year, the amount of the discount amortized on December 31 would be $550, which is the sum of the first two semiannual amortization amounts ($266 and $284) from the preceding table.

Bonds Issued at a Premium

If the market rate of interest is 11% and the contract rate is 12%, the bonds will sell at a premium. The present value of the five-year, $100,000 bonds, with a market rate of 11%, may be calculated as follows:

Present value of $100,000 due in 5 years, at 11% compounded semi-annually: $100,000 × .5854 (present value of $1 for 10 periods at 5 1/2%)	$ 58,540
Present value of 10 semiannual interest payments of $6,000, at 11% compounded semiannually: $6,000 × 7.5376 (present value of an annuity of $1 for 10 periods at 5 1/2%)	45,226
Total present value of bonds......................................	$103,766

The entry to record the issuance of the bonds is as follows:

Jan. 1 Cash	103,766	
Bonds Payable		100,000
Premium on Bonds Payable................		3,766

Procedures for amortization of the premium and determination of the periodic interest expense are basically the same as those used for bonds issued at a discount.

Amortization of Premium by the Straight-Line Method. Application of the straight-line method to the illustration would yield amortization of 1/10 of $3,766, or $376.60 each half year. Just as bond discount can be viewed as additional interest expense, bond premium can be viewed as a reduction in the amount of interest expense. The entry to record the first interest payment and the amortization of the related amount of premium is as follows:

July 1 Interest Expense	5,623.40	
Premium on Bonds Payable	376.60	
Cash......................................		6,000.00

If the amortization of the premium is recorded only at the end of the year, each interest payment would be recorded by debiting Interest Expense and crediting Cash. The amortization of the premium at the end of the year, in the illustration, would then be recorded as follows:

Dec. 31 Premium on Bonds Payable	753.20	
Interest Expense		753.20

The amount of the premium amortized, $753.20, is the sum of the two semiannual amounts of $376.60.

Amortization of Premium by the Interest Method. Application of the interest method of amortization yields the following data:

Interest Payment	A Interest Paid (6% of Face Amount)	B Interest Expense (5½% of Bond Carrying Amount)	C Premium Amortization (A–B)	D Unamortized Premium (D–C)	E Bond Carrying Amount ($100,000 + D)
				$3,766	$103,766
1	$6,000	$5,707(5½% of $103,766)	$293	3,473	103,473
2	6,000	$5,691(5½% of $103,473)	309	3,164	103,164
3	6,000	$5,674(5½% of $103,164)	326	2,838	102,838
4	6,000	$5,657(5½% of $102,838)	343	2,495	102,495
5	6,000	$5,638(5½% of $102,495)	362	2,133	102,133
6	6,000	$5,618(5½% of $102,133)	382	1,751	101,751
7	6,000	$5,597(5½% of $101,751)	403	1,348	101,348
8	6,000	$5,575(5½% of $101,348)	425	923	100,923
9	6,000	$5,551(5½% of $100,923)	449	474	100,474
10	6,000	$5,526(5½% of $100,474)	474	—	100,000

The following important details should be observed:

1. The interest paid (column A) remains constant at 6% of $100,000, the face amount of the bonds.
2. The interest expense (column B) is computed at 5 1/2% of the bond carrying amount at the beginning of each period, yielding a gradually decreasing amount.
3. The excess of the periodic interest payment of $6,000 over the interest expense is the amount of premium to be amortized (column C).
4. The unamortized premium (column D) decreases from the initial balance, $3,766, to a zero balance at the maturity date of the bonds.
5. The carrying amount (column E) decreases from $103,766, the amount received for the bonds, to $100,000 at maturity.

The entry to record the first payment and the amortization of the related amount of premium is as follows:

```
July 1   Interest Expense ...................................   5,707
         Premium on Bonds Payable ......................     293
            Cash.........................................             6,000
```

If the amortization is recorded only at the end of the year, the amount of the premium amortized on December 31 would be $602, which is the sum of the first two semiannual amounts ($293 and $309) from the preceding table.

BOND SINKING FUND *special cash account set aside to retire bonds at maturity*

The bond indenture may provide that funds for the payment of bonds at maturity be accumulated over the life of the issue. The amounts set aside are kept separate from other assets in a special fund called a **sinking fund**. Cash deposited in the fund is usually invested in income-producing securities. The periodic deposits plus the earnings on the investments should approximately equal the face amount of the bonds at maturity. Control over the fund may be exercised by the corporation or by a trustee, which is usually a financial corporation.

When cash is transferred to the sinking fund, an account called Sinking Fund Cash is debited and Cash is credited. The purchase of investments is recorded by a debit to Sinking Fund Investments and a credit to Sinking Fund Cash. As interest or dividends are received, the cash is debited to Sinking Fund Cash and Sinking Fund Income is credited.

To illustrate the accounting for a bond sinking fund, assume that a corporation issues $100,000 of 10-year bonds dated January 1, with the provision that equal annual deposits be made in the bond sinking fund at the end of each of the 10 years. The fund is expected to be invested in securities that will yield approximately 14% per year. Reference to the appropriate mathematical table indicates that annual deposits of $5,171 are sufficient to provide a fund of approximately $100,000 at the end of 10 years. A few of the typical transactions and the related entries affecting the sinking fund during the 10-year period are illustrated as follows:

inquire ? about table ↓ these figures given no table

Deposit of cash in the fund

The first deposit in the sinking fund is recorded. A similar entry would be recorded as deposits are made at the end of each of the 9 remaining years.

Entry: Sinking Fund Cash.............................. 5,171
       Cash 5,171

Purchase of investments

The purchases of securities after the first deposit was made are recorded in a summary entry. The time of purchase and the amount invested at any one time vary, depending upon market conditions and the unit price of securities purchased.

Entry: Sinking Fund Investments.................... 5,000
       Sinking Fund Cash...................... 5,000

Receipt of income from investments

The receipt of income for the year on the securities purchased is recorded in a summary entry. Interest and dividends are received at different times during the year, and the amount earned per year normally increases as the fund increases.

Entry: Sinking Fund Cash..........................   700
       Sinking Fund Income......................   700

Sale of investments

The sale of all securities at the end of the tenth year is recorded. Investments may be sold from time to time and the proceeds reinvested. Prior to maturity, all investments are converted into cash.

Entry: Sinking Fund Cash..........................   85,100
       Sinking Fund Investments..................   82,480
       Gain on Sale of Investments   2,620

Payments of bonds

The payment of the bonds and the transfer of the remaining sinking fund cash to the cash account is recorded. The cash available in the fund at the end of the tenth year is assumed to be composed of the following:

Proceeds from sale of investments................... $ 85,100
Income earned during tenth year....................   11,520
Last annual deposit   5,171
     Total... $101,791

Entry: Bonds Payable   100,000
       Cash......................................   1,791
       Sinking Fund Cash........................   101,791

In the illustration, the amount of the fund exceeded the amount of the liability by $1,791. This excess was transferred to the regular cash account. If the fund had been less than the amount of the liability, $99,500 for example, the regular cash account would have been drawn upon for the $500 deficiency.

Sinking fund income represents earnings of the corporation and is reported in the income statement as "Other income." The cash and the securities making up the sinking fund are classified in the balance sheet as "Investments," which usually appears immediately below the current assets section.

APPROPRIATION FOR BONDED INDEBTEDNESS

The restriction of dividends during the life of a bond issue is another means of increasing the assurance that the obligation will be paid at maturity. Assuming that the corporation in the preceding example is required by the bond indenture to appropriate $10,000 of retained earnings each year for the 10-year life of the bonds, the following entry would be made annually:

Dec. 31	Retained Earnings............................	10,000	
	Appropriation for Bonded Indebtedness		10,000

As was indicated in Chapter 16, an appropriation has no direct relationship to a sinking fund. Each is independent of the other. When there is both a fund and an appropriation for the same purpose, the appropriation may be said to be **funded**.

BOND REDEMPTION

callable bonds can be redeemed at any time. Call price higher than face amount.

Callable bonds are redeemable by the issuing corporation within the period of time and at the price stated in the bond indenture. Usually the call price is above the face value. If the market rate of interest declines after the issuance of the bonds, the corporation may sell new bonds at a lower interest rate and use the funds to redeem the original issue. The reduction of future interest expense is always an incentive for bond redemption. A corporation may also redeem all or a portion of its bonds before maturity by purchasing them on the open market.

When a corporation redeems bonds at a price below their carrying amount, the corporation realizes a gain. If the price is in excess of the carrying amount, a loss is incurred. To illustrate redemption, assume that on June 30 a corporation has a bond issue of $100,000 outstanding, on which there is an unamortized premium of $4,000. The corporation has the option of calling the bonds for $105,000, which it exercises on this date. The entry to record the redemption is:

June 30	Bonds Payable............................	100,000	
	Premium on Bonds Payable	4,000	
	Loss on Redemption of Bonds	1,000	
	Cash....................................		105,000

If the bonds were not callable, the corporation might purchase a portion on the open market. Assuming that the corporation purchases one fourth ($25,000) of the bonds for $24,000 on June 30, the entry to record the redemption would be as follows:

carrying value 26,000

June 30	Bonds Payable............................	25,000	
	Premium on Bonds Payable	1,000	
	Cash....................................		24,000
	Gain on Redemption of Bonds		2,000

Note that only the portion of the premium relating to the bonds redeemed is written off. The excess of the carrying amount of the bonds purchased, $26,000, over the cash paid, $24,000, is recognized as a gain.

BALANCE SHEET PRESENTATION OF BONDS PAYABLE

Bonds payable are usually reported on the balance sheet as long-term liabilities. If there are two or more bond issues, separate accounts should be maintained and the details of each should be reported on the balance sheet or in a supporting schedule or note. When the balance sheet date is within one year of the bond maturity date, the bonds should be transferred to the current liability classification if they are to be paid out of current assets. If they are to be paid with funds that have been set aside or if they are to be replaced with another bond issue, they should remain in the noncurrent category and their anticipated liquidation disclosed in an explanatory note.

The balance in a discount account should be reported in the balance sheet as a deduction from the related bonds payable. Conversely, the balance in a premium account should be reported as an addition to the related bonds payable. Either in the financial statements or in accompanying notes, the description of the bonds (terms, security, due date, etc.) should also include the effective interest rate and the maturities and sinking fund requirements for each of the next five years.[4]

INVESTMENTS IN BONDS *one company buying another company's bond*

The issuance of bonds and related transactions were discussed in the preceding paragraphs from the standpoint of the issuing corporation. Whenever a corporation records a transaction between itself and the owners of its bonds, there is a reciprocal entry in the accounts of the investor.

In the following discussion, attention will be given to the principles underlying the accounting for investments in **debt securities** (bonds and notes) that are identified as long-term investments. **Long-term investments are investments that are not intended as a ready source of cash in the normal operations of the business.** These long-term investments are listed in the balance sheet under the caption "Investments," which usually follows the current assets. By contrast, temporary investments or marketable securities, which were discussed in Chapter 9, are available to meet the needs for additional cash for normal operations and are classified as current assets.

---

[4]*Statement of Financial Accounting Standards, No. 47,* "Disclosure of Long-Term Obligations" (Stamford: Financial Accounting Standards Board, 1981), par. 10.

A business may make long-term investments simply because it has cash that is not needed in its normal operations. As discussed previously, cash and securities in bond sinking funds are considered long-term investments, since they are accumulated for the purpose of paying the bond liability. A corporation may also purchase bonds as a means of establishing or maintaining business relations with the issuing company.

Investments in corporate bonds may be purchased directly from the issuing corporation or from other investors. The services of a broker are usually employed in buying and selling bonds listed on the organized exchanges. The record of transactions on bond exchanges is reported daily in the financial pages of newspapers. This record usually includes data on the bond interest rate, maturity date, volume of sales, and the high, low, and closing prices for each corporation's bonds traded during the day. Prices for bonds are quoted as a percentage of the face amount. Thus, the price of a $1,000 bond quoted at 104 1/2 would be $1,045.

ACCOUNTING FOR INVESTMENTS IN BONDS

A long-term investment in debt securities is customarily carried at cost. The cost of bonds purchased includes the amount paid to the seller plus other costs related to the purchase, such as the broker's commission. When bonds are purchased between interest dates, the buyer pays the seller the interest accrued from the last interest payment date to the date of purchase. The amount of the interest paid should be debited to Interest Income, since it is an offset against the amount that will be received at the next interest date. To illustrate, assume that a $1,000 bond is purchased at 102 plus a brokerage fee of $5.30 and accrued interest of $10.20. The transaction is recorded by the following entry. Note that the cost of the bond is recorded in a single account, i.e., the face amount of the bond and the premium paid are not recorded in separate accounts.

Apr. 2 Investment in Lewis Co. Bonds	1,025.30	*temporary debit*
Interest Income .... *accrued interest*	10.20	
Cash		1,035.50

As discussed previously, the price investors pay for bonds may be much greater or less than the face amount or the original issuance price. When bonds held as long-term investments are purchased at a price other than the face amount, the discount or premium should be amortized over the remaining life of the bonds. The amortization of discount increases the amount of the investment account and interest income. The amortization of premium decreases the amount of the investment account and interest income. The procedures for determining the amount of amortization each period correspond to those described and illustrated on pages 739 to 742.

Interest received on bond investments is recorded by a debit to Cash and a credit to Interest Income. At the end of a fiscal year, the interest accrued should be recorded by a debit to Interest Receivable and a credit to Interest Income. The adjusting entry should be reversed after the accounts are closed, so that all receipts of bond interest during the following year may be recorded without referring to the adjustment data.

As a basis for illustrating the transactions associated with long-term investments in bonds, assume that $50,000 of 8% bonds of Nowell Corporation, due in 8 3/4 years, are purchased on July 1 to yield approximately 11%. The purchase price is $41,706 plus interest of $1,000 accrued from April 1, the date of the last semiannual interest payment. Entries in the accounts of the purchaser at the time of purchase and for the remainder of the fiscal year, ending December 31, are as follows:

July 1 Payment for investment in bonds and accrued interest

Cost of $50,000 of Nowell Corp. bonds.....................	$41,706
Interest accrued on $50,000 at 8%, April 1–July 1 (3 months)..	1,000
Total...	$42,706

Entry: Investment in Nowell Corp. Bonds	41,706	
Interest Income..............................	1,000	
Cash		42,706

October 1 Receipt of semiannual interest

Interest on $50,000 at 8%, April 1–October 1 (6 months), $2,000

Entry: Cash	2,000	
Interest Income..............................		2,000

December 31 Adjusting entries

Interest accrued on $50,000 at 8%, October 1–December 31 (3 months), $1,000

Entry: Interest Receivable...........................	1,000	
Interest Income..............................		1,000

Discount to be amortized by interest method, July 1–December 31 (6 months):

Interest income (5 1/2% of bond carrying amount of $41,706)	$2,294
Less interest received (4% of face amount of $50,000) ...	2,000
Amount to be amortized	$ 294

Entry: Investment in Nowell Corp. Bonds	294	
Interest Income...............................		294

The entries in the interest income account in the above illustration may be summarized as follows:

July   1 Paid accrued interest — 3 months........................ $(1,000)
Oct.   1 Received interest payment — 6 months................... 2,000
Dec. 31 Recorded accrued interest — 3 months 1,000
      31 Recorded amortization of discount — 6 months........... 294
        Interest earned — 6 months.......................... $ 2,294

SALE OF INVESTMENTS IN BONDS

When bonds held as long-term investments are sold, the seller will receive the sales price (less commissions and other selling costs) plus the interest accrued since the last payment date. Before recording the proceeds, the seller should record the appropriate amount of the amortization of discount or premium for the current period, up to the date of sale. Then, in recording the proceeds, any gain or loss incurred on the sale can be recognized. To illustrate the recording of a sale of bonds held as a long-term investment, assume that the Nowell Corporation bonds of the preceding example are sold for $47,350 plus accrued interest on June 30, seven years after their purchase. The carrying amount of the bonds (cost plus amortized discount) as of January 1 of the year of sale is $47,080. The entries to record the amortization of discount for the current year and the sale of the bonds are as follows:

June 30 Amortization of discount for current year

Discount to be amortized by the interest method, January 1–June 30, $589

Entry: Investment in Nowell Corp. Bonds   589
        Interest Income...........................   589

June 30 Receipt of interest and sale of bonds

Interest accrued on $50,000 at 8%, April 1–June 30 (3 months), $1,000

Carrying amount of bonds on January 1 of current year $47,080
Discount amortized in current year   589
Carrying amount of bonds on June 30...................... $47,669
Proceeds of sale..   47,350
Loss on sale .... $ 319

Entry: Cash..   48,350   *includes interest income*
        Loss on Sale of Investments   319
        Interest Income..............................   1,000
        Investment in Nowell Corp. Bonds   47,669

CHAPTER REVIEW

KEY POINTS

1. Financing Corporations.

Business enterprises may raise funds for long-term financing in various ways. They may sell capital stock or issue notes or bonds, which are a form of interest-bearing note. When funds are borrowed through the issuance of bonds, there is a definite commitment to pay periodic interest and to repay the principal at a stated future date. There are many factors that must be considered when different methods of financing are evaluated. One such factor is the impact on the corporation's earnings per share of common stock.

2. Characteristics of Bonds.

When a corporation issues bonds, it executes a contract, known as a bond indenture or trust indenture, with bondholders. The principal amount of each bond is called its face value and is usually in a multiple of $1,000. Different types of bonds that may be issued by a corporation include registered bonds, bearer bonds, coupon bonds, term bonds, serial bonds, convertible bonds, callable bonds, secured bonds, and debenture bonds.

3. Present Value Concepts.

The concept of present value plays an important role in many accounting analyses and business decisions. The concept of present value is that an amount of cash to be received at some date in the future is not the equivalent of the same amount of cash held at an earlier date. In other words, a sum of cash to be received in the future is not as valuable as the same sum on hand today, because cash on hand today can be invested to earn income.

4. Present Value Concepts for Bonds Payable.

When a corporation issues bonds, it incurs two distinct obligations: (1) to pay the face amount of the bonds at a specified maturity date, and (2) to pay periodic interest at a specified percentage of the face amount. A price that a buyer is willing to pay for these future benefits is the sum of (1) the present value of the face amount of the bonds at the maturity date and (2) the present value of the periodic interest payments. The present value of $1 table is used to compute the present value of the face amount of the bonds at the maturity date. The present value of an annuity of $1 table is used to compute the present value of the periodic interest payments on the bonds.

5. Accounting for Bonds Payable.

The interest rate specified in the bond indenture is called the contract or coupon rate, which may differ from the rate prevailing in the market at the time the bonds are issued. If the market or effective rate is higher than the contract rate, the bonds will sell at a discount, or less than their face amount. The discount results because buyers are unwilling to pay the face amount for bonds whose contract rate is lower than the prevailing market rate. If the market rate is lower than the contract rate, the bonds will sell at a premium, or more than their face amount. In this case, buyers are willing to pay more than the face amount for bonds whose contract rate is higher than the market rate.

When bonds are issued at a discount, Discount on Bonds Payable is debited for the amount of the discount. When bonds are issued at a premium, Premium on Bonds Payable is credited for the amount of the premium. The amount of the discount or premium must be allocated to interest expense over the life of the bonds by using either the straight-line method or the interest method. The straight-line method provides for a constant amount of interest expense. The interest method provides for a constant rate of interest. A discount is amortized by crediting Discount on Bonds Payable. A premium is amortized by debiting Premium on Bonds Payable. The amortization of a discount increases interest expense, and the amortization of a premium decreases interest expense. The amortization entry may be recorded at either the date of periodic interest payments or the end of the accounting period.

6. Bond Sinking Fund.

The bond indenture may provide that funds for the payment of bonds at maturity be accumulated over the life of the issue. The amounts set aside are accounted for separately from other assets in a special fund called a sinking fund. Cash deposited in this fund is usually invested in income-producing securities. The periodic deposits plus the earnings on the investments should approximately equal the face amount of the bonds at maturity.

7. Appropriation for Bonded Indebtedness.

The bond indenture may require a board of directors to restrict dividends during the life of a bond issue through the use of an appropriation of retained earnings. This action may also be taken voluntarily. When there is both a bond sinking fund and an appropriation of retained earnings for the purpose of redeeming bonds at maturity, the appropriation is said to be funded.

8. Bond Redemption.

Callable bonds are redeemable by the issuing corporation at the price stated in the bond indenture. If the bonds are not callable, they may be purchased on the open market. When a corporation redeems bonds, any gain or loss on the redemption is recognized in the accounts.

9. Balance Sheet Presentation of Bonds Payable.

Bonds payable are usually reported on the balance sheet as long-term liabilities. When the balance sheet date is within one year of the bond maturity date, the bonds should be transferred to the current liability classification if they are to be paid out of current assets. If they are to be paid with funds that have been set aside or if they are to be replaced with another bond issue, they should remain in the noncurrent category and their anticipated liquidation disclosed in an explanatory note. The balance in a discount account should be reported in the balance sheet as a deduction from the related bonds payable, and the balance in a premium account should be reported as an addition to the related bonds payable.

10. Investments in Bonds.

A corporation may purchase bonds of another corporation as a long-term investment that is not intended as a ready source of cash in the normal operations of the business. These long-term investments are listed in the balance sheet under the caption "Investments," following the current assets section.

11. Accounting for Investments in Bonds.

A long-term investment in debt securities is customarily carried at cost. The cost of the bonds purchased includes the amount paid to the seller plus other costs related to the purchase, such as the broker's commission. When bonds are purchased between interest dates, the buyer pays the seller the interest accrued from the last interest payment date to the date of the purchase. The amount of the interest paid should be debited to Interest Income, since it is an offset against the amount that will be received at the next interest date. When bonds held as long-term investments are purchased at a price other than the face amount, the discount or premium should be amortized over the remaining life of the bonds. The procedures for determining the amount of amortization are similar to those for bonds payable. The amortization of a discount increases the amount of the investment account and interest income. The amortization of a premium decreases the amount of the investment account and interest income.

12. Sale of Investments in Bonds.

When bonds held as long-term investments are sold, the seller will receive the sales price (less commissions and other selling costs) plus the interest accrued since the last payment date. Before recording the proceeds, the seller should record the appropriate amount of the amortization of discount or premium for the current period, up to the date of sale. Then, in recording the proceeds, any gain or loss incurred on the sale can be recognized.

KEY TERMS

bonds 730
bond indenture 732
present value 734
contract rate of interest 736
effective rate of interest 736
bond discount 736

bond premium 736
carrying amount 739
sinking fund 743
debt securities 746 bonds & notes
long-term investments 746

SELF-EXAMINATION QUESTIONS
Answers in Appendix B.

1. If a corporation plans to issue $1,000,000 of 12% bonds at a time when the market rate for similar bonds is 10%, the bonds can be expected to sell:
    A. at their face amount
    B. at a premium
    C. at a discount
    D. at a price below their face amount

2. If the bonds payable account has a balance of $500,000 and the discount on bonds payable account has a balance of $40,000, what is the carrying amount of the bonds?
    A. $460,000
    B. $500,000
    C. $540,000
    D. none of the above

3. The cash and the securities comprising the sinking fund established for the payment of bonds at maturity are classified on the balance sheet as:
    A. current assets
    B. investments
    C. long-term liabilities
    D. none of the above

4. If a firm purchases $100,000 of bonds of X Company at 101 plus accrued interest of $2,000 and pays broker's commissions of $50, the amount debited to Investment in X Company Bonds would be:
    A. $100,000
    B. $101,050
    C. $103,000
    D. none of the above

5. The balance in the discount on bonds payable account would usually be reported in the balance sheet in the:
    A. current assets section
    B. current liabilities section
    C. long-term liabilities section
    D. none of the above

ILLUSTRATIVE PROBLEM

Dent Inc.'s fiscal year ends December 31. Selected transactions for the period 1987 through 1994 involving bonds payable issued by Dent Inc. are as follows:

1987

Nov. 30. Issued $4,000,000 of 25-year, 9% callable bonds dated November 30, 1987, for cash of $3,840,000. Interest is payable semiannually on November 30 and May 31.

Dec. 31. Recorded the adjusting entry for interest payable.
    31. Recorded amortization of $533 discount on the bonds.
    31. Closed the interest expense account.

1988

Jan. 1. Reversed the adjusting entry for interest payable.
May 31. Paid the semiannual interest on the bonds.
Nov. 30. Paid the semiannual interest on the bonds.
Dec. 31. Recorded the adjusting entry for interest payable.
    31. Recorded amortization of $6,400 discount on the bonds.
    31. Closed the interest expense account.

1994

Nov. 30. Recorded the redemption of the bonds, which were called at 102. The balance in the bond discount account is $115,200 after the payment of interest and amortization of discount have been recorded. (Record the redemption only.)

Instructions:

1. Prepare journal entries to record the preceding transactions.
2. Determine the amount of interest expense for 1987 and 1988.
3. Estimate the effective annual interest rate by dividing the interest expense for 1987 by the bond carrying amount at the time of issuance and multiplying by 12.
4. Determine the carrying amount of the bonds as of December 31, 1988.

SOLUTION

(1)
  1987

Nov. 30 Cash	3,840,000	
Discount on Bonds Payable	160,000	
Bonds Payable		4,000,000
Dec. 31 Interest Expense ..... *divided by 12*	30,000	
Interest Payable		30,000
31 Interest Expense	533	
Discount on Bonds Payable		533

One month of annual interest (handwritten note)

Dec. 31 Income Summary	30,533	
Interest Expense		30,533

1988
Jan. 1 Interest Payable	30,000	
Interest Expense		30,000
May 31 Interest Expense	180,000	
Cash		180,000
Nov. 30 Interest Expense	180,000	
Cash		180,000
Dec. 31 Interest Expense	30,000	
Interest Payable		30,000
31 Interest Expense	6,400	
Discount on Bonds Payable		6,400
31 Income Summary	366,400	
Interest Expense		366,400

1994
Nov. 30 Bonds Payable	4,000,000	
Loss on Redemption of Bonds Payable.	195,200	
Discount on Bonds Payable		115,200
Cash		4,080,000

(2) (a) 1987—$ 30,533
    (b) 1988—$366,400   *why is it that 12/31 entry omitted*

(3) $30,533 ÷ $3,840,000 = .8% rate for one month of a year
    .8% × 12 = 9.6% annual rate

(4)
Initial carrying amount of bonds	$3,840,000
Discount amortized on December 31, 1987	533
Discount amortized on December 31, 1988	6,400
Carrying amount of bonds, December 31, 1988	$3,846,933

DISCUSSION QUESTIONS

1. When underwriters are used by the corporation issuing bonds, what function do the underwriters perform?

2. How are interest payments made to holders of (a) bearer or coupon bonds and (b) registered bonds?

3. Explain the meaning of each of the following terms as they relate to a bond issue: (a) secured, (b) convertible, (c) callable, and (d) debenture.

4. Describe the two distinct obligations incurred by a corporation when issuing bonds.

5. A corporation issues $5,000,000 of 12% coupon bonds to yield interest at the rate of 11%. (a) Was the amount of cash received from the sale of the bonds greater or less than $5,000,000? (b) Identify the following terms related to the bond issue: (1) face amount, (2) market or effective rate of interest, (3) contract or coupon rate of interest, and (4) maturity amount.

6. If bonds issued by a corporation are sold at a premium, is the market rate of interest greater or less that the coupon rate?

7. What is the present value of $1,000 due in 2 years, if the market rate of interest is 11%.

8. What is the present value of $1,000 to be received in each of the next 2 years, if the market rate of interest is 11%?

9. If the bonds payable account has a balance of $1,000,000 and the premium on bonds payable account has a balance of $37,420, what is the carrying amount of the bonds?

10. The following data are related to a $500,000, 12% bond issue for a selected semi-annual interest period:

Bond carrying amount at beginning of period $531,000
Interest paid at end of period   30,000
Interest expense allocable to the period   28,450

(a) Were the bonds issued at a discount or at a premium? (b) What is the balance of the discount or premium account at the beginning of the period? (c) How much amortization of discount or premium is allocable to the period?

11. A corporation issues 10%, 20-year debenture bonds, with a face amount of $5,000,000, for 102 1/2 at the beginning of the current year. Assuming that the premium is to be amortized on a straight-line basis, what is the total amount of interest expense for the current year?

12. Indicate the title of (a) the account to be debited and (b) the account to be credited in the entry made at year-end for amortization of (1) discount on bonds payable and (2) premium on bonds payable.

13. When the premium on bonds payable is amortized by the interest method, does the interest expense increase or decrease over the amortization period?

14. What is the purpose of a bond sinking fund?

15. If the amount accumulated in a sinking fund account exceeds the amount of liability at the redemption date, to what account is the excess transferred?

16. How are cash and securities comprising a sinking fund classified on the balance sheet?

17. Bonds Payable has a balance of $300,000 and Premium on Bonds Payable has a balance of $11,400. If the issuing corporation redeems the bonds at 102, what is the amount of gain or loss on redemption?

18. Indicate how the following accounts should be reported in the balance sheet: (a) Premium on Bonds Payable, and (b) Discount on Bonds Payable.

19. Under what caption are "Long-term investments in bonds" listed on the balance sheet?

20. The quoted price of Turpin Corp. bonds on May 1 is 105. On the same day the interest accrued is 4% of the face amount. (a) Does the quoted price include accrued interest? (b) If $20,000 face amount of Turpin Corp. bonds is purchased on May 1 at the quoted price, what is the cost of the bonds, exclusive of commission?

21. An investor sells $20,000 of bonds of ICC Corp. carried at $20,450, for $20,900 plus accrued interest of $200. The broker remits the balance due after deducting a commission of $80. Present the entry to record this transaction.

22. Real World Focus. General Electric Company 8 1/2% debenture bonds due in 2004 were reported in *The Wall Street Journal* as selling for 97 1/2 on March 6, 1986. (a) Were the bonds selling at a premium or at a discount on March 6, 1986? (b) Was the market rate of interest for similar quality bonds higher or lower than 8 1/2% on March 6, 1986?

EXERCISES

Exercise 17–1. Effect of financing on earnings per share. Two companies are financed as follows:

	Sims Inc.	Tone Co.
Bonds payable, 10% (issued at face value)	$2,000,000	$1,000,000
Preferred 9% stock (nonparticipating)	2,000,000	1,000,000
Common stock, $10 par	2,000,000	4,000,000

Income tax is estimated at 50% of income. Determine for each company the earnings per share of common stock, assuming that the income before bond interest and income tax for each company is (a) $600,000, (b) $1,000,000, and (c) $1,600,000.

Exercise 17–2. Entries for issuance and calling of bonds. F. C. Classic Company issued $5,000,000 of 20-year, 12% callable bonds on March 1, 1987, with interest payable on March 1 and September 1. The fiscal year of the company is the calendar year. Present the journal entries to record the following selected transactions:

1987
Mar.   1. Issued the bonds for cash at their face amount.
Sept. 1. Paid the interest on the bonds.
Dec. 31. Recorded accrued interest for four months.
       31. Closed the interest expense account.

1988
Jan. 1. Reversed the adjusting entry for accrued interest.
Mar. 1. Paid the interest on the bonds.
1992
Sept. 1. Called the bond issue at 102, the rate provided in the bond indenture. (Omit entry for payment of interest.)

Exercise 17–3. Entries for bond issuance; amortization of discount by straight-line method. On the first day of its fiscal year, Grant Corporation issued $10,000,000 of 10-year, 10% bonds, interest payable semiannually, at an effective interest rate of 12%, receiving cash of $8,852,950.

(a) Present the journal entries to record the following:
  (1) Sale of the bonds.
  (2) First semiannual interest payment. (Amortization of discount is to be recorded annually.)
  (3) Second semiannual interest payment.
  (4) Amortization of discount at the end of the first year, using the straight-line method.
(b) Determine the amount of the bond interest expense for the first year.

Exercise 17–4. Computation of bond proceeds, entries for bond issuance, and amortization of premium by straight-line method. On March 1, 1987, Allen Corporation issued $5,000,000 of 10-year, 12% bonds at an effective interest rate of 11%. Interest is payable semiannually on March 1 and September 1. Present the journal entries to record the following:

(a) Sale of bonds on March 1, 1987. (Use the tables of present values appearing in the chapter to determine the bond proceeds.)
(b) First interest payment on September 1, 1987, including amortization of bond premium for 6 months, using the straight-line method.

SPREADSHEET PROBLEM

Exercise 17–5. Computation of bond proceeds, amortization of premium by interest method, and interest expense. On the first day of its fiscal year, Harris Co. issued $10,000,000 of 10-year, 12% bonds at an effective interest rate of 10%, with interest payable semiannually. Compute the following, presenting figures used in your computations and rounding to the nearest dollar:

(a) The amount of cash proceeds from the sale of the bonds. (Use the tables of present values appearing in the chapter.)
(b) The amount of premium to be amortized for the first semiannual interest payment period, using the interest method.
(c) The amount of premium to be amortized for the second semiannual interest payment period, using the interest method.
(d) The amount of the bond interest expense for the first year.

Exercise 17–6. Entries for bond sinking fund and appropriation of retained earnings. Yaxley Corporation issued $20,000,000 of 20-year bonds on the first day of the fiscal year. The bond indenture provides that a sinking fund be accumulated by 20 annual deposits of $550,000, beginning at the end of the first year.

Present the journal entries to record the following selected transactions related to the bond issue:

(a) The required amount is deposited in the sinking fund.
(b) Investments in securities from the first sinking fund deposit total $539,100.
(c) Appropriated $1,000,000 of retained earnings for bonded indebtedness.
(d) The sinking fund earned $36,500 during the year following the first deposit (summarizing entry).
(e) The bonds are paid at maturity, and excess cash of $97,750 in the fund is transferred to the cash account.
(f) Transferred the appropriation for bonded indebtedness balance of $20,000,000 back to retained earnings.

Exercise 17–7. Computation of amortization of bond discount by both straight-line and interest methods. On July 1 of the current fiscal year, Rockford Company purchased $500,000 of 10-year, 10% bonds as a long-term investment directly from the issuing company for $442,650. The effective rate of interest is 12%, and the interest is payable semiannually. Compute the amount of discount to be amortized for the first semiannual interest payment period, using (a) the straight-line method and (b) the interest method.

contract rate 10%
market rate 12%

Exercise 17–8. Entries for purchase and sale of investment in bonds. Present journal entries to record the following selected transactions of Hackman Corporation:

(a) Purchased for cash $200,000 of Dirch Co. 11% bonds at 102 plus accrued interest of $5,500.
(b) Received first semiannual interest.
(c) Amortized $360 on the bond investment at the end of the first year.
(d) Sold the bonds at 99 plus accrued interest of $2,775. The bonds were carried at $201,500 at the time of the sale.

PROBLEMS

Series A

Problem 17–1A. Entries for bonds payable transactions. The following transactions were completed by Harlow Co., whose fiscal year is the calendar year:

1987
Oct. 1. Issued $10,000,000 of 10-year, 12% callable bonds dated October 1, 1987, for cash of $11,246,320. Interest is payable semiannually on October 1 and April 1.
Dec. 31. Recorded the adjusting entry for interest payable.

Dec. 31. Recorded bond premium amortization of $18,842, which was determined using the interest method.
31. Closed the interest expense account.

1988
Jan. 1. Reversed the adjusting entry for interest payable.
Apr. 1. Paid the semiannual interest on the bonds.
Oct. 1. Paid the semiannual interest on the bonds.
Dec. 31. Recorded the adjusting entry for interest payable.
31. Recorded bond premium amortization of $79,184, which was determined by using the interest method.
31. Closed the interest expense account.

1994
Oct. 1. Recorded the redemption of the bonds, which were called at 102. The balance in the bond premium account is $507,764 after the payment of interest and amortization of premium have been recorded. (Record the redemption only.)

Instructions:

(1) Prepare journal entries to record the foregoing transactions.
(2) Indicate the amount of the interest expense in (a) 1987 and (b) 1988.
(3) Determine the effective interest rate by dividing the interest expense for 1987 by the bond carrying amount at the time of issuance and converting the result to an annual rate.
(4) Determine the carrying amount of the bonds as of December 31, 1988.

Problem 17–2A.   Entries for bonds payable transactions. On July 1, 1987, Betz Corporation issued $12,000,000 of 10-year, 10% bonds at an effective interest rate of 11%. Interest on the bonds is payable semiannually on December 31 and June 30. The fiscal year of the company is the calendar year.

Instructions:

(1) Present the journal entry to record the amount of the cash proceeds from the sale of the bonds. Use the tables of present values appearing in this chapter to compute the cash proceeds, rounding to the nearest dollar.
(2) Present the journal entries to record the following selected transactions for 1987 and 1988:
  (a) The entry for the payment of interest and the amortization of the bond discount on December 31, 1987, using the interest method.
  (b) The semiannual interest payment on June 30, 1988, including the amortization of the bond discount, using the interest method.
(3) Present the entries for Instruction (2), using the straight-line method of discount amortization.
(4) What is the total interest expense for 1987 for (a) the interest method of discount amortization and (b) the straight-line method of discount amortization? (c) Will the annual interest expense using the interest method of discount amortization always be less than the annual interest expense using the straight-line method of discount amortization?

Problem 17–3A.   Entries for bond and sinking fund transactions, including appropriation of retained earnings. During 1987 and 1988, Watts Company completed the following transactions relating to its $4,500,000 issue of 30-year, 11% bonds dated September 1, 1987. Interest is payable on September 1 and March 1. The corporation's fiscal year is the calendar year.

1987
Sept. 1. Sold the bond issue for $4,197,600.
Dec. 31. Recorded the adjusting entry for interest payable.
Dec. 31. Recorded bond discount amortization of $3,360, which was determined by using the straight-line method.
  31. Deposited $20,000 cash in a bond sinking fund.
  31. Appropriated $50,000 of retained earnings for bonded indebtedness.
  31. Closed the interest expense account.

1988
Jan. 1. Reversed the adjustment for interest payable.
  15. Purchased various securities with sinking fund cash, cost $17,400.
Mar. 1. Paid the semiannual interest on the bonds.
Sept. 1. Paid the semiannual interest on the bonds.
Dec. 15. Recorded the receipt of $1,900 of income on sinking fund securities, depositing the cash in the sinking fund.
  31. Recorded the adjusting entry for interest payable.
  31. Recorded bond discount amortization of $10,080, which was determined by using the straight-line method.
  31. Deposited $60,000 cash in the sinking fund.
  31. Appropriated $150,000 of retained earnings for bonded indebtedness.
  31. Closed the interest expense account.

Instructions:

(1) Prepare journal entries to record the foregoing transactions.
(2) Prepare a columnar table, using the following headings, and list the information for each of the two years.

	Bond Interest Expense for Year	Sinking Fund Income for Year	Bonds Payable	Discount on Bonds	Sinking Fund Cash	Sinking Fund Investments	Appropriation For Bonded Indebtedness
Year	*a*	*b*	*c*	*d*	*e*	*f*	*g*
1987	168,360		4,500,000				
1988	505,080		4,500,000				

Problem 17–4A.   Entries for bond and sinking fund transactions. The following transactions relate to the issuance of $900,000 of 10-year, 8% bonds dated January 1, 1978, and the accumulations in a sinking fund to redeem the bonds at maturity. Interest on the bonds is payable on June 30 and December 31.

1978
Jan. 2. Sold the bond issue at 100.
June 30. Paid semiannual interest on bonds.
Dec. 31. Paid semiannual interest on bonds and deposited $52,000 in a bond sinking fund.

1979

Jan. 13. Purchased $50,100 of investments with bond sinking fund cash.
June 30. Paid semiannual interest on bonds.
Nov. 11. Received $3,890 income on investments.
Dec. 31. Paid semiannual interest on bonds.

(Assume that all intervening transactions have been properly recorded.)

1988

Jan. 2. Sold all investments in the bond sinking fund for $880,500. The sinking fund investments had a book carrying value of $899,200.
      9. Paid the bonds at maturity from the sinking fund cash and the regular cash account. The cash available in the sinking fund at this date was $891,900.

Instructions:

Prepare journal entries to record the foregoing transactions.

Problem 17–5A. Entries for bond investments. The following transactions relate to certain securities acquired by Crawford Company, whose fiscal year ends on December 31:

1987

Nov. 1. Purchased $400,000 of Watson Company 20-year, 9% coupon bonds dated September 1, 1987, directly from the issuing company for $388,100 plus $6,000 accrued interest.
Dec. 31. Recorded the adjustment for interest receivable on the Watson Company bonds.
     31. Recorded bond discount amortization of $100 on the Watson Company bonds. The amortization amount was determined by using the straight-line method.

(Assume that all intervening transactions and adjustments have been properly recorded, and that the number of bonds owned has not changed from December 31, 1987, to December 31, 1991.)

1992

Jan. 1. Reversed the adjustment of December 31, 1991, for interest receivable on the Watson Company bonds.
Mar. 1. Deposited the coupons for semiannual interest on the Watson Company bonds.
June 1. Sold one half of the Watson Company bonds at 98 plus accrued interest. The broker deducted $1,240 for commission, etc., remitting the balance. Before the sale was recorded, $125 of discount on one half of the bonds was amortized, increasing the carrying amount of those bonds to $195,425.
Sept. 1. Deposited coupons for semiannual interest on the Watson Company bonds.

Dec. 31. Recorded the adjustment for interest receivable on the Watson Company bonds.

31. Recorded bond discount amortization of $300 on the Watson Company bonds.

Instructions:

(1) Prepare journal entries to record the foregoing transactions.
(2) Determine the amount of interest earned on the bonds in 1987.
(3) Determine the amount of interest earned on the bonds in 1992.

Problem 17–6A. Work sheet and financial statements for corporation. The accounts in the ledger of Roberts Industries Inc., with the balances on December 31, 1987, the end of the current fiscal year, are as follows:

Cash	$ 56,200
Marketable Securities	30,000
Accounts Receivable	127,660
Allowance for Doubtful Accounts	1,200
Merchandise Inventory	130,000
Prepaid Insurance	9,120
Store Supplies	4,120
Bond Sinking Fund	70,100
Store Equipment	377,600
Accumulated Depreciation — Store Equipment	84,000
Office Equipment	136,000
Accumulated Depreciation — Office Equipment	51,080
Accounts Payable	55,900
Interest Payable	—
First Mortgage 12% Bonds Payable	160,000
Premium on Bonds Payable	9,800
Common Stock, $20 par	200,000
Retained Earnings	232,672
Income Summary	—
Sales	1,638,200
Purchases	1,239,960
Purchases Discounts	14,480
Sales Salaries and Commissions Expense	98,000
Advertising Expense	25,200
Depreciation Expense — Store Equipment	—
Store Supplies Expense	—
Miscellaneous Selling Expense	7,500
Office and Officers Salaries Expense	74,000
Rent Expense	48,000
Depreciation Expense — Office Equipment	—
Uncollectible Accounts Expense	—
Insurance Expense	—
Miscellaneous General Expense	6,380
Interest Expense	16,000
Sinking Fund Income	7,708
Interest Income	800

The data needed for year-end adjustments on December 31, 1987, are as follows:

Merchandise inventory on December 31 (at cost, first-in,
   first-out).. $142,000
Insurance expired during the year.......................... 6,140
Store supplies inventory on December 31................... 1,520
Depreciation (straight-line method) for the current year on:
   Store equipment....................................... 30,800
   Office equipment....................................... 18,720
Uncollectible accounts expense is estimated at 1% of sales.
Bonds payable are due on November 1, 1992. Interest on
   bonds is payable on May 1 and November 1. Premium
   to be amortized on bonds payable, using the straight-
   line method 1,680

Instructions:

(1) Prepare a ten-column work sheet for the fiscal year ended December 31.
(2) Prepare a multiple-step income statement. (Disregard income tax.)
(3) Prepare a report form balance sheet. (The market price of marketable securities is $31,600).

Series B

Problem 17–1B.   Entries for bonds payable transactions. The following transactions were completed by Valdez Industries Inc., whose fiscal year is the calendar year:

1987
Mar. 31. Issued $8,000,000 of 10-year, 10% callable bonds dated March 31, 1987, receiving cash of $7,521,760. Interest is payable semiannually on March 31 and September 30.
Sept. 30. Paid the semiannual interest on the bonds.
Dec. 31. Recorded the adjusting entry for interest payable.
     31. Recorded bond discount amortization of $20,922, which was determined by using the interest method.
     31. Closed the interest expense account.

1988
Jan. 1. Reversed the adjusting entry for interest payable.
Mar. 31. Paid the semiannual interest on the bonds.
Sept. 30. Paid the semiannual interest on the bonds.
Dec. 31. Recorded the adjusting entry for interest payable.
     31. Recorded bond discount amortization of $30,512, which was determined by using the interest method.
     31. Closed the interest expense account.

1995
Mar. 31. Recorded the redemption of the bonds, which were called at 102 1/2. The balance in the bond discount account is $140,738 after the payment of interest and amortization of discount have been recorded. (Record the redemption only.)

Instructions:

(1) Prepare journal entries to record the foregoing transactions.
(2) Indicate the amount of the interest expense in (a) 1987 and (b) 1988.
(3) Determine the effective interest rate by dividing the interest expense for 1987 by the bond carrying amount at the time of issuance and converting the result to an annual rate.
(4) Determine the carrying amount of the bonds as of December 31, 1988.

Problem 17–2B. Entries for bonds payable transactions. On July 1, 1987, Pender Corporation issued $20,000,000 of 10-year, 12% bonds at an effective interest rate of 11%. Interest on the bonds is payable semiannually on December 31 and June 30. The fiscal year of the company is the calendar year.

Instructions:

(1) Present the journal entry to record the amount of the cash proceeds from the sale of the bonds. Use the tables of present values appearing in this chapter to compute the cash proceeds, rounding to the nearest dollar.
(2) Present the journal entries to record the following:
    (a) The first semiannual interest payment on December 31, 1987, including the amortization of the bond premium, using the interest method.
    (b) The interest payment on June 30, 1988, including the amortization of the bond premium, using the interest method.
(3) Present the entries for Instruction (2), using the straight-line method of amortization.
(4) Determine the total interest expense for 1987 under (a) the interest method of premium amortization and (b) the straight-line method of premium amortization. (c) Will the annual interest expense using the interest method of premium amortization always be greater than the annual interest expense using the straight-line method of premium amortization?

Problem 17–3B. Entries for bond and sinking fund transactions, including appropriation of retained earnings. During 1987 and 1988, Carr Company completed the following transactions relating to its $5,000,000 issue of 20-year, 12% bonds dated February 1, 1987. Interest is payable on February 1 and August 1. The corporation's fiscal year is the calendar year.

1987
Feb. 1. Sold the bond issue for $5,402,000 cash.
Aug. 1. Paid the semiannual interest on the bonds.
Dec. 31. Recorded the adjusting entry for interest payable.
     31. Recorded bond premium amortization of $18,425, which was determined by using the straight-line method.
     31. Deposited $264,000 cash in a bond sinking fund.
     31. Appropriated $440,000 of retained earnings for bonded indebtedness.
     31. Closed the interest expense account.

1988
Jan. 1. Reversed the adjustment for interest payable.
      9. Purchased various securities with sinking fund cash, cost $256,500.

Feb. 1. Paid the semiannual interest on the bonds.
Aug. 1. Paid the semiannual interest on the bonds.
Dec. 20. Recorded the receipt of $22,150 of income on sinking fund securities, depositing the cash in the sinking fund.
      31. Recorded the adjusting entry for interest payable.
      31. Recorded bond premium amortization of $20,100, which was determined by using the straight-line method.
      31. Deposited $288,000 cash in the sinking fund.
      31. Appropriated $480,000 of retained earnings for bonded indebtedness.
      31. Closed the interest expense account.

Instructions:

(1) Prepare journal entries to record the foregoing transactions.
(2) Prepare a columnar table, using the following headings, and list the information for each of the two years.

					Account Balances at End of Year		
Year	Bond Interest Expense for Year	Sinking Fund Income for Year	Bonds Payable	Premium on Bonds	Sinking Fund		Appropriation for Bonded Indebtedness
					Cash	Investments	

Problem 17–5B. Entries for bond investments. The following transactions relate to certain securities acquired as a long-term investment by Power Company, whose fiscal year ends on December 31:

1987

May 1. Purchased $100,000 of Bowen Company 15-year, 12% coupon bonds dated April 1, 1987, directly from the issuing company for $101,790 plus accrued interest of $1,000.
Oct. 1. Deposited the coupons for semiannual interest on the Bowen Company bonds.
Dec. 31. Recorded the adjustment for interest receivable on the Bowen Company bonds.
      31. Recorded bond premium amortization of $80 on the Bowen Company bonds. The amortization amount was determined by using the straight-line method.

(Assume that all intervening transactions and adjustments have been properly recorded, and that the number of bonds owned has not changed from December 31, 1987, to December 31, 1992.)

1993

Jan. 1. Reversed the adjustment of December 31, 1992, for interest receivable on the Bowen Company bonds.
Apr. 1. Deposited coupons for semiannual interest on the Bowen Company bonds.

July 1. Sold one half of the Bowen Company bonds at 103 plus accrued interest. The broker deducted $540 for commission, etc., remitting the balance. Before the sale was recorded, $30 of premium on one half of the bonds was amortized, reducing the carrying amount of those bonds to $50,525.

Oct. 1. Deposited coupons for semiannual interest on the Bowen Company bonds.

Dec. 31. Recorded the adjustment for interest receivable on the Bowen Company bonds.

31. Recorded bond premium amortization of $60 on the Bowen Company bonds.

Instructions:

(1) Prepare journal entries to record the foregoing transactions.
(2) Determine the amount of interest earned on the bonds in 1987.
(3) Determine the amount of interest earned on the bonds in 1993.

MINI-CASE 17

You hold a 10% common stock interest in the family-owned business, a soft drink bottling distributorship. Your father, who is the manager, has proposed an expansion of plant facilities at an expected cost of $1,500,000. Two alternative plans have been suggested as methods of financing the expansion. Each plan is briefly described as follows:

Plan 1. Issue an additional 20,000 shares of $20 par common stock at $25 per share, and $1,000,000 of 20-year, 12% bonds at face amount.

Plan 2. Issue $1,500,000 of 20-year, 12% bonds at face amount.

The balance sheet as of the end of the previous fiscal year is as follows:

C-U Bottling Co.
Balance Sheet
December 31, 19--

Assets

Current assets	$1,200,000
Plant assets.............................	5,800,000
Total assets............................	$7,000,000

Liabilities and Stockholders' Equity

Current liabilities..........................	$1,800,000
Common stock, $20.......................	600,000
Premium on common stock.................	150,000
Retained earnings	4,450,000
Total liabilities and stockholders' equity......	$7,000,000

Net income has remained relatively constant over the past several years. The expansion program is expected to increase yearly income before bond interest and income tax from $700,000 to $960,000.

Your father has asked you, as the company treasurer, to prepare an analysis of each financing plan.

Instructions:

(1) Prepare a tabulation indicating the expected earnings per share on the common stock under each plan. Assume an income tax rate of 50%.
(2) List factors other than earnings per share that should be considered in evaluating the two plans.
(3) Which plan offers the greater benefit to the present stockholders? Give reasons for your opinion.

Chapter 18

INVESTMENTS IN STOCKS; CONSOLIDATED STATEMENTS; INTERNATIONAL OPERATIONS

Chapter Objectives:

■ Describe and illustrate the accounting for long-term investments in stocks.

■ Describe alternative methods of combining businesses.

■ Describe and illustrate the accounting for parent-subsidiary affiliations and the preparation of consolidated financial statements.

■ Illustrate a corporate balance sheet for a parent company and its subsidiaries.

■ Describe and illustrate the accounting for international operations.

18

In the preceding chapter, the principles of accounting for long-term investments in bonds were discussed. In this chapter, the principles of accounting for long-term investments in stocks will be presented. Accounting for the combining of the operations of two corporations and the expansion of operations into international markets will also be discussed.

INVESTMENTS IN STOCKS

A business may make long-term investments in **equity securities** (preferred and common shares), simply because it has cash that it does not need for normal operations. A corporation may also purchase stocks as a means of establishing or maintaining business relations with the issuing company. In some cases, a corporation may acquire all or a large part of the voting stock of another corporation in order to control its activities. Similarly, a corporation may organize a new corporation for the purpose of marketing a new product or for some other business reason, receiving stock in exchange for the assets transferred to the new corporation.

Investments in stocks may be purchased directly from the issuing corporation or from other investors. Both preferred and common stocks may be *listed* on an organized stock exchange, or they may be *unlisted,* in which case they are said to be bought or sold *over the counter.* The services of a broker are usually used in buying and selling both listed and unlisted securities.

The record of transactions on the stock exchanges is reported daily by the financial press. This record usually includes, for each stock traded, the high and low price for the past year, the current annual dividend, the volume of sales for the day, and the high, low, and closing price for the day. Prices for stocks are quoted in terms of fractional dollars, with 1/8 of a dollar being the usual minimum fraction, although some low-priced stocks are sold in lower fractions of a dollar, such as 1/16 or 1/32. Thus, a price of 40 3/8 per share means $40.375; a price of 40 1/2 means $40.50.

In the following discussion, attention will be given to the principles underlying the accounting for investments in stocks that are not intended as a ready source of cash in the normal operations of the business. Such investments are identified as long-term investments and are reported in the balance sheet under the caption "Investments." The principles underlying the accounting for investments in stocks that are classified as temporary investments or marketable securities were discussed in Chapter 9.

More Americans Than Ever Before Own Stock

About 47 million Americans own stock, more than ever before, but many are participants through stock mutual funds, according to a New York Stock Exchange survey.

The survey said the 47 million investors tallied as of mid-1985 were an 11 percent increase over the 42 million found in the exchange's last survey in mid-1983.

That means that one in five Americans is now a stock investor, as opposed to one of every six two years ago.

Women account for 57 percent of the new investors, the survey said; typically, she is married, employed in a technical or professional job, has an annual household income of $35,000 and a portfolio of $2,200.

Source: Adapted from "More Americans Than Ever Before Own Stock," *Champaign-Urbana News Gazette,* December 5, 1985. © Associated Press.

ACCOUNTING FOR LONG-TERM INVESTMENTS IN STOCK

There are two methods of accounting for long-term investments in stock: (1) the **cost method** and (2) the **equity method**. The method used depends upon whether the investor owns enough of the voting stock of the investee (company whose stock is owned by the investor) to have a significant influence over its operating and financing policies. If the investor does not have a significant influence, the cost method (with the lower of cost or market rule) must be used. If the investor can exercise a significant influence in a long-term investment situation, the equity method must be used. Evidence of such influence includes, but is not limited to, representation on the board of directors, material intercompany transactions, and interchange of managerial personnel. Guidelines to be applied in making the election are as follows:

In order to achieve a reasonable degree of uniformity in application, the Board concludes that an investment (direct or indirect) of 20% or more of the voting stock of an investee should lead to a presumption that in the absence of evidence to the contrary an investor has the ability to exercise significant influence over an investee. Conversely, an investment of less than 20% of the voting stock of an investee should lead to a presumption that an investor does not have the ability to exercise significant influence unless such ability can be demonstrated.[1]

Cost Method

The cost of stocks purchased includes not only the amount paid to the seller but also other costs related to the purchase, such as the broker's commission and postage charges for delivery. When stocks are purchased between dividend dates, there is no separate charge for the pro rata amount of the dividend. Dividends do not accrue from day to day, since they become an obligation of the issuing corporation only when they are declared by the board of directors. The prices of stocks may be affected by the anticipated dividend as the usual declaration date approaches, but this anticipated dividend is only one of many factors that influence stock prices.

The total cost of stocks purchased should be debited to an investment account. When the cost method is used, cash dividends on capital stock held as an investment may be recorded as an increase in the appropriate income and asset accounts. To illustrate, assume that Ingle Corporation purchases 100 shares of Howe Corporation common stock at 55 plus a brokerage fee of $42. At the end of the year, Howe Corporation declares a $2 per share cash dividend. Entries in the accounts of Ingle Corporation, the investor, are as follows:

Record purchase of Howe Corp. common stock for $5,542 cash

Entry:	Investment in Howe Corp. Stock	5,542	
	Cash		5,542

Record share of cash dividends paid by Howe Corp.

Entry:	Cash	200	
	Dividend Income		200

In the illustration, the dividend was recorded when it became taxable to Ingle Corporation, which occurred when the cash was received. An alternative would be to record the cash dividend when it is declared by the investee corporation. If this alternative had been used, Ingle Corporation would have debited Dividends Receivable and credited Dividend Income when the dividend was declared. When the dividend was paid, Ingle Corporation would have debited Cash and credited the receivable.

---

[1]*Opinions of the Accounting Principles Board, No. 18*, "The Equity Method of Accounting for Investments in Common Stock" (New York: American Institute of Certified Public Accountants, 1971), par. 17.

A dividend in the form of additional shares of stock is usually not income, and therefore no entry is needed beyond a notation as to the additional number of shares acquired. The receipt of a stock dividend does, however, affect the carrying amount of each share of stock. Thus, if a 5-share common stock dividend is received on 100 shares of common stock with a current carrying amount of $4,200 ($42 per share), the unit carrying amount of the 105 shares becomes $4,200 ÷ 105, or $40 per share.

Long-term investments in stocks of a company over which the investor does not exercise significant influence are subject to the lower of cost or market rule. In applying the rule, the carrying amount of a long-term investment in a portfolio of equity securities is the lower of the *total* cost or *total* market price of the portfolio at the date of the balance sheet. Any market value changes that are recognized are not included in net income, but are reported as a separate item in the stockholders' equity section of the balance sheet.[2] If the decline in market value below cost of an individual security as of the balance sheet date is other than temporary, the cost basis of the individual security is written down and the amount of the write-down is accounted for as a realized loss. After the write-down, the carrying amount of the individual security cannot be changed for subsequent recoveries in market value.[3]

Equity Method

When the equity method of accounting is used, a stock purchase is recorded at cost as under the cost method. The features that distinguish the equity method from the cost method relate to the net income and cash dividends of the investee and are summarized as follows:

1. The investor records its share of the periodic net income of the investee as an increase in the investment account and as revenue of the period. Conversely, the investor's share of the investee's periodic loss is recorded as a decrease in the investment and a loss of the period.
2. The investor records its share of cash or property dividends on the stock as a decrease in the investment account and an increase in the appropriate asset accounts.

To illustrate the foregoing, assume that as of the beginning of the fiscal years of Otto Corporation and Parker Corporation, Otto acquires 40% of the common (voting) stock of Parker for $350,000 in cash, that Parker reports net income of $105,000 for the year, and that Parker declared and paid $45,000 in cash dividends during the year. Entries in the accounts of the investor to record these transactions are as follows:

---

[2]*Statement of Financial Accounting Standards, No. 12,* "Accounting for Certain Marketable Securities" (Stamford: Financial Accounting Standards Board, 1975), par. 11.
[3]*Ibid.,* par. 21.

Record purchase of 40% of Parker Corp. common stock for $350,000 cash

Entry: Investment in Parker Corp. Stock	350,000	
Cash		350,000

Record 40% of Parker Corp. net income of $105,000

Entry: Investment in Parker Corp. Stock	42,000	
Income of Parker Corp.		42,000

Record 40% of cash dividends of $45,000 paid by Parker Corp.

Entry: Cash	18,000	
Investment in Parker Corp. Stock		18,000

The combined effect of recording 40% of Parker Corporation's income and the dividends received was to increase Cash by $18,000, Investment in Parker Corp. Stock by $24,000, and Income of Parker Corp. by $42,000.

SALE OF LONG-TERM INVESTMENTS IN STOCKS

When shares of stock held as a long-term investment are sold, the investment account is credited for the carrying amount of the shares sold and the cash or appropriate receivable account is debited for the proceeds (sales price less commission and other selling costs). Any difference between the proceeds and the carrying amount is recorded as a gain or loss on the sale. To illustrate, assume that an investment in Drey Corporation stock has a carrying amount of $15,700. If the proceeds from the sale of the stock are $17,500, the entry to record the transaction is as follows:

Cash	17,500	
Investment in Drey Corp. Stock		15,700
Gain on Sale of Investments		1,800

BUSINESS COMBINATIONS

The history of business organization in the United States has been characterized by continuous growth in the size of business entities and the combining of separate enterprises to form even larger operating units. Over the past several years, the combining of businesses has increased dramatically both in numbers and dollars. In 1985, for example, more than 3,000 combinations took place, involving the exchange of cash, debt obligations, or capital stock of approximately \$180 billion.[4] These combinations were influenced by such objectives as efficiencies of large-scale production, broadening of markets and sales volume, reduction of competition, diversification of product lines, and savings in income taxes.

The combining of businesses is often announced to the public, especially if the businesses are well known. For example, the following advertisement appeared in *Business Week* (January, 27, 1986), announcing the acquisition of Hughes Aircraft Company by General Motors Corporation:

December 27, 1985

General Motors Corporation

has acquired

Hughes Aircraft Company

The undersigned acted as financial advisor to General Motors Corporation in this transaction.

Salomon Brothers Inc

The combining of businesses that are engaged either in similar types of activity or in totally different kinds of pursuits may be effected (1) through a joining of two or more corporations to form a single unit by merger or by consolidation, or (2) through common control of two or more corporations by means of stock ownership that results in a parent-subsidiary affiliation. These methods of combining separate corporations into larger operating units are complex. Therefore, the discussion that follows is intended to be introductory, with major emphasis on the financial statements of business combinations.

---

[4]"New Climate for Mergers," Vartanig G. Varten, *The New York Times*, March 13, 1986.

Mergers and Consolidations

When one corporation acquires the properties of another corporation and the latter then dissolves, the joining of the two enterprises is called a **merger**. Usually, all of the assets of the acquired company, as well as its liabilities, are taken over by the acquiring company, which continues its operations as a single unit. Payment may be in the form of cash, obligations, or capital stock of the acquiring corporation, or there may be a combination of several kinds of consideration. In any event, the consideration received by the dissolving corporation is distributed to its stockholders in final liquidation.

When two or more corporations transfer their assets and liabilities to a corporation which has been created for purposes of the takeover, the combination is called a **consolidation**. The new corporation usually issues its own securities in exchange for the properties acquired, and the original corporations are dissolved.

There are many legal, financial, managerial, and accounting problems associated with mergers and consolidations. Perhaps the most important matter is the determination of the class and amount of securities to be issued to the owners of the dissolving corporations. In resolving this problem, several factors are considered, including the relative value of the net assets contributed, the relative earning capacities, and the market price of the securities of the respective companies. Bargaining between the parties to the combination may also affect the final outcome.

Parent and Subsidiary Corporations

A common means of achieving a business combination is by one corporation owning a controlling share of the outstanding voting stock of one or more other corporations. When this method is used, none of the participants dissolves. All continue as separate legal entities. The corporation owning all or a majority of the voting stock of another corporation is known as the **parent company**. The corporation that is controlled is known as the **subsidiary company**. Two or more corporations closely related through stock ownership are sometimes called **affiliated** or **associated** companies.

The relationship of a parent and a subsidiary may be established by "purchase" or by a "pooling of interests." When a corporation acquires a controlling share of the voting common stock of another corporation in exchange for cash, other assets, issuance of notes or other debt obligations, or by a combination of these items, the transaction is treated as a purchase. It is accounted for by the **purchase method**. When this method of effecting a parent-subsidiary affiliation is used, the stockholders of the acquired company transfer their stock to the parent corporation.

Alternatively, when two corporations become affiliated by means of an exchange of voting common stock of one corporation (the parent) for substantially all (at least 90%) of the voting common stock of the other corporation (the subsidiary), the transaction is termed a pooling of interests. It is accounted for by the **pooling of interests method**. When this method of effecting a parent-subsidiary affiliation is used, the former stockholders of the subsidiary become stockholders of the parent company.

The accounting implications of the two affiliation methods are very different. The method first described is a "sale-purchase" transaction in contrast to the second method, in which there is a "joining of ownership interests" in the two companies.

The Accounting Principles Board established very strict criteria that must be met before the pooling of interests method can be used.[5] As a result, most business combinations are accounted for as a purchase. The 1985 edition of *Accounting Trends & Techniques* reported that, of the applicable companies surveyed, 89% of the business combinations were accounted for by the purchase method and 11% were accounted for by the pooling of interests method.

ACCOUNTING FOR PARENT-SUBSIDIARY AFFILIATIONS

Although the corporations that make up a parent-subsidiary affiliation may operate as a single economic unit, they continue to maintain separate accounting records and prepare their own periodic financial statements. The parent corporation uses the equity method of accounting for its investment in the stock of a subsidiary.

After the parent-subsidiary relationship has been established, the investment account of the parent is periodically increased by its share of the subsidiary's net income and decreased by its share of dividends received from the subsidiary. At the end of each fiscal year, the parent reports the investment account balance on its own balance sheet as a long-term investment, and its current share of the subsidiary's net income on its own income statement as a separate item.

In addition to the interrelationship through stock ownership, there are usually other intercorporate transactions which have an effect on the financial statements of both the parent and the subsidiary. For example, either may own bonds or other evidences of indebtedness issued by the other and either may purchase or sell goods or services to the other.

Because of the central managerial control factor and the intertwining of relationships, it is usually desirable to present the results of operations and the financial position of a parent company and its subsidiaries as if the group were a single company with one or more branches or divisions. Such statements are likely to be more meaningful to stockholders of the parent company than separate statements for each corporation. However, separate statements are preferable for a subsidiary whose operations are totally different from those of

---

[5]*Opinions of the Accounting Principles Board, No. 16,* "Business Combinations" (New York: American Institute of Certified Public Accountants, 1970).

the parent (as when the parent is engaged in manufacturing and the subsidiary is a bank, insurance company, or finance company) or because control over the subsidiary's assets and operations is uncertain (as in a subsidiary that is located outside the United States and that is subject to foreign government controls).

The financial statements resulting from the combining of parent and subsidiary statements are generally called **consolidated statements**. Specifically, such statements may be identified by the addition of "and subsidiary(ies)" to the name of the parent corporation or by modification of the title of the respective statement, as in *consolidated balance sheet* or *consolidated income statement*.[6]

BASIC PRINCIPLES OF CONSOLIDATION OF FINANCIAL STATEMENTS

When the data on the financial statements of the parent corporation and its subsidiaries are combined to form the consolidated statements, special attention should be given to the ties of relationship between the separate corporations. These ties are represented by the intercompany items appearing in their respective ledgers and statements. Examples of such intercompany items include notes receivable and notes payable, accounts receivable and accounts payable, interest receivable and interest payable, sales and purchases (or cost of merchandise sold), and interest expense and interest income. The intercompany items, which are called **reciprocals**, must be eliminated from the statements that are to be consolidated. For example, a note representing a loan by a parent corporation to its subsidiary would appear as a note receivable in the parent's balance sheet and a note payable in the subsidiary's balance sheet. When the two balance sheets are combined, the note receivable and the note payable would be eliminated because the consolidated balance sheet is prepared as if the parent and subsidiary were one operating unit. After the proper eliminations are made, the remaining items on the financial statements of the subsidiary are combined with the like items on the financial statements of the parent.

The intercompany accounts of a parent and its subsidiaries may not be entirely reciprocal in amount. Differences may be caused by the manner in which the parent-subsidiary relationship was created, by the extent of the parent's ownership of the subsidiary, or by the nature of their subsequent intercompany transactions. Such factors must be considered when the financial statements of affiliated corporations are consolidated.

To direct attention to the basic concepts of consolidation, most of the data appearing in financial statements will be omitted from many of the illustrations in the following paragraphs. The term "net assets" will be used as a

---

[6]Examples of consolidated statements are presented in Appendix H.

substitute for the specific assets and liabilities that appear in the balance sheet. Explanations will also be simplified by using the term "book equity" in referring to the monetary amount of the stockholders' equity of the subsidiary acquired by the parent. The illustrative companies will be identified as Parent and Subsidiary.

Purchase Method

When a parent-subsidiary affiliation is effected as a purchase, the parent corporation is deemed to have purchased all or a major part of the subsidiary corporation's net assets. Accordingly, the principles of accounting for a sale-purchase transaction are applied to the consolidation of the parent and the subsidiary.

Consolidated Balance Sheet at Date of Acquisition. At the date of acquisition, the assets of the subsidiary should be reported on the consolidated balance sheet at their cost to the parent, as measured by the amount of the consideration given in acquiring the stock. In the subsidiary's ledger, the reciprocal of the investment account at the date of acquisition is the composite of all of the subsidiary's stockholders' equity accounts. Any difference between the cost to the parent and the amounts reported on the subsidiary's balance sheet must be given recognition on the consolidated balance sheet.

Income from an investment in assets does not accrue to an investor until after the assets have been purchased. Therefore, subsidiary company earnings accumulated prior to the date of the parent-subsidiary purchase affiliation must be excluded from the consolidated balance sheet and the income statement. Only those earnings of the subsidiary realized subsequent to the affiliation are includable in the consolidated statements.

Wholly Owned Subsidiary Acquired at a Cost Equal to Book Equity. Assume that Parent creates Subsidiary, transferring to it $120,000 of assets and $20,000 of liabilities, and taking in exchange 10,000 shares of $10 par common stock of Subsidiary. The effect of the transaction on Parent's ledger is to replace the various assets and liabilities (net assets of $100,000) with a single account: Investment in Subsidiary, $100,000. The effect on the balance sheet of Parent, together with the balance sheet of Subsidiary prepared immediately after the transaction, is as follows:

	Assets	Stockholders' Equity
Parent:		
Investment in Subsidiary, 10,000 shares.......	$100,000	
Subsidiary:		
Net assets.................................	$100,000	
Common stock, 10,000 shares, $10 par		$100,000

When the balance sheets of the two corporations are consolidated, the reciprocal accounts Investment in Subsidiary and Common Stock are offset against each other, or *eliminated*. The individual assets (Cash, Equipment, etc.) and the individual liabilities (Accounts Payable, etc.) making up the $100,000 of net assets on the balance sheet of Subsidiary are then added to the corresponding items on the balance sheet of Parent. The consolidated balance sheet is completed by listing Parent's paid-in capital accounts and retained earnings.

Wholly Owned Subsidiary Acquired at a Cost Above Book Equity. Instead of creating a new subsidiary, a corporation may acquire an already established corporation by purchasing its stock. In such cases, the subsidiary stock's total cost to the parent usually differs from the book equity of such stock. To illustrate, assume that Parent acquires for $180,000 all of the outstanding stock of Subsidiary, a going concern, from Subsidiary's stockholders. Assume further that the stockholders' equity of Subsidiary is made up of common stock of $100,000 (10,000 shares, $10 par) and $50,000 of retained earnings. Parent records the investment at its cost of $180,000, regardless of the amount of the book equity of Subsidiary. It should also be noted that the $180,000 paid to Subsidiary's stockholders has no effect on the assets, liabilities, or stockholders' equity of Subsidiary. The situation immediately after the transaction may be presented as follows:

	Assets	Stockholders' Equity
Parent:		
Investment in Subsidiary, 10,000 shares	$180,000	
Subsidiary:		
Net assets..............................	$150,000	
Common stock, 10,000 shares, $10 par.......		$100,000
Retained earnings		50,000

It is readily apparent that the reciprocal items on the separate balance sheets differ by $30,000. If the reciprocals were eliminated, as in the preceding illustration, and were replaced solely by Subsidiary's net assets of $150,000, the consolidated balance sheet would be out of balance.

The treatment of the $30,000 difference depends upon the reason that Parent paid more than book equity for Subsidiary's stock. When the amount paid above book equity is due to an excess of fair market value over book value of Subsidiary's assets, the values of the appropriate assets should be revised upward by $30,000. For example, if land that Subsidiary had acquired several years previously at a cost of $50,000 (book value) has a current fair market value of $80,000, the book amount should be increased from $50,000 to $80,000 when the asset is reported on the consolidated balance sheet. When Parent has paid more for Subsidiary's stock because Subsidiary has prospects for high future earnings, the $30,000 should be reported on the consolidated balance sheet under a description such as "Goodwill" or "Excess of cost of business acquired over related net assets."

When the amount paid above book equity is due to both an excess of fair market value over book value of assets and high future earnings prospects, the excess of cost over book equity should be allocated accordingly.[7] To illustrate, assume that the $30,000 difference in the illustration is due to a $20,000 excess of fair value over book value of Subsidiary's land and Subsidiary prospects for high future earnings. The book amount of the land, which had cost $50,000, would be increased to $70,000, and goodwill of $10,000 would be reported on the consolidated balance sheet.

Wholly Owned Subsidiary Acquired at a Cost Below Book Equity. All of the stock of a corporation may be acquired from its stockholders at a cost that is less than book equity. To illustrate, assume that the stock in Subsidiary is acquired for $130,000 and that the composition of the stockholders' equity of Subsidiary is the same as in the preceding illustration. Parent records the investment at its cost of $130,000. The situation immediately after the transaction is as follows:

	Assets	Stockholders' Equity
Parent:		
Investment in Subsidiary, 10,000 shares.......	$130,000	
Subsidiary:		
Net assets................................	$150,000	
Common stock, 10,000 shares, $10 par		$100,000
Retained earnings		50,000

Elimination of the reciprocal accounts and reporting the $150,000 of net assets of Subsidiary on the consolidated balance sheet creates an imbalance of $20,000. The possible reasons for the apparent "bargain" purchase and the treatment of the imbalance are generally the reverse of those given in explaining acquisition at a price higher than book equity. The complexities that might arise in some instances are discussed in advanced texts.

Partially Owned Subsidiary Acquired at a Cost Above or Below Book Equity. When one corporation seeks to gain control over another by purchase of its stock, it is not necessary and often not possible to acquire all of the stock. To illustrate this situation, assume that Parent acquires, at a total cost of $190,000, 80% of the stock of Subsidiary, whose book equity is composed of common stock of $100,000 (10,000 shares, $10 par) and $80,000 of retained

---

[7]*Opinions of the Accounting Principles Board, No. 16, op. cit.,* par. 87.

earnings. The relevant data immediately after the acquisition of the stock are as follows:

	Assets	Stockholders' Equity
Parent:		
Investment in Subsidiary, 8,000 shares........	$190,000	
Subsidiary:		
Net assets.................................	$180,000	
Common stock, 10,000 shares, $10 par		$100,000
Retained earnings		80,000

The explanation of the $10,000 imbalance in the reciprocal items in this illustration is more complex than in the preceding illustrations. Two factors are involved: (1) the amount paid for the stock is greater than 80% of Subsidiary's book equity and (2) only 80% of Subsidiary's stock was purchased. Since Parent acquired 8,000 shares or 80% of the outstanding shares of Subsidiary, only 80% of the stockholders' equity accounts of Subsidiary can be eliminated. The remaining 20% of the stock is owned by outsiders, who are called collectively the **minority interest**. The eliminations from the partially reciprocal accounts and the amounts to be reported on the consolidated balance sheet, including the minority interest, are determined as follows:

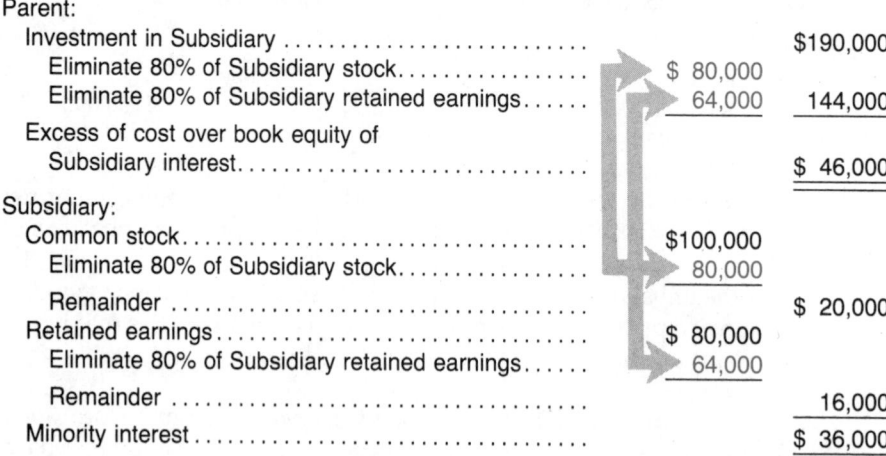

Parent:			
Investment in Subsidiary			$190,000
Eliminate 80% of Subsidiary stock.................		$ 80,000	
Eliminate 80% of Subsidiary retained earnings......		64,000	144,000
Excess of cost over book equity of			
Subsidiary interest..............................			$ 46,000
Subsidiary:			
Common stock....................................		$100,000	
Eliminate 80% of Subsidiary stock.................		80,000	
Remainder			$ 20,000
Retained earnings................................		$ 80,000	
Eliminate 80% of Subsidiary retained earnings......		64,000	
Remainder			16,000
Minority interest....................................			$ 36,000

The excess cost of $46,000 is reported on the consolidated balance sheet as goodwill or the valuation placed on other assets is increased by $46,000, according to the principles explained earlier. The minority interest of $36,000, which is the amount of Subsidiary's book equity allocable to outsiders, is reported on the consolidated balance sheet, usually preceding the stockholders' equity accounts of Parent. The 1985 edition of *Accounting Trends & Techniques* indicates that minority interest is reported in the long-term liabilities section by most of the companies surveyed.

Consolidated Balance Sheet Subsequent to Acquisition. Subsequent to acquisition of a subsidiary, the parent company uses the equity method to account for its investment in the subsidiary. Thus, the parent company's investment account is increased periodically for its share of the subsidiary's earnings and decreased for the related dividends received. Correspondingly, the retained earnings account of the subsidiary will be increased periodically by the amount of its net income and reduced by dividend distributions. Because of these periodic changes in the balances of the reciprocal accounts, the eliminations required in preparing a consolidated balance sheet will change each year.

To illustrate consolidation of balance sheets subsequent to acquisition, assume that Subsidiary in the preceding illustration earned net income of $50,000 and paid dividends of $20,000 during the year subsequent to Parent's acquisition of 80% of its stock. The net effect of the year's transactions on Subsidiary were as follows:

	Net Assets	Common Stock	Retained Earnings
Subsidiary:			
Date of acquisition..................	$180,000	$100,000	$ 80,000
Add net income	50,000		50,000
Deduct dividends	(20,000)		(20,000)
Date subsequent to acquisition.......	$210,000	$100,000	$110,000

Parent's entries to record its 80% share of subsidiary's net income and dividends are as follows:

Parent:

Investment in Subsidiary............................	40,000	
Income of Subsidiary		40,000
Cash	16,000	
Investment in Subsidiary...........................		16,000

The net effect of the foregoing entries on Parent's investment account is to increase the balance by $24,000, as follows:

Parent:
Investment in subsidiary, 8,000 shares:

Date of acquisition..............................		$190,000
Add 80% of Subsidiary's net income.............	$40,000	
Deduct 80% of Subsidiary's dividends............	(16,000)	24,000
One year subsequent to acquisition..............		$214,000

Continuing the illustration, the eliminations from the partially reciprocal accounts and the amounts to be reported on the consolidated balance sheet are determined as follows:

Parent:

Investment in Subsidiary		$214,000
Eliminate 80% of Subsidiary stock	$ 80,000	
Eliminate 80% of Subsidiary retained earnings	88,000	168,000
Excess of cost over book equity of		
Subsidiary interest		$ 46,000

Subsidiary:

Common stock	$100,000	
Eliminate 80% of Subsidiary stock	80,000	
Remainder		$ 20,000
Retained earnings	$110,000	
Eliminate 80% of Subsidiary retained earnings	88,000	
Remainder		22,000
Minority interest		$ 42,000

A comparison of the data with the analysis as of the date of acquisition shows the following:

1. Minority interest increased $6,000 (from $36,000 to $42,000), which is equivalent to 20% of the $30,000 net increase ($50,000 of net income less $20,000 of dividends) in Subsidiary's retained earnings.
2. Excess of cost over book equity of the subsidiary interest remained unchanged at $46,000.

To avoid additional complexities, it was assumed that the $46,000 excess at the date of acquisition was not due to goodwill or to assets subject to depreciation or amortization.[8]

Work Sheet for Consolidated Balance Sheet. The preceding discussion focused on the basic concepts associated with the process of preparing consolidated balance sheets. If the consolidation process becomes quite complex or if the amount of data to be processed is substantial, all of the relevant data for the consolidated statements may be assembled on work sheets. Although a work sheet is not essential, it is used in the following illustration to show an alternate method of accumulating all relevant data for the consolidated balance sheet. Whether or not a work sheet is used, the basic concepts and the consolidated balance sheet would not be affected.

To illustrate the use of the work sheet, assume that (as was the case in the illustration in the preceding section) Parent had purchased 80% of Subsidiary stock for $190,000. For the year since the acquisition, Parent had debited the

---

[8]Any portion of the excess of cost over book equity assigned to goodwill must be amortized according to *Opinions of the Accounting Principles Board No. 17,* "Intangible Assets." Similarly, any excess of cost over book equity assigned to plant assets of limited life must be gradually reduced by depreciation. The application of such amortization and depreciation techniques to consolidated statements goes beyond the scope of the discussion here.

investment account for its share of Subsidiary earnings and had credited the investment account for its share of dividends declared by Subsidiary. Balance sheet data for Parent and Subsidiary as of December 31 of the year subsequent to acquisition appear as follows. Although these data include amounts for land, other assets, and liabilities, the net assets and stockholders' equity for Subsidiary are the same as in the preceding illustration.

	Parent	Subsidiary
Investment in Subsidiary....................	$214,000	
Land	100,000	$ 60,000
Other assets	400,000	200,000
	$714,000	$260,000
Liabilities.................................	$164,000	$ 50,000
Common stock:		
Parent..................................	300,000	
Subsidiary..............................		100,000
Retained earnings:		
Parent..................................	250,000	
Subsidiary..............................		110,000
	$714,000	$260,000

The account balances at December 31 and the eliminations from the reciprocal accounts would be entered on the work sheet. The amounts would be determined for the consolidated balance sheet items as follows (the right margin notations are added as an aid to understanding):

Parent and Subsidiary
Work Sheet for Consolidated Balance Sheet
December 31, 19--

	Parent	Subsidiary	Eliminations Debit	Eliminations Credit	Consolidated Balance Sheet	
Investment in Subsidiary ..	214,000			168,000	46,000	Excess of cost over book equity
Land	100,000	60,000			160,000	
Other Assets............	400,000	200,000			600,000	
	714,000	260,000			806,000	
Liabilities	164,000	50,000			214,000	
Common Stock:						
Parent...............	300,000				300,000	
Subsidiary		100,000	80,000		20,000	minority interest
Retained Earnings:						
Parent...............	250,000				250,000	
Subsidiary		110,000	88,000		22,000	minority interest
	714,000	260,000	168,000	168,000	806,000	

It should be noted that the work sheet is only an aid for accumulating the data for the consolidated balance sheet. It is not the consolidated balance sheet. Also, if there are other intercompany items that must be eliminated from the statements that are to be consolidated, those eliminations would be entered in the eliminations columns of the work sheet. For example, a loan by a parent to its subsidiary on a note would require an elimination of the amount of the note from both notes receivable and notes payable in the work sheet.

When 80% of Subsidiary common stock and Subsidiary retained earnings is eliminated against the Investment in Subsidiary, as indicated in the eliminations columns of the work sheet, (1) the $46,000 excess of cost over book equity of the subsidiary interest can be identified and (2) the minority interest of $42,000 (consisting of $20,000 related to subsidiary common stock and $22,000 related to subsidiary retained earnings) can be identified. The $46,000 excess of cost over book equity is reported on the consolidated balance sheet according to the principles explained earlier.

In the following balance sheet, it is assumed that the $46,000 is due to an excess of fair value over book value of Subsidiary's land. Thus, the amount for land as reported on the consolidated balance sheet would be $206,000, consisting of the parent's amount of $100,000 plus the subsidiary's amount of $106,000 (the $60,000 book amount plus the $46,000 excess of cost over book equity attributable to the land). The minority interest of $42,000 is also reported on the consolidated balance sheet as explained earlier.

Parent and Subsidiary
Consolidated Balance Sheet
December 31, 19--

Assets

Land	$206,000
Other assets	600,000
Total assets	$806,000

Liabilities and Stockholders' Equity

Liabilities	$214,000
Minority interest in subsidiary	42,000
Common stock	300,000
Retained earnings	250,000
Total liabilities and stockholders' equity	$806,000

Pooling of Interests Method

When a parent-subsidiary affiliation is effected as a pooling of interests, the ownership of the two companies is joined together in the parent corporation. The parent deems its investment in the subsidiary to be equal to the carrying amount of the subsidiary's net assets. Any difference that may exist between such carrying amount and the fair value of the subsidiary's assets does not affect the amount recorded by the parent as the investment.

Consolidated Balance Sheet at Date of Affiliation. Since the parent's investment in the subsidiary is equal to the carrying amount of the subsidiary's net assets, no change is needed in the amounts at which the subsidiary's assets should be included in the consolidated balance sheet prepared at the date of affiliation. The subsidiary's assets are reported as they appear in the subsidiary's separate balance sheet.

The credit to the parent company's stockholders' equity accounts for the stock issued in exchange for the subsidiary company's stock corresponds to the amount debited to the investment account. In addition to the common stock account, the paid-in capital accounts may be affected, as well as the retained earnings account. According to the concept of continuity of ownership interests, subsidiary earnings accumulated prior to the affiliation should be combined with those of the parent on the consolidated balance sheet. It is as though there had been a single economic unit from the time the enterprises had begun.

To illustrate the procedure for consolidating the balance sheets of two corporations by the pooling of interests method, their respective financial positions immediately prior to the exchange of stock are assumed to be as follows:

	Assets	Stockholders' Equity
Parent:		
Net assets	$230,000	
Common stock, 4,000 shares, $25 par		$100,000
Retained earnings		130,000
Subsidiary:		
Net assets	$150,000	
Common stock, 10,000 shares, $10 par		$100,000
Retained earnings		50,000

Since poolings must involve substantially all (90% or more) of the stock of the subsidiary, the illustration will assume an exchange of 100% of the stock. It is also assumed that the fair market value of the net assets of both companies is greater than the amounts reported above and that there appears to be an element of goodwill in both cases. Based on recent price quotations, it is agreed that for the purpose of the exchange, Parent's common stock is to be valued at $45 a share and Subsidiary's at $18 a share.[9] According to the agreement, the exchange of stock is brought about as follows:

---

[9] In practice, it may be necessary to pay cash for fractional shares or for subsidiary shares held by dissenting stockholders.

Parent issues 4,000 shares valued at $45 per share $180,000

in exchange for

Subsidiary's 10,000 shares valued at $18 per share $180,000

The excess of the $180,000 value of Parent's stock issued over the $150,000 of net assets of Subsidiary may be ignored and the investment recorded as follows:

Parent:

Investment in Subsidiary	150,000	
Common Stock		100,000
Retained Earnings		50,000

After the foregoing entry has been recorded, the basic balance sheet data of the two companies are as follows:

	Assets	Stockholders' Equity
Parent:		
Investment in Subsidiary, 10,000 shares	$150,000	
Other net assets	230,000	
Common stock, 8,000 shares, $25 par		$200,000
Retained earnings		180,000
Subsidiary:		
Net assets	$150,000	
Common stock, 10,000 shares, $10 par		$100,000
Retained earnings		50,000

To consolidate the balance sheets of the two companies, Parent's investment account and Subsidiary's common stock and retained earnings accounts are eliminated. The net assets of the two companies, $230,000 and $150,000, are combined without any changes in valuation, making a total of $380,000. The consolidated stockholders' equity is composed of common stock of $200,000 and retained earnings of $180,000, for a total of $380,000.

Consolidated Balance Sheet Subsequent to Affiliation. The equity method is used by the parent corporation in recording changes in its investment account subsequent to acquisition. Thus, the account is increased by the parent's share of the subsidiary's earnings and decreased by its share of dividends. Continuing the illustration of the preceding section, assume that Subsidiary's net income and dividends paid during the year subsequent to affiliation with Parent are $20,000 and $5,000 respectively. After Parent has recorded Subsidiary's net income and dividends, the Parent's investment in Subsidiary increases by $15,000, and the Subsidiary's net assets and retained earnings increase by $15,000, yielding the following account balances:

	Assets	Stockholders' Equity
Parent:		
Investment in Subsidiary, 10,000 shares.......	$165,000	
Subsidiary:		
Net assets.....................................	$165,000	
Common stock, 10,000 shares, $10 par		$100,000
Retained earnings		65,000

When the balance sheets of the affiliated corporations are consolidated, the reciprocal accounts are eliminated and the $165,000 of net assets of Subsidiary are combined with those of Parent.

Work Sheet for Consolidated Balance Sheet. To illustrate the use of the work sheet to assemble the relevant data for the consolidated balance sheet for an affiliation effected as a pooling of interests, assume that (as was the case in the illustration in the preceding section) Parent had exchanged 4,000 shares of its common stock for all of the 10,000 shares of Subsidiary common stock. For the year since the acquisition, Parent had debited the investment account for its share (100%) of Subsidiary earnings and had credited the investment account for its share (100%) of dividends declared by Subsidiary. Balance sheet data for Parent and Subsidiary as of December 31 of the year subsequent to acquisition appear as follows. As in the purchase illustration, amounts for land, other assets, and liabilities have been added, but the amounts for net assets and stockholders' equity for Subsidiary are the same as in the preceding illustration.

	Parent	Subsidiary
Investment in Subsidiary....................	$165,000	
Land	80,000	$ 40,000
Other assets	325,000	175,000
	$570,000	$215,000
Liabilities..................................	$140,000	$ 50,000
Common stock:		
Parent.................................	200,000	
Subsidiary.............................		100,000
Retained earnings:		
Parent.................................	230,000	
Subsidiary.............................		65,000
	$570,000	$215,000

The account balances at December 31 and the eliminations from the reciprocal accounts would be entered on the work sheet and the amounts determined for the consolidated balance sheet items as follows:

Parent and Subsidiary
Work Sheet for Consolidated Balance Sheet
December 31, 19--

	Parent	Subsidiary	Eliminations Debit	Eliminations Credit	Consolidated Balance Sheet
Investment in Subsidiary ...	165,000			165,000	
Land.	80,000	40,000			120,000
Other Assets.	325,000	175,000			500,000
	570,000	215,000			620,000
Liabilities	140,000	50,000			190,000
Common Stock:					
Parent.	200,000				200,000
Subsidiary		100,000	100,000		
Retained Earnings:					
Parent.	230,000				230,000
Subsidiary		65,000	65,000		
	570,000	215,000	165,000	165,000	620,000

After 100% of Subsidiary common stock and Subsidiary retained earnings is eliminated against the Investment in Subsidiary, as indicated in the eliminations columns of the work sheet, the amounts for the two companies are combined, without any changes in valuation, and are then reported on the consolidated balance sheet.

As previously discussed, the work sheet is only an aid for accumulating the data for the consolidated balance sheet. These data are the basis for the consolidated balance sheet, which is prepared in the normal manner.

Consolidated Income Statement and Other Statements

Consolidation of income statements and other statements of affiliated companies usually presents fewer difficulties than those encountered in balance sheet consolidations. The difference is largely because of the inherent nature of the statements. The balance sheet reports cumulative effects of all transactions from the very beginning of an enterprise to a current date, whereas the income statement, the retained earnings statement, and the statement of changes in financial position report selected transactions only and are for a limited period of time, usually a year.

The principles used in the consolidation of the income statements of a parent and its subsidiaries are the same, regardless of whether the affiliation is deemed to be a purchase or a pooling of interests. When the income statements are consolidated, all amounts resulting from intercompany transactions, such as management fees or interest on loans charged by one affiliate to another, must be eliminated. Any intercompany profit included in inventories must also be eliminated. The remaining amounts of sales, cost of merchandise sold, operating expenses, and other revenues and expenses reported on the income statements of the affiliated corporations are then combined. The eliminations required in consolidating the retained earnings statement and other statements are based largely on data assembled in consolidating the balance sheet and income statement.

CORPORATION FINANCIAL STATEMENTS

Examples of retained earnings statements and sections of income statements affected by the corporate form of organization have been presented in preceding chapters. A complete balance sheet of a corporation, containing items discussed in this and preceding chapters, is illustrated on pages 792 and 793.

ACCOUNTING FOR INTERNATIONAL OPERATIONS

In an effort to expand operations, many U.S. companies conduct business in foreign countries. If the operations of these multinational companies involve currencies other than the dollar, special accounting problems may arise (1) in accounting for transactions with the foreign companies and (2) in the preparation of consolidated statements for domestic and foreign companies that are affiliated. The basic principles used in such situations are presented in the following paragraphs. Details and complexities are reserved for advanced texts.

Accounting for Transactions with Foreign Companies

If transactions with foreign companies are executed in dollars, no special accounting problems arise. Such transactions would be recorded as illustrated in the text. For example, the sale of merchandise to a Japanese company that is billed in and paid in dollars would be recorded by the U.S. company in the normal manner, using dollar amounts. However, if transactions involve receivables or payables that are to be received or paid in a foreign currency, the U.S. company may incur an exchange gain or loss.

Connor Corporation
Consolidated
December

Assets

Current assets:

Cash		$ 255,000
Marketable securities, at cost (market price, $160,000)		152,500
Accounts and notes receivable	$ 722,000	
Less allowance for doubtful receivables	37,000	685,000
Inventories, at lower of cost (first-in, first-out) or market		917,500
Prepaid expenses		70,000
Total current assets		$2,080,000

Investments:

Bond sinking fund		$ 422,500
Investment in bonds of Dalton Company		240,000
Total investments		662,500

	Cost	Accumulated Depreciation	Book Value	
Plant assets (depreciated by the straight-line method):				
Land	$ 250,000	—	$ 250,000	
Buildings	920,000	$ 379,955	540,045	
Machinery and equipment	2,764,400	766,200	1,998,200	
Total plant assets	$3,934,400	$1,146,155		2,788,245

Intangible assets:

Goodwill		$ 300,000
Organization costs		50,000
Total intangible assets		350,000

Total assets	$5,880,745

and Subsidiaries
Balance Sheet
31, 19--

Liabilities

Current liabilities:

Accounts payable..................	$ 508,810	
Income tax payable	120,500	
Dividends payable	94,000	
Accrued liabilities	81,400	
Total current liabilities............		$ 804,710

Long-term liabilities:

Debenture 8% bonds payable, due December 31, 19--	$1,000,000	
Less unamortized discount........	60,000	$ 940,000
Minority interest in subsidiaries		115,000
Total long-term liabilities		1,055,000

Deferred credits:

Deferred income tax payable........		95,500
Total liabilities......................		$1,955,210

Stockholders' Equity

Paid-in capital:

Common stock, $20 par (250,000 shares authorized, 100,000 shares issued)	$2,000,000	
Premium on common stock.........	320,000	
Total paid-in capital		$2,320,000

Retained earnings:
Appropriated:

For bonded indebtedness........	$250,000	
For plant expansion ...	750,000	$1,000,000
Unappropriated...................		605,535
Total retained earnings............		1,605,535
Total stockholders' equity		3,925,535
Total liabilities and stockholders' equity......................		$5,880,745

Realized Currency Exchange Gains and Losses. When a U.S. company executes a transaction with a company in a foreign country using a currency other than the dollar, one currency needs to be converted into another to settle the transaction. For example, a U.S. company purchasing merchandise from a British company that requires payment in British pounds must exchange dollars ($) for pounds (£) to settle the transaction. This exchange of one currency into another involves the use of an exchange rate. The **exchange rate** is the rate at which one unit of currency (the dollar, for example) can be converted into another currency (the British pound, for example). To continue with the illustration, if the U.S. company had purchased merchandise for £1,000 from a British company on June 1, when the exchange rate was $1.40 per British pound, $1,400 would need to be exchanged for £1,000 to make the purchase.[10] Since the U.S. company maintains its accounts in dollars, the transaction would be recorded as follows:

June 1 Purchases...................................	1,400	
Cash..		1,400
Payment of Invoice No. 1725 from W. A.		
Sterling Co., £1,000; exchange rate, $1.40		
per British pound.		

Special accounting problems arise when the exchange rate fluctuates between the date of the original transaction (such as a purchase on account) and the settlement of that transaction in cash in the foreign currency (such as the payment of an account payable). In practice, such fluctuations are frequent. To illustrate, assume that on July 10, when the exchange rate was $.004 per yen (Y), a purchase for Y100,000 was made from a Japanese company. Since the U.S. company maintains its accounts in dollars, the entry would be recorded at $400 (Y100,000 × $.004), as follows:

July 10 Purchases......................................	400	
Accounts Payable—M. Suzuki and Son..........		400
Invoice No. 818, Y100,000, exchange rate,		
$.004 per yen.		

If on the date of payment, August 9, the exchange rate had increased to $.005 per yen, the Y100,000 account payable must be settled by exchanging $500 (Y100,000 × $.005) for Y100,000. In such a case, the U.S. company incurs

---

[10]Foreign exchange rates are quoted in major financial reporting services. Because the exchange rates are quite volatile, those used in this chapter are assumed rates which do not necessarily reflect current rates.

an exchange loss of $100, because $500 was needed to settle a $400 debt (account payable). The cash payment would be recorded as follows:

```
Aug.  9   Accounts Payable—M. Suzuki and Son............    400
          Exchange Loss.................................    100
              Cash.......................................              500
              Cash paid on Invoice No. 818, for Y100,000, or
              $400, when exchange rate was $.005 per yen.
```

All transactions with foreign companies can be analyzed in the manner described above. For example, assume that on May 1, when the exchange rate was $.25 per Swiss franc (F), a sale on account for $1,000 to a Swiss company was billed in Swiss francs. The transaction would be recorded as follows:

```
May  1    Accounts Receivable—D. W. Robinson Co. ........   1,000
              Sales......................................            1,000
              Invoice No. 9772, F4,000; exchange rate,
              $.25 per Swiss franc.
```

If the exchange rate had increased to $.30 per Swiss franc on May 31, the date of receipt of cash, the U.S. company would realize an exchange gain of $200. The gain was realized because the F4,000, which had a value of $1,000 on the date of sale, had increased in value to $1,200 (F4,000 × $.30) on May 31 when payment was received. The receipt of the cash would be recorded as follows:

```
May 31    Cash.........................................   1,200
              Accounts Receivable—D. W. Robinson Co. ......          1,000
              Exchange Gain..............................            200
              Cash received on Invoice No. 9772, for
              F4,000, or $1,000, when exchange rate was
              $.30 per Swiss franc.
```

Unrealized Currency Exchange Gains and Losses. In the previous illustrations, the transactions were completed by either the receipt or the payment of cash. Therefore, any exchange gain or loss was realized and, in an accounting sense, was "recognized" at the date of the cash receipt or cash payment. However, if financial statements are prepared between the date of the original transaction (sale or purchase on account, for example) and the date of the cash receipt or cash payment, and the exchange rate has changed since the original transaction, an unrealized gain or loss must be recognized in the statements. To illustrate, assume that a sale on account for $1,000 had been made to a

German company on December 20, when the exchange rate was $.50 per deutsche mark (DM), and that the transaction had been recorded as follows:

Dec. 20   Accounts Receivable—T. A. Mueller Inc.   1,000
          Sales.   1,000
            Invoice No. 1793, DM2,000; exchange rate,
            $.50 per deutsche mark.

If the exchange rate had decreased to $.45 per deutsche mark on December 31, the date of the balance sheet, the $1,000 account receivable would have a value of only $900 (DM2,000 × $.45). This "unrealized" loss would be recorded as follows:

Dec. 31   Exchange Loss.   100
          Accounts Receivable—T. A. Mueller Inc.   100
            Invoice No. 1793, DM2,000 × $.05 decrease in
            exchange rate.

Assuming that DM2,000 are received on January 19 in the following year, when the exchange rate is $.42, the additional decline in the exchange rate from $.45 to $.42 per deutsche mark must be recognized. The cash receipt would be recorded as follows:

Jan. 19   Cash.   840
          Exchange Loss ($.03×DM2,000)   60
            Accounts Receivable—T. A. Mueller Inc.   900
            Cash received on Invoice No. 1793, for
            DM2,000, or $900, when exchange rate was
            $.42 per deutsche mark.

If the exchange rate had increased between December 31 and January 19, an exchange gain would be recorded on January 19. For example, if the exchange rate had increased from $.45 to $.47 per deutsche mark during this period, Exchange Gain would be credited for $40 ($.02 × DM2,000).

A balance in the exchange loss account at the end of the fiscal period should be reported in the Other Expense section of the income statement. A balance in the exchange gain account should be reported in the Other Income section.

Consolidated Financial Statements with Foreign Subsidiaries

Before the financial statements of domestic and foreign companies are consolidated, the amounts shown on the statements for the foreign companies must be converted to U.S. dollars. Asset and liability amounts are normally converted to U.S. dollars by using the exchange rates as of the balance sheet date. Revenues and expenses are normally converted by using the exchange rates that were in effect when those transactions were executed. (For practical purposes, a weighted average rate for the period is generally used.) The adjustments (gains or losses) resulting from the conversion are reported as a separate item in the stockholders' equity section of the balance sheets of the foreign companies.[11]

After the foreign company statements have been converted to U.S. dollars, the financial statements of U.S. and foreign subsidiaries are consolidated in the normal manner as described previously in this chapter.

CHAPTER REVIEW

KEY POINTS

1. Investments in Stocks.

A business may make long-term investments in equity securities (preferred and common shares) with cash that it does not need for normal operations. A corporation may also purchase stocks as a means of establishing or maintaining business relations with the issuing company. In other cases, a corporation may acquire all or a large part of the voting stock of another corporation in order to control its activities.

2. Accounting for Long-Term Investments in Stock.

There are two methods of accounting for long-term investments in stock: (1) the cost method and (2) the equity method. The method used depends upon whether the investor owns enough of the voting stock of the investee

---

[11]*Statement of Financial Accounting Standards, No. 52,* "Foreign Currency Translation" (Stamford: Financial Accounting Standards Board, 1981).

(company whose stock is owned by the investor) to have a significant influence over its operating and financing policies. If the investor does not have a significant influence, the cost method (with the lower of cost or market rule) must be used. If the investor can exercise significant influence in a long-term investment situation, the equity method must be used.

The cost of stocks purchased includes not only the amount paid to the seller but also other costs related to the purchase, such as the broker's commission and postage charges for delivery. When the cost method is used, cash dividends on capital stock held as an investment may be recorded as an increase in the appropriate income and asset accounts. Under the cost method, the lower of cost or market rule must be applied to the total cost or total market price of the stock as of the date of the balance sheet. Any market value changes that are recognized are not included in net income, but are reported as a separate item in the stockholders' equity section of the balance sheet. If the decline in market value below cost for an individual security as of the balance sheet date is other than temporary, the cost basis of the individual security is written down and the amount of the write-down is accounted for as a realized loss. After the write-down, the carrying amount of the individual security cannot be changed for subsequent recoveries in market value.

When the equity method of accounting is used, a stock purchase is recorded at cost. The investor records its share of periodic net income of the investee as an increase in the investment account and as revenue of the period. Conversely, the investor's share of the investee's periodic loss is recorded as a decrease in the investment and a loss of the period. In addition, the investor records its share of cash or property dividends on the stock as a decrease in the investment account and as an increase in the appropriate asset accounts.

3. Sale of Long-Term Investments in Stocks.

When shares of stock held as a long-term investment are sold, the investment account is credited for the carrying amount of the shares sold and the cash or appropriate receivable account is debited for the proceeds (sales price less commission and other selling costs). Any difference between the proceeds and the carrying amount is recorded as a gain or loss on the sale.

4. Business Combinations.

Combinations of businesses may be effected (1) through a joining of two or more corporations to form a single unit by either merger or consolidation, or (2) through common control of two or more corporations by means of stock ownership that results in a parent-subsidiary affiliation. When a corporation acquires the properties of another corporation and the latter then dissolves, the joining of the two enterprises is called a merger. When two or more corporations transfer their assets and liabilities to a corporation which has been created for purposes of the takeover, the combination is called a consolidation. When a business combination is effected by one corporation acquiring a controlling share of the outstanding voting stock of one or more other corporations, the corporation owning the majority of the voting stock is known as the parent company. The corporation that is controlled is known as the subsidiary company. When a corporation acquires a controlling share of the voting stock of another corporation in exchange for cash, other assets, issuance of notes or other debt obligations, or by a combination of these items, the transaction is accounted for by the purchase method. When two corporations are combined by exchanging the voting common stock of one corporation (the parent) for substantially all (at least 90%) of the voting common stock of the other corporation (the subsidiary), the transaction is accounted for by the pooling of interests method.

5. Accounting for Parent-Subsidiary Affiliations.

Although the corporations that make up a parent-subsidiary affiliation may operate as a single economic unit, they usually continue to maintain separate accounting records and prepare their own periodic financial statements. The parent corporation uses the equity method of accounting for its investment in the stock of the subsidiary. The financial statements resulting from combining the parent and subsidiary statements are generally called consolidated statements.

6. Basic Principles of Consolidation of Financial Statements.

When the data on the financial statements of the parent corporation and its subsidiaries are combined to form the consolidated statements, special attention should be given to the intercompany items appearing on the separate corporation financial statements. These intercompany items must be eliminated in preparing financial statements for the consolidated entity.

When a parent-subsidiary affiliation is effected as a purchase, the parent corporation is deemed to have purchased all or a major part of the subsidiary corporation's net assets. Accordingly, the assets of the subsidiary should be reported on the consolidated balance sheet at their cost to the parent. In the subsidiary's ledger, the reciprocal of the investment account at the date of acquisition is the composite of all the subsidiary's stockholders' equity accounts. In some cases, a parent corporation may pay an amount above the book equity of a subsidiary because the subsidiary has prospects for high future earnings. The amount of this excess should be identified on the consolidated balance sheet as goodwill. When a parent corporation purchases less than 100% of the subsidiary's stock, the remaining stockholders' equity is identified as minority interest. The minority interest is reported on the consolidated balance sheet, usually preceding the stockholders' equity accounts of the parent.

When a parent-subsidiary affiliation is effected as a pooling of interests, the ownership of the two companies is joined together in the parent corporation. The parent deems its investment in the subsidiary to be equal to the carrying amount of the subsidiary's net assets. Any difference that may exist between such carrying amount and the fair value of the subsidiary's assets does not affect the amount recorded by the parent as the investment. Consequently, no change is needed in the amounts at which the subsidiary's assets should be included in the consolidated balance sheet.

The principles used in the consolidation of income statements of a parent and its subsidiary are the same, regardless of whether the affiliation is deemed to be a purchase or a pooling of interests. When the income statements are consolidated, all amounts resulting from intercompany transactions, such as management fees or interest on loans charged by one affiliate to another, must be eliminated. Any intercompany profit included in inventories must also be eliminated.

7. Accounting for International Operations.

When U.S. companies conduct business in foreign countries, special accounting problems may arise (1) in accounting for transactions with foreign companies and (2) in the preparation of consolidated statements for domestic and foreign companies that are affiliated. When a U.S. company executes a transaction with a company in a foreign country using a currency other than the dollar, an exchange rate should be used to convert one currency into another to settle the transaction. Because of this conversion process, gains and losses on foreign transactions may arise. If a foreign transaction has not been completed by the end of the year, an unrealized currency exchange gain or loss may need to be recognized, depending upon fluctuations in the exchange rates.

Before the financial statements of domestic and foreign countries are consolidated, the statements of the foreign companies must be converted to U.S. dollars. Asset and liability amounts are normally converted to U.S. dollars by using the exchange rates as of the balance sheet date. Revenues and expenses are normally converted by using the exchange rates that were in effect when those transactions were executed.

KEY TERMS

equity securities 770	subsidiary company 776
cost method 771	purchase method 776
equity method 771	pooling of interests method 777
merger 776	consolidated statements 778
consolidation 776	minority interest 782
parent company 776	exchange rate 792

SELF-EXAMINATION QUESTIONS
Answers in Appendix B.

1. Which of the following are characteristic of a parent-subsidiary relationship known as a pooling of interests?
   A. Parent acquires substantially all of the voting stock of subsidiary in exchange for cash
   B. Parent acquires substantially all of the voting stock of subsidiary in exchange for its bonds payable
   C. Parent acquires substantially all of the voting stock of subsidiary in exchange for its voting common stock
   D. All of the above

2. P Co. purchased the entire outstanding stock of S Co. for $1,000,000 in cash. If at the date of acquisition, S Co.'s stockholders' equity consisted of $750,000 of common stock and $150,000 of retained earnings, what is the amount of the difference between cost and book equity of the subsidiary interest?
   A. Excess of cost over book equity of subsidiary interest, $250,000
   B. Excess of cost over book equity of subsidiary interest, $100,000
   C. Excess of book equity over cost of subsidiary interest, $250,000
   D. None of the above

3. If in Question 2, P Co. had purchased 90% of the outstanding stock of S Co. for $1,000,000, what is the amount of the difference between cost and book equity of subsidiary interest?
   A. Excess of cost over book equity of subsidiary interest, $100,000
   B. Excess of cost over book equity of subsidiary interest, $190,000
   C. Excess of cost over book equity of subsidiary interest, $250,000
   D. None of the above

4. Based on the data in Question 3, what is the amount of the minority interest at the date of acquisition?
   A. $15,000   C. $100,000
   B. $75,000   D. None of the above

5. On July 9, 1987, a sale on account for $10,000 to a Mexican company was billed for 250,000 pesos. The exchange rate was $.04 per peso on July 9 and $.05 per peso on August 8, 1987, when the cash was received on account. Which of the following statements identifies the exchange gain or loss for the fiscal year ended December 31, 1987?
   A. Realized exchange loss, $2,500 C. Unrealized exchange loss, $2,500
   B. Realized exchange gain, $2,500 D. Unrealized exchange gain, $2,500

ILLUSTRATIVE PROBLEM

All of Stereophonic Inc.'s outstanding shares of stock were acquired on October 1, 1987, by Piedmont Inc. After lengthy negotiations with Stereophonic Inc.'s major shareholder, it was agreed that (1) the current management of Stereophonic Inc. would be retained for a minimum of five years, (2) Stereophonic Inc. would be operated as an independent subsidiary, and (3) Piedmont Inc. would issue 1,200 of its own $100 par common stock in exchange for all of Stereophonic Inc.'s stock.

The balance sheets of the two corporations on September 30, 1987, were as follows:

	Piedmont Inc.	Stereophonic Inc.
Assets		
Cash....................................	$ 124,200	$ 18,120
Accounts receivable........................	238,150	36,810
Inventory	405,750	61,300
Land....................................	120,000	50,000
Plant and equipment (net)	612,300	120,450
	$1,500,400	$286,680
Liabilities and Stockholders' Equity		
Accounts payable..........................	$ 136,400	$ 41,500
Common stock	900,000	120,000
Retained earnings	464,000	125,180
	$1,500,400	$286,680

Instructions:

1. Prepare the journal entry that should be made by Piedmont Inc. to record the combination as a pooling of interests.
2. Assuming the business combination is to be recorded as a pooling of interests, prepare a consolidated balance sheet for Piedmont Inc. and Stereophonic Inc. as of October 1, 1987.
3. Assume that Piedmont Inc. paid $106,000 in cash and issued 1,500 shares of Piedmont Inc. common stock with a fair market value of $212,000 for all the common stock of Stereophonic Inc. Prepare the journal entry for Piedmont Inc. to record the combination as a purchase.
4. Assuming that the business combination is to be recorded as a purchase and that the book values of the net assets of Stereophonic Inc. are approximately equal to their fair market values, prepare a consolidated balance sheet for Piedmont Inc. and Stereophonic Inc. as of October 1, 1987.

SOLUTION

(1)

Investment in Stereophonic Inc.	245,180	
Common Stock.............................		120,000
Retained Earnings		125,180

(2)

Piedmont Inc. and Subsidiary Stereophonic Inc.
Consolidated Balance Sheet
October 1, 1987

Assets

Current assets:		
Cash	$ 142,320	
Accounts receivable.....................	274,960	
Inventory..............................	467,050	
Total current assets		$ 884,330
Plant assets:		
Land	$ 170,000	
Plant and equipment (net)..............	732,750	
Total plant assets		902,750
Total assets		$1,787,080

Liabilities

Accounts payable........................		$ 177,900

Stockholders' Equity

Common stock..........................	$1,020,000	
Retained earnings	589,180	
Total stockholders' equity		1,609,180
Total liabilities and stockholders' equity		$1,787,080

(3)

Investment in Stereophonic Inc.	318,000	
Cash		106,000
Common Stock.............................		150,000
Premium on Common Stock.................		62,000

(4)   Piedmont Inc. and Subsidiary Stereophonic Inc.
                    Consolidated Balance Sheet
                         October 1, 1987

Assets

Current assets:
Cash*	$ 36,320	
Accounts receivable	274,960	
Inventory	467,050	
Total current assets		$ 778,330

Plant assets:
Land	$ 170,000	
Plant and equipment (net)	732,750	
Total plant assets		902,750

Intangible assets:
Goodwill**		72,820
Total assets		$1,753,900

Liabilities

Accounts payable		$ 177,900

Stockholders' Equity

Common stock	$1,050,000	
Premium on common stock	62,000	
Retained earnings	464,000	
Total stockholders' equity		1,576,000
Total liabilities and stockholders' equity		$1,753,900

*$124,200 + $18,120 − $106,000 = $36,320
**$318,000 − $245,180 = $72,820

DISCUSSION QUESTIONS

1. (a) What are two methods of accounting for long-term investments in stock? (b) Under what caption are long-term investments in stocks reported on the balance sheet?

2. When stocks are purchased between dividend dates, does the purchaser pay the seller the dividend accrued since the last dividend payment date? Explain.

3. A stockholder owning 200 shares of Tone Co. common stock, acquired at a total cost of $5,880, receives a common stock dividend of 10 shares. What is the carrying amount per share after the stock dividend?

4. What terms are applied to the following: (a) a corporation that is controlled by another corporation through ownership of a controlling interest in its stock; (b) a corporation that owns a controlling interest in the voting stock of another corporation; (c) a group of corporations related through stock ownership?

5. What are the two methods by which the relationship of parent-subsidiary may be established?

6. P Company purchases for $5,000,000 the entire common stock of S Corporation. What type of accounts on S's balance sheet are reciprocal to the investment account on P's balance sheet?

7. Are the eliminations of the reciprocal accounts in consolidating the balance sheets of P and S in Question 6 recorded in the respective ledgers of the two companies? Explain.

8. Powers Company purchased from stockholders the entire outstanding stock of Sanders Inc. for a total of $4,500,000 in cash. At the date of acquisition, Sanders Inc. had $2,500,000 of liabilities and total stockholders' equity of $4,000,000. (a) As of the acquisition date, what was the total amount of the assets of Sanders Inc.? (b) As of the acquisition date, what was the amount of the net assets of Sanders Inc.? (c) What is the amount of difference between the investment account and the book equity of the subsidiary interest acquired by Powers Company?

9. What is the possible explanation of the difference determined in Question 8(c) and how will it affect the reporting of the difference on the consolidated balance sheet?

10. If, in Question 8, Powers Company had paid only $3,700,000 for the stock of Sanders Inc., what would the solution to part (c) have been?

11. Parent Corporation owns 90% of the outstanding common stock of Subsidiary Corporation, which has no preferred stock. (a) What is the term applied to the remaining 10% interest? (b) If the total stockholders' equity of Subsidiary Corporation is $700,000, what is the amount of Subsidiary's book equity allocable to outsiders? (c) Where is the amount determined in (b) reported on the consolidated balance sheet?

12. P Corporation owns 85% of the outstanding common stock of S Co., which has no preferred stock. Net income of S Co. was $300,000 for the year, and cash dividends declared and paid during the year amounted to $200,000. What entries should be made by P Corporation to record its share of S Co.'s (a) net income and (b) dividends? (c) What is the amount of the net increase in the equity of the minority interest?

13. (a) What purpose is served by the work sheet for a consolidated balance sheet? (b) Is the work sheet a substitute for the consolidated balance sheet?

14. At the end of the fiscal year, the amount of notes receivable and notes payable reported on the respective balance sheets of a parent and its wholly owned subsidiary are as follows:

	Parent	Subsidiary
Notes Receivable.......	$ 400,000	$50,000
Notes Payable	175,000	45,000

If $25,000 of Subsidiary's notes receivable are owed by Parent, determine the amount of notes receivable and notes payable to be reported on the consolidated balance sheet.

15. Sales and purchases of merchandise by a parent corporation and its wholly owned subsidiary during the year were as follows:

	Parent	Subsidiary
Sales..................	$6,000,000	$910,000
Purchases	3,600,000	595,000

If $500,000 of the sales of Parent were made to Subsidiary, determine the amount of sales and purchases to be reported on the consolidated income statement.

16. The relationships of parent and subsidiary were established by the following transactions. Identify each affiliation as a "purchase" or a "pooling of interests."
   (a) Company P receives 100% of the voting common stock of Company S in exchange for cash and long-term bonds payable.
   (b) Company P receives 95% of the voting common stock of Company S in exchange for voting common stock of Company P.
   (c) Company P receives 95% of the voting common stock of Company S in exchange for cash.
   (d) Company P receives 70% of the voting common stock of Company S in exchange for voting common stock of Company P.

17. Which of the following procedures for consolidating the balance sheet of a parent and wholly owned subsidiary are characteristic of acquisition of control by purchase and which are characteristic of a pooling of interests? (a) Retained earnings of subsidiary at date of acquisition are eliminated. (b) Retained earnings of subsidiary at date of acquisition are combined with retained earnings of parent. (c) Assets are not revalued. (d) Goodwill may not be recognized.

18. On July 31, Penn Corp. issued 10,000 shares of its $20 par common stock, with a total market value of $330,000, to the stockholders of Sands Inc. in exchange for all of Sands' common stock. Penn Corp. records its investment at $300,000. The net assets and stockholders' equities of the two companies just prior to the affiliation are summarized as follows:

	Penn Corp.	Sands Inc.
Net assets	$910,000	$300,000
Common stock	$700,000	$200,000
Retained earnings	210,000	100,000
	$910,000	$300,000

(a) At what amounts would the following be reported on the consolidated balance sheet as of July 31, applying the pooling of interests method: (1) Net assets, (2) Retained earnings?

(b) Assume that, instead of issuing shares of stock, Penn Corp. had given $330,000 in cash and long-term notes. At what amounts would the following be reported on the consolidated balance sheet as of July 31: (1) Net assets, (2) Retained earnings?

19. Can a U.S. company incur an exchange gain or loss because of fluctuations in the exchange rate if its transactions with foreign countries, involving receivables or payables, are executed in (a) dollars, (b) the foreign currency?

20. A U.S. company purchased merchandise for 10,000 francs on account from a French company. If the exchange rate was $.22 per franc on the date of purchase and $.20 per franc on the date of payment of the account, what was the amount of exchange gain or loss realized by the U.S. company?

21. What two conditions give rise to unrealized currency exchange gains and losses from sales and purchases on account that are to be settled in the foreign currency?

22. Real World Focus. The 1984 and 1983 financial statements of Cessna Aircraft Company list the following long-term asset:

	September 30,	
	1984	1983
Investments in unconsolidated companies:		
Finance subsidiaries	144,901,000	134,093,000

The notes to the financial statements indicate that the 100%-owned finance subsidiaries are accounted for by the equity method. The net income of the finance subsidiaries for the fiscal year ending September 30, 1984, is $10,808,000. (a) Prepare the journal entry that Cessna Aircraft would have made to record its interest in the net income of the finance subsidiaries. (b) Did the finance subsidiaries declare any dividends during the fiscal year ending September 30, 1984?

EXERCISES

Exercise 18–1. Entries for investment in stock, receipt of dividends, and sale of shares. On March 2, Linn Corporation acquired 500 shares of the 50,000 outstanding shares of Wills Co. common stock at 53 1/4 plus commission and postage charges of $150. On July 15, a cash dividend of $3 per share and a 5% stock dividend were received. On November 25, 200 shares were sold at 55 1/2 less commission and postage charges of $45. Present entries to record (a) the purchase of the stock, (b) the receipt of the dividends, and (c) the sale of the 200 shares.

Exercise 18–2.   Entries using equity method for stock investment. At a total cost of $2,200,000, Dunn Corporation acquired 100,000 shares of Mini-Systems Co. common stock as a long-term investment. Dunn Corporation uses the equity method of accounting for this investment. Mini-Systems Co. has 250,000 shares of common stock outstanding, including the shares acquired by Dunn Corporation. Present the entries by Dunn Corporation to record the following information:

(a) Mini-Systems Co. reports net income of $600,000 for the current period.
(b) A cash dividend of $.50 per common share is paid by Mini-Systems Co. during the current period.

Exercise 18–3.   Determination and reporting of items related to consolidated statements. On the last day of the fiscal year, Pullen Inc. purchased 85% of the common stock of Starr Company for $600,000, at which time Starr Company reported the following on its balance sheet: assets, $980,000; liabilities, $300,000; common stock, $10 par, $500,000; retained earnings, $180,000. In negotiating the stock sale, it was determined that the book carrying amounts of Starr's recorded assets and equities approximated their current market values.

(a) Indicate for each of the following the section, the title of the item, and the amount to be reported on the consolidated balance sheet as of the date of acquisition:
(1) Difference between cost and book equity of subsidiary interest.
(2) Minority interest.
(b) During the following year, Pullen Inc. realized net income of $810,000, exclusive of the income of the subsidiary, and Starr Company realized net income of $150,000. In preparing a consolidated income statement, indicate in what amounts the following would be reported:
(1) Minority interest's share of net income.
(2) Consolidated net income.

Exercise 18–4.   Consolidated balance sheet from affiliation effected as a purchase. On December 31 of the current year, P Corporation purchased 90% of the stock of S Company. The data reported on their separate balance sheets immediately after the acquisition are as follows:

	P Corporation	S Company
Assets		
Cash...	$ 32,200	$ 21,250
Accounts receivable (net)........................	50,800	35,000
Inventories....................................	141,000	61,750
Investment in S Company	370,000	—
Equipment (net)	400,000	291,500
	$994,000	$409,500
Liabilities and Stockholders' Equity		
Accounts payable..............................	$ 99,000	$ 49,500
Common stock, $10 par	750,000	250,000
Retained earnings	145,000	110,000
	$994,000	$409,500

The fair value of S Company's assets corresponds to their book carrying amounts, except for equipment, which is valued at $325,000 for consolidation purposes. Prepare a consolidated balance sheet as of December 31, in report form, omitting captions for current assets, plant assets, etc. (A work sheet need not be used.)

Exercise 18–5. Consolidated balance sheet from affiliation effected as a pooling. As of July 31 of the current year, Pike Corporation exchanged 5,000 shares of its $10 par common stock for the 1,000 shares of Seed Company $50 par common stock held by Seed stockholders. The separate balance sheets of the two enterprises, immediately after the exchange of shares, are as follows:

	Pike Corporation	Seed Company
Assets		
Cash.......................................	$ 22,500	$ 15,500
Accounts receivable (net)........................	27,250	20,000
Inventories......................................	75,750	32,750
Investment in Seed Company.....................	87,500	—
Equipment (net)	329,000	44,250
	$542,000	$112,500
Liabilities and Stockholders' Equity		
Accounts payable...............................	$ 77,000	$ 25,000
Common stock	300,000	50,000
Retained earnings	165,000	37,500
	$542,000	$112,500

Prepare a consolidated balance sheet as of July 31, in report form, omitting captions for current assets, plant assets, etc. (A work sheet need not be used.)

Exercise 18–6. Consolidated income statement. For the current year ended June 30, the results of operations of Packer Corporation and its wholly owned subsidiary, Sullen Enterprises, are as follows:

	Packer Corporation		Sullen Enterprises	
Sales......................		$990,000		$410,000
Cost of merchandise sold....	$655,000		$245,000	
Selling expenses	155,000		60,000	
General expenses	85,000		40,000	
Interest expense (income) ...	(12,000)	883,000	12,000	357,000
Net income		$107,000		$ 53,000

During the year, Packer sold merchandise to Sullen for $75,000. The merchandise was sold by Sullen to nonaffiliated companies for $100,000. Packer's interest income was realized from a long-term loan to Sullen.

(a) Prepare a consolidated income statement for the current year for Packer and its subsidiary. Use the single-step form and disregard income taxes. (A work sheet need not be used.)

(b) Assuming that none of the merchandise sold by Packer to Sullen had been sold during the year to nonaffiliated companies, and that Packer's cost of the merchandise had been $51,000, determine the amounts that would have been reported for the following items on the consolidated income statement: (1) sales, (2) cost of merchandise sold, (3) net income.

Exercise 18–7. Determination of consolidated balance sheet amounts for affiliation effected as a pooling and as a purchase. Summarized data from the balance sheets of Page Company and Swartz Inc., as of June 30 of the current year, are as follows:

	Page Company	Swartz Inc.
Net assets	$900,000	$120,000
Common stock:		
50,000 shares, $10 par..........................	500,000	
2,500 shares, $20 par..........................		50,000
Retained earnings	400,000	70,000

(a) On July 1 of the current year, the two companies combine. Page Company issues 5,000 shares of its $10 par common stock, valued at $130,000, to Swartz's stockholders in exchange for the 2,500 shares of Swartz's $20 par common stock, also valued at $130,000. Assuming that the affiliation is effected as a pooling of interests, what are the amounts that would be reported for net assets, common stock, and retained earnings as of July 1 of the current year?

(b) Assume that Page Company had paid cash of $130,000 for all of Swartz Inc.'s common stock on July 1 of the current year and that the book value of the net assets of Swartz Inc. is deemed to reflect fair value. (1) What are the amounts that would be reported for net assets, common stock, and retained earnings as of July 1 of the current year, using the purchase method? (2) How much goodwill will be reported on the combined balance sheet?

Exercise 18–8. Entries for sales made in foreign currency. Omar Company makes sales on account to several Mexican companies which it bills in pesos. Record the journal entries for the following selected transactions completed during the current year:

Feb. 2. Sold merchandise on account, 100,000 pesos; exchange rate, $.04 per peso.

Mar. 4. Received cash from sale of February 2, 100,000 pesos; exchange rate, $.05 per peso.

May 30. Sold merchandise on account, 120,000 pesos; exchange rate, $.05 per peso.

June 30. Received cash from sale of May 30, 120,000 pesos; exchange rate, $.04 per peso.

Exercise 18–9. Entries for purchases made in foreign currency. Schoenfeld Company purchases merchandise from a German company that requires payment in deutsche marks. Record the journal entries for the following selected transactions completed during the current year:

June 10. Purchased merchandise on account, net 30, 5,000 deutsche marks; exchange rate, $.51 per deutsche mark.
July 10. Paid invoice of June 10; exchange rate, $.52 per deutsche mark.
Sept. 1. Purchased merchandise on account, net 30, 4,000 deutsche marks; exchange rate, $.52 per deutsche mark.
Oct. 1. Paid invoice of September 1; exchange rate, $.50 per deutsche mark.

PROBLEMS

Series A

Problem 18–1A. Entries for investments in stock. The following transactions relate to certain securities acquired by Griffin Company, whose fiscal year ends on December 31:

1987
Mar. 8. Purchased 1,000 shares of the 10,000 outstanding common shares of Howard Corporation at 35 plus commission and other costs of $175.
May 15. Received the regular cash dividend of 80¢ a share on Howard Corporation stock.
Nov. 15. Received the regular cash dividend of 80¢ a share plus an extra dividend of 10¢ a share on Howard Corporation stock.

(Assume that all intervening transactions have been recorded properly, and that the number of shares of stock owned have not changed from December 31, 1987, to December 31, 1991.)

1992
May 20. Received the regular cash dividend of 80¢ a share and a 5% stock dividend on the Howard Corporation stock.
July 20. Sold 500 shares of Howard Corporation stock at 40. The broker deducted commission and other costs of $125, remitting the balance.
Nov. 18. Received a cash dividend at the new rate of 84¢ a share on the Howard Corporation stock.

Instructions:

Record the journal entries for the foregoing transactions.

SPREADSHEET
PROBLEM

Problem 18–2A. Work sheet and consolidated balance sheet from affiliation effected as a purchase. On May 1 of the current year, Park Company purchased 90% of the stock of Summa Company. On the same date, Park Company loaned

Summa Company $50,000 on a 90-day note. The data reported on their separate balance sheets immediately after the acquisition and loan are as follows:

	Park Company	Summa Company
Assets		
Cash...	$ 50,750	$ 25,750
Accounts receivable (net).........................	48,500	32,000
Notes receivable	50,000	—
Inventories.....................................	164,750	52,250
Investment in Summa Company....................	290,000	—
Equipment (net)	340,000	215,000
	$944,000	$325,000
Liabilities and Stockholders' Equity		
Accounts payable................................	$175,000	$ 29,500
Notes payable...................................	—	50,000
Common stock, $20 par..........................	500,000	—
Common stock, $10 par..........................	—	200,000
Retained earnings	269,000	45,500
	$944,000	$325,000

The fair value of Summa Company's assets corresponds to the book carrying amounts, except for equipment, which is valued at $265,000 for consolidation purposes.

Instructions:

(1) Prepare a work sheet for a consolidated balance sheet as of May 1 of the current year.
(2) Prepare in report form a consolidated balance sheet as of May 1, omitting captions for current assets, plant assets, etc.

Problem 18–3A. Work sheet and consolidated balance sheet; year-end minority interest, increase in investment account during year. On June 30, Pole Company purchased 80% of the outstanding stock of Selma Company for $360,000. Balance sheet data for the two corporations immediately after the transaction are as follows:

	Pole Company	Selma Company
Assets		
Cash and marketable securities	$ 86,700	$ 31,050
Accounts receivable.............................	120,500	59,160
Allowance for doubtful accounts	(9,500)	(1,320)
Inventories......................................	475,000	115,440
Investment in Selma Company....................	360,000	—
Land	100,000	21,000
Building and equipment	990,000	297,000
Accumulated depreciation	(200,000)	(66,000)
	$1,922,700	$456,330

	Pole Company	Selma Company
Liabilities and Stockholders' Equity		
Accounts payable..............................	$ 152,500	$ 42,990
Income tax payable	41,500	5,940
Bonds payable (due in 2005)	500,000	—
Common stock, $20 par........................	900,000	—
Common stock, $10 par	—	300,000
Retained earnings	328,700	107,400
	$1,922,700	$456,330

Instructions:

(1) Prepare a work sheet for a consolidated balance sheet as of the date of acquisition.
(2) Prepare in report form a detailed consolidated balance sheet as of the date of acquisition. The fair value of Selma Company's assets are deemed to correspond to the book carrying amounts, except for land, which is to be increased by $30,000 for consolidation purposes.
(3) Assuming that Selma Company earns net income of $60,000 and pays cash dividends of $40,000 during the ensuing fiscal year and that Pole Company records its share of the earnings and dividends, determine the following as of the end of the year:
   (a) The net amount added to Pole Company's investment account as a result of Selma Company's earnings and dividends.
   (b) The amount of the minority interest.

Problem 18–4A. Consolidated balance sheet from affiliation effected as a purchase. Several years ago, Price Corporation purchased 9,000 shares of the 10,000 outstanding shares of stock of Sax Company. Since the date of acquisition, Price Corporation has debited the investment account for its share of the subsidiary's earnings and has credited the account for its share of dividends declared. Balance sheet data for the two corporations as of December 31 of the current year are as follows:

	Price Corp.	Sax Co.
Assets		
Cash...	$ 57,750	$ 21,050
Notes receivable................................	40,000	15,000
Accounts receivable (net)........................	140,750	49,650
Interest receivable	3,000	600
Dividends receivable	4,500	—
Inventories.....................................	199,500	65,000
Prepaid expenses	5,100	1,700
Investment in Sax Co............................	180,180	—
Land...	75,000	45,000
Buildings and equipment	411,000	240,000
Accumulated depreciation	(200,000)	(95,400)
	$916,780	$342,600

	Price Corp.	Sax Co.
Liabilities and Stockholders' Equity		
Notes payable.....................................	$ 45,000	$ 50,000
Accounts payable................................	99,500	65,500
Income tax payable	35,000	13,900
Dividends payable	15,000	5,000
Interest payable	2,450	3,000
Common stock, $20 par..........................	600,000	—
Common stock, $10 par..........................	—	100,000
Premium on common stock.......................	—	25,000
Retained earnings	119,830	80,200
	$916,780	$342,600

Price Corporation holds $35,000 of short-term notes of Sax Company, on which there is accrued interest of $3,000. Sax Company owes Price Corporation $15,000 for a management advisory fee for the year. It has been recorded by both corporations in their respective accounts payable and accounts receivable accounts.

Instructions:

Prepare in report form a detailed consolidated balance sheet as of December 31 of the current year. (A work sheet is not required.) The excess of book equity in Sax Company over the balance of the Price Corporation's investment account is attributable to overvaluation of Sax Company's land.

Problem 18–5A. Consolidated balance sheet from both pooling and purchase methods. On July 1 of the current year, after several months of negotiations, Peck Company issued 15,000 shares of its own $10 par common stock for all of Scott Inc.'s outstanding shares of stock. The fair market value of the Peck Company shares issued is $22.50 per share, or a total of $337,500. Scott Inc. is to be operated as a separate subsidiary. The balance sheets of the two firms on June 30 of the current year are as follows:

	Peck Company	Scott Inc.
Assets		
Cash...	$ 202,500	$ 23,500
Accounts receivable (net)........................	245,000	41,900
Inventory	428,250	61,450
Land...	120,000	50,000
Plant and equipment (net)	504,250	123,150
	$1,500,000	$300,000
Liabilities and Stockholders' Equity		
Accounts payable..............................	$ 145,000	$ 52,500
Common stock ($10 par)	1,000,000	150,000
Retained earnings	355,000	97,500
	$1,500,000	$300,000

Instructions:

(1) (a) What entry would be made by Peck Company to record the combination as a pooling of interests? (b) Prepare a consolidated balance sheet for Peck Company and Scott Inc. as of July 1 of the current year, assuming that the business combination has been recorded as a pooling of interests. (A work sheet is not required.)

(2) (a) Assume that Peck Company paid $150,000 in cash and issued 12,500 shares of Peck common stock with a fair market value of $187,500 for all the common stock of Scott Inc. What entry would Peck Company make to record the combination as a purchase? (b) Prepare a consolidated balance sheet as of July 1 of the current year, assuming that the business combination has been recorded as a purchase, and that the book values of the net assets of Scott Inc. are deemed to represent fair value. (A work sheet is not required.)

(3) Assume the same situation as in (2), except that the fair value of the land of Scott Inc. was $60,000. Prepare a consolidated balance sheet as of July 1 of the current year. (A work sheet is not required.)

Problem 18–6A. Eliminations for and preparation of consolidated balance sheet and income statement. On January 1 of the current year, Polk Corporation exchanged 25,000 shares of its $10 par common stock for 10,000 shares (the entire issue) of Swain Company's $25 par common stock. Later in the year, Swain purchased from Polk Corporation $100,000 of its $200,000 issue of bonds payable, at face amount. All of the items for "interest" appearing on the balance sheets and income statements of both corporations are related to the bonds.

During the year, Polk Corporation sold merchandise with a cost of $175,000 to Swain Company for $250,000, all of which was sold by Swain Company before the end of the year.

Polk Corporation has correctly recorded the income and dividends reported for the year by Swain Company. Data for the income statements for both companies for the current year are as follows:

	Polk Corporation	Swain Company
Revenues:		
Sales.	$1,900,000	$625,000
Income of subsidiary	125,000	—
Interest income.	—	3,125
	$2,025,000	$628,125
Expenses:		
Cost of merchandise sold.	$1,219,600	$315,750
Selling expenses	185,000	62,275
General expenses	135,000	37,000
Interest expense.	12,500	—
Income tax.	155,100	88,100
	$1,707,200	$503,125
Net income	$ 317,800	$125,000

Data for the balance sheets of both companies as of the end of the current year are as follows:

	Polk Corporation	Swain Company
Assets		
Cash...	$ 86,200	$ 37,150
Accounts receivable (net).......................	138,400	62,800
Dividends receivable...........................	12,500	—
Interest receivable............................	—	3,125
Inventories....................................	549,550	199,000
Investment in Swain Co. (10,000 shares).........	505,800	—
Investment in Polk Corp. bonds (at face amount)...	—	100,000
Plant and equipment...........................	837,850	312,000
Accumulated depreciation	(230,300)	(164,075)
	$1,900,000	$550,000
Liabilities and Stockholders' Equity		
Accounts payable..............................	$ 154,400	$ 26,100
Income tax payable............................	20,000	5,600
Dividends payable.............................	20,000	12,500
Interest payable...............................	6,250	—
Bonds payable, 12 1/2% (due in 2004)...........	200,000	—
Common stock, $10 par........................	1,000,000	—
Common stock, $25 par........................	—	250,000
Premium on common stock.....................	40,000	80,000
Retained earnings.............................	459,350	175,800
	$1,900,000	$550,000

Instructions:

(1) Determine the amounts to be eliminated from the following items in preparing the consolidated balance sheet as of December 31 of the current year: (a) dividends receivable and dividends payable; (b) interest receivable and interest payable; (c) investment in Swain Co. and stockholders' equity; (d) investment in Polk Corp. bonds and bonds payable.

(2) Prepare a detailed consolidated balance sheet as of December 31 in report form.

(3) Determine the amounts to be eliminated from the following items in preparing the consolidated income statement for the current year ended December 31: (a) sales and cost of merchandise sold; (b) interest income and interest expense; (c) income of subsidiary and net income.

(4) Prepare a single-step consolidated income statement, inserting the earnings per share in parentheses on the same line with net income.

(5) Determine the amount of the reduction in consolidated inventories, net income, and retained earnings if Swain Company's inventory had included $75,000 of the merchandise purchased from Polk Corporation.

Problem 18–7A. Foreign currency transactions. Waddell Company sells merchandise to and purchases merchandise from various Canadian and Mexican companies. These transactions are settled in the foreign currency. The following selected transactions were completed during the current fiscal year:

Jan. 10. Purchased merchandise on account from Javier Company, net 30, $10,000 Canadian; exchange rate, $.88 per Canadian dollar.

Feb. 9. Issued check for amount owed to Javier Company; exchange rate, $.90 per Canadian dollar.

Mar. 30. Sold merchandise on account to Valdez Company, net 30, 500,000 pesos; exchange rate, $.045 per Mexican peso.

Apr. 29. Received cash from Valdez Company; exchange rate, $.046 per Mexican peso.

June 1. Purchased merchandise on account from Blume Company, net 30, $30,000 Canadian; exchange rate, $.88 per Canadian dollar.

July 1. Issued check for amount owed to Blume Company; exchange rate, $.87 per Canadian dollar.

Oct. 5. Sold merchandise on account to Osuna Company, net 30, 300,000 pesos; exchange rate, $.044 per Mexican peso.

Nov. 4. Received cash from Osuna Company; exchange rate, $.043 per Mexican peso.

Dec. 15. Sold merchandise on account to Gresky Company, net 30, $50,000 Canadian; exchange rate, $.85 per Canadian dollar.

21. Purchased merchandise on account from Ortega Company, net 30, 250,000 pesos; exchange rate, $.047 per Mexican peso.

31. Recorded unrealized currency exchange gain and/or loss on transactions of December 15 and 21. Exchange rates on December 31: $.84 per Canadian dollar; $.046 per Mexican peso.

Instructions:

(1) Present the journal entries to record the transactions and adjustments for the year.
(2) Present the journal entries to record the payment of the December 21st purchase on January 20, when the exchange rate was $.048 per Mexican peso, and the receipt of cash from the December 15th sale, on January 21, when the exchange rate was $.83 per Canadian dollar.

Series B

Problem 18–2B. Work sheet and consolidated balance sheet from affiliation effected as a purchase. On June 30 of the current year, Putman Company purchased 85% of the stock of Searcy Company. On the same date, Putman Company loaned Searcy Company $50,000 on a 60-day note. The data reported on their separate balance sheets immediately after the acquisition and loan are as follows:

	Putman Company	Searcy Company
Assets		
Cash..	$ 56,500	$ 55,000
Accounts receivable (net).......................	95,250	70,000
Notes receivable	75,000	—
Inventories....................................	179,250	98,000
Investment in Searcy Company	520,000	—
Equipment (net)	425,000	430,000
	$1,351,000	$653,000

	Putman Company	Searcy Company
Liabilities and Stockholders' Equity		
Accounts payable...............................	$ 210,000	$ 45,000
Notes payable..................................	—	50,000
Common stock, $20 par........................	800,000	—
Common stock, $10 par........................	—	400,000
Retained earnings	341,000	158,000
	$1,351,000	$653,000

The fair value of Searcy Company's assets correspond to the book carrying amounts, except for equipment, which is valued at $450,000 for consolidation purposes.

Instructions:

(1) Prepare a work sheet for a consolidated balance sheet as of June 30 of the current year.
(2) Prepare in report form a consolidated balance sheet as of June 30, omitting captions for current assets, plant assets, etc.

Problem 18–3B. Work sheet and consolidated balance sheet; year-end minority interest; increase in investment account during year. On July 31, Perry Company purchased 80% of the outstanding stock of Sims Company for $600,000. Balance sheet data for the two corporations immediately after the transaction are as follows:

	Perry Company	Sims Company
Assets		
Cash and marketable securities	$ 263,200	$ 35,400
Accounts receivable............................	369,225	66,225
Allowance for doubtful accounts	(30,150)	(12,075)
Inventories....................................	735,375	183,150
Investment in Sims Company	600,000	—
Land...	210,000	112,500
Building and equipment	1,093,950	741,900
Accumulated depreciation	(348,600)	(392,850)
	$2,893,000	$734,250
Liabilities and Stockholders' Equity		
Accounts payable..............................	$ 308,575	$106,725
Income tax payable	63,000	9,075
Bonds payable (due in 2007)	600,000	—
Common stock, $20 par........................	1,125,000	—
Common stock, $5 par.........................	—	450,000
Retained earnings	796,425	168,450
	$2,893,000	$734,250

Instructions:

(1) Prepare a work sheet for a consolidated balance sheet as of the date of acquisition.
(2) Prepare in report form a detailed consolidated balance sheet as of the date of acquisition. The fair value of Sims Company's assets are deemed to correspond to the book carrying amounts, except for land, which is to be increased by $70,000.
(3) Assuming that Sims Company earns net income of $135,000 and pays cash dividends of $60,000 during the following fiscal year and that Perry Company records its share of the earnings and dividends, determine the following as of the end of the year:
   (a) The net amount added to Perry Company's investment account as a result of Sims Company's earnings and dividends.
   (b) The amount of the minority interest.

Problem 18–6B. Eliminations for and preparation of consolidated balance sheet and income statement. On January 2 of the current year, Pella Corporation exchanged 15,000 shares of its $20 par common stock for 12,000 shares (the entire issue) of Stein Company's $25 par common stock. Stein purchased from Pella Corporation $150,000 of its $250,000 issue of bonds payable, at face amount. All of the items for "interest" appearing on the balance sheets and income statements of both corporations are related to the bonds.

During the year, Pella Corporation sold merchandise with a cost of $184,000 to Stein Company for $230,000, all of which was sold by Stein Company before the end of the year.

Pella Corporation has correctly recorded the income and dividends reported for the year by Stein Company. Data for the income statements for both companies for the current year are as follows:

	Pella Corporation	Stein Company
Revenues:		
Sales.	$1,600,000	$500,000
Income of subsidiary	110,000	—
Interest income	—	15,000
	$1,710,000	$515,000
Expenses:		
Cost of merchandise sold.	$ 950,000	$280,000
Selling expenses	165,000	52,000
General expenses	125,000	37,000
Interest expense.	25,000	—
Income tax.	195,000	36,000
	$1,460,000	$405,000
Net income	$ 250,000	$110,000

Data for the balance sheets of both companies as of the end of the current year are as follows:

	Pella Corporation	Stein Company
Assets		
Cash..	$ 62,500	$ 25,800
Accounts receivable (net).......................	165,000	51,800
Dividends receivable...........................	50,000	—
Interest receivable.............................	—	7,500
Inventories....................................	275,000	126,300
Investment in Stein Co. (12,000 shares)...........	641,550	—
Investment in Pella Corp. bonds (at face amount)..	—	150,000
Plant and equipment...........................	1,150,000	471,950
Accumulated depreciation......................	(650,000)	(108,350)
	$1,694,050	$725,000
Liabilities and Stockholders' Equity		
Accounts payable..............................	$ 75,200	$ 27,750
Income tax payable............................	20,510	5,700
Dividends payable.............................	30,000	50,000
Interest payable...............................	12,500	—
Bonds payable, 10% (due in 2003)..............	250,000	—
Common stock, $20 par........................	1,000,000	—
Common stock, $25 par........................	—	300,000
Premium on common stock......................	100,000	50,000
Retained earnings.............................	205,840	291,550
	$1,694,050	$725,000

Instructions:

(1) Determine the amounts to be eliminated from the following items in preparing the consolidated balance sheet as of December 31 of the current year: (a) dividends receivable and dividends payable; (b) interest receivable and interest payable; (c) investment in Stein Co. and stockholders' equity; (d) investment in Pella Corp. bonds and bonds payable.

(2) Prepare a detailed consolidated balance sheet as of December 31 in report form.

(3) Determine the amounts to be eliminated from the following items in preparing the consolidated income statement for the current year ended December 31: (a) sales and cost of merchandise sold; (b) interest income and interest expense; (c) income of subsidiary and net income.

(4) Prepare a single-step consolidated income statement, inserting the earnings per share in parentheses on the same line with net income.

(5) Determine the amount of the reduction in consolidated inventories, net income, and retained earnings if Stein Company's inventory had included $50,000 of the merchandise purchased from Pella Corporation.

Problem 18–7B. Foreign currency transactions. Dixon Company sells merchandise to and purchases merchandise from various Canadian and Mexican companies. These transactions are settled in the foreign currency. The following selected transactions were completed during the current fiscal year:

Mar. 15. Sold merchandise on account to Carr Company, net 30, 300,000 pesos; exchange rate, $.048 per Mexican peso.

Apr. 14. Received cash from Carr Company; exchange rate, $.047 per Mexican peso.

May 5. Purchased merchandise on account from Lofgren Company, net 30, $5,000 Canadian; exchange rate, $.82 per Canadian dollar.

June 4. Issued check for amount owed to Lofgren Company; exchange rate, $.81 per Canadian dollar.

Aug. 31. Sold merchandise on account to Sanchez Company, net 30, 300,000 pesos; exchange rate, $.044 per Mexican peso.

Sept. 30. Received cash from Sanchez Company; exchange rate, $.046 per Mexican peso.

Oct. 10. Purchased merchandise on account from Chevalier Company, net 30, $20,000 Canadian; exchange rate, $.83 per Canadian dollar.

Nov. 9. Issued check for amount owed to Chevalier Company; exchange rate, $.84 per Canadian dollar.

Dec. 15. Sold merchandise on account to Adams Company, net 30, $50,000 Canadian; exchange rate, $.85 per Canadian dollar.

16. Purchased merchandise on account from Santos Company, net 30, 250,000 pesos; exchange rate, $.047 per Mexican peso.

31. Recorded unrealized currency exchange gain and/or loss on transactions of December 15 and 16. Exchange rates on December 31: $.86 per Canadian dollar; $.048 per Mexican peso.

Instructions:

(1) Present entries to record the transactions and adjusting entries for the year.
(2) Present entries to record the payment of the December 16 purchase, on January 15, when the exchange rate was $.046 per Mexican peso, and the receipt of cash from the December 15 sale, on January 17, when the exchange rate was $.87 per Canadian dollar.

MINI-CASE 18

Stella Wilkinson

Your grandmother recently retired, sold her home in Kansas City, and moved to a retirement community in Palm Springs. With some of the proceeds from the sale of her home, she is considering investing $150,000 in the stock market.

In the process of selecting among alternative stock investments, your grandmother collected annual reports from twenty different companies. In reviewing these reports, however, she has become confused and has questions concerning several items which appear in the financial reports. She has asked for your help and has written down the following questions for you to answer:

(a) "In reviewing the annual reports, I noticed many references to 'consolidated financial statements.' What are consolidated financial statements?"

(b) " 'Excess of cost of business acquired over related net assets' appears on the consolidated balance sheets in several annual reports. What does this mean? Is it an asset (it appears with other assets)?"

(c) "What is minority interest?"

(d) "A footnote to one of the consolidated statements indicated interest and the amount of a loan from one company to another had been eliminated. Is this good accounting? A loan is a loan. How can a company just eliminate a loan that hasn't been paid off?"

(e) "How can financial statements for an American company (in dollars) be combined with a British subsidiary (in pounds)?"

Instructions:

(1) Briefly respond to each of your grandmother's questions.

(2) While discussing the items in (1) with your grandmother, she asked for your advice on whether she should limit her investment to one stock. What would you advise?

Part

6

ADDITIONAL
STATEMENTS
AND ANALYSES

Chapter 19

STATEMENT OF CHANGES IN FINANCIAL POSITION— CASH AND WORKING CAPITAL

Chapter Objectives:

- Describe the nature of the statement of changes in financial position.

- Describe the two common concepts of funds:
  Cash
  Working capital

- Describe and illustrate the preparation of a statement of changes in financial position based on cash.

- Describe and illustrate the preparation of a statement of changes in financial position based on working capital.

19

The four basic financial statements are the balance sheet, the income statement, the retained earnings statement (statement of owner's equity), and the statement of changes in financial position. The preparation and use of the first three statements were thoroughly discussed in preceding chapters. This chapter is devoted to the statement of changes in financial position, a statement that is especially useful in evaluating past and planning future financing and investing activities.

NATURE OF THE STATEMENT OF CHANGES IN FINANCIAL POSITION

examine change in funds from one period to another

The **statement of changes in financial position**, or **funds statement**,[1] reports a firm's significant financing and investing activities for a period. These activities are generally described in terms of the inflow and outflow of "funds," with **funds** defined as either "cash" or "working capital" (current assets − current liabilities). The statement of changes in financial position, then, can be said to provide a summary of the *sources* from which funds became available and the purposes for which the funds were *applied* during a period. Common inflows (sources) of funds include operations which earn income, the sale of long-term investments and plant assets, and the issuance of bonds and capital stock. Typically, the funds obtained are used for such outflows (applications) as the purchase of long-term investments and plant assets, the retirement of bonds, and the declaration of cash dividends.

Both the acquisition and the subsequent use of funds can affect profitability and solvency (the ability to meet currently maturing debt). For example, the acquisition of funds by issuing bonds commits the firm not only to the payment of periodic interest expense (which affects profitability and solvency), but also to the redemption of the bonds at maturity (which affects solvency). Thus, the statement of changes in financial position is useful in analyzing both past and future profitability and solvency of the firm.

---

[1]Although the formal name of the statement is statement of changes in financial position, the term often used in discussing the statement is funds statement. This shorter term will often be used in the discussion.

Cash Flow and Survival

Businesses generally do not go broke because they lack assets but because they have inadequate cash flow. A number of now defunct companies have gone bankrupt while rich in assets but lacking the necessary cash flow to survive. Thus handicapped, they could not convert assets into cash quickly enough to avoid economic disaster.

Source: From a speech by Harvey Kapnick, chairman of Arthur Andersen & Co., before an American Petroleum Institute Conference, June 11, 1979.

Both a funds statement based on cash and a funds statement based on working capital may be prepared for management's use, but usually only one statement is presented in published financial reports. Although both bases are being widely used, the cash basis funds statement is receiving increasingly more attention by the accounting profession. For example, the Financial Executives Institute now recommends the use of the cash basis for the funds statement. Also, as discussed in Chapter 13, one of the broad objectives of financial reporting set forth by the Financial Accounting Standards Board is to provide financial information that enables users to predict cash flows to the business and subsequently to themselves. Based on this objective, the FASB has proposed that a *statement of cash flows* replace the statement of changes in financial position.

As a result of this attention, the cash basis funds statement is increasing in frequency of use. For example, of the 600 industrial and merchandising companies surveyed and reported in the 1985 edition of *Accounting Trends & Techniques*, 59% of the companies used the cash basis in the current year, compared with 52% in the preceding year.

In the discussion that follows, the cash basis funds statement will be discussed first. Since many companies still report on the working capital basis, this alternative form of the funds statement will then be discussed.

826

FUNDS STATEMENT BASED ON CASH

When the cash basis is used, the funds statement summarizes the inflows and outflows of cash during a period.[2] Cash flowing into an enterprise is classified as to source to form the first section of the funds statement. Cash flowing out of an enterprise is classified according to the manner of use or application and is reported in the second section of the statement. Ordinarily, the totals of the two sections are unequal. If the inflow (sources) has exceeded the outflow (applications), the excess is the amount of the increase in cash. When the reverse situation occurs, the excess of outflow is a measure of the amount by which cash has decreased. Accordingly, the difference between the totals of the sources and the applications sections of the funds statement is identified as an increase or a decrease in cash.

The common inflows (sources) and outflows (applications) of cash are indicated in the following diagram:

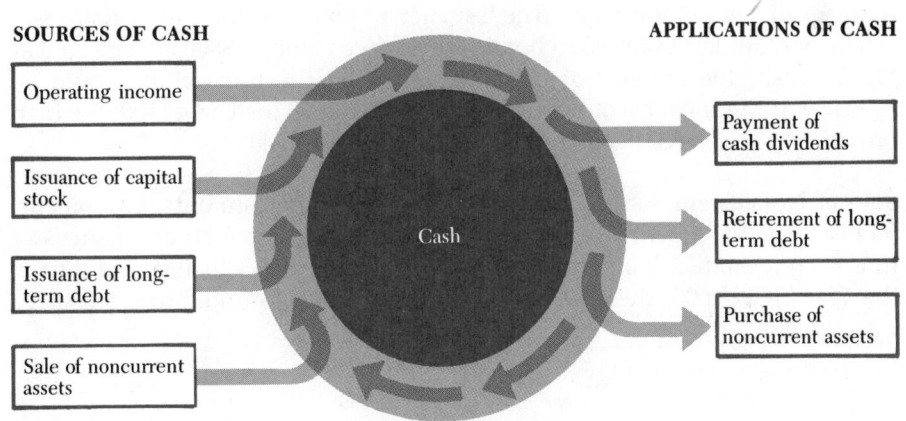

SOURCES OF CASH

- Operating income
- Issuance of capital stock
- Issuance of long-term debt
- Sale of noncurrent assets

Cash

APPLICATIONS OF CASH

- Payment of cash dividends
- Retirement of long-term debt
- Purchase of noncurrent assets

SOURCES AND APPLICA-TIONS OF CASH

Although other sources and applications of cash may be possible, a complete discussion of all sources and applications is left for more advanced texts. The focus in this chapter is to present an understanding of the concept of funds and the preparation, interpretation, and use of the funds statement.

Sources of Cash

As illustrated in the diagram above, the four common sources of cash are (1) operating income, (2) the issuance of capital stock, (3) the issuance of

---

[2]The cash basis is sometimes expanded to include temporary investments that are readily convertible to cash.

long-term debt, and (4) the sale of noncurrent assets. These sources of cash are briefly described in the following paragraphs.

Operating Income. Often the largest and most frequent source of cash is profitable operations. Revenues realized from the sale of goods or services are often accompanied by increases in cash. Conversely, many of the expenses incurred are accompanied by decreases in cash. However, the revenues and expenses, and therefore net income, reported on the income statement are determined on the accrual basis and are not necessarily equivalent to the cash actually flowing from operations. The amount reported as net income must therefore be adjusted upward or downward to determine the amount of cash provided by operations.[3]

Issuance of Capital Stock. If capital stock is sold during the period, cash is provided. For example, if 10,000 shares of $25 par common stock are sold at 40, cash of $400,000 would be provided.

Issuance of Long-Term Debt. The issuance of bonds or long-term notes is a source of cash. For example, if bonds with a face value of $600,000 are sold at 100 for cash, the amount of funds provided by the transaction would be $600,000. If the $600,000 of bonds had been sold at 90 instead of 100, the cash provided would have been $540,000 instead of $600,000.

Sale of Noncurrent Assets. The sale of long-term investments, equipment, buildings, land, patents, or other noncurrent assets for cash are sources of funds. For example, if a patent carried in the ledger at $30,000 is sold during the year for $70,000, the cash provided by the sale amounted to $70,000.

Applications of Cash

The three common applications of cash, as indicated in the diagram on page 827, are (1) the payment of cash dividends, (2) the retirement of long-term debt, and (3) the purchase of noncurrent assets. These uses of cash are briefly described in the following paragraphs.

Payment of cash dividends. One of the most common applications of cash is the payment of cash dividends. For example, if cash dividends of $40,000 were

---

[3]If gains or losses are reported as extraordinary items on the income statement, they should be identified as such on the funds statement. Extraordinary items are discussed in Chapter 16.

declared during the period but only $30,000 in dividends was paid, the funds applied would be $30,000.

Retirement of Long-Term Debt. The liquidation of bonds or long-term notes is an application of cash. For example, if callable bonds issued at their face value of $100,000 are redeemed at 105, the funds applied would be $105,000.

Purchases of Noncurrent Assets. Cash may be applied to the purchase of equipment, buildings, land, long-term investments, patents, or other non-current assets. For example, if equipment is purchased for $75,000, funds applied would be $75,000.

Other Changes in Financial Position

Regardless of which of the bases is used for a specific funds statement, financial position may be affected by transactions that do not involve funds. If such transactions have occurred during the period, their effect, if significant, should also be reported in the funds statement. This broadened concept, termed the "all financial resources concept" is required by generally accepted accounting principles.[4] To illustrate, if an enterprise issues bonds or capital stock in exchange for land and buildings, the transaction has no effect on cash. Nevertheless, because of the significant effect on financial position, both the increase in the plant assets and the increase in long-term liabilities or stockholders' equity should be reported on the funds statement. A complete discussion of the kinds of nonfund transactions that usually have a significant effect on financial position is beyond the scope of the discussion here. The following are illustrative of the many possibilities: preferred or common stock may be issued in liquidation of long-term debt, common stock may be issued in exchange for convertible preferred stock, and long-term investments may be exchanged for machinery and equipment.

Transactions of the type indicated in the preceding paragraph may be reported on the funds statement as though there were two transactions: (1) a source of funds and (2) an application of funds. The relationship of the source and the application should be disclosed by proper wording in the descriptive captions or by footnote. To illustrate, assume that common stock of $200,000 par is issued in exchange for $200,000 face amount of bonds payable, on which there is no unamortized discount or premium. The issuance of the common stock should be reported in the sources section of the statement as follows:

---

[4]*Opinions of the Accounting Principles Board, No. 19,* "Reporting Changes in Financial Position" (New York: American Institute of Certified Public Accountants, 1971), par. 8.

"Issuance of common stock at par in retirement of bonds payable, $200,000."
The other part of the transaction could be described in the applications section
as follows: "Retirement of bonds payable by the issuance of common stock at
par, $200,000." The transaction is reported as if (1) cash had been received
from the issuance of the common stock and (2) cash had been used to retire
the bonds.

ASSEMBLING DATA FOR THE FUNDS STATEMENT BASED ON CASH

To determine the sources and applications of cash, all the cash receipts
and disbursements for a period could be analyzed and then reported by source
or application on the funds statement. However, this procedure would be
expensive and time consuming. A more efficient procedure is to examine the
noncash balance sheet accounts and determine the sources and applications
of cash that lead to changes in these accounts during the period. In performing
this analysis, supplementary explanatory data can be obtained from the income statement and other records as needed. Such a procedure is not only
efficient but also logical, because all transactions eventually affect balance
sheet accounts. For example, although revenues and expenses are not shown
directly on the balance sheet, the retained earnings account on the balance
sheet is affected as revenues and expenses are closed at the end of a period.

Although there is no order in which the noncash balance sheet accounts
must be analyzed, time can be saved and greater accuracy can be achieved by
selecting the accounts in the reverse order in which they appear on the balance
sheet. Therefore, the retained earnings account provides the starting point
for determining the source that normally appears first on the funds
statement—funds provided by operations.

To illustrate this approach to assembling the data for the funds statement
based on cash, the following comparative balance sheet for T. R. Morgan
Corporation for the year ended December 31, 1988, will be used. Selected
ledger accounts will be presented as needed, along with supplementary data
taken from the income statement.[5]

---

[5]When the volume of data is substantial, experienced accountants may first assemble all relevant
facts in working papers designed for the purpose. Specialized working papers are not essential,
however. Because of their complexity, they tend to obscure the basic concepts of funds analysis
for anyone who is not already familiar with the subject. For this reason, special working papers
will not be used in the following discussion. Instead, the emphasis will be on the basic analyses.
The use of a work sheet as an aid in assembling data for the funds statement is presented in
Appendix D.

T. R. Morgan Corporation
Comparative Balance Sheet
December 31, 1988 and 1987

	1988	1987	Increase Decrease*
Assets			
Cash..................................	$ 49,000	$ 26,000	$ 23,000
Trade receivables (net)...............	74,000	65,000	9,000
Inventories..........................	172,000	180,000	8,000*
Prepaid expenses	4,000	3,000	1,000
Investments (long-term)	—	45,000	45,000*
Land.................................	90,000	40,000	50,000
Building	200,000	200,000	—
Accumulated depreciation — building...	(36,000)	(30,000)	(6,000)
Equipment...........................	240,000	142,000	98,000
Accumulated depreciation — equipment.	(43,000)	(40,000)	(3,000)
Total assets.........................	$750,000	$631,000	$119,000
Liabilities			
Accounts payable (merchandise creditors)........................	$ 50,000	$ 32,000	$ 18,000
Income tax payable...................	2,500	4,000	1,500*
Dividends payable....................	15,000	8,000	7,000
Bonds payable.......................	120,000	245,000	125,000*
Total liabilities......................	$187,500	$289,000	$101,500*
Stockholders' Equity			
Preferred stock.......................	$ 50,000	—	$ 50,000
Premium on preferred stock	10,000	—	10,000
Common stock.......................	280,000	$230,000	50,000
Retained earnings	222,500	112,000	110,500
Total stockholders' equity............	$562,500	$342,000	$220,500
Total liabilities and stockholders' equity .	$750,000	$631,000	$119,000

Retained Earnings

According to the comparative balance sheet for T. R. Morgan Corporation, there was an increase of $110,500 in retained earnings during the year. The retained earnings account, as shown below, indicates the nature of the entries made during the year that resulted in this increase.

ACCOUNT RETAINED EARNINGS   ACCOUNT NO.

| Date | | Item | Debit | Credit | Balance | |
					Debit	Credit
1988						
Jan.	1	Balance				112,000
Dec.	31	Net income		140,500		
	31	Cash dividends	30,000			222,500

The retained earnings account indicates net income of $140,500 and cash dividends declared of $30,000. The determination of the amount of cash provided by operations and the cash applied to the payment of dividends is discussed in the following paragraphs. It should be noted that there may be entries in the retained earnings account that do not affect cash, such as a transfer of retained earnings to paid-in capital accounts in the issuance of a stock dividend. Similarly, transfers between the retained earnings account and appropriations accounts have no effect on cash. Such transactions would not be reported on the funds statement.

Cash Provided by Operations. The amount of net income, $140,500, which is reported on the income statement, was determined by the accrual method of accounting. It is therefore necessary to recognize the relationship of the accrual method to the movement of cash. Usually, a part of some of the costs and expenses reported on the income statement, as well as a part of the revenue earned, is not accompanied by cash outflow or inflow.

There is often a period of time between the accrual of a revenue and the receipt of the related cash. Perhaps the most common example is the sale of merchandise or a service on account, for which payment is received at a later point in time. Hence, the amount reported on the income statement as revenue from sales is not likely to correspond with the amount of the related cash inflow for the same period.

Timing differences between the incurrence of an expense and the related cash outflow must also be considered in determining the amount of cash provided by operations. For example, the amount reported on the income statement as insurance expense is the amount of insurance premiums expired rather than the amount of premiums paid during the period. Similarly, supplies paid for in one year may be used and thus converted to an expense in a later year. Conversely, a portion of some of the expenses incurred near the end of one period, such as wages and taxes, may not require a cash outlay until the following period.

Some revenues and expenses related to noncurrent accounts do not provide or use cash. For example, depreciation expense is a proper expense for the purpose of determining net income, but it does not require an outlay of cash.

To determine the amount of cash provided by operations, the accrual basis net income, as reported on the income statement, must be converted to the cash basis. For purposes of illustration, the types of accounts that must be analyzed to convert net income from the accrual basis to the cash basis can be placed in two categories, described as follows:

1. Expenses affecting noncurrent accounts but not cash. For example, depreciation of plant assets and amortization of intangible assets are deducted from revenue but have no effect on cash. Similarly, the amortization of premium on bonds payable, which decreases interest expense and therefore increases operating income, does not affect cash.
2. Revenues and expenses affecting current asset and current liability accounts in amounts that differ from cash flows. For example, a sale of $10,000 on account, on which $8,000 has subsequently been collected, increases revenue by $10,000 but increases cash by only $8,000. In this case, to convert the revenue reported on the income statement ($10,000) to the cash basis, the increase in accounts receivable of $2,000 ($10,000 sale less $8,000 collection) can be deducted from the $10,000 of revenue to yield a cash flow of $8,000.

The conversion of the net income reported on the income statement to cash provided by operations can be summarized as follows:

Net income, per income statement			$XX
Add:	Depreciation of plant assets	$XX	
	Amortization of bond discount and intangible assets	XX	
	Decreases in current assets (receivables, inventories, prepaid expenses)	XX	
	Increases in current liabilities (accounts and notes payable, accrued liabilities)	XX	XX
Deduct:	Amortization of bond premium	$XX	
	Increases in current assets (receivables, inventories, prepaid expenses)	XX	
	Decreases in current liabilities (accounts and notes payable, accrued liabilities)	XX	XX
Cash provided by operations			$XX

Note that two current accounts—cash and dividends payable—are not included in this conversion schedule. Cash is omitted because it is the current asset that is the focus of the analysis. Dividends payable is omitted because dividends are a distribution of earnings and do not affect net income. The treatment of dividends as they affect the funds statement will be discussed later in the chapter. In the following paragraphs, the manner in which the net income reported by T. R. Morgan Corporation is converted to "Cash provided by operations" is discussed.

Depreciation. The comparative balance sheet for T. R. Morgan Corporation indicates that Accumulated Depreciation—Equipment increased by

$3,000, and Accumulated Depreciation—Building increased by $6,000. Reference to these two accounts, shown as follows, indicates that depreciation for the year was $12,000 for the equipment and $6,000 for the building, or a total of $18,000.

ACCOUNT ACCUMULATED DEPRECIATION—EQUIPMENT   ACCOUNT NO.

Date		Item	Debit	Credit	Balance Debit	Balance Credit
1988						
Jan.	1	Balance				40,000
May	9	Discarded, no salvage	9,000			
Dec.	31	Depreciation for year		12,000		43,000

ACCOUNT ACCUMULATED DEPRECIATION—BUILDING   ACCOUNT NO.

Date		Item	Debit	Credit	Balance Debit	Balance Credit
1988						
Jan.	1	Balance				30,000
Dec.	31	Depreciation for year		6,000		36,000

Since the $18,000 of depreciation expense reduces net income but did not require an outlay of cash, $18,000 is added to net income in the process of determining the cash provided by operations, as follows:

> *Source of cash:*
> Operations during the year:
> Net income...................................... $140,500
> Add item not decreasing cash during the year:
> Depreciation.................................... 18,000

Current assets and current liabilities. In the process of determining cash provided by operations, decreases in the noncash current assets and increases in the current liabilities must be added to the amount reported as net income. Conversely, increases in the noncash current assets and decreases in the current liabilities must be deducted from the amount reported as net income. The relevant current asset and current liability accounts of T. R. Morgan Corporation are as follows:

Accounts	December 31 1988	December 31 1987	Increase Decrease*
Trade receivables (net)......................	$ 74,000	$ 65,000	$ 9,000
Inventories .... Add back	172,000	180,000	8,000*
Prepaid expenses	4,000	3,000	1,000
Accounts payable (merchandise creditors).....	50,000	32,000	18,000
Income tax payable.......................	2,500	4,000	1,500*

The additions to *trade receivables* for sales on account during the year were $9,000 more than the deductions for amounts collected from customers on account. The amount reported on the income statement as sales therefore included $9,000 that did not yield cash inflow during the year. Accordingly, $9,000 must be deducted from net income.

The $8,000 decrease in *inventories* indicates that the merchandise sold exceeded the cost of the merchandise purchased by $8,000. The amount reported on the income statement as a deduction from the revenue therefore included $8,000 that did not require cash outflow during the year. Accordingly, $8,000 must be added to net income.

The outlay of cash for *prepaid expenses* exceeded by $1,000 the amount deducted as an expense during the year. Hence, $1,000 must be deducted from net income.

The effect of the increase in *accounts payable*, which is the amount owed creditors for goods and services, was to include in expired costs and expenses the sum of $18,000 for which there had been no cash outlay during the year. Income was thereby reduced by $18,000, though there was no cash outlay. Hence, $18,000 must be added to net income.

The outlay of cash for *income taxes* exceeded by $1,500 the amount of income tax deducted as an expense during the period. Accordingly, $1,500 must be deducted from net income.

The foregoing adjustments to income may be summarized as follows in a format suitable for the funds statement:

Source of cash:

Operations during the year:		
Net income		$140,500
Add items not decreasing cash during the year:		
Depreciation . . (Non cash expenses)	$18,000	
Decrease in inventories	8,000	
Increase in accounts payable	18,000	44,000
		$184,500
Deduct items not increasing cash during the year:		
Increase in trade receivables	$ 9,000	
Increase in prepaid expenses.	1,000	
Decrease in income tax payable	1,500	11,500
Cash provided by operations		$173,000

Cash Applied to Payment of Dividends. According to the retained earnings account of T. R. Morgan Corporation (page 832), cash dividends of $30,000 were declared during the year. However, according to the dividends payable account, shown as follows, dividend payments during the year totaled

$23,000, revealing a timing difference between the declaration and the payment.

ACCOUNT DIVIDENDS PAYABLE   ACCOUNT NO.

Date		Item	Debit	Credit	Balance Debit	Balance Credit
1988						
Jan.	1	Balance				8,000
	10	Cash paid	8,000		—	—
June	20	Dividend declared		15,000		15,000
July	10	Cash paid	15,000		—	—
Dec.	20	Dividend declared		15,000		15,000

The $23,000 of cash applied to dividend payments may be noted on the funds statement as follows:

> *Application of cash:*
> Cash dividends declared....................... $30,000
> Deduct increase in dividends payable 7,000 $23,000

Preferred Stock

The increase of $50,000 in the preferred stock account and the increase of $10,000 in the premium on preferred stock account, shown as follows, is the result of an issuance of preferred stock for $60,000.

ACCOUNT PREFERRED STOCK, $50 PAR   ACCOUNT NO.

Date		Item	Debit	Credit	Balance Debit	Balance Credit
1988						
Nov.	1	1,000 shares issued for cash		50,000		50,000

ACCOUNT PREMIUM ON PREFERRED STOCK   ACCOUNT NO.

Date		Item	Debit	Credit	Balance Debit	Balance Credit
1988						
Nov.	1	1,000 shares issued for cash		10,000		10,000

This change in financial position may be noted on the funds statement as follows:

> *Source of cash:*
> Issuance of $50 par preferred stock at $60................ $60,000

Common Stock

The increase of $50,000 in the common stock account, shown as follows, is the result of stock being issued in exchange for land valued at $50,000.

ACCOUNT COMMON STOCK					ACCOUNT NO.	
					Balance	
Date		Item	Debit	Credit	Debit	Credit
1988 Jan.	1	Balance				230,000
Dec.	28	Issued at par in exchange for land		50,000		280,000

Although cash was not involved, the transaction represents a significant change in financial position and should be reported on the funds statement, as discussed previously. The source of funds portion of the transaction may be noted as follows:

Source of cash:
Issuance of common stock at par for land. $50,000

Bonds Payable

The next item listed on the balance sheet, bonds payable, decreased $125,000 during the year. Examination of the bonds payable account, which appears as follows, indicates that $125,000 of the bonds payable were retired by payment of the face amount.

ACCOUNT BONDS PAYABLE					ACCOUNT NO.	
					Balance	
Date		Item	Debit	Credit	Debit	Credit
1988 Jan.	1	Balance				245,000
June	30	Retired by payment of cash at face amount	125,000			120,000

This transaction's effect on funds is noted as follows:

Application of cash:
Retirement of bonds payable $125,000

Equipment

The comparative balance sheet indicates that the cost of equipment increased $98,000. The following equipment account and the accumulated depreciation account reveal that the net change of $98,000 was the result of two separate transactions—the discarding of equipment that had cost $9,000 and the purchase of equipment for $107,000. The equipment discarded had been fully depreciated, as indicated by the debit of $9,000 in the accumulated depreciation account, and no salvage was realized from its disposal. Hence, the transaction had no effect on cash and is not reported on the funds statement.

ACCOUNT EQUIPMENT   ACCOUNT NO.

Date		Item	Debit	Credit	Balance Debit	Balance Credit
1988						
Jan.	1	Balance			142,000	
May	9	Discarded, no salvage		9,000		
Dec.	7	Purchased for cash	107,000		240,000	

ACCOUNT ACCUMULATED DEPRECIATION—EQUIPMENT   ACCOUNT NO.

Date		Item	Debit	Credit	Balance Debit	Balance Credit
1988						
Jan.	1	Balance				40,000
May	9	Discarded, no salvage	9,000			
Dec.	31	Depreciation for year		12,000		43,000

The effect on funds of the purchase of equipment for $107,000 was as follows:

Application of cash:
Purchase of equipment $107,000

The credit in the accumulated depreciation account had the effect of reducing the book value of equipment by $12,000 but caused no change in cash. This transaction was treated previously as an addition to net income in determining cash provided by operations.

Building

According to the comparative balance sheet, there was no change in the $200,000 balance in the building account between the beginning and end of the year. Reference to the ledger confirms the absence of entries in the building account during the year, and hence the account is not shown here. The credit in the related accumulated depreciation account reduced the book value of the building, but, as indicated previously, cash was not affected.

Land

The comparative balance sheet indicates that land increased by $50,000. The notation in the land account, which follows, indicates that the land was acquired by issuance of common stock at par.

					Balance	
ACCOUNT LAND					ACCOUNT NO.	
Date		Item	Debit	Credit	Debit	Credit
1988 Jan.	1	Balance			40,000	
Dec.	28	Acquired by issuance of common stock at par	50,000		90,000	

Although cash was not involved in this transaction, as indicated previously, the acquisition represents a significant change in financial position. Therefore, the application of funds portion of the transaction may be noted as follows:

Application of cash:
Purchase of land by issuance of common stock at par $50,000

Investments ?

The comparative balance sheet indicates that investments decreased by $45,000. The notation in the following investments account indicates that the investments were sold for $75,000 in cash.

					Balance	
ACCOUNT INVESTMENTS					ACCOUNT NO.	
Date		Item	Debit	Credit	Debit	Credit
1988 Jan.	1	Balance			45,000	
June	8	Sold for $75,000 cash		45,000	—	—

The $30,000 gain on the sale is included in the net income reported on the income statement. It is also necessary to report the book value of the sale of the investments as an additional source of cash. To report the entire proceeds of $75,000 as a source of cash would incorrectly include the gain reported in net income. Accordingly, to avoid a double reporting of the $30,000 gain, the notation in the funds statement is as follows:

Source of cash:
Book value of investments sold (excludes $30,000 gain
reported in net income) $45,000

The proceeds from the sale of investments would appear on the funds statement in two places: (1) book value of investments sold, $45,000, and (2) gain on sale of investments as part of net income, $30,000.

FORM OF THE FUNDS STATEMENT BASED ON CASH

As mentioned previously, the funds statement based on cash is usually divided into two main sections—sources of cash and applications of cash. These two sections may be followed by a listing of the cash balance at the beginning of the period, at the end of the period, and the net change. An alternative is to begin the statement with the beginning cash balance, add the total of the sources section, subtract the total of the applications section, and conclude with the cash balance at the end of the period.

An analysis of the funds statement for T. R. Morgan Corporation, presented on page 841, indicates that the cash position increased by $23,000 during the year. The principal source of cash was operations ($173,000), which indicates that most of the cash acquired during the year was generated internally. The principal uses of cash were the retirement of bonds payable ($125,000) and the purchase of equipment ($107,000).

FUNDS STATEMENT BASED ON WORKING CAPITAL

The excess of an enterprise's total current assets over its total current liabilities at a point in time may be termed its **working capital** or **net current assets**. For T. R. Morgan Corporation, working capital was $231,500 at the end of 1988 and $230,000 at the end of 1987, as indicated in the following schedule prepared from data taken from the comparative balance sheet on page 831:

| | December 31 | | Increase |
	1988	1987	Decrease*
Current assets:			
Cash...............................	$ 49,000	$ 26,000	$23,000
Trade receivables (net)....................	74,000	65,000	9,000
Inventories	172,000	180,000	8,000*
Prepaid expenses	4,000	3,000	1,000
Total......................	$299,000	$274,000	$25,000
Current liabilities:			
Accounts payable	$ 50,000	$ 32,000	$18,000
Income tax payable.......................	2,500	4,000	1,500*
Dividends payable........................	15,000	8,000	7,000
Total......................	$ 67,500	$ 44,000	$23,500
Working capital............................	$231,500	$230,000	$ 1,500

STATEMENT
OF CHANGES
IN FINANCIAL
POSITION—
BASED ON
CASH

T. R. Morgan Corporation
Statement of Changes in Financial Position
For Year Ended December 31, 1988

Sources of cash:
  Operations during the year:

Net income		$140,500	
Add items not decreasing			
cash during the year:			
Depreciation	$18,000		
Decrease in inventories .	8,000		
Increase in accounts			
payable	18,000	44,000	
		$184,500	
Deduct items not increasing			
cash during the year:			
Increase in trade			
receivables	$ 9,000		
Increase in prepaid			
expenses	1,000		
Decrease in income tax			
payable	1,500	11,500	
Cash provided by			
operations		$173,000	
Issuance of preferred stock. .		60,000	
Issuance of common stock			
at par for land		50,000	
Book value of investments			
sold (excludes $30,000 gain			
reported in net income) . . .		45,000	$328,000

Applications of cash:
  Payment of dividends:

Cash dividends declared. .	$ 30,000		
Deduct increase in			
dividends payable	7,000	$ 23,000	
Retirement of bonds			
payable		125,000	
Purchase of land by			
issuance of common			
stock at par		50,000	
Purchase of equipment		107,000	305,000
Increase in cash			$ 23,000

Change in cash balance:

Cash balance,		
December 31, 1988		$ 49,000
Cash balance,		
December 31, 1987		26,000
Increase in cash		$ 23,000

The increase of $25,000 in total current assets during the year increased working capital. The increase of $23,500 in total current liabilities decreased working capital. The combined effect was a $1,500 increase in working capital. Note that working capital is a "net" concept. An increase or decrease in working capital cannot be determined solely by the amount of change in total current assets or solely by the amount of change in total current liabilities.

The amount of most of the items classified as current assets and current liabilities varies from one balance sheet date to another. Many of the items change daily. Inventories are increased by purchases on account, which also increase accounts payable. Accounts payable are reduced by payment, which also reduces cash. As merchandise is sold on account, inventories decrease and accounts receivable increase. In turn, the collections from customers increase cash and reduce accounts receivable. An understanding of this continuous interaction among the various current assets and current liabilities is essential to an understanding of the concept of working capital and analyses related to it. Note that the amount of working capital is neither increased nor decreased by a transaction (1) that affects only current assets (such as a purchase of marketable securities for cash), (2) that affects only current liabilities (such as the issuance of a short-term note to a creditor on account), or (3) that affects only current assets and current liabilities (such as the payment of an account payable).

The working capital schedule on page 840 shows an increase of $1,500 in working capital, which may be significant in evaluating financial position. However, the schedule gives no indication of the inflows (sources) and outflows (applications) of funds (working capital) that resulted in the increase. Working capital could have flowed into the business from operating income, the sale of noncurrent assets, the issuance of long-term debt, the issuance of capital stock, or a combination of these and other sources. Working capital could have flowed out of the business for the purchase of noncurrent assets, the retirement of long-term debt, the declaration of cash dividends, or other similar occurrences. The effects of the most common inflows and outflows of working capital are indicated in the following diagram:

SOURCES OF WORKING CAPITAL

APPLICATIONS OF WORKING CAPITAL

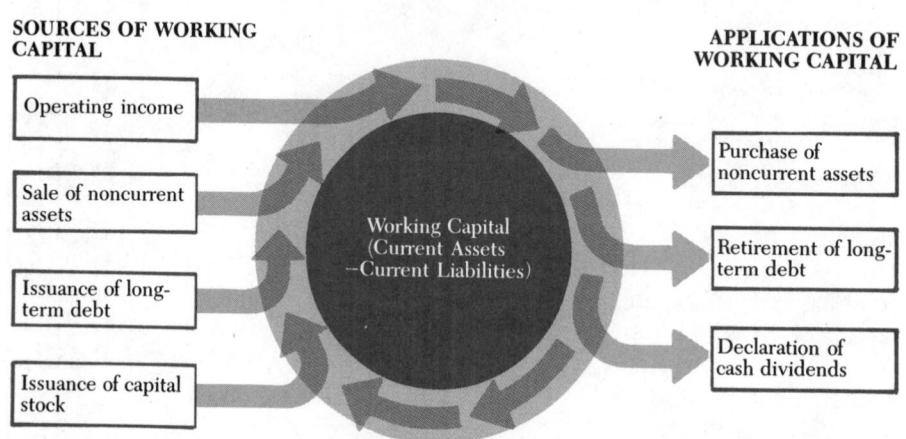

SOURCES AND APPLICATIONS OF WORKING CAPITAL

Comparison of the diagram above with the one on page 827, which illustrated the common sources and applications of cash, indicates that both cash and working capital often flow in from the same source and are used for the same purpose. However, in determining the amount of working capital flows for the funds statement based on working capital, two items must be determined in a manner that differs from that used for the cash basis funds statement. These two differences relate to the determining of (1) the working capital provided by operations and (2) the working capital applied to the declaration of cash dividends. In determining the working capital provided by operations, the reported net income must be adjusted for income statement items that do not decrease or increase working capital. In determining the working capital applied to the declaration of cash dividends, the focus must be on the reduction in working capital resulting from the declaration of the dividends.

ASSEMBLING DATA FOR THE FUNDS STATEMENT BASED ON WORKING CAPITAL

With two exceptions, as noted above, the funds statement based on working capital is prepared by using the same type of analysis as discussed earlier in the chapter for the funds statement based on cash.[6] For determining these two items, which relate to the working capital provided by operations and the working capital applied to the declaration of dividends, an analysis of the retained earnings account is the starting point.

Working Capital Provided by Operations

The retained earnings account for T. R. Morgan Corporation, shown as follows, indicates a credit for $140,500 of net income:

ACCOUNT RETAINED EARNINGS					ACCOUNT NO.	
					Balance	
Date		Item	Debit	Credit	Debit	Credit
1988 Jan.	1	Balance				112,000
Dec.	31	Net income		140,500		
	31	Cash dividends	30,000			222,500

The net income, which is reported on the income statement, must usually be adjusted upward and/or downward to determine the amount of working capital provided by operations. Although most operating expenses either decrease current assets or increase current liabilities, thus affecting working

---

[6]The use of a work sheet as an aid in assembling data for the funds statement is presented in Appendix D.

capital, the depreciation of plant assets and the amortization of intangibles and bond premiums and discounts do not do so. For T. R. Morgan Corporation, the $140,500 of net income understates the amount of working capital provided by operations to the extent that depreciation expense is deducted from revenue. Accordingly, the depreciation expense for the year on the equipment ($12,000) and the building ($6,000), totaling $18,000, must be added back to the net income.

The data to be reported as working capital provided by operations is noted on the funds statement as follows:

Source of working capital:	
Operations during the year:	
Net income..............................	$140,500
Add item not decreasing working	
capital during the year:	
Depreciation..........................	18,000
Working capital provided by operations	$158,500

Working Capital Applied to the Declaration of Dividends

Working capital is applied to cash dividends at the time the current liability is incurred, regardless of when the dividends are actually paid. The effect of the declaration of cash dividends of $30,000, recorded as a debit in the retained earnings account, is indicated on the funds statement as follows:

Application of working capital:	
Declaration of cash dividends	$30,000

Other Sources and Applications of Working Capital

Reference to the earlier analysis for the funds statement based on cash discloses that the sale of preferred stock and investments yielded cash and that there were cash outlays for equipment and the retirement of bonds. These transactions affected working capital and may be noted on the funds statement as follows:

Sources of working capital:	
Issuance of $50 par preferred stock at $60...............	$ 60,000
Book value of investment sold (excludes $30,000 gain	
reported in net income)	45,000
Applications of working capital:	
Purchase of equipment	$ 107,000
Retirement of bonds payable	125,000

The earlier analysis also indicated that land was acquired by the issuance of common stock. Although the transaction did not involve working capital, it resulted in a significant change in financial position and should be reported on the funds statement. The following notation indicates the manner in which the transaction is to be reported on the statement:

Source of working capital:
Issuance of common stock at par for land. $50,000

Application of working capital:
Purchase of land by issuance of common stock at par $50,000

FORM OF THE FUNDS STATEMENT BASED ON WORKING CAPITAL

Although there are many possible variations in the form and the content of the funds statement, the first section is usually devoted to the source of funds, with income from operations presented as the first item. The second section is devoted to the application or use of funds. The difference between the totals of the sources section and the applications section is identified as the increase or the decrease in working capital.

The net change in the amount of working capital reported on the statement should be supported by details of the changes in each of the working capital components.[7] The information may be presented in a third section of the statement, as in the illustration on page 846 for T. R. Morgan Corporation, or it may be presented as a separate tabulation accompanying the statement. The data required in either case can be taken from the comparative balance sheet. The two amounts identified as the increase or decrease in working capital ($1,500 increase in the illustration) must agree.

An analysis of the funds statement for T. R. Morgan Corporation indicates that operations provided the majority of the funds during the year ($158,500). Because there are limits to the amount of funds that can be provided on a continuing basis from other sources, such as a sale of plant assets or an issuance of common stock, the amount of funds provided by operations is often the most significant source of funds.

An analysis of the applications section indicates that $125,000 of bonds were retired, land and equipment were purchased for $157,000, and $30,000 of cash dividends were declared during the year, yet working capital increased by $1,500. The "changes in components of working capital" indicates that the current assets are more liquid at the end of the year than at the beginning. For example, the more liquid assets, cash and receivables, have increased, while the less liquid asset, inventories, has decreased. Also, the increase in the more liquid assets of cash and receivables ($32,000 increase) exceeds the increase in the current liabilities.

---

[7]*Opinions of the Accounting Principles Board, No. 19, op. cit.,* par. 12.

STATEMENT
OF CHANGES
IN FINANCIAL
POSITION—
BASED ON
WORKING
CAPITAL

*Working capital =
difference between
current assets and
current liabilities*

T. R. Morgan Corporation
Statement of Changes in Financial Position
For Year Ended December 31, 1988

Sources of working capital:
  Operations during the year:
    Net income $140,500
    Add item not decreasing working
    capital during the year:
      Depreciation   18,000

    Working capital provided by
      operations $158,500
  Issuance of preferred stock........... 60,000
  Issuance of common stock at par
    for land.......................... 50,000
  Book value of investments sold (excludes
    $30,000 gain reported in net income. .   45,000 $313,500

Applications of working capital:
  Declaration of cash dividends.......... $ 30,000
  Purchase of land by issuance of common
    stock at par....................... 50,000
  Retirement of bonds payable 125,000
  Purchase of equipment................ 107,000   312,000
Increase in working capital .... $ 1,500

Changes in components of working capital:
  Increase (decrease) in current assets:
    Cash............................. $ 23,000
    Trade receivables (net).............. 9,000
    Inventories........................ (8,000)
    Prepaid expenses .... 1,000 $ 25,000
  Increase (decrease) in current liabilities:
    Accounts payable .... $ 18,000
    Income tax payable................. (1,500)
    Dividends payable................. 7,000   23,500
Increase in working capital .... $ 1,500

CHAPTER REVIEW

KEY POINTS

1. Nature of the Statement of Changes in Financial Position.

The statement of changes in financial position (funds statement) reports a firm's significant financing and investing activities for a period, using either a cash definition or a working capital definition of funds. The funds statement is useful in analyzing both past and future profitability and solvency of a firm.

2. Funds Statement Based on Cash.

When the cash basis is used for the funds statement, the statement is divided into two main sections — sources of cash and applications of cash. The common sources of cash are (1) operating income, (2) issuance of capital stock, (3) issuance of long-term debt, and (4) sale of noncurrent assets. The common applications of cash are (1) payment of cash dividends, (2) retirement of long-term debt, and (3) purchase of noncurrent assets. The difference between the total of the sources and the total of the applications is the increase or decrease in cash for the period.

According to the all financial resources concept of funds, significant transactions that affect financial position should be reported, even though they do not affect cash. Thus, a transaction such as the issuance of common stock in redemption of bonds would be reported as both a source and an application of funds.

3. Funds Statement Based on Working Capital.

The excess of an enterprise's total current assets over its total current liabilities at a point in time may be termed its working capital or net current assets. The amount of working capital is neither increased nor decreased by a transaction that affects only current assets and/or only current liabilities.

The funds statement based on working capital is divided into a section for sources of working capital and a section for applications of working capital. There may also be a third section in which changes in the amounts of the current assets and the current liabilities are reported.

KEY TERMS

statement of changes in
   financial position 825
funds statement 825

funds 825
working capital 840

SELF-EXAMINATION QUESTIONS
Answers in Appendix B.

1. Which of the following transactions would provide cash?
    A. Issuance of common stock
    B. Acquisition of land for cash
    C. Payment of cash dividend
    D. None of the above

2. Which of the following transactions represents an application of cash?
    A. Sale of common stock for cash
    B. Issuance of bonds payable for cash
    C. Acquisition of equipment for cash
    D. None of the above

3. The net income reported on the income statement for the year was $55,000 and depreciation on plant assets for the year was $22,000. The balances of the current asset and current liability accounts at the beginning and end of the year are as follows:

	End	Beginning
Cash	$ 65,000	$ 70,000
Trade receivables..........................	100,000	90,000
Inventories	145,000	150,000
Prepaid expenses..........................	7,500	8,000
Accounts payable (merchandise creditors)	51,000	58,000

    The total amount reported for cash provided by operations in the statement of changes in financial position would be:
    A. $33,000   C. $77,000
    B. $55,000   D. none of the above

4. Based on the data presented in Question 3, the total amount reported for the working capital provided by operations in the statement of changes in financial position would be:
    A. $33,000   C. $77,000
    B. $55,000   D. none of the above

5. If an enterprise's total current assets are $225,000 and its total current liabilities are $150,000, its working capital is:
    A. $75,000   C. $375,000
    B. $225,000   D. none of the above

ILLUSTRATIVE PROBLEM

The comparative balance sheet of Jones Inc. for December 31, 1988 and 1987, is as follows:

Assets	1988	1987
Cash..	$ 55,100	$ 42,500
Trade receivables (net)...........................	91,350	61,150
Inventories.......................................	104,500	109,500
Prepaid expenses	3,600	2,700
Land..	50,000	50,000
Buildings	325,000	245,000
Accumulated depreciation—buildings...............	(120,600)	(110,400)
Machinery and equipment	255,000	255,000
Accumulated depreciation—machinery and equipment .	(92,000)	(65,000)
Patents...	35,000	40,000
	$706,950	$630,450

Liabilities and Stockholders' Equity		
Accounts payable (merchandise creditors)..........	$ 61,150	$ 75,000
Dividends payable	15,000	10,000
Salaries payable..................................	6,650	7,550
Mortgage note payable, due 1995	50,000	—
Bonds payable	—	75,000
Common stock, $20 par...........................	300,000	250,000
Premium on common stock.......................	100,000	75,000
Retained earnings	174,150	137,900
	$706,950	$630,450

An examination of the income statement and the accounting records revealed the following additional information applicable to the current year:
(a) Net income, $96,250.
(b) Depreciation expense reported on the income statement: buildings, $10,200; machinery and equipment, $27,000.
(c) Patent amortization reported on the income statement, $5,000.
(d) A mortgage note for $50,000 was issued in connection with the construction of a building costing $80,000; the remainder was paid in cash.
(e) 2,500 shares of common stock were issued at 30 in exchange for the bonds payable.
(f) Cash dividends declared, $60,000.

Instructions:

1. Prepare a statement of changes in financial position based on cash. Include in the statement a summary of the change in the cash balance.
2. Prepare a statement of changes in financial position based on working capital. Include in the statement a section for changes in the components of working capital.

SOLUTION   *cash*

(1)   Jones Inc.
              Statement of Changes in Financial Position
                   For Year Ended December 31, 1988

Sources of cash:
  Operations during the year:
    Net income............... $ 96,250
    Add items not decreasing
    cash during the year:
      Depreciation............. $37,200
      Amortization of patents ..   5,000
      Decrease in inventories...   5,000   47,200
                                                $143,450

    Deduct items not increasing
    cash during the year:
      Increase in trade
        receivables (net) $30,200
      Increase in prepaid
        expenses.............   900
      Decrease in accounts
        payable.............   13,850
      Decrease in salaries
        payable.............   900   45,850
    Cash provided by operations $97,600
    Issuance of common stock
    in exchange for bonds
      payable.................   75,000
    Issuance of mortgage note
      payable on building......   50,000 $222,600

Applications of cash:
  Payment of dividends:
    Cash dividends declared.... $ 60,000
    Less increase in dividends
      payable................   5,000 $55,000
    Retirement of bonds by issuance
      of common stock   75,000
    Construction of building......   80,000   210,000
  Increase in cash............... $ 12,600

Change in cash balance:
  Cash balance,
    December 31, 1988 .... $ 55,100
  Cash balance,
    December 31, 1987   42,500
  Increase in cash............... $ 12,600

Workingcapitl

(2)

Jones Inc.
Statement of Changes in Financial Position
For Year Ended December 31, 1988

Sources of working capital:				
Operations during the year:				
Net income..............		$96,250		
Add items not decreasing working capital during the year:				
Depreciation...........	$37,200			
Amortization of patents .	5,000	42,200		
Working capital provided by operations..........			$138,450	
Issuance of common stock in exchange for bonds payable			75,000	
Issuance of mortgage note payable on building.......			50,000	$263,450
Applications of working capital:				
Declaration of cash dividends			$ 60,000	
Retirement of bonds by issuance of common stock			75,000	
Construction of building...			80,000	215,000
Increase in working capital				$ 48,450
Changes in components of working capital:				
Increase (decrease) in current assets:				
Cash....................			$ 12,600	
Trade receivables (net).....			30,200	
Inventories..............			(5,000)	
Prepaid expenses			900	$ 38,700
Increase (decrease) in current liabilities:				
Accounts payable			$(13,850)	
Dividends payable			5,000	
Salaries payable..........			(900)	(9,750)
Increase in working capital				$ 48,450

DISCUSSION QUESTIONS

1. Which of the four principal financial statements is most useful in evaluating past and planning future financing and investing activities?

2. What are the principal definitions of the term *funds,* as employed in referring to the statement of changes in financial position?

3. What is the shorter term often employed in referring to the statement of changes in financial position?

4. State the effect of each of the following transactions, considered individually, on cash:
   (a) Sold a new issue of $100,000 of bonds at 102.
   (b) Declared cash dividends of $25,000.
   (c) Sold equipment with a book value of $37,500 for $40,000.
   (d) Sold 5,000 shares of $50 par common stock at $45 per share.
   (e) Retired $500,000 of bonds on which there was $2,500 of unamortized bond discount for $501,000.
   (f) Declared a stock dividend of $30,000.
   (g) Purchased land for $250,000, giving a 5-year mortgage note payable.

5. When the total of the sources section exceeds the total of the applications section on a statement of changes in financial position based on cash, is this excess identified as an increase or as a decrease in cash?

6. A long-term investment in bonds with a cost of $70,000 was sold for $75,000 cash. (a) What was the gain or loss on the sale? (b) What was the effect of the transaction on cash? (c) How should the transaction be reported in the funds statement?

7. (a) What is the effect on cash of the declaration and issuance of a stock dividend? (b) Does the stock dividend represent a source or an application of cash?

8. On its income statement for the current year, a company reported a net loss of $50,000 from operations. On its statement of changes in financial position, it reported an increase of $25,000 in cash from operations. Explain the seeming contradiction between the loss and the increase in cash.

9. What is the effect on cash of an appropriation of retained earnings for bonded indebtedness?

10. A retail enterprise, employing the accrual method of accounting, owed merchandise creditors (accounts payable) $295,000 at the beginning of the year and $320,000 at the end of the year. What adjustment for the $25,000 increase must be made to income from operations in determining the amount of cash provided by operations? Explain.

11. If revenue from sales amounted to $940,000 for the year and trade receivables totaled $120,000 and $135,000 at the beginning and end of the year respectively, what was the amount of cash received from customers during the year?

12. If salaries payable was $95,000 and $85,000 at the beginning and end of the year respectively, should $10,000 be added to or deducted from income to determine the amount of cash provided by operations? Explain.

13. The board of directors declared cash dividends totaling $120,000 during the current year. The comparative balance sheet indicates dividends payable of $25,000 at the beginning of the year and $30,000 at the end of the year. What was the amount of cash disbursed to stockholders during the year?

14. (a) What is meant by *working capital*? (b) Name another term, other than "funds," that has the same meaning.

15. State the effect of each of the following transactions, considered individually, on working capital:
    (a) Sold, for $2,500 cash, merchandise that had cost $1,750.
    (b) Received $750 from a customer on account.
    (c) Issued 1,000 shares of $20 par common stock for $22 a share, receiving cash.
    (d) Purchased $25,000 of merchandise on account, terms 2/10, n/30.
    (e) Borrowed $50,000 cash, issuing a 5-year, 13% note.
    (f) Paid $4,000 to a creditor on account.
    (g) Purchased machinery for $22,500 on account.
    (h) Issued a $5,000, 30-day, non-interest-bearing note to a creditor in settlement of an account payable.

16. What is the effect on working capital of writing off $5,000 of uncollectible accounts against Allowance for Doubtful Accounts?

17. A corporation issued $5,000,000 of 20-year bonds for cash at 105. (a) Did the transaction provide funds or apply funds? (b) What was the amount of funds involved? (c) Was working capital affected?

18. Fully depreciated equipment costing $75,000 was discarded. What was the effect of the transaction on working capital if (a) $5,000 cash is received, (b) there is no salvage value?

19. The board of directors declared a cash dividend of $50,000 near the end of the fiscal year, which ends on December 31, payable in January. (a) What was the effect of the declaration on working capital? (b) Did the declaration represent a source or an application of working capital? (c) Did the payment of the dividend in January affect working capital, and if so, how?

20. A net loss of $45,000 from operations is reported on the income statement. The only revenue or expense item reported that did not affect working capital was depreciation expense of $30,000. Will the change in financial position attributed to operations appear in the funds statement as a source or as an application of working capital, and at what amount?

21. Assume that a corporation has net income of $150,000 that included a charge of $3,500 for the amortization of bond discount and depreciation expense of $60,000. What amount should this corporation report on its funds statement for working capital provided by operations?

22. A corporation acquired as a long-term investment all of another corporation's capital stock, valued at $5,000,000, by issuance of $5,000,000 of its own common stock.

Where should the transaction be reported on the statement of changes in financial position (a) if the cash basis is used, and (b) if the working capital basis is used?

23. Real World Focus. Tandy Corporation converted approximately $100 million of 6 1/2% debenture bonds into shares of common stock. How would this transaction be reported on the statement of changes in financial position?

EXERCISES

Exercise 19–1.   Cash provided by operations section. The net income reported on the income statement for the current year was $87,100. Depreciation recorded on equipment and a building amounted to $32,250 for the year. Balances of the current asset and current liability accounts at the beginning and end of the year are as follows:

	End of Year	Beginning of Year
Cash	$ 61,125	$58,725
Trade receivables	87,500	80,000
Inventories	110,000	95,000
Prepaid expenses	6,900	7,650
Accounts payable (merchandise creditors)	77,200	72,700
Salaries payable	3,750	6,250

Prepare the cash provided by operations section of the statement of changes in financial position.

Exercise 19–2.   Reporting changes in equipment on cash basis funds statement. An analysis of the general ledger accounts indicated that office equipment, which had cost $60,000 and on which accumulated depreciation totaled $52,500 on the date of sale, was sold for $7,000 during the year. Using this information, indicate the items to be reported as a source of cash and as an application of cash on the statement of changes in financial position.

Exercise 19–3. Reporting land transactions on cash basis funds statement. On the basis of the details of the following plant asset account, indicate the items to be reported as a source of cash and as an application of cash on the statement of changes in financial position.

ACCOUNT LAND ACCOUNT NO.

Date		Item	Debit	Credit	Balance Debit	Balance Credit
19--						
Jan.	1	Balance			650,000	
Aug.	29	Purchased with long-term mortgage note	200,000			
Nov.	20	Sold for $75,000		40,000	810,000	

Exercise 19–4. Reporting stockholders' equity items on cash basis funds statement. On the basis of the following stockholders' equity accounts, indicate the items, exclusive of net income, to be reported as a source of cash and as an application of cash on the statement of changes in financial position. There were no unpaid dividends at either the beginning or end of the year.

ACCOUNT COMMON STOCK, $10 PAR ACCOUNT NO.

Date		Item	Debit	Credit	Balance Debit	Balance Credit
19--						
Jan.	1	Balance, 50,000 shares				500,000
	20	5,000 shares issued for cash		50,000		
June	25	2,750-share stock dividend		27,500		577,500

ACCOUNT PREMIUM ON COMMON STOCK ACCOUNT NO.

Date		Item	Debit	Credit	Balance Debit	Balance Credit
19--						
Jan.	1	Balance				50,000
	20	5,000 shares issued for cash		10,000		
June	25	Stock dividend		5,000		65,000

ACCOUNT RETAINED EARNINGS ACCOUNT NO.

Date		Item	Debit	Credit	Balance Debit	Balance Credit
19--						
Jan.	1	Balance				225,000
June	25	Stock dividend	32,500			
Dec.	15	Cash dividend	55,000			
	31	Net income		97,500		235,000

SPREADSHEET
PROBLEM

Exercise 19–5. Changes in components of working capital section. Using the following schedule of current assets and current liabilities, prepare the section of the statement of changes in financial position entitled "Changes in components of working capital."

	End of Year	Beginning of Year
Cash	$ 46,500	$ 41,300
Trade receivables (net)	63,100	60,000
Inventories	143,000	147,750
Prepaid expenses..................	4,700	4,850
Accounts payable	55,000	53,000
Dividends payable	15,000	15,500
Salaries payable..................	11,250	12,250

Exercise 19–6. Working capital provided by operations section. The net income reported on the income statement for the current year was $64,500. Adjustments required to determine the amount of working capital provided by operations, as well as some other data used for the year-end adjusting entries, are described as follows:

(a) Uncollectible accounts expense, $5,750.
(b) Depreciation expense, $25,000.
(c) Amortization of patents, $3,500.
(d) Interest accrued on notes payable, $1,250.
(e) Income tax payable, $10,500.
(f) Wages accrued but not paid, $2,900.

Prepare the working capital provided by operations section of the statement of changes in financial position.

Exercise 19–7. Reporting land acquisition for cash and mortgage note on funds statement based on working capital. On the basis of the details of the following plant asset account, indicate the items to be reported as a source of working capital and as an application of working capital on the statement of changes in financial position.

ACCOUNT LAND

ACCOUNT NO.

Date		Item	Debit	Credit	Balance	
					Debit	Credit
19--						
Jan.	1	Balance			750,000	
Mar.	2	Purchased for cash	100,000			
Oct.	29	Purchased with long-term mortgage note	300,000		1,150,000	

Exercise 19–8. Statement of changes in financial position based on cash. The comparative balance sheet of R. N. Corley Inc. for December 31 of the current year and the previous year is as follows:

| | December 31 | |
	Current Year	Preceding Year
Cash	$ 72,000	$ 50,500
Trade receivables (net)	88,000	80,000
Inventories	105,900	91,400
Investments	—	50,000
Land	50,000	—
Equipment	375,000	275,000
Accumulated depreciation.................	(149,000)	(114,000)
	$541,900	$432,900
Accounts payable (merchandise creditors)	$ 57,000	$ 55,000
Dividends payable	15,000	10,000
Common stock, $40 par	320,000	250,000
Premium on common stock	17,000	12,000
Retained earnings.........................	132,900	105,900
	$541,900	$432,900

(handwritten annotations in right margin: "Increase / Decrease"; 21500 +60,000; 8000; 14500 −60,000; *50,000; 50,000; 100,000; 35000; 2000; 5000; 70,000; 5,000; 27,000)*

The following additional information was taken from Corley's records:

    (a) The investments were sold for $60,000 cash.
    (b) Equipment and land were acquired for cash.
    (c) There were no disposals of equipment during the year.
    (d) The common stock was issued for cash.
    (e) There was a $64,500 credit to Retained Earnings for net income.
    (f) There was a $37,500 debit to Retained Earnings for cash dividends declared.

    Using the information and the comparative balance sheet, prepare a statement of changes in financial position based on cash, including a summary of changes in cash.

Exercise 19–9.   Statement of changes in financial position based on working capital. **From the data presented in Exercise 19–8, prepare a statement of changes in financial position based on working capital, including a summary of changes in working capital.**

PROBLEMS

Series A

Problem 19–1A.   Statement of changes in financial position based on cash. The comparative balance sheet of AZCO Company at June 30 of the current year and the preceding year is as follows:

Assets	Current Year	Preceding Year	
Cash	$ 40,750	$ 55,250	(14500)
Trade receivables	85,400	95,000	(9600)
Merchandise inventory.......................	255,300	249,200	6100
Prepaid expenses...........................	3,825	2,700	1125
Plant assets................................	321,500	289,500	32000
Accumulated depreciation — plant assets	(172,100)	(197,500)	(25400)
	$534,675	$494,150	

Liabilities and Stockholders' Equity			
Accounts payable (merchandise creditors)	$ 53,525	$ 49,150	4375
Mortgage note payable	—	75,000	
Common stock, $20 par	250,000	200,000	
Premium on common stock	40,000	25,000	
Retained earnings...........................	191,150	145,000	
	$534,675	$494,150	

Additional data obtained from the income statement and from an examination of the accounts in the ledger are as follows:

(a) Net income, $91,150.
(b) Depreciation reported on the income statement, $28,600.
(c) An addition to the building was constructed at a cost of $86,000, and fully depreciated equipment costing $54,000 was discarded, with no salvage realized.
(d) The mortgage note payable was not due until 1992, but the terms permitted earlier payment without penalty.
(e) 2,500 shares of common stock were issued at 26 for cash.
(f) Cash dividends declared, $45,000.

Instructions:

Prepare a statement of changes in financial position based on cash, including a summary of the change in the cash balance.

Problem 19–2A. Statement of changes in financial position based on working capital. The comparative balance sheet of AZCO Company and other data necessary for the analysis of the company's funds flow are presented in Problem 19–1A.

Instructions:

Prepare a statement of changes in financial position based on working capital, including a section for changes in the components of working capital.

Problem 19–3A. Statement of changes in financial position based on cash. The comparative balance sheet of A. R. Katz Corporation at December 31 of the current year and the preceding year is as follows:

SPREADSHEET
PROBLEM

Decrease

Assets	Current Year	Preceding Year	
Cash.......................................	$ 89,900	$ 82,400	—7500
Trade receivables (net).....................	117,200	132,700	*15500
Inventories................................	260,070	238,070	22000
Prepaid expenses	4,500	3,900	600
Land	100,000	100,000	0
Buildings	622,500	422,500	200,000
Accumulated depreciation—buildings...........	(210,000)	(192,000)	(18,000)
Machinery and equipment	275,000	275,000	0
Accumulated depreciation—machinery and equipment	(130,600)	(108,400)	
Patents....................................	40,500	50,000	
	$1,169,070	$1,004,170	

Liabilities and Stockholders' Equity			
Accounts payable (merchandise creditors).......	$ 36,280	$ 51,780	
Dividends payable	25,000	20,000	
Salaries payable............................	10,550	19,400	
Mortgage note payable, due 1995	150,000	—	
Bonds payable	—	100,000	
Common stock, $15 par......................	550,000	475,000	
Premium on common stock...................	75,000	50,000	
Retained earnings	322,240	287,990	
	$1,169,070	$1,004,170	

An examination of the income statement and the accounting records revealed the following additional information applicable to the current year:

(a) Net income, $84,250.
(b) Depreciation expense reported on the income statement: buildings, $18,000; machinery and equipment, $22,200.
(c) Patent amortization reported on the income statement, $9,500.
(d) A mortgage note for $150,000 was issued in connection with the construction of a building costing $200,000; the remainder was paid in cash.
(e) 5,000 shares of common stock were issued at 20 in exchange for the bonds payable.
(f) Cash dividends declared, $50,000.

18,000
22,200
40,200

Instructions:

Prepare a statement of changes in financial position based on cash, including a summary of the change in the cash balance.

Problem 19–4A.   Statement of changes in financial position based on working capital. The comparative balance sheet of A. R. Katz Corporation and other data necessary for the analysis of the corporation's funds flow are presented in Problem 19–3A.

Instructions:

Prepare a statement of changes in financial position based on working capital, including a section for changes in the components of working capital.

Problem 19–5A.   Statement of changes in financial position based on cash.

The comparative balance sheet of C. R. Lucas Inc. at December 31 of the current year and the preceding year is as follows:

Assets	Current Year	Preceding Year
Cash...	$ 97,600	$ 84,500
Trade receivables (net).........................	140,500	125,250
Income tax refund receivable....................	7,500	—
Inventories.....................................	214,150	225,650
Prepaid expenses	8,100	9,250
Investments....................................	70,000	200,000
Land..	110,000	150,000
Buildings	650,000	375,000
Accumulated depreciation—buildings...........	(173,100)	(161,500)
Equipment.....................................	507,000	392,000
Accumulated depreciation—equipment	(181,620)	(171,420)
	$1,450,130	$1,228,730

Liabilities and Stockholders' Equity		
Accounts payable (merchandise creditors).......	$ 71,400	$ 90,600
Income tax payable............................	—	9,000
Bonds payable	300,000	—
Discount on bonds payable	(24,375)	—
Common stock, $5 par	525,000	500,000
Premium on common stock....................	70,000	60,000
Appropriation for plant expansion..............	200,000	175,000
Retained earnings	308,105	394,130
	$1,450,130	$1,228,730

The noncurrent asset, the noncurrent liability, and the stockholders' equity accounts for the current year are as follows:

ACCOUNT INVESTMENTS   ACCOUNT NO.

Date		Item	Debit	Credit	Balance Debit	Balance Credit
19--						
Jan.	1	Balance			200,000	
May	5	Realized $155,000 cash from sale		130,000	70,000	

ACCOUNT LAND   ACCOUNT NO.

Date		Item	Debit	Credit	Balance Debit	Balance Credit
19--						
Jan.	1	Balance			150,000	
Aug.	15	Realized $50,000 from sale		40,000	110,000	

ACCOUNT BUILDINGS   ACCOUNT NO.

Date		Item	Debit	Credit	Balance Debit	Balance Credit
19--						
Jan.	1	Balance			375,000	
June	30	Acquired with bonds payable	275,000		650,000	

ACCOUNT ACCUMULATED DEPRECIATION — BUILDINGS   ACCOUNT NO.

Date		Item	Debit	Credit	Balance Debit	Balance Credit
19--						
Jan.	1	Balance				161,500
Dec.	31	Depreciation for year		11,600		173,100

ACCOUNT EQUIPMENT   ACCOUNT NO.

Date		Item	Debit	Credit	Balance Debit	Balance Credit
19--						
Jan.	1	Balance			392,000	
Apr.	4	Discarded, no salvage		40,000		
July	11	Purchased for cash	80,000			
Oct.	10	Purchased for cash	75,000		507,000	

ACCOUNT ACCUMULATED DEPRECIATION — EQUIPMENT   ACCOUNT NO.

Date		Item	Debit	Credit	Balance Debit	Balance Credit
19--						
Jan.	1	Balance				171,420
Apr.	4	Equipment discarded	40,000			
Dec.	31	Depreciation for year		50,200		181,620

ACCOUNT BONDS PAYABLE   ACCOUNT NO.

Date		Item	Debit	Credit	Balance Debit	Balance Credit
19--						
June	30	Issued 20-year bonds		300,000		300,000

ACCOUNT DISCOUNT ON BONDS PAYABLE   ACCOUNT NO.

Date		Item	Debit	Credit	Balance Debit	Balance Credit
19--						
June	30	Bonds issued	25,000		25,000	
Dec.	31	Amortization		625	24,375	

ACCOUNT COMMON STOCK, $5 PAR   ACCOUNT NO.

Date		Item	Debit	Credit	Balance Debit	Balance Credit
19--						
Jan.	1	Balance				500,000
July	1	Stock dividend		25,000		525,000

ACCOUNT PREMIUM ON COMMON STOCK   ACCOUNT NO.

Date		Item	Debit	Credit	Balance Debit	Balance Credit
19--						
Jan.	1	Balance				60,000
July	1	Stock dividend		10,000		70,000

ACCOUNT APPROPRIATION FOR PLANT EXPANSION   ACCOUNT NO.

Date		Item	Debit	Credit	Balance Debit	Balance Credit
19--						
Jan.	1	Balance				175,000
Dec.	31	Appropriation		25,000		200,000

ACCOUNT RETAINED EARNINGS   ACCOUNT NO.

Date		Item	Debit	Credit	Balance Debit	Balance Credit
19--						
Jan.	1	Balance				394,130
July	1	Stock dividend	35,000			
Dec.	31	Net loss	1,025			
	31	Cash dividends	25,000			
	31	Appropriated	25,000			308,105

Instructions:

Prepare a statement of changes in financial position based on cash, including a summary of the change in the cash balance.

Problem 19–6A. Statement of changes in financial position based on working capital. The comparative balance sheet of C. R. Lucas Inc. and other data necessary for the analysis of the corporation's funds flow are presented in Problem 19–5A.

Instructions:

Prepare a statement of changes in financial position based on working capital, including a section for changes in the components of working capital.

Problem 19–7A. Statements of changes in financial position based on cash and working capital. An income statement and a comparative balance sheet for Lee Company are as follows:

Lee Company
Income Statement
For Current Year Ended December 31

Sales..		$962,500
Cost of merchandise sold........................		617,500
Gross profit....................................		$345,000
Operating expenses (including depreciation of $32,200).		220,600
Income from operations		$124,400
Other income:		
Gain on sale of land	$15,000	
Gain on sale of investments	7,500	
Interest income..............................	1,600	24,100
		$148,500
Interest expense...............................		24,000
Income before income tax		$124,500
Income tax.....................................		43,000
Net income		$ 81,500

Lee Company
Comparative Balance Sheet
December 31, Current and Preceding Year

Assets	Current Year	Preceding Year
Cash..	$ 39,900	$ 46,600
Trade receivables (net).........................	109,750	94,250
Inventories....................................	169,200	152,100
Prepaid expenses	4,150	4,900
Investments...................................	27,600	75,000
Land	70,000	60,000
Buildings	330,000	180,000
Accumulated depreciation — buildings...............	(73,000)	(65,000)
Equipment....................................	395,000	350,000
Accumulated depreciation — equipment	(143,800)	(119,600)
Total assets................................	$928,800	$778,250

Liabilities and Stockholders' Equity		
Accounts payable (merchandise creditors)...........	$ 64,750	$ 50,400
Income tax payable	5,000	7,800
Dividends payable	12,500	10,000
Mortgage note payable..........................	150,000	—
Bonds payable	100,000	200,000
Common stock, $25 par..........................	350,000	300,000
Premium on common stock.......................	38,000	33,000
Retained earnings	208,550	177,050
Total liabilities and stockholders' equity...........	$928,800	$778,250

The following additional information on funds flow during the year was obtained from an examination of the ledger:

(a) Investments (long-term) were purchased for $27,600.
(b) Investments (long-term) were sold for $82,500.
(c) Equipment was purchased for $45,000. There were no disposals.
(d) A building valued at $150,000 and land valued at $50,000 were acquired by a cash payment of $50,000 and issuance of a five-year mortgage note payable for the balance.
(e) Land which cost $40,000 was sold for $55,000 cash.
(f) Bonds payable of $100,000 were retired by the payment of their face amount.
(g) 2,000 shares of common stock were issued for cash at 27 1/2.
(h) Cash dividends of $50,000 were declared.

Instructions:

(1) Prepare a statement of changes in financial position on the cash basis, including a summary of the change in the cash balance.
(2) Prepare a statement of changes in financial position on the working capital basis, including a section for changes in the components of working capital.

Problem 19–8A.   Real World Focus. The current asset and current liability sections of the December 31, 1984 and 1983 balance sheets of Gibson Greetings Inc. are as follows (dollars in thousands):

	1984	1983
Current assets:		
Cash and equivalents	$ 3,064	$ 836
Trade receivables (net)	83,681	69,335
Inventories	71,853	51,142
Prepaid expenses..........................	1,564	1,003
Deferred income taxes.....................	13,655	11,733
Total current assets	$173,817	$134,049
Current liabilities:		
Debt due within one year	$ 29,500	$ 23,674
Accounts payable..........................	8,633	8,422
Income taxes payable	9,266	19,412
Other accrued liabilities....................	23,214	19,272
Total current liabilities	$ 70,613	$ 70,780

Gibson Greetings Inc.'s "sources of funds from operations" section of the statement of changes in financial position based on working capital is as follows (dollars in thousands):

Sources of funds:	
From operations:	
Net income...	$28,347
Items not affecting funds:	
Depreciation and amortization	2,653
Deferred income taxes..............................	1,566
Total funds from operations	$32,566

Instructions:

Prepare the "sources of funds from operations" section of the statement of changes in financial position for Gibson Greetings Inc., assuming that "cash and equivalents" had been used as the basis for the statement. Use the format illustrated above in preparing this section.

Series B

Problem 19–1B. Statement of changes in financial position based on cash.
The comparative balance sheet of AIA Corporation at December 31 of the current year and the preceding year is as follows:

Assets	Current Year	Preceding Year
Cash...	$ 62,600	$ 51,250
Trade receivables...............................	55,800	58,500
Merchandise inventory	97,500	77,300
Prepaid expenses	5,300	4,650
Plant assets....................................	375,000	337,500
Accumulated depreciation — plant assets	(110,000)	(125,000)
	$486,200	$404,200

Liabilities and Stockholders' Equity		
Accounts payable (merchandise creditors)...........	$ 55,600	$ 40,100
Mortgage note payable...........................	—	50,000
Common stock, $25 par..........................	250,000	200,000
Premium on common stock.......................	55,000	25,000
Retained earnings	125,600	89,100
	$486,200	$404,200

Additional data obtained from the income statement and from an examination of the accounts in the ledger are as follows:

(a) Net income, $72,500.
(b) Depreciation reported on the income statement, $27,500.
(c) An addition to the building was constructed at a cost of $80,000, and fully depreciated equipment costing $42,500 was discarded, with no salvage realized.
(d) The mortgage note payable was not due until 1993, but the terms permitted earlier payment without penalty.
(e) 2,000 shares of common stock were issued at 40 for cash.
(f) Cash dividends declared, $36,000.

Instructions:

Prepare a statement of changes in financial position based on cash, including a summary of the change in the cash balance.

Problem 19–2B. Statement of changes in financial position based on working capital. The comparative balance sheet of AIA Corporation and other data necessary for the analysis of the corporation's funds flow are presented in Problem 19–1B.

Instructions:

Prepare a statement of changes in financial position based on working capital, including a section for changes in the components of working capital.

Problem 19–3B. Statement of changes in financial position based on cash. The comparative balance sheet of Dina Corporation at December 31 of the current year and the preceding year is as follows:

Assets	Current Year	Preceding Year
Cash...	$ 53,400	$ 46,200
Trade receivables (net)..........................	82,100	67,450
Inventories.....................................	110,500	119,750
Prepaid expenses	4,000	2,900
Land..	60,000	60,000
Buildings	345,000	265,000
Accumulated depreciation—buildings...............	(140,600)	(130,400)
Machinery and equipment	275,000	275,000
Accumulated depreciation—machinery and equipment	(92,000)	(65,000)
Patents.......................................	30,000	35,000
	$727,400	$675,900

Liabilities and Stockholders' Equity		
Accounts payable (merchandise creditors)...........	$ 52,750	$ 80,000
Dividends payable	10,000	7,500
Salaries payable................................	4,500	4,950
Mortgage note payable, due 1992	50,000	—
Bonds payable	—	100,000
Common stock, $20 par..........................	380,000	300,000
Premium on common stock.......................	80,000	60,000
Retained earnings	150,150	123,450
	$727,400	$675,900

An examination of the income statement and the accounting records revealed the following additional information applicable to the current year:

(a) Net income, $66,700.

(b) Depreciation expense reported on the income statement: buildings, $10,200; machinery and equipment, $27,000.

(c) Patent amortization reported on the income statement, $5,000.

(d) A mortgage note for $50,000 was issued in connection with the construction of a building costing $80,000; the remainder was paid in cash.

(e) 4,000 shares of common stock were issued at 25 in exchange for the bonds payable.

(f) Cash dividends declared, $40,000.

Instructions:

Prepare a statement of changes in financial position based on cash, including a summary of the change in the cash balance.

Problem 19–4B. Statement of changes in financial position based on working capital. The comparative balance sheet of Dina Corporation and other data necessary for the analysis of the corporation's funds flow are presented in Problem 19–3B.

Instructions:

Prepare a statement of changes in financial position based on working capital, including a section for changes in the components of working capital.

Problem 19–5B. Statement of changes in financial position based on cash. The comparative balance sheet of ACF Inc. at December 31 of the current year and the preceding year is as follows:

Assets	Current Year	Preceding Year
Cash..	$ 56,125	$ 60,525
Trade receivables (net)...........................	110,500	99,400
Inventories.....................................	218,750	192,700
Prepaid expenses	6,400	6,750
Investments....................................	—	75,000
Land..	47,500	47,500
Buildings	305,000	210,000
Accumulated depreciation—buildings..............	(76,400)	(69,000)
Equipment.....................................	470,500	395,500
Accumulated depreciation—equipment	(143,500)	(129,000)
	$994,875	$889,375

Liabilities and Stockholders' Equity		
Accounts payable (merchandise creditors)...........	$ 64,500	$ 80,500
Income tax payable..............................	5,900	4,800
Bonds payable	100,000	—
Discount on bonds payable	(4,875)	—
Common stock, $20 par..........................	550,000	500,000
Premium on common stock.......................	67,000	55,000
Appropriation for plant expansion..................	75,000	50,000
Retained earnings	137,350	199,075
	$994,875	$889,375

The noncurrent asset, the noncurrent liability, and the stockholders' equity accounts for the current year are as follows:

ACCOUNT INVESTMENTS   ACCOUNT NO.

Date		Item	Debit	Credit	Balance Debit	Balance Credit
19--						
Jan.	1	Balance			75,000	
Aug.	3	Realized $67,500 cash from sale		75,000	—	—

ACCOUNT LAND   ACCOUNT NO.

Date		Item	Debit	Credit	Balance Debit	Balance Credit
19--						
Jan.	1	Balance			47,500	

ACCOUNT BUILDINGS   ACCOUNT NO.

Date		Item	Debit	Credit	Balance Debit	Balance Credit
19--						
Jan.	1	Balance			210,000	
July	1	Acquired with bonds payable	95,000		305,000	

ACCOUNT ACCUMULATED DEPRECIATION — BUILDINGS   ACCOUNT NO.

Date		Item	Debit	Credit	Balance Debit	Balance Credit
19--						
Jan.	1	Balance				69,000
Dec.	31	Depreciation for year		7,400		76,400

ACCOUNT EQUIPMENT   ACCOUNT NO.

Date		Item	Debit	Credit	Balance Debit	Balance Credit
19--						
Jan.	1	Balance			395,500	
Mar.	28	Discarded, no salvage		35,000		
Sept.	12	Purchased for cash	65,000			
Nov.	21	Purchased for cash	45,000		470,500	

ACCOUNT ACCUMULATED DEPRECIATION — EQUIPMENT   ACCOUNT NO.

Date		Item	Debit	Credit	Balance Debit	Balance Credit
19--						
Jan.	1	Balance				129,000
Mar.	28	Equipment discarded	35,000			
Dec.	31	Depreciation for year		49,500		143,500

ACCOUNT BONDS PAYABLE   ACCOUNT NO.

Date		Item	Debit	Credit	Balance Debit	Balance Credit
19-- July	1	Issued 20-year bonds		100,000		100,000

ACCOUNT DISCOUNT ON BONDS PAYABLE   ACCOUNT NO.

Date		Item	Debit	Credit	Balance Debit	Balance Credit
19-- July	1	Bonds issued	5,000		5,000	
Dec.	31	Amortization		125	4,875	

ACCOUNT COMMON STOCK, $20 PAR   ACCOUNT NO.

Date		Item	Debit	Credit	Balance Debit	Balance Credit
19-- Jan.	1	Balance				500,000
July	22	Stock dividend		50,000		550,000

ACCOUNT PREMIUM ON COMMON STOCK   ACCOUNT NO.

Date		Item	Debit	Credit	Balance Debit	Balance Credit
19-- Jan.	1	Balance				55,000
July	22	Stock dividend		12,000		67,000

ACCOUNT APPROPRIATION FOR PLANT EXPANSION   ACCOUNT NO.

Date		Item	Debit	Credit	Balance Debit	Balance Credit
19-- Jan.	1	Balance				50,000
Dec.	31	Appropriation		25,000		75,000

ACCOUNT RETAINED EARNINGS   ACCOUNT NO.

Date		Item	Debit	Credit	Balance Debit	Balance Credit
19-- Jan.	1	Balance				199,075
July	22	Stock dividend	62,000			
Dec.	31	Net income		100,275		
	31	Cash dividends	75,000			
	31	Appropriated	25,000			137,350

Instructions:

Prepare a statement of changes in financial position based on cash, including a summary of the change in the cash balance.

Problem 19–6B.   Statement of changes in financial position based on working capital. The comparative balance sheet of ACF Inc. and other data necessary for the analysis of the corporation's funds flow are presented in Problem 19–5B.

Instructions:

Prepare a statement of changes in financial position based on working capital, including a section for changes in the components of working capital.

MINI-CASE 19

A.J. JENKINS
INC.

Ann Jenkins is the president and majority shareholder of A. J. Jenkins Inc., a small retail store chain. Recently, Jenkins submitted a loan application for A. J. Jenkins Inc. to Paxton State Bank. It called for a $150,000, 13%, 10-year loan to help finance the construction of a building and the purchase of store equipment costing a total of $200,000 to enable A. J. Jenkins Inc. to open another store in Paxton. Land for this purpose was acquired last year. The bank's loan officer requested a statement of changes in financial position based on cash in addition to the most recent income statement, balance sheet, and retained earnings statement that Jenkins had submitted with the loan application.

As a close family friend, Jenkins asked you to prepare a statement of changes in financial position. From the records provided, you prepared the following statement:

A. J. Jenkins Inc.
Statement of Changes in Financial Position
For Year Ended December 31, 19--

Based on cash

Sources of cash:
Operations during the year:

Net income		$ 82,500		
Add items not decreasing cash during the year:				
Depreciation	$25,500			
Decrease in trade receivables	9,000	34,500		
		$117,000		
Deduct items not increasing cash during the year:				
Increase in inventory	$ 7,500			
Increase in prepaid expenses	500			
Decrease in accounts payable	2,000	10,000		
Cash provided by operations			$107,000	
Issuance of common stock at par for land			40,000	
Book value of investments sold (excludes $5,000 gain)			30,000	$177,000

Applications of cash:

Payment of dividends			$ 50,000	
Purchase of land by issuance of common stock at par			40,000	
Purchase of store equipment			30,000	120,000
Increase in cash				$ 57,000

Change in cash balance:

Cash balance, December 31, current year				$ 97,000
Cash balance, December 31, preceding year				40,000
Increase in cash				$ 57,000

After reviewing the statement, Jenkins telephoned you and commented, "Are you sure this statement is right?" Jenkins then raised the following questions:

(a) "How can depreciation be a source of cash?"

(b) "The issuance of common stock for the land is listed both as a source and as an application of cash. This transaction has nothing to do with cash! Shouldn't the two items related to this transaction be eliminated from both the sources and applications sections?"

(c) "Why did you list only the $30,000 book value of the investments sold, excluding the gain of $5,000, as a source of funds? We actually received cash of $35,000 from the sale. Shouldn't the $35,000 be included as a source of cash?"

(d) "Why does the bank need this statement anyway? They can compute the increase in cash from the balance sheets for the last two years."

After jotting down Jenkins' questions, you assured her that this statement was "right". However, to alleviate Jenkins' concern, you arranged a meeting for the following day.

Instructions:

(1) How would you respond to each of Jenkins' questions?

(2) Do you think that the statement of changes in financial position enhances the chances of A. J. Jenkins Inc. receiving the loan? Discuss.

Chapter **20**

FINANCIAL
STATEMENT
ANALYSIS AND
ANNUAL REPORTS

Chapter Objectives:

■ Describe the need for financial statement analysis.

■ Describe the types of financial statement analysis.

■ Describe basic financial statement analytical procedures.

■ Illustrate the application of financial statement analysis in assessing solvency and profitability.

■ Identify and illustrate the content of corporate annual reports.

Rich's -- Annual Report
Financial Statement

T he financial condition and the results of operations
of business enterprises are of interest to many groups, including owners,
managers, creditors, governmental agencies, employees, and prospective
owners and creditors. The principal financial statements, together with supplementary statements and schedules, present much of the basic information
needed to make sound economic decisions regarding business enterprises. In
this chapter, the various ways in which financial statement data can be analyzed to assist in making these decisions will be discussed. In addition, annual
reports that are issued by corporations and that contain the basic financial
statements, a summary of activities for the past year, and an indication of
plans for the future are discussed. These annual reports often contain some
financial analyses as well as much of the basic information needed for additional analyses that can be used to make economic decisions regarding business enterprises.

TYPES OF FINANCIAL STATEMENT ANALYSIS

Most of the items in the principal financial statements are of limited
significance when considered individually. Users of financial statements often
gain a clearer picture through studying relationships and comparisons of
items (1) within a single year's statements, (2) in a succession of statements,
(3) with other enterprises, and (4) with industry averages. The selection and
the preparation of analytical aids are a part of the work of the accountant.

Certain aspects of financial condition or of operations are of greater importance to some interested groups than to others. In general, all groups are
interested in the ability of a business to pay its debts as they come due and to
earn a reasonable amount of income. These two aspects of the status of an

enterprise are called factors of **solvency** and **profitability**. An enterprise that cannot meet its obligations to its creditors on a timely basis may experience difficulty in obtaining credit, which may lead to a decline in its profitability, and it may even be forced into bankruptcy. Similarly, an enterprise whose earnings are less than those of its competitors is likely to be at a disadvantage in obtaining credit or new capital from stockholders. In addition to this inter-relationship between solvency and profitability, it is important to recognize that analysis of historical data is useful in assessing the past performance of an enterprise and in forecasting its future performance.

The basic analytical procedures and the various types of financial analysis useful in evaluating the solvency and profitability of an enterprise are discussed in the following paragraphs.

BASIC ANALYTICAL PROCEDURES

The analytical measures obtained from financial statements are usually expressed as ratios or percentages. For example, the relationship of $150,000 to $100,000 ($150,000/$100,000 or $150,000:$100,000) may be expressed as 1.5, 1.5:1, or 150%. This ease of computation and simplicity of form for expressing financial relationships are major reasons for the widespread use of ratios and percentages in financial analysis.

Analytical procedures may be used to compare the amount of specific items on a current statement with the corresponding amounts on earlier statements. For example, in comparing cash of $150,000 on the current balance sheet with cash of $100,000 on the balance sheet of a year earlier, the current amount may be expressed as 1.5 or 150% of the earlier amount. The relationship may also be expressed in terms of change, that is, the increase of $50,000 may be stated as a 50% increase.

Analytical procedures are also widely used to show the relationships of individual items to each other and of individual items to totals on a single statement. To illustrate, assume that included in the total of $1,000,000 of assets on a balance sheet are cash of $50,000 and inventories of $250,000. In relative terms, the cash balance is 5% of total assets and the inventories represent 25% of total assets. Individual items in the current asset group could also be related to total current assets. Assuming that the total of current assets in the example is $500,000, cash represents 10% of the total and inventories represent 50% of the total.

Increases or decreases in items may be expressed in percentage terms only when the base figure is positive. If the base figure is zero or a negative value, the amount of change cannot be expressed as a percentage. For example, if comparative balance sheets indicate no liability for notes payable on the first, or base, date and a liability of $10,000 on the later date, the increase of $10,000 cannot be stated as a percent of zero. Similarly, if a net loss of $10,000 in a particular year is followed by a net income of $5,000 in the next year, the increase of $15,000 cannot be stated as a percent of the loss of the base year.

In the following discussion and illustrations of analytical procedures, the basic significance of the various measures will be emphasized. The measures developed are not ends in themselves; they are only guides to the evaluation of financial and operating data. Many other factors, such as trends in the industry, changes in price levels, and general economic conditions and prospects, may also need consideration in order to arrive at sound conclusions.

Horizontal Analysis

The percentage analysis of increases and decreases in corresponding items in comparative financial statements is called **horizontal analysis**. The amount of each item on the most recent statement is compared with the corresponding item on one or more earlier statements. The increase or decrease in the amount of the item is then listed, together with the percent of increase or decrease. When the comparison is made between two statements, the earlier statement is used as the base. If the analysis includes three or more statements, there are two alternatives in the selection of the base: the earliest date or period may be used as the basis for comparing all later dates or periods, or each statement may be compared with the immediately preceding statement. The two alternatives are illustrated as follows:

BASE: EARLIEST YEAR

Increase (Decrease*)

| | | | | 1987–88 | | 1987–89 | |
Item	1987	1988	1989	Amount	Percent	Amount	Percent
A	$100,000	$150,000	$200,000	$ 50,000	50%	$100,000	100%
B	100,000	200,000	150,000	100,000	100%	50,000	50%

BASE: PRECEDING YEAR

Increase (Decrease*)

| | | | | 1987–88 | | 1988–89 | |
Item	1987	1988	1989	Amount	Percent	Amount	Percent
A	$100,000	$150,000	$200,000	$ 50,000	50%	$ 50,000	33%
B	100,000	200,000	150,000	100,000	100%	50,000*	25%*

Comparison of the amounts in the last two columns of the first analysis with the amounts in the corresponding columns of the second analysis reveals the effect of the base year on the direction of change and the amount and percent of change.

A condensed comparative balance sheet for two years, with horizontal analysis, is illustrated as follows:

COM-
PARATIVE
BALANCE
SHEET—
HORIZONTAL
ANALYSIS

Chung Company Comparative Balance Sheet December 31, 1988 and 1987			Increase (Decrease*)	
	1988	1987	Amount	Percent
Assets				
Current assets	$ 550,000	$ 533,000	$ 17,000	3.2%
Long-term investments	95,000	177,500	82,500*	46.5%*
Plant assets (net)	444,500	470,000	25,500*	5.4%*
Intangible assets	50,000	50,000	—	
Total assets	$1,139,500	$1,230,500	$ 91,000*	7.4%*
Liabilities				
Current liabilities	$ 210,000	$ 243,000	$ 33,000*	13.6%*
Long-term liabilities	100,000	200,000	100,000*	50.0%*
Total liabilities	$ 310,000	$ 443,000	$133,000*	30.0%*
Stockholders' Equity				
Preferred 6% stock,				
$100 par	$ 150,000	$ 150,000	—	—
Common stock, $10 par . . .	500,000	500,000	—	—
Retained earnings	179,500	137,500	$ 42,000	30.5%
Total stockholders' equity . .	$ 829,500	$ 787,500	$ 42,000	5.3%
Total liabilities and stockholders' equity	$1,139,500	$1,230,500	$ 91,000*	7.4%*

The significance of the various increases and decreases in the items shown cannot be fully determined without additional information. Although total assets at the end of 1988 were $91,000 (7.4%) less than at the beginning of the year, liabilities were reduced by $133,000 (30%) and stockholders' equity increased $42,000 (5.3%). It would appear that the reduction of $100,000 in long-term liabilities was accomplished, for the most part, through the sale of long-term investments. A statement of changes in financial position would provide more definite information about the changes in the composition of the balance sheet items.

The foregoing balance sheet may be expanded to include the details of the various categories of assets and liabilities, or the details may be presented in separate schedules. Opinions differ as to which method presents the clearer picture. A supporting schedule with horizontal analysis is illustrated by the following comparative schedule of current assets:

COM-
PARATIVE
SCHEDULE
OF CURRENT
ASSETS—
HORIZONTAL
ANALYSIS

Chung Company Comparative Schedule of Current Assets December 31, 1988 and 1987			Increase (Decrease*)	
	1988	1987	Amount	Percent
Cash....................	$ 90,500	$ 64,700	$25,800	39.9%
Marketable securities	75,000	60,000	15,000	25.0%
Accounts receivable (net) .	115,000	120,000	5,000*	4.2%*
Inventories..............	264,000	283,000	19,000*	6.7%*
Prepaid expenses	5,500	5,300	200	3.8%
Total current assets.......	$550,000	$533,000	$17,000	3.2%

The reduction in accounts receivable may have come about through changes in credit terms or improved collection policies. Similarly, a reduction in inventories during a period of increased sales probably indicates an improvement in the management of inventories.

The changes in the current assets would appear to be favorable, particularly in view of the 24.8% increase in net sales, shown in the following comparative income statement with horizontal analysis:

COM-
PARATIVE
INCOME
STATE-
MENT—
HORIZONTAL
ANALYSIS

Chung Company Comparative Income Statement For Years Ended December 31, 1988 and 1987			Increase (Decrease*)	
	1988	1987	Amount	Percent
Sales....................	$1,530,500	$1,234,000	$296,500	24.0%
Sales returns and allowances.............	32,500	34,000	1,500*	4.4%*
Net sales	$1,498,000	$1,200,000	$298,000	24.8%
Cost of goods sold	1,043,000	820,000	223,000	27.2%
Gross profit.............	$ 455,000	$ 380,000	$ 75,000	19.7%
Selling expenses	$ 191,000	$ 147,000	$ 44,000	29.9%
General expenses	104,000	97,400	6,600	6.8%
Total operating expenses..	$ 295,000	$ 244,400	$ 50,600	20.7%
Operating income	$ 160,000	$ 135,600	$ 24,400	18.0%
Other income	8,500	11,000	2,500*	22.7%*
	$ 168,500	$ 146,600	$ 21,900	14.9%
Other expense	6,000	12,000	6,000*	50.0%*
Income before income tax..	$ 162,500	$ 134,600	$ 27,900	20.7%
Income tax	71,500	58,100	13,400	23.1%
Net income	$ 91,000	$ 76,500	$ 14,500	19.0%

An increase in net sales, considered alone, is not necessarily favorable. The increase in Chung Company's net sales was accompanied by a somewhat greater percentage increase in the cost of goods (merchandise) sold, which indicates a narrowing of the gross profit margin. Selling expenses increased markedly and general expenses increased slightly, making an overall increase in operating expenses of 20.7%, as contrasted with a 19.7% increase in gross profit.

Although the increase in operating income and in the final net income figure is favorable, it would be incorrect for management to conclude that its operations were at maximum efficiency. A study of the expenses and additional analysis and comparisons of individual expense accounts should be made.

The income statement illustrated is in condensed form. Such a condensed statement usually provides enough information for all interested groups except management. If desired, the statement may be expanded or supplemental schedules may be prepared to present details of the cost of goods sold, selling expenses, general expenses, other income, and other expense.

A comparative retained earnings statement with horizontal analysis is illustrated as follows:

COM-PARATIVE RETAINED EARNINGS STATE-MENT— HORIZONTAL ANALYSIS

Chung Company Comparative Retained Earnings Statement For Years Ended December 31, 1988 and 1987			Increase (Decrease*)	
	1988	1987	Amount	Percent
Retained earnings, January 1..............	$137,500	$100,000	$37,500	37.5%
Net income for year.......	91,000	76,500	14,500	19.0%
Total	$228,500	$176,500	$52,000	29.5%
Dividends: On preferred stock	$ 9,000	$ 9,000	—	—
On common stock......	40,000	30,000	$10,000	33.3%
Total	$ 49,000	$ 39,000	$10,000	25.6%
Retained earnings, December 31	$179,500	$137,500	$42,000	30.5%

Examination of the statement reveals an increase of 30.5% in retained earnings for the year. The increase was attributable to the retention of $42,000 of the net income for the year ($91,000 net income − $49,000 dividends paid).

Vertical Analysis

Percentage analysis may also be used to show the relationship of the component parts to the total in a single statement. This type of analysis is called **vertical analysis**. As in horizontal analysis, the statements may be prepared in either detailed or condensed form. In the latter case, additional details of the changes in the various categories may be presented in supporting schedules. If such schedules are prepared, the percentage analysis may be based on either the total of the schedule or the balance sheet total. Although vertical analysis is confined within each individual statement, the significance of both the amounts and the percentages is increased by preparing comparative statements.

In vertical analysis of the balance sheet, each asset item is stated as a percent of total assets, and each liability and stockholders' equity item is stated as a percent of total liabilities and stockholders' equity. A condensed comparative balance sheet with vertical analysis is illustrated as follows:

COM-PARATIVE BALANCE SHEET— VERTICAL ANALYSIS

	1988		1987	
Chung Company Comparative Balance Sheet December 31, 1988 and 1987				
	Amount	Percent	Amount	Percent
Assets				
Current assets	$ 550,000	48.3%	$ 533,000	43.3%
Long-term investments	95,000	8.3	177,500	14.4
Plant assets (net)	444,500	39.0	470,000	38.2
Intangible assets	50,000	4.4	50,000	4.1
Total assets	$1,139,500	100.0%	$1,230,500	100.0%
Liabilities				
Current liabilities	$ 210,000	18.4%	$ 243,000	19.7%
Long-term liabilities	100,000	8.8	200,000	16.3
Total liabilities	$ 310,000	27.2%	$ 443,000	36.0%
Stockholders' Equity Preferred 6% stock,				
$100 par	$ 150,000	13.2%	$ 150,000	12.2%
Common stock, $10 par . . .	500,000	43.9	500,000	40.6
Retained earnings	179,500	15.7	137,500	11.2
Total stockholders' equity . .	$ 829,500	72.8%	$ 787,500	64.0%
Total liabilities and stockholders' equity	$1,139,500	100.0%	$1,230,500	100.0%

The major relative changes in Chung Company's assets were in the current asset and long-term investment groups. In the lower half of the balance sheet, the greatest relative change was in long-term liabilities and retained earnings. Stockholders' equity increased from 64% of total liabilities and stockholders' equity at the end of 1987 to 72.8% at the end of 1988, with a corresponding decrease in the claims of creditors.

In vertical analysis of the income statement, each item is stated as a percent of net sales. A condensed comparative income statement with vertical analysis is illustrated as follows:

Chung Company Comparative Income Statement For Years Ended December 31, 1988 and 1987				
	1988		1987	
	Amount	Percent	Amount	Percent
Sales..................	$1,530,500	102.2%	$1,234,000	102.8%
Sales returns and allowances............	32,500	2.2	34,000	2.8
Net sales	$1,498,000	100.0%	$1,200,000	100.0%
Cost of goods sold	1,043,000	69.6	820,000	68.3
Gross profit	$ 455,000	30.4%	$ 380,000	31.7%
Selling expenses	$ 191,000	12.8%	$ 147,000	12.3%
General expenses	104,000	6.9	97,400	8.1
Total operating expenses..	$ 295,000	19.7%	$ 244,400	20.4%
Operating income	$ 160,000	10.7%	$ 135,600	11.3%
Other income	8,500	.6	11,000	.9
	$ 168,500	11.3%	$ 146,600	12.2%
Other expense	6,000	.4	12,000	1.0
Income before income tax.	$ 162,500	10.9%	$ 134,600	11.2%
Income tax	71,500	4.8	58,100	4.8
Net income	$ 91,000	6.1%	$ 76,500	6.4%

COM-PARATIVE INCOME STATEMENT —VERTICAL ANALYSIS

Care must be used in judging the significance of differences between percentages for the two years. For example, the decline of the gross profit rate from 31.7% in 1987 to 30.4% in 1988 is only 1.3 percentage points. In terms of dollars of potential gross profit, however, it represents a decline of approximately $19,500 (1.3% × $1,498,000).

Common-Size Statements

Horizontal and vertical analyses with both dollar and percentage figures are helpful in disclosing relationships and trends in financial condition and operations of individual enterprises. Vertical analysis with both dollar and percentage figures is also useful in comparing one company with another or with industry averages. Such comparisons may be made easier by the use of **common-size statements**, in which all items are expressed only in relative terms.

Common-size statements may be prepared in order to compare percentages of a current period with past periods, to compare individual businesses, or to compare one business with industry percentages published by trade associations and financial information services. A comparative common-size income statement for two enterprises is illustrated as follows:

COMMON-
SIZE INCOME
STATEMENT

Chung Company and Ross Corporation Condensed Common-Size Income Statement For Year Ended December 31, 1988		
	Chung Company	Ross Corporation
Sales..........................	102.2%	102.3%
Sales returns and allowances	2.2	2.3
Net sales	100.0%	100.0%
Cost of goods sold	69.6	70.0
Gross profit................................	30.4%	30.0%
Selling expenses	12.8%	11.5%
General expenses	6.9	4.1
Total operating expenses......................	19.7%	15.6%
Operating income	10.7%	14.4%
Other income	.6	.6
	11.3%	15.0%
Other expense	.4	.5
Income before income tax.....................	10.9%	14.5%
Income tax..................................	4.8	5.5
Net income	6.1%	9.0%

Examination of the statement reveals that although Chung Company has a slightly higher rate of gross profit than Ross Corporation, the advantage is more than offset by its higher percentage of both selling and general expenses. As a consequence, the operating income of Chung Company is 10.7% of net sales as compared with 14.4% for Ross Corporation, an unfavorable difference of 3.7 percentage points.

Other Analytical Measures

In addition to the percentage analyses previously discussed, there are a number of other relationships that may be expressed in ratios and percentages. The items used in the measures are taken from the financial statements of the current period and hence are a further development of vertical analysis. Comparison of the items with corresponding measures of earlier periods is an extension of horizontal analysis.

Some of the more important ratios useful in the evaluation of solvency and profitability are discussed in the sections that follow. The examples are based on the illustrative statements presented earlier. In a few instances, data from a company's statements of the preceding year and from other sources are also used.

stop

SOLVENCY ANALYSIS

Solvency is the ability of a business to meet its financial obligations as they come due. Solvency analysis, therefore, focuses mainly on balance sheet relationships that indicate the ability to liquidate current and noncurrent liabilities. Major analyses used in assessing solvency include (1) current position analysis, (2) accounts receivable analysis, (3) inventory analysis, (4) the ratio of plant assets to long-term liabilities, (5) the ratio of stockholders' equity to liabilities, and (6) the number of times interest charges are earned.

Current Position Analysis

To be useful, ratios relating to a firm's solvency must show the firm's ability to liquidate its liabilities. The use of ratios showing the ability to liquidate current liabilities is called **current position analysis** and is of particular interest to short-term creditors.

Working Capital. The excess of the current assets of an enterprise over its current liabilities at a certain moment of time is called working capital. The absolute amount of working capital and the flow of working capital during a period of time as reported by a statement of changes in financial position are often used in evaluating a company's ability to meet currently maturing obligations. Although useful for making intra-period comparisons for a company, these absolute amounts are difficult to use in comparing companies of different sizes or in comparing such amounts with industry figures. For example, working capital of $250,000 may be very adequate for a small building contractor specializing in residential construction, but it may be completely inadequate for a large building contractor specializing in industrial and commerical construction.

Current Ratio. Another means of expressing the relationship between current assets and current liabilities is through the current ratio, sometimes referred to as the **working capital ratio** or **bankers' ratio**. The ratio is computed by dividing the total of current assets by the total of current liabilities. The determination of working capital and the current ratio for Chung Company is illustrated as follows:

	1988	1987
Current assets	$550,000	$533,000
Current liabilities	210,000	243,000
Working capital	$340,000	$290,000
Current ratio	2.6:1	2.2:1

The current ratio is a more dependable indication of solvency than is working capital. To illustrate, assume that as of December 31, 1988, the working capital of a competing corporation is much greater than $340,000, but its current ratio is only 1.3:1. Considering these factors alone, Chung Company, with its current ratio of 2.6:1, is in a more favorable position to obtain short-term credit than the corporation with the greater amount of working capital.

Acid-Test Ratio. The amount of working capital and the current ratio are two solvency measures that indicate a company's ability to meet currently maturing obligations. However, these two measures do not take into account the composition of the current assets. To illustrate the significance of this additional factor, the following current position data for Chung Company and Randall Corporation as of December 31, 1988, are as follows:

	Chung Company	Randall Corporation
Current assets:		
Cash	$ 90,500	$ 45,500
Marketable securities	75,000	25,000
Accounts receivable (net)	115,000	90,000
Inventories	264,000	380,000
Prepaid expenses	5,500	9,500
Total current assets	$550,000	$550,000
Current liabilities	210,000	210,000
Working capital	$340,000	$340,000
Current ratio	2.6:1	2.6:1

Both companies have working capital of $340,000 and a current ratio of 2.6:1. But the ability of each company to meet its currently maturing debts is vastly different. Randall Corporation has more of its current assets in inventories, which must be sold and the receivables collected before the current liabilities can be paid in full. A considerable amount of time may be required to convert these inventories into cash. Declines in market prices and a reduction in demand could also impair the ability to pay current liabilities. Conversely, Chung Company has enough cash and current assets (marketable securities and accounts receivable) which can generally be converted to cash rather quickly to meet its current liabilities.

A ratio that measures the "instant" debt-paying ability of a company is called the acid-test ratio or **quick ratio**. It is the ratio of the total **quick assets**, which are the cash, the marketable securities, and the receivables, to the total current liabilities. The acid-test ratio data for Chung Company are as follows:

	1988	1987
Quick assets:		
Cash	$ 90,500	$ 64,700
Marketable securities......................	75,000	60,000
Accounts receivable (net)	115,000	120,000
Total.....................................	$280,500	$244,700
Current liabilities...........................	$210,000	$243,000
Acid-test ratio	1.3:1	1.0:1

A thorough analysis of a firm's current position would include the determination of the amount of working capital, the current ratio, and the acid-test ratio. The current and acid-test ratios are most useful when viewed together and when compared with similar ratios for previous periods and with those of other firms in the industry.

Accounts Receivable Analysis

The size and composition of accounts receivable change continually during business operations. The amount is increased by sales on account and reduced by collections. Firms that grant long credit terms tend to have relatively greater amounts tied up in accounts receivable than those granting short credit terms. Increases or decreases in the volume of sales also affect the amount of outstanding accounts receivable.

Accounts receivable yield no revenue, hence it is desirable to keep the amount invested in them at a minimum. The cash made available by prompt collection of receivables improves solvency and may be used for purchases of merchandise in larger quantities at a lower price, for payment of dividends to stockholders, or for other purposes. Prompt collection also lessens the risk of loss from uncollectible accounts.

Accounts Receivable Turnover. The relationship between credit sales and accounts receivable may be stated as the **accounts receivable turnover**. It is computed by dividing net sales on account by the average net accounts receivable. It is preferable to base the average on monthly balances, which gives effect to seasonal changes. When such data are not available, it is necessary to use the average of the balances at the beginning and the end of the year. If there are trade notes receivable as well as accounts, the two should be combined. The accounts receivable turnover data for Chung Company are as follows. All sales were made on account.

	1988	1987
Net sales on account......................	$1,498,000	$1,200,000
Accounts receivable (net):		
Beginning of year	$ 120,000	$ 140,000
End of year	115,000	120,000
Total......................................	$ 235,000	$ 260,000
Average	$ 117,500	$ 130,000
Accounts receivable turnover...............	12.7	9.2

The increase in the accounts receivable turnover for 1988 indicates that there has been an acceleration in the collection of receivables, due perhaps to improvement in either the granting of credit or the collection practices used, or both.

Number of Days' Sales in Receivables. Another means of expressing the relationship between credit sales and accounts receivable is the **number of days' sales in receivables**. This measure is determined by dividing the net accounts receivable at the end of the year by the average daily sales on account (net sales on account divided by 365), illustrated as follows for Chung Company:

	1988	1987
Accounts receivable (net), end of year.......	$ 115,000	$ 120,000
Net sales on account......................	$1,498,000	$1,200,000
Average daily sales on account.............	$ 4,104	$ 3,288
Number of days' sales in receivables........	28.0	36.5

The number of days' sales in receivables gives a rough measure of the length of time the accounts receivable have been outstanding. A comparison of this measure with the credit terms, with figures for comparable firms in the same industry, and with figures of Chung Company for prior years will help reveal the efficiency in collecting receivables and the trends in the management of credit.

Inventory Analysis

Although an enterprise must maintain sufficient inventory quantities to meet the demands of its operations, it is desirable to keep the amount invested in inventory to a minimum. Inventories in excess of the needs of business reduce solvency by tying up funds. Excess inventories may also cause increases in the amount of insurance, property taxes, storage, and other related expenses, further reducing funds that could be used to better advantage. There is also added risk of loss through price declines and deterioration or obsolescence of the inventory.

Inventory Turnover. The relationship between the volume of goods (merchandise) sold and inventory may be stated as the inventory turnover. It is computed by dividing the cost of goods sold by the average inventory. If monthly data are not available, it is necessary to use the average of the inventories at the beginning and the end of the year. The inventory turnover data for Chung Company are as follows:

	1988	1987
Cost of goods sold	$1,043,000	$820,000
Inventories:		
Beginning of year	$ 283,000	$311,000
End of year	264,000	283,000
Total.	$ 547,000	$594,000
Average	$ 273,500	$297,000
Inventory turnover.	3.8	2.8

The improvement in the turnover resulted from an increase in the cost of goods sold, combined with a decrease in average inventory. The variation in types of inventories is too great to permit any broad generalizations as to what is a satisfactory turnover. For example, a firm selling food should have a much higher turnover than one selling furniture or jewelry, and the perishable foods department of a supermarket should have a higher turnover than the soaps and cleansers department. However, for each business or each department within a business, there is a reasonable turnover rate. A turnover below this rate means that the company or the department is incurring extra expenses such as those for administration and storage, is increasing its risk of loss because of obsolescence and adverse price changes, is incurring interest charges in excess of those considered necessary, and is failing to free funds for other uses.

Number of Days' Sales in Inventory. Another means of expressing the relationship between the cost of goods sold and inventory is the number of days' sales in inventory. This measure is determined by dividing the inventories at the end of the year by the average daily cost of goods sold (cost of goods sold divided by 365), illustrated as follows for Chung Company:

	1988	1987
Inventories, end of year.	$ 264,000	$283,000
Cost of goods sold	$1,043,000	$820,000
Average daily cost of goods sold.	$ 2,858	$ 2,247
Number of days' sales in inventory.	92.4	125.9

The number of days' sales in inventory gives a rough measure of the length of time it takes to acquire, sell, and then replace the average inventory. Although there was a substantial improvement in the second year, comparison of the measure with those of earlier years and of comparable firms is an essential element in judging the effectiveness of Chung Company's inventory control.

As with many attempts to analyze financial data, it is possible to determine more than one measure to express the relationship between the cost of goods sold and inventory. Both the inventory turnover and number of days' sales in inventory are useful for evaluating the efficiency in the management of inventory. Whether both measures are used or whether one measure is preferred over the other is a matter for the individual analyst to decide.

Ratio of Plant Assets to Long-Term Liabilities

Long-term notes and bonds are often secured by mortgages on plant assets. *The* **ratio of total plant assets to long-term liabilities** *provides a solvency measure that shows the margin of safety of the noteholders or bondholders. It also gives an indication of the potential ability of the enterprise to borrow additional funds on a long-term basis.* The ratio of plant assets to long-term liabilities of Chung Company is as follows:

	1988	1987
Plant assets (net)	$444,500	$470,000
Long-term liabilities	$100,000	$200,000
Ratio of plant assets to long-term liabilities	4.4 : 1	2.4 : 1

The marked increase in the ratio at the end of 1988 was mainly due to the liquidation of one half of Chung Company's long-term liabilities. If the company should need to borrow additional funds on a long-term basis, it is in a stronger position to do so.

Ratio of Stockholders' Equity to Liabilities

Claims against the total assets of an enterprise are divided into two basic groups, those of the creditors and those of the owners. *The relationship between the total claims of the creditors and owners provides a solvency measure that indicates the margin of safety for the creditors and the ability of the enterprise to withstand adverse business conditions.* If the claims of the creditors are large in proportion to the equity of the stockholders, there are likely to be substantial charges for interest payments. If earnings decline to the point where the company is unable to meet its interest payments, control of the business may pass to the creditors.

The relationship between stockholder and creditor equity is shown in the vertical analysis of the balance sheet. For example, the balance sheet of Chung Company presented on page 880 indicates that on December 31, 1988, stockholders' equity represented 72.8% and liabilities represented 27.2% of the sum of the liabilities and stockholders' equity (100.0%). Instead of expressing each item as a percent of the total, the relationship may be expressed as a ratio of one to the other, as follows:

	1988	1987
Total stockholders' equity	$829,500	$787,500
Total liabilities	$310,000	$443,000
Ratio of stockholders' equity to liabilities	2.7:1	1.8:1

The balance sheet of Chung Company shows that the major factor affecting the change in the ratio was the $100,000 reduction in long-term liabilities during 1988. The ratio at both dates shows a large margin of safety for the creditors.

Number of Times Interest Charges Earned

Some corporations, such as railroads and public utilities, have a high ratio of debt to stockholders' equity. In analyzing such corporations, it is customary to express *the solvency measure that shows the relative risk of the debtholders in terms of the* **number of times the interest charges are earned** during the year. The higher the ratio, the greater the assurance of continued interest payments in case of decreased earnings. *The measure also provides an indication of general financial strength,* which is of concern to stockholders and employees, as well as to creditors.

In the following data, the amount available to meet interest charges is not affected by taxes on income because interest is deductible in determining taxable income.

	1988	1987
Income before income tax.	$ 900,000	$ 800,000
Add interest charges	300,000	250,000
Amount available to meet interest charges .	$1,200,000	$1,050,000
Number of times interest charges earned	4	4.2

Analyses like the above can be applied to dividends on preferred stock. In such cases, net income would be divided by the amount of preferred dividends to yield the number of times preferred dividends were earned. This measure gives an indication of the relative assurance of continued dividend payments to preferred stockholders.

stop

PROFITABILITY ANALYSIS

Profitability is the ability of an entity to earn income. It can be assessed by computing various relevant measures, including (1) the ratio of net sales to assets, (2) the rate earned on total assets, (3) the rate earned on stockholders' equity, (4) the rate earned on common stockholders' equity, (5) earnings per share on common stock, (6) the price-earnings ratio, and (7) dividend yield.

Ratio of Net Sales to Assets

The **ratio of net sales to assets** *is a profitability measure that shows how effectively a firm utilizes its assets.* Assume that two competing enterprises have equal amounts of assets, but the amount of the sales of one is double the amount of the sales of the other. Obviously, the former is making better use of its assets. In computing the ratio, any long-term investments should be excluded from total assets because they are wholly unrelated to sales of goods or services. Assets used in determining the ratio may be the total at the end of the year, the average at the beginning and the end of the year, or the average of the monthly totals. The basic data and the ratio of net sales to assets for Chung Company are as follows:

	1988	1987
Net sales	$1,498,000	$1,200,000
Total assets (excluding long-term investments):		
Beginning of year	$1,053,000	$1,010,000
End of year	1,044,500	1,053,000
Total	$2,097,500	$2,063,000
Average	$1,048,750	$1,031,500
Ratio of net sales to assets	1.4:1	1.2:1

The ratio improved to a minor degree in 1988, largely due to the increased sales volume. A comparison of the ratio with those of other enterprises in the same industry would be helpful in assessing Chung Company's effectiveness in the utilization of assets.

Rate Earned on Total Assets

The **rate earned on total assets** *is a measure of the profitability of the assets, without regard to the equity of creditors and stockholders in the assets.* The rate is therefore not affected by differences in methods of financing an enterprise.

The rate earned on total assets is derived by adding interest expense to net income and dividing this sum by total assets. By adding interest expense to net income, the profitability of the assets is determined without considering the means of financing the acquisition of the assets. The rate earned by Chung Company on total assets is determined as follows:

	1988	1987
Net income..............................	$ 91,000	$ 76,500
Plus interest expense......................	6,000	12,000
Total.....................................	$ 97,000	$ 88,500
Total assets:		
Beginning of year.......................	$1,230,500	$1,187,500
End of year	1,139,500	1,230,500
Total.....................................	$2,370,000	$2,418,000
Average	$1,185,000	$1,209,000
Rate earned on total assets...............	8.2%	7.3%

The rate earned on total assets of Chung Company for 1988 indicates an improvement over that for 1987. A comparison with other companies and with industry averages would also be useful in evaluating the effectiveness of management performance.

It is sometimes preferable to determine the rate of operating income (income before nonoperating income, nonoperating expense, extraordinary items, and income tax) to total assets. If nonoperating income is not considered, the investments yielding such income should be excluded from the assets. The use of income before income tax eliminates the effect of changes in the tax structure on the rate of earnings. When considering published data on rates earned on assets, the reader should note the exact nature of the measure.

Rate Earned on Stockholders' Equity

Another relative measure of profitability is obtained by dividing net income by the total stockholders' equity. In contrast to the rate earned on total assets, the rate earned on stockholders' equity *emphasizes the income yield in relationship to the amount invested by the stockholders*.

The amount of the total stockholders' equity throughout the year varies for several reasons—the issuance of additional stock, the retirement of a class of stock, the payment of dividends, and the gradual accrual of net income. If monthly figures are not available, the average of the stockholders' equity at the beginning and the end of the year is used, as in the following illustration:

	1988	1987
Net income..............................	$ 91,000	$ 76,500
Stockholders' equity:		
Beginning of year	$ 787,500	$ 750,000
End of year	829,500	787,500
Total.................................	$1,617,000	$1,537,500
Average	$ 808,500	$ 768,750
Rate earned on stockholders' equity	11.3%	10.0%

The rate earned by a thriving enterprise on the equity of its stockholders is usually higher than the rate earned on total assets. The reason for the difference is that the amount earned on assets acquired through the use of funds provided by creditors is more than the interest charges paid to creditors. This tendency of the rate on stockholders' equity to vary disproportionately from the rate on total assets is sometimes called **leverage**. The Chung Company rate on stockholders' equity for 1988, 11.3%, compares favorably with the rate of 8.2% earned on total assets, as reported on the preceding page. The leverage factor of 3.1% (11.3% − 8.2%) for 1988 also compares favorably with the 2.7% (10.0% − 7.3%) differential for the preceding year. These leverage factors for Chung Company are illustrated graphically in the following charts:

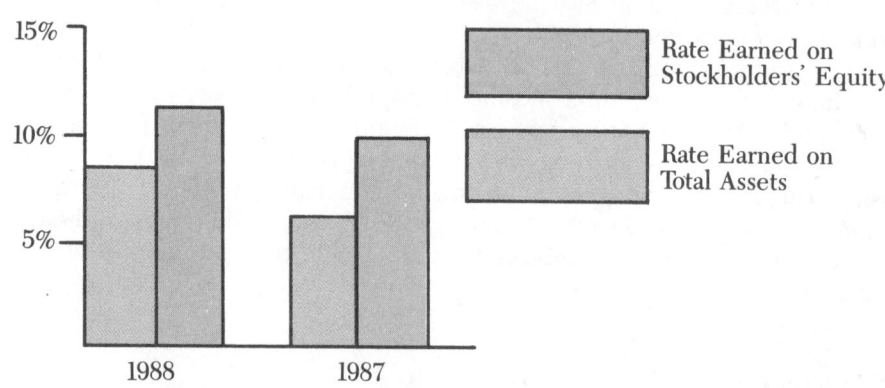

Rate Earned on Common Stockholders' Equity

When a corporation has both preferred and common stock outstanding, the holders of the common stock have the residual claim on earnings. The **rate earned on common stockholders' equity** is the net income less preferred dividend requirements for the period, stated as a percent of the average equity of the common stockholders.

Chung Company has $150,000 of 6% nonparticipating preferred stock outstanding at both balance sheet dates, hence annual preferred dividends amount to $9,000. The common stockholders' equity is the total stockholders' equity, including retained earnings, reduced by the par of the preferred stock ($150,000). The basic data and the rate earned on common stockholders' equity are as follows:

	1988	1987
Net income................................	$ 91,000	$ 76,500
Preferred dividends	9,000	9,000
Remainder — identified with common stock...	$ 82,000	$ 67,500
Common stockholders' equity:		
Beginning of year	$ 637,500	$ 600,000
End of year	679,500	637,500
Total.................................	$1,317,000	$1,237,500
Average	$ 658,500	$ 618,750
Rate earned on common stockholders' equity .	12.5%	10.9%

The rate earned on common stockholders' equity differs from the rates earned by Chung Company on total assets and total stockholders' equity. This situation will occur if there are borrowed funds and also preferred stock outstanding, which rank ahead of the common shares in their claim on earnings. Thus the concept of leverage, as discussed in the preceding section, can be applied to the use of funds from the sale of preferred stock as well as from borrowing. Funds from both sources can be used in an attempt to increase the return on common stockholders' equity.

Earnings per Share on Common Stock

One of the profitability measures most commonly quoted by the financial press and included in the income statement in corporate annual reports is **earnings per share on common stock**. If a company has issued only one class of stock, the earnings per share are determined by dividing net income by the number of shares of stock outstanding. If there are both preferred and common stock outstanding, the net income must first be reduced by the amount necessary to meet the preferred dividend requirements.

Any changes in the number of shares outstanding during the year, such as would result from stock dividends or stock splits, should be disclosed in quoting earnings per share on common stock. Also if there are any nonrecurring (extraordinary, etc.) items in the income statement, as discussed in Chapter 16, the income per share before such items should be reported along with net income per share. In addition, if there are convertible bonds or convertible preferred stock outstanding, also discussed in Chapter 16, the amount reported as net income per share should be stated without considering the conversion privilege, followed by net income per share assuming conversion had occurred.

The data on the earnings per share of common stock for Chung Company are as follows:

	1988	1987
Net income.	$91,000	$76,500
Preferred dividends	9,000	9,000
Remainder—identified with common stock	$82,000	$67,500
Shares of common stock outstanding	50,000	50,000
Earnings per share on common stock	$1.64	$1.35

Since earnings form the primary basis for dividends, earnings per share and dividends per share on common stock are commonly used by investors in weighing the merits of alternative investment opportunities. Earnings per share data can be presented in conjunction with dividends per share data to indicate the relationship between earnings and dividends and the extent to which the corporation is retaining its earnings for use in the business. The following chart shows this relationship for Chung Company:

CHART OF
EARNINGS
AND
DIVIDENDS
PER SHARE
OF COMMON
STOCK

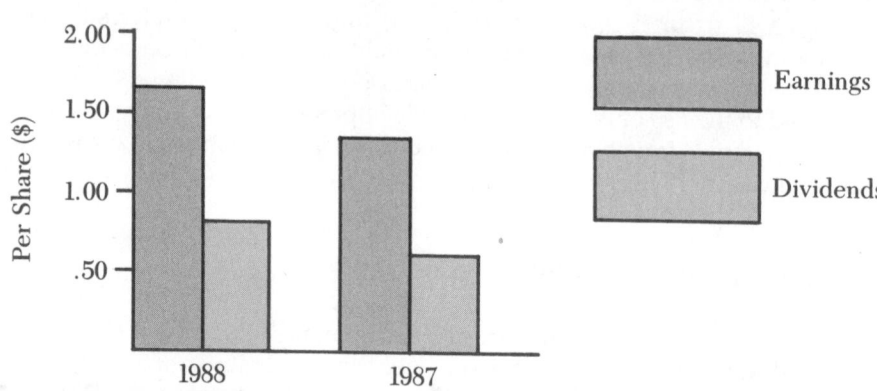

Price-Earnings Ratio

A profitability measure commonly quoted by the financial press is the **price-earnings (P/E) ratio** on common stock. *The price-earnings ratio is used as an indicator of a firm's future earnings prospects.* It is computed by dividing the market price per share of common stock at a specific date by the annual earnings per share. Assuming market prices per common share of 20 1/2 at the end of 1988 and 13 1/2 at the end of 1987, the price-earnings ratio on common stock of Chung Company is as follows:

	1988	1987
Market price per share of common stock.	$20.50	$13.50
Earnings per share on common stock	$ 1.64	$ 1.35
Price-earnings ratio on common stock	12.5	10.0

The price-earnings ratio indicates that a share of common stock of Chung Company was selling for 12.5 and 10 times the amount of earnings per share at the end of 1988 and 1987 respectively.

Dividend Yield

The **dividend yield** on common stock is a profitability measure that shows the rate of return to common stockholders in terms of cash dividend distributions. It is of special interest to investors whose main investment objective is to receive a current return on the investment rather than an increase in the market price of the investment. The dividend yield is computed by dividing the annual dividends paid per share of common stock by the market price per share at a specific date. Assuming dividends of $.80 and $.60 per common share and market prices per common share of 20 1/2 and 13 1/2 at the end of 1988 and 1987 respectively, the dividend yield on common stock of Chung Company is as follows:

	1988	1987
Dividends per share on common stock	$ .80	$ .60
Market price per share of common stock............	$20.50	$13.50
Dividend yield on common stock...................	3.9%	4.4%

SUMMARY OF ANALYTICAL MEASURES

The following presentation is a summary of the method of computation and use of the analytical measures discussed in this chapter:

	Method of Computation	Use
Solvency measures		
Working capital	Current assets − current liabilities	To indicate the ability to meet currently maturing obligations
Current ratio	$\dfrac{\text{Current assets}}{\text{Current liabilities}}$	
Acid-test ratio	$\dfrac{\text{Quick assets}}{\text{Current liabilities}}$	To indicate instant debt-paying ability
Accounts receivable turnover	$\dfrac{\text{Net sales on account}}{\text{Average accounts receivable}}$	To assess the efficiency in collecting receivables and in the management of credit
Number of days' sales in receivables	$\dfrac{\text{Accounts receivable, end of year}}{\text{Average daily sales on account}}$	

	Method of Computation	Use
(handwritten: balance sheet)		
Inventory turnover	$\dfrac{\text{Cost of goods sold}}{\text{Average inventory}}$	**To assess the efficiency in the management of inventory**
Number of days' sales in inventory	$\dfrac{\text{Inventory, end of year}}{\text{Average daily cost of goods sold}}$ *(handwritten: ÷ 365)*	
Ratio of plant assets to long-term liabilities	$\dfrac{\text{Plant assets (net)}}{\text{Long-term liabilities}}$	**To indicate the margin of safety to long-term creditors**
Ratio of stockholders' equity to liabilities	$\dfrac{\text{Total stockholders' equity}}{\text{Total liabilities}}$	**To indicate the margin of safety to creditors**
Number of times interest charges earned	$\dfrac{\text{Income before income tax + interest expense}}{\text{Interest expense}}$	**To assess the risk to debtholders in terms of number of times interest charges were earned**

Profitability measures

Ratio of net sales to assets	$\dfrac{\text{Net sales}}{\text{Average total assets (excluding long-term investments)}}$	**To assess the effectiveness in the use of assets**
Rate earned on total assets	$\dfrac{\text{Net income + interest expense}}{\text{Average total assets}}$	**To assess the profitability of the assets**
Rate earned on stockholders' equity	$\dfrac{\text{Net income}}{\text{Average stockholders' equity}}$	**To assess the profitability of the investment by stockholders**
Rate earned on common stockholders' equity *(handwritten: 16)*	$\dfrac{\text{Net income − preferred dividends}}{\text{Average common stockholders' equity}}$	**To assess the profitability of the investment by common stockholders**
Earnings per share on common stock *(handwritten: 17)*	$\dfrac{\text{Net income − preferred dividends}}{\text{Shares of common stock outstanding}}$ *(handwritten: − preferred equity)*	
Dividends per share of common stock *(handwritten: must know outstanding shares)*	$\dfrac{\text{Dividends}}{\text{Shares of common stock outstanding}}$	**To indicate the extent to which earnings are being distributed to common stockholders**
Price-earnings ratio	$\dfrac{\text{Market price per share of common stock}}{\text{Earnings per share on common stock}}$	**To indicate future earnings prospects, based on the relationship between market value of common stock and earnings**
Dividend yield	$\dfrac{\text{Dividends per common share}}{\text{Market price per common share}}$	**To indicate the rate of return to common stockholders in terms of dividends**

Perceptions of Financial Ratios

Financial statements serve as the primary financial reporting mechanism of an entity, both internally and externally. An analysis of the financial information communicated by these statements should include the computation and interpretation of financial ratios.

A survey of the views of financial executives on important issues relating to financial ratios indicated that financial ratios are an important tool in analyzing the financial results of a company and in managing a company. In addition, 93 of the 100 respondents to the survey indicated that their firms use financial ratios as part of their corporate objectives. The ratios most significant to the respondents are those that measure the ability of the firm to earn a profit.

Source: Adapted from Charles H. Gibson, "How Industry Perceives Financial Ratios," *Management Accounting* (April, 1982), pp. 13–19.

Financial ratios are often more useful when they are compared with similar ratios of other companies or groups of companies. For this purpose, average ratios for many industries are compiled by various financial services and trade associations. In this process, however, it should be remembered that averages are just that—averages—and care should be taken in their use. The danger in interpreting averages was graphically illustrated by Eldon Grimm, a Wall Street analyst who said: "A statistician is an individual who has his head in the refrigerator, his feet in the oven and on the average feels comfortable."

Source: Quotation from "Twenty-Five Years Ago in *Forbes*," *Forbes* (August 16, 1982), p. 107.

The analytical measures that have been discussed and illustrated are representative of many that can be developed for a medium-size merchandising enterprise. Some of them might well be omitted in analyzing a specific firm, or additional measures could be developed. The type of business activity, the capital structure, and the size of the enterprise usually affect the measures used.

Percentage analyses, ratios, turnovers, and other measures of financial position and operating results are useful analytical devices. They are helpful in appraising the present performance of an enterprise and in forecasting its future. They are not, however, a substitute for sound judgment, nor do they provide definitive guides to action. In selecting and interpreting analytical indexes, proper consideration should be given to any conditions peculiar to the enterprise or to the industry of which the enterprise is a part. The possible influence of the general economic and business environment should also be weighed.

To determine trends, the interrelationship of the measures used in appraising a certain enterprise should be carefully studied, as should comparable indexes of earlier fiscal periods. Data from competing enterprises may also be compared in order to determine the relative efficiency of the firm being analyzed. In making such comparisons, however, it is essential to consider the potential effects of any significant differences in the accounting methods used by the enterprises.

CORPORATE ANNUAL REPORTS

Corporations ordinarily issue to their stockholders and other interested parties annual reports summarizing activities of the past year and any significant plans for the future. Although there are many differences in the form and sequence of the major sections of annual reports, one section is always devoted to the financial statements, including the accompanying notes. In addition, annual reports usually include (a) selected data referred to as financial highlights, (b) a letter from the president of the corporation, which is sometimes also signed by the chairperson of the board of directors, (c) the independent auditors' report, (d) the management report, and (e) a five- or ten-year historical summary of financial data. As a way to strengthen the relationship with stockholders, many corporations also include pictures of their products and officers or other materials. The following subsections describe the portions of annual reports commonly related to financial matters, with the exception of the principal financial statements, examples of which appear in Appendix H.

Financial Highlights

This section, sometimes called *Results in Brief,* typically summarizes the major financial results for the last year or two. It is usually presented on the first one or two pages of the annual report. Such items as sales, income before income taxes, net income, net income per common share, cash dividends, cash dividends per common share, and the amount of capital expenditures are typically presented. An example of a financial highlights section from a corporation's annual report is as follows:

FINANCIAL HIGHLIGHTS

(Dollars in thousands except per share amounts)

For the Year	Current Year	Preceding Year
Sales....................................	$1,336,750	$ 876,400
Income before income tax....................	149,550	90,770
Net income	105,120	66,190
Per common share	4.03	2.62
Dividends declared on common stock	34,990	33,150
Per common share	1.48	1.40
Capital expenditures and investments	265,120	157,050

At Year-End

	Current Year	Preceding Year
Working capital...............................	$ 415,410	$ 423,780
Total assets..................................	1,712,170	1,457,240
Long-term debt...............................	440,680	457,350
Stockholders' equity	840,350	692,950

FINANCIAL HIGHLIGHTS SECTION

There are many variations in format and content of the financial highlights section of the annual report. In addition to the selected income statement data, information about the financial position at year end, such as the amount of working capital, total assets, long-term debt, and stockholders' equity, is often provided. Other year-end data often reported are the number of common and preferred shares outstanding, number of common and preferred stockholders, and number of employees.

President's Letter

A letter by the president to the stockholders, discussing such items as reasons for an increase or decrease in net income, changes in existing plant or purchase or construction of new plants, significant new financing commitments, attention given to social responsibility issues, and future prospects, is also found in most annual reports. A condensed version of a president's letter adapted from a corporation's annual report is as follows:

To the Stockholders:

FISCAL YEAR REVIEWED

The record net income in this fiscal year resulted from very strong product demand experienced for about two thirds of the fiscal year, more complete utilization of plants, and a continued improvement in sales mix. Income was strong both domestically and internationally during this period.

PLANT EXPANSION CONTINUES

Capital expenditures during the year were $14.5 million. Expansions were in progress or completed at all locations. Portions of the Company's major new expansion at one of its West Coast plants came on stream in March of this year and will provide much needed capacity in existing and new product areas. Capital expenditures will be somewhat less during next year.

ENVIRONMENTAL CONCERN

The Company recognizes its responsibility to provide a safe and healthy environment at each of its plants. The Company expects to spend approximately $1 million in the forthcoming year to help continue its position as a constructive corporate citizen.

OUTLOOK

During the past 10 years the Company's net income and sales have more than tripled. Net income increased from $3.1 million to $10.7 million, and sales from $45 million to $181 million.

The Company's employees are proud of this record and are determined to carry the momentum into the future. The current economic slowdown makes results for the new fiscal year difficult to predict. However, we are confident and enthusiastic about the Company's prospects for continued growth over the longer term.

Respectfully submitted,

Frances B. Davis

Frances B. Davis
President

March 24, 1988

During recent years, corporate enterprises have become increasingly active in accepting environmental and other social responsibilities. In addition to the brief discussion that may be contained in the president's letter, a more detailed analysis of the company's social concerns may be included elsewhere in the annual report. Knowledgeable investors recognize that the failure of a business enterprise to meet acceptable social norms can have long-run unfavorable implications. In the near future, an important function of accounting may be to assist management in developing a statement covering the social responsibilities of corporate enterprises and what management is doing about them.

Independent Auditors' Report

Before issuing annual statements, all publicly held corporations, as well as many other corporations, engage independent public accountants, usually CPAs, to conduct an *examination* of the financial statements. Such an examination is for the purpose of adding credibility to the statements that have been prepared by management. Upon completion of the examination, which for large corporations may engage many accountants for several weeks or longer, an **independent auditors' report** is prepared. This report accompanies the financial statements. A typical report briefly describes, in two paragraphs, (1) the scope of the auditors' examination and (2) their opinion as to the fairness of the statements. The wording used in the following report for General Motors Corporation conforms with general usage.[1]

**Deloitte
Haskins + Sells**
CERTIFIED PUBLIC ACCOUNTANTS

1114 Avenue of the Americas
New York, New York 10036

February 3, 1986

General Motors Corporation, its Directors and Stockholders:

We have examined the Consolidated Balance Sheet of General Motors Corporation and consolidated subsidiaries as of December 31, 1985 and 1984 and the related Statements of Consolidated Income and Changes in Consolidated Financial Position for each of the three years in the period ended December 31, 1985. Our examinations were made in accordance with generally accepted auditing standards and, accordingly, included such tests of the accounting records and such other auditing procedures as we considered necessary in the circumstances.

In our opinion, these financial statements present fairly the financial position of the companies at December 31, 1985 and 1984 and the results of their operations and the changes in their financial position for each of the three years in the period ended December 31, 1985, in conformity with generally accepted accounting principles applied on a consistent basis.

Deloitte Haskins + Sells

INDEPEN-
DENT
AUDITORS'
REPORT
SECTION

non qualified opinion

---

[1]*Codification of Statements on Auditing Standards* (New York: American Institute of Certified Public Accountants, 1986), par. 509.07.

In most instances, the auditors can render a report such as the one illustrated, which may be said to be "unqualified." However, it is possible that accounting methods used by a client do not conform with generally accepted accounting principles or that a client has not been consistent in the application of principles. In such cases, a "qualified" opinion must be rendered and the exception briefly described. If the effect of the departure from accepted principles is sufficiently material, an "adverse" or negative opinion must be issued and the exception described. In rare circumstances, the auditors may be unable to perform sufficient auditing procedures to enable them to reach a conclusion as to the fairness of the financial statements. In such circumstances, the auditors must issue a "disclaimer" and briefly describe the reasons for their failure to be able to reach a decision as to the fairness of the statements.

Professional accountants cannot disregard their responsibility in attesting to the fairness of financial statements without seriously jeopardizing their reputations. This responsibility is described as follows:

> *The report shall either contain an expression of opinion regarding the financial statements, taken as a whole, or an assertion to the effect that an opinion cannot be expressed. When an overall opinion cannot be expressed, the reasons therefor should be stated. In all cases where an auditor's name is associated with financial statements, the report should contain a clear-cut indication of the character of the auditor's examination, if any, and the degree of responsibility he is taking.[2]*

Management Report

Responsibility for the accounting system and the resultant financial statements rests mainly with the principal officers of a corporation. In the **management report**, the chief financial officer or other representative of management (1) states that the financial statements are management's responsibility and that they have been prepared according to generally accepted accounting principles, (2) presents management's assessment of the company's internal accounting control system, and (3) comments on any other pertinent matters related to the accounting system, the financial statements, and the examination by the independent auditor.

Although the concept of a management report is relatively new, an increasing number of corporations are including such a report in the annual report. An example of such a report for Alcoa is as follows:

---

[2]*Ibid.*, par. 509.04.

Management's Report to Alcoa Shareholders

The accompanying financial statements of Alcoa and consolidated subsidiaries were prepared by management, which is responsible for their integrity and objectivity. The statements were prepared in accordance with generally accepted accounting principles and include amounts that are based on management's best judgments and estimates. The other financial information included in this annual report is consistent with that in the financial statements.

The company maintains a system of internal controls, including accounting controls, and a strong program of internal auditing. The system of controls provides for appropriate division of responsibility and the application of policies and procedures that are consistent with high standards of accounting and administration. The company believes that its system of internal controls provides reasonable assurance that assets are safeguarded against losses from unauthorized use or disposition and that financial records are reliable for use in preparing financial statements.

The Audit Committee of the Board of Directors, composed solely of directors who are not officers or employees, meets regularly with management, with the company's internal auditors, and with its independent certified public accountants, to discuss their evaluation of internal accounting controls and the quality of financial reporting. The independent auditors and the internal auditors have free access to the Audit Committee, without management's presence.

Management also recognizes its responsibility for conducting the company's affairs according to the highest standards of personal and corporate conduct. This responsibility is characterized and reflected in key policy statements issued from time to time regarding, among other things, conduct of its business activities within the laws of the host countries in which the company operates and potentially conflicting outside business interests of its employees. The company maintains a systematic program to assess compliance with these policies.

Charles W. Parry
Chairman of the Board
and Chief Executive Officer

James W. Wirth
Senior Vice President--Finance

Historical Summary

This section, for which there are many variations in title, reports selected financial and operating data of past periods, usually for five or ten years. It is usually presented in close proximity to the financial statements for the current year, and the types of data reported are varied. An example of a portion of such a report is as follows:

*usually
10 yrs*

Five-Year Consolidated Financial and Statistical Summary for Years Ended December 31 (Dollar amounts in millions except for per share data)			
For the Year	1987	1986	1983
Net sales	$1,759.7	$1,550.1	$ 997.4
Gross profit	453.5	402.8	270.8
Percent to net sales.	25.8%	26.0%	27.2%
Interest expense.	33.9	21.3	15.0
Income before income tax	172.7	163.4	87.5
Income tax.	82.8	77.8	40.2
Net income	89.9	85.6	47.3
Percent to net sales.	5.1%	5.5%	4.7%
Per common share:			
Net income	5.19	4.84	2.54
Dividends.	1.80	1.65	1.40
Return on stockholders' equity	15.9%	16.4%	11.2%
Common share market price:			
High	31	41 ½	40 ⅝
Low.	18	22 ⅜	22 ¼
Depreciation and amortization	43.3	41.0	23.6
Capital expenditures	98.5	72.1	55.5
At Year End			
Working capital.	$ 443.9	$ 434.8	$ 254.6
Plant assets — gross	704.7	620.3	453.7
Plant assets — net	420.0	362.7	263.4
Stockholders' equity	594.3	536.9	447.6
Stockholders' equity per common share. .	33.07	29.69	23.02
Number of holders of common shares . . .	39,503	39,275	43,852
Number of employees.	50,225	50,134	42,826

Other Information

The preceding paragraphs described the most commonly presented sections of annual reports related to financial matters. Some annual reports may include other financial information, such as forecasts which indicate financial plans and expectations for the year ahead, and supplemental statements reporting the effects of price-level changes on financial statements.

CHAPTER REVIEW

KEY POINTS

1. Types of Financial Statement Analysis.

Users of financial statements often gain a clearer picture of the economic condition of an entity by studying relationships and comparisons of items (1) within a single year's statements, (2) in a succession of statements, and (3) with other enterprises. Users are especially interested in solvency and profitability. Analysis of historical data in financial statements is useful in assessing the past performance of an enterprise and in forecasting its future performance.

2. Basic Analytical Procedures.

The analytical measures obtained from financial statements are usually expressed as ratios or percentages. The basic measures developed through the use of analytical procedures are not ends in themselves. They are only guides to the evaluation of financial and operating data. Many other factors, such as trends in the industry, changes in price levels, and general economic conditions and prospects, may also need consideration in order to arrive at sound conclusions.

The percentage analysis of increases and decreases in corresponding items in comparative financial statements is called horizontal analysis. Percentage analysis may also be used to show the relationship of the component parts to the total in a single statement. This type of analysis is called vertical analysis. Although vertical analysis is confined within each individual statement, the significance of both the amounts and the percentages is increased by preparing comparative statements. Vertical analysis with both dollar and percentage figures is also useful in comparing one company with another or with industry averages. Such comparisons may be made easier by the use of common-size statements, in which all items are expressed only in relative terms.

3. Solvency Analysis.

Solvency is the ability of a business to meet its financial obligations as they come due. Solvency analysis, therefore, focuses mainly on balance sheet relationships that indicate the ability to liquidate liabilities. Major analyses used in assessing solvency include (1) current position analysis, (2) accounts receivable analysis, (3) inventory analysis, (4) the ratio of plant assets to long-term liabilities, (5) the ratio of stockholders' equity to liabilities, and (6) the number of times interest charges are earned.

Current position analysis includes the assessment of working capital, the current ratio, and the acid-test ratio. Accounts receivable analysis includes the assessment of accounts receivable turnover and number of days' sales in receivables. Inventory analysis includes the assessment of inventory turnover and number of days' sales in inventory. The ratio of plant assets to long-term liabilities shows the margin of safety for the creditors. The ratio of stockholders' equity to liabilities indicates the margin of safety for the creditors and the ability of the enterprise to withstand adverse business conditions. The number of times interest charges are earned indicates the relative risk of the debtholders' continuing to receive interest payments.

4. Profitability Analysis.

Profitability is the ability of an entity to earn income. It can be assessed by computing various relevant measures, including (1) the ratio of net sales to assets, (2) the rate earned on total assets, (3) the rate earned on stockholders' equity, (4) the rate earned on common stockholders' equity, (5) earnings per share on common stock, (6) the price-earnings ratio, and (7) dividend yield.

5. Summary of Analytical Measures.

The type of business activity, the capital structure, and the size of the enterprise usually affect the measures used in financial statement analysis. These analytical measures, however, are not a substitute for sound judgment, nor do they provide definitive guides to action. In selecting and interpreting analytical indexes, proper consideration should be given to any conditions peculiar to the enterprise or to the industry of which the enterprise is a part.

6. Corporate Annual Reports.

Corporations ordinarily issue to their stockholders and other interested parties annual reports summarizing activities of the past year and any significant plans for the future. These reports normally include the financial highlights section, the president's letter, the independent auditors' report, the management report, and a historical summary of operations.

KEY TERMS

solvency 875	common-size statements 882
profitability 875	working capital 883
horizontal analysis 876	current ratio 883
vertical analysis 880	acid-test ratio 885

SELF-EXAMINATION QUESTIONS
Answers in Appendix B.

1. What type of analysis is indicated by the following?

	Amount	Percent
Current assets	$100,000	20%
Plant assets	400,000	80
Total assets	$500,000	100%

A. Vertical analysis
B. Horizontal analysis
C. Differential analysis
D. None of the above

2. Which of the following measures is useful as an indication of the ability of a firm to liquidate current liabilities?
A. Working capital
B. Current ratio
C. Acid-test ratio
D. All of the above

3. The ratio determined by dividing total current assets by total current liabilities is:
A. current ratio
B. working capital ratio
C. bankers' ratio
D. all of the above

4. The ratio of the quick assets to current liabilities, which indicates the "instant" debt-paying ability of a firm, is:
A. current ratio
B. working capital ratio
C. acid-test ratio
D. none of the above

5. A measure useful in evaluating the efficiency in the management of inventories is:
A. inventory turnover
B. number of days' sales in inventory
C. both A and B
D. none of the above

ILLUSTRATIVE PROBLEM

Fleming Inc.'s comparative financial statements for the years ending December 31, 1988 and 1987, are as follows. The market price of Fleming Inc.'s common stock was $30 on December 31, 1987, and $25 on December 31, 1988.

Fleming Inc.
Comparative Income Statement
For Years Ended December 31, 1988 and 1987

	1988	1987
Sales (all on account)	$5,125,000	$3,257,600
Sales returns and allowances	125,000	57,600
Net sales	$5,000,000	$3,200,000
Cost of goods sold	3,400,000	2,080,000
Gross profit	$1,600,000	$1,120,000
Selling expenses	$ 650,000	$ 464,000
General expenses	325,000	224,000
Total operating expenses	$ 975,000	$ 688,000
Operating income	$ 625,000	$ 432,000
Other income	25,000	19,200
	$ 650,000	$ 451,200
Other expense (interest)	105,000	64,000
Income before income tax	$ 545,000	$ 387,200
Income tax	300,000	176,000
Net income	$ 245,000	$ 211,200

Fleming Inc.
Comparative Retained Earnings Statement
For Years Ended December 31, 1988 and 1987

	1988	1987
Retained earnings, January 1	$ 723,000	$ 581,800
Add net income for year	245,000	211,200
Total	$ 968,000	$ 793,000
Deduct dividends:		
On preferred stock	$ 40,000	$ 40,000
On common stock	45,000	30,000
Total	$ 85,000	$ 70,000
Retained earnings, December 31	$ 883,000	$ 723,000

Fleming Inc.
Comparative Balance Sheet
December 31, 1988 and 1987

Assets	1988	1987
Current assets:		
Cash..	$ 175,000	$ 125,000
Marketable securities.........................	150,000	50,000
Accounts receivable (net).....................	425,000	325,000
Inventories..................................	720,000	480,000
Prepaid expenses	30,000	20,000
Total current assets.......................	$1,500,000	$1,000,000
Long-term investments	250,000	225,000
Plant assets.................................	2,093,000	1,948,000
Total assets.................................	$3,843,000	$3,173,000
Liabilities		
Current liabilities............................	$ 750,000	$ 650,000
Long-term liabilities:		
Mortgage note payable, 10%, due 1993	$ 410,000	—
Bonds payable, 8%, due 1995	800,000	$ 800,000
Total long-term liabilities...................	$1,210,000	$ 800,000
Total liabilities	$1,960,000	$1,450,000
Stockholders' Equity		
Preferred 8% stock, $100 par	$ 500,000	$ 500,000
Common stock, $10 par	500,000	500,000
Retained earnings	883,000	723,000
Total stockholders' equity....................	$1,883,000	$1,723,000
Total liabilities and stockholders' equity...........	$3,843,000	$3,173,000

Instructions:

Determine the following measures for 1988:
    (1) Working capital.
    (2) Current ratio.
    (3) Acid-test ratio.
    (4) Accounts receivable turnover.
    (5) Number of days' sales in receivables.
    (6) Inventory turnover.
    (7) Number of days' sales in inventory.
    (8) Ratio of plant assets to long-term liabilities.
    (9) Ratio of stockholders' equity to liabilities.
    (10) Number of times interest charges earned.
    (11) Number of times preferred dividends earned.
    (12) Ratio of net sales to assets.

(continued)

(13) Rate earned on total assets.
(14) Rate earned on stockholders' equity.
(15) Rate earned on common stockholders' equity.
(16) Earnings per share on common stock.
(17) Price-earnings ratio.
(18) Dividend yield.

SOLUTION

(1) Working capital: $750,000
$1,500,000 − $750,000

(2) Current ratio: 2.0:1
$1,500,000 ÷ $750,000

(3) Acid-test ratio: 1.0:1
$750,000 ÷ $750,000

(4) Accounts receivable turnover: 13.3

$$\$5,000,000 \div \frac{\$425,000 + \$325,000}{2}$$

(5) Number of days' sales in receivables: 31 days
$5,000,000 ÷ 365 = $13,699
$ 425,000 ÷ $13,699

(6) Inventory turnover: 5.7

$$\$3,400,000 \div \frac{\$720,000 + \$480,000}{2}$$

(7) Number of days' sales in inventory: 77.3 days
$3,400,000 ÷ 365 = $9,315
$ 720,000 ÷ $9,315

(8) Ratio of plant assets to long-term liabilities: 1.7:1
$2,093,000 ÷ $1,210,000

(9) Ratio of stockholders' equity to liabilities: 1.0:1
$1,883,000 ÷ $1,960,000

(10) Number of times interest charges earned: 6.2
($545,000 + $105,000) ÷ $105,000

(11) Number of times preferred dividends earned: 6.1
$245,000 ÷ $40,000

(12) Ratio of net sales to assets: 1.5:1

$$\$5,000,000 \div \frac{\$3,593,000 + \$2,948,000}{2}$$

(13) Rate earned on total assets: 10.0%

$$(\$245,000 + \$105,000) \div \frac{\$3,843,000 + \$3,173,000}{2}$$

(14) Rate earned on stockholders' equity: 13.6%

$$\$245,000 \div \frac{\$1,883,000 + \$1,723,000}{2}$$

(15) Rate earned on common stockholders' equity: 15.7%

$$(\$245,000 - \$40,000) \div \frac{\$1,383,000 + \$1,223,000}{2}$$

(16) Earnings per share on common stock: $4.10
$($245,000 - $40,000) \div 50,000$

(17) Price-earnings ratio: 6.1   *market price / earnings*
$25 \div $4.10   *per share*

(18) Dividend yield: 3.6%

$$\frac{(\$45,000 \div 50,000 \text{ shares})}{\$25}$$

DISCUSSION QUESTIONS

1. In the analysis of the financial status of an enterprise, what is meant by *solvency* and *profitability*?

2. Using the following data taken from a comparative balance sheet, illustrate (a) horizontal analysis and (b) vertical analysis.

	Current Year	Preceding Year
Accounts payable........................	$ 600,000	$ 400,000
Total current liabilities	1,250,000	1,000,000

3. What is the advantage of using comparative statements for financial analysis rather than statements for a single date or period?

4. The current year's amount of net income (after income tax) is 20% larger than that of the preceding year. Does this indicate an improved operating performance? Discuss.

5. What are common-size financial statements?

6. (a) Name the major ratios useful in assessing solvency and profitability.
   (b) Why is it important not to rely on only one ratio or measure in assessing the solvency or profitability of an enterprise?

7. Identify the measure of current position analysis described by each of the following: (a) the excess of the current assets over current liabilities, (b) the ratio of current assets to current liabilities, (c) the ratio of quick assets to current liabilities.

8. Selected condensed data taken from the balance sheet of Young Corporation at June 30, the end of the current fiscal year, are as follows:

Cash, marketable securities, and receivables..............	$300,000
Other current assets.....................................	450,000
Total current assets	$750,000
Current liabilities.......................................	$250,000

At June 30, what are (a) the working capital, (b) the current ratio, and (c) the acid-test ratio?

9. For Stapp Company, the working capital at the end of the current year is $75,000 greater than the working capital at the end of the preceding year, reported as follows. Does this mean that the current position has improved? Explain.

	Current Year	Preceding Year
Current assets:		
Cash, marketable securities, and receivables .	$360,000	$300,000
Inventories...............................	540,000	325,000
Total current assets.....................	$900,000	$625,000
Current liabilities............................	450,000	250,000
Working capital.............................	$450,000	$375,000

10. A company that grants terms of n/30 on all sales has an accounts receivable turnover for the year, based on monthly averages, of 6. Is this a satisfactory turnover? Discuss.

11. What does an increase in the number of days' sales in receivables ordinarily indicate about the credit and collection policy of the firm?

12. (a) Why is it advantageous to have a high inventory turnover? (b) Is it possible for the inventory turnover to be too high? Discuss. (c) Is it possible to have a high inventory turnover and a high number of days' sales in inventory? Discuss.

13. What does the following data taken from a comparative balance sheet indicate about the company's current ability to borrow additional funds on a long-term basis as compared to the preceding year?

	Current Year	Preceding Year
Plant assets (net)	$1,800,000	$1,700,000
Long-term liabilities.	600,000	850,000

14. What does an increase in the ratio of stockholders' equity to liabilities indicate about the margin of safety for the firm's creditors and the ability of the firm to withstand adverse business conditions?

15. In computing the ratio of net sales to assets, why are long-term investments excluded in determining the amount of the total assets?

16. In determining the number of times interest charges are earned, why are interest charges added to income before income tax?

17. In determining the rate earned on total assets, why is interest expense added to net income before dividing by total assets?

18. (a) Why is the rate earned on stockholders' equity by a thriving enterprise ordinarily higher than the rate earned on total assets?
    (b) Should the rate earned on common stockholders' equity normally be higher or lower than the rate earned on total stockholders' equity? Explain.

19. The net income (after income tax) of Olson Company was $20 per common share in the latest year and $30 per common share for the preceding year. At the beginning of the latest year, the number of shares outstanding was doubled by a stock split. There were no other changes in the amount of stock outstanding. What were the earnings per share in the preceding year, adjusted to place them on a comparable basis with the latest year?

20. The price-earnings ratio for the common stock of Daytona Company was 12 at December 31, the end of the current fiscal year. What does the ratio indicate about the selling price of the common stock in relation to current earnings?

21. Why would the dividend yield differ significantly from the rate earned on common stockholders' equity?

22. Favorable business conditions may bring about certain seemingly unfavorable ratios, and unfavorable business operations may result in apparently favorable ratios. For example, Almond Company increased its sales and net income substantially for the current year, yet the current ratio at the end of the year is lower than at the beginning of the year. Discuss some possible causes of the apparent weakening of the current position while sales and net income have increased substantially.

23. (a) What are the major components of an annual report? (b) Indicate the purpose of the financial highlights section and the president's letter.

24. (a) The typical independent auditors' report expressing an unqualified opinion consists of two paragraphs. What is reported in each paragraph? (b) Under what conditions does an auditor give a qualified opinion?

25. Real World Focus. Tandy Corporation's 1985 annual report contains supplementary data which indicates that the rate earned on total assets was 10.6% for the year ended June 30, 1985. For the same period, the rate earned on stockholders' equity was 18.4%. What is the explanation for the difference in the two rates?

EXERCISES

Exercise 20–1.   Vertical analysis of income statement. Revenue and expense data for P. A. Good Company are as follows:

	1988	1987
Sales	$900,000	$800,000
Cost of goods sold	531,000	464,000
Selling expenses	135,000	144,000
General expenses	63,000	64,000
Income tax	72,000	56,000

(a) Prepare an income statement in comparative form, stating each item for both 1988 and 1987 as a percent of sales.
(b) Comment on the significant changes disclosed by the comparative income statement.

Exercise 20–2.   Horizontal analysis of balance sheet. Balance sheet data for Dennis Company on December 31, the end of the fiscal year, are as follows:

	1988	1987
Current assets	$451,000	$410,000
Plant assets	449,000	413,800
Intangible assets	50,000	56,200
Current liabilities	100,000	90,000
Long-term liabilities	250,000	275,000
Common stock	400,000	350,000
Retained earnings	200,000	165,000

Prepare a comparative balance sheet with horizontal analysis, indicating the increase (decrease) for 1988 when compared with 1987.

SPREADSHEET
PROBLEM

Exercise 20–3.   Current position analysis. The following data were abstracted from the balance sheet of Concepcion Company:

	Current Year	Preceding Year
Cash	$ 95,500	$112,500
Marketable securities......................	45,000	50,000
Accounts and notes receivable (net)...........	189,500	187,500
Inventories................................	279,500	189,000
Prepaid expenses..........................	20,500	11,000
Accounts and notes payable (short-term)	275,000	222,500
Accrued liabilities	25,000	27,500

(a) Determine for each year (1) the working capital, (2) the current ratio, and (3) the acid-test ratio. (Present figures used in your computations.)

(b) What conclusions can be drawn from these data as to the company's ability to meet its currently maturing debts?

Exercise 20–4.   Accounts receivable analysis. The following data are taken from the financial statements for Shula Company:

	Current Year	Preceding Year
Accounts receivable, end of year	$ 662,100	$ 601,350
Monthly average accounts receivable (net)...	627,000	550,100
Net sales on account.....................	5,016,000	3,850,700

Terms of all sales are 1/10, n/60.

(a) Determine for each year (1) the accounts receivable turnover and (2) the number of days' sales in receivables.

(b) What conclusions can be drawn from these data concerning the composition of the accounts receivable?

Exercise 20–5.   Inventory analysis. The following data were abstracted from the income statement of McHale Corporation:

compute cost of goods sold

	Current Year	Preceding Year
Sales..	$4,275,500	$4,160,000
Beginning inventories... *less ending inventory*	648,000	558,000
Purchases	2,664,000	2,790,000
Ending inventories	672,000	648,000

(a) Determine for each year (1) the inventory turnover and (2) the number of days' sales in inventory.

(b) What conclusions can be drawn from these data concerning the composition of the inventories?

Exercise 20–6. Six measures of solvency or profitability. The following data were taken from the financial statements of John Britz and Co. for the current fiscal year:

Plant assets (net)	$1,250,000

Liabilities:

Current liabilities	$ 400,000
Mortgage note payable, 10%, issued 1982, due 1992...............	500,000
Total liabilities...	$ 900,000

Stockholders' equity:

Preferred 8% stock, $100 par, cumulative, nonparticipating (no change during year)..		$ 200,000
Common stock, $10 par (no change during year)..................		1,000,000

Retained earnings:

Balance, beginning of year	$687,500		
Net income	193,500	$881,000	
Preferred dividends.....................	$ 16,000		
Common dividends	65,000	81,000	
Balance, end of year..			800,000
Total stockholders' equity.......................................			$2,000,000

Net sales..	$3,975,000
Interest expense	50,000

[handwritten: ending total assets 2,900,000]

Assuming that long-term investments totaled $150,000 throughout the year and that total assets were $2,700,000 at the beginning of the year, determine the following, presenting figures used in your computations: (a) ratio of plant assets to long-term liabilities, (b) ratio of stockholders' equity to liabilities, (c) ratio of net sales to assets, (d) rate earned on total assets, (e) rate earned on stockholders' equity, (f) rate earned on common stockholders' equity.

Exercise 20–7. Five measures of solvency or profitability. The balance sheet for Culp Corporation at the end of the current fiscal year indicated the following:

Bonds payable, 12% (issued in 1975, due in 1995).........	$2,000,000
Preferred 8% stock, $100 par...........................	1,000,000
Common stock, $50 par	2,500,000

Income before income tax was $720,000, and income taxes were $320,000 for the current year. Cash dividends paid on common stock during the current year totaled $300,000. The common stock was selling for $64 per share at the end of the year. Determine each of the following: (a) number of times bond interest charges were earned, (b) number of times preferred dividends were earned, (c) earnings per share on common stock, (d) price-earnings ratio, and (e) dividend yield.

Exercise 20–8. Earnings per share. The net income reported on the income statement of Burger and Co. was $2,900,000. There were 500,000 shares of $10 par common stock and 100,000 shares of $8 preferred stock outstanding throughout the current year. The income statement included two extraordinary items: a $900,000 gain from condemnation of land and a $300,000 loss arising from flood damage, both after applicable income tax. Determine the per share figures for common stock for (a) income before extraordinary items and (b) net income.

Exercise 20–9.   Real World Focus. The following comparative income statement (in thousands of dollars) for the years ending December 31, 1984 and 1983, was adapted from the 1984 annual report of William Wrigley Jr. Company:

	1984	1983
Revenues.....................................	$596,781	$588,942
Costs and expenses:		
Cost of sales.............................	$286,189	$277,536
Selling, distribution, and general		
administrative...........................	238,737	237,082
Interest....................................	823	695
Total costs and expenses.....................	$525,749	$515,313
Earnings before income taxes.................	$ 71,032	$ 73,629
Income taxes...............................	31,370	34,465
Net earnings	$ 39,662	$ 39,164

(a) Prepare a comparative income statement for 1984 and 1983 in vertical form, stating each item as a percent of revenues. (b) Based upon (a), which 1984 income statement item(s) might warrant additional investigation?

PROBLEMS

Series A

Problem 20–1A.   Horizontal analysis for income statement. For 1988, Talman Company reported its most significant increase in net income in years. At the end of the year, Ann Talman, the president, is presented with the following condensed comparative income statement:

Talman Company
Comparative Income Statement
For Years Ended December 31, 1988 and 1987

	1988	1987
Sales.....................................	$909,000	$804,500
Sales returns and allowances	9,000	4,500
Net sales	$900,000	$800,000
Cost of goods sold.........................	548,000	480,000
Gross profit	$352,000	$320,000
Selling expenses............................	$117,000	$144,000
General expenses...........................	81,000	65,000
Total operating expenses	$198,000	$209,000
Operating income..........................	$154,000	$111,000
Other income..............................	2,000	1,000
Income before income tax....................	$156,000	$112,000
Income tax................................	58,000	42,000
Net income................................	$ 98,000	$ 70,000

Instructions:

(1) Prepare a comparative income statement with horizontal analysis for the two-year period, using 1987 as the base year.
(2) To the extent the data permit, comment on the significant relationships revealed by the horizontal analysis prepared in (1).

SPREADSHEET PROBLEM

Problem 20–2A. Vertical analysis for income statement. For 1988, Knight Company initiated an extensive sales promotion campaign that included the expenditure of an additional $75,000 for advertising. At the end of the year, John Knight, the president, is presented with the following condensed comparative income statement:

Knight Company
Comparative Income Statement
For Years Ended December 31, 1988 and 1987

	1988	1987
Sales.....................................	$841,500	$687,480
Sales returns and allowances	16,500	7,480
Net sales	$825,000	$680,000
Cost of goods sold.........................	519,750	435,200
Gross profit	$305,250	$244,800
Selling expenses............................	$198,000	$102,000
General expenses...........................	36,300	40,800
Total operating expenses	$234,300	$142,800
Operating income..........................	$ 70,950	$102,000
Other expense.............................	2,475	2,720
Income before income tax....................	$ 68,475	$ 99,280
Income tax................................	14,850	24,480
Net income................................	$ 53,625	$ 74,800

Instructions:

(1) Prepare a comparative income statement for the two-year period, presenting an analysis of each item in relationship to net sales for each of the years.
(2) To the extent the data permit, comment on the significant relationships revealed by the vertical analysis prepared in (1).

Problem 20–3A.   Common-size income statement. Revenue and expense data for the current calendar year for Regal Publishing Company and for the publishing industry are as follows. The Regal Publishing Company data are expressed in dollars; the publishing industry averages are expressed in percentages.

	Regal Publishing Company	Publishing Industry Average
Sales....................................	$8,080,000	100.6%
Sales returns and allowances	80,000	.6%
Cost of goods sold.......................	5,760,000	69.0%
Selling expenses.........................	656,000	9.0%
General expenses........................	496,000	8.2%
Other income...........................	40,000	.6%
Other expense..........................	96,000	1.4%
Income tax.............................	464,000	6.0%

Instructions:

(1) Prepare a common-size income statement comparing the results of operations for Regal Publishing Company with the industry average.
(2) As far as the data permit, comment on significant relationships revealed by the comparisons.

Problem 20–4A.   Effect of transactions on current position analysis. Data pertaining to the current position of Mullins Company are as follows:

Cash.....................................	$ 90,000
Marketable securities	40,000
Accounts and notes receivable (net)..........	120,000
Inventories	225,000
Prepaid expenses	25,000
Accounts payable	140,000
Notes payable (short-term)	75,000
Accrued liabilities.........................	35,000

Instructions:

(1) Compute (a) the working capital, (b) the current ratio, and (c) the acid-test ratio.
(2) List the following captions on a sheet of paper:

| Transaction | Working Capital | Current Ratio | Acid-Test Ratio |

Compute the working capital, the current ratio, and the acid-test ratio after each of the following transactions, and record the results in the appropriate columns. Consider each transaction separately and assume that only that transaction affects the data given above.

(a) Declared a cash dividend, $50,000.
(b) Issued additional shares of stock for cash, $100,000.
(c) Purchased goods on account, $50,000.
(d) Paid accounts payable, $60,000.
(e) Borrowed cash from bank on a long-term note, $50,000.
(f) Paid cash for office supplies, $20,000.
(g) Received cash on account, $75,000.
(h) Paid notes payable, $75,000.
(i) Declared a common stock dividend on common stock, $100,000.
(j) Sold marketable securities, $40,000.

Problem 20–5A. Effect of errors on current position analysis. Prior to approving an application for a short-term loan, Tolono National Bank required that Morgan Company provide evidence of working capital of at least $300,000, a current ratio of at least 1.5:1, and an acid-test ratio of at least 1.0:1. The chief accountant of Morgan Company compiled the following data pertaining to the current position:

Morgan Company
Schedule of Current Assets and Current Liabilities
December 31, 1987

Current assets:
Cash	$ 54,750
Marketable securities	72,500
Accounts receivable	341,500
Notes receivable	125,000
Interest receivable	6,250
Inventories	188,250
Supplies	11,750
Total current assets	$800,000

Current liabilities:
Accounts payable	$300,000
Notes payable	100,000
Total current liabilities	$400,000

Instructions:

(1) Compute (a) the working capital, (b) the current ratio, and (c) the acid-test ratio.
(2) At the request of the bank, a firm of independent auditors was retained to examine data submitted with the loan application. This examination disclosed several errors. Prepare correcting entries for each of the following errors:
  (a) A canceled check indicates that a bill for $28,750 for repairs on factory equipment had not been recorded in the accounts.
  (b) Accounts receivable of $41,500 are uncollectible and should be immediately written off. In addition, it was estimated that of the remaining receivables, 5% would eventually become uncollectible. An allowance should be made for these future uncollectible accounts.

125,000   + 2083.33

(c) Six months' interest had been accrued on the $125,000, 10%, six-month note receivable dated October 1, 1987.

(d) Supplies on hand at December 31, 1987, total $4,750.

(e) The marketable securities portfolio includes $50,000 of Dixon Company stock that is held as a long-term investment.

(f) The notes payable account consists of a 12%, 90-day note dated November 1, 1987. No interest had been accrued on the note.   *753583*

(g) Accrued wages as of December 31, 1987, totaled $30,000.

(h) Rental Income had been credited upon receipt of $72,000, which was the full *Unearned Rent* amount of a year's rent for warehouse space leased to C. A. Cox Inc., effective *Rent Income* July 1, 1987.

(3) Giving effect to each of the preceding errors separately and assuming that only that error affects the current position of Morgan Company, compute (a) the working capital, (b) the current ratio, and (c) the acid-test ratio. Use the following column headings for recording your answers:

Error	Working Capital	Current Ratio	Acid-Test Ratio

(4) Prepare a revised schedule of working capital as of December 31, 1987, and recompute the current ratio and the acid-test ratio, giving effect to the corrections of all of the preceding errors.

(5) Discuss the action you would recommend that the bank take regarding the pending loan application.

Problem 20–6A.   Eighteen measures of solvency and profitability. The comparative financial statements of C. L. Ames Inc. are as follows. The market price of C. L. Ames Inc.'s common stock was $60.50 on December 31, 1987, and $51 on December 31, 1988.

C. L. Ames Inc.
Comparative Income Statement
For Years Ended December 31, 1988 and 1987

	1988	1987
Sales (all on account)	$9,396,750	$8,024,000
Sales returns and allowances	46,750	24,000
Net sales	$9,350,000	$8,000,000
Cost of goods sold	5,984,000	4,800,000
Gross profit	$3,366,000	$3,200,000
Selling expenses	$1,496,000	$1,232,000
General expenses	673,200	658,000
Total operating expenses	$2,169,200	$1,890,000
Operating income	$1,196,800	$1,310,000
Other income	149,600	136,000
	$1,346,400	$1,446,000
Other expense (interest)	240,000	210,000
Income before income tax	$1,106,400	$1,236,000
Income tax	506,400	596,000
Net income	$ 600,000	$ 640,000

C. L. Ames Inc.
Comparative Retained Earnings Statement
For Years Ended December 31, 1988 and 1987

	1988	1987
Retained earnings, January 1	$2,770,000	$2,420,000
Add net income for year	600,000	640,000
Total.	$3,370,000	$3,060,000
Deduct dividends:		
On preferred stock	$ 90,000	$ 90,000
On common stock.	210,000	200,000
Total.	$ 300,000	$ 290,000
Retained earnings, December 31	$3,070,000	$2,770,000

C. L. Ames Inc.
Comparative Balance Sheet
December 31, 1988 and 1987

Assets	1988	1987
Current assets:		
Cash	$ 412,500	$ 363,000
Marketable securities	137,500	132,000
Accounts receivable (net)	550,000	495,000
Inventories	792,000	726,000
Prepaid expenses	88,000	44,000
Total current assets	$1,980,000	$1,760,000
Long-term investments	275,000	220,000
Plant assets	5,665,000	5,280,000
Total assets	$7,920,000	$7,260,000
Liabilities		
Current liabilities	$1,100,000	$ 990,000
Long-term liabilities:		
Mortgage note payable, 12%, due 1990	$ 250,000	—
Bonds payable, 14%, due 2007	1,500,000	$1,500,000
Total long-term liabilities	$1,750,000	$1,500,000
Total liabilities	$2,850,000	$2,490,000
Stockholders' Equity		
Preferred 9% stock, $100 par	$1,000,000	$1,000,000
Common stock, $10 par	1,000,000	1,000,000
Retained earnings	3,070,000	2,770,000
Total stockholders' equity	$5,070,000	$4,770,000
Total liabilities and stockholders' equity	$7,920,000	$7,260,000

Instructions:

Determine the following measures for 1988, presenting the figures used in your computations:
 (1) Working capital.
 (2) Current ratio.
 (3) Acid-test ratio.
 (4) Accounts receivable turnover.
 (5) Number of days' sales in receivables.
 (6) Inventory turnover.
 (7) Number of days' sales in inventory.
 (8) Ratio of plant assets to long-term liabilities.
 (9) Ratio of stockholders' equity to liabilities.
(10) Number of times interest charges earned.
(11) Number of times preferred dividends earned.
(12) Ratio of net sales to assets.
(13) Rate earned on total assets.
(14) Rate earned on stockholders' equity. ✗
(15) Rate earned on common stockholders' equity. ✗
(16) Earnings per share on common stock.
(17) Price-earnings ratio.
(18) Dividend yield.

Problem 20–7A. Report on detailed financial analysis. Ralph Lamor is considering making a substantial investment in C. L. Ames Inc. The company's comparative financial statements for 1988 and 1987 are given in Problem 20–6A. To assist in the evaluation of the company, Lamor secured the following additional data taken from the balance sheet at December 31, 1986:

Accounts receivable (net) .... $ 440,000
Inventories 674,000
Long-term investments 100,000
Total assets 6,700,000
Total stockholders' equity (preferred and common stock
  outstanding same as in 1987) 4,200,000

Instructions:

Prepare a report for Lamor, based on an analysis of the financial data presented. In preparing your report, include all ratios and other data that will be useful in arriving at a decision regarding the investment.

Series B

Problem 20–2B. Vertical analysis for income statement. For 1988, Paret Company initiated an extensive sales promotion campaign that included the expenditure of an additional $50,000 for advertising. At the end of the year, Ray Paret, the president, is presented with the following condensed comparative income statement:

Paret Company
Comparative Income Statement
For Years Ended December 31, 1988 and 1987

	1988	1987
Sales....................................	$609,000	$361,800
Sales returns and allowances	9,000	1,800
Net sales	$600,000	$360,000
Cost of goods sold.........................	372,000	216,000
Gross profit	$228,000	$144,000
Selling expenses............................	$108,000	$ 57,600
General expenses..........................	24,000	16,200
Total operating expenses	$132,000	$ 73,800
Operating income..........................	$ 96,000	$ 70,200
Other income..............................	1,800	1,440
Income before income tax....................	$ 97,800	$ 71,640
Income tax................................	24,000	18,000
Net income................................	$ 73,800	$ 53,640

Instructions:

(1) Prepare a comparative income statement for the two-year period, presenting an analysis of each item in relationship to net sales for each of the years.
(2) To the extent the data permit, comment on the significant relationships revealed by the vertical analysis prepared in (1).

Problem 20–4B. Effect of transactions on current position analysis. Data pertaining to the current position of D. Ellis Inc. are as follows:

Cash.....................................	$132,500
Marketable securities	50,000
Accounts and notes receivable (net)..........	297,500
Inventories	482,500
Prepaid expenses..........................	37,500
Accounts payable	302,500
Notes payable (short-term)	75,000
Accrued liabilities..........................	22,500

Instructions:

(1) Compute (a) the working capital, (b) the current ratio, and (c) the acid-test ratio.
(2) List the following captions on a sheet of paper:

Transaction	Working Capital	Current Ratio	Acid-Test Ratio

Compute the working capital, the current ratio, and the acid-test ratio after each of the following transactions, and record the results in the appropriate columns. Consider each transaction separately and assume that only that transaction affects the data given above.
(a) Paid accounts payable, $100,000.

(b) Sold marketable securities, $50,000.
(c) Purchased goods on account, $80,000.
(d) Paid notes payable, $75,000.
(e) Declared a cash dividend, $50,000.
(f) Declared a common stock dividend on common stock, $72,500.
(g) Borrowed cash from bank on a long-term note, $200,000.
(h) Received cash on account, $150,000.
(i) Issued additional shares of stock for cash, $150,000.
(j) Paid cash for office supplies, $30,000.

Problem 20–6B. Eighteen measures of solvency and profitability. The comparative financial statements of A. B. Peters Company are as follows. The market price of A. B. Peters Company's common stock was $64 on December 31, 1987, and $82 on December 31, 1988.

A.B. Peters Company
Comparative Income Statement
For Years Ended December 31, 1988 and 1987

	1988	1987
Sales (all on account)	$6,860,000	$4,880,000
Sales returns and allowances	110,000	80,000
Net sales	$6,750,000	$4,800,000
Cost of goods sold	4,590,000	3,120,000
Gross profit	$2,160,000	$1,680,000
Selling expenses	$ 877,500	$ 741,000
General expenses	438,750	336,000
Total operating expenses	$1,316,250	$1,077,000
Operating income	$ 843,750	$ 603,000
Other income	33,750	30,000
	$ 877,500	$ 633,000
Other expense (interest)	193,800	120,000
Income before income tax	$ 683,700	$ 513,000
Income tax	316,200	226,500
Net income	$ 367,500	$ 286,500

A.B. Peters Company
Comparative Retained Earnings Statement
For Years Ended December 31, 1988 and 1987

	1988	1987
Retained earnings, January 1	$1,084,500	$ 903,000
Add net income for year	367,500	286,500
Total	$1,452,000	$1,189,500
Deduct dividends:		
On preferred stock	$ 60,000	$ 60,000
On common stock	67,500	45,000
Total	$ 127,500	$ 105,000
Retained earnings, December 31	$1,324,500	$1,084,500

par value

par

outstanding shares

A. B. Peters Company
Comparative Balance Sheet
December 31, 1988 and 1987

Assets	1988	1987
Current assets:		
Cash	$ 337,500	$ 262,500
Marketable securities....................	150,000	—
Accounts receivable (net)	637,500	487,500
Inventories	1,080,000	720,000
Prepaid expenses.......................	45,000	30,000
Total current assets	$2,250,000	$1,500,000
Long-term investments	375,000	337,500
Plant assets.............................	3,139,500	2,922,000
Total assets	$5,764,500	$4,759,500

Liabilities		
Current liabilities.........................	$1,125,000	$ 975,000
Long-term liabilities:		
Mortgage note payable, 12%, due 1997....	$ 615,000	—
Bonds payable, 10%, due 1995..........	1,200,000	$1,200,000
Total long-term liabilities	$1,815,000	$1,200,000
Total liabilities	$2,940,000	$2,175,000

Stockholders' Equity		
Preferred $8 stock, $100 par	$ 750,000	$ 750,000
Common stock, $25 par	750,000	750,000
Retained earnings.......................	1,324,500	1,084,500
Total stockholders' equity	$2,824,500	$2,584,500
Total liabilities and stockholders' equity	$5,764,500	$4,759,500

Instructions:

Determine the following measures for 1988, presenting the figures used in your computations:
(1) Working capital.
(2) Current ratio.
(3) Acid-test ratio.
(4) Accounts receivable turnover.
(5) Number of days' sales in receivables.
(6) Inventory turnover. ← (times) 5.1 times
(7) Number of days' sales in inventory.
(8) Ratio of plant assets to long-term liabilities.   fixed assets   1.73 ; 1
(9) Ratio of stockholders' equity to liabilities.   .96 ; 1

$$\frac{877500}{193800} = 4.53 \text{ times}$$

(10) Number of times interest charges earned.
(11) Number of times preferred dividends earned. —— $367500 \div 60000 = 6.125$
(12) Ratio of net sales to assets. — $1.25 : 1$
(13) Rate earned on total assets. ————→ $367,500 \div 5,764,500 = 6.37\%$
(14) Rate earned on stockholders' equity.
(15) Rate earned on common stockholders' equity.
(16) Earnings per share on common stock.
(17) Price-earnings ratio.
(18) Dividend yield.

MINI-CASE 20

You and your sister are both presidents of companies in the same industry, CDP Inc. and RST Inc., respectively. Both companies were originally operated as a single-family business; but, shortly after your father's death in 1975, the business was divided into two companies. Your sister took over CDP Inc., located in Indianapolis, while you took over RST Inc., located in Cincinnati.

During a recent family reunion, your sister referred to the much larger rate of return to her stockholders than was the case in your company and suggested that you consider rearranging the method of financing your corporation. The difference is highlighted by the following chart, which compares the rates earned on the stockholders' equity and the assets of the two companies:

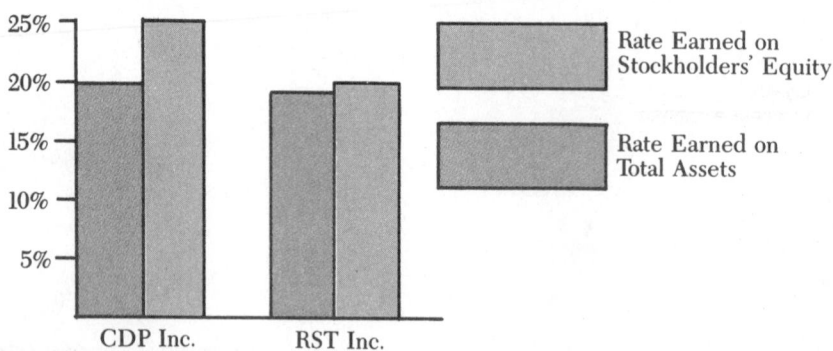

Since 1975, the growth in your sister's company has been financed largely through borrowing and yours largely through the issuance of additional common stock. Both companies have about the same volume of sales, gross profit, operating income, and total assets.

The income statements for the year ended December 31, 1988, and the balance sheets at December 31, 1988, for both companies are shown on the next page.

In addition to the 1988 financial statements, the following data were taken from the balance sheet at December 31, 1987:

	CDP Inc.	RST Inc.
Total assets	$ 800,000	$ 860,000
Total stockholders' equity	495,000	740,000

Income Statements

	CDP Inc.	RST Inc.
Sales.....................................	$2,029,500	$1,952,500
Sales returns and allowances	29,500	22,500
Net sales	$2,000,000	$1,930,000
Cost of goods sold.......................	1,225,000	1,179,000
Gross profit	$ 775,000	$ 751,000
Selling expenses.........................	$ 335,000	$ 305,750
General expenses........................	195,000	175,250
Total operating expenses	$ 530,000	$ 481,000
Operating income........................	$ 245,000	$ 270,000
Interest expense.........................	31,000	10,500
Income before income tax.................	$ 214,000	$ 259,500
Income tax	86,000	103,500
Net income..............................	$ 128,000	$ 156,000

Balance Sheets

Assets	CDP Inc.	RST Inc.
Current assets............................	$ 62,500	$ 65,000
Plant assets (net)	775,000	810,000
Intangible assets.........................	12,500	25,000
Total assets	$ 850,000	$ 900,000
Liabilities		
Current liabilities.........................	$ 25,000	$ 40,000
Long-term liabilities......................	310,000	100,000
Total liabilities	$ 335,000	$ 140,000
Stockholders' Equity		
Common stock ($10 par)..................	$ 100,000	$ 400,000
Retained earnings........................	415,000	360,000
Total stockholders' equity	$ 515,000	$ 760,000
Total liabilities and stockholders' equity	$ 850,000	$ 900,000

utilizing more plant assets

Instructions:

(1) Determine for 1988 the following ratios and other measures for both companies.
    (a) Ratio of plant assets to long-term liabilities.
    (b) Ratio of stockholders' equity to liabilities.
    (c) Ratio of net sales to assets. *she has edge on sales*
    (d) Rate earned on total assets.
    (e) Rate earned on stockholders' equity.
(2) For both CDP Inc. and RST Inc., the rate earned on stockholders' equity is greater than the rate earned on total assets. Explain. *more assets*
(3) Why is the rate of return on stockholders' equity for CDP Inc. approximately 20% greater than for RST Inc.?
(4) Comment on your sister's suggestion for rearranging the financing of RST Inc.

7 Part

ACCOUNTING FOR DECENTRALIZED OPERATIONS AND MANUFACTURING OPERATIONS

Chapter 21

RESPONSIBILITY ACCOUNTING

Chapter Objectives:

- Describe managerial accounting and distinguish managerial accounting from financial accounting.

- Describe the management process and the role of managerial accounting in this process.

- Describe the typical organization of the managerial accounting function in a business enterprise.

- Describe the nature of responsibility accounting.

- Describe the nature of decentralized operations and the special accounting needs of management of such operations.

- Describe and illustrate responsibility accounting for cost centers.

- Describe and illustrate responsibility accounting for profit centers.

- Describe and illustrate responsibility accounting for investment centers.

Accounting, as described in Chapter 1, can be viewed as an information system that provides essential data about the financial activities of an entity to various users to aid them in making informed judgments and decisions. One important user of accounting information is management, who has the responsibility of directing the operations of an enterprise. The types of information needed and the use of this information by management in directing operations are the focus of most of the remainder of this text.

The preceding chapters focused on the concepts and principles of financial accounting and their application in the analysis of transactions and the preparation and interpretation of the financial statements. This chapter begins with a general description of the nature of managerial accounting and its relationship to financial accounting. The chapter concludes with a discussion of managerial accounting concepts and principles that are appropriate for planning and controlling businesses with operations separated into departments or other organizational units.

The discussions of this chapter apply to service, merchandising, and manufacturing enterprises. A service enterprise provides services to its customers. A merchandising enterprise purchases merchandise for resale to its customers. A manufacturing enterprise converts materials into finished products through the use of labor and machinery. Accounting and reporting for manufacturing enterprises is discussed in Chapter 22.

FINANCIAL ACCOUNTING AND MANAGERIAL ACCOUNTING

Although economic information can be classified in many ways, accountants often divide accounting information into two types: financial and managerial. A brief discussion of each of these is useful in understanding the nature of the information needed by management.

Financial accounting information is presented in periodic statements that are prepared according to **generally accepted accounting principles (GAAP)**. These statements, which report the results of past financial activities, are intended primarily for the use of persons who are "outside" or external to the enterprise, such as shareholders, creditors, governmental agencies, and the general public. However, these statements are also useful to management in directing the operations of the enterprise. For example, in planning future operations, management often begins by evaluating the results of relevant past activities as reported in the basic financial statements.

Managerial accounting information includes both historical and estimated data, which management uses in conducting daily operations and in planning future operations. For example, in controlling inflows and outflows of cash, management relies upon accounting to provide information concerning the amount owed to each creditor, the amount owed by each customer, and the date each amount is due. Production managers, by comparing past performances with planned objectives, can take steps to accelerate favorable trends and reduce those trends that are unfavorable.

As indicated in the following diagram, managerial accounting overlaps financial accounting to the extent that management uses the financial statements in directing current operations and planning future operations. However, managerial accounting extends beyond financial accounting by providing additional information and reports for management's use. In providing this additional information, the accountant is *not* governed by generally accepted accounting principles. Since these data are used only by management, the accountant provides the data in the format that is most useful for management. The principle of "usefulness," then, is dominant in guiding the accountant in preparing management reports.

FINANCIAL
AND
MANAGERIAL
ACCOUNTING
FUNCTIONS

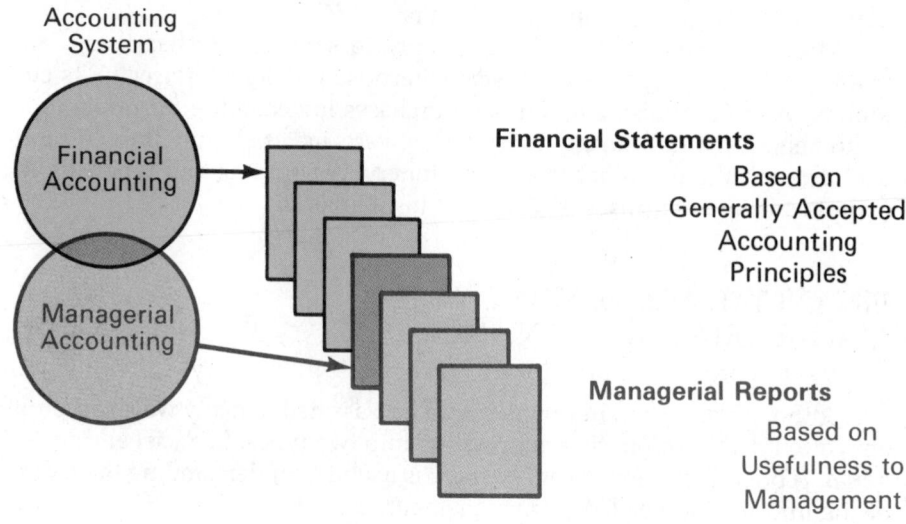

THE MANAGEMENT PROCESS

Managerial accountants supply accounting information to assist management in the basic functions of planning and control. **Planning** is the process of setting goals for the use of an organization's resources and of developing ways to achieve these goals. Accountants provide information to enable management to plan effectively. For example, accountants provide information to assist management in setting product selling prices. In this context, projections indicating the anticipated results of alternate selling prices can be useful to management in deciding among alternatives.

Control is the process of directing operations to achieve the organization's goals and plans. For example, accounting reports comparing the actual costs with the planned costs of producing products provide management with the basis for making decisions to control costs.

A common ingredient of both planning and control is decision making, and accountants provide information useful to management in making decisions. For example, decisions need to be made in selecting from among alternate proposed plans. Decisions also need to be made to keep actual costs within the bounds of proposed costs. The relationship between managerial accounting, the management process, and decision making is shown in the following diagram:

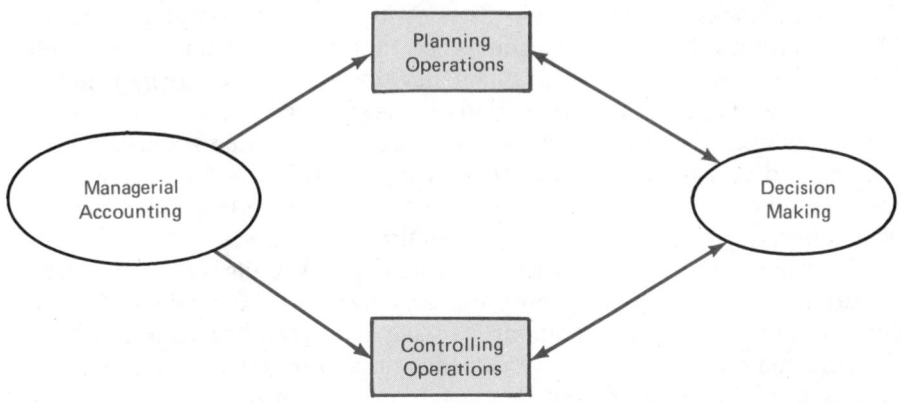

MANAGERIAL
ACCOUNTING
AND THE
BASIC
FUNCTIONS
OF
MANAGEMENT

As indicated in the diagram, decisions must be made by management in planning and controlling operations. As the results of these decisions evolve and are reviewed, additional decisions may be necessary to revise plans and modify steps taken to control operations. For example, if accounting information indicates that actual performance is below planned performance, the plans may be revised or the controls modified in an attempt to improve performance. Thus, the interrelationships of the planning and control functions of management may be viewed as an endless loop, with the managerial accountant providing input for the use of management in carrying out both functions.

In most business organizations, the chief managerial accountant is called the **controller**. The controller's function might be compared to that of an airplane's navigator. The navigator, with special skills and training, assists the pilot, but the pilot is responsible for flying the airplane. Likewise, the controller, with special accounting training and skills, advises management, but management is responsible for planning and controlling operations.

NATURE OF RESPONSIBILITY ACCOUNTING

A completely centralized business organization is one in which all major planning and operating decisions are made by the top echelon of management. In a small owner-manager-operated business, centralization is possible and may be desirable, since the owner-manager's close supervision ensures that the business will be operated in conformity with the owner-manager's wishes and desires. As a business grows or its operations become more diverse, it becomes difficult, if not impossible, for one individual to make all decisions. In a one-person real estate agency, for example, the responsibility for planning and controlling operations is clear. If the agency expands by opening an office in a distant city, some of the authority and responsibility for planning and decision making might be delegated to others. In other words, if centralized operations become unwieldy as a business grows, the need to delegate responsibility for portions of operating areas arises.

The separation of a business into more manageable units is termed **decentralization**. In a decentralized business organization, the reponsibility for planning and controlling operations is delegated among managers. These managers have the authority to make decisions without first seeking the approval of higher management. The level of decentralization varies significantly, and there is no one best level of decentralization for all businesses. In some companies, department managers have authority over all departmental operations. In other companies, a department manager may only have authority for controlling costs. The proper level of decentralization for a company depends on the specific, unique circumstances of that company.

In a decentralized business, an important function of the managerial accountant is to assist individual managers in the process of measuring and reporting operating data by their areas of responsibility, called **responsibility accounting**. Concepts and principles useful in responsibility accounting are presented in the remainder of this chapter.

Thinking Small

NCR (formerly National Cash Register Co.) is a Dayton-based multinational electronics and computer manufacturing corporation. In 1979, NCR was a troubled company. Examining its problems, management began to wonder whether its very structure was inhibiting its ability to innovate and adapt.

As a part of this reevaluation process, NCR commissioned the McKinsey & Co. consulting group to study the attributes of a number of highly successful companies. The researchers looked at such corporations as Sperry, IBM, and Hewlett-Packard, to determine what they had done that might be applied to NCR.

Using this study as background, NCR developed a plan for restructuring itself. Analyzing the path of a product from idea to implementation, it discovered some obvious impediments. The development, production, and marketing of a new product involved three separate divisions. This cumbersome system created opportunities for false starts and misinterpreting the market. It took a long time to get a product through this entire process, and sometimes products got lost in translation.

So NCR proceeded to break up its product-management organization and move the parts to units that would develop, manufacture, and market products. In consulting jargon, this is called shifting from a "functional" to a "divisional" organization, and it has been done many times before in other industries.

These changes transformed NCR Corp. from a highly centralized operation into a series of stand-alone or decentralized units. Today there is no requirement that one unit buy components from another NCR unit if it can find better or cheaper products outside the company. Moreover, based upon the nature of their products, the different divisions make their own decisions about how they want to structure themselves with regard to such activities as marketing.

Source: Adapted from Eugene Linden, "Let a Thousand Flowers Bloom," *Inc.,* April, 1984, pp. 64–76.

TYPES OF DECENTRALIZED OPERATIONS

Decentralized operations can be classified by the scope of responsibility assigned and the decision making authority given to individual managers. The three common types of decentralized operations are referred to as cost centers, profit centers, and investment centers. Each of these types of decentralized operations is briefly described in the following paragraphs. Responsibility accounting for each type is then discussed and illustrated in the remainder of this chapter.[1]

Cost Centers

In a **cost center**, the department or division manager has responsibility for the control of costs incurred and the authority to make decisions that affect these costs. For example, the marketing manager has responsibility for the costs of the Marketing Department, and the supervisor of the Power Department has responsibility for the costs incurred in providing power. The department manager does not make decisions concerning sales of the cost center's output, nor does the department manager have control over the plant assets available to the cost center.

Cost centers are the most widely used type of decentralization, because the organization and operation of most businesses allow for an easy identification of areas where managers can be assigned responsibility for and authority over costs. Cost centers may vary in size from a small department with a few employees to an entire manufacturing plant. In addition, cost centers may exist within other cost centers. For example, a manager of a manufacturing plant organized as a cost center may treat individual departments within the plant as separate cost centers, with the department managers reporting directly to the plant manager.

Profit Centers

In a **profit center**, the manager has the responsibility and the authority to make decisions that affect both costs and revenues (and thus profits) for the department or division. For example, a retail department store might decentralize its operations by product line. The manager of each product line would have responsibility for the cost of merchandise and decisions regarding revenues, such as the determination of sales prices. The manager of a profit center

---

[1]Accounting for branch operations is described in Appendix E.

does not make decisions concerning the plant assets available to the center. For example, the manager of the Sporting Goods Department does not make the decision to expand the available floor space for that department.

Profit centers are widely used in businesses in which individual departments or divisions sell products or services to those outside the company. A partial organization chart for a department store decentralized by retail departments as profit centers is as follows:

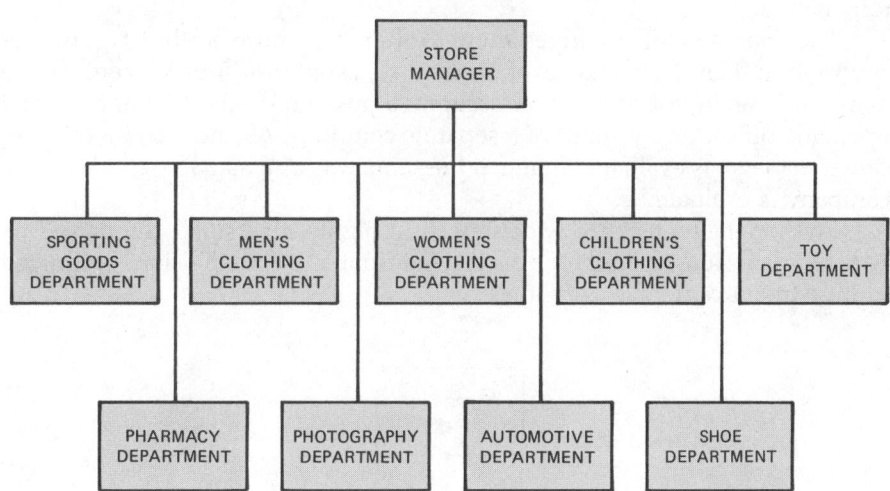

PARTIAL ORGANIZATION CHART FOR DEPARTMENT STORE WITH PROFIT CENTERS

Occasionally, profit centers are established when the center's product or service is consumed entirely within the company. For example, a Repairs and Maintenance Department of a manufacturing plant could be treated as a profit center if its manager were allowed to bill other departments, such as the various production departments, for services rendered. Likewise, the Data Processing Department of a company might bill each of the company's administrative and operating units for computing services.

In a sense, a profit center may be viewed as a business within a business. While the primary concern of a cost center manager is the control of costs, the profit center is concerned with both revenues and costs.

Profit centers are often viewed as an excellent training assignment for new managers. For example, Lester B. Korn, Chairman and Chief Executive Officer of Korn/Ferry International, recently offered the following strategy for young executives enroute to top management positions:

Get Profit-Center Responsibility—Obtain a position where you can prove yourself as both a specialist with particular expertise and a generalist who can exercise leadership, authority, and inspire enthusiasm among colleagues and subordinates.

Investment Centers

In an **investment center**, the manager has the responsibility and the authority to make decisions that affect not only costs and revenues, but also the plant assets available to the center. For example, a plant manager sets selling prices of products and establishes controls over costs. In addition, the plant manager could, within general constraints established by top management, expand production facilities through equipment acquisitions and retirements.

The manager of an investment center has more authority and responsibility than the manager of either a cost center or a profit center. The manager of an investment center occupies a position similar to that of a chief operating officer or president of a separate company. As such, an investment center manager is evaluated in much the same way as a manager of a separate company is evaluated.

Investment centers are widely used in highly diversified companies. A partial organizational chart for a diversified company with divisions organized as investment centers is as follows:

PARTIAL ORGANIZA-TION CHART FOR DIVERSIFIED COMPANY WITH INVESTMENT CENTERS

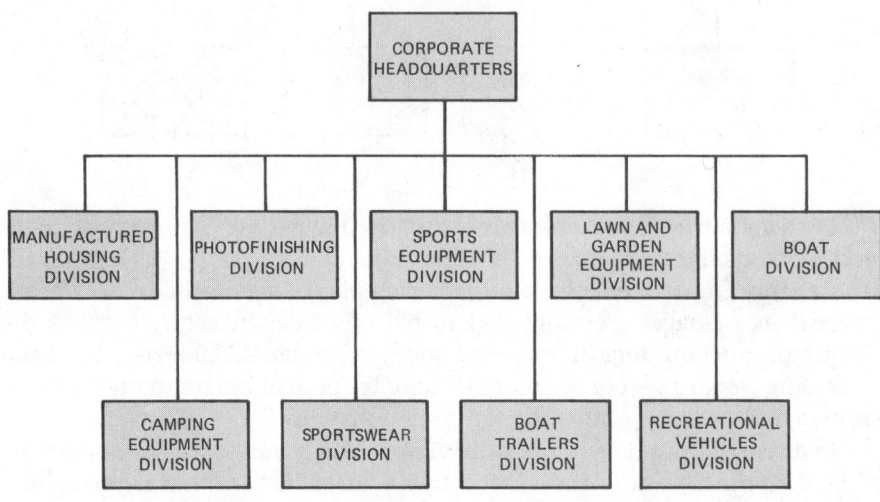

RESPONSIBILITY ACCOUNTING FOR COST CENTERS

Managers of cost centers have the responsibility and the authority to make decisions regarding costs. This responsibility and authority are illustrated in the following organization chart for a manufacturing enterprise with two plants:

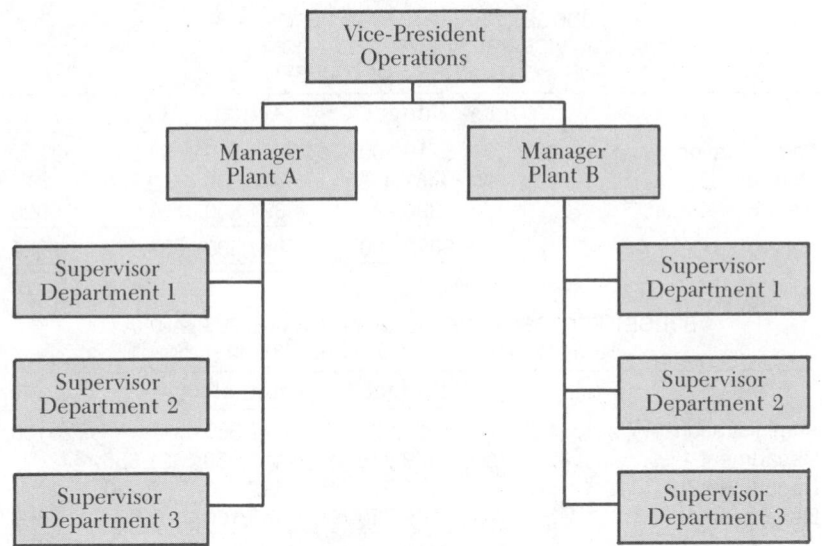

ORGANIZA-
TION CHART
DEPICTING
MANAGE-
MENT RE-
SPONSIBILITY
FOR
OPERATIONS

Within the organizational structure illustrated, there are three levels of cost centers. At the operating level, each department is a cost center, with the department supervisors responsible for controlling costs within their departments. At the next level of the organization, each plant is a cost center, with each plant manager responsible for controlling plant administrative costs as well as supervising the control of costs in the plant departments. Finally, at the top level, the office of the vice-president of operations is a cost center with responsibility for controlling the administrative costs of the office as well as supervising the control of costs in each plant.

The primary accounting tool for planning and controlling costs is a budget. A **budget** is a formal written statement of management's plans for the future, expressed in financial terms. A budget for a cost center should, therefore, set forth a statement of expected costs, based on management's plans. Thus, in the budgetary process, which is discussed in greater detail in Chapter 24, all factors that influence future operations should be carefully studied and investigated.

Managerial accounting reports aid each level of management in carrying out its assigned responsibilities for the control of costs. The managerial accounting report that compares actual results with budgeted figures is called a **budget performance report**. This report enables management to identify significant differences between the budget and the actual cost of individual items. Management can then investigate the differences in those items to determine their cause and to seek means of preventing their recurrence. To illustrate, the following budget performance reports are part of the responsibility accounting system for the manufacturing enterprise described in the previous organization chart:

BUDGET PERFORMANCE REPORT—
VICE-PRESIDENT, OPERATIONS
FOR MONTH ENDED OCTOBER 31, 19--

	Budget	Actual	Over	Under
Administration..............	$ 19,500	$ 19,700	$ 200	
Plant A....................	467,475	470,330	2,855	
Plant B...................	395,225	394,300		$925
	$882,200	$884,330	$3,055	$925

BUDGET PERFORMANCE REPORT—MANAGER, PLANT A
FOR MONTH ENDED OCTOBER 31, 19--

	Budget	Actual	Over	Under
Administration..............	$ 17,500	$ 17,350		$150
Department 1	109,725	111,280	$1,555	
Department 2	190,500	192,600	2,100	
Department 3	149,750	149,100		650
	$467,475	$470,330	$3,655	$800

BUDGET PERFORMANCE REPORT—SUPERVISOR,
DEPARTMENT 1-PLANT A
FOR MONTH ENDED OCTOBER 31, 19--

	Budget	Actual	Over	Under
Factory wages	$ 58,100	$ 58,000		$100
Materials	32,500	34,225	$1,725	
Supervisory salaries	6,400	6,400		
Power and light............	5,750	5,690		60
Depreciation of plant and equipment	4,000	4,000		
Maintenance	2,000	1,990		10
Insurance and property taxes...........	975	975		
	$109,725	$111,280	$1,725	$170

The amount of detail presented in the budget performance report depends upon the level of management to which the report is directed. The reports prepared for the department supervisors present details of the budgeted and actual manufacturing costs for their departments. Each supervisor can then concentrate on the individual items that resulted in significant variations. In the illustration, the budget performance report for Department 1-Plant A indicates a significant variation between the budget and actual amounts for materials. It is clear that supplemental reports providing detailed data on the causes of the variation would aid the supervisor in taking corrective action. One such report, a scrap report, is illustrated as follows. This report indicates the cause of a significant part of the variation.

SCRAP
REPORT

MATERIALS SCRAP REPORT—DEPARTMENT 1-PLANT A
FOR MONTH ENDED OCTOBER 31, 19--

Material No.	Units Spoiled	Unit Cost	Dollar Loss	Remarks
A392	50	$3.10	$ 155.00	Machine malfunction
C417	76	.80	60.80	Inexperienced employee
G118	5	1.10	5.50	
J510	120	8.25	990.00	Substandard materials
K277	2	1.50	3.00	
P719	7	2.10	14.70	
V112	22	4.25	93.50	Machine malfunction
			$1,322.50	

The scrap report is one example of the type of supplemental report that can be provided to department supervisors. Other examples would include reports on factory wages and the cost of idle time.

The budget performance reports for the plant managers contain summarized data on the budgeted and actual costs for the departments under their jurisdiction. These reports enable them to identify the department supervisors responsible for significant variances. The report for the vice-president in charge of operations summarizes the data by plant. The persons responsible for plant operations can thus be held accountable for significant variations from predetermined objectives.

RESPONSIBILITY ACCOUNTING FOR PROFIT CENTERS

Since managers of profit centers have responsibility for and authority to make decisions regarding expenses and revenues, responsibility accounting reports for profit centers are normally in the form of income statements. These income statements for individual profit centers report expenses and revenues by departments through either gross profit or operating income. Alternatively, profit center income statements may include a breakdown of revenues and expenses by responsibility for their incurrence, and may identify contributions made by each department to overall company profit.

Since profit centers are widely used by merchandising enterprises, such as department stores, a merchandising enterprise is used as the basis for the following discussion and illustration of responsibility accounting for profit centers. Although the degree to which profit centers are used by a merchandising enterprise varies, profit centers are typically established for each major retail department. The enterprise in the illustrations, Garrison Company, has established Departments A and B as profit centers.

Gross Profit by Departments

To compute gross profit by departments, it is necessary to determine by departments each element entering into gross profit. An income statement showing gross profit by departments for Garrison Company appears below. For illustrative purposes, the operating expenses are shown in condensed form. Usually they would be listed in detail.

For a merchandising enterprise, the gross profit is one of the most significant figures in the income statement. Since the sales and the cost of goods sold are both controlled by departmental management, the reporting of gross profit by departments is useful in cost analysis and control. In addition, such reports aid management in directing its efforts toward obtaining a mix of sales that will maximize profits. For example, after studying the reports, management may decide to change sales or purchases policies to achieve a higher gross profit for each department. Caution must be exercised in the use of such reports to insure that proposed changes affecting gross profit do not have an

INCOME STATEMENT DEPARTMENTALIZED THROUGH GROSS PROFIT

		Garrison Income For Year Ended
	Department A		
Revenue from sales:			
Sales	....	$630,000	....
Less sales returns and allowances	....	15,300	....
Net sales	....	....	$614,700
Cost of goods sold:			
Inventories, January 1, 19--	....	$ 80,150	....
Purchases	$334,550	....	....
Less purchases discounts	6,200	328,350	....
Goods available for sale	....	$408,500	....
Less inventories, December 31, 19--	....	85,150	....
Cost of goods sold	....	....	323,350
Gross profit	....	....	$291,350
Operating expenses:			
Selling expenses	....	....	....
General expenses	....	....	....
Total operating expenses	....	....	....
Income from operations	....	....	....
Other expense:			
Interest expense	....	....	....
Income before income tax	....	....	....
Income tax	....	....	....
Net income	....	....	....

adverse effect on net income. A change that increases gross profit could result in an even greater increase in operating expenses and thereby decrease net income.

Operating Income by Departments

Departmental reporting may be extended to operating income. In such cases, each department must be assigned not only the related revenues and the cost of goods sold (as in the preceding illustration), but also that part of operating expenses incurred for its benefit. Some of these expenses may be easily identified with the department benefited. For example, if each sales-person is restricted to a certain sales department, the sales salaries may be assigned to the proper departmental salary accounts each time the payroll is prepared. On the other hand, the salaries of company officers, executives, and office personnel are not identifiable with specific sales departments and must therefore be allocated if an equitable and reasonable basis for allocation exists.

Company
Statement
December 31, 19--

Department B			Total		
. . . .	$270,000	. . . .	. . . .	$900,000	. . . .
. . . .	7,100	. . . .	. . . .	22,400	. . . .
. . . .	. . . .	$262,900	. . . .	. . . .	$877,600
. . . .	$ 61,750	. . . .	. . . .	$141,900	. . . .
$200,350	. . . .	. . . .	$534,900	. . . .	. . . .
2,400	197,950	. . . .	8,600	526,300	. . . .
. . . .	$259,700	. . . .	. . . .	$668,200	. . . .
. . . .	78,950	. . . .	. . . .	164,100	. . . .
. . . .	. . . .	180,750	. . . .	. . . .	504,100
. . . .	. . . .	$ 82,150	. . . .	. . . .	$373,500
. . . .	. . . .	. . . .	. . . .	$113,000	. . . .
. . . .	. . . .	. . . .	. . . .	110,200	. . . .
. . . .	. . . .	. . . .	. . . .	. . . .	223,200
. . . .	. . . .	. . . .	. . . .	. . . .	$150,300
. . . .	. . . .	. . . .	. . . .	. . . .	2,500
. . . .	. . . .	. . . .	. . . .	. . . .	$147,800
. . . .	. . . .	. . . .	. . . .	. . . .	64,444
. . . .	. . . .	. . . .	. . . .	. . . .	$ 83,356

When operating expenses are allocated, they should be apportioned to the respective departments as nearly as possible in accordance with the cost of services rendered to them. Determining the amount of an expense chargeable to each department is not always a simple matter. In the first place, it requires the exercise of judgment; and accountants of equal ability may well differ in their opinions as to the proper basis for the apportionment of operating expenses. Second, the cost of collecting data for use in making an apportionment must be kept within reasonable bounds. Consequently, information that is readily available and is substantially reliable may be used instead of more accurate information that would be more costly to collect.

To illustrate the apportionment of operating expenses, assume that Garrison Company extends its departmental reporting through income from operations. The company's operating expenses for the year and the methods used in apportioning them are presented in the paragraphs that follow.

Sales Salaries Expense is apportioned to the two departments according to the distributions shown in the payroll records. Of the $84,900 total in the account, $54,000 is chargeable to Department A and $30,900 is chargeable to Department B.

Advertising Expense, covering billboard advertising and newspaper advertising, is apportioned according to the amount of advertising incurred for each department. The billboard advertising totaling $5,000 emphasizes the name and the location of the company. This expense is allocated on the basis of sales, the assumption being that this basis represents a fair allocation of billboard advertising to each department. Analysis of the newspaper space costing $14,000 indicates that 65% of the space was devoted to Department A and 35% to Department B. The computations of the apportionment of the total advertising expense are as follows:

	Total	Department A	Department B
Sales—dollars.........	$900,000	$630,000	$270,000
Sales—percent........	100%	70%	30%
Billboard advertising ..	$ 5,000	$ 3,500	$ 1,500
Newspaper space— percent..............	100%	65%	35%
Newspaper advertising.........	14,000	9,100	4,900
Advertising expense	$19,000	$12,600	$6,400

Depreciation Expense—Store Equipment is apportioned according to the average cost of the equipment in each of the two departments. The computations for the apportionment of the depreciation expense are as follows:

	Total	Department A	Department B
Cost of store equipment:			
January 1...............	$28,300	$16,400	$11,900
December 31	31,700	19,600	12,100
Total	$60,000	$36,000	$24,000
Average	$30,000	$18,000	$12,000
Percent.................	100%	60%	40%
Depreciation expense........	$ 4,400	$ 2,640	$ 1,760

Officers' Salaries Expense and **Office Salaries Expense** are apportioned on the basis of the relative amount of time devoted to each department by the officers and by the office personnel. Obviously, this can be only an approximation. The number of sales transactions may have some bearing on the matter, as may billing and collection procedures and other factors such as promotional campaigns that might vary from period to period. Of the total officers' salaries of $52,000 and office salaries of $17,600, it is estimated that 60%, or $31,200 and $10,560 respectively, is chargeable to Department A and that 40%, or $20,800 and $7,040 respectively, is chargeable to Department B.

Rent Expense and **Heating and Lighting Expense** are usually apportioned on the basis of floor space devoted to each department. In apportioning rent expense for a multistory building, differences in the value of the various floors and locations may be taken into account. For example, the space near the main entrance of a department store is more valuable than the same amount of floor space located far from the elevator on the sixth floor. For Garrison Company, rent expense is apportioned on the basis of floor space used because there is no significant difference in the value of the floor areas used by each department. In allocating heating and lighting expense, it is assumed that the number of lights, their wattage, and the extent of use are uniform throughout the sales departments. If there are major variations and the total lighting expense is material, further analysis and separate apportionment may be advisable. The rent expense and the heating and lighting expense are apportioned as follows:

	Total	Department A	Department B
Floor space, square feet.....	160,000	104,000	56,000
Percent.................	100%	65%	35%
Rent expense	$15,400	$10,010	$ 5,390
Heating and lighting expense	$ 5,100	$ 3,315	$ 1,785

Property Tax Expense and **Insurance Expense** are related primarily to the cost of the inventories and the store equipment. Although the cost of these assets may differ from their assessed value for tax purposes and their value for insurance purposes, the cost is most readily available and is considered to be satisfactory as a basis for apportioning these expenses. The computations of the apportionment of the personal property tax expense and the insurance expense are as follows:

	Total	Department A	Department B
Inventories:			
January 1...............	$141,900	$ 80,150	$ 61,750
December 31	164,100	85,150	78,950
Total	$306,000	$165,300	$140,700
Average	$153,000	$ 82,650	$ 70,350
Average cost of store equipment (computed previously).....	30,000	18,000	12,000
Total	$183,000	$100,650	$ 82,350
Percent.................	100%	55%	45%
Property tax expense	$ 6,800	$ 3,740	$ 3,060
Insurance expense	$ 3,900	$ 2,145	$ 1,755

Uncollectible Accounts Expense, Miscellaneous Selling Expense, and **Miscellaneous General Expense** are apportioned on the basis of sales. Although the uncollectible accounts expense may be apportioned on the basis of an analysis of accounts receivable written off, it is assumed that the expense is closely related to sales. The miscellaneous selling and general expenses are apportioned on the basis of sales, which are assumed to be a reasonable measure of the benefit to each department. The computation of the apportionment is as follows:

	Total	Department A	Department B
Sales.....................	$900,000	$630,000	$270,000
Percent.................	100%	70%	30%
Uncollectible accounts expense................	$ 4,600	$ 3,220	$ 1,380
Miscellaneous selling expense................	$ 4,700	$ 3,290	$ 1,410
Miscellaneous general expense................	$ 4,800	$ 3,360	$ 1,440

An income statement presenting income from operations by departments for Garrison Company appears on pages 950 and 951. The amounts for sales and the cost of goods sold are presented in condensed form. Details could be reported if desired, in the manner illustrated on pages 944 and 945.

Departmental Margin

In a recent research study, 85% of the companies surveyed indicated that they allocate some operating expenses to profit centers (departments), as discussed in the preceding section.[2] Caution should be used, however, in relying on income statements departmentalized through income from operations, since the use of arbitrary bases in allocating operating expenses is likely to yield incorrect amounts of departmental operating income. In addition, the reporting of operating income by departments may be misleading, since the departments are not independent operating units. The departments are segments of a business enterprise, and no single department of a business can earn an income independently. For these reasons, income statements of segmented businesses may follow a somewhat different format than the one illustrated on pages 950 and 951. The alternative format emphasizes the contribution of each department to overall company net income and to covering the overall operating expenses incurred on behalf of the business. Income statements prepared in this alternative format are said to follow the **departmental margin** or **contribution margin** approach to responsibility accounting.

Prior to the preparation of an income statement in the departmental margin format, it is necessary to differentiate between operating expenses that are direct and those that are indirect. The two categories may be described in general terms as follows:

1. **Direct expense** — Operating expenses directly traceable to or incurred for the sole benefit of a specific department and usually subject to the control of the department manager.
2. **Indirect expense** — Operating expenses incurred for the entire enterprise as a unit and hence not subject to the control of individual department managers.

The details of departmental sales and the cost of goods sold are presented on the income statement in the usual manner. The direct expenses of each department are then deducted from the related departmental gross profit, yielding balances which are identified as the departmental margin. The remaining expenses, including the indirect operating expenses, are not departmentalized. They are reported separately below the total departmental margin.

---

[2]James M. Fremgen and Shu S. Liao, *The Allocation of Corporate Indirect Costs* (New York: National Association of Accountants, 1981), pp. 33–34.

INCOME
STATEMENT
DEPART-
MENTALIZED
THROUGH
INCOME
FROM
OPERATIONS

Garrison

Income

For Year Ended

	Department A		
Net sales	....	....	$614,700
Cost of goods sold	....	....	323,350
Gross profit	....	....	$291,350
Operating expenses:			
Selling expenses:			
Sales salaries expense	$ 54,000	....	....
Advertising expense	12,600	....	....
Depreciation expense—store equipment	2,640	....	....
Miscellaneous selling expense	3,290	....	....
Total selling expenses	....	$ 72,530	....
General expenses:			
Officers' salaries expense	$ 31,200	....	....
Office salaries expense	10,560	....	....
Rent expense	10,010	....	....
Property tax expense	3,740	....	....
Heating and lighting expense	3,315	....	....
Uncollectible accounts expense	3,220	....	....
Insurance expense	2,145	....	....
Miscellaneous general expense	3,360	....	....
Total general expenses	....	67,550	....
Total operating expenses	....	....	140,080
Income (loss) from operations	....	....	$151,270
Other expense:			
Interest expense	....	....	....
Income before income tax	....	....	....
Income tax	....	....	....
Net income	....	....	....

Company
Statement
December 31, 19--

Department B			Total		
. . . .	. . . .	$262,900	. . . .	. . . .	$877,600
. . . .	. . . .	180,750	. . . .	. . . .	504,100
. . . .	. . . .	$ 82,150	. . . .	. . . .	$373,500
$ 30,900	. . . .	. . . .	$ 84,900	. . . .	. . . .
6,400	. . . .	. . . .	19,000	. . . .	. . . .
1,760	. . . .	. . . .	4,400	. . . .	. . . .
1,410	. . . .	. . . .	4,700	. . . .	. . . .
. . . .	$ 40,470	. . . .	. . . .	$113,000	. . . .
$ 20,800	. . . .	. . . .	$ 52,000	. . . .	. . . .
7,040	. . . .	. . . .	17,600	. . . .	. . . .
5,390	. . . .	. . . .	15,400	. . . .	. . . .
3,060	. . . .	. . . .	6,800	. . . .	. . . .
1,785	. . . .	. . . .	5,100	. . . .	. . . .
1,380	. . . .	. . . .	4,600	. . . .	. . . .
1,755	. . . .	. . . .	3,900	. . . .	. . . .
1,440	. . . .	. . . .	4,800	. . . .	. . . .
. . . .	42,650	. . . .	. . . .	110,200	. . . .
. . . .	. . . .	83,120	. . . .	. . . .	223,200
. . . .	. . . .	$ (970)	. . . .	. . . .	$150,300
. . . .	. . . .	. . . .	. . . .	. . . .	2,500
. . . .	. . . .	. . . .	. . . .	. . . .	$147,800
. . . .	. . . .	. . . .	. . . .	. . . .	64,444
. . . .	. . . .	. . . .	. . . .	. . . .	$ 83,356

An income statement in the departmental margin format for Garrison Company is presented on the following page. The basic revenue, cost, and expense data for the period are identical with those reported in the earlier illustration. The expenses identified as "direct" are sales salaries, property tax, uncollectible accounts, insurance, depreciation, and the newspaper advertising portion of advertising. The billboard portion of advertising, which is for the benefit of the business as a whole, as well as officers' and office salaries, and the remaining operating expenses, are identified as "indirect." Although a $970 net loss from operations is reported for Department B on page 951, a departmental margin of $38,395 is reported for the same department on the statement on page 953.

With departmental margin income statements, the manager of each department can be held responsible for operating expenses traceable to the department. A reduction in the direct expenses of a department will have a favorable effect on that department's contribution to the net income of the enterprise.

The departmental margin income statement may also be useful to management in making plans for future operations. For example, this type of analysis can be used when the discontinuance of a certain operation or department is being considered. If a specific department yields a departmental margin, it generally should be retained, even though the allocation of the indirect operating expenses would result in a net loss for that department. This observation is based upon the assumption that the department in question represents a relatively small segment of the enterprise. Its termination, therefore, would not cause any significant reduction in the amount of indirect expenses.

RESPONSIBILITY ACCOUNTING FOR INVESTMENT CENTERS

Since investment center managers have responsibility for revenues and expenses, operating income is an essential part of investment center reporting. In addition, because the investment center manager also has responsibility for the assets invested in the center, two additional measures of performance are often used. These additional measures are the rate of return on investment and residual income. In practice, most companies use some combination of all these measures. In the following paragraphs, each measure of investment center performance is described and illustrated for Marsh Company, a diversified company with three operating divisions, A, B, and C.

Garrison Company
Income Statement
For Year Ended December 31, 19--

	Department A		Department B		Total	
Net sales	. . . . . .	$614,700	. . . . . .	$262,900	. . . . . .	$877,600
Cost of goods sold.	. . . . . .	323,350	. . . . . .	180,750	. . . . . .	504,100
Gross profit	. . . . . .	$291,350	. . . . . .	$ 82,150	. . . . . .	$373,500
Direct departmental expenses:						
Sales salaries expense	$54,000	. . . .	$30,900	. . . .	$84,900	. . . .
Advertising expense	9,100	. . . .	4,900	. . . .	14,000	. . . .
Property tax expense.	3,740	. . . .	3,060	. . . .	6,800	. . . .
Uncollectible accounts expense	3,220	. . . .	1,380	. . . .	4,600	. . . .
Depreciation expense—store equipment	2,640	. . . .	1,760	. . . .	4,400	. . . .
Insurance expense.	2,145	. . . .	1,755	. . . .	3,900	. . . .
Total direct departmental expenses	. . . . . .	74,845	. . . . . .	43,755	. . . . . .	118,600
Departmental margin.	. . . . . .	$216,505	. . . . . .	$ 38,395	. . . . . .	$254,900
Indirect expenses:						
Officers' salaries expense.	. . . . . .	. . . .	. . . . . .	. . . .	$52,000	. . . .
Office salaries expense.	. . . . . .	. . . .	. . . . . .	. . . .	17,600	. . . .
Rent expense	. . . . . .	. . . .	. . . . . .	. . . .	15,400	. . . .
Heating and lighting expense .	. . . . . .	. . . .	. . . . . .	. . . .	5,100	. . . .
Advertising expense	. . . . . .	. . . .	. . . . . .	. . . .	5,000	. . . .
Miscellaneous selling expense	. . . . . .	. . . .	. . . . . .	. . . .	4,700	. . . .
Miscellaneous general expense	. . . . . .	. . . .	. . . . . .	. . . .	4,800	. . . .
Total indirect expenses	. . . . . .	. . . .	. . . . . .	. . . .	. . . . . .	104,600
Income from operations	. . . . . .	. . . .	. . . . . .	. . . .	. . . . . .	$150,300
Other expense:						
Interest expense.	. . . . . .	. . . .	. . . . . .	. . . .	. . . . . .	2,500
Income before income tax	. . . . . .	. . . .	. . . . . .	. . . .	. . . . . .	$147,800
Income tax.	. . . . . .	. . . .	. . . . . .	. . . .	. . . . . .	64,444
Net income.	. . . . . .	. . . .	. . . . . .	. . . .	. . . . . .	$ 83,356

INCOME STATEMENT DEPARTMENTALIZED THROUGH DEPARTMENTAL MARGIN

Operating Income

Because investment centers are evaluated as if they were separate companies, traditional financial statements are normally prepared for each center. For purposes of assessing profitability, operating income is the focal point of analysis. Since the determination of operating income for decentralized operations was described and illustrated in the preceding paragraphs, only condensed divisional income statements will be used for illustrative purposes. The condensed divisional income statements for Marsh Company are as follows:

Marsh Company
Divisional Income Statements
For Year Ended December 31, 19--

	Division A	Division B	Division C
Sales.......................	$560,000	$672,000	$750,000
Cost of goods sold	336,000	470,400	562,500
Gross profit.......................	$224,000	$201,600	$187,500
Operating expenses	154,000	117,600	112,500
Operating Income	$ 70,000	$ 84,000	$ 75,000

Based on the amount of divisional operating income, Division B is the most profitable of Marsh Company's divisions, with income from operations of $84,000. Divisions A and C are less profitable, with Division C reporting $5,000 more operating income than Division A.

Although operating income is a useful measure of investment center profitability, it does not reflect the amount of investment in assets committed to each center. For example, if the amount of assets invested in Division B is twice that of the other divisions, then Division B is the least profitable of the divisions in terms of the rate of return on investment. Since investment center managers also control the amount of assets invested in their centers, they should be held accountable for the use of invested assets.

Rate of Return on Investment

One of the most widely used measures of divisional performance for investment centers is the **rate of return on investment (ROI)**, or **rate of return on assets**. This rate is computed as follows:

$$\text{Rate of Return on Investment (ROI)} = \frac{\text{Operating Income}}{\text{Invested Assets}}$$

The rate of return on investment is useful because the three factors subject to control by divisional managers (revenues, expenses, and invested assets) are considered in its computation. By measuring profitability relative to the amount of assets invested in each division, the rate of return on investment can be used to compare divisions. The higher the rate of return on investment, the more effectively the division is utilizing its assets in generating income. To illustrate, the rate of return on investment for each division of Marsh Company, based on the book value of invested assets, is as follows:

	Operating Income	Invested Assets	Rate of Return on Investment
Division A............	$70,000	$350,000	20%
Division B............	84,000	700,000	12
Division C............	75,000	500,000	15

Although Division B generated the largest operating income, its rate of return on investment (12%) is the lowest. Hence, relative to the assets invested, Division B is the least profitable division. In comparison, the rates of return on investment of Divisions A and C are 20% and 15% respectively. These differences in the rates of return on investment may be analyzed by restating the expression for the rate of return on investment in expanded form, as follows:

$$\text{Rate of Return on Investment (ROI)} = \frac{\text{Operating Income}}{\text{Sales}} \times \frac{\text{Sales}}{\text{Invested Assets}}$$

In the expanded form, the rate of return on investment is the product of two factors: (1) the ratio of operating income to sales, often termed the **profit margin**, and (2) the ratio of sales to invested assets, often termed the **investment turnover**. As shown in the following computation, the use of this expanded expression yields the same rate of return for Division A, 20%, as the previous expression for the rate of return on investment:

$$\text{Rate of Return on Investment (ROI)} = \frac{\text{Operating Income}}{\text{Sales}} \times \frac{\text{Sales}}{\text{Invested Assets}}$$

$$\text{ROI} = \frac{\$70,000}{\$560,000} \times \frac{\$560,000}{\$350,000}$$

$$\text{ROI} = 12.5\% \times 1.6$$

$$\text{ROI} = 20\%$$

The expanded expression for the rate of return on investment is useful in management's evaluation and control of decentralized operations because the profit margin and the investment turnover focus on the underlying operating relationships of each division. The profit margin component focuses on profitability by indicating the rate of profit earned on each sales dollar. When efforts are aimed at increasing a division's profit margin by changing the division's sales mix, for example, the division's rate of return on investment may increase.

The investment turnover component focuses on efficiency in the use of assets and indicates the rate at which sales are being generated for each dollar of invested assets. The more sales per dollar invested, the greater the efficiency in the use of the assets. When efforts are aimed at increasing a division's investment turnover through special sales promotions, for example, the division's rate of return on investment may increase.

The rate of return on investment, using the expanded expression for each division of Marsh Company, is summarized as follows:

$$\text{Rate of Return on Investment (ROI)} = \text{Profit Margin} \times \text{Investment Turnover}$$

$$\text{ROI} = \frac{\text{Operating Income}}{\text{Sales}} \times \frac{\text{Sales}}{\text{Invested Assets}}$$

Division A:
$$\text{ROI} = \frac{\$70,000}{\$560,000} \times \frac{\$560,000}{\$350,000}$$
$$\text{ROI} = 12.5\% \times 1.6$$
$$\text{ROI} = 20\%$$

Division B:
$$\text{ROI} = \frac{\$84,000}{\$672,000} \times \frac{\$672,000}{\$700,000}$$
$$\text{ROI} = 12.5\% \times .96$$
$$\text{ROI} = 12\%$$

Division C:
$$\text{ROI} = \frac{\$75,000}{\$750,000} \times \frac{\$750,000}{\$500,000}$$
$$\text{ROI} = 10\% \times 1.5$$
$$\text{ROI} = 15\%$$

Although Divisions A and B have the same profit margins, Division A's investment turnover is larger than that of Division B (1.6 to .96). Thus, by more efficiently utilizing its invested assets, Division A's rate of return on investment is higher than Division B's. Division C's profit margin of 10% and investment turnover of 1.5 are lower than the corresponding factors for Division A. The product of these factors results in a return on investment of 15% for Division C, as compared to 20% for Division A.

To determine possible ways of increasing the rate of return on investment, the profit margin and investment turnover for a division should be analyzed. For example, if Division A is in a highly competitive industry where the profit margin cannot be easily increased, the division manager should concentrate on increasing the investment turnover. To illustrate, assume that sales of Division A could be increased by $56,000 through changes in advertising expenditures. The cost of goods sold is expected to be 60% of sales, and operating expenses will increase to $169,400. If the advertising changes are undertaken, Division A's operating income would increase from $70,000 to $77,000, as shown in the following condensed income statement:

Sales ($560,000 + $56,000)	$616,000
Cost of goods sold ($616,000 × 60%)	369,600
Gross profit	$246,400
Operating expenses	169,400
Operating income	$ 77,000

The rate of return on investment for Division A, using the expanded expression, is recomputed as follows:

$$\text{Rate of Return on Investment (ROI)} = \frac{\text{Operating Income}}{\text{Sales}} \times \frac{\text{Sales}}{\text{Invested Assets}}$$

$$\text{ROI} = \frac{\$77,000}{\$616,000} \times \frac{\$616,000}{\$350,000}$$

$$\text{ROI} = 12.5\% \times 1.76$$

$$\text{ROI} = 22\%$$

Although Division A's profit margin remains the same (12.5%), the division's investment turnover has increased from 1.6 to 1.76, an increase of 10% (.16 ÷ 1.6). The 10% increase in investment turnover has the effect of also increasing the rate of return on investment by 10% (from 20% to 22%).

The major advantage of the use of the rate of return on investment instead of operating income as a divisional performance measure is that the amount of divisional investment is directly considered. Thus, divisional performances can be compared, even though the sizes of the divisions may vary significantly.

In addition to its use as a performance measure, the rate of return on investment can assist management in other ways. For example, in considering a decision to expand the operations of Marsh Company, management should consider giving priority to Division A because it earns the highest rate of return on investment. If the current rates of return on investment can be maintained in the future, an investment in Division A will return 20 cents

(20%) on each dollar invested, while investments in Divisions B and C will return only 12 cents and 15 cents respectively.

A major disadvantage of the rate of return on investment as a performance measure is that it may lead divisional managers to reject new investment proposals, even though the rate of return on these investments exceeds the minimum considered acceptable by the company. For example, a division might have an overall rate of return on investment of 25%, and the company might have an overall rate of return on investment of 15%. If the division accepts a new investment that would earn a 20% rate of return on investment, the overall rate of return for the division would decrease, but the overall rate of return for the company as a whole would increase. Thus, the division manager might reject the proposal, even though its acceptance would be in the best interests of the company.

Residual Income

In the previous illustration for Marsh Company, two measures of evaluating divisional performance were discussed and illustrated. The advantages and disadvantages of both measures were also discussed. An additional measure, residual income, is useful in overcoming some of the disadvantages associated with the operating income and rate of return on investment measures.

Residual income is the excess of divisional operating income over a minimum amount of desired operating income. The minimum amount of desired divisional operating income is set by top management by establishing a minimum rate of return for the invested assets and then multiplying this rate by the amount of divisional assets. To illustrate, assume that the top management of Marsh Company has established 10% as the minimum rate of return on divisional assets. The residual incomes for Divisions A, B, and C are computed as follows:

	Division A	Division B	Division C
RESIDUAL INCOME BY DIVISION			
Divisional operating income	$70,000	$84,000	$75,000
Minimum amount of divisional operating income:			
$350,000 × 10%.................	35,000		
$700,000 × 10%.................		70,000	
$500,000 × 10%.................			50,000
Residual income	$35,000	$14,000	$25,000

The major advantage of residual income as a performance measure is that it gives consideration not only to a minimum rate of return on investment, but also to the total magnitude of the operating income earned by each division.

For example, Division A has more residual income than the other divisions of Marsh Company, even though it has the least operating income. Also, Division C earns $11,000 more residual income than Division B, even though Division B generates more operating income than Division C. The reason for this difference is that Division B has $200,000 more assets than Division C. Hence, Division B's operating income is reduced by $20,000 ($200,000 × 10%) more than Division C's operating income in determining residual income.

CHAPTER REVIEW

KEY POINTS

1. Financial Accounting and Managerial Accounting.

Financial accounting information is presented in periodic statements that are prepared according to generally accepted accounting principles. These statements are intended primarily for the use of persons who are outside or external to the enterprise. Managerial accounting information includes both historical and estimated data for management's use in conducting daily operations and in planning future operations. Since these data are used only by management, the principle of usefulness is dominant in guiding the accountant in preparing management reports.

2. The Management Process.

Managerial accountants supply accounting information to assist management in the basic functions of planning and control. A common ingredient of both planning and control is decision making, and managerial accountants provide information useful to management in making decisions. The chief managerial accountant, called the controller, provides advice and assistance to management, but is not responsible for the operations of the business.

3. Nature of Responsibility Accounting.

In a decentralized business organization, the responsibility for planning and controlling operations is delegated among managers who have authority to make decisions without first seeking the approval of higher management. In a decentralized business, an important function of the managerial accountant is to assist managers in the process of measuring and reporting operating data by their areas of responsibility, called responsibility accounting.

4. Types of Decentralized Operations.

Decentralized operations can be classified by the scope of the responsibility assigned and the decision making authority given to individual managers. In a cost center, the manager has responsibility for the control of costs incurred and the authority to make decisions that affect these costs. In a profit center, the manager has the responsibility and the authority to make decisions that affect both costs and revenue (and thus profits) for the department or division. In an investment center, the manager has the responsibility and the authority to make decisions that affect not only costs and revenues, but also the plant assets available to the center.

5. Responsibility Accounting for Cost Centers.

The primary accounting tool for planning and controlling costs for a cost center is a budget. A budget is a formal written statement of management's plans for the future, expressed in financial terms. A budget performance report enables management to compare actual results with budgeted figures.

6. Responsibility Accounting for Profit Centers.

Since managers of profit centers have responsibility for and authority to make decisions regarding expenses and revenues, responsibility accounting reports for profit centers are normally in the form of income statements. One such statement determines gross profit by departments. Departmental reporting may be extended to operating income, in which case the operating expenses incurred by the company must be allocated to the departments. These expenses are usually allocated on the basis of the departmental benefit received from the expenditure. Some accountants, who consider the allocation of operating expenses to be arbitrary, advocate the preparation of departmental income statements based upon departmental margin or contribution margin. Departmental margin is determined by deducting the direct expenses of each department from departmental gross profit. The remaining expenses are not allocated to a department, but are reported in the income statement separately below the total departmental margin.

7. Responsibility Accounting for Investment Centers.

Because investment centers are evaluated as if they were separate companies, traditional financial statements which report operating income are normally prepared for each center. A measure of performance for investment centers is the rate of return on investment. The rate of return on investment is computed by dividing operating income by invested assets. In addition, the rate of return on investment may be considered as the product of two factors: (1) the profit margin, and (2) the investment turnover. An additional measure of investment center performance, residual income, is the excess of divisional operating income over a minimum amount of desired operating income.

KEY TERMS

financial accounting 934
managerial accounting 934
planning 935
control 935
controller 936
decentralization 936
responsibility accounting 936
cost center 938
profit center 938
investment center 940
budget 941

budget performance report 941
departmental margin 949
contribution margin 949
direct expense 949
indirect expense 949
rate of return on investment
 (ROI) 954
profit margin 955
investment turnover 955
residual income 958

SELF-EXAMINATION QUESTIONS
Answers in Appendix B.

1. When the manager has the responsibility for and authority to make decisions that affect costs and revenues, but no responsibility for or authority over assets invested in the department, the department is referred to as:
   A. a cost center
   B. a profit center
   C. an investment center
   D. none of the above

2. Which of the following would be the most appropriate basis for allocating rent expense for use in arriving at operating income by departments?
   A. Departmental sales
   B. Physical space occupied
   C. Cost of inventory
   D. Time devoted to departments

3. The term used to describe the excess of departmental gross profit over direct departmental expenses is:
   A. income from operations
   B. net income
   C. departmental margin
   D. none of the above

4. Division A of Kern Co. has sales of $350,000, cost of goods sold of $200,000, operating expenses of $30,000, and invested assets of $600,000. What is the rate of return on investment for Division A?
   A. 20%
   B. 25%
   C. 40%
   D. None of the above

5. Division L of Liddy Co. has a rate of return on investment of 24% and an investment turnover of 1.6. What is the profit margin?
   A. 6%
   B. 15%
   C. 24%
   D. None of the above

ILLUSTRATIVE PROBLEM

Perry Home Appliances operates two sales departments—Department F for freezers and refrigerators, and Department R for ranges and ovens. The trial balance shown on page 963 was prepared as of April 30, the end of the current fiscal year, after all adjustments, including those for inventories, were recorded and posted.

Inventories at the beginning of the year were as follows: Department F, $17,200; Department R, $36,000.

The bases to be used in apportioning expenses, together with other essential information, are as follows:

Sales salaries—payroll records: Department F, $17,300; Department R, $26,100.

Advertising expense—usage: Department F, $4,000; Department R, $6,800.

Depreciation expense—average cost of equipment. Equipment balances at beginning of year: Department F, $17,000; Department R, $26,000. Equipment balances at end of year: Department F, $18,200; Department R, $26,800.

Store supplies expense—requisitions: Department F, $550; Department R, $700.

Office salaries—Department F, 30%; Department R, 70%.

Rent expense and heating and lighting expense—floor space: Department F, 1,200 sq. ft.; Department R, 2,800 sq. ft.

Property tax expense and insurance expense—average cost of equipment plus average cost of inventories.

Uncollectible accounts expense, miscellaneous selling expense, and miscellaneous general expense—volume of gross sales.

Perry Home Appliances
Trial Balance
April 30, 19--

Cash.	72,650	
Accounts Receivable.	97,450	
Inventories—Department F.	17,600	
Inventories—Department R.	41,200	
Prepaid Insurance	4,400	
Store Supplies	625	
Store Equipment.	45,000	
Accumulated Depreciation—Store Equipment		25,800
Accounts Payable		34,300
Income Tax Payable		6,400
Common Stock.		100,000
Retained Earnings		80,375
Cash Dividends	25,000	
Income Summary.	53,200	58,800
Sales—Department F.		350,000
Sales—Department R		650,000
Sales Returns and Allowances—Department F	6,400	
Sales Returns and Allowances—Department R	10,200	
Purchases—Department F	280,600	
Purchases—Department R	532,000	
Sales Salaries.	43,400	
Advertising Expense	10,800	
Depreciation Expense—Store Equipment	8,800	
Store Supplies Expense	1,250	
Miscellaneous Selling Expense.	800	
Office Salaries	10,000	
Rent Expense.	9,800	
Heating and Lighting Expense.	4,000	
Property Tax Expense.	3,000	
Insurance Expense	1,800	
Uncollectible Accounts Expense.	1,100	
Miscellaneous General Expense.	900	
Interest Income.		1,000
Income Tax	24,700	
	1,306,675	1,306,675

Instructions:

Prepare an income statement departmentalized through income from operations.

SOLUTION

PERRY HOME
Income
For Year Ended

		Department F	
Revenue from sales:			
Sales.........................	....	$350,000	....
Less sales returns and allowances	....	6,400	....
Net sales.......................	....	......	$343,600
Cost of goods sold:			
Inventories, May 1, 19--	....	$ 17,200	....
Purchases.....................	....	280,600	....
Goods available for sale	....	$297,800	....
Less inventories, April 30, 19-- ...	....	17,600	....
Cost of goods sold	....	......	280,200
Gross profit	....	......	$ 63,400
Operating expenses:			
Selling expenses:			
Sales salaries	$17,300	......	....
Advertising expense	4,000	......	....
Depreciation expense—			
store equipment	3,520	......	....
Store supplies expense	550	......	....
Miscellaneous selling expense..	280	......	....
Total selling expenses	....	$ 25,650	....
General expenses:			
Office salaries	$ 3,000	......	....
Rent expense..................	2,940	......	....
Heating and lighting expense ..	1,200	......	....
Property tax expense	1,050	......	....
Insurance expense	630	......	....
Uncollectible accounts expense .	385	......	....
Miscellaneous general expense .	315	......	....
Total general expenses	....	9,520	....
Total operating expenses	....	......	35,170
Income from operations	....	......	$ 28,230
Other income:			
Interest income	....	......	....
Income before income tax.........	....	......	....
Income tax	....	......	....
Net income......................	....	......	....

APPLIANCES
Statement
April 30, 19--

Department R			Total		
......	$650,000	......	......	$1,000,000	......
......	10,200	......	......	16,600	......
......	......	$639,800	......	......	$983,400
......	$ 36,000	......	......	$ 53,200	......
......	532,000	......	......	812,600	......
......	$568,000	......	......	$ 865,800	......
......	41,200	......	......	58,800	......
......	......	526,800	......	......	807,000
......	......	$113,000	......	......	$176,400
$26,100	......	......	$43,400	......	......
6,800	......	......	10,800	......	......
5,280	......	......	8,800	......	......
700	......	......	1,250	......	......
520	......	......	800	......	......
......	$ 39,400	......	......	$ 65,050	......
$ 7,000	......	......	$10,000	......	......
6,860	......	......	9,800	......	......
2,800	......	......	4,000	......	......
1,950	......	......	3,000	......	......
1,170	......	......	1,800	......	......
715	......	......	1,100	......	......
585	......	......	900	......	......
......	21,080	......	......	30,600	......
......	......	60,480	......	......	95,650
......	......	$ 52,520	......	......	$ 80,750
......	......	......	......	......	1,000
......	......	......	......	......	$ 81,750
......	......	......	......	......	24,700
......	......	......	......	......	$ 57,050

DISCUSSION QUESTIONS

1. In preparing reports for the management's use, must the managerial accountant use generally accepted accounting principles? Discuss.

2. What is the dominant principle that guides the managerial accountant in preparing management reports?

3. Briefly describe the two basic functions of management.

4. What is the role of the controller in a business organization?

5. What is a decentralized business organization?

6. What is responsibility accounting?

7. Name three common types of responsibility centers for decentralized operations.

8. Differentiate between a cost center and a profit center.

9. In what major respect would budget performance reports prepared for the use of plant managers of a manufacturing enterprise with cost centers differ from those prepared for the use of the various department supervisors who report to the plant managers?

10. The newly appointed manager of the Appliance Department in a department store is studying the income statements presenting gross profit by departments in an attempt to adjust operations to achieve the highest possible gross profit for the department. (a) Suggest ways in which an income statement departmentalized through gross profit can be used in achieving this goal. (b) Suggest reasons why caution must be exercised in using such statements.

11. Describe the underlying principle of apportionment of operating expenses to departments for income statements departmentalized through income from operations.

12. For each of the following types of expenses listed in the left column, select the allocation basis listed in the right column that is most appropriate for use in arriving at operating income by departments.

Expense:	Basis of allocation:
(a) Sales salaries	(1) Cost of inventory and equipment
(b) Rent expense	(2) Departmental sales
(c) Advertising expense	(3) Time devoted to departments
(d) Property tax expense on inventory and equipment	(4) Physical space occupied

13. Differentiate between a direct and an indirect operating expense.

14. Indicate whether each of the following operating expenses incurred by a department store is a direct or an indirect expense:
    (a) Insurance expense on office building
    (b) Uncollectible accounts expense
    (c) Sales commissions
    (d) Heating and lighting expense
    (e) General manager's salary
    (f) Depreciation of store equipment

15. What term is applied to the dollar amount representing the excess of departmental gross profit over direct departmental expenses?

16. Name three performance measures useful in evaluating investment centers.

17. What is the major shortcoming of using operating income as a performance measure for investment centers?

18. Why should the factors under the control of the investment center manager (revenues, expenses, and invested assets) be considered in the computation of the rate of return on investment?

19. Halbert Co. has $300,000 invested in Division R, which earned $81,000 of operating income. What is the rate of return on investment for Division R?

20. If Halbert Co. in Question 19 had sales of $540,000, what is (a) the profit margin and (b) the investment turnover for Division R?

21. In a decentralized company in which the divisions are organized as investment centers, how could a division be considered the least profitable, even though it earned the largest amount of operating income?

22. Division C of Austin Co. has a rate of return on investment of 20%. (a) If Division C increases its investment turnover by 15%, what would be the new rate of return on investment? (b) If Division C also increases its profit margin from 10% to 12%, what would be the new rate of return on investment?

23. The rates of return on investment for Horn Co.'s three divisions, X, Y, and Z, are 22%, 18%, and 12%, respectively. In expanding operations, which of Horn Co.'s divisions should be given priority? Explain.

24. What term is used to describe the excess of divisional operating income over a minimum amount of desired operating income?

25. Division M of Jones Co. reported operating income of $260,000, based on invested assets of $800,000. If the minimum rate of return on divisional investments is 15%, what is the residual income for Division M?

26. Real World Focus. Tandy Corporation's annual report for the year ended June 30, 1985, reports a profit margin of 6.7% and an investment turnover rate of 1.58. (a) What was the rate of return on investment for the year ended June 30, 1985? (b) If the investment turnover rate does not change for the year ended June 30, 1986, what must the profit margin be to earn a rate of return on investment of 15%? (Round to the nearest tenth of one percent.)

EXERCISES

Exercise 21–1. Budget performance report. The budget for Department P of Plant 11 for the current month ended April 30 is as follows:

Factory wages	$168,000
Materials	147,000
Power and light	51,000
Supervisory salaries	36,000
Depreciation of plant and equipment	21,300
Maintenance	19,300
Insurance and property taxes	12,000

During April, the costs incurred in Department P of Plant 11 were: factory wages, $168,750; materials, $152,150; power and light, $50,400; supervisory salaries, $36,000; depreciation of plant and equipment, $21,300; maintenance, $19,180; insurance and property taxes, $12,000. (a) Prepare a budget performance report for the supervisor of Department P, Plant 11, for the month of April. (b) For what significant variations in costs might the supervisor be expected to request supplemental reports?

Exercise 21–2. Apportionment of rent expense to departments. Hobbs Company occupies a two-story building. The departments and the floor space occupied by each department are as follows:

Receiving and Storage	basement	1,800 sq. ft.
Department 1	basement	4,200
Department 2	first floor	3,500
Department 3	first floor	6,500
Department 4	second floor	1,000
Department 5	second floor	1,600
Department 6	second floor	1,400

The building is leased at an annual rental of $100,000, allocated to the floors as follows: basement, 30%; first floor, 50%; second floor, 20%. Determine the amount of rent to be apportioned to each department.

Exercise 21–3. Apportionment of depreciation and property tax expense to departments. In income statements prepared for Beeman Company, depreciation expense on equipment is apportioned on the basis of the average cost of the equipment, and property tax expense is apportioned on the basis of the combined total of the average cost of the equipment and the average cost of the inventories. Depreciation expense on equipment amounted to $150,000, and property tax expense amounted to $30,000 for the year. Determine the apportionment of the depreciation expense and the property tax expense, based on the following data:

| | Average Cost | |
Departments	Equipment	Inventories
Service:		
A...........	$ 360,000	
B...........	240,000	
Sales:		
X...........	720,000	$360,000
Y...........	480,000	120,000
Z...........	600,000	120,000
Total..........	$2,400,000	$600,000

Exercise 21–4. Departmental income statement. The following data were summarized from the accounting records for Crow Company for the current year ended October 31:

Cost of goods sold:
    Department E............................ $166,800
    Department F............................ 237,000

Direct expenses:
    Department E............................ 88,000
    Department F............................ 119,200

Income tax 38,400
Indirect expenses 76,400
Interest Income 16,000

Net sales:
    Department E............................ 328,400
    Department F............................ 466,200

Prepare an income statement departmentalized through departmental margin.

Exercise 21–5. Determination of missing items on income statements. One item is omitted from each of the following condensed divisional income statements of Bormann Company:

	Division G	Division H	Division I
Sales...........................	$450,000	$640,000	(e)
Cost of goods sold..............	270,000	(c)	320,000
Gross profit	(a)	$330,000	$260,000
Operating expenses..............	30,000	(d)	100,000
Operating income...............	(b)	$130,000	(f)

(a) Determine the amount of the missing items, identifying them by letter. (b) Based on operating income, which division is the most profitable?

Exercise 21–6. Rate of return on investment. The operating income and the amount of invested assets in each division of Enders Company are as follows:

	Operating Income	Invested Assets
Division A	$221,000	$850,000
Division B	158,400	480,000
Division C	136,800	720,000

(a) Compute the rate of return on investment for each division. (b) Which division is the most profitable per dollar invested?

Exercise 21–7.   Residual income. Based on the data in Exercise 21–6, assume that management has established a minimum rate of return for invested assets of 15%. (a) Determine the residual income for each division. (b) Based on residual income, which of the divisions is the most profitable?

Exercise 21–8.   Determination of missing items for computations of rate of return on investment. One item is omitted from each of the following computations of the rate of return on investment:

Rate of Return on Investment	=	Profit Margin	×	Investment Turnover
26%		20%		(a)
(b)		12%		1.5
36%		(c)		2.4
24%		15%		(d)
(e)		15%		.8

Determine the missing items, identifying each by the appropriate letter.

Exercise 21–9.   Profit margin, investment turnover, and rate of return on investment. The condensed income statement for Division E of Farmer Company is as follows:

Sales	$600,000
Cost of goods sold	360,000
Gross profit.	$240,000
Operating expenses	144,000
Operating income	$ 96,000

The manager of Division E is considering ways to increase the rate of return on investment. (a) Using the expanded expression, determine the profit margin, investment turnover, and rate of return on investment of Division E, assuming that $400,000 of assets have been invested in Division E. (b) If expenses could be reduced by $12,000 without decreasing sales, what would be the impact on the profit margin, investment turnover, and rate of return on investment for Division E?

Exercise 21–10. Determination of missing items for computations of rate of return on investment and residual income. One or more items is missing from the following tabulation of rate of return on investment and residual income:

Invested Assets	Operating Income	Rate of Return on Investment	Minimum Rate of Return	Minimum Amount of Operating Income	Residual Income
$750,000	$150,000	(a)	16%	(b)	(c)
$420,000	(d)	15%	(e)	$42,000	$21,000
$600,000	(f)	(g)	(h)	$72,000	$36,000
$900,000	$216,000	(i)	20%	(j)	(k)

Determine the missing items, identifying each item by the appropriate letter.

PROBLEMS

Series A

If the working papers correlating with the textbook are not used, omit Problem 21–1A.

Problem 21–1A. Budget performance reports. The organization chart for the manufacturing operations of Hubble Inc. is presented in the working papers, along with the completed budget performance reports for the Machine Shop and Assembly Departments of Plant 2. Partially completed budget performance reports for the Painting Department of Plant 2 and the vice-president in charge of operations are also presented.

Instructions:

(1) Complete the budget performance report for the supervisor of the Painting Department of Plant 2.
(2) Prepare a budget performance report for the use of the manager of Plant 2, detailing the relevant data from the three departments in the plant. Assume that the budgeted and actual administration expenses for the plant were $22,600 and $23,850, respectively.
(3) Complete the budget performance report for the vice-president in charge of operations.

Problem 21–2A. Departmental income statement through income from operations. Waller Appliances operates two sales departments—Department S for small appliances, such as radios and televisions, and Department L for large appliances, such as refrigerators and washing machines. The following trial balance was prepared as of October 31, the end of the current fiscal year, after all adjustments, including those for inventories, were recorded and posted.

Cash	27,500	
Accounts Receivable	60,700	
Inventories — Department S	12,240	
Inventories — Department L	42,760	
Prepaid Insurance.	1,360	
Store Supplies.	1,330	
Store Equipment	55,320	
Accumulated Depreciation — Store Equipment.		12,750
Accounts Payable.		10,600
Income Tax Payable.		3,310
Common Stock		50,000
Retained Earnings		29,260
Cash Dividends.	6,000	
Income Summary	65,000	55,000
Sales — Department S.		280,000
Sales — Department L		520,000
Sales Returns and Allowances — Department S	2,800	
Sales Returns and Allowances — Department L.	4,200	
Purchases — Department S	168,000	
Purchases — Department L.	338,000	
Sales Salaries Expense.	33,900	
Advertising Expense.	12,090	
Depreciation Expense — Store Equipment.	6,200	
Store Supplies Expense	1,620	
Miscellaneous Selling Expense	2,600	
Office Salaries Expense	30,000	
Rent Expense	12,000	
Heating and Lighting Expense.	10,200	
Property Tax Expense	3,800	
Insurance Expense.	1,800	
Uncollectible Accounts Expense	1,500	
Miscellaneous General Expense	1,700	
Interest Expense.	1,800	
Income Tax	56,500	
	960,920	960,920

Inventories at the beginning of the year were as follows: Department S, $15,600; Department L, $49,400.

The bases to be used in apportioning expenses, together with other essential information, are as follows:

Sales salaries expense — payroll records: Department S, $11,800; Department L, $22,100.

Advertising expense — usage: Department S, $4,250; Department L, $7,840.

Depreciation expense — average cost of equipment. Equipment balances at beginning of year: Department S, $19,360; Department L, $29,320. Equipment balances at end of year: Department S, $22,240; Department L, $33,080.

Store supplies expense — requisitions: Department S, $580; Department L, $1,040.

Office salaries expense — Department S, 32%; Department L, 68%.

Rent expense and heating and lighting expense — floor space: Department S, 4,200 sq. ft.; Department L, 10,800 sq. ft.

Property tax expense and insurance expense—average cost of equipment plus average cost of inventories.

Uncollectible accounts expense, miscellaneous selling expense, and miscellaneous general expense—volume of gross sales.

Instructions:

Prepare an income statement departmentalized through income from operations.

Problem 21–3A. Departmental income statement through departmental margin. Wilson Corporation consists of two departments, J and M. The bases to be used in apportioning expenses between the two departments, together with other essential data, are as follows:

Sales salaries and commissions expense—basic salary plus 5% of sales. Basic salaries for Department J, $40,800; Department M, $18,200.

Advertising expense for brochures—usage within each department advertising specific products: Department J, $9,400; Department M, $4,350.

Depreciation expense—average cost of store equipment: Department J, $63,800, Department M, $46,200.

Insurance expense—average cost of store equipment plus average cost of inventories. Average cost of inventories was $49,950 for Department J and $15,050 for Department M.

Uncollectible accounts expense—.4% of sales. Departmental managers are responsible for the granting of credit on the sales made by their respective departments.

The following data are obtained from the ledger on May 31, the end of the current fiscal year:

Sales—Department J		550,000
Sales—Department M		220,000
Cost of Goods Sold—Department J	357,500	
Cost of Goods Sold—Department M	145,200	
Sales Salaries and Commissions Expense	97,500	
Advertising Expense	13,750	
Depreciation Expense—Store Equipment	9,500	
Miscellaneous Selling Expense	1,520	
Administrative Salaries Expense	32,800	
Rent Expense	18,000	
Utilities Expense	11,200	
Insurance Expense	4,800	
Uncollectible Accounts Expense	3,080	
Miscellaneous General Expense	720	
Interest Income		5,000
Income Tax	24,200	

Instructions:

(1) Prepare an income statement departmentalized through departmental margin.
(2) Determine the rate of gross profit for each department.
(3) Determine the rate of departmental margin to sales for each department.

Problem 21–4A. Divisional income statements and rate of return on investment analysis. Mitchell Company is a diversified company with three operating divisions organized as investment centers. Condensed data taken from the records of the three divisions for the year ended August 31 are as follows:

	Division A	Division B	Division C
Sales......................	$1,000,000	$1,500,000	$1,800,000
Cost of goods sold...........	600,000	975,000	1,350,000
Operating expenses..........	280,000	345,000	252,000
Invested assets..............	800,000	1,000,000	1,200,000

The management of Mitchell Company is evaluating each division as a basis for planning a future expansion of operations.

Instructions:

(1) Prepare condensed divisional income statements for Divisions A, B, and C.
(2) Using the expanded expression, compute the profit margin, investment turnover, and rate of return on investment for each division.
(3) If available funds permit the expansion of operations of only one division, which of the divisions would you recommend for expansion, based on (1) and (2)?

Problem 21–5A. Effect of proposals on divisional performance. A condensed income statement for Division H of Searcy Company for the year ended October 31 is as follows:

Sales	$2,400,000
Cost of goods sold	1,440,000
Gross profit.............................	$ 960,000
Operating expenses	660,000
Operating income	$ 300,000

The president of Searcy Company is concerned with Division H's rate of return on invested assets of $2,000,000, and has indicated that the division's rate of return on investment must be increased to at least 18% by the end of the next year if operations are to continue. The division manager is considering the following three proposals:

Proposal 1: Transfer equipment with a book value of $400,000 to other divisions at no gain or loss and lease similar equipment. The annual lease payments would exceed the amount of depreciation expense on the old equipment by $16,800. This increase in expense would be included as part of the cost of goods sold. Sales would remain unchanged.

Proposal 2: Reduce invested assets by discontinuing a product line. This action would eliminate sales of $150,000, cost of goods sold of $120,000, and operating expenses of $45,000. Assets of $200,000 would be transferred to other divisions at no gain or loss.

Proposal 3: Purchase new and more efficient machinery and thereby reduce the cost of goods sold by $134,400. Sales would remain unchanged, and the old machinery, which has no remaining book value, would be scrapped at no gain or loss. The new machinery would increase invested assets by $400,000 for the year.

Instructions:

(1) Using the expanded expression, determine the profit margin, investment turnover, and rate of return on investment for Division H for the past year.
(2) Prepare condensed estimated income statements for Division H for each proposal.
(3) Using the expanded expression, determine the profit margin, investment turnover, and rate of return on investment for Division H under each proposal.
(4) Which of the three proposals would meet the required 18% rate of return on investment?
(5) If Division H were in an industry where the investment turnover could not be increased, how much would the profit margin have to increase to meet the president's required 18% rate of return on investment?

Problem 21–6A. Determination of missing items from computations. Data for Divisions A, B, C, D, and E of Young Company are as follows:

	Sales	Operating Income	Invested Assets	Rate of Return on Investment	Profit Margin	Investment Turnover
Division A ...	$750,000	$120,000	$500,000	(a)	(b)	(c)
Division B ...	(d)	(e)	$600,000	12%	(f)	1.25
Division C ...	$420,000	(g)	(h)	(i)	15%	1.2
Division D ...	$375,000	(j)	(k)	(l)	16%	1.25
Division E ...	(m)	$ 88,000	(n)	22%	11%	(o)

Instructions:

(1) Determine the missing items, identifying each by letters (a) through (o).
(2) Determine the residual income for each division, assuming that the minimum rate of return established by management is 10%.
(3) Which division is the most profitable?

Problem 21–7A. Divisional performance analysis and evaluation. The vice-president of operations of Carney Company is evaluating the performance of two divisions organized as investment centers. Division F generates the largest amount of operating income but has the lowest rate of return on investment. Division E has the highest rate of return on investment but generates the smallest operating income. Invested assets and condensed income statement data for the past year for each division are as follows:

	Division E	Division F
Sales	$5,000,000	$6,750,000
Cost of goods sold	3,000,000	4,320,000
Operating expenses	1,200,000	1,620,000
Invested assets	4,000,000	4,500,000

Instructions:

(1) Prepare condensed divisional income statements for each division for the year ended October 31.
(2) Using the expanded expression, determine the profit margin, investment turnover, and rate of return on investment for each division.
(3) If management desires a minimum rate of return of 12%, determine the residual income for each division.
(4) Discuss the evaluation of Divisions E and F, using the performance measures determined in (1), (2), and (3).

Problem 21–8A.   Divisional performance analysis and evaluation. The vice-president of operations of Swann Inc. recently resigned, and the president is considering which one of two division managers to promote to the vacated position. Both division managers have been with the company approximately ten years. Operating data for each division for the past three years are as follows:

	1987	1986	1985
Division M:			
Sales.....................	$ 1,520,000	$ 1,360,000	$ 1,200,000
Cost of goods sold...........	900,000	800,000	720,000
Gross profit.................	$ 620,000	$ 560,000	$ 480,000
Operating expenses..........	460,400	410,400	345,600
Operating income............	$ 159,600	$ 149,600	$ 134,400
Invested assets..............	$ 950,000	$ 800,000	$ 600,000
Total industry sales	$15,200,000	$10,880,000	$ 8,000,000
Division N:			
Sales.....................	$ 900,000	$ 770,000	$ 500,000
Cost of goods sold...........	540,000	460,000	300,000
Gross profit.................	$ 360,000	$ 310,000	$ 200,000
Operating expenses..........	216,000	194,500	128,000
Operating income............	$ 144,000	$ 115,500	$ 72,000
Invested assets..............	$ 600,000	$ 550,000	$ 400,000
Total industry sales	$11,250,000	$11,000,000	$10,000,000

Instructions:

(1) For each division for each of the three years, use the expanded expression to determine the profit margin, investment turnover, and rate of return on investment.
(2) Assuming that 15% has been established as a minimum rate of return, determine the residual income for each division for each of the three years.
(3) Determine each division's market share (division sales divided by total industry sales) for each of the three years.
(4) Based on (1), (2), and (3), which division manager would you recommend for promotion to vice-president of operations?
(5) What other factors should be considered in the promotion decision?

Problem 21–9A.   Real World Focus. The following data (in millions) for the four primary business segments of Rockwell International Corporation were taken from Rockwell International's 1985 financial statements:

	Sales	Operating Income	Assets
Aerospace	$5,309	$493.8	$1,499
Electronics	3,412	354.2	3,457
Automotive..................	1,722	225.9	963
General Industries	895	104.3	572

Instructions:

(1) For each of the four segments, use the expanded expression to determine the profit margin, investment turnover, and rate of return on investment. Round the profit margin to one decimal place, round the investment turnover to two decimal places, and determine the rate of return on investment by multiplying the profit margin by the investment turnover.
(2) Rank the segments from the highest to the lowest in terms of rate of return on investment.

Series B

If the working papers correlating with the textbook are not used, omit Problem 21–1B.

Problem 21–1B.   Budget performance reports. The organization chart for the manufacturing operations of Hubble Inc. is presented in the working papers, along with the completed budget performance reports for the Machine Shop and Assembly Departments of Plant 2. Partially completed budget performance reports for the Painting Department of Plant 2 and the vice-president in charge of operations are also presented.

Instructions:

(1) Complete the budget performance report for the supervisor of the Painting Department of Plant 2.
(2) Prepare a budget performance report for the use of the manager of Plant 2, detailing the relevant data from the three departments in the plant. Assume that the budgeted and actual administration expenses for the plant were $15,800 and $14,300, respectively.
(3) Complete the budget performance report for the vice-president in charge of operations.

Problem 21–2B.   Departmental income statement through income from operations. Sparkman Co. operates two sales departments — Department S for sporting goods and Department T for camping equipment. The following trial balance was prepared as of June 30, the end of the current fiscal year, after all adjustments, including the adjustments for inventories, were recorded and posted:

Cash	18,520	
Accounts Receivable	36,100	
Inventories—Department S	24,300	
Inventories—Department T	16,400	
Prepaid Insurance	1,500	
Store Supplies	1,400	
Store Equipment	83,200	
Accumulated Depreciation—Store Equipment		22,200
Accounts Payable		17,300
Income Tax Payable		2,700
Common Stock		50,000
Retained Earnings		57,170
Cash Dividends	5,000	
Income Summary	41,500	40,700
Sales—Department S		280,000
Sales—Department T		120,000
Sales Returns and Allowances—Department S	2,500	
Sales Returns and Allowances—Department T	1,700	
Purchases—Department S	131,600	
Purchases—Department T	70,400	
Sales Salaries Expense	70,000	
Advertising Expense	11,000	
Depreciation Expense—Store Equipment	5,500	
Store Supplies Expense	3,600	
Miscellaneous Selling Expense	3,000	
Office Salaries Expense	30,000	
Rent Expense	10,000	
Heating and Lighting Expense	6,000	
Property Tax Expense	3,200	
Insurance Expense	2,800	
Uncollectible Accounts Expense	2,200	
Miscellaneous General Expense	1,050	
Interest Expense	1,100	
Income Tax	6,500	
	590,070	590,070

Inventories at the beginning of the year were as follows: Department S, $26,730; Department T, $14,770.

The bases to be used in apportioning expenses, together with other essential information, are as follows:

Sales salaries expense—payroll records: Department S, $45,000; Department T, $25,000.

Advertising expense—usage: Department S, $7,200; Department T, $3,800.

Depreciation expense—average cost of equipment. Balances of equipment at beginning of year: Department S, $48,490; Department T, $26,110. Balances at end of year: Department S, $54,080; Department T, $29,120.

Store supplies expense—requisitions: Department S, $2,420; Department T, $1,180.

Office salaries expense—Department S, 80%; Department T, 20%.

Rent expense and heating and lighting expense—floor space: Department S, 14,400 sq. ft.; Department T, 5,600 sq. ft.

Property tax expense and insurance expense—average cost of equipment plus average cost of inventories.

Uncollectible accounts expense, miscellaneous selling expense, and miscellaneous general expense—volume of gross sales.

Instructions:

Prepare an income statement departmentalized through income from operations.

Problem 21–4B. Divisional income statements and rate of return on investment analysis. Zavor Company is a diversified company with three operating divisions organized as investment centers. Condensed data taken from the records of the three divisions for the year ended August 31 are as follows:

	Division X	Division Y	Division Z
Sales......................	$960,000	$1,875,000	$1,350,000
Cost of goods sold...........	624,000	1,200,000	810,000
Operating expenses...........	192,000	525,000	324,000
Invested assets..............	800,000	750,000	900,000

The management of Zavor Company is evaluating each division as a basis for planning a future expansion of operations.

Instructions:

(1) Prepare condensed divisional income statements for Divisions X, Y, and Z.
(2) Using the expanded expression, compute the profit margin, investment turnover, and rate of return on investment for each division.
(3) If available funds permit the expansion of operations of only one division, which of the divisions would you recommend for expansion, based on (1) and (2)?

Problem 21–6B. Determination of missing items from computations. Data for Divisions M, N, O, P, and Q of Reid Company are as follows:

	Sales	Operating Income	Invested Assets	Rate of Return on Investment	Profit Margin	Investment Turnover
Division M ..	$ 500,000	$ 60,000	$400,000	(a)	(b)	(c)
Division N ..	$1,080,000	(d)	$600,000	18%	(e)	(f)
Division O ..	(g)	$174,000	(h)	(i)	24%	1.25
Division P ..	$ 840,000	(j)	(k)	24%	20%	(l)
Division Q ..	(m)	$ 75,600	$360,000	(n)	(o)	1.5

Instructions:

(1) Determine the missing items, identifying each by letters (a) through (o).
(2) Determine the residual income for each division, assuming that the minimum rate of return established by management is 12%.
(3) Which division is the most profitable?

Problem 21–7B.   Divisional performance analysis and evaluation. The vice-president of operations of Eaton Company is evaluating the performance of two divisions organized as investment centers. Division Y has the highest rate of return on investment, but generates the smallest amount of operating income. Division X generates the largest operating income, but has the lowest rate of return on investment. Invested assets and condensed income statement data for the past year for each division are as follows:

	Division X	Division Y
Sales	$3,375,000	$3,840,000
Cost of goods sold	2,025,000	2,496,000
Operating expenses	756,000	768,000
Invested assets	2,700,000	2,400,000

Instructions:

(1) Prepare condensed divisional income statements for each division for the year ended October 31.
(2) Using the expanded expression, determine the profit margin, investment turnover, and rate of return on investment for each division.
(3) If management desires a minimum rate of return of 16%, determine the residual income for each division.
(4) Discuss the evaluation of Divisions X and Y, using the performance measures determined in (1), (2), and (3).

MINI-CASE 21

Your father is the president of Newman Company, a privately held, diversified company with five separate divisions organized as investment centers. A condensed income statement for the Sporting Goods Division for the past year is as follows:

Newman Company — Sporting Goods Division
Income Statement
For Year Ended December 31, 19--

Sales.	$22,500,000
Cost of goods sold.	13,500,000
Gross profit	$ 9,000,000
Operating expenses.	5,400,000
Operating income.	$ 3,600,000

The manager of the Sporting Goods Division was recently presented with the opportunity to add an additional product line, which would require invested assets of $5,000,000. A projected income statement for the new product line is as follows:

New Product Line
Projected Income Statement
For Year Ended December 31, 19--

Sales.	$ 6,000,000
Cost of goods sold.	3,600,000
Gross profit	$ 2,400,000
Operating expenses.	1,500,000
Operating income.	$ 900,000

The Sporting Goods Division currently has $15,000,000 in invested assets, and Newman Company's overall rate of return on investment, including all divisions, is 15%. Each division manager is evaluated on the basis of divisional rate of return on investment, and a bonus equal to $4,000 for each percentage point by which the division's rate of return on investment exceeds the company average is awarded each year.

Your father is concerned that the manager of the Sporting Goods Division rejected the addition of the new product line, when all estimates indicated that the product line would be profitable and would increase overall company income. You have been asked to analyze the possible reasons why the Sporting Goods Division manager rejected the new product line.

Instructions:

(1) Determine the rate of return on investment for the Sporting Goods Division for the past year.
(2) Determine the Sporting Goods Division manager's bonus for the past year.
(3) Determine the estimated rate of return on investment for the new product line.
(4) Why might the manager of the Sporting Goods Division decide to reject the new product line?
(5) Can you suggest an alternative performance measure for motivating division managers to accept new investment opportunities that would increase the overall company income and rate of return on investment?

Chapter 22

MANUFACTURING OPERATIONS AND JOB ORDER COST SYSTEMS

Chapter Objectives:

■ Describe the concepts, principles, and terminology used in accounting for manufacturing operations.

■ Describe a general accounting system for a manufacturing operation.

■ Describe and illustrate the preparation of a statement of cost of goods manufactured.

■ Describe the basic characteristics of cost accounting systems.

■ Describe and illustrate the flow of data through a cost accounting system of a manufacturing enterprise.

■ Describe alternative cost accounting systems for manufacturing operations.

■ Describe and illustrate a job order cost accounting system.

Job order process

anagerial accounting has evolved in response to the changing informational needs of management. Perhaps the most important single event in this evolutionary process was the Industrial Revolution, which occurred in England from the mid-eighteenth to the mid-nineteenth centuries. As a result of the Industrial Revolution, the production of marketable goods changed from the handicraft method, in which a relatively small number of items were made individually, to the factory system, in which many identical products could be made in large volumes. Manufacturing enterprises became larger and more complex, and competition among manufacturers increased. In turn, these changes brought about a greater need for information that would be useful to management in planning and controlling operations.

In this and later chapters, attention is directed to concepts and principles for measuring the efficiency of a manufacturer's current operations and for planning future operations. Although these concepts and principles are presented in the context of a manufacturing enterprise, many of them can be applied to merchandising and service enterprises.

MANUFACTURING OPERATIONS

Manufacturers employ labor and use machinery to change materials into finished products. In thus changing the form of goods, their activities differ from those of merchandisers. The furniture manufacturer, for example, changes lumber and other materials into furniture. The furniture dealer in turn purchases the finished goods from the manufacturer and sells them without additional processing.

Some functions of manufacturing companies, such as selling, administration, and financing, are like those of merchandising organizations. The accounting procedures related to these functions are the same for both types of enterprises. The production function of a manufacturing company, however, requires accounting procedures that provide for the accumulation of data identified with the production processes. These procedures involve additional ledger accounts and the establishment of internal controls over the manufacturing operations.

The cost of merchandise acquired by a merchandising business for resale to customers is a composite of invoice prices and various additions and deductions to cover such items as delivery charges, allowances, and cash discounts. When this merchandise is sold rather than consumed, the cost is called the **cost of merchandise sold**. The cost of manufacturing a product, however, includes not only the cost of tangible materials but also the many costs incurred in changing the materials into a finished product ready for sale. The cost of manufactured products sold is called the **cost of goods sold**.

Cost of Manufactured Products

Unlike a merchandising enterprise, which maintains one inventory account, manufacturing businesses maintain three inventory accounts for (1) goods in the state in which they are to be sold, (2) goods in the process of manufacture, and (3) goods in the state in which they were acquired. These inventories are called **finished goods**, **work in process**, and **materials**, respectively. The balances in the inventory accounts may be presented in the balance sheet in the following manner:

Inventories:		
Finished goods	$300,000	
Work in process	55,000	
Materials	123,000	$478,000

The finished goods inventory and the work in process inventory are composed of three manufacturing costs: **direct materials** cost, which is the delivered cost of the materials that enter directly into the finished product; **direct labor** cost, which is the wages of the factory workers who change the materials into a finished product; and **factory overhead** cost, which includes all of the remaining costs of operating the factory. Some examples of factory overhead costs are wages for factory supervision, supplies used in the factory but not entering directly into the finished product, and taxes, insurance, depreciation, and maintenance related to factory plant and equipment.

The direct materials, direct labor, and factory overhead costs incurred in the process of manufacturing are reported on the balance sheet as work in process inventory until the goods are completed. After the goods are completed, they are reported as finished goods inventory on the balance sheet. The goods that have been sold are reported on the income statement as cost of goods sold. The relationship between the costs incurred in the manufacturing process, inventories, and the cost of goods sold is illustrated in the top portion of the diagram on page 986. The relationship between purchases of merchandise, merchandise inventory, and the cost of merchandise sold is illustrated in the bottom portion of the diagram.

INVENTORY
COST FLOWS
FOR MANU-
FACTURING
AND MER-
CHANDISING
ENTERPRISES

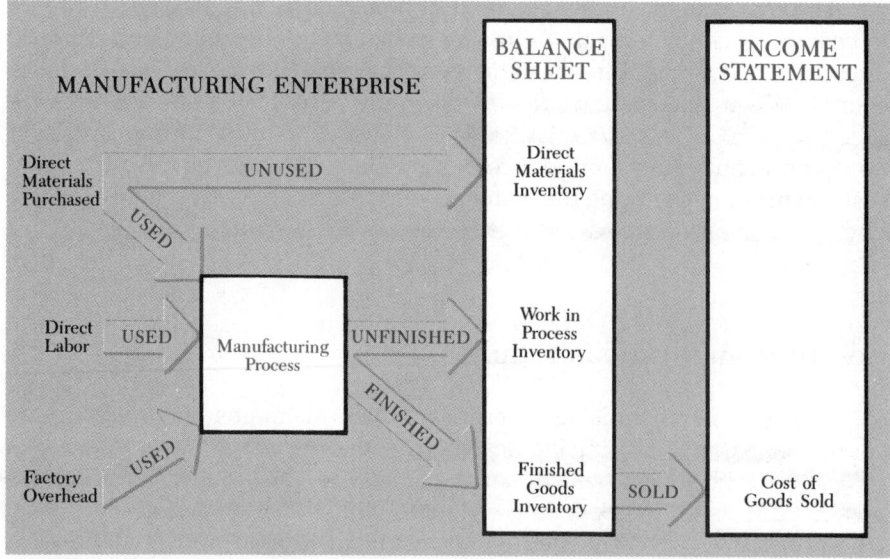

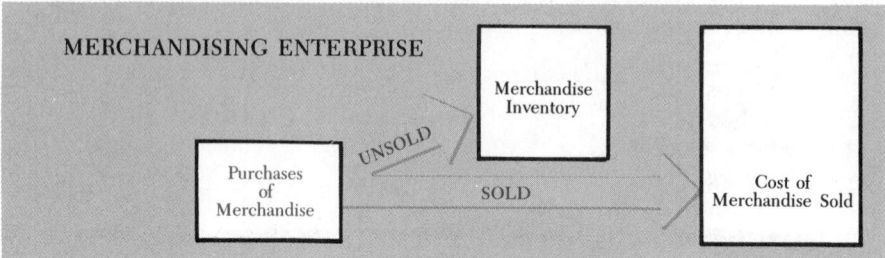

Accounting Systems

Two basic accounting systems are commonly used by manufacturers: general accounting systems and cost accounting systems. A general accounting system is essentially an extension to manufacturing operations of the common system for merchandising enterprises which use periodic inventory procedures. A cost accounting system uses perpetual inventory procedures and provides more detailed information concerning costs of production.

In the remainder of this chapter, a general accounting system is described, followed by a discussion and illustration of one of the two main types of cost accounting systems. The other main type of cost accounting system is discussed in Chapter 23.

GENERAL ACCOUNTING SYSTEM FOR MANUFACTURING OPERATIONS

Although the accounting procedures for manufacturing operations are likely to be more complex than those used in merchandising operations, the complexity of such procedures varies widely. If only a single product or several similar products are manufactured, and if the manufacturing processes are neither complicated nor numerous, the accounting system may be fairly simple. In such cases, the periodic system of inventory accounting used in merchandising may be extended to the three manufacturing inventories, and the manufacturing accounts may be summarized periodically in an account entitled Manufacturing Summary. It is to such a simple situation that attention will first be directed.

Statement of Cost of Goods Manufactured

Since manufacturing activities differ greatly from selling and general administration activities, it is customary to separate the two groups of accounts in the summarizing process at the end of an accounting period. In addition, the manufacturing group is usually reported in a separate **statement of cost of goods manufactured** in order to avoid a long, complicated income statement. An income statement and its supporting statement of cost of goods manufactured are illustrated on page 988.

In the statement of cost of goods manufactured, the amount listed for the work in process inventory at the beginning of the period is composed of the estimated cost of the direct materials, the direct labor, and the factory overhead applicable to the inventory of partially processed products at the end of the preceding period. The cost of the direct materials placed in production is determined by adding the beginning inventory of materials and the net cost of the direct materials purchased and deducting the ending inventory. The amount listed for direct labor is determined by referring to the direct labor account. The factory overhead costs, which are determined by referring to the ledger, are listed individually in the statement of cost of goods manufactured or in a separate schedule. The sum of the costs of direct materials placed in production, the direct labor, and the factory overhead represents the total manufacturing costs incurred during the period. Addition of this amount to the beginning inventory of work in process yields the total cost of the work that has been in process during the period. The estimated cost of the ending inventory of work in process is then deducted to yield the cost of goods manufactured. It should be noted that the "cost of goods manufactured" reported in the statement of cost of goods manufactured and in the income statement is comparable to the "purchases" reported by a merchandising enterprise.

INCOME
STATEMENT

Ming Manufacturing Company
Income Statement
For Year Ended December 31, 1987

Sales.		$915,800
Cost of goods sold:		
Finished goods inventory, January 1, 1987.	$ 78,500	
Cost of goods manufactured	550,875	
Cost of finished goods available for sale.	$629,375	
Less finished goods inventory, December 31, 1987 . .	91,000	
Cost of goods sold.		538,375

STATEMENT
OF COST OF
GOODS
MANU-
FACTURED

internal statement for mangement use only

Ming Manufacturing Company
Statement of Cost of Goods Manufactured
For Year Ended December 31, 1987

Work in process inventory, January 1, 1987 . ?			$ 55,000
Direct materials:			
Inventory, January 1, 1987.	$ 62,000		
Purchases	220,800		
Cost of materials available for use.	$282,800		
Less inventory, December 31, 1987.	58,725		
Cost of materials placed in production		$224,075	
Direct labor		218,750	
Factory overhead:			
Indirect labor.	$ 49,300		
Depreciation of factory equipment.	22,300		
Heat, light, and power	21,800		
Property taxes.	9,750		
Depreciation of buildings.	6,000		
Insurance expired	4,750		
Factory supplies used.	2,900		
Miscellaneous factory costs.	2,050		
Total factory overhead		118,850	
Total manufacturing costs			561,675
Total work in process during period			$616,675
Less work in process inventory,			
December 31, 1987. . ?			65,800
Cost of goods manufactured.			$550,875

goes into income statement

Periodic Inventory Procedures

The process of adjusting the periodic inventory and other accounts of a manufacturing business is like that for a merchandising enterprise. Adjustments to the merchandise inventory account are replaced by adjusting entries for direct materials, work in process, and finished goods. The first two accounts are adjusted through Manufacturing Summary, and the third is adjusted through Income Summary.

At the end of the accounting period, the temporary accounts that appear in the statement of cost of goods manufactured are closed to Manufacturing Summary. This account's final balance, which represents the cost of goods manufactured during the period, is then closed to Income Summary. The remaining temporary accounts (sales, expenses, etc.) are then closed to Income Summary in the usual manner.

The relationship of the manufacturing summary account to the income summary account is illustrated as follows:

Manufacturing Summary

Dec. 31 Work in process inventory, Jan. 1	55,000	Dec. 31 Work in process inventory, Dec. 31	65,800
31 Direct materials inventory, Jan. 1	62,000	31 Direct materials inventory, Dec. 31	58,725
31 Direct materials purchases	220,800	31 To Income Summary	550,875
31 Direct labor	218,750		
31 Factory overhead	118,850		
	675,400		675,400

Income Summary

Dec. 31 Finished goods inventory, Jan. 1	78,500	Dec. 31 Finished goods inventory, Dec. 31	91,000
31 From Manufacturing Summary	550,875		

COST OF GOODS MANUFACTURED CLOSED TO INCOME SUMMARY

To simplify the illustration, the individual overhead accounts are presented as a total. Note that the balance transferred from the manufacturing summary account to the income summary account, $550,875, is the same as the final figure reported on the statement of cost of goods manufactured.

A work sheet may be used in preparing financial statements for a manufacturing enterprise which uses periodic inventory procedures. A description and illustration of such a work sheet is presented in Appendix F.

COST ACCOUNTING SYSTEM FOR MANUFACTURING OPERATIONS

Through the use of perpetual inventory procedures, a cost accounting system achieves greater accuracy in the determination of costs than is possible with a general accounting system that uses periodic inventory procedures. Cost accounting procedures also permit far more effective control by supplying data on the costs incurred by each factory department and the unit cost of manufacturing each type of product. Such procedures provide not only data useful to management in minimizing costs but also other valuable information about production methods to use, quantities to produce, product lines to promote, and sales prices to charge.

Perpetual Inventory Procedures

Perpetual inventory controlling accounts and subsidiary ledgers are maintained for materials, work in process, and finished goods in cost accounting systems. Each of these accounts is debited for all additions and is credited for all deductions. The balance of each account thus represents the inventory on hand.

All expenditures incidental to manufacturing move through the work in process account, the finished goods account, and eventually into the cost of goods sold account. The flow of costs through the perpetual inventory accounts and into the cost of goods sold account is illustrated as follows:

FLOW OF COSTS THROUGH PERPETUAL INVENTORY ACCOUNTS

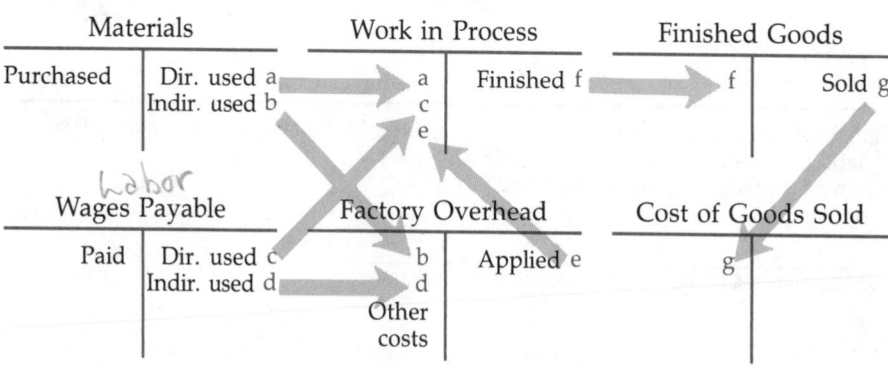

Materials and factory labor used in production are classified as direct and indirect. The materials and the factory labor used directly in the process of manufacturing are debited to Work in Process (a and c in the diagram). The materials and the factory labor used that do not enter directly into the finished product are debited to Factory Overhead (b and d in the diagram). Examples of indirect materials are oils and greases, abrasives and polishes, cleaning supplies, gloves, and brushes. Examples of indirect labor are salaries of supervisors, inspectors, material handlers, security guards, and janitors. The proper amount of factory overhead costs are transferred to Work in Process (e in the diagram). The costs of the goods finished are transferred from Work in Process to Finished Goods (f in the diagram). When the goods are sold, their costs are transferred from Finished Goods to Cost of Goods Sold (g in the diagram).

The number of accounts presented in the flowchart was limited in order to simplify the illustration. In practice, manufacturing operations may require many processing departments, each requiring separate work in process and factory overhead accounts.

Types of Cost Accounting Systems

There are two main types of cost systems for manufacturing operations — job order cost and process cost. Each of the two systems is widely used, and a manufacturer may use a job order cost system for some of its products and a process cost system for others. The basic concepts of job order cost systems are illustrated in this chapter, while process cost systems are discussed in Chapter 23.

A job order cost system provides for a separate record of the cost of each particular quantity of product that passes through the factory. It is best suited to industries that manufacture goods to fill special orders from customers and to industries that produce different lines of products for stock. It is also appropriate when standard products are manufactured in batches rather than on a continuous basis. In a job order cost system, a summary such as the following would show the cost incurred in completing a job:

Job 565
1,000 Units of Product X200

Direct materials used........................	$2,380
Direct labor used............................	4,400
Factory overhead applied	3,080
Total cost	$9,860
Unit cost ($9,860 ÷ 1,000).................	$ 9.86

Under a process cost system, the costs are accumulated for each of the departments or processes within the factory. A process system is best used by manufacturers of like units of product that are not distinguishable from each other during a continuous production process.

JOB ORDER COST SYSTEMS

In the following paragraphs, the discussion of job order cost systems refers to the source documents that serve as the basis for the entries to record the materials, labor, and overhead costs. The managerial uses of cost accounting in planning and controlling operations are also highlighted.

Materials

Procedures used in the procurement and issuance of materials differ considerably among manufacturers and even among departments of a particular manufacturer. The discussion that follows is confined to the basic principles, however, and will disregard relatively minor variations and details.

Some time in advance of the date that production of a certain commodity is to begin, the department responsible for scheduling informs the purchasing department, by means of **purchase requisitions**, of the materials that will be needed. The purchasing department then issues the necessary **purchase orders** to suppliers. After the goods have been received and inspected, the receiving department personnel prepare a **receiving report**, showing the quantity received and its condition. Quantities, unit costs, and total costs of the goods billed, as reported on the supplier's invoice, are then compared with the purchase order and the receiving report to make sure that the amounts billed agree with the materials ordered and received. After such verifications, the invoice is recorded as a debit to Materials and a credit to Accounts Payable.

The account Materials in the general ledger is a controlling account. A separate account for each type of material is maintained in a subsidiary ledger called the **materials ledger**. Details as to quantity and cost of materials received are recorded in the materials ledger on the basis of the purchase invoices, or receiving reports. A typical form of materials ledger account is illustrated as follows:

MATERIALS
LEDGER
ACCOUNT

MATERIAL NO. 23								ORDER POINT 1,000	
RECEIVED			**ISSUED**				**BALANCE**		
REC. REPORT NO.	QUAN- TITY	AMOUNT	MAT. REQ. NO.	QUAN- TITY	AMOUNT	DATE	QUAN- TITY	AMOUNT	UNIT PRICE
						JAN. 1	1,200	600.00	.50
			672	500	250.00	4	700	350.00	.50
196	3,000	1,620.00				8	700	350.00	.50
							3,000	1,620.00	.54
			704	800	404.00	18	2,900	1,566.00	.54

The accounts in the materials ledger may also be used as an aid in maintaining proper inventory quantities of stock items. Frequent comparisons of quantity balances with predetermined order points enable management to avoid costly idle time caused by lack of materials. The subsidiary ledger form may also include columns for recording quantities ordered and dates of the purchase orders.

Materials are transferred from the storeroom to the factory in response to **materials requisitions**, which may be issued by the manufacturing department concerned or by a central scheduling department. Storeroom personnel record the issuances on the materials requisition by inserting the physical quantity data. Transfer of responsibility for the materials is evidenced by the signature or initials of the storeroom and factory personnel concerned. The requisition is then routed to the materials ledger clerk, who inserts unit prices and amounts. A typical materials requisition is illustrated as follows:

MATERIALS
REQUISITION

MATERIALS REQUISITION				
Job No. 62			Requisition No. 704	
Authorized by R. A. Sanders			Date January 18, 19--	
Description	Quantity Authorized	Quantity Issued	Unit Price	Amount
Material No. 23	800	700 100	$.50 .54	$350 54
Total issued				$404
Issued by M. K.		Received by J. B.		

The completed requisition serves as the basis for posting quantities and dollar data to the materials ledger accounts. In the illustration, the first-in, first-out costing method was used. A summary of the materials requisitions completed during the month serves as the basis for transferring the cost of the materials from the controlling account in the general ledger to the controlling accounts for work in process and factory overhead. The flow of materials into production is illustrated by the following entry:

Work in Process.....................................	13,000	
Factory Overhead	840	
Materials		13,840

The perpetual inventory system for materials has three important advantages: (1) it provides for prompt and accurate charging of materials to jobs and factory overhead, (2) it permits the work of inventory-taking to be spread out rather than concentrated at the end of a fiscal period, and (3) it aids in the disclosure of inventory shortages or other irregularities. As physical quantities of the various materials are determined, the actual inventories are compared with the balances of the respective subsidiary ledger accounts. The causes of significant differences between the two should be determined and the responsibility for the differences assigned to specific individuals. Remedial action can then be taken.

Factory Labor

Unlike materials, factory labor is not tangible, nor is it acquired and stored in advance of its use. Hence, there is no perpetual inventory account for labor. The two main objectives in accounting for labor are (1) determination of the correct amount to be paid each employee for each payroll period, and (2) appropriate allocation of labor costs to factory overhead and individual job orders.

The amount of time spent by an employee in the factory is usually recorded on **clock cards**, which are also called **in-and-out cards**. The amount of time spent by each employee and the labor cost incurred for each individual job, or for factory overhead, are recorded on **time tickets**. A typical time ticket form is illustrated as follows:

TIME TICKET

Time Ticket				
Employee Name Gail Berry		No. 4521		
Employee No. 240		Date January 18, 19--		
Description of work Finishing		Job No. 62		
Time Started	Time Stopped	Hours Worked	Hourly Rate	Cost
10:00	12:00	2	$6.50	$13.00
1:00	2:00	1	6.50	6.50
Total cost				$19.50
Approved by T. D.				

The times reported on an employee's time tickets are compared with the related clock cards as an internal check on the accuracy of payroll disbursements. A summary of the time tickets at the end of each month serves as the basis for recording the direct and indirect labor costs incurred. The flow of labor costs into production is illustrated by the following entry:

Work in Process....................................	10,000	
Factory Overhead	2,200	
Wages Payable....................................		12,200

Factory Overhead

Factory overhead includes all manufacturing costs, except direct materials and direct labor. Examples of factory overhead costs, in addition to indirect materials and indirect labor, are depreciation, electricity, fuel, insurance, and property taxes. It is customary to have a factory overhead controlling account in the general ledger. Details of the various types of cost are accumulated in a subsidiary ledger.

Debits to Factory Overhead come from various sources. For example, the cost of indirect materials is obtained from the summary of the materials requisitions, the cost of indirect labor is obtained from the summary of the time tickets, costs of electricity and water are obtained from invoices, and the cost of depreciation and expired insurance may be recorded as adjustments at the end of the accounting period.

Although factory overhead cannot be specifically identified with particular jobs, it is as much a part of manufacturing costs as direct materials and direct labor. As the use of machines and automation has increased, factory overhead has represented an ever larger part of total costs. Many items of factory overhead cost are incurred for the entire factory and cannot be directly related to the finished product. The problem is further complicated because some items of factory overhead cost are relatively fixed in amount while others tend to vary according to changes in productivity.

To wait until the end of an accounting period to allocate factory overhead to the various jobs would be quite acceptable from the standpoint of accuracy but highly unsatisfactory in terms of timeliness. If the cost system is to be of maximum usefulness, it is imperative that cost data be available as each job is completed, even though there is a sacrifice in accuracy. It is only through timely reporting that management can make whatever adjustments seem necessary in pricing and manufacturing methods to achieve the best possible combination of revenue and cost on future jobs. Therefore, in order that job costs may be available currently, it is customary to apply factory overhead to production by using a **predetermined factory overhead rate**.

balance in account

Predetermined Factory Overhead Rate. The factory overhead rate is determined by relating the estimated amount of factory overhead for the forthcoming year to some common activity base, one that will equitably apply the factory overhead costs to the goods manufactured. The common bases include direct labor costs, direct labor hours, and machine hours. For example, if it is estimated that the total factory overhead costs for the year will be $100,000 and that the total direct labor cost will be $125,000, an overhead rate of 80% ($100,000 ÷ $125,000) will be applied to the direct labor cost incurred during the year.

close out to cost of goods sold

As factory overhead costs are incurred, they are debited to the factory overhead account. The factory overhead costs applied to production are periodically credited to the factory overhead account and debited to the work in process account. The application of factory overhead costs to production (80% of direct labor cost of $10,000) is illustrated by the following entry:

Work in Process...	8,000	
Factory Overhead		8,000

Inevitably, factory overhead costs applied and actual factory overhead costs incurred during a particular period will differ. If the amount applied exceeds the actual costs, the factory overhead account will have a credit balance and the overhead is said to be **overapplied** or **overabsorbed**. If the amount applied is less than the actual costs, the account will have a debit balance and the overhead is said to be **underapplied** or **underabsorbed**. Both cases are illustrated in the following account:

ACCOUNT FACTORY OVERHEAD   ACCOUNT NO.

Date		Item	Debit	Credit	Balance Debit	Balance Credit
May	1	Balance				200
	31	Costs incurred	8,320			
	31	Cost applied		8,000	120	

Underapplied Balance ⬅

Overapplied Balance ⬅

Disposition of Factory Overhead Balance. The balance in the factory overhead account is carried forward from month to month until the end of the year. The amount of the balance is reported on interim balance sheets as a deferred item.

The Implications of Automation for Allocating Factory Overhead — A Case Study

For some departments at Amerock Corporation, the allocation of overhead on the basis of direct labor became less accurate and less useful as manufacturing processes became more automated. The solution was to change from direct labor hours to machine hours for these departments.

Amerock Corporation, a manufacturer of cabinet and decorative hardware, found that the only disadvantages to using machine hours as a basis for allocating factory overhead were the time it would take to develop the system and the need for additional reporting by the machine operators. The potential benefits clearly outweighed any disadvantages. In the accounting area, a major advantage would be the ability to allocate overhead when one worker tended several machines. Better cost estimating would also be possible because overhead allocation would be more accurate. Forecasting and the calculation of actual costs would be easier. In the manufacturing area, machine utilization information would be more useful in understanding and controlling production and reporting.

Amerock Corporation's change in its overhead allocation basis has made it possible for accounting to capture costs accurately and for manufacturing to measure performance efficiently. The results have been so successful that Amerock plans to convert most of its departments to a machine hour basis as more of its plants become automated.

Source: Adapted from Gregory Hakala, "Measuring Costs with Machine Hours," *Management Accounting* (October, 1985), pp. 57–61.

The nature of the balance in the factory overhead account (underapplied or overapplied), as well as the amount, will change during the year. If there is a decided trend in either direction and the amount is substantial, the reason should be determined. If the variation is caused by alterations in manufacturing methods or by substantial changes in production goals, it may be advisable to revise the factory overhead rate. The accumulation of a large underapplied balance is more serious than a trend in the opposite direction and may indicate inefficiencies in production methods, excessive expenditures, or a combination of factors.

Despite any corrective actions that may be taken to avoid an underapplication or overapplication of factory overhead, the account will usually have a balance at the end of the fiscal year. Since the balance represents the underapplied or overapplied factory overhead applicable to the operations of the year just ended, it is not proper to report it in the year-end balance sheet as a deferred item.

There are two main alternatives for disposing of the balance of factory overhead at the end of the year: (1) by allocation of the balance among work in process, finished goods, and cost of goods sold accounts on the basis of the total amounts of applied factory overhead included in those accounts at the end of the year, or (2) by transfer of the balance to the cost of goods sold account. Theoretically, only the first alternative is sound because it represents a correction of the estimated overhead rate and brings the accounts into agreement with the costs actually incurred. On the other hand, much time and expense may be required to make the allocation and to revise the unit costs of the work in process and finished goods inventories. Furthermore, in most manufacturing enterprises, a very large part of the total manufacturing costs for the year passes through the work in process and the finished goods accounts into the cost of goods sold account before the end of the year. Therefore, unless the total amount of the underapplied or overapplied balance is great, it is satisfactory to transfer it to Cost of Goods Sold.

Work in Process

Costs incurred for the various jobs are debited to Work in Process. The job costs described in the preceding sections may be summarized as follows:

Direct materials, $13,000 — Work in Process debited and Materials credited; data obtained from summary of materials requisitions.

Direct labor, $10,000 — Work in Process debited and Wages Payable credited; data obtained from summary of time tickets.

Factory overhead, $8,000 — Work in process debited and Factory Overhead credited; data obtained by applying overhead rate to direct labor cost (80% of $10,000).

The work in process account to which these costs were charged is illustrated as follows:

ACCOUNT WORK IN PROCESS   ACCOUNT NO.

Date		Item	Debit	Credit	Balance Debit	Balance Credit
May	1	Balance			3,000	
	31	Direct materials	13,000		16,000	
	31	Direct labor	10,000		26,000	
	31	Factory overhead	8,000		34,000	
	31	Jobs completed		31,920	2,080	

The work in process account is a controlling account that contains summary information only. The details concerning the costs incurred on each job order are accumulated in a subsidiary ledger known as the **cost ledger**. Each cost ledger account, called a **job cost sheet**, has spaces for recording all direct materials and direct labor chargeable to the job and for applying factory overhead at the predetermined rate. Postings to the job cost sheets are made from materials requisitions and time tickets or from summaries of these documents.

The four cost sheets in the subsidiary ledger for the work in process account illustrated are summarized as follows:

COST LEDGER

Job 71 (Summary)	
Balance..................	3,000
Direct materials............	2,000
Direct labor...............	2,400
Factory overhead	1,920
	9,320

Job 73 (Summary)	
Direct materials............	6,000
Direct labor...............	4,000
Factory overhead	3,200
	13,200

Job 72 (Summary)	
Direct materials............	4,000
Direct labor...............	3,000
Factory overhead	2,400
	9,400

Job 74 (Summary)	
Direct materials............	1,000
Direct labor...............	600
Factory overhead	480
	2,080

The relationship between the work in process controlling account on page 999 and the subsidiary cost ledger may be observed in the following tabulation:

Work in Process (Controlling)		Cost Ledger (Subsidiary)	
Beginning balance.........	$ 3,000 ⟷	Beginning balance	
		Job 71	$ 3,000
		Direct materials	
		Job 71.................	$ 2,000
Direct materials	$13,000 ⟷	Job 72.................	4,000
		Job 73.................	6,000
		Job 74.................	1,000
			$13,000
		Direct labor	
		Job 71.................	$ 2,400
Direct labor...............	$10,000 ⟷	Job 72.................	3,000
		Job 73.................	4,000
		Job 74.................	600
			$10,000
		Factory overhead	
		Job 71.................	$ 1,920
Factory overhead..........	$ 8,000 ⟷	Job 72.................	2,400
		Job 73.................	3,200
		Job 74.................	480
			$ 8,000
		Jobs completed	
		Job 71.................	$ 9,320
Jobs completed	$31,920 ⟷	Job 72.................	9,400
		Job 73.................	13,200
			$31,920
Ending balance	$ 2,080 ⟷	Ending balance	
		Job 74	$ 2,080

The data in the cost ledger were presented in summary form for illustrative purposes. A job cost sheet for Job 72, providing for the current accumulation of cost elements entering into the job order and for a summary when the job is completed, is as follows:

Job No. 72

Item 5,000 Type C Containers

For Stock

Date May 7, 19--

Date wanted May 23, 19--

Date completed May 21, 19--

Direct Materials		Direct Labor				Summary	
Mat. Req. No.	Amount	Time Summary No.	Amount	Time Summary No.	Amount	Item	Amount
834	800.00	2202	83.60	2248	122.50	Direct	
838	1,000.00	2204	208.40	2250	187.30	materials	4,000.00
841	1,400.00	2205	167.00	2253	155.40	Direct labor	3,000.00
864	800.00	2210	229.00		3,000.00	Factory	
	4,000.00	2211	198.30			overhead	
		2213	107.20			(80% of	
		2216	110.00			direct	
		2222	277.60			labor cost)	2,400.00
		2224	217.40				
		2225	106.30			Total cost	9,400.00
		2231	153.20				
		2234	245.20			No. of units	
		2237	170.00			finished	5,000
		2242	261.60			Cost per unit	1.88

When Job 72 was completed, the direct materials costs and the direct labor costs were totaled and entered in the Summary column. Factory overhead was added at the predetermined rate of 80% of the direct labor cost, and the total cost of the job was determined. The total cost of the job, $9,400, divided by the number of units produced, 5,000, yielded a unit cost of $1.88 for the Type C Containers produced.

Upon the completion of Job 72, the job cost sheet was removed from the cost ledger and filed for future reference. At the end of the accounting period, the sum of the total costs on all cost sheets completed during the period is determined and the following entry is made:

Finished Goods 31,920

Work in Process......................................   31,920

The remaining balance in the work in process account represents the total cost charged to the uncompleted job cost sheets.

Finished Goods and Cost of Goods Sold

The finished goods account is a controlling account. The related subsidiary ledger, which has an account for each kind of commodity produced, is called the **finished goods ledger** or **stock ledger**. Each account in the subsidiary finished goods ledger provides columns for recording the quantity and the cost of goods manufactured, the quantity and the cost of goods shipped, and the quantity, the total cost, and the unit cost of goods on hand. An account in the finished goods ledger is illustrated as follows:

FINISHED GOODS LEDGER ACCOUNT

ITEM: TYPE C CONTAINER

JOB ORDER NO.	QUAN-TITY	AMOUNT	SHIP ORDER NO.	QUAN-TITY	AMOUNT	DATE	QUAN-TITY	AMOUNT	UNIT COST
	MANUFACTURED			SHIPPED			BALANCE		
						May 1	2,000	3,920.00	1.96
			643	2,000	3,920.00	8	—	—	—
72	5,000	9,400.00				21	5,000	9,400.00	1.88
			646	2,000	3,760.00	23	3,000	5,640.00	1.88

Just as there are various methods of costing materials entering into production, there are various methods of determining the cost of the finished goods sold. In the illustration, the first-in, first-out method is used. The quantities shipped are posted to the finished goods ledger from a copy of the shipping order or other memorandum. The finished goods ledger clerk then records on the copy of the shipping order the unit cost and the total amount of the commodity sold. A summary of the cost data on these shipping orders becomes the basis for the following entry:

Cost of Goods Sold....................................	30,168	
Finished Goods		30,168

If goods are returned by a buyer and are put back in stock, it is necessary to debit Finished Goods and credit Cost of Goods Sold for the cost.

Sales

For each sale of finished goods, it is necessary to maintain a record of both the cost price and the selling price of the goods sold. As previously stated, the cost data may be recorded on the shipping orders. As each sale occurs, the cost of the goods billed is recorded by debiting Cost of Goods Sold and crediting Finished Goods. The selling price of the goods sold is recorded by debiting Accounts Receivable (or Cash) and crediting Sales.

ILLUSTRATION OF JOB ORDER COST ACCOUNTING

To illustrate further a job order cost accounting system, assume that Spencer Co. has the following general ledger trial balance on January 1, the first day of the fiscal year:

Spencer Co.
Trial Balance
January 1, 19--

Cash...	85,000	
Accounts Receivable	73,000	
Finished Goods	40,000	
Work in Process................................	20,000	
Materials	30,000	
Prepaid Expenses...............................	2,000	
Plant Assets	850,000	
Accumulated Depreciation—Plant Assets..........		473,000
Accounts Payable		70,000
Wages Payable.................................		15,000
Common Stock..................................		500,000
Retained Earnings...............................		42,000
	1,100,000	1,100,000

Although in practice the transactions for Spencer Co. would be recorded daily in various journals, the January transactions and adjustments are summarized as follows, along with the related journal entries:

(a) Materials purchased and prepaid expenses incurred.

Summary of invoices and receiving reports:

Material A............................	$ 29,000
Material B............................	17,000
Material C............................	16,000
Material D............................	4,000
Total...............................	$ 66,000

Entry: Materials....................................	66,000	
Prepaid Expenses	1,000	
Accounts Payable...........................		67,000

(b) Materials requisitioned for use.

Summary of requisitions:

By Use

Job 1001.................	$12,000	
Job 1002.................	26,000	
Job 1003.................	22,000	$ 60,000
Factory Overhead...........		3,000
Total.....................		$ 63,000

By Types

Material A.................	$27,000
Material B.................	18,000
Material C.................	15,000
Material D.................	3,000
Total.....................	$ 63,000

Entry: Work in Process...........................	60,000	
Factory Overhead..........................	3,000	
Materials.................................		63,000

(c) Factory labor used.

Summary of time tickets:

Job 1001.................	$60,000	
Job 1002.................	30,000	
Job 1003.................	10,000	$100,000
Factory Overhead...........		20,000
Total.....................		$120,000

Entry: Work in Process...........................	100,000	
Factory Overhead..........................	20,000	
Wages Payable............................		120,000

(d) Other costs incurred.

Entry: Factory Overhead..........................	56,000	
Selling Expenses	25,000	
General Expenses	10,000	
Accounts Payable..........................		91,000

(e) Expiration of prepaid expenses.

Entry: Factory Overhead..........................	1,000	
Selling Expenses	100	
General Expenses	100	
Prepaid Expenses		1,200

(f) Depreciation.

Entry: Factory Overhead. 7,000
     Selling Expenses 200
     General Expenses 100
     Accumulated Depreciation—Plant Assets . . .   7,300

(g) Application of factory overhead costs to jobs. The predetermined rate was 90% of direct labor cost.

Summary of factory overhead applied:

    Job 1001 (90% of $60,000). . . . . $ 54,000
    Job 1002 (90% of $30,000).   27,000
    Job 1003 (90% of $10,000).   9,000
    Total. . . . . $ 90,000

Entry: Work in Process. 90,000
     Factory Overhead.   90,000

(h) Jobs completed.

Summary of completed job cost sheets:

    Job 1001. . . . . $146,000
    Job 1002.   83,000
    Total. $229,000

Entry: Finished Goods. 229,000
     Work in Process   229,000

(i) Sales and cost of goods sold.

Summary of sales invoices and shipping orders:

	Sales Price	Cost Price
Product X	$ 19,600	$ 15,000
Product Y	165,100	125,000
Product Z	105,300	80,000
Total.	$290,000	$220,000

Entry: Accounts Receivable. 290,000
     Sales.   290,000

Entry: Cost of Goods Sold 220,000
     Finished Goods.   220,000

(j) Cash received.

Entry: Cash 300,000
     Accounts Receivable.   300,000

(k) Cash disbursed

Entry: Accounts Payable.......................... 190,000
　　　　 Wages Payable............................ 125,000
　　　　　　 Cash.................................. 　　　　　 315,000

The flow of costs through the manufacturing accounts, together with summary details of the subsidiary ledgers, is illustrated below. Entries in the accounts are identified by letters to facilitate comparisons with the foregoing summary journal entries.

GENERAL LEDGER

FLOW OF COSTS THROUGH JOB ORDER COST ACCOUNTS

The trial balance taken from the general ledger of Spencer Co. on January 31 is as follows:

Spencer Co.
Trial Balance
January 31, 19--

Cash	70,000	
Accounts Receivable	63,000	
Finished Goods	49,000	
Work in Process	41,000	
Materials	33,000	
Prepaid Expenses	1,800	
Plant Assets	850,000	
Accumulated Depreciation—Plant Assets		480,300
Accounts Payable		38,000
Wages Payable		10,000
Common Stock		500,000
Retained Earnings		42,000
Sales		290,000
Cost of Goods Sold	220,000	
Factory Overhead		3,000
Selling Expenses	25,300	
General Expenses	10,200	
	1,363,300	1,363,300

The balances of the three inventory accounts—Finished Goods, Work in Process, and Materials—represent the respective ending inventories on January 31. The balances of the general ledger controlling accounts are compared with their respective subsidiary ledgers as follows:

Controlling Accounts		Subsidiary Ledgers		
Account	Balance	Account	Balance	
Finished Goods	$49,000 ⟷	Product X	$ 5,000	
		Product Y	26,000	
		Product Z	18,000	$49,000
Work in Process	$41,000 ⟷	Job 1003		$41,000
Materials	$33,000 ⟷	Material A	$17,000	
		Material B	7,000	
		Material C	6,000	
		Material D	3,000	$33,000

CON-
TROLLING
AND
SUBSIDIARY
ACCOUNTS
COMPARED

To simplify the Spencer Co. illustration, only one work in process account and one factory overhead account were used. Usually, a manufacturing business has several processing departments, each requiring separate work in process and factory overhead accounts. In the illustration, one predetermined rate was used in applying the factory overhead to jobs. In a factory with several processing departments, a single factory overhead rate may not provide accurate product costs and effective cost control. A single rate for the entire factory cannot take into consideration such factors as differences among departments in the nature of their operations and in amounts of factory overhead incurred. In such cases, each factory department should have a separate factory overhead rate. For example, in a factory with twenty distinct operating departments, one department might have an overhead rate of 110% of direct labor cost, another a rate of $4 per direct labor hour, and another a rate of $3.50 per machine hour.

The following financial statements are based on the data for Spencer Co. It should be noted that the overapplied factory overhead on January 31 is reported on the balance sheet as a deferred item.

Spencer Co.
Income Statement
For Month Ended January 31, 19--

Sales		$290,000
Cost of goods sold		220,000
Gross profit		$ 70,000
Operating expenses:		
Selling expenses	$25,300	
General expenses	10,200	
Total operating expenses		35,500
Income from operations		$ 34,500

Spencer Co.
Retained Earnings Statement
For Month Ended January 31, 19--

Retained earnings, January 1, 19--	$42,000
Income for the month	34,500
Retained earnings, January 31, 19--	$76,500

Spencer Co.
Balance Sheet
January 31, 19--

Assets

Current assets:

Cash...........................		$ 70,000	
Accounts receivable...................		63,000	
Inventories:			
Finished goods.....................	$49,000		
Work in process....................	41,000		
Materials	33,000	123,000	
Prepaid expenses		1,800	
Total current assets..................			$257,800
Plant assets.........................		$850,000	
Less accumulated depreciation.........		480,300	369,700
Total assets..........................			$627,500

Liabilities

Current liabilities:

Accounts payable....................	$38,000		
Wages payable......................	10,000		
Total current liabilities...............		$ 48,000	
Deferred credits:			
Factory overhead....................		3,000	
Total liabilities......................			$ 51,000

Stockholders' Equity

Common stock.......................		$500,000	
Retained earnings....................		76,500	
Total stockholders' equity.............			576,500
Total liabilities and stockholders' equity			$627,500

CHAPTER REVIEW

KEY POINTS

1. Manufacturing Operations.

Manufacturers employ labor and use machinery to change materials into finished products. The cost of manufactured products sold is called the cost of goods sold. The three inventory accounts of a manufacturing business are finished goods, work in process, and materials. The finished goods and work in process inventories are composed of three types of manufacturing costs:

direct materials, direct labor, and factory overhead. All expenditures incidental to manufacturing move through the work in process account, to the finished goods account and eventually into the cost of goods sold account.

2. General Accounting System for Manufacturing Operations.

A general accounting system is an extension to manufacturing operations of the periodic inventory procedures used by merchandising enterprises. The manufacturing accounts are summarized periodically in an account entitled Manufacturing Summary. At the end of the accounting period, the manufacturing summary account is closed to Income Summary. To avoid a long, complicated income statement, a separate statement of cost of goods manufactured is usually prepared.

3. Cost Accounting System for Manufacturing Operations.

A cost accounting system uses perpetual inventory procedures, with controlling accounts and subsidiary ledgers for materials, work in process, and finished goods. The two main types of cost accounting systems for manufacturing operations are the job order cost and process cost systems.

4. Job Order Cost Systems.

A job order cost system provides for a separate record of the cost of each particular quantity of product that passes through the factory. The details concerning the costs incurred on each job order are accumulated in a subsidiary ledger known as the cost ledger. Each cost ledger account, called a job cost sheet, has spaces for recording all direct materials and direct labor chargeable to the job and for applying factory overhead at the predetermined rate. Work in Process is the controlling account for the cost ledger. As a job is finished, it is transferred to the finished goods ledger, for which Finished Goods is the controlling account.

KEY TERMS

cost of merchandise sold 985
cost of goods sold 985
finished goods 985
work in process 985
materials 985
direct materials 985
direct labor 985
factory overhead 985
statement of cost of goods
   manufactured 987
job order cost system 991
process cost system 991
purchase requisitions 992

purchase orders 992
receiving report 992
materials ledger 992
materials requisitions 993
time tickets 994
predetermined factory
   overhead rate 995
overapplied overhead 996
underapplied overhead 996
cost ledger 999
job cost sheet 999
finished goods ledger 1002

SELF-EXAMINATION QUESTIONS

Answers in Appendix B.

1. The account maintained by a manufacturing business for inventory of goods in the process of manufacture is:
   A. Finished Goods
   B. Materials
   C. Work in Process
   D. None of the above

2. For a manufacturing business, finished goods inventory includes:
   A. direct materials costs
   B. direct labor costs
   C. factory overhead costs
   D. all of the above

3. An example of a factory overhead cost is:
   A. wages of factory assembly-line workers
   B. salaries for factory plant supervisors
   C. bearings for electric motors being manufactured
   D. all of the above

4. For which of the following would the job order cost system be appropriate?
   A. Antique furniture repair shop
   B. Rubber manufacturer
   C. Coal manufacturer
   D. All of the above

5. If the factory overhead account has a credit balance, factory overhead is said to be:
   A. underapplied
   B. overapplied
   C. underabsorbed
   D. none of the above

ILLUSTRATIVE PROBLEM

Shelton Signs Inc. specializes in the production of neon signs and uses a job order cost system. The following data summarize the operations related to production for November, the first month of operations:

(a) Materials purchased on account, $21,750.
(b) Materials requisitioned and factory labor used:

	Materials	Factory Labor
Job No. 1	$2,750	$1,700
Job No. 2	3,800	2,000
Job No. 3	2,990	1,450
Job No. 4	5,950	3,800
Job No. 5	3,250	1,900
Job No. 6	900	600
For general factory use	595	500

(c) Factory overhead costs incurred on account, $4,300.
(d) Depreciation of machinery, $1,450.

(e) The factory overhead rate is 60% of direct labor cost.

(f) Jobs completed: Nos. 1, 2, 4, and 5.

(g) Jobs Nos. 1, 2, and 4 were shipped and customers were billed for $7,900, $10,500, and $18,100, respectively.

Instructions:

1. Prepare entries to record the foregoing summarized operations.
2. Determine the account balances for Work in Process and Finished Goods.
3. Prepare a schedule of unfinished jobs to support the balance in the work in process account.
4. Prepare a schedule of completed jobs on hand to support the balance in the finished goods account.

SOLUTION

(1)

(a)	Materials	21,750	
	Accounts Payable		21,750
(b)	Work in Process...............................	31,090	
	Factory Overhead	1,095	
	Materials		20,235
	Wages Payable...............................		11,950
(c)	Factory Overhead	4,300	
	Accounts Payable		4,300
(d)	Factory Overhead	1,450	
	Accumulated Depreciation—Machinery......		1,450
(e)	Work in Process................................	6,870	
	Factory Overhead (60% of $11,450)...........		6,870
(f)	Finished Goods	30,790	
	Work in Process..............................		30,790

Computation of the cost of jobs finished:

Job	Direct Materials	Direct Labor	Overhead	Total
Job No. 1............	$2,750	$1,700	$1,020	$ 5,470
Job No. 2............	3,800	2,000	1,200	7,000
Job No. 4............	5,950	3,800	2,280	12,030
Job No. 5............	3,250	1,900	1,140	6,290
				$30,790

(g) Accounts Receivable.......................... 36,500

      Sales.....................................   36,500

    Cost of Goods Sold......................... 24,500

        Finished Goods   24,500

Computation of the cost of jobs sold:

Job No. 1	$ 5,470
Job No. 2	7,000
Job No. 4	12,030
	$24,500

(2) Work in Process: $7,170 ($31,090 + $6,870 − $30,790)

    Finished Goods: $6,290 ($30,790 − $24,500)

(3)

Schedule of Unfinished Jobs

	Direct Materials	Direct Labor	Factory Overhead	Total
Job No. 3	$2,990	$1,450	$870	$5,310
Job No. 6	900	600	360	1,860
Balance of Work in Process, November 30				$7,170

(4)

Schedule of Completed Jobs

Job No. 5:	Direct materials	$3,250
	Direct labor..................................	1,900
	Factory overhead...........................	1,140
Balance of Finished Goods, November 30.................		$6,290

DISCUSSION QUESTIONS

1. Name the three inventory accounts for a manufacturing business and describe what each balance represents at the end of an accounting period.

2. What are the three categories of manufacturing costs included in the cost of finished goods and the cost of work in process?

3. For a manufacturing enterprise, what is the description of the amount that is comparable to a merchandising concern's net cost of merchandise purchased?

4. Which of the following amounts is not closed to Manufacturing Summary?
   (a) direct materials inventory as of the beginning of the year
   (b) direct materials inventory as of the end of the year
   (c) finished goods inventory as of the beginning of the year
   (d) factory overhead

5. (a) Name the two principal types of cost accounting systems. (b) Which system provides for a separate record of each particular quantity of product that passes through the factory? (c) Which system accumulates the costs for each department or process within the factory?

6. Distinguish between the purchase requisition and the purchase order used in the procurement of materials.

7. Briefly discuss how the purchase order, purchase invoice, and receiving report can be used to assist in controlling cash disbursements for materials acquired.

8. What document is the source for (a) debiting the accounts in the materials ledger, and (b) crediting the accounts in the materials ledger?

9. Briefly discuss how the accounts in the materials ledger can be used as an aid in maintaining appropriate inventory quantities of stock items.

10. How does use of the materials requisition help control the issuance of materials from the storeroom?

11. Discuss the major advantages of a perpetual inventory system over a periodic system for materials.

12. (a) Differentiate between the clock card and the time ticket. (b) Why should the total time reported on an employee's time tickets for a payroll period be compared with the time reported on the employee's clock cards for the same period?

13. Which of the following items are properly classified as part of factory overhead?
    (a) factory supplies used   (d) property taxes on factory buildings
    (b) interest expense   (e) sales commissions
    (c) amortization of factory patents (f) direct materials

14. Discuss how the predetermined factory overhead rate can be used in job order cost accounting to assist management in pricing jobs.

15. (a) How is a predetermined factory overhead rate calculated? (b) Name three common bases used in calculating the rate.

16. (a) What is (1) overapplied factory overhead and (2) underapplied factory overhead? (b) If the factory overhead account has a debit balance, was factory overhead underapplied or overapplied? (c) If the factory overhead account has a credit balance at the end of the first month of the fiscal year, where will the amount of this balance be reported on the interim balance sheet?

17. At the end of a fiscal year, there was a relatively minor balance in the factory overhead account. What is the simplest satisfactory procedure for the disposition of the balance in the account?

18. What name is given to the individual accounts in the cost ledger?

19. What document serves as the basis for posting to (a) the direct materials section of the job cost sheet, and (b) the direct labor section of the job cost sheet?

20. Describe the source of the data for debiting Work in Process for (a) direct materials, (b) direct labor, and (c) factory overhead.

21. What account is the controlling account for (a) the materials ledger, (b) the cost ledger, and (c) the finished goods ledger or stock ledger?

22. Real World Focus. Inventory data taken from the financial statements of three different types of businesses are as follows:

Emery Air Freight Corporation (December 31, 1985):
No inventories are shown on the balance sheet.

Family Dollar Stores, Inc. (August 31, 1985):
Merchandise inventories $100,784,767

La-Z-Boy Chair Company (April 27, 1985):
Materials. $12,209,463
Work in process   11,629,767
Finished goods   4,096,476

Explain the differences in the makeup of the inventories for the companies shown above.

EXERCISES

Exercise 22–1. Statement of cost of goods manufactured. The following accounts were selected from the pre-closing trial balance of Jarvis Co. at July 31, 1988, the end of the current fiscal year:

Direct Labor	$192,000
Direct Materials Inventory	51,600
Direct Materials Purchases	230,100
Factory Overhead (control)	76,800
Finished Goods Inventory	76,500
General Expense (control).	54,750
Interest Expense	8,500
Sales	717,600
Selling Expense (control).	76,500
Work in Process Inventory.	55,500

Inventories at July 31 were as follows:

Finished Goods	$81,000
Work in Process	59,550
Direct Materials	54,000

Prepare a statement of cost of goods manufactured.

Exercise 22–2. Adjusting and closing entries.

On the basis of the data presented in Exercise 22–1, prepare journal entries on July 31 to:

(a) Adjust the inventory accounts.
(b) Close the appropriate accounts to Manufacturing Summary.
(c) Close Manufacturing Summary.

Exercise 22–3. Cost of materials issuances by fifo and lifo methods.

The balance of Material G on April 1 and the receipts and issuances during April are as follows:

Balance:	April	1	240 units at $40.00
Received:	April	6	600 units at $42.00
		14	480 units at $42.60
		26	360 units at $43.20
Issued:	April	7	360 units for Job 410
		17	300 units for Job 415
		28	420 units for Job 430

Determine the cost of each of the three issuances under a perpetual system, using (a) the first-in, first-out method and (b) the last-in, first-out method.

Exercise 22–4. Entry for issuance of materials.

The issuances of materials for the current month are as follows:

Requisition No.	Material	Job No.	Amount
841	F-10	1020	$5,140
842	H-60	1060	1,690
843	W-3	1035	3,860
844	A-16	General factory use	750
845	J-48	1018	4,320

Present the journal entry to record the issuances of materials.

Exercise 22–5. Entry for factory labor costs.

A summary of the time tickets for the current month follows:

Job No.	Amount	Job No.	Amount
673	$1,250	677	$ 800
674	8,100	Indirect labor	1,180
675	2,670	678	6,250
676	4,500	679	5,200

Present the journal entry to record the factory labor costs.

Exercise 22–6. *Factory overhead rates, entries, and account balance.* Logan Company, which maintains departmental accounts for work in process and factory overhead, applies factory overhead to jobs on the basis of machine hours in Department 30 and on the basis of direct labor costs in Department 40. Estimated factory overhead costs, direct labor costs, and machine hours for January are as follows:

	Department 30	Department 40
Estimated factory overhead cost for year	$65,000	$243,600
Estimated direct labor costs for year		$580,000
Estimated machine hours for year	20,000	
Actual factory overhead costs for January	$ 6,050	$ 20,100
Actual direct labor costs for January		$ 48,500
Actual machine hours for January	1,800	

(a) Determine the factory overhead rate for Department 30. (b) Determine the factory overhead rate for Department 40. (c) Prepare the journal entries to apply factory overhead to production for January. (d) Determine the balances of the departmental factory overhead accounts as of January 31 and indicate whether the amounts represent overapplied or underapplied factory overhead.

Exercise 22–7. *Entry for jobs completed; cost of unfinished jobs.* The following account appears in the ledger after only part of the postings have been completed for November:

Work in Process		
Balance, November 1	17,150	
Direct Materials	43,100	
Direct Labor	67,500	
Factory Overhead	37,000	

Jobs finished during November are summarized as follows:

Job 1320............	$25,400	Job 1327............	$40,800
Job 1326............	45,600	Job 1330............	26,100

(a) Prepare the journal entry to record the jobs completed and (b) determine the cost of the unfinished jobs at November 30.

Exercise 22–8.   Entries for factory costs and jobs completed. Hill Enterprises Inc. began manufacturing operations on February 1. Jobs 201 and 202 were completed during the month, and all costs applicable to them were recorded on the related costs sheets. Jobs 203 and 204 are still in process at the end of the month, and all applicable costs except factory overhead have been recorded on the related cost sheets. In addition to the materials and labor charged directly to the jobs, $10,500 of indirect materials and $25,200 of indirect labor were used during the month. The cost sheets for the four jobs entering production during the month are as follows, in summary form:

Job 201	
Direct materials	15,750
Direct labor.................	12,600
Factory overhead...........	7,560
Total....................	35,910

Job 202	
Direct materials.............	28,200
Direct labor.................	20,160
Factory overhead	12,096
Total....................	60,456

Job 203	
Direct materials	21,400
Direct labor.................	17,640
Factory overhead...........	60 %

_10 584_

Job 204	
Direct materials.............	5,500
Direct labor.................	7,800
Factory overhead	60%

_4680_

Prepare an entry to record each of the following operations for the month (one entry for each operation):

(a) Direct and indirect materials used.
(b) Direct and indirect labor used.
(c) Factory overhead applied (a single overhead rate is used, based on direct labor cost).
(d) Completion of Jobs 201 and 202.

_7560 ÷ 12600 =_
_60 %_

PROBLEMS

Series A

If the working papers correlating with the textbook are not used, omit Problem 22–1A.

Problem 22–1A.   Manufacturing work sheet and income statement. The work sheet for Thaxton Manufacturing Company, for the current year ended March 31, 1988, is presented in the working papers. Data concerning account titles, trial balance amounts, and selected adjustments have been entered on the work sheet.

Instructions:

(1) Enter the six adjustments required for the inventories on the work sheet. Additional adjustment data are:

Finished goods inventory at March 31 . . . . $54,600
Work in process inventory at March 31 39,500
Direct materials inventory at March 31 35,200

The adjustments for finished goods inventory should be entered as adjustments to the income summary account, and the work in process and direct materials inventory adjustments should be entered as adjustments to the manufacturing summary account.

(2) Complete the work sheet. The data for the manufacturing summary account and the other manufacturing accounts should be extended to the statement of cost of goods manufactured columns. After all of these data have been extended, the two cost of goods manufactured columns should be totaled and the difference determined. This difference, which is labeled "cost of goods manufactured" in the account title column, is transferred to the income statement columns by entries in the statement of cost of goods manufactured credit column and the income statement debit column. The remainder of the work sheet is completed in the same manner as is followed for a merchandising business. (Appendix F further describes and illustrates the use of a work sheet for manufacturing operations.)

(3) Prepare a statement of cost of goods manufactured.
(4) Prepare a multiple-step income statement.

Problem 22–2A. Entries and schedules for unfinished and completed jobs.
Logan Printing Company uses a job order cost system. The following data summarize the operations related to production for June, the first month of operations:

   (a) Materials purchases on account, $110,160.
   (b) Materials requisitioned and factory labor used:

	Materials	Factory Labor
Job 601	$15,840	$9,500
Job 602	10,380	7,040
Job 603	13,900	5,100
Job 604	20,950	13,380
Job 605	11,440	6,680
Job 606	7,100	2,900
For general factory use	2,300	1,760

   (c) Factory overhead costs incurred on account, $21,200.
   (d) Depreciation of machinery and equipment, $7,760.
   (e) The factory overhead rate is 75% of direct labor cost.
   (f) Jobs completed: 601, 602, 603, and 605.
   (g) Jobs 601, 602, and 605 were shipped and customers were billed for $49,250, $31,100, and $31,280 respectively.

Instructions:

(1) Prepare entries to record the foregoing summarized operations.
(2) Open T accounts for Work in Process and Finished Goods and post the appropriate entries, using the identifying letters as dates. Insert memorandum account balances as of the end of the month.
(3) Prepare a schedule of unfinished jobs to support the balance in the work in process account.
(4) Prepare a schedule of completed jobs on hand to support the balance in the finished goods account.

If the working papers correlating with the textbook are not used, omit Problem 22–3A.

Problem 22–3A.   Job order cost sheet. Stein Furniture Company repairs, refinishes, and reupholsters furniture. A job order cost system was installed recently to facilitate (1) the determination of price quotations to prospective customers, (2) the determination of actual costs incurred on each job, and (3) cost reductions.

In response to a prospective customer's request for a price quotation on a job, the estimated cost data are inserted on an unnumbered job cost sheet. If the offer is accepted, a number is assigned to the job and the costs incurred are recorded in the usual manner on the job cost sheet. After the job is completed, reasons for the variances between the estimated and actual costs are noted on the sheet. The data are then available to management in evaluating the efficiency of operations and in preparing quotations on future jobs.

On June 10, an estimate of $665 for reupholstering a couch was given to Nancy Westbrook. The estimate was based on the following data:

Estimated direct materials:	
10 meters at $8.50 per meter.....................................	$ 85
Estimated direct labor:	
20 hours at $13 per hour	260
Estimated factory overhead (50% of direct labor cost)...........	130
Total estimated costs......................................	$475
Markup (40% of production costs)...........................	190
Total estimate	$665

On June 14, the couch was picked up from the residence of Nancy Westbrook, 2408 Bobolink Way, Tampa, with a commitment to return it on June 28.

The job was completed on June 24. The related materials requisitions and time tickets are summarized as follows:

Materials Requisition No.	Description	Amount
3480	10 meters at $8.50	$ 85
3492	2 meters at $8.50	17

Time Ticket No.	Description	Amount
H143	15 hours at $13	$195
H151	7 hours at $13	91

Instructions:

(1) Complete that portion of the job order cost sheet that would be prepared when the estimate is given to the customer.
(2) Assign number R6-18 to the job, record the costs incurred, and complete the job order cost sheet. In commenting upon the variances between actual costs and estimated costs, assume that 2 meters of materials were spoiled, the factory overhead rate has been proved to be satisfactory, and an inexperienced employee performed the work.

Problem 22–4A. Posting of entries to accounts; preparation of financial statements. The trial balance of F. R. Conrad Inc., at the beginning of the current fiscal year, is as follows:

F. R. Conrad Inc.
Trial Balance
May 1, 19--

Cash...	46,300	
Accounts Receivable................................	70,260	
Finished Goods	66,500	
Work in Process......................................	24,360	
Materials	32,200	
Prepaid Expenses	8,600	
Plant Assets	582,400	
Accumulated Depreciation—Plant Assets		330,500
Accounts Payable		23,700
Wages Payable.......................................		—
Common Stock..		100,000
Retained Earnings...................................		376,420
Sales...		—
Cost of Goods Sold.................................	—	
Factory Overhead	—	
Selling Expenses	—	
General Expenses...................................	—	
	830,620	830,620

Transactions completed during May and adjustments required on May 31 are summarized as follows:

(a) Materials purchased on account		$27,480
(b) Materials requisitioned for factory use:		
Direct...	$25,800	
Indirect...	320	26,120
(c) Factory labor costs incurred:		
Direct...	$12,960	
Indirect...	1,840	14,800
(d) Other costs and expenses incurred on account:		
Factory overhead	$ 6,750	
Selling expenses..............................	6,570	
General expenses.............................	4,800	18,120

(e) Cash disbursed:

Accounts payable	$49,200	
Wages payable	13,300	62,500

(f) Depreciation charged:

Factory equipment	$ 4,320	
Office equipment.............................	360	4,680

(g) Prepaid expenses expired:

Chargeable to factory.........................	$ 640	
Chargeable to selling expenses.................	150	
Chargeable to general expenses................	140	930

(h) Applied factory overhead at a predetermined rate:
110% of direct labor cost.

(i) Total cost of jobs completed......................	51,600

(j) Sales, all on account:

Selling price	67,200
Cost...	43,600
(k) Cash received on account........................	68,400

Instructions:

(1) Open T accounts and record the initial balances indicated in the May 1 trial balance, identifying each as "Bal."
(2) Record the transactions directly in the accounts, using the identifying letters in place of dates.
(3) Prepare an income statement for the month ended May 31, 19--.
(4) Prepare a retained earnings statement for the month ended May 31, 19--.
(5) Prepare a balance sheet as of May 31, 19--.

Problem 22–5A.   Entries, trial balance, and financial statements. The trial balance of the general ledger of R. Staub Co. as of March 31, the end of the first month of the current fiscal year, is as follows:

R. Staub Co.
Trial Balance
March 31, 19--

Cash	92,000	
Accounts Receivable	185,300	
Finished Goods.............................	187,600	
Work in Process	62,000	
Materials....................................	72,900	
Plant Assets................................	810,000	
Accumulated Depreciation—Plant Assets......		360,000
Accounts Payable............................		125,000
Wages Payable..............................		15,000
Capital Stock................................		100,000
Retained Earnings		738,700
Sales.......................................		280,000
Cost of Goods Sold	168,000	
Factory Overhead............................	900	
Selling and General Expenses................	40,000	
	1,618,700	1,618,700

As of the same date, balances in the accounts of selected subsidiary ledgers are as follows:

Finished goods ledger:
Commodity X, 2,000 units, $40,000; Commodity Y, 6,000 units, $90,000; Commodity Z, 3,200 units, $57,600.
Cost ledger:
Job 700, $62,000.
Materials ledger:
Material R15, $38,600; Material Z10, $31,600; Material W01, $2,700.

The transactions completed during April are summarized as follows:

(a) Materials were purchased on account as follows:

Material R15 . . . . $55,000
Material Z10   38,500
Material W01   1,500

(b) Materials were requisitioned from stores as follows:

Job 700, Material R15, $21,040; Material Z10, $16,800 . . . . $37,840
Job 701, Material R15, $27,000; Material Z10, $23,120   50,120
Job 702, Material R15, $13,800; Material Z10, $6,130.   19,930
For general factory use, Material W01   1,600

(c) Time tickets for the month were chargeable as follows:

Job 700	$19,600	Job 702	$16,400
Job 701	16,800	Indirect labor.	5,000

(d) Factory payroll checks for $59,400 were issued.
(e) Various factory overhead charges of $11,200 were incurred on account.
(f) Selling and general expenses of $38,200 were incurred on account.
(g) Payments on account were $140,000.
(h) Depreciation of $10,300 on factory plant and equipment was recorded.
(i) Factory overhead was applied to jobs at 60% of direct labor cost.
(j) Jobs completed during the month were as follows: Job 700 produced 6,400 units of Commodity X; Job 701 produced 5,000 units of Commodity Y.
(k) Total sales on account were $383,200. The goods sold were as follows (use first-in, first-out method): 4,600 units of Commodity X; 7,500 units of Commodity Y; 2,000 units of Commodity Z.
(l) Cash of $250,000 was received on accounts receivable.

Instructions:

(1) Open T accounts for the general ledger, the finished goods ledger, the cost ledger, and the materials ledger. Record directly in these accounts the balances as of March 31, identifying them as "Bal." Record the quantities as well as the dollar amounts in the finished goods ledger.

(continued)

(2) Prepare entries to record the April transactions. After recording each transaction, post to the T accounts, using the identifying letters as dates. When posting to the finished goods ledger, record quantities as well as dollar amounts.

(3) Prepare a trial balance.

(4) Prepare schedules of the account balances in the finished goods ledger, the cost ledger, and the materials ledger.

(5) Prepare an income statement for the two months ended April 30.

Problem 22–6A. Determination of amounts missing from selected accounts in job cost system. Following are selected accounts for Watson Products. For the purposes of this problem, some of the debits and credits have been omitted.

Sept sales

Accounts Receivable

| Oct. 1 | Balance | 47,600 | Oct. 31 | Collections | 102,000 |
| Oct. 31 | Sales | (A) | | | |

54400 +52000 *- 47,600*

Materials

| Oct. 1 | Balance | 11,500 | Oct. 31 | Requisitions | (B) |
| Oct. 31 | Purchases | 16,900 | | | |

28400 -9500   *all materials*   *18900*

Work in Process

Oct. 1	Balance	21,000	Oct. 31	Goods finished	(E)
Oct. 31	Direct materials	(C)			
Oct. 31	Direct labor	22,400			
Oct. 31	Factory overhead	(D)			

18900 -500 = 18400   *61920*   *80% → 17920*

Finished Goods

| Oct. 1 | Balance | 38,900 | Oct. 31 | Cost of goods sold | (G) |
| Oct. 31 | Goods finished | (F) | | | |

61920   *24000*   *76820*

Factory Overhead

| Oct. 1 | Balance | 120 | Oct. 31 | Applied (80% of direct labor cost) | (H) |
| 1–31 | Costs incurred | 17,500 | | | |

17920

Cost of Goods Sold

| Oct. 31 | | (I) | | | |

76820

Sales

| | | | Oct 31 | | (J) |

106,400

Selected balances at October 31:

Accounts receivable $52,000
Finished goods 24,000
Work in process .... 17,800 *ending*
Materials .... *on hand* 9,500

Materials requisitions for October included $500 of materials issued for general factory use. All sales are made on account, terms n/30.

└Factory overhead

Instructions:

(1) Determine the amounts represented by the letters (A) through (J), presenting your computations.
(2) Determine the amount of factory overhead overapplied or underapplied as of October 31.

over 30 U

Series B

If the working papers correlating with the textbook are not used, omit Problem 22–1B.

Problem 22–1B.   Manufacturing work sheet and income statement. **The work sheet for Thaxton Manufacturing Company, for the current year ended March 31, 1988, is presented in the working papers. Data concerning account titles, trial balance amounts, and selected adjustments have been entered on the work sheet.**

Instructions:

(1) Enter the six adjustments required for the inventories on the work sheet. Additional adjustment data are:
   Finished goods inventory at March 31 .... $56,100
   Work in process inventory at March 31 40,600
   Direct materials inventory at March 31 30,900
   The adjustments for finished goods inventory should be entered as adjustments to the income summary account, and the work in process and direct materials inventory adjustments should be entered as adjustments to the manufacturing summary account.
(2) Complete the work sheet. The data for the manufacturing summary account and the other manufacturing accounts should be extended to the statement of cost of goods manufactured columns. After all of these data have been extended, the two cost of goods manufactured columns should be totaled and the difference determined. This difference, which is labeled "cost of goods manufactured" in the account title column, is transferred to the income statement columns by entries in the statement of cost of goods manufactured credit column and the income statement debit column. The remainder of the work sheet is completed in the same manner as is followed for a merchandising business. (Appendix F further describes and illustrates the use of a work sheet for manufacturing operations.)
(3) Prepare a statement of cost of goods manufactured.
(4) Prepare a multiple-step income statement.

Problem 22–2B.   Entries and schedules for unfinished and completed jobs.
Owens Printing Company uses a job order cost system. The following data summarize the operations related to production for November, the first month of operations:

(a) Materials purchased on account, $57,420.
(b) Materials requisitioned and factory labor used:

	Materials	Factory Labor
Job 101	$11,600	$9,150
Job 102	3,400	1,960
Job 103	8,520	4,690
Job 104	4,280	1,900
Job 105	6,830	2,800
Job 106	6,180	4,610
For general factory use	1,310	3,000

(c) Factory overhead costs incurred on account, $11,300.
(d) Depreciation of machinery and equipment, $5,400.
(e) The factory overhead rate is 70% of direct labor cost. — 7910
(f) Jobs completed: 101, 102, 104, and 105.
(g) Jobs 101, 102, and 104 were shipped and customers were billed for $36,200, $8,400, and $10,350 respectively.

Instructions:

(1) Prepare entries to record the foregoing summarized operations.
(2) Open T accounts for Work in Process and Finished Goods and post the appropriate entries, using the identifying letters as dates. Insert memorandum account balances as of the end of the month.
(3) Prepare a schedule of unfinished jobs to support the balance in the work in process account.
(4) Prepare a schedule of completed jobs on hand to support the balance in the finished goods account.

If the working papers correlating with the textbook are not used, omit Problem 22–3B.

Problem 22–3B.   Job order cost sheet. Katz Furniture Company repairs, refinishes, and reupholsters furniture. A job order cost system was installed recently to facilitate (1) the determination of price quotations to prospective customers, (2) the determination of actual costs incurred on each job, and (3) cost reductions.

In response to a prospective customer's request for a price quotation on a job, the estimated cost data are inserted on an unnumbered job cost sheet. If the offer is accepted, a number is assigned to the job and the costs incurred are recorded in the usual manner on the job cost sheet. After the job is completed, reasons for the variances between the estimated and actual costs are noted on the sheet. The data are then available to management in evaluating the efficiency of operations and in preparing quotations on future jobs.

On February 6, an estimate of $360 for reupholstering a chair and couch was given to John Bergman. The estimate was based on the following data:

Estimated direct materials:	
12 meters at $10 per meter	$120
Estimated direct labor:	
8 hours at $15 per hour......................................	120
Estimated factory overhead (40% of direct labor cost)	48
Total estimated costs.......................................	$288
Markup (25% of production costs)............................	72
Total estimate	$360

On February 10, the chair and couch were picked up from the residence of John Bergman, 1454 Spartan Lane, Des Moines, with a commitment to return it on February 21. The job was completed on February 19.

The related materials requisitions and time tickets are summarized as follows:

Materials Requisition No.	Description	Amount
U642	12 meters at $10	$120
U651	3 meters at $10	30

Time Ticket No.	Description	Amount
1519	6 hours at $15	$ 90
1520	3 hours at $15	45

Instructions:

(1) Complete that portion of the job order cost sheet that would be prepared when the estimate is given to the customer.
(2) Assign number 89-10-1 to the job, record the costs incurred, and complete the job order cost sheet. In commenting upon the variances between actual costs and estimated costs, assume that 3 meters of materials were spoiled, the factory overhead rate has been proved to be satisfactory, and an inexperienced employee performed the work.

Problem 22–5B. Entries, trial balance, and financial statements. The trial balance of the general ledger of Thurman Corporation as of January 31, the end of the first month of the current fiscal year, is shown at the top of page 1028.

As of the same date, balances in the accounts of selected subsidiary ledgers are as follows:

Finished goods ledger:
    Commodity E, 3,500 units, $42,000; Commodity F, 1,800 units, $27,000; Commodity G, 1,400 units, $37,800.
Cost ledger:
    Job 580, $36,840.
Materials ledger:
    Material M, $17,700; Material N, $22,140; Material O, $4,500.

Thurman Corporation
Trial Balance
January 31, 19--

Cash	54,840	
Accounts Receivable	111,180	
Finished Goods.	106,800	
Work in Process	36,840	
Materials.	44,340	
Plant Assets.	474,600	
Accumulated Depreciation — Plant Assets.		211,740
Accounts Payable.		79,780
Wages Payable.		9,000
Capital Stock		200,000
Retained Earnings		311,700
Sales.		160,980
Cost of Goods Sold	120,000	
Factory Overhead.	1,200	
Selling and General Expenses.	23,400	
	973,200	973,200

The transactions completed during February are summarized as follows:

(a) Materials were purchased on account as follows:

Material M.	$33,000
Material N	23,100
Material O	900

(b) Materials were requisitioned from stores as follows:

Job 580, Material M, $16,200; Material N, $14,178	$30,378
Job 581, Material M, $8,280; Material N, $3,324	11,604
Job 582, Material M, $12,720; Material N, $10,118	22,838
For general factory use, Material O.	960

(c) Time tickets for the month were chargeable as follows:

Job 580	$11,760	Job 582	$9,840
Job 581	10,080	Indirect labor	3,600

(d) Factory payroll checks for $38,640 were issued.

(e) Various factory overhead charges of $13,425 were incurred on account.

(f) Depreciation of $5,400 on factory plant and equipment was recorded.

(g) Factory overhead was applied to jobs at 70% of direct labor cost.

(h) Jobs completed during the month were as follows: Job 580 produced 5,700 units of Commodity F; Job 582 produced 1,460 units of Commodity G.

(i) Selling and general expenses of $22,920 were incurred on account.

(j) Payments on account were $85,800.

(k) Total sales on account were $167,800. The goods sold were as follows (use first-in, first-out method): 1,500 units of Commodity E; 3,200 units of Commodity F; 1,600 units of Commodity G.

(l) Cash of $150,600 was received on accounts receivable.

Instructions:

(1) Open T accounts for the general ledger, the finished goods ledger, the cost ledger, and the materials ledger. Record directly in these accounts the balances as of January 31, identifying them as "Bal." Record the quantities as well as the dollar amounts in the finished goods ledger.

(2) Prepare entries to record the February transactions. After recording each transaction, post to the T accounts, using the identifying letters as dates. When posting to the finished goods ledger, record quantities as well as dollar amounts.

(3) Prepare a trial balance.

(4) Prepare schedules of the account balances in the finished goods ledger, the cost ledger, and the materials ledger.

(5) Prepare an income statement for the two months ended February 28.

Problem 22–6B. Determination of amounts missing from selected accounts in job cost system. Following are selected accounts for Nowell Products. For the purposes of this problem, some of the debits and credits have been omitted.

Accounts Receivable

Mar.	1	Balance	81,600	Mar. 31	Collections	120,500
	31	Sales	(A)			

Materials

Mar.	1	Balance	21,000	Mar. 31	Requisitions	(B)
	31	Purchases	41,500			

Work in Process

Mar.	1	Balance	24,000	Mar. 31	Goods finished	(E)
	31	Direct materials	(C)			
	31	Direct labor	48,200			
	31	Factory overhead	(D)			

Finished Goods

Mar.	1	Balance	12,800	Mar. 31	Cost of goods sold	(G)
	31	Goods finished	(F)			

Factory Overhead

Mar.	1	Balance	300	Mar. 31	Applied (60% of	
	1–31	Costs incurred	28,800		direct labor cost)	(H)

Cost of Goods Sold

Mar. 31	(I)	

Sales

	Mar. 31	(J)

Selected balances at March 31:

Accounts receivable	$78,750
Finished goods.	22,000
Work in process.	27,300
Materials	15,000

   Materials requisitions for March included $1,300 of materials issued for general factory use. All sales are made on account, terms n/30.

Instructions:

(1) Determine the amounts represented by the letters (A) through (J), presenting your computations.
(2) Determine the amount of factory overhead overapplied or underapplied as of March 31.

MINI-CASE 22

   As an assistant cost accountant for Atkinson Industries, you have been assigned to review the activity base for the predetermined factory overhead rate. The president, J. C. Atkinson, has expressed concern that the over- or underapplied overhead has fluctuated excessively over the years.

An analysis of the company's operations and use of the current overhead base (direct materials usage) have narrowed the possible alternative overhead bases to direct labor cost and machine hours. For the past five years, the following data have been gathered:

	1987	1986	1985	1984	1983
Actual overhead ..	$ 840,000	$ 820,000	$ 900,000	$ 735,000	$ 705,000
Applied overhead ..	812,000	847,500	921,000	750,000	656,000
(Over) under-applied overhead	$ 28,000	$ (27,500)	$ (21,000)	$ (15,000)	$ 49,000
Direct labor cost.......	$3,350,000	$3,300,000	$3,625,000	$2,925,000	$2,800,000
Machine hours......	663,000	645,000	726,000	597,000	569,000

Handwritten annotations above Direct labor cost: 25% 25% 25% 25% 25%

Handwritten annotations below Machine hours: 127% 127% 124% 123% 124%

Instructions:

(1) Calculate a predetermined factory overhead rate for each alternative base, assuming that the rates would have been determined by relating the amount of factory overhead for the past five years to the base. *25%*

(2) For each of the past five years, determine the over- or underapplied overhead, based on the two predetermined overhead rates developed in (1).

(3) Which predetermined overhead rate would you recommend? Discuss the basis for your recommendation.

Chapter 23

PROCESS COST SYSTEMS

Chapter Objectives:

- ■ Distinguish process cost accounting systems from job order cost accounting systems.

- ■ Describe and illustrate the basic concepts for a process cost accounting system.

- ■ Describe and illustrate the preparation and the use of a cost of production report.

- ■ Describe and illustrate the accounting for joint products.

- ■ Describe and illustrate the accounting for by-products.

I n many industries, job orders as described in Chapter 22 are not suitable for scheduling production and accumulating the manufacturing costs. Companies manufacturing cement, flour, or paint, for example, do so on a continuous basis. The principal product is a homogeneous mass rather than a collection of distinct units. No useful purpose would be served by maintaining job orders for particular amounts of a product as the material passes through the several stages of production.

PROCESS COST AND JOB ORDER COST SYSTEMS DISTINGUISHED

Many of the methods, procedures, and managerial applications presented in the preceding chapter in the discussion of job order cost systems apply equally to process cost systems. For example, perpetual inventory accounts with subsidiary ledgers for materials, work in process, and finished goods are requisites of both systems. In job order cost accounting, however, the costs of direct materials, direct labor, and factory overhead are charged directly to job orders. In process cost accounting, the costs are charged to processing departments, and the cost of a finished unit is determined by dividing the total cost incurred in each process by the number of units produced. Since all goods produced in a department are identical units, it is not necessary to classify production into job orders.

In factories with departmentalized operations, costs are accumulated in factory overhead and work in process accounts maintained for each department. If there is only one processing department in a factory, the cost accounting procedures are simple. The manufacturing cost elements are charged to the single work in process account, and the unit cost of the finished product is determined by dividing the total cost by the number of units produced.

A New Way To Build Cars

When the General Motors Corporation opens assembly plants in Kansas City, Kan., and Doraville, Ga., in the fall of 1987, they will be largely missing a key element of traditional mass production: an assembly line. Instead, the company plans to assemble cars using hundreds of motorized, unmanned carriers called automated guided vehicles, which will carry a car as it goes through the assembly process.

With the carriers, G.M. is breaking away from the auto industry's traditional method of operation, which is centered on a relentlessly moving assembly line that insures high productivity. But company officials describe the carriers as the heart of a new assembly system that they say will improve auto quality and greatly increase plant flexibility.

Although other companies are using the carriers in limited applications, such as materials handling, G.M. is the first American car company to use them as the basis for a production system.

When Henry Ford perfected the assembly line, he was making only one type of car, the Model T, which came in just one color, black. Since then, options have proliferated and today there can be as much as a 30 percent difference in the content of a stripped-down model and one fully loaded.

Because current lines move at a constant speed, regardless of the model mix, plant managers have had to hire enough workers to build the most complex car in the assigned amount of time. This means that some people are idle when base models come down the line. And because stopping the line to fix something would idle thousands, most workers only tag an incorrectly fitting part and hope it will be repaired at the end of the line.

With the carriers, the notion of a "line" begins to fade, although the vehicles generally follow a prescribed path, receiving their instructions from wires buried in the plant floor. If a particular car has a heavy load of options, though, the vehicle may be directed to move out of the main path to have those parts installed, while less heavily equipped models continue along the route. G.M. engineers call this "decoupling the line." With this flexibility, plant managers will be able to balance the work force more closely with the workload.

The carriers also fit into the modular assembly concept that G.M. officials have called one of the keys to cutting manufacturing costs in its Saturn program. Instead of installing thousands of parts, one by one, on a car, a whole module, such as an instrument panel, will be built off the line, tested and only installed if it passes the tests. Since a carrier can be programmed to stop and go as needed, it could roll to the completed instrument panels and then stop to ease the installation.

"We couldn't have done this a few years ago," said David D. Campbell, the director of operations for G.M.'s Chevrolet-Pontiac-Canada group. "We need computers that can keep track of hundreds of carriers and decide on a minute-by-minute basis what station to assign them to, based on variations in the model mix."

Source: Adapted from John Holusha, "A New Way to Build Cars," *The New York Times,* March 13, 1986.

When the manufacturing procedure requires a sequence of different processes, the output of Process 1 becomes the direct materials of Process 2, the output of Process 2 becomes the direct materials of Process 3, and so on until the finished product emerges. Additional direct materials requisitioned from stores may also be introduced during subsequent processes.

A work in process account for a departmentalized factory is illustrated as follows. In this illustration, the total cost of $96,000 is divided by the output, 10,000 units, to obtain a unit cost of $9.60.

Work in Process — Assembly Department

Direct materials	32,000	To Sanding Dept., 10,000 units	96,000
Direct labor	40,000	Cost per unit:	
Factory overhead	24,000	$96,000 ÷ 10,000 = $9.60	
	96,000		96,000

SERVICE DEPARTMENTS AND PROCESS COSTS

In a factory with several processes, there may be one or more **service departments** that do not process the materials directly. Examples of service departments are the factory office, the power plant, and the maintenance and repair shop. These departments perform services for the benefit of other production departments. The costs that they incur, therefore, are part of the total manufacturing costs and must be charged to the processing departments.

The services performed by a service department give rise to internal transactions with the processing departments benefited. These internal transactions are recorded periodically in order to charge the factory overhead accounts of the processing departments with their share of the costs incurred by the service departments. The period usually chosen is a month, although a different period of time may be used. To illustrate, assume that the Power Department produced 500 000 kilowatt-hours (kwh) during the month at a total cost of $30,000, or 6¢ per kilowatt-hour ($30,000 ÷ 500 000). The factory overhead accounts for the departments that used the power are accordingly charged for power at the 6¢ rate. Assuming that during the month the Assembly Department used 200 000 kwh and the Sanding Department used 300 000 kwh, the accounts affected by the interdepartmental transfer of cost would appear as follows:

SERVICE
DEPARTMENT
COSTS
CHARGED TO
PROCESSING
DEPART-
MENTS

Power Department

Fuel	12,000	To Factory Overhead— Assembly Dept.	12,000
Wages	8,500		
Depreciation	3,000	To Factory Overhead— Sanding Dept.	18,000
Maintenance	2,500		
Insurance	2,000		
Taxes	1,500		
Miscellaneous	500		
	30,000		30,000

| Factory Overhead—Assembly Dept. | | Factory Overhead—Sanding Dept. | |
| Power | 12,000 | Power | 18,000 |

Some service departments render services to other service departments. For example, the power department may supply electric current to light the factory office and to operate data processing equipment. At the same time, the factory office provides general supervision for the power department, maintains its payroll records, buys its fuel, and so on. In such cases, the costs of the department rendering the greatest service to other service departments may be distributed first, despite the fact that it receives benefits from other service departments.

PROCESSING COSTS

The accumulated costs transferred from preceding departments and the costs of direct materials and direct labor incurred in each processing department are debited to the related work in process account. Each work in process account is also debited for the factory overhead applied. The costs incurred are summarized periodically, usually at the end of the month. The costs related to the output of each department during the month are then transferred to the next processing department or to Finished Goods, as the case may be. This flow of costs through a work in process account is illustrated as follows:

Work in Process—Sanding Department

10,000 units at $9.60 from Assembly Dept.		96,000	To Polishing Dept., 10,000 units	160,000
Direct labor	36,800		Cost per unit:	
Factory overhead	27,200	64,000	$160,000 ÷ 10,000 = $16	
		160,000		160,000

The three debits in the preceding account may be grouped into two separate categories: (1) direct materials or partially processed materials received from another department, which in this case is composed of 10,000 units received from the Assembly Department, with a total cost of $96,000, and (2) direct labor and factory overhead applied in the Sanding Department, which in this case totaled $64,000. This second group of costs is called the **processing cost**.

Again referring to the illustration, all of the 10,000 units were completely processed in the Sanding Department and were passed on to the Polishing Department. The $16 unit cost of the product transferred to the Polishing Department is made up of Assembly Department cost of $9.60 ($96,000 ÷ 10,000 units) and processing cost of $6.40 ($64,000 ÷ 10,000 units) incurred in the Sanding Department.

INVENTORIES OF PARTIALLY PROCESSED MATERIALS

In the preceding illustration, all materials entering a process were completely processed at the end of the accounting period. In such a case, the determination of unit costs is quite simple. The total of the costs transferred from other departments, the direct materials, the direct labor, and the factory overhead charged to a department is divided by the number of units completed and passed on to the next department or to finished goods. Often, however, some partially processed materials remain in various stages of production in a department at the end of a period. In this case, the costs in work in process must be allocated between the units that have been completed and transferred to the next process or to finished goods and those that are only partially completed and remain within the department.

To allocate direct materials and transferred costs between the output completed and transferred to the next process and inventory of goods within the department, it is necessary to determine the manner in which materials are placed in production. For some products, all materials must be on hand before any work begins. For other products, materials may be added to production in about the same proportion as processing costs are incurred. In still other situations, materials may enter the process at relatively few points, which may or may not be evenly spaced throughout the process.

To allocate processing costs between the output completed and transferred to the next process and the inventory of goods within the process, it is necessary to determine (1) the number of *equivalent units* of production during the period and (2) the *processing cost per equivalent unit* for the same period. The **equivalent units of production** are the number of units that could have been manufactured from start to finish during the period. To illustrate, assume that there is no inventory of goods in process in a certain processing department at the beginning of the period, that 1,000 units of materials enter the process during the period, and that at the end of the period all of the units are 75% completed. The equivalent production in the processing department for the period would be 750 units (75% of 1,000). Assuming further that the processing costs incurred during the period totaled $15,000, the processing cost per equivalent unit would be $20 ($15,000 ÷ 750).

Usually there is an inventory of partially processed units in the department at the beginning of a period. These units are normally completed during the period and transferred to the next department along with units started and completed in the current period. Other units started in the period are only partially processed and thus make up the ending inventory. To illustrate the computation of equivalent units under such circumstances, the following data are assumed for the Polishing Department of Haworth Manufacturing Company:

Inventory within Polishing Department on March 1	600 units, 1/3 completed
Completed in Polishing Department and transferred to finished goods during March.	9,800 units, completed
Inventory within Polishing Department on March 31	800 units, 2/5 completed

The equivalent units of production are determined as follows:

DETER- MINATION OF EQUIVALENT UNITS OF PRODUCTION

To process units in inventory on March 1 . . . . 600 units × 2/3	400
To process units started and completed in March . . . . 9,800 units − 600 units	9,200
To process units in inventory on March 31 . . . . 800 units × 2/5	320
Equivalent units of production in March	9,920

The 9,920 equivalent units of production represent the number of units that would have been produced if there had been no inventories within the process either at the beginning or at the end of the period.

Continuing with the illustration, the next step is to allocate the costs incurred in the Polishing Department between the units completed during March and those remaining in process at the end of the month. If materials (including transferred costs) were used and processing costs were incurred uniformly throughout the month, the total costs of the process would be divided by 9,920 units to obtain the unit cost. On the other hand, if all materials were introduced at the beginning of the process, the full materials cost per unit must be assigned to the uncompleted units. The processing costs would then be allocated to the finished and the uncompleted units on the basis of equivalent units of production. Entries in the following account are based on the latter assumption:

ACCOUNT WORK IN PROCESS—POLISHING DEPARTMENT   ACCOUNT NO.

Date		Item	Debit	Credit	Balance Debit	Balance Credit
Mar.	1	Bal., 600 units, 1/3 completed			10,200	
	31	Sanding Dept., 10,000 units at $16	160,000		170,200	
	31	Direct labor	26,640		196,840	
	31	Factory overhead	18,000		214,840	
	31	Goods finished, 9,800 units		200,600		
	31	Bal., 800 units, 2/5 completed			14,240	

The processing costs incurred in the Polishing Department during March total $44,640 ($26,640 + $18,000). The equivalent units of production for March, determined above, is 9,920. The processing cost per equivalent unit is therefore $4.50 ($44,640 ÷ 9,920). Of the $214,840 debited to the Polishing Department, $200,600 was transferred to Finished Goods and $14,240 remained in the account as work in process inventory. The computation of the allocations to finished goods and to inventory is as follows:

Goods Finished During March

600 units:	Inventory on March 1, 1/3 completed..........	$ 10,200	
	Processing cost in March:		
	600 × 2/3, or 400 units at $4.50............	1,800	
	Total		$ 12,000
	(Unit cost: $12,000 ÷ 600 = $20)		
9,200 units:	Materials cost in March, at $16 per unit........	$147,200	
	Processing cost in March:		
	9,200 at $4.50 per unit....................	41,400	
	Total		188,600
	(Unit cost: $188,600 ÷ 9,200 = $20.50)		
9,800 units:	Goods finished during March.................		$200,600

ALLOCATION OF DEPARTMENTAL CHARGES TO FINISHED GOODS AND INVENTORY

Polishing Department Inventory on March 31

800 units:	Materials cost in March, at $16 per unit........	$ 12,800	
	Processing cost in March:		
	800 × 2/5, or 320 at $4.50.................	1,440	
800 units:	Polishing Department inventory on March 31 ...		$ 14,240

COST OF PRODUCTION REPORT

A report prepared periodically for each processing department summarizes (1) the units for which the department is accountable and the disposition of these units, and (2) the costs charged to the department and the allocation of these costs. This report, termed the **cost of production report**, may be used as the source of the computation of unit production costs and the allocation of the processing costs in the general ledger to the finished and the uncompleted units. More importantly, the report is used to control costs. Each department head is held responsible for the units entering production and the costs incurred in the department. Any differences in unit product costs from one month to another are studied carefully and the causes of significant differences are determined.

The cost of production report based on the data presented in the preceding section for the Polishing Department of Haworth Manufacturing Company is shown on page 1040.

Haworth Manufacturing Company
Cost of Production Report — Polishing Department
For the Month Ended March 31, 19--

Quantities:
Charged to production:

In process, March 1		600
Received from Sanding Department		10,000
Total units to be accounted for		10,600

Units accounted for:

Transferred to finished goods...................		9,800
In process, March 31		800
Total units accounted for		10,600

Costs:
Charged to production:

In process, March 1		$ 10,200
March costs:		
Direct materials from Sanding Department ($16 per unit)		160,000
Processing costs:		
Direct labor..............................	$ 26,640	
Factory overhead..........................	18,000	
Total processing costs ($4.50 per unit).......		44,640
Total costs to be accounted for		$214,840

Costs allocated as follows:
Transferred to finished goods:

600 units at $20.............................	$ 12,000	
9,200 units at $20.50........................	188,600	
Total cost of finished goods...................		$200,600
In process, March 31:		
Direct materials (800 units at $16)	$ 12,800	
Processing costs (800 units × 2/5 × $4.50)....	1,440	
Total cost of inventory in process, March 31....		14,240
Total costs accounted for.......................		$214,840

Computations:
Equivalent units of production:

To process units in inventory on March 1: 600 units × 2/3	400
To process units started and completed in March: 9,800 units − 600 units	9,200
To process units in inventory on March 31: 800 units × 2/5	320
Equivalent units of production...............	9,920

Unit processing cost: $44,640 ÷ 9,920	$ 4.50

JOINT PRODUCTS AND BY-PRODUCTS

In some manufacturing processes, more than one product is produced. In processing cattle, for example, the meat packer produces dressed beef, hides, and other products. In processing logs, the lumber mill produces several grades of lumber in addition to scraps and sawdust. When the output of a manufacturing process consists of two or more different products, the products may be joint products, or one or more of the products may be a by-product.

When two or more goods of significant value are produced from a single principal direct material, the products are termed **joint products**. Similarly, the costs incurred in the manufacture of joint products are called **joint costs**. Common examples of joint products are gasoline, naphtha, kerosene, paraffin, benzine, and other related goods, all of which come from the processing of crude oil.

If one of the products resulting from a process has little value in relation to the main product or joint products, it is known as a **by-product**. The emergence of a by-product is only incidental to the manufacture of the main product or joint products. By-products may be leftover materials, such as sawdust and scraps of wood in a lumber mill, or they may be separated from the material at the beginning of production, as in the case of cottonseed from raw cotton.

Accounting for Joint Products

In management decisions concerning the production and sale of joint products, only the relationship of the total revenue to be derived from the entire group to their total production cost is relevant. Nothing is to be gained from an allocation of joint costs to each product because one product cannot be produced without the others. A decision to produce a single joint product is in effect a decision to produce all of the joint products.

Since joint products come from the processing of a common parent material, the assignment of cost to each separate product cannot be based on actual expenditures. It is impossible to determine the amount of cost incurred in the manufacture of each separate product. However, for purposes of inventory valuation, it is necessary to allocate joint costs among the joint products.

One method of allocation commonly used is the **market (sales) value method**. Its main feature is the assignment of costs to the different products according to their relative sales values. To illustrate, assume that 10,000 units of Product X and 50,000 units of Product Y were produced at a total cost of $63,000. The sales values of the two products and the allocation of the joint costs are as follows:

Joint Costs	Joint Product	Units Produced	Sales Value per Unit	Total Sales Value
$63,000	X	10,000	$3.00	$30,000
	Y	50,000	1.20	60,000
Total sales value....................................				$90,000

Allocation of joint costs:

X: $\dfrac{\$30,000}{\$90,000} \times \$63,000$ $21,000

Y: $\dfrac{\$60,000}{\$90,000} \times \$63,000$ 42,000

Unit cost:
X: $21,000 ÷ 10,000 units......................... $2.10
Y: $42,000 ÷ 50,000 units......................... .84

Accounting for By-Products

The amount of manufacturing cost usually assigned to a by-product is the sales value of the by-product reduced by any additional costs necessary to complete and sell it. The amount of cost thus determined is removed from the proper work in process account and transferred to a finished goods inventory account. To illustrate, assume that for a certain period the costs accumulated in Department 4 total $24,400, and during the same period of time, 1,000 units of by-product B emerge from the processing in Department 4. If the estimated value of the by-product is $200, after estimated completion and selling costs have been deducted, Finished Goods — Product B would be debited for $200 and Work in Process — Department 4 would be credited for the same amount, as illustrated in the following accounts:

Work in Process — Department 4		Finished Goods — Product B	
24,400	200	200	

ILLUSTRATION OF PROCESS COST ACCOUNTING

To illustrate further the basic procedures of the process costing system, assume that Conway Company manufactures Product A. The manufacturing activity begins in Department 1, where all materials enter production. The materials remain in Department 1 for a relatively short time, and there is usually no inventory of work in process in that department at the end of the accounting period. From Department 1, the materials are transferred to

Department 2. In Department 2, there are usually inventories at the end of the accounting period. Separate factory overhead accounts are maintained for Departments 1 and 2. Factory overhead is applied at 80% and 50% of direct labor cost for Departments 1 and 2 respectively. There are two service departments, Maintenance and Power.

The trial balance of the general ledger on January 1, the first day of the fiscal year, is as follows:

Conway Company
Trial Balance
January 1, 19--

Cash..	39,400	
Accounts Receivable	45,000	
Finished Goods—Product A (1,000 units at $36.50).....	36,500	
Work in Process—Department 2		
(800 units, 1/2 completed)	24,600	
Materials	32,000	
Prepaid Expenses................................	6,150	
Plant Assets	510,000	
Accumulated Depreciation—Plant Assets..............		295,000
Accounts Payable................................		51,180
Wages Payable..................................		3,400
Common Stock...................................		250,000
Retained Earnings...............................		94,070
	693,650	693,650

To reduce the illustrative entries to a manageable number and to avoid repetition, the transactions and the adjustments for January are stated as summaries. In practice, the transactions would be recorded from day to day in various journals. The descriptions of the transactions, followed in each case by the entry, are as follows:

(a) Materials purchased and prepaid expenses incurred.

Entry: Materials.....................................	80,500	
Prepaid Expenses	3,300	
Accounts Payable...........................		83,800

(b) Materials requisitioned for use.

Entry: Maintenance Department	1,200	
Power Department............................	6,000	
Factory Overhead—Department 1..............	3,720	
Factory Overhead—Department 2..............	2,700	
Work in Process—Department 1	58,500	
Materials....................................		72,120

(c) Factory labor used.

Entry:		
Maintenance Department	3,600	
Power Department	4,500	
Factory Overhead — Department 1	2,850	
Factory Overhead — Department 2	2,100	
Work in Process — Department 1	24,900	
Work in Process — Department 2	37,800	
Wages Payable		75,750

(d) Other costs incurred.

Entry:		
Maintenance Department	600	
Power Department	900	
Factory Overhead — Department 1	1,800	
Factory Overhead — Department 2	1,200	
Selling Expenses	15,000	
General Expenses	13,500	
Accounts Payable		33,000

(e) Expiration of prepaid expenses.

Entry:		
Maintenance Department	300	
Power Department	750	
Factory Overhead — Department 1	1,350	
Factory Overhead — Department 2	1,050	
Selling Expenses	900	
General Expenses	600	
Prepaid Expenses		4,950

(f) Depreciation.

Entry:		
Maintenance Department	300	
Power Department	1,050	
Factory Overhead — Department 1	1,800	
Factory Overhead — Department 2	2,700	
Selling Expenses	600	
General Expenses	300	
Accumulated Depreciation — Plant Assets		6,750

(g) Distribution of Maintenance Department costs.
The portion of services rendered was 5%, 45%, and 50% for the Power Department, Department 1, and Department 2, respectively.

Entry:		
Power Department	300	
Factory Overhead — Department 1	2,700	
Factory Overhead — Department 2	3,000	
Maintenance Department		6,000

(h) Distribution of Power Department costs.
Power was provided at 5¢ per kwh for 108 000 and 162 000 kwh for Departments 1 and 2, respectively.

Entry: Factory Overhead—Department 1   5,400
       Factory Overhead—Department 2   8,100
         Power Department   13,500

(i) Application of factory overhead costs to work in process.
The predetermined rates were 80% and 50% of direct labor cost for Departments 1 and 2 respectively. See transaction (c) for the monthly direct labor costs.

Entry: Work in Process—Department 1   19,920
       Work in Process—Department 2   18,900
         Factory Overhead—Department 1   19,920
         Factory Overhead—Department 2   18,900

(j) Transfer of production costs from Department 1 to Department 2.
4,100 units were fully processed, and there is no work in process in Department 1 at the beginning or at the end of the month.

Total costs charged to Department 1:	
Direct materials	$ 58,500
Direct labor	24,900
Factory overhead	19,920
Total costs	$103,320

Unit cost of product transferred to Department 2:	
$103,320 ÷ 4,100	$ 25.20

Entry: Work in Process—Department 2   103,320
       Work in Process—Department 1   103,320

(k) Transfer of production costs from Department 2 to Finished Goods.
4,000 units were completed, and the remaining 900 units were 2/3 completed at the end of the month.

Equivalent units of production:	
To process units in inventory on January 1:	
800 × 1/2	400
To process units started and completed in January:	
4,000 − 800	3,200
To process units in inventory on January 31:	
900 × 2/3	600
Equivalent units of production in January	4,200

Processing costs:	
Direct labor [transaction (c)]	$ 37,800
Factory overhead [transaction (i)]	18,900
Total processing costs	$ 56,700

Unit processing cost:
$56,700 ÷ 4,200. . . . . $ 13.50

Allocation of costs of Department 2:
   Units started in December, completed in January:

Inventory on January 1, 800 units 1/2 completed.	$ 24,600	
Processing costs in January, 400 at $13.50	5,400	
Total ($30,000 ÷ 800 = $37.50 unit cost). . . .		$ 30,000

   Units started and completed in January:

From Department 1, 3,200 units at $25.20	$ 80,640	
Processing costs, 3,200 at $13.50	43,200	
Total ($123,840 ÷ 3,200 = $38.70 unit cost) . . .		123,840
Total transferred to Product A		$153,840

   Units started in January, 2/3 completed:

From Department 1, 900 units at $25.20	$ 22,680	
Processing costs, 600 at $13.50	8,100	
Total work in process — Department 2		30,780
Total costs charged to Department 2		$184,620

Entry: Finished Goods — Product A   153,840
        Work in Process — Department 2   153,840

(l) Cost of goods sold.

Product A, 3,800 units:

1,000 units at $36.50	$ 36,500
800 units at $37.50	30,000
2,000 units at $38.70	77,400
Total cost of goods sold	$143,900

Entry: Cost of Goods Sold   143,900
        Finished Goods — Product A   143,900

(m) Sales.

Entry: Accounts Receivable   210,500
        Sales   210,500

(n) Cash received.

Entry: Cash   200,000
        Accounts Receivable   200,000

(o) Cash disbursed.

Entry: Accounts Payable   120,000
        Wages Payable   72,500
        Cash   192,500

A chart of the flow of costs from the service and processing department accounts into the finished goods account and then to the cost of goods sold account is as follows. Entries in the accounts are identified by letters to aid the comparison with the summary journal entries.

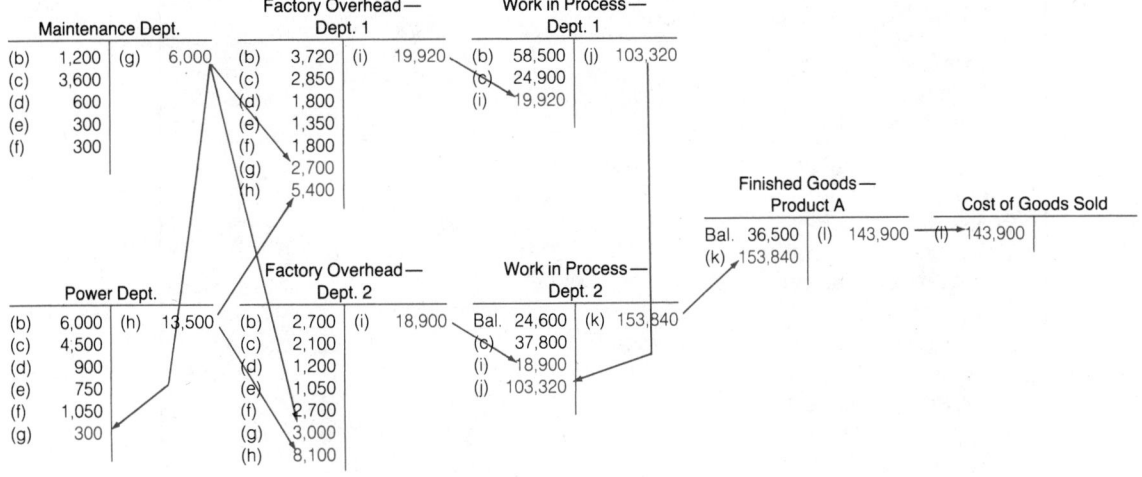

FLOW OF COSTS THROUGH PROCESS COST ACCOUNTS

Cost of Production Reports

The cost of production reports for Departments 1 and 2 are as follows:

Conway Company Cost of Production Report — Department 1 For Month Ended January 31, 19--	
Quantities:	
Units charged to production and to be accounted for	4,100
Units accounted for and transferred to Department 2...........	4,100
Costs:	
Costs charged to production in January:	
Direct materials	$ 58,500
Direct labor..	24,900
Factory overhead.......................................	19,920
Total costs to be accounted for	$103,320
Total costs accounted for and transferred to Department 2	
(4,100 units × $25.20).................................	$103,320

Conway Company
Cost of Production Report — Department 2
For Month Ended January 31, 19--

Quantities:
  Charged to production:
    In process, January 1 800
    Received from Department 1 4,100

    Total units to be accounted for 4,900

  Units accounted for:
    Transferred to finished goods 4,000
    In process, January 31 900

    Total units accounted for 4,900

Costs:
  Charged to production:
    In process, January 1 .... $ 24,600
  January costs:
    Direct materials from Department 1
      ($25.20 per unit) 103,320
    Processing costs:
      Direct labor .... $ 37,800
      Factory overhead 18,900

      Total processing costs ($13.50 per unit) 56,700

    Total costs to be accounted for $184,620

Costs allocated as follows:
  Transferred to finished goods:
    800 units at $37.50 .... $ 30,000
    3,200 units at $38.70 123,840

    Total cost of finished goods $153,840
  In process, January 31:
    Direct materials (900 units at $25.20) .... $ 22,680
    Processing costs (900 units × 2/3 × $13.50) ... 8,100

    Total cost of inventory in process, January 31 .. 30,780

    Total costs accounted for $184,620

Computations:
  Equivalent units of production:
    To process units in inventory on January 1:
      800 units × 1/2 400
    To process units started and completed in January:
      4,000 units − 800 units 3,200
    To process units in inventory on January 31:
      900 units × 2/3 600

    Equivalent units of production 4,200

  Unit processing cost:
    $56,700 ÷ 4,200 .... $13.50

Financial Statements

The financial statements for process cost systems are similar to those for job order cost systems. To illustrate, the trial balance and the condensed financial statements for Conway Company are presented as follows. Note that the net underapplied factory overhead of $1,650 ($1,950 − $300) on January 31 is reported on the balance sheet as a deferred item.

Conway Company
Trial Balance
January 31, 19--

Cash	46,900	
Accounts Receivable	55,500	
Finished Goods — Product A (1,200 units at $38.70)	46,440	
Work in Process — Department 2 (900 units, 2/3 completed)	30,780	
Materials	40,380	
Prepaid Expenses	4,500	
Plant Assets	510,000	
Accumulated Depreciation — Plant Assets		301,750
Accounts Payable		47,980
Wages Payable		6,650
Common Stock		250,000
Retained Earnings		94,070
Sales		210,500
Cost of Goods Sold	143,900	
Factory Overhead — Department 1		300
Factory Overhead — Department 2	1,950	
Selling Expenses	16,500	
General Expenses	14,400	
	911,250	911,250

Conway Company
Income Statement
For Month Ended January 31, 19--

Sales		$210,500
Cost of goods sold		143,900
Gross profit		$ 66,600
Operating expenses:		
Selling expenses	$16,500	
General expenses	14,400	
Total operating expenses		30,900
Income from operations		$ 35,700

Conway Company
Retained Earnings Statement
For Month Ended January 31, 19--

Retained earnings, January 1, 19--	$ 94,070
Income for the month	35,700
Retained earnings, January 31, 19--	$129,770

Conway Company
Balance Sheet
January 31, 19--

Assets

Current assets:			
Cash..................................		$ 46,900	
Accounts receivable		55,500	
Inventories:			
Finished goods......................	$46,440		
Work in process	30,780		
Materials	40,380	117,600	
Prepaid expenses		4,500	
Total current assets.................			$224,500
Plant assets.........................		$510,000	
Less accumulated depreciation		301,750	208,250
Deferred debits:			
Factory overhead underapplied			1,650
Total assets.............................			$434,400

Liabilities

Current liabilities:			
Accounts payable		$ 47,980	
Wages payable.......................		6,650	
Total liabilities			$ 54,630

Stockholders' Equity

Common stock.........................		$250,000	
Retained earnings		129,770	
Total stockholders' equity................			379,770
Total liabilities and stockholders' equity			$434,400

CHAPTER REVIEW

KEY POINTS

1. Process Cost and Job Order Cost Systems Distinguished.

No useful purpose would be served for companies manufacturing a homogeneous product, such as cement, flour, or paint, to maintain job orders for each particular amount of product. In these cases, a process cost system is normally utilized. In process cost accounting, costs are charged to processing departments, and the cost of the finished unit is determined by dividing the total cost incurred in each process by the number of units produced.

2. Service Departments and Process Costs.

In a factory with several processes, there may be one or more service departments that do not process the materials directly. Examples include the factory office, the power plant, and the maintenance and repair shop. Periodically, the costs incurred by service departments are allocated to the factory overhead accounts of the processing departments.

3. Processing Costs.

The accumulated costs transferred from preceding departments and the costs of direct materials and direct labor incurred in each processing department are debited to the related work in process account. Each work in process account is also debited for the factory overhead applied. The direct labor and the factory overhead applied are referred to as the processing costs.

4. Inventories of Partially Processed Materials.

Frequently, partially processed materials remain in various stages of production in a department at the end of a period. In this case, the manufacturing costs must be allocated between the units that have been completed and those that are only partially completed and remain within the department. To allocate processing costs between the output completed and the inventory of goods within the department, it is necessary to determine (1) the number of equivalent units of production during the period and (2) the processing cost per equivalent unit for the same period. The equivalent units of production are the number of units that could have been manufactured from start to finish during the period.

5. Cost of Production Report.

A report prepared periodically for each processing department summarizes (1) the units for which the department is accountable and the disposition of these units and (2) the costs charged to the department and the allocation of these costs. This report, termed the cost of production report, may be used as the source of the computation of unit production costs and the allocation of the processing costs to the finished and the uncompleted units. More importantly, the report is used to control costs.

6. Joint Products and By-Products.

In some manufacturing processes, more than one product is produced. When the output of a manufacturing process consists of two or more different products, the products are either joint products or by-products. When two or more goods of significant value are produced from a single principal direct material, the products are termed joint products. Similarly, the costs incurred in the manufacture of joint products are called joint costs. If one of the products resulting from a process has little value in relation to the main product or joint products, it is known as a by-product.

Since joint products come from the processing of a common parent material, the assignment of cost to each separate product cannot be based on actual expenditures. The allocation of joint costs among the joint products is usually performed using the market (sales) value method. The amount of manufacturing cost usually assigned to a by-product is the sales value of the by-product reduced by any additional costs necessary to complete and sell it.

KEY TERMS

service departments 1035
processing cost 1037
equivalent units of production 1037
cost of production report 1039

joint products 1041
joint costs 1041
by-product 1041
market (sales) value method 1041

SELF-EXAMINATION QUESTIONS
Answers in Appendix B.

1. For which of the following businesses would the process cost system be most appropriate?
    A. Custom furniture manufacturer   C. Crude oil refinery
    B. Commercial building contractor   D. None of the above

2. The group of manufacturing costs referred to as *processing costs* includes:
   A. direct materials and direct labor
   B. direct materials and factory overhead
   C. direct labor and factory overhead
   D. none of the above

3. Information relating to production in Department A for May is as follows:

May	1	Balance, 1,000 units, 3/4 completed................	$22,150
	31	Direct materials, 5,000 units	75,000
	31	Direct labor..	32,500
	31	Factory overhead.................................	16,250

If 500 units were 1/4 completed at May 31 and 5,500 units were completed during May, what was the number of equivalent units of production for May?
   A. 4,500   C. 5,500
   B. 4,875   D. None of the above

4. Based on the data presented in Question 3, what is the unit processing cost?
   A. $10   C. $25
   B. $15   D. None of the above

5. If one of the products resulting from a process has little value in relation to the principal products, it is known as a:
   A. joint product   C. direct material
   B. by-product   D. none of the above

ILLUSTRATIVE PROBLEM

Tate Company manufactures Product A by a series of four processes, all materials being introduced in Department 1. From Department 1 the materials pass through Departments 2, 3, and 4, emerging as finished Product A. All inventories are costed by the first-in, first-out method.

The balances in the accounts Work in Process—Department 4 and Finished Goods were as follows on May 1:

Work in Process—Department 4 (1,000 units, 1/4 completed)......	$17,800
Finished Goods (1,800 units at $23.50 a unit)....................	42,300

The following costs were charged to Work in Process—Department 4 during May:

Direct materials transferred from Department 3: 4,700 units at	
$16 a unit..	$75,200
Direct labor	25,500
Factory overhead...	15,300

During May, 5,000 units of A were completed and 4,800 units were sold. Inventories on May 31 were as follows:

Work in Process—Department 4: 700 units, 1/2 completed
Finished Goods: 2,000 units

Instructions:

Determine the following, presenting the computations in good order:
(a) Equivalent units of production for Department 4 during May.
(b) Unit processing cost for Department 4 for May.
(c) Total and unit cost of Product A started in a prior period and finished in May.
(d) Total and unit cost of Product A started and finished in May.
(e) Total cost of goods transferred to finished goods.
(f) Work in process inventory for Department 4, May 31.
(g) Cost of goods sold (indicate number of units and unit costs.)
(h) Finished goods inventory, May 31.

SOLUTION

to be completed

(a) Equivalent units of production:
    To process units in inventory on May 1:
        1,000 units × 3/4.   750
    To process units started and completed
        in May: 5,000 units − 1,000 units   4,000
    To process units in inventory on May 31:
        700 units × 1/2   350
    Equivalent units of production in May   5,100

(b) Unit processing cost: $\dfrac{\$25,500 + \$15,300}{5,100} = \$8$

(c) Cost of Product A started in a prior period and
    finished in May:
        1,000 units: Inventory on May 1, 1/4 completed . . . . . $ 17,800
                     Processing cost in May, 750 × $8.   6,000
                     Total. . . . . $ 23,800

        Unit cost: $23,800 ÷ 1,000 = $23.80

(d) Cost of Product A started and finished in May:
        4,000 units: Materials from Department 3,
                     4,000 × $16 . . . . $ 64,000
                     Processing cost in May, 4,000 × $8   32,000
                     Total. . . . . $ 96,000

        Unit cost: $96,000 ÷ 4,000 = $24

(e) Total cost of goods transferred to finished goods:

Cost of Product A started in a prior period and finished in May (1,000 units at $23.80)	$ 23,800
Cost of Product A started and finished in May (4,000 units at $24)	96,000
Total	$119,800

(f) Work in process inventory, May 31:

700 units: Materials cost, 700 × $16	$ 11,200
Processing costs in May, 350 × $8	2,800
Work in process inventory, May 31	$ 14,000

(g) Cost of goods sold:

1,800 units at $23.50	$ 42,300
1,000 units at $23.80	23,800
2,000 units at $24.00	48,000
4,800 units	$114,100

(h) Finished goods inventory, May 31:

2,000 units at $24	$ 48,000

DISCUSSION QUESTIONS

1. Which type of cost system, process or job order, would be best suited for each of the following: (a) paint manufacturer, (b) oil refinery, (c) furniture upholsterer, (d) building contractor, (e) refrigerator manufacturer? Give reasons for your answers.

2. Are perpetual inventory accounts for materials, work in process, and finished goods generally used for (a) job order cost systems and (b) process cost systems?

3. In job order cost accounting, the three elements of manufacturing cost are charged directly to job orders. Why is it not necessary to charge manufacturing costs in process cost accounting to job orders?

4. (a) How does a service department differ from a processing department? (b) Give two examples of a service department.

5. Cowen Company maintains a cafeteria for its employees at a cost of $2,250 per month. On what basis would the company most likely allocate the cost of the cafeteria among the production departments?

6. What two groups of manufacturing costs are referred to as processing costs?

7. In the manufacture of 1,000 units of a product, direct materials cost incurred was $20,000, direct labor cost incurred was $8,000, and factory overhead applied was $4,000. (a) What is the total processing cost? (b) What is the processing cost per unit? (c) What is the total manufacturing cost? (d) What is the manufacturing cost per unit?

8. What is meant by the term "equivalent units"?

9. If Department A had no work in process at the beginning of the period, 5,000 units were completed during the period, and 1,000 units were 25% completed at the end of the period, what was the number of equivalent units of production for the period?

10. The following information concerns production in Department C for January. All direct materials are placed in process at the beginning of production. Determine the number of units in work in process inventory at the end of the month.

WORK IN PROCESS — DEPARTMENT C

Date		Item	Debit	Credit	Balance Debit	Balance Credit
Jan.	1	Bal., 6,000 units, ¾ completed			9,500	
	31	Direct materials, 15,000 units	7,500			
	31	Direct labor	14,450			
	31	Factory overhead	7,225			
	31	Goods finished, 13,500 units		28,550		
	31	Bal., _____ units, ½ completed			10,125	

11. For Question No. 10., determine the equivalent units of production for January.

12. What data are summarized in the two principal sections of the cost of production report?

13. What is the most important purpose of the cost of production report?

14. Distinguish between a joint product and a by-product.

15. Department 7 produces two products. How should the costs be allocated (a) if the products are joint products and (b) if one of the products is a by-product?

16. Factory employees in Department 4 of Farr Co. are paid widely varying wage rates. In such circumstances, would direct labor hours or direct labor cost be the more equitable base for applying factory overhead to the production of the department? Explain.

17. In a factory with several processing departments, a separate factory overhead rate may be determined for each department. Why is a single factory overhead rate often inadequate in such circumstances?

18. Real World Focus. As production processes become more and more automated in what many see as the "age of robotics," materials may enter into and leave a

production process without human intervention. For example, in the manufacture of automobiles, General Motors uses state-of-the-art paint systems, which are operated from an automated video control room. The control room supervisor monitors the preparation of the bare metal body of the automobile as it is submerged in a primer. Next, the body passes through nine pairs of robot painters teamed with other robot devices that open and close doors and paint inside surfaces. (a) In this type of production environment, would direct labor hours be an appropriate base for allocation of predetermined factory overhead? (b) Can you suggest other possible factory overhead bases?

EXERCISES

Exercise 23–1. Flowchart of accounts related to service and processing departments. Yates Co. manufactures two products. The entire output of Department 1 is transferred to Department 2. Part of the fully processed goods from Department 2 are sold as Product P and the remainder of the goods are transferred to Department 3 for further processing into Product Q. The service department, Factory Office, provides services for each of the processing departments.

Prepare a chart of the flow of costs from the service and processing department accounts into the finished goods accounts and then into the cost of goods sold account. The relevant accounts are as follows:

Cost of Goods Sold
Factory Office
Factory Overhead — Department 1
Factory Overhead — Department 2
Factory Overhead — Department 3

Finished Goods — Product P
Finished Goods — Product Q
Work in Process — Department 1
Work in Process — Department 2
Work in Process — Department 3

Exercise 23–2. Entry for allocation of service department costs. The Maintenance and Repair Department provides services to processing departments C, D, and E. During July of the current year, the total cost incurred by the Maintenance and Repair Department was $80,000. During July, it was estimated that 60% of the services were provided to Department C, 25% to Department D, and 15% to Department E.

Prepare an entry to record the allocation of the Maintenance and Repair Department cost for July to the processing departments.

Exercise 23–3.   Entries for flow of factory costs for process cost system. Lunn Company manufactures a single product by a continuous process, involving four production departments. The records indicate that $65,000 of direct materials were issued to and $90,000 of direct labor was incurred by Department 1 in the manufacture of the product; the factory overhead rate is 60% of direct labor cost; work in process in the department at the beginning of the period totaled $37,500; and work in process at the end of the period totaled $35,000.

Prepare entries to record (a) the flow of costs into Department 1 during the period for (1) direct materials, (2) direct labor, and (3) factory overhead; (b) the transfer of production costs to Department 2.

Exercise 23–4.   Factory overhead rate, entry for application of factory overhead, and factory overhead account balance. The chief cost accountant for R. D. Evans Co. estimates total factory overhead cost for Department F for the year at $72,000 and total direct labor costs at $96,000. During March, the actual direct labor cost totaled $8,100, and factory overhead cost incurred totaled $6,250. (a) What is the predetermined factory overhead rate based on direct labor cost? (b) Prepare the entry to apply factory overhead to production for March. (c) What is the March 31 balance of the account Factory Overhead—Department F? (d) Does the balance in (c) represent overapplied or underapplied factory overhead?

Exercise 23–5.   Equivalent units of production and related costs. The charges to Work in Process—Department 1 for a period, together with information concerning production, are as follows. All direct materials are placed in process at the beginning of production.

400 remaining)   *no ending inventory*

Work in Process—Department 1			
2,000 units, 80% completed	49,100	To Dept. 2, 6,200 units	169,600
Direct materials, 4,200 at $15	63,000		
Direct labor	46,000		
Factory overhead	11,500		

everything sent out

Determine the following, presenting your computations: (a) equivalent units of production, (b) processing cost per equivalent unit of production, (c) total and unit cost of product started in prior period and completed in the current period, and (d) total and unit cost of product started and completed in the current period.

Exercise 23–6.   Cost of production report. Prepare a cost of production report for the Assembly Department of Cohen Company for May of the current fiscal year, using the following data:

Inventory, May 1, 5,000 units, 40% completed $120,000
Materials from the Sanding Department, 15,000 units . @ 22.50 . .   337,500
Direct labor for May.   51,875
Factory overhead for May   31,125
Goods finished during May (includes units in process, May 1)
    16,500 units . . . .   —
Inventory, May 31, 3,500 units, 60% completed . . . .   —

Exercise 23–7. Allocation of costs for by-product and joint products. The charges to Work in Process—Department 4, together with units of product completed during the period, are indicated in the following account:

Work in Process—Department 4

From Department 3	125,600	By-product A, 1,000 units
Direct labor	30,300	Joint product P, 4,000 units
Factory overhead	10,100	Joint product Q, 10,000 units

There is no inventory of goods in process at either the beginning or the end of the period. The value of A is $1 a unit; P sells at $25 a unit, and Q sells at $15 a unit.

Allocate the costs to the three products and determine the unit cost of each, presenting your computations.

PROBLEMS

Series A

Problem 23–1A. Entries for process cost system. Sellers Company manufactures Product Z. Material A is placed in process in Department 1, where it is ground and partially refined. The output of Department 1 is transferred to Department 2, where Material B is added at the beginning of the process and the refining is completed. On June 1, Sellers Company had the following inventories:

Finished goods (6,150 units)	$107,625
Work in process—Department 1	—
Work in process—Department 2 (3,150 units, 2/3 completed)	51,345
Materials	61,470

Departmental accounts are maintained for factory overhead, and there is one service department, Factory Office. Manufacturing operations for June are summarized as follows:

(a) Materials purchased on account. $32,700

(b) Materials requisitioned for use:
Material A $51,705
Material B   9,840
Indirect materials — Department 1   2,160
Indirect materials — Department 2   540

(c) Labor used:
Direct labor — Department 1 . . . . $73,050
Direct labor — Department 2   29,175
Indirect labor — Department 1   4,200
Indirect labor — Department 2   1,920
Factory Office   3,450

(d) Depreciation charged on plant assets:
Department 1 . . . . $29,850
Department 2   14,400
Factory Office   1,650

(e) Miscellaneous costs incurred on account:
Department 1 . . . . $ 5,535
Department 2   3,465
Factory Office   1,800

(f) Expiration of prepaid expenses:
Department 1 . . . . $ 3,420
Department 2   735
Factory Office   1,125

(g) Distribution of Factory Office costs:
Department 1 . . . .   60% of total Factory Office costs
Department 2 . . . .   40% of total Factory Office costs

(h) Application of factory overhead costs:
Department 1 . . . .   70% of direct labor cost
Department 2 . . . .   80% of direct labor cost

(i) Production costs transferred from Department 1 to Department 2:
12,300 units were fully processed, and there was no inventory of work in process in Department 1 at June 30.

(j) Production costs transferred from Department 2 to finished goods:
11,250 units, including the inventory at June 1, were fully processed. There were 4,200 units 3/5 completed at June 30.

(k) Cost of goods sold during June:
12,000 units (Use the first-in, first-out method in crediting the finished goods account.)

Instructions:

(1) Prepare entries to record the foregoing operations. Identify each entry by letter.
(2) Compute the June 30 work in process inventory for Department 2.

Problem 23–2A. Cost of production report. The data related to production during June of the current year for Department 2 of Sellers Company are presented in Problem 23–1A.

Instructions:

Prepare a cost of production report for Department 2 for June.

Problem 23–3A. Financial statements for process cost system. The trial balance of Sarnoff Inc. at January 31, the end of the first month of the current fiscal year, is as follows:

Sarnoff Inc.
Trial Balance
January 31, 19--

Cash...	80,600	
Marketable Securities	60,000	
Accounts Receivable.............................	245,000	
Allowance for Doubtful Accounts		9,900
Finished Goods — Product A1......................	91,600	
Finished Goods — Product A2......................	155,000	
Work in Process — Department 1	17,750	
Work in Process — Department 2	33,150	
Work in Process — Department 3	29,400	
Materials	60,500	
Prepaid Insurance	14,750	
Office Supplies.................................	5,250	
Land...	105,000	
Buildings	660,000	
Accumulated Depreciation — Buildings		319,200
Machinery and Equipment	342,000	
Accumulated Depreciation—Machinery and Equipment.		216,600
Office Equipment	59,400	
Accumulated Depreciation — Office Equipment.......		25,560
Patents..	66,000	
Accounts Payable		122,150
Wages Payable.................................		19,750
Income Tax Payable		6,500
Mortgage Note Payable (due 1995)................		120,000
Common Stock ($15 par)		600,000
Retained Earnings		518,220
Sales..		755,500
Cost of Goods Sold.............................	502,300	
Factory Overhead — Department 1..................	400	
Factory Overhead — Department 2..................	370	
Factory Overhead — Department 3..................		290
Selling Expenses...............................	99,750	
General Expenses...............................	68,800	
Interest Expense	1,000	
Interest Income.................................		350
Income Tax	16,000	
	2,714,020	2,714,020

Instructions:

(1) Prepare an income statement.
(2) Prepare a retained earnings statement.
(3) Prepare a balance sheet.

Problem 23–4A. Equivalent units and related costs; cost of production report. Drysdale Company manufactures Product C by a series of four processes, all materials being introduced in Department 1. From Department 1, the materials pass through Departments 2, 3, and 4, emerging as finished Product C. All inventories are costed by the first-in, first-out method.

The balances in the accounts Work in Process—Department 4 and Finished Goods were as follows on July 1:

4500

Work in Process—Department 4 (6,000 units, 3/4 completed) . $ 66,300
Finished Goods (8,000 units at $13 a unit)   104,000

The following costs were charged to Work in Process—Department 4 during July:

Direct materials transferred from Department 3: 26,000 units
    at $5.20 a unit. $135,200
Direct labor.   144,000
Factory overhead   72,000
During July, 25,000 units of C were completed and 26,800 units were sold.

Inventories on July 31 were as follows:

Work in Process—Department 4: 7,000 units, 1/2 completed
Finished Goods: 6,200 units

Instructions:

(1) Determine the following, presenting computations in good order:
    (a) Equivalent units of production for Department 4 during July.
    (b) Unit processing cost for Department 4 for July.
    (c) Total and unit cost of Product C started in a prior period and finished in July.
    (d) Total and unit cost of Product C started and finished in July.
    (e) Total cost of goods transferred to finished goods.
    (f) Work in process inventory for Department 4, July 31.
    (g) Cost of goods sold (indicate number of units and unit costs).
    (h) Finished goods inventory, July 31.
(2) Prepare a cost of production report for Department 4 for July.

Problem 23–5A. Entries for process cost system, including joint products. I.C. Han Products manufactures joint products A and B. Materials are placed in production in Department 1, and after processing, are transferred to Department 2, where more materials are added. The finished products emerge from Department 2. There are two service departments: Factory Office, and Maintenance and Repair.

There were no inventories of work in process at the beginning or at the end of January. Finished goods inventories at January 1 were as follows:

Product A, 2,500 units	$75,000
Product B, 900 units........................	45,000

Transactions related to manufacturing operations for January are summarized as follows:

(a) Materials purchased on account, $91,750.

(b) Materials requisitioned for use: Department 1, $47,000 ($42,540 entered directly into the products); Department 2, $31,385 ($27,320 entered directly into the products); Maintenance and Repair, $1,990.

(c) Labor costs incurred: Department 1, $36,100 ($31,500 entered directly into the products); Department 2, $38,800 ($33,600 entered directly into the products); Factory Office, $5,850; Maintenance and Repair, $13,650.

(d) Miscellaneous costs and expenses incurred on account: Department 1, $5,570; Department 2, $4,150; Factory Office, $1,400; and Maintenance and Repair, $2,170.

(e) Depreciation charged on plant assets: Department 1, $6,900; Department 2, $5,360; Factory Office, $900; and Maintenance and Repair, $980.

(f) Expiration of various prepaid expenses: Department 1, $450; Department 2, $330; Factory Office, $350; and Maintenance and Repair, $490.

(g) Factory office costs allocated on the basis of hours worked: Department 1, 2,200 hours; Department 2, 1,760 hours; Maintenance and Repair, 440 hours.

(h) Maintenance and repair costs allocated on the basis of services rendered: Department 1, 60%; Department 2, 40%.

(i) Factory overhead applied to production at the predetermined rates: 120% and 90% of direct labor cost for Departments 1 and 2 respectively.

(j) Output of Department 1: 8,100 units.

(k) Output of Department 2: 4,000 units of Product A and 1,600 units of Product B. Unit selling price is $45 for Product A and $75 for Product B.

(l) Sales on account: 4,500 units of Product A at $45 and 1,700 units of Product B at $75. Credits to the finished goods accounts are to be made according to the first-in, first-out method.

Instructions:

Present entries in general journal form to record the transactions, identifying each by letter. Include as an explanation for entry (k) the computations for the allocation of the production costs for Department 2 to the joint products, and as an explanation for entry (l) the number of units and the unit costs for each product sold.

Problem 23–6A.   Work in process account data for two months and determination of difference in unit product cost between months. A process cost system is used to record the costs of manufacturing Product C, which requires a series of three processes. The inventory of Work in Process—Department 3 on July 1 and debits to the account during July were as follows:

Balance, 1,200 units, 2/3 completed	$11,640
From Department 2, 5,250 units	9,450
Direct labor	50,676
Factory overhead	12,669

During July, the 1,200 units in process on July 1 were completed, and of the 5,250 units entering the department, all were completed except 2,000 units, which were 3/4 completed.

Charges to Work in Process—Department 3 for August were as follows:

From Department 2, 6,100 units	$10,675
Direct labor	63,500
Factory overhead	15,875

During August, the units in process at the beginning of the month were completed, and of the 6,100 units entering the department, all were completed except 500 units, which were 1/2 completed.

Instructions:

(1) Set up an account for Work in Process—Department 3. Enter the balance as of July 1 and record the debits and credits in the account for July. Present computations for the determination of (a) equivalent units of production, (b) unit processing cost, (c) cost of goods finished, differentiating between units started in the prior period and units started and finished in July, and (d) work in process inventory.

(2) Record the transactions for August in the account. Present the computations listed in (1).

(3) Determine the difference in unit cost between the product started and completed in July and the product started and completed in August. Determine also the amount of the difference attributable collectively to operations in Departments 1 and 2 and the amount attributable to operations in Department 3.

Series B

Problem 23–1B.   Entries for process cost system. Ryan Company manufactures Product W. Material E is placed in process in Department 1, where it is ground and partially refined. The output of Department 1 is transferred to Department 2, where Material F is added at the beginning of the process and the refining is completed. On April 1, Ryan Company had the following inventories:

Finished goods (7,000 units)	$169,400
Work in process—Department 1	—
Work in process—Department 2 (1,400 units, 3/4 completed)	28,140
Materials	37,650

Departmental accounts are maintained for factory overhead, and there is one service department, Factory Office. Manufacturing operations for April are summarized as follows:

(a) Materials purchased on account............................ $68,500
(b) Materials requisitioned for use:

Material E	$37,114
Material F	30,800
Indirect materials—Department 1	2,460
Indirect materials—Department 2	1,770

(c) Labor used:

Direct labor—Department 1	$77,000
Direct labor—Department 2	54,950
Indirect labor—Department 1	2,900
Indirect labor—Department 2	2,750
Factory Office	2,618

(d) Miscellaneous costs incurred on account:

Department 1	$ 9,950
Department 2	7,250
Factory Office	2,996

(e) Expiration of prepaid expenses:

Department 1	$ 1,490
Department 2	975
Factory Office	420

(f) Depreciation charged on plant assets:

Department 1	$20,500
Department 2	17,500
Factory Office	1,330

(g) Distribution of Factory Office costs:

Department 1	75% of total Factory Office costs
Department 2	25% of total Factory Office costs

(h) Application of factory overhead costs:

Department 1	55% of direct labor cost
Department 2	60% of direct labor cost

(i) Production costs transferred from Department 1 to Department 2:
   12,320 units were fully processed, and there was no inventory of work in process in Department 1 at April 30.

(j) Production costs transferred from Department 2 to finished goods:
     11,200 units, including the inventory at April 1, were fully processed. 2,520
     units were 1/3 completed at April 30.
(k) Cost of goods sold during April:
     13,300 units (Use the first-in, first-out method in crediting the finished goods
     account.)

Instructions:

(1) Prepare entries to record the foregoing operations. Identify each entry by letter.
(2) Compute the April 30 work in process inventory for Department 2.

Problem 23–4B.   Equivalent units and related costs; cost of production
report. Bowers Company manufactures Product Z by a series of three processes, all
materials being introduced in Department 1. From Department 1, the materials pass
through Departments 2 and 3, emerging as finished Product Z. All inventories are costed
by the first-in, first-out method.

The balances in the accounts Work in Process—Department 3 and Finished
Goods were as follows on March 1:

Work in Process—Department 3 (7,000 units, 1/2 completed) . $212,100
Finished Goods (12,000 units at $36.20 a unit)   434,400

The following costs were charged to Work in Process—Department 3 during
March:

Direct materials transferred from Department 2: 37,000 units
    at $24 a unit. $888,000
Direct labor.   232,600
Factory overhead   140,000

During March, 35,000 units of Z were completed and 37,200 units were sold.
Inventories on March 31 were as follows:

Work in Process—Department 3: 9,000 units, 1/3 completed
Finished Goods: 9,800 units

Instructions:

(1) Determine the following, presenting computations in good order:
    (a) Equivalent units of production for Department 3 during March.
    (b) Unit processing cost for Department 3 for March.

(c) Total and unit cost of Product Z started in a prior period and finished in March.

(d) Total and unit cost of Product Z started and finished in March.

(e) Total cost of goods transferred to finished goods.

(f) Work in process inventory for Department 3, March 31.

(g) Cost of goods sold (indicate number of units and unit costs).

(h) Finished goods inventory, March 31.

(2) Prepare a cost of production report for Department 3 for March.

Problem 23–6B. Work in process account data for two months and determination of difference in unit product cost between months. A process cost system is used to record the costs of manufacturing Product F10, which requires a series of four processes. The inventory of Work in Process—Department 4 on June 1 and debits to the account during June were as follows:

Balance, 800 units, 1/4 completed.	$13,040
From Department 3, 4,600 units	51,520
Direct labor.	77,000
Factory overhead	19,250

During June, the 800 units in process on June 1 were completed, and of the 4,600 units entering the department, all were completed except 1,100 units, which were 1/4 completed.

Charges to Work in Process—Department 4 for July were as follows:

From Department 3, 4,125 units	$47,850
Direct labor.	83,448
Factory overhead	20,862

During July, the units in process at the beginning of the month were completed, and of the 4,125 units entering the department, all were completed except 750 units, which were 1/2 completed.

Instructions:

(1) Set up an account for Work in Process—Department 4. Enter the balance as of June 1 and record the debits and the credits in the account for June. Present computations for the determination of (a) equivalent units of production, (b) unit processing cost, (c) cost of goods finished, differentiating between units started in the prior period and units started and finished in June, and (d) work in process inventory.

(2) Record the transactions for July in the account. Present the computations listed in (1).

(3) Determine the difference in unit cost between the product started and completed in June and the product started and completed in July. Determine also the amount of the difference attributable collectively to operations in Departments 1 through 3 and the amount attributable to operations in Department 4.

MINI-CASE 23

H and S Inc. manufactures product 3D by a series of four processes. All materials are placed in production in the Die Casting Department and, after processing, are transferred to the Tooling, Assembly, and Polishing Departments, emerging as a finished product 3D.

On June 1, the balance in the account Work in Process — Polishing was $201,960, determined as follows:

Direct materials: 12,000 units...........................	$122,040
Direct labor: 12,000 units, 3/4 completed..................	64,530
Factory overhead: 12,000 units, 3/4 completed............	15,390
Total..	$201,960

The following costs were charged to Work in Process — Polishing during June:

Direct materials transferred from Assembly Dept., 136,000 units.......................................	$1,428,000
Direct labor...	988,920
Factory overhead	217,080

During June, 138,000 units of 3D were completed and transferred to Finished Goods. On June 30, the inventory in the Polishing Department consisted of 10,000 units, one-half completed.

As a new cost accountant for H and S Inc., you have just received a phone call from Ann Pearlstein, the superintendent of the Polishing Department. She was extremely upset with the cost of production report, which she says does not balance. In addition, she commented:

"I give up! These reports are a waste of time. My department has always been the best department in the plant, so why should I bother with these reports? Just what purpose do they serve?"

The report to which Pearlstein referred is as follows:

H and S Inc.
Cost of Production Report—Polishing Department
For Month Ended June 30, 19--

Quantities:		
Charged to production:		
In process, June 1.........................		9,000
Received from Assembly Department		136,000
Total units to be accounted for		145,000
Units accounted for:		
Transferred to finished goods		138,000
In process, June 30........................		5,000
Total units accounted for		143,000
Costs:		
Charged to production:		
In process, June 1.........................		$ 201,960
June costs:		
Direct materials from Assembly Department		
($9.42 per unit)...........................		1,428,000
Processing costs:		
Direct labor	$988,920	
Factory overhead........................	217,080	
Total processing costs ($8.04 per unit)		1,206,000
Total costs to be accounted for................		$2,835,960
Costs allocated as follows:		
Transferred to finished goods:		
138,000 units at $17.46 ($9.42 + $8.04)		$2,409,480
In process, June 30:		
Materials (5,000 units × $9.42)..............	$ 47,100	
Processing costs (5,000 units × $8.04)	40,200	
Total cost of inventory in process...........		87,300
Total costs accounted for.....................		$2,496,780
Computations:		
Equivalent units of production:		
To process units in inventory on June 1:		
12,000 units × 3/4		9,000
To process units started and completed in June.		136,000
To process units in inventory on June 30:		
10,000 units × 1/2		5,000
Equivalent units of production		150,000
Unit processing cost:		
$1,206,000 ÷ 150,000		$8.04

Instructions:

(1) Based upon the data for June, prepare a revised cost of production report for the Polishing Department.
(2) Assume that for May, the unit direct materials cost was $10.17 and the unit processing cost was $8.88. Determine the change in the direct materials unit cost and unit processing cost for June.
(3) Based on (2), what are some possible explanations for the changing unit costs?
(4) Describe how you would explain to Pearlstein that cost of production reports are useful.

Part **8**

PLANNING,
CONTROL, AND
DECISION MAKING

Chapter 24

BUDGETING AND STANDARD COST SYSTEMS

Chapter Objectives:

■ Describe the nature and objectives of budgeting and the budget process.

■ Identify the components of the master budget and illustrate the preparation of a master budget for a small manufacturing enterprise.

■ Describe and illustrate budget performance reports and flexible budgets.

■ Describe the use of standard costs in planning and controlling operations.

■ Illustrate the use of variance analysis for direct materials, direct labor, and factory overhead.

■ Describe and illustrate how standards may be incorporated into the accounts of a manufacturing enterprise.

Effective planning and control are requisites of successful operations. Various uses of accounting data by management in performing these functions have been described and illustrated in earlier chapters. For example, the role of cost accounting in planning production and controlling costs has been discussed and illustrated. This chapter is devoted to budgeting and standard costs, two additional accounting devices that aid management in planning and controlling the operations of the business.

NATURE AND OBJECTIVES OF BUDGETING

As mentioned in Chapter 21, a **budget** is a formal written statement of management's plans for the future, expressed in financial terms. A budget charts the course of future action. Thus, it serves management's primary functions in the same manner that the architect's blueprints aid the builder and the navigator's flight plan aids the pilot.

A budget, like a blueprint and flight plan, should contain sound, attainable objectives. If the budget is to contain such objectives, planning must be based on careful study, investigation, and research. Management's reliance on data thus obtained lessens the role of guesswork and intuition in managing a business enterprise.

In a recent survey, the corporate boards of directors of 600 of the 1,000 largest U.S. corporations emphasized the importance of planning to the success of a business. The results of this survey, which asked the boards to identify the most important issues facing them now, and five years from now, are as follows:[1]

---

[1]Deloitte Haskins & Sells, "Major Issues Facing Boards of Directors," *DH+S Review,* September 2, 1985, p. 6.

Relative Importance of Issues
Facing Boards of Directors of
Major U.S. Corporations

Issue	Currently Ranking as No. 1 In Importance	Ranking as No. 1 In Importance Five Years from Now
Financial results	50%	37%
Strategic planning	20	44
Day-to-day operations	10	—
Managerial succession	7	17
Mergers/acquisitions	2	—

The essentials of budgeting are (1) the establishment of specific goals for future operations and (2) the periodic comparison of actual results with these goals. The establishment of specific goals for future operations encompasses the planning function of management. The periodic comparison of actual results with these goals encompasses the control function of management.

Although budgets are commonly associated with profit-making enterprises, they play an important role in operating most instrumentalities of government, ranging from rural school districts and small villages to gigantic agencies of the federal government. They are also an important part of the operations of churches, hospitals, and other nonprofit institutions. Individuals and family units often use budgeting techniques as an aid to careful management of resources. In this chapter, the principles of budgeting are discussed in the context of profit-making enterprises.[2]

BUDGET PERIOD

Budgets of operating activities usually include the fiscal year of an enterprise. A year is short enough to make possible fairly dependable estimates of future operations, and yet long enough to make it possible to view the future in a reasonably broad context. However, to achieve effective control, the annual budgets must be subdivided into shorter time periods, such as quarters of the year, months, or weeks. It is also necessary to review the budgets

---

[2]The application of the basic budgeting principles to individuals and nonprofit organizations is presented in Chapter 28.

from time to time and make any changes that become necessary as a result of unforeseen changes in general business conditions, in the particular industry, or in the individual enterprise.

A frequent variant of fiscal-year budgeting, sometimes called **continuous budgeting**, provides for maintenance of a twelve-month projection into the future. At the end of each time interval used, the twelve-month budget is revised by removing the data for the period just ended and adding the newly estimated budget data for the same period next year.

BUDGETING PROCEDURES

The details of budgeting systems are affected by the type and degree of complexity of a particular company, the amount of its revenues, the relative importance of its various divisions, and many other factors. Budget procedures used by a large manufacturer of automobiles would obviously differ in many ways from a system designed for a small manufacturer of paper products. The differences between a system designed for factory operations of any type and a financial enterprise such as a bank would be even more marked.

The development of budgets for a following fiscal year usually begins several months prior to the end of the current year. The responsibility for their development is ordinarily assigned to a committee made up of the budget director and such high-level executives as the controller, treasurer, production manager, and sales manager. The process is started by requesting estimates of sales, production, and other operating data from the various administrative units concerned. It is important that all levels of management and all departments participate in the preparation and submission of budget estimates. The involvement of all supervisory personnel fosters cooperation both within and among departments and also heightens awareness of each department's importance in the overall processes of the company. All levels of management are thus encouraged to set goals and to control operations in a manner that strengthens the possibilities of achieving the goals.

The process of developing budget estimates differs among enterprises. One method is to require all levels of management to start from zero and estimate sales, production, and other operating data as though operations were being started for the first time. Although this concept, called **zero-base budgeting**, has received wide attention in regard to budgeting for governmental units, it is equally useful to commercial enterprises. Another method of developing estimates is for each level of management to modify last year's budgeted amounts in light of last year's operating results and expected changes for the coming year.

The various estimates received by the budget committee are revised, reviewed, coordinated, cross-referenced, and finally put together to form the **master budget**. The estimates submitted should not be substantially revised by the committee without first giving the originators an opportunity to defend their proposals. After agreement has been reached and the master budget has been adopted by the budget committee, copies of the pertinent sections are distributed to the proper personnel in the chain of accountability. Periodic reports comparing actual results with the budget should likewise be distributed to all supervisory personnel.

As a framework for describing and illustrating budgeting, a small manufacturing enterprise will be assumed. The major parts of its master budget are as follows:

COM-PONENTS OF MASTER BUDGET

Budgeted income statement
  Sales budget
  Cost of goods sold budget
    Production budget
    Direct materials purchases budget
    Direct labor cost budget
    Factory overhead cost budget
  Operating expenses budget

Budgeted balance sheet
  Capital expenditures budget
  Cash budget

Sales Budget

The first budget to be prepared is usually the sales budget. An estimate of the dollar volume of sales revenue serves as the foundation upon which the other budgets are based. Sales volume will have a significant effect on all of the factors entering into the determination of operating income.

The sales budget ordinarily indicates (1) the quantity of forecasted sales for each product and (2) the expected unit selling price of each product. These data are often classified by areas and/or sales representatives.

In forecasting the quantity of each product expected to be sold, the starting point is generally past sales volumes. These amounts are revised for various factors expected to affect future sales, such as a backlog of unfilled sales orders, planned advertising and promotion, expected industry and general economic conditions, productive capacity, projected pricing policy, and market research study findings. Statistical analysis can be used in this process to evaluate the effect of these factors on past sales volume. Such analysis can provide a mathematical association between past sales and the several variables expected to affect future sales.

Once the forecast of sales volume is completed, the anticipated sales revenue is then determined by multiplying the volume of forecasted sales by the expected unit sales price, as shown in the following sales budget:

Bowers Company
Sales Budget
For Year Ending December 31, 19--

Product and Area	Unit Sales Volume	Unit Selling Price	Total Sales
Product X:			
Area A	208,000	$ 9.90	$2,059,200
Area B	162,000	9.90	1,603,800
Area C	158,000	9.90	1,564,200
Total	528,000		$5,227,200
Product Y:			
Area A	111,600	$16.50	$1,841,400
Area B	78,800	16.50	1,300,200
Area C	89,600	16.50	1,478,400
Total	280,000		$4,620,000
Total revenue from sales			$9,847,200

Frequent comparisons of actual sales with the budgeted volume, by product, area, and/or sales representative, will show differences between the two. Management is then able to investigate the probable cause of the significant differences and attempt corrective action.

Production Budget

The number of units of each commodity expected to be manufactured to meet budgeted sales and inventory requirements is set forth in the production budget. The budgeted volume of production is based on the sum of (1) the expected sales volume and (2) the desired year-end inventory, less (3) the inventory expected to be available at the beginning of the year. A production budget is illustrated as follows:

Bowers Company
Production Budget
For Year Ending December 31, 19--

	Units Product X	Units Product Y
Sales	528,000	280,000
Plus desired ending inventory, December 31, 19--	80,000	60,000
Total	608,000	340,000
Less estimated beginning inventory, January 1, 19--	88,000	48,000
Total production	520,000	292,000

The production needs must be carefully coordinated with the sales budget to assure that production and sales are kept in balance during the period. Ideally, manufacturing operations should be maintained at capacity, and inventories should be neither excessive nor insufficient to fill sales orders.

Direct Materials Purchases Budget

The production needs shown by the production budget, combined with data on direct materials needed, provide the data for the direct materials purchases budget. The quantities of direct materials purchases necessary to meet production needs is based on the sum of (1) the materials expected to be needed to meet production requirements and (2) the desired year-end inventory, less (3) the inventory expected to be available at the beginning of the year. The quantities of direct materials required are then multiplied by the expected unit purchase price to determine the total cost of direct materials purchases.

In the following direct materials purchases budget, materials A and C are required for Product X, and materials A, B, and C are required for Product Y.

DIRECT
MATERIALS
PURCHASES
BUDGET

Bowers Company
Direct Materials Purchases Budget
For Year Ending December 31, 19--

	Direct Materials		
	A	B	C
Units required for production:			
Product X	390,000	—	520,000
Product Y	146,000	292,000	294,200
Plus desired ending inventory, Dec. 31, 19--	80,000	40,000	120,000
Total	616,000	332,000	934,200
Less estimated beginning inventory, Jan. 1, 19--..	103,000	44,000	114,200
Total units to be purchased	513,000	288,000	820,000
Unit price	$ .60	$ 1.70	$ 1.00
Total direct materials purchases	$307,800	$489,600	$820,000

The timing of the direct materials purchases requires close coordination between the purchasing and production departments so that inventory levels can be maintained within reasonable limits.

Direct Labor Cost Budget

The needs indicated by the production budget provide the starting point for the preparation of the direct labor cost budget. The direct labor hours necessary to meet production needs are multiplied by the estimated hourly rate to yield the total direct labor cost. The manufacturing operations for both Products X and Y are performed in Departments 1 and 2. A direct labor cost budget is illustrated as follows:

Bowers Company
Direct Labor Cost Budget
For Year Ending December 31, 19--

	Department 1	Department 2
Hours required for production:		
Product X	75,000	104,000
Product Y	46,800	116,800
Total	121,800	220,800
Hourly rate	$10	$8
Total direct labor cost	$1,218,000	$1,766,400

The direct labor requirements must be carefully coordinated with available labor time to assure that sufficient labor will be available to meet production needs. Efficient manufacturing operations minimize idle time and labor shortages.

Factory Overhead Cost Budget

The factory overhead costs estimated to be necessary to meet production needs are presented in the factory overhead cost budget. For use as part of the master budget, the factory overhead cost budget usually presents the total estimated cost for each item of factory overhead. A factory overhead cost budget is illustrated as follows:

Bowers Company
Factory Overhead Cost Budget
For Year Ending December 31, 19--

Indirect factory wages	$ 732,800
Supervisory salaries	360,000
Power and light	306,000
Depreciation of plant and equipment	288,000
Indirect materials	182,800
Maintenance	140,280
Insurance and property taxes	79,200
Total factory overhead cost	$2,089,080

Supplemental schedules are often prepared to present the factory overhead cost for each individual department. Such schedules enable department supervisors to direct attention to those costs for which each is solely responsible. They also aid the production manager in evaluating performance in each department.

Cost of Goods Sold Budget

The budget for the cost of goods sold is prepared by combining data on estimated inventories with the relevant estimates of quantities and costs in the budgets for (1) direct materials purchases, (2) direct labor costs, and (3) factory overhead costs. A cost of goods sold budget is illustrated as follows:

COST OF
GOODS SOLD
BUDGET

Bowers Company
Cost of Goods Sold Budget
For Year Ending December 31, 19--

Finished goods inventory, January 1, 19--...			$1,095,600
Work in process inventory, January 1, 19-- ..		$ 214,400	
Direct materials:			
Direct materials inventory, January 1, 19--....................	$ 250,800		
Direct materials purchases.............	1,617,400		
Cost of direct materials available for use..	$1,868,200		
Less direct materials inventory, December 31, 19--	236,000		
Cost of direct materials placed in production......................	$1,632,200		
Direct labor...........................	2,984,400		
Factory overhead	2,089,080		
Total manufacturing costs		6,705,680	
Total work in process during period		$6,920,080	
Less work in process inventory, December 31, 19--		220,000	
Cost of goods manufactured			6,700,080
Cost of finished goods available for sale...			$7,795,680
Less finished goods inventory, December 31, 19--			1,195,000
Cost of goods sold			$6,600,680

Operating Expenses Budget

Based on past experiences, which are adjusted for future expectations, the estimated selling and general expenses are set forth in the operating expenses budget. For use as part of the master budget, the operating expenses budget ordinarily presents the expenses by nature or type of expenditure, such as sales salaries, rent, insurance, and advertising. An operating expenses budget is illustrated as follows:

Bowers Company Operating Expenses Budget For Year Ending December 31, 19--		
Selling expenses:		
Sales salaries expense	$595,000	
Advertising expense	360,000	
Travel expense	115,000	
Telephone expense — selling	95,000	
Miscellaneous selling expense	25,000	
Total selling expenses		$1,190,000
General expenses:		
Officers salaries expense	$360,000	
Office salaries expense	105,000	
Heating and lighting expense	75,000	
Taxes expense	60,000	
Depreciation expense — office equipment	27,000	
Telephone expense — general	18,000	
Insurance expense	17,500	
Office supplies expense	7,500	
Miscellaneous general expense	25,000	
Total general expenses		695,000
Total operating expenses		$1,885,000

Detailed supplemental schedules based on departmental responsibility are often prepared for major items in the operating expenses budget. The advertising expense schedule, for example, should include such details as the advertising media to be used (newspaper, direct mail, television), quantities (column inches, number of pieces, minutes), cost per unit, frequency of use, and sectional totals. A realistic budget is prepared through careful attention to details, and effective control is achieved through assignment of responsibility to departmental supervisors.

Budgeted Income Statement

A budgeted income statement can usually be prepared from the estimated data presented in the budgets for sales, cost of goods sold, and operating expenses, with the addition of data on other income, other expense, and income tax. A budgeted income statement is illustrated as follows:

Bowers Company
Budgeted Income Statement
For Year Ending December 31, 19--

Revenue from sales		$9,847,200
Cost of goods sold		6,600,680
Gross profit		$3,246,520
Operating expenses:		
Selling expenses	$1,190,000	
General expenses	695,000	
Total operating expenses		1,885,000
Income from operations		$1,361,520
Other income:		
Interest income	$ 98,000	
Other expense:		
Interest expense	90,000	8,000
Income before income tax		$1,369,520
Income tax		610,000
Net income		$ 759,520

The budgeted income statement brings together in condensed form the projection of all profit-making phases of operations and enables management to weigh the effects of the individual budgets on the profit plan for the year. If the budgeted net income in relationship to sales or to stockholders' equity is disappointingly low, additional review of all factors involved should be undertaken in an attempt to improve the plans.

Capital Expenditures Budget

The capital expenditures budget summarizes future plans for acquisition of plant facilities and equipment.[3] Substantial expenditures may be needed to replace machinery and other plant assets as they wear out, become obsolete, or for other reasons fall below minimum standards of efficiency. In addition, an expansion of plant facilities may be planned to keep pace with increasing demand for a company's product or to provide for additions to the product line.

---

[3] The methods of evaluating alternate capital expenditure proposals are discussed in Chapter 27.

The useful life of many plant assets extends over relatively long periods of time, and the amount of the expenditures for such assets usually changes a great deal from year to year. The customary practice, therefore, is to project the plans for a number of years into the future in preparing the capital expenditures budget. A five-year capital expenditures budget is illustrated as follows:

CAPITAL EX-
PENDITURES
BUDGET

Bowers Company
Capital Expenditures Budget
For Five Years Ending December 31, 1991

Item	1987	1988	1989	1990	1991
Machinery— Department 1	$400,000			$280,000	$360,000
Machinery— Department 2	180,000	$260,000	$560,000	200,000	
Office equipment		90,000			60,000
Total	$580,000	$350,000	$560,000	$480,000	$420,000

The various proposals recognized in the capital expenditures budget must be considered in preparing certain operating budgets. For example, the expected amount of depreciation on new equipment to be acquired in the current year must be taken into consideration when the budgets for factory overhead and operating expenses are prepared. The manner in which the proposed expenditures are to be financed will also affect the cash budget.

Cash Budget

The cash budget presents the expected inflow and outflow of cash for a day, week, month, or longer period. Receipts are classified by source and disbursements by purpose. The expected cash balance at the end of the period is then compared with the amount established as the minimum balance and the difference is the anticipated excess or deficiency for the period.

The minimum cash balance represents a safety buffer for mistakes in cash planning and for emergencies. However, the amount stated as the minimum balance need not remain fixed. It should perhaps be larger during periods of "peak" business activity than during the "slow" season. In addition, for effective cash management, much of the minimum cash balance can often be deposited in interest-bearing accounts.

Getting the Most out of Your Cash

Most businesses could reduce their interest expenses if they would improve cash management. The goal of cash management is to use the company's money to maximize earnings while meeting all obligations and maintaining adequate liquidity.

Two of the most efficient cash management tools are the wire transfer and the lockbox. Wire transfers are the safest and fastest way to move large sums of money quickly. Identify customers who pay you large amounts monthly. Have them wire the money directly to your bank.

A lockbox is a system that has your customer remittance checks mailed directly to a post office box in the name of your company. You authorize your bank to collect the customers' payments. Each item is deposited directly to the bank, according to your instructions. A lockbox greatly accelerates the transformation of your receivables into cash and eliminates delay from mail and processing.

Every morning, through phone calls or through a third party, you can receive information on your previous night's bank balances, credits, and disbursements in order to determine what you have available for investments that day. You can arrange for your bank to "sweep" the money out of your account and into investments every day.

If you are borrowing from a bank and not using your cash as effectively as you can, you are losing interest every day. If you don't need the money on a day-by-day basis, you can get good return by investing the excess money in overnight, one- or two-week or 30-day instruments. If you are required to keep a compensating balance, monitor the account so that you do not keep more than the required amount.

Accelerating your collections, delaying your disbursements and getting the needed information concerning your cash status are what cash management is all about.

Source: Adapted from Allen E. Fishman, "Getting the Most out of Your Cash," *St. Louis Post-Dispatch* (May 5, 1986), p. 14A.

The interrelationship of the cash budget with other budgets may be seen from the following illustration. Data from the sales budget, the various budgets for manufacturing costs and operating expenses, and the capital expenditures budget affect the cash budget. Consideration must also be given to dividend policies, plans for equity or long-term debt financing, and other projected plans that will affect cash.

CASH BUDGET

Bowers Company
Cash Budget
For Three Months Ending March 31, 19--

	January	February	March
Estimated cash receipts from:			
Cash sales	$168,000	$185,000	$115,000
Collections of accounts receivable	699,000	712,800	572,000
Other sources (issuance of securities,			
interest, etc.)	—	—	27,000
Total cash receipts	$867,000	$897,800	$714,000
Estimated cash disbursements for:			
Manufacturing costs	$541,200	$557,000	$536,000
Operating expenses	150,200	151,200	140,800
Capital expenditures	—	144,000	80,000
Other purposes (notes, income tax, etc.). . . .	47,000	20,000	160,000
Total cash disbursements	$738,400	$872,200	$916,800
Cash increase (decrease)	$128,600	$ 25,600	$(202,800)
Cash balance at beginning of month	280,000	408,600	434,200
Cash balance at end of month	$408,600	$434,200	$231,400
Minimum cash balance	300,000	300,000	300,000
Excess (deficiency)	$108,600	$134,200	$ (68,600)

In some cases, it is useful to present supplemental schedules to indicate the details of some of the amounts in the cash budget. For example, the following schedule illustrates the determination of the estimated cash receipts arising from collections of accounts receivable. For the illustration, it is assumed that the accounts receivable balance was $295,800 on January 1, and sales for each of the three months ending March 31 are $840,000, $925,000, and $575,000, respectively. Bowers Company expects to sell 20% of its merchandise for cash. Of the sales on account, 60% are expected to be collected in the month of the sale and the remainder in the following month.

Bowers Company
Schedule of Collections of Accounts Receivable
For Three Months Ending March 31, 19--

	January	February	March
January 1 balance	$295,800		
January sales on account (80% × $840,000):			
Collected in January (60% × $672,000)	403,200		
Collected in February (40% × $672,000)		$268,800	
February sales on account (80% × $925,000):			
Collected in February (60% × $740,000)		444,000	
Collected in March (40% × $740,000)........			$296,000
March sales on account (80% × $575,000):			
Collected in March (60% × $460,000)........			276,000
Totals....................................	$699,000	$712,800	$572,000

The importance of accurate cash budgeting can scarcely be over-emphasized. An unanticipated lack of cash can result in loss of discounts, unfavorable borrowing terms on loans, and damage to the credit rating. On the other hand, an excess amount of idle cash also shows poor management. When the budget shows periods of excess cash, such funds can be used to reduce loans or purchase investments in readily marketable income-producing securities. Reference to the Bowers Company cash budget shows excess cash during January and February and a deficiency during March.

Budgeted Balance Sheet

The budgeted balance sheet presents estimated details of the financial condition at the end of a budget period, assuming that all budgeted operating and financing plans are fulfilled. It need not differ in form and arrangement from a balance sheet based on actual data in the accounts and hence is not illustrated. If the budgeted balance sheet shows weaknesses in financial position, such as an abnormally large amount of current liabilities in relation to current assets, or excessive long-term debt in relation to stockholders' equity, the relevant factors should be given further study, so that corrective action may be taken.

BUDGET PERFORMANCE REPORTS

A budget performance report comparing actual results with the budgeted figures should be prepared periodically for each budget. This "feedback" enables management to determine the cause of significant differences and to seek means of preventing their recurrence. If corrective action cannot be taken because of changed conditions that have occurred since the budget was prepared, future budget figures should be revised accordingly.

Budget performance reports for enterprises decentralized into cost centers were illustrated in Chapter 21. A budget performance report for Bowers Company is illustrated as follows:

BUDGET PERFOR-MANCE REPORT

Bowers Company
Budget Performance Report—Factory Overhead Cost, Department 1
For Month Ended June 30, 19--

	Budget	Actual	Over	Under
Indirect factory wages	$30,200	$30,400	$200	
Supervisory salaries	15,000	15,000		
Power and light	12,800	12,750		$ 50
Depreciation of plant and equipment	12,000	12,000		
Indirect materials	7,600	8,250	650	
Maintenance	5,800	5,700		100
Insurance and property taxes	3,300	3,300		
	$86,700	$87,400	$850	$150

The amounts reported in the "Budget" column were obtained from supplemental schedules accompanying the master budget. The amounts in the "Actual" column are the costs actually incurred. The last two columns show the amounts by which actual costs exceeded or were below budgeted figures. As shown in the illustration, there were differences between the actual and budgeted amounts for some of the items of overhead cost. The cause of the significant difference in indirect materials cost should be investigated, and an attempt to find means of corrective action should be made. For example, if the difference in indirect materials cost were found to be caused by a marketwide increase in the price of materials used, a corrective action may not be possible. On the other hand, if the difference resulted from the inefficient use of materials in the production process, it may be possible to eliminate the inefficiency and effect a savings in future indirect materials costs.

BUDGETING AND HUMAN BEHAVIOR

In the budgeting process, overall goals of the business as well as specific goals for individual units within the business are established. Significant human behavior problems can develop if managers view these goals as unrealistic or unachievable. In such a case, managers may become discouraged as well as uncommitted to the achievement of the goals. As a result, the budget becomes less effective as a tool for planning and controlling operations. On the other hand, goals set within a range that managers consider attainable are likely to inspire managers to achieve the goals. Therefore, it is important that all levels of management be involved in establishing the goals which they will be expected to achieve. In such an environment, the budget is a planning tool that will favorably affect human behavior and increase the possibility of achieving the goals.

Human behavior problems can also arise when the budgeted and actual results are compared in budget performance reports. These problems can be minimized if budgets are revised when substantial changes in expectations occur during a budget period. Otherwise, the budgets will be of questionable value as incentives and instruments for controlling costs and expenses.

FLEXIBLE BUDGETS

The effect of changes in volume of activity can be "built in" to the budget system by what are termed **flexible budgets**. Particularly useful in estimating and controlling factory overhead costs and operating expenses, a flexible budget is in reality a series of budgets for varying rates of activity. To illustrate, assume that because of extreme variations in demand and other uncontrollable factors, the output of a particular manufacturing enterprise fluctuates widely from month to month. In such circumstances, the total factory overhead costs incurred during periods of high activity are certain to be greater than during periods of low activity. It is equally certain, however, that fluctuations in total factory overhead costs will not be exactly proportionate to the volume of production. For example, if $100,000 of factory overhead costs are usually incurred during a month in which production totals 10,000 units, the factory overhead for a month in which only 5,000 units are produced would unquestionably be more than $50,000.

Items of factory cost and operating expense that tend to remain constant in amount regardless of changes in volume of activity may be said to be **fixed**. Real estate taxes, property insurance, and depreciation expense on buildings are examples of fixed costs. The amounts incurred are substantially independent of the level of operations. Costs and expenses which tend to fluctuate in amount according to changes in volume of activity are called **variable**. Supplies and indirect materials used and sales commissions are examples of variable costs and expenses. The degree of variability is not the same for all variable items; few, if any, vary in exact proportion to sales or production. The terms **semivariable** or **semifixed** are sometimes applied to items that have both fixed and variable characteristics to a significant degree. An example is electric power, for which there is often an initial flat fee and a rate for additional usage. For example, the charge for electricity used might be $700 for the first 10 000 kwh consumed during a month and $.05 per kwh used above 10 000.

Although there are many approaches to the preparation of a flexible budget, the first step is to identify the fixed and variable components of the various factory overhead and operating expenses being budgeted. The costs and expenses can then be presented in variable and fixed categories. For example, in the following flexible budget for factory overhead cost for one department and one product, "electric power" is broken down into its fixed and variable cost components for three different levels of production. The fixed portion is $10,000 for all levels of production. The variable portion is $30,000 for 10,000 units of product, $27,000 ($30,000 × 9,000/10,000) for 9,000 units of product, and $24,000 ($30,000 × 8,000/10,000) for 8,000 units of product.

Collins Manufacturing Company Monthly Factory Overhead Cost Budget				FLEXIBLE BUDGET FOR FACTORY OVERHEAD COST
Units of product............................	8,000	9,000	10,000	
Variable cost:				
Indirect factory wages	$ 32,000	$ 36,000	$ 40,000	
Electric power	24,000	27,000	30,000	
Indirect materials...........................	12,000	13,500	15,000	
Total variable cost........................	$ 68,000	$ 76,500	$ 85,000	
Fixed cost:				
Supervisory salaries	$ 40,000	$ 40,000	$ 40,000	
Depreciation of plant and equipment	25,000	25,000	25,000	
Property taxes	15,000	15,000	15,000	
Insurance	12,000	12,000	12,000	
Electric power	10,000	10,000	10,000	
Total fixed cost..........................	$102,000	$102,000	$102,000	
Total factory overhead cost..................	$170,000	$178,500	$187,000	

(handwritten notes in margin: "flexible" beside variable cost section, "static" beside fixed cost section)

In practice, the number of production levels and the interval between levels in a flexible budget will vary with the range of production volume. For example, instead of budgeting for 8,000, 9,000, and 10,000 units of product, it might be necessary to provide for levels, at intervals of 500, from 6,000 to 12,000 units. Alternative bases, such as machine hours or direct labor hours, may also be used in measuring the volume of activity.

In preparing budget performance reports, the actual results would be compared with the flexible budget figures for the level of operations achieved. For example, if Collins Manufacturing Company manufactured 10,000 units during a month, the budget figures reported in the budget performance report would be those appearing in the "10,000 units" column of Collins' flexible budget.

AUTOMATED BUDGETING PROCEDURES

Many firms use computers in the budgeting process. Computers can not only speed up the budgeting process, but they can also reduce the cost of budget preparation when large quantities of data need to be processed. Computers are especially useful in preparing flexible budgets and in continuous budgeting. Budget performance reports can also be prepared on a timely basis by the use of the computer.

By using computerized simulation models, which are mathematical statements of the relationships among various operating activities, management can determine the impact of various operating alternatives on the master budget. For example, if management wishes to evaluate the impact of a proposed change in direct labor wage rates, the computer can quickly provide a revised master budget that reflects the new rates. If management wishes to evaluate a proposal to add a new product line, the computer can quickly update current budgeted data and indicate the effect of the proposal on the master budget.

STANDARD COSTS   *budgets in unit*

The determination of the unit cost of products manufactured is basic to cost accounting. The process cost and job order cost systems discussed in the preceding chapters were designed to determine *actual* or *historical* unit costs. The aim of both systems is to provide management with timely data on actual manufacturing costs and to aid in cost control and profit maximization.

The use of budgetary control procedures is often extended to the point of unit cost projections for each commodity produced. Cost systems using detailed estimates of each element of manufacturing cost entering into the finished product are sometimes called **standard cost systems**. Such systems enable management to determine how much a product should cost (standard), how much it does cost (actual), and the causes of any difference (variance) between the two. Standard costs thus serve as a measuring device for determination of efficiency. If the standard cost of a product is $5 per unit and its current actual cost is $5.50 per unit, the factors responsible for the excess cost can be determined and remedial measures taken. Thus, supervisors have a device for controlling the costs for which they are responsible, and employees become more cost conscious.

Standard costs may be used in either the process type of production or the job order type of production. For more effective control, standard costs should be used for each department or cost center in the factory. It is possible, however, to use standard costs in some departments and actual costs in others.

A wide variety of management skills are needed in setting standards, and the joint effort of accounting, engineering, personnel administration, and other managerial areas is also needed. Time and motion studies of each operation are made, and the work force is trained to use the most efficient methods. Direct materials and productive equipment are subjected to detailed study and tests in an effort to achieve maximum productivity for a given level of costs.

VARIANCES FROM STANDARDS

One of the primary purposes of a standard cost system is to facilitate control over costs by comparing actual costs with standard costs. Control is achieved by the action of management in investigating significant deviations of performance from standards and taking corrective action. Differences between the standard costs of a department or product and the actual costs incurred are termed variances. If the actual cost incurred is less than the standard cost, the variance is favorable. If the actual cost exceeds the standard cost, the variance is unfavorable. When actual costs are compared with standard costs, only the "exceptions" or variances are reported to the person responsible for cost control. This reporting by the "principle of exceptions" enables the one responsible for cost control to concentrate on the cause and correction of the variances.

When manufacturing operations are automated, standard cost data can be integrated with the computer that directs operations. Variances can then be detected and reported automatically by the computer system, and adjustments can be made to operations in progress.

The total variance for a certain period is usually made up of several variances, some of which may be favorable and some unfavorable. There may be variances from standards in direct materials costs, in direct labor costs, and in factory overhead costs. Illustrations and analyses of these variances for Ballard Company, a manufacturing enterprise, are presented in the following paragraphs. For illustrative purposes, it is assumed that only one type of direct material is used, that there is a single processing department, and that Product X is the only commodity manufactured by the enterprise. The standard costs for direct materials, direct labor, and factory overhead for a unit of Product X are as follows:

Direct materials:	
2 pounds at $1 per pound..................	$ 2.00
Direct labor:	
.4 hour at $16 per hour	6.40
Factory overhead:	
.4 hour at $8.40 per hour...................	3.36
Total per unit	$11.76

Direct Materials Cost Variance

Two major factors enter into the determination of standards for direct materials cost: (1) the quantity (usage) standard and (2) the price standard. If the actual quantity of direct materials used in producing a commodity differs from the standard quantity, there is a **quantity variance**. If the actual unit price of the materials differs from the standard price, there is a **price variance**. To illustrate, assume that the standard direct materials cost of producing 10,000 units of Product X and the direct materials cost actually incurred during June were as follows:

Actual:	20,600 pounds at $1.04	$21,424
Standard:	20,000 pounds at $1.00	20,000

The unfavorable variance of $1,424 resulted in part from an excess usage of 600 pounds of direct materials and in part from an excess cost of $.04 per pound. The analysis of the direct materials cost variance is as follows:

<table>
<tr><td rowspan="11">DIRECT
MATERIALS
COST
VARIANCE</td><td colspan="3">Quantity variance:</td></tr>
<tr><td>Actual quantity . . . .</td><td>20,600 pounds</td><td></td></tr>
<tr><td>Standard quantity . . . .</td><td>20,000 pounds</td><td></td></tr>
<tr><td>Variance — unfavorable .</td><td>600 pounds × standard price, $1 . . . . . .</td><td>$ 600</td></tr>
<tr><td colspan="3">Price variance:</td></tr>
<tr><td>Actual price . . . .</td><td>$1.04 per pound</td><td></td></tr>
<tr><td>Standard price . . . .</td><td>1.00 per pound</td><td></td></tr>
<tr><td>Variance — unfavorable .</td><td>$ .04 per pound × actual quantity, 20,600 .</td><td>824</td></tr>
<tr><td colspan="2">Total direct materials cost variance — unfavorable . . . .</td><td>$1,424</td></tr>
</table>

Direct Materials Quantity Variance. The direct materials quantity variance is the difference between the actual quantity used and the standard quantity, multiplied by the standard price per unit. If the standard quantity exceeds the actual quantity used, the variance is favorable. If the actual quantity of materials used exceeds the standard quantity, the variance is unfavorable, as shown for Ballard Company in the following illustration:

<table>
<tr><td rowspan="5">DIRECT
MATERIALS
QUANTITY
VARIANCE</td><td>Direct Materials
Quantity Variance</td><td>=</td><td>Actual Quantity Used −
Standard Quantity</td><td>×</td><td>Standard Price
per Unit</td></tr>
<tr><td colspan="5">Quantity variance = (20,600 pounds − 20,000 pounds) × $1.00 per pound</td></tr>
<tr><td colspan="5">Quantity variance = 600 pounds   × $1.00 per pound</td></tr>
<tr><td colspan="5">Quantity variance = $600 unfavorable</td></tr>
</table>

Direct Materials Price Variance. The direct materials price variance is the difference between the actual price per unit and the standard price per unit, multiplied by the actual quantity used. If the standard price per unit exceeds the actual price per unit, the variance is favorable. If the actual price per unit exceeds the standard price per unit, the variance is unfavorable, as shown for Ballard Company in the following illustration:

$$\begin{array}{l}\text{Direct Materials} \\ \text{Price Variance}\end{array} = \begin{array}{c}\text{Actual Price per Unit} - \\ \text{Standard Price}\end{array} \times \begin{array}{c}\text{Actual Quantity} \\ \text{Used}\end{array}$$

Price variance = ($1.04 per pound − $1.00 per pound) × 20,600 pounds
Price variance = $.04 per pound   × 20,600 pounds
Price variance = $824 unfavorable

DIRECT MATERIALS PRICE VARIANCE

Reporting Direct Materials Cost Variance. The physical quantity and the dollar amount of the quantity variance should be reported to the factory superintendent and other personnel responsible for production. If excessive amounts of direct materials were used because of the malfunction of equipment or some other failure within the production department, those responsible should correct the situation. However, an unfavorable direct materials quantity variance is not necessarily the result of inefficiency within the production department. If the excess usage of 600 pounds of materials in the example above had been caused by inferior materials, the purchasing department should be held responsible.

The unit price and the total amount of the materials price variance should be reported to the purchasing department, which may or may not be able to control this variance. If materials of the same quality could have been purchased from another supplier at the standard price, the variance was controllable. On the other hand, if the variance resulted from a marketwide price increase, the variance was not subject to control.

Direct Labor Cost Variance

As in the case of direct materials, two major factors enter into the determination of standards for direct labor cost: (1) the time (usage or efficiency) standard, and (2) the rate (price or wage) standard. If the actual direct labor hours spent producing a product differ from the standard hours, there is a time variance. If the wage rate paid differs from the standard rate, there is a rate variance. The standard cost and the actual cost of direct labor in the production of 10,000 units of Product X during June are assumed to be as follows:

Actual: 3,950 hours at $16.40 . . . . $64,780
Standard: 4,000 hours at 16.00   64,000

The unfavorable direct labor variance of $780 is made up of a favorable time variance and an unfavorable rate variance, determined as follows:

Time variance:

Actual time	3,950 hours
Standard time	4,000 hours
Variance — favorable. . . .	−50 hours × standard rate, $16 . . . . $ 800

Rate variance:

Actual rate.	$16.40 per hour
Standard rate	16.00 per hour
Variance — unfavorable .	$ .40 per hour × actual time, 3,950 hours 1,580

Total direct labor cost variance — unfavorable. . . . . $ 780

Direct Labor Time Variance. The direct labor time variance is the difference between the actual hours worked and the standard hours, multiplied by the standard rate per hour. If the actual hours worked exceed the standard hours, the variance is unfavorable. If the actual hours worked are less than the standard hours, the variance is favorable, as shown for Ballard Company in the following illustration:

$$\frac{\text{Direct Labor}}{\text{Time Variance}} = \frac{\text{Actual Hours Worked} -}{\text{Standard Hours}} \times \frac{\text{Standard Rate}}{\text{per Hour}}$$

Time variance = (3,950 hours − 4,000 hours) × $16 per hour
Time variance = −50 hours   × $16 per hour
Time variance = $800 favorable

In the illustration, when the standard hours (4,000) are subtracted from the actual hours worked (3,950), the difference is "−50 hours." The minus sign indicates that the variance of 50 hours, or $800 (50 hours × $16), is favorable.

Direct Labor Rate Variance. The direct labor rate variance is the difference between the actual rate per hour and the standard rate per hour, multiplied by the actual hours worked. If the standard rate per hour exceeds the actual rate per hour, the variance is favorable. If the actual rate per hour exceeds the standard rate per hour, the variance is unfavorable, as shown for Ballard Company in the following illustration:

$$\frac{\text{Direct Labor}}{\text{Rate Variance}} = \frac{\text{Actual Rate per Hour} -}{\text{Standard Rate}} \times \frac{\text{Actual Hours}}{\text{Worked}}$$

Rate variance = ($16.40 per hour − $16.00 per hour) × 3,950 hours
Rate variance = $.40 per hour   × 3,950 hours
Rate variance = $1,580 unfavorable

Reporting Direct Labor Cost Variance. The control of direct labor cost is often in the hands of production supervisors. To aid them, periodic reports analyzing the cause of any direct labor variance may be prepared. A comparison of standard direct labor hours and actual direct labor hours will provide the basis for an investigation into the efficiency of direct labor (time variance). A comparison of the rates paid for direct labor with the standard rates highlights the efficiency of the supervisors or the personnel department in selecting the proper grade of direct labor for production (rate variance).

Factory Overhead Cost Variance

Some of the difficulties encountered in allocating factory overhead costs among products manufactured have been considered in Chapter 22. These difficulties stem from the great variety of costs that are included in factory overhead and their nature as indirect costs. For the same reasons, the procedures used in determining standards and variances for factory overhead cost are more complex than those used for direct materials cost and direct labor cost.

A flexible budget is used to establish the standard factory overhead rate and to aid in determining subsequent variations from standard. The standard rate is determined by dividing the standard factory overhead costs by the standard amount of productive activity, generally expressed in direct labor hours, direct labor cost, or machine hours. A flexible budget showing the standard factory overhead rate for a month is as follows:

<table>
<tr><td colspan="5">Ballard Company
Factory Overhead Cost Budget
For Month Ending June 30, 19--</td></tr>
<tr><td>Percent of productive capacity ....</td><td>80%</td><td>90%</td><td>100%</td><td>110%</td></tr>
<tr><td>Direct labor hours....................</td><td>4,000</td><td>4,500</td><td>5,000</td><td>5,500</td></tr>
<tr><td>Budgeted factory overhead:</td><td></td><td></td><td></td><td></td></tr>
<tr><td>Variable cost:</td><td></td><td></td><td></td><td></td></tr>
<tr><td>Indirect factory wages ....</td><td>$12,800</td><td>$14,400</td><td>$16,000</td><td>$17,600</td></tr>
<tr><td>Power and light ....</td><td>5,600</td><td>6,300</td><td>7,000</td><td>7,700</td></tr>
<tr><td>Indirect materials.................</td><td>3,200</td><td>3,600</td><td>4,000</td><td>4,400</td></tr>
<tr><td>Maintenance......................</td><td>2,400</td><td>2,700</td><td>3,000</td><td>3,300</td></tr>
<tr><td>Total variable cost..............</td><td>$24,000</td><td>$27,000</td><td>$30,000</td><td>$33,000</td></tr>
<tr><td>Fixed cost:</td><td></td><td></td><td></td><td></td></tr>
<tr><td>Supervisory salaries ....</td><td>$ 5,500</td><td>$ 5,500</td><td>$ 5,500</td><td>$ 5,500</td></tr>
<tr><td>Depreciation of plant and equipment</td><td>4,500</td><td>4,500</td><td>4,500</td><td>4,500</td></tr>
<tr><td>Insurance and property taxes.......</td><td>2,000</td><td>2,000</td><td>2,000</td><td>2,000</td></tr>
<tr><td>Total fixed cost..................</td><td>$12,000</td><td>$12,000</td><td>$12,000</td><td>$12,000</td></tr>
<tr><td>Total factory overhead cost...........</td><td>$36,000</td><td>$39,000</td><td>$42,000</td><td>$45,000</td></tr>
<tr><td>Factory overhead rate per direct labor hour ($42,000 ÷ 5,000)...</td><td colspan="4">$8.40</td></tr>
</table>

FACTORY OVERHEAD COST BUDGET INDICATING STANDARD FACTORY OVERHEAD RATE

The standard factory overhead cost rate is determined on the basis of the projected factory overhead costs at 100% of productive capacity, where this level of capacity represents the general expectation of business activity under normal operating conditions. In the illustration, the standard factory overhead rate is $8.40 per direct labor hour. This rate can be subdivided into $6 per hour for variable factory overhead ($30,000 ÷ 5,000 hours) and $2.40 per hour for fixed factory overhead ($12,000 ÷ 5,000 hours).

Variances from standard for factory overhead cost result (1) from operating at a level above or below 100% of capacity and (2) from incurring a total amount of factory overhead cost greater or less than the amount budgeted for the level of operations achieved. The first factor results in the **volume variance**, which is a measure of the penalty of operating at less than 100% of productive capacity or the benefit from operating at a level above 100% of productive capacity. The second factor results in the **controllable variance**, which is the difference between the actual amount of factory overhead incurred and the amount of factory overhead budgeted for the level of production achieved during the period. To illustrate, assume that the actual cost and standard cost of factory overhead for Ballard Company's production of 10,000 units of Product X during June were as follows:

Actual:	Variable factory overhead	$24,600	
	Fixed factory overhead.................	12,000	$36,600
Standard: 4,000 hours at $8.40..................			33,600

The unfavorable factory overhead cost variance of $3,000 is made up of a volume variance and a controllable variance, determined as follows:

FACTORY OVERHEAD COST VARIANCE		
Volume variance:		
Productive capacity of 100%........................	5,000 hours	
Standard for amount produced.......................	4,000 hours	
Productive capacity not used	1,000 hours	
Standard fixed factory overhead cost rate	×$2.40	
Variance — unfavorable		$2,400
Controllable variance:		
Actual factory overhead cost incurred................	$36,600	
Budgeted factory overhead for standard product produced	36,000	
Variance — unfavorable		600
Total factory overhead cost variance — unfavorable......................		$3,000

Factory Overhead Volume Variance. The factory overhead volume variance is the difference between the productive capacity at 100% and the standard productive capacity, multiplied by the standard fixed factory overhead rate. If the standard capacity for the amount produced exceeds the productive capacity at 100%, the variance is favorable. If the productive capacity at 100%

exceeds the standard capacity for the amount produced, the variance is unfavorable, as shown for Ballard Company in the following illustration:

FACTORY
OVERHEAD
VOLUME
VARIANCE

$$\frac{\text{Factory Overhead}}{\text{Volume Variance}} = \frac{\text{Productive Capacity at 100\%} -}{\text{Standard Capacity for Amount Produced}} \times \frac{\text{Standard Fixed Factory}}{\text{Overhead Rate}}$$

Volume variance = (5,000 hours − 4,000 hours)   × $2.40 per hour
Volume variance = 1,000 hours   × $2.40 per hour
Volume variance = $2,400 unfavorable

In the illustration, the unfavorable volume variance of $2,400 can be viewed as the cost of the available but unused productive capacity (1,000 hours). It should also be noted that the variable portion of the factory overhead cost rate was ignored in determining the volume variance. Variable factory overhead costs vary with the level of production. Thus, a curtailment of production should be accompanied by a comparable reduction of such costs. On the other hand, fixed factory overhead costs are not affected by changes in the volume of production. The fixed factory overhead costs represent the costs of providing the capacity for production, and the volume variance measures the amount of the fixed factory overhead cost due to the variance between capacity used and 100% of capacity.

The idle time that resulted in a volume variance may be due to such factors as failure to maintain an even flow of work, machine breakdowns or repairs causing work stoppages, and failure to obtain enough sales orders to keep the factory operating at full capacity. Management should determine the causes of the idle time and should take corrective action. A volume variance caused by failure of supervisors to maintain an even flow of work, for example, can be remedied. Volume variances caused by lack of sales orders may be corrected through increased advertising or other sales effort, or it may be advisable to develop other means of using the excess plant capacity.

Factory Overhead Controllable Variance. The factory overhead controllable variance is the difference between the actual factory overhead and the budgeted factory overhead for the standard amount produced. If the budgeted factory overhead for the standard amount produced exceeds the actual factory overhead, the variance is favorable. If the actual factory overhead exceeds the budgeted factory overhead for the standard amount produced, the variance is unfavorable. For Ballard Company, the standard direct labor hours for the amount produced during June was 4,000 (80% of productive capacity). Therefore, the factory overhead budgeted at this level of production, according to the budget on page 1095, was $36,000. When this budgeted factory overhead is compared with the actual factory overhead, as shown in the following illustration for Ballard Company, an unfavorable variance results.

FACTORY
OVERHEAD
CONTROL-
LABLE
VARIANCE

$$\frac{\text{Factory Overhead}}{\text{Controllable Variance}} = \frac{\text{Actual Factory}}{\text{Overhead}} - \frac{\text{Budgeted Factory Overhead for}}{\text{Standard Amount Produced}}$$

Controllable variance = $36,600   − $36,000
Controllable variance = $600 unfavorable

The amount and the direction of the controllable variance show the degree of efficiency in keeping the factory overhead costs within the limits established by the budget. Most of the controllable variance is related to the cost of the variable factory overhead items because generally there is little or no variation in the costs incurred for the fixed factory overhead items. Therefore, responsibility for the control of this variance generally rests with department supervisors.

Reporting Factory Overhead Cost Variance. The best means of presenting standard factory overhead cost variance data is through a factory overhead cost variance report. Such a report, illustrated as follows, can present both the controllable variance and the volume variance in a format that pinpoints the causes of the variances and aids in placing the responsibility for control.

FACTORY
OVERHEAD
COST
VARIANCE
REPORT

Ballard Company
Factory Overhead Cost Variance Report
For Month Ended June 30, 19--

Productive capacity for the month....................... 5,000 hours
Actual production for the month........................ 4,000 hours

	Budget	Actual	Variances Favorable	Variances Unfavorable
Variable cost:				
Indirect factory wages	$12,800	$13,020		$ 220
Power and light	5,600	5,550	$50	
Indirect materials..............	3,200	3,630		430
Maintenance..................	2,400	2,400		
Total variable cost...........	$24,000	$24,600		
Fixed cost:				
Supervisory salaries	$ 5,500	$ 5,500		
Depreciation of plant and				
equipment..................	4,500	4,500		
Insurance and property taxes....	2,000	2,000		
Total fixed cost..............	$12,000	$12,000		
Total factory overhead cost........	$36,000	$36,600		
Total controllable variances			$50	$ 650

Net controllable variance—unfavorable .... $ 600
Volume variance—unfavorable:
  Idle hours at the standard rate for fixed factory overhead—
  1,000 × $2.40 2,400
Total factory overhead cost variance—unfavorable $3,000

The variance in many of the individual cost items in factory overhead can be subdivided into quantity and price variances, as were the variances in direct materials and direct labor. For example, the indirect factory wages variance may include both time and rate variances, and the indirect materials variance may be made up of both a quantity variance and a price variance.

The foregoing brief introduction to analysis of factory overhead cost variance suggests the many difficulties that may be encountered in actual practice. The rapid increase of automation in factory operations has been accompanied by increased attention to factory overhead costs. The use of predetermined standards and the analysis of variances from such standards provides management with the best possible means of establishing responsibility and controlling factory overhead costs.

STANDARDS IN THE ACCOUNTS

Although standard costs can be used solely as a statistical device apart from the ledger, it is generally considered preferable to incorporate them in the accounts. One approach, when this plan is used, is to debit the work in process account for the actual cost of direct materials, direct labor, and factory overhead entering into production. The same account is credited for the standard cost of the product completed and transferred to the finished goods account. The balance remaining in the work in process account is then made up of the ending inventory of work in process and the variances of actual cost from standard cost. In the following illustrative accounts, there is assumed to be no ending inventory of work in process. The balance in the account is the sum of the variances (unfavorable) between standard and actual costs.

ACCOUNT WORK IN PROCESS   ACCOUNT NO.   **STANDARD COSTS IN ACCOUNTS**

Date		Item	Debit	Credit	Balance Debit	Balance Credit
June	30	Direct materials (actual)	21,424		21,424	
	30	Direct labor (actual)	64,780		86,204	
	30	Factory overhead (actual)	36,600		122,804	
	30	Units finished (standard)		117,600		
	30	Balance (variances)			5,204	

ACCOUNT FINISHED GOODS   ACCOUNT NO.

Date		Item	Debit	Credit	Balance Debit	Balance Credit
June	1	Inventory (standard)			88,800	
	30	Units finished (standard)	117,600		206,400	
	30	Units sold (standard)		113,500	92,900	

Variances from standard costs are usually not reported to stockholders and others outside of management. However, it is customary to disclose the variances on income statements prepared for management. An interim monthly income statement prepared for Ballard Company's internal use is illustrated as follows:

VARIANCES
FROM
STANDARDS
IN INCOME
STATEMENT

Ballard Company
Income Statement
For Month Ended June 30, 19--

	Favorable	Unfavorable	
Sales..............................			$185,400
Cost of goods sold—at standard			113,500
Gross profit—at standard			$ 71,900
Less variances from standard cost:			
Direct materials quantity...........		$ 600	
Direct materials price		824	
Direct labor time..................	$800		
Direct labor rate..................		1,580	
Factory overhead volume..........		2,400	
Factory overhead controllable.......	___	600	5,204
Gross profit.......................			$ 66,696
Operating expenses:			
Selling expenses		$22,500	
General expenses		19,225	41,725
Income before income tax...........			$ 24,971

At the end of the fiscal year, the variances from standard are usually transferred to the cost of goods sold account. However, if the variances are significant or if many of the products manufactured are still on hand, the variances should be allocated to the work in process, finished goods, and cost of goods sold accounts. The result of such an allocation is to convert these account balances from standard cost to actual cost.

REVISION OF STANDARDS

Standard costs should be continuously reviewed, and when they no longer represent the conditions that were present when the standards were set, they should be changed. Standards should not be revised merely because they differ from actual costs, but because they no longer reflect the conditions that they were intended to measure. For example, the direct labor cost standard would not be revised simply because workers were unable to meet properly determined standards. On the other hand, standards should be revised when prices, product designs, labor rates, manufacturing methods, or other circumstances change to such an extent that the current standards no longer represent a useful measure of performance.

CHAPTER REVIEW

KEY POINTS

1. Nature and Objectives of Budgeting.

The essentials of budgeting are (1) the establishment of specific goals for future operations and (2) the periodic comparison of actual results with these goals. The establishment of specific goals for future operations encompasses the planning function of management. The periodic comparison of actual results with these goals encompasses the control function of management.

2. Budget Period.

Although budgets may be prepared for quarters of the year, months, or weeks, budgets of operating activities usually include the fiscal year of an enterprise. A variant of fiscal-year budgeting, continuous budgeting, provides for maintenance of a twelve-month projection into the future.

3. Budgeting Procedures.

All levels of management should be encouraged to participate in the budgeting process. Usually a budget committee has final responsibility for preparation of the master budget.

The sales budget is usually the first component of the master budget that is prepared. The production budget sets forth the number of units of each commodity expected to be manufactured to meet budgeted sales and inventory requirements. The direct materials budget is based on the needs shown by the production budget. The production budget also serves as a starting point for the preparation of the direct labor cost budget and factory overhead cost budget. The cost of goods sold budget is prepared by combining data on estimated inventories with the relevant estimates of quantities and costs in the budgets for (1) direct materials purchases, (2) direct labor costs, and (3) factory overhead costs. After the operating expenses budget is prepared, the budgeted income statement can be prepared.

The capital expenditures budget summarizes future plans for the acquisition of plant facilities and equipment, while the cash budget represents the expected inflow and outflow of cash for a day, week, month, or a longer period. The budgeted balance sheet presents estimated details of financial condition at the end of a budget period, assuming that all the budgeted operating and financing plans are fulfilled.

4. Budget Performance Reports.

A budget performance report provides feedback to management by reporting actual results compared with budgeted figures. Significant differences can then be investigated and corrective action taken.

5. Budgeting and Human Behavior.

Significant human behavior problems can develop if managers view a budget as unrealistic or unachievable. Human behavior problems can also arise when budgeted and actual results are compared. These problems can be minimized if managers are involved in establishing budgets initially and budgets are revised for changes and expectations that occur during a budget period.

6. Flexible Budgets.

Through the use of flexible budgets, the effect of changes in volume of activity can be built into the budgetary system. The preparation of flexible budgets requires the separation of costs and expenses into fixed and variable components. The use of flexible budgets facilitates the preparation of budget performance reports based on the actual level of operations achieved.

7. Automated Budgeting Procedures.

Computers can be useful in speeding up the budgetary process and in preparing timely budget performance reports. In addition, through the use of simulation models, management can determine the impact of operating alternatives on the various budgets.

8. Standard Costs.

Standard cost systems use detailed estimates of each element of manufacturing cost to measure efficiency. The establishment of standards requires a joint effort by management, accounting, engineering, personnel, administration, and other managerial areas.

9. Variances from Standards.

One of the primary purposes of a standard cost system is to facilitate control over costs by comparing actual costs with standard costs and thus determining variances. The two major variances for direct materials cost are the (1) direct materials quantity variance and (2) direct materials price variance. The two major variances for direct labor costs are the (1) direct labor time variance and (2) direct labor rate variance. The two major variances for factory overhead costs are the (1) factory overhead volume variance and (2) factory overhead controllable variance.

10. Standards in the Accounts.

It is generally preferable to incorporate standards in the accounts. One approach is to debit the work in process account for the actual costs of direct materials, direct labor, and factory overhead entering into production. The same account is then credited for the standard costs of the product completed and transferred to the finished goods account. Thus, the variances of actual costs from standard costs are isolated along with the ending inventory in the work in process account. At the end of the fiscal year, the variances are usually transferred to the cost of goods sold account.

11. Revision of Standards.

Established standards should be continually reviewed. If the standards no longer represent present conditions, they should be revised.

KEY TERMS

budget 1073
continuous budgeting 1075
zero-base budgeting 1075
master budget 1076
capital expenditures budget 1082
budget performance report 1086
flexible budgets 1088
fixed costs and expenses 1088
variable costs and expenses 1088
semivariable costs 1088
standard costs 1090

variances 1091
direct materials quantity
   variance 1092
direct materials price
   variance 1092
direct labor time variance 1093
direct labor rate variance 1093
factory overhead volume
   variance 1096
factory overhead controllable
   variance 1096

SELF-EXAMINATION QUESTIONS

Answers in Appendix B.

1. The budget that summarizes future plans for acquisition of plant facilities and equipment is the:
    A. cash budget
    B. sales budget
    C. capital expenditures budget
    D. none of the above

2. The system that "builds in" the effect of fluctuations in volume of activity into the various budgets is termed:
    A. budget performance reporting
    B. continuous budgeting
    C. flexible budgeting
    D. none of the above

3. The actual and standard direct labor costs for producing a specified quantity of product are as follows:

Actual:	990 hours at $10.90.	$10,791
Standard:	1,000 hours at $11.00.	11,000

The direct labor cost time variance is:

A. $99 favorable   C. $110 favorable

B. $99 unfavorable   D. $110 unfavorable

4. The actual and standard factory overhead costs for producing a specified quantity of product are as follows:

Actual:	Variable factory overhead........	$72,500	
	Fixed factory overhead..........	40,000	$112,500
Standard:	19,000 hours at $6		
	($4 variable and $2 fixed)........		114,000

If 1,000 hours of productive capacity were unused, the factory overhead volume variance would be:

A. $1,500 favorable   C. $4,000 unfavorable

B. $2,000 unfavorable   D. none of the above

5. Based on the data in Question 4, the factory overhead controllable variance would be:

A. $3,500 favorable   C. $1,500 favorable

B. $3,500 unfavorable   D. none of the above

ILLUSTRATIVE PROBLEM

Hamilton Company prepared the following factory overhead cost budget for the Finishing Department for June of the current year:

Hamilton Company
Factory Overhead Cost Budget—Finishing Department
For Month Ending June 30, 19--

Direct labor hours:		
Normal productive capacity.....................		10,000
Hours budgeted...............................		9,000
Variable cost:		
Indirect factory wages	$9,450	
Indirect materials............................	6,750	
Power and light..............................	5,400	
Total variable cost...........................		$21,600
Fixed cost:		
Supervisory salaries...........................	$8,000	
Indirect factory wages	3,300	
Depreciation of plant and equipment	3,100	
Insurance	1,500	
Power and light...............................	1,200	
Property taxes................................	900	
Total fixed cost		18,000
Total factory overhead cost......................		$39,600

Instructions:

1. Prepare a flexible budget for the month of July, indicating capacities of 8,000, 9,000, 10,000, and 11,000 direct labor hours and the determination of a standard factory overhead rate per direct labor hour.
2. Prepare a standard factory overhead cost variance report for July. The Finishing Department was operated for 8,000 direct labor hours and the following factory overhead costs were incurred:

Indirect factory wages	$11,500
Supervisory salaries......................................	8,000
Power and light...	6,350
Indirect materials..	6,050
Depreciation of plant and equipment	3,100
Insurance	1,500
Property taxes..	900
Total factory overhead costs incurred....................	$37,400

SOLUTION

(1)

Hamilton Company
Factory Overhead Cost Budget—Finishing Department
For Month Ending July 31, 19--

Percent of normal productive capacity.......................	80%	90%	100%	110%
Direct labor hours................	8,000	9,000	10,000	11,000
Budgeted factory overhead:				
Variable cost:				
Indirect factory wages.........	$ 8,400	$ 9,450	$10,500	$11,550
Indirect materials	6,000	6,750	7,500	8,250
Power and light	4,800	5,400	6,000	6,600
Total variable cost..........	$19,200	$21,600	$24,000	$26,400
Fixed cost:				
Supervisory salaries...........	$ 8,000	$ 8,000	$ 8,000	$ 8,000
Indirect factory wages.........	3,300	3,300	3,300	3,300
Depreciation of plant and equipment	3,100	3,100	3,100	3,100
Insurance	1,500	1,500	1,500	1,500
Power and light	1,200	1,200	1,200	1,200
Property taxes	900	900	900	900
Total fixed cost	$18,000	$18,000	$18,000	$18,000
Total factory overhead cost	$37,200	$39,600	$42,000	$44,400

Factory overhead rate per direct labor hour
($42,000 ÷ 10,000 hours)................................. $4.20

(2)   Hamilton Company
     Factory Overhead Cost Variance Report—Finishing Department
                    For Month Ended July 31, 19--

Normal productive capacity for the month ....   10,000 hours
Actual production for the month ....   8,000 hours

| | | | Variances | |
	Budget	Actual	Favorable	Unfavorable
Variable cost:				
Indirect factory wages	$ 8,400	$ 8,200	$200	
Indirect materials	6,000	6,050		$ 50
Power and light	4,800	5,150		350
Total variable cost......	$19,200	$19,400		
Fixed cost:				
Supervisory salaries	$ 8,000	$ 8,000		
Indirect factory wages	3,300	3,300		
Depreciation of plant and				
equipment	3,100	3,100		
Insurance	1,500	1,500		
Power and light	1,200	1,200		
Property taxes	900	900		
Total fixed cost	$18,000	$18,000		
Total factory overhead cost .	$37,200	$37,400		

Total controllable variances .... $200 $ 400

Net controllable variance—unfavorable..................... $ 200
Volume variance—unfavorable:
   Idle hours at standard rate for fixed factory overhead—
      2,000 × $1.80..   3,600
Total factory overhead cost variance—unfavorable............ $3,800

DISCUSSION QUESTIONS

1. What is a budget?

2. (a) Name the two basic functions of management in which accounting is involved.
   (b) How does a budget aid management in the discharge of these basic functions?

3. What is meant by *continuous budgeting*?

4. Why should all levels of management and all departments participate in the preparation and submission of budget estimates?

5. Which budgetary concept requires all levels of management to start from zero and estimate sales, production, and other operating data as though the operations were being initiated for the first time?

6. Why should the production requirements as set forth in the production budget be carefully coordinated with the sales budget?

7. Why should the timing of direct materials purchases be closely coordinated with the production budget?

8. What is a capital expenditures budget?

9. (a) Discuss the purpose of the cash budget. (b) If the cash budget for the first quarter of the fiscal year indicates excess cash at the end of each of the first two months, how might the excess cash be used?

10. What is a budget performance report?

11. Briefly discuss the type of human behavior problem that might arise if goals used in developing budgets are unrealistic or unachievable.

12. What is a flexible budget?

13. Distinguish between (a) fixed costs and (b) variable costs.

14. Which of the following costs incurred by a manufacturing enterprise tend to be fixed and which tend to be variable: (a) cost of direct materials entering into finished product, (b) salary of factory superintendent, (c) indirect materials, (d) rent on factory building, (e) depreciation on factory building, (f) property taxes on factory building, (g) direct labor entering into finished product?

15. What is a semivariable (or semifixed) cost?

16. Drake Corporation uses flexible budgets. For each of the following variable operating expenses, indicate whether there has been a saving or an excess of expenses, assuming that actual sales were $500,000.

Expense Item	Actual Amount	Budget Allowance Based on Sales
Factory supplies expense.........	$15,800	3%
Uncollectible accounts expense....	9,500	2%

17. What are the basic objectives in the use of standard costs?

18. As the term is used in reference to standard costs, what is a *variance*?

19. What is meant by reporting by the "principle of exceptions" as the term is used in reference to cost control?

20. (a) What are the two variances between the actual cost and the standard cost for direct materials? (b) Discuss some possible causes of these variances.

21. (a) What are the two variances between the actual cost and the standard cost for direct labor? (b) Who generally has control over the direct labor cost?

22. (a) Describe the two variances between the actual costs and the standard costs for factory overhead. (b) What is a factory overhead cost variance report?

23. If standards are recorded in the accounts and Work in Process is debited for the actual manufacturing costs and credited for the standard cost of products produced, what does the balance in Work in Process represent?

24. Are variances from standard costs usually reported in financial statements issued to stockholders and others outside the firm?

25. Assuming that the variances from standards are not significant at the end of the period, to what account are they transferred?

26. Real World Focus. The following ten-year summary of the ratio of cost of sales to net sales for PepsiCo Inc. was taken from PepsiCo's annual reports:

	Cost of Sales ÷ Net Sales
1976	49.8%
1977	48.2
1978	48.4
1979	47.0
1980	46.8
1981	45.4
1982	43.3
1983	40.9
1984	39.9
1985	39.1

During this period, the net sales of PepsiCo increased by more than 300%. As sales increase, why would management normally expect the ratio of cost of sales to net sales to decline?

EXERCISES

SPREADSHEET
PROBLEM

Exercise 24–1.   Sales and production budgets. Husley Company manufactures two models of humidifiers, M3 and P4. Based on the following production and sales data for June of the current year, prepare (a) a sales budget and (b) a production budget.

	M3	P4
Estimated inventory (units), June 1..................	45,000	27,600
Desired inventory (units), June 30..................	54,000	24,000
Expected sales volume (units):		
Region A.......................................	81,500	40,800
Region B.......................................	66,200	24,800
Unit sales price......................................	$14.50	$20

Exercise 24–2. Schedule of cash collections of accounts receivable. Mattox Company was organized on August 1 of the current year. Projected sales for each of the first three months of operations are as follows:

August	$160,000
September...................	200,000
October	280,000

The company expects to sell 25% of its merchandise for cash. Of sales on account, 60% are expected to be collected in the month of the sale, 30% in the month following the sale, and the remainder in the following month. Prepare a schedule indicating cash collections of accounts receivable for August, September, and October.

Exercise 24–3. Schedule of cash disbursements. Sirmons Company was organized on February 28 of the current year. Projected operating expenses for each of the first three months of operations are as follows:

March	$ 98,000
April.......................	122,000
May........................	136,000

Depreciation, insurance, and property taxes represent $18,000 of the estimated monthly operating expenses. Insurance was paid on February 28, and property taxes will be paid in December. Three fourths of the remainder of the operating expenses are expected to be paid in the month in which they are incurred, with the balance to be paid in the following month. Prepare a schedule indicating cash disbursements for operating expenses for March, April, and May.

Exercise 24–4. Flexible budget for operating expenses. Daniel Company uses flexible budgets that are based on the following data:

Sales commissions	6% of sales
Advertising expense	$10,000 for $200,000 of sales
	$15,000 for $300,000 of sales
	$20,000 for $400,000 of sales
Miscellaneous selling expense	$1,000 plus 1/2% of sales
Office salaries expense....................	$15,000
Office supplies expense	2% of sales
Miscellaneous general expense	$500 plus 1/4% of sales

Prepare a flexible operating expenses budget for November of the current year for sales volumes of $200,000, $300,000, and $400,000.

Exercise 24–5. Budget performance report. The operating expenses incurred during November of the current year by Daniel Company were as follows:

Sales commissions	$23,800
Advertising expense	22,600

Miscellaneous selling expense	$ 3,050
Office salaries expense	15,000
Office supplies expense	7,810
Miscellaneous general expense	1,620

Assuming that the total sales for November were $400,000, prepare a budget performance report for operating expenses on the basis of the data presented above and in Exercise 24–4.

Exercise 24–6.   Direct materials variances. The following data relate to the direct materials cost for the production of 30,000 units of product:

Actual:	78,000 pounds at $1.82	$141,960
Standard:	75,000 pounds at 1.80	135,000

Determine the quantity variance, price variance, and total direct materials cost variance.

Exercise 24–7.   Standard direct materials cost per unit from variance data. The following data relating to direct materials cost for July of the current year are taken from the records of J. Ledbetter Company:

Quantity of direct materials used	16,000 pounds
Unit cost of direct materials	$2.50 per pound
Units of finished product manufactured	20,625 units
Standard direct materials per unit of finished product	.8 pounds
Direct materials quantity variance — favorable	$1,200
Direct materials price variance — unfavorable	$1,600

Determine the standard direct materials cost per unit of finished product, assuming that there was no inventory of work in process at either the beginning or the end of the month. Present your computations.

Exercise 24–8.   Direct labor variances. The following data relate to direct labor cost for the production of 15,000 units of product:

Actual:	42,500 hours at $15.80	$671,500
Standard:	42,000 hours at $16.00	672,000

Determine the time variance, rate variance, and total direct labor cost variance.

Exercise 24–9.   Factory overhead cost variances. The following data relate to factory overhead cost for the production of 40,000 units of product:

Actual:	Variable factory overhead	$152,000
	Fixed factory overhead	120,000
Standard:	60,000 hours at $4	240,000

If productive capacity of 100% was 80,000 hours and the factory overhead costs budgeted at the level of 60,000 standard hours was $270,000, determine the volume variance, controllable variance, and total factory overhead cost variance. The fixed factory overhead rate was $1.50 per hour.

Exercise 24–10. Income statement indicating standard cost variances. The following data were taken from the records of Watkins Company for May of the current year:

Cost of goods sold (at standard).........................	$390,000
Direct materials quantity variance—unfavorable...........	2,560
Direct materials price variance—favorable................	1,320
Direct labor time variance—unfavorable..................	3,270
Direct labor rate variance—favorable	900
Factory overhead volume variance—unfavorable..........	10,000
Factory overhead controllable variance—favorable	1,600
General expenses.....................................	25,000
Sales...	500,000
Selling expenses.....................................	42,000

Prepare an income statement for presentation to management.

PROBLEMS

Series A

Problem 24–1A. Sales, production, direct materials, and direct labor budgets. The budget director of Greaves Company requests estimates of sales, production, and other operating data from the various administrative units every month. Selected information concerning sales and production for August of the current year are summarized as follows:

(a) Estimated sales for August by sales territory:
   Northeast:
      Product A: 24,000 units at $45 per unit
      Product B: 20,000 units at $60 per unit
   Southeast:
      Product A: 15,000 units at $45 per unit
      Product B: 27,000 units at $60 per unit
   Southwest:
      Product A: 32,000 units at $45 per unit
      Product B: 43,000 units at $60 per unit

(b) Estimated inventories at August 1:
   Direct materials:
      Material W: 21,000 lbs.   Material Y: 21,500 lbs.
      Material X: 15,600 lbs.   Material Z: 27,600 lbs.
   Finished products:
      Product A: 10,000 units   Product B: 15,000 units

(c) Desired inventories at August 31:
   Direct materials:
      Material W: 18,000 lbs.   Material Y: 28,000 lbs.
      Material X: 22,000 lbs.   Material Z: 20,000 lbs.
   Finished products:
      Product A: 12,000 units   Product B: 25,000 units

(d) Direct materials used in production:
   In manufacture of Product A:
      Material X: 1.2 lbs. per unit of product
      Material Y: .8 lbs. per unit of product
      Material Z: 1.0 lb. per unit of product
   In manufacture of Product B:
      Material W: 1.5 lbs. per unit of product
      Material Y: .9 lbs. per unit of product
      Material Z: 1.4 lbs. per unit of product

(e) Anticipated purchase price for direct materials:
      Material W: $1.40 per lb.   Material Y: $2.00 per lb.
      Material X: $ .50 per lb.   Material Z: $1.75 per lb.

(f) Direct labor requirements:
   Product A:
      Department 20: 1.0 hour at $14 per hour
      Department 30: .6 hours at $20 per hour
   Product B:
      Department 10: 1.4 hours at $15 per hour
      Department 20: .5 hours at $14 per hour

Instructions:

(1) Prepare a sales budget for August.
(2) Prepare a production budget for August.
(3) Prepare a direct materials purchases budget for August.
(4) Prepare a direct labor cost budget for August.

Problem 24–2A. Budgeted income statement and supporting budgets. **The budget director of Martin Inc., with the assistance of the controller, treasurer, production manager, and sales manager, has gathered the following data for use in developing the budgeted income statement for July:**

(a) Estimated sales for July:
   Product J: 50,000 units at $120 per unit
   Product K: 30,000 units at $90 per unit

(b) Estimated inventories at July 1:
   Direct materials: Finished products:
      Material A: 5,000 lbs.   Product J: 10,000 units at $92 per unit
      Material B: 40,000 lbs.   Product K: 7,000 units at $75 per unit
      Material C: 8,000 lbs.

(c) Desired inventories at July 31:
   Direct materials: Finished products:
      Material A: 8,000 lbs.   Product J: 15,000 units at $92 per unit
      Material B: 35,000 lbs.   Product K: 9,000 units at $75 per unit
      Material C: 10,000 lbs.

(d) Direct materials used in production:
   In manufacture of Product J:
      Material A: .75 lbs. per unit of product
      Material B: 1.5 lbs. per unit of product
   In manufacture of Product K:
      Material B: 1.0 lb. per unit of product
      Material C: 1.2 lbs. per unit of product

(e) Anticipated cost of purchases and beginning and ending inventory of direct materials:
      Material A: $14.00 per lb.
      Material B: $ .80 per lb.
      Material C: $20.00 per lb.

(f) Direct labor requirements:
   Product J:
      Department 100: 3.0 hours at $15 per hour
      Department 200: 1.0 hour at $20 per hour
   Product K:
      Department 200:   .5 hours at $20 per hour
      Department 300: 2.0 hours at $18 per hour

(g) Estimated factory overhead costs for July:

Indirect factory wages.	$250,000
Depreciation of plant and equipment.	220,000
Supervisory salaries	125,000
Power and light	115,700
Indirect materials	81,000
Maintenance	33,400
Insurance and property taxes	25,900

(h) Estimated operating expenses for July:

Sales salaries expense	$462,000
Officers salaries expense.	300,000
Advertising expense	286,000
Office salaries expense	125,000
Depreciation expense—office equipment	84,500
Telephone expense—selling	47,900
Telephone expense—general	22,000
Travel expense—selling	14,500
Travel expense—general	8,300
Office supplies expense.	4,000
Miscellaneous selling expense	11,200
Miscellaneous general expense	7,500

(i) Estimated other income and expense for July:

Interest income	$180,000
Interest expense	145,000

(j) Estimated tax rate: 30%.

Instructions:

(1) Prepare a sales budget for July.
(2) Prepare a production budget for July.
(3) Prepare a direct materials purchases budget for July.
(4) Prepare a direct labor cost budget for July.
(5) Prepare a factory overhead cost budget for July.
(6) Prepare a cost of goods sold budget for July. Work in process at the beginning of July is estimated to be $140,000, and work in process at the end of July is estimated to be $150,000.
(7) Prepare an operating expenses budget for July. Classify the expenses as either selling or general expenses.
(8) Prepare a budgeted income statement for July.

Problem 24–3A.   Cash budget. The treasurer of Flores Company instructs you to prepare a monthly cash budget for the next three months. You are presented with the following budget information:

	April	May	June
Sales	$600,000	$550,000	$700,000
Manufacturing costs	390,000	360,000	450,000
Operating expenses	125,000	115,000	145,000
Capital expenditures	—	160,000	—

The company expects to sell about 25% of its merchandise for cash. Of sales on account, 60% are expected to be collected in full in the month following the sale and the remainder the following month. Depreciation, insurance, and property taxes represent $30,000 of the estimated monthly manufacturing costs and $5,000 of the probable monthly operating expenses. Insurance and property taxes are paid in December. Of the remainder of the manufacturing costs and operating expenses, 70% are expected to be paid in the month in which they are incurred and the balance in the following month.

Current assets as of April 1 are composed of cash of $70,200, marketable securities of $60,000, and accounts receivable of $570,000 ($442,000 from March sales and $128,000 from February sales). Current liabilities as of April 1 are composed of a $100,000, 12%, 120-day note payable due June 20, $105,000 of accounts payable incurred in March for manufacturing costs, and accrued liabilities of $30,200 incurred in March for operating expenses.

It is expected that $4,000 in dividends will be received in May. An estimated income tax payment of $31,200 will be made in June. Flores Company's regular semiannual dividend of $20,000 is expected to be declared in May and paid in June. Management desires to maintain a minimum cash balance of $60,000.

Instructions:

(1) Prepare a monthly cash budget for April, May, and June.
(2) On the basis of the cash budget prepared in (1), what recommendation should be made to the treasurer?

Problem 24–4A. Budgeted income statement and balance sheet. As a preliminary to requesting budget estimates of sales, costs, and expenses for the fiscal year beginning January 1, 1987, the following tentative trial balance as of December 31 of the preceding year is prepared by the accounting department of Calmer Company:

Cash..	85,000	
Accounts Receivable............................	90,000	
Finished Goods	150,000	
Work in Process.................................	78,800	
Materials	52,200	
Prepaid Expenses	10,200	
Plant and Equipment.............................	800,000	
Accumulated Depreciation—Plant and Equipment....		320,000
Accounts Payable		100,000
Notes Payable		60,000
Common Stock, $20 par..........................		150,000
Retained Earnings...............................		636,200
	1,266,200	1,266,200

Factory output and sales for 1987 are expected to total 60,000 units of product, which are to be sold at $20 per unit. The quantities and costs of the inventories (lifo method) at December 31, 1987, are expected to remain unchanged from the balances at the beginning of the year.

Budget estimates of manufacturing costs and operating expenses for the year are summarized as follows:

	Estimated Costs and Expenses	
	Fixed (Total for Year)	Variable (Per Unit Sold)
Cost of goods manufactured and sold:		
Direct materials	—	$2.50
Direct labor	—	6.00
Factory overhead:		
Depreciation of plant and equipment ...	$25,000	—
Other factory overhead	18,000	1.95
Selling expenses:		
Sales salaries and commissions	30,000	.60
Advertising	15,000	—
Miscellaneous selling expense	1,000	.05
General expenses:		
Office and officers salaries	40,000	.30
Supplies	2,000	.10
Miscellaneous general expense	1,000	.04

Balances of accounts receivable, prepaid expenses, and accounts payable at the end of the year are expected to differ from the beginning balances by only inconsequential amounts.

For purposes of this problem, assume that federal income tax of $160,500 on 1987 taxable income will be paid during 1987. Regular quarterly cash dividends of $.30 a share are expected to be declared and paid in March, June, September, and December. It is anticipated that plant and equipment will be purchased for $200,000 cash in November.

Instructions:

(1) Prepare a budgeted income statement for 1987.
(2) Prepare a budgeted balance sheet as of December 31, 1987.

Problem 24–5A.   Direct materials, direct labor, and factory overhead cost variance analysis. Standard costs and actual costs for direct materials, direct labor, and factory overhead incurred for the manufacture of 5,000 units of product were as follows:

	Standard Costs	Actual Costs
Direct materials	7,000 pounds at $12	7,200 pounds at $11.50
Direct labor	2,000 hours at $15	1,850 hours at $15.50
Factory overhead	Rates per direct labor, based on 100% of capacity of 2,500 labor hours:	
	Variable cost, $13.20	$28,000 variable cost
	Fixed cost, $8.00	$20,000 fixed cost

Instructions:

Determine (a) the quantity variance, price variance, and total direct materials cost variance; (b) the time variance, rate variance, and total direct labor cost variance; and (c) the volume variance, controllable variance, and total factory overhead cost variance.

Problem 24–6A. Flexible factory overhead cost budget and variance report. Yates Company prepared the following factory overhead cost budget for the Painting Department for October of the current year:

Yates Company
Factory Overhead Cost Budget — Painting Department
For Month Ending October 31, 19--

Direct labor hours:		
Productive capacity of 100%......................		20,000
Hours budgeted		16,000
Variable cost:		
Indirect factory wages............................	$24,000	
Indirect materials	9,600	
Power and light...................................	4,800	
Total variable cost		$38,400
Fixed cost:		
Supervisory salaries	$18,000	
Indirect factory wages............................	12,400	
Depreciation of plant and equipment................	7,500	
Insurance..	6,200	
Power and light...................................	4,100	
Property taxes....................................	3,800	
Total fixed cost		52,000
Total factory overhead cost		$90,400

During October, the Painting Department was operated for 16,000 direct labor hours, and the following factory overhead costs were incurred:

Indirect factory wages	$38,000
Supervisory salaries......................................	18,000
Indirect materials..	9,400
Power and light..	9,100
Depreciation of plant and equipment	7,500
Insurance	6,200
Property taxes...	3,800
Total factory overhead cost incurred.....................	$92,000

Instructions:

(1) Prepare a flexible budget for October, indicating capacities of 14,000, 16,000, 18,000, and 20,000 direct labor hours and the determination of a standard factory overhead rate per direct labor hour.

(2) Prepare a standard factory overhead cost variance report for October.

Problem 24–7A. Entries and standard cost variance analysis. Walters Inc. maintains perpetual inventory accounts for materials, work in process, and finished goods and uses a standard cost system based on the following data:

	Standard Cost per Unit
Direct materials: 4 kilograms at $1.25 per kg	$ 5
Direct labor: 3 hours at $15 per hour	45
Factory overhead: $1.00 per direct labor hour	3
Total.	$53

There was no inventory of work in process at the beginning or end of January, the first month of the current fiscal year. The transactions relating to production completed during January are summarized as follows:

(a) Materials purchased on account, $75,600.
(b) Direct materials used, $36,400. The amount represented 28 000 kilograms at $1.30 per kilogram.
(c) Direct labor paid, $315,700. This amount represented 20,500 hours at $15.40 per hour. There were no accruals at either the beginning or the end of the period.
(d) Factory overhead incurred during the month was composed of depreciation on plant and equipment, $8,500; indirect labor, $7,400; insurance, $4,750; and miscellaneous factory costs, $4,150. The indirect labor and miscellaneous factory costs were paid during the period, and the insurance represents an expiration of prepaid insurance. Of the total factory overhead of $24,800, fixed costs amounted to $12,000 and variable costs were $12,800.
(e) Goods finished during the period, 6,900 units.

Instructions:
(1) Prepare entries to record the transactions, assuming that the work in process account is debited for actual production costs and credited with standard costs for goods finished.
(2) Prepare a T account for Work in Process and post to the account, using the identifying letters as dates.
(3) Prepare schedules of variances for direct materials cost, direct labor cost, and factory overhead cost. Productive capacity for the plant is 30,000 direct labor hours.
(4) Total the amount of the standard cost variances and compare this total with the balance of the work in process account.

Series B

Problem 24–3B.   Cash budget. The treasurer of Inman Company instructs you to prepare a monthly cash budget for the next three months. You are presented with the following budget information:

	October	November	December
Sales.	$240,000	$360,000	$410,000
Manufacturing costs.	140,000	220,000	250,000
Operating expenses.	38,000	54,000	62,000
Capital expenditures	—	90,000	—

The company expects to sell about 30% of its merchandise for cash. Of sales on account, 80% are expected to be collected in full in the month following the sale and the remainder the following month. Depreciation, insurance, and property taxes represent $20,000 of the estimated monthly manufacturing costs and $8,000 of the probable monthly operating expenses. Insurance and property taxes are paid in March and August respectively. Of the remainder of the manufacturing costs and operating expenses, 65% are expected to be paid in the month in which they are incurred and the balance in the following month.

Current assets as of May 1 are composed of cash of $28,500, marketable securities of $40,000, and accounts receivable of $176,400 ($140,000 from September sales and $36,400 from August sales). Current liabilities as of October 1 are composed of a $50,000, 10%, 90-day note payable due November 5, $42,500 of accounts payable incurred in September for manufacturing costs, and accrued liabilities of $10,200 incurred in September for operating expenses.

It is expected that $2,000 in dividends will be received in October. An estimated income tax payment of $15,000 will be made in November. Inman Company's regular quarterly dividend of $10,000 is expected to be declared in November and paid in December. Management desires to maintain a minimum cash balance of $25,000.

Instructions:

(1) Prepare a monthly cash budget for October, November, and December.
(2) On the basis of the cash budget prepared in (1), what recommendation should be made to the treasurer?

Problem 24–5B. Direct materials, direct labor, and factory overhead cost variance analysis. Standard costs and actual costs for direct materials, direct labor, and factory overhead incurred for the manufacture of 2,000 units of product were as follows:

	Standard Costs	Actual Costs
Direct materials	3,000 pounds at $8	3,100 pounds at $8.20
Direct labor.............	6,200 hours at $12	6,000 hours at $13.25
Factory overhead........	Rates per direct labor hour, based on 100% of capacity of 8,000 labor hours:	
	Variable cost, $1.20	$8,200 variable cost
	Fixed cost, $3.50	$28,000 fixed cost

Instructions:

Determine (a) the quantity variance, price variance, and total direct materials cost variance; (b) the time variance, rate variance, and total direct labor cost variance; and (c) the volume variance, controllable variance, and total factory overhead cost variance.

Problem 24–6B. Flexible factory overhead cost budget and variance report. Wooten Inc. prepared the following factory overhead cost budget for the Polishing Department for March of the current year:

Wooten Inc.
Factory Overhead Cost Budget—Polishing Department
For Month Ending March 31, 19--

Direct labor hours:		
Productive capacity of 100%........................		25,000
Hours budgeted		28,750
Variable cost:		
Indirect factory wages.............................	$16,100	
Indirect materials	9,430	
Power and light...................................	7,360	
Total variable cost		$32,890
Fixed cost:		
Supervisory salaries	$13,500	
Indirect factory wages............................	7,780	
Depreciation of plant and equipment	5,220	
Insurance..	3,160	
Power and light...................................	2,800	
Property taxes....................................	1,940	
Total fixed cost.................................		34,400
Total factory overhead cost		$67,290

During March, the Polishing Department was operated for 28,750 direct labor hours, and the following factory overhead costs were incurred:

Indirect factory wages	$25,780
Supervisory salaries......................................	13,500
Power and light..	10,000
Indirect materials..	9,700
Depreciation of plant and equipment	5,220
Insurance	3,160
Property taxes...	1,940
Total factory overhead cost incurred.....................	$69,300

Instructions:

(1) Prepare a flexible budget for March, indicating capacities of 17,500, 21,250, 25,000, and 28,750 direct labor hours and the determination of a standard factory overhead rate per direct labor hour.
(2) Prepare a standard factory overhead cost variance report for March.

Problem 24–7B.   Entries and standard cost variance analysis. Duckworth Inc. maintains perpetual inventory accounts for materials, work in process, and finished goods and uses a standard cost system based on the following data:

	Standard Cost per Unit
Direct materials: 4 kilograms at $2.50 per kg	$10
Direct labor: 2 hours at $16.50 per hour	33
Factory overhead: $2.50 per direct labor hour	5
Total..	$48

There was no inventory of work in process at the beginning or end of August, the first month of the current fiscal year. The transactions relating to production completed during August are summarized as follows:

(a) Materials purchased on account, $120,600.
(b) Direct materials used, $49,920. This represented 20 800 kilograms at $2.40 per kilogram.
(c) Direct labor paid, $169,320. This represented 10,200 hours at $16.60 per hour. There were no accruals at either the beginning or the end of the period.
(d) Factory overhead incurred during the month was composed of depreciation on plant and equipment, $13,700; indirect labor, $9,480; insurance, $2,400; and miscellaneous factory costs, $5,320. The indirect labor and miscellaneous factory costs were paid during the period, and the insurance represents an expiration of prepaid insurance. Of the total factory overhead of $30,900, fixed costs amounted to $18,000, and variable costs were $12,900.
(e) Goods finished during the period, 5,000 units.

Instructions:

(1) Prepare entries to record the transactions, assuming that the work in process account is debited for actual production costs and credited with standard costs for goods finished.
(2) Prepare a T account for Work in Process and post to the account, using the identifying letters as dates.
(3) Prepare schedules of variances for direct materials cost, direct labor cost, and factory overhead cost. Productive capacity for the plant is 15,000 direct labor hours.
(4) Total the amount of the standard cost variances and compare this total with the balance of the work in process account.

MINI-CASE 24

BARNES MANUFACTURING COMPANY

Your father is president and chief operating officer of Barnes Manufacturing Company and has hired you as a summer intern to assist the controller. The controller has asked you to visit with the production supervisor of the Polishing Department and evaluate the supervisor's concern with the budgeting process. After this evaluation, you are to meet with the controller to discuss suggestions for improving the budgeting process.

This morning, you met with the supervisor, who expressed dissatis-faction with the budgets and budget performance reports prepared for the factory overhead costs for the Polishing Department. Specifically, July's budget performance report was mentioned as an example. The supervisor indicated that this report is not useful in evaluating the efficiency of the department, because most of the overages for the individual factory overhead items are not caused by inefficiencies, but by variations in the volume of activity between actual and budget. Although you were not provided with a copy of the budget for July, the supervisor indicated that it is standard practice for the plant manager to prepare a budget based on the production of 20,000 units. Actual production varies widely, however, with approximately 22,000 to 24,000 units being produced each month for the past several months. You are provided with the following budget performance report for July of the current year, when actual production was 24,000 units. All of the overages relate to variable costs, and the other costs are fixed.

Barnes Manufacturing Company
Budget Performance Report — Factory Overhead Cost, Polishing Department
For Month Ended July 31, 19--

	Budget	Actual	Over	Under
Indirect factory wages	$18,000	$21,800	$3,800	
Electric power	15,000	17,500	2,500	
Supervisory salaries	12,000	12,000		
Depreciation of plant assets.	8,100	8,100		
Indirect materials	7,500	9,100	1,600	
Insurance and property taxes	5,000	5,000		
	$65,600	$73,500	$7,900	$0

In your discussion, you learned that the department supervisor has little faith in the budgeting process. The supervisor views the budgets as worthless and the budget performance reports as a waste of time, because they require an explanation of the budget overages, which, for the most part, are not departmentally controlled.

Instructions:

Prepare a list of suggestions for improving the budgeting process. Include any reports that you might find useful when you meet with the controller to discuss your suggestions.

Chapter 25

PROFIT REPORTING FOR MANAGEMENT ANALYSIS

Chapter Objectives:

- Describe the characteristics of accounting reports prepared for use by management.

- Describe and illustrate gross profit analysis.

- Describe and illustrate absorption costing concepts.

- Describe and illustrate variable costing concepts.

- Describe and illustrate managerial uses of variable costing.

The basic concepts of accounting systems that provide management with information useful in planning and controlling operations were described and illustrated in previous chapters. In this chapter, attention will be focused on an end product of the accounting system — accounting reports for use by management. The discussion will begin with a presentation of the general characteristics of these reports and their use in establishing profit goals and developing plans for achieving these goals. Following this general discussion, accounting reports evolving from gross profit analysis and variable costing — two concepts especially useful in planning and controlling operations — will be discussed and illustrated.

CHARACTERISTICS OF MANAGERIAL ACCOUNTING REPORTS

As discussed in Chapter 21, the managerial accountant can be viewed as the observer and reporter of the business's operations. In this role, the accountant extracts the essential data from the accounting system and presents it in a format that best meets the needs of management. The usefulness of accounting reports for management depends on the characteristics presented in the following diagram:

CHARACTERISTICS OF USEFUL MANAGERIAL ACCOUNTING REPORTS

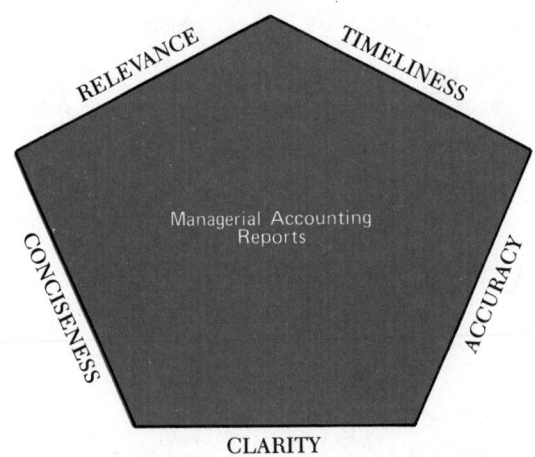

Relevance

Relevance means that the economic information reported must be pertinent to the specific action being considered by management. In applying this concept, the accountant must be familiar with the operations of the firm and the needs of management in order to select what is important from the masses of data that are available. Especially in this modern age of the information explosion, this selection process can be difficult. To accomplish this task, the accountant must determine the needs of management for the decision at hand, examine the available data, and select only the relevant data for reporting to management. To illustrate, assume that management is considering the replacement of fully depreciated equipment, which cost $100,000, with new equipment costing $150,000. It is the $150,000 that is relevant for an analysis of financing the replacement. The original cost, $100,000, is irrelevant.

In applying the concept of relevance, it is important to recognize that some accounting information may have little or no relevance for one use but may have a high degree of relevance for another use. For example, in the previous illustration, the $100,000 was irrelevant for purposes of evaluating the financing of the replacement equipment. For tax purposes, however, the $100,000 (and its accumulated depreciation) would be relevant for determining the amount of the gain from the sale or trade-in of the old equipment and the amount of the income tax due on any gain.

Timeliness

Timeliness refers to the need for accounting reports to contain the most up-to-date information. In many cases, outdated data can lead to unwise decisions. For example, if prior years' costs are relied upon in setting the selling price of a product, the resulting selling price may not be sufficient to cover the current year's costs and to provide a satisfactory profit.

In some cases, the timeliness concept may require the accountant to prepare reports on a prearranged schedule, such as daily, weekly, or monthly. For example, daily reports of cash receipts and disbursements assist management in effectively managing the use of cash on a day-to-day basis. On the other hand, weekly reports of the cost of products manufactured may be satisfactory to assist management in the control of costs. In other cases, reports are prepared on an irregular basis or only when needed. For example, if management is evaluating a proposed advertising promotion for the month of May, a report of current costs and other current relevant data for this specific proposal would be needed in sufficient time for management to make and implement the decision.

Accuracy

Accuracy refers to the need for the report to be correct within the constraints of the use of the report and the inherent inaccuracies in the measurement process. If the report is not accurate, management's decision may not be prudent. For example, if an inaccurate report on a customer's past payment practices is presented to management, an unwise decision in granting credit may be made.

As previously indicated, the concept of accuracy must be applied within the constraint of the use to be made of the report. In other words, there are occasions when accuracy should be sacrificed for less precise data that are more useful to management. For example, in planning production, estimates (forecasts) of future sales may be more useful than more accurate data from past sales. In addition, it should be noted that there are inherent inaccuracies in accounting data that are based on estimates and approximations. For example, in determining the unit cost of a product manufactured, an estimate of depreciation expense on factory equipment used in the manufacturing process must be made. Without this estimate, the cost of the product would be of limited usefulness in establishing the product selling price.

Clarity

Clarity refers to the need for reports to be clear and understandable in both format and content. Reports that are clear and understandable will enable management to focus on significant factors in planning and controlling operations. For example, for management's use in controlling the costs of manufacturing a product, a report that compares actual costs with expected costs and clearly indicates the differences enables management to give its attention to significant differences and to take any necessary corrective action.

Conciseness

Conciseness refers to the requirement that the report should be brief and to the point. Although the report must be complete and include all relevant information, the inclusion of unnecessary information wastes management's time and makes it more difficult for management to focus on the significant factors related to a decision. For example, reports prepared for the top level of management should usually be broad in scope and present summaries of data rather than small details.

Cost-Benefit Balance

The characteristics of managerial accounting reports provide general guidelines for the preparation of reports to meet the various needs of management. In applying these guidelines, consideration must be given to the specific needs of each manager, and the reports should be tailored to meet these needs. In preparing reports, costs are incurred, and a primary consideration is that the value of the management reports must at least equal the cost of producing them. This overriding cost-benefit evaluation must be considered, no matter how informational a report may be. A report should not be prepared if its cost exceeds the benefits derived by users.

GROSS PROFIT ANALYSIS

Gross profit is often considered the most significant intermediate figure in the income statement. It is common to determine its percentage relationship to sales and to make comparisons with prior periods. However, the mere knowledge of the percentages and the degree and direction of change from prior periods is insufficient. Management needs information about the causes. The procedure used in developing such information is termed **gross profit analysis**.

Since gross profit is the excess of sales over the cost of goods sold, a change in the amount of gross profit can be caused by (1) an increase or decrease in the amount of sales and (2) an increase or decrease in the amount of the cost of goods sold. An increase or decrease in either element may in turn be due to (1) a change in the number of units sold and (2) a change in the unit price. The effect of these two factors on either sales or cost of goods sold may be stated as follows:

1. **Quantity factor**. The effect of a change in the number of units sold, assuming no change in unit price.
2. **Price factor**. The effect of a change in unit price on the number of units sold.

1127

The following data are to be used as the basis for illustrating gross profit analysis. For the sake of simplicity, a single commodity is assumed. The amount of detail entering into the analysis would be greater if a number of different commodities were sold, but the basic principles would not be affected.

	1988	1987	Increase Decrease*
Sales..........................	$900,000	$800,000	$100,000
Cost of goods sold..............	650,000	570,000	80,000
Gross profit	$250,000	$230,000	$ 20,000
Number of units sold.............	125,000	100,000	25,000
Unit sales price..................	$7.20	$8.00	$.80*
Unit cost price...................	$5.20	$5.70	$.50*

The following analysis of these data shows that the favorable increase in the number of units sold was partially offset by a decrease in unit selling price. Also, the increase in the cost of goods sold due to increased quantity was partially offset by a decrease in unit cost.

GROSS
PROFIT
ANALYSIS
REPORT

Analysis of Increase in Gross Profit
For Year Ended December 31, 1988

Increase in amount of sales attributed to:
  Quantity factor:
    Increase in number of units sold
      in 1988......................   25,000
    Unit sales price in 1987 ....   × $8 $200,000

  Price factor:
    Decrease in unit sales price in 1988 . $.80
    Number of units sold in 1988 ....   ×125,000   100,000

  Net increase in amount of sales....... $100,000
Increase in amount of cost of goods sold
attributed to:
  Quantity factor:
    Increase in number of units sold
      in 1988......................   25,000
    Unit cost price in 1987 ....   × $5.70 $142,500

  Price factor:
    Decrease in unit cost price in 1988.. $.50
    Number of units sold in 1988 ....   ×125,000   62,500

  Net increase in amount of cost of
    goods sold   80,000
Increase in gross profit................ $ 20,000

The data presented in the report may be useful both in evaluating past performance and in planning for the future. The importance of the cost reduction of $.50 a unit is quite clear. If the unit cost had not changed from the preceding year, the net increase in the amount of sales ($100,000) would have been more than offset by the increase in the cost of goods sold ($142,500), causing a decrease of $42,500 in gross profit. The $20,000 increase in gross profit actually attained was made possible, therefore, by the ability of management to reduce the unit cost of the commodity.

The means by which the $.50 reduction in the unit cost of the commodity was accomplished is also significant. If it was due to the spreading of fixed factory overhead costs over the larger number of units produced, the decision to reduce the sales price in order to achieve a larger volume was probably wise. On the other hand, if the $.50 reduction in unit cost was due to operating efficiencies entirely unrelated to the increased production, the $.80 reduction in the unit sales price was unwise. The accuracy of the conclusion can be demonstrated by comparing actual results with hypothetical results. The hypothetical results are based on (1) a sales volume that did not change from the 1987 level and (2) a unit cost reduction to $5.20 due to operating efficiencies. The following analysis shows the possible loss of an opportunity to have realized an additional gross profit of $30,000 ($280,000 − $250,000).

	Actual		Hypothetical	
Number of units sold	125,000		100,000	
Unit sales price	$7.20		$8.00	
Sales		$900,000		$800,000
Unit cost price	$5.20		$5.20	
Cost of goods sold		650,000		520,000
Gross profit		$250,000		$280,000

If the reduction in unit cost had been achieved by a combination of spreading the fixed factory overhead over more production units and achieving operating efficiencies related to the increased production, the approximate effects of each could be determined by additional analyses. The methods used in gross profit analysis may also be extended, with some changes, to the analysis of changes in selling and general expenses.

ABSORPTION COSTING AND VARIABLE COSTING

In the preceding illustration of gross profit analysis, the importance of the cost of goods sold in determining income was emphasized. In determining the cost of goods sold, two alternate costing concepts can be used. These two costing concepts are absorption costing and variable costing.

The cost of manufactured products consists of direct materials, direct labor, and factory overhead. All such costs become a part of the finished goods inventory and remain there as an asset until the goods are sold. This conventional treatment of manufacturing costs is sometimes called absorption costing because all costs are "absorbed" into finished goods. Although the concept is necessary in determining historical costs and taxable income, another costing concept may be more useful to management in making decisions.

In **variable costing**, which is also termed **direct costing**, the cost of goods manufactured is composed only of variable costs—those manufacturing costs that increase or decrease as the volume of production rises or falls. These costs are the direct materials, direct labor, and only those factory overhead costs which vary with the rate of production. The remaining factory overhead costs, which are the fixed or nonvariable items, are related to the productive capacity of the manufacturing plant and are not affected by changes in the quantity of product manufactured. Accordingly, the fixed factory overhead does not become a part of the cost of goods manufactured, but is considered an expense of the period.

The distinction between absorption costing and variable costing is illustrated in the following diagram. Note that the difference between the two costing concepts is in the treatment of the fixed manufacturing costs, which consist of the fixed factory overhead costs.

ABSORPTION
COSTING
COMPARED
WITH
VARIABLE
COSTING

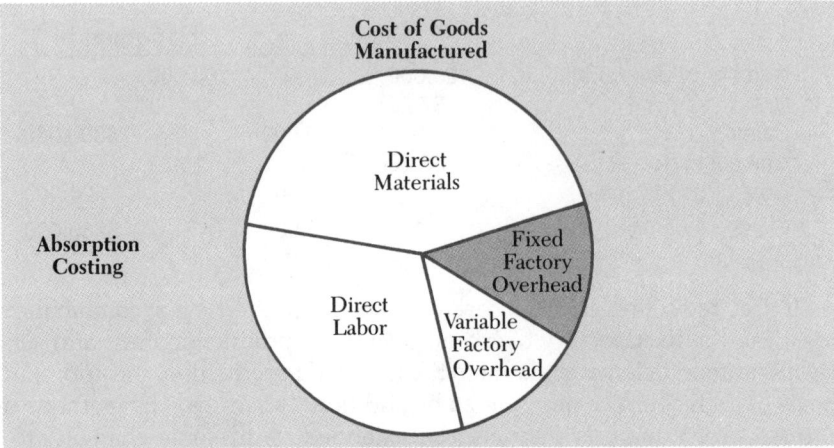

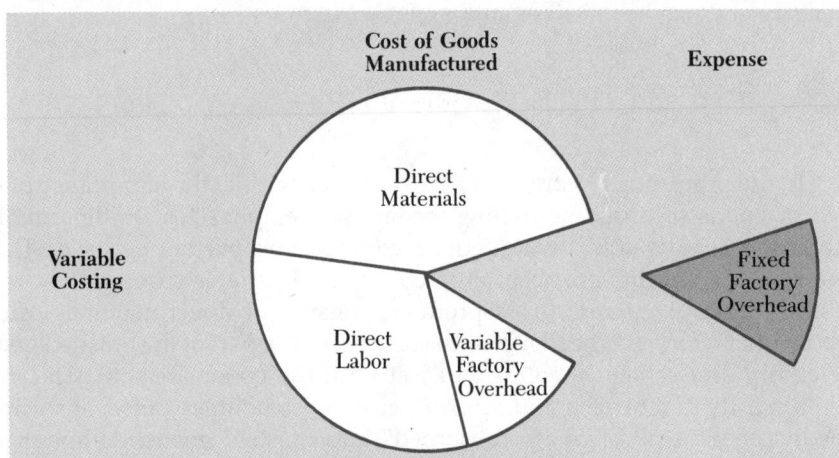

Variable Costing and the Income Statement

The arrangement of data in the variable costing income statement differs considerably from the format of the conventional income statement. Variable costs and expenses are presented separately from fixed costs and expenses, with significant summarizing amounts inserted at intermediate points. As a basis for illustrating the differences between the two forms, assume that 15,000 units were manufactured and sold at a unit price of $50 and the costs and expenses were as follows:

	Total Cost or Expense	Number of Units	Unit Cost
Manufacturing costs:			
Variable........................	$375,000	15,000	$25
Fixed..........................	150,000	15,000	10
Total........................	$525,000		$35
Selling and general expenses:			
Variable ($5 per unit sold)	$ 75,000		
Fixed..........................	50,000		
Total........................	$125,000		

The two income statements prepared from this information are as follows. The computations in parentheses are shown as an aid to understanding.

ABSORPTION COSTING INCOME STATEMENT

Absorption Costing Income Statement	
Sales (15,000 × $50)	$750,000
Cost of goods sold (15,000 × $35)	525,000
Gross profit...	$225,000
Selling and general expenses ($75,000 + $50,000)	125,000
Income from operations	$100,000

VARIABLE COSTING INCOME STATEMENT

Variable Costing Income Statement		
Sales (15,000 × $50)		$750,000
Variable cost of goods sold (15,000 × $25)		375,000
Manufacturing margin..................................		$375,000
Variable selling and general expenses		75,000
Contribution margin...................................		$300,000
Fixed costs and expenses:		
Fixed manufacturing costs.........................	$150,000	
Fixed selling and general expenses	50,000	200,000
Income from operations		$100,000

The absorption costing income statement does not distinguish between variable and fixed costs and expenses. All manufacturing costs are included in the cost of goods sold. The deduction of the cost of goods sold from sales yields the intermediate amount, gross profit. Deduction of selling and general expenses then yields income from operations.

In contrast, the variable costing income statement includes only the variable manufacturing costs in the cost of goods sold. Deduction of the cost of goods sold from sales yields an intermediate amount, termed **manufacturing margin**. Deduction of the variable selling and general expenses yields the **contribution margin**, or **marginal income**. The fixed costs and expenses are then deducted from the contribution margin to yield income from operations.

Units Manufactured Equal Units Sold. In the preceding illustration, 15,000 units were manufactured and sold. Both the absorption and the variable costing income statements reported the same income from operations of $100,000. Assuming no other changes, this equality of income will always be the case when the number of units manufactured and the number of units sold are equal. Only when the number of units manufactured and the number of units sold are not equal, which creates a change in the quantity of finished goods in inventory, will the income from operations differ under the two concepts.

Units Manufactured Exceed Units Sold. For any period in which the number of units manufactured exceeds the number of units sold, the operating income reported under the absorption costing concept will be larger than the operating income reported under the variable costing concept. To illustrate, assume that in the preceding example only 12,000 units of the 15,000 units manufactured were sold. The two income statements that result are as follows. Computations are inserted parenthetically as an aid to understanding.

ABSORPTION
COSTING
INCOME
STATEMENT

Absorption Costing Income Statement		
Sales (12,000 × $50)		$600,000
Cost of goods sold:		
Cost of goods manufactured (15,000 × $35)	$525,000	
Less ending inventory (3,000 × $35)	105,000	
Cost of goods sold		420,000
Gross profit		$180,000
Selling and general expenses ($60,000 + $50,000)		110,000
Income from operations		$ 70,000

Variable Costing Income Statement		
Sales (12,000 × $50)...............................		$600,000
Variable cost of goods sold:		
Variable cost of goods manufactured		
(15,000 × $25).................................	$375,000	
Less ending inventory (3,000 × $25)	75,000	
Variable cost of goods sold.....................		300,000
Manufacturing margin.............................		$300,000
Variable selling and general expenses		60,000
Contribution margin..............................		$240,000
Fixed costs and expenses:		
Fixed manufacturing costs........................	$150,000	
Fixed selling and general expenses	50,000	200,000
Income from operations		$ 40,000

The $30,000 difference in the amount of income from operations ($70,000 − $40,000) is due to the different treatment of the fixed manufacturing costs. The entire amount of the $150,000 of fixed manufacturing costs is included as an expense of the period in the variable costing statement. The ending inventory in the absorption costing statement includes $30,000 (3,000 × $10) of fixed manufacturing costs. This $30,000, by being included in inventory on hand, is thus excluded from the current cost of goods sold and instead is deferred to another period.

Units Manufactured Less Than Units Sold. For any period in which the number of units manufactured is less than the number of units sold, the operating income reported under the absorption costing concept will be less than the operating income reported under the variable costing concept. To illustrate, assume that 5,000 units of inventory were on hand at the beginning of a period, 10,000 units were manufactured during the period, and 15,000 units were sold (10,000 units manufactured during the period plus the 5,000 units on hand at the beginning of the period) at $50 per unit. The manufacturing costs and selling and general expenses are as follows:

	Total Cost or Expense	Number of Units	Unit Cost
Beginning inventory:			
Manufacturing costs:			
Variable.................	$125,000	5,000	$25
Fixed	50,000	5,000	10
Total..................	$175,000		$35

	Total Cost or Expense	Number of Units	Unit Cost
Current period:			
Manufacturing costs:			
Variable	$250,000	10,000	$25
Fixed	150,000	10,000	15
Total	$400,000		$40
Selling and general expenses:			
Variable ($5 per unit sold).	$ 75,000		
Fixed	50,000		
Total	$125,000		

The two income statements prepared from this information are as follows. Computations are inserted parenthetically as an aid to understanding.

Absorption Costing Income Statement

Sales (15,000 × $50)		$750,000
Cost of goods sold:		
Beginning inventory (5,000 × $35)	$175,000	
Cost of goods manufactured (10,000 × $40)	400,000	
Cost of goods sold		575,000
Gross profit		$175,000
Selling and general expenses ($75,000 + $50,000) . . .		125,000
Income from operations		$ 50,000

Variable Costing Income Statement

Sales (15,000 × $50)		$750,000
Variable cost of goods sold:		
Beginning inventory (5,000 × $25)	$125,000	
Variable cost of goods manufactured		
(10,000 × $25)	250,000	
Variable cost of goods sold		375,000
Manufacturing margin		$375,000
Variable selling and general expenses		75,000
Contribution margin		$300,000
Fixed costs and expenses:		
Fixed manufacturing costs	$150,000	
Fixed selling and general expenses	50,000	200,000
Income from operations		$100,000

The $50,000 difference ($100,000 − $50,000) in the amount of income from operations is attributable to the different treatment of the fixed manufacturing costs. The beginning inventory in the absorption costing income statement includes $50,000 (5,000 units × $10) of fixed manufacturing costs incurred in the preceding period. By being included in the beginning inventory, this $50,000 is included in the cost of goods sold for the current period. Under variable costing, however, this $50,000 was included as an expense in an income statement of a prior period. Therefore, none of it is included as an expense in the current period variable costing income statement.

Comparison of Income Reported Under the Two Concepts

The examples presented in the preceding sections illustrated the effects of the absorption costing and variable costing concepts on income from operations when the level of inventory changes during a period. These effects may be summarized as follows:

Units manufactured:

Equal units sold	Absorption costing income equals variable costing income.
Exceed units sold.	Absorption costing income is greater than variable costing income.
Less than units sold.	Absorption costing income is less than variable costing income

Income Analysis Under Absorption Costing

As was illustrated in the preceding examples, changes in the quantity of the finished goods inventory, caused by differences in the levels of sales and production, directly affect the amount of income from operations reported under absorption costing. Management should therefore be aware of the possible effects of changing inventory levels on operating income reported under absorption costing in analyzing and evaluating operations. To illustrate, assume that the following two proposed production levels are being evaluated by the management of Brownstein Manufacturing Company:

Proposal 1: 20,000 Units To Be Manufactured

	Total Cost or Expense	Number of Units	Unit Cost
Manufacturing costs:			
Variable.	$ 700,000	20,000	$35
Fixed	400,000	20,000	20
Total.	$1,100,000		$55
Selling and general expenses:			
Variable ($5 per unit sold). . .	$ 100,000		
Fixed	100,000		
Total.	$ 200,000		

Proposal 2: 25,000 Units To Be Manufactured

	Total Cost or Expense	Number of Units	Unit Cost
Manufacturing costs:			
Variable	$ 875,000	25,000	$35
Fixed	400,000	25,000	16
Total	$1,275,000		$51
Selling and general expenses:			
Variable ($5 per unit sold) . . .	$ 100,000		
Fixed	100,000		
Total	$ 200,000		

Brownstein Manufacturing Company has no beginning inventory, and sales are estimated to be 20,000 units at $75 per unit, regardless of production levels. If the company manufactures 20,000 units, which is an amount equal to the estimated sales, income from operations under absorption costing would be $200,000. However, the reported income from operations could be increased by $80,000 by manufacturing 25,000 units and adding 5,000 units to the finished goods inventory. The absorption costing income statements illustrating this effect are as follows:

ABSORPTION COSTING INCOME STATEMENTS

Absorption Costing Income Statements		
	20,000 Units Manufactured	25,000 Units Manufactured
Sales (20,000 units × $75)	$1,500,000	$1,500,000
Cost of goods sold:		
Cost of goods manufactured:		
(20,000 units × $55)	$1,100,000	
(25,000 units × $51)		$1,275,000
Less ending inventory:		
(5,000 units × $51)		255,000
Cost of goods sold	$1,100,000	$1,020,000
Gross profit	$ 400,000	$ 480,000
Selling and general expenses ($100,000 + $100,000)	200,000	200,000
Income from operations	$ 200,000	$ 280,000

The $80,000 increase in operating income would be caused by the allocation of the fixed manufacturing costs of $400,000 over a greater number of units of production. Specifically, an increase in production from 20,000 units to 25,000 units meant that the fixed manufacturing costs per unit decreased from $20 ($400,000 ÷ 20,000 units) to $16 ($400,000 ÷ 25,000 units). Thus, the cost of goods sold when 25,000 units are manufactured would be $4 per unit less, or $80,000 less in total (20,000 units sold times $4). Since the cost of goods sold is less, operating income is $80,000 more when 25,000 units are manufactured rather than 20,000 units.

Under the variable costing concept, income from operations would have been $200,000, regardless of the amount by which units manufactured exceeded sales, because no fixed manufacturing costs are allocated to the units manufactured. To illustrate, the following variable costing income statements are presented for Brownstein for the production of 20,000 units, 25,000 units, and 30,000 units. In each case, the income from operations is $200,000.

VARIABLE COSTING INCOME STATEMENTS

Variable Costing Income Statements			
	20,000 Units Manufactured	25,000 Units Manufactured	30,000 Units Manufactured
Sales (20,000 units × $75) ..	$1,500,000	$1,500,000	$1,500,000
Variable cost of goods sold:			
Variable cost of goods manufactured:			
(20,000 units × $35)....	$ 700,000		
(25,000 units × $35)....		$ 875,000	
(30,000 units × $35)....			$1,050,000
Less ending inventory:			
(0 units × $35).........	0		
(5,000 units × $35).....		175,000	
(10,000 units × $35)....			350,000
Variable cost of goods sold................	$ 700,000	$ 700,000	$ 700,000
Manufacturing margin.......	$ 800,000	$ 800,000	$ 800,000
Variable selling and general expenses...............	100,000	100,000	100,000
Contribution margin........	$ 700,000	$ 700,000	$ 700,000
Fixed costs and expenses:			
Fixed manufacturing costs..	$ 400,000	$ 400,000	$ 400,000
Fixed selling and general expenses..............	100,000	100,000	100,000
Total fixed costs and expenses..............	$ 500,000	$ 500,000	$ 500,000
Income from operations	$ 200,000	$ 200,000	$ 200,000

As illustrated, if absorption costing is used, management should be careful in analyzing income from operations when large changes in inventory levels occur. Otherwise, increases or decreases in income from operations due to changes in inventory levels could be misinterpreted to be the result of operating efficiencies or inefficiencies.

MANAGEMENT'S USE OF VARIABLE COSTING AND ABSORPTION COSTING

Both variable costing and absorption costing serve useful purposes for management. However, there are limitations to the use of both concepts in certain circumstances. Therefore, managerial accountants must carefully analyze each situation in evaluating whether variable costing reports or absorption costing reports would be more useful. In many situations, the preparation of reports under both concepts will provide useful insights. Such reports and their advantages and disadvantages are discussed in the following paragraphs.

Cost Control

All costs are controllable by someone within a business enterprise, but they are not all controllable at the same level of management. For example, plant supervisors, as members of operating management, are responsible for controlling the use of direct materials in their departments. They have no control, however, of the amount of insurance coverage or premium costs related to the buildings housing their departments. For a specific level of management, **controllable costs** are costs that it controls directly, and **uncontrollable costs** are costs that another level of management controls. This distinction, as applied to specific levels of management, is useful in fixing the responsibility for incurrence of costs and then for reporting the cost data to those responsible for cost control.

Variable manufacturing costs are controlled at the operating level because the amount of such costs varies with changes in the volume of production. By including only variable manufacturing costs in the cost of the product, variable costing provides a product cost figure that can be controlled by operating management. The fixed factory overhead costs are ordinarily the responsibility of a higher level of management. When the fixed factory overhead costs are reported as a separate item in the variable costing income statement, they are easier to identify and control than when they are spread among units of product as they are under absorption costing.

As is the case with the fixed and variable manufacturing costs, the control of the variable and fixed operating expenses is usually the responsibility of different levels of management. Under variable costing, the variable selling and general expenses are reported in a separate category from the fixed selling and general expenses. Because they are reported in this manner, both types of operating expenses are easier to identify and control than is the case under absorption costing, where they are not reported separately.

Product Pricing

Many factors enter into the determination of the selling price of a product. The cost of making the product is clearly significant. Microeconomic theory deduces, from a set of restrictive assumptions, that income is maximized by expanding output to the volume where the revenue realized by the sale of the final unit (marginal revenue) equals the cost of that unit (marginal cost). Although the degree of exactness assumed in economic theory is rarely attainable, the concepts of marginal revenue and marginal cost are useful in setting selling prices.

In the short run, an enterprise is committed to the existing capacity of its manufacturing facilities. The pricing decision should be based upon making the best use of such capacity. The fixed costs and expenses cannot be avoided, but the variable costs and expenses can be eliminated if the company does not manufacture the product. The selling price of a product, therefore, should at least be equal to the variable costs and expenses of making and selling it. Any price above this minimum selling price contributes an amount toward covering fixed costs and expenses and providing operating income. Variable costing procedures yield data that emphasize these relationships.

In the long run, plant capacity can be increased or decreased. If an enterprise is to continue in business, the selling prices of its products must cover all costs and expenses and provide a reasonable operating income. Hence, in establishing pricing policies for the long run, information provided by absorption costing procedures is needed.

The results of a recent research study sponsored by the National Association of Accountants indicated that the companies studied used absorption costing in making routine pricing decisions. However, these companies regularly used variable costing as a basis for setting prices in many short-run situations.[1]

There are no simple solutions to most pricing problems. Consideration must be given to many factors of varying importance. Accounting can contribute by preparing analyses of various pricing plans for both the short run and the long run.

---

[1]Thomas M. Bruegelmann, Gaile A. Haessly, Michael Schiff, and Clarie P. Wolfangel, *The Use of Variable Costing in Pricing Decisions*, National Association of Accountants (Montvale, New Jersey, 1986), p. vii.

Production Planning

Production planning also has both short-run and long-run implications. In the short run, production is limited to existing capacity, and operating decisions must be made quickly before opportunities are lost. For example, a company manufacturing products with a seasonal demand may have an opportunity to obtain an off-season order that will not interfere with its production schedule nor reduce the sales of its other products. The relevant factors for such a short-run decision are the revenues and the variable costs and expenses. If the revenues from the special order will provide a contribution margin, the order should be accepted because it will increase the company's operating income. For long-run planning, management must also consider the fixed costs and expenses.

Sales Analysis

The primary objective of the marketing and sales functions is to offer the company's products for sale at prices that will result in an adequate amount of income relative to the total assets employed. To evaluate these functions properly, management needs information concerning the profitability of various types of products and sales mixes, sales territories, and salespersons. Variable costing can make a significant contribution to management decision making in such areas.

Sales Mix Analysis. Sales mix, sometimes referred to as product mix, is generally defined as the relative distribution of sales among the various products sold. Some products are more profitable than others, and management should concentrate its sales efforts on those that will provide the maximum total operating income.

Sales mix studies are based on assumptions, such as the ability to sell one product in place of another and the ability to convert production facilities to accommodate the manufacture of one product instead of another. Proposed changes in the sales mix often affect only small segments of a company's total operations. In such cases, changes in sales mix may be possible within the limits of existing capacity, and the presentation of cost and revenue data in the variable costing form is useful in achieving the most profitable sales mix.

Two very important factors that should be determined for each product are (1) the production facilities needed for its manufacture and (2) the amount of contribution margin to be gained from its manufacture. If two or more products require equal use of limited production facilities, then management should concentrate its sales and production efforts on the product or products with the highest contribution margin per unit. The following report, which focuses on product contribution margins, is an example of the type of data needed for an evaluation of sales mix. The enterprise, which manufactures two products and is operating at full capacity, is considering whether to change the emphasis of its advertising and other promotional efforts.

Contribution Margin by Unit of Product
April 15, 19--

	Product A	Product B
Sales price	$6.00	$8.50
Variable cost of goods sold	3.50	5.50
Manufacturing margin	$2.50	$3.00
Variable selling and general expenses	1.00	1.00
Contribution margin	$1.50	$2.00

CONTRI-BUTION MARGIN STATE-MENT— UNIT OF PRODUCT

The statement indicates that Product B yields a greater amount of contribution margin per unit than Product A. Therefore, Product B provides the larger contribution to the recovery of fixed costs and expenses and realization of operating income. If the amount of production facilities used for each product is assumed to be equal, it would be desirable to increase the sales of Product B.

If two or more products require unequal use of production resources, management should concentrate its sales and production efforts on that product or products with the highest contribution margin per unit of resource. For example, assume that in the above illustration, to manufacture Product B requires twice the machine hours required for Product A. Specifically, Product B requires 2 machine hours per unit, while Product A requires only 1 machine hour per unit. Under this assumption, the contribution margin per unit of resource (machine hours) is $1.50 ($1.50 contribution margin ÷ 1 machine hour) for Product A and $1 ($2 contribution margin ÷ 2 machine hours) for Product B. Under such circumstances, a change in sales mix designed to increase sales of Product A would be desirable.

To illustrate, if 2,000 additional units of Product A (requiring 2,000 machine hours) could be sold in place of 1,000 units of Product B (also requiring 2,000 machine hours), the total company contribution margin would increase by $1,000, as follows:

Additional contribution margin from sale of additional 2,000 units of Product A ($1.50 × 2,000 units)	$3,000
Less contribution margin from forgoing production and sale of 1,000 units of Product B ($2 × 1,000 units)	2,000
Increase in total contribution margin	$1,000

Sales Territory Analysis. An income statement presenting the contribution margin by sales territories is often useful to management in appraising past performance and in directing future sales efforts. The following income statement is prepared in such a format, in abbreviated form:

CONTRI-
BUTION
MARGIN
STATE-
MENT—
SALES
TERRITORIES

Contribution Margin Statement by Sales Territory
For Month Ended July 31, 19--

	Territory A	Territory B	Total
Sales................................	$315,000	$502,500	$817,500
Less variable costs and expenses......	189,000	251,250	440,250
Contribution margin..................	$126,000	$251,250	$377,250
Less fixed costs and expenses.........			242,750
Income from operations			$134,500

In addition to the contribution margin, the **contribution margin ratio** (contribution margin divided by sales) for each territory is useful in evaluating sales territories and directing operations toward more profitable activities. For Territory A, the contribution margin ratio is 40% ($126,000 ÷ $315,000), and for Territory B the ratio is 50% ($251,250 ÷ $502,500). Consequently, more profitability could be achieved by efforts to increase the sales of Territory B relative to Territory A.

Salespersons' Analysis. A report to management for use in evaluating the sales performance of each salesperson could include total sales, gross profit, gross profit percentage, total selling expenses, and contribution to company profit. Such a report is illustrated as follows:

Salespersons' Analysis
For Six Months Ended June 30, 19--

Sales-person	Total Sales	Gross Profit	Gross Profit Percentage	Total Selling Expenses	Contribution to Company Profit
A	$300,000	$120,000	40%	$24,000	$ 96,000
B	250,000	75,000	30	22,500	52,500
C	500,000	125,000	25	35,000	90,000
D	180,000	72,000	40	18,000	54,000
E	460,000	197,800	43	27,600	170,200
F	320,000	112,000	35	22,400	89,600

The preceding report illustrates that the total sales figure is not the only consideration in evaluating a salesperson. For example, although salesperson C has the highest total sales, C's sales are not contributing as much to overall company profits as are the sales of A and E, primarily because C's sales have the lowest gross profit percentage. Of the six salespersons, E is generating the highest dollar contribution to company profit and is selling the most profitable mix of products, as measured by a gross profit percentage of 43%.

Other factors should also be considered in evaluating the performance of salespersons. For example, sales growth rates, years of experience, and actual performance compared to budgeted performance may be more important than total sales.

CHAPTER REVIEW

KEY POINTS

1. Characteristics of Managerial Accounting Reports.

The usefulness of an accounting report for management depends upon the relevance of the economic information reported, and the timeliness, the accuracy, the clarity, and the conciseness of the report. In applying the preceding characteristics, the cost of preparing a report should not exceed the benefit derived from it by its users.

2. Gross Profit Analysis.

A change in the amount of gross profit can be caused by (1) an increase or decrease in the amount of sales and (2) an increase or decrease in the amount of the cost of goods sold. An increase or decrease in either element may in turn be due to (1) a change in the number of units sold and (2) a change in the unit price. These two factors are known as the quantity factor and the price factor respectively.

3. Absorption Costing and Variable Costing.

The costs of manufacturing are direct materials, direct labor, and factory overhead. Under absorption costing, all such costs become part of the cost of goods manufactured. Under variable costing, the cost of goods manufactured is composed of only variable costs — those manufacturing costs that increase or decrease as the volume of production rises or falls. These costs are the direct materials, direct labor, and only those factory overhead costs which vary with the rate of production. The fixed factory overhead costs do not become a part of the cost of goods manufactured, but are considered an expense of the period. In the variable costing income statement, the deduction of the cost of goods sold from sales yields an intermediate amount, termed manufacturing margin. Deduction of the variable selling and general expenses yields the contribution margin. Fixed costs and expenses are then deducted from the contribution margin to yield income from operations.

A comparison of income reported under the absorption costing and variable costing concepts when the level of inventory changes during the period is summarized in the following table:

Units manufactured:

Equal units sold	Absorption costing income equals variable costing income.
Exceed units sold.	Absorption costing income is greater than variable costing income.
Less than units sold.	Absorption costing income is less than variable costing income.

The possible effects of any changes in inventory levels on operating income should be considered when management analyzes and evaluates operations.

4. Management's Use of Variable Costing and Absorption Costing.

Variable costing is especially useful at the operating level of management because the amount of variable manufacturing costs varies with changes in the volume of production and thus is controllable at this level. The fixed factory overhead costs are ordinarily controllable by a higher level of management.

In the short run, variable costing may be useful in establishing the selling price of a product. This price should be at least equal to the variable costs and expenses of making and selling the product. In the long run, however, absorption costing procedures are useful in establishing selling prices, in that all costs and expenses and a reasonable amount of operating income must be earned.

Variable costing can make a significant contribution to management decision making in analyzing and evaluating sales. Management should concentrate its sales efforts on those products that will provide the maximum total operating income. Sales mix studies emphasize the contribution margin of each product in evaluating sales territories and directing operations towards more profitable activities. In addition, a salespersons' analysis report may be useful to management in evaluating the sales performance of each salesperson. Such a report emphasizes the contribution of each salesperson to the overall company profit.

KEY TERMS

gross profit analysis 1127
absorption costing 1129
variable costing 1130
manufacturing margin 1132

contribution margin 1132
sales mix 1140
contribution margin ratio 1142

SELF-EXAMINATION QUESTIONS
Answers in Appendix B.

1. If sales totaled $800,000 for the current year (80,000 units at $10 each) and $765,000 for the preceding year (85,000 units at $9 each), the effect of the quantity factor on the change in sales is:
   A. a $50,000 increase
   B. a $35,000 decrease
   C. a $45,000 decrease
   D. none of the above

2. The concept that considers the cost of products manufactured to be composed only of those manufacturing costs that vary with the rate of production is known as:
   A. absorption costing
   B. variable costing
   C. replacement cost
   D. none of the above

3. In an income statement prepared under the variable costing concept, the deduction of the variable cost of goods sold from sales yields an intermediate amount referred to as:
   A. gross profit
   B. contribution margin
   C. manufacturing margin
   D. none of the above

4. Sales were $750,000, variable cost of goods sold was $400,000, variable selling and general expenses were $90,000, and fixed costs and expenses were $200,000. The contribution margin was:
   A. $60,000
   B. $260,000
   C. $350,000
   D. none of the above

5. During a year in which the number of units manufactured exceeded the number of units sold, the operating income reported under the absorption costing concept would be:
   A. larger than the operating income reported under the variable costing concept
   B. smaller than the operating income reported under the variable costing concept
   C. the same as the operating income reported under the variable costing concept
   D. none of the above

ILLUSTRATIVE PROBLEM

During the current period, McLaughlin Company sold 60,000 units of product at a selling price of $30 per unit. At the beginning of the period, there were 10,000 units in inventory and McLaughlin Company manufactured 50,000 units during the period. The manufacturing costs and selling and general expenses were as follows:

	Total Cost or Expense	Number of Units	Unit Cost
Beginning inventory:			
Direct materials............................	$ 67,000	10,000	$ 6.70
Direct labor................................	155,000	10,000	15.50
Variable factory overhead.................	18,000	10,000	1.80
Fixed factory overhead....................	20,000	10,000	2.00
Total......................................	$ 260,000		$26.00
Current period costs:			
Direct materials............................	$ 350,000	50,000	$ 7.00
Direct labor................................	810,000	50,000	16.20
Variable factory overhead.................	90,000	50,000	1.80
Fixed factory overhead....................	100,000	50,000	2.00
Total......................................	$1,350,000		$27.00
Selling and general expenses:			
Variable	$ 65,000		
Fixed.....................................	45,000		
Total......................................	$ 110,000		

Instructions:

1. Prepare an income statement based on the absorption costing concept.
2. Prepare an income statement based on the variable costing concept.
3. Explain the reason for the difference in the amount of operating income reported in *1* and *2*.

SOLUTION

(1)   Absorption Costing Income Statement

Sales (60,000 × $30)		$1,800,000
Cost of goods sold:		
Beginning inventory (10,000 × $26)	$ 260,000	
Cost of goods manufactured (50,000 × $27)	1,350,000	
Cost of goods sold....................		1,610,000
Gross profit.............................		$ 190,000
Selling and general expenses ($65,000 + $45,000)		110,000
Income from operations..................		$ 80,000

(2)

Variable Costing Income Statement		
Sales (60,000 × $30)		$1,800,000
Variable cost of goods sold:		
Beginning inventory (10,000 × $24)	$ 240,000	
Variable cost of goods manufactured		
(50,000 × $25)................,........	1,250,000	
Variable cost of goods sold		1,490,000
Manufacturing margin		$ 310,000
Variable selling and general expenses		65,000
Contribution margin.....................		$ 245,000
Fixed costs and expenses:		
Fixed manufacturing costs...............	$ 100,000	
Fixed selling and general expenses	45,000	145,000
Income from operations..................		$ 100,000

(3) The difference of $20,000 ($100,000 − $80,000) in the amount of income from operations is attributable to the different treatment of the fixed manufacturing costs. The beginning inventory in the absorption costing income statement includes $20,000 (10,000 units × $2) of fixed manufacturing costs incurred in the preceding period. This $20,000 was included as an expense in a variable costing income statement of a prior period, however. Therefore, none of it is included as an expense in the current period variable costing income statement.

DISCUSSION QUESTIONS

1. What is the dominant principle that guides the managerial accountant in preparing management reports?

2. What are the five characteristics of useful managerial accounting reports?

3. In planning production, forecasts are often used rather than data from past operations. (a) What general characteristics of managerial accounting reports support the use of forecast data? (b) What general characteristic of managerial accounting reports is sacrificed when forecasted data rather than past data are used?

4. Farnell Company is contemplating the expansion of its operations through the purchase of the assets of Jaffe Lumber Company. Included among the assets of Jaffe Lumber Company is lumber purchased for $300,000 and having a current replacement cost of $350,000. Which cost ($300,000 or $350,000) is relevant for the decision to be made by Farnell Company? Briefly explain the reason for your answer.

5. A bank loan officer is evaluating a request for a loan that is to be secured by a mortgage on the borrower's property. The property cost $380,000 twenty years ago and has a current market value of $520,000. Which figure, $380,000 or $520,000, is relevant for the loan officer's use in evaluating the request for the loan? Discuss.

6. What is meant by cost-benefit balance as it relates to the preparation of management reports?

7. Discuss the two factors affecting both sales and cost of goods sold to which a change in gross profit can be attributed.

8. The analysis of increase in gross profit for a company includes the effect that an increase in the quantity of goods sold has had on the cost of goods sold. How is this figure determined?

9. What types of costs are customarily included in the cost of manufactured products under (a) the *absorption costing* concept and (b) the *variable costing* concept?

10. Which type of manufacturing cost (direct materials, direct labor, variable factory overhead, fixed factory overhead) is included in the cost of goods manufactured under the absorption costing concept but is excluded from the cost of goods manufactured under the variable costing concept?

11. At the end of the first year of operations, 500 units remained in the finished goods inventory. The unit manufacturing costs during the year were as follows:

Direct materials............................ $ 3.00
Direct labor................................ 24.00
Fixed factory overhead 1.50
Variable factory overhead .... .50

What would be the cost of the finished goods inventory reported on the balance sheet under (a) the absorption costing concept and (b) the variable costing concept?

12. Which of the following costs would be included in the cost of a manufactured product according to the variable costing concept: (a) electricity purchased to operate factory equipment, (b) property taxes on factory building, (c) direct labor, (d) salary of factory supervisor, (e) direct materials, (f) depreciation on factory building, and (g) rent on factory building?

13. In the following equations, based on the variable costing income statement, identify the items designated by **X**:
(a) Net sales − **X** = manufacturing margin
(b) Manufacturing margin − **X** = contribution margin
(c) Contribution margin − **X** = income from operations

14. In the variable costing income statement, how are the fixed manufacturing costs reported and how are the fixed selling and general expenses reported?

15. If the quantity of the ending inventory is larger than that of the beginning inventory, will the amount of income from operations determined by absorption costing be more than or less than the amount determined by variable costing? Explain.

16. Since all costs of operating a business are controllable, what is the significance of the term *uncontrollable cost*?

17. Discuss how financial data prepared on the basis of variable costing can assist management in the development of short-run pricing policies.

18. What term is used to refer to the relative distribution of sales among the various products manufactured?

19. A company, operating at full capacity, manufactures two products, with Product E requiring three times the production facilities as Product F. The contribution margin is $50 per unit for Product E and $15 per unit for Product F. How much would the total contribution margin be increased or decreased for the coming year if the sales of Product E could be increased by 1,000 units by changing the emphasis of promotional efforts?

20. Explain why rewarding sales personnel on the basis of total sales might not be in the best interests of an enterprise whose goal is to maximize profits.

21. Real World Focus. Dutch Pantry Inc. operates 53 full-service family restaurants in 12 eastern states. To assure consistent quality, many of the items served in the restaurants are prepared in a central food processing plant. Classify each of the following costs and expenses of the food processing plant as either variable or fixed.
   (a) Cooking oil
   (b) Office salaries
   (c) Electricity
   (d) Experimental costs and expenses
   (e) Depreciation on equipment (straight-line method)
   (f) Garbage collection expense
   (g) Water
   (h) Cleaning supplies
   (i) Property taxes
   (j) Salad dressing
   (k) Spices

EXERCISES

SPREADSHEET PROBLEM

Exercise 25–1. Gross profit analysis report. The following data for Driscoll Company are available:

	For Year Ended March 31			
	1988		1987	
Sales	60,000 units at $20	$1,200,000	40,000 units at $25.00	$1,000,000
Cost of goods sold........	60,000 units at $14	840,000	40,000 units at $13.50	540,000
Gross profit...		$ 360,000		$ 460,000

Prepare an analysis of the decrease in gross profit for the year ended March 31, 1988.

Exercise 25–2. Income statements under absorption costing and variable costing. Casey Company began operations on July 1 and operated at 100% of capacity during the first month. The following data summarize the results for July:

Sales (12,000 units)........................		$600,000
Production costs (15,000 units):		
Direct materials...........................	$150,000	
Direct labor..............................	180,000	
Variable factory overhead..................	45,000	
Fixed factory overhead	30,000	405,000
Selling and general expenses:		
Variable selling and general expenses........	$ 60,000	
Fixed selling and general expenses	18,000	78,000

(a) Prepare an income statement in accordance with the absorption costing concept. (b) Prepare an income statement in accordance with the variable costing concept. (c) What is the reason for the difference in the amount of operating income reported in (a) and (b)?

Exercise 25–3. Cost of goods manufactured, using variable costing and absorption costing. On October 31, the end of the first year of operations, Kanter Company manufactured 40,000 units and sold 35,000 units. The following income statement was prepared, based on the variable costing concept:

Kanter Company
Income Statement
For Year Ended October 31, 19--

Sales...		$700,000
Variable cost of goods sold:		
Variable cost of goods manufactured..............	$480,000	
Less ending inventory...........................	60,000	
Variable cost of goods sold		420,000
Manufacturing margin		$280,000
Variable selling and general expenses		70,000
Contribution margin		$210,000
Fixed costs and expenses:		
Fixed manufacturing costs.......................	$ 60,000	
Fixed selling and general expenses................	50,000	110,000
Income from operations		$100,000

Determine the unit cost of goods manufactured, based on (a) the variable costing concept and (b) the absorption costing concept.

Exercise 25–4. Variable costing income statement. On June 30, the end of the first month of operations, Lloyd Company prepared the following income statement, based on the absorption costing concept:

Lloyd Company
Income Statement
For Month Ended June 30, 19--

Sales (4,400 units).............................		$66,000
Cost of goods sold:		
Cost of goods manufactured	$45,000	
Less ending inventory (600 units)...................	5,400	
Cost of goods sold............................		39,600
Gross profit		$26,400
Selling and general expenses.......................		15,800
Income from operations		$10,600

If the fixed manufacturing costs were $15,000 and the variable selling and general expenses were $7,700, prepare an income statement in accordance with the variable costing concept.

Exercise 25–5. Absorption costing income statement. On April 30, the end of the first month of operations, Moyer Company prepared the following income statement, based on the variable costing concept:

Moyer Company
Income Statement
For Month Ended April 30, 19--

Sales (18,000 units)...............................		$360,000
Variable cost of goods sold:		
Variable cost of goods manufactured..............	$200,000	
Less ending inventory (2,000 units)	20,000	
Variable cost of goods sold		180,000
Manufacturing margin		$180,000
Variable selling and general expenses		36,000
Contribution margin.................................		$144,000
Fixed costs and expenses:		
Fixed manufacturing costs........................	$ 50,000	
Fixed selling and general expenses...............	29,000	79,000
Income from operations		$ 65,000

Prepare an income statement in accordance with the absorption costing concept.

Exercise 25–6. Estimated income statements, using absorption and variable costing. Prior to the first month of operations ending January 31, Lester Company estimated the following operating results:

Sales (1,000 × $50)..	$50,000
Manufacturing costs (1,000 units):	
Direct materials.......................................	15,000
Direct labor..	10,000
Variable factory overhead.............................	7,000
Fixed factory overhead	4,800
Fixed selling and general expenses	6,500
Variable selling and general expenses....................	2,000

The company is evaluating a proposal to manufacture 1,200 units instead of 1,000 units.

(a) Assuming no change in sales, unit variable manufacturing costs, and fixed factory overhead and total selling and general expenses, prepare an estimated income statement, comparing operating results if 1,000 and 1,200 units are manufactured, in the (1) absorption costing format and (2) variable costing format. (b) What is the reason for the difference in income from operations reported for the two levels of production by the absorption costing income statement?

Exercise 25–7.   Change in sales mix and contribution margin. Van Cleave Company manufactures Products A and B and is operating at full capacity. To manufacture Product A requires four times the number of machine hours as required for Product B. Market research indicates that 2,000 additional units of Product B could be sold. The contribution margin by unit of product is as follows:

	Product A	Product B
Sales price.................................	$120	$50
Variable cost of goods sold..................	70	36
Manufacturing margin	$ 50	$14
Variable selling and general expenses........	32	9
Contribution margin	$ 18	$ 5

Prepare a tabulation indicating the increase or decrease in total contribution margin if 2,000 additional units of Product B are produced and sold.

Exercise 25–8.   Real World Focus. The following data were adapted from the income statement of General Electric Company for the year ended December 31, 1985:

	In Millions
Sales of products and services to customers	$28,285
Operating costs:	
Cost of goods sold.....................................	19,775
Selling, general, and administrative expense	4,349
Depreciation and amortization	1,226
Operating costs......................................	$25,350
Income from operations................................	$ 2,935

Assume that the variable amount of each category of operating costs is as follows:

Cost of goods sold	$15,820
Selling, general, and administrative expense	2,200
Depreciation and amortization	-0-

Based on the above data, prepare a variable costing income statement for General Electric Company for the year ended December 31, 1985.

PROBLEMS

Series A

Problem 25–1A. Gross profit analysis report. Towns Company manufactures only one product. In 1987, the plant operated at full capacity. At a meeting of the board of directors on November 17, 1987, it was decided to raise the price of this product from $60, which had prevailed last year, to $65, effective January 1, 1988. Although the cost price was expected to rise about $2.40 per unit in 1988 because of increases in the cost of direct materials and direct labor, the increase in selling price was expected to cover these increases and also add to operating income. The comparative income statement for 1987 and 1988 is as follows:

	1988		1987	
Sales		$227,500		$240,000
Cost of goods sold: variable	$120,400		$128,000	
fixed	14,000	134,400	14,000	142,000
Gross profit		$ 93,100		$ 98,000
Operating expenses: variable	$ 16,800		$ 19,200	
fixed	40,000	56,800	40,000	59,200
Operating income		$ 36,300		$ 38,800

Instructions:

(1) Prepare a gross profit analysis report for the year 1988.
(2) At a meeting of the board of directors on April 3, 1989, the president, after reading the gross profit analysis report, made the following comment:
> It looks as if the increase in unit cost price was $2.90 and not the anticipated $2.40. The failure of operating management to keep these costs within the bounds of those in 1987, except for the anticipated $2.40 increase in direct materials and direct labor cost, was a major factor in the decrease in gross profit.

Do you agree with this analysis of the increase in unit cost price? Explain.

Problem 25–2A. Absorption and variable costing income statements. During the first month of operations ended October 31, Woodruff Company manufactured 150,000 units, of which 120,000 were sold. Operating data for the month are summarized as follows:

Sales.....................................		$840,000
Manufacturing costs:		
Direct materials..........................	$150,000	
Direct labor..............................	330,000	
Variable factory overhead..................	120,000	
Fixed factory overhead	60,000	660,000
Selling and general expenses:		
Variable..................................	$ 72,000	
Fixed....................................	48,000	120,000

Instructions:

(1) Prepare an income statement based on the absorption costing concept.
(2) Prepare an income statement based on the variable costing concept.
(3) Explain the reason for the difference in the amount of operating income reported in (1) and (2).

Problem 25–3A. Income statements under absorption costing and variable costing. The demand for Product H, one of numerous products manufactured by Sommer Inc., has dropped sharply because of recent competition from a similar product. The company's chemists are currently completing tests of various new formulas, and it is anticipated that the manufacture of a superior product can be started on June 1, one month hence. No changes will be needed in the present production facilities to manufacture the new product because only the mixture of the various materials will be changed.

The controller has been asked by the president of the company for advice on whether to continue production during May or to suspend the manufacture of Product H until June 1. The controller has assembled the following pertinent data:

Sommer Inc.
Estimated Income Statement—Product H
For Month Ending April 30, 19--

Sales (20,000 units)	$800,000
Cost of goods sold	760,500
Gross profit................................	$ 39,500
Selling and general expenses...............	84,000
Loss from operations	$ 44,500

The estimated production costs and selling and general expenses, based on a production of 20,000 units, are as follows:

Direct materials....................................	$14.50 per unit
Direct labor.......................................	18.00 per unit
Variable factory overhead.........................	2.50 per unit
Variable selling and general expenses..............	3.00 per unit
Fixed factory overhead	$60,500 for April
Fixed selling and general expenses	24,000 for April

Sales for May are expected to drop about 30% below those of the preceding month. No significant changes are anticipated in the production costs or operating expenses. No extra costs will be incurred in discontinuing operations in the portion of the plant associated with Product H. The inventory of Product H at the beginning and end of May is expected to be inconsequential.

Instructions:

(1) Prepare an estimated income statement in absorption costing form for May for Product H, assuming that production continues during the month.
(2) Prepare an estimated income statement in variable costing form for May for Product H, assuming that production continues during the month.
(3) State the estimated operating loss arising from the activities associated with Product H for May if production is temporarily suspended.
(4) Prepare a brief statement of the advice the controller should give.

Problem 25–4A.   Salespersons' report and analysis. Lin Company employs seven salespersons to sell and distribute its product throughout the state. Data extracted from reports received from the salespersons during the current year ended December 31 are as follows:

Salesperson	Total Sales	Cost of Goods Sold	Total Selling Expenses
Barr	$900,000	$585,000	$217,500
Farmer	675,000	418,500	175,500
Griffith	560,000	341,600	118,400
Murray	600,000	372,000	141,000
Owens	375,000	225,000	78,000
Thom	480,000	278,400	112,500
York	525,000	315,000	114,000

Instructions:

(1) Prepare a report for the year, indicating total sales, gross profit, gross profit percentage, total selling expenses, and contribution to company profit by salesperson.
(2) Which salesperson contributed the highest dollar amount to company profit during the year?
(3) Briefly list factors other than contribution to company profit that should be considered in evaluating the performance of salespersons.

Problem 25–5A. Variable costing income statement and effect on income of change in operations. T. E. Collins Company manufactures three styles of folding chairs, A, B, and C. The income statement has consistently indicated a net loss for Style B, and management is considering three proposals: (1) continue Style B, (2) discontinue Style B and reduce total output accordingly, or (3) discontinue Style B and conduct an advertising campaign to expand the sales of Style A so that the entire plant capacity can continue to be used.

If Proposal 2 is selected and Style B is discontinued and production curtailed, the annual fixed production costs and fixed operating expenses could be reduced by $22,500 and $12,000 respectively. If Proposal 3 is selected, it is anticipated that an additional annual expenditure of $40,000 for advertising Style A would yield an increase of 40% in its sales volume, and that the increased production of Style A would utilize the plant facilities released by the discontinuance of Style B.

The sales, costs, and expenses have been relatively stable over the past few years, and they are expected to remain so for the foreseeable future. The income statement for the past year ended August 31 is:

| | Style | | | |
	A	B	C	Total
Sales	$650,000	$190,000	$600,000	$1,440,000
Cost of goods sold:				
Variable costs	$370,000	$132,300	$330,000	$ 832,300
Fixed costs	125,000	40,700	120,000	285,700
Total cost of goods sold	$495,000	$173,000	$450,000	$1,118,000
Gross profit	$155,000	$ 17,000	$150,000	$ 322,000
Less operating expenses:				
Variable expenses	$ 64,800	$ 18,900	$ 60,000	$ 143,700
Fixed expenses	36,000	16,000	35,000	87,000
Total operating expenses	$100,800	$ 34,900	$ 95,000	$ 230,700
Income from operations	$ 54,200	$(17,900)	$ 55,000	$ 91,300

Instructions:

(1) Prepare an income statement for the past year in the variable costing format. Use the following headings:

| | Style | | | |
| | A | B | C | Total |

Data for each style should be reported through contribution margin. The fixed costs and expenses should be deducted from the total contribution margin, as reported in the "Total" column, to determine income from operations.

(2) Based on the income statement prepared in (1) and the other data presented above, determine the amount by which total annual operating income would be reduced below its present level if Proposal 2 is accepted.

(3) Prepare an income statement in the variable costing format, indicating the projected annual operating income if Proposal 3 is accepted. Use the following headings:

	Style		
	A	C	Total

Data for each style should be reported through contribution margin. The fixed costs and expenses should be deducted from the total contribution margin as reported in the "Total" column. For purposes of this problem, the additional expenditure of $40,000 for advertising can be added to the fixed operating expenses.

(4) By how much would total annual income increase above its present level if Proposal 3 is accepted? Explain.

Series B

Problem 25–1B. Gross profit analysis report. Ayers Company manufactures only one product. In 1987, the plant operated at full capacity. At a meeting of the board of directors on December 1, 1987, it was decided to raise the price of this product from $36, which had prevailed for the past few years, to $40, effective January 1, 1988. Although the cost price was expected to rise about $2 per unit in 1988 because of a direct materials and direct labor wage increase, the increase in selling price was expected to cover this increase and also add to operating income. The comparative income statement for 1987 and 1988 is as follows:

	1988		1987	
Sales		$640,000		$720,000
Cost of goods sold: variable	$377,600		$432,000	
fixed...........	48,000	425,600	48,000	480,000
Gross profit.......................		$214,400		$240,000
Operating expenses: variable	$ 96,000		$120,000	
fixed..........	50,000	146,000	50,000	170,000
Operating income		$ 68,400		$ 70,000

Instructions:

(1) Prepare a gross profit analysis report for the year 1988.
(2) At a meeting of the board of directors on March 10, 1989, the president, after reading the gross profit analysis report, made the following comment:

It looks as if the increase in unit cost price was $2.60 and not the anticipated $2. The failure of operating management to keep these costs within the bounds of those in 1987, except for the anticipated $2 increase in direct materials and direct labor cost, was a major factor in the decrease in gross profit.

Do you agree with this analysis of the increase in unit cost price? Explain.

Problem 25–2B. Absorption and variable costing income statements. During the first month of operations ended April 30, Hyatt Company manufactured 80,000 units, of which 60,000 were sold. Operating data for the month are summarized as follows:

Sales.......................................		$480,000
Manufacturing costs:		
Direct materials...........................	$ 96,000	
Direct labor..............................	192,000	
Variable factory overhead..................	60,000	
Fixed factory overhead	120,000	468,000
Selling and general expenses:		
Variable..................................	$ 66,000	
Fixed.....................................	35,000	101,000

Instructions:

(1) Prepare an income statement based on the absorption costing concept.
(2) Prepare an income statement based on the variable costing concept.
(3) Explain the reason for the difference in the amount of operating income reported in (1) and (2).

Problem 25–3B. Income statements under absorption costing and variable costing. The demand for Product X, one of numerous products manufactured by Engel Inc., has dropped sharply because of recent competition from a similar product. The company's chemists are currently completing tests of various new formulas, and it is anticipated that the manufacture of a superior product can be started on August 1, one month hence. No changes will be needed in the present production facilities to manufacture the new product because only the mixture of the various materials will be changed.

The controller has been asked by the president of the company for advice on whether to continue production during July or to suspend the manufacture of Product X until August 1. The controller has assembled the following pertinent data:

Engel Inc.
Estimated Income Statement—Product X
For Month Ending June 30, 19--

Sales (10,000 units)	$200,000
Cost of goods sold	157,000
Gross profit..............................	$ 43,000
Selling and general expenses..............	50,000
Loss from operations	$ 7,000

The estimated production costs and selling and general expenses, based on a production of 10,000 units, are as follows:

Direct materials.................................	$4.50 per unit
Direct labor....................................	6.00 per unit
Variable factory overhead.......................	1.20 per unit
Variable selling and general expenses............	2.00 per unit
Fixed factory overhead	$40,000 for June
Fixed selling and general expenses	30,000 for June

Sales for July are expected to drop about 50% below those of the preceding month. No significant changes are anticipated in the production costs or operating expenses. No extra costs will be incurred in discontinuing operations in the portion of the plant associated with Product X. The inventory of Product X at the beginning and end of July is expected to be inconsequential.

Instructions:

(1) Prepare an estimated income statement in absorption costing form for July for Product X, assuming that production continues during the month.
(2) Prepare an estimated income statement in variable costing form for July for Product X, assuming that production continues during the month.
(3) State the estimated operating loss arising from the activities associated with Product X for July if production is temporarily suspended.
(4) Prepare a brief statement of the advice the controller should give.

MINI-CASE 25

SCHOOLCRAFT MOTORS

Your father operates a family-owned automotive dealership. Recently, the city government has requested bids on the purchase of 10 sedans for use by the city police department. Although the city prefers to purchase from local dealerships, state law requires the acceptance of the lowest bid. The past several contracts for automotive purchases have been granted to dealerships from surrounding communities.

The following data were taken from the dealership records for the normal sale of the automobile for which current bids have been requested:

Retail list price of sedan	$13,600
Cost allocated to normal sale:	
Dealer cost from manufacturer.	10,800
Fixed overhead	500
Shipping charges from manufacturer	420
Preparation charges.	100
Sales commission based on selling price	6%

Your father has asked you to help him in arriving at a "winning" bid price for this contract. In the past, your father has always bid $300 above the total cost (including fixed overhead). No sales commissions will be paid if the bid is accepted, and your father has indicated that the bid price must contribute at least $300 per car to the profits of the dealership.

Instructions:

(1) Do you think that your father has used good bidding procedures for prior contracts? Explain.
(2) What should be the bid price, based upon your father's profit objectives?
(3) Explain why the bid price determined in (2) would not be an acceptable price for normal customers.

Chapter 26

COST-VOLUME-
PROFIT ANALYSIS

Chapter Objectives:

- Describe the use of analyses of cost-volume-profit relationships in planning operations.

- Describe and illustrate the mathematical approach to costvolume-profit analysis.

- Describe and illustrate the graphic approach to cost-volumeprofit analysis.

- Describe and illustrate special cost-volume-profit relationships.

- Describe the general use of quantitative techniques by management.

- Describe and illustrate the use of quantitative techniques for inventory control.

In Chapter 25, three forms of profit analysis useful in planning and controlling operations—gross profit analysis, absorption costing, and variable costing—were discussed and illustrated. Cost-volume-profit analysis, described in this chapter, is another tool for management's use in making decisions that affect the profitability of the business. This chapter also discusses quantitative techniques, which rely on sophisticated mathematical relationships and statistical methods. The application of these techniques to inventory control is illustrated.

COST-VOLUME-PROFIT RELATIONSHIPS

Cost-volume-profit analysis is the systematic examination of the interrelationships between selling prices, volume of sales and production, costs, expenses, and profits. This analysis is a complex matter, since these relationships are often affected by forces entirely or partially beyond management's control. For example, the determination of the selling price of a product is often affected by not only the costs of production, but also by uncontrollable factors in the marketplace. On the other hand, the cost of producing the product is affected by such controllable factors as the efficiency of operations and the volume of production.

Accountants can play an important role in cost-volume-profit analysis by providing management with information on the relative profitability of its various products, the probable effects of changes in selling price, and other variables. Such information can help management improve the relationship between these variables. For example, an analysis of sales and cost data can be helpful in determining the level of sales volume necessary for the business to earn a satisfactory profit.

Costs represent one of the most significant factors in cost-volume-profit analysis. For this purpose, all operating costs and expenses must be subdivided into two categories: (1) variable and (2) fixed. In this chapter, the term "cost" is often used as a convenience to represent both "costs" and "expenses."

Variable Costs

Variable costs are costs that change, in total, as the volume of activity changes. For example, assume that Product Q requires $5 of direct materials per unit. The total direct materials cost of manufacturing 10,000 units is $50,000; 20,000 units require direct materials of $100,000; and so on. Note that the unit cost of the direct materials ($5) remains constant with changes in volume. These variable cost relationships are shown in the following graphs:

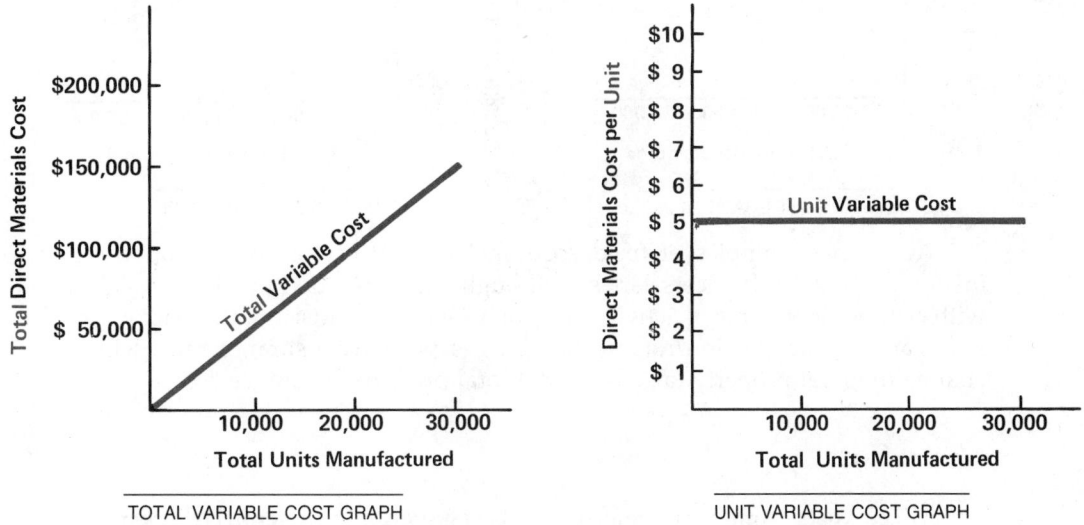

TOTAL VARIABLE COST GRAPH UNIT VARIABLE COST GRAPH

Direct labor, as well as direct materials, is a variable cost. Similarly, items such as supplies, electricity, indirect materials, and sales commissions are additional examples of variable costs and expenses.

Fixed Costs

Fixed costs remain constant, in total, as the volume of activity changes. For example, straight-line depreciation of $200,000 on factory buildings and equipment will not change, regardless of whether 10,000 units or 20,000 units of product are manufactured. Although fixed costs do not vary in total with changes in volume of activity, the unit cost will change with changes in activity. If volume increases, the unit cost will decrease, and if volume decreases, the unit cost will increase. For example, the unit cost of straight-line depreciation of $200,000 for 10,000 units is $20, and for 20,000 units of product, the unit cost is $10. These fixed cost relationships are shown in the following graphs:

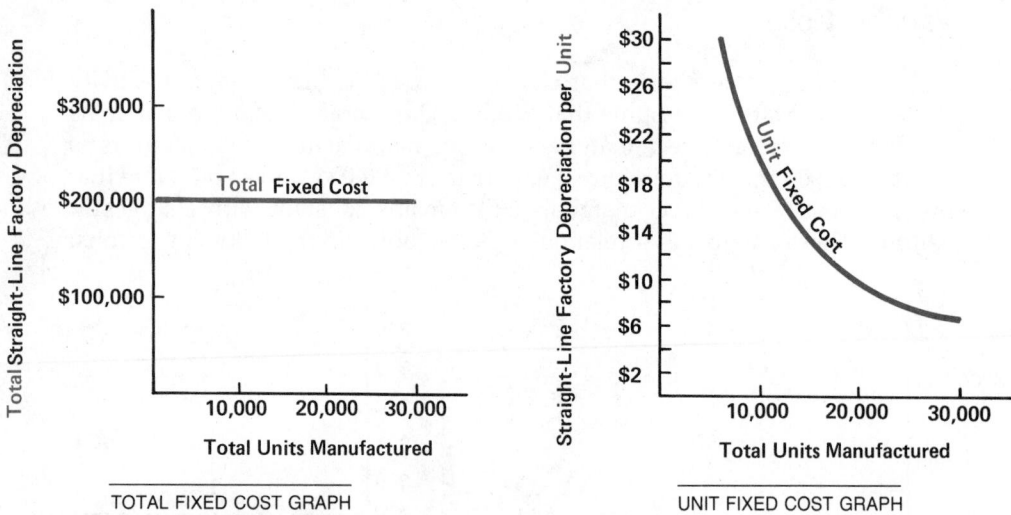

TOTAL FIXED COST GRAPH   UNIT FIXED COST GRAPH

Additional examples of fixed costs include real estate taxes, property insurance, rent, and office salaries. Although such costs do not vary in total with changes in volume of activity, they may change because of other factors. For example, changes in property tax rates or property insurance rates will change the total property tax cost or the total property insurance cost.

Mixed Costs

Mixed costs, sometimes referred to as **semivariable** or **semifixed** costs, are costs that have both variable and fixed characteristics. For example, the rental of manufacturing equipment may require a fixed charge plus a rate for each hour of use above a specified amount. To illustrate, assume that the rental cost for an item of equipment is $15,000, plus $1 per unit of production in excess of 10,000 units to a maximum of 30,000 units. This cost relationship is shown in the following graph:

MIXED COST
GRAPH

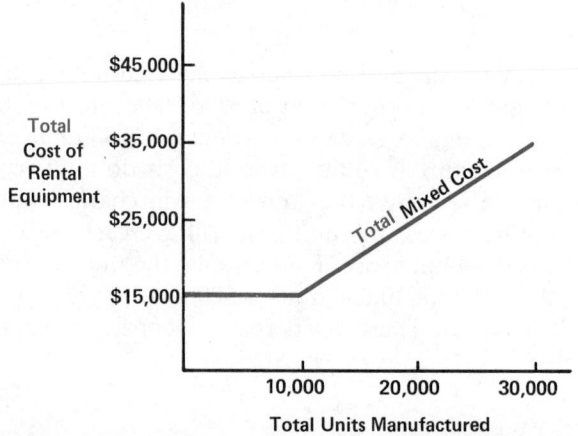

For purposes of analysis, mixed costs can generally be separated into variable and fixed components. In the remainder of this chapter, the variable and fixed components of mixed costs are used in describing and illustrating cost-volume-profit analysis.

MATHEMATICAL APPROACH TO COST-VOLUME-PROFIT ANALYSIS

After the costs and expenses have been classified into fixed and variable components, the effect on profit of these costs and expenses, along with revenues and volume, can be expressed in the form of cost-volume-profit analysis. Although accountants have proposed various approaches for cost-volume-profit analysis, the mathematical approach is one of two common approaches described and illustrated in this chapter.

The mathematical approach to cost-volume-profit analysis generally uses equations (1) to indicate the revenues necessary to achieve the break-even point in operations or (2) to indicate the revenues necessary to achieve a desired or target profit. These two equations and their use by management in profit planning are described and illustrated in the paragraphs that follow.

Break-Even Point

The level of operations of an enterprise at which revenues and expired costs are exactly equal is called the **break-even point**. At this level of operations, an enterprise will neither realize an operating income nor incur an operating loss. Break-even analysis can be applied to past periods, but it is most useful when applied to future periods as a guide to business planning, particularly if either an expansion or a curtailment of operations is expected. In such cases, it is concerned with future prospects and future operations and hence relies upon estimates. The reliability of the analysis is greatly influenced by the accuracy of the estimates.

The break-even point can be computed by means of a mathematical formula which indicates the relationship between revenue, costs, and capacity. The data required are (1) total estimated fixed costs for a future period, such as a year, and (2) the total estimated variable costs for the same period, stated as a percent of net sales. To illustrate, assume that fixed costs are estimated at $90,000 and that variable costs are expected to be 60% of sales. The break-even point is $225,000 of sales, computed as follows:

Break-Even Sales (in $) = Fixed Costs (in $) + Variable Costs (as % of Break-Even Sales)

$$S = \$90,000 + 60\%S$$
$$40\%S = \$90,000$$
$$S = \$225,000$$

The validity of the preceding computation is shown in the following income statement:

Sales......................................		$225,000
Expenses:		
Variable costs ($225,000 × 60%)............	$135,000	
Fixed costs...............................	90,000	225,000
Operating profit............................		-0-

The break-even point can be expressed either in terms of total sales dollars, as in the preceding illustration, or in terms of units of sales. For example, in the preceding illustration, if the unit selling price is $25, the break-even point can be expressed as either $225,000 of sales or 9,000 units ($225,000 ÷ $25).

The break-even point can be affected by changes in the fixed costs, unit variable costs, and unit selling price. The effect of each of these factors on the break-even point is briefly described in the following paragraphs.

Effect of Changes in Fixed Costs. Although fixed costs do not change in total with changes in volume of activity, they may change because of other factors, such as changes in property tax rates and salary increases given to factory supervisors. Increases in fixed costs will raise the break-even point. Similarly, decreases in fixed costs will lower the break-even point.

To illustrate, assume that Bishop Co. is evaluating a proposal to budget an additional $100,000 for advertising. Fixed costs (before the additional expenditure of $100,000 is considered) are estimated at $600,000, and variable costs are estimated at 75% of sales. The break-even point (before the additional expenditure is considered) is $2,400,000, computed as follows:

Break-Even Sales (in $) = Fixed Costs (in $) + Variable Costs (as % of Break-Even Sales)
  S = $600,000 + 75%S
  25%S = $600,000
  S = $2,400,000

If advertising expense is increased by $100,000, the break-even point is raised to $2,800,000, computed as follows:

Break-Even Sales (in $) = Fixed Costs (in $) + Variable Costs (as % of Break-Even Sales)
  S = $700,000 + 75%S
  25%S = $700,000
  S = $2,800,000

The increased fixed cost of $100,000 increases the break-even point by $400,000 of sales, since 75 cents of each sales dollar must cover variable costs. Hence, $4 of additional sales are needed for each $1 increase in fixed costs if the operating profit for Bishop Co. is to remain unchanged.

Effect of Changes in Variable Costs. Although unit variable costs do not change with changes in volume of activity, they may change because of other factors, such as changes in the price of direct materials and salary increases given to factory workers providing direct labor. Increases in unit variable costs will raise the break-even point. Similarly, decreases in unit variable costs will lower the break-even point.

To illustrate, assume that Park Co. is evaluating a proposal to pay an additional 2% sales commission to its sales representatives as an incentive to increase sales. Fixed costs are estimated at $84,000, and variable costs are estimated at 58% of sales (before the additional 2% commission is considered). The break-even point (before the additional commission is considered) is $200,000, computed as follows:

Break-Even Sales (in $) = Fixed Costs (in $) + Variable Costs (as % of Break-Even Sales)
$$S = \$84{,}000 + 58\%S$$
$$42\%S = \$84{,}000$$
$$S = \$200{,}000$$

If the sales commission proposal is adopted, the break-even point is raised to $210,000, computed as follows:

Break-Even Sales (in $) = Fixed Costs (in $) + Variable Costs (as % of Break-Even Sales)
$$S = \$84{,}000 + 60\%S$$
$$40\%S = \$84{,}000$$
$$S = \$210{,}000$$

The additional 2% sales commission (a variable cost) increases the break-even point by $10,000 of sales. If the proposal is adopted, 2% less of each sales dollar is available to cover the fixed costs of $84,000.

Effect of Changing Unit Selling Price. Increases in the unit selling price will lower the break-even point, while decreases in the unit selling price will raise the break-even point. To illustrate the effect of changing the unit selling price, assume that Graham Co. is evaluating a proposal to increase the unit selling price of its product from its current price of $50 to $60 and has accumulated the following relevant data:

	Current	Proposed
Unit selling price	$50	$60
Unit variable cost	$30	$30
Variable costs (as % of break-even sales):		
$30 unit variable cost ÷ $50 unit selling price	60%	
$30 unit variable cost ÷ $60 unit selling price		50%
Total fixed costs	$600,000	$600,000

The break-even point based on the current selling price is $1,500,000, computed as follows:

Break-Even Sales (in $) = Fixed Costs (in $) + Variable Costs (as % of Break-Even Sales)
$$S = \$600{,}000 + 60\%S$$
$$40\%S = \$600{,}000$$
$$S = \$1{,}500{,}000$$

If the selling price is increased by $10 per unit, the break-even point is decreased to $1,200,000, computed as follows:

Break-Even Sales (in $) = Fixed Costs (in $) + Variable Costs (as % of Break-Even Sales)
$$S = \$600,000 + \$50\%S$$
$$50\%S = \$600,000$$
$$S = \$1,200,000$$

The increase in selling price of $10 per unit decreases the break-even point by $300,000 (from $1,500,000 to $1,200,000). In terms of units of sales, the decrease is from 30,000 units ($1,500,000 ÷ $50) to 20,000 units ($1,200,000 ÷ $60).

Desired Profit

At the break-even point, sales and costs are exactly equal. However, business enterprises do not use the break-even point as their goal for future operations. Rather, they seek to achieve the largest possible volume of sales above the break-even point. By modifying the break-even equation, the sales volume required to earn a desired amount of profit may be estimated. For this purpose, a factor for desired profit is added to the standard break-even formula. To illustrate, assume that fixed costs are estimated at $200,000, variable costs are estimated at 60% of sales, and the desired profit is $100,000. The sales volume is $750,000, computed as follows:

Sales (in $) = Fixed Costs (in $) + Variable Costs (as % of Sales) + Desired Profit
$$S = \$200,000 + 60\%S + \$100,000$$
$$40\%S = \$300,000$$
$$S = \$750,000$$

The validity of the preceding computation is shown in the following income statement:

Sales......................................		$750,000
Expenses:		
Variable costs ($750,000 × 60%)............	$450,000	
Fixed costs.............................	200,000	650,000
Operating profit.............................		$100,000

GRAPHIC APPROACH TO COST-VOLUME-PROFIT ANALYSIS

Cost-volume-profit analysis can be presented graphically as well as in equation form. Many managers prefer the graphic format because the operating profit or loss for any given level of capacity can be readily determined, without the necessity of solving an equation. The following paragraphs describe two graphic approaches which managers find useful.

Cost-Volume-Profit (Break-Even) Chart

A **cost-volume-profit chart**, sometimes called a **break-even chart**, is used to assist management in understanding the relationships between costs, sales, and operating profit or loss. To illustrate the cost-volume-profit chart, assume that fixed costs are estimated at $90,000, and variable costs are estimated as 60% of sales. The maximum sales at 100% of capacity is $400,000. The following cost-volume-profit chart is based on the foregoing data:

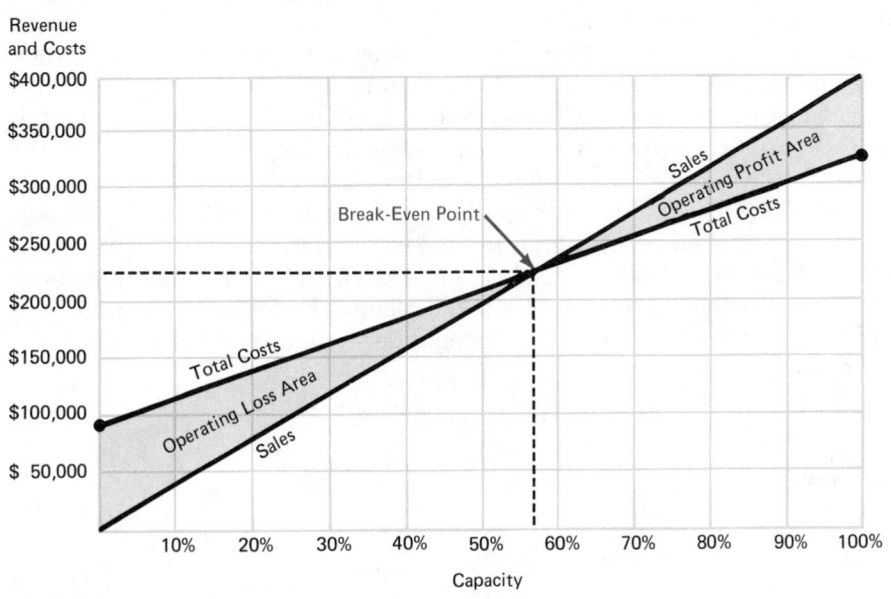

COST-VOLUME-PROFIT CHART

The cost-volume-profit chart is constructed in the following manner:

1. Percentages of capacity of the enterprise are spread along the horizontal axis, and dollar amounts representing operating data are spread along the vertical axis. The outside limits of the chart represent 100% of capacity and the maximum sales potential at that level of capacity.
2. A diagonal line representing sales is drawn from the lower left corner to the upper right corner.
3. A point representing fixed costs is plotted on the vertical axis at the left, and a point representing total costs at maximum capacity is plotted at the

right edge of the chart. A diagonal line representing total costs at various percentages of capacity is then drawn connecting these two points.

4. Horizontal and vertical lines are drawn at the point of intersection of the sales and cost lines, which is the break-even point, and the areas representing operating profit and operating loss are identified.

In the illustration, the total costs at maximum capacity are $330,000 (fixed costs of $90,000 plus variable costs of $240,000, which is 60% of $400,000). The dotted line drawn from the point of intersection to the vertical axis identifies the break-even sales amount of $225,000. The dotted line drawn from the point of intersection to the horizontal axis identifies the break-even point in terms of capacity of approximately 56%. Operating profits will be earned when sales levels are to the right of the break-even point (operating profit area), and operating losses will be incurred when sales levels are to the left of the break-even point (operating loss area).

Changes in the unit selling price, total fixed costs, and unit variable costs can also be analyzed using a cost-volume-profit chart. To illustrate, using the preceding example, assume that a proposal to reduce fixed costs by $42,000 is to be evaluated. In this situation, the total fixed costs would be $48,000 ($90,000 − $42,000), and the total costs at maximum capacity would amount to $288,000 ($48,000 of fixed costs plus variable costs of $240,000). The preceding cost-volume-profit chart is revised by plotting the points representing the total fixed cost and the total cost and drawing a line between the two points, indicating the proposed total cost line. The following revised chart indicates that the break-even point would decrease to $120,000 of sales (30% of capacity).

**REVISED
COST-
VOLUME-
PROFIT
CHART**

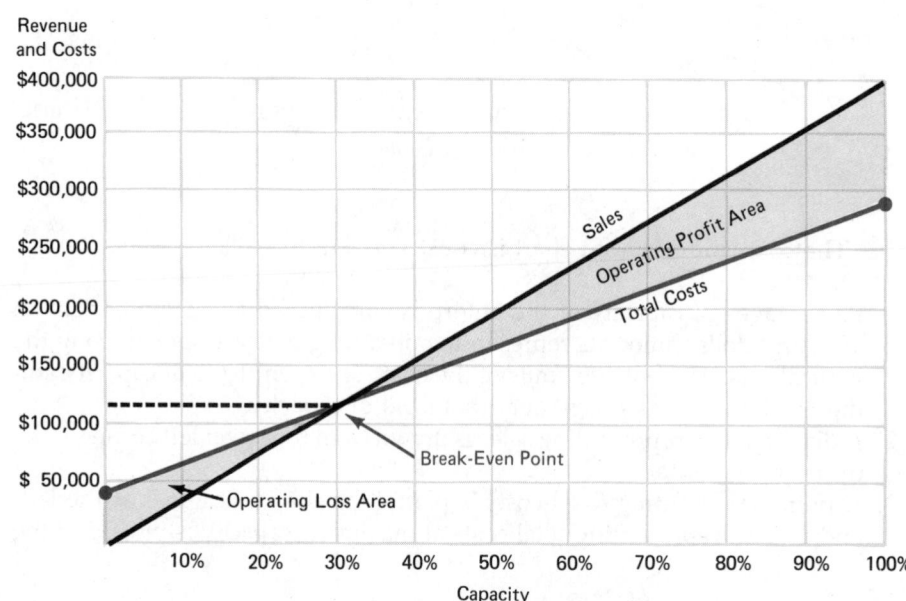

Profit-Volume Chart

Rather than focusing on sales revenues and costs, as was the case for the cost-volume-profit chart, another graphic approach to cost-volume-profit analysis, called the **profit-volume chart**, focuses on profitability. On the profit-volume chart, only the difference between total sales revenues and total costs is plotted, which enables management to determine the operating profit (or loss) for various levels of operations.

To illustrate the profit-volume chart, assume that fixed costs are estimated at $50,000, variable costs are estimated at 75% of sales, and the maximum capacity is $500,000 of sales. The maximum operating loss is equal to the fixed costs of $50,000, and the maximum operating profit at 100% of capacity is $75,000, computed as follows:

Sales......................................		$500,000
Expenses:		
Variable costs ($500,000 × 75%)............	$375,000	
Fixed costs...............................	50,000	425,000
Operating profit.............................		$ 75,000

The following profit-volume chart is based on the foregoing data:

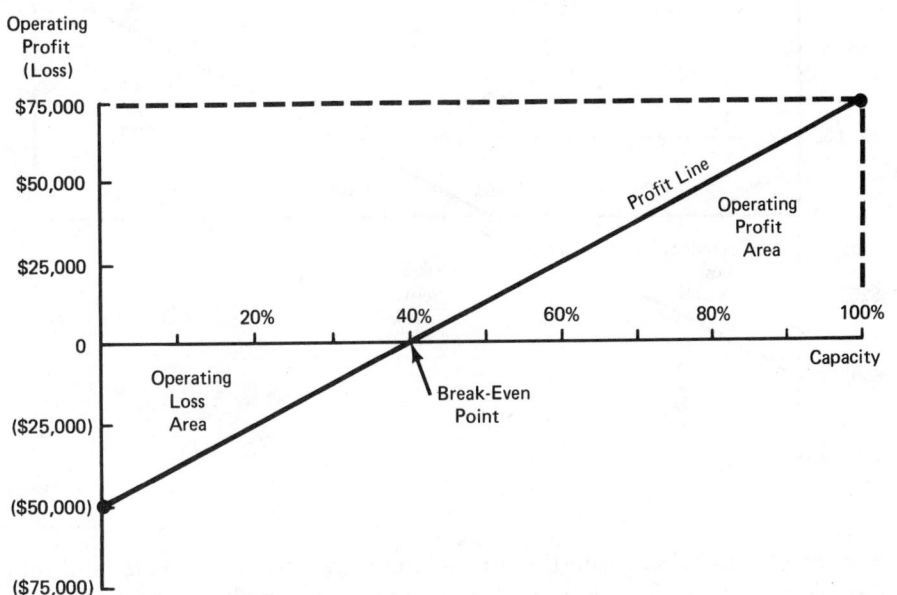

The profit-volume chart is constructed in the following manner:

1. Percentages of capacity of the enterprise are spread along the horizontal axis, and dollar amounts representing operating profits and losses are spread along the vertical axis.

2. A point representing the maximum operating loss is plotted on the vertical axis at the left. This loss is equal to the total fixed costs at 0% of capacity.
3. A point representing the maximum operating profit at 100% of capacity is plotted on the right.
4. A diagonal profit line is drawn connecting the maximum operating loss point with the maximum operating profit point.
5. The profit line intersects the horizontal axis at the break-even point expressed as a percentage of capacity, and the areas representing operating profit and operating loss are identified.

In the illustration, the break-even point is 40% of productive capacity, which can be converted to $200,000 of total sales (maximum capacity of $500,000 × 40%). Operating profit will be earned when sales levels are to the right of the break-even point (operating profit area), and operating losses will be incurred when sales levels are to the left of the break-even point (operating loss area). For example, at 60% of productive capacity, an operating profit of $25,000 will be earned, as indicated in the following profit-volume chart:

**PROFIT-
VOLUME
CHART**

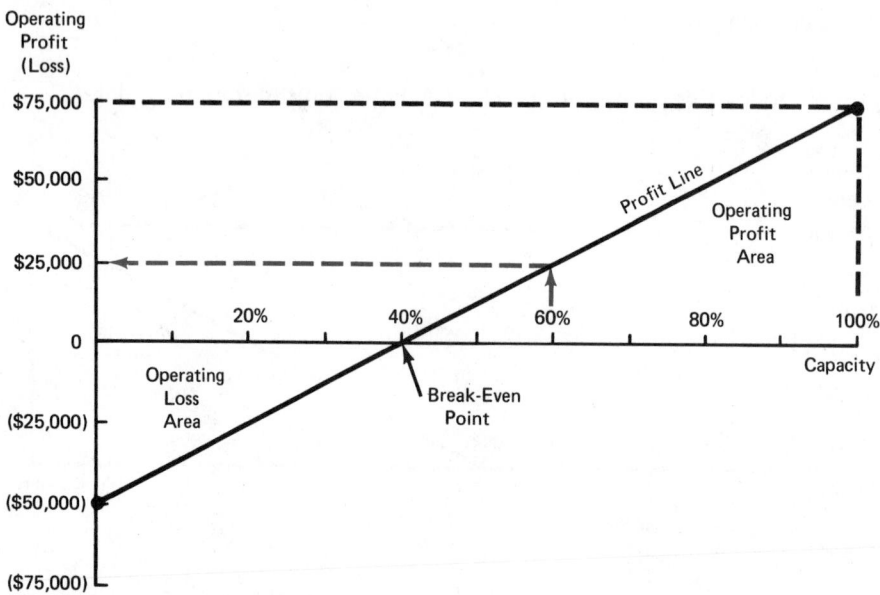

The effect of changes in the unit selling price, total fixed costs, and unit variable costs on profit can be analyzed using a profit-volume chart. To illustrate, using the preceding example, assume that the effect on profit of an increase of $25,000 in fixed costs is to be evaluated. In this case, the total fixed costs would be $75,000 ($50,000 + $25,000), and the maximum operating loss at 0% of capacity would be $75,000. The maximum operating profit at 100% of capacity would be $50,000, computed as follows:

Sales...................................		$500,000
Expenses:		
Variable costs ($500,000 × 75%)............	$375,000	
Fixed costs...............................	75,000	450,000
Operating profit..........................		$ 50,000

A revised profit-volume chart is constructed by plotting the maximum operating loss and maximum operating profit points and drawing a line between the two points, indicating the revised profit line. The original and the revised profit-volume charts are as follows:

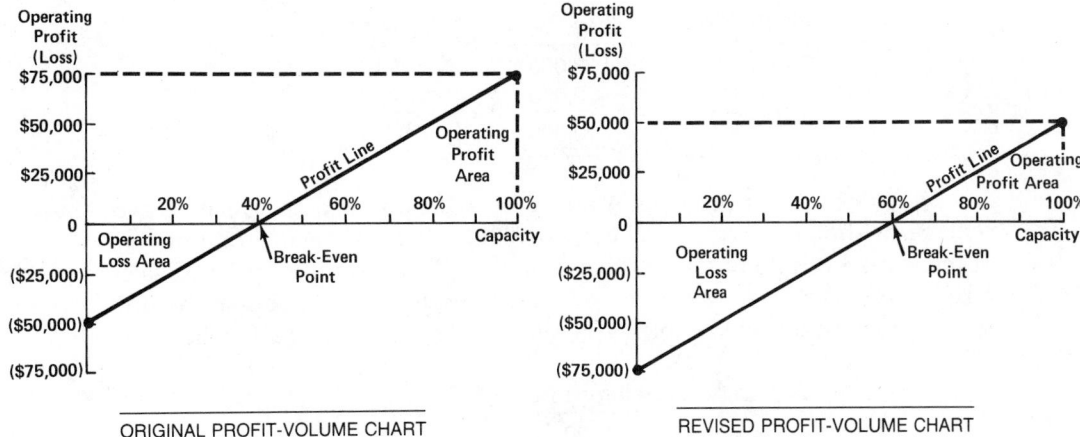

ORIGINAL PROFIT-VOLUME CHART

REVISED PROFIT-VOLUME CHART

The revised profit-volume chart indicates that the break-even point is 60% of capacity, which can be converted to total sales of $300,000 (maximum capacity of $500,000 × 60%). Note that the operating loss area of the chart has increased, while the operating profit area has decreased under the proposed change in fixed costs.

USE OF COMPUTERS IN COST-VOLUME-PROFIT ANALYSIS

In the preceding paragraphs, the use of the mathematical approach to cost-volume-profit analysis and the use of the cost-volume-profit chart and the profit-volume chart for analyzing the effect of changes in selling price, costs, and volume on profits have been demonstrated. Both the mathematical and graphic approaches are becoming increasingly popular and easy to use when managers have access to a computer terminal or a microcomputer. With the wide variety of computer software that is available, managers can vary assumptions regarding selling prices, costs, and volume and can instantaneously analyze the effects of each assumption on the break-even point and profit.

SALES MIX CONSIDERATIONS

In many businesses, more than one product is sold at varying selling prices. In addition, the products often have different unit variable costs, and each product makes a different contribution to profits. Thus, the total business profit, as well as the break-even point, depends upon the proportions in which the products are sold.

Sales mix is the relative distribution of sales among the various products sold by an enterprise. For example, assume that the sales for Cascade Company during the past year, a typical year for the company, are as follows:

Product	Units Sold	Sales Mix
A	8,000	80%
B	2,000	20
	10,000	100%

The sales mix for products A and B can be expressed as a relative percentage, as shown above, or as the ratio of 80:20. To illustrate the computation of the break-even point for Cascade Company, based on this specified sales mix, assume that fixed costs are $200,000. In addition, assume that the unit selling prices and unit variable costs for products A and B are as follows:

Product	Selling Price	Variable Cost
A	$ 90	$70
B	140	95

To compute the break-even point when several products are sold, it is useful to think of the individual products as components of one overall enterprise product. For Cascade Company, assume that this overall enterprise product is arbitrarily labeled E. The unit selling price of E can be thought of as equal to the total of the unit selling prices of the individual products A and B, each multiplied by the respective sales mix percentages. Likewise, the unit variable cost of E can be thought of as equal to the total of the unit variable costs of products A and B, multiplied by the respective sales mix percentages. These computations are as follows:

Unit selling price of E: ($90 × .8) + ($140 × .2) = $100
Unit variable cost of E: ($70 × .8) + ($95 × .2) = $75

The variable costs for enterprise product E are therefore expected to be 75% of sales ($75 ÷ $100). The break-even point can be determined in the normal manner, using the equation, as follows:

Break-Even Sales (in $) = Fixed costs (in $) + Variable Costs (as % of Break-Even Sales)
S = $200,000 + 75%S
25%S = $200,000
S = $800,000

The break-even point of $800,000 of sales of enterprise product E is equivalent to 8,000 total sales units ($800,000 ÷ $100). Since the sales mix for products A and B is 80% and 20% respectively, the break-even quantity of A is 6,400 (8,000 × 80%) and B is 1,600 (8,000 × 20%) units.

The validity of the preceding analysis can be verified by preparing the following income statement:

Cascade Company
Income Statement
For Year Ended December 31, 19--

	Product A	Product B	Total
Sales:			
6,400 units × $90	$576,000		$576,000
1,600 units × $140		$224,000	224,000
Total sales	$576,000	$224,000	$800,000
Variable costs:			
6,400 units × $70	$448,000		$448,000
1,600 units × $95		$152,000	152,000
Total variable costs	$448,000	$152,000	$600,000
Fixed costs			200,000
Total costs			$800,000
Operating profit			-0-

The effects of changes in the sales mix on the break-even point can be determined by repeating the preceding analysis, assuming a different sales mix.

SPECIAL COST-VOLUME-PROFIT RELATIONSHIPS

Additional relationships can be developed from the information presented in both the mathematical and graphic approaches to cost-volume-profit analysis. Two of these relationships that are especially useful to management in decision making are discussed in the following paragraphs.

Margin of Safety

The difference between the current sales revenue and the sales at the break-even point is called the **margin of safety**. It represents the possible decrease in sales revenue that may occur before an operating loss results, and it may be stated either in terms of dollars or as a percentage of sales. For example, if the volume of sales is $250,000 and sales at the break-even point amount to $200,000, the margin of safety is $50,000 or 20%, as shown by the following computation:

$$\text{Margin of Safety} = \frac{\text{Sales} - \text{Sales at Break-Even Point}}{\text{Sales}}$$

$$\text{Margin of Safety} = \frac{\$250,000 - \$200,000}{\$250,000} = 20\%$$

The margin of safety is useful in evaluating past operations and as a guide to business planning. For example, if the margin of safety is low, management should carefully study forecasts of future sales because even a small decline in sales revenue will result in an operating loss.

Contribution Margin Ratio

Another relationship between cost, volume, and profits that is especially useful in business planning because it gives an insight into the profit potential of a firm is the **contribution margin ratio**, sometimes called the **profit-volume ratio**. This ratio, which was introduced in Chapter 25, indicates the percentage of each sales dollar available to cover the fixed expenses and to provide operating income. For example, if the volume of sales is $250,000 and variable expenses amount to $175,000, the contribution margin ratio is 30%, as shown by the following computation:

$$\text{Contribution Margin Ratio} = \frac{\text{Sales} - \text{Variable Expenses}}{\text{Sales}}$$

$$\text{Contribution Margin Ratio} = \frac{\$250,000 - \$175,000}{\$250,000} = 30\%$$

The contribution margin ratio permits the quick determination of the effect on operating income of an increase or a decrease in sales volume. To illustrate, assume that the management of a firm with a contribution margin ratio of 30% is studying the effect on operating income of adding $25,000 in sales orders. Multiplying the ratio (30%) by the change in sales volume ($25,000) indicates an increase in operating income of $7,500 if the additional orders are obtained. In using the analysis in such a case, factors other than sales volume, such as the amount of fixed expenses, the percentage of variable expenses to sales, and the unit sales price, are assumed to remain constant. If these factors are not constant, the effect of any change must be considered in applying the analysis.

The contribution margin ratio is also useful in setting business policy. For example, if the contribution margin ratio of a firm is large and production is at a level below 100% capacity, a comparatively large increase in operating income can be expected from an increase in sales volume. On the other hand, a comparatively large decrease in operating income can be expected from a decline in sales volume. A firm in such a position might decide to devote more effort to additional sales promotion because of the large change in operating income that will result from changes in sales volume. On the other hand, a firm with a small contribution margin ratio will probably want to give more attention to reducing costs and expenses before concentrating large efforts on additional sales promotion.

LIMITATIONS OF COST-VOLUME-PROFIT ANALYSIS

The reliability of cost-volume-profit analysis depends upon the validity of several assumptions. One major assumption is that there is no change in inventory quantities during the year; that is, the quantity of units in the beginning inventory equals the quantity of units in the ending inventory. When changes in inventory quantities occur, the computations for cost-volume-profit analysis become more complex.

For cost-volume-profit analysis, a relevant range of activity is assumed, within which all costs can be classified as either fixed or variable. Within the relevant range, which is usually a range of activity within which the company is likely to operate, the unit variable costs and the total fixed costs will not change. For example, within the relevant range of activity, factory supervisory salaries are fixed. For cost-volume-profit analysis, it is assumed that a significant change in activity that would cause these salaries to change, such as adding a night shift that would double production, will not occur.

These assumptions simplify cost-volume-profit relationships, and since substantial variations in the assumptions are often uncommon in practice, cost-volume-profit analysis can be used quite effectively in decision making. Under conditions of substantial variations from the assumptions, the analysis of the cost-volume-profit relationships must be used cautiously.

MANAGERIAL USES OF QUANTITATIVE TECHNIQUES

Each of the previously discussed uses of accounting data in planning and controlling business operations have involved a limited number of objectives or variables. In recent years, more sophisticated quantitative techniques have been developed to assist management in solving problems. This framework of quantitative techniques, sometimes called **operations research**, uses mathematical and statistical models with a large number of interdependent variables. The accounting system is the source of much of the quantitative data needed by many operations research techniques.

The use of quantitative techniques often leads to a clarification of management decision alternatives and their expected effects on the business enterprise. For example, the most economical plan for purchasing materials for a single plant may be easily determined, based on the lowest overall cost per unit of materials. However, the most economical plan for purchasing materials for several plants may not be as easily determined, because transportation costs to the various plant locations may be different, and the amount of purchases from any one supplier may be limited. In this latter case, a quantitative technique known as linear programming may be useful in determining the most economical plan for purchasing materials.

The primary disadvantages of quantitative techniques are their complexity and their reliance on mathematical relationships and statistical methods which may be understood by only the most highly trained experts. When computers are used, however, these complexities can be programmed into the computer, so that quantitative techniques can be used by all levels of management.

QUANTITATIVE TECHNIQUES FOR INVENTORY CONTROL

For a business enterprise that needs large quantities of inventory to meet sales orders or production requirements, inventory is one of its most important assets. The lack of sufficient inventory can result in lost sales, idle production facilities, production bottlenecks, and additional purchasing costs due to placing special orders or rush orders. On the other hand, excess inventory can result in large storage costs and large spoilage losses, which reduce the profitability of the enterprise. Thus, it is important for a business enterprise to know the ideal quantity to be purchased in a single order and the minimum and maximum quantities to be on hand at any time. Such factors as economies of large-scale buying, storage costs, work interruption due to shortages, and seasonal and cyclical changes in production schedules need to be considered. Three quantitative techniques that are especially useful in inventory control are (1) the economic order quantity formula, (2) the inventory order point formula, and (3) linear programming.

Economic Order Quantity

The optimum quantity of inventory to be ordered at one time is termed the **economic order quantity (EOQ)**. Important factors to be considered in determining the optimum quantity are the costs involved in processing an order for the materials and the costs involved in storing the materials.

The annual cost of processing orders for a specified material (cost of placing orders, verifying invoices, processing payments, etc.) increases as the number of orders placed increases. On the other hand, the annual cost of storing the materials (taxes, insurance, occupancy of storage space, etc.) decreases as the number of orders placed increases. The economic order quantity is therefore that quantity that will minimize the combined annual costs of ordering and storing materials.

The combined annual cost incurred in ordering and storing materials can be computed under various assumptions as to the number of orders to be placed during a year. To illustrate, assume the following data for an inventoriable material which is used at the same rate during the year:

Units required during the year   1,200
Ordering cost, per order placed $10.00
Annual storage cost, per unit 60

If a single order were placed for the entire year's needs, the cost of ordering the 1,200 units would be $10. The average number of units held in inventory during the year would therefore be 600 (1,200 units ÷ 2) and would result in an annual storage cost of $360 (600 units × $.60). The combined order and storage costs for placing only one order during the year would thus be $370 ($10 + $360). If, instead of a single order, two orders were placed during the year, the order cost would be $20 (2 × $10), 600 units would need to be purchased on each order, the average inventory would be 300 units, and the annual storage cost would be $180 (300 units × $.60). Accordingly, the combined order and storage costs for placing two orders during the year would be $200 ($20 + $180). Successive computations will disclose the EOQ when the combined cost reaches its lowest point and starts upward. The following table shows an optimum of 200 units of materials per order, with 6 orders per year, at a combined cost of $120:

| Number of Orders | Number of Units per Order | Average Units in Inventory | Order and Storage Costs | | | TABULATION OF ECONOMIC ORDER QUANTITY |
			Order Cost	Storage Cost	Combined Cost	
1	1,200	600	$10	$360	$370	
2	600	300	20	180	200	
3	400	200	30	120	150	
4	300	150	40	90	130	
5	240	120	50	72	122	
6	200	100	60	60	120	
7	171	86	70	52	122	

The economic order quantity may also be determined by a formula based on differential calculus. The formula and its application to the illustration is as follows:

$$EOQ = \sqrt{\frac{2 \times \text{Annual Units Required} \times \text{Cost per Order Placed}}{\text{Annual Storage Cost per Unit}}}$$

$$EOQ = \sqrt{\frac{2 \times 1,200 \times \$10}{\$.60}}$$

$$EOQ = \sqrt{40,000}$$

$$EOQ = 200 \text{ units}$$

Inventory Order Point

The **inventory order point**, usually expressed in units, is the level to which inventory is allowed to fall before an order for additional inventory is placed. The inventory order point depends on the (1) daily usage of inventory that is expected to be consumed in production or sold, (2) number of production days that it takes to receive an order for inventory, termed the **lead time**, and (3) **safety stock**, which is the amount of inventory that is available for use when unforeseen circumstances arise, such as delays in receiving ordered inventory as a result of a national truckers' strike. Once the order point is reached, the most economical quantity should be ordered.

The inventory order point is computed by using the following formula:

Inventory Order Point = (Daily Usage × Days of Lead Time) + Safety Stock

To illustrate, assume that Beacon Company, a printing company, estimates daily usage of 3,000 pounds of paper and a lead time of 30 days to receive an order of paper. Beacon Company desires a safety stock of 10,000 pounds. The inventory order point for the paper is 100,000 pounds, computed as follows:

Inventory Order Point = (Daily Usage × Lead Time) + Safety Stock
Inventory Order Point = (3,000 lbs. × 30 days) + 10,000 lbs.
Inventory Order Point = 90,000 lbs. + 10,000 lbs.
Inventory Order Point = 100,000 lbs.

In this illustration, a safety stock of 10,000 pounds of paper was assumed. This level of safety stock should be established by management after considering many factors, such as the uncertainty in the estimates of daily inventory usage and lead time. If management were 100% certain that estimates of the daily usage and lead time were correct, no safety stock would be required. As the uncertainty in these estimates increases, the amount of safety stock normally increases. In addition, the level of safety stock carried by an enterprise will also depend on the costs of carrying inventory and the costs of being out of inventory when materials are needed for production or sales. If the costs of carrying inventory are low and the costs of being out of inventory are high, then relatively large amounts of safety stock would normally be carried by a business enterprise.

And The Computer Said...

As competition has become more and more intense in the retail industry, retailers have begun to rely more and more heavily on quantitative techniques and computers to cut expenses, to reduce inventory requirements, and to improve sales. Three examples of the use of quantitative techniques and computers in the retail industry are given in the following paragraphs.

Dylex Ltd., a Toronto operator of apparel stores, uses IBM's Inforem inventory program, which helps restock more than 1,000 stores from Vancouver to Cornerbrook, Newfoundland. "It allows you to keep track of inventory in each store by size and color and the rate at which it is selling, and then forecasts the estimated inventory," explains Chris Schwartz, a vice president of Dylex. "So if a particular store is in a Chinese neighborhod and sells a lot of small sizes, the computer will know that. And when new merchandise arrives, it will automatically allocate small sizes to that store." In addition, such systems help retailers adjust quickly when a product is selling poorly, says Gordon Edelstone, a vice president of Dylex's Tip Top division. "We can identify an item that looks like a dog and mark it down immediately and sell it even before (competitors) recognize the product isn't selling well."

In the next three years, K Mart Corp., with headquarters in Troy, Michigan, expects to spend $300 million to install computerized, laser-scanning registers that will automatically reorder certain merchandise when stock gets low. A similar retailer reduced the time it takes to replenish inventory because purchase orders are electronically transmitted to more than 500 suppliers. In addition, the same company figures that average inventory investment has been reduced by about 17% for some products.

New York-based J. C. Penney Co. automatically reorders products accounting for 50% of its $12 billion in annual sales from 281 suppliers, cutting lead time by at least 10 days, says Robert Capone, director of systems and data processing. "There are two ways of getting purchase orders into the Penney system," he explains. "Orders are generated automatically based on reorder points and quantities, and other orders are entered into terminals at Penney stores. The order goes directly into the computer and right to the vendor. It isn't approved in New York."

Source: Adapted from Hank Gilman, "The Technology Edge," *The Wall Street Journal*, September 16, 1985, p. 55C.

Quantitative techniques using statistics and probability theory may be useful to managers in establishing order point and safety stock levels. Such techniques are described in advanced texts.

Linear Programming for Inventory Control

Linear programming is a quantitative method that can provide data for solving a variety of business problems in which management's objective is to minimize costs or maximize profits, subject to several limiting factors. Although a thorough discussion of linear programming is appropriate for more advanced courses, the following simplified illustration demonstrates the way in which linear programming can be applied to determine the most economical purchasing plan. In this situation, management's objective is to minimize the total cost of purchasing materials for several branch locations, subject to the availability of materials from suppliers.

Assume that a manufacturing company purchases Part P for use at both its West Branch and East Branch. Part P is available in limited quantities from two suppliers. The total unit cost price varies considerably for parts acquired from the two suppliers mainly because of differences in transportation charges. The relevant data for the decision regarding the most economical purchase arrangement are summarized in the following diagram:

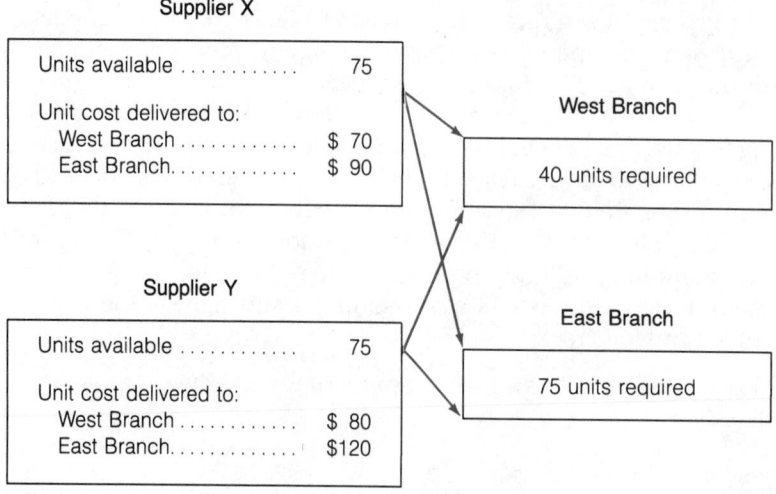

It might appear that the most economical course of action would be to purchase (1) the 40 units required by West Branch from Supplier X at $70 a unit, (2) 35 units for East Branch from Supplier X at $90 a unit, and (3) the remaining 40 units required by East Branch from Supplier Y at $120 a unit. If this course of action were followed, the total cost of the parts needed by the two branches would amount to $10,750, as indicated by the following computation:

| | Cost of Purchases | | |
	By West Branch	By East Branch	Total
From Supplier X:			
40 units at $70	$2,800		$ 2,800
35 units at $90		$3,150	3,150
From Supplier Y:			
40 units at $120		4,800	4,800
Total.	$2,800	$7,950	$10,750

Although many different purchasing programs are possible, the most economical course of action would be to purchase (1) the 75 units required by East Branch from Supplier X at $90 a unit and (2) the 40 units required by West Branch from Supplier Y at $80 a unit. If this plan were used, no units would be purchased at the lowest available unit cost, and the total cost of the parts would be $9,950, calculated as follows:

| | Cost of Purchases | | |
	By West Branch	By East Branch	Total
From Supplier X:			
75 units at $90		$6,750	$6,750
From Supplier Y:			
40 units at $80	$3,200		3,200
Total.	$3,200	$6,750	$9,950

Linear programming can be applied to this situation by using a mathematical equation approach. This approach, called the **simplex method**, uses algebraic equations and is often used more practically with a computer. The simplex method is described in advanced texts.

CHAPTER REVIEW

KEY POINTS

1. Cost-Volume-Profit Relationships.

Cost-volume-profit analysis is the systematic examination of the interrelationships between selling prices, volume of sales and production, costs, expenses, and profits. Accountants can play an important role in cost-volume-profit analysis by providing management with information on the relative profitability of its various products, the probable effects of changes in selling price, and other variables.

In cost-volume-profit analysis, costs are subdivided into two categories: (1) variable and (2) fixed. Variable costs are costs that change, in total, as the volume of activity changes. Fixed costs remain constant, in total, as the volume of activity changes. Mixed costs are costs that have both variable and fixed characteristics. For purposes of analysis, mixed costs can generally be separated into variable and fixed components.

2. Mathematical Approach to Cost-Volume-Profit Analysis.

The mathematical approach to cost-volume-profit analysis uses equations (1) to indicate the revenues necessary to achieve the break-even point in operations or (2) to indicate the revenues necessary to achieve a desired or target profit. The level of operations of an enterprise at which revenues and expired costs are exactly equal is called the break-even point. The break-even point can be determined using the following equation:

Break-Even Sales (in $) = Fixed Costs (in $) + Variable Costs (as % of Break-Even Sales)

The break-even point is raised by increases in fixed costs, increases in variable costs, or decreases in the unit selling price. The break-even point is lowered by decreases in fixed costs, decreases in variable costs, or increases in the unit selling price. By modifying the break-even equation and adding a factor for desired profit, the sales volume required to earn a desired amount of profit may be estimated.

3. Graphic Approach to Cost-Volume-Profit Analysis.

Many managers prefer to use a graphic format for cost-volume-profit analysis because the operating profit or loss for any given level of capacity can be readily determined, without the necessity of solving an equation. A cost-volume-profit chart is used to assist management in understanding the relationships between costs, sales, and operating profit or loss. Changes in the unit selling price, total fixed costs, and unit variable costs can also be analyzed using a cost-volume-profit chart. Another graphic approach to cost-volume-profit analysis, called the profit-volume chart, focuses on profitability rather than on sales revenues and costs. The effect of changes in unit selling price, total fixed costs, and unit variable costs on profit can also be analyzed using a profit-volume chart.

4. Use of Computers in Cost-Volume-Profit Analysis.

Both the mathematical and graphic approaches to cost-volume-profit analysis are becoming increasing popular and easy to use when managers have access to a computer terminal or a microcomputer. With the wide variety of computer software that is available, managers can vary assumptions regarding selling prices, costs, and volume and can instantaneously analyze the effects of each assumption on the break-even point and profit.

5. Sales Mix Considerations.

The break-even point for an enterprise selling two or more products must be calculated on the basis of a specified sales mix. If the sales mix is assumed to be constant, the break-even point can be computed using the standard approaches.

6. Special Cost-Volume-Profit Relationships.

The difference between the current sales revenue and the sales at the break-even point is called the margin of safety. The margin of safety is useful in evaluating past operations and as a guide to business planning. Another relationship between costs, volume, and profits that is especially useful in business planning because it gives an insight into the profit potential of a firm is the contribution margin ratio. This ratio indicates the percentage of each sales dollar available to cover the fixed costs and expenses and to provide operating income. The contribution margin ratio permits the quick determination of the effect on operating income of an increase or a decrease in sales volume.

7. Limitations of Cost-Volume-Profit Analysis.

The reliability of cost-volume-profit analysis depends upon the validity of several assumptions. One major assumption is that there is no change in inventory quantities during the year. Another assumption is that the analysis is conducted within a relevant range of activity within which all costs can be classified as fixed or variable. These assumptions simplify cost-volume-profit relationships, and since substantial variations in the assumptions are often uncommon in practice, cost-volume-profit analysis can be used quite effectively in decision making.

8. Managerial Uses of Quantitative Techniques.

In recent years, sophisticated quantitative techniques have been developed to assist management in solving problems. This framework of quantitative techniques is called operations research and uses mathematical and statistical models with a large number of interdependent variables. The use of quantitative techniques often leads to a clarification of management decision alternatives and their expected effects on the business enterprise. The primary disadvantages of quantitative techniques are their complexity and their reliance on mathematical relationships and statistical methods which may be understood by only the most highly trained experts. When computers are used, however, these disadvantages become less important.

9. Quantitative Techniques for Inventory Control.

For a business enterprise that needs large quantities of inventory to meet sales orders or production requirements, inventory is one of its most important assets. One quantitative technique useful in inventory control is the economic order quantity. This quantitative technique uses a formula for determining the optimum quantity of inventory to be ordered at one time. Another quantitative technique for inventory control is the inventory order point formula. This technique determines the inventory order point based on daily usage of the inventory, the lead time to receive inventory, and the amount of safety stock desired by management. Linear programming is another quantitative technique that can provide data for solving a variety of business problems in which management's objective is to minimize costs or maximize profits, subject to several limiting factors. Linear programming can be useful in inventory control in determining the most economical plan for purchasing materials for one or more locations.

KEY TERMS

cost-volume-profit analysis 1162
variable costs 1163
fixed costs 1163
mixed costs 1164
semivariable costs 1164
break-even point 1165
cost-volume-profit chart 1169
profit-volume chart 1171
sales mix 1174
margin of safety 1175

contribution margin ratio 1176
operations research 1177
economic order quantity
  (EOQ) 1178
inventory order point 1180
lead time 1180
safety stock 1180
linear programming 1182
simplex method 1183

SELF-EXAMINATION QUESTIONS

Answers in Appendix B.

1. For cost-volume-profit analysis, costs must be classified as either fixed or variable. Variable costs:
   A. change in total as the volume of activity changes
   B. do not change in total as the volume of activity changes
   C. change on a per unit basis as the volume of activity changes
   D. none of the above

2. If variable costs are 40% of sales and fixed costs are $240,000, what is the break-even point?
   A. $200,000   C. $400,000
   B. $240,000   D. None of the above

3. Based on the data presented in Question 2, how much sales would be required to realize operating profit of $30,000?
   A. $400,000   C. $600,000
   B. $450,000   D. None of the above

4. If sales were $500,000, variable costs are $200,000, and fixed costs are $240,000, what is the margin of safety?
   A. 20%   C. 60%
   B. 40%   D. None of the above

5. In determining the economic order quantity, which, if any, of the following factors are important to consider?
   A. Storage cost per unit   C. Cost per order placed
   B. Annual units required   D. All of the above

ILLUSTRATIVE PROBLEM

Nissat Company expects to maintain the same inventories at the end of the year as at the beginning of the year. The estimated fixed costs and expenses for the year are $360,000 and the estimated variable costs and expenses per unit are $9. It is expected that 75,000 units will be sold at a selling price of $15 per unit. Capacity output is 80,000 units.

Instructions:

1. Determine the break-even point (a) in dollars of sales, (b) in units, and (c) in terms of capacity.
2. Construct a cost-volume-profit chart, indicating the break-even point in dollars of sales.
3. Construct a profit-volume chart, indicating the break-even point as a percentage of capacity.
4. What is the expected margin of safety?
5. What is the contribution margin ratio?

SOLUTION

(1) (a) Break-even point in dollars of sales:
$$S = \$360,000 + 60\%S$$
$$S - 60\%S = \$360,000$$
$$S = \$900,000$$

(b) Break-even point in units:
$$\$900,000 \div \$15 = 60,000 \text{ units}$$

(c) Break-even point in terms of capacity:
$$60,000 \div 80,000 = 75\%$$

(2)

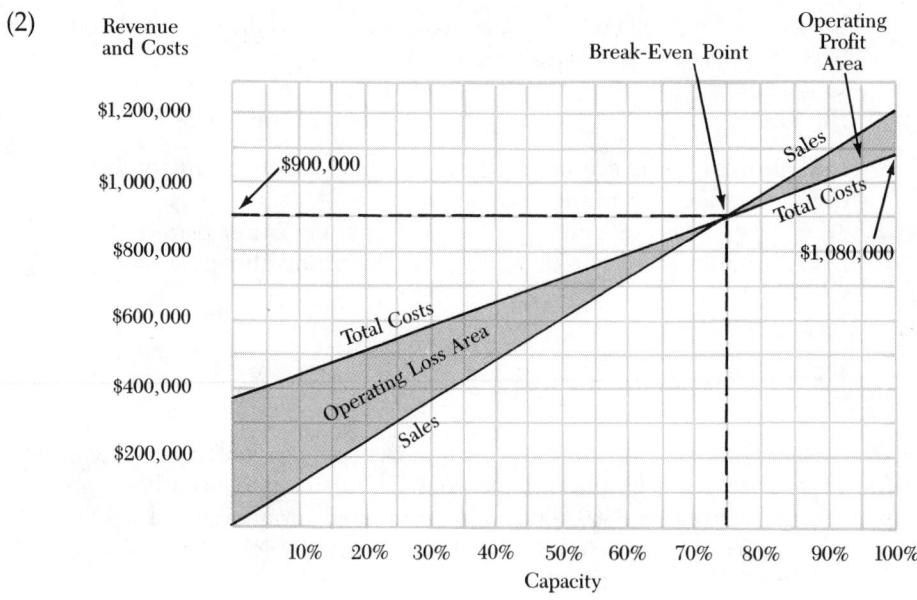

(3)

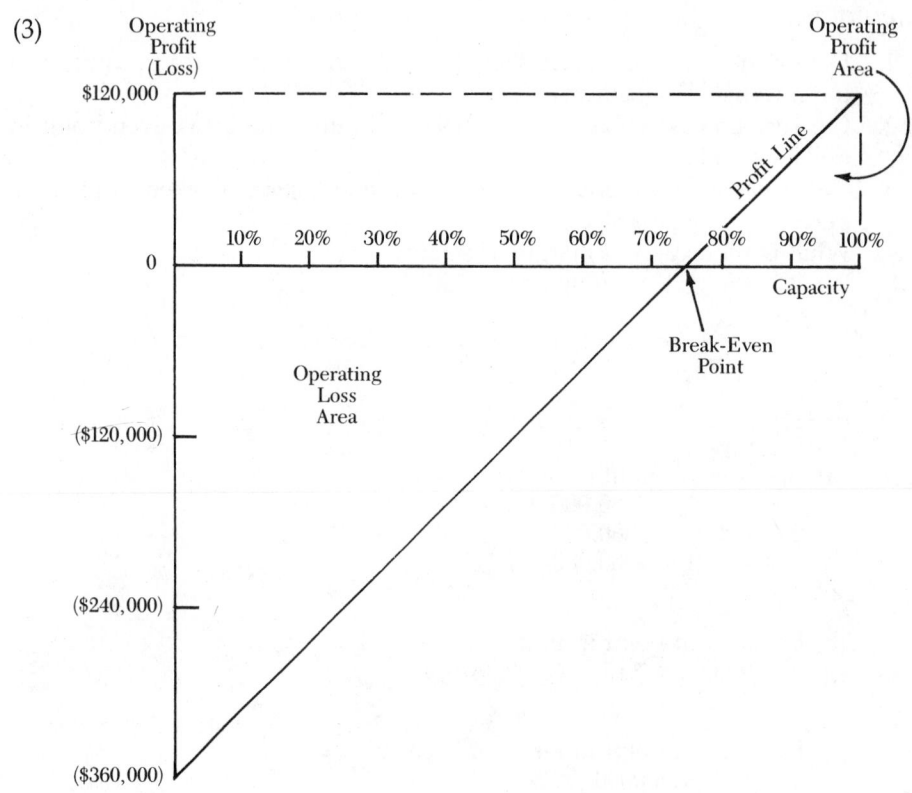

(4) Margin of safety:

Expected sales (75,000 units @ $15) $1,125,000
Break-even point 900,000
Margin of safety............................. $ 225,000 or 20%

(5) Contribution margin ratio $= \dfrac{\text{Sales} - \text{Variable Expenses}}{\text{Sales}}$

$$= \frac{\$1,125,000 - (75,000 \times \$9)}{\$1,125,000}$$

$$= \frac{\$450,000}{\$1,125,000}$$

$$= 40\%$$

DISCUSSION QUESTIONS

1. How do changes in volume of activity affect (a) total variable costs and (b) total fixed costs?

2. If total fixed costs are $84,000, what is the unit fixed cost if production is (a) 20,000 units and (b) 35,000 units?

3. (a) What are mixed costs? (b) If a leased copying machine costs $50 per month plus 1¢ per copy, and 10,500 copies were made during April, what was the total cost for April?

4. (a) What is the break-even point? (b) What equation can be used to determine the break-even point?

5. If sales are $800,000, variable costs are $520,000, and fixed costs are $175,000, what is the break-even point?

6. If fixed costs are $320,000 and variable costs are 60% of sales, what is the break-even point?

7. If the unit cost of direct materials is decreased, what effect will this change have on the break-even point?

8. If the property tax rates are increased, what effect will this change in fixed costs have on the break-even point?

9. If fixed costs are $250,000 and variable costs are 65% of sales, what sales are required to realize an operating profit of $100,000?

10. What is the advantage of presenting cost-volume-profit analysis in the chart form over the equation form?

11. Name the following chart and identify the items represented by the letters a through f.

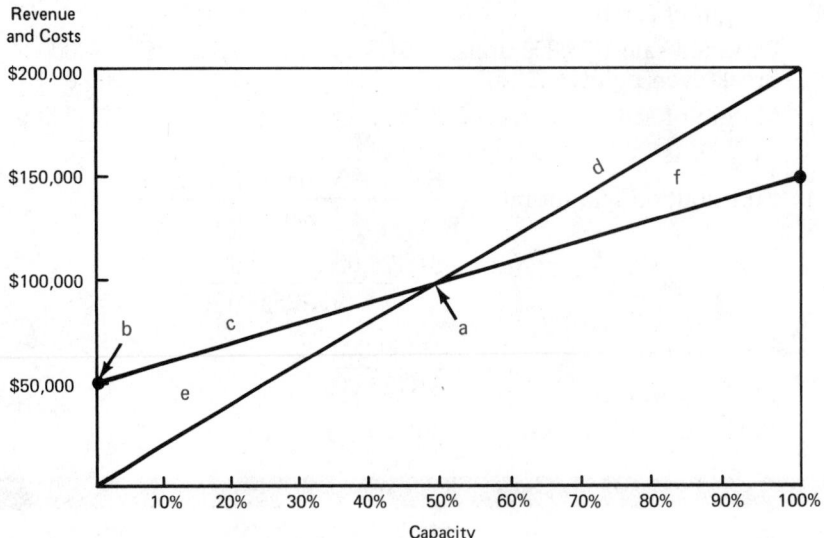

12. Name the following chart and identify the items represented by the letters *a* through *f*.

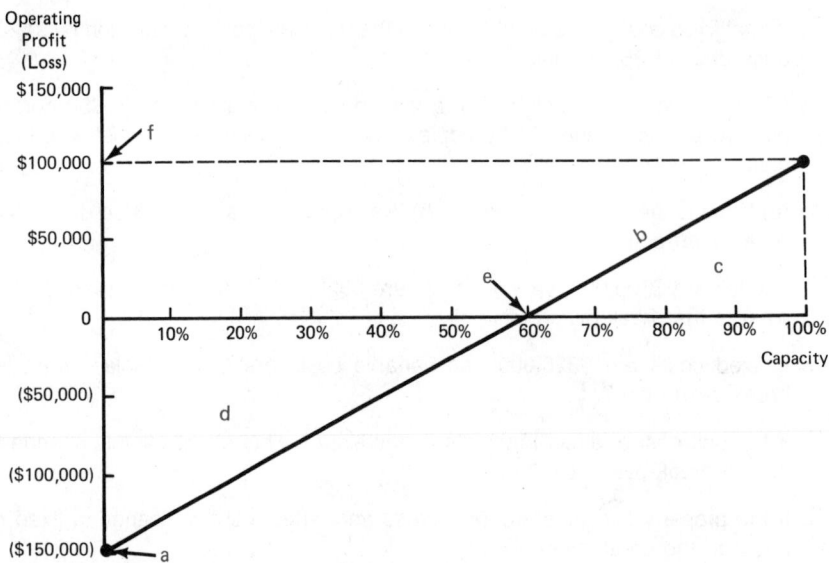

13. Both Harris Company and Lammers Company had the same sales, total costs, and operating profit for the current fiscal year, yet Harris Company had a lower break-even point than Lammers Company. Explain the reason for this difference in break-even points.

14. (a) What is meant by *sales mix?* (b) For conventional break-even analysis, is the sales mix assumed to be constant?

15. (a) What is meant by the term *margin of safety*? (b) If sales are $600,000, net income is $50,400, and sales at the break-even point are $480,000, what is the margin of safety?

16. What ratio indicates the percentage of each sales dollar that is available to cover fixed costs and to provide a profit?

17. (a) If sales are $180,000 and variable costs are $126,000, what is the contribution margin ratio? (b) What is the contribution margin ratio if variable costs are 65% of sales?

18. An examination of the accounting records of Cardel Company disclosed a high contribution margin ratio and production at a level below maximum capacity. Based on this information, suggest a likely means of improving operating profit. Explain.

19. What is operations research?

20. For a business enterprise that needs large quantities of inventories to meet sales orders or production requirements, what can result from insufficient inventory?

21. What term is used to describe the optimum quantity of inventory to be ordered at one time?

22. The inventory order point depends on what factors?

23. Assuming that Parish Co. estimates daily usage of 1,200 pounds of Material X, the lead time to receive an order of Material X is 10 days, and a safety stock of 3,600 pounds is desired, what is the inventory order point?

24. If everything else remains the same, as the cost of carrying inventory decreases, would the level of safety stock normally carried by a company increase or decrease?

25. What quantitative technique is often useful in determining the most economical plan for purchasing materials for several locations?

26. Real World Focus. The 1985 annual report of William Wrigley Jr. Company indicates that, compared to the previous year, net sales were approximately $30,000,000 higher, and income from operations was approximately $9,500,000 higher. The William Wrigley Jr. Company has operated above the break-even point throughout the 1980s. Assuming that fixed costs and expenses did not change significantly from the prior year, what is the estimated contribution margin for William Wrigley Jr. Company?

EXERCISES

Exercise 26–1.   Break-even point and sales to realize operating profit. For the current year ending October 31, Duval Company expects fixed costs and expenses of $72,000 and variable costs and expenses equal to 64% of sales.

(a) Compute the anticipated break-even point.
(b) Compute the sales required to realize operating profit of $43,200.

SPREADSHEET
PROBLEM

Exercise 26-2. Break-even point. For the past year, DeLong Company had fixed costs of $342,000 and variable costs equal to 55% of sales. All revenues and costs are expected to remain constant for the coming year, except that property taxes are expected to increase by $27,000 during the year.

(a) Compute the break-even point for the past year.
(b) Compute the anticipated break-even point for the coming year.

Exercise 26-3. Break-even point. For the current year ending May 31, Lynch Company expects fixed costs of $420,000 and variable costs equal to 65% of sales. For the coming year, a new wage contract will increase variable costs to 70% of sales.

(a) Compute the break-even point for the current year.
(b) Compute the anticipated break-even point for the coming year, assuming that all revenues and costs are to remain constant, with the exception of the costs represented by the new wage contract.

Exercise 26-4. Break-even point. Currently the unit selling price of a product is $40, the unit variable cost is $27, and the total fixed costs are $52,000. A proposal is being evaluated to increase the unit selling price to $45.

(a) Compute the current break-even point.
(b) Compute the anticipated break-even point, assuming that the unit selling price is increased and all costs remain constant.

Exercise 26-5. Profit-volume chart. For the coming year, Inwood Inc. anticipates fixed costs of $200,000, variable costs equal to 60% of sales, and maximum capacity of $1,000,000 of sales.

(a) What is the maximum possible operating loss?
(b) Compute the maximum possible operating profit.
(c) Construct a profit-volume chart.
(d) Determine the break-even point as a percentage of capacity by using the profit-volume chart constructed in (c).

Exercise 26-6. Margin of safety. (a) If Tucker Company, with a break-even point at $420,000 of sales, has actual sales of $700,000, what is the margin of safety expressed (1) in dollars and (2) as a percentage of sales? (b) If the margin of safety for Faust Company was 25%, fixed costs were $240,000, and variable costs were 60% of sales, what was the amount of actual sales?

Exercise 26-7. Contribution margin ratio. (a) Woodall Company budgets sales of $750,000, fixed costs and expenses of $120,000, and variable costs and expenses of $480,000, what is the anticipated contribution margin ratio? (b) If the contribution margin ratio for Austin Company is 28%, sales were $850,000, and fixed costs and expenses were $88,000, what was the operating profit?

Exercise 26–8. Computation of break-even point, variable and fixed costs, and operating profit. For the past year, Gonzales Company had sales of $1,200,000, a margin of safety of 15%, and a contribution margin ratio of 40%. Compute:

(a) The break-even point.
(b) The variable costs and expenses.
(c) The fixed costs and expenses.
(d) The operating profit.

Exercise 26–9. Computation of break-even point, sales, and operating profit. For 1987, a company had sales of $1,800,000, fixed costs of $300,000, and a contribution margin ratio of 25%. During 1988, the variable costs were 75% of sales, the fixed costs did not change from the previous year, and the margin of safety was 20%.

(a) What was the operating profit for 1987?
(b) What was the break-even point for 1988?
(c) What was the amount of sales for 1988?
(d) What was the operating profit for 1988?

Exercise 26–10. Economic order quantity and inventory order point. Jewell Company estimates that 4,080 units of Material W will be required during the coming year. The materials will be used at the rate of 15 units per day throughout the 272-day period of budgeted production for the year. Past experience indicates that the annual storage cost is $.15 per unit, the cost to place an order is $34, the lead time to receive an order is 30 days, and the desired amount of safety stock is 225 units. Determine (a) the economic order quantity, (b) the inventory order point, and (c) the number of units to be purchased when the inventory order point is reached.

Exercise 26–11. Real World Focus. The following income statement data were taken from the 1985 financial statements of Pillsbury Company:

	(In millions)
Net sales	$4,670.6
Costs and expenses:	
Cost of sales	$3,292.7
Selling, general, and administrative expenses	984.7
Interest expense	53.0
	$4,330.4
Income before income tax	$ 340.2

Assume that the costs and expenses have been classified into the following fixed and variable components:

	Fixed	Variable
Cost of sales	20%	80%
Selling, general, and administrative expenses	40%	60%
Interest expense	100%	0%

Based on the above data, determine (a) the break-even point for Pillsbury Company and (b) the margin of safety expressed in sales dollars and as a percentage of 1985 sales. Round computations to one decimal place.

PROBLEMS

Series A

Problem 26–1A. Break-even point and cost-volume-profit chart. For the coming year, Peak Company anticipates fixed costs of $300,000 and variable costs equal to 70% of sales.

Instructions:

(1) Compute the anticipated break-even point.
(2) Compute the sales required to realize an operating profit of $90,000.
(3) Construct a cost-volume-profit chart, assuming sales of $2,000,000 at full capacity.
(4) Determine the probable operating profit if sales total $1,600,000.

Problem 26–2A. Break-even point and cost-volume-profit chart. Hooper Company operated at 80% of capacity last year, when sales were $800,000. Fixed costs were $240,000, and variable costs were 60% of sales. Hooper Company is considering a proposal to spend an additional $40,000 on billboard advertising during the current year in an attempt to increase sales and utilize additional capacity.

Instructions:

(1) Construct a cost-volume-profit chart indicating the break-even point for last year.
(2) Using the cost-volume-profit chart prepared in (1), determine (a) the operating profit for last year and (b) the maximum operating profit that could have been realized during the year.
(3) Construct a cost-volume-profit chart indicating the break-even point for the current year, assuming that a noncancelable contract is signed for the additional billboard advertising. No changes are expected in unit selling price or other costs.
(4) Using the cost-volume-profit chart prepared in (3), determine (a) the operating profit if sales total $800,000 and (b) the maximum operating profit that could be realized during the year.

Problem 26–3A. Break-even point and profit-volume chart. Last year, Randall Company had sales of $300,000, fixed costs of $50,000, and variable costs of $225,000. Randall Company is considering a proposal to spend $12,500 to hire a public relations firm, hoping that the company's image can be improved and sales increased. Maximum operating capacity is $500,000 of sales.

Instructions:

(1) Construct a profit-volume chart for last year.
(2) Using the profit-volume chart prepared in (1), determine for last year (a) the break-even point, (b) the operating profit, and (c) the maximum operating profit that could have been realized.
(3) Construct a profit-volume chart for the current year, assuming that the additional $12,500 expenditure is made and there is no change in unit selling price or other costs.
(4) Using the profit-volume chart prepared in (3), determine (a) the break-even point, (b) the operating profit if sales total $300,000, and (c) the maximum operating profit that could be realized.

Problem 26–4A. Sales mix and break-even point. Data related to the expected sales of products A and B for Gowdy Company for the current year, which is typical of recent years, are as follows:

Product	Selling Price per Unit	Variable Cost per Unit	Sales Mix
A	$160	$ 88	75%
B	200	144	25

The estimated fixed costs for the current year are $544,000.

Instructions:

(1) Determine the estimated sales revenues necessary to reach the break-even point for the current year.
(2) Based on the break-even point in (1), determine the unit sales of both A and B for the current year.

Problem 26–5A. Break-even point and cost-volume-profit chart, margin of safety, and contribution margin ratio. Joyce Company expects to maintain the same inventories at the end of 1987 as at the beginning of the year. The total of all production costs for the year is therefore assumed to be equal to the cost of goods sold. With this in mind, the various department heads were asked to submit estimates of the expenses for their departments during 1987. A summary report of these estimates is as follows:

	Estimated Fixed Expense	Estimated Variable Expense (per unit sold)
Production costs:		
Direct materials...................	—	$ 5.40
Direct labor......................	—	12.60
Factory overhead	$150,000	2.00
Selling expenses:		
Sales salaries and commissions	50,000	.60
Advertising......................	25,400	—
Travel	5,600	—
Miscellaneous selling expense.......	1,200	.15
General expenses:		
Office and officers' salaries	30,000	—
Supplies	5,100	.20
Miscellaneous general expense......	2,700	.05
	$270,000	$21.00

It is expected that 40,000 units will be sold at a selling price of $30 a unit. Capacity output is 50,000 units.

Instructions:

(1) Determine the break-even point (a) in dollars of sales, (b) in units, and (c) in terms of capacity.
(2) Prepare an estimated income statement for 1987.
(3) Construct a cost-volume-profit chart, indicating the break-even point in dollars of sales.
(4) What is the expected margin of safety?
(5) What is the expected contribution margin ratio?

Problem 26–6A. Break-even point under present and proposed conditions. Fain Company operated at full capacity during 1987. Its income statement for 1987 is as follows:

Sales.....................................		$4,000,000
Cost of goods sold.........................		2,400,000
Gross profit		$1,600,000
Operating expenses:		
Selling expenses.........................	$850,000	
General expenses........................	250,000	
Total operating expenses		1,100,000
Operating profit...........................		$ 500,000

The division of costs and expenses between fixed and variable is as follows:

	Fixed	Variable
Cost of goods sold......	15%	85%
Selling expenses	10%	90%
General expenses	22%	78%

Management is considering a plant expansion program that will permit an increase of $800,000 in yearly sales. The expansion will increase fixed costs and expenses by $150,000, but will not affect the relationship between sales and variable costs and expenses.

Instructions:

(1) Determine for present capacity (a) the total fixed costs and expenses and (b) the total variable costs and expenses.
(2) Determine the percentage of total variable costs and expenses to sales.
(3) Compute the break-even point under present conditions.
(4) Compute the break-even point under the proposed program.
(5) Determine the amount of sales that would be necessary under the proposed program to realize the $500,000 of operating profit that was earned in 1987.
(6) Determine the maximum operating profit possible with the expanded plant.
(7) If the proposal is accepted and sales remain at the 1987 level, what will the operating profit or loss be for 1988?
(8) Based on the data given, would you recommend accepting the proposal? Explain.

Problem 26–7A. Economic order quantity and inventory order point. McCay Company has recently decided to implement a policy designed to control inventory better. Based on past experience, the following data have been gathered for materials, which are used at a uniform rate throughout the year:

Units required during the year	2,760
Units of safety stock	180
Days of scheduled production	230
Days of lead time to receive an order	25
Ordering cost, per order placed	$34.50
Annual storage cost, per unit	$ .40

Instructions:

(1) Complete the following table for "number of orders" of 1 through 6.

Number of Orders	Number of Units per Order	Average Units in Inventory	Order and Storage Costs		
			Order Cost	Storage Cost	Combined Cost
1	2,760	1,380	$34.50	$552.00	$586.50

(2) Determine the economic order quantity, based on the table completed in (1).
(3) Determine the economic order quantity, using the formula on page 1180.
(4) Determine the inventory order point.

Problem 26–8A. Economic order quantity under present and proposed conditions. Based on the data presented in Problem 26–7A, assume that McCay Company is considering the purchase of new automated storage equipment to facilitate access to materials and to increase storage capacity. In addition, the manager of the purchasing department has requested authorization to purchase five microcomputers to expedite the processing of purchase orders.

Instructions:

(1) Assuming that the new storage equipment will increase the storage cost from $.40 to $1.60 per unit, determine the economic order quantity for McCay Company, using the formula on page 1180.
(2) Assuming that the new storage equipment is not purchased and the acquisition of the microcomputer equipment will decrease the cost per order placed from $34.50 to $5.52, determine the economic order quantity, using the formula on page 1180.
(3) Assuming that both the new storage equipment and the microcomputer equipment are purchased, determine the economic order quantity, using the formula on page 1180. As indicated in (1) and (2), the purchase of the storage equipment is expected to increase the storage cost per unit from $.40 to $1.60, and the microcomputer equipment is expected to decrease the cost per order placed from $34.50 to $5.52.
(4) Based on the answers to Problem 26–7A and (1), (2), and (3) above, what generalizations can be made concerning how changes in the cost per order placed and the storage cost per unit affect the economic order quantity?

Series B

Problem 26–1B. Break-even point and cost-volume-profit chart. For the coming year, Reece Company anticipates fixed costs of $140,000 and variable costs equal to 60% of sales.

Instructions:

(1) Compute the anticipated break-even point.
(2) Compute the sales required to realize an operating profit of $40,000.
(3) Construct a cost-volume-profit chart, assuming sales of $500,000 at full capacity.
(4) Determine the probable operating profit if sales total $400,000.

Problem 26–2B. Break-even point and cost-volume-profit chart. Chadwick Company operated at 70% of capacity last year, when sales totaled $700,000. Fixed costs were $125,000, and variable costs were 75% of sales. Chadwick Company is considering a proposal to spend an additional $25,000 on billboard advertising during the current year in an attempt to increase sales and utilize additional capacity.

Instructions:

(1) Construct a cost-volume-profit chart indicating the break-even point for last year.
(2) Using the cost-volume-profit chart prepared in (1), determine (a) the operating profit for last year and (b) the maximum operating profit that could have been realized during the year.
(3) Construct a cost-volume-profit chart indicating the break-even point for the current year, assuming that a noncancelable contract is signed for the additional billboard advertising. No changes are expected in unit selling price or other costs.
(4) Using the cost-volume-profit chart prepared in (3), determine (a) the operating profit if sales total $700,000 and (b) the maximum operating profit that could be realized during the year.

Problem 26–3B. *Break-even point and profit-volume chart.* Last year, Coggins Company had sales of $400,000, fixed costs of $50,000, and variable costs of $320,000. Coggins Company is considering a proposal to spend $10,000 to hire a public relations firm, hoping that the company's image can be improved and sales increased. Maximum operating capacity is $500,000 of sales.

Instructions:

(1) Construct a profit-volume chart for last year.
(2) Using the profit-volume chart prepared in (1), determine for last year (a) the break-even point, (b) the operating profit, and (c) the maximum operating profit that could have been realized.
(3) Construct a profit-volume chart for the current year, assuming that the additional $10,000 expenditure is made and there is no change in unit selling price or other costs.
(4) Using the profit-volume chart prepared in (3), determine (a) the break-even point, (b) the operating profit if sales total $400,000, and (c) the maximum operating profit that could be realized.

SPREADSHEET PROBLEM

Problem 26–5B. *Break-even point and cost-volume-profit chart, margin of safety, and contribution margin ratio.* Spencer Company expects to maintain the same inventories at the end of 1987 as at the beginning of the year. The total of all production costs for the year is therefore assumed to be equal to the cost of goods sold. With this in mind, the various department heads were asked to submit estimates of the expenses for their departments during 1987. A summary report of these estimates is as follows:

	Estimated Fixed Expense	Estimated Variable Expense (per unit sold)
Production costs:		
Direct materials.....................	—	$ 3.25
Direct labor........................	—	8.70
Factory overhead	$120,000	1.80
Selling expenses:		
Sales salaries and commissions	60,000	.80
Advertising........................	35,200	—
Travel	21,800	—
Miscellaneous selling expense.......	7,000	.20
General expenses:		
Office and officers' salaries	40,000	—
Supplies	11,600	.15
Miscellaneous general expense......	4,400	.10
	$300,000	$15.00

It is expected that 50,000 units will be sold at a selling price of $25 a unit. Capacity output is 60,000 units.

Instructions:

(1) Determine the break-even point (a) in dollars of sales, (b) in units, and (c) in terms of capacity.
(2) Prepare an estimated income statement for 1987.
(3) Construct a cost-volume-profit chart, indicating the break-even point in dollars of sales.
(4) What is the expected margin of safety?
(5) What is the expected contribution margin ratio?

Problem 26–7B.   Economic order quantity and inventory order point. Colson Company has recently decided to implement a policy designed to control inventory better. Based on past experience, the following data have been gathered for materials, which are used at a uniform rate throughout the year:

Units required during the year	3,960
Units of safety stock.......................................	270
Days of scheduled production	220
Days of lead time to receive an order	20
Ordering cost, per order placed............................	$33.00
Annual storage cost, per unit................................	$ .15

Instructions:

(1) Complete the following table for "number of orders" of 1 through 6.

Number of Orders	Number of Units per Order	Average Units in Inventory	Order and Storage Costs		
			Order Cost	Storage Cost	Combined Cost
1	3,960	1,980	$33.00	$297.00	$330.00

(2) Determine the economic order quantity, based on the table completed in (1).
(3) Determine the economic order quantity, using the formula on page 1180.
(4) Determine the inventory order point.

MINI-CASE 26

Owens Company manufactures product M, which sold for $45 per unit in 1987. For the past several years, sales and operating profit have been declining. On sales of $495,000 in 1987, the company operated near the break-even point and used only 55% of its productive capacity. Bill Owens, your father-in-law, is considering several proposals to reverse the trend of declining sales and operating profit, and to more fully use production facilities. One proposal under consideration is to reduce the unit selling price to $40.

Your father-in-law has asked you to aid him in assessing the proposal to reduce the sales price by $5. For this purpose, he provided the following summary of the estimated fixed and variable costs and expenses for 1988, which are unchanged from 1987:

Variable costs and expenses:

Production costs..........................	$18.60 per unit
Selling expenses	6.20 per unit
General expenses	4.00 per unit

Fixed costs and expenses:

Production costs..........................	$120,000
Selling expenses	30,000
General expenses	26,400

Instructions:

(1) Determine the break-even point for 1988 in dollars, assuming (a) no change in sales price and (b) the proposed sales price.

(2) How much additional sales are necessary for Owens Company to break even in 1988 under the proposal?

(3) Determine the operating profit for 1988, assuming (a) no change in sales price and volume from 1987 and (b) the new sales price and no change in volume from 1987.

(4) Determine the maximum operating profit for 1988, assuming the proposed sales price.

(5) Briefly list factors that you would discuss with your father-in-law in evaluating the proposal.

Chapter 27

DIFFERENTIAL ANALYSIS AND CAPITAL INVESTMENT ANALYSIS

Chapter Objectives:

■ Describe the nature of differential analysis and illustrate its application to decisions involving:
> Leasing or selling
> Discontinuing an unprofitable segment
> Making or buying
> Replacing equipment
> Processing or selling
> Accepting business at a special price

■ Describe the nature of capital investment analysis and illustrate the evaluation of capital investment proposals by the following methods:
> Average rate of return
> Cash payback
> Discounted cash flow
> Discounted internal rate of return

■ Describe and illustrate the capital rationing process.

■ Describe the use of a capital expenditures budget for planning and controlling capital investment expenditures.

A primary objective of accounting is to provide management with analyses and reports that will be useful in resolving current problems and in planning for the future. The types of analyses and reports depend on the nature of the decisions to be made. In this chapter, two types of analyses—differential analysis and capital investment analysis—are discussed and illustrated. Differential analysis provides management with data on the differences between total revenues and total costs associated with alternative courses of action. Capital investment analysis is the process by which accounting aids management in planning, evaluating, and controlling long-term investments involving property, plant, and equipment.

DIFFERENTIAL ANALYSIS

Planning for future operations is chiefly decision making. For some decisions, revenue and cost information drawn from the general ledger and other basic accounting records is very useful. For example, historical cost data in the absorption costing format are helpful in planning production for the long run. Historical cost data in the variable costing format are useful in planning production for the short run. However, the revenue and cost data needed to evaluate courses of future operations or to choose among competing alternatives are often not available in the basic accounting records.

The relevant revenue and cost data in the analysis of future possibilities are the differences between the alternatives under consideration. The amounts of such differences are called **differentials** and the area of accounting concerned with the effect of alternative courses of action on revenues and costs is called **differential analysis**.

Differential revenue is the amount of increase or decrease in revenue expected from a particular course of action as compared with an alternative. To illustrate, assume that certain equipment is being used to manufacture a product that provides revenue of $150,000. If the equipment could be used to make another product that would provide revenue of $175,000, the differential revenue from the alternative would be $25,000.

Differential cost is the amount of increase or decrease in cost that is expected from a particular course of action as compared with an alternative. For example, if an increase in advertising expenditures from $100,000 to $150,000 is being considered, the differential cost of the action would be $50,000.

The main advantage of differential analysis is its selection of relevant revenues and costs related to alternative courses of action. Differential analysis reports emphasize the significant factors bearing on the decision, help to clarify the issues, and save the time of the reader.

Differential analysis can aid management in making decisions on a variety of alternatives, including (1) whether equipment should be leased or sold, (2) whether to discontinue an unprofitable segment, (3) whether to manufacture or purchase a needed part, (4) whether to replace usable plant assets, (5) whether to process further or sell an intermediate product, and (6) whether to accept additional business at a special price. The following discussion relates to the use of differential analysis in analyzing these alternatives.

Lease or Sell

Management often has a choice between leasing or selling a piece of equipment that is no longer needed in the business. In deciding which option is best, management can use differential analysis. To illustrate, assume that Company A is considering the disposal of equipment that originally cost $200,000 and has been depreciated a total of $120,000 to date. Company A can sell the equipment through a broker for $100,000 less a 6% commission. Alternatively, Company B has tentatively offered to lease the equipment for a number of years for a total of $160,000, after which Company A would sell it for a small amount as scrap. During the period of the lease, Company A would incur repair, insurance, and property tax expenses estimated at $35,000. Company A's analysis of whether to lease or sell the equipment is as follows:

Proposal To Lease or Sell Equipment
June 22, 19--

Differential revenue from alternatives:		
Revenue from lease................................	$160,000	
Revenue from sale.................................	100,000	
Differential revenue from lease		$60,000
Differential cost of alternatives:		
Repair, insurance, and property tax expenses........	$ 35,000	
Commission expense on sale	6,000	
Differential cost of lease.........................		29,000
Net advantage of lease alternative..................		$31,000

DIFFERENTIAL
ANALYSIS
REPORT—
LEASE OR
SELL

It should be noted that it was not necessary to consider the $80,000 book value ($200,000 − $120,000) of the equipment. The $80,000 is a **sunk cost**; that is, it is a cost that will not be affected by later decisions. In the illustration, the expenditure to acquire the equipment had already been made, and the choice is now between leasing or selling the equipment. The relevant factors to be considered are the differential revenues and differential costs associated with the lease or sell decision. The undepreciated cost of the equipment is irrelevant. The validity of the foregoing report can be shown by the following conventional analysis:

Lease alternative:

Revenue from lease		$160,000
Depreciation expense	$80,000	
Repair, insurance, and property tax expenses	35,000	115,000
Net gain		$45,000

Sell alternative:

Sale price		$100,000
Book value of equipment	$80,000	
Commission expense	6,000	86,000
Net gain		14,000
Net advantage of lease alternative		$31,000

The alternatives presented in the illustration were relatively uncomplicated. Regardless of the number and complexity of the additional factors that may be involved, the approach to differential analysis remains basically the same. Two factors that often need to be considered are (1) the differential revenue from investing the funds generated by the alternatives and (2) the income tax differential. In the example, there would undoubtedly be a differential advantage to the immediate investment of the $94,000 net proceeds ($100,000 − $6,000) from the sale over the investment of the net proceeds from the lease arrangement, which would become available over a period of years. The income tax differential would be that related to the differences in timing of the income from the alternatives and the differences in the amount of investment income.

Discontinuance of an Unprofitable Segment

When a department, branch, territory, or other segment of an enterprise has been operating at a loss, management should consider eliminating the unprofitable segment. It might be natural to assume (sometimes mistakenly) that the total operating income of the enterprise would be increased if the operating loss could be eliminated. Discontinuance of the unprofitable segment will usually eliminate all of the related variable costs and expenses. However, if the segment represents a relatively small part of the enterprise, the fixed costs and expenses (depreciation, insurance, property taxes, etc.)

will not be reduced by its discontinuance. It is entirely possible in this situation for the total operating income of a company to be reduced rather than increased by eliminating an unprofitable segment. As a basis for illustrating this type of situation, the following income statement is presented for the year just ended, which was a normal year. For purposes of the illustration, it is assumed that discontinuance of Product A, on which losses are incurred annually, will have no effect on total fixed costs and expenses.

Condensed Income Statement
For Year Ended August 31, 19--

| | Product | | | |
	A	B	C	Total
Sales	$100,000	$400,000	$500,000	$1,000,000
Cost of goods sold:				
Variable costs..............	$ 60,000	$200,000	$220,000	$ 480,000
Fixed costs................	20,000	80,000	120,000	220,000
Total cost of goods sold.....	$ 80,000	$280,000	$340,000	$ 700,000
Gross profit..................	$ 20,000	$120,000	$160,000	$ 300,000
Operating expenses:				
Variable expenses...........	$ 25,000	$ 60,000	$ 95,000	$ 180,000
Fixed expenses	6,000	20,000	25,000	51,000
Total operating expenses....	$ 31,000	$ 80,000	$120,000	$ 231,000
Income (loss) from operations ...	$ (11,000)	$ 40,000	$ 40,000	$ 69,000

Data on the estimated differential revenue and differential cost related to discontinuing Product A, on which an operating loss of $11,000 was incurred during the past year, may be assembled in a report such as the following. This report emphasizes the significant factors bearing on the decision.

Proposal To Discontinue Product A
September 29, 19--

Differential revenue from annual sales of product:		
Revenue from sales................................		$100,000
Differential cost of annual sales of product:		
Variable cost of goods sold	$60,000	
Variable operating expenses.......................	25,000	85,000
Annual differential income from sales of Product A......		$ 15,000

DIFFERENTIAL ANALYSIS REPORT— DISCONTINUANCE OF UNPROFITABLE SEGMENT

Instead of an increase in annual operating income to $80,000 (Product B, $40,000; Product C, $40,000) that might seem to be indicated by the income statement, the discontinuance of Product A would reduce operating income to an estimated $54,000 ($69,000 − $15,000). The validity of this conclusion can be shown by the following conventional analysis:

Proposal To Discontinue Product A
September 29, 19--

	Current Operations			Discontinuance of Product A
	Product A	Products B and C	Total	
Sales	$100,000	$900,000	$1,000,000	$900,000
Cost of goods sold:				
Variable costs	$ 60,000	$420,000	$ 480,000	$420,000
Fixed costs	20,000	200,000	220,000	220,000
Total cost of goods sold	$ 80,000	$620,000	$ 700,000	$640,000
Gross profit	$ 20,000	$280,000	$ 300,000	$260,000
Operating expenses:				
Variable expenses	$ 25,000	$155,000	$ 180,000	$155,000
Fixed expenses	6,000	45,000	51,000	51,000
Total operating expenses	$ 31,000	$200,000	$ 231,000	$206,000
Income (loss) from operations	$ (11,000)	$ 80,000	$ 69,000	$ 54,000

For purposes of the illustration, it was assumed that the discontinuance of Product A would not cause any significant reduction in the volume of fixed costs and expenses. If plant capacity made available by discontinuance of a losing operation can be used in some other manner or if plant capacity can be reduced, with a resulting reduction in fixed costs and expenses, additional analysis would be needed.

In decisions involving the elimination of an unprofitable segment, management must also consider such other factors as its effect on employees and customers. If a segment of the business is discontinued, some employees may have to be laid off and others may have to be relocated and retrained. Also important is the possible decline in sales of the more profitable products to customers who were attracted to the firm by the discontinued product.

Make or Buy

The assembly of many parts is often a substantial element in manufacturing operations. Many of the large factory complexes of automobile manufacturers are specifically called assembly plants. Some of the parts of the finished automobile, such as the motor, are produced by the automobile manufacturer, while other parts, such as tires, are often purchased from other manufacturers. Even in manufacturing the motors, such items as spark plugs and nuts and bolts may be acquired from suppliers in their finished state. When parts or components are purchased, management has usually evaluated the question of "make or buy" and has concluded that a savings in cost results from buying the part rather than manufacturing it. However, "make or buy" options are likely to arise anew when a manufacturer has excess productive capacity in the form of unused equipment, space, and labor.

As a basis for illustrating such alternatives, assume that a manufacturer has been purchasing a component, Part X, for $5 a unit. The factory is currently operating at 80% of capacity, and no significant increase in production is anticipated in the near future. The cost of manufacturing Part X, determined by absorption costing methods, is estimated at $1 for direct materials, $2 for direct labor, and $3 for factory overhead (at the predetermined rate of 150% of direct labor cost), or a total of $6. The decision based on a simple comparison of a "make" price of $6 with a "buy" price of $5 is obvious. However, to the extent that unused capacity could be used in manufacturing the part, there would be no increase in the total amount of fixed factory overhead costs. Hence, only the variable factory overhead costs need to be considered. Variable factory overhead costs such as power and maintenance are determined to amount to approximately 65% of the direct labor cost of $2, or $1.30. The cost factors to be considered are summarized in the following report:

DIFFERENTIAL
ANALYSIS
REPORT—
MAKE OR
BUY

Proposal To Manufacture Part X
February 15, 19--

Purchase price of part.		$5.00
Differential cost to manufacture part:		
Direct materials	$1.00	
Direct labor	2.00	
Variable factory overhead.	1.30	4.30
Cost reduction from manufacturing Part X		$ .70

Other possible effects of a change in policy should also be considered, such as the possibility that a future increase in volume of production would require the use of the currently idle capacity of 20%. The possible effect of the alternatives on employees and on future business relations with the supplier of the part, who may be providing other essential components, are additional factors that might need study.

Equipment Replacement

The usefulness of plant assets may be impaired long before they are considered to be "worn out." Equipment may no longer be ideally adequate for the purpose for which it is used, but on the other hand it may not have reached the point of complete inadequacy. Similarly, the point in time when equipment becomes obsolete may be difficult to determine. Decisions to replace usable plant assets should be based on studies of relevant costs rather than on whims or subjective opinions. The costs to be considered are the alternative future costs of retention as opposed to replacement. The book values of the plant assets being replaced are sunk costs and are irrelevant.

To illustrate some of the factors involved in replacement decisions, assume that an enterprise is considering the disposal of several identical machines having a total book value of $100,000 and an estimated remaining life of five years. The old machines can be sold for $25,000. They can be replaced by a single high-speed machine at a cost of $250,000, with an estimated useful life of five years and no residual value. Analysis of the specifications of the new machine and of accompanying changes in manufacturing methods indicate an estimated annual reduction in variable manufacturing costs from $225,000 to $150,000. No other changes in the manufacturing costs or the operating expenses are expected. The basic data to be considered are summarized in the following report:

DIFFERENTIAL
ANALYSIS
REPORT—
EQUIPMENT
REPLACE-
MENT

Proposal To Replace Equipment November 28, 19--		
Annual variable costs — present equipment	$225,000	
Annual variable costs — new equipment	150,000	
Annual differential decrease in cost	$ 75,000	
Number of years applicable	× 5	
Total differential decrease in cost	$375,000	
Proceeds from sale of present equipment	25,000	$400,000
Cost of new equipment		250,000
Net differential decrease in cost, 5-year total		$150,000
Annual differential decrease in cost — new equipment		$ 30,000

Complicating features could be added to the foregoing illustration, such as a disparity between the remaining useful life of the old equipment and the estimated life of the new equipment, or possible improvement in the product due to the new machine, with a resulting increase in selling price or volume of sales. Another factor that should be considered is the importance of alternative uses for the cash outlay needed to obtain the new equipment. The amount of income that would result from the best available alternative to the proposed use of cash or its equivalent is sometimes called **opportunity cost**. If, for example, it is assumed that the cash outlay of $250,000 for the new equipment, less the $25,000 proceeds from the sale of the present equipment, could be used to yield a 10% return, the opportunity cost of the proposal would amount to 10% of $225,000, or $22,500.

The term "opportunity cost" introduces a new concept of "cost." In reality, it is not a cost in any usual sense of the word. Instead, it represents the forgoing of possible income associated with a lost opportunity. Although opportunity cost computations do not appear as a part of historical accounting data, they are unquestionably useful in analyses involving choices between alternative courses of action.

Process or Sell

When a product is manufactured, it progresses through various stages of production. Often, a product can be sold at an intermediate stage of production, or it can be processed further and then sold. In deciding whether to sell a product at an intermediate stage or to process it further, the differential revenues that would be provided and the differential costs that would be incurred from further processing must be considered. Since the costs of producing the intermediate product do not change, regardless of whether the intermediate product is sold or processed further, these costs are not differential costs and are not considered.

To illustrate, assume that an enterprise produces Product Y in batches of 4,000 gallons by processing standard quantities of 4,000 gallons of direct materials, which cost $1.20 per gallon. Product Y can be sold without further processing for $2 per gallon. It is possible for the enterprise to process Product Y further to yield Product Z, which can be sold for $5 per gallon. Product Z will require additional processing costs of $5,760 per batch, and 20% of the gallons of Product Y will evaporate during production. The differential revenues and costs to be considered in deciding whether to process Product Y to produce Product Z are summarized in the following report:

DIFFERENTIAL
ANALYSIS
REPORT—
PROCESS
OR SELL

Proposal To Process Product Y Further
October 1, 19--

Differential revenue from further processing per batch:		
Revenue from sale of Product Z [(4,000 gallons−800 gallons evaporation) × $5]	$16,000	
Revenue from sale of Product Y (4,000 gallons × $2) . . .	8,000	
Differential revenue		$8,000
Differential cost per batch:		
Additional cost of producing Product Z.		5,760
Net advantage of further processing Product Y per batch .		$2,240

The net advantage of further processing Product Y into Product Z is $2,240 per batch. Note that the initial cost of producing the intermediate Product Y, $4,800 (4,000 gallons × $1.20), is not considered in deciding whether to process Product Y further. This initial cost will be incurred regardless of whether Product Z is produced.

Acceptance of Business at a Special Price

In determining whether to accept additional business at a special price, management must consider the differential revenue that would be provided and the differential cost that would be incurred. If the company is operating at full capacity, the additional production will increase both fixed and variable production costs. But if the normal production of the company is below full capacity, additional business may be undertaken without increasing fixed production costs. In the latter case, the variable costs will be the differential cost of the additional production. Variable costs are the only costs to be considered in making a decision to accept or reject the order. If the operating expenses are likely to increase, these differentials must also be considered.

To illustrate, assume that the usual monthly production of an enterprise is 10,000 units of a certain commodity. At this level of operation, which is well below capacity, the manufacturing cost is $20 per unit, composed of variable costs of $12.50 and fixed costs of $7.50. The normal selling price of the product in the domestic market is $30. The manufacturer receives an offer from an exporter for 5,000 units of the product at $18 each. Production costs can be spread over a three-month period without interfering with normal production or incurring overtime costs. Pricing policies in the domestic market will not be affected. Comparison of a sales price of $18 with the present unit cost of $20 would indicate that this offer should be rejected. However, if attention is limited to the differential cost, which in this case is composed of the variable costs and expenses, the conclusion is quite different. The essentials of the analysis are presented in the following brief report:

DIFFERENTIAL
ANALYSIS
REPORT—
SALE AT
SPECIAL
PRICE

Proposal To Sell to Exporter
March 10, 19--

Differential revenue from acceptance of offer:
Revenue from sale of 5,000 additional units at $18 . . . . $90,000

Differential cost of acceptance of offer:
Variable costs and expenses of 5,000 additional units at $12.50   62,500

Gain from acceptance of offer $27,500

Proposals to sell an increased output in the domestic market at a reduction from the normal price may require additional considerations of a difficult nature. It would clearly be unwise to increase sales volume in one territory by means of a price reduction if sales volume would thereby be jeopardized in other areas. Manufacturers must also exercise care to avoid violations of the Robinson-Patman Act, which prohibits price discrimination within the United States unless the difference in price can be justified by a difference in the cost of serving different customers.

NATURE OF CAPITAL INVESTMENT ANALYSIS

With the accelerated growth of American industry, increasing attention has been given to long-term investment decisions involving property, plant, and equipment. The process by which management plans, evaluates, and controls such investments is called **capital investment analysis**, or **capital budgeting**. This analysis may involve thousands, millions, or even billions of dollars. In addition, capital investment decisions normally involve a long-term commitment of funds and thus affect operations for many years. These funds must earn a reasonable rate of return, so that the enterprise can meet its obligations to creditors and provide dividends to stockholders. Because capital investment decisions are some of the most important decisions that management makes, the systems and procedures for planning, evaluating, and controlling capital investments must be carefully developed and implemented.

A capital investment program should include a plan for encouraging employees at all levels of an enterprise to submit proposals for capital investments. The plan should provide for communicating to the employees the long-range goals of the enterprise, so that useful proposals are submitted. In addition, the plan may provide for rewarding employees whose proposals are implemented. All reasonable proposals should be given serious consideration, and the effects of the economic implications expected from these proposals should be identified.

The essentials of the most commonly used methods of evaluating capital investment proposals are described in the following sections. The similarities and differences between the methods, as well as the uses of each method, are emphasized. Finally, considerations complicating capital investment analyses, the process of allocating available investment funds among competing proposals (capital rationing), and planning and controlling capital expenditures are briefly discussed.

METHODS OF EVALUATING CAPITAL INVESTMENT PROPOSALS

The methods of evaluating capital investment proposals can be grouped into two general categories: (1) methods that ignore present value and (2) present value methods. The characteristic that distinguishes one category from the other is the way in which the concept of the time value of money is treated. Because cash on hand can be invested to earn more cash, while cash to be received in the future cannot, money has a time value. However, the methods that ignore present value do not give consideration to the fact that cash on hand is more valuable than cash to be received in the future. The two methods in this category are (1) the average rate of return method and (2) the cash payback method.

By converting dollars to be received in the future into current dollars, using the concept of present value, the present value methods take into consideration the fact that money has a time value. The two common present value methods used in evaluating capital investment proposals are (1) the discounted cash flow method and (2) the discounted internal rate of return method.

Each of the four methods of analyzing capital investment proposals has both advantages and limitations. Often management will use some combination of the four methods in evaluating the various economic aspects of capital investment proposals.

Methods That Ignore Present Value

The average rate of return and the cash payback methods of evaluating capital investment proposals are simple to use and are especially useful in screening proposals. Management often establishes a minimum standard, and proposals not meeting this minimum standard are dropped from further consideration. When several alternative proposals meet the minimum standard, management will often rank the proposals from the most desirable to the least desirable.

The methods that ignore present value are also useful in evaluating capital investment proposals that have relatively short useful lives. In such situations, the timing of the cash flows is less important, and management generally focuses its attention on the amount of income to be earned from the investment and the total net cash flows to be received from the investment.

Average Rate of Return Method. The expected **average rate of return**, sometimes referred to as the **accounting rate of return**, is a measure of the expected profitability of an investment in plant assets. The amount of income expected to be earned from the investment is stated as an annual average over the number of years the asset is to be used. The amount of the investment may be considered to be the original cost of the plant asset, or recognition may be given to the effect of depreciation on the amount of the investment. According to the latter view, the investment gradually declines from the original cost to the estimated residual value at the end of its useful life. If straight-line depreciation and no residual value are assumed, the average investment would be equal to one half of the original expenditure.

To illustrate, assume that management is considering the purchase of a certain machine at a cost of $500,000. The machine is expected to have a useful life of 4 years, with no residual value, and its use during the 4 years is expected to yield total income of $200,000. The estimated average annual income is therefore $50,000 ($200,000 ÷ 4), and the average investment is $250,000 [($500,000 + $0 residual value) ÷ 2]. Accordingly, the expected average rate of return on the average investment is 20%, computed as follows:

$$\text{Average Rate of Return} = \frac{\text{Estimated Average Annual Income}}{\text{Average Investment}}$$

$$\text{Average Rate of Return} = \frac{\$200,000 \div 4}{(\$500,000 + \$0) \div 2}$$

$$\text{Average Rate of Return} = 20\%$$

The expected average rate of return of 20% should be compared with the rate established by management as the minimum reward for the risks involved in the investment. The attractiveness of the proposed purchase of additional equipment is indicated by the difference between the expected rate and the minimum desired rate.

When several alternative capital investment proposals are being considered, the proposals can be ranked by their average rates of return. The higher the average rate of return of 25%, the more desirable the proposal. For example, assume that management is considering the following alternative capital investment proposals and has computed the indicated average rates of return:

	Proposal A	Proposal B
Estimated average annual income	$ 30,000	$ 36,000
Average investment	$120,000	$180,000
Average rate of return:		
$30,000 ÷ $120,000	25%	
$36,000 ÷ $180,000		20%

If only the average rate of return is considered, Proposal A, based on its average rate of return of 25%, would be preferred over Proposal B.

The primary advantages of the average rate of return method are its ease of computation and the fact that it emphasizes the amount of income earned over the entire life of the proposal. Its main disadvantages are its lack of consideration of the expected cash flows from the proposal and the timing of these cash flows. These cash flows are important because cash coming from an investment can be reinvested in other income-producing activities. Therefore, the more funds and the sooner the funds become available, the more income that can be generated from their reinvestment.

Cash Payback Method. The expected period of time that will pass between the date of a capital investment and the complete recovery in cash (or equivalent) of the amount invested is called the **cash payback period**. To simplify the analysis, the revenues and the out-of-pocket operating expenses expected to be associated with the operation of the plant assets are assumed to be entirely in the form of cash. The excess of the cash flowing in from revenue over the cash flowing out for expenses is termed **net cash flow**. The time required for the net cash flow to equal the initial outlay for the plant asset is the payback period.

For purposes of illustration, assume that the proposed investment in a plant asset with an 8-year life is $200,000 and that the annual net cash flow is expected to be $40,000. The estimated cash payback period for the investment is 5 years, computed as follows:

$$\frac{\$200,000}{\$40,000} = \text{5-year cash payback period}$$

In the preceding illustration, the annual net cash flows were equal ($40,000 per year). If these annual net cash flows are not equal, the cash payback period is determined by summing the annual net cash flows until the cumulative sum equals the amount of the proposed investment. To illustrate, assume that for a proposed investment of $400,000, the annual net cash flows and cumulative net cash flows over the proposal's 6-year life are as follows:

Year	Net Cash Flow	Cumulative Net Cash Flow
1	$ 60,000	$ 60,000
2	80,000	140,000
3	105,000	245,000
4	155,000	400,000
5	140,000	540,000
6	90,000	630,000

The cumulative net cash flow at the end of the fourth year equals the amount of the investment, $400,000. Therefore, the payback period is 4 years.

The cash payback method is widely used in evaluating proposals for expansion and for investment in new projects. A relatively short payback period is desirable, because the sooner the cash is recovered the sooner it becomes available for reinvestment in other projects. In addition, there is likely to be less possibility of loss from changes in economic conditions, obsolescence, and other unavoidable risks when the commitment is short-term. The cash payback concept is also of interest to bankers and other creditors who may be dependent upon net cash flow for the repayment of claims associated with the initial capital investment. The sooner the cash is recovered, the sooner the debt or other liabilities can be paid. Thus, the cash payback method would be especially useful to managers whose primary concern is liquidity.

One of the primary disadvantages of the cash payback method as a basis for decisions is its failure to take into consideration the expected profitability of a proposal. A project with a very short payback period, coupled with relatively poor profitability, would be less desirable than one with a longer payback period but with satisfactory profitability. Another disadvantage of the cash payback method is that the cash flows occurring after the payback period are ignored. A 5-year project with a 3-year payback period and two additional years of substantial cash flows is more desirable than a 5-year project with a 3-year payback period that has lower cash flows in the last two years.

Present Value Methods

An investment in plant and equipment may be viewed as the acquisition of a series of future net cash flows composed of two elements: (1) recovery of the initial investment and (2) income. The period of time over which these net cash flows will be received may be an important factor in determining the value of an investment.

As discussed in Chapter 17, the concept of present values is that any specified amount of cash to be received at some date in the future is not the equivalent of the same amount of cash held at an earlier date. A sum of cash to be received in the future is not as valuable as the same sum on hand today, because cash on hand today can be invested to earn income. For example, $10,000 on hand today would be more valuable than $10,000 to be received a year from today. In other words, if cash can be invested to earn 10% per year, the $10,000 on hand today will accumulate to $11,000 ($10,000 plus $1,000 earnings) by one year from today. The $10,000 on hand today can be referred to as the present value amount that is equivalent to $11,000 to be received a year from today.

Discounted Cash Flow Method. The **discounted cash flow method**, sometimes referred to as the **net present value method**, uses present value concepts to compute the present value of the cash flows expected from a proposal. To illustrate, if the rate of earnings is 12% and the cash to be received in one year is $1,000, the present value amount is $892.86 ($1,000 ÷ 1.12). If the cash is to be received one year later (two years in all), with the earnings compounded at the end of the first year, the present value amount would be $797.20 ($892.86 ÷ 1.12).

Instead of determining the present value of future cash flows by a series of divisions in the manner just illustrated, it is customary to find the present value of $1 from a table of present values and to multiply it by the amount of the future cash flow. Reference to the following partial table indicates that the present value of $1 to be received two years hence, with earnings at the rate of 12% a year, is .797. Multiplication of .797 by $1,000 yields $797, which is the same amount that was determined in the preceding paragraph by two successive divisions. The small difference is due to rounding the present value factors in the table to three decimal places.

Year	6%	10%	12%	15%	20%
1	.943	.909	.893	.870	.833
2	.890	.826	.797	.756	.694
3	.840	.751	.712	.658	.579
4	.792	.683	.636	.572	.482
5	.747	.621	.567	.497	.402
6	.705	.564	.507	.432	.335
7	.665	.513	.452	.376	.279
8	.627	.467	.404	.327	.233
9	.592	.424	.361	.284	.194
10	.558	.386	.322	.247	.162

PRESENT VALUE OF $1 AT COMPOUND INTEREST

The particular rate of return selected in discounted cash flow analysis is affected by the nature of the business enterprise and its relative profitability, the purpose of the capital investment, the cost of securing funds for the investment, the minimum desired rate of return, and other related factors. If the present value of the net cash flow expected from a proposed investment, at the selected rate, equals or exceeds the amount of the investment, the proposal is desirable. For purposes of illustration, assume a proposal for the acquisition of $200,000 of equipment with an expected useful life of 5 years and a minimum desired rate of return of 10%. The anticipated net cash flow for each of the 5 years and the analysis of the proposal are as follows. The calculation shows that the proposal is expected to recover the investment and provide more than the minimum rate of return.

Year	Present Value of $1 at 10%	Net Cash Flow	Present Value of Net Cash Flow
1	.909	$ 70,000	$ 63,630
2	.826	60,000	49,560
3	.751	50,000	37,550
4	.683	40,000	27,320
5	.621	40,000	24,840
Total....................		$260,000	$202,900

Amount to be invested	200,000
Excess of present value over amount to be invested	$ 2,900

When several alternative investment proposals of the same amount are being considered, the one with the largest excess of present value over the amount to be invested is the most desirable. If the alternative proposals involve different amounts of investment, it is useful to prepare a relative ranking of the proposals by using a **present value index**. The present value index for the previous illustration is computed by dividing the total present value of the net cash flow by the amount to be invested, as follows:

$$\text{Present Value Index} = \frac{\text{Total Present Value of Net Cash Flow}}{\text{Amount To Be Invested}}$$

$$\text{Present Value Index} = \frac{\$202,900}{\$200,000}$$

$$\text{Present Value Index} = 1.01$$

To illustrate the ranking of the proposals by use of the present value index, assume that the total present values of the net cash flow and the amounts to be invested for three alternative proposals are as follows:

	Proposal A	Proposal B	Proposal C
Total present value of net cash flow...	$107,000	$86,400	$93,600
Amount to be invested..............	100,000	80,000	90,000
Excess of present value over amount to be invested......................	$ 7,000	$ 6,400	$ 3,600

The present value index for each proposal is as follows:

	Present Value Index
Proposal A	1.07 ($107,000 ÷ $100,000)
Proposal B	1.08 ($ 86,400 ÷ $ 80,000)
Proposal C	1.04 ($ 93,600 ÷ $ 90,000)

The present value indexes indicate that although Proposal A has the largest excess of present value over the amount to be invested, it is not as attractive as Proposal B in terms of the amount of present value per dollar invested. It should be noted, however, that Proposal B requires an investment of only $80,000, while Proposal A requires an investment of $100,000. The possible use of the $20,000 if B is selected should be considered before a final decision is made.

The primary advantage of the discounted cash flow method is that it gives consideration to the time value of money. A disadvantage of the method is that the computations are more complex than those for the methods that ignore present value. In addition, this method assumes that the cash received from the proposal during its useful life will be reinvested at the rate of return used to compute the present value of the proposal. Because of changing economic conditions, this assumption may not always be reasonable.

Discounted Internal Rate of Return Method. The **discounted internal rate of return method**, sometimes called the **internal rate of return** or **time-adjusted rate of return method**, uses present value concepts to compute the rate of return from the net cash flows expected from capital investment proposals. Thus, it is similar to the discounted cash flow method, in that it focuses on the present value of the net cash flows. However, the discounted internal rate of return method starts with the net cash flows and, in a sense, works backwards to determine the discounted rate of return expected from the proposal. The discounted cash flow method requires management to specify a minimum rate of return, which is then used to determine the excess (deficiency) of the present value of the net cash flow over the investment.

To illustrate the use of the discounted internal rate of return method, assume that management is evaluating a proposal to acquire equipment costing $33,530, which is expected to provide annual net cash flows of $10,000 per year for 5 years. If a rate of return of 12% is assumed, the present value of the net cash flows can be computed using the present value of $1 table on page 1217, as follows:

Year	Present Value of $1 at 12%	Net Cash Flow	Present Value of Net Cash Flow
1	.893	$10,000	$ 8,930
2	.797	10,000	7,970
3	.712	10,000	7,120
4	.636	10,000	6,360
5	.567	10,000	5,670
Total........................		$50,000	$36,050

Since the present value of the net cash flow based on a 12% rate of return, $36,050, is greater than the $33,530 to be invested, 12% is obviously not the discounted internal rate of return. The following analysis indicates that 15% is the rate of return that equates the $33,530 cost of the investment with the present value of the net cash flows.

Year	Present Value of $1 at 15%	Net Cash Flow	Present Value of Net Cash Flow
1	.870	$10,000	$ 8,700
2	.756	10,000	7,560
3	.658	10,000	6,580
4	.572	10,000	5,720
5	.497	10,000	4,970
Total.........................		$50,000	$33,530

In the illustration, the discounted internal rate of return was determined by trial and error. A rate of 12% was assumed before the discounted internal rate of return of 15% was identified. Such procedures are tedious and time consuming. When equal annual net cash flows are expected from a proposal, as in the illustration, the computations can be simplified by using a table of the present value of an annuity.[1]

A series of equal cash flows at fixed intervals is termed an **annuity**. The **present value of an annuity** is the sum of the present values of each cash flow. From another point of view, the present value of an annuity is the amount of cash that would be needed today to yield a series of equal cash flows at fixed intervals in the future. For example, reference to the following table of the present value of an annuity of $1 shows that the present value of cash flows at the end of each of five years, with a discounted internal rate of return of 15% per year, is 3.353. Multiplication of $10,000 by 3.353 yields the same amount ($33,530) that was determined in the preceding illustration by five successive multiplications.

PRESENT VALUE OF AN ANNUITY OF $1 AT COMPOUND INTEREST

Year	6%	10%	12%	15%	20%
1	.943	.909	.893	.870	.833
2	1.833	1.736	1.690	1.626	1.528
3	2.673	2.487	2.402	2.283	2.106
4	3.465	3.170	3.037	2.855	2.589
5	4.212	3.791	3.605	3.353	2.991
6	4.917	4.355	4.111	3.785	3.326
7	5.582	4.868	4.564	4.160	3.605
8	6.210	5.335	4.968	4.487	3.837
9	6.802	5.759	5.328	4.772	4.031
10	7.360	6.145	5.650	5.019	4.192

The procedures for using the present value of an annuity of $1 table to determine the discounted internal rate of return are as follows:

[1]In the illustration, equal annual net cash flows are assumed, so that attention can be focused on the basic concepts. If the annual net cash flows are not equal, the procedures are more complex, but the basic concepts are not affected. In such cases, computers can be used to perform the computations.

1. A present value factor for an annuity of $1 is determined by dividing the amount to be invested by the annual net cash flow, as expressed in the following formula:

$$\text{Present Value Factor for an Annuity of \$1} = \frac{\text{Amount To Be Invested}}{\text{Annual Net Cash Flow}}$$

2. The present value factor determined in (1) is located in the present value of an annuity of $1 table by first locating the number of years of expected useful life of the investment in the Year column and then proceeding horizontally across the table until the present value factor determined in (1) is found.
3. The discounted internal rate of return is then identified by the heading of the column in which the present value factor in (2) is located.

To illustrate the use of the present value of an annuity of $1 table, assume that management is considering a proposal to acquire equipment costing $97,360, which is expected to provide equal annual net cash flows of $20,000 for 7 years. The present value factor for an annuity of $1 is 4.868, computed as follows:

$$\text{Present Value Factor for an Annuity of \$1} = \frac{\text{Amount To Be Invested}}{\text{Annual Net Cash Flow}}$$

$$\text{Present Value Factor for an Annuity of \$1} = \frac{\$97,360}{\$20,000}$$

$$\text{Present Value Factor for an Annuity of \$1} = 4.868$$

For a period of 7 years, the following table for the present value of an annuity of $1 indicates that the factor 4.868 is associated with a percentage of 10%. Thus, 10% is the discounted internal rate of return for this proposal.

Year	6%	10%	12%
1	.943	.909	.893
2	1.833	1.736	1.690
3	2.673	2.487	2.402
4	3.465	3.170	3.037
5	4.212	3.791	3.605
6	4.917	4.355	4.111
7	5.582	4.868	4.564
8	6.210	5.335	4.968
9	6.802	5.759	5.328
10	7.360	6.145	5.650

PRESENT VALUE OF AN ANNUITY OF $1 AT COMPOUND INTEREST

If the minimum acceptable rate of return for similar proposals is 10% or less, then the proposed equipment acquisition should be considered desirable. When several proposals are under consideration, management often ranks the proposals by their discounted internal rates of return, and the proposal with the highest rate is considered the most attractive.

The Discounted Internal Rate of Return Method — An Application Using the Microcomputer

The complexity of using the present value methods of evaluating capital investment proposals can be significantly reduced by using a microcomputer. The following computer program, which was written in the BASIC programming language, computes the discounted internal rate of return for an investment proposal with a series of equal net cash flows.

```
10   INPUT "periods";N: INPUT "investment";I: INPUT "annual net cash flow";C
20   INPUT "guess";G
30   X=(X+G)/100+1:S=I
40   FOR J=1 TO N:S=S+C/X^J:NEXT:X=(X-1)*100
50   IF ABS(Y-X)<=.001 THEN END
60   LPRINT X:Y=X:RESTORE:IF S>0 THEN 30
70   X=X-G:G=G/3:GOTO 30
```

To run this program, the user must have access to the BASIC programming system. The manual accompanying this system will describe the procedures for calling up the system and entering, saving, loading, and running a program. In using the above program, the program steps must be keyboarded exactly as shown. When the program is run, the user will be required to input (1) the number of periods for which the proposed capital investment will yield annual cash inflows, (2) the cost of the investment expressed as a negative initial cash flow, (3) the annual net cash flows, and (4) an initial guess as to the approximate discounted internal rate of return. The initial guess does not necessarily have to be close to the true value, since the computer will estimate the true value regardless of the accuracy of the initial guess. The initial guess only adds efficiency to the estimation process. An example of the use of this computer program for the illustration presented on page 1221 is as follows:

```
periods? 7
investment? -97360
annual net cash flow? 20000
guess? 15
  15
 4.999995
 9.999991
 14.99999
 11.66666
 10.55554
 10.18517
 10.06172
 10.02057
 10.00685
 10.00227
 10.00456
 10.00303
```

The program will stop computing the estimated discounted internal rate of return when successive estimates are reasonably close to one another and additional precision is not warranted. In the above example, the approximate discounted internal rate of return is 10%. Note that the difference between the above estimate and the illustration in the text is due to rounding within the computer program.

Note: This program was written for the BASIC programming language using the IBM personal computer.

The primary advantage of the discounted internal rate of return method is that the present values of the net cash flows over the entire useful life of the proposal are considered. An additional advantage of the method is that by determining a rate of return for each proposal, all proposals are automatically placed on a common basis for comparison, without the need to compute a present value index as was the case for the discounted cash flow method. The primary disadvantage of the discounted internal rate of return method is that the computations are somewhat more complex than for some of the other methods. In addition, like the discounted cash flow method, this method assumes that the cash received from a proposal during its useful life will be reinvested at the discounted internal rate of return. Because of changing economic conditions, this assumption may not always be reasonable.

FACTORS THAT COMPLICATE CAPITAL INVESTMENT ANALYSIS

In the preceding paragraphs, the basic concepts for four widely used methods of evaluating capital investment proposals were discussed. In practice, additional factors may have an impact on the outcome of a capital investment decision. Some of the most important of these factors, which are described in the following paragraphs, are the federal income tax, the leasing alternative, uncertainty, and changes in price levels.

Income Tax

In many cases, the impact of the federal income tax on capital investment decisions can be very significant. One provision of the Internal Revenue Code (IRC) which should be considered in capital investment analysis is depreciation.

For determining depreciation for federal income tax purposes, useful lives that are much shorter than the actual useful lives can often be used. Also, depreciation can be calculated by methods that approximate the 150–200 percent declining-balance method. Thus, depreciation for tax purposes often exceeds the depreciation for financial statement purposes in the early years of an asset's use. The tax reduction in these early years is offset by higher taxes as the annual cost recovery allowance decreases, so that accelerated depreciation does not effect a long-run saving in taxes.

Lease Versus Capital Investment

Leasing of plant assets has become common in many industries in recent years. Leasing allows an enterprise to acquire the use of plant assets without the necessity of using large amounts of cash to purchase them. In addition, if management believes that a plant asset has a high degree of risk of becoming obsolete before the end of its useful life, then leasing rather than purchasing the asset may be more attractive. By leasing the asset, management reduces the risk of suffering a loss due to obsolescence. Finally, the Internal Revenue Code provisions which allow the lessor (the owner of the asset) to pass tax deductions on to the lessee (the party leasing the asset) have increased the popularity of leasing in recent years. For example, a company that leases for its use a $200,000 plant asset with a life of 8 years for $50,000 per year is permitted to deduct the annual lease payments of $50,000.

In many cases, before a final decision is made, management should consider the possibility of leasing assets instead of purchasing them. Ordinarily, leasing assets is more costly than purchasing because the lessor must include in the rental price not only the costs associated with owning the assets but also a profit. Nevertheless, using the methods of evaluating capital investment proposals, management should consider whether or not the profitability and cash flows from the lease alternative with its risks compares favorably to the profitability and cash flows from the purchase alternative with its risks.

Uncertainty

All capital investment analyses rely on factors that are uncertain; that is, the accuracy of the estimates involved, including estimates of expected revenues, expenses, and cash flows, are uncertain. Although the estimates are subject to varying degrees of risk or uncertainty, the long-term nature of capital investments suggests that many of the estimates are likely to involve considerable uncertainty. Errors in one or more of the estimates could lead to unwise decisions.

Changes in Price Levels

The past three decades, which have been characterized by increasing price levels, are described as periods of **inflation**. In recent years, the rates of inflation have fluctuated widely, making the estimation of future revenues, expenses, and cash flows more difficult. Therefore, management should consider the expected future price levels and their likely effect on the estimates used in capital investment analyses. Fluctuations in the price levels assumed could significantly affect the analyses.

CAPITAL RATIONING

Capital rationing refers to the process by which management allocates available investment funds among competing capital investment proposals.

Generally, management will use various combinations of the evaluation methods described in this chapter in developing an effective approach to capital rationing.

In capital rationing, an initial screening of alternative proposals is usually performed by establishing minimum standards for the cash payback and the average rate of return methods. The proposals that survive this initial screening are subjected to the more rigorous discounted cash flow and discounted internal rate of return methods of analysis. The proposals that survive this final screening are evaluated in terms of nonfinancial factors, such as employee morale. For example, the acquisition of new, more efficient equipment which eliminates several jobs could lower employee morale to a level that could decrease overall plant productivity.

The final step in the capital rationing process is a ranking of the proposals and a comparison of proposals with the funds available to determine which proposals will be funded. The unfunded proposals are reconsidered if funds subsequently become available. The flowchart on page 1226 portrays the capital rationing decision process.

CAPITAL EXPENDITURES BUDGET

Once capital investment expenditures for a period have been approved, a **capital expenditures budget** should be prepared and procedures should be established for controlling the expenditures. After the assets are placed in service, the actual results of operations should be compared to the initial projected results to determine whether the capital expenditures are meeting management's expectations.

The capital expenditures budget facilitates the planning of operations and the financing of capital expenditures. A capital expenditures budget, which is integrated with the master budget as discussed in Chapter 24, summarizes acquisition decisions for a period typically ranging from one to five years. The following capital expenditures budget was prepared for Sealy Company:

Sealy Company
Capital Expenditures Budget
For Five Years Ending December 31, 1991

Item	1987	1988	1989	1990	1991
Machinery—Department A...	$240,000	—	—	$168,000	$216,000
Machinery—Department B...	108,000	$156,000	$336,000	120,000	—
Delivery equipment.........	—	54,000	—	—	36,000
Total..................	$348,000	$210,000	$336,000	$288,000	$252,000

CAPITAL
RATIONING
DECISION
PROCESS

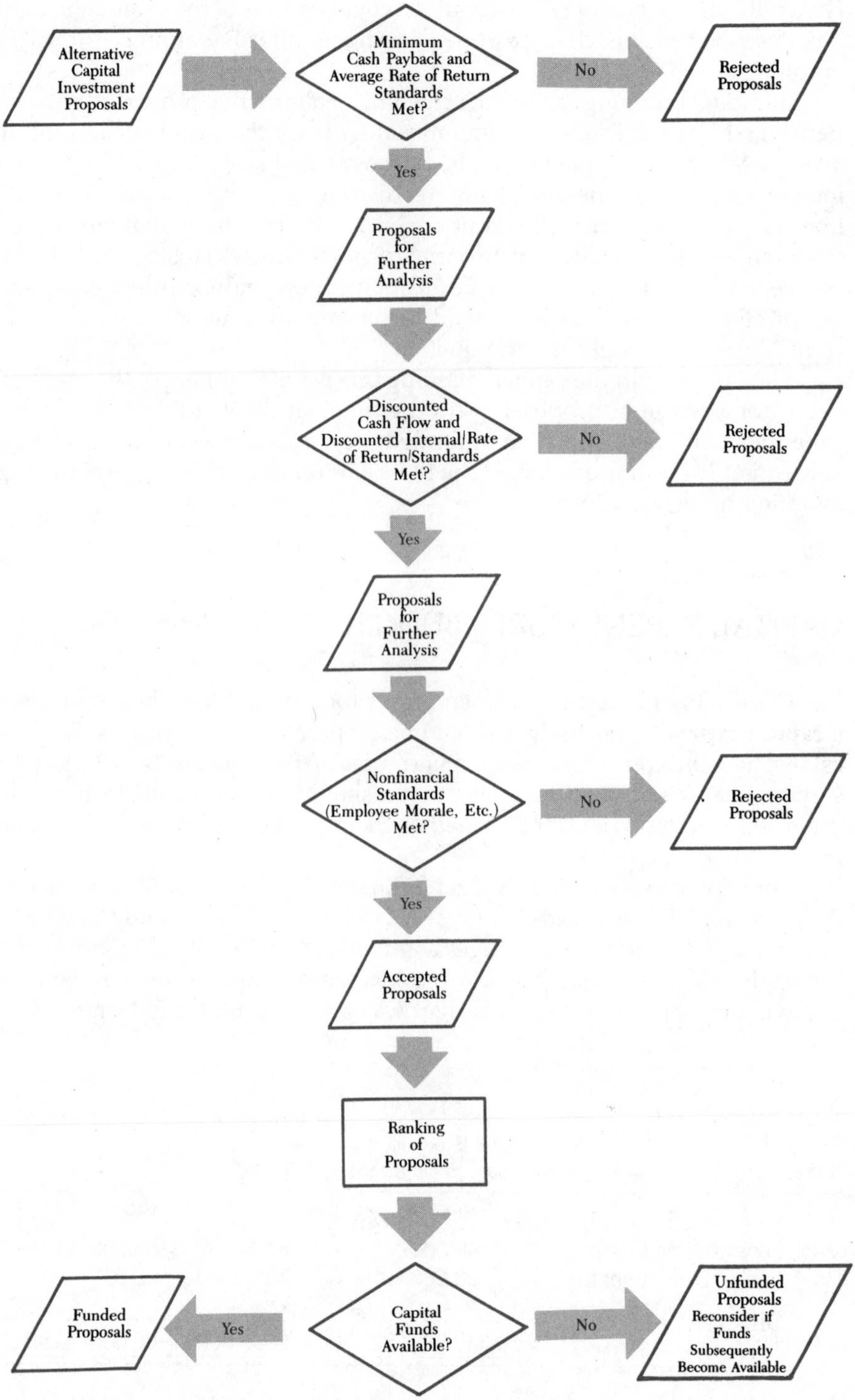

Alternative
Capital
Investment
Proposals

Minimum
Cash Payback and
Average Rate of Return
Standards
Met?

No → Rejected
Proposals

Yes

Proposals
for
Further
Analysis

Discounted
Cash Flow and
Discounted Internal Rate
of Return Standards
Met?

No → Rejected
Proposals

Yes

Proposals
for
Further
Analysis

Nonfinancial
Standards
(Employee Morale, Etc.)
Met?

No → Rejected
Proposals

Yes

Accepted
Proposals

Ranking
of
Proposals

Capital
Funds
Available?

Funded
Proposals ← Yes

No → Unfunded
Proposals
Reconsider if
Funds
Subsequently
Become Available

The capital expenditures budget does not authorize the acquisition of plant assets. Rather, it serves as a planning device to determine the effects of the capital expenditures on operations after management has evaluated the alternative proposals, using the methods described in this chapter. Final authority for capital expenditures must come from the proper level of management. In some corporations, large capital expenditures must be approved by the board of directors.

Once the capital expenditures have been approved, control must be established over the costs of acquiring the assets, including the costs of installation and testing before the assets are placed in service. Throughout this period of acquiring the assets and readying them for use, actual costs should be compared to planned (budgeted) costs. Timely reports should be prepared, so that management can take corrective actions as quickly as possible and thereby minimize cost overruns and operating delays.

After the assets have been placed in service, attention should be focused on comparisons of actual operating expenses with budgeted operating expenses. Such comparisons provide opportunities for management to follow up on successful expenditures or to terminate or otherwise attempt to salvage failing expenditures.

USE OF COMPUTERS IN CAPITAL INVESTMENT ANALYSIS

Some of the computations for the capital investment evaluation methods discussed in this chapter can become rather complex. By use of the computer, the calculations can be performed easily and quickly. The most important use of the computer, however, is in developing various models which indicate the effect of changes in key factors on the results of capital investment proposals. For example, the effect of various potential changes in future price levels on a proposal could be simulated and the results presented to management for its use in decision making.

CHAPTER REVIEW

KEY POINTS

1. Differential Analysis.

The area of accounting concerned with the effect of alternative courses of action on revenues and costs is called differential analysis. Differential revenue is the amount of increase or decrease in revenue expected from a particular course of action as compared with an alternative. Differential cost is the amount of increase or decrease in cost that is expected from a particular course of action as compared with an alternative.

Differential analysis can aid management in making decisions on a variety of alternatives, including (1) whether equipment should be leased or sold, (2) whether to discontinue an unprofitable segment, (3) whether to manufacture or purchase a needed part, (4) whether to replace plant assets, (5) whether to process further or sell an intermediate product, and (6) whether to accept additional business at a special price.

2.   Nature of Capital Investment Analysis.

The process by which management plans, evaluates, and controls investments involving property, plant, and equipment is called capital investment analysis. A capital investment program should include a plan for encouraging employees at all levels of an enterprise to submit proposals for capital investments. All reasonable proposals should be given serious consideration, and the effects of the economic implications expected from these proposals should be identified.

3.   Methods of Evaluating Capital Investment Proposals.

The methods of evaluating capital investment proposals can be grouped into two general categories: (1) methods that ignore present value and (2) present value methods. The methods that ignore present value include (1) the average rate of return method and (2) the cash payback method. Methods that use present values in evaluating capital investment proposals are (1) the discounted cash flow method and (2) the discounted internal rate of return method.

The expected average rate of return is a measure of the expected profitability of an investment in plant assets. When several alternative capital investment proposals are being considered, the proposals can be ranked by their average rates of return. The higher the average rate of return, the more desirable the proposal. The primary advantage of the average rate of return method is its simplicity, and its primary disadvantage is its lack of consideration of expected cash flows from a proposal and the timing of those cash flows.

The cash payback method measures the cash payback period, which is the expected period of time that will pass between the date of a capital investment and the complete recovery in cash (or equivalent) of the amount invested. The cash payback method is especially useful to managers whose primary concern is liquidity. The primary disadvantage of the cash payback method is its failure to take into consideration the expected profitability of a proposal. Another disadvantage of the cash payback method is that the cash flows occurring after the payback period are ignored.

The discounted cash flow method uses present value concepts to compute the present value of the cash flows expected from a proposal. When several alternative investment proposals of the same amount are being considered, the one with the largest excess of present value over the amount to be invested is the most desirable. If the alternative proposals involve different amounts of investment, it is useful to prepare a ranking of the proposals by using a present value index. The primary advantage of the discounted cash flow method is that it gives consideration to the time value of money. A disadvantage of the method is that the computations are more complex than those for the methods that ignore present value. In addition, it assumes that the cash received from the proposal during its useful life will be reinvested at the rate of return used to compute the present value of·the proposal.

The discounted internal rate of return method uses present value concepts to compute the rate of return from the net cash flows expected from capital investment proposals. When several proposals are under consideration, management often ranks proposals by their discounted internal rates of return, and the proposal with the highest rate is considered the most attractive. The primary advantage of the discounted internal rate of return method is that the present values of the net cash flows over the entire useful life of the proposal are considered. The primary disadvantage of the discounted internal rate of return method is that the computations are somewhat more complex than for some of the other methods. In addition, like the discounted cash flow method, this method assumes that the cash received from a proposal during its useful life will be reinvested at the discounted internal rate of return.

4. Factors that Complicate Capital Investment Analysis.

Factors that may complicate capital investment analysis include the impact of the federal income tax, the leasing alternative, uncertainty, and changes in price levels.

5. Capital Rationing.

Capital rationing refers to the process by which management allocates available investment funds among competing capital investment proposals. In capital rationing, an initial screening of alternative proposals is usually performed by establishing minimum standards for the cash payback and the average rate of return methods. The final step in the capital rationing process is a ranking of the proposals and a comparison of proposals with the funds available to determine which proposals will be funded.

6. Capital Expenditures Budget.

Once capital investment expenditures for a period have been approved, a capital expenditures budget should be prepared and procedures should be established for controlling the expenditures. These procedures include the preparation of timely reports which compare actual costs with planned (budgeted) costs.

7. Use of Computers in Capital Investment Analysis.

Some of the computations for the capital investment evaluation methods can become complex. By the use of the computer, the calculations can be performed easily and quickly. In addition, the computer can be used in developing various models which indicate the effect of changes in key factors on the results of capital investment proposals.

KEY TERMS

differential analysis 1204
differential revenue 1204
differential cost 1204
sunk cost 1205
opportunity cost 1210
capital investment analysis 1212
average rate of return 1214
cash payback period 1215
discounted cash flow method 1217

present value index 1218
discounted internal rate of
   return method 1219
annuity 1220
present value of an annuity 1220
inflation 1224
capital rationing 1224
capital expenditures budget 1225

SELF-EXAMINATION QUESTIONS
Answers in Appendix B.

1. The amount of increase or decrease in cost that is expected from a particular course of action as compared with an alternative is referred to as:
    A. differential cost   C. sunk cost
    B. replacement cost   D. none of the above

2. Victor Company is considering the disposal of equipment that was originally purchased for $200,000 and has accumulated depreciation to date of $150,000. The same equipment would cost $310,000 to replace. What is the sunk cost?
    A. $50,000   C. $200,000
    B. $150,000   D. None of the above

3. Management is considering a $100,000 investment in a project with a 5-year life and no residual value. If the total income from the project is expected to be $60,000 and recognition is given to the effect of straight-line depreciation on the investment, the average rate of return is:
    A. 12%   C. 60%
    B. 24%   D. none of the above

4. As used in the analysis of proposed capital investments, the method that determines the expected period of time that will elapse between the date of a capital investment and the complete recovery of the amount of cash invested is called:
   A. the average rate of return method
   B. the cash payback method
   C. the discounted cash flow method
   D. none of the above

5. Which method of analyzing capital investment proposals determines the total present value of the cash flows expected from the investment and compares this value with the amount to be invested?
   A. Average rate of return
   B. Cash payback
   C. Discounted cash flow
   D. Discounted internal rate of return

ILLUSTRATIVE PROBLEM

The capital investment committee of Bormann Company is currently considering two projects. The estimated operating income and net cash flows expected from each project are as follows:

	Project A		Project B	
Year	Operating Income	Net Cash Flow	Operating Income	Net Cash Flow
1	$ 9,000	$19,000	$ 5,000	$15,000
2	7,000	17,000	6,000	16,000
3	6,000	16,000	8,000	18,000
4	5,000	15,000	7,000	17,000
5	3,000	13,000	4,000	14,000
	$30,000	$80,000	$30,000	$80,000

Each project requires an investment of $50,000. Straight-line depreciation will be used, and no residual value is expected. The committee has selected a rate of 15% for purposes of the discounted cash flow analysis.

Instructions:

1. Compute the following:
   a. The average rate of return for each project, giving effect to depreciation on the investment.
   b. The excess or deficiency of present value over the amount to be invested, as determined by the discounted cash flow method for each project. Use the present value of $1 table appearing in this chapter.
2. Prepare a brief report for the capital investment committee, advising it on the relative merits of the two projects.

SOLUTION

(1) (a) Average annual rate of return for both projects:

$$\frac{\$30,000 \div 5}{(\$50,000 + \$0) \div 2} = 24\%$$

(b) Discounted cash flow analysis:

Year	Present Value of 1 at 15%	Net Cash Flow Project A	Net Cash Flow Project B	Present Value of Net Cash Flow Project A	Present Value of Net Cash Flow Project B
1	.870	$19,000	$15,000	$16,530	$13,050
2	.756	17,000	16,000	12,852	12,096
3	.658	16,000	18,000	10,528	11,844
4	.572	15,000	17,000	8,580	9,724
5	.497	13,000	14,000	6,461	6,958
Total		$80,000	$80,000	$54,951	$53,672
Amount to be invested				50,000	50,000
Excess of present value over amount to be invested				$ 4,951	$ 3,672

(2) (a) Both projects offer the same average annual rate of return.
   (b) Although both projects exceed the selected rate established for dis-counted cash flows, Project A offers a larger excess of present value over the amount to be invested. Thus, if only one of the two projects can be accepted, Project A would be the more attractive.

DISCUSSION QUESTIONS

1. What term is applied to the type of analysis that emphasizes the difference between the revenues and costs for proposed alternative courses of action?

2. Explain the meaning of (a) *differential revenue* and (b) *differential cost.*

3. Phillips Lumber Company incurs a cost of $80 per thousand board feet in process-ing a certain "rough-cut" lumber which it sells for $120 per thousand board feet. An alternative is to produce a "finished-cut" at a total processing cost of $96 per thousand board feet, which can be sold for $160 per thousand board feet. What is the amount of (a) the differential revenue and (b) the differential cost associated with the alternative?

4. (a) What is meant by *sunk costs?* (b) A company is contemplating replacing an old piece of machinery which cost $320,000 and has $280,000 accumulated depreciation to date. A new machine costs $400,000. What is the sunk cost in this situation?

5. The condensed income statement for Irving Company for the current year is as follows:

| | Product | | | |
	A	B	C	Total
Sales	$200,000	$170,000	$ 80,000	$450,000
Less variable costs and expenses. .	120,000	100,000	60,000	280,000
Contribution margin.	$ 80,000	$ 70,000	$ 20,000	$170,000
Less fixed costs and expenses.	40,000	31,000	30,000	101,000
Income (loss) from operations	$ 40,000	$ 39,000	$(10,000)	$ 69,000

Management decided to discontinue the manufacture and sale of Product C. Assuming that the discontinuance will have no effect on the total fixed costs and expenses or on the sales of Products A and B, has management made the correct decision? Explain.

6. (a) What is meant by *opportunity cost?* (b) Lieu Company is currently earning 10% on $200,000 invested in marketable securities. It proposes to use the $200,000 to acquire plant facilities to manufacture a new product that is expected to add $30,000 annually to net income. What is the opportunity cost involved in the decision to manufacture the new product?

7. Which two methods of capital investment analysis ignore present value?

8. Which two methods of capital investment analysis can be described as present value methods?

9. What is the "time value of money" concept?

10. (a) How is the average rate of return computed for capital investment analysis, assuming that consideration is given to the effect of straight-line depreciation on the amount of the investment? (b) If the amount of an 8-year investment is $100,000, the straight-line method of depreciation is used, there is no residual value, and the total income expected from the investment is $140,000, what is the average rate of return?

11. What are the principal objections to the use of the average rate of return method in evaluating capital investment proposals?

12. (a) As used in analyses of proposed capital investments, what is the cash payback period? (b) Discuss the principal limitations of the cash payback method for evaluating capital investment proposals.

13. What is the present value of $6,720 to be received one year from today, assuming an earnings rate of 12%?

14. Which method of evaluating capital investment proposals reduces their expected future net cash flows to present values and compares the total present values to the amount of the investment?

15. A discounted cash flow analysis used to evaluate a proposed equipment acquisition indicated an $18,000 excess of present value over the amount to be invested. What is the meaning of the $18,000 as it relates to the desirability of the proposal?

16. How is the present value index for a proposal determined?

17. What are the major disadvantages of the use of the discounted cash flow method of analyzing capital investment proposals?

18. What is an annuity?

19. What are the major disadvantages of the use of the discounted internal rate of return method of analyzing capital investment proposals?

20. What provision of the Internal Revenue Code is especially important for consideration in analyzing capital investment proposals?

21. What are the major advantages of leasing a plant asset rather than purchasing it.

22. What is capital rationing?

23. Real World Focus. Mead Corporation reported in its 1984 annual report the following loss on its industrial manufacturing and distribution operations for the year ended December 31, 1983:

	(in millions)
Net sales..................................	$246.8
Costs and expenses......................	265.0
Loss from operations	$ (18.2)

Would Mead Corporation increase its income from operations by $18,200,000 if the industrial manufacturing and distribution operations were discontinued? Discuss.

EXERCISES

Exercise 27–1.   Differential analysis report for discontinuance of product. A condensed income statement by product line for Chow Co. indicated the following for Product H for the past year:

Sales	$120,000
Cost of goods sold	70,000
Gross profit..............................	$ 50,000
Operating expenses	60,000
Loss from operations	$ (10,000)

It is estimated that 20% of the cost of goods sold represents fixed factory overhead costs and that 40% of operating expenses is fixed. Since Product H is only one of many products, the fixed costs and expenses will not be materially affected if the product is discontinued. (a) Prepare a differential analysis report, dated January 3 of the current year, for the proposed discontinuance of Product H. (b) Should Product H be retained? Explain.

Exercise 27–2. Make or buy decision. Hernandez Company has been purchasing carrying cases for its portable typewriters at a delivered cost of $20 per unit. The company, which is currently operating below full capacity, charges factory overhead to production at the rate of 40% of direct labor cost. The direct materials and direct labor costs per unit to produce comparable carrying cases are expected to be $7 and $10 respectively. If Hernandez Company manufactures the carrying cases, fixed factory overhead costs will not increase and variable factory overhead costs associated with the cases are expected to be 15% of direct labor costs. (a) Prepare a differential analysis report, dated May 10 of the current year, for the make or buy decision. (b) On the basis of the data presented, would it be advisable to make or to continue buying the carrying cases? Explain.

Exercise 27–3. Differential analysis report for machine replacement. Elmore Company produces a commodity by applying a machine and direct labor to the direct material. The original cost of the machine is $270,000, the accumulated depreciation is $160,000, its remaining useful life is 10 years, and its salvage value is negligible. On February 10, a proposal was made to replace the present manufacturing procedure with a fully automatic machine that will cost $500,000. The automatic machine has an estimated useful life of 10 years and no significant salvage value. For use in evaluating the proposal, the accountant accumulated the following annual data on present and proposed operations:

	Present Operations	Proposed Operations
Sales.....................................	$650,000	$650,000
Direct materials..........................	277,200	277,200
Direct labor	118,800	—
Power and maintenance	20,400	47,200
Taxes, insurance, etc.	13,200	19,200
Selling and general expenses	52,800	52,800

(a) Prepare a differential analysis report for the proposal to replace the machine. Include in the analysis both the net differential decrease in costs and expenses anticipated over the 10 years and the annual differential decrease in costs and expenses anticipated. (b) Based only on the data presented, should the proposal be accepted? (c) What are some of the other factors that should be considered before a final decision is made?

Exercise 27–4. Decision on acceptance of additional business. Bailey Company has a plant capacity of 60,000 units, and current production is 40,000 units.

Monthly fixed costs and expenses are $130,000, and variable costs and expenses are $14.20 per unit. The present selling price is $25 per unit. On November 23, the company received an offer from EMI Company for 10,000 units of the product at $16 each. The EMI Company will market the units in a foreign country under its own brand name. The additional business is not expected to affect the regular selling price or quantity of sales of Bailey Company. (a) Prepare a differential analysis report for the proposed sale to EMI Company. (b) Briefly explain the reason why the acceptance of this additional business will increase operating income. (c) What is the minimum price per unit that would produce a contribution margin?

Exercise 27–5. Average rate of return. The following data are accumulated by Frantz Company in evaluating two competing capital investment proposals:

	Proposal E	Proposal F
Amount of investment	$450,000	$180,000
Useful life.................................	6 years	8 years
Estimated residual value..................	-0-	-0-
Estimated total income	$243,000	$108,000

Determine the expected average rate of return for each proposal, giving effect to straight-line depreciation on each investment.

Exercise 27–6. Cash payback period. Burke Company is evaluating two capital investment proposals, each requiring an investment of $150,000 and each with an 8-year life and expected total net cash flows of $240,000. Proposal 1 is expected to provide equal annual net cash flows of $30,000, and Proposal 2 is expected to have the following unequal annual net cash flows:

Year 1................	$60,000
Year 2................	50,000
Year 3................	40,000
Year 4................	20,000
Year 5................	20,000
Year 6................	20,000
Year 7................	20,000
Year 8................	10,000

Determine the cash payback period for both proposals.

Exercise 27–7. Discounted cash flow method. The following data are accumulated by Auerbach Company in evaluating the purchase of $120,000 of equipment having a 4-year useful life:

	Net Income	Net Cash Flow
Year 1	$25,000	$55,000
Year 2	10,000	40,000
Year 3	6,000	36,000
Year 4	4,000	34,000

(a) Assuming that the desired rate of return is 12%, determine the excess (deficiency) of present value over the amount to be invested for the proposal. Use the table of the present value of $1 appearing in this chapter. (b) Would management be likely to look with favor on the proposal? Explain.

Exercise 27–8. Present value index. Grayson Company has computed the excess of present value over the amount to be invested for capital expenditure proposals P and Q, using the discounted cash flow method. Relevant data related to the computation are as follows:

	Proposal P	Proposal Q
Total present value of net cash flow	$318,000	$441,000
Amount to be invested	300,000	420,000
Excess of present value over amount to be invested	$ 18,000	$ 21,000

Determine the present value index for each proposal.

Exercise 27–9. Average rate of return, cash payback period, discounted cash flow method. Linston Company is considering the acquisition of machinery at a cost of $400,000. The machinery has an estimated life of 5 years and no residual value. It is expected to provide yearly income of $40,000 and yearly net cash flows of $120,000. The company's minimum desired rate of return for discounted cash flow analysis is 10%. Compute the following:

(a) The average rate of return, giving effect to straight-line depreciation on the investment.
(b) The cash payback period.
(c) The excess (deficiency) of present value over the amount to be invested, as determined by the discounted cash flow method. Use the table of the present value of $1 appearing in this chapter.

Exercise 27–10. Discounted internal rate of return method. The discounted internal rate of return method is used by Ramsey Company in analyzing a capital expenditure proposal that involves an investment of $342,600 and annual net cash flows of $120,000 for each of the 4 years of useful life. (a) Determine a "present value factor for an annuity of $1" which can be used in determining the discounted internal rate of return. (b) Using the factor determined in (a) and the present value of an annuity of $1 table appearing in this chapter, determine the discounted internal rate of return for the proposal.

Exercise 27–11. Discounted cash flow method and discounted internal rate of return method. Emerson Inc. is evaluating a proposed expenditure of $121,480 on a 4-year project whose estimated net cash flows are $40,000 for each of the four years.

(a) Compute the excess (deficiency) of present value over the amount to be invested, using the discounted cash flow method and an assumed rate of return of 15%. (b) Based on the analysis prepared in (a), is the rate of return (1) more than 15%, (2) 15%, or (3) less than 15%? Explain. (c) Determine the discounted internal rate of return by computing a "present value factor for an annuity of $1" and using the table of the present value of an annuity of $1 presented in the text.

PROBLEMS

Series A

Problem 27–1A.   Differential analysis report involving opportunity costs.
On August 1, Waters Company is considering leasing a building and purchasing the necessary equipment to operate a public warehouse. The project would be financed by selling $800,000 of 9% U.S. Treasury bonds that mature in 20 years. The bonds were purchased at face value and are currently selling at face value. The following data have been assembled:

Cost of equipment..	$800,000
Life of equipment..	20 years
Estimated residual value of equipment................................	$200,000
Yearly costs to operate the warehouse, in addition to depreciation of equipment..	$ 50,000
Yearly expected revenues—first 8 years.............................	$180,000
Yearly expected revenues—next 12 years	$150,000

Instructions:

(1) Prepare a differential analysis report presenting the differential revenue and the differential cost associated with the proposed operation of the warehouse for the 20 years as compared with present conditions.
(2) Based on the results disclosed by the differential analysis, should the proposal be accepted?
(3) If the proposal is accepted, what is the total estimated income from operation of the warehouse for the 20 years?

Problem 27–2A.   Differential analysis report for machine replacement proposal. Lee Company is considering the replacement of a machine that has been used in its factory for three years. Relevant data associated with the operations of the old machine and the new machine, neither of which has any residual value, are as follows:

Old Machine

Cost of machine, 9-year life	$300,000
Annual depreciation	33,333
Annual manufacturing costs, exclusive of depreciation..................	510,000
Related annual operating expenses	320,000
Associated annual revenue...	1,120,000
Current estimated selling price.......................................	180,000

New Machine

Cost of machine, 6-year life	$630,000
Annual depreciation	105,000
Estimated annual manufacturing costs, exclusive of depreciation.........	380,000

Annual operating expenses and revenue are not expected to be affected by purchase of the new machine.

Instructions:

(1) Prepare a differential analysis report as of October 4 of the current year, comparing operations utilizing the new machine with operations using the present equipment. The analysis should indicate the total differential decrease or increase in costs that would result over the 6-year period if the new machine is acquired.
(2) List other factors that should be considered before a final decision is reached.

Problem 27–3A. Differential analysis report for sales promotion proposal.
Gorksi Company is planning a one-month campaign for June to promote sales of one of its two products. A total of $35,000 has been budgeted for advertising, contests, redeemable coupons, and other promotional activities. The following data have been assembled for their possible usefulness in deciding which of the products to select for the campaign:

	Product D	Product E
Unit selling price	$50	$60
Unit production costs:		
Direct materials	$14	$18
Direct labor	10	14
Variable factory overhead	8	8
Fixed factory overhead	6	6
Total unit production costs	$38	$46
Unit variable operating expenses	5	5
Unit fixed operating expenses	3	3
Total unit costs and expenses	$46	$54
Operating income per unit	$ 4	$ 6

No increase in facilities would be necessary to produce and sell the increased output. It is anticipated that 10,000 additional units of Product D or 8,000 additional units of Product E could be sold without changing the unit selling price of either product.

Instructions:

(1) Prepare a differential analysis report as of May 5 of the current year, presenting the additional revenue and additional costs and expenses anticipated from the promotion of Product D and Product E.
(2) The sales manager had tentatively decided to promote Product E, estimating that operating income would be increased by $13,000 ($6 operating income per unit for 8,000 units, less promotion expenses of $35,000). It was also believed that the selection of Product D would increase operating income by only $5,000 ($4 operating income per unit for 10,000 units, less promotion expenses of $35,000). State briefly your reasons for supporting or opposing the tentative decision.

Problem 27–4A. **Differential analysis report for further processing.** The management of Beeman Company is considering whether to process further Product X into Product Y. Product Y can be sold for $50 per pound, and Product X can be sold without further processing for $10 per pound. Product X is produced in batches of 300 pounds by processing 400 pounds of raw material, which costs $7 per pound. Product Y will require additional processing costs of $2.50 per pound of Product X, and 3 pounds of Product X will produce 1 pound of Product Y.

Instructions:

(1) Prepare a differential analysis report as of April 10, presenting the differential revenue and differential cost per batch associated with the further processing of Product X to produce Product Y.
(2) Briefly report your recommendations.

Problem 27–5A. **Differential analysis report for further processing.** Childers Refining Inc. refines Product V in batches of 100,000 gallons, which it sells for $4.80 per gallon. The associated unit costs and expenses are currently as follows:

Direct materials	$2.70
Direct labor	.72
Variable factory overhead	.28
Fixed factory overhead	.18
Sales commissions	.48
Fixed selling and general expenses	.12

The company is presently considering a proposal to put Product V through several additional processes to yield Products V and W. Although the company had determined such further processing to be unwise, new processing methods have now been developed. Existing facilities can be used for the additional processing, but since the factory is operating at full 8-hour-day capacity, the processing would have to be performed at night. Additional costs of processing would be $6,500 per batch, and there would be an evaporation loss of 10%, with 65% of the processed material evolving as Product V and 25% as Product W. The selling price of Product W is $7.20 per gallon. Sales commissions are a uniform percentage based on the sales price.

Instructions:

(1) Prepare a differential analysis report as of January 20, presenting the differential revenue and the differential cost per batch associated with the processing to produce Products V and W, compared with processing to produce Product V only.
(2) Briefly report your recommendations.

Problem 27–6A. **Average rate of return method, discounted cash flow method, and analysis.** The capital investments budget committee is considering two projects. The estimated operating income and net cash flows from each project are as follows:

	Project G		Project H	
Year	Operating Income	Net Cash Flow	Operating Income	Net Cash Flow
1	$15,000	$ 39,000	$ 7,000	$ 31,000
2	10,000	34,000	9,000	33,000
3	8,000	32,000	10,000	34,000
4	6,000	30,000	10,000	34,000
5	6,000	30,000	9,000	33,000
Total	$45,000	$165,000	$45,000	$165,000

Each project requires an investment of $120,000. Straight-line depreciation will be used, and no residual value is expected. The committee has selected a rate of 10% for purposes of the discounted cash flow analysis.

Instructions:

(1) Compute the following:
   (a) The average rate of return for each project, giving effect to depreciation on the investment.
   (b) The excess (deficiency) of present value over the amount to be invested, as determined by the discounted cash flow method for each project. Use the present value of $1 table appearing in this chapter.
(2) Prepare a brief report for the capital investment committee, advising it on the relative merits of the two projects.

Problem 27–7A.   Cash payback period, discounted cash flow method, and analysis. Enders Company is considering two projects. The estimated net cash flows from each project are as follows:

Year	Project L	Project M
1	$ 50,000	$200,000
2	250,000	100,000
3	100,000	100,000
4	50,000	80,000
5	50,000	20,000
Total	$500,000	$500,000

Each project requires an investment of $300,000, with no residual value expected. A rate of 20% has been selected for the discounted cash flow analysis.

Instructions:

(1) Compute the following for each project:
   (a) Cash payback period.
   (b) The excess (deficiency) of present value over the amount to be invested, as determined by the discounted cash flow method. Use the present value of $1 table appearing in this chapter.

(continued)

(2) Prepare a brief report advising management on the relative merits of each of the two projects.

Problem 27–8A.   Discounted cash flow method, present value index, and analysis. Farmer Company wishes to evaluate three capital investment proposals by using the discounted cash flow method. Relevant data related to the proposals are summarized as follows:

	Proposal A	Proposal B	Proposal C
Amount to be invested.........	$100,000	$100,000	$150,000
Annual net cash flows:			
Year 1.....................	60,000	45,000	75,000
Year 2.....................	45,000	40,000	70,000
Year 3.....................	30,000	30,000	60,000

Instructions:

(1) Assuming that the desired rate of return is 15%, prepare a discounted cash flow analysis for each proposal. Use the present value of $1 table appearing in this chapter.
(2) Determine a present value index for each proposal.
(3) Which proposal offers the largest amount of present value per dollar of investment? Explain.

Problem 27–9A.   Discounted cash flow method, discounted internal rate of return method, and analysis. Management is considering two capital investment proposals. The estimated net cash flows from each proposal are as follows:

Year	Proposal A	Proposal B
1	$50,000	$160,000
2	50,000	160,000
3	50,000	160,000
4	50,000	160,000

Proposal A requires an investment of $129,450, while Proposal B requires an investment of $456,800. No residual value is expected from either proposal.

Instructions:

(1) Compute the following for each proposal:
   (a) The excess (deficiency) of present value over the amount to be invested, as determined by the discounted cash flow method. Use a rate of 12% and the present value of $1 table appearing in this chapter.
   (b) A present value index.

(2) Determine the discounted internal rate of return for each proposal by (a) computing a "present value factor for an annuity of $1" and (b) using the present value of an annuity of $1 table appearing in this chapter.

(3) What advantage does the discounted internal rate of return method have over the discounted cash flow method in comparing proposals?

Series B

Problem 27–1B. Differential analysis report involving opportunity costs. On July 1, Stuart Company is considering leasing a building and purchasing the necessary equipment to operate a public warehouse. The project would be financed by selling $750,000 of 8% U.S. Treasury bonds that mature in 10 years. The bonds were purchased at face value and are currently selling at face value. The following data have been assembled:

Cost of equipment...	$750,000
Life of equipment..	10 years
Estimated residual value of equipment.................................	$ 50,000
Yearly costs to operate the warehouse, in addition to depreciation of equipment..	$ 74,000
Yearly expected revenues—first 6 years.............................	$220,000
Yearly expected revenues—next 4 years	$200,000

Instructions:

(1) Prepare a differential analysis report presenting the differential revenue and the differential cost associated with the proposed operation of the warehouse for the 10 years as compared with present conditions.

(2) Based on the results disclosed by the differential analysis, should the proposal be accepted?

(3) If the proposal is accepted, what is the total estimated income from operation of the warehouse for the 10 years?

Problem 27–2B. Differential analysis report for machine replacement proposal. Greeley Company is considering the replacement of a machine that has been used in its factory for four years. Relevant data associated with the operations of the old machine and the new machine, neither of which has any residual value, are as follows:

Old Machine

Cost of machine, 9-year life	$585,000
Annual depreciation	65,000
Annual manufacturing costs, exclusive of depreciation..................	375,000
Related annual operating expenses	138,500
Associated annual revenue...	920,000
Current estimated selling price......................................	210,000

New Machine

Cost of machine, 5-year life $750,000
Annual depreciation 150,000
Estimated annual manufacturing costs, exclusive of depreciation......... 220,000

Annual operating expenses and revenue are not expected to be affected by purchase of the new machine.

Instructions:

(1) Prepare a differential analysis report as of April 2 of the current year, comparing operations utilizing the new machine with operations using the present equipment. The analysis should indicate the total differential decrease or increase in costs that would result over the 5-year period if the new machine is acquired.
(2) List other factors that should be considered before a final decision is reached.

Problem 27–6B. Average rate of return method, discounted cash flow method, and analysis. The capital investments budget committee is considering two projects. The estimated operating income and net cash flows from each project are shown as follows:

	Project J		Project K	
Year	Operating Income	Net Cash Flow	Operating Income	Net Cash Flow
1	$ 25,000	$ 75,000	$ 40,000	$ 90,000
2	25,000	75,000	30,000	80,000
3	25,000	75,000	20,000	70,000
4	15,000	65,000	6,000	56,000
5	10,000	60,000	4,000	54,000
Total	$100,000	$350,000	$100,000	$350,000

Each project requires an investment of $250,000. Straight-line depreciation will be used, and no residual value is expected. The committee has selected a rate of 12% for purposes of the discounted cash flow analysis.

Instructions:

(1) Compute the following:
   (a) The average rate of return for each project, giving effect to depreciation on the investment.
   (b) The excess (deficiency) of present value over the amount to be invested, as determined by the discounted cash flow method for each project. Use the present value of $1 table appearing in this chapter.
(2) Prepare a brief report for the capital investment committee, advising it on the relative merits of the two projects.

Problem 27–8B. **Discounted cash flow method, present value index, and analysis.** J. Wilson Company wishes to evaluate three capital investment projects by using the discounted cash flow method. Relevant data related to the projects are summarized as follows:

	Project P	Project Q	Project R
Amount to be invested.........	$480,000	$240,000	$240,000
Annual net cash flows:			
Year 1....................	300,000	180,000	60,000
Year 2....................	240,000	120,000	120,000
Year 3....................	180,000	60,000	180,000

Instructions:

(1) Assuming that the desired rate of return is 20%, prepare a discounted cash flow analysis for each project. Use the present value of $1 table appearing in this chapter.
(2) Determine a present value index for each project.
(3) Which project offers the largest amount of present value per dollar of investment? Explain.

Problem 27–9B. **Discounted cash flow method, discounted internal rate of return method, and analysis.** Management is considering two capital investment projects. The estimated net cash flows from each project are as follows:

Year	Project S	Project T
1	$120,000	$30,000
2	120,000	30,000
3	120,000	30,000
4	120,000	30,000

Project S requires an investment of $364,440, while Project T requires an investment of $85,650. No residual value is expected from either project.

Instructions:

(1) Compute the following for each project:
   (a) The excess (deficiency) of present value over the amount to be invested, as determined by the discounted cash flow method. Use a rate of 10% and the present value of $1 table appearing in this chapter.
   (b) A present value index.
(2) Determine the discounted internal rate of return for each project by (a) computing a "present value factor for an annuity of $1" and (b) using the present value of an annuity of $1 table appearing in this chapter.
(3) What advantage does the discounted internal rate of return method have over the discounted cash flow method in comparing projects?

MINI-CASE 27

PLUNKETT INDUSTRIES INC.

Your father is considering an investment of $400,000 in either Project X or Project Y. In discussing the two projects with an advisor, it was decided that, for the risk involved, a return of 12% on the cash investment would be required. For this purpose, your father estimated the following economic factors for the projects:

	Project X	Project Y
Useful life.	4 years	4 years
Residual value	-0-	-0-
Net income:		
Year 1.	$ 20,000	$ 55,000
2.	30,000	40,000
3.	35,000	15,000
4.	43,000	10,000
Net cash flows:		
Year 1.	$120,000	$155,000
2.	130,000	140,000
3.	135,000	115,000
4.	143,000	110,000

Although the average rate of return exceeded 12% on both projects, your father has tentatively decided to invest in Project X because the rate was higher for Project X. Although he doesn't fully understand the importance of cash flow, he has heard others talk about its importance in evaluating investments. In this respect, he noted that the total net cash flow from Project X is $528,000, which exceeds that from Project Y by $8,000.

Instructions:

(1) Determine the average rate of return for both projects.
(2) How would you explain the importance of net cash flows in the analysis of investment projects? Include a specific example to demonstrate the importance of net cash flows and their timing to these two projects.

Part **9**

INDIVIDUALS AND NONPROFIT ORGANIZATIONS

Chapter 28

ACCOUNTING FOR INDIVIDUALS AND NONPROFIT ORGANIZATIONS

Chapter Objectives:

- Describe accounting systems for individuals.
- Describe and illustrate the preparation of budgets and budget performance records for individuals.
- Describe the primary financial statements for individuals.
- Illustrate the preparation of the statement of financial condition for an individual.
- Describe the characteristics of nonprofit organizations.
- Describe and illustrate the concepts and principles of fund accounting for nonprofit organizations.
- Describe and illustrate the preparation and use of the principal financial statements for a nonprofit organization.

28

receding chapters have discussed accounting concepts and procedures used by business enterprises organized to make a profit. Although many of these concepts and procedures apply to individuals and nonprofit organizations, there are also many differences.

The term **individuals**, as used in the chapter title, may refer to a person or to a family unit, such as a husband, wife, and children. **Nonprofit**, or **not-for-profit**, entities are usually organized as informal associations or as corporations in accordance with applicable laws and regulations. Such organizations may be classified as either (1) governmental units or (2) charitable, religious, or philanthropic units (hereafter referred to simply as "charitable"). The first category includes the federal government and state, county, and city governments. The second category includes churches, hospitals, private schools and universities, medical research facilities, and many other types of organizations that are financed wholly or in part by donations.

ACCOUNTING SYSTEMS FOR INDIVIDUALS

Accounting systems for individuals differ widely. Some individuals may use a system based on the accrual method and double-entry accounting, with a complete set of journals, ledgers, and reports. Such an elaborate system is needed by individuals who have complex reporting obligations and many financial transactions of large amounts. For other individuals, a rather simple system based on the cash method is sufficient. The basics of such a system are described briefly in the sections that follow.

Budgets for Individuals

The use of budgets by an individual or a family unit is an important part of successful financial planning. A budget provides a systematic and orderly method of managing money. It enables individuals to spend their money wisely and to live within their income. The cash basis is ordinarily used in preparing budgets for individuals because most of their transactions are cash transactions evidenced by bank deposits and checks. In addition, the cash basis is required for an individual's reports to state taxing authorities and to the Internal Revenue Service for income taxes and FICA taxes.

The first step in preparing a budget is to determine as accurately as possible the cash income expected during a certain period of time, ordinarily a calendar year. Money to be received from salary or wages (net take-home pay), interest on bonds or savings accounts, dividends on shares of stock, and any other cash income should be included in the estimate. The second step is to develop a realistic plan for allocating the estimated income among the various goods and services most wanted by the individual or family and to provide for savings. There is no magic formula for determining the amount to be saved or the allocation of expenditures among various "essentials" and "luxuries." Much depends on such factors as the size of the family unit, its needs, tastes, wants, and the priorities assigned to each.

The process of estimating income and expenditures is often complicated by the fact that not all income is received on a regularly recurring basis and not all expenditures are incurred on a regularly recurring basis. Some income may be received on a weekly, biweekly, monthly, quarterly, or semiannual basis. For example, if salary is received biweekly, twenty-six amounts are used in determining the yearly amount. On the other hand, dividends on shares of stock are ordinarily received quarterly and four amounts would be used in estimating the yearly amount. Heating and lighting expenses ordinarily vary as the seasons change, thus requiring the consideration of twelve different monthly estimates to determine the yearly amount.

After the estimate of total income and expenditures for the year has been completed, the next step is to divide total income and each category of expenditure by 12, which provides the data for the monthly budget. Such a budget for a family composed of husband and wife and two children is illustrated as follows:

MONTHLY BUDGET

	Susan and Henry Rice Monthly Budget	
Income.		$1,950
Allocations for expenditures:		
Housing and house operation.	$675	
Food and sundries.	560	
Transportation.	200	
Clothing	130	
Medical care.	90	
Recreation and education	80	
Contributions and gifts	70	
Savings	70	
Miscellaneous.	75	
Total allocations for expenditures.		$1,950

Basic to the budgeting process is the requirement that the budget balance, that is, that the allocations among planned expenditures and savings do not exceed cash income. The need to maintain a balanced budget requires that priorities on spending be established if the individual or family unit is to be able to do those things that give it the most satisfaction. Thus, if the preliminary budget shows an excess of cash outflow over cash income, as is often the case, consideration should be given to possibilities of increasing earnings, reducing expenditures, omitting savings, borrowing money, or drawing upon accumulated savings from earlier periods. If the reverse situation occurs, the excess cash income may be added to savings or used to reduce outstanding liabilities.

Budget Performance Record for Individuals

An essential part of budgeting is the necessity of keeping a record of actual expenditures and making frequent comparisons with budgeted amounts. This record, termed the **budget performance record**, is then used to help control expenditures and to help the individuals to live within their budget.

The budget performance record is a multicolumn form that shows (1) the monthly budget allocations for each category of expenditures, (2) the actual individual expenditures made during the month and the end-of-month total of each category, and (3) the amount by which each total is over or under the budgeted amounts. Budget performance records for January, the first month of the budget period, and for a portion of February are illustrated as follows. The budget allocations are based on the budget appearing on the preceding page.

Susan and Henry Rice
Budget Performance Record—January, 19--

	Housing & house operation	Food & sundries	Trans-portation	Clothing	Medical care	Recrea-tion & education	Contri-butions & gifts	Savings	Miscella-neous
January allocation.........	675	560	200	130	90	80	70	70	75
January payments:									
January 1.................			15			18			8
2.................		57							7
4.................					12				
5.................		41							
7.................		25							11
8.................	15		16		10	12			
9.................	83	80		65					
10................	55						50		
12................		47							5
14................		32				9			
15................	156	38	14						
17................		35							15
19................		45	49			5			
21................						11			18
23................	30	27	15	22					
26................	75								
27................		52					30		
29................		38	12						
30................	360				35			70	
31................		58	51	18		24			8
Total.................	774	575	172	105	57	79	80	70	72
Over* or under budget, February 1...........	99*	15*	28	25	33	1	10*	—	3

Susan and Henry Rice
Budget Performance Record—February, 19--

	Housing & house operation	Food & sundries	Trans-portation	Clothing	Medical care	Recrea-tion & education	Contri-butions & gifts	Savings	Miscella-neous
Over* or under budget, February 1	99*	15*	28	25	33	1	10*	—	3
February allocation	675	560	200	130	90	80	70	70	75
Total budget, February	576	545	228	155	123	81	60	70	78
February payments:									
February 1	. . . .	15	. . . .	. . . .	. . . .	17	. . . .	. . . .	. . . .
2	. . . .	. . . .	14	18	. . . .	. . . .	. . . .	. . . .	16
3	. . . .	19	. . . .	. . . .	. . . .	. . . .	. . . .	. . . .	8
5	. . . .	62	. . . .	. . . .	. . . .	. . . .	. . . .	. . . .	. . . .
7	14	. . . .	. . . .	. . . .	. . . .	. . . .	10	. . . .	. . . .
8	. . . .	25	12	. . . .	. . . .	24	. . . .	. . . .	. . . .
9	82	. . . .	. . . .	. . . .	5	. . . .	. . . .	. . . .	7
10	. . . .	41	. . . .	40	. . . .	. . . .	. . . .	. . . .	5

The January payments were recorded during the month and totaled at the end of the month for each category. These totals were then subtracted from the budget allocations to determine the over or under budget amounts as of February 1. For example, the allocation for housing and house operation for January was $675, and the total payments made during January amounted to $774. The payments exceeded the budgeted amount by $99. An investigation determined that this budget variance was the result of seasonal fluctuations in expenditures, namely, higher than average expenditures necessary for heat and light during the month and payment of a semiannual premium on property insurance. The over budget amount of $99, therefore, was carried forward to the budget performance record for February.

The actual expenditures will often vary from the monthly allocations, and the causes of the "over budget" amounts should be carefully examined. If they are fairly small in amount and are the result of seasonal fluctuations in expenditures, as in the illustration, the balances should be carried forward to the next month and no revisions of the monthly budget are necessary. On the other hand, if the balances are significant and cannot be attributed to seasonal fluctuations, the monthly budget for the succeeding months should be revised accordingly. For example, a large expenditure for medical care that had not been anticipated may require a revision of the budgeted allocations for expenditures and savings for the next several months.

Records for Individuals

In addition to the budget performance record described in the preceding section, the record keeping system ordinarily consists of (1) a checkbook,

(2) a file for bills and statements of account representing unpaid liabilities, (3) a file for documents supporting cash payments, and (4) a property inventory record.

As cash is received, it is deposited in the checking account and the amount is recorded in the checkbook, either on a "stub" or "check register" provided by the bank for the purpose of keeping a record of deposits, checks, and cash balance. As each check is written, the amount of the disbursement and its purpose should be entered on the stub or check register and the remaining balance recorded. The disbursement should be entered in the budget performance record. The checkbook "cash balance" should be reconciled with the monthly bank statement as described in Chapter 8.

Individuals, like business enterprises, often need to make small expenditures. Payment by check in such cases would result in delay, annoyance, and excessive writing of checks. Instead, a check for a moderate sum can be "cashed" and the money used for small disbursements in a manner similar to a business enterprise's use of a petty cash fund. A pocket note pad may be carried for purposes of recording such expenditures. As a check is written to replenish the "pocket" cash, the memoranda recorded in the note pad may be summarized for recording on the stub or check register and in the budget performance record.

A simple but effective method of handling unpaid liabilities is to maintain a file box or folder in which bills and statements of account are placed. When the liabilities are paid, the documents are marked with the number of the check written to make the payment and are filed in a paid file. This file should be retained as long as is legally required for such purposes as verification of income tax deductions claimed, or as long as it may be needed for informational purposes.

The property inventory record contains detailed information, including description and cost data, about valuable pieces of property, such as personal residence (including improvements), investments, jewelry, silverware, and china. Such a record is especially useful for insurance purposes and for establishing gain or loss on sale of property.

FINANCIAL STATEMENTS FOR INDIVIDUALS

Financial statements are often prepared for an individual or for related individuals, such as a husband and wife as a family unit. Such statements may be used in arranging a loan of a large amount, as an aid in planning for retirement, for estate and income tax planning, or for disclosure by public officials or candidates for public office.

Financial statements for individuals should be prepared according to generally accepted accounting principles for personal financial statements.[1]

---

[1]*Statement of Position, No. 82-1*, "Accounting and Financial Reporting for Personal Financial Statements" (New York: American Institute of Certified Public Accountants, 1982).

These principles primarily focus on an individual's assets and liabilities, which are reported at estimated current values rather than historical costs.

Statement of Financial Condition

The main financial statement for individuals is the **statement of financial condition**, sometimes called the statement of assets and liabilities. This statement, illustrated below and on pages 1255–1256 presents the (1) estimated current values of assets, (2) estimated current amounts of liabilities, (3) estimated income tax on unrealized appreciation of assets, and (4) estimated net worth.

The assets and liabilities are reported on the accrual basis. Current and noncurrent classifications are not used, because working capital is generally not relevant to users of personal financial statements. The notes accompanying the statement describe the methods used in determining the current values and other relevant details.

Bruce A. and Jennifer S. McCord Statement of Financial Condition December 31, 19--	
Assets	
Cash (Note 2)	$ 18,250
Marketable securities (Note 3)	115,600
Cash value of life insurance ($300,000 face value)	36,500
Investment in real estate (Note 4)	130,000
Equity interest in McCord and Associates (Note 5)	183,000
Automobiles	17,000
Residence, pledged against mortgage (Note 4)	225,000
Household furnishings	28,500
Jewelry and paintings (Note 4)	50,000
Vested interest in AB Corp. pension trust	49,700
Total assets	$853,550
Liabilities	
Accounts payable and accrued liabilities	$ 7,700
Income tax payable	8,775
Note payable, 12%, due May 31, 19--	40,000
Mortgage note payable, 11%, final payment due July 1, 19-- (Note 6)	148,500
Total liabilities	$204,975
Estimated income tax on unrealized appreciation of assets (Note 7)	28,000
Net worth	620,575
Total liabilities, estimated income tax on unrealized appreciation of assets, and net worth	$853,550

Note 1–Current values and amounts

The accompanying statement of financial condition includes the assets and liabilities of Bruce A. and Jennifer S. McCord. Assets are stated at their estimated current values and liabilities at their estimated current amounts.

Note 2–Cash

The cash amount of $18,250 includes $17,500 deposited in money market accounts. These accounts allow unrestricted withdrawal without penalty.

Note 3–Marketable securities

Marketable securities consist of the following (estimated current value is the quoted market price on December 31, 19--, less estimated broker commissions):

	Shares or Face Amount	Current Value
Stocks:		
American Manufacturing	500	$ 48,700
Jackson Tool Company	200	9,800
Pontiac Power Company	100	5,500
United Products Inc.	50	20,900
Bonds:		
Pontiac Power Company, 10⅛%, due 20--	$ 5,000	10,300
U.S. Government, 9½%, due 19--	10,000	20,400
Total		$115,600

Note 4–Investment in real estate and residence and personal effects

The estimated market price of investment in real estate and residence, jewelry, and paintings is based on independent appraisals made by Hunt and Associates.

Note 5–Equity interest in McCord and Associates

The estimated market price of the equity interest of Bruce A. McCord in McCord and Associates partnership is based on an offer made on October 10, 19-- to purchase the net assets of the partnership. The offer was rejected.

Note 6–Mortgage note payable

The terms of the mortgage note provide for monthly payments of $760, which includes the interest accrued on the loan.

Note 7–Estimated income tax on unrealized appreciation of assets

Estimated income taxes have been provided on the unrealized appreciation of the estimated current values of assets over their tax bases as if the estimated current values of the assets had been realized on the statement date, using applicable tax laws and regulations. This estimate will probably differ from the amounts of income taxes that eventually might be paid because of possible changes in the current values of the assets and in the tax laws which might be in effect at the time of disposal of the assets.

Assets. Assets, such as real estate and securities, are reported in the order of liquidity at their estimated current values. The current values of most assets other than listed securities may be estimated by examining recent transactions involving similar assets or by using appraisals by independent experts in particular fields, such as art or jewelry. Any estimated costs of disposal of an asset, such as commissions, are deducted in arriving at estimated current values.

Investments. The estimated current values of corporate securities, real estate, interests in sole proprietorships or partnerships, and life insurance must be determined as accurately as possible. Quoted market prices of marketable securities are usually available in the financial press. The estimated current market value of real estate can be obtained from a competent real estate appraiser. Data on recent sales of similar real estate may also be available. An offer to purchase the net assets of a sole proprietorship or other business unit or an estimate of liquidation values may be used as the estimated market price of such investments. Life insurance is reported at its cash surrender value, which is obtainable from the policy contract or from the insurer, less the amount of any loans against it. The face amount of life insurance should also be disclosed.

Residences and personal effects. Ordinarily, a residence and household furnishings, automobiles, objects of art, and jewelry are reported in the statement of financial condition if their value is material in relation to total assets. The estimated current values of especially significant assets may be determined by independent appraisers or estimated on the basis of advertised prices of similar items.

Future interests. Individuals may have future interests in pensions, profit-sharing plans, trusts, or similar future rights. If the individual has a definite (rather than contingent) legal right to future benefits, such a right is said to be "vested" in the individual. The present value of such interests should be reported on the statement.

Liabilities. Commitments to pay future sums that are fixed in amount are listed on the statement of financial condition at their present values in the order of dates of maturity. Examples of such commitments include fixed amounts of alimony and charitable pledges. Commitments that depend upon a future contingency or the rendering of services by others should be disclosed in a note.

Estimated Income Tax on Unrealized Appreciation of Assets. An estimate of the income tax that could be owed if the assets were sold at their current values should be reported as a separate item below the total liabilities. This provision is necessary because the current values of the assets cannot be realized without the incurrence of a tax liability.

Net Worth. The equity of the individual(s) is called **net worth**. At the financial statement date, net worth can be determined as the difference between (1) the total assets and (2) the total of the liabilities plus the estimated income tax on the unrealized appreciation of the assets. On the statement of financial condition, net worth is reported below the estimated income tax on unrealized appreciation of assets.

Other Financial Statements for Individuals

For most uses, a single statement of financial condition is sufficient. In some situations, comparative statements for at least two years may be useful. When comparative statements are presented, an additional statement is often included. This statement, referred to as the statement of changes in net worth, presents the major sources of increases and decreases in net worth.

Although personal financial statements are presented on the basis of estimated current values, users may sometimes request certain historical cost data. Such data may be included as supplementary information in the statements.

Steve Henrich — A Financial Profile and Analysis

Steve Henrich has been successful financially by following that easier-said-than-done investment strategy of buying low and selling high. But at the moment he's in a quandary. "Stocks and bonds seem to have stabilized at a high, and I don't know where to go. I know there must be other opportunities out there but I'm just not familiar with them," he said.

At age 39, Henrich earns $54,200 as a lieutenant colonel in the U.S. Air Force. He is divorced, with daughters aged 13 and 5.

The following is a statement of financial condition for Colonel Henrich, who participated in a program, sponsored by *USA Today*, in which professional financial planners offer advice:

Assets

Checking account	$ 500
Savings account	2,500
Money market fund	5,200
Life insurance, cash value	1,370
Municipal bond fund	1,200
Penny stocks	800
Rental property	52,500
IRA (CD and money fund)	6,100
Foreign currency CD	4,200
Annuity	5,600
Condominium (residence)	83,500
Furnishings	20,000
Car ('86 Trans Am)	16,000
Total	$199,470

Liabilities

Mortgage for residence	$ 75,000
Car loan	16,000
Mortgage on rental property	42,500
Total	$133,500
Net worth	$ 65,970

"With the big run-up we've had in stocks and bonds, it's easy to feel the opportunities are all behind us—but they're not," said financial planner Patrick Renn of Atlanta's Consolidated Planning Corp. Renn said Henrich should move back into the stock market.

To get into stocks, Renn recommends that Henrich should:

- Take his profit on the foreign currency certificate of deposit, sell his penny stocks and put the money in higher-quality stock investments.
- Invest new money using dollar cost-averaging. That's a systematic plan by which you invest a set amount on a regular basis—say, every month—no matter what the stock market is doing.
- Switch the $5,600 in his deferred annuity to a so-called variable annuity.

Source: Adapted from Jim Henderson, "Investor Seeks Bargains in a Bull Market," *USA Today*, June 30, 1986.

CHARACTERISTICS OF NONPROFIT ORGANIZATIONS

Entities engaged in business transactions may be classified as profit-making or nonprofit. Profit-making organizations respond to a demand for a product or a service with the expectation of earning net income. The accounting concepts and procedures applicable to such organizations were discussed in preceding chapters. The distinguishing characteristics of nonprofit organizations are: (1) there is neither a conscious profit motive nor an expectation of earning net income; (2) no part of any excess of revenues over expenditures is distributed to those who contributed support through taxes or voluntary donations; and (3) any excess of revenues over expenditures that results from operations in the short run is ordinarily used in later years to further the purposes of the organization.

Nonprofit organizations provide goods or services that fulfill a social need, often for those who do not have the purchasing power to acquire these goods or services for themselves.

Some nonprofit organizations, such as a government-owned electric utility or a public transportation company, are created to provide services to the citizens of the area for a fee that is close to the cost of providing the service. After the initial investment, they tend to be self-sustaining; that is, the revenues earned support their operations. Because the activities of such organizations are financed mainly by charges to the customers using the services, the accounting concepts and procedures used are those appropriate to a commercial enterprise. Most nonprofit organizations, however, are established to provide a service to society without levying against the user a direct charge equal to the full cost of the service. The concepts and procedures applicable to nonprofit organizations of the latter type are discussed in the remainder of the chapter. The explanations and illustrations presented are necessarily brief and relatively free of the complexities encountered in actual practice.

ACCOUNTING FOR NONPROFIT ORGANIZATIONS

With the increase in the sense of social responsibility in society has come a corresponding increase in the number of nonprofit organizations and in the volume of their activities. Approximately one third of the volume of business in the United States is conducted by governmental units and charitable organizations. As such organizations play an increasingly significant role, accounting for these organizations is receiving more and more attention. For example, the Governmental Accounting Standards Board (GASB), similar to the Financial Accounting Standards Board (FASB), was established in 1984. This body is responsible for establishing accounting standards for state and local governmental units.[2] Accounting for other nonprofit organizations, such

---

[2]*Statement No. 1*, "Authoritative Status of NCGA Pronouncements and AICPA Industry Audit Guide" (Stamford: Governmental Accounting Standards Board, 1984).

On Governmental Accounting

"I think it an object of great importance . . . to simplify our system of finance, and to bring it within the comprehension of every member of Congress . . . the whole system [has been] involved in impenetrable fog. [T]here is a point . . . on which I should wish to keep my eye . . . a simplification of the form of accounts . . . so as to bring everything to a single center[;] we might hope to see the finances of the Union as clear and intelligible as a merchant's books, so that every member of Congress, and every man of any mind in the Union, should be able to comprehend them to investigate abuses, and consequently to control them."

Thomas Jefferson
April 1802

Source: *Sound Financial Reporting In the U.S. Government* (Chicago: Arthur Andersen & Co, 1986).

as churches and hospitals, is also receiving attention by the American Institute of Certified Public Accountants and other professional accounting groups.

The accounting systems for all nonprofit organizations must provide financial data to internal management for use in planning and controlling operations and to external parties, such as taxpayers and donors, for use in determining the effectiveness of operations. The basic double-entry system, an effective system of internal control, and the periodic determination of and reporting of financial position and results of operations are essential for nonprofit organizations. In addition, accounting systems for nonprofit organizations should include mechanisms (1) to ensure that management observes the restrictions imposed upon it by law, charter, by-laws, etc., and (2) to provide for reports to taxpayers and donors that such restrictions have been respected. For these reasons, a nonprofit organization often applies the concept of "fund accounting" in conjunction with a budget and appropriations technique to account for the assets received by the organization and to ensure that expenditures are made only for authorized purposes.

Fund Accounting

In this book, the term "fund" has been used with a variety of meanings. Fund has been used to denote segregations of cash for a special purpose, for example, in "petty cash fund," or to designate the amount of cash and marketable securities segregated in a "sinking fund" to pay long-term obligations at maturity. The term was also used in the context of the funds statement, where funds can be interpreted broadly to mean "working capital" or more narrowly to mean "cash".

In accounting for nonprofit organizations, **fund** is defined as an accounting entity with accounts maintained for recording assets, liabilities, **fund equity** (the excess of assets over liabilities), revenues, and expenditures for a particular purpose according to specified restrictions or limitations. The following description of fund accounting appeared in an annual report for the District of Columbia:

> The accounts of the District are organized in funds and account groups, each of which is considered a separate accounting entity. The accompanying financial statements include all funds and account groups of the District.
>
> The operations of each fund are accounted for with a separate set of self-balancing accounts that comprise its assets, liabilities, fund equity, revenues, and expenditures or expenses, as appropriate. Government resources are allocated to and accounted for in individual funds based upon the purposes for which they are to be spent.

Funds may be established by law, provisions of a charter, administrative action, or by a special contribution to a charitable organization. Cities usually maintain a "General Fund" for recording transactions related to many community services, such as fire and police protection, street lighting and repairs, and maintenance of water and sewer mains. Additional funds may be maintained for special tax assessments, bond redemption, and for other specified purposes. It is possible to have transactions between funds, as when one fund borrows money from another fund, in which case the transaction is recorded in the accounts of both funds.

Both public and private universities usually maintain a number of separate funds in addition to a General Fund. For example, there may be a number of scholarship funds, named for alumni or other donors, with many restrictions concerning the recipients, such as high scholastic attainment, residence in a specified area, and enrollment in a particular course of study.

Charitable organizations often have a number of funds, sometimes called "endowment funds," from which only the income may be spent. The amounts contributed to such funds are often invested in various income-yielding bonds and stocks. For fund balances of modest amount, however, it is not feasible to identify each bond or share with a particular fund. In such situations, the investments are commingled, each fund having a claim on the investment pool equal to its fund balance. The income is periodically divided among the various participating funds in proportion to the respective fund balances at the beginning of the period. The same technique is used by governmental units, such as state universities, for the temporary investment of large amounts of cash that would otherwise yield no income.

Estimated Revenues and Appropriations. Budgeting is an important part of an accounting system for nonprofit organizations. The budget is prepared by management and subsequently reviewed, revised, and approved by the governing body (council, directors, trustees, etc.) of the organization. The official budget sets the specific goals for the fiscal period and, through appropriations, designates the manner in which the revenues of each fund are to be used to accomplish these goals. The estimated revenues may be viewed as potential assets and the **appropriations** as potential liabilities.

Many governmental units apply the concept of **zero-base budgeting** in developing budget estimates. This concept requires all levels of management to start from zero and estimate revenues and appropriations as if there had been no previous activities in their unit.

After the budget for the General Fund has been approved by the governing body, the estimated revenues and appropriations are recorded in controlling accounts. Any difference between the estimated revenues and appropriations is recorded in the fund equity account, Fund Balance. The amount in the fund balance account represents unrestricted, spendable resources of the General Fund. An example of such an entry is as follows:

Estimated Revenues	1,900,000	
Appropriations		1,850,000
Fund Balance		50,000

The effect of the recording of the budgeted amounts in the General Fund accounts is presented in the following diagram:

GENERAL FUND ACCOUNTS

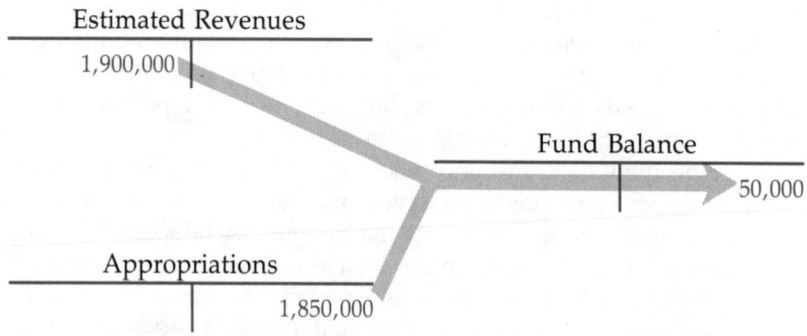

When the budget shows an excess of estimated revenues over appropriations, as in the preceding illustration, Fund Balance is credited. If the budget had shown an excess of appropriations over estimated revenues, the excess would be debited to Fund Balance. The subsidiary ledgers for Estimated Revenues and Appropriations contain accounts for the various sources of expected revenue (property taxes, sales taxes, etc.) and the various purposes of appropriations (general government, streets and roads, libraries, etc.). By recording this budgetary information in the accounts, periodic reports comparing actual amounts with budgeted amounts can be prepared readily.

Revenues. The realization of revenues requires an entry debiting accounts for the assets acquired and crediting the revenues account. For example, a portion of the estimated revenues from property taxes, sales taxes, etc., may be realized in the form of cash during the first month of the fiscal year. To summarize these receipts, an entry would be made as follows:

Cash...	152,500	
Revenues..		152,500

Revenues is a controlling account. In practice, it is customary to use a single subsidiary ledger, called the **revenue ledger**, for both Estimated Revenues and Revenues. Each subsidiary account is used for recording the estimated revenues and the actual revenues. The relationship between the general ledger accounts and the subsidiary revenue ledger is illustrated in the following diagram:

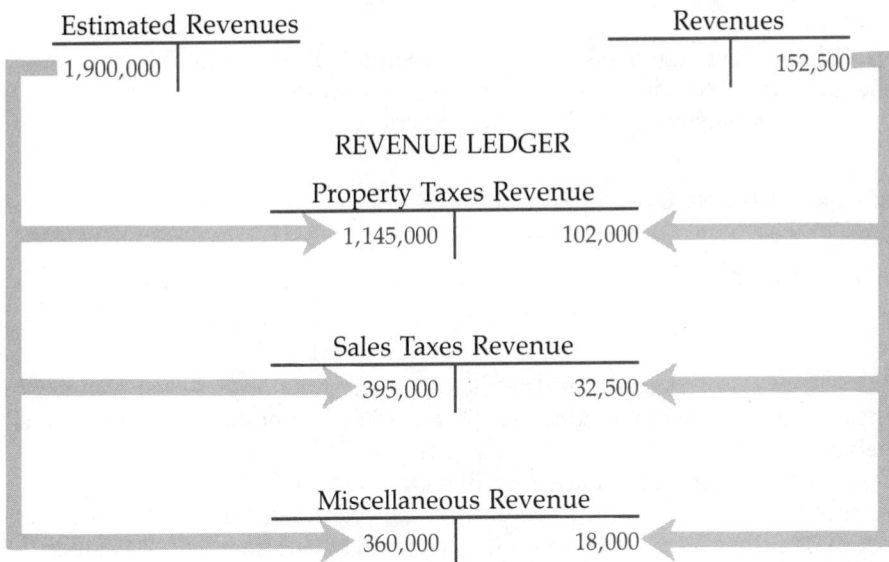

GENERAL LEDGER ACCOUNTS

At any point in time, the difference between the two general ledger controlling accounts, Estimated Revenues and Revenues, would be equal to the sum of the balances of the accounts in the subsidiary revenue ledger. A debit balance in a subsidiary ledger account indicates the amount of the excess of estimated revenues over actual revenues. If actual revenues exceed the amount estimated, the account balance would be a credit.

Expenditures. As regularly recurring expenditures, such as payrolls, are incurred, the account Expenditures is debited and the appropriate liability accounts or cash are credited. For example, the entry for the biweekly payroll would be as follows:

Expenditures...	31,200	
Wages Payable.....................................		31,200

Encumbrances. There is usually a lapse of time between the placing of an order and delivery of the goods or services ordered. When contracts such as those for road or building construction are executed, the time lag may extend over relatively long periods. All legally binding commitments to pay money eventually become expenditures. These commitments, called **encumbrances**, should be recorded in the accounts when a contract is entered into in order to ensure that expenditures do not exceed amounts appropriated. The means of preventing overexpenditures is illustrated by the following entry:

Encumbrances	10,000	
Fund Balance Reserved for Encumbrances.............		10,000

When orders are filled or contracts completed for amounts encumbered, the entry that recorded the encumbrance is reversed and the expenditure is recorded, as illustrated by the following entries:

Fund Balance Reserved for Encumbrances..............	10,000	
Encumbrances		10,000
Expenditures...	10,000	
Accounts Payable		10,000

The effect of these two entries is to (1) cancel the original entry in which the encumbrance was recorded and (2) record the expenditure and the related liability.

When encumbrances are recorded, the sum of the balances of the accounts Encumbrances and Expenditures can be viewed as offsets to the account Appropriations. The difference obtained by subtracting the balances of Encumbrances and Expenditures from the amount of Appropriations is the amount of commitments that can still be made. For example, if appropriations of $1,850,000 were approved when the budget was adopted and $1,500,000 and $240,000 have been recorded in Expenditures and Encumbrances, respectively, only $110,000 is available for commitment during the remainder of the fiscal year.

Expenditure Ledger. Appropriations, Encumbrances, and Expenditures are controlling accounts. In practice, it is customary to use a single subsidiary ledger, called the **expenditure ledger**, in which each account indicates appropriations, encumbrances, and expenditures.

When a budget is approved, appropriations are recorded in the proper accounts in the expenditure ledger to indicate the unencumbered or uncommitted balance. As order commitments are made, the amounts of the encumbrances are recorded in the proper expenditure ledger account (by a debit) and the unencumbered balance is adjusted accordingly. When orders are filled, the expenditure and the credit to encumbrances are recorded in the proper columns. At any point in time, the accounts in the expenditure ledger indicate the balance of the encumbrances outstanding and the unencumbered balance.

In the following illustration of an account in the expenditure ledger, the budget appropriation for police department supplies is $250,000 as of July 1. On July 5, a purchase order that encumbered $10,000 was recorded and the encumbrances balance of $10,000 and the unencumbered balance of $240,000 were recorded. When the invoice of $10,000 was received on July 17, the encumbrances balance was reduced to zero and the $10,000 expenditure was recorded.

ACCOUNT POLICE DEPARTMENT — SUPPLIES   ACCOUNT NO. 200-21

Date		Item	Encumbrances			Expenditures		Unencumbered Balance
			Debit	Credit	Balance	Item	Total	
July	1	Budget appropriation						250,000
	5	Purchase order	10,000		10,000			240,000
	17	Invoice		10,000	—	10,000	10,000	240,000
	30	Purchase order	7,500		7,500			232,500

Long-Lived Assets. When long-lived assets are purchased, they are usually recorded as debits to the account Expenditures in the same manner as supplies and other ordinary expenses. A separate record of the individual assets can be maintained for the purpose of assigning responsibility for the custody and use of these assets.

The practice of recording the purchase of long-lived assets as an expenditure and the related failure to record depreciation expense has been severely criticized for many years. Most governmental units and charitable organizations still fail to differentiate between long-lived assets and ordinary recurring expenses. This practice is supported by the fact that the acquisition of plant assets is often authorized by a special appropriation, perhaps financed by a bond issue for a local government unit or by donations or special fund-raising drives for a charitable organization.

Periodic Reporting

A nonprofit organization should prepare interim statements comparing actual revenues and expenditures with the related budgeted amounts. Variations between the two should be investigated immediately to determine their cause and to consider possible corrective actions.

At the end of the fiscal year, closing entries are recorded and the operating data are summarized and reported. The entry to close the revenues and estimated revenues accounts is illustrated as follows:

Revenues	1,920,000	
Estimated Revenues		1,900,000
Fund Balance		20,000

In the illustration, actual revenues exceeded the amount estimated. If the actual revenues had been less than the amount estimated, the fund equity account, Fund Balance, would have been decreased by a debit. The effect of this entry is to adjust Fund Balance to the actual amount of the revenues for the period.

The entry to close the appropriations and expenditures accounts is illustrated as follows:

Appropriations	1,850,000	
Expenditures		1,825,000
Fund Balance		25,000

In the illustration, appropriations exceeded the actual expenditures. If the appropriations had been less than the actual expenditures, Fund Balance would have been decreased by a debit. The effect of this entry is to adjust Fund Balance to the actual amount of the expenditures for the period.

The entry to close the encumbrances account, which represents the commitments outstanding at the end of the year, is illustrated as follows:

Fund Balance	20,000	
Encumbrances		20,000

Inevitably, some orders placed during the year will remain unfilled at the end of the year. To indicate the commitment to pay for these orders, Fund Balance Reserved for Encumbrances is not closed and is included in the fund equity section of the year-end balance sheet. When the orders are filled in the next year, Fund Balance Reserved for Encumbrances will be debited and Accounts Payable credited.

Financial statements for each fund and combined financial statements for all funds should be prepared periodically. The principal financial statements prepared at the end of each fiscal year are: (1) a balance sheet, which is similar to a commercial enterprise balance sheet, and (2) a statement of revenues, expenditures, and changes in fund balance. The objective of the **statement of revenues, expenditures, and changes in fund balance** is to provide users with information on a nonprofit entity's operating performance for a period. The nature of this statement emphasizes the absence of the profit motive and the importance of controlling expenditures within the revenue limits imposed by law or the dictate of donors. The first part of the statement presents a comparison of the budgeted and actual revenues and expenditures, but not a net income amount. The second part, which is similar to the retained earnings statement for a commercial enterprise, presents the effects of operations and encumbrances on the unreserved fund balance. Both the balance sheet and the statement of revenues, expenditures, and changes in fund balance are illustrated in the following section.

The financial statements for the funds should also be accompanied by adequate disclosures, including a summary of significant accounting policies. Two excerpts from the summary of significant accounting policies section of the District of Columbia's annual report are as follows:

Encumbrances

Encumbrances are commitments to acquire goods and services. The recording of purchase orders and contracts in order to reserve that portion of the applicable appropriation is employed as an extension of allocation in the General Fund.

Fixed Assets

Costs to acquire fixed assets used in governmental funds are charged as current expenditures in the General Fund.

ILLUSTRATION OF NONPROFIT ACCOUNTING

To illustrate further the concepts and procedures that have been described, assume that the trial balance of the General Fund of the City of Lewiston, as of July 1, 1987, the beginning of the fiscal year, is as follows:

City of Lewiston — General Fund
Trial Balance
July 1, 1987

Cash..	242,500	
Savings Accounts	250,000	
Property Taxes Receivable	185,000	
Investment in U.S. Treasury Notes................	350,000	
Accounts Payable		162,600
Wages Payable................................		30,000
Fund Balance		834,900
	1,027,500	1,027,500

The transactions completed during the year for the General Fund are summarized and recorded as follows, in general journal form. In practice, the transactions would be recorded from day to day in various journals.

(a) *Estimated revenues and appropriations.*

   Entry: Estimated Revenues   9,100,000
               Appropriations   9,070,000
               Fund Balance   30,000

(b) *Revenues from property tax levy.*

   Entry: Property Taxes Receivable...........   6,500,000
               Revenues......................   6,500,000

(c) *Collection of property taxes and other taxes on a cash basis, such as sales taxes, motor vehicle license fees, municipal court fines, etc.*

   Entry: Cash   9,105,000
               Property Taxes Receivable.........   6,470,000
               Revenues......................   2,635,000

(d) *Expenditures for payrolls.*

   Entry: Expenditures   3,280,000
               Wages Payable..................   3,280,000

(e) *Expenditures encumbered.*

   Entry: Encumbrances.....................   5,800,000
               Fund Balance Reserved for
                  Encumbrances.................   5,800,000

(f) *Liquidation of encumbrances and receipt of invoices.*

   Entry: Fund Balance Reserved for
               Encumbrances.....................   5,785,000
                  Encumbrances..................   5,785,000

           Expenditures   5,785,000
               Accounts Payable.................   5,785,000

(g) *Cash disbursed.*

   Entry: Accounts Payable..................   5,800,000
               Wages Payable....................   3,270,000
               Cash   9,070,000

(h) Revenues and estimated revenues accounts closed.

Entry: Revenues........................ 9,135,000
          Estimated Revenues   9,100,000
          Fund Balance   35,000

(i) Appropriations and expenditures accounts closed.

Entry: Appropriations..................... 9,070,000
          Expenditures   9,065,000
          Fund Balance   5,000

(j) Encumbrances account closed.

Entry: Fund Balance   15,000
          Encumbrances....................   15,000

After the foregoing entries have been posted, the general ledger accounts and the trial balance for the General Fund appear as follows. Entries in the accounts are identified by letters to facilitate comparison with the summary journal entries.

Cash

Balance	242,500	(g)	9,070,000
(c)	9,105,000	Balance	277,500
	9,347,500		9,347,500
Balance	277,500		

Savings Accounts

Balance	250,000

Property Taxes Receivable

Balance	185,000	(c)	6,470,000
(b)	6,500,000	Balance	215,000
	6,685,000		6,685,000
Balance	215,000		

Investment in U.S. Treasury Notes

Balance	350,000

Accounts Payable

(g)	5,800,000	Balance	162,600
Balance	147,600	(f)	5,785,000
	5,947,600		5,947,600
		Balance	147,600

Wages Payable

(g)	3,270,000	Balance	30,000
Balance	40,000	(d)	3,280,000
	3,310,000		3,310,000
		Balance	40,000

Fund Balance Reserved for Encumbrances

(f)	5,785,000	(e)	5,800,000
Balance	15,000		
	5,800,000		5,800,000
		Balance	15,000

Fund Balance				Appropriations			
(j)	15,000	Balance	834,900	(i)	9,070,000	(a)	9,070,000
Balance	889,900	(a)	30,000				
		(h)	35,000				
		(i)	5,000		Appropriations subtotal		
	904,900		904,900				
		Balance	889,900				

Estimated Revenues				Expenditures			
(a)	9,100,000	(h)	9,100,000	(d)	3,280,000	(i)	9,065,000
				(f)	5,785,000		
					9,065,000		9,065,000

Encumbrances

Revenues				Encumbrances			
(h)	9,135,000	(b)	6,500,000	(e)	5,800,000	(f)	5,785,000
		(c)	2,635,000			(j)	15,000
	9,135,000		9,135,000		5,800,000		5,800,000

City of Lewiston—General Fund
Trial Balance
June 30, 1988

Cash.	277,500	
Savings Accounts	250,000	
Property Taxes Receivable.	215,000	
Investment in U.S. Treasury Notes	350,000	
Accounts Payable		147,600
Wages Payable.		40,000
Fund Balance Reserved for Encumbrances.		15,000
Fund Balance		889,900
	1,092,500	1,092,500

The balance sheet for the City of Lewiston General Fund, as of June 30, 1988, is as follows. On the balance sheet, the fund balance reserved for encumbrances is reported as a separate item in the fund equity section. The balance of the account Fund Balance, $889,900, is described as "Unreserved fund balance." As mentioned previously, this amount represents the unrestricted, spendable resources of the General Fund.

City of Lewiston—General Fund
Balance Sheet
June 30, 1988

Assets

Cash	$ 277,500
Savings accounts[3]	250,000
Property taxes receivable	215,000
Investment in U.S. Treasury notes	350,000
Total assets	$1,092,500

Liabilities

Accounts payable	$147,600	
Wages payable	40,000	
Total liabilities		$ 187,600

Fund Equity

Fund balance reserved for encumbrances	$ 15,000	
Unreserved fund balance	889,900	
Total fund equity		904,900
Total liabilities and fund equity		$1,092,500

Although there are many variations in form, the statement of revenues, expenditures, and changes in fund balance reports the following:

1. Differences (in terms of over or under budget) between budgeted revenues and actual revenues.
2. Differences (in terms of over or under budget) between budgeted expenditures and actual expenditures.
3. The excess or deficiency of revenues (both actual and budgeted) over expenditures.
4. The fund balance at the beginning of the year and the amount of the encumbrances closed to fund balance at the end of the year.
5. The fund balance at the end of the year.

The statement of revenues, expenditures, and changes in fund balance for the City of Lewiston General Fund is as follows:

[3]*Statement No. 3,* "Deposits with Financial Institutions, Investments (including Repurchase Agreements), and Reverse Repurchase Agreements" (Stamford: Governmental Accounting Standards Board, 1986), requires specific disclosures about deposits with financial institutions. A discussion of these disclosures is beyond the scope of this chapter.

STATEMENT
OF
REVENUES,
EXPEN-
DITURES,
AND
CHANGES
IN FUND
BALANCE

City of Lewiston — General Fund
Statement of Revenues, Expenditures, and Changes in Fund Balance
For Year Ended June 30, 1988

	Budget	Actual	Over	Under
Revenues:				
General property taxes	$6,480,000	$6,500,000	$20,000	
Sales taxes	1,835,500	1,850,500	15,000	
Motor vehicle licenses	312,250	310,250		$ 2,000
Municipal court fines	257,000	255,750		1,250
Interest	35,000	35,000		
Building permits	27,100	27,500	400	
Miscellaneous	153,150	156,000	2,850	
Total revenues	$9,100,000	$9,135,000	$38,250	$ 3,250
Expenditures:				
General government	$2,450,000	$2,465,250	$15,250	
Police department— personnel services	1,250,000	1,256,000	6,000	
Police department—supplies	299,000	290,500		$ 8,500
Police department—equipment	190,000	182,750		7,250
Police department— other charges	30,000	27,500		2,500
Fire department— personnel services	1,035,000	1,039,000	4,000	
Fire department—supplies	320,600	315,600		5,000
Fire department—equipment	200,500	197,750		2,750
Fire department— other charges	16,400	18,200	1,800	
Streets and roads	1,530,000	1,521,850		8,150
Sanitation	741,000	739,500		1,500
Public welfare	630,000	632,600	2,600	
Libraries	377,500	378,500	1,000	
Total expenditures	$9,070,000	$9,065,000	$30,650	$35,650
Excess of revenues over expenditures	$ 30,000	$ 70,000		
Fund balance, July 1, 1987		834,900		
		$ 904,900		
Less encumbrances		15,000		
Fund balance, June 30, 1988		$ 889,900		

The data for the preparation of the preceding statement would be provided by the various subsidiary ledgers for the City of Lewiston General Fund. These ledgers were not presented in order to simplify the illustration.

CHAPTER REVIEW

KEY POINTS

1. Accounting Systems for Individuals.

Although accounting systems for individuals differ widely, the most commonly used system is based on the cash method. Under the cash method, the use of budgets is an important part of successful financial planning. Monthly budgets of income and expenditures should be prepared. For control purposes, actual expenditures should be compared frequently with budgeted amounts through the use of a budget performance record.

In addition to the budget performance record, the record keeping system for individuals ordinarily consists of a checkbook, a file for bills and statements of account representing unpaid liabilities, a file for documents supporting cash payments, and a property inventory record.

2. Financial Statements for Individuals.

The main financial statement for individuals or for related individuals, such as a husband and wife as a family unit, is the statement of financial condition. This statement presents the estimated current values of assets, estimated current amounts of liabilities, estimated income tax on unrealized appreciation of assets, and estimated net worth. The notes accompanying the statement describe the methods used in determining the current values and other relevant details.

When comparative statements of financial condition are presented, an additional statement is often included. This statement, the statement of changes in net worth, presents the major sources of increases and decreases in net worth.

3. Characteristics of Nonprofit Organizations.

The distinguishing characteristics of nonprofit organizations are: (1) there is neither a conscious profit motive nor an expectation of earning net income; (2) no part of any excess of revenues over expenditures is distributed to those who contributed support through taxes or voluntary donations; and (3) any excess of revenues over expenditures that results from operations in the short run is ordinarily used in later years to further the purposes of the organization.

4. Accounting for Nonprofit Organizations.

The Governmental Accounting Standards Board (GASB) is responsible for establishing accounting standards for state and local governmental units.

Accounting for nonprofit organizations, sometimes referred to as fund accounting, is based upon double-entry accounting. It includes procedures to ensure that the management of the organization observes restrictions imposed upon it by law, charter, bylaws, etc. Fund is defined as an accounting entity with accounts maintained for recording assets, liabilities, fund equity, revenues, and expenditures for a particular purpose according to specified restrictions or limitations.

Budgeting is an important part of an accounting system for nonprofit organizations. The concept of zero-base budgeting requires management to start from zero and estimate revenues and expenditures. Estimated revenues, viewed as potential assets, and appropriations, viewed as potential liabilities, are recorded directly in the accounts. Any excess or deficiency of estimated revenues over appropriations is recorded in the fund balance account. The receipt of revenues is recorded by debiting an asset account and crediting the revenues controlling account. Recurring expenditures are recorded by debiting the expenditures controlling account and crediting an asset or liability account. When there is a lapse of time between the placing of an order and the delivery of the goods or services ordered, expenditures are recorded by use of encumbrances and fund balance reserved for encumbrances accounts. When encumbrances are recorded, the sum of the balances of the accounts Encumbrances and Expenditures can be viewed as offsets to the account Appropriations. The difference is the amount of commitments that can still be made. Appropriations, Expenditures, and Encumbrances are controlling accounts.

When long-lived assets are purchased, they are usually recorded as debits to the account Expenditures. A separate record is maintained for the purpose of assigning responsibility for the custody and use of these assets.

At the end of a reporting period, actual revenues and expenditures should be compared with the related budgeted amounts. The revenues, estimated revenues, appropriations, expenditures, and encumbrances accounts are closed to the fund balance account. The fund balance reserved for encumbrances account is not closed and appears in the year-end balance sheet.

The principal financial statements for a nonprofit organization are: (1) a balance sheet and (2) a statement of revenues, expenditures, and changes in fund balance.

KEY TERMS

statement of financial condition 1254
fund 1261
fund equity 1261
appropriations 1262
zero-base budgeting 1262

encumbrances 1264
statement of revenues,
  expenditures, and changes
  in fund balance 1267

SELF-EXAMINATION QUESTIONS

Answers in Appendix B.

1. Assets in the statement of financial condition for individuals are reported at:
   A. cost
   B. estimated current values
   C. lower of cost or market
   D. none of the above

2. The caption for the equity of the individual in the statement of financial condition is:
   A. proprietorship
   B. capital
   C. net worth
   D. none of the above

3. In accounting for nonprofit organizations, the term employed to represent an accounting entity with accounts for assets, liabilities, fund equity, revenues, and expenditures for a particular purpose is:
   A. fund
   B. appropriation
   C. encumbrance
   D. none of the above

4. In accounting for nonprofit organizations, the account that represents the fund equity of an accounting entity is:
   A. Retained Earnings
   B. Accumulated Earnings
   C. Fund Balance
   D. none of the above

5. The principal financial statements for a nonprofit organization are a balance sheet and a (an):
   A. statement of revenues, expenditures, and changes in fund balance
   B. trial balance
   C. income statement
   D. none of the above

ILLUSTRATIVE PROBLEM

The City of Yatesville's fiscal period ends June 30. The trial balance of the General Fund as of July 1, 1987, was as follows:

City of Yatesville — General Fund
Trial Balance
July 1, 1987

Cash	12,600	
Savings Accounts	66,800	
Property Taxes Receivable	480,600	
Accounts Payable		7,300
Wages Payable		4,450
Fund Balance		548,250
	560,000	560,000

The operations for the year ended June 30, 1988, are summarized as follows:

(a) Estimated revenues, $2,400,000; appropriations, $2,350,000.
(b) Revenues from property tax levy, $1,925,500.
(c) Cash received from property taxes, $2,005,600, and other revenues, $485,700.
(d) Expenditures encumbered and evidenced by purchase orders, $1,760,000.
(e) Liquidation of encumbrances and vouchers prepared for purchase order billings, $1,755,000.
(f) Expenditures for payrolls, $602,000.
(g) Cash disbursed for vouchers, $1,740,000; for payment of wages, $598,000; for savings accounts, $150,000.

Instructions:

1. Open T accounts for the accounts appearing in the trial balance and enter the balances as of July 1, 1987, identifying them as "Bal."
2. Open T accounts for Fund Balance Reserved for Encumbrances, Estimated Revenues, Revenues, Appropriations, Expenditures, and Encumbrances.
3. Prepare the journal entries to record the foregoing summarized operations.
4. Post the entries recorded in 3 to the accounts, using the identifying letters in place of dates.
5. Prepare the appropriate entries to close the accounts as of June 30, 1988, and post to the accounts using the letter "C" to identify the postings.
6. Prepare a balance sheet as of June 30, 1988.

SOLUTION

(1), (2), (4), and (5)

	Cash		
Bal.	12,600	(g)	2,488,000
(c)	2,491,300		

	Accounts Payable		
(g)	1,740,000	Bal.	7,300
		(e)	1,755,000

	Savings Accounts	
Bal.	66,800	
(g)	150,000	

	Wages Payable		
(g)	598,000	Bal.	4,450
		(f)	602,000

	Property Taxes Receivable		
Bal.	480,600	(c)	2,005,600
(b)	1,925,500		

	Fund Balance Reserved for Encumbrances		
(e)	1,755,000	(d)	1,760,000

Fund Balance			
C	7,000	Bal.	548,250
C	5,000	(a)	50,000
		C	11,200

Appropriations			
C	2,350,000	(a)	2,350,000

Estimated Revenues			
(a)	2,400,000	C	2,400,000

Expenditures			
(e)	1,755,000	C	2,357,000
(f)	602,000		

Revenues			
C	2,411,200	(b)	1,925,500
		(c)	485,700

Encumbrances			
(d)	1,760,000	(e)	1,755,000
		C	5,000

(3)

(a) Estimated Revenues 2,400,000
    Appropriations....................... 2,350,000
    Fund Balance 50,000

(b) Property Taxes Receivable............... 1,925,500
    Revenues............................ 1,925,500

(c) Cash..................................... 2,491,300
    Property Taxes Receivable............. 2,005,600
    Revenues............................ 485,700

(d) Encumbrances 1,760,000
    Fund Balance Reserved for
        Encumbrances 1,760,000

(e) Fund Balance Reserved for Encumbrances . 1,755,000
    Encumbrances 1,755,000

    Expenditures 1,755,000
    Accounts Payable 1,755,000

(f) Expenditures 602,000
    Wages Payable....................... 602,000

(g) Accounts Payable 1,740,000
    Wages Payable........................ 598,000
    Savings Accounts 150,000
    Cash................................ 2,488,000

(5)

Revenues................................. 2,411,200
    Estimated Revenues 2,400,000
    Fund Balance 11,200

(continued)

Appropriations...............................	2,350,000	
Fund Balance	7,000	
Expenditures.............................		2,357,000
Fund Balance	5,000	
Encumbrances		5,000

(6)

City of Yatesville — General Fund
Balance Sheet
June 30, 1988

Assets

Cash	$ 15,900
Savings accounts	216,800
Property taxes receivable....................	400,500
Total assets	$633,200

Liabilities

Accounts payable...........................	$ 22,300
Wages payable	8,450
Total liabilities..............................	$ 30,750

Fund Equity

Fund balance reserved for encumbrances	$ 5,000
Unreserved fund balance....................	597,450
Total fund equity	602,450
Total liabilities and fund equity	$633,200

DISCUSSION QUESTIONS

1. How does the use of budgets assist an individual or family unit in financial planning?

2. If the preliminary monthly budget for an individual indicates an excess of cash outflow over cash income, what courses of action might the individual consider to achieve a balanced budget?

3. What name is given to the record that indicates the relationship between actual expenditures made by an individual and the allocations for expenditures provided in the budget?

4. In addition to a budget performance record, what four other records are ordinarily included in an individual's record keeping system?

5. In what respects does the statement of financial condition prepared for individuals differ from the conventional balance sheet prepared for commercial enterprises?

6. In what order are (a) assets and (b) liabilities listed in the statement of financial condition?

7. Why should the statement of financial condition include an amount for estimated income tax on unrealized appreciation of assets?

8. In the statement of financial condition, what caption is used to identify the equity of an individual?

9. What entity is responsible for establishing accounting standards for state and local governmental units?

10. What characteristics distinguish commercial enterprises from nonprofit organizations?

11. As the term is used in reference to accounting for nonprofit organizations, what is meant by "fund accounting"?

12. What concept requires all levels of management of a governmental unit to start from zero and estimate revenues and appropriations as if there had been no previous activities in their unit?

13. In recording estimated revenues and appropriations as expressed in the budget, would Fund Balance be debited or credited if appropriations exceed estimated revenues?

14. If an account in the revenue ledger indicated that estimated revenues exceeded revenues, will the account have a debit balance or a credit balance?

15. What is the purpose of recording encumbrances in the accounts?

16. If the appropriations, expenditures, and encumbrances accounts have balances of $950,000, $750,000, and $125,000 respectively, what amount is available for commitments during the remainder of the fiscal year?

17. In the subsidiary expenditure ledger, the libraries account shows an unencumbered balance. Does this balance indicate that appropriations for the year exceed the sum of encumbrances outstanding and expenditures incurred to date?

18. (a) What account in the general ledger of a nonprofit organization is debited for purchases of long-lived assets? (b) Is depreciation generally recorded on such assets?

19. When the closing entry for the appropriations and expenditures accounts is prepared, in what account is the difference between the balances in the two accounts recorded?

20. In which financial statements will the year-end balance of the following accounts appear: (a) Expenditures and (b) Fund Balance Reserved for Encumbrances?

21. Real World Focus. The following General Fund items are included in the annual report for the City of Athens, Georgia, for the year ended June 30, 1985:

Total assets	$1,952,756
Liabilities	204,352
Encumbrances	277,269

What is the unreserved fund balance as of June 30, 1985?

EXERCISES

Exercise 28–1. Statement of financial condition. Jennifer and Charles Sanders applied to the Atlantic National Bank for a loan. The bank requested a statement of financial condition. Summary financial data accumulated as of July 1 are as follows:

(a) Present value of accounts payable and accrued liabilities, $15,200.
(b) Automobiles: cost, $30,800; estimated market price, $17,500.
(c) Cash, including money market funds, $22,350.
(d) Cash value of $300,000 face value life insurance policy, $30,500.
(e) Household furnishings: cost, $102,200; estimated market price, $78,000.
(f) Marketable securities: cost, $230,000; estimated current value, $310,000.
(g) Present value of 12% mortgage note payable, final payment due August 1, 19--, $134,100.
(h) Residence (pledged against mortgage note): cost $200,000; estimated market price, $250,000.

Prepare a statement of financial condition (exclusive of notes to the statement) as of July 1. Assume that the estimated income tax on unrealized appreciation of assets is $16,000.

Exercise 28–2. Entries from budget for nonprofit enterprise. The budget approved for the fiscal year by the city council of Marble Hill for the General Fund indicated appropriations of $1,850,000 and estimated revenues of $1,910,000. Present the journal entry to record the financial data indicated by the budget.

Exercise 28–3. Entries for placement of orders and their receipt for nonprofit enterprise. An order was placed by a nonprofit organization for $8,560 of supplies. Subsequently, $7,110 of the supplies were received and $1,450 were back ordered. Present entries to record (a) the placement of the order and (b) the receipt of the supplies and the invoice of $7,110, terms n/eom.

Exercise 28–4. Closing entries for nonprofit enterprise. Selected account balances from the General Fund ledger of McNair Foundation at the end of the current fiscal year are as follows:

Appropriations	$580,000
Encumbrances	35,000
Estimated Revenues	600,000
Expenditures	542,000
Fund Balance	71,300
Fund Balance Reserved for Encumbrances	35,000
Revenues	605,500

Prepare the appropriate closing entries.

Exercise 28–5. Balance sheet for General Fund of university. Selected account balances from the ledger of the University of San Antonio Alumni Association — General Fund are as follows:

Accounts Payable	$ 12,700
Cash in Bank	15,600
Fund Balance	198,550
Marketable Securities	180,000
Petty Cash	650
Fund Balance Reserved for Encumbrances	10,000
Savings Accounts	25,000

Prepare a balance sheet as of July 31.

Exercise 28–6. Statement of revenues, expenditures, and changes in fund balance. Data from two subsidiary ledgers of Cumberland College — Intercollegiate Athletics Fund, at August 31, 1988, are as follows:

Revenue Ledger

	Debits	Credits
Basketball	100,000	102,100
Football	350,000	334,800
Other	10,000	12,200

Expenditure Ledger

	Expenditures	Budget Appropriations
Administration	55,600	50,000
Basketball	75,300	75,000
Football	235,900	240,000
Maintenance of facilities . .	38,750	40,000
Publicity	15,800	13,200
Other	27,400	30,000

The beginning balance of the fund balance account as of September 1, 1987, was $187,500. Assuming that the encumbrances account has a balance of $5,000 on August 31, 1988, prepare a statement of revenues, expenditures, and changes in fund balance for the year ended August 31, 1988.

Exercise 28–7. Computation of unreserved fund balance. Selected account balances before closing on June 30, the end of the current fiscal year for S. L. Rankin Foundation—General Fund, are as follows. The fund balance account had a balance of $396,400 on July 1, 1987, the beginning of the current year.

Appropriations	$2,080,000
Encumbrances	10,000
Estimated Revenues	2,120,000
Expenditures	2,008,000
Revenues	2,060,000

Compute the balance of the fund balance account as of June 30, 1988, the end of the current fiscal year.

PROBLEMS

Series A

Problem 28–1A. Statement of financial condition. Gail Hill is a partner in the firm of Wells, Young, and Associates, and Edward Hill owns and manages Western Motor Inn. They applied to the Texas National Bank for a loan to be used to build an apartment complex. The bank requested a statement of financial condition, and they assembled the following data for this purpose at April 30:

(a) Cash in bank, savings, and money market accounts, $30,000. (Unrestricted withdrawals are allowed without penalty.)
(b) Marketable securities (current value is quoted market price on April 30, 19--, less estimated broker commissions):

	Cost	Current Value
Stocks:		
Ramos Manufacturing Inc., 500 shares	$10,000	$15,000
WCT Industries, 1,000 shares	25,000	32,000
Irving Food Stores Inc., 600 shares	60,000	72,000
Bonds:		
U.S. Treasury, 10%, $40,000 face amount, due 19--.	30,000	34,500
Dooley Motors Inc., 15%, $30,000 face amount, due 19--	25,000	32,800

(c) Gail Hill's equity interest in Wells, Young, and Associates: cost, $60,000; estimated market, $180,000. Edward Hill's equity interest in Western Motor Inn: cost $100,000; estimated market, $120,000. The estimated market prices were determined by an independent appraisal made by Choi Realty.

(d) Cash value of $200,000 face value life insurance policy, $45,500.

(e) Residence: cost, $250,000; estimated market, $300,000. The estimated market price was determined by an independent appraisal made by Stuart and Associates. The residence is pledged against an 11% mortgage note payable, final installment due February 1, 19--. The present value of the monthly mortgage payments of $1,800, including interest, is $140,000.

(f) Household furnishings: cost, $86,800; estimated market, $62,700.

(g) Automobiles: cost, $38,500; estimated market, $21,000.

(h) Jewelry and paintings: cost, $15,500; estimated market, $20,000. The estimated market price was determined by an independent appraisal made by Stuart and Associates.

(i) Present value of vested interest in Marlowe Corporation Pension Trust, $17,200.

(j) Present value of accounts payable and accrued liabilities, $8,500.

(k) Income tax payable, $12,400.

(l) Present value of 14% note payable, due May 1, 19--, $18,000.

(m) Estimated income tax on unrealized appreciation of salable assets, $48,500.

Instructions:

Prepare a statement of financial condition as of April 30 of the current year. Notes to the statement should be presented as appropriate.

Problem 28–2A. Budget performance record for individual. Susan and William Faber maintain a budget performance record. The over-under budget amounts as of September 1 and the monthly allocations for expenditures as indicated by the monthly budget were as follows:

	Over*-Under Budget	Allocations
Housing and house operation.	$150	$1,800
Food and sundries	50	480
Transportation	30*	200
Clothing..................	40*	100
Medical care..............	50	80
Recreation and education ...	10	50
Contributions and gifts	20*	60
Savings	—	200
Miscellaneous.............	10*	40

The expenditures for September are summarized as follows:

Sept. 1. Food and sundries, $36.
3. Medical care, $20; miscellaneous, $15.
5. Food and sundries, $82; recreation and education, $30.
7. Transportation, $40; miscellaneous, $6.

Sept. 10. Food and sundries, $58; clothing, $60.
    12. Housing and house operation, $600; food and sundries, $74; transportation, $35.
    14. Transportation, $18; recreation and education, $15.
    16. Housing and house operation, $220; food and sundries, $110; miscellaneous, $5.
    18. Food and sundries, $30; transportation, $40.
    19. Clothing, $30; miscellaneous, $12.
    22. Housing and house operation, $150; recreation and education, $14.
    23. Food and sundries, $43; transportation, $10; contributions, $50.
    25. Transportation, $25; clothing, $20.
    27. Housing and house operation, $300; food and sundries, $27.
    28. Food and sundries, $40; medical care, $45; miscellaneous, $10.
    30. Housing and house operation, $550; transportation, $30; savings, $200.

Instructions:

Prepare a budget performance record for September.

If the working papers correlating with the textbook are not used, omit Problem 28–3A.

Problem 28–3A.   Statements for nonprofit enterprise. After the closing entries were posted, the accounts in the ledger of the General Fund for Santa Rosa on July 31, 1988, the end of the current fiscal year, are as follows:

Accounts Payable	$ 63,000
Cash in Bank	22,000
Savings Accounts	60,000
Cash on Hand	6,750
Fund Balance	204,100
Fund Balance Reserved for Encumbrances	50,000
Investments in Marketable Securities	180,000
Property Taxes Receivable	87,150
Wages Payable	38,800

Estimated revenues, revenues, appropriations, and expenditures from the respective subsidiary ledgers have been entered in the working papers in the statement of revenues, expenditures, and changes in fund balance. The fund balance account had a balance of $243,500 on August 1, 1987, the beginning of the current fiscal year. The amount of encumbrances closed to fund balance at July 31, 1988, was $50,000.

Instructions:

(1) Complete the statement of revenues, expenditures, and changes in fund balance for the year ended July 31, 1988.
(2) Prepare a balance sheet.

Problem 28–4A.   Entries for summarized operations and closing for nonprofit enterprise; accounts; trial balance. The trial balance for the City of San Angelo—General Fund at the beginning of the current fiscal year is as follows:

City of San Angelo—General Fund
Trial Balance
July 1, 19--

Cash	110,000	
Savings Accounts	300,000	
Property Taxes Receivable	250,000	
Investment in U.S. Treasury Notes	120,000	
Accounts Payable		105,800
Wages Payable		42,100
Fund Balance		632,100
	780,000	780,000

The following data summarize the operations for the current year:

(a) Estimated revenues, $7,000,000; appropriations, $6,850,000.
(b) Revenues from property tax levy, $5,000,000.
(c) Cash received from property taxes, $4,910,000, and other revenues, $2,150,000.
(d) Expenditures encumbered and evidenced by purchase orders, $4,000,000.
(e) Expenditures for payrolls, $2,775,000.
(f) Liquidation of encumbrances and vouchers prepared for purchase order billings, $3,900,000.
(g) Cash disbursed for vouchers, $3,800,000; for payment of wages, $2,760,000; for savings accounts, $475,000.

Instructions:

(1) Open T accounts for the accounts appearing in the trial balance and enter the balances as of July 1, identifying them as "Bal."
(2) Open T accounts for Fund Balance Reserved for Encumbrances, Estimated Revenues, Revenues, Appropriations, Expenditures, and Encumbrances.
(3) Prepare journal entries to record the foregoing summarized operations.
(4) Post the entries recorded in (3) to the accounts, using the identifying letters in place of dates.
(5) Prepare the appropriate entries to close the accounts as of June 30 and post to the accounts, using the letter "C" to identify the postings.
(6) Prepare a trial balance as of June 30.

Problem 28–5A. Statements for nonprofit enterprise. The account balances in the General Fund ledger of the City of Irving on June 30, 1988, the end of the current fiscal year, are as follows:

Cash on Hand	$	3,600
Cash in Bank		245,000
Savings Accounts		300,000
Property Taxes Receivable		120,000
Accounts Payable		48,200
Wages Payable		30,900
Fund Balance Reserved for Encumbrances		13,500

Estimated Revenues	$4,045,400
Revenues	4,068,000
Appropriations	4,020,700
Expenditures	4,023,800
Encumbrances	13,500

The total of the debits and credits in the revenue ledger are as follows:

	Debits	Credits
General property taxes	$3,090,000	$3,120,000
Sales taxes	735,000	721,200
Motor vehicle licenses	140,000	141,600
Interest on savings accounts	30,000	31,800
Miscellaneous	50,400	53,400

Data from the expenditure ledger are as follows:

	Expenditures	Budget Appropriations
General government	$1,348,200	$1,332,000
Police department	792,000	800,000
Fire department	617,500	633,500
Streets and roads	597,600	578,400
Sanitation	423,700	424,800
Public welfare	244,800	252,000

The encumbrances balances in the expenditure ledger are as follows:

General government	$5,200
Fire department	3,000
Sanitation	5,300

Instructions:

(1) Prepare a statement of revenues, expenditures, and changes in fund balance for the year ended June 30, 1988. The fund balance account had a balance of $545,300 on July 1, 1987, the beginning of the current fiscal year.
(2) Prepare a balance sheet as of June 30, 1988.

Series B

Problem 28–1B.   Statement of financial condition. Tim Enders is a partner in the firm of Enders and Associates, and Pam Enders owns and manages The Loft. They applied to First City Bank for a loan to be used to build an apartment complex. The bank requested a statement of financial condition, and they assembled the following data for this purpose at August 31:

(a) Cash in bank, savings, and money market accounts, $22,300. (Unrestricted withdrawals are allowed without penalty.)

(b) Marketable securities (current value is quoted market price on August 31, 19--, less estimated broker commissions):

	Cost	Current Value
Stocks:		
FHI Industries, 400 shares......................	$12,500	$14,200
Hickman Manufacturing Inc., 200 shares	5,200	6,050
Person Food Stores Inc., 800 shares	18,000	21,800
Bonds:		
U.S. Treasury, 8%, $50,000 face amount, due 19-- .	46,300	48,100
Keefe Motors Inc., 10%, $20,000 face amount, due 20--...................................	20,000	22,600

(c) Tim Enders' equity interest in Enders and Associates: cost, $50,000; estimated market, $140,000. Pam Enders' equity interest in The Loft: cost, $20,000; estimated market, $35,000. Estimated market prices were determined by an independent appraisal made by Fender Realty.

(d) Cash value of $500,000 face value life insurance policy, $84,000.

(e) Residence: cost $175,000; estimated market, $240,000. The estimated market price was determined by an independent appraisal made by Reynolds and Associates. The residence is pledged against a 9 1/2% mortgage note payable, final installment due November 1, 19--. The present value of the monthly mortgage payments of $1,250, including interest, is $97,600.

(f) Household furnishings: cost, $81,000; estimated market, $49,000.

(g) Automobiles: cost, $32,600; estimated market, $16,000.

(h) Jewelry and paintings: cost, $28,000; estimated market, $33,000. The estimated market price was determined by an independent appraisal made by Reynolds and Associates.

(i) Present value of vested interest in Momper Inc. Pension Trust, $12,900.

(j) Present value of accounts payable and accrued liabilities, $8,900.

(k) Income tax payable, $7,500.

(l) Present value of 12% note payable, due March 1, 19--, $24,000.

(m) Estimated income tax on unrealized appreciation of salable assets, $27,600.

Instructions:

Prepare a statement of financial condition as of August 31 of the current year. Notes to the statement should be presented as appropriate.

If the working papers correlating with the textbook are not used, omit Problem 28–3B.

Problem 28–3B. Statements for nonprofit enterprise. After the closing entries were posted, the account balances in the ledger of the General Fund for Santa Rosa on July 31, 1988, the end of the current fiscal year, are as follows:

Accounts Payable.......................................	$ 57,500
Cash in Bank...	28,700
Cash on Hand...	8,400
Fund Balance	205,300

Fund Balance Reserved for Encumbrances	$ 40,000
Investments in Marketable Securities	150,000
Property Taxes Receivable	92,000
Savings Accounts	45,800
Wages Payable	22,100

Estimated revenues, revenues, appropriations, and expenditures from the respective subsidiary ledgers have been entered in the working papers in the statement of revenues, expenditures, and changes in fund balance. The fund balance account had a balance of $234,700 on August 1, 1987, the beginning of the current fiscal year. The amount of encumbrances closed to fund balance at July 31, 1988, was $40,000.

Instructions:

(1) Complete the statement of revenues, expenditures, and changes in fund balance for the year ended July 31, 1988.
(2) Prepare a balance sheet.

Problem 28–4B.   Entries for summarized operations and closing for nonprofit enterprise; accounts; trial balance. The trial balance for the City of Maple Heights — General Fund at the beginning of the current fiscal year is as follows:

Maple Heights — General Fund
Trial Balance
July 1, 19--

Cash	225,000	
Savings Accounts	80,000	
Property Taxes Receivable	122,500	
Investment in U.S. Treasury Notes	100,000	
Accounts Payable		52,700
Wages Payable		19,200
Fund Balance		455,600
	527,500	527,500

The following data summarize the operations for the current year:

(a) Estimated revenues, $2,180,000; appropriations, $2,150,000.
(b) Revenues from property tax levy, $1,450,000.
(c) Cash received from property taxes, $1,460,000, and other revenues, $760,000.
(d) Expenditures for payrolls, $1,150,000.
(e) Expenditures encumbered and evidenced by purchase orders, $1,210,000.
(f) Liquidation of encumbrances and vouchers prepared for purchase order billings, $1,050,000.
(g) Cash disbursed for vouchers, $1,065,000; for payment of wages, $1,155,800; for savings accounts, $40,000.

Instructions:

(1) Open T accounts for the accounts appearing in the trial balance and enter the balances as of July 1, identifying them as "Bal."
(2) Open T accounts for Fund Balance Reserved for Encumbrances, Estimated Revenues, Revenues, Appropriations, Expenditures, and Encumbrances.
(3) Prepare journal entries to record the foregoing summarized operations.
(4) Post the entries recorded in (3) to the accounts, using the identifying letters in place of dates.
(5) Prepare the appropriate entries to close the accounts as of June 30 and post to the accounts, using the letter "C" to identify the postings.
(6) Prepare a trial balance as of June 30.

MINI-CASE 28

Margie Phelps

Margie Phelps, a former college art professor, is running for the office of state representative of the eighth legislative district. A major campaign issue has been the incumbent's challenge that Phelps disclose her personal financial statement, even though state law does not require such disclosures. Phelps has decided to meet this challenge and has asked you to prepare such a statement. Phelps has assembled the following data at October 15:

(a) Cash in bank, savings, and money market accounts, $18,400. (Unrestricted withdrawals are allowed without penalty.)

(b) Marketable securities (current value is quoted market price on October 15, 19--, less estimated broker commissions):

	Cost	Current Value
Stocks:		
CDF Industries, 500 shares..	$15,000	$ 18,300
Weber Manufacturing Inc.,		
25,000 shares	50,000	240,000
Bonds:		
U.S. Treasury, 9%, $100,000		
face amount, due 19--	71,600	78,500

(c) Margie Phelps' equity interest in Phelps & Associates: cost, $200,000; estimated market value, $750,000. Estimated market prices were determined by independent appraisal made by Bleau Realty.

(d) Cash value of $200,000 face value life insurance policy, $15,600.

(e) Residence: cost, $350,000; estimated market, $400,000. The estimated market price was determined by an independent appraisal made by Borman and Associates. The residence is pledged against a 10 1/2% mortgage note payable, final installment due July 1, 19--. Present value of monthly mortgage payments of $2,400, including interest, is $150,000.

(f) Household furnishings: cost, $50,000; estimated market, $28,000.

(g) Automobiles: cost, $45,000; estimated market, $31,200.

(h) Jewelry and paintings; cost $42,000; estimated market, $65,000. The estimated market price was determined by an independent appraisal made by Borman and Associates.

(i) Vested interest in Morgan Corporation Pension Trust: estimated market, $30,000.

(j) Present value of accounts payable and accrued liabilities, $17,500.

(k) Income tax payable, $10,000.

(l) Present value of 10 1/2% note payable, due January 31, 19--, $85,000.

(m) Estimated income tax on unrealized appreciation of salable assets, $280,000.

Instructions:

(1) Prepare a statement of financial condition as of October 15. Notes to the statement should be presented as appropriate.

(2) After reviewing the statement of financial condition prepared in (1), Phelps objects to the caption "Estimated income tax on unrealized appreciation of assets." She argues that this disclosure will give voters the impression that she is delinquent on payment of her taxes. How would you respond?

(3) If Phelps publishes the statement of financial condition prepared in (1), how could it embarrass her in the eyes of the voters and possibly reduce her chances of election?

APPENDIXES

A

Absorption costing. The concept that considers the cost of manufactured products to be composed of direct materials, direct labor, and factory overhead.

Accelerated depreciation method. A depreciation method that provides for a high depreciation charge in the first year of use of an asset and gradually declining periodic charges thereafter.

Account. The form used to record additions and deductions for each individual asset, liability, owner's equity, revenue, and expense.

Account form of balance sheet. A balance sheet with assets on the left-hand side and liabilities and owner's equity on the right-hand side.

Accounting. The process of identifying, measuring, and communicating economic information to permit informed judgments and decisions by users of the information.

Accounting cycle. The sequence of principal accounting procedures employed to process transactions during a fiscal period.

Accounting equation. The expression of the relationship between assets, liabilities, and owner's equity; most commonly stated as Assets = Liabilities + Owner's Equity.

Accounting system. The system that provides the information for use in conducting the affairs of the business and reporting to owners, creditors, and other interested parties.

Account payable. A liability created by a purchase made on credit.

Account receivable. A claim against a customer for sales made on credit.

Accounts payable ledger. The subsidiary ledger containing the individual accounts with suppliers (creditors).

Accounts receivable ledger. The subsidiary ledger containing the individual accounts with customers (debtors).

Accounts receivable turnover. The relationship between credit sales and accounts receivable, computed by dividing net sales on account by the average net accounts receivable.

Accrual. An expense or a revenue that gradually increases with the passage of time.

Accrual basis. Revenues are recognized in the period earned and expenses are recognized in the period incurred in the process of generating revenues.

Accrued asset (accrued revenue) or accrued liability (accrued expense). An asset (revenue) or a liability (expense) that gradually increases with the passage of time and that is recorded at the end of the accounting period by an adjusting entry.

Accumulated depreciation account. The contra asset account used to accumulate the depreciation recognized to date on plant assets.

Acid-test ratio. The ratio of the sum of cash, receivables, and marketable securities to current liabilities.

Adequate disclosure. The concept that financial statements and their accompanying footnotes should contain all of the pertinent data believed essential to the reader's understanding of an enterprise's financial status.

Adjusting entry. An entry required at the end of an accounting period to record an internal transaction and to bring the ledger up to date.

Aging the receivables. The process of analyzing the accounts receivable and classifying them according to various age groupings, with the due date being the base point for determining age.

Allowance method. The method of accounting for uncollectible receivables, by which advance provision for the uncollectibles is made.

American Institute of Certified Public Accountants (AICPA). The national professional organization of CPAs.

Amortization. The periodic expense attributed to the decline in usefulness of an intangible asset or the allocation of bond premium or discount over the life of a bond issue.

Annuity. A series of equal cash flows at fixed intervals.

Appropriation. A designated use of revenues for which a potential liability is recognized by nonprofit organizations.

Appropriation of retained earnings. The amount of a corporation's retained earnings that has been restricted and therefore is not available for distribution to shareholders as dividends.

Articles of partnership. The formal written contract creating a partnership.

Asset. Property owned by a business enterprise.

Average cost method. The method of inventory costing that is based on the assumption that costs should be charged against revenue in accordance with the weighted average unit costs of the commodities sold.

Average rate of return. A method of evaluating capital investment proposals that focuses on the expected profitability of the investment.

B

Balance of an account. The amount of difference between the debits and the credits that have been entered into an account.

Balance sheet. A financial statement listing the assets, liabilities, and owner's equity of a business entity as of a specific date.

Bank reconciliation. The method of analysis that details the items that are responsible for the difference between the cash balance reported in the bank statement and the balance of the cash account in the ledger.

Bond. A form of interest-bearing note employed by corporations to borrow on a long-term basis.

Bond indenture. The contract between a corporation issuing bonds and the bondholders.

Bookkeeping. The recording of business data in a prescribed manner.

Boot. The balance owed the supplier when an old asset is traded for a new asset.

Break-even point. The level of operations of an enterprise at which revenues and expired costs are equal.

Budget. A formal written statement of management's plans for the future, expressed in financial terms.

Budget performance report. A report comparing actual results with budget figures.

Business entity concept. The concept that assumes that accounting applies to individual economic units and that each unit is separate and distinct from the persons who supply its assets.

Business transaction. The occurrence of an event or of a condition that must be recorded in the accounting records.

By-product. A product resulting from a manufacturing process and having little value in relation to the principal product or joint products.

C

Capital. The rights (equity) of the owners in a business enterprise.

Capital expenditure. A cost that adds to the utility of an asset for more than one accounting period.

Capital expenditures budget. The budget summarizing future plans for acquisition of plant facilities and equipment.

Capital investment analysis. The process by which management plans, evaluates, and controls long-term capital investments involving property, plant, and equipment.

Capital lease. A lease which includes one or more of four provisions that result in treating the leased asset as a purchased asset in the accounts.

Capital rationing. The process by which management allocates available investment funds among competing capital investment proposals.

Capital stock. Shares of ownership of a corporation.

Carrying amount. The amount at which a temporary or a long-term investment or a long-term liability is reported on the balance sheet; also called basis or book value.

Cash. Any medium of exchange that a bank will accept at face value.

Cash basis. Revenue is recognized in the period cash is received, and expenses are recognized in period cash is paid.

Cash discount. The deduction allowable if an invoice is paid by a specified date.

Cash dividend. A cash distribution of earnings by a corporation to its shareholders.

Cash payback period. The expected period of time that will elapse between the date of a capital expenditure and the complete recovery in cash (or equivalent) of the amount invested.

Cash payments journal. The journal in which all cash payments are recorded.

Cash receipts journal. The journal in which all cash receipts are recorded.

Certified Public Accountant (CPA). An accountant who meets state licensing requirements for engaging in the practice of public accounting as a CPA.

Chart of Accounts. A listing of all the accounts used by a business enterprise.

Check register. A modified form of the cash payments journal used to record all transactions paid by check.

Closing entry. An entry necessary to eliminate the balance of a temporary account in preparation for the following accounting period.

Codes of professional ethics. Standards of conduct established by professional organizations of CPAs to guide CPAs in the conduct of their practices.

Common-size statement. A financial statement in which all items are expressed only in relative terms.

Common stock. The basic ownership class of corporate capital stock.

Completed-contract method. The method that recognizes revenue from long-term construction contracts when the project is completed.

Composite-rate depreciation method. A method of depreciation based on the use of a single rate that applies to entire groups of assets.

Conservatism. The concept that dictates that in selecting among alternatives, the method or procedure that yields the lesser amount of net income or asset value should be selected.

Consistency. The concept that assumes that the same generally accepted accounting principles have been applied in the preparation of successive financial statements.

Consolidated statement. A financial statement resulting from combining parent and subsidiary company statements.

Consolidation. The creation of a new corporation by the transfer of assets and liabilities from two or more existing corporations.

Constant dollar. Historical costs that have been converted into dollars of constant value through the use of a price-level index.

Contingent liability. A potential obligation that will materialize only if certain events occur in the future.

Continuous budgeting. A method of budgeting that provides for maintenance of a twelve-month projection into the future.

Contra account. An account that is offset against another account.

Contract rate of interest. The interest rate specified on a bond.

Contribution margin. Sales less variable cost of goods sold and variable selling and general expenses.

Contribution margin ratio. The percentage of each sales dollar that is available to cover the fixed expenses and provide an operating income.

Control. The process of directing operations to achieve the organization's goals and plans.

Controller. The chief managerial accountant of an organization.

Controlling account. The account in the general ledger that summarizes the balances of a subsidiary ledger.

Corporation. A separate legal entity that is organized in accordance with state or federal statutes and in which ownership is divided into shares of stock.

Cost center. A decentralized unit in which the department or division manager has responsibility for control of costs incurred and the authority to make decisions that affect these costs.

Cost ledger. A subsidiary ledger employed in a job order cost system and which contains an account for each job order.

Cost method. A method of accounting for an investment in stock, by which the investor recognizes as income its share of cash dividends of the investee.

Cost of goods sold. The cost of the manufactured product sold.

Cost of merchandise sold. The cost of the merchandise purchased by a merchandise enterprise and sold.

Cost of production report. A report prepared periodically by a processing department, summarizing (1) the units for which the department is accountable and the disposition of these units and (2) the costs charged to the department and the allocation of these costs.

Cost principle. The principle that assumes that the monetary record for properties and services purchased by a business should be maintained in terms of cost.

Cost-volume-profit analysis. The systematic examination of the interrelationships between selling prices, volume of sales and production, costs, expenses, and profits.

Cost-volume-profit chart. A chart used to assist management in understanding the relationships between costs, expenses, sales, and operating profit or loss.

Credit. (1) The right side of an account; (2) the amount entered on the right side of an account; (3) to enter an amount on the right side of an account.

Credit memorandum. The form issued by a seller to inform a debtor that a credit has been posted to the debtor's account receivable.

Cumulative preferred stock. Preferred stock that is entitled to current and past dividends before dividends may be paid on common stock.

Current asset. Cash or another asset that may reasonably be expected to be realized in cash or sold or consumed, usually within a year or less, through the normal operations of a business.

Current cost. The amount of cash that would have to be paid currently to acquire assets of the same age and in the same condition as existing assets.

Current liability. A liability that will be due within a short time (usually one year or less) and that is to be paid out of current assets.

Current ratio. The ratio of current assets to current liabilities.

D

Debit. (1) The left side of an account; (2) the amount entered on the left side of an account; (3) to enter an amount on the left side of an account.

Debit memorandum. The form issued by a buyer to inform a creditor that a debit has been posted to the creditor's account payable.

Debt security. A bond or a note payable.

Decentralization. The separation of a business into more manageable units.

Declining-balance depreciation method. A method of depreciation that provides declining periodic depreciation charges to expense over the estimated life of an asset.

Deferral. A postponement of the recognition of an expense already paid or a revenue already received.

Deficiency. The debit balance in the owner's equity account of a sole proprietor or a partner.

Deficit. A debit balance in the retained earnings account.

Departmental margin. Departmental gross profit less direct departmental expenses.

Depletion. The cost of metal ores and other minerals removed from the earth.

Depreciation. The decrease in usefulness of all plant assets except land.

Differential analysis. The area of accounting concerned with the effect of alternative courses of action on revenues and costs.

Differential cost. The amount of increase or decrease in cost that is expected from a particular course of action compared with an alternative.

Differential revenue. The amount of increase or decrease in revenue expected from a particular course of action as compared with an alternative.

Direct expense. An expense directly traceable to or incurred for the sole benefit of a specific department and ordinarily subject to the control of the department manager.

Direct labor. Wages of factory workers who convert materials into a finished product.

Direct labor rate variance. The cost associated with the difference between the standard rate and the actual rate paid for direct labor used in producing a commodity.

Direct labor time variance. The cost associated with the difference between the standard hours and actual hours of direct labor spent producing a commodity.

Direct materials. The cost of materials that enter directly into the finished product.

Direct materials price variance. The cost associated with the difference between the standard price and the actual price of direct materials used in producing a commodity.

Direct materials quantity variance. The cost associated with the difference between the standard quantity and the actual quantity of direct materials used in producing a commodity.

Direct write-off method. A method of accounting for uncollectible receivables, whereby an expense is recognized only when specific accounts are judged to be uncollectible.

Discontinued operations. The operations of a business segment that has been disposed of.

Discount. (a) The interest deducted from the maturity value of a note; (b) excess of par value of stock over its sales price; (c) excess of the face amount of bonds over their issue price.

Discounted cash flow method. A method of analysis of proposed capital investments that focuses on the present value of the cash flows expected from the investment.

Discounted internal rate of return method. A method of analysis of proposed capital investments that focuses on using present value concepts to compute the rate of return from the net cash flows expected from the investment.

Discount rate. The rate used in computing the interest to be deducted from the maturity value of a note.

Dishonored note receivable. A note which the maker fails to pay on the due date.

Dividend. A distribution of earnings of a corporation to its owners (stockholders).

Double-entry accounting. A system for recording transactions based on recording increases and decreases in accounts so that debits always equal credits.

Drawing account. The account used to record distributions to a sole proprietor or partner.

E

Earnings per share (EPS) on common stock. The profitability ratio of net income available to common shareholders to the number of common shares outstanding.

Economic order quantity (EOQ). The optimum quantity of specified inventoriable materials to be ordered at one time.

Effective rate of interest. The market rate of interest at the time bonds are issued.

Electronic data processing (EDP). The term applied to the processing of data by electronic equipment.

Electronic funds transfer (EFT). A payment system that uses computerized electronic impulses rather than paper (money, checks, etc.) to effect a cash transaction.

Employee's earnings record. A detailed record of each employee's earnings.

Encumbrance. A commitment by a nonprofit organization to incur expenditures in the future.

Equity. The right or claim to the properties of a business enterprise.

Equity method. A method of accounting for investments in common stock, by which the investment account is adjusted for the investor's share of periodic net income and property dividends of the investee.

Equity per share. The ratio of stockholders' equity to the related number of shares of stock outstanding.

Equity security. Preferred or common stock.

Equivalent units of production. The number of units that could have been manufactured from start to finish during a period.

Exchange rate. The rate at which one unit of currency can be converted into another currency.

Expense. The amount of assets consumed or services used in the process of earning revenue.

Extraordinary item. An event or transaction that is unusual and infrequent.

F

Factory overhead. All of the costs of operating the factory except for direct materials and direct labor.

Factory overhead controllable variance. The difference between the actual amount of factory overhead cost incurred and the amount of factory overhead budgeted for the level of operations achieved.

Factory overhead volume variance. The cost or benefit associated with operating at a level above or below 100% of productive capacity.

FICA tax. Federal Insurance Contributions Act tax used to finance federal programs for old-age and disability benefits and health insurance for the aged.

Financial accounting. The branch of accounting that is concerned with the recording of transactions using generally accepted accounting principles (GAAP) for a business enterprise or other economic unit and with a periodic preparation of various statements from such records.

Financial Accounting Standards Board (FASB). The current authoritative body for the development of accounting principles for all entities except state and municipal governments.

Finished goods. Goods in the state in which they are to be sold.

Finished goods ledger. The subsidiary ledger that contains the individual accounts for each kind of commodity produced.

First-in, first-out (fifo) method. A method of inventory costing based on the assumption that the costs of merchandise sold should be charged against revenue in the order in which the costs were incurred.

Fiscal year. The annual accounting period adopted by an enterprise.

Fixed expense (cost). An expense (cost) that tends to remain constant in amount regardless of variations in volume of activity.

Flexible budget. A series of budgets for varying rates of activity.

FOB destination. Terms of agreement between buyer and seller, whereby ownership passes when merchandise is received by the buyer, and the seller absorbs the transportation costs.

FOB shipping point. Terms of agreement between buyer and seller, whereby ownership passes when merchandise is delivered to the shipper, and the buyer absorbs the transportation costs.

Fund. A term with multiple meanings, including (1) segregations of cash for a special purpose, (2) cash or working capital as reported in the funds statement, (3) in accounting for nonprofit organizations, an accounting entity with accounts maintained for recording assets, liabilities, fund equity, revenues, and expenditures for a particular purpose.

Funded. An appropriation of retained earnings accompanied by a segregation of cash or marketable securities.

Fund equity. The excess of assets over liabilities in a nonprofit organization.

Funds statement. The statement of changes in financial position.

G-H

General expense. Expense incurred in the general operation of a business.

General journal. The two-column form used to record journal entries that do not "fit" in any special journals.

General ledger. The principal ledger, when used in conjunction with subsidiary ledgers, that contains all of the balance sheet and income statement accounts.

Generally accepted accounting principles (GAAP). Generally accepted guidelines for the preparation of financial statements.

Going concern concept. The concept that assumes that a business entity has a reasonable expectation of continuing in business at a profit for an indefinite period of time.

Goodwill. An intangible asset that attaches to a business as a result of such favorable factors as location, product superiority, reputation, and managerial skill.

Government Accounting Standards Board (GASB). The current authoritative body for the development of accounting principles for state and municipal governments.

Gross pay. The total earnings of an employee for a payroll period.

Gross profit. The excess of net revenue from sales over the cost of merchandise sold.

Gross profit analysis. The procedure used to develop information concerning the effect of changes in quantities and unit prices on sales and cost of goods sold.

Gross profit method. A means of estimating inventory on hand without the need for a physical count.

Horizontal analysis. The percentage of increases and decreases in corresponding items in comparative financial statements.

I

Income from operations. The excess of gross profit over total operating expenses.

Income statement. A summary of the revenues and expenses of a business entity for a specific period of time.

Income summary account. The account used in the closing process for summarizing the revenue and expense accounts.

Indirect expense. An expense that is incurred for an entire business enterprise as a unit and that is not subject to the control of individual department managers.

Inflation. A period when prices in general are rising and the purchasing power of money is declining.

Installment method. The method of recognizing revenue, whereby each receipt of cash from installment sales is considered to be composed of partial payment of cost of merchandise sold and gross profit.

Intangible asset. A long-lived asset that is useful in the operations of an enterprise, is not held for sale, and is without physical qualities.

Interim statement. A financial statement issued for a period covering less than a fiscal year.

Internal accounting controls. Procedures and records that are mainly concerned with the reliability of financial records and reports and with the safeguarding of assets.

Internal administrative controls. Procedures and records that aid management in achieving business goals.

Internal controls. The detailed procedures adopted by an enterprise to control its operations.

Internal Revenue Service (IRS). The branch of the U.S. Treasury Department concerned with enforcement and collection of the income tax.

Inventory order point. The level to which inventory is allowed to fall before an order for additional inventory is placed.

Inventory turnover. The relationship between the volume of goods sold and inventory, computed by dividing the cost of goods sold by the average inventory.

Investment center. A decentralized unit in which the manager has the responsibility and authority to make decisions that affect not only cost and revenues, but also the plant assets available to the center.

Investment turnover. A component of the rate of return on investment, computed as the ratio of sales to invested assets.

Invoice. The bill provided by the seller (who refers to it as a sales invoice) to a buyer (who refers to it as a purchase invoice) for items purchased.

J

Job cost sheet. An account in the cost ledger in which the costs charged to a particular job order are recorded.

Job order cost system. A type of cost system that provides for a separate record of the cost of each particular quantity of product that passes through the factory.

Joint cost. The cost common to the manufacture of two or more products (joint products).

Joint products. Two or more commodities of significant value produced from a single principal direct material.

Journal. The initial record in which the effects of a transaction on accounts are recorded.

Journalizing. The process of recording a transaction in a journal.

L

Last-in, first-out (lifo) method. A method of inventory costing based on the assumption that the most recent merchandise costs incurred should be charged against revenue.

Lead time. The time, usually expressed in days, that it takes to receive an order for inventory.

Ledger. The group of accounts used by an enterprise.

Leverage. The tendency of the rate earned on stockholders' equity to vary from the rate earned on total assets because the amount earned on assets acquired through the use of funds provided by creditors varies from the interest paid to these creditors.

Liability. A debt of a business enterprise.

Linear Programming. A quantitative method that can be used in providing data for solving a variety of business problems in which management's objective is to minimize cost or maximize profits, subject to several limiting factors.

Liquidating dividend. A distribution out of paid-in capital when a corporation permanently reduces its operations or winds up its affairs completely.

Liquidation. The winding-up process when a partnership goes out of business.

Long-term investment. An investment that is not intended to be a ready source of cash in the normal operations of a business and that is listed in the "investments" section of the balance sheet.

Long-term liability. A liability that is not due for a comparatively long time (usually more than one year).

Lower of cost or market. A method of costing inventory or valuing temporary investments that carries those assets at the lower of their cost or current market prices.

M

Managerial accounting. The branch of accounting that uses both historical and estimated data in providing information which management uses in conducting daily operations and in planning future operations.

Manufacturing margin. Sales less variable cost of goods sold.

Margin of safety. The difference between current sales revenue and the sales at the break-even point.

Marketable security. An investment in a security that can be readily sold when cash is needed.

Market (sales) value method. A method of allocating joint costs among products according to their relative sales values.

Master budget. The comprehensive budget plan encompassing all the individual budgets related to sales, cost of goods sold, operating expenses, capital expenditures, and cash.

Matching. The principle of accounting that all revenues should be matched with the expenses incurred in earning those revenues during a period of time.

Materiality. The concept that recognizes the practicality of ignoring small or insignificant deviations from generally accepted accounting principles.

Materials. Goods in the state in which they were acquired for use in manufacturing operations.

Materials ledger. The subsidiary ledger containing the individual accounts for each type of material.

Materials requisition. The form used by the appropriate manufacturing department to authorize the issuance of materials from the storeroom.

Maturity value. The amount due at the maturity or due date of a note.

Merchandise inventory. Merchandise on hand and available for sale.

Merger. The fusion of two corporations by the acquisition of the properties of one corporation by another, with the dissolution of one of the corporations.

Minority interest. The portion of a subsidiary corporation's capital stock that is not owned by the parent corporation.

Mixed cost. A cost with both variable and fixed characteristics, sometimes referred to as semivariable or semifixed cost.

Multiple-step income statement. An income statement with numerous sections and subsections with several intermediate balances before net income.

N

Natural business year. A year that ends when a business's activities have reached the lowest point in its annual operating cycle.

Net income. The final figure in the income statement when revenues exceed expenses.

Net loss. The final figure in the income statement when expenses exceed revenues.

Net pay. Gross pay less payroll deductions; the amount the employer is obligated to pay the employee.

Net realizable value. The amount at which merchandise that can be sold only at prices below cost should be valued, determined as the estimated selling price less any direct cost of disposition.

Net worth. The owner's equity in a business.

Nominal account. A revenue or expense account periodically closed to the income summary account; a temporary owner's equity account.

Note payable. A written promise to pay, representing an amount owed by a business.

Note receivable. A written promise to pay, representing an amount to be received by a business.

Number of days' sales in inventory. The relationship between the volume of sales and inventory, computed by dividing the inventory at the end of the year by the average daily cost of goods sold.

O

Operating lease. A lease which does not meet the criteria for a capital lease, and thus which is accounted for as an operating expense, so that neither future lease obligations nor future rights to use the leased asset are recognized in the accounts.

Operations research. Quantitative techniques which often utilize mathematical and statistical models encompassing a large number of interdependent variables and which assist management in planning and controlling business operations.

Opportunity cost. The amount of income that would result from the best available alternative to a proposed use of cash or its equivalent.

Other expense. An expense that cannot be associated definitely with operations.

Other income. Revenue from sources other than the principal activity of a business.

Overapplied factory overhead. The amount of factory overhead applied in excess of the actual factory overhead costs incurred for production during a period.

Owner's equity. The rights of the owners in a business enterprise.

P-Q

Paid-in capital. The capital acquired from stockholders.

Par. The arbitrary monetary figure printed on a stock certificate.

Parent company. The company owning all or a majority of the voting stock of another corporation.

Participating preferred stock. Preferred stock that could receive dividends in excess of the specified amount granted by its preferential rights.

Partnership. An unincorporated business owned by two or more individuals.

Payroll. The total amount paid to employees for a certain period.

Payroll register. A multi-column form used to assemble and summarize payroll data at the end of each payroll period.

Percentage-of-completion method. The method of recognizing revenue from long-term contracts over the entire life of the contract.

Periodic inventory system. A system of inventory accounting in which only the revenue from sales is recorded each time a sale is made; the cost of merchandise on hand at the end of a period is determined by a detailed listing (physical inventory) of the merchandise on hand.

Perpetual inventory system. A system of inventory accounting that employs records that continually disclose the amount of the inventory on hand.

Petty cash fund. A special cash fund used to pay relatively small amounts.

Physical inventory. The detailed listing of merchandise on hand.

Planning. The process of setting goals for the use of an organization's resources and developing ways to achieve these goals.

Plant asset. A tangible asset of a relatively fixed or permanent nature owned by a business enterprise.

Point of sale method. The method of recognizing revenue, whereby the revenue is determined to be realized at the time that title passes to the buyer.

Pooling of interests method. A method of accounting for an affiliation of two corporations resulting from an exchange of voting stock of one corporation for substantially all of the voting stock of the other corporation.

Post-closing trial balance. A trial balance prepared after all of the temporary accounts have been closed.

Posting. The process of transferring debits and credits from a journal to the accounts.

Predetermined factory overhead rate. The rate used to apply factory overhead costs to the goods manufactured.

Preemptive right. The right of each shareholder to maintain the same fractional interest in the corporation by purchasing a proportionate number of shares of any additional issuances of stock.

Preferred stock. A class of stock with preferential rights over common stock.

Premium. (a) The excess of the sales price of stock over its par amount; (b) excess of the issue price of bonds over the face amount.

Prepaid expense. A purchased commodity or service that has not been consumed at the end of an accounting period.

Present value. The estimated present worth of an amount of cash to be received (or paid) in the future.

Present value index. An index computed by dividing the total present value of the net cash flow to be received from a proposed capital investment by the amount to be invested.

Present value of an annuity. The sum of the present values of a series of equal cash flows to be received at fixed intervals.

Price-earnings (P/E) ratio. The ratio of the market price per share of common stock, at a specific date, to the annual earnings per share.

Price-level index. The ratio of the total cost of a group of commodities prevailing at a particular time to the total cost of the same group of commodities at an earlier base time.

Prior period adjustment. Correction of a material error related to a prior period or periods, excluded from the determination of net income.

Private accounting. The profession whose members are accountants employed by a business firm or nonprofit organization.

Proceeds. The net amount available from discounting a note.

Process cost system. A type of cost system that accumulates costs for each of the various departments or processes within a factory.

Processing cost. The direct labor and factory overhead costs associated with the manufacture of a product.

Profitability. The ability of a firm to earn income.

Profit center. A decentralized unit in which the manager has the responsibility and the authority to make decisions that affect both cost and revenues (and thus profits).

Profit margin. A component of the rate of return on investment, computed as the ratio of operating income to sales.

Profit-volume chart. A chart used to assist management in understanding the relationship between profit and volume.

Promissory note. A written promise to pay a sum in money on demand or at a definite time.

Public accounting. The profession whose members render accounting services on a fee basis.

Purchase method. The accounting method employed when a parent company acquires a controlling share of the voting stock of a subsidiary other than by the exchange of voting common stock.

Purchase order. The form issued by the purchasing department to suppliers, requesting the delivery of materials.

Purchase requisition. The form used to inform the purchasing department that items are needed by a business.

Purchases discounts. An available discount taken by the purchaser for early payment of an invoice; a contra account to Purchases.

Purchases journal. The journal in which all items purchased on account are recorded.

Purchases returns and allowances. Reduction in purchases, resulting from merchandise returned to the vendor or from the vendor's reduction in the original purchase price; a contra account to Purchases.

Quick assets. The sum of cash, receivables, and marketable securities.

R

Rate earned on common stockholders' equity. A measure of profitability computed by dividing net income, reduced by preferred dividend requirements, by common stockholders' equity.

Rate earned on stockholders' equity. A measure of profitability computed by dividing net income by total stockholders' equity.

Rate earned on total assets. A measure of the profitability of assets, without regard to the equity of creditors and stockholders in the assets.

Rate of return on investment (ROI). A measure of managerial efficiency in the use of investments in assets.

Real account. A balance sheet account.

Realization. The sale of assets when a partnership is being liquidated.

Receiving report. The form used by the receiving department to indicate that materials have been received and inspected.

Report form of balance sheet. The form of balance sheet with the liability and owner's equity sections presented below the asset section.

Residual income. The excess of divisional operating income over a "minimum" amount of desired operating income.

Residual value. The estimated recoverable cost of a depreciable asset as of the time of its removal from service.

Responsibility accounting. The process of measuring and reporting operating data by areas of responsibility.

Retail inventory method. A method of inventory costing based on the relationship of the cost and retail price of merchandise.

Retained earnings. Net income retained in a corporation.

Retained earnings statement. A statement for a corporate enterprise, summarizing the changes in retained earnings during a specific period of time.

Revenues. The gross increases in owner's equity as a result of business and professional activities entered into for the purpose of earning income.

Revenue expenditure. An expenditure that benefits only the current period.

Reversing entry. An entry that reverses a specific adjusting entry to facilitate the recording of routine transactions in the subsequent period.

S

Safety stock. The amount of inventory that serves as a reserve for unforeseen circumstances, and therefore is not normally used in regular operations.

Sales discounts. An available discount granted by the seller for early payment of an invoice; a contra account to Sales.

Sales journal. The journal in which all sales of merchandise on account are recorded.

Sales mix. The relative distribution of sales among the various products available for sale.

Sales returns and allowances. Reductions in sales, resulting from merchandise returned by customers or from the seller's reduction in the original sales price; a contra account to Sales.

Securities and Exchange Commission (SEC). The federal agency that exercises a dominant influence over the development of accounting principles for most companies whose securities are traded in interstate commerce.

Selling expense. An expense incurred directly and entirely in connection with the sale of merchandise.

Service department. A factory department that does not process materials directly but renders services for the benefit of production departments.

Simplex method. A mathematical equation approach to linear programming, which is often used more practically with a computer.

Single-step income statement. An income statement with the total of all expenses deducted from the total of all revenues.

Sinking fund. Assets set aside in a special fund to be used for a specific purpose.

Slide. The erroneous movement of all digits in a number, one or more spaces to the right or the left, such as writing $542 as $5,420.

Sole proprietorship. A business owned by one individual.

Solvency. The ability of a firm to pay its debts as they come due.

Special journal. A journal designed to record a single type of transaction.

Standard costs. Detailed estimates of what a product should cost.

Stated value. An amount assigned by the board of directors to each share of no-par stock.

Statement of changes in financial position. A basic financial statement devoted exclusively to reporting changes in financial position for a specified period of time.

Statement of cost of goods manufactured. A separate statement for a manufacturer that reports the cost of goods manufactured during a period.

Statement of financial condition. The principal financial statement for individuals, presenting the estimated current values of assets, current amounts of liabilities, estimated income tax on unrealized appreciation of assets, and net worth.

Statement of owner's equity. A summary of the changes in the owner's equity of a business entity that have occurred during a specific period of time.

Statement of revenues, expenditures, and changes in fund balance. The statement for a nonprofit enterprise that provides a comparison of budgeted and actual revenues and expenditures along with the effect of operations on the unreserved fund balance.

Stock dividend. Distribution of a company's own stock to its shareholders.

Stockholders. The owners of a corporation.

Stockholders' equity. The equity of the shareholders in a corporation.

Stock outstanding. The stock in the hands of the stockholders.

Stock split. A reduction in the par or stated value of a share of common stock and the issuance of a proportionate number of additional shares.

Straight-line depreciation method. A method of depreciation that provides for equal periodic charges to expense over the estimated life of an asset.

Subsidiary company. The corporation that is controlled by a parent company.

Subsidiary ledger. A ledger containing individual accounts with a common characteristic.

Sum-of-the-years-digits depreciation method. A method of depreciation that provides for declining periodic depreciation charges to expense over the estimated life of an asset.

Sunk cost. A cost that is not affected by subsequent decisions.

T

T account. A form of account resembling the letter T.

Taxable income. The base on which the amount of income tax is determined.

Temporary account. A revenue or expense account periodically closed to the income summary account; a nominal account.

Temporary investment. An investment in securities that can be readily sold when cash is needed.

Time tickets. The form on which the amount of time spent by each employee and the labor cost incurred for each individual job, or for factory overhead, are recorded.

Trade discount. The reduction allowable from the list price of goods offered for sale.

Transposition. The erroneous arrangement of digits in a number, such as writing $542 as $524.

Treasury stock. A corporation's own outstanding stock that has been reacquired.

Trial balance. A summary listing of the balances and the titles of the accounts.

U-V

Underapplied factory overhead. The amount of actual factory overhead in excess of the factory overhead applied to production during a period.

Unearned revenue. Revenue received in advance of its being earned.

Units-of-production depreciation method. A method of depreciation that provides for depreciation expense based on the expected productive capacity of an asset.

Variable costing. The concept that considers the cost of products manufactured to be composed only of those manufacturing costs that increase or decrease as the volume of production rises or falls (direct materials, direct labor, and variable factory overhead).

Variable expense (cost). An expense (cost) that tends to fluctuate in amount in accordance with variations in volume of activity.

Variances from standard. Difference between standard cost and actual cost.

Vertical analysis. The percentage analysis of component parts in relation to the total of the parts in a single financial statement.

Voucher. A document that serves as evidence of authority to pay cash.

Voucher register. The journal in which all vouchers are recorded.

Voucher system. Records, methods, and procedures employed in verifying and recording liabilities and paying and recording cash payments.

W-Z

Working capital. The excess of total current assets over total current liabilities at some point in time.

Work in process. Goods in the process of manufacture.

Work sheet. A working paper used to assist in the preparation of financial statements.

Zero-base budgeting. A concept of budgeting that requires all levels of management to start from zero and estimate budget data as if there had been no previous activities in their unit.

ANSWERS TO SELF-EXAMINATION QUESTIONS

CHAPTER 1

1. **D** A corporation, organized in accordance with state or federal statutes, is a separate legal entity in which ownership is divided into shares of stock (answer D). A sole proprietorship, sometimes referred to as a single proprietorship (answers A and B), is an unincorporated business enterprise owned by one individual. A partnership (answer C) is an unincorporated business enterprise owned by two or more individuals.

2. **A** The properties owned by a business enterprise are referred to as assets (answer A). The debts of the business are called liabilities (answer B), and the equity of the owners is called stockholders' equity or owner's equity (answers C and D).

3. **A** The balance sheet is a listing of the assets, liabilities, and owner's equity of a business entity at a specific date (answer A). The income statement (answer B) is a summary of the revenue and expenses of a business entity for a specific period of time. The statement of owner's equity (answer C) summarizes the changes in owner's equity for a sole proprietorship or partnership during a specific period of time. The retained earnings statement (answer D) summarizes the changes in retained earnings for a corporation during a specific period of time.

4. **C** The accounting equation is:

   Assets = Liabilities + Owner's Equity

   Therefore, if assets increased by $20,000 and liabilities increased by $12,000, owner's equity must have increased by $8,000 (answer C) as indicated in the following computation.

   Assets = Liabilities + Owner's Equity
   $20,000 = $12,000 + Owner's Equity
   $20,000 − $12,000 = Owner's Equity
   $ 8,000 = Owner's Equity

5. **B** Net income is the excess of revenue over expenses, or $7,500 (answer B). If expenses exceed revenue, the difference is a net loss. Withdrawals by the owner are the opposite of the owner's investing in the business and do not affect the amount of net income or net loss.

CHAPTER 2

1. **A** A debit may signify an increase in asset accounts (answer A) or a decrease in liability and owner's capital accounts. A credit may signify a decrease in asset accounts (answer B) or an increase in liability and owner's capital accounts (answers C and D).

2. **C** Liability, capital, capital stock, retained earnings, and revenue (answer C) accounts have normal credit balances. Asset (answer A), drawing (answer B), dividend, and expense (answer D) accounts have normal debit balances.

3. **D** The current asset category includes cash and other assets that may reasonably be expected to be realized in cash or sold or consumed usually within a year or less, and therefore would include cash (answer A), accounts receivable (answer B), and supplies on hand (answer C).

4. **A** The receipt of cash from customers on account increases the asset Cash and decreases the asset Accounts Receivable as indicated by answer A. Answer B has the debit and credit reversed, and answers C and D involve transactions with creditors (accounts payable) and not customers (accounts receivable).

5. **D** The trial balance (answer D) is a listing of the balances and the titles of the accounts in the ledger on a given date, so that the equality of the debits and credits in the ledger can be verified. The income statement (answer A) is a summary of revenue and expenses for a period of time, the balance sheet (answer B) is a presentation of the assets, liabilities, and owner's equity on a given date, and the retained earnings statement (answer C) is a summary of the changes in retained earnings for a corporation over a period of time.

CHAPTER 3

1. **D** The balance in the supplies account, before adjustment, represents the amount of supplies available. From this amount ($2,250) is subtracted the amount of supplies on hand ($950) to determine the supplies used ($1,300). Since

increases in expense accounts are recorded by debits and decreases in asset accounts are recorded by credits, answer D is the correct entry.

2. C Since increases in expense accounts (such as depreciation expense) are recorded by debits and it is customary to record the decreases in usefulness of plant assets as credits to accumulated depreciation accounts, answer C is the correct entry.

3. D The book value of a plant asset is the difference between the balance in the asset account and the balance in the related accumulated depreciation account, or $22,500 − $14,000, as indicated by answer D ($8,500).

4. C Since all revenue and expense accounts are closed at the end of the period, both Sales (revenue) and Salary Expense (expense) would be closed to Income Summary (answer C).

5. A Since the post-closing trial balance includes only balance sheet accounts (all of the revenue, expense, and drawing accounts have been previously closed), Cash (answer A) would appear on the trial balance. Both Sales (answer B) and Salary Expense (answer C) are temporary accounts that are closed prior to the preparation of the post-closing trial balance.

CHAPTER 4

1. A A debit memorandum (answer A), issued by the buyer, indicates the amount the buyer proposes to debit to the accounts payable account. A credit memorandum (answer B), issued by the seller, indicates the amount the seller proposes to credit to the accounts receivable account. An invoice (answer C) or a bill (answer D), issued by the seller, indicates the amount and terms of the sale.

2. C The amount of discount for early payment is $10 (answer C), or 1% of $1,000. Although the $50 of transportation costs paid by the seller are debited to the customer's account, the customer is not entitled to a discount on that amount.

3. B The customer is entitled to a discount of $9 (answer B) for early payment. This amount is 1% of $900, which is the sales price of $1,000 less the return of $100. The $50 of transportation costs is an expense of the seller.

4. D Purchases discounts (answer A), purchases returns and allowances (answer B), and merchandise inventory at the end of the period (answer C) are all subtracted from the sum of merchandise inventory at the beginning of the period and purchases in determining the cost of merchandise sold.

5. A The amount of merchandise inventory appearing in the trial balance columns of the work sheet represents the inventory at the beginning of the period (answer A). This amount and the amount of the merchandise inventory at the end of the period (answer B) are included on the work sheet as inventory adjustments. These two adjustments and the net cost of merchandise purchased provide the data to determine the cost of merchandise sold (answer C).

CHAPTER 5

1. B The single-step form of income statement (answer B) is so named because the total of all expenses is deducted from the total of all revenues. The multiple-step form (answer A) includes numerous sections and subsections with several intermediate balances before arriving at net income. The account form (answer C) and the report form (answer D) are two common forms of the balance sheet.

2. C Gross profit (answer C) is the excess of net sales over the cost of merchandise sold. Operating income (answer A) or income from operations (answer B) is the excess of gross profit over operating expenses. Net income (answer D) is the final figure on the income statement after all revenues and expenses have been reported.

3. D Expenses such as interest expense (answer D) that cannot be associated definitely with operations are identified as other expense or non-operating expense. Depreciation expense — office equipment (answer A) is a general expense. Sales salaries expense (answer B) is a selling expense. Insurance expense (answer C) is a mixed expense with elements of both selling expense and general expense. For small businesses, however, insurance expense is usually reported as a general expense.

4. B The salaries paid on July 3, $21,700 (answer C), includes salary expense incurred prior to July 1, $5,500 (answer A). Therefore, the salary expense for July 1–3 is the difference between the amount paid and the credit balance in Salary Expense on July 1, or $16,200 (answer B).

5. D The omission of the adjustment for accrued salaries at the end of the year understates expenses (answer A) and consequently overstates net income (answer B) for the year. The liability for salaries payable is also omitted and results in understating liabilities at the end of the year (answer C).

CHAPTER 6

1. D Every adjusting entry affects both a balance sheet account and an income statement account. Therefore if the debit portion of an adjusting entry increases an asset (balance sheet) account, the credit portion of the entry must affect an income statement account, as would be the case for a decrease in an expense account (answer D).

2. A Deferred expenses are assets, and those expected to benefit a relatively short period of time are listed on the balance sheet among the current assets (answer A).

3. B Unearned revenues are revenues received in advance that will be earned in the future. They represent a liability (answer B) of the business to furnish goods or services in a future period.

4. A Under the system of initially recording office supplies as an expense, the office supplies expense account would have a balance of $2,910 ($660 plus $2,250) before adjustment, representing the combined cost of office supplies on hand at the beginning of the year and the cost of office supplies purchased during the year. The accounts are therefore adjusted by debiting Office Supplies and crediting Office Supplies Expense for $595 (answer A). The adjustment transfers $595, representing the unconsumed supplies on hand at the end of the year, to the asset account.

5. B The $500 credit balance in salary expense on January 1, the beginning of the fiscal year, before any transactions have occurred, resulted from a reversing entry that transferred the credit balance in the salaries payable account at the end of the preceding year to the salary expense account. This credit balance is a liability (answer B) that will be paid as a portion of the first salary payment of the fiscal year. Therefore, the first salary payment of the fiscal year will discharge the liability of $500 and the remainder of the payment will represent salary expense incurred.

CHAPTER 7

1. C The task of revising an accounting system is composed of three phases. Systems analysis (answer A) is the initial phase involving the determination of the informational needs, sources of such information, and deficiencies in the processing methods currently employed. Systems design (answer B) is the phase in which proposals for changes are developed. Systems implementation (answer C) is the final phase involving carrying out or implementing the proposals for changes.

2. A The detailed procedures adopted by management to control operations are collectively termed internal controls (answer A). Internal controls are classified as administrative controls (answer C) and accounting controls (answer B). Internal administrative controls consist of procedures and records that assist management in achieving business objectives. Internal accounting controls consist of procedures and records that are primarily concerned with the reliability of financial records and reports and with the safeguarding of assets.

3. B All payments of cash for any purpose are recorded in the cash payments journal (answer B). Only purchases of merchandise or other items *on account* are recorded in the purchases journal (answer A). All sales of merchandise on account are recorded in the sales journal (answer C), and all receipts of cash are recorded in the cash receipts journal (answer D).

4. A The general term used to describe the type of separate ledger that contains a substantial number of individual accounts with a common characteristic is subsidiary ledger (answer A). The creditors ledger (answer B), sometimes called the accounts payable ledger (answer C), is a specific subsidiary ledger containing only individual accounts with creditors. Likewise, the accounts receivable ledger (answer D), also referred to as the customers ledger, is a specific subsidiary ledger containing only individual accounts with customers.

5. B The controlling account for the customers ledger (the ledger that contains the individual accounts with customers) is Accounts Receivable (answer B). The accounts payable account (answer A) is the controlling account for the creditors ledger. There are no subsidiary ledgers for the sales (answer C) and purchases (answer D) accounts.

CHAPTER 8

1. B On any specific date, the cash in bank account in a depositor's ledger may not agree with the reciprocal account in the bank's ledger because of delays and/or errors by either party in recording transactions. The purpose of a bank reconciliation, therefore, is to determine the reasons for any discrepancies between the two account balances. All errors should then be corrected by the depositor or the bank as appropriate. In arriving at the adjusted (correct) balance according to the bank statement, outstanding checks must be deducted (answer B) to adjust for checks that have been written by the depositor but that have not yet been presented to the bank for payment.

2. **C** All reconciling items that are added to and deducted from the "balance per depositor's records" on the bank reconciliation (answer C) require that journal entries be made by the depositor to correct errors made in recording transactions or to bring the cash account up to date for delays in recording transactions.

3. **D** A voucher (answer A) is the form on which is recorded pertinent data about a liability. After a voucher is approved by the designated official, it is recorded in the voucher register (answer D). The voucher is filed in an unpaid vouchers file (answer B) until it is due for payment. It is then removed from the file and a check is issued in payment and an entry is made in the check register (answer C).

4. **D** A major advantage of recording purchases at the net amount (answer A) is that the cost of failing to take discounts is recorded in the accounts (answer B) and then reported as an expense on the income statement (answer C).

5. **D** To avoid the delay, annoyance, and expense that is associated with paying all obligations by check, relatively small amounts (answer A) are paid from a petty cash fund. The fund is established by estimating the amount of cash needed to pay these small amounts during a specified period (answer B) and it is then reimbursed when the amount of money in the fund is reduced to a predetermined minimum amount (answer C).

CHAPTER 9

1. **C** Maturity value is the amount that is due at the maturity or due date. The maturity value of $10,300 (answer C) is determined as follows:

Face amount of note	$10,000
Plus interest ($10,000 × 12/100 × 90/360)	300
Maturity value of note	$10,300

2. **B** The proceeds of $15,021.25 (answer B) are determined as follows:

Face value of note dated June 1	$15,000.00
Interest on note (60 days at 10%)	250.00
Maturity value of note due July 31	$15,250.00
Discount on maturity value (45 days, from June 16 to July 31 at 12%)	228.75
Proceeds	$15,021.25

3. **B** The estimate of uncollectible accounts, $8,500 (answer C), is the amount of the desired balance of Allowance for Doubtful Accounts *after adjustment*. The amount of the current provision to be made for uncollectible accounts expense is thus $6,000 (answer B), which is the amount that must be added to the Allowance for Doubtful Accounts credit balance of $2,500 (answer A), so that the account will have the desired balance of $8,500.

4. **B** The amount expected to be realized from accounts receivable is the balance of Accounts Receivable, $100,000, less the balance of Allowance for Doubtful Accounts, $7,000, or $93,000 (answer B).

5. **A** Securities held as temporary investments are classified on the balance sheet as current assets (answer A).

CHAPTER 10

1. **C** The overstatement of inventory by $7,500 at the end of a period will cause the cost of merchandise sold for the period to be understated by $7,500, the gross profit for the period to be overstated by $7,500, and the net income for the period to be overstated by $7,500 (answer C).

2. **B** The perpetual system (answer B) continuously discloses the amount of inventory. The periodic inventory system (answer A) relies upon a detailed listing of the merchandise on hand, called a physical inventory (answer C), to determine the cost of inventory at the end of a period. The retail inventory method (answer D) is employed in connection with the periodic system and is based on the relationship of the cost of merchandise available for sale to the retail price of the same merchandise.

3. **A** The fifo method (answer A) is based on the assumption that costs are charged against revenue in the order in which they were incurred. The lifo method (answer B) charges the most recent costs incurred against revenue, and the average cost method (answer C) charges a weighted average of unit costs of commodities sold against revenue. The perpetual inventory system (answer D) is a system that continuously discloses the amount of inventory.

4. **D** The fifo method of costing is based on the assumption that costs should be charged against revenue in the order in which they were incurred (first-in, first-out). Thus the most recent costs are assigned to inventory. The 35 units would be assigned a unit cost of $23 (answer D).

5. **B** When the price level is steadily rising, the earlier unit costs are lower than recent unit costs. Under the fifo method (answer B), these earlier costs

are matched against revenue to yield the highest possible net income. The periodic inventory system (answer D) is a system and not a method of costing.

CHAPTER 11

1. C All expenditures necessary to get a plant asset (such as machinery) in place and ready for use are proper charges to the asset account. In the case of machinery acquired, the transportation costs (answer A) and the installation costs (answer B) are both (answer C) proper charges to the machinery account.

2. A The periodic charge for depreciation under the sum-of-the-years-digits method is determined by multiplying a fraction by the original cost of the asset after the estimated residual value has been subtracted. The denominator of the fraction, which remains constant, is the sum of the digits representing the years of life, or 6 (3 + 2 + 1), in the question. The numerator of the fraction, which changes each year, is the number of years of life remaining at the beginning of the year for which depreciation is being computed, or 3 for the first year, 2 for the second year, and 1 for the third year in the question. The $4,500 (answer A) of depreciation for the first year is determined as follows:

$$\frac{\text{Years of Life Remaining at Beginning of Year}}{\text{Sum of Digits for Years of Life}} \times \left[\text{Cost} - \begin{array}{l}\text{Estimated}\\ \text{Residual Value}\end{array} \right]$$

$$\frac{3}{3 + 2 + 1} \times (\$9,500 - \$500)$$

$$= \frac{1}{2} \times \$9,000 = \$4,500$$

3. B Depreciation methods that provide for a higher depreciation charge in the first year of the use of an asset and a gradually declining periodic charge thereafter are referred to as accelerated depreciation methods. Examples of such methods are the sum-of-the years-digits (answer B) and the declining balance methods.

4. D The acceptable method of accounting for an exchange of similar assets in which the trade-in allowance ($30,000) exceeds the book value of the old asset ($25,000) requires that the cost of the new asset be determined by adding the amount of boot given ($70,000) to the book value of the old asset ($25,000), which totals $95,000.

5. D Long-lived assets that are useful in operations, not held for sale, and without physical qualities are referred to as intangible assets. Patents, goodwill, and copyrights are examples of intangible assets (answer D).

CHAPTER 12

1. B The amount of net pay of $693 (answer B) is determined as follows:

Gross pay:		
40 hours at $20	$800	
5 hours at $30	150	$950
Deductions:		
Federal income tax withheld . .	$212	
FICA ($600 × .075).	45	257
Net pay.		$693

2. A Employers are usually required to withhold a portion of the earnings of their employees for payment of federal income taxes (answer A). Generally, federal (answer B) and state (answer C) unemployment compensation taxes are levied against the employer only and thus are not deducted from employee earnings.

3. D The employer incurs operating costs for FICA tax (answer A), federal unemployment compensation tax (answer B), and state unemployment compensation tax (answer C). These costs add significantly to the total labor costs for most businesses.

4. C Liabilities due within a year should be presented as current liabilities, and those with a more distant future due date should be presented as long-term liabilities on the balance sheet. Therefore, the 12 monthly payments of $1,000 each, for a total of $12,000, represent a current liability, and the remaining $38,000 is a long-term liability (answer C).

5. B The net amount available to a borrower from discounting a note payable is termed the proceeds. The proceeds of $4,900 (answer B) is determined as follows:

Face amount of note.	$5,000
Less discount ($5,000 × 12/100	
× 60/360)	100
Proceeds	$4,900

CHAPTER 13

1. D In the balance sheet, the equipment should be reported at its cost less accumulated depreciation, $100,000. The effect of the declining value of

the dollar on plant assets, the market value of plant assets, and the replacement cost of plant assets are not recognized in the basic historical cost statements.

2. A Under the installment basis of accounting, gross profit is realized in accordance with the amount of cash collected in each year, based on the percent of gross profit to sales. For the question, the amount of gross profit to be realized for the current year is $22,500 (answer A), determined as follows:

Percent of gross profit to sales:
$60,000 ÷ $200,000 = 30%

Gross profit realized:
$75,000 × 30% = $22,500

3. A Under the percentage-of-completion method of accounting, the amount of revenue to be recognized during a period is determined on the basis of the estimated percentage of the contract that has been completed during the period. The costs incurred during the period are deducted from this revenue to yield the income from the contract. The $950,000 of income for the question is determined as follows:

Revenue to be recognized (40% × $20,000,000)	$8,000,000
Costs incurred	7,050,000
Income	$ 950,000

4. D In some situations, there are a number of accepted alternative principles that could be used. To assure a high degree of comparability of the financial statements between periods, appropriate disclosure should be made when a change is made from one accepted principle to another. A change in method of inventory pricing (answer A), a change in depreciation method for previously recorded plant assets (answer B), and a change in method of accounting for installment sales (answer C) are examples of changes in accepted alternative principles that should be appropriately disclosed.

5. D The concept of materiality (answer D) relates to the acceptance of a procedure that deviates from absolute accuracy for insignificant or immaterial items, such as reporting cents on financial statements.

CHAPTER 14

1. B Noncash assets contributed to a partnership should be recorded at the amounts agreed upon by the partners. The preferable practice is to record the office equipment at $9,000 (answer B).

2. C Net income and net loss are divided among the partners in accordance with their agreement. In the absence of any agreement, all partners share equally (answer C).

3. C X's share of the $45,000 of net income is $19,000 (answer C), determined as follows:

	X	Y	Total
Interest allowance.	$10,000	$ 5,000	$15,000
Salary allowance .	12,000	24,000	36,000
Total	$22,000	$29,000	$51,000
Excess of allowances over income	3,000	3,000	6,000
Net income distribution.....	$19,000	$26,000	$45,000

4. A When an additional person is admitted to a partnership by purchasing an interest from one or more of the partners, the purchase price is paid directly to the selling partner(s). The amount of capital transferred from the capital account(s) of the selling partner(s) to the capital account of the incoming partner is the capital interest acquired from the selling partner(s). In the question, the amount is $32,500 (answer A), which is one half of X's capital balance of $65,000.

5. B Partnership cash would be equal to the net balance in the partners' capital accounts, or $8,000. This cash would be distributed in accordance with the credit balances in the partners' capital accounts, after considering the potential loss that might result from the inability to collect from a deficient partner. Therefore the $8,000 (answer B) would be distributed to X (X's $10,000 capital balance less the potential loss from Y's $2,000 deficiency).

CHAPTER 15

1. D The owners' equity in a corporation is commonly called stockholders' equity (answer A), shareholders' investment (answer B), capital (answer C), or shareholders' equity.

2. C If a corporation has cumulative preferred stock outstanding, dividends that have been passed for prior years plus the dividend for the current year must be paid before dividends may be declared on common stock. In this case, dividends of $27,000 ($9,000 × 3) have been passed for the preceding three years and the current year's dividends are $9,000, making a total of $36,000

(answer C) that must be paid to preferred stock-holders before dividends can be declared on common stock.

3. D The stockholders' equity section of corporate balance sheets is divided into two principal sub-sections: (1) investments contributed by the stockholders and (2) net income retained in the business. Included as part of the investments by stockholders is the excess of par over issued price of stock, such as discount on common stock (answer A); the par of stock subscribed, such as common stock subscribed (answer B); and the excess of issued price of stock over par, such as premium on preferred stock (answer C).

4. C Reacquired stock, known as treasury stock, should be listed in the stockholders' equity section (answer C) of the balance sheet. The price paid for the treasury stock is deducted from the total of all of the stockholders' equity accounts.

5. B The total stockholders' equity is determined as follows:

Preferred stock.	$1,000,000
Common stock	2,000,000
Premium on common stock	100,000
Retained earnings	540,000
Total equity	$3,640,000

The amount allocated to common stock is deter-mined as follows:

Total equity		$3,640,000
Allocated to preferred stock:		
Liquidation price . . .	$1,100,000	
Dividends in arrears	240,000	1,340,000
Allocated to common stock.		$2,300,000

The equity per common share is determined as follows:

$2,300,000 ÷ 100,000 shares = $23 per share

CHAPTER 16

1. D Paid-in capital is one of the two major subdivisions of the stockholders' equity of a corporation. It may result from many sources, including the receipt of donated real estate (answer A), the redemption of a corporation's own stock (answer B), and the sale of a corporation's treasury stock (answer C).

2. A The amount of income tax deferred to future years is $18,000 (answer A), determined as follows:

Depreciation expense, sum-of-the-years-digits method	$100,000
Depreciation expense, straight-line method	60,000
Excess expense in determination of taxable income	$ 40,000
Income tax rate.	× 45%
Income tax deferred to future years .	$ 18,000

3. C The correction of a material error related to a prior period should be excluded from the deter-mination of net income of the current period and reported as an adjustment of the balance of re-tained earnings at the beginning of the current period (answer C).

4. A Events and transactions that are distinquished by their unusual nature and by the infrequency of their occurrence, such as a gain on condemnation of land for public use, are reported in the income statement as extraordinary items (answer A).

5. C An appropriation for plant expansion is a portion of total retained earnings and would be reported in the stockholders' equity section of the balance sheet (answer C).

CHAPTER 17

1. B Since the contract rate on the bonds is higher than the prevailing market rate, a rational investor would be willing to pay more than the face amount, or a premium (answer B), for the bonds. If the contract rate and the market rate were equal, the bonds could be expected to sell at their face amount (answer A). Likewise, if the market rate is higher than the contract rate, the bonds would sell at a price below their face amount (answer D) or at a discount (answer C).

2. A The bond carrying amount, sometimes called the book value, is the face amount plus unamortized premium or less unamortized discount. For this question, the carrying amount is $500,000 less $40,000, or $460,000 (answer A).

3. B Although the sinking fund may consist of cash as well as securities, the fund is listed on the balance sheet as an investment (answer B) because it is to be used to pay the long-term liability at maturity.

4. B The amount debited to the investment account is the cost of the bonds, which includes the amount paid to the seller for the bonds (101% × $100,000) plus broker's commissions ($50), or $101,050 (answer B). The $2,000 of accrued interest that is paid to the seller should be debited to Interest Income, since it is an offset against the

amount that will be received as interest at the next interest date.

5. C The balance of Discount on Bonds Payable is usually reported as a deduction from Bonds Payable in the long-term liabilities section (answer C) of the balance sheet. Likewise, a balance in a premium on bonds payable account would usually be reported as an addition to Bonds Payable in the long-term liabilities section of the balance sheet.

CHAPTER 18

1. C When parent acquires substantially all of the voting stock of subsidiary in exchange for its voting common stock (answer C), the affiliation is termed a "pooling of interests." When parent acquires substantially all of the voting stock of subsidiary in exchange for cash (answer A), other assets, issuances of debt obligations (answer B), or a combination of the foregoing, it is termed a "purchase."

2. B The excess of cost over book equity of interest in S Co. is $100,000 (answer B), determined as follows:

Investment in S Co. (cost)	$1,000,000
Eliminate 100% of S Co. stock .	(750,000)
Eliminate 100% of S Co. retained earnings	(150,000)
Excess of cost over book equity of subsidiary interest	$ 100,000

3. B The excess of cost over book equity of interest in S Co. is $190,000 (answer B), determined as follows:

Investment in S Co. (cost)	$1,000,000
Eliminate 90% of S Co. stock .	(675,000)
Eliminate 90% of S Co. retained earnings	(135,000)
Excess of cost over book equity of subsidiary interest	$ 190,000

4. D The 10% of the stock owned by outsiders is referred to as the minority interest. It amounts to $90,000, determined as follows:

10% of common stock.	$75,000
10% of retained earnings	15,000
Total minority interest	$90,000

5. B The 250,000 pesos ($10,000 ÷ $.04) representing the billed price, which had a value of $10,000 on July 9, 1987, had increased in value to $12,500 (250,000 pesos × $.05) on August 8, 1987, when payment was received. The gain, which was realized because the transaction was completed by the receipt of cash, was $2,500 (answer B).

CHAPTER 19

1. A Cash is provided by the issuance of common stock (answer A). Transactions that decrease cash (answers B and C) are applications of cash.

2. C The acquisition of equipment for cash (answer C) decreases cash and is therefore an application of cash. The sale of common stock for cash (answer A) and the issuance of bonds payable for cash (answer B) both increase cash and therefore are sources of cash.

3. D The operations section of the statement of changes in financial position would report a total of $65,500 for the cash provided by operations, determined as follows:

Operations during the year:		
Net income		$55,000
Add items not decreasing cash during the year:		
Depreciation	$22,000	
Decrease in inventories .	5,000	
Decrease in prepaid expenses	500	27,500
		$82,500
Deduct items not increasing cash during the year:		
Increase in trade receivables	$10,000	
Decrease in accounts payable.	7,000	17,000
Cash provided by operations.		$65,500

4. C The operations section of the statement of changes in financial position would report a total of $77,000 (answer C) for the working capital provided by operations, determined as follows:

Operations during the year:		
Net income	$55,000	
Add item not decreasing working capital during the year:		
Depreciation	22,000	$77,000

5. A Working capital is the excess of total current assets over total current liabilities; that is, $225,000 less $150,000, or $75,000 (answer A) in the question.

CHAPTER 20

1. A Percentage analysis indicating the relationship of the component parts to the total in a financial statement, such as the relationship of current assets to total assets (20% to 100%) in the question, is called vertical analysis (answer A). Percentage analysis of increases and decreases in corresponding items in comparative financial statements is called horizontal analysis (answer B). An example of horizontal analysis would be the presentation of the amount of current assets in the preceding balance sheet along with the amount of current assets at the end of the current year, with the increase or decrease in current assets between the periods expressed as a percentage. Differential analysis (answer C), as discussed in Chapter 27, is the area of accounting concerned with the effect of alternative courses of action on revenue and expenses.

2. D Various solvency measures, categorized as current position analysis, indicate a firm's ability to meet currently maturing obligations. Each measure contributes in the analysis of a firm's current position and is most useful when viewed with other measures and when compared with similar measures for other periods and for other firms. Working capital (answer A) is the excess of current assets over current liabilities; the current ratio (answer B) is the ratio of current assets to current liabilities; and the acid-test ratio (answer C) is the ratio of the sum of cash, receivables, and marketable securities to current liabilities.

3. D The ratio of current assets to current liabilities is usually referred to as the current ratio (answer A) and is sometimes referred to as the working capital ratio (answer B) or bankers' ratio (answer C).

4. C The ratio of the sum of cash, receivables, and marketable securities (sometimes called quick assets) to current liabilities is called the acid-test ratio (answer C) or quick ratio. The current ratio (answer A) and working capital ratio (answer B) are two terms that describe the ratio of current assets to current liabilities.

5. C As with many attempts at analyzing financial data, it is possible to determine more than one measure that is useful for evaluating the efficiency in the management of inventories. Both the inventory turnover (answer A), which is determined by dividing the cost of goods sold by the average inventory, and the number of days' sales in inventory (answer B), which is determined by dividing the inventories at the end of the year by the average daily cost of goods sold, express the relationship between the cost of goods sold and inventory.

CHAPTER 21

1. B The manager of a profit center (answer B) has responsibility for and authority over costs and revenues. If the manager has responsibility and authority for only costs, the department is referred to as a cost center (answer A). If the responsibility and authority extend to the investment in assets as well as costs and revenues, it is referred to as an investment center (answer C).

2. B Operating expenses should be apportioned to the various departments as nearly as possible in accordance with the cost of services rendered to them. For rent expense, generally the most appropriate basis is the floor space devoted to each department (answer B).

3. C When the departmental margin approach to income reporting is employed, the direct departmental expenses for each department are deducted from the gross profit for each department to yield departmental margin for each department (answer C). The indirect expenses are deducted from the total departmental margin to yield income from operations (answer A). The final total income is identified as net income (answer B).

4. A The rate of return on investment for Division A is 20% (answer A), computed as follows:

$$\text{Rate of Return on Investment (ROI)} = \frac{\text{Operating Income}}{\text{Invested Assets}}$$

$$\text{ROI} = \frac{\$350,000 - \$200,000 - \$30,000}{\$600,000}$$

$$\text{ROI} = \frac{\$120,000}{\$600,000}$$

$$\text{ROI} = 20\%$$

5. B The profit margin for Division L of Liddy Co. is 15% (answer B), computed as follows:

$$\text{Rate of Return on Investment (ROI)} = \text{Profit Margin} \times \text{Investment Turnover}$$

$$24\% = \text{Profit Margin} \times 1.6$$

$$15\% = \text{Profit Margin}$$

CHAPTER 22

1. C Three inventory accounts are maintained by manufacturing businesses for (1) goods in the process of manufacture (Work in Process—answer C), (2) goods in the state in which they are

to be sold (Finished Goods — answer A), and (3) goods in the state in which they were acquired (Materials — answer B).

2. D The finished goods inventory is composed of three categories of manufacturing costs: direct materials (answer A), direct labor (answer B), and factory overhead (answer C).

3. B Factory overhead includes all manufacturing costs, except direct materials and direct labor. Salaries of plant supervisors (answer B) is an example of a factory overhead item. Wages of factory assembly-line workers (answer A) is a direct labor item, and bearings for electric motors (answer C) are direct materials.

4. A Job order cost systems are best suited to businesses manufacturing for special orders from customers, such as would be the case for a repair shop for antique furniture (answer A). A process cost system is best suited for manufacturers of homogeneous units of product, such as rubber (answer B) and coal (answer C).

5. B If the amount of factory overhead applied during a particular period exceeds the actual overhead costs, the factory overhead account will have a credit balance and is said to be overapplied (answer B) or overabsorbed. If the amount applied is less than the actual costs, the account will have a debit balance and is said to be underapplied (answer A) or underabsorbed (answer C).

CHAPTER 23

1. C The process cost system is most appropriate for a business where manufacturing is conducted by continuous operations and involves a series of uniform production processes, such as the processing of crude oil (answer C). The job order cost system is most appropriate for a business where the product is made to customers' specifications, such as custom furniture manufacturing (answer A) and commercial building construction (answer B).

2. C The manufacturing costs that are necessary to convert direct materials into finished products are referred to as processing costs. The processing costs include direct labor and factory overhead (answer C).

3. B The number of units that could have been produced from start to finish during a period is termed equivalent units. The 4,875 equivalent units (answer B) is determined as follows:

To process units in inventory on May 1: 1,000 units × 1/4	250
To process units started and completed in May: 5,500 units − 1,000 units...	4,500
To process units in inventory on May 31: 500 units × 1/4	125
Equivalent units of production in May .	4,875

4. A The processing costs (direct labor and factory overhead) totaling $48,750 are divided by the number of equivalent units (4,875) to determine the unit processing cost of $10 (answer A).

5. B The product resulting from a process that has little value in relation to the principal product or joint products is known as a by-product (answer B). When two or more commodities of significant value are produced from a single direct material, the products are termed joint products (answer A). The raw material that enters directly into the finished product is termed direct material (answer C).

CHAPTER 24

1. C The capital expenditures budget (answer C) summarizes the plans for the acquisition of plant facilities and equipment for a number of years into the future. The cash budget (answer A) presents the expected inflow and outflow of cash for a budget period, and the sales budget (answer B) presents the expected sales for the budget period.

2. C Flexible budgeting (answer C) provides a series of budgets for varying rates of activity and thereby builds into the budgeting system the effect of fluctuations in volume of activity. Budget performance reporting (answer A) is a system of reports that compares actual results with budgeted figures. Continuous budgeting (answer B) is a variant of fiscal-year budgeting that provides for continuous twelve-month projections into the future. This twelve-month projection is achieved and maintained by periodically deleting from the current budget the data for the elapsed period and adding newly estimated budget data for the same period next year.

3. C The favorable direct labor cost time variance of $110 (answer C) is determined as follows:

Actual time	990 hours
Standard time	1,000 hours
Time variance — favorable	−10 hours
10 hours × $11 standard	$110

4. B The unfavorable factory overhead volume variance of $2,000 (answer B) is determined as follows:

Productive capacity not used....	1,000 hours
Standard fixed factory overhead cost rate....................	× $2
Factory overhead volume variance —unfavorable...............	$2,000

5. A A favorable factory overhead controllable variance of $3,500 (answer A) is determined as follows:

Actual factory overhead cost incurred	$112,500
Budgeted factory overhead for standard product produced [(19,000 hours at $4 variable) + (20,000 hours at $2 fixed)]......	116,000
Factory overhead controllable variance—favorable	$ −3,500

CHAPTER 25

1. C A change in sales revenue from one period to another can be attributed to (1) a change in the number of units sold—quantity factor and (2) a change in the unit price—price factor. The $45,000 decrease (answer C) attributed to the quantity factor is determined as follows:

Decrease in number of units sold in current year....................	5,000
Unit sales price in preceding year ..	× $9
Quantity factor—decrease.........	$45,000

The price factor can be determined as follows:

Increase in unit sales price in current year..........................	$1
Number of units sold in current year	×80,000
Price factor—increase	$80,000

The increase of $80,000 attributed to the price factor less the decrease of $45,000 attributed to the quantity factor accounts for the $35,000 increase in total sales for the current year.

2. B Under the variable costing concept (answer B), the cost of products manufactured is composed of only those manufacturing costs that increase or decrease as the volume of production rises or falls. These costs include direct materials, direct labor, and variable factory overhead. Under the absorption costing concept (answer A), all manufacturing costs become a part of the cost of the products manufactured. The absorption costing concept is required in the determination of historical cost and taxable income. The variable costing concept is often useful to management in making decisions.

3. C In the variable costing income statement, the deduction of the variable cost of goods sold from sales yields the manufacturing margin (answer C). Deduction of the variable selling and general expenses from manufacturing margin yields the contribution margin (answer B).

4. B The contribution margin of $260,000 (answer B) is determined by deducting all of the variable costs and expenses ($400,000 + $90,000) from sales ($750,000).

5. A In a period in which the number of units manufactured exceeds the number of units sold, the operating income reported under the absorption costing concept is larger than the operating income reported under the variable costing concept (answer A) because a portion of the fixed manufacturing costs are deferred when the absorption costing concept is used. This deferment has the effect of excluding a portion of the fixed manufacturing costs from the current cost of goods sold.

CHAPTER 26

1. A Variable costs change in total as the volume of activity changes (answer A) or, expressed in another way, the unit variable cost remains constant with changes in volume.

2. C The break-even point of $400,000 (answer C) is that level of operations at which revenue and expired costs are exactly equal and is determined as follows:

$$\text{Break-Even Sales (in \$)} = \text{Fixed Costs (in \$)} + \text{Variable Costs (as \% of Sales)}$$
$$S = \$240,000 + 40\%S$$
$$60\%S = \$240,000$$
$$S = \$400,000$$

3. B $450,000 of sales (answer B) would be required to realize operating profit of $30,000, computed as follows:

$$\text{Sales (in \$)} = \text{Fixed Costs (in \$)} + \text{Variable Costs (as \% of Sales)} + \text{Desired Profit}$$
$$S = \$240,000 + 40\%S + \$30,000$$
$$60\%S = \$270,000$$
$$S = \$450,000$$

4. A The margin of safety of 20% (answer A) represents the possible decrease in sales revenue that may occur before an operating loss results and is determined as follows:

$$\text{Margin of Safety} = \frac{\text{Sales} - \text{Break-Even Point}}{\text{Sales}}$$

$$= \frac{\$500,000 - \$400,000}{\$500,000}$$

$$= 20\%$$

The margin of safety can also be expressed in terms of dollars and would amount to $100,000, determined as follows:

Sales..........................	$500,000
Less sales at break-even point	400,000
Margin of safety	$100,000

5. D Storage cost per unit (answer A), annual units required (answer B), and cost per order (answer C) are all important in the determination of economic order quantity.

CHAPTER 27

1. A Differential cost (answer A) is the amount of increase or decrease in cost that is expected from a particular course of action compared with an alternative. Replacement cost (answer B) is the cost of replacing an asset at current market prices, and sunk cost (answer C) is a past cost that will not be affected by subsequent decisions.

2. A A sunk cost is not affected by later decisions. For Victor Company, the sunk cost is the $50,000 (answer A) book value of the equipment, which is equal to the original cost of $200,000 (answer C) less the accumulated depreciation of $150,000 (answer B).

3. B The average rate of return is 24% (answer B), determined by dividing the expected average annual earnings by the average investment, as follows:

$$\frac{\$60,000 \div 5}{(\$100,000 + \$0) \div 2} = 24\%$$

4. B Of the three methods of analyzing proposals for capital investments, the cash payback method (answer B) refers to the expected period of time required to recover the amount of cash to be

invested. The average rate of return method (answer A) is a measure of the anticipated profitability of a proposal. The discounted cash flow method (answer C) reduces the expected future net cash flows originating from a proposal to their present values.

5. C The discounted cash flow method (answer C) uses the concept of present value to determine the total present value of the cash flows expected from a proposal and compares this value with the amount to be invested. The average rate of return method (answer A) and the cash payback method (answer B) ignore present value. The discounted internal rate of return method (answer D) uses the present value concept to determine the discounted internal rate of return expected from the proposal.

CHAPTER 28

1. B Personal financial statements are used for many purposes, such as income tax planning and arranging for a loan. For such multiple purposes, reporting of assets at estimated current values (answer B) is most useful.

2. C The caption "net worth" (answer C) is used in the statement of financial condition for the individual's equity. Titles such as proprietorship (answer A) and capital (answer B) are usually associated with commercial enterprises.

3. A In accounting for nonprofit organizations, the term used to represent an accounting entity with appropriate accounts for a particular purpose is "fund" (answer A). Potential liabilities of a fund are referred to as appropriations (answer B), and a fund's binding commitments to pay money eventually are referred to as encumbrances (answer C).

4. C The account that represents the equity for a nonprofit organization is termed Fund Balance (answer C). For a commercial enterprise, the equity resulting from earnings retained in the enterprise is referred to by various terms, including Retained Earnings (answer A) and Accumulated Earnings (answer B).

5. A One of the two principal financial statements for a nonprofit organization is the statement of revenues, expenditures, and changes in fund balance (answer A). The trial balance (answer B) is not a financial statement. Because of the lack of a profit motive or the expectation of earning net income, an income statement (answer C) is normally not prepared for a nonprofit organization.

C ALTERNATIVE METHOD OF RECORDING MERCHANDISE INVENTORIES

The recording of adjusting entries for merchandise inventory at the end of the accounting period is described and illustrated in Chapters 4 and 5. The alternative method presented in this appendix classifies the entries for the beginning and the ending merchandise inventories as *closing* entries instead of *adjusting* entries. The difference in viewpoint has a minor effect on the work sheet, the sequence of entries in the journal, and the income summary account. It does not alter the financial statements in any way.

WORK SHEET

The merchandise inventory at the beginning of the period is to be reported on the income statement as a part of the cost of merchandise sold. On the work sheet, merchandise inventory at the beginning of the period is therefore extended from the Trial Balance Debit column to the Adjusted Trial Balance Debit column and the Income Statement Debit column.

The merchandise inventory at the end of the period is to be reported on the balance sheet as an asset and on the income statement as a deduction from the cost of merchandise available for sale. The ending merchandise inventory is therefore entered on the work sheet as a debit in the Balance Sheet Debit column and as a credit in the Income Statement Credit column. Both the debit and the credit amounts are placed on the same line as that used for the beginning merchandise inventory.

All adjustments are recorded in the Adjustments columns of the work sheet in the same manner as was illustrated on pages 176 and 177, except that by this method no entries are required in the Adjustments columns for merchandise inventory. The balances are then extended to the Income Statement and Balance Sheet columns, and the work sheet is completed. A work sheet employing this alternative procedure is illustrated on page C-2. Note that the Income Statement and Balance Sheet columns, including column totals and the amount of net income, are the same as those on the work sheet on pages 176 and 177.

Midtown Electric Corporation
Work Sheet
For Year Ended December 31, 1987

ACCOUNT TITLE	TRIAL BALANCE		ADJUSTMENTS		ADJUSTED TRIAL BALANCE		INCOME STATEMENT		BALANCE SHEET	
	DEBIT	CREDIT	DEBIT	CREDIT	DEBIT	CREDIT	DEBIT	CREDIT	DEBIT	CREDIT
Cash	62,950				62,950				62,950	
Notes Receivable	40,000				40,000				40,000	
Accounts Receivable	60,880				60,880				60,880	
Merchandise Inventory	59,700				59,700		59,700	62,150	62,150	
Office Supplies	1,090			(a) 610	480				480	
Prepaid Insurance	4,560			(b) 1,910	2,650				2,650	
Store Equipment	27,100				27,100				27,100	
Accumulated Depreciation—Store Equipment		12,600		(c) 3,100		15,700				15,700
Office Equipment	15,570				15,570				15,570	
Accumulated Depreciation—Office Equipment		7,230		(d) 2,490		9,720				9,720
Accounts Payable		22,420				22,420				22,420
Salaries Payable				(e) 1,140		1,140				1,140
Mortgage Note Payable		25,000				25,000				25,000
Capital Stock		100,000				100,000				100,000
Retained Earnings		41,200				41,200				41,200
Dividends	18,000				18,000				18,000	
Sales		720,185				720,185		720,185		
Sales Returns and Allowances	6,140				6,140		6,140			
Sales Discounts	5,790				5,790		5,790			
Purchases	521,980				521,980		521,980			
Purchases Returns and Allowances		9,100				9,100		9,100		
Purchases Discounts		2,525				2,525		2,525		
Transportation In	17,400				17,400		17,400			
Sales Salaries Expense	59,250		(e) 780		60,030		60,030			
Advertising Expense	10,860				10,860		10,860			
Depreciation Expense—Store Equipment			(d) 3,100		3,100		3,100			
Miscellaneous Selling Expense	630				630		630			
Office Salaries Expense	20,660		(e) 360		21,020		21,020			
Rent Expense	8,100				8,100		8,100			
Depreciation Expense—Office Equipment			(d) 2,490		2,490		2,490			
Insurance Expense			(b) 1,910		1,910		1,910			
Office Supplies Expense			(a) 610		610		610			
Miscellaneous General Expense	760				760		760			
Interest Income		3,600				3,600		3,600		
Interest Expense	2,440				2,440		2,440			
	943,860	943,860	9,250	9,250	950,590	950,590	722,960	797,560	289,780	215,180
Net Income							74,600			74,600
							797,560	797,560	289,780	289,780

ADJUSTING ENTRIES

The adjusting entries made from the alternative work sheet are illustrated as follows. They are exactly the same as those illustrated on page 208, except for the exclusion of adjustments for inventory.

	DATE		DESCRIPTION	POST. REF.	DEBIT	CREDIT	
1			Adjusting Entries				1
2	1987 Dec.	31	Office Supplies Expense	717	6 1 0 00		2
3			Office Supplies	116		6 1 0 00	3
4							4
5		31	Insurance Expense	716	1 9 1 0 00		5
6			Prepaid Insurance	117		1 9 1 0 00	6
7							7
8		31	Depreciation Expense — Store Equip.	613	3 1 0 0 00		8
9			Accumulated Depr. — Store Equip.	122		3 1 0 0 00	9
10							10
11		31	Depreciation Expense — Office Equip.	715	2 4 9 0 00		11
12			Accumulated Depr. — Office Equip.	124		2 4 9 0 00	12
13							13
14		31	Sales Salaries Expense	611	7 8 0 00		14
15			Office Salaries Expense	711	3 6 0 00		15
16			Salaries Payable	213		1 1 4 0 00	16
17							17
18							18

JOURNAL — PAGE 28

CLOSING ENTRIES

All accounts with balances in the Income Statement Credit column of the work sheet are closed in one compound journal entry by debiting each account and crediting Income Summary. All accounts with balances in the Income Statement Debit column are closed in one entry by debiting Income Summary and crediting each account. The Income Summary and the dividends accounts are then closed to the retained earnings account. All of the closing entries for the alternative procedure are as follows:

JOURNAL   PAGE 29

	DATE		DESCRIPTION	POST. REF.	DEBIT	CREDIT	
1			Closing Entries				1
2	1987 Dec.	31	Merchandise Inventory	114	62 1 5 0 00		2
3			Sales	411	720 1 8 5 00		3
4			Purchases Returns and Allowances	512	9 1 0 0 00		4
5			Purchases Discounts	518	2 5 2 5 00		5
6			Interest Income	812	3 6 0 0 00		6
7			Income Summary	313		797 5 6 0 00	7
8							8
9		31	Income Summary	313	722 9 6 0 00		9
10			Merchandise Inventory	114		59 7 0 0 00	10
11			Sales Returns and Allowances	412		6 1 4 0 00	11
12			Sales Discounts	413		5 7 9 0 00	12
13			Purchases	511		521 9 8 0 00	13
14			Transportation In	514		17 4 0 0 00	14
15			Sales Salaries Expense	611		60 0 3 0 00	15
16			Advertising Expense	612		10 8 6 0 00	16
17			Depreciation Exp.—Store Equip.	613		3 1 0 0 00	17
18			Miscellaneous Selling Expense	619		6 3 0 00	18
19			Office Salaries Expense	711		21 0 2 0 00	19
20			Rent Expense	712		8 1 0 0 00	20
21			Depreciation Exp.—Office Equip.	715		2 4 9 0 00	21
22			Insurance Expense	716		1 9 1 0 00	22
23			Office Supplies Expense	717		6 1 0 00	23
24			Miscellaneous General Expense	719		7 6 0 00	24
25			Interest Expense	911		2 4 4 0 00	25
26							26
27		31	Income Summary	313	74 6 0 0 00		27
28			Retained Earnings	311		74 6 0 0 00	28
29							29
30		31	Retained Earnings	311	18 0 0 0 00		30
31			Dividends	312		18 0 0 0 00	31

The income summary account, as it will appear after the merchandise inventory adjustments and the closing entries have been posted, is as follows:

ACCOUNT Income Summary   ACCOUNT NO. 313

DATE		ITEM	POST. REF.	DEBIT	CREDIT	BALANCE DEBIT	BALANCE CREDIT
1987 Dec.	31	Revenue, etc.	29		797 5 6 0 00		797 5 6 0 00
	31	Expenses, etc.	29	722 9 6 0 00			74 6 0 0 00
	31	Net Income	29	74 6 0 0 00			

D

WORK SHEET FOR STATEMENT OF CHANGES IN FINANCIAL POSITION

Some accountants prefer to use a work sheet to assist them in assembling data for the statement of changes in financial position (funds statement). Although a work sheet is not essential, it is especially useful when a large number of transactions must be analyzed. Also, whether or not a work sheet is used, the concepts of funds and the funds statement are not affected.

The following sections describe and illustrate the use of the work sheet. Attention is directed to its use in preparing the funds statement (1) based on cash and (2) based on working capital. The data that appear in Chapter 19 for T. R. Morgan Corporation are used for the illustrations.

WORK SHEET PROCEDURES FOR FUNDS STATEMENT BASED ON CASH

The comparative balance sheet and additional data obtained from the accounts of T. R. Morgan Corporation are presented on page D-2. The work sheet prepared from these data is presented on page D-3. The procedures to prepare the work sheet for the funds statement based on cash are outlined as follows:

1. List the title of each *noncash* account in the Description column. For each account, enter the debit or credit representing the change (increase or decrease) in the account balance for the year in the Change During Year column.
2. Add the debits and credits in the Change During Year column and determine the subtotals. Enter the change (increase or decrease) in cash during the year in the appropriate column to balance the totals of the debits and credits.
3. Provide space in the bottom portion of the work sheet for later use in identifying the various (1) sources of cash and (2) applications of cash.
4. Analyze the change during the year in each noncash account to determine the sources and/or applications of cash related to the transactions recorded in each account. Record these sources and applications in the bottom portion of the work sheet by means of entries in the Work Sheet Entries columns.
5. Complete the work sheet.

These procedures are explained in detail in the following paragraphs.

Noncash Accounts

Since the analysis of transactions recorded in the noncash accounts reveals the sources and applications of cash, the work sheet focuses on noncash accounts. For this purpose, the titles of the noncash accounts are entered in the Description column. To facilitate reference in the illustration, noncash current accounts are listed first, followed by the noncurrent accounts. The order of the listing is not important. Next, the debit or credit change for the year in each account balance is entered in the Change During Year column. For example, the beginning and ending balances of Trade Receivables were $65,000 and $74,000, respectively. Thus, the change for the year was an increase, or debit, of $9,000. The beginning and ending balances of Inventories were $180,000 and $172,000, respectively. Thus, the change for the year was a decrease, or credit, of $8,000. The changes in the other accounts are determined in a like manner.

T. R. Morgan Corporation
Comparative Balance Sheet
December 31, 1988 and 1987

	1988	1987	Increase Decrease*
Assets			
Cash..............................	$ 49,000	$ 26,000	$ 23,000
Trade receivables (net)................	74,000	65,000	9,000
Inventories..........................	172,000	180,000	8,000*
Prepaid expenses	4,000	3,000	1,000
Investments (long-term)	—	45,000	45,000*
Land..............................	90,000	40,000	50,000
Building	200,000	200,000	—
Accumulated depreciation—building....	(36,000)	(30,000)	(6,000)
Equipment..........................	240,000	142,000	98,000
Accumulated depreciation—equipment..	(43,000)	(40,000)	(3,000)
Total assets.........................	$750,000	$631,000	$119,000
Liabilities.			
Accounts payable (merchandise creditors)	$ 50,000	$ 32,000	$ 18,000
Income tax payable...................	2,500	4,000	1,500*
Dividends payable....................	15,000	8,000	7,000
Bonds payable.......................	120,000	245,000	125,000*
Total liabilities	$187,500	$289,000	$101,500*
Stockholders' Equity			
Preferred stock.......................	$ 50,000	—	$ 50,000
Premium on preferred stock	10,000	—	10,000
Common stock.......................	280,000	$230,000	50,000
Retained earnings	222,500	112,000	110,500
Total stockholders' equity..............	$562,500	$342,000	$220,500
Total liabilities and stockholders' equity ..	$750,000	$631,000	$119,000

Additional data:

(1) Net income, $140,500.
(2) Cash dividends declared, $30,000.
(3) Common stock issued at par for land, $50,000.
(4) Preferred stock issued for cash, $60,000.
(5) Bonds payable retired for cash, $125,000.
(6) Depreciation for year: equipment, $12,000; building, $6,000.
(7) Fully depreciated equipment discarded, $9,000.
(8) Equipment purchased for cash, $107,000.
(9) Book value of investments sold for $75,000 cash, $45,000.

WORK SHEET
FOR STATE-
MENT OF
CHANGES IN
FINANCIAL
POSITION—
BASED ON
CASH

T. R. Morgan Corporation
Work Sheet for Statement of Changes in Financial Position
For Year Ended December 31, 1988

Description	Change During Year Debit	Change During Year Credit	Work Sheet Entries Debit		Work Sheet Entries Credit	
Trade receivables	9,000				(q)	9,000
Inventories		8,000	(p)	8,000		
Prepaid expenses	1,000				(o)	1,000
Accounts payable		18,000	(n)	18,000		
Income tax payable	1,500				(m)	1,500
Dividends payable		7,000	(l)	7,000		
Investments		45,000	(k)	45,000		
Land	50,000				(j)	50,000
Building	—	—				
Accumulated depreciation—building		6,000	(i)	6,000		
Equipment	98,000		(g)	9,000	(h)	107,000
Accumulated depreciation— equipment		3,000	(f)	12,000	(g)	9,000
Bonds payable	125,000				(e)	125,000
Preferred stock		50,000	(d)	50,000		
Premium on preferred stock		10,000	(d)	10,000		
Common stock		50,000	(c)	50,000		
Retained earnings		110,500	(a)	140,500	(b)	30,000
	284,500	307,500				
Increase in cash	23,000					
Totals	307,500	307,500				

Sources of cash:		
Operations:		
Net income	(a)	140,500
Depreciation of equipment	(f)	12,000
Depreciation of building	(i)	6,000
Decrease in income tax payable	(m) 1,500	
Increase in accounts payable	(n)	18,000
Increase in prepaid expenses	(o) 1,000	
Decrease in inventories	(p)	8,000
Increase in trade receivables	(q) 9,000	
Issuance of preferred stock	(d)	60,000
Issuance of common stock for land	(c)	50,000
Book value of investments sold	(k)	45,000
Applications of cash:		
Declaration of cash dividends	(b) 30,000	
Increase in dividends payable	(l)	7,000
Retirement of bonds	(e) 125,000	
Purchase of equipment	(h) 107,000	
Purchase of land by issuance of common stock	(j) 50,000	
Totals	679,000	679,000

Change in Cash

Since transactions that result in changes in cash also result in changes in the noncash accounts, the change in cash for the period will equal the change in the noncash accounts for the period. Thus, if a subtotal of the debits and credits for the noncash accounts (as indicated in the Change During Year column) is determined, the increase or decrease in cash for the period can be inserted in the appropriate column and the two columns will balance. In the illustration, the subtotal of the credit column ($307,500) exceeds the subtotal of the debit column ($284,500) by $23,000, which is identified as the increase in cash. By entering the $23,000 as a debit in the Change During Year column, the debit and credit columns are balanced. This $23,000 increase in cash will be reported on the funds statement as the difference between the total of the sources section and the total of the applications section.

If the subtotals in the Change During Year columns indicate that the debits exceed the credits, the balancing figure would be identified as a decrease in cash.

Sources and Applications of Cash

After the Change During Year columns are totaled and ruled, "Sources of cash" is written in the Description column. Several lines are skipped, so that at a later time the various sources of cash can be entered, and "Applications of cash" is written in the Description column. When the work sheet is completed, this bottom portion will contain the data necessary to prepare the sources section and the applications section of the funds statement.

To determine the various sources and applications of cash for the year, the changes in the noncash accounts are analyzed. As each account is analyzed, entries made in the work sheet relate specific sources or applications of cash to the noncash accounts. For purposes of discussion, the noncash accounts can be classified as (1) noncurrent accounts and (2) current accounts (except cash).

Analysis of Noncurrent Accounts

As was discussed on pages 827–829, transactions that increase or decrease noncurrent accounts often result in sources and applications of cash. Therefore, the changes in the noncurrent accounts are analyzed to determine the various sources and applications of cash for the year. As each account is analyzed, entries that relate specific sources or applications of cash to the noncurrent account are made in the work sheet. It should be noted that the work sheet entries are not entered into the accounts. They are, as is the entire work sheet, strictly an aid in assembling the data for later use in preparing the funds statement.

The sequence in which the noncurrent accounts are analyzed is unimportant. However, because it is more convenient and efficient, and the chance for errors is reduced, the analysis illustrated will begin with the retained earnings account and proceed upward in the listing in sequential order.

Retained Earnings. The work sheet indicates that there was an increase of $110,500 in retained earnings for the year. The additional data, taken from an examination of the account, indicate that the increase was the result of two factors: (1) net income of $140,500 and (2) declaration of cash dividends of $30,000. To identify the sources and applications of cash, two entries are made on the work sheet. These entries also serve to account for, or explain, the increase of $110,500.

Net income. In closing the accounts at the end of the year, the retained earnings account was credited for $140,500, representing the net income. The $140,500 is also reported on the funds statement as a source of cash. An entry on the work sheet to debit retained earnings and to credit "Sources of cash—operations: net income" accomplishes the following: (1) the credit portion of the closing entry (to retained earnings) is accounted for, or in effect canceled, and (2) the source of cash is identified in the bottom portion of the work sheet. The entry on the work sheet is as follows:

(a) Retained Earnings..............................	140,500	
Sources of Cash—Operations:		
Net Income.....................................		140,500

The cash provided by operations is affected by expenses that did not decrease cash. It is also affected by differences between the time an expense is incurred and the time cash flows out, and differences between the time a revenue is recognized and the time cash flows in to the business. These effects are discussed later in this appendix.

Dividends. In closing the accounts at the end of the year, the retained earnings account was debited for $30,000, representing the cash dividends declared. The $30,000 is also reported on the funds statement as an application of cash. An entry on the work sheet to debit "Applications of cash—declaration of cash dividends" and to credit retained earnings accomplishes the following: (1) the debit portion of the closing entry (to retained earnings) is accounted for, or in effect canceled, and (2) the application of cash is identified in the bottom portion of the work sheet. The entry on the work sheet is as follows:

(b) Applications of Cash—Declaration		
of Cash Dividends................................	30,000	
Retained Earnings..............................		30,000

The cash applied to the payment of dividends is affected by a difference between the time a dividend is declared and the time it is paid. This effect is discussed later in this appendix.

Common Stock. The next noncurrent item on the work sheet, common stock, increased by $50,000 during the year. The additional data, taken from an examination of the account, indicate that the stock was exchanged for land. The work sheet entry to account for this increase and to identify the source of cash is as follows:

(c) Common Stock	50,000	
Sources of Cash—Issuance of Common Stock		
for Land..		50,000

It should be noted that the effect of the exchange will also be analyzed when the land account is examined.

Preferred Stock. The work sheet indicates that the preferred stock account increased by $50,000 and the premium on preferred stock account increased by $10,000. The additional data indicate that these increases resulted from the sale of preferred stock for $60,000. The work sheet entry to account for these increases and to identify the source of cash is as follows:

(d) Preferred Stock	50,000	
Premium on Preferred Stock.......................	10,000	
Source of Cash—Issuance of Preferred Stock		60,000

Bonds Payable. The decrease of $125,000 in the bonds payable account during the year resulted from the retirement of the bonds for cash. The work sheet entry to record the effect of this transaction on cash is as follows:

(e) Applications of Cash—Retirement of Bonds Payable. .   125,000
    Bonds Payable...............................   125,000

Accumulated Depreciation—Equipment. The work sheet indicates that the accumulated depreciation—equipment account increased by $3,000 during the year. The additional data indicate that the increase resulted from (1) depreciation expense of $12,000 (credit) for the year and (2) discarding $9,000 (debit) of fully depreciated equipment. Since depreciation expense does not affect cash but does decrease the amount of net income, it should be added to net income to determine the amount of cash from operations. This effect is indicated on the work sheet by the following entry:

(f) Accumulated Depreciation—Equipment   12,000
    Sources of Cash—Operations:
    Depreciation of Equipment   12,000

It should be noted that the notation in the Description column is placed so that the $12,000 can be added to "Sources of cash—operations: net income."

Since the discarding of the fully depreciated equipment did not affect cash, the following entry is made on the work sheet in order to fully account for the change of $3,000 in the accumulated depreciation—equipment account:

(g) Equipment......................................   9,000
    Accumulated Depreciation—Equipment   9,000

It should be noted that this entry, like the transaction that was recorded in the accounts, does not affect cash. It serves only to complete the accounting for all transactions that resulted in the change in the account during the year and thus helps assure that no transactions affecting cash are overlooked in the analysis.

Equipment. The work sheet indicates that the equipment account increased by $98,000 during the year. The additional data, determined from an examination of the ledger account, indicates that the increase resulted from (1) discarding $9,000 of fully depreciated equipment and (2) purchasing $107,000 of equipment. The discarding of the equipment was included in, or accounted for, in (g) and needs no additional attention. The application of cash to the purchase of equipment is recognized by the following entry on the work sheet:

(h) Applications of Cash—Purchase of Equipment   107,000
    Equipment......................................   107,000

Accumulated Depreciation—Building. The $6,000 increase in the accumulated depreciation—building account during the year resulted from the entry to record depreciation expense. Since depreciation expense does not affect cash but does decrease the amount of net income, it should be added to net income to determine the amount of cash from operations. This effect is accomplished by the following entry on the work sheet:

(i) Accumulated Depreciation—Building...............   6,000
    Sources of Cash—Operations:
    Depreciation of Building........................   6,000

Building. There was no change in the balance of the building account during the year, and reference to the account confirms that no entries were made in it during the year. Hence, no entry is necessary on the work sheet.

Land. As indicated in the analysis of the common stock account, the $50,000 increase in land resulted from a purchase by issuance of common stock. The work sheet entry to indicate this application of cash is as follows:

(j)	Applications of Cash—Purchase of Land by	
	Issuance of Common Stock	50,000
	Land...		50,000

Investments. The work sheet indicates that investments decreased by $45,000. The examination of the ledger account indicates that investments were sold for $75,000. As was explained on page 839, the $30,000 gain on the sale is already included in net income and consequently has already been accounted for as a source of cash. Only the $45,000 book value of the investments sold would be reported as a source of cash. To indicate this source on the work sheet, the following entry is made:

(k)	Investments	45,000
	Sources of Cash—Book Value of Investments Sold. .		45,000

Analysis of Current Accounts (Except Cash)

The amount of cash used to pay dividends may differ from the amount of cash dividends declared. Timing differences between the incurrence of an expense and the related cash outflow and between the recognition of revenue and the receipt of cash must be considered in determining the amount of cash provided by operations. Therefore, the current accounts (other than cash) are analyzed to determine (1) cash applied to payment of dividends and (2) cash provided by operations.

Cash Applied to Payment of Dividends. The additional data indicate that $30,000 of dividends had been declared, which was identified as an application in entry (b). The $7,000 credit in the Change During Year column of the work sheet for Dividends Payable reveals a timing difference between the declaration and the payment. In other words, the $7,000 increase in Dividends Payable for the year indicates that dividends paid were $7,000 less than dividends declared. The work sheet entry to adjust the dividends declared of $30,000 to reflect the dividends paid of $23,000 is as follows:

(l)	Dividends Payable	7,000
	Applications of Cash—Declaration of Cash	
	Dividends: Increase in Dividends Payable.........		7,000

When the $7,000, which represents the increase in dividends payable, is deducted from the $30,000 of "application of cash—declaration of cash dividends," $23,000 is subsequently reported on the funds statement as an application of cash.

Cash Provided by Operations. The starting point in the analysis of the effect of operations on cash is net income for the period. The effect of this amount, $140,500, is indicated by entry (a). As indicated in the earlier analysis, depreciation expense of $18,000 must be added [(f) and (i)] to the $140,500 because depreciation expense did not decrease the amount of cash. In addition, it is necessary to recognize the relationship of the accrual method of accounting to the movement of cash. Ordinarily, a portion of some of the other costs and expenses reported on the income statement, as well as a portion of the revenue earned, is not accompanied by cash outflow or inflow.

The effect of timing differences is indicated by the amount and the direction of change in the balances of the asset and liability accounts affected by operations. Decreases in such assets and increases in such liabilities during the period must be added to the amount reported as net income to determine the amount of cash provided by operations. Conversely, increases in such assets and decreases in such liabilities must be deducted from the amount reported as net income.

The noncash current accounts (except Dividends Payable) provide the following data that indicate the effect of timing differences on the amount of cash inflow and outflow from operations:

Accounts	Increase Decrease*
Trade receivables (net)	$ 9,000
Inventories	8,000*
Prepaid expenses.....................................	1,000
Accounts payable (merchandise creditors)	18,000
Income tax payable	1,500*

The sequence in which the noncash current accounts are analyzed is unimportant. However, to continue the sequence used in analyzing preceding accounts, the analysis illustrated will begin with the income tax payable account and proceed upward in the listing in sequential order.

Income tax payable decrease. The outlay of cash for income taxes exceeded by $1,500 the amount of income tax deducted as an expense during the period. Accordingly, $1,500 must be deducted from income to determine the amount of cash provided by operations. This procedure is indicated on the work sheet by the following entry:

(m) Sources of Cash — Operations: Decrease in Income
      Tax Payable 1,500
         Income Tax Payable................................   1,500

Accounts payable increase. The effect of the increase in the amount owed creditors for goods and services was to include in expired costs and expenses the sum of $18,000. Income was thereby reduced by $18,000 for which there had been no cash outlay during the year. Hence, $18,000 must be added to income to determine the amount of cash provided by operations. The work sheet entry is as follows:

(n) Accounts Payable 18,000
    Sources of Cash — Operations: Increase in
      Accounts Payable   18,000

Prepaid expenses increase. The outlay of cash for prepaid expenses exceeded by $1,000 the amount deducted as an expense during the year. Hence $1,000 must be deducted from income to determine the amount of cash provided by operations. The work sheet entry is as follows:

(o) Sources of Cash — Operations: Increase in Prepaid
    Expenses 1,000
      Prepaid Expenses...................................   1,000

Inventories decrease. The $8,000 decrease in inventories indicates that the merchandise sold exceeded the cost of the merchandise purchased by $8,000. The amount reported on the income statement as a deduction from the revenue therefore included $8,000 that did not require cash outflow during the year. Accordingly, $8,000 must be added to income to determine the amount of cash provided by operations. The work sheet entry is as follows:

(p) Inventories 8,000
      Sources of Cash—Operations: Decrease in Inventories ..   8,000

Trade receivables (net) increase. The additions to trade receivables for sales on account during the year exceeded by $9,000 the deductions for amounts collected from customers on account. The amount reported on the income statement as sales therefore included $9,000 that did not yield cash inflow during the year. Accordingly, $9,000 must be deducted from income to determine the amount of cash provided by operations. The work sheet entry is as follows:

(q) Sources of Cash—Operations: Increase in Trade
     Receivables 9,000
      Trade Receivables   9,000

Completing the Work Sheet

After all of the noncash accounts have been analyzed, all of the sources and applications are identified in the bottom portion of the work sheet. To assure the equality of the work sheet entries, the last step is to total the Work Sheet Entries columns.

Preparation of the Funds Statement

The data for the sources section and the applications section of the funds statement are obtained from the bottom portion of the work sheet. Some modifications are made to the work sheet data for presentation on the statement. For example, in presenting the cash provided by operations, the additions to (deductions from) net income are labeled "Add (deduct) items not decreasing (increasing) cash during the year." Another example is the reporting of the total depreciation expense ($18,000) instead of the two separate amounts ($12,000 and $6,000). The increase (or decrease) in cash that is reported on the statement is also identified on the work sheet. The funds statement prepared from the work sheet, including the details of the changes in the cash account, is illustrated on page D-10.

WORK SHEET PROCEDURES FOR FUNDS STATEMENT BASED ON WORKING CAPITAL

The work sheet used to assemble the data for the funds statement based on cash is also used to assemble data for the funds statement based on working capital. The work sheet procedures differ in that the focus changes from *noncash* accounts, as was the case when the funds statement was based on cash, to *noncurrent* accounts. In other words, *only* the changes in the noncurrent accounts need to be analyzed in preparing the work sheet for the funds statement based on working capital. To illustrate such a work sheet, the data for T. R. Morgan Corporation presented on page D-2 are used. The work sheet prepared from these data is presented on page D-11.

The procedures to prepare the work sheet for the funds statement based on working capital are outlined as follows:

1. List the title of each noncurrent account in the Description column. For each account, enter that debit or credit representing the change (increase or decrease) in the account balance for the year in the Change During Year column.
2. Add the debits and credits in the Change During Year column and determine the subtotals. Enter the change (increase or decrease) in working capital during the year in the appropriate column to balance the totals of the debits and credits. *(continued on page D-11)*

STATEMENT
OF CHANGES
IN FINANCIAL
POSITION—
BASED ON
CASH

T. R. Morgan Corporation
Statement of Changes in Financial Position
For Year Ended December 31, 1988

Sources of cash:
  Operations during the year:
    Net income $140,500
    Add items not decreasing
    cash during the year:
      Depreciation $18,000
      Decrease in inventories .   8,000
      Increase in accounts
        payable   18,000   44,000
                                                       $184,500

    Deduct items not increasing
    cash during the year:
      Increase in trade
        receivables .... $ 9,000
      Increase in prepaid
        expenses............   1,000
      Decrease in income tax
        payable   1,500   11,500

    Cash provided by
      operations $173,000
  Issuance of preferred stock..   60,000
  Issuance of common stock
    at par for land............   50,000
  Book value of investments
    sold (excludes $30,000 gain
    reported in net income) ...   45,000 $328,000

Applications of cash:
  Payment of dividends:
    Cash dividends declared.. $ 30,000
    Deduct increase in
      dividends payable......   7,000 $ 23,000
  Retirement of bonds
    payable   125,000
  Purchase of land by
    issuance of common
    stock at par.............   50,000
  Purchase of equipment......   107,000   305,000
Increase in cash............. $ 23,000

Change in cash balance:
  Cash balance,
    December 31, 1988....... $ 49,000
  Cash balance,
    December 31, 1987.......   26,000
Increase in cash............. $ 23,000

WORK SHEET
FOR STATE-
MENT OF
CHANGES IN
FINANCIAL
POSITION—
BASED ON
WORKING
CAPITAL

T. R. Morgan Corporation
Work Sheet for Statement of Changes in Financial Position
For Year Ended December 31, 1988

Description	Change During Year Debit	Change During Year Credit	Work Sheet Entries Debit	Work Sheet Entries Credit
Investments		45,000	(k) 45,000	
Land...............................	50,000			(j) 50,000
Building...........................	—	—		
Accumulated depreciation—building .		6,000	(i) 6,000	
Equipment.........................	98,000		(g) 9,000	(h) 107,000
Accumulated depreciation— equipment.......................		3,000	(f) 12,000	(g) 9,000
Bonds payable.....................	125,000			(e) 125,000
Preferred stock		50,000	(d) 50,000	
Premium on preferred stock.........		10,000	(d) 10,000	
Common stock.....................		50,000	(c) 50,000	
Retained earnings.................		110,500	(a) 140,500	(b) 30,000
	273,000	274,500		
Increase in working capital..........	1,500			
Totals	274,500	274,500		

Sources of working capital:
  Operations:

Net income..		(a) 140,500
Depreciation of equipment		(f) 12,000
Depreciation of building............................		(i) 6,000
Issuance of preferred stock		(d) 60,000
Issuance of common stock for land		(c) 50,000
Book value of investments sold		(k) 45,000
Applications of working capital:		
Declaration of cash dividends	(b) 30,000	
Retirement of bonds................................	(e) 125,000	
Purchase of equipment	(h) 107,000	
Purchase of land by issuance of common stock	(j) 50,000	
Totals	634,500	634,500

3. Provide space in the bottom portion of the work sheet for later use in identifying the various (1) sources of working capital and (2) applications of working capital.
4. Analyze the change during the year in each noncurrent account in order to determine the sources and/or applications of working capital related to the transactions recorded in each account. Record these sources and applications in the bottom portion of the work sheet by means of entries in the Work Sheet Entries columns.
5. Complete the work sheet.

   These procedures are explained in detail in the following paragraphs.

Noncurrent Accounts

Since the analysis of transactions recorded in the noncurrent accounts reveals the sources and applications of working capital, the work sheet focuses on the noncurrent accounts. For this purpose, the titles of the noncurrent accounts are entered in the Description column. To facilitate reference in the illustration, the noncurrent asset accounts are listed first, followed by the noncurrent liability accounts. The order of the listing is not important.

The debit or credit change for the year in each account balance is entered in the Change During Year column. For example, the beginning and ending balances of Investments were $45,000 and zero, respectively. Thus, the change for the year was a decrease, or credit, of $45,000. The changes in the other accounts are determined in a like manner.

Change in Working Capital

Since transactions that result in changes in working capital (the current accounts) also result in changes in the noncurrent accounts, the change in working capital for the period will equal the change in the noncurrent accounts for the period. Thus, if a subtotal of the debits and credits for the noncurrent accounts (as indicated in the Change During Year column) is determined, the increase or decrease in working capital for the period can be inserted in the appropriate column and the two columns will balance. In the illustration, the subtotal of the credit column ($274,500) exceeds the subtotal of the debit column ($273,000) by $1,500, which is identified as the increase in working capital. By entering the $1,500 as a debit in the Change During Year column, the debit and credit columns are balanced. This $1,500 increase in working capital will be reported on the funds statement as the difference between the total of the sources section and the total of the applications section. This change is supported by details of the change in each of the working capital components, as follows:

<table>
<tr><td>Changes in components of working capital:</td><td></td><td></td></tr>
<tr><td> Increase (decrease) in current assets:</td><td></td><td></td></tr>
<tr><td>   Cash</td><td>$23,000</td><td></td></tr>
<tr><td>   Trade receivables (net)</td><td>9,000</td><td></td></tr>
<tr><td>   Inventories</td><td>(8,000)</td><td></td></tr>
<tr><td>   Prepaid expenses</td><td>1,000</td><td>$25,000</td></tr>
<tr><td> Increase (decrease) in current liabilities:</td><td></td><td></td></tr>
<tr><td>   Accounts payable</td><td>$18,000</td><td></td></tr>
<tr><td>   Income tax payable</td><td>(1,500)</td><td></td></tr>
<tr><td>   Dividends payable</td><td>7,000</td><td>23,500</td></tr>
<tr><td>Increase in working capital</td><td></td><td>$ 1,500</td></tr>
</table>

CHANGES IN COMPONENTS OF WORKING CAPITAL

If the subtotals in the Change During Year columns indicate that the debits exceed the credits, the balancing figure would be identified as a decrease in working capital.

Sources and Applications Sections

After the Change During Year columns are totaled and ruled, "Sources of working capital" is written in the Description column. Several lines are skipped, so that at a later time the various sources of working capital can be entered, and "Applications of working capital" is written in the Description column. When the work sheet is completed, this bottom portion will contain the data necessary to prepare the sources section and the applications section of the funds statement.

Analysis of Noncurrent Accounts

The analysis of the noncurrent accounts, discussed on pages D-4 to D-7, revealed various sources and applications of cash. The effect of these transactions on both cash and working capital is the same. Therefore, the entries on the work sheet for the funds statement based on working capital will be identical to entries (a)–(k), as shown on pages D-5 to D-7, except that they would be adjusted to reflect the working capital basis. The entries for the work sheet for the funds statement based on working capital for T. R. Morgan Corporation are summarized as follows:

(a) Retained Earnings.............................. 140,500
    Sources of Working Capital—Operations:
    Net Income..................................... 140,500

(b) Applications of Working Capital—Declaration of Cash
    Dividends 30,000
    Retained Earnings.............................. 30,000

(c) Common Stock 50,000
    Sources of Working Capital—Issuance of Common
    Stock for Land 50,000

(d) Preferred Stock 50,000
    Premium on Preferred Stock...................... 10,000
    Sources of Working Capital—Issuance of
    Preferred Stock 60,000

(e) Applications of Working Capital—Retirement of
    Bonds Payable................................. 125,000
    Bonds Payable................................. 125,000

(f) Accumulated Depreciation—Equipment 12,000
    Sources of Working Capital—Operations:
    Depreciation of Equipment 12,000

(g) Equipment.. 9,000
    Accumulated Depreciation—Equipment 9,000

(h) Applications of Working Capital—Purchase of
    Equipment..................................... 107,000
    Equipment..................................... 107,000

(i) Accumulated Depreciation—Building 6,000
    Sources of Working Capital—Operations:
    Depreciation of Building......................... 6,000

(j) Applications of Working Capital—Purchase of Land
    by Issuance of Common Stock.................... 50,000
    Land.. 50,000

(k) Investments 45,000
    Sources of Working Capital—Book Value of
    Investments Sold............................... 45,000

Completing the Work Sheet

After all of the noncurrent accounts have been analyzed, all of the sources and applications are identified in the bottom portion of the work sheet. To assure the equality of the work sheet entries, the last step is to total the Work Sheet Entries columns.

Preparation of the Funds Statement

The data for the sources section and the applications section of the funds statement are obtained from the bottom portion of the work sheet. The increase (or decrease) in working capital that is reported on the statement is also identified on the work sheet. The funds statement prepared from the work sheet, including the details of the changes in each working capital component, is as follows:

STATEMENT OF CHANGES IN FINANCIAL POSITION— BASED ON WORKING CAPITAL

T. R. Morgan Corporation
Statement of Changes in Financial Position
For Year Ended December 31, 1988

Sources of working capital:			
Operations during the year:			
Net income	$140,500		
Add item not decreasing working capital during the year:			
Depreciation	18,000		
Working capital provided by operations		$158,500	
Issuance of preferred stock...........		60,000	
Issuance of common stock at par for land........................		50,000	
Book value of investments sold (excludes $30,000 gain reported in net income) .		45,000	$313,500
Applications of working capital:			
Declaration of cash dividends..........		$ 30,000	
Purchase of land by issuance of common stock at par.......................		50,000	
Retirement of bonds payable		125,000	
Purchase of equipment................		107,000	312,000
Increase in working capital			$ 1,500
Changes in components of working capital:			
Increase (decrease) in current assets:			
Cash.............................		$ 23,000	
Trade receivables (net).............		9,000	
Inventories........................		(8,000)	
Prepaid expenses		1,000	$ 25,000
Increase (decrease) in current liabilities:			
Accounts payable		$ 18,000	
Income tax payable.................		(1,500)	
Dividends payable..................		7,000	23,500
Increase in working capital			$ 1,500

E BRANCH ACCOUNTING

In an effort to increase sales and income, a business enterprise may open new stores (branches) in different locations. Among the types of retail businesses in which branch operations were first successfully developed on a major scale were variety, grocery, and drug stores. There are a number of large corporations with hundreds or thousands of retail branches distributed over a wide area. In addition to the national chain store organizations, there are many of a regional or local nature. The growth of suburban shopping centers has added significantly to the number of firms, especially department stores, that have expanded through the opening of branches. For example, such retailers as Sears, J. C. Penney, and K-Mart each operate thousands of stores throughout the United States.

Although commonly associated with retailing, branch operations are also carried on by banking institutions, service organizations, and many kinds of manufacturing enterprises. Regardless of the nature of the business, each branch ordinarily has a branch manager. Within the framework of general policies set by top management, the branch manager may be given freedom in conducting the business of the branch. Data concerning the amount of business handled and the profitability of operations at each location are essential as a basis for decisions by executive management. It is also necessary to maintain a record of the assets and liabilities of each branch.

This appendix deals with the accounting concepts and principles for a single branch of a merchandising business. The fundamental considerations are not greatly affected, however, by the number of branches or by the par-ticular type of business.

SYSTEMS FOR BRANCH ACCOUNTING

There are various systems of accounting for branch operations. The system may be highly centralized, with the accounting for the branch done at the home office. Or the system may be almost completely decentralized, with the branch responsible for the detailed accounting and only summary accounts carried for the branch by the home office. Using some of the elements of both extremes is also common. Many variations are possible, but the two methods of branch accounting described in the following paragraphs are typical.

Centralized System

The branch may prepare only the basic records of its transactions, such as sales invoices, time tickets for employees, and vouchers for liabilities incurred. Copies of all such documents are forwarded to the home office, where they are recorded in proper journals in the usual manner. When this system is used, the branch has no journals or ledgers. If the operating results of the branch are to be determined separately, which is normally the case, separate branch accounts for sales, cost of merchandise sold, and expenses must be main-tained in the home office ledger.

One important result of centralizing the record keeping activities at one location may be sub-stantial savings in office expense. There is also greater assurance of uniformity in accounting methods used. On the other hand, there is some likelihood of delays and inaccuracies in submitting data to the home office, with the result that periodic reports on the operations of a branch may not be available when needed.

Decentralized System

When the accounting for branches is decentralized, each branch maintains its own accounting system with journals and ledgers. The account classification for assets, liabilities, revenues, and expenses in the branch ledger conforms to the classification used by the home office. The account-ing processes are like those of an independent business, except that the branch does not have owner's equity accounts. A special account entitled Home Office takes the place of the owner's equity accounts. The process of pre-paring financial statements and adjusting and closing the accounts is substantially the same as for an independent enterprise. It is this system of branch accounting to which the remainder of the appendix is devoted.

UNDERLYING PRINCIPLES OF DECENTRALIZED BRANCH ACCOUNTING

When the branch has a ledger with a full set of accounts except owner's equity accounts, there must be some tie-in between the branch ledger and the general ledger at the home office. The properties at the branch are a part of the assets of the entire enterprise, and liabilities incurred at the branch are liabilities of the entire enterprise. Although the accounting system at the branch is much like that of an independent company, the branch is not con-sidered a separate entity but only a segment of the business.

The tie-in between the home office and the branch is accomplished by the subsidiary ledger technique, with an added modification that makes the branch ledger a self-contained unit. The basic features of the system are shown in the following chart:

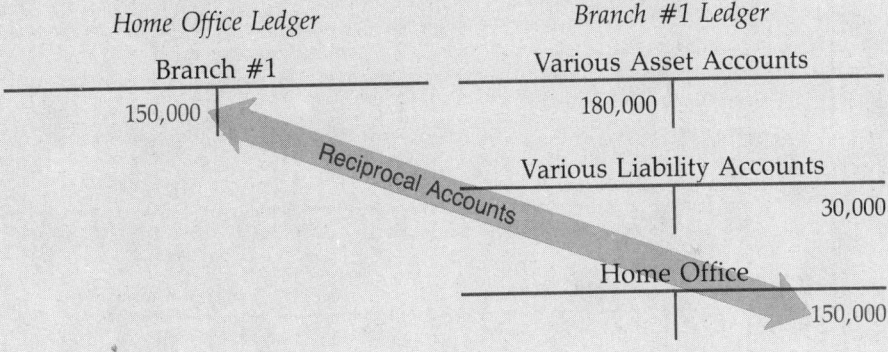

In the home office ledger, the account Branch #1 has a debit balance of $150,000. This balance represents the sum of the assets minus the sum of the liabilities recorded in the ledger at the branch. The various asset and liability accounts in the branch ledger are represented in the chart by one account for all assets ($180,000) and one account for all liabilities ($30,000). To make the branch ledger self-balancing, the account Home Office is added. It has a credit balance of $150,000. The two accounts, Branch #1 in the home office ledger and Home Office in the branch ledger, have equal but opposite balances and are known as **reciprocal accounts**. The home office account in the branch ledger replaces the owner's equity accounts that would be used if the branch were a separate entity. Actually, the account represents the portion of the owner's equity of the home office that is invested in the branch.

When the home office sends assets to the branch, it debits Branch #1 for the total and credits the proper asset accounts. Upon receiving the assets, the branch debits the proper asset accounts and credits Home Office. To illustrate, assume that the home office begins branch operations by sending $20,000 in cash to the newly appointed branch manager. The entries in the two ledgers are illustrated as follows:

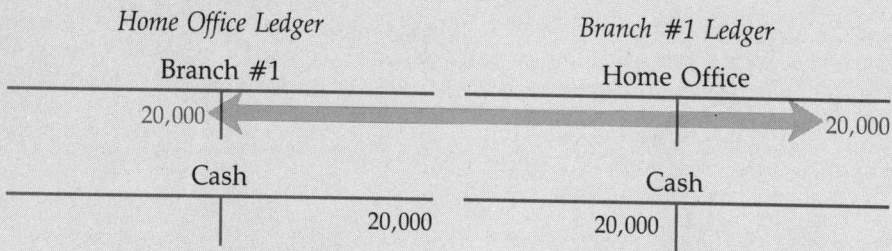

Home Office Ledger

Branch #1

| 20,000 | |

Branch #1 Ledger

Home Office

| | 20,000 |

Cash

| | 20,000 |

Cash

| 20,000 | |

When the branch disburses the cash, it records the transactions as though it were an independent entity. For example, if the branch purchases office equipment for $9,000, paying cash, it debits Office Equipment and credits Cash. No entry is required by the home office because there is no change in the amount of the investment at the branch.

As the branch incurs expenses and earns revenue, it records the transactions in the usual manner. Although such transactions affect the amount of the home office investment at the branch, recognition of the change is delayed until the accounts are closed at the end of the accounting period. At that time, the income summary account in the branch ledger is closed to the account Home Office. If operations have resulted in an operating income, the account Home Office will be credited. In the home office, an operating income at the branch is recorded by a debit to Branch #1 and a credit to Branch Operating Income. For an operating loss, the entries would be just the reverse.

In a merchandising enterprise, all or a large part of the stock in trade of the branch may be supplied by the home office. A shipment of merchandise from the home office is recorded by the home office by debiting Branch #1 and crediting Shipments to Branch #1. The branch records the transaction by debiting Shipments from Home Office and crediting Home Office. It is evident from the following accounts that the two shipments accounts are also reciprocal accounts.

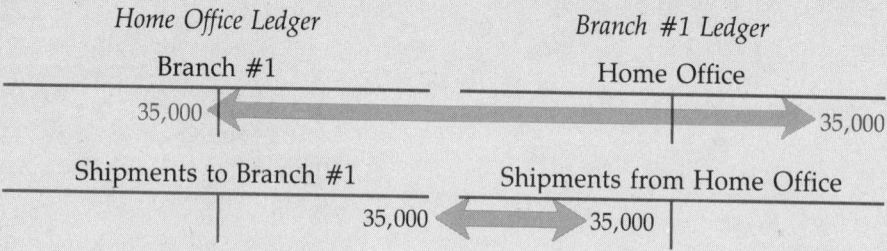

Home Office Ledger

Branch #1

| 35,000 | |

Branch #1 Ledger

Home Office

| | 35,000 |

Shipments to Branch #1

| | 35,000 |

Shipments from Home Office

| 35,000 | |

The account Shipments to Branch #1 is a contra account representing a reduction in Merchandise Inventory and Purchases in the home office ledger. Shipments from Home Office, in the branch ledger, is like a purchases account. Both accounts are temporary in nature and are periodically closed to the respective income summary accounts.

ILLUSTRATION OF DECENTRALIZED BRANCH ACCOUNTING

A series of entries illustrating the underlying principles applicable to branch accounting on a decentralized basis is presented on pages E-4 and E-5. The illustration begins with the opening of a branch and continues with a summary of operations during the remainder of the accounting period. Typical transactions between the home office and the branch are considered, as well as those between the branch and other business enterprises. These transactions are recorded in general journal form. The adjusting and closing entries of the branch and the entry required by the home office to record the operating income of the branch are also presented.

Home Office Entries[1]	Branch Entries

TRANSACTIONS:

(1) The home office established Branch #1 near the end of the fiscal year, sending $20,000 in cash and $40,000 in merchandise.

Branch #1	60,000		Cash	20,000	
Cash		20,000	Shipments from H.O.	40,000	
Shipments to Br. #1		40,000	Home Office		60,000

(2) The branch purchased on account $20,000 of merchandise, $30,000 of equipment, and $1,500 of prepaid insurance.

No entry.	Purchases	20,000	
	Equipment	30,000	
	Prepaid Insurance	1,500	
	Accounts Payable		51,500

(3) The branch sold merchandise for $36,000 in cash and $21,000 on account.

No entry.	Cash	36,000	
	Accounts Receivable	21,000	
	Sales		57,000

(4) The branch paid operating expenses of $11,300.

No entry.	Operating Expenses	11,300	
	Cash		11,300

(5) The branch collected $12,000 on accounts receivable.

No entry.	Cash	12,000	
	Accounts Receivable		12,000

(6) The branch paid $32,000 on accounts payable.

No entry.	Accounts Payable	32,000	
	Cash		32,000

(7) The branch sent $10,000 in cash to the home office.

Cash	10,000		Home Office	10,000	
Branch #1		10,000	Cash		10,000

ADJUSTING:

(a) To record the branch ending merchandise inventory.

No entry.	Merchandise Inventory	22,000	
	Income Summary		22,000

(continued)

[1] Only the entries and accounts affecting Branch #1 are presented.

Home Office Entries	Branch Entries

(b) To record the branch insurance and depreciation expense.

No entry.	Operating Expenses 700
	Prepaid Insurance 200
	Accum. Depreciation 500

CLOSING:

(c) To close the branch sales account.

No entry.	Sales 57,000
	Income Summary 57,000

(d) To close the branch cost and expense accounts.

No entry.	Income Summary 72,000
	Shipments from H.O. 40,000
	Purchases 20,000
	Operating Expenses 12,000

(e) To close the branch income summary account and to record the operating income of the branch in the accounts of the home office.

Branch #1 7,000	Income Summary 7,000
Branch #1 Operating	Home Office 7,000
Income 7,000	

After the foregoing entries have been posted, the home office accounts affected and the branch ledger accounts appear as shown below and on pages E-6 and E-7.

Home Office Ledger	Branch Ledger

Cash (Home Office Ledger)

(7)	10,000	(1)	20,000

Cash (Branch Ledger)

(1)	20,000	(4)	11,300
(3)	36,000	(6)	32,000
(5)	12,000	(7)	10,000
		Balance	14,700
	68,000		68,000
Balance	14,700		

Accounts Receivable

(3)	21,000	(5)	12,000
		Balance	9,000
	21,000		21,000
Balance	9,000		

| Home Office Ledger | | Branch Ledger | |

Merchandise Inventory

| (a) | 22,000 | |

Prepaid Insurance

(2)	1,500	(b)	200
		Balance	1,300
	1,500		1,500
Balance	1,300		

Equipment

| (2) | 30,000 | |

Accumulated Depreciation

| | | (b) | 500 |

Accounts Payable

(6)	32,000	(2)	51,500
Balance	19,500		
	51,500		51,500
		Balance	19,500

Branch #1

(1)	60,000	(7)	10,000
(e)	7,000	Balance	57,000
	67,000		67,000
Balance	57,000		

Home Office

(7)	10,000	(1)	60,000
Balance	57,000	(e)	7,000
	67,000		67,000
		Balance	57,000

Branch #1 Operating Income

| | | (e) | 7,000 |

Branch Operating Income will be
closed to the income summary account.

Income Summary

(d)	72,000	(a)	22,000
(e)	7,000	(c)	57,000
	79,000		79,000

Sales

| (c) | 57,000 | (3) | 57,000 |

| Home Office Ledger | | | Branch Ledger | | |

Shipments to Branch #1

		(1)	40,000

Shipments from Home Office

(1)	40,000	(d)	40,000

Shipments to Branch #1 is deducted from the sum of the beginning inventory and purchases. It will be closed to the income summary account.

Purchases

(2)	20,000	(d)	20,000

Operating Expenses

(4)	11,300	(d)	12,000
(b)	700		
	12,000		12,000

FINANCIAL STATEMENTS FOR HOME OFFICE AND BRANCH

Branch financial statements differ from those of a separate business entity in two minor respects. In the branch income statement, shipments from the home office appear in the cost of merchandise sold section following purchases. In the branch balance sheet, the account Home Office takes the place of the owner's equity accounts.

The home office income statement reports details of sales, cost of merchandise sold, expenses, and income or loss from home office operations in the usual manner. The operating income or loss of each branch is then listed, and the operating results for the entire enterprise are reported. The assets section of the balance sheet prepared from the home office ledger will include the controlling accounts for the various branches. The nature and the amounts of the various assets and liabilities at the branch locations will not be disclosed.

The home office statements, together with financial statements for each individual branch, serve a useful purpose for management. They are not usually issued to stockholders and creditors. Accordingly, it is necessary to combine the data on the income statements of the home office and the branches to form one overall income statement. The data on the balance sheets of the home office and of the various branches are also combined to form one balance sheet for the enterprise. The preparation of the combined statements is made easier by the use of work sheets. The work sheets for both statements are similar in that each has a column for the home office account balances, a column for the account balances of each branch, a set of columns headed "Eliminations," and a final column to which the combined figures are extended.

The combined income statement and the related work sheet for Keller Corporation are shown on page E-8.

The account Shipments from Home Office is canceled by a credit in the Eliminations column, and the account Shipments to Branch #1 is canceled by a debit in the Eliminations column. These eliminations are necessary in the preparation of a combined statement reporting the home office and the branch as a single operating unit. The two accounts merely record a change in location of merchandise within the company.

The combined balance sheet and the related work sheet for Keller Corporation are shown on page E-9. The reciprocal account Branch #1 is canceled by a credit elimination; the reciprocal account Home Office is canceled by a debit elimination.

Keller Corporation
Work Sheet for Combined Income Statement
For Year Ended March 31, 19--

	Home Office	Branch #1	Eliminations		Combined Income Statement
			Debit	Credit	
Sales	897,000	57,000			954,000
Cost of merchandise sold:					
Mdse. inv., April 1............	141,000				141,000
Purchases....................	652,000	20,000			672,000
	793,000				
Shipments from home office....		40,000		40,000	
Less shipments to Branch #1 ..	40,000		40,000		
Mdse. available for sale........	753,000	60,000			813,000
Less mdse. inv., March 31	150,000	22,000			172,000
Cost of merchandise sold......	603,000	38,000			641,000
Gross profit....................	294,000	19,000			313,000
Operating expenses............	150,500	12,000			162,500
Income before income tax........	143,500	7,000	40,000	40,000	150,500
Income tax					60,500
Net income					90,000

Keller Corporation
Income Statement
For Year Ended March 31, 19--

Sales...		$954,000
Cost of merchandise sold:		
Merchandise inventory, April 1, 19--	$141,000	
Purchases	672,000	
Merchandise available for sale....................	$813,000	
Less merchandise inventory, March 31, 19--........	172,000	
Cost of merchandise sold		641,000
Gross profit......................................		$313,000
Operating expenses		162,500
Income before income tax..........................		$150,500
Income tax.......................................		60,500
Net income (per common share, $4.50).............		$ 90,000

Keller Corporation
Work Sheet for Combined Balance Sheet
March 31, 19--

	Home Office	Branch #1	Eliminations		Combined Balance Sheet
			Debit	Credit	
Debit balances:					
Cash.........................	62,000	14,700			76,700
Accounts receivable...........	81,000	9,000			90,000
Merchandise inventory.........	150,000	22,000			172,000
Prepaid insurance.............	8,200	1,300			9,500
Branch #1	57,000			57,000	
Equipment....................	195,000	30,000			225,000
Total......................	553,200	77,000			573,200
Credit balances:					
Accumulated depreciation	87,000	500			87,500
Accounts payable.............	110,000	19,500			129,500
Home office		57,000	57,000		
Common stock................	200,000				200,000
Retained earnings.............	156,200				156,200
Total	553,200	77,000	57,000	57,000	573,200

Keller Corporation
Balance Sheet
March 31, 19--

Assets

Cash..		$ 76,700
Accounts receivable		90,000
Merchandise inventory		172,000
Prepaid insurance		9,500
Equipment.....................................	$225,000	
Less accumulated depreciation	87,500	137,500
Total assets...................................		$485,700

Liabilities and Stockholders' Equity

Accounts payable		$129,500
Common stock, $10 par.........................	$200,000	
Retained earnings	156,200	356,200
Total liabilities and stockholders' equity		$485,700

SHIPMENTS TO BRANCH BILLED AT SELLING PRICE

In the foregoing discussion and illustrations, the billing for merchandise shipped to the branch has been assumed to be at cost price. When all or most of the merchandise handled by the branch is supplied by the home office, billings are usually made at selling price. An advantage of this procedure is that it provides a convenient control over inventories at the branch. The branch merchandise inventory at the beginning of a period (at selling price), plus shipments during the period (at selling price), less sales for the period yields the ending inventory (at selling price). Comparison of the book amount with the physical inventory taken at selling prices discloses any differences. A significant difference between the physical and the book inventories indicates a need for remedial action by the management.

When shipments to the branch are billed at selling prices, no gross profit will be reported on the branch income statement. The merchandise inventory on the branch balance sheet will also be stated at the billed (selling) price of the merchandise on hand. In combining the branch statements with the home office statements, it is necessary to convert the data back to cost by eliminating the markup from both the shipments accounts and the inventory accounts.

PROBLEMS

Problem E–1. Branch and home office entries. Davis Department Stores Inc. established its first branch store, the Maysville Branch, on October 1. Selected transactions related to the Maysville Branch for October are as follows:

Oct. 1. The home office sent to the branch: cash, $10,000; equipment, $19,500; merchandise at cost, $58,200.
6. The branch purchased merchandise on account from outside firms, $11,900.
10. The branch sold merchandise: for cash, $7,700; on account, $4,300.
15. The branch collected $2,200 on account.
18. The branch paid accounts payable, $8,400.
20. The branch paid operating expenses, $950.
21. The branch purchased merchandise on account from outside firms, $6,700.
24. The branch sold merchandise: for cash, $12,300; on account, $5,500.
27. The branch sent $8,000 to the home office.
30. The branch received merchandise at cost from the home office, $16,700.
31. The branch reported an operating income of $5,750.

Instructions:

(1) Prepare the journal entries for the Maysville Branch to record the preceding transactions.
(2) Prepare the journal entries for the home office to record the preceding transactions.

Problem E–2. Entries for two branches and home office. Jones Inc. maintains retail branches (outlets) for its products. During April, the following selected transactions occurred between the home office and two of the branches:

April 1. The home office sent cash to establish two branches: Tucker Branch, $16,000; Crawford Branch, $20,000.

6. The home office sent merchandise at cost to each of the branches: Tucker Branch, $120,000; Crawford Branch, $136,000.

18. The home office instructed the Tucker Branch to ship to the Crawford Branch merchandise costing $35,000. Shipping costs of $800 paid by the Tucker Branch are to be debited to the home office account in Tucker Branch's records. The $800 shipping costs should not be added to the cost of shipments to the Crawford Branch, since the home office has agreed to bear these shipping charges, which it will record by debiting Transportation Costs.

30. The home office sent cash to the branch offices to replenish the branch cash funds after receiving the following disbursement reports. Each branch should record (1) the cash disbursements and (2) the replenishment of its cash fund.

Tucker Branch: sales salaries, $8,100; office salaries, $4,500; rent, $1,600; utilities expense, $420; miscellaneous general expense, $260.

Crawford Branch: sales salaries, $10,200; office salaries, $4,500; rent, $1,800; utilities expense, $380; miscellaneous general expense, $200.

Instructions:

(1) Prepare the journal entries for the Tucker Branch to record the preceding transactions.
(2) Prepare the journal entries for the Crawford Branch to record the preceding transactions.
(3) Prepare the journal entries for the home office to record the preceding transactions.

If the working papers correlating with the textbook are not used, omit Problem E–3.

Problem E–3. Work sheet and combined financial statements for branch and home office. A work sheet for a combined income statement and a work sheet for a combined balance sheet for C. W. Powell Co. and its Oakland Branch for the current fiscal year ended August 31 are presented in the working papers. Data concerning account titles and amounts have been entered on the work sheets. The amounts on the work sheet for the combined income statement were taken from the adjusted trial balance, and the income of the branch had not been recognized in the revenue accounts of the home office. On the work sheet for the combined balance sheet, the amount in the Oakland Branch account was adjusted to give effect to the income of the branch for the current year.

Instructions:

(1) Enter the proper amounts in the "Eliminations" columns and complete the work sheets.
(2) Prepare a combined income statement and a combined balance sheet.

Problem E–4.   Branch entries and accounts; branch income statement and balance sheet; home office entries. Sara A. Chambers and Co. opened a branch office in Yatesville on January 1 of the current year. Summaries of transactions, adjustments, and year-end closing for branch operations of the current year ended December 31 are as follows:

(a) Received cash advance, $20,000, and merchandise (billed at cost), $120,000, from the home office.
(b) Purchased equipment on account, $43,500.
(c) Purchased merchandise on account, $83,000.
(d) Sales on account, $205,000; cash sales, $35,000.
(e) Received cash from customers on account, $178,000.
(f) Paid creditors on account, $101,200.
(g) Paid operating expenses, $51,800 (all expenses are charged to Operating Expenses, a controlling account).
(h) Sent $50,000 cash to home office.
(i) Recorded accumulated depreciation, $5,000, and allowance for doubtful accounts, $1,200.
(j) Merchandise inventory at December 31, $52,000.
(k) Closed revenue, expense, and income summary.

Instructions:

(1) Present the entries for the branch to record the foregoing transactions. Post to the following T accounts: Cash, Accounts Receivable, Allowance for Doubtful Accounts, Merchandise Inventory, Equipment, Accumulated Depreciation, Accounts Payable, Home Office, Income Summary, Sales, Shipments from Home Office, Purchases, and Operating Expenses.
(2) Prepare an income statement for the year and a balance sheet as of December 31 for the branch.
(3) Present the entries required on the home office records. Post to a T account entitled Yatesville Branch.

F   MANUFACTURING WORK SHEET

Many accountants use a work sheet to assist them in the preparation of financial statements. The use of a work sheet for a merchandising enterprise was illustrated in Chapter 4. In a like manner, a work sheet may be used for a manufacturing enterprise. Such a work sheet was not illustrated in Chapter 22, so that the discussion could focus on the basic concepts applicable to accounting for manufacturing operations.

The following sections describe and illustrate the use of a work sheet for manufacturing operations. The illustration is based on the presentation of a general accounting system, which is described on pages 987–989.

WORK SHEET PROCEDURES

The work sheet used in preparing financial statements for a merchandising business, which was illustrated in Chapter 4, is expanded for manufacturing enterprises using periodic inventory procedures by adding a pair of columns for the statement of cost of goods manufactured as shown on page F-3. All items that enter into the determination of the cost of goods manufactured are extended to these two columns. After all these data have been extended, the two cost of goods manufactured columns should be totaled and the difference determined. This difference, which is labeled "Cost of Goods Manufactured" in the account title column, is transferred to the income statement columns by entries in the statement of cost of goods manufactured credit column and the income statement debit column. The remainder of the work sheet is completed in the same manner as is followed for a merchandising business.

To illustrate the use of a work sheet for a manufacturing enterprise, data are taken from the accounts and records of Ming Manufacturing Company, which uses periodic inventory procedures. The unadjusted trial balance at the end of 1987 is reported in the first two columns of the work sheet presented on page F-3. The data needed for year-end adjustments on December 31, 1987, are summarized as follows:

Inventories on December 31, 1987:
Finished goods	$91,000
Work in process	65,800
Direct materials	58,725
Factory supplies	1,800

Depreciation for the year:
Factory buildings	6,000
Factory equipment	22,300

Accruals on December 31, 1987:
Wages and salaries:
Direct labor	4,500
Indirect labor	950

Adjusting Entries

The adjusting entries are recorded on the work sheet in the usual manner illustrated in the merchandising enterprise chapters, except for inventories of work in process and direct materials. Each of the adjusting entries pertaining to the inventories of finished goods, work in process, and direct materials is briefly described below.

The finished goods inventory account is adjusted through the income summary account in the same manner as the merchandise inventory of a merchandising enterprise. The beginning finished goods inventory is transferred to the income summary account by crediting Finished Goods and debiting Income Summary for $78,500 (entry (a) on the work sheet). The ending finished goods inventory is recorded by debiting Finished Goods and crediting Income Summary for $91,000 (entry (b) on the work sheet).

As explained in Chapter 22, the work in process inventory account is adjusted through Manufacturing Summary. The inventory of work in process at the beginning of the period is transferred to the manufacturing summary account by crediting Work in Process and by debiting Manufacturing Summary for $55,000 (entry (c) on the work sheet). The ending work in process inventory is recorded by debiting Work in Process and by crediting Manufacturing Summary for $65,800 (entry (d) on the work sheet).

Like the work in process inventory, the direct materials inventory at the beginning of the fiscal period is transferred to the manufacturing summary account by crediting Direct Materials and by debiting Manufacturing Summary for $62,000 (entry (e) on the work sheet). The direct materials inventory at the end of the period is recorded by debiting Direct Materials and crediting Manufacturing Summary for $58,725 (entry (f) on the work sheet).

Completing the Work Sheet

After all the adjustments have been entered on the work sheet, each account balance, as adjusted, is then extended to the appropriate column. In this illustration, the adjusted trial balance columns which appear in the work sheets illustrated in Chapters 3, 4, and 5 have been eliminated. Experienced accountants often omit these columns in order to save time in preparing the work sheet. Under this approach, the adjusted account balances are entered directly into the proper financial statement columns. The temporary accounts that appear in the statement of cost of goods manufactured are extended to the statement of cost of goods manufactured columns. The other accounts are extended to the income statement and balance sheet columns in the usual manner. Note that the beginning and ending inventory amounts appearing opposite Income Summary and Manufacturing Summary in the adjustments column are extended individually rather than as the net figure, since both amounts will be used in preparing the statements.

After all of the amounts have been extended to the appropriate columns, the work sheet is completed in the following manner:

(1) The statement of cost of goods manufactured columns are totaled. In the illustration, the total of the Dr. column is $675,400 and the total of the Cr. column is $124,525.
(2) The amount of the difference between the two statement of cost of goods manufactured columns is determined and entered in the statement of cost of goods manufactured Cr. column and the income statement Dr. column. This amount ($550,875 in the illustration) is the cost of goods manufactured for the period.
(3) The totals of the columns are entered. The statement of cost of goods manufactured columns should now be in balance.
(4) The amount of net income is determined and is recorded in the income statement Dr. column and in the balance sheet Cr. column.
(5) The totals of the last four columns, which should now be in balance, are entered.

Financial Statements

The completed work sheet provides the information necessary for preparing the financial statements. For Ming Manufacturing Company, the income statement, statement of cost of goods manufactured, retained earnings statement, and balance sheet are shown on pages F-4 and F-5. It should be noted that the factory overhead items are listed separately in the statement of cost of goods manufactured. An alternative would be to report the items in a separate schedule and list only the total in the statement of cost of goods manufactured.

Ming Manufacturing Company
Work Sheet
For Year Ended December 31, 1987

ACCOUNT TITLE	TRIAL BALANCE DEBIT	TRIAL BALANCE CREDIT	ADJUSTMENTS DEBIT	ADJUSTMENTS CREDIT	STATEMENT OF COST OF GOODS MANUFACTURED DEBIT	STATEMENT OF COST OF GOODS MANUFACTURED CREDIT	INCOME STATEMENT DEBIT	INCOME STATEMENT CREDIT	BALANCE SHEET DEBIT	BALANCE SHEET CREDIT
Cash	18,200								18,200	
Accounts Receivable	66,100								66,100	
Allowance for Doubtful Accounts		1,500								1,500
Finished Goods	78,500		(b) 91,000	(a) 78,500					91,000	
Work in Process	55,000		(d) 65,800	(c) 55,000					65,800	
Direct Materials	62,000		(f) 58,725	(e) 62,000					58,725	
Factory Supplies	4,700			(g) 2,900					1,800	
Prepaid Insurance	1,250								1,250	
Land	50,000								50,000	
Factory Buildings	240,000								240,000	
Accumulated Depreciation — Factory Buildings		30,000		(h) 6,000						36,000
Factory Equipment	446,000								446,000	
Accumulated Depreciation — Factory Equipment		111,500		(i) 22,300						133,800
Accounts Payable		45,600								45,600
Wages and Salaries Payable				(j) 5,450						5,450
Income Tax Payable		13,200								13,200
Common Stock ($10 par)		200,000								200,000
Retained Earnings		537,325								537,325
Dividends	40,000								40,000	
Income Summary			(a) 78,500	(b) 91,000			78,500	91,000 *		
Manufacturing Summary			(c) 55,000 (e) 62,000	(d) 65,800 (f) 58,725	55,000 62,000	65,800 58,725				
Sales		915,800						915,800		
Direct Materials Purchases	220,800				220,800					
Direct Labor	214,250		(j) 4,500		218,750					
Indirect Factory Labor	48,350		(j) 950		49,300					
Depreciation — Factory Equipment			(i) 22,300		22,300					
Factory Heat, Light, and Power	21,800				21,800					
Factory Property Taxes	9,750				9,750					
Depreciation — Factory Buildings			(h) 6,000		6,000					
Insurance Expense — Factory	4,750				4,750					
Factory Supplies Expense			(g) 2,900		2,900					
Miscellaneous Factory Expense	2,050				2,050					
Selling Expenses	130,500						130,500			
General Expenses	88,700						88,700			
Income Tax	52,225						52,225			
	1,854,925	1,854,925	447,675	447,675	675,400	124,525				
Cost of Goods Manufactured						550,875	550,875			
					675,400	675,400	900,800	1,006,800	1,078,875	972,875
Net Income							106,000			106,000
							1,006,800	1,006,800	1,078,875	1,078,875

F-3

Ming Manufacturing Company
Income Statement
For Year Ended December 31, 1987

Sales.		$915,800
Cost of goods sold:		
Finished goods inventory, January 1, 1987	$ 78,500	
Cost of goods manufactured.	550,875	
Cost of finished goods available for sale	$629,375	
Less finished goods inventory, December 31, 1987. .	91,000	
Cost of goods sold		538,375
Gross profit		$377,425
Operating expenses:		
Selling expenses	$130,500	
General expenses	88,700	
Total operating expenses.		219,200
Income before income tax.		$158,225
Income tax.		52,225
Net income (per share, $5.30)		$106,000

Ming Manufacturing Company
Statement of Cost of Goods Manufactured
For Year Ended December 31, 1987

Work in process inventory, January 1, 1987. .			$ 55,000
Direct materials:			
Inventory, January 1, 1987.		$ 62,000	
Purchases		220,800	
Cost of materials available for use.		$282,800	
Less inventory, December 31, 1987.		58,725	
Cost of materials placed in production. .		$224,075	
Direct labor		218,750	
Factory overhead:			
Indirect labor.	$49,300		
Depreciation of factory equipment.	22,300		
Heat, light, and power	21,800		
Property taxes.	9,750		
Depreciation on buildings	6,000		
Insurance expired	4,750		
Factory supplies used.	2,900		
Miscellaneous factory costs.	2,050		
Total factory overhead		118,850	
Total manufacturing costs			561,675
Total work in process during period			$616,675
Less work in process inventory,			
December 31, 1987.			65,800
Cost of goods manufactured.			$550,875

Ming Manufacturing Company
Retained Earnings Statement
For Year Ended December 31, 1987

Retained earnings, January 1, 1987		$537,325
Net income for year.	$106,000	
Less dividends.	40,000	
Increase in retained earnings		66,000
Retained earnings, December 31, 1987		$603,325

Ming Manufacturing Company
Balance Sheet
December 31, 1987

Assets

Current assets:			
Cash.		$ 18,200	
Accounts receivable	$ 66,100		
Less allowance for doubtful accounts .	1,500	64,600	
Inventories:			
Finished goods.	$ 91,000		
Work in process	65,800		
Direct materials	58,725	215,525	
Factory supplies.		1,800	
Prepaid insurance		1,250	
Total current assets			$301,375
Plant assets:			
Land		$ 50,000	
Buildings	$240,000		
Less accumulated depreciation	36,000	204,000	
Factory equipment.	$446,000		
Less accumulated depreciation	133,800	312,200	
Total plant assets.			566,200
Total assets.			$867,575

Liabilities

Current liabilities:			
Accounts payable	$ 45,600		
Wages and salaries payable.	5,450		
Income tax payable.	13,200		
Total current liabilities		$ 64,250	

Stockholders' Equity

Common stock, $10 par.	$200,000		
Retained earnings	603,325		
Total stockholders' equity.		803,325	
Total liabilities and stockholders' equity . . .		$867,575	

ADJUSTING ENTRIES

At the end of the accounting period, the adjusting entries appearing in the work sheet are recorded in the journal and posted to the ledger, bringing the ledger into agreement with the data reported in the financial statements. The adjusting entries for Ming Manufacturing Company are as follows:

Adjusting Entries

(a)	Income Summary	78,500	
	Finished Goods		78,500
(b)	Finished Goods	91,000	
	Income Summary		91,000
(c)	Manufacturing Summary	55,000	
	Work in Process		55,000
(d)	Work in Process	65,800	
	Manufacturing Summary		65,800
(e)	Manufacturing Summary	62,000	
	Direct Materials		62,000
(f)	Direct Materials	58,725	
	Manufacturing Summary		58,725
(g)	Factory Supplies Expense	2,900	
	Factory Supplies		2,900
(h)	Depreciation—Factory Buildings	6,000	
	Accumulated Depreciation—Factory Buildings		6,000
(i)	Depreciation—Factory Equipment	22,300	
	Accumulated Depreciation—Factory Equipment		22,300
(j)	Direct Labor	4,500	
	Indirect Factory Labor	950	
	Wages and Salaries Payable		5,450

CLOSING ENTRIES

The closing entries are recorded in the journal immediately following the adjusting entries, illustrated as follows:

Closing Entries

Manufacturing Summary	558,400	
Direct Materials Purchases		220,800
Direct Labor		218,750
Indirect Factory Labor		49,300
Depreciation—Factory Equipment		22,300
Factory Heat, Light, and Power		21,800
Factory Property Taxes		9,750
Depreciation—Factory Buildings		6,000
Insurance Expense—Factory		4,750
Factory Supplies Expense		2,900
Miscellaneous Factory Expense		2,050

Sales..	915,800	
Income Summary.................................		915,800
Income Summary....................................	822,300	
Selling Expenses.................................		130,500
General Expenses................................		88,700
Income Tax......................................		52,225
Manufacturing Summary............................		550,875
Income Summary....................................	106,000	
Retained Earnings................................		106,000
Retained Earnings..................................	40,000	
Dividends.......................................		40,000

The manufacturing accounts are closed to Manufacturing Summary. The revenue account, Sales, is closed to Income Summary. The expense accounts, including the balance in Manufacturing Summary ($550,875, which represents the cost of goods manufactured), are also closed to Income Summary. The final steps in the closing process are to close the balances in Income Summary (representing the net income) and Dividends to Retained Earnings.

PROBLEMS

Problem F–1. **Manufacturing work sheet and financial statements.** The accounts in the ledger of Randall Manufacturing Inc., with unadjusted balances on December 31, the end of the current year, are as follows:

Cash..	30,550
Accounts Receivable.............................	47,450
Allowance for Doubtful Accounts..................	900
Finished Goods..................................	55,800
Work in Process.................................	32,100
Direct Materials.................................	42,000
Prepaid Expenses (Controlling)...................	10,000
Land...	50,000
Factory Buildings................................	260,000
Accumulated Depreciation—Factory Buildings.......	90,000
Factory Equipment...............................	172,650
Accumulated Depreciation—Factory Equipment.....	97,950

Office Equipment	30,000
Accumulated Depreciation—Office Equipment	10,000
Accounts Payable	40,400
Income Tax Payable	—
Wages Payable	—
Common Stock ($60 par)	300,000
Retained Earnings	126,450
Dividends	20,000
Income Summary	—
Manufacturing Summary	—
Sales	668,500
Direct Materials Purchases	197,000
Direct Labor	178,900
Factory Overhead (Controlling)	65,150
Selling Expenses (Controlling)	70,275
General Expenses (Controlling)	45,825
Interest Expense	3,500
Income Tax	23,000

The data needed for the year-end adjustments on December 31 are as follows:

Inventories on December 31:		
Finished goods	$60,000	
Work in process	35,600	
Direct materials	39,400	$135,000
Income tax owed at December 31		9,000
Doubtful accounts at December 31 from analysis of accounts receivable		3,000
Prepaid insurance expired during year:		
Factory overhead	$ 4,200	
General expenses	1,100	5,300
Accrued wages at December 31:		
Direct labor	$ 2,500	
Indirect labor	500	3,000
Depreciation expense for year:		
Factory building	$ 8,000	
Factory equipment	16,700	
Office equipment	2,600	27,300

Instructions:

(1) Prepare a manufacturing work sheet. (Leave one extra line after Manufacturing Summary and two extra lines after Factory Overhead and General Expenses for use in recording the adjusting entries.)
(2) Prepare a statement of cost of goods manufactured.
(3) Prepare an income statement.
(4) Prepare a retained earnings statement.
(5) Prepare a balance sheet.

Problem F–2. Manufacturing financial statements. The chief accountant for Stiles Co. prepared the following manufacturing work sheet for the current year:

Stiles
Work
For Year Ended

ACCOUNT TITLE	TRIAL BALANCE		ADJUSTMENTS	
	DEBIT	CREDIT	DEBIT	CREDIT
Cash	20,450			
Accounts Receivable	75,500			
Allowance for Doubtful Accounts		1,800		
Finished Goods	90,000		(b) 95,000	(a) 90,000
Work in Process	72,000		(d) 68,000	(c) 72,000
Direct Materials	58,500		(f) 65,200	(e) 58,500
Prepaid Insurance	8,700			(g) 5,900
Factory Supplies	8,250			(h) 5,250
Land	75,000			
Factory Buildings	290,000			
Accumulated Depreciation—Factory Buildings		170,000		(i) 16,000
Factory Equipment	446,000			
Accumulated Depreciation—Factory Equipment		211,500		(j) 22,300
Accounts Payable		55,900		
Wages Payable				(k) 4,550
Income Tax Payable		8,200		
Common Stock ($20 par)		300,000		
Retained Earnings		325,225		
Dividends	60,000			
Income Summary			(a) 90,000	(b) 95,000
Manufacturing Summary			(c) 72,000	(d) 68,000
			(e) 58,500	(f) 65,200
Sales		785,500		
Direct Materials Purchases	184,800			
Direct Labor	174,250		(k) 3,800	
Indirect Factory Labor	47,250		(k) 750	
Depreciation—Factory Equipment			(j) 22,300	
Factory Heat, Light, and Power	31,800			
Factory Property Taxes	12,750			
Depreciation—Factory Buildings			(i) 16,000	
Insurance Expense—Factory			(g) 5,900	
Factory Supplies Expense			(h) 5,250	
Miscellaneous Factory Expense	3,650			
Selling Expenses	100,500			
General Expenses	58,500			
Income Tax	40,225			
	1,858,125	1,858,125	502,700	502,700
Cost of Goods Manufactured				
Net Income				

Instructions:

(1) Prepare a statement of cost of goods manufactured.
(2) Prepare an income statement.
(3) Prepare a retained earnings statement.
(4) Prepare a balance sheet.

Co.
Sheet
December 31, 19--

STATEMENT OF COST OF GOODS MANUFACTURED		INCOME STATEMENT		BALANCE SHEET	
DEBIT	CREDIT	DEBIT	CREDIT	DEBIT	CREDIT
				20,450	
				75,500	
					1,800
				95,000	
				68,000	
				65,200	
				2,800	
				3,000	
				75,000	
				290,000	
					186,000
				446,000	
					233,800
					55,900
					4,550
					8,200
					300,000
					325,225
				60,000	
		90,000	95,000		
72,000	68,000				
58,500	65,200				
			785,500		
184,800					
178,050					
48,000					
22,300					
31,800					
12,750					
16,000					
5,900					
5,250					
3,650					
		100,500			
		58,500			
		40,225			
639,000	133,200				
	505,800	505,800			
639,000	639,000	795,025	880,500	1,200,950	1,115,475
		85,475			85,475
		880,500	880,500	1,200,950	1,200,950

Problem F–3   Statement of cost of goods manufactured; adjusting entries and closing entries. The following accounts related to manufacturing operations were selected from the pre-closing trial balance of Corbin Co. at December 31, the end of the current fiscal year:

Depreciation of Factory Buildings	$ 20,000
Depreciation of Factory Equipment	29,000
Direct Labor	210,600
Direct Materials Inventory	60,000
Direct Materials Purchases	290,500
Factory Supplies Expense	6,150
Finished Goods Inventory	90,000
Heat, Light, and Power Expense	28,750
Indirect Labor	47,250
Insurance Expense	9,000
Miscellaneous Factory Costs	4,850
Property Taxes Expense	12,500
Work in Process Inventory	56,800

Inventories at December 31 were as follows:

Finished Goods	$102,300
Work in Process	66,500
Direct Materials	71,400

Instructions:

(1) Prepare a statement of cost of goods manufactured.
(2) Prepare journal entries to adjust the work in process and direct materials inventories.
(3) Prepare journal entries to close the appropriate accounts to Manufacturing Summary.
(4) Prepare the journal entry to close Manufacturing Summary.

G INCOME TAXES

The federal government and more than three-fourths of the states levy an income tax. In addition, some of the states permit municipalities or other political subdivisions to levy income taxes. In operating a business or determining one's personal income tax, it is only good management to plan to keep these taxes to a minimum. This idea was expressed by Judge Learned Hand in *Newman* [35 AFTR 857], as follows:

> Over and over again courts have said that there is nothing sinister in so arranging one's affairs as to keep taxes as low as possible. Everybody does so, rich or poor; and all do right, for nobody owes any public duty to pay more than the law demands; taxes are enforced exactions, not voluntary contributions. To demand more in the name of morals is mere cant.

An understanding of any but the simplest aspects of income taxes is almost impossible without some knowledge of accounting concepts. Conversely, an understanding of the basic concepts of income taxes enable an individual or business to minimize taxes. In many cases, this understanding of the basic concepts leads one to seek the advice and assistance of profes-sional accountants who specialize in determining the tax or developing plans to minimize the tax.

The explanations and illustrations of the federal system presented in this appendix are illustrative of the nature of income taxes. They are brief and relatively free of the many complexities encountered in actual practice. In addition, it should be noted that the federal tax laws are often changed, and that major tax bills have been enacted on the average of every 18 months since the original tax law was passed in 1913. The tax law upon which this discussion is based was changed significantly by the Tax Reform Act of 1986, and the provisions of this act will not be fully implemented until 1991. Therefore, the current tax law and the current tax rates should be examined before tax-related decisions are made.

FEDERAL INCOME TAX SYSTEM

The present system of federal income tax began with the Revenue Act of 1913, which was enacted soon after the ratification of the Sixteenth Amendent to the Constitution. All current income tax statutes, as well as other federal tax laws, are now codified in the Internal Revenue Code (IRC).

The Treasury Department is charged with responsibility in federal tax matters. The division of the Department concerned specifically with enforcement and collection of the income tax is the Internal Revenue Service (IRS), headed by the Commissioner of Internal Revenue. Interpretations of the law and directives formulated according to express provisions of the IRC are issued in various forms. The most important and comprehensive are the "Regulations," which extend to more than two thousands pages.

The data required for the determination of income tax liability are supplied by the taxpayer on official forms and supporting schedules that are referred to collectively as a tax return. Failure to receive the forms from the IRS or failure to maintain adequate records does not relieve taxpayers of their legal obligations to file annual tax returns. Willful failure to comply with the income tax laws may result in the imposition of severe civil and criminal penalties.

Taxpayers alleged by the IRS to be deficient in reporting or paying their tax may, if they disagree with the determination, present their case in informal conferences at district and regional levels. Unresolved disputes may be taken to the federal courts for settlement. The taxpayer may seek relief in the Tax Court or may pay the disputed amount and sue to recover it.

The income tax is not imposed upon business units as such, but upon taxable entities. The principal taxable entities are individuals, corporations, estates, and trusts. Business enterprises organized as sole proprietorships are not taxable entities. The revenues and expenses of such business enterprises are reported in the individual tax returns of the owners. Partnerships are not taxable entities but are required to report on an informational return the details of their revenues, expenses, and allocations to partners. The partners then report on their individual tax returns the amount of net income and other special items allocated to them on the partnership return.

Corporations engaged in business for profit are generally treated as distinct taxable entities. However, it is possible for two or more corporations with common ownership to join in filing a consolidated return. Subchapter S of the IRC also permits a nonpublic corporation that conforms to specified requirements to elect to be treated in a manner similar to a partnership. The effect of the election is to tax the shareholders on their distributive shares of the net income instead of taxing the corporation.

ACCOUNTING METHODS

Although neither the IRC nor the Regulations provide uniform systems of accounting for use by all taxpayers, detailed procedures are prescribed in certain cases. In addition, the IRS has the authority to prescribe accounting methods where those used by a taxpayer fail to yield a fair determination of taxable income. In general, taxpayers have the option of using either the cash basis or the accrual basis.

Cash Basis

Because of its greater simplicity, the cash basis of determining taxable income is usually used by individuals whose sources of income are limited to salary, dividends, and interest. Professional and other service enterprises (e.g., physicians, attorneys, insurance agencies) also ordinarily use the cash basis in determining taxable income. One of the advantages is that the fees charged to clients or customers are not considered to be earned until payment is received. Similarly, it is not necessary to accrue expenses incurred but not paid within the tax year. It is not permissible, however, to treat the entire cost of long-lived assets as an expense of the period in which the cash payment is made.[1] Deductions for depreciation on equipment and buildings used for business purposes may be claimed in the same manner as under the accrual basis, regardless of when payment is made.

Recognition of revenue according to the cash basis is not always contingent upon the actual receipt of cash. In some cases, revenue is said to be constructively received at the time it becomes available to the taxpayer, regardless of when it is actually converted to cash. For example, a check for services rendered which is received before the end of a taxable year is income of that year, even though the check is not deposited or cashed until the following year. Other examples of constructive receipt are bond interest coupons due within the taxable year and interest credited to a savings account as of the last day of the taxable year.

Accrual Basis

For businesses in which production or trading in merchandise is an important factor, purchases and sales must be accounted for on the accrual basis. Thus, revenues from sales must be reported in the year in which the goods are sold, regardless of when the cash is received. Similarly, the cost of goods purchased must be reported in the year in which the liabilities are incurred, regardless of when payment is made. The usual adjustments must also be made for the beginning and ending inventories in order to determine the cost of goods sold and the gross profit. However, manufacturing and merchandising enterprises are not required to extend the accrual basis to every other phase of

---

[1]The current tax law allows small businesses to write off as an expense as much as $10,000 of annual equipment purchases.

their operations. A mixture of the cash and accrual methods of accounting is permissible, if it yields reasonable results and is used consistently from year to year.

INCOME TAX ON INDIVIDUALS

Methods of accounting in general, as well as many of the regulations affecting the determination of net business or professional income, are not affected by the legal nature or the organizational structure of the taxpayer. On the other hand, the tax base and the tax rate structure for individuals differ markedly from those which apply to corporations.

The individual's tax base, upon which the amount of income tax is determined, is called taxable income. Taxable income is gross income less certain deductions as specified by the IRC. It is determined as follows:

GROSS INCOME
minus
DEDUCTIONS FROM GROSS INCOME
equals
ADJUSTED GROSS INCOME
minus
ITEMIZED DEDUCTIONS AND EXEMPTIONS
equals
TAXABLE INCOME

DETER-
MINATION OF
TAXABLE
INCOME FOR
INDIVIDUALS

The basic concepts underlying the determination of taxable income are discussed in the paragraphs that follow.

Gross Income

Items of gross income subject to tax are sometimes called taxable gross income. Some of the taxable and nontaxable items of gross income of indi-viduals are as follows:

TAXABLE ITEMS	NONTAXABLE ITEMS	
Wages and other remuneration from employer.	All or portions of federal old-age pension benefits, depending on amounts of other income.	PARTIAL LIST OF TAXABLE AND NONTAXABLE GROSS INCOME ITEMS
Tips and gratuities for services rendered.		
Cash dividends.	Value of property received as a gift.	
Rents and royalties.	Value of property received by bequest, devise, or inheritance.	
Income from a business or profession.		
Gains from the sale of real estate, securities, and other property.	Life insurance proceeds received because of death of insured.	
Distributive share of partnership income.	Interest on most obligations of a state or political subdivision.	
Income from an estate or trust.		
Prizes won in contests.	Scholarships for tuition and fees.	
Gambling winnings.	Compensation for injuries or for damages related to personal or family rights.	
Jury fees.		
Gains from illegal transactions.	Worker's compensation insurance for sickness or injury.	
Unemployment compensation.		

Deductions from Gross Income

Business expenses and other expenses related to earning revenue are deductible in full or in part from gross income to yield adjusted gross income. For example, ordinary and necessary expenses incurred in the operations of a sole proprietorship are deductible from gross income. Also, expenses that are directly connected with earning rent or royalty income are allowable as deductions from gross income.

A self-employed individual may establish a qualified retirement fund (called a Keogh plan) and deduct the annual contribution from gross income in determining adjusted gross income. Also, certain employees may deduct contributions to plans provided by employers (called 401K plans), and low- and middle-income workers can deduct contributions to individual retirement accounts (called IRAs). The IRC and related regulations state many limitations on the amount of such deductions from gross income.

Adjusted Gross Income

The expenses described in the preceding section are deducted from an amount of related gross income. The resulting figure is the adjusted gross income. The amount of adjusted gross income is used in determining the amount of some of the deductions described in the following section. For example, the medical deduction is limited to the portion of total medical expenses which exceed 7 1/2% of adjusted gross income.

Itemized Deductions, the Standard Deduction, and Exemptions

After the amount of adjusted gross income of an individual is determined, two categories of deductions are subtracted to yield taxable income: (1) itemized deductions or the standard deduction and (2) exemptions. These two deductions from adjusted gross income are described in the following paragraphs.

Itemized Deductions. Certain specified expenditures and losses may be *itemized* and deducted from adjusted gross income. The deductions that are generally available to individuals who itemize deductions are described in the paragraphs that follow.

Charitable contributions. Contributions made by an individual to domestic organizations created exclusively for religious, charitable, scientific, literary, or educational purposes, or for the prevention of cruelty to children or animals are deductible, provided the organization is nonprofit and does not devote a substantial part of its activities to influencing legislation. Contributions to domestic governmental units and to organizations of war veterans are also deductible.

The limitation on the amount of qualified contributions that may be deducted ranges from 20% of adjusted gross income for contributions to private foundations to 50% of adjusted gross income for contributions to public charities, with 50% being the overall maximum. There are other intermediate limitations related to contributions of various types of property other than cash.

Interest expense. Interest expense on indebtedness for the taxpayer's principal and second residences is deductible, subject to certain limitations. Interest expense on indebtedness used for investment purposes is fully deductible up to an amount equal to investment income.

Taxes. Most of the taxes levied by the federal government are *not* deductible from adjusted gross income. Some of the taxes of a nonbusiness or personal nature levied by states or their political subdivisions are deductible from adjusted gross income. The common deductible state and local taxes are real estate, personal property, and income taxes.

Medical expenses. Amounts paid for prescription drugs and insulin and other medical expenses are generally deductible to the extent that they exceed 7 1/2% of adjusted gross income. Other medical expenses deductible in total or in part include medical care insurance, doctors' fees, hospital expenses, etc.

Standard Deduction. As an alternative to itemizing deductions, the taxpayer may take a standard deduction. The amount of the deduction depends upon whether the taxpayer is filing as a single taxpayer, as a head of household, or with a spouse (joint return). In 1988, for example, the standard deduction for a single taxpayer is $3,000.

Exemptions. In general, each taxpayer is entitled to a personal exemption.[2] An additional exemption is allowed for each dependent. The amount of the personal exemption is $1,900 in 1987, $1,950 in 1988, and $2,000 in 1989. Beginning in 1990, the exemption is adjusted annually for inflation.

Taxable Income and Determination of Income Tax

After the taxable income is determined, the taxpayer uses various tax rate schedules to determine the amount of the income tax. For example, the individual tax rates for a single taxpayer are as follows for 1988:

Taxable Income	Tax Rate[3]
$0– $17,850	15%
Over $17,850	28%

To illustrate the use of the tax rate schedules, assume that a single taxpayer has taxable income of $27,850. The tax is determined as follows:

Tax on $17,850 at 15%. . . . . $2,678 (rounded)
Tax on   10,000 at 28%.   2,800
Total on $27,850. . . . . $5,478

INDIVIDUAL TAX RATES— SINGLE TAXPAYER

Credits Against the Tax

After the amount of the income tax has been determined, the tax may be reduced on a dollar-for-dollar basis by the amount of various credits. These credits are therefore quite different from deductions and exemptions, which are reductions of the income subject to tax. The most common credits are described in the paragraphs that follow.

Credit for the Elderly. Some elderly taxpayers receive nontaxable retirement income, while others receive taxable retirement income. The credit for the elderly is an attempt to overcome this perceived inequity. The formula for determining the credit is complex and the IRC should be consulted for the details.

---

[2]Certain high-income taxpayers are not eligible for the personal exemption. For single taxpayers, the personal exemption is phased out by applying a surtax to taxable income that exceeds $89,560.

[3]For certain high-income taxpayers, a surtax is added to offset the benefit of the 15% tax rate.

Child and Disabled Dependent Care Expenses Credit. Taxpayers who maintain a household are allowed a tax credit for expenses, including household expenses, involved in the care of a dependent child under age 15 or a physically or mentally incapacitated dependent or spouse, provided the expenses were incurred to enable the taxpayer to be gainfully employed. The amount of the credit is on a sliding scale, depending on the amount of adjusted gross income and the number of dependents.

Earned Income Credit. This credit against the tax is available to low-income workers who maintain a household for at least one of their dependent chil-dren and who have earned income (wages and self-employment income). Unlike the other credits, which cannot exceed the amount of the tax before applying the credit, if the earned income credit reduces the tax liability below zero, the negative amount is paid to the taxpayer. For example, if a worker's tax liability before applying the credit is $150 and the earned income credit is $375, the taxpayer will receive a direct payment of $225. Direct payments of tax revenues to individuals who have no liability for federal income tax is a concept with significant socioeconomic implications. The concept is often called a "negative income tax."

Filing Returns; Payment of Tax

The income tax withheld from an employee's earnings by an employer represents current payments on account. An individual whose income is not subject to withholding, or only partially so, or an individual whose income is fairly large must estimate the income tax in advance. The estimated tax for the year, after deducting the estimated amount to be withheld and any credit for overpayment from prior years, must be paid currently, usually in quarterly installments.

Annual income tax returns must be filed at the appropriate Internal Revenue Service office within 3 1/2 months following the end of the taxpayer's taxable year. Any balance owed must accompany the return. If there has been an overpayment of the tax liability, the taxpayer may request that the overpayment be refunded or credited against the estimated tax for the following year.

INCOME TAX ON CORPORATIONS

The taxable income of a corporation is determined, in general, by deducting its ordinary business expenses from the total amount of its includable gross income. The corporate tax rates, in general, are as follows for 1988:

CORPORATE
INCOME
TAX RATES

Taxable Income	Tax Rate[4]
$0– $50,000	15%
$50,001–$75,000	25%
Over $75,000	34%

TAX PLANNING TO MINIMIZE INCOME TAXES

There are various legal means of minimizing or reducing federal income taxes, some of which are of broader applicability than others. Much depends upon the volume and the sources of

---

[4]The benefits of the 15% and 25% tax rates would be phased out for companies whose income exceeds $100,000. For those companies, a 5% tax on income over $100,000 would be added until the tax is equal to a flat rate of 34%.

a taxpayer's gross income, the nature of the expenses and other deductions, and the accounting methods used. Examples of means to minimize income taxes are presented in the following paragraphs.

Alternative Accounting Principles

There are many cases in which an enterprise may choose from among two or more optional accounting principles in determining the amount of its taxable income. The particular principle chosen may have an effect on the amount of income tax, not only in the year in which the choice is made but also in later years. To illustrate, the tax law generally permits an enterprise to choose its method of determining the cost of inventory. Two widely used methods are fifo (first-in, first-out) and lifo (last-in, first-out). The more traditional method is fifo, while the more widely used method is lifo. The method chosen may have a significant effect on income and the tax on income in periods of changing price levels.

Under fifo, the first goods purchased during a year are assumed to be the first goods sold. During a period of rising prices, the first goods purchased are the least costly. If the least costly goods are sold, they are charged against revenue, and the most costly goods are included in inventory. Under lifo, however, the last goods purchased during a year are assumed to be the first goods sold. During a period of rising prices, the last goods purchased are the most costly. If the most costly goods are sold, they are charged against revenue, and the least costly goods are included in inventory. Thus, in periods of rising prices, lifo results in higher cost of goods sold, lower income, and lower taxes than fifo.

To illustrate the effects of fifo and lifo on the cost of goods sold and gross profit (and consequently net income and income taxes) in a period of rising prices, assume the following activity for a year for a firm that sells one product:

Sales, 1,000 units at $200...........................	$200,000
Beginning inventory, 500 units at $150................	75,000
Purchases, 1,000 units at $160	160,000
Ending inventory, 500 units..........................	—

The effect of using fifo and lifo on the year's gross profit is as follows:

	Fifo	Lifo
Sales......................	$200,000	$200,000
Cost of goods sold:		
Beginning inventory........	$ 75,000	$ 75,000
Purchases	160,000	160,000
Goods available for sale....	$235,000	$235,000
Ending inventory:		
500 units at $160........	80,000	
500 units at $150........		75,000
Cost of goods sold........	155,000	160,000
Gross profit	$ 45,000	$ 40,000

Under fifo, the 1,000 units sold include the 500 in beginning inventory at $150, or $75,000, plus 500 of those purchased at $160, or $80,000, for a total of $155,000. Under lifo, the 1,000 units sold would be the 1,000 purchased at $160, or $160,000. Thus, using lifo results in a $5,000 higher cost of goods sold (and lower gross profit). From another view, the $5,000 difference in gross profit can be viewed as the difference in the ending inventory amounts ($80,000 − $75,000).

The income tax effect of using fifo versus lifo during periods of declining prices would be the reverse of that illustrated. During periods of declining prices, gross profit (and net income and income taxes) under lifo would exceed that of fifo.

In times of inflation, which has been the long-term trend in the United States since World War II, the use of lifo not only results in a lower annual income tax, but it also permits the taxpayer to retain more funds, by lowering tax payments, to replace goods sold with higher-priced goods. Clearly, this advantage is one of the most important reasons for lifo's popularity.

Use of Corporate Debt

If a corporation is in need of relatively permanent funds, it generally considers borrowing money on a long-term basis or issuing stock. Since interest on debt is a deductible expense in determining taxable income and dividends paid on stock are not, this impact on income tax is one of the important factors to consider in evaluating the two methods of financing. To illustrate, assume that a corporation which expects a tax rate of 34% is considering issuing (1) $1,000,000 of 10% bonds or (2) $1,000,000 of 10% cumulative preferred stock. If the bonds are issued, the deduction of the yearly $100,000 of interest in determining taxable income results in an annual net borrowing cost of $66,000 ($100,000 less tax savings of 34% of $100,000). If the preferred stock is issued, the dividends are not deductible in determining taxable income and the net annual outlay for this method of financing is $100,000. Thus, issuing bonds instead of preferred stock reduced the annual financing expenditures by $34,000 ($100,000 − $66,000).

Nontaxable Investment Income

Interest on bonds issued by a state or political subdivision is exempt from the federal income tax. To illustrate, the following table compares the income after tax on a $100,000 investment in a 10% industrial bond and a $100,000 investment in an 8% municipal bond for a corporation with a tax rate of 34%.

	Taxable 10% Industrial Bond	Nontaxable 8% Municipal Bond
Income	$10,000	$8,000
Tax (34% of $10,000)	3,400	—
Income after tax	$ 6,600	$8,000

Although the interest rate on the municipal bond (8%) is less than the rate on the industrial bond (10%), the aftertax income is larger from the investment in the municipal bond.

GENERAL IMPACT OF INCOME TAXES

The foregoing description of the federal income tax system and discussion of tax minimization demonstrates the importance of income taxes to individuals and to business enterprises. Many accountants, in both private and public practice, devote their entire attention to tax planning for their employers or their clients. The statutes and the administrative regulations, which are often changed, must be studied continuously by anyone who engages in this phase of accounting.

DISCUSSION QUESTIONS

1. (a) Does the failure to receive the tax forms from the IRS qualify as a legitimate means of tax avoidance? (b) Does the failure to maintain adequate records qualify as a legitimate means of tax avoidance?

2. (a) What are the principal taxable entities subject to the federal income tax? (b) How is the income of a sole proprietorship taxed?

3. Describe briefly the system employed in subjecting the income of partnerships to the federal income tax.

4. The adjusted gross income of a sole proprietorship for the year was $60,000, of which the owner withdrew $45,000. What amount of income from the business enterprise must be reported on the owner's income tax return?

5. Do corporations electing partnership treatment (Subchapter S) pay federal income tax? Discuss.

6. Which of the two methods of accounting, cash or accrual, is more commonly used by individual taxpayers?

7. Describe constructive receipt of gross income as it applies to (a) a salary check received from an employer, (b) interest credited to a savings account, and (c) bond interest coupons.

8. Arrange the following items in their proper sequence for the determination of taxable income of an individual.
   (a) Adjusted gross income
   (b) Gross income
   (c) Itemized deductions and exemptions
   (d) Taxable income
   (e) Expenses related to business or specified revenue

9. Which inventory method (lifo or fifo) would result in the lower income tax during a period of rising prices? Explain.

EXERCISES

Exercise G-1. Determination of income using cash method and accrual method. Nancy Young, DDS, opened her dental office after graduation from dental school in early January of the current year. On December 30, the accounting records indicated the following for the current year to date:

	Total	Cash Received	Cash Paid
Fees earned	$92,000	$79,000	—
Lease of dental office and equipment	24,000	—	$22,000
Dental assistant salary	18,000	—	16,500
Dental supplies, utilities, etc.	9,000	—	7,400

(a) Determine the amount of net income Young would report from her dental practice for the current year under the (a) cash method and (b) accrual method.

(b) List the advantages of using the cash method rather than the accrual method in accounting for Young's dental practice.

(c) What is the principal advantage of using the accrual method rather than the cash method in accounting for Young's dental practice?

Exercise G–2. Determination of corporation income tax. During the current year, three corporations realized the following taxable income:

Corporation A...............................	$ 10,000
Corporation B...............................	60,000
Corporation C...............................	100,000

Using the tax rates indicated in the chapter, determine the amount of income tax owed by each corporation.

Exercise G–3. Effects of using fifo and lifo for inventory costing. On January 10 of the current year, Linda Marie Fell opened the Old Fashioned Ice Cream Parlor. During the year, ice cream was purchased at three different prices, as follows:

	Price per Gallon
January 10–May 1	$1.50
May 2–August 20	1.55
August 21–December 31.............	1.65

Sales averaged 400 gallons of ice cream per month, and 150 gallons were on hand at December 31.

(a) Assuming the use of the fifo (first-in, first-out) inventory method, determine the cost of the inventory at December 31.

(b) Assuming the use of the lifo (last-in, first-out) inventory method, determine the cost of the inventory at December 31.

(c) Which inventory method, fifo or lifo, will result in the lower net income, and by how much will the income be lower?

Exercise G–4. Effects of using fifo and lifo for inventory costing. Acme Limousine Sales sold 25 limousines for $22,500 each during the first year of operations. Data related to purchases during the year are as follows:

	Quantity	Unit Cost
January 3	5	$20,000
April 10	4	20,100
June 30	7	20,250
August 22	10	20,300
November 5	5	20,500

Sales of limousines are the company's only source of income, and operating expenses for the current year are $19,750.

(a) Determine the net income for the current year, using the fifo (first-in, first-out) inventory method.

(b) Determine the net income for the current year, using the lifo (last-in, first-out) inventory method.

(c) Which method of inventory costing, fifo or lifo, would you recommend for tax purposes? Discuss.

Exercise G–5.   Effects of corporation income tax on two financing plans. The board of directors of Highland Inc. is planning an expansion of plant facilities expected to cost $2,000,000. The board is undecided about the method of financing this expansion and is considering two plans:

Plan 1. Issue 20,000 shares of $100, 10% cumulative preferred stock at par.
Plan 2. Issue $2,000,000 of 20-year, 12% bonds at face amount.

The condensed balance sheet of the corporation at the end of the most recent fiscal year is as follows:

Highland Inc.
Balance Sheet
December 31, 19--

Assets		Liabilities and Stockholders' Equity	
Current assets	$1,400,000	Current liabilities	$1,140,000
Plant assets	4,600,000	Common stock, $25 par...	2,500,000
		Premium on common stock	1,000,000
		Retained earnings........	1,360,000
		Total liabilities and stock-	
Total assets	$6,000,000	holders' equity	$6,000,000

Net income has remained relatively constant over the past several years. As a result of the expansion program, yearly income after tax but before bond interest and related income tax is expected to increase to $450,000.

(a) Prepare a tabulation indicating the net annual outlay (dividends and interest after tax) for financing under each plan. (Use the 34% income tax rate indicated in the chapter.)

(b) List factors other than the net cost of financing that the board should consider in evaluating the two plans.

H SPECIMEN FINANCIAL STATEMENTS

This appendix contains selected statements and notes for real companies.

CONSOLIDATED STATEMENTS OF INCOME
(In thousands except per share data)

The Coca-Cola Company

Year Ended December 31,	1985	1984	1983
Net Operating Revenues	$7,903,904	$7,151,826	$6,640,759
Cost of goods and services	4,193,557	3,822,637	3,617,699
Gross Profit	3,710,347	3,329,189	3,023,060
Selling, administrative and general expenses	2,664,945	2,287,041	2,041,257
Operating Income	1,045,402	1,042,148	981,803
Interest income	147,523	128,823	82,877
Interest expense	167,822	122,983	72,145
Other income (deductions)—net	67,746	6,841	(2,025)
Income From Continuing Operations Before Income Taxes	1,092,849	1,054,829	990,510
Income taxes	415,283	433,071	437,566
Income From Continuing Operations	677,566	621,758	552,944
Income from discontinued operations (net of applicable income taxes of $7,870 in 1985, $6,144 in 1984 and $4,920 in 1983)	9,000	7,060	5,843
Gain on disposal of discontinued operations (net of applicable income taxes of $20,252)	35,733	—	—
Net Income	$ 722,299	$ 628,818	$ 558,787
Per Share			
Continuing operations	$ 5.17	$ 4.70	$ 4.06
Discontinued operations	.34	.06	.04
Net income	$ 5.51	$ 4.76	$ 4.10
Average Shares Outstanding	131,118	132,210	136,222

See Notes to Consolidated Financial Statements.

CONSOLIDATED BALANCE SHEETS
(In thousands except share data)

The Coca-Cola Company

		December 31,	
		1985	1984
Assets			
Current	Cash	$ 495,672	$ 307,564
	Marketable securities, at cost (approximates market)	369,491	474,575
		865,163	782,139
	Trade accounts receivable, less allowances of $19,479 in 1985 and $20,670 in 1984	897,200	872,332
	Inventories and film costs	913,293	740,063
	Prepaid expenses and other assets	294,628	241,326
	Total Current Assets	2,970,284	2,635,860
Investments, Film Costs and Other Assets	Investments (principally investments in affiliates)	470,575	334,220
	Film costs	536,112	341,662
	Receivables and other assets	364,581	408,324
		1,371,268	1,084,206
Property, Plant and Equipment	Land	139,450	130,883
	Buildings and improvements	771,088	645,150
	Machinery and equipment	1,742,118	1,518,264
	Containers	358,354	337,993
		3,011,010	2,632,290
	Less allowances for depreciation	1,127,301	1,009,715
		1,883,709	1,662,575
Goodwill and Other Intangible Assets		672,445	615,428
		$6,897,706	$5,958,069

Liabilities and Shareholders' Equity			
Current	Accounts payable and accrued expenses	$1,108,964	$1,020,807
	Loans and notes payable	391,629	502,216
	Current maturities of long-term debt	34,495	120,300
	Entertainment obligations	215,249	192,537
	Accrued taxes—including income taxes	253,507	186,942
	Total Current Liabilities	2,003,844	2,022,802
Entertainment Obligations		270,676	175,234
Long-Term Debt		889,201	740,001
Deferred Income Taxes		320,832	241,966
Deferred Entertainment Revenue		434,096	—
Shareholders' Equity	Common stock, no par value— Authorized: 180,000,000 shares in 1985 and 1984; Issued: 137,699,566 shares in 1985 and 137,263,936 shares in 1984	69,227	69,009
	Capital surplus	602,617	532,186
	Reinvested earnings	3,092,255	2,758,895
	Foreign currency translation adjustment	(181,440)	(234,811)
		3,582,659	3,125,279
	Less treasury stock, at cost (9,039,031 shares in 1985; 6,438,837 shares in 1984)	603,602	347,213
		2,979,057	2,778,066
		$6,897,706	$5,958,069

See Notes to Consolidated Financial Statements.

The Procter & Gamble Company And Subsidiaries
Years Ended June 30, 1985, 1984 and 1983

Millions of Dollars Except Per Share Amounts

Consolidated Statement Of Earnings

	1985	1984	1983
INCOME			
Net sales	$13,552	$12,946	$12,452
Interest and other income	193	179	129
	13,745	13,125	12,581
COSTS AND EXPENSES			
Cost of products sold	9,099	8,533	8,020
Marketing, administrative, and other expenses	3,477	3,026	2,903
Interest expense	165	139	108
	12,741	11,698	11,031
EARNINGS BEFORE INCOME TAXES	1,004	1,427	1,550
INCOME TAXES	369	537	684
NET EARNINGS	$ 635	$ 890	$ 866

Per Common Share

	1985	1984	1983
Net earnings	$3.80	$5.35	$5.22

Average shares outstanding (in millions):
1985—167.2
1984—166.4
1983—165.9

	1985	1984	1983
Dividends	$2.60	$2.40	$2.25

See Notes to Consolidated Financial Statements.

The Procter & Gamble Company And Subsidiaries
June 30, 1985 and 1984

Millions of Dollars

Consolidated Balance Sheet	1985	1984
ASSETS		
CURRENT ASSETS		
Cash	$ 19	$ 39
Marketable securities	459	702
Accounts receivable, less allowance for doubtful accounts	1,205	1,058
Inventories	1,754	1,540
Prepaid expenses and other current assets	379	317
	3,816	3,656
PROPERTY, PLANT, AND EQUIPMENT	7,466	6,646
Less accumulated depreciation	2,174	1,978
	5,292	4,668
OTHER ASSETS, PRIMARILY GOODWILL	575	574
TOTAL	$9,683	$8,898
LIABILITIES AND SHAREHOLDERS' EQUITY		
CURRENT LIABILITIES		
Accounts payable—trade	$ 981	$ 963
Accounts payable—other	250	252
Accrued liabilities	740	637
Taxes payable	219	165
Debt due within one year	399	357
	2,589	2,374
LONG-TERM DEBT	877	630
DEFERRED INCOME TAXES	945	814
SHAREHOLDERS' EQUITY		
Common shares	167	167
Additional paid-in capital	328	299
Currency translation adjustments	(293)	(265)
Retained earnings	5,070	4,879
	5,272	5,080
TOTAL	$9,683	$8,898

See Notes to Consolidated Financial Statements.

The Procter & Gamble Company

Notes to Consolidated Financial Statements

1. Summary of Significant Accounting Policies

PRINCIPLES OF CONSOLIDATION: The financial statements include the accounts of The Procter & Gamble Company and its majority-owned subsidiaries. Investments in 20% to 50% owned affiliates in which significant management control is exercised are included at original cost adjusted for the change in equity since acquisition. Other investments in affiliates are carried at cost.

CURRENCY TRANSLATION: Assets and liabilities denominated in most foreign currencies are translated into U.S. dollars at year-end exchange rates. Gains or losses from these translations are excluded from net earnings and reflected in shareholders' equity.

MARKETABLE SECURITIES: Substantially all of the marketable securities are government and corporate debt instruments which are carried at cost which approximates market.

INVENTORY VALUATION: Inventories are valued at the lower of cost or market. Cost for most inventories is determined by the last-in, first-out method. For the remaining inventories, cost is determined primarily by the average cost method.

Futures contracts are purchased primarily to hedge certain agricultural commodity requirements. Gains and losses on these contracts are included in earnings when the related products are sold.

Toys "R" Us, Inc. and Subsidiaries

Statements of Consolidated Stockholders' Equity

	Issued	
(In thousands except shares information)	Shares	Amount
Balance, January 30, 1983	36,004,858	$3,600
Three-for-two stock split effected in the form of a 50% stock dividend payable July 26, 1983	18,000,699	1,800
Net earnings for year	—	—
Exercise of stock options	48,737	5
Tax benefit from exercise of non-qualified stock options	—	—
Balance, January 29, 1984	54,054,294	5,405
Three-for-two stock split effected in the form of a 50% stock dividend payable January 8, 1985	27,473,693	2,747
Net earnings for year	—	—
Exercise of stock options	1,625,937	163
Tax benefit from exercise of non-qualified stock options		
Foreign currency translation loss	—	—
Balance, February 3, 1985	83,153,924	8,315
Net earnings for year	—	—
Exercise of stock options and other	899,992	90
Tax benefit from exercise of non-qualified stock options		
Foreign currency translation gain	—	—
Balance, February 2, 1986	84,053,916	$8,405

GOODWILL: The excess of the purchase price over the value ascribed to net tangible assets of businesses acquired after October 31, 1970 is amortized on a straight-line basis over forty years. Goodwill arising prior to that date is not amortized.

DEPRECIATION: For financial accounting purposes, depreciation is calculated on a straight-line basis over the estimated useful lives of the properties.

INCOME TAXES: Provision is made for the income tax effects of all transactions in the consolidated statement of earnings, including those for which actual tax payment or tax relief is deferred to future years. These deferrals result primarily from the use of shorter equipment lives and accelerated methods of depreciation for tax purposes.

Investment tax credits are recognized as a reduction of the tax expense in the year in which the related assets are placed in service or earlier where permitted by tax regulations.

OTHER EXPENSES: Advertising and research and development costs are charged against earnings in the year incurred.

| | Common stock | | Additional paid-in capital | Retained earnings | Foreign currency translation adjustments | Receivable from exercise of stock options | Total |
| | In treasury | | | | | | |
Shares	Amount						
(751,275)	$(4,352)		$147,745	$183,750	$ —	$(7,267)	$323,476
(375,637)	—		—	(1,862)	—	—	(62)
—	—		—	92,317	—	—	92,317
—	—		394	—	—	—	399
—	—		43,593	—	—	—	43,593
(1,126,912)	(4,352)		191,732	274,205	—	(7,267)	459,723
(563,456)	—		—	(2,808)	—	—	(61)
—	—		—	111,424	—	—	111,424
—	—		5,779	—	—	(344)	5,598
—	—		2,812	—	—	—	2,812
—	—		—	—	(383)	—	(383)
(1,690,368)	(4,352)		200,323	382,821	(383)	(7,611)	579,113
—	—		—	119,774	—	—	119,774
(1,903)	(71)		5,713	—	—	(554)	5,178
—	—		10,894	—	—	—	10,894
—	—		—	—	2,435	—	2,435
(1,692,271)	$(4,423)		$216,930	$502,595	$2,052	$(8,165)	$717,394

HERSHEY FOODS CORPORATION
Consolidated Statements of Changes in Financial Position

(in thousands of dollars)

For the years ended December 31,	1985	1984	1983
Cash Provided from (Used by) Continuing Operations			
Income from continuing operations	$ 120,649	$ 110,435	$ 100,972
Depreciation and amortization	52,351	42,770	37,095
Deferred income taxes	30,268	22,454	12,150
Working capital provided from continuing operations	203,268	175,659	150,217
Changes in working capital (excluding cash and short-term investments and debt):			
Inventories	(6,725)	8,713	(16,081)
Accounts receivable	4,360	(24,521)	8,673
Accounts payable	(8,579)	29,271	5,136
Other	(9,602)	3,167	12,232
Other long-term liabilities	6,136	2,713	13,017
Cash provided from continuing operations	188,858	195,002	173,194
Cash Provided from Discontinued Operations	12,062	638	1,198
Cash Dividends Paid	(43,942)	(38,680)	(34,470)
Cash Provided from (Used for) Investment Transactions			
Capital additions	(114,449)	(87,049)	(105,244)
Business acquisitions, net of working capital acquired	(6,479)	(52,199)	—
Sale and leaseback transactions, net of deferred gain	—	—	25,480
Other	(1,117)	(931)	4,298
Cash (used for) investment transactions	(122,045)	(140,179)	(75,466)
Reduction of Debt, net	(12,214)	(1,955)	(25,868)
Increase in Cash and Short-Term Investments	22,719	14,826	38,588
Cash and Short-Term Investments at January 1	87,917	73,091	34,503
Cash and Short-Term Investments at December 31	$ 110,636	$ 87,917	$ 73,091

The notes to consolidated financial statements are an integral part of these statements.

INDEX

I-1